Features of
Exploring *Human Sexuality*

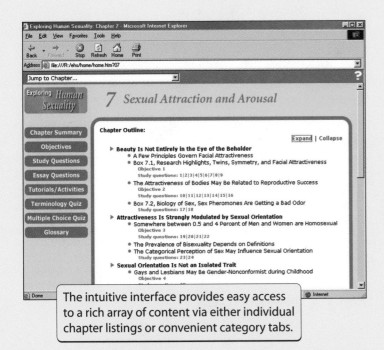

The intuitive interface provides easy access to a rich array of content via either individual chapter listings or convenient category tabs.

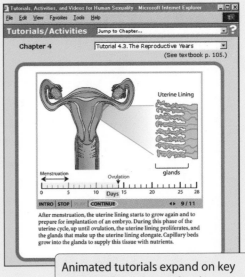

Animated tutorials expand on key concepts from the textbook.
All tutorials include an introduction, an animation, and a quiz.

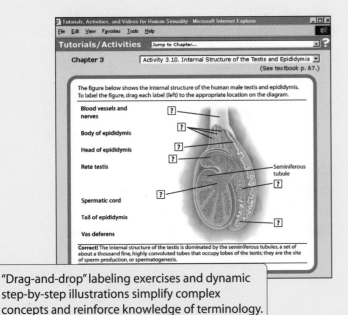

"Drag-and-drop" labeling exercises and dynamic step-by-step illustrations simplify complex concepts and reinforce knowledge of terminology.

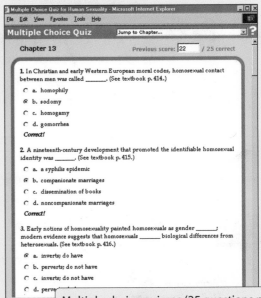

Multiple choice quizzes (25 questions per chapter) include answers and a reference to the textbook for each question.

Additional highlights...

Objectives (10 per chapter) – these learning objectives help you focus on the important topics in the chapter. Each is referenced to a specific heading in the textbook.

Study Questions (50 per chapter) – a comprehensive set of self-study questions that covers the full range of content in every chapter. Each question is referenced to an objective and to pages in the textbook for further study.

Essay Questions (10 per chapter) – these essay-style questions will help you synthesize and apply what you have learned in the chapter.

Terminology Quiz – all the important terms from each chapter are presented in a self-quiz format for quick study.

Glossary – a searchable glossary of important terminology introduced in the textbook.

Exploring *Human Sexuality*
Activities

The following activities are available on the Exploring *Human Sexuality* CD included with this textbook.
Page numbers indicate where in the textbook the topic is covered.

Human Sexuality

Human Sexuality

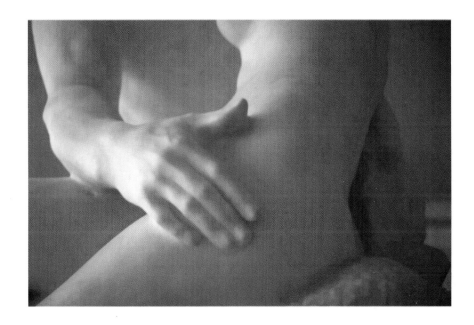

Simon LeVay

Sharon M. Valente
University of Southern California
Veterans Affairs Greater Los Angeles Healthcare System

Sinauer Associates, Inc., Publishers
Sunderland, Massachusetts, U.S.A.

The Cover

Lovers by Dawn Csutoros (www.csutoros.com), 1999.
© 2002 Artists Rights Society (ARS), New York/VISCOPY, Sydney.

About the book

Editor: Peter Farley
Project Editor: Kerry Falvey
Production Manager: Christopher Small
Book Layout and Production: Joan Gemme, Jefferson Johnson, and Janice Holabird
Illustration Program: Dragonfly Media Group
Book Design and Cover: Jefferson Johnson
Photo Editor: David McIntyre
Color Separations: Burt Russell Litho
Book and Cover Manufacture: Courier Companies, Inc.

Human Sexuality

Sinauer Associates
23 Plumtree Road
Sunderland, MA 01375 U.S.A.
FAX: 413-549-1118
E-mail: publish@sinauer.com
Internet: www.sinauer.com

Library of Congress Cataloging-in-Publication Data
LeVay, Simon.
    Human sexuality / Simon LeVay, Sharon M. Valente.
      p.   cm.
    Includes bibliographical references and index.
    ISBN 0-87893-454-5
    1. Sex (Psychology) 2. Sex (Biology) 3. Sex--Social aspects. 4. Sexual disorders.
      I. Valente, Sharon McBride, 1945- II. Title.
BF692 .L48 2002
306.7--dc21   2002014403

About the Authors

Simon LeVay earned a B.A. in Natural Sciences from Cambridge University and a doctorate in Neuroanatomy from the University of Göttingen, Germany. Focusing his research on the visual system, and more recently on the brain basis of human sexuality, he served on the faculties of Harvard Medical School (1971–1984) and the Salk Institute for Biological Studies (1984–1992), before turning his attention full-time to writing. His previous books are: *The Sexual Brain* (MIT Press, 1993); *City of Friends* (with Elisabeth Nonas, MIT Press, 1995); *Queer Science* (MIT Press, 1996); *Albrick's Gold* (Richard Kasak Books, 1997); *The Earth in Turmoil* (with Kerry Sieh, W.H. Freeman, 1998); *Here Be Dragons* (with David Koerner, Oxford University Press, 2000); and *Healing the Brain* (with Curt Freed, Times Books, 2002). Dr. LeVay has also published over 40 research papers as well as numerous popular articles and columns.

Sharon M. Valente is an Assistant Professor of Clinical Nursing at the University of Southern California and a Research Fellow in the Veterans Affairs Greater Los Angeles Healthcare system. Dr. Valente earned a Bachelor of Science in Nursing from Mt. St. Mary's College, a Master's in Psychiatric Nursing from the University of California, Los Angeles, and a doctorate in Counseling Psychology from the University of Southern California. The recipient of several awards for excellence in both research and teaching, Dr. Valente has co-taught (with Vern Bullough) a popular course in Human Sexuality at the University of Southern California since the mid-1990s. She is coeditor (with Corinne Hatton) of *Suicide: Assessment and Intervention*, Second Edition (Appleton Century Crofts, 1984). Her research interests include psychiatric/mental health, suicide, HIV, end-of-life issues, sexuality, and psychosocial oncology.

Brief Contents

Contents

chapter *3* Sexual Bodies 49

chapter *4* Sex Hormones and the Menstrual Cycle 89

chapter *5* Sexual Development 121

chapter 6 Gender 161

chapter 7 Sexual Attraction and Arousal 191

chapter *10* *Fertility, Pregnancy, and Childbirth* 293

chapter *11* *Preventing Childbirth* 333

chapter *17 Sex, Illness, and Disability* 541

chapter *18 Sexual Assault, Harassment, and Partner Violence* 569

chapter *19* Sex as a Commodity 599

Preface

Unlike the topics of many other college courses, sexuality is one that you will be quite familiar with, in one way or another, before you read the first page of this textbook or attend your first class. Here are some statistics (for the United States) to illustrate the point:

- Among 18- to 24-year olds, 94 percent of women and 89 percent of men have experienced coitus (penile-vaginal intercourse) (Laumann et al., 1994).
- In the age range of 14 to 25, thirty-nine percent of women and 52 percent of men say that they have thought about sex within the previous five minutes (Cameron & Biber, 1973).
- Over 90 percent of college students have experienced "unrequited love," both as the suitor and as the rejector (Baumeister et al., 1993).
- The typical American teenager is exposed to about 14,000 references to sex on television per year (American Academy of Pediatrics, 1995).

It's likely, in other words, that you are coming to this book and the course it accompanies with a considerable degree of personal experience, knowledge, and opinion, as well as the curiosity that motivates you to learn more.

One might think that such "advance preparation" for a course would be an unqualified benefit, yet it can also bring problems. For one thing, your "knowledge" about human sexuality may not be knowledge at all, but misconception. Typical American schoolchildren receive far less education in sexual matters than do children in many European countries. In some regions of the UnitedStates, sex education is limited to some very basic biological facts accompanied by a stress on the importance of sexual abstinence. In this vacuum, sexual "knowledge" is absorbed by a kind of social diffusion, in which peer networks and the mass media are the leading sources, but unreliable ones at best. Thus, to derive the most benefit from this course, you may need to abandon some erroneous beliefs that you had assumed to be "common knowledge." For instance, here are some statistics that you may find surprising, that might not be part of the body of knowledge you carry with you:

- Sixty-five million Americans are living with an incurable sexually transmitted disease (Centers for Disease Control, 2001m).
- Forty-three percent of all U.S. women have had an induced abortion by age 45, and most of these abortions are done early in a woman's reproductive years (Alan Guttmacher Institute, 2000b).
- Seventy percent of Americans believe that abortion for reasons of mere convenience (such as career advancement) should be illegal (Goldberg & Elder, 1998).
- Seventy-three percent of Americans are personally acquainted with someone who is openly gay (Rubin, 2000).

Also, because nearly all college-age women and men have sexual feelings, and since most have been in one or more sexual relationships, they may come to believe that sexuality is a topic in which everyone is a natural expert. This can lead to the view that normal scientific standards should, to some degree, give way to a learning environment favoring self-affirmation and esteem-building over critical thinking or the absorption of factual knowledge.

Finally, your "advance preparation" has been specific to your own particular background and interests. Depending on whether you are a woman or a man, whether your skin is black or white or brown, whether you are religiously observant or not, whether you are sexually attracted to men or women or both, and whether or not you have ever been sexually molested or assaulted, these and countless other details of your identity and life history imbue you with a uniquely personal viewpoint on sexuality. That is, of course, a good thing in one respect: it means that you and your fellow students are contributing unique and diverse perspectives to the class, thus potentially enriching the learning experience for all. It also means, however, that there are likely to be significant gaps in your knowledge and understanding. If you're a man, you may not know much about women's sex organs or the disorders that can affect them. If you're gay and never engage in heterosexual sex, or if you're sexually abstinent, you may never have thought about techniques for preventing childbirth. If you're straight, you may know little or nothing about the history or political concerns of gay people or other sexual minorities. If you're American, you may know little about sexual customs or attitudes beyond America's shores. Whatever your background, we hope that reading this book broadens your perspective

One of our main aims in writing this book was to "normalize" the place of human sexuality within the academic curriculum; that is, to help establish it as a focus of study equivalent to any other. That meant concentrating on aspects of sexuality that are amenable to rational inquiry and critical analysis. Although we certainly hope that what you learn from this book will enrich your own sex life and help you form opinions that appropriately express your core values, we have (as much as possible) avoided dispensing advice or expressing our own opinions on moral issues. In fact, we probably use the words "we" and "you" quite a bit less than do some other sexuality textbooks.

On the few occasions where we give "you" explicit advice, it is in the context of highly practical issues such how to use a condom, how to examine "your" breasts for lumps, or how to minimize "your" risk of being raped. In reading passages like these, you may get the impression that only some of them require your attention: for example, that only men need to know how to use a condom or that only women need to know how to examine their breasts or how to reduce the risk of rape. We disagree: these and comparable topics are relevant to all of you. As a result of taking this course you will probably become one of the most knowledgeable people on sexual matters in the communities to which you belong: your understanding will be useful not only for yourself, but also for your sex partner or partners, your friends and relatives, your present or future children, and possibly your clients or students. We urge you to read this book as a sex expert in the making, not merely as someone concerned simply about your own sex life.

The study of human sexuality cuts across many disciplines—that is a large part of what makes it so fascinating a subject, in addition to the intrinsic allure of sex itself. Students who enroll in human sexuality courses are also highly diverse in terms of their academic backgrounds and career goals. This challenges textbook authors to present the various topics in a fashion that is comprehensible to all and yet not tediously elementary to some. We have attempted to meet this challenge in a variety of ways. We have made sure to define **key terms** (indicated by boldface type) and to include most of them in an extensive Glossary. Where necessary, background material that may be elementary to some readers (such as basic facts about the nervous system, or key statistical concepts) have been placed in boxes or in well-delineated paragraphs so that the student who is more knowledgeable in such material can easily recognize and bypass it.

Another way that we have attempted to maintain both comprehensibility and interest is through the illustrations. You might think that it would be a simple matter to illustrate a book on human sexuality. In reality it is a significant challenge. Illustrating some of the concepts discussed in this book, especially in its more biologically oriented sections, requires a great deal of thought and design skill. Luckily our publisher, Sinauer Associates, is an industry leader in the use of art as a pedagogical medium. Thanks to their efforts, in conjunction with the art studio, many complex topics, such as the regulation of the menstrual cycle and the replication cycle of the AIDS virus, have been given a visual representation that gracefully parallels and clarifies the accompanying text.

Boxes are another important pedagogical feature of the book. There are over 100 boxes, organized into 7 themes: Biology of Sex, Cultural Diversity, Research Highlights, Sexual Health, Sex in History, Personal Points of View, and Society, Values and the Law. Within each theme, the individual boxes range from the serious (Mormon Polygamy, Hatred in the Hallways) to the lighthearted (The Flirting Academy, The Blackout Babies), but they all attempt to expand your horizons with a slightly more in-depth look at a topic than is possible within the main text. We hope that you will find the boxes both entertaining and informative.

Besides the book itself, the electronic study guide included with it is an invaluable learning aid. Assembled by Neil V. Watson of Simon Fraser University, *Exploring Human Sexuality* parallels the text with numerous animations, activities, and other materials. These items are listed on the front pages of the book.

Acknowledgments

Producing a modern college textbook like this one demands the combined efforts of a much larger group of people than the two of us who are privileged to have our names on the front cover. The most heavily involved have been the staff members of Sinauer Associates, who have produced, with great efficiency and good humor, what we consider a book of outstanding visual quality and educational value. Those with whom we have had the most enduring contacts are Editor Peter Farley, Production Editor Kerry Falvey, and Photo Editor David McIntyre, but many others have labored behind the scenes to produce the book, and we are very grateful to all of them. We also thank Norma Roche for her skillful copy editing, and Dragonfly Media Group for producing the excellent drawings and other graphical material.

We also acknowledge with gratitude the extensive and constructive comments made by the following persons who reviewed parts or all of the book:

Veanne N. Anderson, *Indiana State University*
J. Michael Bailey, *Northwestern University*
M. Betsy Bergen, *Kansas State University*
S. Marc Breedlove, *Michigan State University*
Vern L. Bullough, *California State University, Northridge (Emeritus)*
Ann W. Burgess, *University of Pennsylvania*
Amanda Collings, *University of Massachusetts, Amherst*
Robert J. Contreras, *The Florida State University*
David Crews, *University of Texas*
Karen Ericksen, *University of California, Davis*
Michelle S. Eslami, *UCLA*
Jamie Goldenberg, *Boise State University*
Roger A. Gorski, *UCLA*
Kathleen M. Greaves, *Oregon State University*
Scott Hershberger, *California State University, Long Beach*
Victor S. Johnston, *New Mexico State University*
Peter J. Katsufrakis, *University of Southern California*
Doreen Kimura, *Simon Fraser University*
Martin L. Lalumière, *University of Toronto*
Larry Lance, *University of North Carolina, Charlotte*
Philippa Levine, *University of Southern California*
Joseph LoPiccolo, *University of Missouri*
Pauline M. Maki, *National Institutes of Health*
James J. Ponzetti, Jr., *University of British Columbia*
Ritch C. Savin-Williams, *Cornell University*
Louanne Watson, *Silverton Hospital, Salem, Oregon*
Midge Wilson, *DePaul University*

SIMON LEVAY and SHARON VALENTE, September, 2002

chapter 1

Exploring human sexuality benefits from a broad perspective and an open mind.

Perspectives on Sexuality

*B*efore plunging into a detailed discussion of human sexuality, we ask some basic preliminary questions: Why study sexuality? What is sexuality "about"? And how best can we study it? Sexuality is such a central and all-pervasive aspect of our being that, to do it justice, we must study it with almost all the modes of inquiry that have been used to illuminate human nature.

Why Study Human Sexuality?

There are many possible reasons why you have chosen to take a course in human sexuality. Maybe you're simply curious about a topic that is often treated with embarrassment, evasion, or flippancy. Maybe you are looking for ways to improve your own sex life, or feel you have sexual problems that need to be solved. Maybe you are planning a career that requires an understanding of human sexuality.

Whatever your personal motives, we applaud your choice. For beyond the specific reasons that may have caused you and your fellow students to select this course, there are two aspects of human sexuality that make it a rewarding object of study for anyone. First is the fact that sexuality is a central part of who we are: we can hardly hope to understand ourselves unless we know something of our nature as sexual beings. Second, because sex colors so many aspects of our lives, studying sex means integrating knowledge from many different areas of inquiry. We are compelled to go beyond the narrow bounds of particular academic disciplines and research techniques. In the process, we may hope to develop some sense of the unity of human knowledge.

The Meaning of the Word "Sex" Has Changed

We can get some idea of the broad significance of sex by tracing the meaning of the word **sex** over the centuries. Originally, "sex" meant simply "the categories of male or female, based on anatomical characteristics." That is the only way in which Shakespeare used the word, for example. He would not have understood modern expressions such as "to have sex" or "sex is fun."

Shakespeare (like most people across the ages) believed that there was a lot one could say about people based on knowledge of their sex. Men and women tended to have differing qualities; for example, men were more aggressive and women were gentler. Shakespeare was well aware that individual men and women could go against these stereotypes, but he portrayed these exceptions as violations of sexual norms—violations that might be consciously chosen. When Lady Macbeth was plotting Duncan's murder, for example, he had her say:

> Come, you spirits
> *That tend on mortal thoughts,* unsex me *here,*
> *And fill me from the crown to the toe top-full*
> *Of direst cruelty!*
>   (*Macbeth,* Act 1, scene 5, lines 44–47; emphasis added.)

The meaning of "sex" as "the categories of male or female" persists today, of course. Innumerable bureaucratic forms ask: "Sex: M/F (Circle one)." There are some people—such as intersexes and transexuals* (see Chapter 13)—for whom this question may pose a real conundrum, but for most of us our sex is an obvious biological given, a reference point on which everything else depends. The anatomical and physiological differences between the sexes, and their development, are primary themes in human sexuality and are discussed in Chapters 2–4 of this book.

To encompass the things that we can say—or think we can say—*about* the sexes (such as that "direst cruelty" is not a womanly trait), another term, **gender,** was introduced in the mid-twentieth century (Money et al., 1957). "Gender" means the constellation of cognitive, behavioral, and personality traits that differ (to a greater or lesser degree) between the sexes. The nature of gender differences, and how they arise, is an important and controversial theme in human sexuality; these questions are discussed in Chapter 6.

Meanwhile, the meaning of the word "sex" gradually broadened. By the late nineteenth century it was applied to the whole topic of genital anatomy and function, as well as to differences between males and females. By the mid-twentieth century "sex" was used commonly to mean sexual attraction and sexual behavior; in other words, the word referred no longer just to a category but also to a phenomenon and a process. People now

---

*Although the word "transexual" is commonly spelled "transsexual," the spelling with one "s" is etymologically preferable—see the Glossary.

"had sex" when earlier they "copulated," "engaged in sexual intercourse," or (in the language of four-letter words) "fucked." As we'll see in Chapter 8, people still don't agree on the precise meaning of "having sex," but they do agree that it means getting together for some sexual purpose. Words and phrases such as "sexiness," "sex-crazed," "sex education," and "sex therapy" have become commonplace, and most of these words relate to sexual attraction and behavior, not to the categories of male or female.

As the meaning of "sex" became focused on sexual behavior, it became a bit of a "dirty word"—even though it has only three letters, rather than four. Toward the end of the twentieth century, therefore, there was a marked trend toward using the word "gender" as a kind of euphemism for the original meaning of "sex"—the categories of male or female. People began to use phrases such as "persons of either gender" as a genteel alternative to "persons of either sex." Besides being euphemistic, this trend may also be a kind of salute to 1970s feminists, who used the word "gender" a great deal. But it actually undermined the feminist use of the word, because it implied that gender was a biological given—the opposite of what most 1970s feminists believed (see Chapter 6).

The trend toward using "gender" in this fashion has invaded the sciences, including biology and medicine (Figure 1.1). Thus, phrases such as "the patient's age and gender" are now common. So it has become important for sex researchers and educators to spell out the particular meaning of the word "gender" they are using, and we do so in Chapter 6.

The word **sexuality** may also be used as a euphemism for "sex," in the same way that "elderly" is a euphemism for "old." But "sexuality" emphasizes the fact that to understand sex fully, we must study much more than just "having sex." We must understand sexual relationships and sexual identities as well.

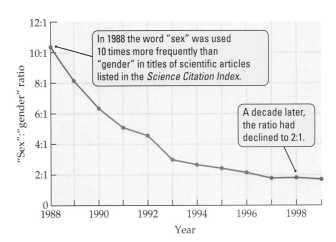

In 1988 the word "sex" was used 10 times more frequently than "gender" in titles of scientific articles listed in the *Science Citation Index*.

A decade later, the ratio had declined to 2:1.

Figure 1.1 Is "sex" necessary? (From Haig, 2000.)

Sex Is About Relationships

Most sexual behavior takes place in the context of **relationships.** Not all, of course. Masturbation is a common form of sexual expression that doesn't require a partner. Even with masturbation, however, there may be an *imagined* partner: men and women who masturbate often fantasize about a desirable partner as an aid to sexual arousal (see Chapter 8).

Sexual relationships are central to many, perhaps most, people's lives. Even in a sizable textbook like this one, we can only scratch the surface of this topic, but we will attempt to make several general points. First, sexual relationships are extremely *diverse*:

- They may last a few minutes or several decades.
- They may be motivated by physical attraction, emotional bonding, a sense of duty, a desire to be a parent, a desire to conform or rebel, or a need to make money.
- They may be mutually fulfilling, one-sided, unhappy, or abusive.
- They may involve very similar or very dissimilar partners.
- They may involve two individuals or several.
- They may be centered around sex or have sex as a mere incidental feature.
- They may be recognized and approved by society, or they may be hidden, disapproved of, or illegal.
- Sometimes, relationships that the outside world assumes to be sexual are not sexual at all.

Second, real sexual relationships are not ideal relationships. We do not get exactly what we want in this world, and we must count ourselves lucky when we come close. Whether we are looking for a partner for a night or for a life-

Although most people would not call an interaction between a prostitute and her customer a "relationship," we use the word to refer to any sexual interaction, from a one-time visit with a streetwalker to a lifelong marriage.

time, we consciously or unconsciously shop around for the best partner we can get, where "best" refers to all kinds of tangible and intangible qualities that influence our desires. People choose and are chosen. The net result is a matching that confers varying degrees of satisfaction. Almost always, though, there will be some degree of mismatch or *conflict* that tests the partners' adaptability and communication skills.

When sexual relationships are challenged by interpersonal difficulties or external forces, some endure and some fall apart. Many studies have been conducted, and many volumes written, about what makes the difference between these outcomes. Our treatment of these issues (in Chapters 8 and 11) must necessarily be more superficial than their importance warrants.

Third, sexual behavior and sexual relationships take place in a *moral context.* We all have a sense of what is right or wrong, a sense that is influenced by our upbringing, our life experiences, our religious beliefs (or lack or them), our ability to reason, and perhaps even by our genes. People do not share exactly the same moral sense, nor do they necessarily agree on whether some universal code of ethics governs all human behavior and all situations.

The authors of this book claim no special knowledge of what is right or wrong, in the sexual domain or any other. Thus, we steer clear of telling you how you should behave, except in a few practical matters where the goal is agreed upon (e.g., the use of a condom in such a way that it does its job properly). Still, we acknowledge the importance of moral questions in the sexual domain, and we bring up these questions at many points in the book, even if we don't attempt to answer them. Many of the discussion questions at the end of each chapter present opportunities for you to consider the moral aspects of the topics covered in the book. Learning more about sex may help you make sexual choices appropriate to your own moral code. It may even lead you to reconsider some of your moral positions.

Sex Is About Identity

Sexuality strongly influences people's sense of who they are. Most obviously, this is true of a person's sex. Nearly all women have a strong sense of identity as women, and nearly all men as men. This subjective sense of belonging to a particular sex—a trait called **gender identity**—shows itself as a suite of sex-typed social behaviors (**gender role**). It also forms a basis for group action, especially by women, who have historically been disadvantaged in a variety of ways. The women's movement of the 1970s sought to correct these historical injustices and thus gave many women a political identity as members of the female sex.

A small minority of males and females have a gender identity that is discordant with their anatomical sex. The identity of such **transgendered** or **transexual** individuals may be twofold: first, as a member of the sex they feel they belong to (as a woman, for example, in the case of a male-to-female transexual), but also as a transgendered person. This is because the social experience of being transgendered imposes a sense of difference from conventionally gendered men and women and a sense of commonality with other transgendered persons. Transgendered men and women form a group that is socially and politically active to a far greater extent than one might imagine possible on the basis of their small numbers.

Sexual orientation—meaning whether an individual is predominantly attracted to persons of the same sex, the other sex, or both sexes—is also often perceived as an aspect of identity. Again, it is largely people belonging to the socially disadvantaged orientation who are conscious of their sexual orientation

Transgendered men and women identify with the sex opposite to their anatomical sex. In addition, however, their transgendered status may itself offer them a unique identity, providing a focus for social life, mutual support, and political action.

as a central aspect of their identity. **Homosexual** men and women—those who are attracted to people of their own sex—often reach out to one another for sexual fulfillment, social engagement, and political action. **Bisexual** people, who are attracted to both sexes, do not necessarily have to meet other bisexuals for the purposes of sexual fulfillment, but bisexuals are also socially disadvantaged, in that both heterosexual and homosexual people are liable to have negative beliefs about them (see Chapter 13). Thus, bisexuals have a more conscious identity as bisexual than heterosexuals do as heterosexual.

Other aspects of people's sexuality may also confer a sense of identity:

- People who have group sexual relationships ("polyamorists")
- "Swingers" and others who engage in sex outside of lasting relationships
- People who engage in sadomasochistic practices
- People who prefer very young or very old sex partners
- Prostitutes and others whose work involves sex
- People who choose to defer sex until marriage
- People who sacrifice their sexuality in favor of a lifelong religious vocation
- Sex offenders
- People who have experienced rape or childhood molestation
- Parents
- People with sexually transmitted diseases (including AIDS)
- People with medical conditions or disabilities that affect sexual expression

All of these people are likely to have some sense of identity and community with others like them. These groups of people may have newsletters and newsgroups, meeting places, organizations and political goals, and a shared outlook. In other words, our sexual feelings, behaviors, and experiences help establish our place in society, making us sympathetic to people who share our traits and less sympathetic—sometimes downright hostile—to those who do not. We can hardly do justice to all these sexual identities in this book, but we touch on some of them in Chapters 13–19.

There Are Many Approaches to the Study of Sexuality

Because sexuality affects so many aspects of our lives, it can be studied with the tools of many different disciplines. Practitioners of these different disciplines tend to make different assumptions about the purpose, the mechanisms, and the development of sexual feelings and behavior. Let's take a look at some of the diverse approaches to sexuality that will occupy us later in the book.

Medicine Is Concerned with "Health" and "Sickness"

Over the years, medical research has gathered vital knowledge about the physical basis of sexuality—in particular, about the structure, function, and development of the male and female genital and reproductive systems. Starting at the time of the Renaissance, **anatomists** made detailed studies of the internal reproductive tracts of men and women. In the twentieth century, **endocrinologists** and **reproductive physiologists** explored the hormonal systems that make men's and women's bodies so different from each other and that give women something that men don't have: a menstrual cycle and the capacity to nurture a fetus. **Neuroscientists** began to lay out the neural control mechanisms that mediate sexual arousal and sexual behavior. **Geneticists** explored how sex is determined and how this process of sex determination can go awry. **Pathologists** and **microbiologists** discovered the causes of sexually transmitted diseases. All these spheres of knowledge, though far from complete, are central to our present-day understanding of human sexuality, and we make no apology for devoting a great deal of space to them in this book.

Medicine has also explored the *mental* aspects of sexuality, and here its record is more controversial, for several reasons. For one thing, we still have only a very limited understanding of how the brain generates mental states. Thus, theories have tended to be high-

Box 1.1 *Sex in History*

Freud and Hirschfeld: Contrasting Theories on Sexual Orientation

About a century ago, two German-speaking doctors proposed radically different theories to account for why some people are sexually attracted predominantly to members of the other sex while others are attracted to members of the same sex or to both sexes—a characteristic we now call sexual orientation. In Vienna, Sigmund Freud developed a theory that was based on the concept of an **unconscious mind,** whose operations could supposedly be probed by **psychoanalytic techniques** such as free association, the interpretation of dreams, and slips of the tongue. The unconscious mind, though hidden from view and free from moral restraints, nevertheless resembled the conscious mind in many respects, being capable of rational thought, planning, memory, and emotion.

Sigmund Freud (1856–1939)

In Freud's conception, the unconscious mind was more broadly focused in its sexual desires than was the conscious mind. This was particularly true during early childhood, which he believed included autoerotic and homosexual phases as well as incestuous desires directed toward one or the other parent. As we'll detail in Chapter 7, Freud thought that the "normal" progression to adult heterosexuality could be derailed in various ways, often involving unconscious emotional processes such as a hostile, too-close, or jealous relationship with a parent or sibling. These phenomena could lead to what Freud called **perversions;** that is, mental states in which adult sexual desires were directed toward atypical targets, such as

persons of the same sex (homosexuality), inanimate objects (fetishism), and so on. Or they could lead to **neuroses,** in which the sexual element was supposedly repressed from consciousness altogether and reemerged in the form of nonsexual traits and disorders, such as obsessive-compulsive behaviors, depression, or "hysteria."

In Berlin, Magnus Hirschfeld took a radically different view. Hirschfeld proposed the existence of two **neural centers** in the brain that were responsible for sexual attraction to men and to women. During early fetal life, he suggested, all humans possessed both centers, but later one center grew and dominated, while the other regressed. In men, of course, it was usually the center for attraction to women that persisted, while in women it was the center for attraction to men. Only in the minority of homosexual individuals did development take the opposite course. Hirschfeld believed that **sex hormones** (then understood in only a very rudimentary way) channeled development in one direction or another, and that people also had a **genetic predisposition** to same-sex or opposite-sex attraction.

In many ways, the views of Freud and Hirschfeld represented opposite approaches to understanding the mind and sexuality. Freud tried to understand the mind in terms of processes that, though hidden, were inherently *mental*—unconscious thoughts. And he saw interpersonal relationships as holding the key to sexual orientation and other aspects of adult sexuality. To Freud, getting to your adult sexuality was a long, sometimes chaotic drama in which you yourself took the leading role. Hirschfeld, on the other hand, tried to reduce the mind to relatively simple *nonmental* phenomena such as the growth and activity of nerve cells, hormone secretion, and information encoded in the genes. In Hirschfeld's view, these phenomena controlled sexual development in a fashion that was largely independent of family relationships and other aspects of life experience. To Hirschfeld, getting to your adult sexuality

was a process that unfolded mechanistically without your active participation—it simply happened to you.

Freud's theories came to dominate most people's ideas about the mind through the early and middle part of the twentieth century, while Hirschfeld's theories languished in obscurity. Toward the end of the century, however, there was a noticeable shift of views. To some people, Freud's theories began to seem capricious, poorly substantiated, or inspired by prejudice (against women, especially). Meanwhile, scientific advances tended to bolster a reductionistic view of sexuality. Studies in animals showed that prenatal hormone levels do indeed influence sexual behavior in adulthood, and family studies supported the idea that genes do have some influence on sexual orientation in humans.

Probably the dominant view at present is that both approaches offer potential insights into human sexuality. There must be some biological underpinnings to all our thoughts and behaviors, and exploring these underpinnings is likely to tell us a lot about why people differ from one another sexually. On the other hand, it seems likely that there are aspects of human sexuality that need to be studied at the level of thoughts—in other words, by a **cognitive approach**. Thus, even if neither Freud's nor Hirschfeld's theories turn out to be right, they may both have contributed useful styles of thinking to the discussion.

Magnus Hirschfeld (1868–1935)

ly speculative, and wildly disparate theories have been put forward by different doctors, even at the same time and place (Box 1.1)

An even more controversial aspect of the medical approach has been the tendency of doctors to view sexual issues in terms of health and disease. An early example of this approach was the work of the German physician Richard von Krafft-Ebing (1840–1902), who wrote a best-selling treatise on sexual disorders titled *Psychopathia Sexualis* (1886). This book was a compendium of 237 case histories illustrating all kinds of sexual "deviations," including masturbation, homosexuality, transvestism, fetishism, exhibitionism, pedophilia, bestiality, sadism, masochism, necrophilia (sexual fixation on corpses), coprophilia (sexual fixation on feces), and sexual murder (Jack the Ripper was one of the case histories). A great part of the book's appeal was in the graphic accounts of these deviations, some of which are shocking even today.

Krafft-Ebing claimed the right to "name" sexual disorders and to "diagnose" persons who suffered from them (Davis, 1996). But in doing so, was he responding to a plea for understanding and treatment from deeply disturbed individuals, or was he seeking to impose his own code of sexual propriety on people who would otherwise have had perfectly harmless and satisfying sex lives? Looking at the "deviations" listed above, there may be some that you practice yourself with no sense of guilt or sickness, some that you have no problem with if other people want to practice them, and some that you think should be prevented at all costs, whether through medical or legal means. But do doctors have the right to decide which is which?

Among the most eloquent critics of Krafft-Ebing, and of others like him, have been the French philosopher Michel Foucault (1926–1984) and the American psychiatrist (or "anti-psychiatrist") Thomas Szasz (born 1920). Foucault saw psychiatry as an instrument of the state, whose tyrannical gaze "inscribed" people with mental illness, just as the judicial system "inscribed" people with criminality (Foucault, 1978). Szasz saw (and still sees) all psychiatric diagnoses as inventions, phrased to resemble the diagnosis of physical diseases but actually having no objective basis. Back in the time when homosexuality was considered a mental illness, Szasz commented that the psychiatric perspective on this condition was nothing but "a thinly disguised replica of the religious perspective which it replaced" (Szasz, 1970). In a recent article, Szasz dismissed *Psychopathia Sexualis* as "the first modern pornographic tract successfully merchandised as medical science" (Szasz, 2000).

In spite of such criticisms, the idea that sexual aberrations can be named and diagnosed has been codified in the American Psychiatric Association's *Diagnostic and Statistical Manual of Mental Disorders* (or *DSM*), which is revised periodically (American Psychiatric Association, 2000). The APA underwent a paroxysmal struggle in the early 1970s over the question of whether homosexuality should continue to be listed as a mental disorder (Bayer, 1981). Thanks in part to the efforts of gay activists both inside and outside the psychiatric profession, this diagnostic category was removed in 1973 (see Chapter 13).

Many other questionable sexual "disorders" are still listed in the *DSM*, however; these include "gender identity disorder of childhood" (boys who feel and act like girls, and vice versa), as well as several disorders that are straight out of *Psychopathia Sexualis*. There is a difference, though: the *DSM* now emphasizes that (with some exceptions) a sexual condition is not a disorder unless it causes distress to the person who experiences it. In a sense, then, the affected person must participate in the diagnostic process.

The question of what constitutes a sexual disorder in need of treatment comes up in many places in this book, especially in the discussion of homosexuality, transexuality, pedophilia, and other atypical forms of sexual expression (see Chapters 12 and 13). In reviewing this material, we suggest that you look beyond the Greek-sounding terminology (the "philias" and "phobias"). Ask yourself what criteria you would use to distinguish between traits that should be medically treated or legally restrained and traits that can be accepted as part of the diverse tapestry of human sexual expression.

Contrary to the impression created by Foucault or Szasz, many psychiatrists are actually out to help their patients, not to force them into conformity. Richard Pillard, a Boston University psychiatrist, played an early role in getting the APA to remove homosexuality from the *DSM*. When we asked him whether "gender identity disorder of childhood" should also be delisted, he replied: "I think it's a cultural diagnosis. If these same kids grew up in a culture that had a place for them, they would not be in conflict or distress, and no diagnosis would be relevant. That said, these children are still suffering and can benefit from sensitive treatment." And, Pillard points out, diagnoses are a necessary part of the medical process, since insurance companies require them to reimburse physicians for treatment (Pillard, personal communication).

The Biological Approach Emphasizes Our Animal Nature

There is a great deal of overlap between the biological and medical perspectives. Both emphasize an evidence-based approach, and both are rooted in an understanding of the body's physical systems. These days, M.D.s and Ph.D.s work side by side to solve clinical problems and to elucidate questions of more general human significance. This collaboration is summarized in the phrase "biomedical research." Still, there are a couple of differences between these two approaches that are worth noting.

Unlike doctors, biologists are not particularly concerned with deciding what is "normal" or "abnormal." In fact, many biologists believe that the use of these terms involves value judgments that cannot be made on the basis of purely scientific criteria. Biologists simply try to describe and understand what is out there. This neutral perspective has been helpful in the study of sexual function and sexual behavior.

Also, biologists are especially aware that *Homo sapiens* is just one of millions of animal species on this planet, albeit a species of particular interest to ourselves. They know that humans and other animals evolved from common ancestors. The common ancestors of humans and chimpanzees, for example, lived about 8 million years ago—a very brief period of time in comparison with the overall history of life on Earth (Smithsonian Institution, 2002). Thus, biologists expect to find similarities in the basic sexual and reproductive functions of humans and other animals, especially those that are closely related to us. This viewpoint has been rewarded with important discoveries about the biological basis of human sexuality, as we'll see in several sections of this book.

Biologists do not ignore differences between us and other animals. As we'll see in Chapter 2, evolution has led to a great deal of diversity in sexual function. Different species use entirely different mechanisms to determine whether an embryo becomes male or female, for example. And sexual behavior differs quite markedly even between two of our closest relatives, chimpanzees and gorillas. What biology teaches us is that each species is a unique variation on a common theme.

Humans are unique in their intelligence, language skills, and moral sense, and these traits are brought into play in the sexual domain. Even these traits, though, are ultimately the product of evolution. Therefore, understanding how human mental phenomena, such as jealousy, affect our sex lives may require a consideration of our long evolutionary history (Buss, 1995).

Frogs may produce a hundred offspring from a single reproductive embrace (amplexus). Contemporary humans may have hundreds of sexual encounters without producing a single offspring. With such striking differences in reproductive efficiency, it is unlikely that sex serves the same purposes or is governed by the same mechanisms in frogs and humans.

Psychologists Have Taken Diverse Approaches to Sexuality

Psychology—the study of the mind—has splintered into all kinds of overlapping subdisciplines, several of which have their own unique perspectives on sexuality. Probably the most significant branch in the study of sexuality is **social psychology**—the study of interpersonal relations (Plous, 2002). Social psychologists concern themselves with all kinds of sexual matters, such as sexual attraction and sexual relationships, gender differences, homosexuality, sexual assault, intimate-partner violence, and anti-gay prejudice. Social psychology may be descriptive or experimental. An example of the latter approach would be a study in which people are made to experience varying levels of anxiety or arousal in order to see what effects these mental states have on their sexual responsiveness (see Chapter 7).

In general, of course, social psychologists seek to understand sexual phenomena in terms of interpersonal relations. Imitation, competition, rewards and punishments, role modeling, reciprocity, family dynamics, love, peer pressure, conflict resolution, and the victim-perpetrator cycle are all important concepts in social psychology, and we touch on many of these in this book. Social psychologists do not usually focus on the possible biological underpinnings of sexual expression.

Psychobiologists or **biological psychologists** occupy the interface between psychology and the biological sciences, especially neuroscience and endocrinology. Psychobiologists interested in sexual behaviors often study these behaviors in laboratory animals rather than in humans, because their experiments may involve risk to their subjects or may require killing the animals in order to analyze their brains or other systems.

An example of the psychobiological approach is the work of Donald Pfaff at Rockefeller University. In a series of over 400 papers published over several decades, Pfaff and his colleagues have dissected the neural, hormonal, and molecular genetic bases of sexual behavior in rats, especially female rats. In spite of the wide evolutionary gap between rodents and humans, Pfaff's work may have important implications for women's sexual and reproductive health (Pfaff et al., 2000).

Cultural (or **cross-cultural**) **psychologists** concern themselves with the influence of ethnic and cultural diversity on thought, behavior, and interpersonal relationships. Where cultural psychology focuses on differences between entire societies, it overlaps extensively with **anthropology.** Margaret Mead, for example, pioneered the study of sexual attitudes and gender differences in Pacific Island societies in the early part of the twentieth century (Mead, 1928, 1935). Mead called herself an anthropologist, but people doing similar research today may refer to themselves as cultural psychologists. The comparison of sexual behaviors and attitudes between different societies helps us understand which elements of human sexuality are universal—and therefore possibly "hardwired" into our brains—and which are culture-bound (Box 1.2).

Of course, many diverse ethnic and cultural traditions exist in the United States, so there is ample room for cultural studies of sexuality and gender within our own society. Some Native Americans, for example, preserve an ancient tradition that assigned a special, spiritual role to homosexual or transgendered individuals (Williams, 1986). Hispanics, on the other hand, may be influenced by the Latin American culture of *machismo,* which emphasizes stereotypical masculinity. Sexual behavior differs greatly among different groups: only 27 percent of Asian-American high school students have ever engaged in penile-vaginal intercourse (coitus), for example, compared with 72 percent of African-American students (Schuster et al., 1998) (see Chapter 12). Understanding the roots of such cultural differences could aid efforts to reduce unwanted pregnancy and sexually transmitted diseases among teenagers.

Clinical psychologists deal with emotional, behavioral, and personality problems—problems that quite often have a sexual element. They may treat patients or do research. A related group is **sex therapists,** who deal with problems that interfere with the enjoyment of sex—problems such as premature ejaculation or lack of sexual desire. **Marriage and family counselors** deal with problems affecting marriages and other intimate relationships—problems that may arise out of sexual difficulties or that, conversely, may arise in nonsexual areas of the relationship but interfere with sexual relations. These three groups of professionals do not generally have M.D.s; instead, they usually have Ph.D.s or master's degrees. Thus they are not usually able to prescribe drugs, and they tend to focus on the nonbiological roots of sexual dysfunctions, such as childhood experiences, relationship difficulties, and the like. To some extent there is a tension between the medical and psychological perspectives on sexual problems, as we'll see in Chapter 15.

Social Scientists Focus on the Connection between Sex and Society

Social science is a catch-all phrase that covers scientific studies of humankind as a social species—that is to say, pretty much everything about us that is interesting. Social psychology and cultural psychology, discussed above, can be viewed as branches of social science. Social scientists make a unique contribution to the study of sexuality, however, by linking the sexual feelings and behaviors of individuals to larger social structures.

One way social scientists accomplish this is by taking a **demographic** approach to sexuality—by examining, in other words, how sexual expression varies with age, race, national origin, religious and political beliefs, place of residence, educational level, and so on. Such studies are often carried out by means of **sex surveys.**

CULTURAL DIVERSITY

The Fattening Room

There's an old saying, attributed to the Duchess of Windsor, that "you can never be too rich or too thin." To judge by the rail-thin models and actresses that Americans see on film and TV every day, thinness is the ultimate in female beauty (Figure A). Yet there are societies in which the other end of the size spectrum—outright obesity—is preferred.

(A) In the United States, thin is beautiful.

Case in point: the Annang people of south-eastern Nigeria.

Annang women have to engage in considerable physical labor, yet calorie-rich food is scarce, so most women are very lean. Before a girl is married off, however, she is secluded in a "fattening room" for several months—sometimes for more than a year. While in the room, the girl is called a *mbobo*. She does no work and has few visitors, but she is fed three large meals every day. The meals consist of high-calorie foods such as yams and rice—expensive luxuries for the Annang, who generally depend on nutrient-poor cassava. Between meals, the mbobo is instructed in the duties and skills of womanhood. She may also undergo circumcision (see Chapter 3). At the conclusion of the fattening period there is a festival. All the mbobo in the village have their bodies painted, and they dance nude in public to display their fatness. The ceremony includes a great deal of feasting, the food being provided by the mbobos' families.

A young man in search of a bride may select one of the mbobo, but he will have to make a substantial bridal payment to her father. The fatter the mbobo, the higher the payment, for all Annang people agree that fat women are the most attractive and desirable as brides.

Why is there such a striking difference between American culture and that of the Annang in the estimation of female attractiveness? According to Pamela Brink of the University of Alberta, who has done fieldwork among the Annang, two related factors make fatness attractive in that culture (Brink, 1989). First, the general scarcity of food and the occurrence of periodic droughts and famines make it difficult for an Annang woman to complete a pregnancy and nurse her baby successfully. A woman who is markedly overweight when she marries is carrying energy reserves that will see her through her first pregnancy—an assurance that is valuable to a potential husband.

The fattening process is also a form of "conspicuous consumption"—a demonstration of wealth on the part of the mbobo's family. To fatten a mbobo, the family not only must provide her with expensive foodstuffs, but must also do without her labor during the time she is secluded. The festival at the conclusion of the fattening process is also very expensive. Thus a fat mbobo and a lavish feast are proof of the family's resources and status. Many families cannot afford to fatten a mbobo, and they must marry their daughters off to less desirable men.

Although the traditional fattening-room practices are on the decline, fatness is still idealized, both among the Annang and more widely in West Africa (Smith, 2001) (Figure B). In some localities, women of limited means put on weight by consuming animal feed or by the use of corticosteroids, even though these drugs produce an unnatural-looking obesity and can be toxic.

In the contemporary United States almost anyone can obtain enough food to gain weight, so obesity does not demonstrate any particular wealth or status. For many women it is more of a challenge to remain thin than to become fat. Perhaps for this reason, obesity is devalued as a measure of attractiveness, and thinness is preferred.

The marked difference between the Annang and ourselves in the judgment of female attractiveness suggests that these judgments are not genetically programmed or "hardwired" into our brains. Instead, they depend on cultural tradition and social circumstances. Still, there do seem to be some aspects of physical appearance whose attractiveness is judged in a consistent way across cultures, as we will see in Chapter 7.

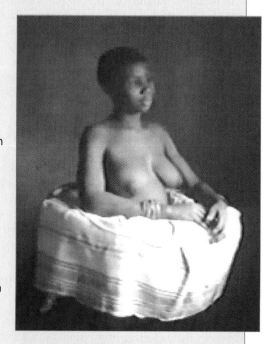

(B) In West Africa, fatness is preferred. This video still, taken from the documentary film *Becoming a Woman in Okrika*, by Judith Gleason and Elisa Mereghetti, shows an *iriabo* (the Okrika equivalent of a *mbobo*) in a fattening room wearing many layers of fabric to accentuate her hips—and her fertility.

The most famous sex survey was conducted by zoologist Alfred Kinsey and his colleagues at Indiana University in the middle years of the twentieth century. Kinsey's group interviewed about 17,000 Americans about their sex lives, and the results were published in two thick, data-rich volumes—one on men and one on women (Kinsey et al., 1948, 1953). The Kinsey reports, as they are usually called, created a sensation when they appeared, because they documented a much wider prevalence of unconventional sexual practices than most people expected. For example, the reports stated that 37 percent of men had had at least one sexual contact with another male resulting in orgasm at some time between adolescence and old age. This finding challenged the then-prevailing view of homosexual relationships as some kind of rare aberration. The reports also found marked class differences in sexual behavior and attitudes: better-educated, professional people masturbated much more frequently than those with little education or those who worked as laborers, for example.

Sex survey pioneer Alfred Kinsey (1894–1956) (left, seated), and his colleagues (from left to right) Clyde Martin, Paul Gebhard, and Wardell Pomeroy, interviewed over 17,000 men and women between 1938 and 1956.

With the onset of the AIDS epidemic around 1980, the need for detailed information about sexual practices and attitudes spurred a host of new sex surveys. Most notable among them was the National Health and Social Life Survey (NHSLS), led by social scientists at the University of Chicago and elsewhere (Laumann et al., 1994). Although the NHSLS data are now more than a decade old, they still provide a key source of demographic information about sexuality in the United States, and they are cited frequently in this book. Besides being more up-to-date than the Kinsey survey, the NHSLS was technically superior in a number of respects, especially in its use of modern population sampling methods.

On the other hand, funding difficulties caused the NHSLS to be limited to only about 3400 interviewees—too few to draw reliable conclusions about small minorities such as, say, black lesbians. It also failed to include persons younger than 18 (a group whose sexual activity is of great significance from a public policy perspective) or older than 59 (the group whose sex lives we know the least about). Finally, some critics have argued that the NHSLS and other recent surveys failed to elicit completely forthright responses from the interviewees, and therefore underestimated the prevalence of stigmatized traits and behaviors such as promiscuity, homosexuality, and abortion (Lewontin, 1995). All in all, the demographic approach to sexuality is vitally important, but it will not fully succeed in its aims until the topic of sex no longer elicits embarrassment on the part of interviewees or aversion on the part of funding agencies.

Social scientists are particularly interested in how social structures such as the family, friendship networks, mass media, the law, and the economy mold individual sexual feelings and behaviors. One dominant idea is that these structures, as they impinge on individuals, promote a kind of role-playing behavior, in which people are like performers in a play—perhaps a play that is the product of a collective rather than a single playwright. Leading exponents of this **script-theory** approach have been William Simon (of the University of Houston), John Gagnon (of the State University of New York), and Ira Reiss (now retired from the University of Minnesota) (Reiss, 1986; Simon & Gagnon, 1987). Script theorists do not deny the importance of the self or individual responsibility in sexual expression, but they assert that the meaning of sexual acts is highly context-dependent and is assessed by reference to social expectations. We discuss their ideas in Chapter 6 and elsewhere.

The Law Sets Limits on Sexual Expression

Laws have regulated sexual behavior and sexual relationships since the dawn of civilization. In the ancient Jewish societies described in the Torah and the Christian Old Testament, the legal regulation of sexuality fell to religious authorities (see Chapter 9). Some of those ancient proscriptions, such as the ban on sex during a woman's menstrual period, may have had an entirely spiritual significance. Others, such as the ban on adultery, served a more obvious practical purpose by reducing (or attempting to reduce) social conflicts.

In the contemporary United States, the laws are not written by clerics, nor are they supposed to enforce particular religions' codes of behavior. Still, religious beliefs do persist in American law. For example, many states still have laws that ban homosexual behavior, anal sex, and the like ("sodomy statutes"). These laws have no practical purpose, but they enforce moral attitudes that can be traced back to Christian and ancient Jewish teachings. Such laws are still sporadically enforced, or their mere existence may be used to set sexual minorities at a disadvantage (see Chapter 13).

Much more significant are laws that regulate the age of consent, marriage, divorce, abortion, sexual assault, pornography, and prostitution. The theoretical basis and function of these laws is a fertile area of study and, of course, political debate. One legal scholar who has made a special study of this field is Richard Posner of the University of Chicago Law School (and retired Chief Justice of the U.S. Court of Appeals for the Seventh Circuit).

Posner argues that most or all sexual behaviors involve costs and benefits to society as a whole ("externalities"), and not just for the individual who engages in them (Posner, 1992). A man who visits a prostitute, for example, is using up resources that might otherwise have supported his children, thus increasing the potential costs that those children will impose on society. He may also be spreading diseases that will affect others. On the other hand, he is helping the prostitute avoid becoming a welfare burden. According to Posner, the rational analysis of all these externalities could provide a logical basis for the criminalization of prostitution, or conversely for its legalization, without any appeal to purely moral or religious arguments. In a sense, Posner seeks to reduce sexual law to economics (Posner, 1998), but an economics that factors in all kinds of difficult-to-value phenomena, such as the public's happiness or unhappiness when faced with the reality of prostitution.

U.S. laws regulating sexuality are complex and vary greatly with locality. In California alone, for example, there are well over a hundred offenses for which a convicted person must register as a sex offender (Office of the Attorney General, 2001). For this reason, we do not attempt a systematic presentation of sex laws in this book. We do discuss the legal aspects of several specific areas of sexuality, however; these areas include abortion (see Chapter 11), homosexual behavior and gay rights (see Chapter 13), sex between adults and minors (see Chapters 12, 13, and 14), sexual violence and harassment (see Chapter 18), and prostitution and pornography (see Chapter 19).

Feminists Emphasize Women's Sexual Rights

Feminism—the belief that women are entitled to the same social, economic, and political rights as men, and the organized pursuit of these goals—has had a profound influence on how Americans think about sexuality.

There have been two major periods of feminism in the United States. In the early period, which ran from the mid-nineteenth century until the ratification of the Nineteenth Amendment to the U.S. Constitution in 1920, the focus was on women's right to vote. Some sexual issues were also debated during this period, however. Most notable was the issue of **contraception** (see Chapter 11). Realizing that many women were trapped in poverty and ill health by an endless cycle of reproduction, feminist Margaret Sanger (1879–1966) campaigned tirelessly for women's right to learn about and use contraceptives. In the face of fierce opposition—Sanger spent a month in jail at one point—she and her colleagues opened birth control clinics and helped develop new contraceptive technologies. The Planned Parenthood Federation, a leading provider of contraceptive and abortion services, traces its origins to Sanger's movement.

The second period of feminism began in the 1960s and had its heyday in the 1970s. This wave of feminism was a much more broadly based ferment of ideas centered on women's equality in every field. It pitted feminists (of both sexes) against "male chauvinists"—men who attempted to defend the bastions of male privilege in employment, politics, and social life. In the sexual domain, central issues were a woman's entitlement to sexual pleasure, her right to terminate a pregnancy, and freedom from sexual assault and harassment. During the 1970s, feminists rejected the notion that women should mold their bodies or behavior in the service of men's sexual desire. "Burning one's bra" was considered the ultimate feminist protest, though probably no more than a handful of women literally did so.

A dominant idea in 1970s feminism was that differences between the sexes are established by learning and culture—that boys are **socialized** to be sexually aggressive, for example, whereas girls are socialized to be submissive. The notion that there might be biological predispositions underlying gender differences was generally downplayed or dismissed altogether. These feminist ideas became very influential in academe, and still are. Some leading contemporary textbooks on human sexuality (e.g., Hyde & DeLamater, 2003), are grounded in traditional feminist theories of sexuality and gender.

Current thinking about women's issues is highly diverse, and these contrasting strands of thought are sometimes referred to collectively as **postfeminism.** One postfeminist scholar whose ideas are markedly at odds with traditional feminism is cultural critic Camille Paglia of the University of the Arts in Philadelphia (Paglia, 1990, 1994). Paglia sees gender differences as

Tennis legend Billie Jean King is carried into the Houston Astrodome on the day of her 1973 victory over ex-Wimbledon champion and self-described "male chauvinist pig" Bobby Riggs.

largely innate, and the influence of culture as reining them in rather than creating them. Socialization, according to Paglia, is the reason why women can walk the streets with some expectation of safety, not the reason why men commit rape.

In this book, we present both feminist views of sexuality and contrasting ideas. Because the roots of human sexuality are still largely unexplained, we do not attempt to decide between rival theories in most cases. In fact, it is likely that biological predispositions, socialization, and other processes all combine to generate our unique sexual identities.

Ethical Systems Can Be Sex-Negative or Sex-Positive

People's sense of right and wrong behavior, in sex as in other spheres of action, derives from many sources: religious teachings, secular humanist ideas, upbringing, past sexual interactions, reasoned thought, and even from ethical "instincts" that we inherit from our evolutionary past. At the risk of oversimplifying the matter, one can say that there are "sex-negative" and "sex-positive" ethical traditions.

Sex-negative traditions label many—perhaps all—sexual behaviors as wrong. Early Christianity was dominated by sex-negative ideas: abstention from sexual activity was the only truly virtuous state, according to Saint Augustine (see Chapter 9). Among the most sex-positive traditions, on the other hand, are those of some Pacific islands, such as Mangaia in the Cook Islands. Mangaian girls and boys are given instruction in sexual techniques and encouraged to put what they learned into practice, even in the form of casual liaisons (see Chapter 8). Our own contemporary U.S. culture contains a mixture of sex-positive and sex-negative elements—elements that are often at war with each other.

Sexual ethics may be founded on authority ("homosexuality is against God's law"), on agreed-upon principles such as honesty ("you should tell your partner if you have herpes"), or on an analysis of consequences ("if teens have sex, we'll all have to support the unwanted babies that result"). Because of these varied modes of ethical thought, people (including professional ethicists) have diverging views on what is right and wrong, and sexual ethics may change over time.

To illustrate this point: Bernadette Brooten of Brandeis University leads a group that is concerned with the reworking of Jewish and Christian sexual ethics in the light of feminist theory (Brooten, 2002). Saint Paul roundly condemned sex between women in his Epistle to the Romans, for example. According to Brooten, Paul's condemnation was rooted in his belief in the importance of distinct social roles for men and women, with women in a subordinate position. This distinction was threatened by lesbian relationships (Brooten, 1996). Feminism and other social forces have brought the justification for strict gender roles into question, so Paul's denunciation of female homosexuality may have lost some of its moral relevance to contemporary society.

Our most extended discussion of sexual ethics is in the context of sexual relationships (see Chapter 9), but we also bring up moral questions in several other chapters, sometimes in the form of boxes titled "Society, Values, and the Law."

Artists Explore the Intangible Aspects of Sexuality

Sex has been a central theme in art, literature, and music across the ages. We do not attempt any kind of systematic treatment of this vast field in this book, but we do focus on a few themes.

Wandering minstrels of medieval Europe celebrated romantic love in narrative poems and short lyrics.

First, art and literature offer a window onto the sexual lives of people in cultures far removed from our own. Is romantic love a human universal, for example, or is it a product of modern Western culture (see Chapter 9)? To find the answer, one can search for evidence of romantic love in writings from ancient times and remote locations, such as the songs of the wandering minstrels (troubadours and minnesinger) in the Age of Chivalry. Here is a famous German example, written by an unknown poet about 800 years ago:

> *Du bist min, ich bin din*
> *—des solt du gewis sin.*
> *du bist beslozzen in minem herzen;*
> *verloren ist das slüzzelin*
> *—du muost och iemer drinne sin.*

> ("You are mine, I am yours/ Of that you should be aware/ You are locked in my heart/ Lost is the little key/ You must stay in there forever.")

How did people feel about the human body in antiquity, during the Middle Ages, or after the Renaissance? Sculptures and paintings that survive from those periods can help us answer that question (see Chapter 7). What did people actually do in bed? Greek vase paintings and the Indian sex treatise, the *Kama Sutra,* provide explicit information on this point (see Chapter 8).

Second, there is an immense body of art, literature, and film that is intended to stimulate sexual desire. This work is referred to as **pornography,** often with the implication that it is a "low" form of art, lacks serious aesthetic value, or is immoral. Critical attitudes toward pornography often reflect sex-negative traditions in our society and are often expressed by conservative Christian groups. Since the 1970s, however, some feminists have also attacked pornography, representing it as demeaning to women or as promoting violence against them (Dworkin, 1981). Others have rebutted such charges or have defended pornography on a free-speech basis (Strossen, 1995). As we'll discuss in Chapter 19, researchers have conducted numerous studies to evaluate the effects of pornography, yet conclusive answers have been hard to reach.

Educators Have Struggled to Communicate Basic Knowledge about Sexuality

Since you have enrolled in a college course on human sexuality and you are reading this book—probably without having to fight any particular battles to do so—it may seem odd that we use the term "struggle" to refer to education about sexuality. Yet we have already mentioned how much opposition Margaret Sanger faced when she attempted to disseminate knowledge about birth control in the early part of the twentieth century. Similar difficulties have plagued education in all aspects of human sexuality and continue to the present day (Box 1.3).

Box 1.3 *Sex in History*

Mary Calderone and Sex Education

Mary Calderone (1904–1998)

One sex educator who faced more than her share of opposition was physician Mary Steichen Calderone. Calderone was the daughter (and frequent model) of famed photographer Edward Steichen. As such, she grew up in a bohemian atmosphere that celebrated the human body. On the other hand, Calderone recounted that her

Victorian mother made her wear metal "mittens" at night to discourage masturbation. Perhaps these beginnings helped foster her lifelong interest in sex and sex education.

Calderone graduated from Vassar College and the University of Rochester Medical School. In 1941 she married a leading public health expert, Frank Calderone. This marriage, as well as her lifelong Quaker faith, may have helped concentrate her attention on social issues. In 1953 she became medical director of the Planned Parenthood Federation. In that position she was able, in 1964, to get the American Medical Association to reverse its long-standing policy opposing birth control.

In 1964 Calderone became the director of a new organization, the Sexuality Information and Education Council of the United States (SIECUS). Among other efforts, SIECUS became involved in sex education programs for children. Calderone wrote or co-authored several popular books on this theme, with titles such as *The Family Book about Sexuality* (1981) and *Talking with Your Child about Sex* (1982), as well as books about family planning and marital happiness. (Most are now out of print.)

Before Calderone's time, sex education was largely a matter of warning young people about the dangers of sex, such as sexually transmitted diseases and unwanted preg-

nancy. Calderone took a different view. "We must block our habit of considering sex as a problem to be controlled," she said. "Emphasis must be on sex as a vital life force to be utilized." She encouraged educators to look beyond the nitty-gritty of sexual behavior. "Sex is not just something you do in marriage, in bed, in the dark, in one position," she declared. "Sex is what it means to be a man or a woman."

SIECUS had a major effect on sex education in schools. Its success triggered a noisy reaction from conservative groups, including the John Birch Society and the Christian Crusade. By the late 1960s every speech that Calderone gave was interrupted by hecklers, and organizations with names such as Mothers Organized for Moral Stability accused SIECUS of promoting teen sex and they described Calderone as an "aging libertine."

Although Calderone may have contributed to the sexual revolution of the 1960s, she herself was no sexual radical. She believed that coitus should take place only in the context of marriage, and while she advocated tolerance of homosexuality, she also hoped for a "cure." Thus, in her later years, she was somewhat left behind by changes in sexual attitudes. Still, her struggle to present young people with positive education about sexuality goes on today.

Sources: Moran, 2000; More, 2001.

Religious conservatives may oppose sex education programs in schools for a number of reasons. They may see sex education as a private matter that should be the prerogative of parents, not governments. They may feel that not enough emphasis is placed on abstinence from sexual activity. They may believe that, whatever the content of sex education programs, the effect will be to legitimize and promote sexual activity among teenagers, with associated harmful consequences.

Because of pressure from conservatives, which may be exerted by local communities as well as via financial incentives by the federal government, there is a strong emphasis on abstinence in school sex education today. According to a study by the Alan Guttmacher Institute, an organization that promotes research and education on family planning and reproductive health, 86 percent of school districts that have a policy on sex education mandate an emphasis on abstinence, and 35 percent prohibit all mention of contraceptive techniques except to stress their failure rates. Only 14 percent of sex education policies could be described as comprehensive, meaning that they teach about both abstinence and contraception as part of a broader program designed to prepare adolescents to become sexually healthy adults. Districts in the South are almost five times more likely to have an abstinence-only policy than are districts in the Northeast (Landry et al., 1999).

Box 1.4 *Society, Values, and the Law*

The World Association for Sexology's "Declaration of Sexual Rights"

The World Association for Sexology (WAS) represents 118 national sex-research organizations. At its 1999 World Congress, held in Hong Kong, WAS approved the following Declaration of Sexual Rights. Bear in mind while reading this document that, although it may reflect a consensus among the members of WAS, it touches on topics, such as gay rights and female circumcision (alluded to here as "mutilation"), on which there are differing views in different cultures around the world (see Box 3.1 and Chapter 13).

Sexuality is an integral part of the personality of every human being. Its full development depends upon the satisfaction of basic human needs such as the desire for contact, intimacy, emotional expression, pleasure, tenderness and love. Sexuality is constructed through the interaction between the individual and social structures. Full development of sexuality is essential for individual, interpersonal, and societal well being. Sexual rights are universal human rights based on the inherent freedom, dignity, and equality of all human beings. Since health is a fundamental human right, so must sexual health be a basic human right. In order to assure that human beings and societies develop healthy sexuality, the following sexual rights must be recognized, promoted, respected, and defended by all societies through all means. Sexual health is the result of an environment that recognizes, respects and exercises these sexual rights.

1. **The right to sexual freedom.** Sexual freedom encompasses the possibility for individuals to express their full sexual potential. However, this excludes all forms of sexual coercion, exploitation and abuse at any time and situations in life.

2. **The right to sexual autonomy, sexual integrity, and safety of the sexual body.** This right involves the ability to make autonomous decisions about one's sexual life within a context of one's own personal and social ethics. It also encompasses control and enjoyment of our own bodies free from torture, mutilation and violence of any sort.

3. **The right to sexual privacy.** This involves the right for individual decisions and behaviors about intimacy as long as they do not intrude on the sexual rights of others.

4. **The right to sexual equity.** This refers to freedom from all forms of discrimination regardless of sex, gender, sexual orientation, age, race, social class, religion, or physical and emotional disability.

5. **The right to sexual pleasure.** Sexual pleasure, including autoeroticism, is a source of physical, psychological, intellectual and spiritual well being.

6. **The right to emotional sexual expression.** Sexual expression is more than erotic pleasure or sexual acts. Individuals have a right to express their sexuality through communication, touch, emotional expression and love.

7. **The right to sexually associate freely.** This means the possibility to marry or not, to divorce, and to establish other types of responsible sexual associations.

8. **The right to make free and responsible reproductive choices.** This encom-passes the right to decide whether or not to have children, the number and spacing of children, and the right to full access to the means of fertility regulation.

9. **The right to sexual information based upon scientific inquiry.** This right implies that sexual information should be generated through the process of unencumbered and yet scientifically ethical inquiry, and disseminated in appropriate ways at all societal levels.

10. **The right to comprehensive sexuality education.** This is a lifelong process from birth throughout the life cycle and should involve all social institutions.

11. **The right to sexual health care.** Sexual health care should be available for prevention and treatment of all sexual concerns, problems and disorders.

Clara Haignere is a health education specialist at Temple University who has undertaken a detailed review of studies on the effectiveness of school sex education programs. According to her analysis, abstinence-only programs have little or no effect on teens' sexual behavior. Comprehensive programs, on the other hand, do cause teens to delay sexual activity and make them more likely to use contraception when they do become sexually active (Haignere et al., 1999). As we'll see in Chapter 16, successful sex education programs are those that start young and that take into account the social networks that mold and validate young people's opinions and behaviors.

Sex Research Is Becoming a Discipline in Its Own Right

As we have seen throughout this chapter, women and men in a variety of academic disciplines and other walks of life have made important contributions to our understanding of human sexuality. Increasingly, however, there is a perception that sex research is an academic discipline in its own right. This discipline is an unusual one in that it demands a training that crosses most of the intellectual boundaries that tradition has established.

The study of sex is sometimes referred to as **sexology,** although people who label themselves sexologists tend to be those who focus on sexual dysfunctions. **Sex research** is probably a broader and more widely understood term. However it is named, sex research is now fostered by numerous organizations at local, international, and global levels. In the United States, the Society for the Scientific Study of Sexuality (SSSS or "Quad-S") organizes national and regional meetings and publishes the *Journal of Sex Research* and other periodicals. The American Association of Sex Educators, Counselors, and Therapists (AASECT) certifies educational programs in sex education and therapy. There are also institutes devoted to research or training in issues of sexuality, such as the Kinsey Institute (which is affiliated with Indiana University), and special-purpose organizations such as the Alan Guttmacher Institute and the Sexuality Information and Education Council of the United States (SIECUS).

At an international level, two organizations stand out. The International Academy of Sex Research (IASR) organizes an annual meeting and publishes the *Archives of Sexual Behavior.* The World Association for Sexology (WAS) also holds an annual meeting and has promulgated a Universal Declaration of Sexual Rights (Box 1.4). The abstracts of WAS and IASR meetings are available online and offer an overview of current trends in sex research.

Summary

1. The word "sex" means the categories of male or female, or (in more recent usage) the entire phenomenon of sexual attraction and behavior. The word "gender" means the constellation of mental and behavioral traits that differ between males and females.

2. Sexual relationships are highly diverse: they may be motivated by a variety of different factors, they may be brief or durable, and they may be socially approved or stigmatized. Most sexual relationships involve some degree of mismatch or conflict that challenges the participants' adaptability and communication skills. Engaging in sexual relationships also requires ethical decisions—decisions that, while influenced by knowledge and reason, are based ultimately on a personal sense of what is right and wrong.

3. Many aspects of sex influence our sense of who we are—our identity. These include characteristics such as male, female, lesbian, gay, bisexual, heterosexual, transgendered, and many others. Sexual identities influence our place in society far beyond the sphere of persons with whom we have actual sexual contact.

4. Sexuality can be studied with a wide variety of approaches. The medical approach has elucidated many of the anatomical structures and physiological processes that underlie sexual and reproductive life. It has also sought to characterize and treat disorders of sexual desire and behavior, but this effort has involved controversial judgments as to the normality or abnormality of various forms of sexual expression.

5. The biological approach is grounded in the recognition that humans are animals who have evolved under natural selection. Biologists seek commonalities between the sexuality of human and nonhuman animals, but also look for unique features of human sexuality that reflect our particular niche as an intelligent and socially complex species.

6. The psychological approach falls into several subdisciplines. Social psychologists concern themselves with the diverse ways in which sex influences interpersonal relations. Psychobiologists focus on the biological underpinnings of sexual behavior, and often study this behavior in laboratory animals rather than humans. Cultural psy-

chologists study how cultural diversity affects sexual expression. Clinical psychologists and sex therapists deal with problems affecting sexual desire or performance.

7. Social scientists are concerned with the interactions between the sexuality of individuals and larger demographic groupings. Sex surveys are an important tool in this approach. An example of a theoretical social-science approach is sexual script theory: the notion that, as a result of constant interaction with others, people learn to play certain sexual roles.

8. The law regulates and limits sexual expression. In part, sex laws reflect a traditional or religion-based sexual morality. Although much sexual expression is essentially private, there are some consequences of sexual behavior that affect society as a whole. There may therefore be a practical or "economic" basis for the legal regulation of sex.

9. Feminists have greatly influenced attitudes about sex. Feminist ideas that have entered mainstream thinking include the notion that women are capable of and entitled to sexual pleasure, have a right to contraception and abortion, are entitled to protection from sexual violence, and are as capable as men in all spheres of life. Feminists have generally favored the idea that sexual attitudes—especially insofar as they differ between the sexes—result from socialization rather than from innate differences.

10. Ethical traditions can be broadly characterized as sex-negative (such as early Christian views on sex) or sex-positive (such as the attitudes of some Polynesian societies.) The basis for ethical judgments may change over time, leading to a revision of beliefs concerning what is right and wrong in the sphere of sexual behavior.

11. Sex has long been the subject of literature, art, and other modes of creative expression. Works that are intended to be sexually arousing constitute pornography; such works may be deemed obscene and subjected to legal restrictions. The regulation of pornography is a contentious sociopolitical issue.

12. Educators have faced a difficult struggle to communicate basic information about sex. Even today, there is a widespread fear that instruction in sexual matters, including techniques to avoid sexually transmitted diseases and unwanted pregnancy, may be seen as permitting or even encouraging sexual behavior by teenagers, but research suggests that the opposite may be true.

13. Sexology or sex research is gradually asserting itself as an independent and multidisciplinary field of study. National and international organizations, conferences, and journals are devoted to a rational, evidence-based approach to human sexuality.

Discussion Questions

1. After reading the "Declaration of Sexual Rights" (see Box 1.4), do you agree with everything in it? Do you think there are important topics that the Declaration fails to address? Should these rights be incorporated into the laws of all countries, or should local cultural standards (concerning homosexuality and female circumcision, for example) be respected?

2. According to its mission statement, the Sexuality Information and Education Council of the United States (SIECUS) "advocates the right of individuals to make responsible sexual choices." Should people also have the right to make *irresponsible* sexual choices? Where would you draw the line between sexual behaviors that should be permitted and those that should be outlawed, and on what grounds?

Web Resources

Kinsey Institute for Research in Sex, Gender, and Reproduction www.kinseyinstitute.org

American Association of Sex Educators, Counselors, and Therapists www.aasect.org

Society for the Scientific Study of Sexuality www.sexscience.org

International Academy of Sex Research www.iasr.org

World Association for Sexology www.worldsexology.org

Alan Guttmacher Institute www.guttmacher.org

Sexuality Information and Education Council of the United States www.siecus.org

Archive for Sexology—English language "megasite" at the University of Berlin
www2.hu-berlin.de/sexology/

Recommended Reading

Bullough, V. L. (1994). *Science in the bedroom: A history of sex research.* New York: Basic
Books.
Bullough, V. L., & Bullough, B. (1994). *Human sexuality: An encyclopedia.* New York:
Garland.
Francoeur, R. T. (1997–2001). *The international encyclopedia of sexuality.* New York:
Continuum.
(All three of these books are available online at the Archive for Sexology—see "Web
Resources" above.)

chapter 2

Like humans and countless other animals, these copulating common blue damselflies have evolved to reproduce sexually.

Sex and Evolution

*O*ur sexuality evolved from the sex lives of nonhuman creatures that preceded us in the long history of life on Earth. By studying this evolutionary process, we can hope to find clues to some very basic "Why?" questions about ourselves: Why are we sexual beings? Why are there two sexes? Why are there approximately equal numbers of men and women? Why do we find some people more attractive than others? Why don't all sex acts lead to pregnancy? Why are men more interested in casual sex than women? Why do we sometimes cheat on our partners? And why do we sometimes remain faithful? The study of evolution may not provide complete answers to these questions, but it does remind us that answers are needed, for nothing about human sexuality is as obvious as it may seem at first glance.

Most of the examples and research studies described in this chapter feature nonhuman animals. This may seem an odd way to begin a textbook on human sexuality. Later in the book, however, we will often have cause to compare ourselves with other animals and to consider human sexuality against the background of the evolutionary principles discussed here.

A Variety of Methods of Reproduction Has Evolved

Evolution has led not just to humans, but to over a million other species that currently inhabit Earth, plus millions more that are now extinct. Although we humans like to think of ourselves as the high point of evolution—perhaps even its ultimate goal—scientists have discovered nothing special about our position on the evolutionary tree that would support this notion. Instead, we seem to be just one leaf out of many. And the sex lives of humans, remarkably diverse though they are, still occupy just a tiny corner of the range of sexual behavior that exists or has existed on this planet.

The principles of evolution were laid out by Charles Darwin in *The Origin of Species* (1859). Individuals within a single species differ slightly from one another—whether it be in the length of their noses, the speed of their running, or their preference for one food over another. In part, these differences are **heritable**—they are passed down from parent to offspring. If circumstances favor the survival and reproduction of animals with a certain heritable trait (such as the ability to run fast), that trait will be passed on to more offspring and will become more prevalent in succeeding generations. If a trait is disadvantageous, it will be passed on to fewer offspring and will tend to die out. This process is **natural selection,** and it is the essential kernel of evolution.

We now know that heritable traits are encoded by **genes,** and that genes are linear stretches of a polymer called **deoxyribonucleic acid (DNA)** that is strung out along **chromosomes** within the nucleus of each cell in an organism. There are an estimated 30,000–60,000 genes in the human **genome** (the exact number is not yet known), and any two people will show differences in many of these genes. It is the combined instructions contained in all these genes, interacting with the diverse environments in which we develop, that make each of us uniquely human.

The main ingredient in evolution is time—lots of it (Figure 2.1). It is now about 4.6 billion years since the formation of our Earth, about 3.9 billion years since it became hospitable to life, and at least 3.7 billion years since life actually arose (Rosing, 1999). Thus, evolution has had at least 3.7 billion years to create the diversity of species that exists on Earth today.

The nature of the very earliest life forms is a matter of speculation, but the earliest organisms to use DNA as their genetic repository were microscopic, single-celled organisms without nuclei that reproduced by binary fission (splitting in two). They also readily swapped DNA between individuals. This early form of gene swapping was probably quite disorganized; it may have simply involved the uptake of fragments of DNA released by dead organisms.

Present-day bacteria also swap DNA, but they do so through a specific mechanism called **conjugation** (Figure 2.2). Two bacteria become connected by a fine hairlike tube called a *pilus,* and a short piece of DNA called a *plasmid* passes through the pilus from the donor to the recipient bacterium. The plasmid may later become integrated into the recipient bacterium's main genome. One way in which bacterial conjugation affects humans is that it offers a means by which genes conferring resistance to antibiotics can pass from one strain of bacteria to another, thus complicating our efforts to treat infectious diseases.

Organisms composed of nucleated cells—**eukaryotes**—probably appeared between 3 billion and 2 billion years ago. Initially they were all single-celled organisms, like present-day amoebas, but multicellular eukaryotes (both animals and plants) appeared about 1.5 billion years ago. Eukaryotic animals greatly diversified in the so-called Cambrian explosion, 545 million years ago, when all the main kinds of body plans that now exist—arthropod, vertebrate, sponge, and so on—first appeared.

Eukaryotic cells divide by **mitosis** (Box 2.1). Mitosis is the commonest form of reproduction by single-celled eukaryotic organisms. Many multicellular animals are also capable of

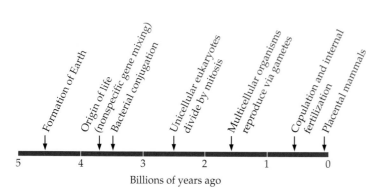

Figure 2.1 A brief history of sex. Dates are approximate.

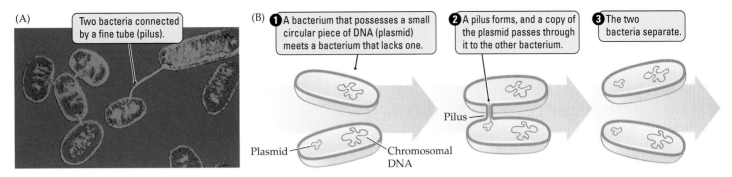

(A) Two bacteria connected by a fine tube (pilus).

(B) ❶ A bacterium that possesses a small circular piece of DNA (plasmid) meets a bacterium that lacks one.

❷ A pilus forms, and a copy of the plasmid passes through it to the other bacterium.

❸ The two bacteria separate.

Pilus

Plasmid

Chromosomal DNA

Figure 2.2 Bacterial conjugation.

reproduction by mitosis: a single cell or collection of cells from one organism undergoes repeated mitosis, creating an entire new organism. This new organism is genetically identical to its parent. One example that you may have heard about is the reproduction of hydra and other microscopic animals by a simple budding process; another is the propagation of plants from cuttings. Reproduction by means of mitosis is **asexual.**

Nearly all eukaryotic organisms also have the capacity for **sexual reproduction**. The key feature of sexual reproduction is the mixing of genes from two individuals. This mixing occurs through the fusion of two specialized cells known as **gametes** (Figure 2.3), each of which contributes chromosomes to the new organism. In order to keep the number of chromosomes constant from one generation to the next, the gametes are usually **haploid;** that is, they contain half the number of chromosomes contained in the regular, **diploid** cells of the same organism. Haploid gametes are produced by a special sequence of cell divisions known as **meiosis** (see Box 2.1) that takes place within reproductive tissues (**gonads**).

Except for Dolly the sheep and other animals that have been produced in the laboratory by artificial cloning techniques, all mammals are the products of sexual reproduction. In fact, most vertebrates reproduce exclusively by sexual means. Among invertebrate animals and plants, many species have the capacity to reproduce either sexually or asexually. The propagation of flowering plants either from seeds or from cuttings is a well-known example. It is rare, however, to find eukaryotic organisms that rely exclusively on asexual reproduction.

Rival Theories Offer Explanations for Sexual Reproduction

The fact that nearly all multicellular organisms are capable of sexual reproduction, and that most vertebrates rely on it exclusively, tells us that the capacity for this form of reproduction must be **adaptive;** that is, it must help the organism that uses it to perpetuate its genes in future generations. How does it do so?

Surprisingly, the answer to this very basic question is a bit of a mystery. On the face of it, asexual reproduction is more adaptive than sexual reproduction. That's because an animal that reproduces asexually devotes all its resources to passing on its own genes, and those genes are perpetuated in any and all of its descendants. An animal that reproduces sexually, on the other hand, willingly dilutes its genes with those of another animal, thus reducing the representation of its own genes in future generations. It seems like a pointless self-sacrifice. This paradox is particularly striking in species in which one sex—usually the female—invests far more in reproduction than the other. In such species, it would seem that females would do better to give birth **parthenogenetically** (by asexual "virgin birth") rather than to give some male's genes a free ride into the next generation. Yet, with a few exceptions, females in such species engage in sexual reproduction some or all of the time.

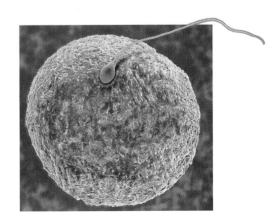

Figure 2.3 Gametes. A sperm and an ovum.

Box 2.1 Biology of Sex

The Cellular Basis of Reproduction

Many organisms can reproduce either asexually, by means of mitosis (Figure A), or sexually, by means of meiosis and fertilization (Figure B). Unicellular organisms, and simple multicellular invertebrates such as Hydra, reproduce asexually most of the time and sexually less often. Most vertebrates, including humans as well as all other mammals, reproduce only sexually, so their gametes are produced by meiosis (we'll describe an interesting exception in Box 2.2). All other cells in the body are produced by mitosis.

(A) Asexual reproduction by mitosis. Only selected phases are shown here.

A diploid cell contains several pairs of homologous chromosomes. One pair is shown here.

Interphase   Mitosis

G1 Phase
Chromosomes prepare for DNA replication.

S Phase
DNA of each chromosome is replicated to form sister chromatids.

G2 Phase
Each chromosome now consists of two sister chromatids. There is no interaction between homologous chromosomes.

Metaphase
Nuclear membrane breaks down and mitotic spindle forms.

Anaphase
Sister chromatids are pulled apart.

Cell division
Each daughter cell has a copy of every chromosome, so is diploid like its parent.

(B) Sexual reproduction involves meiosis. Only the key phases are shown here.

Mother

Diploid parental cells contain several pairs of homologous chromosomes. One pair is shown here in each cell.

DNA replication. Each chromosome becomes two sister chromatids.

Meiosis I
Homologous chromosomes join to form tetrads.

Genetic exchange takes place between homologous chromosomes…

…which are pulled apart at anaphase.

After cell division, each daughter cell is haploid—it contains half the number of parental chromosomes, each of which consists of two sister chromatids.

Father

Sexual Reproduction May Limit Harmful Mutations

One theory suggests that sexual reproduction is adaptive because it helps organisms deal with the problem of harmful **mutations.** Mutations are random changes in an organism's genome caused by errors in the copying of DNA or by damaging chemicals, sunlight, or radiation. Many mutations are neutral—they have no effect on an organism's ability to survive and reproduce—but of those that are not neutral, far more are harmful than beneficial, just as random changes in computer software, for example, would be far more likely to degrade its performance than to improve it.

When organisms reproduce asexually, harmful mutations tend to accumulate over the generations. Because all the descendants of a given animal possess all of that animal's genes, there is no way to get rid of a harmful mutation short of eliminating that entire lineage. When organisms reproduce sexually, on the other hand, harmful mutations *can* be eliminated. That's because offspring receive a randomly selected half of their mother's genes and half of their father's genes. If one parent carries a particular damaged gene, about half of that parent's offspring will not inherit it—they will inherit the normal version of the gene from the other parent instead.

In reality, most organisms carry numerous harmful mutations. Thus each offspring is likely to inherit some harmful mutations from each parent. But because of the lottery-like nature of sexual reproduction, some of the offspring will receive a greater total load of harmful mutations, and other offspring will receive fewer. Natural selection will, of course, favor the survival and reproduction of the offspring with fewer harmful mutations. Thus, sexual reproduction may help maintain an equilibrium state in a population of organisms, in which the appearance of new harmful mutations is balanced by the gradual elimination of old ones.

This advantage of sexual reproduction should outweigh the disadvantage mentioned above (the dilution of an organism's genes), but only if certain conditions apply (Kondrashov, 1988). The rate of appearance of new harmful mutations has to be high enough (more than about one new mutation per generation), and the harmful mutations have to interact syn-

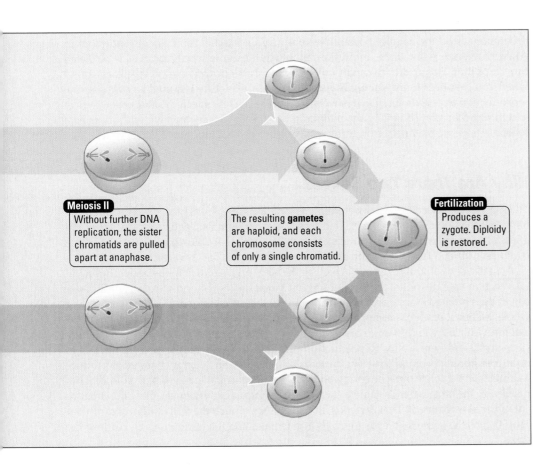

Meiosis II
Without further DNA replication, the sister chromatids are pulled apart at anaphase.

The resulting **gametes** are haploid, and each chromosome consists of only a single chromatid.

Fertilization
Produces a zygote. Diploidy is restored.

ergistically (i.e., two mutations must be more than twice as bad as one). Only then will there be sufficient differences among offspring that natural selection can effectively weed out those carrying many mutations. There is dispute about whether these conditions generally apply (Lynch et al., 1999; Keightley & Eyre-Walker, 2000), and for that reason it is not known whether this theory adequately explains why sexual reproduction is so common.

Sexual Reproduction May Generate Beneficial Gene Combinations

Another theory ignores the matter of harmful mutations and attributes the value of sexual reproduction to the novel combinations of genes that it produces. Having offspring with different combinations of genes might be useful because those offspring would have different ways of utilizing the resources available in the environment (eating different foods, for example). In this case, the offspring would compete less with one another for available resources, so that their parents could have more surviving offspring than otherwise possible. Alternatively, the mixing of genes might be useful in dealing with changes in the environment. For example, many species engage in an endless war with parasites, in which the parasites are constantly evolving new ways to outwit the host's defenses. Gene mixing may be an effective way for the host species to rapidly develop new defenses against these ever-changing attacks (Hamilton et al., 1981). Finally, gene mixing provides a means to take advantage of the occasional *beneficial* mutation. With asexual reproduction, such beneficial mutations are forever coupled with the harmful mutations preexisting in the same animal, but with sexual reproduction, beneficial mutations can be separated from harmful ones.

Future Research May Resolve the Puzzle

We don't know which of these theories is correct—perhaps *both* of them are. Several avenues of future research may help clarify the issue. One avenue is that of in vitro evolution, in which researchers observe evolution happening within a laboratory population of fast-breeding organisms. In such a setting, it is possible to breed the organisms in different environments (with and without parasites, for example) to see whether these differences affect the balance between sexually and asexually reproducing individuals. Another avenue is "in silico" evolution, in which the evolutionary process is modeled by a computer. This approach can test whether theories—however good they may sound when you first hear them—actually have the logical structure required to cause sexual reproduction to persist. Finally, it is worth studying the few species that *never* engage in sexual reproduction (Box 2.2). By analyzing how these species survive without sexual reproduction, we may better understand why sex is so essential for the rest of us.

Why Are There Two Sexes?

The theories just discussed offer potential explanations for why organisms reproduce sexually, but they don't explain the existence of males and females. After all, why shouldn't a sexually reproducing species consist of individuals that are all alike, any two of which could pair off and fuse their gametes ("sex without sexes," as it were)?

Actually, sex without sexes might well be the ideal arrangement for a species. But natural selection operates not at the level of species, but at the level of individuals. For that reason, it does not necessarily produce arrangements that would be ideal for the species as a whole. Rather, it produces compromises—states in which the conflicting interests of countless individuals are in dynamic equilibrium. Sex without sexes is not generally an equilibrium state, and here's why. Reproduction requires an **investment**—a commitment of resources. For many organisms, that investment is the time and energy required to produce a gamete. That gamete must be endowed with enough nutrient material so that, once it has fused with the other parent's gamete, it can develop into a new organism. How much nutrient material is required? That depends, in part, on how much the *other* parent contributes. Thus begins the game that leads to males and females and the never-ending "battle of the sexes."

Box 2.2   Biology of Sex

The Paradox of Sexless Species

Cnemidophorus uniparens is a slender whiptail lizard that lives in arid environments in the southwestern United States. Remarkably, this species consists entirely of females, who reproduce parthenogenetically. Although they never reproduce sexually, the lizards do in engage in sexual behavior (Figure A). In these encounters, one female takes the "female" role and another takes the "male" role. Any particular lizard may show either "female" or "male" behavior, depending on where she is in her ovarian cycle (see Chapter 4). If she is in the preovulatory phase (when eggs are maturing in her ovary), she will show "female" behavior, but if she is in the postovulatory phase (when the eggs are moving down her oviduct and acquiring their shells) she will show "male" behavior. Because neither animal has a testis or penis, however, there is no actual sexual penetration or transfer of sperm. The females' eggs are generated by mitosis rather than meiosis, and they do not require fertilization to develop into offspring.

According to zoologist David Crews of the University of Texas at Austin, the *C. uniparens* species has arisen recently by hybridization between two other, sexually reproducing *Cnemidophorus* species, and it has inherited their patterns of sexual behavior. The sexual encounters between females, although not involving the transfer of sperm, do facilitate reproduction: the encounters trigger hormonal changes that promote egg development and ovulation (Crews et al., 1986).

If the ability to reproduce sexually is beneficial, how does *C. uniparens* do without it? A key factor may be the recent origin of the species. In the short term, an organism that reproduces asexually may be favored, because its offspring expand clonally and therefore can rapidly fill its ecological niche. Without sexual reproduction, however, *C. uniparens* may accumulate an increasing load of harmful mutations as the generations go by. If so, it may eventually be outcompeted and driven to extinction by sexually reproducing *Cnemidophorus* species.

An even greater puzzle is presented by a group of animals called bdelloid rotifers (Figure B). These tiny tubelike creatures can be found in almost any freshwater environment, and they move around like leeches ("bdelloid" means "leechlike"). They are known to have existed for at least 40 million years, because they have been found preserved in amber of that age. And they are not just one species, but an entire class of invertebrates, with at least 352 member species. Yet no one has seen a bdelloid reproduce sexually—in fact, no one has ever come across a male bdelloid. Of course, sex can be hard to spot—an anthropologist from Mars might not catch *humans* having sex for quite a while. There are many species that usually reproduce parthenogenetically but occasionally engage in sex, and many scientists suspected that the bdelloid rotifers might do the same. According to this idea, even one in a thousand sexual births might be enough to reap the benefits that sexual reproduction is supposed to confer.

That theory was tested by Harvard molecular biologist Matthew Meselson and his postdoctoral student David Mark Welch (Mark Welch & Meselson, 2000). Meselson and Mark Welch analyzed the DNA of several species of bdelloids. They found exactly the patterns that would be expected in organisms that stopped mixing their genes tens of millions of years ago. Essentially, they proved that bdelloids have been totally celibate all this time and are none the worse for it.

How, then, have bdelloids done without sex? If the benefit of sex lies in the generation of new, beneficial combinations of genes to combat environmental threats such as parasites, it may be that the bdelloids have found other means to combat those threats. Alternatively, if the benefit of sex lies in the elimination of harmful mutations, the bdelloids may have found ways to prevent those mutations or to correct them once they occur. These alternative strategies presumably have costs of their own. Thus, the further study of bdelloids could help explain why the rest of us find sex so necessary.

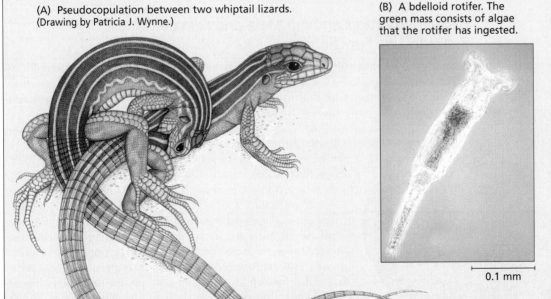

(A) Pseudocopulation between two whiptail lizards. (Drawing by Patricia J. Wynne.)

(B) A bdelloid rotifer. The green mass consists of algae that the rotifer has ingested.

0.1 mm

Isogametes

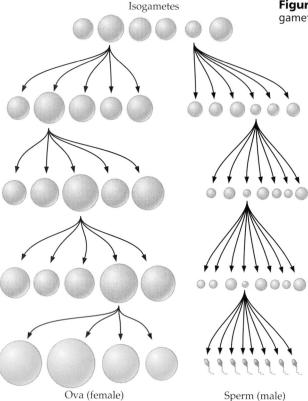

Ova (female)

Sperm (male)

Figure 2.4 Disruptive selection splits a single population of medium-sized gametes into large (female) and small (male) types.

Let's consider a hypothetical sex without sexes species, in which the gametes of all individuals are roughly similar in size and nutrient content (Figure 2.4). Even so, there will be some natural variation, so that some individuals will produce slightly larger gametes and some will produce slightly smaller ones. Individuals that produce larger gametes, containing more nutrients, will be favored by natural selection because those gametes stand a better chance of developing into offspring. But individuals that produce smaller gametes will also be favored, because such gametes require a smaller investment. And as long as there are some larger gametes around to fuse with, those smaller gametes can still develop into offspring. The only individuals that are not especially favored are those that produce middle-sized gametes, so those individuals tend to die out. Thus the population gradually diverges into two groups pursuing different strategies. One group follows a "nurturing" strategy and produces large, nutrient-loaded gametes (**ova** or eggs); the other follows an "exploitative" strategy and produces small, nutrient-poor gametes (**sperm**) (see Figure 2.3). This process whereby natural selection divides one population into two is called **disruptive selection.** The two groups that result are females and males, respectively.

There are several other factors that come into play. For one thing, there is the question of mobility. To fuse, gametes need to come together, which usually means that at least one of the gametes has to be motile. It is much easier for small gametes to move than large ones, so gametes produced by males are usually the motile ones. There is also the matter of numbers. Because each sperm requires so little investment to produce, males can produce many more sperm than females can produce ova. Indeed, some factors that we'll consider below often make it essential for males to produce large numbers of sperm. Thus, the total investment in gamete production may end up being similar in the two sexes.

Hermaphrodites Combine Male and Female Reproductive Functions

Although we usually think of males and females as being two different kinds of individuals within a species, it is not uncommon for individuals to combine male and female reproductive functions within a single body. Such individuals are called **hermaphrodites**. In some species, including most flowering plants and trees as well as some invertebrate animals such as worms and mollusks, all the individuals are hermaphrodites, and there are no pure males or females.

One might imagine that hermaphrodites would fertilize themselves. Such self-fertilization, however, would nullify much of the advantage that sexual reproduction is thought to confer. Thus, in hermaphroditic species, there generally exist mechanisms to prevent the fusion of male and female gametes from the same individual. Male and female gametes may be generated at different times, or at distant locations on the organism. In many plants, self-fertilization is prevented by molecular genetic tricks that make male and female gametes from the same plant incompatible. In hermaphroditic animals, there are often behavioral mechanisms that prevent self-fertilization.

About one in a hundred thousand human babies is born with gonadal tissue of both sexes. Such persons are sometimes called "true hermaphrodites." They do not have the external genitalia of both sexes, however, and they are not able to reproduce both as females and as males. In fact, most are infertile except

This banana slug (*Aeolidiella glauca*) is a simultaneous hermaphrodite: it produces both sperm and eggs at the same time. It does not fertilize itself, however, so it must find another slug to mate with.

with medical assistance. The condition is better termed "gonadal intersexuality," and it is considered an error of sexual differentiation (see Chapter 5).

Can There Be More Than Two Sexes?

Imaginative writers have envisioned species with multiple sexes: William Tenn, for example, wrote a book titled *The Seven Sexes* (Tenn, 1968). No one has actually found a species with more than two sexes on Earth, however, so we may have to wait until we make contact with extraterrestrial beings before we find out whether multiple sexes are a workable arrangement.

Although no species has more than two sexes in the usual sense, there are species in which individuals of the same sex can have different reproductive roles. For example, some individuals of one sex may be temporarily or permanently sterile or reproductively inactive. A well-known example is found among bees, ants, and termites, in which only a single female in a colony (the queen) is fertile; the rest are sterile workers. In the African cichlid fish *Haplochromis burtoni*, large, brightly colored males do all the mating with females, while small, drab males remain sexually inactive. If the reproductive male in a group dies, one of the inactive males is transformed physically and behaviorally into a reproductive male (Fernald, 1993). Among domesticated sheep, some rams (male sheep) have a strong preference for engaging in sex with other rams, and there are differences between the brain organization of these "homosexual" rams and that of "heterosexual" rams (Perkins et al., 1995). Whether homosexual rams exist in wild populations, and what the evolutionary significance of such behavior may be, remains unknown.

There are two main kinds of individuals in a termite nest: fertile "reproductives" (the single queen and king), and sterile workers and soldiers, who may be of either sex. In this photo, workers attend to the queen, the large object in the center. A soldier can be seen at the bottom right.

Why Are There Equal Numbers of Males and Females?

From a human perspective, the reason for an equal sex ratio seems obvious. After all, since most of us desire to form sexual partnerships with a member of the other sex, any significant imbalance in the numbers of males and females would leave a lot of people without partners. So it seems only right and proper that about half of all babies are boys and half are girls.

However, roughly equal numbers of males and females are also seen in species in which males and females don't partner up, or do so in very unequal proportions. Among langur monkeys, for example, a dominant male controls a harem of a dozen or so female partners. Among elks, a single bull controls up to sixty females. This leaves most males with no partners; unless they can displace the dominant male, they have little chance of reproducing. In species like these, wouldn't it be better to have more females than males? In fact, given that males of most species can inseminate large numbers of females, wouldn't it be the best arrangement generally to have an excess of females? That way, resources would be consumed primarily by the sex that needs them to keep the species going.

Again, we have to understand that evolution doesn't necessarily lead to the "ideal arrangement" for the species, but to a compromise between the conflicting interests of individuals. Let's imagine that the "ideal arrangement" actually existed, so that among langur monkeys, for example, a female typically gave birth to ten daughters for every son, and there were therefore ten times as many

A single dominant bull elk controls a harem of many females, so many subordinate males are left without sex partners.

female langurs as males. For a while, things would be idyllic: each male would have his harem, every female would have all the offspring she was capable of, and resources would be distributed efficiently.

This situation would not last, however. If a particular female underwent a genetic change such that she produced more sons than daughters, she would gain a tremendous advantage. Each of her sons would be able to mate with numerous females, so she would have far more grandchildren than if she produced mostly daughters. Obviously, the genes for producing an excess of sons would spread through the population, and the sex ratio would drift toward equality. Conversely, if there were a species in which females produced a dozen sons for every daughter, so that there was a vast excess of males in the population, genes for producing *females* would be advantageous and would spread, and again the sex ratio would drift toward equality. So, in practice, the sex ratio usually remains near equality.

This general principle is liable to be modified by a variety of factors, however, so one doesn't always get a sex ratio of exactly 1:1 (Godfray & Werren, 1996). Among humans, for example, males are more vulnerable than females: at every phase of life, starting with conception, males are more likely to die. This higher death rate among males results both from greater disease susceptibility and from behavioral factors such as greater risk-taking. Thus, if equal numbers of males and females were conceived, there would be a marked excess of females during the reproductive years. This in turn could make bearing sons a more attractive option. In reality, the sex ratio at birth does slightly favor males: about 104–107 boys are born for every 100 girls (Chahnazarian, 1991).

Evolution Has Led to Diverse Methods of Sex Determination

Seeing that so many species throughout the animal kingdom have settled on the two-sex system, one might expect that the mechanisms of **sex determination**—of controlling whether an embryo becomes male or female—would also have become fixed early in evolution, and would now be universal. The truth, however, is quite the opposite: Evolution has seen fit to develop a variety of mechanisms of sex determination, even among related species of animals (Mittwoch, 1996).

Sex May Be Determined by Chromosomes

In humans, and in most mammals, an embryo's sex is determined by the chromosomes it possesses (Figure 2.5). Forty-four of our 46 chromosomes are known as **autosomes;** they come in 22 homologous (corresponding) pairs, regardless of a person's sex. With the remaining two chromosomes, the **sex chromosomes,** the situation is more complicated. Females do possess a homologous pair of sex chromosomes, termed **X chromosomes,** but males possess one X chromosome and one much smaller chromosome, called a **Y chromosome.**

Now recall that gametes are produced by meiosis, in which the number of chromosomes is halved. Thus, ova receive 22 autosomes and one X chromosome. Sperm, on the other hand, receive 22 autosomes and either one X or one Y. Thus, when the ovum and sperm fuse at fertilization, the resulting **zygote** receives an X from the ovum and either an X or a Y from the sperm. If an X, the zygote will develop as a female; if a Y, as a male. Since there are roughly equal numbers of X-bearing and Y-bearing sperm, the chances of an offspring being female or male are approximately equal.

It turns out that in humans and nearly all mammals, it is the tiny Y chromosome that determines sex. If one studies the occasional humans who possess unusual combinations of sex chromosomes, such as X, XXX, XXY, or XYY, one finds that any individual possessing at least one Y chromosome will be male; all others will be female. This finding suggests that there is a sex-determining gene on the Y chromosome and that the effect of this gene is to confer maleness; in its absence, zygotes develop as females.

Rare individuals are exceptions to the rule just mentioned. For example, there are a very few XX individuals who are nevertheless male. In these individuals, the sex-determining gene is located on an X rather than a Y chromosome. Molecular genetic analysis of these individuals led to the discovery of the actual sex-determining gene, which has been called *SRY*. This discovery, made by a British research group in 1990 (Sinclair et al., 1990), was a landmark in sex research. Its significance is discussed further in Chapter 5.

Some species of reptiles, amphibians, and fish use a chromosomal mechanism of sex determination very similar to what is seen in mammals, but other mechanisms exist as well. In birds, sex is determined by chromosomes, but it is the females, rather than the males, that possess dissimilar sex chromosomes (they are called Z and W); the males possess two Z's. Thus it may be that the W chromosome carries a gene conferring femaleness and that individuals without this gene develop as males.

In the fruit fly (*Drosophila*), females are XX and males are XY, as in humans, but there the similarity ends. If one creates XXY fruit flies in the laboratory, they turn out to be female, showing that the Y chromosome doesn't confer maleness. It turns out that genes predisposing fruit flies to femaleness are located on the X chromosome, but genes predisposing them to maleness are located on the autosomes. The actual sex of a fly depends on the ratio of the two kinds of genes, so flies with one X are male, and flies with two X's are female.

There is another important difference between sex determination in flies and mammals. In flies, sexual differentiation is *cell-autonomous*—each cell develops according to its own chromosomal makeup. In mammals, by contrast, sexual differentiation is controlled largely by circulating sex hormones (see Chapter 5).

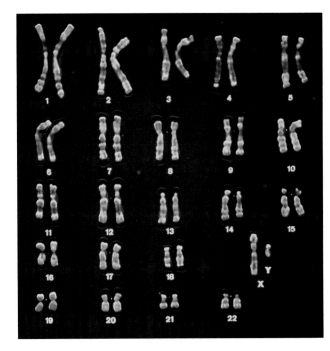

Figure 2.5 Human chromosomes. Men and women have the same autosomes (chromosome pairs 1–22), but different sex chromosomes: women have two X's, men have 1 X and 1 Y (as shown here at lower right).

Sex May Be Determined by Temperature

In many species of reptiles, amphibians, and fish, sex is not determined by chromosomal patterns at all, but by the temperature at which the eggs are incubated. Thus, in a turtle known as the red-eared slider (*Trachemys scripta*), clutches of eggs incubated at 26°C develop as all males, clutches incubated at 31°C develop as all females, and clutches incubated at intermediate temperatures develop as a mixture of males and females. Among lizards and alligators it's the other way around: low temperatures produce females and high temperatures produce males. And in the snapping turtle (*Chelydra serpentina*), both low and high temperatures produce females, whereas intermediate temperatures produce males.

It's not clear whether there is any rhyme or reason to this diversity. Obviously, mammals such as ourselves cannot use the temperature-dependent sex determination mechanism, because the uterine environment in which we develop is kept at a fixed temperature. There may be some basic similarities between the temperature-dependent and the chromosomal mechanisms, however: both influence the rate of development, especially of gonadal tissue, and the differentiation of the gonads into **ovaries** (in females) or **testes** (in males). The gonads, in turn, secrete sex hormones that affect the sexual differentiation of other regions of the body (see Chapter 5).

Sexual Selection Produces Anatomical and Behavioral Differences between Males and Females

In many respects, natural selection acts similarly on females and males. It has ensured that women and men are both adapted to life on land, for example, and that female and male fish are both adapted to life in water. Yet marked differences can develop between males and females of a single species. Think of peacocks and peahens, for example: the males strut to and fro and rustle their gorgeous tail feathers, while the plain females watch silently, evaluate their prospective mates, and decide which male to mate with. Such differences in the appearance and behavior of males and females result from competition for mates. Charles Darwin called this process **sexual selection.**

Males and Females Follow Different Reproductive Strategies

Two common, though not universal, features of sexual selection are competition among males and choice by females. These features result from the differing strategies adopted by males and females at the very origin of the two sexes. Females, as mentioned above, commit themselves to a "nurturing" strategy by virtue of their investment in large, nutrient-rich ova, while males commit themselves to an "exploitative" strategy by virtue of their production of small, nutrient-poor sperm. In some animals, the continuation of these strategies has led to very marked differences in the roles played by the two sexes in reproduction.

Female mammals, for example, carry the burden of **internal fertilization** followed by a prolonged period of **gestation** (pregnancy), which may last from 2 or 3 weeks (in rodents) to 22 months (in elephants). Following **parturition** (delivery of their young), female mammals continue to nourish them through **lactation** (milk production), and usually provide most or all of the care and protection that mammalian infants require. This prolonged investment results in offspring that have a far greater chance of surviving to adulthood than the young of other vertebrates, but it also greatly limits the total number of offspring that female mammals can produce in a lifetime. A female frog can produce hundreds or thousands of tadpoles; a woman can produce only about a dozen children.

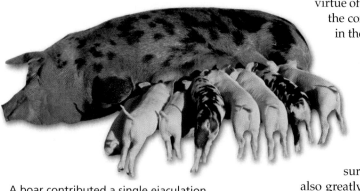

A boar contributed a single ejaculation to the production of this litter of piglets; the sow must fully provide for them from conception through weaning.

Males, on the other hand, can often get away with a very small investment in reproduction—a few drops of **semen** containing sperm. In theory, a male mammal could father as many offspring as a female frog produces tadpoles, simply by inseminating female after female and walking away from each. But that is reckoning without two practical constraints: competition from other males, and the ability of females to choose whom they mate with, as we'll see below.

Females and Males Are Exposed to Different Reproductive Risks

Females and males typically experience different kinds of risks in their reproductive lives. For a female, the maximum number of potential offspring is rather low, but her chances of having close to this number are quite good, since there are plenty of males willing to mate with her. The variation in the number of offspring that females produce is therefore quite limited. The risk for a female is not so much that she will produce few offspring, but that her offspring will fail to survive and reproduce in their turn. To maximize the likelihood that her offspring will survive, she needs not only to invest her own resources in them, but also to ensure that they are fathered by the best available male. (What "best" means, we'll discuss in a moment.)

For a male, the reproductive risks are different. Males, as just mentioned, can have enormous numbers of offspring, but they can all too easily end up having none. Earlier, we mentioned the langur monkeys and elks, in which dominant males control large harems of females, leaving subordinate males without mates. A dominant male fathers many offspring every year, at least so long as he can maintain his position. Subordinate males will have no offspring at all unless they can displace a dominant male or evade his surveillance. Although there are wide differences among species, it is rather typical that males face a great risk of having few or no offspring. Choosing among females tends to be a lesser concern.

Males Often Compete for Access to Females

Because of these differing reproductive risks, males often compete with one another for access to females, while females often choose among males. We should emphasize right away, though, that words such as "compete" and "choose" are really figures of speech. We don't mean to imply that animals consciously try to achieve certain goals—we don't know enough about animals' minds to make such assertions. All we are saying is that, for one reason or another, animals behave *as if* they have certain goals in mind.

What traits are influenced by sexual selection? Competition among males naturally leads to selection for traits that confer success in competition. The most obvious such traits are large size and physical strength; males are commonly larger and stronger than females, especially among mammals. Along with these physical traits goes the behavioral trait of aggressiveness—the willingness to engage in the interminable bouts of roaring, barking, head-butting, biting, kicking, clawing, and general mayhem that establish a male animal's dominance position, and hence his ability to mate with females.

Competition among males also favors traits that assist males in getting to receptive females before other males do. Such traits may include well-developed sensory skills that aid them in finding females, such as the ability to detect sexually attractive odors (**pheromones**) and to home in on their source. Another trait that helps males get to females quickly is early sexual maturation—early in life or early in the breeding season.

Male walruses compete with one another for access to females, so evolution has favored large males.

Yet another trait favored by male–male competition is sexual endurance—the ability to remain reproductively active for a long time. In some species of birds, for example, large numbers of males and females gather at a common mating site, or **lek.** A male bird that can remain sexually active at a lek longer than his competitors will have greater mating success, so males are selected for the ability to mate repeatedly over a long period of time. For females, on the other hand, the ability to mate repeatedly is less important (though it does have a role, as we'll see later).

Females Often Choose among Males

What about female choice? One obvious choice that females can make is to mate with healthy, genetically favored males. How can they identify such males? Just the fact that a male has battered other males into submission speaks volumes about his health and fitness, of course. Not all species engage in such male–male contests, however. If not, females may choose among males on the basis of their physical appearance or behavior.

Choice based on appearance   One aspect of males' appearance to which females often pay attention is their bodily symmetry. Vertebrates are roughly bilaterally symmetrical, at least in outward appearance. The developmental reason for this symmetry is that, aside from obviously asymmetrical structures such as the heart, a single set of genetic instructions directs the development of both sides of the body. Good genes operating in a good environment will therefore produce a highly symmetrical organism. Poor genes, or a poor environment, will disturb this process, leading to slight asymmetries. This kind of perturbation, in which the direction of asymmetry is random, is called **fluctuating asymmetry.** A high degree of fluctuating asymmetry has been correlated with a number of disadvantageous characteristics, such as chromosomal defects, infections, exposure to toxins, and environmental stress (Manning & Chamberlain, 1994; Polak & Trivers, 1994).

It turns out that animals are very good at assessing the symmetry of their **conspecifics** (other animals of the same species), and that they prefer to mate with highly symmetrical individuals. For example, manipulating the tail feathers of male barn swallows to make them less symmetrical renders those males less attractive to females (Møller, 1992). Thus there is sexual selection for symmetry, especially in males. In addition, females are selected for the cognitive skills required to evaluate symmetry.

Besides symmetry, females often look for other anatomical characteristics in males. Female barn swallows, for example, prefer those males whose outermost tail feathers are not just symmetrical, as just mentioned, but are also longer than those of other males. Female deer prefer the males with the largest antlers, female fish often prefer the most brightly colored males, and so on. Generally, the rule is: The bigger and brighter, the better—especially with regard to features that are obviously related to sexual display.

A close-up of a male atlas moth (*Attacus atlas*), showing the feathery antennae that can detect the female moth's sex pheromone at extremely low concentrations.

This peacock's ornate tail feather display is used by females to judge his general health and the quality of his genes.

Interestingly, this demand for "bigger and brighter" seems to be open-ended. If one exaggerates the features that females pay attention to—giving a male barn swallow an artificial tail longer than *any* male normally possesses, for example—such males will be preferred over any "natural" males. Because of this open-ended quality, sexual selection tends to lead to a runaway process in which the display characteristics of males become highly exaggerated. Nevertheless, something holds this process in check. The tails of male barn swallows are not getting longer, for example, even though a male with a super-long tail would attract a lot of females. The most plausible reason why the runaway process comes to a halt is that these displays have a *cost* for males. It takes an investment of food to grow long tail feathers. Large antlers hamper a stag's ability to move through the forest. Bright coloration attracts predators. At some point, the cost of these display features balances their reproductive advantage, so an equilibrium situation is reached.

Indeed, it is precisely the fact that these attractive features have a cost that makes them attractive (Zahavi and Zahavi, 1997). Only a peacock that is genetically well endowed, healthy, and has had ample access to food can sustain the cost of a tail ornate enough to attract peahens. What these displays say is, "I have been able to take on the incredible burden of this tail (or antlers or coloration) and still survive—so I must be a superior animal."

Choice based on behavior Besides choosing males on the basis of anatomical features, females also choose on the basis of **courtship behavior.** Sometimes this behavior is of obviously practical use to the female in producing young. Female spiders, for example, often demand that their suitors provide some food, such as a dead insect (failing which, the suitor himself may be eaten). Some female birds demand that the male provide a nesting site or actually construct a nest.

Besides the direct value of such gifts to the female, there's another, more subtle benefit. Demanding that a male provide resources tests his genetic fitness in the same way that demanding anatomical features such as ornate tail feathers does. Thus, it may be beneficial to the female to make the male spend resources, even if that expenditure does not benefit her in any direct way.

In fact, there are numerous instances in which courtship by males seems to involve useless make-work. Male bowerbirds, for example, have to construct elaborate thatched structures—bowers—and decorate them with all kinds of hard-to-find items, such as colored shells, berries, and bottle tops, before females will pay attention to their advances. The bowers have no practical value to the females—they are not nests—but they do have the indirect value of testing the male's fitness. Courtship song is another example: singing for hours at a time offers no practical benefit to anyone, but by doing so, a male bird advertises the fact that he is not foraging—and if he can survive so long without foraging, he must be a well-favored animal. Much courtship behavior has this flavor: males are forced to inflict handicaps on themselves—the behavioral equivalent of peacock's tails—just to prove that they are fit enough to withstand them.

So far, we've given the impression that females choose among males simply by passively assessing their courtship behavior. In fact, however, females often begin the whole thing. If you have ever been kept awake by caterwauling from your neighbor's rooftop, for example, you will know that female mammals advertise when they are sexually receptive. At around the time when they ovulate (see Chapter 4), when **copulation** (penile–vaginal sex) can result in fertilization, hor-

The male satin bowerbird (at right) is not as eye-catching as a peacock, but he makes up for it by building an elaborate bower and decorating its entrances with blue-colored objects, such as shells, berries, or bottle tops. If a female approves of his work, sex will take place within the avenue of the bower.

monal changes cause females to undergo **estrus,** or heat. Besides complex internal processes connected with ovulation, estrus involves the production of auditory, olfactory, or visual signals intended to alert males to the female's receptive state.

Females also may approach individual males and show **proceptive behavior**—behavior designed to elicit reciprocal courtship. Estrous female mice and rats, for example, perform a hopping, darting, and ear-wiggling routine that may induce the male to attempt a mount. During the remainder of their ovarian cycle, when fertilization is not possible, females do not make these displays or approach males, and they forcefully reject male courtship.

When rodents are observed in seminatural conditions, females can be seen to control the details of mating in an even more precise way. A male rat needs to copulate with a female several times before he ejaculates, and he ejaculates most readily if the copulations are spaced close together—less than a minute apart. Females, on the other hand, are more likely to become pregnant if the copulations are spaced further apart. That's because, in rats, sensory stimuli produced in the vagina during copulation evoke the release of hormones from the pituitary gland, and these hormones are necessary for the establishment of pregnancy. Each individual female has her own "best frequency" of copulation, the frequency that is most likely to elicit the hormonal conditions necessary for pregnancy (Adler & Toner, 1986). This frequency has been described as a **vaginal code.** By her pattern of approach and escape behavior, she ensures that the male, whether he likes it or not, conforms to her vaginal code (Erskine, 1989; McClintock, 1984).

Sometimes Males Make Significant Investments in Reproduction

Insofar as females force males to make an investment in reproduction, they may restore some balance between female and male reproductive strategies. The more that males are compelled to invest, the more interest they will have in ensuring that their investment is not wasted. If a male has to spend days or weeks wooing a female, or if he has to provide expensive nuptial gifts or accomplish burdensome tasks, he may become as committed as the female to seeing that the offspring of their union survive. Otherwise, he will have to start all over again with another female. His life, or the mating season, may simply not be long enough to allow that.

Thus, while there are plenty of species in which males make little or no contribution to the care of their offspring, there are others in which they make contributions as great as those made by females. This kind of cooperative investment can allow for the evolution of lifestyles that would otherwise be impossible. Pairs of seagulls, for example, take alternating shifts at the nest (incubating eggs or protecting hatchlings) and away from the nest (foraging). A single bird cannot accomplish both tasks, so male investment has been essential to the evolution of seagulls, as well as many other species of birds.

In a few species, males take on the entire responsibility of care for eggs or young. A male stickleback fish, for example, constructs an underwater nest in which females lay eggs; after fertilizing them, the male spends about 2 weeks guarding the eggs and the newly hatched fry (Kynard, 1978). Some male water birds, such as phalaropes and jacanas, also take on the entire responsibility for incubating eggs and feeding the hatchlings. Very occasionally, males take over tasks that seem biologically fated to be handled by females, such as pregnancy itself, as in the curious group of fishes known as sea horses and pipefishes (Box 2.3).

If Males Invest, Sexual Selection May Work Differently

If males and females invest about equally in reproduction, sexual selection may not lead to any marked anatomical or behavioral differences between the sexes. Male and female seagulls, for example, are nearly the same size, and neither has any special display feathers or other sexually distinct characteristics. In fact, the only reliable way to tell the sex of a seagull is to examine its internal anatomy.

If males invest *more* than females in reproduction, and thus are limited in how many offspring they can produce, the usual effects of sexual selection on the two sexes can actually be reversed. Among phalaropes and jacanas, for example, females compete for the sexual favors of males, and males choose among females. Consistent with this pat-

Box 2.3   Biology of Sex

When Males Get Pregnant

The sea horses comprise about 35 species of fish belonging to the genus *Hippocampus*. (The hippocampus was a horse-headed sea monster in Greek mythology.) Sea horses break all the rules. Their anatomy is peculiar: a horselike head sits atop a strangely ribbed body and a reptilian tail. Their posture is bizarre: they hold themselves vertically in the water, rather than horizontally like most fishes. But oddest of all is their sex life: like Arnold Schwarzenegger in the movie *Junior*, the *males* get pregnant and give birth to young.

Female and male sea horses form closely bonded, monogamous pairs. The female produces ova in the normal way—that is what defines her as female. But she then deposits the ova in a deep pouchlike cavity in the body of the male, where they are fertilized by the male's sperm. This is the only known example in nature in which fertilization occurs within a male animal's body. After fertilization, the opening of the pouch closes, and the eggs remain sealed off for about 10 days. At the end of that period the pouch reopens, and the young—now tiny sea horses—emerge to face the world (see figure). The female, meanwhile, has prepared another load of ova to deposit in the male's pouch. In the course of a single sea-

son, a male may go through a dozen cycles of fertilization, pregnancy, and parturition, giving birth to a total of several hundred fry.

Because males make the investment of pregnancy, you might think that sexual selection would have effects on sea horses opposite to those it has in most species. That is, one might expect female sea horses to compete for males, and for males to choose among females. But that's not the case, according to Heather Masonjones of Amherst College. Masonjones found that males fight one another for access to females, just as happens in so many other species. To understand the reason for this, Masonjones undertook a detailed study of how much energy female and male sea horses expend on reproduction (Masonjones, 2001). Surprisingly, she found that females expend more energy than males. It appears that, even though sea horse embryos develop inside their father, most or all of the nutrients they consume come from the yolk that their mother packs into the eggs. In terms of investment, their father does little more than provide a safe haven. And because the females do most of the investing, sexual selection acts primarily on males to make them compete for mates, just as it does in the majority of species.

tern, female phalaropes and jacanas are larger and more brightly colored than males.

Among sticklebacks, on the other hand, this reversal doesn't happen: males continue to compete and females continue to choose, in spite of the fact that males provide all the parental care. The reason for this is that several females lay their eggs in one male's nest. The total investment of all those females in producing their eggs is probably greater than the male's investment in caring for them, and a successful male is capable of leaving more offspring than any individual female can.

Sometimes, males choose among females because females vary in how much they can invest in reproduction. This variation is most obvious in species in which

Among birds, the sex that invests less in parenting tends to be larger and more brightly colored. Usually that sex is the male. Occasionally, however, that sex is the female, as in the red phalarope. Naturalist John James Audubon (1785–1851), who painted these phalaropes, assumed wrongly that the brightly colored bird (right) was the male.

individuals continue to grow after reaching reproductive maturity. Whereas humans stop growing soon after the end of puberty, some animals, such as tortoises, grow throughout their lives. In such species, the oldest and largest females are capable of laying the largest clutches of eggs, so males mate preferentially with the oldest females.

Among some primate species, males invest considerably in reproduction, even if not to the same degree as females. For that reason, there may be competition and choosing by both sexes. Take baboons, for example. Male baboons are larger than females and compete intensely for mates, as is true in so many other species. In addition, however, female baboons compete for the sexual attention of males. They do this by means of "sexual swellings"—patches of pigmented genital and perianal skin that swell up around the time of ovulation (Figure 2.6). The females with the largest swellings seem to be genetically favored: they have more offspring than other females, and their offspring are more likely to survive. Thus, males try to copulate with the females with the largest swellings (Domb & Pagel, 2001).

Figure 2.6 Sexual swellings of female baboons appear at the time of ovulation, and thus inform the males that they are ready to mate. In addition, the size of each female's swelling is an indicator of her reproductive fitness, so males try to mate with the females with the largest swellings.

Diverse Relationship Styles Have Evolved

Evolution has led to a bewildering variety of sexual relationships, from sexual free-for-alls to lifelong, sexually exclusive pairings. Understanding the basis for this diversity can be quite a challenge. Still, we can start with the basic assumption that evolution is at work. In other words, animals' genes are likely to promote sexual behavior and relationships that offer them the best prospects for leaving copies of those genes in future generations.

Social and Sexual Arrangements Are Not Necessarily the Same

In looking at animal liaisons, we need to distinguish carefully between two phenomena: *social arrangements* and *sexual reality*. In the past, people (including biologists) have tended to take animals' social arrangements at face value—as if these arrangements tell us unambiguously who is having sex with whom. Sometimes they do. It turns out, however, that humans are not the only species in which social arrangements and sexual reality are imperfectly aligned.

In many species, individuals are essentially solitary or belong to same-sex groups, and they reproduce by mating with strangers (either one or many) whom they never see again. This pattern is seen in the majority of invertebrates, fishes, amphibians, and reptiles. Among mammals, there is considerable diversity in relationship styles, even between related species. For example, mountain voles (*Microtus montanus*) mate with strangers and immediately go their separate ways, whereas their prairie cousins (*Microtus ochrogaster*) form stable pair bonds (Carter & Getz, 1993). (The brain mechanisms that may underlie these differences are discussed in Chapter 9.)

When reproduction does involve social relationships, we see two basic patterns: **monogamy** and **polygamy.** In socially monogamous relationships, two animals (usually of the opposite sex) form a **pair bond** for the duration of the breeding season or even for their entire lifetimes. Many birds, such as the seagulls mentioned earlier, pair up for a season. Swans are famous for forming lifelong pair bonds. The belief that bereaved swans die of grief is a myth, however; they actually go searching for a new mate.

In socially polygamous relationships, one animal forms a relationship with several individuals of the other sex. In most polygamous species, single males form relationships with multiple females. This is the "harem" arrangement described earlier for langur monkeys, and it is technically called **polygyny** ("many wives"). The opposite arrangement—a single female with a harem of males—is called **polyandry** ("many husbands"). It is a rare arrangement, but one animal that does adopt it is the jacana, the water bird we have already mentioned on account of its unusual "females compete, males choose" behavior. In southern Texas one may come across a pond occupied by a single female jacana and several males in a loose social group.

That polygyny is commoner than polyandry is consistent with the greater investment in reproduction by females. It simply would not be possible for females of most species to mate with multiple males and have offspring with all of them. Only when the balance of investment is reversed, as with jacanas, does polyandry crop up.

Some animals, such as lions and chimpanzees, practice a more balanced polygamy in which social groups contain more than one sexually mature adult of each sex, and both males and females mate with multiple partners of the other sex. In such groups, a male's ability to mate is still influenced by his dominance rank. For example, lower-ranking males may have the opportunity to mate with females only at times when the females are unlikely to conceive.

Male Promiscuity Offers Obvious Evolutionary Benefits

As mentioned, social monogamy and social polygamy do not necessarily define who has sex with whom. A male lion will readily mate with a female from outside his pride, for example, if he can get to her before the female members of his pride drive her off. Even males of socially monogamous species commonly take advantage of any extra-pair mating opportunity that offers itself. We'll call this willingness to engage in sex outside of an animal's established relationship or relationships **promiscuity.** Male promiscuity is more or less to be expected in evolutionary terms: the investment in the extra-pair mating is probably so slight that it is "worth it" for the male, even if the chances of that mating leading to viable offspring are not very great.

In this context, one has to wonder not why males of many species are disposed to promiscuity, but why some are not. Sexual monogamy may be imposed on males by females' refusal to engage in extra-pair matings, as in some species of birds. Sometimes males mate with only one female simply because they mate only once—period. An extreme example is offered by deep-sea anglerfishes. In these species, a male homes in on a female and partially fuses with her. His eyes degenerate, and he remains permanently attached to the female, providing her with sperm whenever required. Once attached to his mate in this fashion, he is ill-equipped to embark on extramarital affairs!

Why Are Females Promiscuous?

Male promiscuity makes evolutionary sense, but what about female promiscuity? At first glance, it seems there is no reason for it, since females can usually produce all the offspring they are capable of producing with the aid of a single male. But in fact, female promiscuity may be fairly common, even in species that have long been considered sexually monogamous.

Mate guarding   One reason for suspecting that females are capable of promiscuity is that males often act as if they're concerned about that possibility. A common behavior of this type is **mate guarding:** a male remains close to a female throughout the period when she is fertile and keeps other males away from her. Among birds called sand martins, for example, the female is fertile for a period of about 8 days. During this time, the male follows her wherever she goes, never letting her get more than a few body lengths away from him.

That mate guarding is indeed aimed at deterring female promiscuity was shown by David Westneat (now at the University of Kentucky), who studied red-winged blackbirds, a polygynous species (Westneat, 1994). Male redwings guard their mates as best they can, but they are limited by the fact that they may have more than one female to guard at a time, as well as by their need to spend some time foraging. Westneat removed male redwings from their territories for hour-long periods. During these periods he observed that males from neighboring territories flew in and began to court the females. These courtships often culminated in sex.

To establish whether the females actually had offspring by the neighboring males, Westneat used the method that has become the gold standard in both human and animal studies: DNA analysis. This procedure depends on the fact that individuals of the same species have numerous differences in their DNA. These differences, called **DNA polymorphisms,** can be detected with simple enzymatic tests. Animals inherit their particular DNA sequences from their parents, so by comparing these sequences from an offspring and the individuals who are candidates to be its parents, the true parents can be identified. Since it is usually the identity of the father that is in doubt, the procedure (which is also performed with human DNA) is generally called **paternity testing** (Figure 2.7).

Westneat found that female redwings whose mates were removed for an hour gave birth to significant numbers of offspring fathered by neighboring males—a much higher proportion that that seen in females whose mates remained on guard. In other words, mate guarding really does have the effect of limiting a female's ability to engage in extra-pair sex.

In Westneat's study, even the females whose mates were not removed had some offspring by neighboring males. Apparently, the male's need to forage takes him away from his mates often enough to allow extra-pair sex. Indeed, when Westneat supplemented the food supply of some males, so that they no longer needed to go on foraging trips, they were cuckolded (cheated on) significantly less often than other males. All in all, it appears that male redwings face an unenviable choice—between a full belly and a faithful mate.

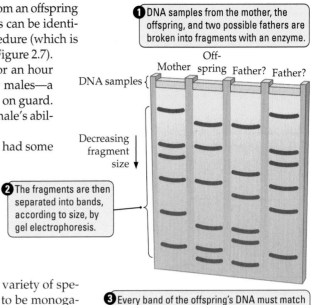

Figure 2.7 Paternity testing. Which male fathered this offspring?

DNA evidence　DNA paternity testing has now been done on a wide variety of species, with a wide variety of results. Some species traditionally thought to be monogamous, such as swans, really are so. Yet among socially monogamous birds, the fraction of offspring that are not fathered by the female's social mate can range as high as 35 percent (in indigo buntings), 55 percent (in reed buntings), or even 76 percent (in Australian superb fairy wrens) (Birkhead, 1998). In general, DNA testing has revealed that female promiscuity is widespread among all vertebrate groups, as well as many invertebrate groups, but there are exceptions. In the polygynous hamadryas baboon, for example, females apparently never cheat on their male partners, even when their partners are sterile (Birkhead, 2000). Among chimpanzees, on the other hand, limited DNA testing has suggested that as many as half of all chimpanzee offspring are fathered by males from outside the group to which the mother belongs (Gagneux et al., 1997).

Sperm competition　When females are promiscuous, competition between males may continue after mating—courtesy of their sperm. The notion that sperm from different males compete with one another is a strange one, but it happens, and in a wide variety of ways. In some species, **intromission** (insertion of the penis) causes the ejection of sperm already present in the female's reproductive tract from a previous mating. Or, part of the male's ejaculate may coagulate into a dense plug that prevents later insemination by other males. Sometimes, females store sperm in crypts in their reproductive tracts; the sperm from several males may be stored in layers within these crypts, and the female generally utilizes the most recently received sperm to fertilize her ova.

The existence of sperm competition can promote the development of a variety of anatomical and behavioral specializations. In species in which sperm competition is rife, penises tend to be long and testes large, so that a large number of sperm can be produced. If we compare our close relatives, the chimpanzee and the gorilla, for example, sperm competition is much more intense among chimpanzees. A female chimpanzee may copulate as many as 1000 times, with many different males, for each time she actually becomes pregnant. Female gorillas, in contrast, copulate no more than about 30 times per pregnancy, and with only one or two males. Corresponding to this difference in sperm competition, the testes of chimpanzees are much larger, and their penises longer (in relation to overall body size), than those of gorillas. Neither chimpanzee nor gorilla can hold a candle to the pig, however. Pigs mate promiscuously, so sperm competition is probably very strong. Boars (male pigs) have penises long enough to deposit semen directly into the female's uterus (rather than into the vagina, as in humans), and a single ejaculate can measure a pint or more in volume and contains an average of 750 billion sperm (compared with a mere 350 *million* in men).

Possible reasons for female promiscuity　It is clear at this point that females of many species, including many socially monogamous or polygynous ones, are promiscuous. But why do females engage in this behavior, if they are unlikely to increase the number of their offspring by doing so?

There are a number of possible reasons for female promiscuity, which may differ among species. In species in which males offer resources such as gifts of food as an incentive to mating, those gifts may make promiscuous mating worthwhile for a female. Her nutritional status may be enhanced to a degree that will allow her to have more or healthier offspring.

In some circumstances, mating with multiple males may in itself increase the total number of a female's offspring, contrary to our previous assumption. In fruit flies, for example, poor nutrition among males may cause this to be the case. Male fruit flies that are well fed deposit enough sperm in one intromission to supply all the female's reproductive needs, but if food supplies are limited, the number of sperm may not be sufficient, in which case a female increases the number of her offspring by mating with multiple males (Bateman, 1948) (Figure 2.8). Similar arguments have been made to account for female promiscuity in primates (Small, 1988), although the data are inconclusive.

Another possibility is that socially monogamous females are promiscuous not in order to have more offspring, but to obtain sperm from higher-quality males than their social partners. After all, if males differ in quality, most females are not going to be partnered with the very best males. There are a few studies supporting this idea. For example, Susan Smith of Mount Holyoke College observed the mating behavior of black-capped chickadees (Smith, 1988). She found that when a female engages in extra-pair sex, she usually does so with a male who was dominant over her social mate during the previous winter. This finding suggests that promiscuous females are shopping for better genes than their regular mates can provide.

Yet another possibility is that a female is promiscuous not to obtain sperm that are "better" in any absolute sense, but to obtain sperm that are better *for her.* This could involve selecting extra-pair partners who are genetically dissimilar to herself. Female mice, for example, mate preferentially with males whose "MHC" genes (genes that affect tissue matching) are different from their own. This kind of selection may occur even within the female's reproductive tract. In mice, for example, there is some evidence that sperm carrying MHC genes different from the female's fertilize the female's ova more readily than those carrying similar genes (Wedekind et al., 1996).

Finally, a truly devious reason for female promiscuity may come into play. When the dominant male in a polygynous species is displaced by a new male, the new male may kill the young born to harem females over the following few months. This infanticidal behavior benefits him because the young he eliminates were fathered by the previous dominant male; once they are out of the way, the females will quickly become pregnant by the new male. Among langurs (Hrdy, 1977), and probably among other polygynous species, pregnant females will solicit sex with the new dominant male even though, being pregnant already, they cannot conceive young with him. The benefit of doing so is that the new male protects the offspring of those females that mate with him, rather than killing them. In essence, the females have fooled the male into thinking that the offspring are his. (Again, "fooled" and "thinking" are figures of speech. We don't know whether the langurs' behavior is controlled by thought processes of the kind humans experience.)

One unexpected consequence of female promiscuity is that, on occasion, it can facilitate homosexual relationships. A few pages ago, when we began our discussion of monogamous relationships, we described such relationships as "usually" being between animals of the opposite sex. Surely same-sex monogamous relationships would never happen, you may have thought, because they would never give rise to offspring. If females are promiscuous, however, then socially monogamous relationships between

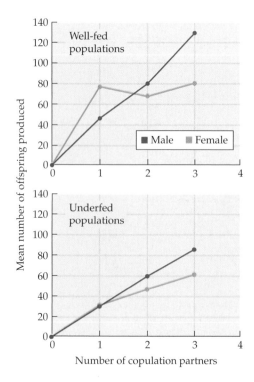

Figure 2.8 The payoff for promiscuity. These graphs plot the number of offspring produced by male and female fruit flies as a function of the number of sex partners they have. The upper graph is for well-fed populations; the lower is for underfed populations. For males, increasing the number of sex partners increases the number of their offspring under either feeding condition. For females in well-fed populations, copulating with a single male suffices to produce the maximum number of offspring. Females in underfed populations increase the number of their offspring by copulating with several males. This is presumably because a single underfed male does not produce enough sperm to fertilize all of a female's eggs. (Data from Angus Bateman; after Birkhead 2000.)

two females may indeed give rise to offspring, because one or both of the females may be inseminated in extra-pair matings.

Socially monogamous female–female relationships have in fact been described in a variety of species. Among seagulls, for example, occasional female–female nesting pairs are found (Hunt & Warner Hunt, 1977). The two females behave very much like a male–female pair, engaging in sex with each other and alternating the duties of foraging and incubation in the usual way. A good fraction of the eggs produced by these pairings are fertile, indicating that extra-pair sex has indeed taken place. Although these female–female pairs are usually in a very small minority, their numbers may rise dramatically if there is an excess of females in a breeding colony.

Males May Copulate with Females by Force

We have seen that the reproductive interests of males and females can be in conflict, and we've already mentioned one grisly consequence of such conflict: infanticide by males who take over harems. Another such consequence is **forced copulation**—the equivalent of what in humans would be called **rape.** Forced copulation is seen in a wide variety of animals, from insects to primates, and in some of these animals it is clearly an adaptive behavior; that is, it persists because it helps those animals who engage in it have more offspring than they would have otherwise.

Perhaps the most detailed study of forced copulation has been done on scorpionflies by evolutionary psychologist Randy Thornhill of the University of New Mexico (Thornhill, 1980). In these insects, a male is able to mate with a female by one of two strategies. In one strategy, he offers the female a nuptial gift, such as a dead insect; the female approaches the gift-bearing male, and they mate. If a male approaches a female without a gift, the female will attempt to flee. In this case, however, the male may grasp the female and hold her immobile with a special appendage called a notal organ, which enables him to obtain a forced mating. Because the notal organ has no use other than for forced copulation (it is not required for consensual sex, for example), Thornhill concluded that forced copulation is not some random byproduct of scorpionfly evolution, but an adaptive behavior resulting from countless generations of sexual selection.

Only a couple of other species (also insects) have anatomical adaptations that facilitate forced copulation. In fact, quite a few species have the opposite—arrangements of the female anatomy that make copulation impossible without her active collaboration. It is likely that these arrangements are adaptations to prevent forced copulation.

Most animals do not have anatomical specializations that either facilitate or prevent this behavior, but attempts at forced copulation by males, and resistance by females, have been observed in numerous species (Figure 2.9), including primates. Whether the behavioral proclivity to forced copulation is an adaptation, or whether it is merely the by-product of selection for other traits, such as aggressiveness, is not always clear. What is certain is that the capacity for forced copulation is not an exclusively human trait (Box 2.4). We take up this topic again in Chapter 18.

Sometimes, Helping Relatives Reproduce Is a Good Strategy

Genes act, of course, within the individual who possesses them. At first thought, then, genes should make individuals focus 100 percent of their efforts on reproducing themselves. Genes are basically selfish, so individuals should be selfish too.

It's no news that there is a lot of selfish behavior in this world, especially in the realm of sexual and reproductive behavior. The topic we

(A)

(B)

Figure 2.9 Consensual and coercive sex in the beetle *Tegrodera aloga*. (A) The male (right) courts the female by drawing her antennae into grooves on his head. The female may or may not respond by copulating with him. (B) In an alternative strategy, the male (below) runs up to the female, throws her on her side, and inserts his genitalia as she struggles to free herself from his grasp. (Photographs courtesy of John Alcock.)

Box 2.4 *Society, Values, and the Law*

Does the Study of Evolution Teach Us How Humans Should Behave?

Reading this chapter may have given you some idea of the diversity of sexual behaviors and sexual relationships among nonhuman species, and of the evolutionary forces that have produced them. This may, in turn, help you to gain a deeper perspective on human sexuality as you read through the rest of the book. But many writers since ancient times have used animal sexuality or evolutionary theories not merely to understand our own sex lives, but to judge them.

Here's one example: The thirteenth-century Catholic theologian St. Thomas Aquinas taught that sex was morally acceptable only within the context of marriage, and this principle has remained the centerpiece of Catholic sexual ethics ever since. Aquinas based his argument on a discussion of what is "natural," and this led him to consider animal sexuality. He knew, however, that not all animals are monogamous. He therefore drew a distinction between what is "natural" for different kinds of animals:

> We see in fact that among all those animals for whom the care of a male and female is required for the upbringing of the offspring, there is no promiscuity but only one male with one female, or several females; this is the case among all birds. It is different, however, among those animals for whom the female alone is sufficient for the upbringing of the offspring, among whom there is

promiscuity, as is evident in the case of dogs and other similar animals.

> (Boswell, 1980; translation by John Boswell)

Aquinas believed that a father and a mother were necessary for the upbringing of a human child, which put humans in the class of creatures for whom promiscuity was unnatural, and therefore wrong.

Another example: The nineteenth-century German lawyer Karl Heinrich Ulrichs was the first modern gay rights activist (see Chapter 13). He wrote:

> Supporting the notion that [homosexuality] is "inborn by a law of nature" is also the fact that sexual acts occur between male beetles. My opponents have to separate this phenomenon from the general field of natural history. They put it in the class of animal diseases, specifically, into the section of animal psychiatry devoted to mentally ill beetles.

> (Translation modified from Kennedy, 1988)

In considering the merits of arguments such as these, you may wish to ask yourself the following questions:

Among the range of sexual behaviors that humans can engage in, some are broadly applauded (e.g., heterosexual monogamy), some are broadly condemned (e.g., rape) and some are morally controversial (e.g.,

polygamy, homosexual contacts). Does the fact that some animals do or do not engage in these behaviors tell us what is morally proper for humans? Are some animals better "role models" for humans than others, and if so, why?

If rape were proved to have been adaptive during human evolution—that is, if genes conferring the capacity to rape persisted because men possessing those genes left more offspring—should that influence our view on whether rape is morally acceptable? Should it influence how we treat convicted rapists or the strategies we use to prevent rape?

Among our close primate relatives, we find one species (the chimpanzee) whose gender-related behavior promotes a male-dominated society, and another (the bonobo) in which the opposite is true. Should we (1) figure out which kind of social structure evolution has intended for us, and design our society in that fashion; (2) take evolved gender differences into account, but try to compensate for them by, for example, affirmative action; (3) ignore our evolutionary history and work toward an egalitarian society; or (4) let society do its own thing?

We will return to some of these moral questions in later chapters, when we have had the opportunity to study these various aspects of human sexuality—monogamy and promiscuity, rape, homosexuality, and gender-related traits—in greater detail.

have just discussed—forced copulation—is an extreme example of that selfishness. But selfless, altruistic behavior is also quite common. Paradoxically, it turns out that unselfish behavior can be the product of selfish genes.

One kind of altruistic behavior with an obvious adaptive value is parental care. In evolutionary terms, it's no good having offspring if those offspring don't have offspring in their turn, so it may pay to help one's offspring survive and become sexually mature, even if that limits the number of offspring one can have oneself. Mammals and birds, in particular, have followed that strategy, but even some insects devote considerable resources to protecting their young. Genes promoting parental care (or at least maternal care) are evidently widespread, and in Chapter 10 we'll discuss some of the biological processes that those genes may regulate.

Genes promoting altruistic behavior toward one's offspring survive because the offspring have a good chance of possessing those same genes. (Specifically, any gene in a parent has a 50 percent chance of being handed down to each offspring.) Therefore, genes for altruism toward one's offspring are helping *themselves* get handed on to the third and future generations. Obviously, genes for *harmfulness* toward one's offspring would not be perpetuated in the same way. Nor would genes for altruism toward *strangers*, because those strangers, being unrelated, would have no special likelihood of possessing the same genes.

Parents and offspring are not the only kinds of relatives who share genes, however. Siblings share approximately 50 percent of their genes. Aunts/uncles share about 25 percent of their genes with their nephews/nieces. First cousins share about 12.5 percent of their genes, and so on. Thus selfish genes may lead an individual to act altruistically toward a variety of close relatives.

The logic behind this theory was laid out by the British evolutionary theorist William Hamilton in the 1960s (Hamilton, 1964). Hamilton proposed that natural selection causes individuals to devote resources to helping their relatives reproduce, to an extent determined by the degree of relatedness. For example, an individual might be willing to give up on having *one* offspring herself if by doing so she enables her sister to have *two* offspring beyond what she would otherwise produce. In terms of genes, it's a toss-up: either a single 50 percent copy (a child) or two 25 percent copies (nephews or nieces). To help a cousin reproduce, on the other hand, an individual should sacrifice one offspring's worth of resources only if that sacrifice helps that cousin have *eight* extra offspring—not a likely eventuality.

Hamilton's theory is known as **kin selection,** and the central concept of kin selection is **inclusive fitness.** You're probably familiar with the use of the phrase "survival of the fittest" to describe the evolutionary process. What kin selection theory says is that, in considering an individual's "fitness," one has to consider not just how many offspring that individual produces, but all the copies of that individual's genes that persist into future generations, whether in direct descendants or in the descendants of siblings or other relatives.

Kin Selection Explains Some Altruistic Animal Behavior

Kin selection theory does seem to explain quite a lot of social and sexual behavior in the animal kingdom. For example, subordinate males in lion prides and other groups may have few or no offspring of their own, at least as long as they are subordinate. If the dominant male is their brother or other close relative, however, it may still be worth it for them to remain in the group and help him reproduce, for by doing so they are propagating copies of some of their own genes. Kin selection also favors the development of "aunting" behavior in primates—the tendency of females to share maternal duties—because the females who share these duties are likely to be sisters or other close relatives.

Probably the most successful application of kin selection theory has been to social insects such as bees and ants. As mentioned earlier, many individuals in these species are sterile worker females, who are unable to reproduce directly. These individuals work tirelessly to help their fertile sister, the queen, produce enormous numbers of offspring. Why do they do this? It turns out that, due to a peculiarity of inheritance in most social insects, workers are more closely related to the queen than they are to any offspring they might have themselves. Undoubtedly, this close relatedness fosters the unusual degree of altruistic behavior in these species (Trivers & Hare, 1976).

Kin selection doesn't explain all altruistic behavior. Females may adopt orphans who are completely unrelated to them, for example; such behavior is not predicted by kin selection theory. It may still be an adaptation—it might have value as a "rehearsal" for parenting one's own offspring—but it could also be a valueless or even deleterious by-product of other adaptations. For example, it could be adaptive for females to nurture infants in their vicinity because those infants are usually their own offspring—so sometimes they nurture the "wrong" infants. While all animals (including ourselves) are products of evolution, it does not follow that *every* behavior has been fine-tuned by natural or sexual selection.

Male and Female Sexualities Evolve Together

Sexual reproduction necessarily involves an interaction between males and females of the same species, so male and female sexual traits evolve together. Genes that promote the development of large sexual swellings in female baboons coevolve with genes that promote a preference for large swellings on the part of male baboons. Genes that promote bower building in male bowerbirds coevolve with genes that promote mating with bower builders in female bowerbirds. Genes that promote promiscuity in female birds coevolve with genes that promote mate guarding behavior in males. What evolves is an interactive system, not an isolated physical or behavioral trait in either sex.

Box 2.5 Biology of Sex

The Battle of the Sexes at the Molecular Level: Genomic Imprinting

Male and female animals must cooperate to produce offspring, but their reproductive interests may not precisely coincide. In general, it benefits the father if the pregnant mother devotes all possible resources to the growth of her fetus or fetuses. It doesn't matter much to him if she thereby reduces her ability to have subsequent offspring, because those later offspring will quite likely be fathered by some other male. For the mother, on the other hand, it makes sense to ration the nourishment she delivers to each litter, so that she has a good chance of producing more healthy offspring at a later time. In mammals, these conflicting interests are translated into molecular mechanisms affecting fetal growth by a process called **genomic imprinting** (Moore & Haig, 1991; Tilghman, 1999).

Recall that mammals, like most organisms, are diploid, meaning that they carry two versions of each gene on homologous chromosomes, one inherited from the mother and one from the father. In general, whether a gene comes from the mother or the father has no effect on the gene's activity (**expression**): both the maternally and paternally derived versions are expressed. For a couple of dozen genes, however, it *does* matter. For some of these **imprinted genes,** the version derived from the mother is expressed and the version derived from the father is silenced. For others, it's the other way around. Imprinted genes receive chemical tags during the production of gametes in the ovary or testis, labeling them as being of female or male origin. After fertilization, the tags are "read," and only the genes bearing the tags of one parental sex are expressed (Pfeifer, 2000) (Figure A). In the figure, genes 2 and 4 are subject to imprinting. In the case of gene 2, only the copy inherited from the father (P2) is expressed. In the case of gene 4, only the copy inherited from the mother (M4) is expressed. Genes 1 and 3 are not imprinted, so both copies are expressed.

It turns out that many of the imprinted genes in which the father's version is expressed act to increase the rate at which the fetus grows. Many of the genes in which the mother's version is expressed have the opposite effect, slowing fetal growth. In other words, fathers and mothers send their fetal offspring conflicting genetic instructions concerning how fast they should grow. The fetus's actual growth rate is a compromise between the instructions supplied by its two parents (Figure B).

Not all the data are consistent with these ideas. For one thing, one might expect there to be less parental conflict over fetal growth rates in mammalian species that are sexually monogamous, because in such species the father should be as concerned as the mother about her prospects for future offspring. Thus one might expect weaker effects of imprinted genes on fetal growth in monogamous species. So far, this doesn't appear to be the case (Vrana et al., 1998). Research on genomic imprinting is still at an early stage, however; further studies may clarify this apparent discrepancy.

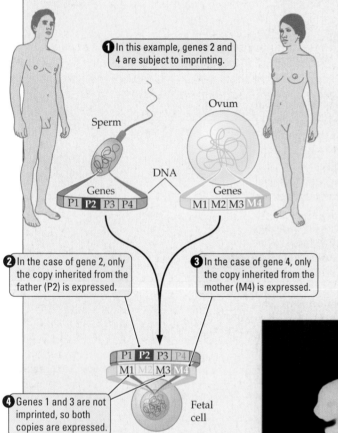

❶ In this example, genes 2 and 4 are subject to imprinting.

Sperm

Ovum

DNA

Genes
| P1 | P2 | P3 | P4 |

Genes
| M1 | M2 | M3 | M4 |

❷ In the case of gene 2, only the copy inherited from the father (P2) is expressed.

❸ In the case of gene 4, only the copy inherited from the mother (M4) is expressed.

| P1 | P2 | P3 | P4 |
| M1 | M2 | M3 | M4 |

Fetal cell

❹ Genes 1 and 3 are not imprinted, so both copies are expressed.

(A) Genomic imprinting

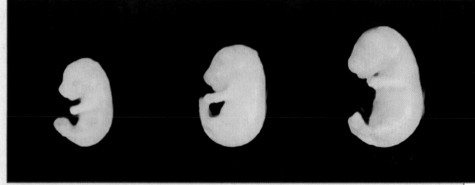

(B) Effects of imprinted genes on growth. The middle panel shows a normal mouse embryo. The embryo on the left has been deprived (by genetic engineering) of the growth-promoting action of a paternally expressed imprinted gene (*Ifg2*), and is therefore dwarfed. The embryo at right has been deprived of the growth-inhibiting effect of a maternally expressed imprinted gene (*Igf2r*), and is therefore oversized. (Courtesy of Jonathan Eggenschwiler, Thomas Ludwig, and Argiris Efstratiadis.)

Of course, coevolution occurs between different species as well (genes for sharp eye-sight in a predator species and genes for protective coloration in its prey, for example). What's different about the coevolution of traits in males and females of the *same* species is that the evolutionary process takes place within a single genome that (with the exception of the Y chromosome) is possessed and handed down by both sexes. So, for example, it may be advantageous for a female sand martin to have genes promoting female promiscuity (because she may have better-quality offspring as a result), but it may also be advantageous for that same female to have genes promoting male mate guarding behavior (because they may help her sons have more offspring). At the level of *behavior,* in other words, there may be a "battle of the sexes," but at the level of the *genome* there may be no battle at all. (The phenomenon of genomic imprinting, discussed in Box 2.5, offers a partial exception to this generalization.)

Sex May Acquire Other Functions Beyond Reproduction

While reproduction is the original and most obvious function of sexual behavior, some species have found uses for sex that have no direct connection with producing young. Notable among these species is our close relative, the bonobo (*Pan paniscus*).

The bonobo is an endangered species of ape that lives along the Zaire River in central Africa. Bonobos split off from chimpanzees (*Pan troglodytes*) about 3 million years ago; our own ancestors diverged from the common ancestors of chimpanzees and bonobos about 8 million years ago. Human DNA is about 98.5 percent identical to that of bonobos and chimpanzees.

Female and Male Bonobos Engage in Nonreproductive Sex

Like most female mammals, female bonobos advertise when they are willing to copulate (estrous). Bonobos, like baboons, do so by means of their genital swellings. In striking contrast to mammals such as mice, however, the estrus of a bonobo extends over about two-thirds of her entire ovarian cycle, which lasts about 2 months (Figure 2.10). In fact, the bonobo is out of estrus only for a few days around the time of **menstruation** (the periodic shedding of the lining of the uterus—see Chapter 4). Although the bonobo ovulates at some point during her estrus, the ovum is viable for only a day or two, and sperm does not survive in her reproductive tract for more than a day or two either. In other words, for most of the time when the female bonobo is willing to have sex, there is no chance that sex will result in pregnancy.

Not only are female bonobos sexually receptive for most of the ovarian cycle, but they are also receptive when they are not cycling at all. Bonobo mothers nurse their young for several years after they are born, and lactation suppresses ovulation. Thus, bonobos cannot become pregnant while they are still nursing previous offspring. Even so, they are sexually receptive throughout this period.

Bonobos have two basic positions for heterosexual copulation. In one, the male mounts the female from the rear, as in nearly all other mammalian species. In the other position, the two animals face each other. The female bonobo seems well adapted for this evolutionary novelty because her **vulva** (external genitalia—see Chapter 3) faces forward. Although copulation is brief—no more than about 10–15 seconds—both the male and the female may experience orgasm, to judge from their grimaces and squeals at climax.

Figure 2.10 Sexual receptivity and the ovarian cycle in a bonobo (above) and a chimpanzee (below). Each graph shows the extent of genital swelling (an indicator of sexual receptivity) on each day of the ovarian cycle, which lasts about 60 days in bonobos and 36 days in chimpanzees. The bonobo is receptive for most of her ovarian cycle, except for a few days around menstruation. The chimpanzee is receptive for a more restricted period in the middle of each cycle, around the time of ovulation. (Data from Jeremy Dahl, Yerkes Primate Center; after deWaal, 1995.)

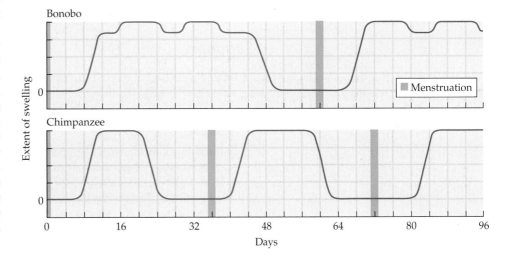

Front-to-front copulation is rare among mammals, but does occur in bonobos and humans.

Further accentuating the nonreproductive nature of much bonobo sex, both female and male bonobos engage in frequent homosexual encounters. When two females have sex, they embrace face to face, and each rubs her swollen **clitoris** (the erectile component of the external female genitalia that mediates sexual pleasure—see Chapter 3) sideways against the other's until both females reach orgasm. This behavior, called genito–genital rubbing, is unique to female–female encounters.

Sexual encounters between males are of two kinds. In one kind, the males face away from each other, and one male rubs his **scrotum** (the sac containing the testes—see Chapter 3) against the other male's buttocks. In the other, the two males rub their penises together while hanging from a tree branch.

Bonobos Use Sex for Conflict Resolution and Alliance Formation

All this nonreproductive sexual activity raises an obvious question—why? Close observation of bonobo colonies in captivity (de Waal, 1995; Parish & de Waal, 2000) and in the wild (Kano, 1992) indicates that bonobos use sex for the prevention and resolution of conflicts. Two bonobos who are faced with a conflict in food allocation, for example, will engage in sex and then divide the food peacefully. This happens regardless of the sex or age of the two animals. Alternatively, one animal may take food from another and "pay" with the currency of sex. When an entire troop of bonobos comes upon a food source—a situation that triggers wild fighting in other species such as chimpanzees—the bonobos engage in extensive bouts of sex with one another before dividing up the food. The bonobo's motto seems to be "Make love, not war."

A related function of sex in bonobos is the cementing of social relationships and the formation of alliances. This function is particularly important for females. Bonobo females leave their natal (birth) groups and join new ones, whereas males stay in their natal groups. Females joining a group are initially unwelcome, but they solidify their position by forming close alliances with high-ranking females. The activity that bonds females in these alliances is genito–genital rubbing. So effective are these sex-mediated alliances that female bonobos have largely taken control of bonobo society away from males. In fact, a male's rank depends in large part on the rank of his mother.

Because bonobos, like many humans, see more to sex than making babies, we might imagine that the bonobo's sexuality is ancestral to our own. But such an assumption would be risky, for chimpanzees—who are about equally closely related to us—are far more restricted in their use of nonreproductive sex. What is remarkable about the *Hominoidea*—the superfamily that includes gibbons, orangutans, gorillas, chimpanzees, bonobos, and humans—is the diversity of their sexual and social arrangements. Gibbons are monogamous, orangutans are solitary, gorillas are polygynous, chimpanzees are polygamous and male-dominated, bonobos are polygamous and female-dominated, and humans—well, that is the topic of the remainder of this book.

Summary

1. The original function of sex—and its only function in many species—is reproduction. The reasons why many species rely on sexual rather than asexual reproduction are disputed. Two general kinds of theories have been presented. First, sex may promote the elimination of harmful mutations. Second, by mixing genes from different individuals, sex may foster the selection of advantageous traits.

2. Natural selection has caused gametes to diverge into female and male forms. Female gametes are large and contain nutrients, male gametes are small and motile. Natural selection also acts to keep the ratio of the sexes near equality in most species, because any imbalance favors animals that have offspring of the minority sex.

3. Sex may be determined by chromosomal mechanisms, as in mammals, or by the temperature at which eggs are incubated, as in many reptiles.

4. Sexual selection, driven by competition for mates, has led to different morphological and behavioral traits in males and females. Because females generally invest more than males in reproduction, males often compete among themselves for access to females. This competition may select for large, aggressive individuals.

5. Females often choose among males. Their choices may be based on morphological features such as symmetry, display feathers, antlers, and the like, or on behavioral traits such as provision of gifts. Some female choice seems aimed at forcing males to make a greater investment in reproduction than they otherwise would. In species in which males do make significant investments, males become more choosy and females more competitive.

6. A wide variety of relationship styles exist. Animals may engage in sex without establishing any social bond, or they may bond in socially monogamous or polygamous relationships. Polygamy usually involves one male and several females (polygyny); the reverse arrangement (polyandry) is rare.

7. In many socially monogamous or polygynous species, both males and females engage in sex outside these social structures. Promiscuity has obvious benefits for males in terms of increased numbers of offspring. For a female, promiscuity may offer a range of benefits: it may help her gain resources from males, it may give her access to high-quality genes, or it may favorably influence the behavior of males toward her or her offspring.

8. Forced copulation has been observed in many species. In a few species, this behavior is clearly adaptive, increasing the male's likelihood of having offspring.

9. Because close relatives share many genes, evolution has led to altruistic behavior among relatives, including behavior in the reproductive domain. Some altruistic reproductive behavior, such as adoption of orphans, is less easily explained in evolutionary terms.

10. Sexual behavior has developed other functions besides reproduction. Bonobos offer a striking example: in this species, much sex takes place when the female is incapable of becoming pregnant, or between individuals of the same sex. Bonobo sex is directed not only toward reproduction, but also toward the avoidance or resolution of conflicts and the establishment of social bonds.

Discussion Questions

1. Do you think that the sexual behavior of nonhuman animals, as discussed in this chapter, is likely or unlikely to be relevant to an understanding of human sexuality? Why?

2. If the technique of reproductive cloning (as with Dolly the sheep) were perfected and universally adopted by humans, would that affect future human evolution? How would it affect people's moral views about sexual behavior?

Web Resources

Genomic Imprinting Web site http://www.geneimprint.com

The Talk.Origins Archive: Exploring the Creation/Evolution Controversy
www.talkorigins.org

Recommended Reading

Birkhead, T. (2000). *Promiscuity: An evolutionary history of sperm competition.* Cambridge, MA: Harvard University Press.

Buss, D. M. (1994). *The evolution of desire: Strategies of human mating.* New York: Basic Books.

Dawkins, R. (1989). *The selfish gene.* 2nd edition. Oxford: Oxford University Press.

Diamond, J. M. (1997). *Why is sex fun? The evolution of human sexuality.* New York: HarperCollins.

chapter 3

Men's and women's bodies are obviously different, but there are important similarities as well.

Sexual Bodies

*J*ust as the word "sex" has two meanings—sexual behavior, and the categories of male or female—our bodies and minds are sexual in those same two senses. First, they are equipped for sexual behavior in terms of anatomical features, hormones, neuronal pathways, and psychological traits. These systems may or may not differ between the sexes: male and female external genitalia are very different, for example, but the physiological basis of sexual arousal is quite similar in men and women.

Second, there are a multitude of differences between female and male bodies and minds that have no direct connection with sexual behavior. Men, on average, are taller than women, for example, and men and women tend to use different strategies in finding their way around unfamiliar environments. To the extent that such sex differences are influenced by our genes, however, we may suspect that they do have some connection to sexual behavior, even though this connection may be indirect or buried in our evolutionary past. Thus, in this and the following chapters, we will cast our net widely, looking at how our bodies are equipped for sexual behavior as well as at some of the broader respects in which men and women differ.

External Genital Anatomy Is the Usual Arbiter of a Person's Sex

We humans are obsessed with knowing the sex of our conspecifics. Indeed, the primacy of sex is built into most human languages, so much so that we may have difficulty talking about a person unless we know whether they are male or female. (In American English, the use of "they" as a means to refer to a single person without specifying their sex is rapidly replacing the traditional "he" and the formal "he or she." We follow that usage in this book.)

All of us know enormous numbers of other people—some intimately, some slightly, some only through the media. Yet if we know a person at all, we nearly always know (or think we know) their sex. How do we know? If we see them face-to-face, we may judge on the basis of body size and shape or facial appearance or manner of movement, or a combination of all of these. If we talk with them on the phone, we may judge on the basis of voice quality. If need be, we can judge by touch or even by smell. And we also often rely on the other person's telling us their sex, either in so many words or by means of cultural cues such as sex-specific names, dress, hairstyles, group affiliations, and the like.

Curiously, most of us consider all these cues to a person's sex mere proxies for the one criterion that we may never get the chance to check on: the morphology of the person's external genitals. Medicine and the law also generally focus on the external genitals as the defining criterion of maleness or femaleness, so the external genitals are described as **primary sexual characteristics.** A person with a penis, scrotum, and testicles is a man; a person with labia, a vaginal opening, and a clitoris is a woman. If these anatomical features do not match what we expect on the basis of all the other cues, we are liable to feel that we have been deceived.

There is something arbitrary about the supremacy of the genitals in the assignment of sex. The reality is that different criteria may be appropriate for different purposes. In the context of reproduction, for example, chromosomal sex, gonadal sex, and the sex of the internal reproductive tract are paramount. In the context of sexual behavior, external anatomical sex (including genital sex) is important. In the context of nonsexual interactions, social sex (sometimes called gender role—see Chapter 6) is really all that matters, if it matters at all.

One advantage of using the external genitalia to decide a person's sex, however, is that there is little overlap in the appearance of male and female genitalia. For example, if we measure the length of the external portion of the clitoris or penis (the "phallus") of many individuals, we get a bimodal (two-peaked) curve. Most clitorises are less than 2 centimeters in length (Verkauf et al., 1992) and most flaccid (nonerect) penises are more than 4 centimeters in length (Wessells et al., 1996b). That's quite different from the pattern we would find if we measured other sex-linked attributes such as body height: even though we may use height as a clue to assigning sex, the overall distribution of heights in the population is unimodal (single-peaked).

In this chapter we follow convention in giving primacy to the external genitalia as the determinants of a person's sex. Still, it's important to realize that there are significant numbers of people whose bodies are in some respect intermediate between the typical female and typical male designs. Such people—**intersexes**—tend to suffer as a consequence of society's compulsion to divide the population into males and females. We'll discuss intersexes further in Chapters 5 and 13.

A Woman's Vulva Includes Her Mons, Outer and Inner Labia, Vaginal Opening, and Clitoris

Many girls and women have little understanding of their sexual anatomy. Partly, that's because the female external genitalia are not as prominent as those of men. In addition, girls often learn that it's not nice to inquire or talk about these body parts. Vague phrases such as "down there" or "your bottom" may substitute for specific terminology. There are plenty of adult women who do not know what the word "vagina" means. Thus the "naming of parts" is the crucial first stage of sex education (Figure 3.1).

The **vulva** is a scientific term used to mean the entire external genital area in a woman or female mammal. You rarely see the word used outside books like this one, which is a pity because there is no common word with exactly the same meaning ("crotch" is close, though it can be used for either sex).

The **mons veneris** (meaning "mountain of Venus"; also called the **mons pubis,** or just the **mons**) is a pad of fatty tissue covered by skin and **pubic hair.** It lies immediately in front of the **pubic symphysis**—the median line of fusion between the left and right pubic bones. The mons may act as a cushion for the woman's pubic area during sex. The hair serves to wick and volatilize odors arising in the woman's vagina and nearby glands—odors that were considered sexually attractive before we became so concerned with "feminine hygiene." The mons may also be a visual trigger for sexual arousal, since it is the most easily visible portion of the vulva.

The **labia majora** or **outer lips** are two folds of skin that run down from the mons on either side of the vulva. Like the mons, they are padded with fatty tissue, and are hairy on the surfaces nearest to the thighs. The skin of the labia majora is often darker than the skin elsewhere.

The **labia minora** or **inner lips** are two thin folds of hairless skin that lie between the two labia majora. In some women the labia minora are visible only after parting the labia majora; in others they protrude to variable degrees (Figure 3.1B–D).

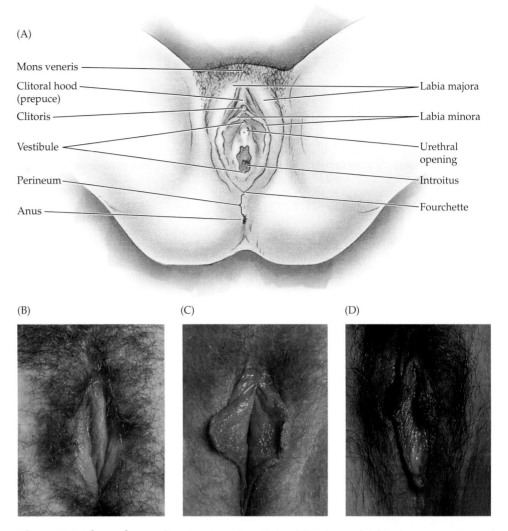

Figure 3.1 The vulva, or female external genitalia. (A) Vulva with labia drawn apart to show the vestibule, urethral opening, and introitus. The perineum and anus are not part of the vulva.(B–D) The labia minora are quite variable in shape and color from woman to woman.

They meet at the front, forming the **clitoral hood** or **clitoral prepuce,** and at the back, forming the **fourchette.** The labia minora generally touch each other, but they enclose a potential space, the **vestibule.**

The labia minora are amply supplied with nerve endings, blood vessels, and glands. The appearance of the labia minora varies greatly from woman to woman, even in the natural state. In some cultures, the labia minora are not left in their natural state, but are stretched, from childhood onward, with the aim of making the vulva more attractive. In others, they are completely cut away before puberty (Box 3.1).

There Is More to the Clitoris than Meets the Eye

Within the vestibule are three important structures: the clitoris, the urethral opening, and the vaginal opening. The **clitoris** is a complex organ, only a portion of which is visible from the exterior. The visible portion is the clitoral **glans.** The glans is a small but erectile and highly sensitive knob of tissue positioned at the front of the vestibule. It is covered, or partly covered, by the clitoral hood or **prepuce,** but can be made visible by gently retracting the hood. The shaft of the clitoris, which is about 2–3 centimeters long, runs upward from the glans, under the hood. Although it cannot be seen directly, its outline is visible through the skin of the hood. The shaft, like the glans, is erectile. The erectile tissue is contained in two **corpora cavernosa,** or **cavernous bodies,** which also extend into the glans. These structures expand by filling with blood during sexual arousal. (We will

Box 3.1   *Society, Values, and the Law*

Female Circumcision

An estimated 80–120 million women worldwide have been subjected to some form of cutting of their external genitals during childhood or at puberty. The various procedures are referred to collectively as **female circumcision** or **female genital mutilation** (World Health Organization, 1998). The practice is prevalent in 29 countries, most of them in Africa. Ninety percent or more of the women in Djibouti, Egypt, Eritrea, Guinea, Mali, Sierra Leone, and Somalia are believed to have been circumcised. Female circumcision is also practiced in the Middle East, Indonesia, and elsewhere (World Health Organization, 2001a). It is particularly associated with Islamic cultures, and although female circumcision is not prescribed in the Qur'an, it is referred to favorably in later Islamic texts and is often perceived to have religious significance.

There are three principal types of female circumcision. In the least invasive version, known as **sunnah** (an Arabic word referring to a traditional religious obligation), the clitoral hood is incised or removed. This procedure is roughly analogous to male circumcision as we know it in the United States (see Box 3.4). In practice, however, some part of the clitoris itself is often removed during sunnah circumcision.

In the second procedure, known as **clitoridectomy** or **excision,** the entire clitoral glans and shaft are removed, along with the hood and sometimes nearby portions of the labia minora.

The third procedure, known as **infibulation** or **pharaonic circumcision,** is the most invasive. It is widely practiced in the Sudan. The procedure includes clitoridectomy, but goes beyond it to include removal of the entire labia minora and the inner parts of the labia majora. The cut or abraded edges of the two labia majora are then stitched together to cover the vestibule. Only a small opening is left for the passage of urine and menstrual blood. The small opening has to be enlarged when the woman first has coitus.

Another form of female circumcision, called **introcision,** was traditionally performed in Australian aboriginal cultures. In this procedure the vagina was enlarged by cutting down into the perineum. The procedure parallels the **subincision** ritual performed on males in the same cultures.

Female circumcision is generally performed by traditional practitioners who lack medical training. It may be done with crude instruments and without anesthesia or attention to sanitary conditions, so that there is a risk of potentially fatal complications, including hemorrhage and infection. There has been a recent trend toward the "medicalization" of female circumcision—that is, its performance by trained medical personnel. This trend could reduce the rate of complications. The trend is controversial, however, since it may been seen as legitimizing the practice.

The long-term effects of female circumcision are also controversial. In some cases, especially with infibulation, it can cause serious problems with urination, menstruation, intercourse, childbirth, and fertility. But some recent studies have suggested that the harmful effects have been exaggerated (Shell-Duncan & Hernlund, 2000).

Female circumcision may be done simply because it is a tradition in a given culture. A woman who retains her clitoris may be considered ritually unclean or dangerous to the health of a man who has sex with her. However, there may be a second purpose to the procedures: the reduction of female sexual activity, especially outside of or before marriage. This reduction is achieved either by decreasing the pleasure of sexual acts (especially by removal of the clitoris) or by making them physically impossible (as with infibulation). In many cultures in which female circumcision is practiced, a woman who has not undergone the procedure is not marriageable—which often means that she is condemned to a life of poverty.

In the United States, circumcision of female children has been illegal since 1996. Nevertheless, it has been performed historically to discourage masturbation and other supposedly unhealthful behaviors. Also, significant numbers of immigrant women have been subjected to circumcision in their countries of birth, so Western medical professionals need to be aware of the phenomenon. Some circumcision of the daughters of immigrants does occur in the United States, but the prevalence of this illegal activity is hard to estimate. In addition, legal but controversial surgeries such as **clitoral reduction** are performed on girls with ambiguous genitalia (see Chapter 13).

The practice of female circumcision has been strongly condemned by many Americans on several grounds: that it interferes with women's right to self-expression, especially in the sexual domain; that it subjugates women's interests to the purported interests of men, and that it makes irreversible decisions for children before they are able to make those decisions for themselves.

It's not surprising that many Americans have made efforts to have female circumcision banned and eliminated in countries around the world. Organizations such as The Research, Action & Information Network for Bodily Integrity of Women (RAINBO) and The National Organization of Circumcision Information Resource Centers (NOCIRC) campaign for the elimination of these practices. (NOCIRC campaigns against male circumcision as well.) Novelist Alice Walker wrote a novel (*Possessing the Secret of Joy*) and produced a documentary film (*Warrior Marks*) about circumcision and its consequences for women in Africa. Patricia Schroeder (then a U.S. Representative from Colorado) was instrumental in the enactment of the 1996 U.S. ban on the practice. And, through their membership in the World Health Organization and UNICEF, the United States and other Western nations have helped put pressure on the governments of countries where female circumcision is practiced. Some African governments have in fact banned or strictly limited the practice, but it is questionable what effect the bans have had so far.

Although campaigning against female circumcision may seem like an entirely praiseworthy activity, it does potentially conflict with another value that some Americans hold dear, which is respect for cultural diversity and autonomy. While *we* may be tempted to use words such as "mutilation," "barbarity," or "atrocity" to describe female circumcision, women in the countries concerned have mostly positive views about the practice, and many girls *want* to have it done as a token of their womanhood and their membership in the culture. Who are we to tell African mothers what to do or not to do with their daughters' genitals, particularly when we consider how little most of us know about their cultures, and how little we concern ourselves with the much graver issues that many of them face—problems such as warfare, poverty, and AIDS?

Balancing these twin goals—of ending a seemingly abusive practice and of respect-

ing cultural diversity—is a difficult ethical exercise (James, 1994; Davis, 1998; Schweder, 2000). As a matter of practicality, efforts by Americans to end the practice may be limited by the low esteem in which Americans and their culture are held in some of the countries where female circumcision is most prevalent. It may be that the greatest progress will come from the work of activist organizations within the cultures concerned. Such organizations now exist in countries such as Burkina Faso, Kenya, Somalia, Nigeria, Sudan, and Gambia (see figure). One possible avenue for change is the institution of "ritual without cutting," in which the traditional rites are preserved but the actual circumcision is omitted. This poster was created by the Foundation for Research on Women's Health, Productivity and the Environment (BAFROW), a Gambian organization dedicated to ending female genital mutilation and replacing the rite with one that does not involve cutting.

discuss the mechanisms of erection in more detail below.) In some cultures, the visible portion of the clitoris is excised or surgically altered before puberty (see Box 3.1).

Completely invisible from the exterior are two extensions of the clitoris, the **crura** (singular **crus**). In a dissected body (Figure 3.2), they can be seen to diverge backward and downward from the clitoral shaft, giving the entire clitoris a wishbone structure. The crura are about 7 centimeters long and partially enwrap the urethra. Yet another pair of structures, the **vestibular bulbs,** are closely associated with the clitoris (O'Connell et al., 1998). They are curved masses of erectile tissue that surround the vestibule and underlie the labia minora.

Two muscles are associated with the clitoris. An **ischiocavernosus muscle** surrounds each crus of the clitoris. Contraction of these muscles during sexual arousal elevates the clitoral shaft and glans, causing the glans to disappear under the clitoral hood. The **bulbospongiosus** (sometimes called **bulbocavernosus**) muscle forms a sling around the clitoral shaft and then runs downward and backward to surround the vaginal opening. The contraction of this muscle tightens the vaginal opening, increases clitoral erection, and may also help increase the erotic sensations of vaginal penetration by transferring mechanical excitation to the clitoris.

The clitoris, especially the glans, is richly innervated with sensory nerve fibers that are specialized for the mediation of sexual arousal. Indeed, the only certain function of the clitoris is sexual pleasure, and its stimulation can lead to orgasm. As we'll discuss later, however, orgasm in women may aid the retention of sperm, so a role for the clitoris in reproduction is possible.

The Appearance of the Vaginal Opening Is Variable

The **vaginal opening** or **introitus** occupies the rear portion of the vestibule. In newborn girls, the introitus is usually covered by an incomplete membranous fold of skin, the

Figure 3.2 Dissection of the vulva to show internal portions of the clitoris and the pelvic floor muscles.

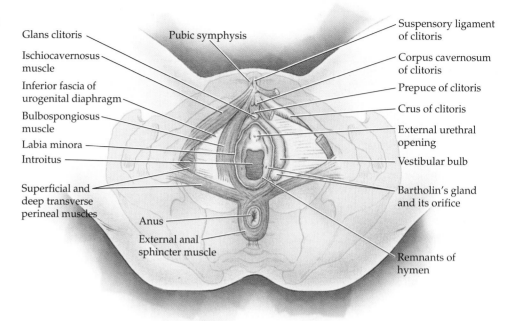

hymen (also known as the maidenhead or "cherry"). Rarely, the hymen is imperforate; that is, it completely blocks the vaginal opening. More commonly it has one or several openings that are large enough to allow for menstrual flow after a girl begins to menstruate, and for the insertion of tampons (Figure 3.3). Sometimes the hymen is absent altogether.

The hymen may rupture when a woman first has sexual intercourse, leading to some pain and bleeding. This phenomenon has led to the traditional notion that the state of a woman's hymen indicates whether or not she is a virgin. One can certainly debate whether a woman's virginity, or lack of it, should be a matter of concern to anyone besides herself. Even if it is, however, the state of her hymen is a fallible indicator. It may be absent, it may rupture during athletic activity or tampon insertion, or she may deliberately stretch the opening with the intention of facilitating first intercourse. Intercourse may also occur without rupture of the hymen. In fact, a woman can become pregnant without vaginal penetration at all, if a man ejaculates onto the general area of her vaginal opening.

In some Mediterranean cultures, it is traditional for a bride's mother or other relative to display the bloodstained sheets from a window after her wedding night, thereby documenting that the marriage was consummated and that the bride was indeed a virgin. Of course, there may be no stain, for any number of reasons—the bride was not a virgin, she was a virgin but didn't have an intact hymen, the couple achieved coitus without rupture of the hymen or without sufficient bleeding to stain the sheets, or they

Figure 3.3 The hymen is highly variable in structure. Most commonly it is annular (A); that is, it has a round central opening that is large enough for passage of the menstrual flow and insertion of a tampon, but usually not large enough for coitus. The opening may be crossed by a band of tissue (septate hymen, [B]), or by several bands that leave numerous small openings (cribriform hymen, [C]). If the openings are very small (microperforate hymen) or are absent entirely (imperforate hymen), the outflow of vaginal secretions and menstrual fluids may be blocked. First intercourse often tears the hymen but leaves it partially intact. Vaginal childbirth removes all but small remnants of the structure ("parous" refers to a woman who has had at least one child) (D). Familiarity with variations in hymen structure is important for professionals who evaluate sexual assaults on girls.

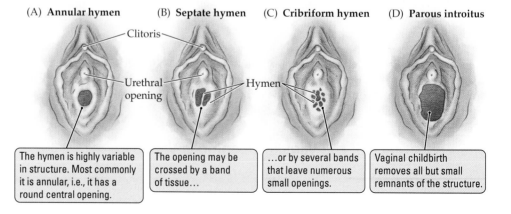

didn't engage in coitus because the man ejaculated prematurely or because one or both parties were too anxious, too drunk, too tired, or too gay to attempt the feat. To guard against any of these eventualities, the mother brings a vial of chicken blood with her.

The **urethral opening,** through which urine is excreted, is located between the vaginal opening and the clitoris. It opens directly to the exterior, not into the vagina as sometimes misconceived.

Small glands of unknown function—**Bartholin's glands**—lie on either side of the vaginal opening. They secrete a few drops of fluid prior to orgasm, but they play little if any role in the lubrication of the vagina.

The **perineum** is the area between the vaginal opening and the anus (or between the scrotum and the anus in males).* During childbirth, an obstetrician or nurse-midwife may extend the vaginal opening by cutting backward into the perineum; this procedure is known as **episiotomy** (see Chapter 10).

There are important structures underlying the vulva. We have already mentioned the deep extensions of the clitoris and the two muscles associated with it, the ischiocavernosus and bulbospongiosus muscles. Other muscles of the **pelvic floor,** including the transverse perineal and pubococcygeal muscles, have important roles during sex. The tonic (steady mild) contraction of these muscles stiffens the walls of the vagina during sex, thus increasing sexual sensations for both participants. The muscles contract more strongly at orgasm, during which they increase pleasure, prevent urinary and fecal leakage, and possibly help to retain semen. Exercises to increase the tone of these muscles have been recommended for the treatment of sexual dysfunction and incontinence (see Chapter 17).

A Woman's Internal Sex Organs Include Her Vagina, Uterus, Oviducts, and Ovaries

The female internal sex organs are the ovaries and a T-shaped passageway, the **reproductive tract.** The stem of the T is formed by the vagina, the cervix, and the body of the uterus. The two horizontal arms of the T are formed by the oviducts, whose ends are near or apposed to the two ovaries. The reproductive tract serves for transport of sperm and ova, fertilization, pregnancy, and passage of the fetus during childbirth.

The Vagina Is the Outermost Portion of the Female Reproductive Tract

The **vagina** is a potential space in the form of a collapsed tube that runs about 8 to 10 centimeters upward and backward from the vaginal opening (Figure 3.4). Penetration of the vagina by the penis constitutes **coitus** or **sexual intercourse.** (Of course, there are plenty of other sexual behaviors that don't involve coitus, as we will see in Chapter 8.) The vagina plays a role in sperm transport and (along with the cervix) forms the **birth canal** through which a fetus is delivered.

The vaginal wall is highly elastic, and consists of three layers: an inner mucosal layer, an intermediate muscular layer, and an outermost fibro-elastic layer. The mucosal layer can be seen by parting the labia minora. When a woman is in a nonaroused state, the mucosa is pink in color. It resembles the mucous membrane lining the inside of the mouth, but it is thrown into folds, or **rugae,** that run around the circumference of the vagina. The mucosal surface is normally mildly acidic (pH 4.0–5.0), and this acidity helps to prevent the growth of harmful bacteria. These secretions may also contain **sex pheromones**—volatile compounds that are distributed in the air and are unconsciously sensed by the olfactory system of other persons, who may then become sexually aroused. The existence of sex pheromones has been well documented in macaque monkeys, but the role of pheromones in human sexuality is still controversial (see Chapters 4 and 7).

---

*This is the meaning of the word "perineum" as it is used by clinicians, and we follow this usage throughout the book. Anatomists use it to refer to the entire territory between the pubic symphysis and the tailbone, thus including the external genitalia and the anus.

(A) **Sagittal (midline) view**

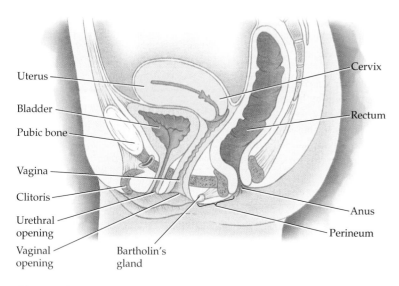

(B) **Frontal view**

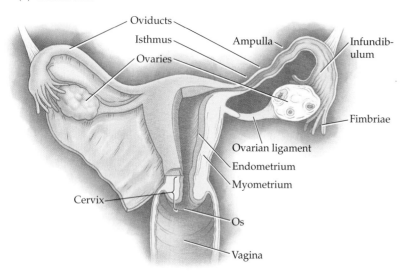

Figure 3.4 The female reproductive tract.

Some women **douche** their vaginas; that is, they rinse them with a jet of water or other liquid as a cleansing or deodorizing procedure, or to treat a vaginal discharge. Gynecologists generally discourage douching, as it may cause more problems than it prevents. A clear, odorless vaginal discharge is normal and does not call for treatment. Other vaginal conditions are discussed in Chapters 16 and 17.

The outer third of the vagina, near the vaginal opening, has a different developmental origin than the remainder (see Chapter 5), and has a different structure. It is tighter and more muscular, and also more richly innervated, than the deeper portion. Thus most of the sensation during coitus—for both partners—derives from contact between the penis and this outer portion of the vagina.

Perhaps the most famous and controversial feature of the vagina is the **Gräfenberg spot**, or **G spot**, named for the sexologist Ernst Gräfenberg, who described it in the early 1950s. Only a minority of women say that they have a G spot, but for those that do, it is an area of heightened sensitivity on the front wall of the vagina, about 3–5 centimeters from the vaginal entrance (Figure 3.5). Deep pressure at that point can trigger the desire to urinate, but it is also said to be sexually arousing and to trigger an orgasm that is different in quality from an orgasm caused by stimulation of the clitoris.

What is the structural basis of the G spot? The best candidate is probably a set of small glands known as **paraurethral glands** or **Skene's glands**. These glands are located just in front of the anterior wall of the vagina and next to the urethra; their ducts open into the urethra. The paraurethral glands are thought to be homologous (developmentally equivalent) to the much larger prostate gland in men (Zaviacic & Whipple, 1993). Besides being located in the right place, the paraurethral glands are good candidates for the G spot because, in

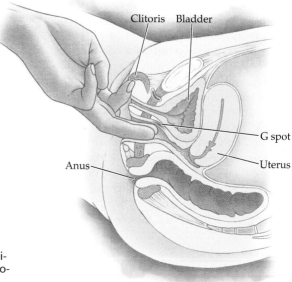

Figure 3.5 Finding the G spot. The G spot is an area of heightened sensitivity on the front wall of the vagina. Not all women have a G spot, and some sexologists question its existence altogether.

some women, orgasms triggered by stimulation of this area are accompanied by ejaculation of fluid from the glands (see below). However, there are other possible explanations for the erotic sensitivity in the region of the G spot: it might be due to stimulation of nerve fibers in the wall of the vagina itself, of the urethra, or of erectile tissue surrounding it.

Some researchers have claimed that every woman has a G spot and that those who are unaware of its existence can be helped to identify it (Ladas et al., 1982). Some believe that it is a vague term that may be used for any erotically sensitive region within the vagina. Others believe that the G spot is a complete myth (Hines, 2001). Debate about the G spot is related to a controversy about vaginal versus clitoral orgasms, which will be considered further below.

The Uterus Serves a Double Duty

The **uterus** or **womb**—the inward continuation of the female reproductive tract beyond the vagina—is a hollow organ that lies within the **pelvic cavity** (the portion of the abdominal cavity that is surrounded by the bones of the **pelvis**). In a nonpregnant woman the uterus is about the shape and size of a small upside-down pear (see Figure 3.4). The narrow part of the pear, the **cervix,** bulges into the deep end of the vagina. A woman can feel her own cervix by inserting two fingers deeply into the vagina while in a squatting position, and she can see her cervix with the help of a mirror, a flashlight, and a speculum (an instrument that holds open the walls of the vagina: Box 3.2).

A constricted opening—the **external os**—connects the vagina to a short canal that runs through the cervix. In the cervical canal are numerous glands that secrete **mucus.** The consistency of this mucus changes with the menstrual cycle (the more commonly used term for the ovarian cycle in humans). Only around the time of ovulation is its consistency optimal for passage of sperm through the cervix (see Chapter 10).

The cervical canal passes through a second constriction—the **internal os**—and opens into the cavity (**lumen**) of the uterus proper. The wall of the uterus has three layers: the inner lining (**endometrium**), the muscular wall (**myometrium**), and a thin outer peritoneal layer (the lining that separates the uterus from the abdominal cavity).

The endometrium must switch periodically between two reproductive functions—the transport of sperm up the reproductive tract toward the site of fertilization, and the implantation and nourishment of a **conceptus.** (The conceptus is the cluster of cells derived from the fertilized ovum, part of which becomes an embryo and ultimately a baby.) Because these two functions require a very different organization, the structure of the endometrium changes over the menstrual cycle. **Menstruation** is the shedding of part of the endometrial lining and its discharge, along with some blood, through the cervix and vagina (see Chapter 4).

The myometrium is composed primarily of so-called **smooth muscle.** Unlike the muscles of the pelvic floor, which are composed of **striated muscle,** the uterine musculature is under the control of the autonomic nervous system and cannot be caused to contract by an effort of will. Involuntary contractions of the myometrium during labor play a vital role in delivery of the fetus (see Chapter 10). Myometrial contractions (often perceived as menstrual cramps; see Chapter 4) also aid in the shedding and expulsion of the endometrial lining at menstruation.

The Oviducts Are the Site of Fertilization

At the upper end, or **fundus,** of the uterus, the reproductive tract divides into two bilaterally symmetrical branches, the **oviducts,** also called **fallopian tubes** or simply **tubes.** (Fallopius was the sixteenth-century Italian anatomist who described them.) Each oviduct is about 10 centimeters long, and forms a pathway between the uterus and the left or right ovary.

The cells lining the lumen of the oviducts carry **cilia,** microscopic hairlike structures that beat in a coordinated fashion toward the uterus. Sperm moving from the uterus toward the ovary have to swim against a current set up by the beating cilia, rather like salmon swimming upstream, but this current is too slow to offer a serious impediment

Box 3.2 *Sexual Health*

Cervical Self-Examination

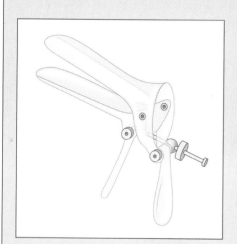

(A) A speculum

A woman can inspect her vulva with the help of a small mirror and a flashlight. To see her cervix, she will also need a vaginal speculum, a two-bladed "duck-billed" device made of plastic that holds the walls of the vagina apart (Figure A). (Specula can be obtained through women's health organizations. They come in three sizes; a small is probably right unless the woman has reason to think she needs a larger one.) The woman should first wash the speculum and practice opening, locking, unlocking, and closing it. Then she lubricates the blades with a water-based lubricant (or just water). With her knees apart, she uses the fingers of one hand to separate the labia. With the other hand, she holds the speculum, with handle up and blades closed, and slides it gently into her vagina (Figure B). (Sometimes it is easier to hold the speculum sideways for the insertion and turn it handle-up once it is fully in place.) Any discomfort should be a signal to stop and relax, and if comfortable insertion isn't possible, the woman should desist. Once the speculum is fully in place, the woman opens and locks the blades, so that she now has both hands free to hold the mirror and flashlight. By shining the flashlight onto the mirror, she should be able to illuminate and see her cervix, which looks like a rounded knob with a central hole or slit (the external os). The appearance of the cervix varies around the menstrual cycle (due to changes in cervical mucus) and from woman to woman. Some women may see fluid-filled sacs on the cervix or polyps protruding through the os; these are usually harmless. To remove the speculum, the woman first unlocks and closes the blades, then gently withdraws it. The speculum should be carefully washed with soap and water, rinsed, and put away in a clean place. It's not a good idea to share a speculum with others. Self-examination is an adjunct to regular professional checkups, not a replacement for them.

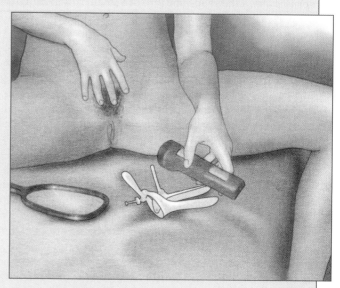

(B) Cervical self-exam

to healthy, fast-moving sperm. Muscular contractions of the walls of the oviducts may also help propel the sperm forward.

The portion of each oviduct near the uterus is relatively narrow and is known as the **isthmus.** The portion nearer the ovary is wider and is called the **ampulla;** this is the usual site of fertilization. The very end of the oviduct flares out into a funnel-like structure called the **infundibulum,** whose rim is fringed by fingerlike extensions known as **fimbria.** The fimbria are near, but not actually fused with, the ovary. At the infundibulum, the lumen of the reproductive tract opens into the abdominal cavity. Thus there is a continuous pathway from a woman's abdominal cavity, down her reproductive tract, to the outside of her body. No comparable pathway exists in men.

The Ovaries Produce Ova and Sex Hormones

The **ovaries**—a woman's gonads—are paired organs located on either side of the uterus. They are ovoid structures measuring about 3 centimeters in their long axis. They are about the same size and shape as a man's testicles, but less regular in outline.

Under the microscope (Figure 3.6), an adult woman's ovary can be seen to contain a large number of **follicles** at various stages of development. Each follicle consists of a central **oocyte,** or developing egg cell, surrounded by supporting cells known as **gran-**

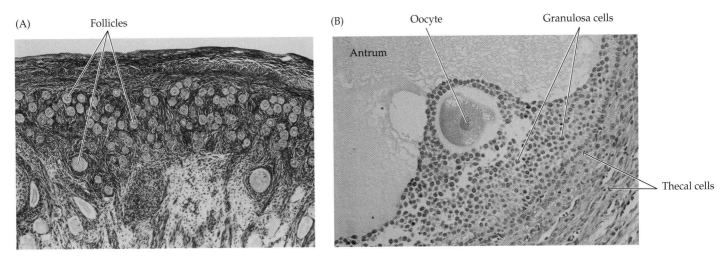

(A) Follicles

(B) Oocyte   Granulosa cells

Antrum

Thecal cells

Figure 3.6 Microscopic structure of the ovary. (A) Low-power view of ovary, showing a number of follicles. (B) Higher-power view of part of a single follicle, showing the central antrum and the oocyte surrounded by granulosa cells.

ulosa cells. Outside of these are some more loosely arranged cells called **thecal cells.** The more mature follicles have a central cavity or **antrum**.

The ovary has two distinct functions. The first is the release of oocytes (**ovulation**). A newborn female has about a million oocytes in each ovary. No new oocytes are generated after birth, and in fact, their numbers decline throughout life. By puberty a woman has about 200,000 in each ovary. During her reproductive life she typically releases only one mature oocyte from one or the other ovary per menstrual cycle. Thus only a tiny fraction of a woman's oocytes are actually ovulated during her lifetime. Much greater numbers of oocytes die in the process of maturation and are never ovulated.

Ovulation occurs by rupture of the wall of the ovary and release of the oocyte and its surrounding cells (collectively called an **ovum**) into the abdominal cavity. The nearby fimbria of the oviduct catch the ovum, and ciliary movement propels it down into the ampulla, where fertilization occurs if sperm are present. We will have much more to say about all these ovarian processes in later chapters.

The second function of the ovary is the production and secretion of **sex hormones**. The granulosa and thecal cells play key roles in the production of these hormones, as we'll see in Chapter 4.

The Breasts Have Both Erotic and Reproductive Significance

The **breasts** (or **mammary glands**) are considered **secondary sexual characteristics,** meaning that they are not components of the genitals, but do differ between the sexes. Although both men and women have **nipples,** and some men have a certain amount of breast tissue, breasts of significant size are generally a feature of women's anatomy, not men's. Occasionally, women or men may have extra nipples or breasts (Box 3.3).

The breasts lie between the skin and the muscles of the anterior (front) chest wall; some breast tissue extends up into the **axillae** (armpits). Each breast consists of about 15 to 20 **lobes** that are separated from one another by fibrous and fatty (adipose) tissue (Figure 3.7). The lobes are subdivided into **lobules,** and (in women who are producing milk) each lobule comprises numerous small cavities called **alveoli.** Each alveolus

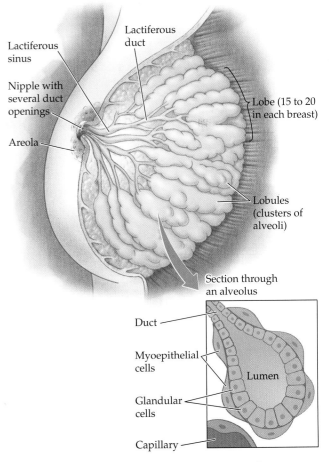

Lactiferous sinus

Lactiferous duct

Nipple with several duct openings

Areola

Lobe (15 to 20 in each breast)

Lobules (clusters of alveoli)

Section through an alveolus

Duct

Myoepithelial cells

Glandular cells

Lumen

Capillary

Figure 3.7 Internal structure of the lactating breast. When the breast is not lactating, the alveoli regress to a rudimentary state.

Biology of Sex

Extra Nipples and Breasts

Ancient goddesses of fertility, such as the Greek Artemis, were portrayed as possessing numerous breasts where most mortal women have but two. Still, occasional men and women can boast extra nipples (**polythelia**—also called **supernumerary nipples**) or breasts (**polymastia**).

Small extra patches of areolar skin, sometimes with miniature nipples at their center, are found in about 6 percent of people—more commonly in men than in women and more commonly on the left side of the body than on the right (Schmidt, 1998). These extra nipples are usually found along the "milk lines"—embryological ridges that run from the armpits to the groin. Mammary glands and nipples originate from characteristic portions of the milk lines in each mammalian species, but can also arise from anomalous portions of the lines. An Israeli study reported that 40 percent of children with polythelia also had congenital anomalies of the renal or urinary systems (Varsano et al., 1984).

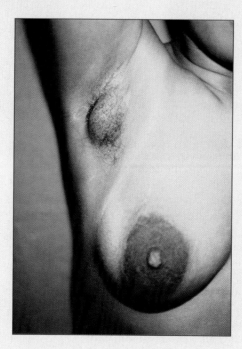

Extra breasts in women can become fully functional at puberty. A nineteenth-century Frenchwoman named Therese Ventre nursed her children from a breast on the side of her left thigh—a highly unusual location off the milk lines—as well as from her two normally located breasts. There has been a traditional (but incorrect) belief that women with extra breasts are unusually fertile. This may be why Anne Boleyn was chosen by King Henry VIII of England as his second wife—but unfortunately for her, the extra breast did not save her from execution after she failed to produce a son (Grossl, 2000). The record number of medically verified breasts in a single person is ten (Deaver & McFarland, 1917).

Extra nipples and breasts may cause discomfort (e.g., if located in the armpits; see figure) or embarrassment. Extra breasts are also subject to the same diseases as regular breasts. For any of these reasons, surgical excision is an option.

consists of a central space, or lumen, lined by a rim of cells that can be stimulated to produce and secrete milk by the appropriate hormonal signals (see Chapter 10). Surrounding the milk-secreting cells are contractile cells called **myoepithelial cells**, as well as blood capillaries and fat cells. The coordinated contraction of the myoepithelial cells causes "milk letdown," the passage of milk from the alveoli into the **lactiferous ducts.** Near the nipple, each lactiferous duct expands into a space known as a **lactiferous sinus.** A dozen or so ducts lead from the sinuses of each breast to the surface of the nipple.

When the sinuses fill with milk, the pressure within the breast increases and milk may actually be ejected from the nipples. A suckling infant probably removes milk by compressing the nipple between its tongue and palate, rather than by actually sucking (i.e., generating negative pressure within its mouth) as commonly believed. By suckling, the infant can remove whatever milk is present within the lactiferous sinuses, but a much larger quantity of milk can be made available by a hormonally controlled **milk letdown reflex** (see Chapter 4).

The nipples are situated at the tip of the breasts in the center of circular patches of darker skin known as **areolae** (singular: areola). The nipples are capable of erection in response to sexual arousal, oral or digital stimulation, or cold. Erection is caused by contraction of smooth muscles beneath the nipple, which push the nipple outward.

As with all secondary sexual characteristics, the breasts vary considerably among individuals. Variation in breast size is due largely to differences in the amount of fatty tissue in the breast; women with small breasts usually have adequate glandular tissue to nurse an infant. (Breast-feeding is discussed further in Chapter 10.)

There is commonly a slight difference in size between a woman's left and right breasts. Although this difference has no functional significance, it is not a completely random phenomenon, since the left breast is the larger one in the majority of women. Furthermore, it has been reported that the direction of breast asymmetry is related to a woman's perform-

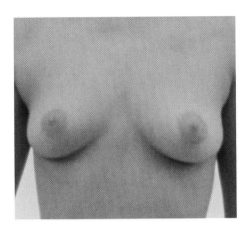 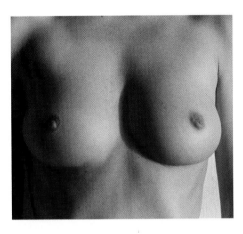 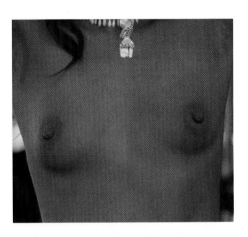

Breasts vary greatly in appearance. There is also commonly some difference in size between a woman's left and right breast.

ance on certain cognitive tests (Kimura, 1994). This finding suggests that some underlying factor, such as hormone levels, influences both breast asymmetry and cognitive development.

The breasts are of great erotic significance to many people. For women, tactile or oral stimulation of the breasts (especially the nipples) in the appropriate circumstances is sexually arousing. The appearance or feel of the breasts is also an important erotic stimulus to women's sex partners, especially in contemporary Western culture. Probably for this reason, many women are unhappy with their breasts; they may seek to alter their appearance through the wearing of various kinds of brassieres (bras) or by plastic surgery. The attractiveness of breasts is discussed further in Chapter 7. Health issues related to the breasts are covered in Chapter 17.

The Male External Genitalia Are the Penis and Scrotum

The parts of a man's reproductive system that can be seen from the outside are the penis, the scrotum or scrotal sac, and the testicles ("balls"), whose twin bulges give the scrotum its shape (Figure 3.8). The testicles are usually considered parts of a man's internal reproductive system, however, not part of the external genitalia.

Actually, men have another genital structure that is rarely mentioned: a pad of fat covered in pubic hair that protects the pubic symphysis. It is very similar to a woman's mons veneris, and if there were any gender parity in the world, it would be called the "mons martis" or "mountain of Mars." Its actual name is the **prepubic fat pad**.

The Penis Combines Erotic, Reproductive, and Excretory Functions

The **penis** is the center of most men's sex lives in a way that no single body part is for women. In much male discourse, the remaining parts of a man's body are reduced to a set of appendages for getting his penis to the right place at the right time.

Developmentally, the penis is homologous with the clitoris (see Chapter 5), but in a functional sense, the penis corresponds to the clitoris, urethra, and vagina all rolled into one, because it is involved in sexual arousal, excretion of urine, and the transfer of gametes from the male to the female. No wonder men focus so much attention on the penis and are so gravely concerned when it fails to perform as advertised (see Chapter 15).

The penis in its natural (i.e., uncircumcised) condition has three visible portions: a **shaft;** a head, or **glans;** and a loose, tubular fold of skin known as the **prepuce** or **foreskin,** which partially or completely covers the glans. The foreskin can be readily pulled back to expose the glans. **Circumcision** is the surgical removal of the foreskin (Box 3.4).

The shaft of the penis contains three erectile structures (Figure 3.9): two **corpora cavernosa,** which lie side by side and account for the bulk of the penis's erectile capacity, and a thinner **corpus spongiosum,** which lies at the midline near the undersurface of the penis. The corpus spongiosum extends from the shaft into the glans, where it balloons out and fills the entire volume of the glans. Both the corpora cavernosa and the corpus

(A)

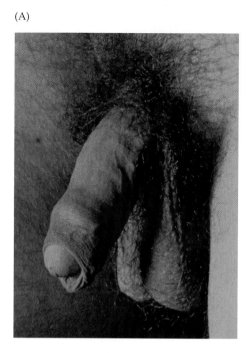

(B)

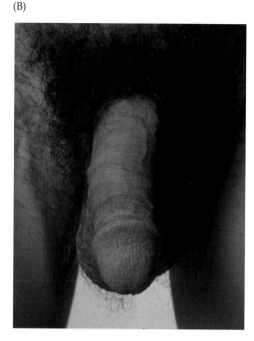

(C)

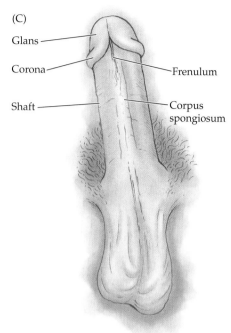

Glans

Corona

Shaft

Frenulum

Corpus spongiosum

Figure 3.8 The male external genitalia. (A) A flaccid uncircumcised penis. (B) A flaccid circumcised penis. (C) An erect circumcised penis seen from below, showing the glans, corona, and frenulum—the most erotically sensitive portions of the penis.

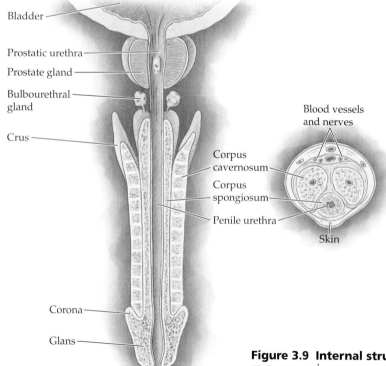

Bladder

Prostatic urethra

Prostate gland

Bulbourethral gland

Crus

Corona

Glans

Urethral meatus

Blood vessels and nerves

Corpus cavernosum

Corpus spongiosum

Penile urethra

Skin

spongiosum extend backward into the body under the pubic symphysis, forming the **root** of the penis, which is about 5 centimeters long. The root is attached to the pubic symphysis via a **suspensory ligament.**

At the inner end of the root of the penis, the corpus spongiosum expands into a bulbous mass of erectile tissue underneath the prostate gland. The corpora cavernosa diverge, forming two **crura** similar to those of a woman's clitoris. As in the clitoris, there are two muscles associated with the root of the penis, the **ischiocavernosus** and **bulbospongiosus** (also called **bulbocavernosus**) **muscles.** These muscles are considerably larger in males, and they assist with erection of the penis and with ejaculation. The bulbospongiosus muscle is an integral part of the external anal sphincter muscle; thus the anal sphincter goes into spasm during ejaculation.

The **urethra,** which discharges urine from the bladder and semen from internal reproductive glands (see below), enters the root of the penis and traverses its length to emerge at the tip of the glans. Within the penis, the urethra runs close to its undersurface and is entirely contained within the corpus spongiosum. The orifice of the urethra is known as the **urethral meatus.**

The shaft of the penis contains other structures, most notably nerves and blood vessels, that play an important role in sexual arousal and erection. The deep structures of

Figure 3.9 Internal structure of the erect penis and the urethra. Note that the corpus spongiosum surrounds the penile urethra and expands at the tip of the penis to form the glans. Unlike the corpora cavernosa, the corpus spongiosum does not have a tough outer fascia, so it is less rigid when erect.

Box 3.4 **CULTURAL DIVERSITY**

Male Circumcision

Circumcision in men means the surgical removal of the prepuce or foreskin of the penis (see figure). Worldwide, about a quarter of all men are circumcised (Moses et al., 1998). Circumcision is an ancient practice that is religiously prescribed for Muslims and Jews. It has also been practiced as a nonreligious tradition in many countries. Currently, about one-third of all male infants born in the United States are circumcised. In the adult U.S. population, circumcision is common among non-Hispanic whites (approximately 80 percent) and less common among African-Americans and Hispanics (about 50 percent and 40 percent, respectively) (Laumann et al., 1997). In Europe, circumcision rates have fallen dramatically over recent decades: a survey conducted in Britain around 1990 revealed that 32 percent of men aged 45–59 had been circumcised, while only 12 percent of men aged 16–24 had been circumcised (Wellings et al., 1994). A less marked decline in the rate of circumcision has been noted in the United States (Wiswell et al., 1987).

Circumcision offers some medical benefits, but also carries slight risks. Probably the most significant medical benefit is a tenfold or greater reduction in the incidence of urinary tract infections in infancy (Herzog, 1989) (Wiswell et al., 1987). Circumcision also prevents (or effectively treats) a condition known as **phimosis,** in which the foreskin is so tight that it cannot be pulled back from the glans (see Chapter 17). Circumcision greatly reduces the risk of cancer of

the penis later in life, but this is a rare cancer even among uncircumcised men.

Worldwide, circumcision is associated with a lower risk of acquiring ulcerative sexually transmitted diseases and AIDS (Moses et al., 1998), and it has been suggested that increasing the practice of circumcision could be a useful measure to curb the AIDS pandemic. Finally, circumcised men are less likely than uncircumcised men to become infected with a common sexually transmitted virus, human papillomavirus (HPV; see Chapter 16). Thus they are less likely to infect their female partners with HPV. This is important because HPV infection in women is the major cause of cervical cancer (see Chapter 17). The female partners of circumcised men have a lower risk of developing cervical cancer than the female partners of uncircumcised men (Castellsague et al., 2002).

Besides its medical benefits, circumcision facilitates hygiene. In uncircumcised men, a cheesy substance called **smegma** builds up under the foreskin, and can develop a rancid smell and taste—something that a man's sex partner may find off-putting, especially when performing oral sex. Microorganisms in smegma may also be responsible for some vaginal infections. Both of these problems can easily be avoided, however, if a man cleans under his foreskin whenever he takes a bath or shower. (This practice may also reduce the risk of penile cancer.)

The risks of circumcision include hemorrhage, infection, and—extremely rarely—damage to the penis. (The story of one boy whose penis was destroyed in a circumcision

accident, and who was subsequently reared as a girl, is told in Chapter 6.) Some opponents of circumcision have suggested that the operation reduces the erotic sensitivity of the penis. However, one national study found that circumcision is associated with a lower incidence of sexual dysfunction (Laumann et al., 1997).

The American Academy of Pediatrics has issued a position statement laying out the benefits and risks of circumcision and suggesting that parents make an informed decision in consultation with their doctors (American Academy of Pediatrics, 1999a). The Academy does urge doctors to end the traditional practice of performing circumcision without anesthesia. The Academy's neutral stance on male circumcision contrasts with its strong opposition to female circumcision.

While male circumcision is in no way comparable to female circumcision in terms of its negative effects, groups such as NOCIRC are ardently opposed to the practice. There is even a self-help book and Web sites, aimed at circumcised men, that purport to explain how to regrow a foreskin. Even if the loss of the foreskin may seem like a trivial or even humorous matter to many people, an ethical question remains: Given that circumcision can be performed at any age, should one preempt a person's right to choose or reject the procedure simply in order to bestow a fairly limited benefit during childhood?

Two other operations on the penis are practiced by certain ethnic groups. In some Polynesian cultures as well as in parts of the Philippines, a slit is made along the top of a boy's foreskin at or before puberty. This operation, called **superincision,** exposes the top surface of the glans and lets the foreskin droop below the glans, but no tissue is removed. Australian aborigines and some other cultures traditionally made a slit along the underside of the penis, exposing the urethra and allowing the glans and part of the shaft to flare outward, giving the penis a flat appearance. This procedure is called **subincision.** For those with strong stomachs, photographs of the procedure (as performed by U.S. body modification enthusiasts) can easily be found on the Web.

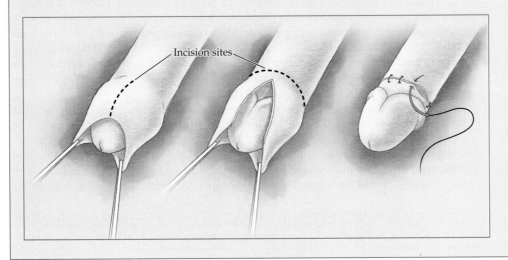

Incision sites

the penile shaft are enclosed in a tough, fibrous sheath of connective tissue, or **fascia.** The skin of the penis is hairless and only loosely attached to the underlying fascia.

The glans has a rim, or **corona,** that circles the penis. On the undersurface of the penis the corona comes closer to the tip of the glans than on the dorsal surface. In this area lies a loose strip of skin named the **frenulum** that runs between the glans and the shaft. Although stimulation anywhere on the penis can be sexually arousing, the corona and the frenulum are usually the most erotically sensitive regions.

The size of the penis—both in the flaccid and erect states—varies considerably among men. Some men are concerned about the size of their penis, but size variations rarely have any practical effect on sexual performance (Box 3.5).

The Scrotum Regulates the Temperature of the Testicles

The **scrotum** or **scrotal sac** is a loose bag of skin that hangs down behind the penis and contains the two testicles. In adult men it is lightly covered with hair, and it possesses numerous sweat glands that help to regulate the temperature of the scrotal contents. Stimulation of the scrotal skin is sexually arousing in most men, though not to the same degree as the most sensitive areas of the penis. Underneath the scrotal skin lies a sheet-like smooth muscle known as the **dartos.** Contraction of the dartos in response to cold (and also during sexual arousal, especially near orgasm) thickens the scrotal skin and throws it into wrinkles. This makes the skin a more effective insulator and also brings the testicles closer to the body, warming them.

The Male Internal Sex Organs Produce and Deliver Semen and Secrete Sex Hormones

The male internal sex organs (Figure 3.10) have two functions that are similar to those of the corresponding female organs: they produce gametes (**sperm**) and secrete sex hormones. As in women, these two tasks are accomplished by the gonads, which in men are called the **testes.*** Men do not become pregnant, so they have no structures corresponding to the uterus or oviducts. However, they do need to store large numbers of sperm, mix them with other secretions, and deliver the resulting **semen** to the urethral meatus for ejaculation. These functions require a number of structures, including several specialized glands and assorted pieces of tubing to connect everything together.

The Testes Secrete Sex Hormones and Manufacture Sperm

The testicles are twin ellipsoidal structures that can easily be seen or felt within the scrotal sac (Figure 3.11). The testicles are not completely symmetrical: one (usually the left) hangs lower, and one (usually the right) is slightly larger. As with women's breasts, there is reported to be a relationship between the direction of testicular asymmetry and men's performance on some cognitive tests (Kimura, 1994).

Each testis weighs about 10–15 grams and lies within a protective capsule, the **tunica albuginea.** Behind each testis is an **epididymis,** through which sperm pass after leaving the testis. The testis and epididymis can easily be moved around within the scrotal sac because they lie within a membranous sac, the **tunica vaginalis,** which, developmentally speaking, is an extension of the abdominal cavity.

Before considering the structure of the testis, let's take a look at the **spermatic cord.** This structure is the testis's "lifeline"—a bundle of structures that connect the testis with organ systems within the abdominal cavity. It runs through a 4-centimeter-long canal—the **inguinal canal**—that passes through the abdominal wall in the region of the groin.

The spermatic cord has a sheetlike covering, or fascia, and a layer of striated ("voluntary") muscle tissue known as the **cremaster muscle.** When it reaches the testicle, the

---

*The terms "testes" and "testicles" denote the same structures, but are generally used in different contexts: "testicles" in the context of gross anatomy or surgery, "testes" in the context of microscopic anatomy or function.

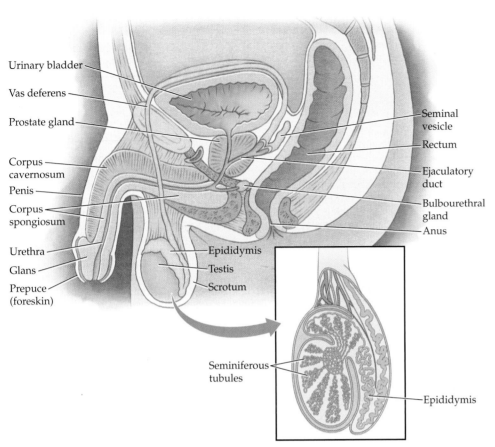

Figure 3.10 The male reproductive tract. Note how the prostate gland surrounds the urethra as it exits the bladder. Enlargement of the prostate can interfere with urination.

Urinary bladder

Vas deferens

Prostate gland

Corpus cavernosum

Penis

Corpus spongiosum

Urethra

Glans

Prepuce (foreskin)

Seminal vesicle

Rectum

Ejaculatory duct

Bulbourethral gland

Anus

Epididymis

Testis

Scrotum

Seminiferous tubules

Epididymis

cremaster forms a sling around the gland. It contracts automatically in response to cold, pulling the testis toward the body and thus, like the dartos muscle, helping to regulate the temperature of the testis.

Within the spermatic cord runs the **vas deferens,** which conveys mature sperm away from the epididymis. In addition, the cord contains arteries, veins, and nerves that supply the testicle. The arteries and veins are closely apposed to each other in a fashion that facilitates the transfer of heat from the arterial to the venous circulation. This arrangement helps keep the temperature of the testicle below the temperature of the remainder of the body.

With all these temperature-regulating elements, it's no surprise to learn that the production of sperm by the human testis requires a specific temperature range: 4°–7°C below core body temperature. That seems to be why the male gonads migrate out of the abdomen into the scrotum during development (see Chapter 5). Increasing the temperature of the testes to 37°C for prolonged periods decreases a man's sperm count. Failure of the testicles to descend into the scrotum may cause infertility and also raises the risk of testicular cancer (see Chapter 17). Increased temperature does not affect the other function of the testes—hormone production—to any significant extent.

It is something of a mystery why sperm production in men should require such low temperatures. Some other mammals, such as elephants, keep their testes inside their abdomen and suffer no adverse consequences. It's possible that the testes were originally exteriorized for some other reason and that the temperature-regulating mechanisms developed secondarily. It is also possible that it is not so much the production as the *storage* of sperm that requires low temperatures:

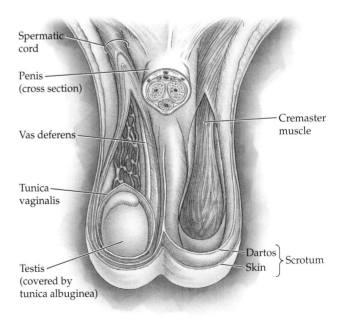

Spermatic cord

Penis (cross section)

Vas deferens

Tunica vaginalis

Testis (covered by tunica albuginea)

Cremaster muscle

Dartos

Skin

} Scrotum

Figure 3.11 The scrotum and its contents.

Box 3.5 # Research Highlights

How Big Should a Penis Be?

Many men fear that they are underendowed—specifically, that their penis is too small to arouse or physically satisfy their partners, or that its small size will provoke ridicule from their peers. Let's take a look at some objective data. The most reliable study of penis size is probably one published in 1996 by three urologists at San

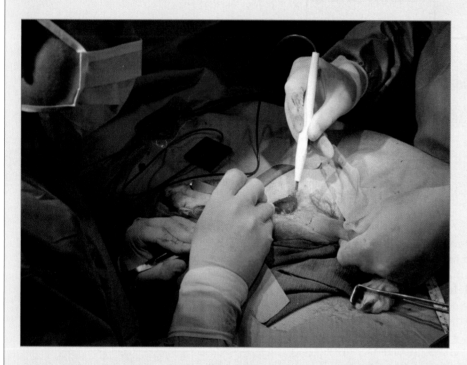

Francisco General Hospital (Wessells et al., 1996b). They measured the flaccid and erect penises of 80 physically normal men. They first measured along the top surface of the flaccid penis, from the skin crease between the penis and the abdominal wall to the tip of the penis. They got a mean length of 8.9 centimeters, with a standard deviation of ±2.4 centimeters. Measuring the erect penis the same way, they got a mean length of 12.9 ±2.9 centimeters. By pushing the end of the tape measure into the prepubic fat pad until it rested against the pubic symphysis, they got a mean "functional erect length" of 15.7 ±2.6 centimeters. The mean circumference of the shaft of the erect penis was 12.3 ±1.3 centimeters. The researchers found no correlation between the length of a man's penis when flaccid and the same penis when erect. However,

the length of a man's flaccid penis when stretched out was about the same as the length of the same penis when erect.

So much for the "hard" data, but what does it say about what is normal? A common medical rule of thumb is that anything within two standard deviations of the mean is "normal." (This range includes 96 percent of the population if the data follow the usual bell-shaped distribution.) According to this criterion, a penis has to have a flaccid length of less than 4 cm, or an erect length of less than 7 cm, to be considered abnormally short.

These figures may give male readers some perspective against which to judge their own anatomy. It is also important, though, to realize that a penis smaller than the "normal" limit just mentioned is still likely to work just fine in most sexual situations. In vaginal penetration, the dimensions of the penis are pretty much irrelevant, because the elasticity of the vaginal wall makes it a "one-size-fits-all" organ. In anal penetration, a small penis may actually be an advantage. The same is true for oral penetration, since a long penis may cause gagging. In general, the significance of

penis size lies only in the mind. Not that the mind isn't important, but it is surely at least as adaptable as the vagina.

There does exist a small industry, centered in Southern California, devoted to the surgical augmentation of the penis. The penis may be lengthened by cutting of the suspensory ligament (see figure), followed by many weeks of traction (hanging weights from the penis). This procedure causes the penis to protrude farther from the body. The procedure lengthens only the flaccid penis, however, not the erect penis. It also drags hairy skin onto the shaft of the penis, which may be considered unsightly.

The girth of the penis can be increased by fat injections, or by transplanting slabs of fatty tissue from the buttocks under the skin of the penis. The procedure leaves visible scars, and the penis often comes to look lumpy or otherwise abnormal over time. At least one man has died from complications of penis enlargement surgery. Men who undergo the surgery are, on average, more dissatisfied than satisfied with the outcome, and they do not experience improved sex lives afterward (Wessells et al., 1996a; Klein, 1999).

Perhaps the most interesting fact about penis augmentation surgery is that the men who request it have average-sized, not small, penises. This fact makes us wonder whether the money spent on the surgery (about $7500 for "the works") would be better invested in psychotherapy to help men understand why they are unhappy with their natural endowment. (For an ancient method of penis enlargement, see Chapter 8.)

Some men complain that their flaccid penis retracts inside their bodies. This can be a consequence of obesity: the prepubic fat pad may become so thick that the flaccid penis is barely long enough to protrude through it. Weight loss or liposuction may alleviate this problem (Adham et al., 2000). Psychological factors may also be at work, however. In fact, epidemics of delusional penile retraction sweep across some Asian countries (especially southern China) from time to time (Cheng, 1997). This condition is known as **koro**, and its victims attach clamps, strings, and other devices to the penis to prevent its complete disappearance, which they are convinced will be accompanied by their own death.

in animals with internal testes, the sperm storage area (the epididymis—see below) is at or near the body surface (Bedford, 1977).

The internal structure of the testis (Figure 3.12) is dominated by the **seminiferous tubules,** a set of about a thousand fine, highly convoluted tubes that occupy lobes of the testis; they are the site of sperm production, or **spermatogenesis.** Unlike oocytes, all of which are present in the ovaries when a girl is born, sperm are not found in the testes until puberty, when **stem cells** begin dividing. The resulting sperm develop while embedded within **Sertoli cells** that line the tubules. Besides developing the highly specialized structures that characterize mature sperm, spermatogenesis involves **meiosis,** a pair of cell divisions that results in the halving of the complement of chromosomes from 46 (the **diploid** number characteristic of most human cells) to 23 (the **haploid** number). Meiosis also involves genetic recombination—a shuffling of the DNA that ensures that each gamete is genetically unique (see Chapter 2).

It takes 64 days for a mature sperm to develop from a stem cell. Of course, huge numbers of sperm are developing simultaneously. About 5 million sperm are produced per gram of testicular tissue per day—day after day for several decades. Out of this gigantic total, perhaps two or three sperm will be lucky enough to contribute their genes to the next generation!

Besides nurturing the developing sperm, the Sertoli cells produce peptide hormones. (A peptide is a chain of several amino acids, similar to a protein but shorter—see Chapter 4.) One of these hormones plays a role in embryonic sex determination (see Chapter 5); the others help regulate testicular function in adult men (see Chapter 4). The spaces between the seminiferous tubules are occupied by **Leydig cells** (or **interstitial cells**), which secrete steroid hormones. The Leydig cells also secrete peptide hormones that control the process of spermatogenesis. We'll examine the roles of all of these hormones in Chapter 4.

(A)

(B)

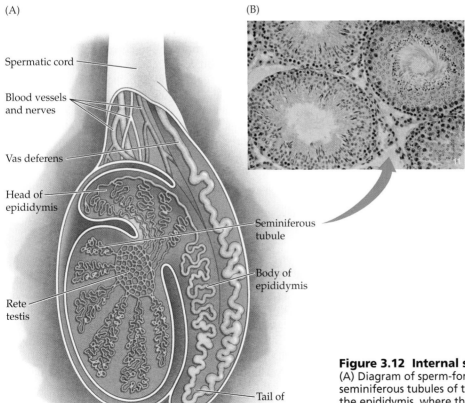

Spermatic cord

Blood vessels
and nerves

Vas deferens

Head of
epididymis

Seminiferous
tubule

Body of
epididymis

Rete
testis

Tail of
epididymis

Figure 3.12 Internal structure of the testis and epididymis.
(A) Diagram of sperm-forming pathway. Sperm initially develop in the seminiferous tubules of the testis, then pass through the rete testis to the epididymis, where they mature further and are stored. They then pass through the vas deferens to the urethra. (B) Cross-section of seminiferous tubules. The sperm develop while embedded in the cells lining the tubules (Sertoli cells). The cells scattered between the tubules (Leydig cells) secrete sex hormones.

After leaving the seminiferous tubules, the sperm pass through a network of spaces known as the **rete testis** and then enter the epididymis. The epididymis has the form of a letter C and is attached to the back surface of the testis. It is actually formed by a single but extremely convoluted tubule. Sperm spend about a week traversing this tubule, during which time they become about a hundredfold more concentrated. They also mature functionally, gaining the capacity for forward motion.

Other Glands Contribute Their Secretions to the Semen

The sperm pass from the lower end of the C of each epididymis into the vas deferens (or vas) on that side. Each vas passes up through the spermatic cord into the abdomen, past the bladder, and down toward the prostate gland (see Figure 3.10). As it enters the prostate, each vas joins with a short duct that adds the secretions of the seminal vesicle on that side; thereafter, the vas changes its name to the **ejaculatory duct.** While still within the prostate, the left and right ejaculatory ducts join the urethra, which conveys urine from the bladder. From that junction on, the urethra serves for the passage of both urine and semen.

The vasa deferentia, along with the epididymis, are storage reservoirs for mature sperm, which have been concentrated by the epididymis into a pastelike mass. Further progress of the sperm occurs not by fluid flow nor by their own motility, but by muscular contractions of the walls of the vasa, each of which squeezes a small volume of sperm into the urethra. These contractions occur just before ejaculation.

The **prostate gland** is a single chestnut-sized gland located immediately below the bladder; it completely surrounds the urethra as it exits the bladder. The secretion of the prostate is a cloudy alkaline fluid; at ejaculation, this fluid is pumped into the urethra by the contraction of muscle fibers within the gland.

The **seminal vesicles** are two small glands that lie behind the bladder, close to the vasa deferentia. Their name is misleading: they are glands that add their secretions to the semen, not storage areas for semen. As with the prostate, the fluid secreted by the seminal vesicles is expelled from the glands at ejaculation.

The last set of glands in this collection are the **bulbourethral** or **Cowper's glands.** These two pea-sized glands lie below the prostate gland, and their secretion—a clear mucous fluid—is expelled into the urethra. In many men, secretion from the bulbourethral glands begins early during sexual arousal and can be seen as a drop or two of slippery liquid that appears at the urethral meatus sometime between erection and ejaculation; hence its colloquial name, "pre-cum." Bulbourethral secretions can contain living sperm; this happens chiefly when a man has sex for a second time without urinating between times. In those circumstances, remnants of the first ejaculate that have remained behind in the urethra get mixed in with the bulbourethral secretions from the second episode. This is of no consequence unless the man is practicing the "withdrawal method" of contraception (withdrawing his penis from his partner's vagina before he ejaculates—see Chapter 11). In that case, he may unwittingly impregnate his partner before he withdraws.

What Is Semen?

Semen or seminal fluid, or "cum" in colloquial English, is the thick, cloudy, off-white liquid ejaculated from the male urethra at sexual climax. The volume of a single ejaculate usually ranges between 2 and 5 milliliters. The most important component of semen is, of course, the sperm (Figure 3.13). Each milliliter of semen contains 50–150 million sperm, and a normal ejaculate contains between 100 and 700 million sperm.

Each sperm (or **spermatozoon**) has the well-known tadpole-like structure: a head, containing the cell's nucleus with its all-important DNA, and a motile tail, or **flagellum,** that propels the spermatozoon forward. When we look a little more closely, two other structures become apparent. Capping the nucleus is an **acrosome,** which contains a complex suite of receptors and enzymes that are necessary for successful fertilization of an ovum (see Chapter 10). The part of the tail nearest to the head, which is slightly thicker than the remainder, is called the **midpiece.** This section contains mitochondria tightly wound around the tail in a spiral fashion. These mitochondria supply chemical energy for propulsion of the sperm.

In spite of the importance of the sperm, they occupy only an insignificant proportion (around 1 percent) of the volume of the semen (Figure 3.14). The remainder, called **seminal plasma,** is a mixture of the secretions of the seminal vesicles (about 70 percent of the total volume) and the prostate gland (about 30 percent), plus small contributions from the epididymis and from the bulbourethral glands. Among the constituents of seminal plasma are water and salts, plus the following:

- The sugar **fructose,** which the sperm use as an energy source.
- **Buffers** that keep the pH alkaline (between about 7.2 and 7.8). These buffers protect the sperm from the acidic environment that they encounter if they are deposited in the vagina.
- **Fibrinogen,** a protein that can be broken down enzymatically to produce the coagulating agent **fibrin.**
- Calcium binders such as **citric acid** that prevent premature coagulation of the semen.
- **Enzymes** derived from the prostate gland. These include an enzyme that converts fibrinogen to fibrin, causing rapid coagulation of the ejaculated semen, as well as another enzyme that slowly breaks down fibrin, re-liquefying the coagulated semen. Yet another prostatic enzyme, **acid phosphatase,** breaks down **glycerylphosphorylcholine** to produce **choline,** which is important for the lipid metabolism of the sperm.
- Antioxidants such as **ascorbic acid** protect the sperm from the damage they might suffer on exposure to air.
- In men infected with pathogenic viruses such as **human immunodeficiency virus** (HIV) or **hepatitis B virus,** these viruses may be present at high concentrations in seminal plasma.

The Anus Can Also Be a Sex Organ

Like the penis, the **anus** is used more frequently for excretion than for sex, but significant numbers of men and women do make use of the anus for sexual purposes (see Chapter 8), so we shall describe it here.

The anal orifice is located at the back end of the perineum (see Figure 3.10). It is kept tightly closed most of the time by tonic contraction of the **external** and **internal anal sphincters.** Beyond the sphincters lies the **rectum,** the lowermost portion of the gastrointestinal tract. The rectum is a more capacious space than the anus, so most of the sensation generated during anal sex (for both partners) derives from penetration of the anus itself (which is both relatively tight and richly innervated), rather than from penetration of the rectum. In men, the prostate gland is located just in front of the rectum; its outline can be felt by inserting a finger through the anus and

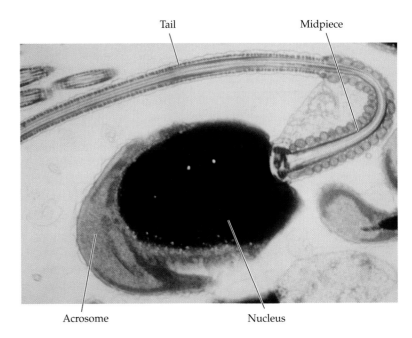

Figure 3.13 Human sperm. Electron micrographic view of a single spermatozoon, showing the acrosome, nucleus, midpiece, and part of the flagellum or tail.

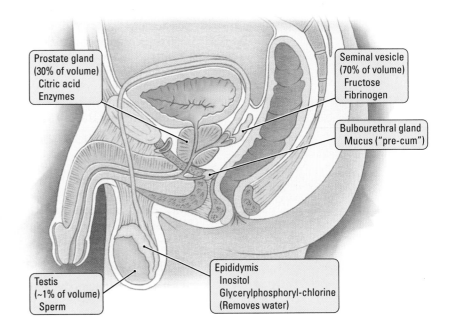

Figure 3.14 Glandular contributions to semen. Sperm make up less than 1 percent of the volume of semen; the rest, known as seminal plasma, comes from various glands.

feeling the front part of the rectum. In women, the structure in front of the rectum is the vagina. Stimulation of these and other nearby structures during anal sex may also contribute to sexual arousal.

The anus and rectum are lined by mucosa, but this surface does not provide significant amounts of lubrication in the way the walls of the vagina do. Thus, most people who engage in anal sex use some kind of lubricant (see Chapter 8). And although we are postponing discussion of sexually transmitted diseases (STDs) to Chapter 16, we should stress right now that condoms offer significant protection from STDs during anal sex, just as they do during vaginal sex.

There Are Numerous Differences between the Sexes beyond the Genitals

We have already discussed one secondary sexual characteristic: the breasts. The bodies of men and women differ in many other respects. The average man is taller, heavier, and more muscular than the average woman; women have (on average) a higher percentage of body fat and wider hips than men. Men (after puberty) are usually hairier than women, especially on the face, but they are also more prone to balding as they age. Women have a smaller larynx, giving them a higher-pitched voice. There are also important sex differences in the nervous and endocrine systems and in mental traits, which we will cover later in this book.

The ultimate reason why all of these traits differ between the sexes is that they are influenced by genes located on the sex chromosomes. This genetic influence is mediated by a variety of routes, but the most important route involves sex hormones, as we'll see in the next chapter. In spite of these genetic influences, secondary sexual characteristics are quite variable among individuals. Whenever one measures such a characteristic, such as height, one finds substantial overlap between the measurements for men and women: it's only the *average* that differs reliably.

Other factors can play a role in either diminishing or exaggerating the differences between the sexes. In some cultures, for example, boys are better fed than girls; this practice increases the sex differences in height and weight. Men are often expected to participate in more strenuous physical activity than women, which makes them stronger and leaner; on the other hand, a woman who undergoes physical training can easily outperform the average untrained man. Shaving is a culture-driven activity that eliminates or diminishes the sex difference in facial hairiness. Finally, there are racial differences in the degree to which these secondary sexual characteristics are expressed. Facial and body hair is generally sparser in East Asians than in Europeans, for example, so hairiness doesn't constitute such a marked difference between the sexes among East Asians.

The Nervous System Orchestrates Sexual Arousal and Response

Sexual behavior is under control of two of the body's three major communication networks, the nervous system and the endocrine system. (The third—the immune system—plays little role in sex.) Here we consider the role of the nervous system, focusing on "low-level" functions that are controlled largely by **spinal reflexes.** Box 3.6 offers a brief refresher course on the organization of the nervous system.

Erection Can Be Mediated by a Spinal Reflex

One simple behavior that illustrates the role of the nervous system in sex is the **erection** of the penis or clitoris in response to tactile stimulation of the genital area. This behavior requires five elements: sensory elements that detect the stimulation, nerves that convey the sensory information to the spinal cord, a processing center in the spinal cord, nerves that carry an output signal to the penis or clitoris, and vascular elements that are responsible for the actual erection. Although the brain also plays a significant role in promoting or inhibiting erection, as we'll see later, this role is not essential. Persons who

Box 3.6 Biology of Sex

The Nervous System

The elementary units of the nervous system are nerve cells, or **neurons** (Figure A; see also Figure D). A typical neuron has a **cell body,** where its nucleus and part of its cytoplasm are located, plus two kinds of cytoplasmic extensions: **dendrites,** which receive and integrate numerous input signals from other neurons or from sensory receptors, and an **axon** or **nerve fiber,** which transmits the neuron's output signals in the form of electrochemical **action potentials** or **nerve impulses.** The axon may span many centimeters (e.g., from the spinal cord to the foot), or it may end in the same region as the cell body. (In the latter case, the neuron is called an **interneuron.**) The terminals of the axon form **synapses** with the dendrites

of other neurons or with muscle fibers. (In the latter case, the neurons are called **motor neurons** and the synapses are called **neuromuscular junctions.**) When action potentials reach synapses, they cause the release of chemical **neurotransmitters,** which are small molecules such as amino acids (e.g., glutamate), catecholamines (e.g., norepinephrine), or acetylcholine. Neurotransmitters diffuse rapidly across the narrow **synaptic cleft** and raise or decrease the excitability of the postsynaptic neuron or muscle fiber.

The nervous system is divided into three subsystems, the central nervous system, the peripheral nervous system, and the autonomic nervous system. (There is also an

enteric nervous system that controls the gut, which will not concern us here.) The **central nervous system** (or **CNS**) comprises the spinal cord and the brain. Most regions of the CNS consist of gray matter and white matter. The **gray matter** is where the CNS carries out its all-important computations; it contains a mix of neuronal cell bodies, dendrites, synapses, and supporting non-neuronal cells, and is organized either into sheets (**cortex**) or clumps (**nuclei**). The **white matter** contains only axons interconnecting various parts of the CNS, along with supporting cells.

The **spinal cord,** although it is a continuous structure, is conventionally divided into **segments;** these segments are defined by the vertebrae through which the bundles of nerve fibers enter and leave the spinal cord. Counting from the upper end, there are eight **cervical,** twelve **thoracic,** five **lumbar,** and five **sacral** segments (see Figure E). The gray matter of the spinal cord can be divided into two **dorsal horns** and two **ventral horns,** one on each side of the cord. Axons enter and leave these areas through the

(A) The structure of a typical neuron

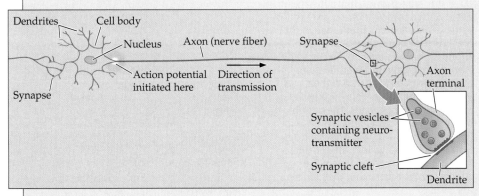

(B) Cross-section of the spinal cord and spinal roots

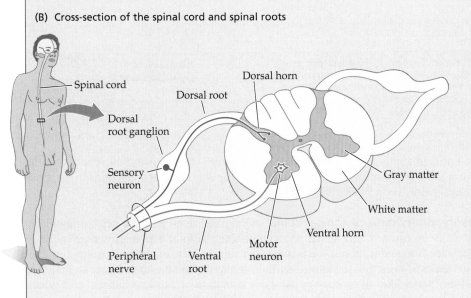

(C) Major subdivisions of the brain

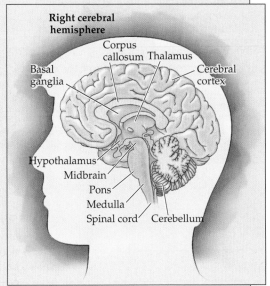

Box 3.6 (continued)

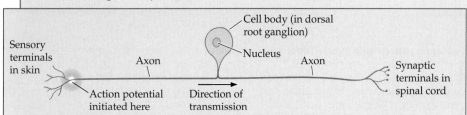

(D) The structure of a sensory neuron, which has no dendrites, but rather a single, T-shaped axon

Sensory terminals in skin

Axon

Cell body (in dorsal root ganglion)

Nucleus

Axon

Synaptic terminals in spinal cord

Action potential initiated here

Direction of transmission

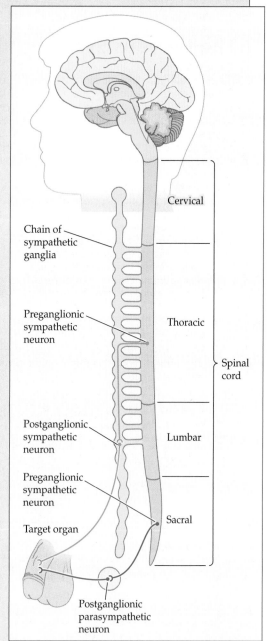

dorsal and ventral roots, respectively (Figure B).

The brain (Figure C) is divided, not into segments, but into two general regions, the cerebral hemispheres and the brain stem. The left and right cerebral hemispheres are each composed of several lobes of cerebral cortex, with underlying white matter. The two hemispheres are interconnected via the corpus callosum. The brain stem includes several subregions: starting from the lower end, they are the medulla, the pons with the attached cerebellum, the midbrain, the thalamus with the underlying hypothalamus, and the basal ganglia. Several of these regions contain cell groups involved in sexual functions.

The peripheral nervous system is the set of motor axons that leaves the CNS to innervate striated (voluntary) muscles, plus the sensory axons that bring information into the CNS. These two kinds of axons are also called efferent (i.e., carrying signals away from the CNS) and afferent (bringing signals into the CNS) fibers, respectively. The motor axons belong to motor neurons whose cell bodies are located in the ventral horn of the spinal cord. The sensory axons belong to neurons whose cell bodies are located in ganglia within the dorsal roots. Sensory neurons are unusual in that they have no dendrites, but rather a T-shaped axon that conveys impulses from the body into the dorsal horn of the spinal cord (Figure D).

The autonomic nervous system (Figure E) controls—largely without our volition—the activity of smooth muscles, heart muscle, and glands throughout the body. Within the autonomic nervous system are two further subsystems, the sympathetic and parasympathetic nervous systems, which often act in opposition to each other. (For example, activity in the sympathetic nerves of the heart causes the heartbeat to speed up, while activity in the parasympathetic nerves causes it to slow down.) Both subsystems consist of two sets of neurons: a set of preganglionic neurons that reside in the spinal cord and send their axons to autonomic ganglia outside the cord, and a set of postganglionic neurons that reside in the ganglia and send their axons to peripheral targets, such as smooth muscle and glands. The ganglia for the sympathetic nervous system lie in a chain next to the spinal cord as well as in other locations, while those for the parasympathetic nervous system are near the target organs that they innervate.

(E) The autonomic nervous system comprises sympathetic (orange) and parasympathetic (green) neurons that often work in opposition to each other.

Cervical

Chain of sympathetic ganglia

Preganglionic sympathetic neuron

Thoracic

Spinal cord

Postganglionic sympathetic neuron

Lumbar

Preganglionic sympathetic neuron

Target organ

Sacral

Postganglionic parasympathetic neuron

have suffered spinal injuries that prevent communication between the brain and the lower reaches of the spinal cord are usually still capable of having erections in response to genital stimulation (see Chapter 17).

Sensory innervation of the genitalia One often reads that the penis and clitoris are "richly innervated," as if that were somehow the total explanation of why these regions are "erogenous zones." If it were that simple, our fingertips, or even our eyeballs, would be as erogenous as our genitals. In reality, one has to consider two further questions: what kind of sensory apparatus exists in the penis and clitoris, and where in the central nervous system are the sensory signals sent?

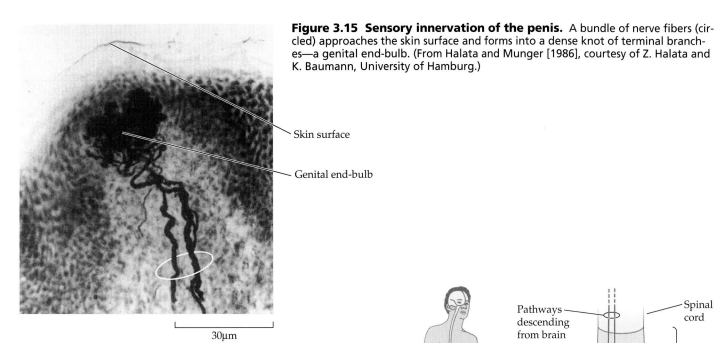

Figure 3.15 Sensory innervation of the penis. A bundle of nerve fibers (circled) approaches the skin surface and forms into a dense knot of terminal branches—a genital end-bulb. (From Halata and Munger [1986], courtesy of Z. Halata and K. Baumann, University of Hamburg.)

Skin surface

Genital end-bulb

30μm

The penis and clitoris possess a unique class of sensory nerve endings termed **genital end-bulbs** (Halata & Munger, 1986) (Figure 3.15). In these structures, the nerve fibers form tangled knots or skeins in the dermis (the deeper part of the skin), either immediately under the epidermis (as in the figure) or deeper in the skin. Numerous genital end-bulbs are found in the skin of the glans, but they are also found in the remaining parts of the penis or clitoris and throughout the genital area. In the penis, the highest density of end-bulbs is around the corona of the glans and in the frenulum—the two zones that are generally the most erotically sensitive regions of the penis.

The clitoris and penis do possess other kinds of nerve endings, some of which are closely associated with the erectile tissue itself. However, they possess few or no nerve endings of the types that are found in other sensitive body areas, such as the fingertips. Correspondingly, the skin of the penis, though erotically sensitive, lacks the ability to make the kinds of fine discriminations that we can easily perform with our fingers. In other words, it appears that the innervation of the penis and clitoris is specialized for just one function: erotic sensation. The exact nature of the stimuli that best activate the genital end-bulbs remains to be studied.

The pudendal and pelvic nerves   If we trace the sensory nerve fibers back out of the penis or clitoris, we find that they travel toward the spinal cord in the left and right **pudendal nerves** (Figure 3.16). The sensory fibers enter the sacral segments of the spinal cord by passing through the dorsal roots. The cell bodies of the sensory fibers are located within the dorsal roots, but no synaptic connections occur there.

The endings of the sensory nerve fibers in the gray matter of the spinal cord form synaptic connections with interneurons. These interneurons, in turn, form synaptic connections with preganglionic

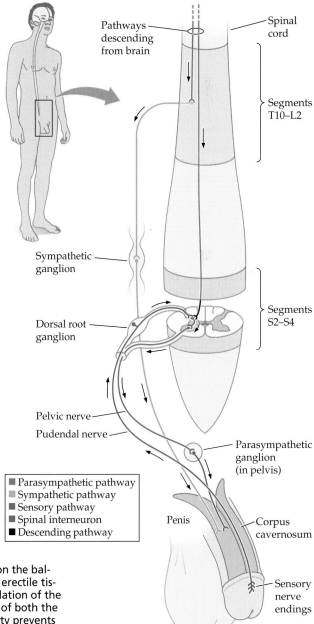

Pathways descending from brain

Spinal cord

Segments T10–L2

Sympathetic ganglion

Dorsal root ganglion

Segments S2–S4

Pelvic nerve

Pudendal nerve

Parasympathetic ganglion (in pelvis)

Penis

Corpus cavernosum

Sensory nerve endings

■ Parasympathetic pathway
■ Sympathetic pathway
■ Sensory pathway
■ Spinal interneuron
■ Descending pathway

Figure 3.16 Nerve pathways involved in erection. Erection depends on the balance of activity in the sympathetic and parasympathetic fibers innervating the erectile tissue. Parasympathetic activity (promoting erection) is triggered by tactile stimulation of the penis (a spinal reflex). Descending inputs from the brain modulate the activity of both the parasympathetic fibers and the countervailing sympathetic fibers, whose activity prevents erection.

Figure 3.17 The mechanism of penile (or clitoral) erection.
(A) Cross-section of the penis, showing the appearance of erectile tissue (in the flaccid state) within the corpora cavernosa. Sinusoids (small white spaces) are separated by trabeculae. (B) Diagram of the erectile mechanism. Note that for simplicity, the illustration shows the penis as if it contains a single large sinusoid. In reality, thousands of microscopic sinusoids make up the erectile tissue of the corpora cavernosa and the corpus spongiosum.

neurons of the parasympathetic nervous system. The cell bodies of these neurons are located in the sacral segments of the spinal cord, and their efferent axons leave the cord in the ventral roots and travel toward the genitalia in the **pelvic nerves.** On reaching ganglia near the bladder, they form synapses with postganglionic parasympathetic neurons, whose axons in turn travel to the erectile tissues in the penis and clitoris.

Before considering how erection occurs, we need to mention another set of nerve fibers that also innervate the erectile tissues. These fibers are components of the **sympathetic nervous system.** This system also originates in preganglionic neurons in the spinal cord, but its neurons are situated at higher levels of the cord—in the lower thoracic and upper lumbar segments. The axons of these neurons pass out of the cord and travel to sympathetic ganglia, where they form synaptic connections with postganglionic neurons. The postganglionic neurons send their axons to the erectile tissues of the penis and clitoris. The parasympathetic and sympathetic nerve fibers work in opposition to each other in controlling the state of the erectile tissue.

The Erectile Tissue Forms a Hydraulic System

Now let's take a look at the erectile tissue itself (Figure 3.17). Here we will focus on the corpora cavernosa of the penis, which have been the object of the most study. The tissue within the corpora cavernosa is like a sponge: it consists of irregular, collapsible spaces (**sinusoids**) separated by walls of connective tissue (**trabeculae**). The sinusoids are part of the vascular system; blood enters them via arterioles and exits via veins. The trabeculae contain smooth muscle cells, and the contraction of these cells shrinks the spaces, thus diminishing the volume of the erectile tissue as a whole. (It's a "self-squeezing" sponge, as it were.) The other major control element consists of smooth muscle cells in the walls of the arterioles. Contraction of these cells constricts the arterioles, diminishing the flow of blood into the sinusoids.

(A)

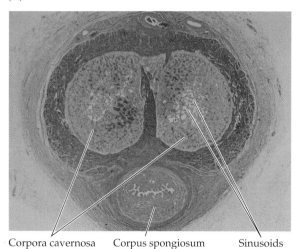

Corpora cavernosa   Corpus spongiosum   Sinusoids

(B)

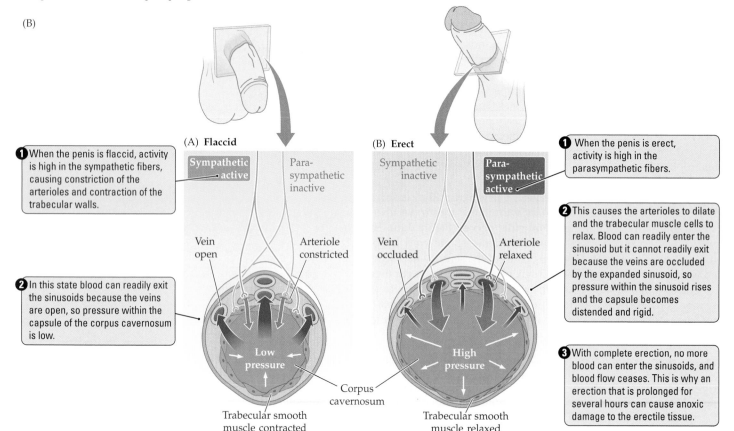

❶ When the penis is flaccid, activity is high in the sympathetic fibers, causing constriction of the arterioles and contraction of the trabecular walls.

❷ In this state blood can readily exit the sinusoids because the veins are open, so pressure within the capsule of the corpus cavernosum is low.

(A) Flaccid

Sympathetic active

Parasympathetic inactive

Vein open

Arteriole constricted

Low pressure

Trabecular smooth muscle contracted

(B) Erect

Sympathetic inactive

Parasympathetic active

Vein occluded

Arteriole relaxed

High pressure

Corpus cavernosum

Trabecular smooth muscle relaxed

❶ When the penis is erect, activity is high in the parasympathetic fibers.

❷ This causes the arterioles to dilate and the trabecular muscle cells to relax. Blood can readily enter the sinusoid but it cannot readily exit because the veins are occluded by the expanded sinusoid, so pressure within the sinusoid rises and the capsule becomes distended and rigid.

❸ With complete erection, no more blood can enter the sinusoids, and blood flow ceases. This is why an erection that is prolonged for several hours can cause anoxic damage to the erectile tissue.

The flaccid state of the penis and clitoris is not simply an inactive condition in which the erectile tissue receives no input from the nervous system. Rather, it is actively maintained by a continuous flow of impulses in the sympathetic nerve fibers. These impulses, on reaching the nerve terminals in the erectile tissue, cause the release of the sympathetic neurotransmitter norepinephrine. This transmitter, in turn, causes a tonic contraction of the smooth muscle of the arterioles (thus restricting the flow of blood into the sinusoids) and of the trabecular walls (thus keeping the volume of the sinusoids low).

When activity in the parasympathetic nerve fibers increases (as, for example, in response to tactile stimulation of the genital area), neurotransmitters are released from their nerve terminals in the erectile tissue. These include three different substances: **acetylcholine, vasoactive intestinal polypeptide (VIP),** and a dissolved gas, **nitric oxide** (Hedlund et al., 2000). Of these three compounds, nitric oxide appears to be the most important. It causes the levels of **cyclic guanosine monophosphate (cGMP),** a signaling molecule, to rise within the smooth muscle cells of the arterioles and the trabecular walls. The cGMP causes the smooth muscle cells to relax, so that the arterioles dilate and more blood flows into sinusoids; thus the erectile tissue as a whole expands. The expansion of the tissue compresses and closes the veins that receive the outflow from the sinusoids; this outflow blockage helps to raise the volume of the erectile tissue. With complete erection, no more blood can enter the sinusoids, so blood flow ceases. (That is why an erection that is prolonged for several hours can cause anoxic damage to the erectile tissue.)

The ability of the corpora cavernosa to expand is limited by the tough connective tissue capsules that enclose them. It is this resistance to expansion that causes the rigidity of the erect penis. Although both the corpora cavernosa and the corpus spongiosum expand during erection, the corpus spongiosum has a less well-developed capsule, so it does not make much contribution to stiffness. The difference can be appreciated by feeling an erect penis: the corpus spongiosum, which forms the ridge along the underside of the penis and also occupies the entire glans, is much softer to the touch than the rest of the organ. Indeed, if the corpus spongiosum were as rigid as the rest of the penis during erection, the urethra would be compressed, and ejaculation might be impossible.

Striated Muscles Are Also Involved in Erection

The two striated muscles, the ischiocavernosus and bulbospongiosus, are also involved in erection of the penis and clitoris (Figure 3.18). This reflex action is most obvious in the case of the penis. If a man's penis is already erect but hanging down from the body, a light

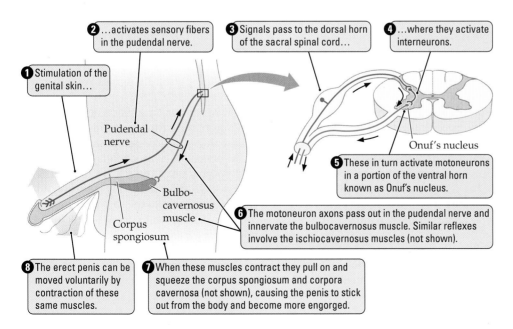

❷ ...activates sensory fibers in the pudendal nerve.

❸ Signals pass to the dorsal horn of the sacral spinal cord...

❹ ...where they activate interneurons.

❶ Stimulation of the genital skin...

Pudendal nerve

Onuf's nucleus

❺ These in turn activate motoneurons in a portion of the ventral horn known as Onuf's nucleus.

Bulbo-cavernosus muscle

Corpus spongiosum

❻ The motoneuron axons pass out in the pudendal nerve and innervate the bulbocavernosus muscle. Similar reflexes involve the ischiocavernosus muscles (not shown).

❽ The erect penis can be moved voluntarily by contraction of these same muscles.

❼ When these muscles contract they pull on and squeeze the corpus spongiosum and corpora cavernosa (not shown), causing the penis to stick out from the body and become more engorged.

Figure 3.18 The ischiocavernosus and bulbocavernosus muscles are involved in erectile reflexes.

touch on the sensitive areas of the penis, or even on nearby skin, will cause the penis to jump up and project directly forward. It is also possible to produce the same movement voluntarily, without any stimulation of the genitals. At the same time, the glans of the penis becomes more enlarged. These responses are caused by contraction of the two muscles, which pull on and squeeze the corpora cavernosa and corpus spongiosum in the root of the penis.

This reflex has the same afferent pathway we described earlier—the sensory fibers running to the spinal cord through the pudendal nerve—but the efferent pathway is different, and does not involve the autonomic nervous system. Instead, the terminals of the sensory fibers in the sacral segments of the spinal cord activate a set of interneurons, which in turn connect with a set of motor neurons in the ventral horn of the cord. These motor neurons form a cell group known as **Onuf's nucleus.** Onuf's nucleus is significantly larger—and contains more motor neurons—in men than in women (Forger & Breedlove, 1986). This difference is one of many **sexual dimorphisms,** or anatomical differences between the sexes, in the human central nervous system; we will be describing others later in this book.

The axons of the motor neurons of Onuf's nucleus run back down the pudendal nerves to the genitalia, where some of them innervate the ischiocavernosus and bulbospongiosus muscles. (Others innervate the anal sphincter, the bladder, and other muscles of the pelvic floor.) When impulses reach the endings of the nerves in the muscles (the neuromuscular junctions), they cause the release of the neurotransmitter acetylcholine, which in turn causes the muscles to contract.

The Brain Also Influences Erection

So far, we have discussed erection as if it were only a spinal reflex triggered by genital stimulation. In fact, however, erection can occur without any tactile stimulation. For example, erections commonly occur during rapid-eye-movement (REM) sleep (the phase of sleep that is accompanied by vivid dreams). They can also occur in response to erotically arousing sights or sounds or just to erotic thoughts.

These nonreflexive influences on erection are mediated by higher levels of the CNS (Figure 3.19). For example, we have mentioned the role of the preganglionic sympathetic neurons in the lumbar section of the spinal cord in keeping the penis flaccid. These preganglionic neurons receive ongoing (tonic) signals from the **locus coeruleus,** a nucleus in the division of the brain known as the pons. During REM sleep, the activity of the neurons in the locus coeruleus decreases, and this, in turn, allows the activity of the sympathetic neurons in the lumbar cord to drop. This change shifts the balance of inputs to the erectile tissue in favor of the parasympathetic nervous system, so an erection occurs. (Very similar episodes occur in women during REM sleep; they involve erection of the clitoris and engorgement of the labia and the walls of the vagina.) The function of these **nocturnal erections** is not certain, but it is suspected that they allow for oxygenation of the genitals and (like stretching exercises in athletics) prevent fibrosis and loss of elasticity in the erectile tissue.

What about erections caused by sexually arousing sights or thoughts? We'll discuss the role of the cerebral cortex in sexual arousal in more detail in Chapter 7. There are some pathways from the cerebral cortex to the spinal cord that are concerned with erection. Specifically, Onuf's nucleus receives inputs from the cortex (probably via at least one synaptic relay station), and it is this pathway that allows a man to move his erect penis voluntarily. However, most of the high-level control of erection is mediated by lower centers in the brain, especially by the hypothalamus (which we'll discuss in Chapter 4) and by cell groups in the brain stem, including the **paragigantocellular nucleus.** The neurons in this nucleus send their axons down to the sacral segments of the spinal cord, where they form synapses with the preganglionic parasympathetic neurons. Activity in this pathway causes the release of the neurotransmitter **serotonin,** which *decreases* the excitability of the parasympathetic neurons. By modulating the activity of the paragigantocellular neurons, the brain can affect the balance between the sympathetic and parasympathetic inputs to the erectile tissues, thus promoting or preventing erections.

Figure 3.19 Some brain regions involved in the regulation of genital function. The locus coeruleus (in the pons) triggers nocturnal erections. The cerebral cortex and certain cell groups in the hypothalamus regulate erection, ejaculation, and vaginal engorgement and lubrication in response to a variety of sensory stimuli, thoughts, and emotional states. The paragigantocellular nucleus and other cell groups in the brain stem exert an inhibitory influence on erection and ejaculation. All these cell groups send axons to the spinal cord; activity in these axons facilitates or suppresses the spinal reflexes controlling physiological arousal.

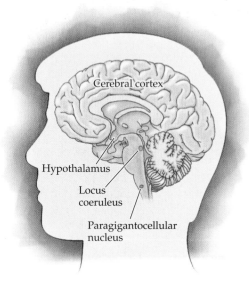

Cerebral cortex

Hypothalamus

Locus coeruleus

Paragigantocellular nucleus

Neurotransmitter-Related Drugs Influence Erection

We have mentioned a number of neurotransmitters—norepinephrine, acetylcholine, VIP, nitric oxide, and serotonin—involved in the regulation of erection. Drugs that interact with these transmitters can affect the ability to obtain and maintain an erection. Sometimes, these interactions are unwanted side effects of drugs used for other purposes. For example, drugs such as the antidepressant **fluoxetine** (**Prozac**), which raise the level of serotonin at synapses, tend to strengthen the inhibitory influence of the paragigantocellular neurons on the parasympathetic neurons in the sacral cord. Thus, in some people, these drugs interfere with the ability to achieve erection (and ejaculation). These unwanted side effects of Prozac can actually be useful in some men; namely, those who suffer from premature ejaculation.

Conversely, several drugs interact with neurotransmitters to facilitate erection. The best-known of these is **sildenafil** (**Viagra**). This drug inhibits the enzyme **phosphodiesterase-5,** which normally breaks down cGMP. Thus, in the presence of sildenafil, the release of nitric oxide causes a greater than usual buildup of cGMP, and so blood flow into the erectile tissue is increased. Sildenafil (at its normally prescribed levels) does not cause an erection in the *absence* of neural input, so there must still be some kind of physical or mental stimulation for an erection to occur.

Erections may also be facilitated by drugs that block the action of norepinephrine at the sympathetic nerve terminals (so called **α-adrenergic blockers**). By interfering with the effects of the sympathetic inputs, these drugs throw the balance toward the parasympathetic inputs, thus favoring erection. Finally, there are drugs that act directly on the smooth muscle of the arterioles and trabeculae of the erectile tissue. One such drug is **prostaglandin E_1:** when injected directly into the penis, or applied via the urethra, it relaxes the arterioles and thus causes an erection. The use of these drugs in erectile dysfunction is discussed in Chapter 15.

Vasocongestion and Vaginal Lubrication Accompany Sexual Arousal in Women

Among the physiological signs of sexual arousal in women are engorgement of the labia and vaginal walls with blood (**vasocongestion**) and **lubrication** of the vaginal mucosa. Vasocongestion causes the vaginal walls to change color from a pinkish to a purplish hue, as the pooled blood loses its oxygen and takes on the color of venous blood. One way that sex researchers monitor physiological arousal in women is to place a photocell in the vagina to track this color change. This technique is called **photoplethysmography** (Figure 3.20). Lubrication of the vagina may be partly due to secretion from the Bartholin's glands, but the major source is a **transudation** (or diffuse seepage) of fluid through all parts of the walls of the vagina.

Vasocongestion and lubrication seem to be controlled by means similar to those that control erection of the penis and clitoris. That is, sympathetic nerve fibers tend to constrict blood vessels and prevent engorgement, while parasympathetic fibers tend to dilate vessels and promote engorgement. Like erection, the labial and vaginal responses can be induced by genital stimulation or by higher-level phenomena such as erotic thoughts or images. As far as lubrication is concerned, VIP seems to be the major parasympathetic neurotransmitter involved: infusion of VIP into the bloodstream of a nonaroused woman provokes vaginal lubrication within a few minutes (Ottesen et al., 1987).

Ejaculation Requires Coordination of Muscles and Glands

Ejaculation in men is the forceful ejection of semen from the urethral meatus at sexual climax. It is actually quite a complex process that requires careful coordination of glands and muscles; luckily, the spinal cord takes care of most of the details and lets the man concentrate on enjoying the sensation of intense sexual pleasure and release—**orgasm**—that usually accompanies ejaculation.

Figure 3.20 A photoplethysmograph is used to measure female sexual arousal. A small photocell is placed against the vaginal wall: it tracks the change in color from pink to purple as the tissue becomes engorged with blood.

As sexual climax approaches, the sympathetic nervous system begins to make itself felt by causing an increase in heart rate, blood pressure, and rate of breathing. Rashes may appear on the front of the body, the neck, or the face, and muscle spasms may also occur. Increased contraction of the ischiocavernosus and bulbospongiosus muscles causes further swelling of the penis, especially of the glans, and the pooling of blood within the glans turns it a purplish color. The cremaster muscle draws the testes upward, sometimes to the point that they disappear from view, and the dartos muscle throws the scrotal skin into wrinkles.

Seminal Emission Is the Loading of Semen into the Urethra

Immediately prior to ejaculation, the various components of the semen are expelled from their reservoirs into the posterior portion of the urethra (Figure 3.21A). This process is called **seminal emission,** and can be felt as a pulsing or flowing sensation at the root of the penis. Seminal emission is triggered by activity in the sympathetic nerve fibers innervating the prostate, the seminal vesicles, and the vasa deferentia, which causes contraction of the smooth muscle in these organs. Once seminal emission occurs, the man has the sense that ejaculation is inevitable, although some men are in fact able to halt the process even at this late stage. In that case, the semen simply flows out of the urethral meatus, rather than being forcefully ejaculated.

During seminal emission, the first component to be loaded into the urethra is the fluid secreted by the prostate gland. This is followed by sperm (and a small amount of fluid) from the vasa deferentia, and finally by the most voluminous component, the secretion of the seminal vesicles. This sequential loading of the urethra is of some functional significance, because the secretions of the prostate gland and the seminal vesicle, when mixed, cause the semen to turn from a liquid to a gel (coagulate) (Finney et al., 1992), a process that normally occurs after ejaculation (e.g., in the vagina). Premature coagulation of the semen within the urethra is prevented by the physical separation of its components.

Ejaculation Is Caused by Contractions of Many Muscles in the Pelvic Floor

Ejaculation itself (Figure 3.21B) is caused by a series of spasmodic contractions of smooth muscle in the walls of the urethra (in response to sympathetic activation) and of the ischiocavernosus and bulbospongiosus muscles and other striated muscles of the pelvic floor (in response to a burst of activity in the sacral motor neurons). These muscles violently squeeze the semen-loaded urethra, especially in the region between the prostate gland and the root of the penis. Each contraction lasts about 0.8 seconds, and the intervals between contractions are about 0.7 seconds in duration (Shafik, 1998).

The urethral sphincter at the outflow of the bladder is usually closed, and it constricts even more tightly at ejaculation in order to prevent the pressurized semen from flowing

Figure 3.21 Seminal emission and ejaculation.

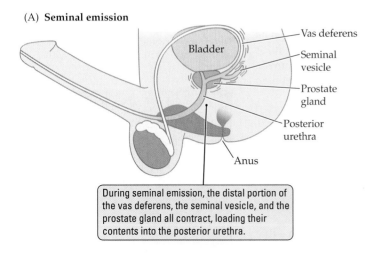

(A) **Seminal emission**

Vas deferens
Bladder
Seminal vesicle
Prostate gland
Posterior urethra
Anus

During seminal emission, the distal portion of the vas deferens, the seminal vesicle, and the prostate gland all contract, loading their contents into the posterior urethra.

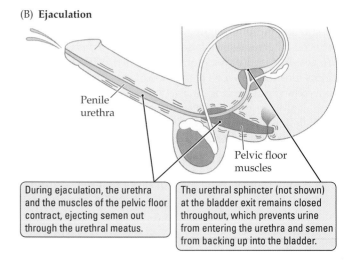

(B) **Ejaculation**

Penile urethra
Pelvic floor muscles

During ejaculation, the urethra and the muscles of the pelvic floor contract, ejecting semen out through the urethral meatus.

The urethral sphincter (not shown) at the bladder exit remains closed throughout, which prevents urine from entering the urethra and semen from backing up into the bladder.

retrogradely into the bladder (Bohlen et al., 2000). (Such retrograde flow may occur if the function of the sphincter has been compromised, leading to a "dry orgasm"; see Chapter 17.) Thus, with nowhere else to go, the semen is expelled from the urethral meatus in a series of spurts of decreasing force. If the man ejaculates into free space, the semen may be propelled a half-meter or so from the body (although this projectile ability is quite variable from person to person and declines with age). If he ejaculates within a woman's vagina, the semen may be propelled against the cervix, but not into the cervical canal.

The proper coordination of all these events requires the activity of several centers in the spinal cord. In addition, animal experiments suggest that the brain plays an important role in the triggering of ejaculation. For example, electrical stimulation of a cell group in the hypothalamus called the paraventricular nucleus causes penile erection and ejaculation in rats (Chen et al., 1997). The evidence in humans is inconclusive: the majority of quadriplegic men (who have suffered an interruption of the pathways from the brain to the spinal cord) report that they never ejaculate under any circumstances, but a substantial minority (about 40 percent) do ejaculate (Alexander et al., 1993). This finding suggests that, while spinal circuitry for ejaculation exists, it requires activation from the brain in most men. It's probably an oversimplification to call ejaculation a "spinal reflex."

Some Women Also Ejaculate

One might think that ejaculation would be a purely male prerogative, but in fact about 40 percent of women also experience a discharge of fluid at sexual climax (Darling et al., 1990). Although first described in the Western scientific literature in 1950 (Grafenberg, 1950), female ejaculation was described in Indian manuscripts dealing with sex as early as the eleventh century (Syed, 1999).

As with male ejaculation, the fluid is discharged from the urethra. The discharge seems to be of two kinds. In one kind of ejaculation, a small amount (a few drops to a teaspoonful or so) of an opalescent fluid is discharged, usually without great force. In another kind, a larger quantity of clear fluid is discharged, sometimes with sufficient force to project the fluid away from the woman's body. By and large, different women report experiencing the two different kinds of ejaculation, but laboratory studies (see below) suggest that they can occur simultaneously in the same woman.

The low-volume, opalescent ejaculate appears to be a secretion from the paraurethral or Skene's glands. As mentioned earlier, these small glands, which are probably homologous to the male prostate, lie just in front of the anterior wall of the vagina, in close proximity to the urethra. The ducts of these glands open into the urethra a centimeter or two back from the urethral opening. Consistent with this interpretation, this kind of ejaculate contains an enzyme characteristic of secretions from the male prostate gland: prostatic acid phosphatase (Belzer et al., 1984). The functional role of this kind of ejaculation in women, if any, is unknown.

The high-volume, clear ejaculate has been much more controversial, with some sexologists doubting the reality of the phenomenon or dismissing it as urine. To solve the riddle, sexologist Gary Schubach (then at the Institute for Advanced Study of Human Sexuality in San Francisco) recruited volunteers who stated that they experienced large-volume ejaculations (Schubach, 1996). Schubach observed that these women did indeed expel large volumes (100 ml or more) of watery fluid from the urethra at orgasm.

To investigate the origin of this fluid, Schubach passed a fine rubber tube (catheter) through the urethras of some of the women, past the ducts of the Skene's glands and into the bladder (Figure 3.22). The women then masturbated (or were stimulated by their partners) to orgasm. The idea was that if the fluid was urine, it should exit the urethra via the inside of the catheter, but if it was a secretion from the Skene's glands or other nearby glands, it should exit the urethra *outside* the catheter. In all cases, all the high-volume fluid expelled at orgasm exited via the inside of the catheter. Schubach's conclu-

Figure 3.22 Female ejaculation.
Gary Schubach performed an experiment (Schubach, 1996) to determine the origin of fluids ejaculated by some women at orgasm. A catheter was inserted into the bladder, and the women masturbated to orgasm.

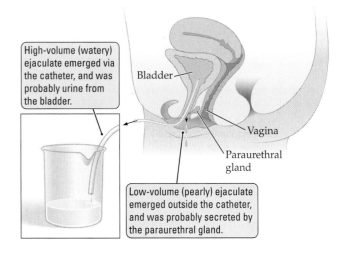

High-volume (watery) ejaculate emerged via the catheter, and was probably urine from the bladder.

Bladder

Vagina

Paraurethral gland

Low-volume (pearly) ejaculate emerged outside the catheter, and was probably secreted by the paraurethral gland.

sion: high-volume female ejaculation involves the expulsion of urine from the bladder. The urine was very dilute, suggesting that the kidney produces dilute urine during sexual arousal. Some of the women also released the low-volume, opalescent ejaculate, and this fluid emerged outside the catheter, consistent with an origin in the Skene's glands.

Given Schubach's results, one might be tempted to dismiss high-volume female ejaculation as no more than brief urinary incontinence associated with the stress of orgasm. Whatever the nature of the fluid ejaculated, however, some women experience this high-volume ejaculation as an intensely erotic event. This is one more reminder that the divide between sexual and nonsexual bodily functions is not as sharp as one might imagine.

Orgasm Is a Subjective Sensation with Physiological Correlates

Since orgasm is, by definition, a subjective experience, we cannot have direct knowledge of anyone's orgasms except our own. Within this limitation, it does seem that the experience of orgasm is fairly uniform from person to person, and in particular, that the orgasms of men and women are similar. In one study, researchers took men's and women's descriptions of their own orgasms, edited them to remove sex-specific references, and gave them to various experts to sort out by sex. It turned out to be impossible (Vance & Wagner, 1976) (Box 3.7).

In general, men and women perceive orgasm as a sequence of intensely pleasurable spasms in the genital area, although the sensation often radiates out to involve other parts of the body. It is also usually experienced as a relief of tension, followed by calm.

In men, the spasms of orgasm have an obvious correlate in the individual spurts of semen that occur during ejaculation. In both sexes, however, the spasms can be recorded by means of pressure transducers placed in the anus or the vagina, or by electrical recordings from the muscles involved (Gerstenberg et al., 1990) (Figure 3.23). The spasms are caused by intense contractions of most of the muscles of the pelvic floor, including the ischiocavernosus and bulbospongiosus muscles and the anal sphincter. In women, the contraction of the bulbospongiosus muscle and other nearby muscles is experienced as a spasmodic tightening of the outer portion of the vagina. The uterus and even the oviducts may also undergo contractions.

There has been speculation that the contractions accompanying female orgasm may (in the case of coitus) help retain semen in the vagina or even facilitate the transfer of sperm to the cervix and uterus (Baker & Bellis, 1995). Also, it is known that the attractiveness of a woman's partner influences whether she experiences orgasm during sex or not (Thornhill et al., 1995). Putting these ideas together, one can speculate that female orgasm should be seen not just as a source of sexual pleasure, but as having reproductive significance. It may be a component of sperm competition (see Chapter 2)—that is, a means by which a woman influences which partner will be the father of her children (Thornhill & Palmer, 2000). Orgasm is not necessary for sperm retention or pregnancy, however.

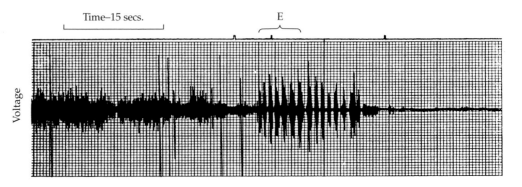

Figure 3.23 Orgasmic contractions recorded in a man. This recording was obtained from an electrode placed in the bulbospongiosus muscle. The man was masturbating to orgasm. Seven spurts of ejaculation (E) occurred in synchrony with the first seven contractions of the muscle. (Courtesy of Roy Levin.)

Box 3.7 *Personal Points of View*

Women and Men Describe Their Orgasms

Here are some descriptions of orgasms written by students (some male, some female) in an introductory psychology course in the 1970s. Some sex-specific words, such as "penis" or "clitoris" have been changed to "genitals."

- "Feels like tension building up until you think it can't build up any more, then release. The orgasm is both the highest point of tension and the release almost at the same time. Also feeling contractions in the genitals. Tingling all over."

- "An orgasm... located (originating) in the genital area, capable of spreading out further... legs, abdomen. A sort of pulsating feeling—very nice if it can extend itself beyond the immediate genital area."

- "Begins with tensing and tingling in anticipation, rectal contractions starting series of chills up spine. Tingling and buzzing sensations grow suddenly to explosion in genital area, some sensation of dizzying and weakening—almost loss of conscious sensation, but not really. Explosion sort of flowers out to varying distance from genital area, depending on intensity."

- "A heightened feeling of excitement with severe, muscular tension especially through the back and legs, rigid straightening of the entire body for about 5 seconds, and a strong and general relaxation and very tired relieved feeling."

- "Tension builds up to an extremely high level—muscles are tense, etc. There is a sudden expanding feeling in the pelvis and muscle spasms throughout the body followed by release of tension. Muscles relax and consciousness returns."

- "Intense excitement of entire body. Vibrations in stomach—mind can consider only your own desires at the moment of climax. After, you feel like you're floating—a sense of joyful tiredness."

- "A building of tension, sometimes, and frustration until the climax. A tightening inside, palpitating rhythm, explosion, and warmth and peace."

- "Often loss of contact with reality. All senses acute. Sight becomes patterns of color, but often very difficult to explain because words were made to fit in the real world."

- "Has a buildup of pressure in genitals with involuntary thrusting of hips and twitching of thigh muscles. Also contracting and releasing of the genital muscles. The pressure becomes quite intense—like there is something underneath the skin of the genitals pushing out. Then there is a sudden release of the tension with contraction of genitals with a feeling of release and relaxation."

- "Spasm of the abdominal and groin area, tingling sensation in limbs, and throbbing at the temples on each side of my head."

Source: Vance and Wagner, 1976.

Physiological correlates of orgasm are also measurable outside the genital area. Respiration rate, heart rate, and blood pressure all reach peak levels. Muscle spasms may occur anywhere in the body, and the person may groan or shout involuntarily.

Are There Two Kinds of Female Orgasm?

There has long been debate about whether women experience two different kinds of orgasm, one triggered by stimulation of the clitoris and another by stimulation of the vagina, especially the G spot. The debate goes back to 1905, when Sigmund Freud, the founder of psychoanalysis, discussed the sexual maturation of women in his influential book *Three Essays on the Theory of Sexuality*. Freud suggested that the clitoris was the main erogenous zone in female children, but that after puberty the vagina normally became the main sexual focus. The function of the clitoris in adult women was merely to start the process of arousal, "just as pine shavings can be kindled in order to set a log of harder wood on fire" (Freud, 1975).

Freud's views were challenged by sexologists William Masters and Virginia Johnson, who conducted extensive laboratory studies of human sexuality starting in the late 1950s (Masters & Johnson, 1966). They reported that the key physiological sign of orgasm in women—spasmodic contractions of the muscles around the outer part of the vagina—was the same no matter how orgasm was reached—whether through coitus, through manual stimulation of the clitoris, or by other means. They pointed out that penetration of the vagina does indirectly stimulate the clitoris, thanks to the labia minora, the bulbospongiosus muscle, and other structures that connect the two organs. Masters and Johnson placed relatively little emphasis on erotic sensitivity within the vagina itself.

The work of Masters and Johnson was liberating for many women because it allowed them to acknowledge the importance of the clitoris without feeling that they were somehow sexually immature or abnormal. Yet there have also been continuing claims for the existence of more than one kind of female orgasm. According to Josephine and Irving Singer (Singer & Singer, 1972), a "uterine orgasm" occurs in response to deep vaginal penetration when the penis (or other penetrating object) makes direct contact with the cervix. This contact, they claimed, causes the uterus to move slightly, thus stimulating nerve endings in the peritoneum (the lining of the abdominal organs). The most obvious sign of a uterine orgasm, according to the Singers, is a characteristic gasping pattern of breathing as the orgasm approaches, followed by an involuntary holding of breath and then an explosive release of breath at the climax itself. The Singers also reported that there were "blended orgasms" that had features of both the uterine orgasm and the regular, "vulval" orgasm described by Masters and Johnson.

Researchers who study the G spot also claim that stimulation of that spot (see Figure 3.5) triggers an orgasm different from the kind that results from clitoral stimulation. While both kinds of orgasms involve contraction of the pelvic floor muscles, only a G-spot orgasm involves major contractions of the uterine musculature, it is claimed (Ladas et al., 1982).

The Hormone Oxytocin May Be Involved in the Subjective Feelings of Orgasm

None of the physiological correlates of orgasm that we've just discussed really explain why orgasm is pleasurable. After all, there are physiological similarities between orgasm and other paroxysmal processes, such as vomiting, but orgasm is distinctly more enjoyable than vomiting. Why?

Although we can't yet answer this question in any detail, it's worth emphasizing one obvious fact: even if the pleasure of orgasm seems to be focused in the genitals, the actual experience of pleasure is a function of the brain. So we would do well to look for brain mechanisms that mediate the orgasmic experience.

One molecule that may play a role in orgasm is **oxytocin,** a hormone secreted by the pituitary gland. (We'll have more to say about this hormone and its mechanism of secretion in Chapter 4.) In both men and women, a surge of oxytocin secretion occurs just before and during orgasm, and this surge raises the concentration of the hormone in the blood to three or four times its normal level (Carmichael et al., 1994). The higher the level of oxytocin, the greater the perceived intensity of the orgasm.

In part, the connection between oxytocin release and the sensation of orgasm may be that oxytocin helps trigger the contraction of smooth muscle in the genital area (e.g., in the walls of the uterus), and that these contractions increase the perceived intensity of the orgasm. However, oxytocin seems to play a more direct role in triggering the subjective sensations of orgasm. If the secretion of oxytocin is blocked pharmacologically, the physiological events of orgasm occur more or less normally, but the pleasurable quality of the orgasm is greatly reduced (Murphy et al., 1990). For that reason, it is suspected that oxytocin acts directly on the brain to give the genital sensations of orgasm their intensely pleasurable coloration. In Chapter 9 we will discuss evidence that oxytocin released during sexual activity does have marked and prolonged effects on brain function.

Brain Imaging Suggests Where Orgasm May Be Experienced

Where in the brain is orgasm actually experienced? To study this question, a Finnish group (Tiihonen et al., 1994) used a functional brain imaging technique known as **single-photon emission computed tomography** (**SPECT**). This technique depends on the fact that the blood flow through a given region of the brain varies with the neural activity in that region—the more active it is, the more blood is required to supply that region with its energy source, glucose. Thus, mapping the blood flow in the brain amounts to mapping brain activity. To visualize blood flow, a short-lived radioactive isotope (technetium-99) is linked to an organic compound and injected into the bloodstream. The technetium-99 emits gamma rays (high-energy photons), and these gamma rays are detected outside the head by an array of sodium iodide crystals, which emit light ("scintillate") when struck by gamma rays. The detector revolves around the head, and a computer generates a three-dimensional map of blood flow. Typically, the data for the experimental condition (in this case, experiencing orgasm) is digitally subtracted from an image acquired during some control condition (e.g., with the subject doing nothing). The resulting "difference image" is taken to represent the changes in neural activity related to the function being studied.

The Finnish group found that male orgasm was accompanied by a *decrease* in blood flow throughout almost the entire cerebral cortex. Just one cortical region—the frontmost portion of the right hemisphere (right **prefrontal cortex**) experienced a significant *increase* in blood flow during orgasm (Figure 3.24). This finding does not mean that the right prefrontal cortex is involved *only* in orgasm: on the contrary, it seems to be involved in a number of emotional states. The main significance of the Finnish report was to show that the brain's involvement in sexual functions can be studied in living subjects. The use of brain imaging in the study of other sex-related states (sexual arousal, romantic love) is described later in this book.

Normal   During orgasm

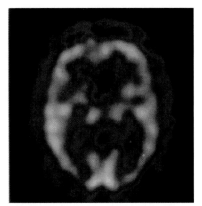 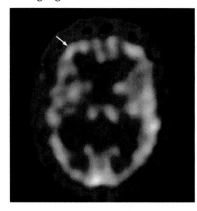

Figure 3.24 Activity changes in the male brain during orgasm as shown by SPECT imaging. There is a region of increased activity in the right prefrontal cortex (arrow); activity in other brain regions decreases. (From Tiihonen et al., 1994.)

There Are Similarities and Differences in the Sexual Response Cycles of Women and Men

So far, we have described a number of events that may occur during sexual activity—erection, lubrication, vaginal engorgement, ejaculation, and orgasm—but we have not tied them together into a sequence or process. The best-known description of the overall process of sexual response is the one developed by Masters and Johnson, in which they divide the process into four phases: excitement, plateau, orgasm, and resolution (Figure 3.25).

The **excitement phase** is just what it sounds like: the period during which sexual arousal begins. In men it is marked principally by erection of the penis, thickening and wrinkling of the scrotal skin, raising of the testes, and an increase in heart rate and blood pressure. In women it is marked by swelling and opening up of the labia minora, vaginal lubrication, a deepening in the color of the labia minora and the vaginal walls, erection of the clitoris and nipples, swelling of the breasts, and an increase in heart rate and blood pressure. Of course, all these signs don't always occur together.

The term **plateau phase** is difficult to define and has been used in different senses. Sometimes it is taken to mean the physiological state close to orgasm in which, in men, the penis reaches its state of fullest erection, marked by the expansion of the girth of the glans at the corona, the pulling of the testes tightly up against the body, and the appearance of bulbourethral secretions at the urethral meatus. In women, the physiological changes close to orgasm include the tightening of the outer third of the vagina, the expansion and lengthening of the inner part of the vagina, the raising of the uterus into a near-vertical position, and the disappearance of the clitoral glans under its hood.

Other writers use the term "plateau phase" simply to refer to the fact that a person may continue to engage in sexual behavior, such as coitus or masturbation, for some time without reaching orgasm. This time may be marked

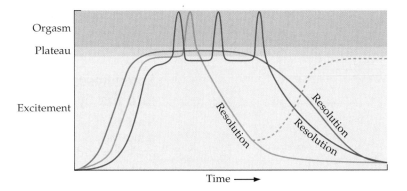

Figure 3.25 Patterns of sexual response. In the pattern shown in blue, the person passes through excitement to the plateau phase, and then experiences more than one orgasm, returning to the plateau phase between orgasms. This pattern is almost exclusively seen in women, not in men. In the pattern shown in orange, only a single orgasm is experienced before loss of arousal (resolution), but a new cycle of arousal may begin after resolution (dashed line). This pattern may be seen in either sex. In the pattern shown in red, the person experiences the plateau phase, but no orgasm.

by essentially no change in psychological or physiological arousal, or by a gradual increase in arousal. Alternatively, a person may approach orgasm on several occasions during this phase, but may deliberately back off on each occasion by reducing physical stimulation for a short period. This may be done with the idea of prolonging the person's own sexual pleasure or that of a partner.

The **orgasm phase,** already described in some detail, is a sense of climactic sexual pleasure and release, usually accompanied by ejaculation in men and by spasmodic contractions of the pelvic floor muscles in both sexes.

The **resolution phase** is the period during which the physiological signs of arousal reverse themselves—for example, erection and vasocongestion subside. If the person has just experienced orgasm, resolution may take only a few minutes. If the person desists from sexual activity without reaching orgasm, resolution may take as much as an hour or more, especially in men. In this case, the resolution phase can be experienced as an unpleasant throbbing sensation in the genital area, sometimes described by men as "blue balls."

Although it is not described as a specific phase, most men experience a **refractory period** after orgasm, during which further sexual stimulation does not lead to renewed erection or a second orgasm. According to Masters and Johnson, the refractory period lasts between 30 and 90 minutes. The length of the refractory period varies greatly with age, however, being negligible in some boys around the age of puberty but extending over a day or more in some older men. While the early part of the refractory period may be *absolute*—that is, the man cannot be physiologically aroused by any means—it may be followed by a *relative* refractory period during which the man can be aroused by stronger than usual stimuli, such as a novel sex partner. This latter effect has been well documented in laboratory animals, and is referred to as the **Coolidge effect.***

Many Women Can Experience Multiple Orgasms

Women do not generally have a clear-cut refractory period after an orgasm. This means that many women can experience **multiple orgasms** without an intervening resolution phase. This is the most striking difference between the sexual response cycles of women and men. One survey of college-educated U.S. nurses found that about 43 percent of them usually experienced multiple orgasms during sex (Darling et al., 1991). No doubt many more women could experience multiple orgasms if they had the cooperation of their partners. Because male fatigue is a factor in limiting the orgasms of women during coitus, most reports of large numbers of sequential orgasms—up to 50 or so—concern women who are masturbating.

A minority of men are also capable of multiple orgasms (Dunn & Trost, 1989). Often, one orgasm in the series is accompanied by ejaculation, while others preceding or following it are "dry." Some sexologists believe that all men are capable of learning to have multiple orgasms (Hartman & Fithian, 1984).

Some Researchers Have Incorporated Mental Processes into the Cycle

Masters and Johnson's four-phase model of the sexual response cycle is descriptive rather than explanatory. So, for example, it doesn't help us understand why the plateau phase can lead either to the orgasmic phase or directly to the resolution phase, or why women can experience multiple orgasms but men cannot. Another limitation of this model is that it sees the response cycle primarily as a physiological rather than a psy-

---

*This calls for a brief digression to explain how the phenomenon of arousal by a novel sex partner came to be associated with the name of Calvin Coolidge—yes, the twenty-ninth president of the United States. According to legend, the President and Mrs. Coolidge were once touring a farm. Soon after their arrival they were taken off on separate tours. When Mrs. Coolidge passed the chicken pens she paused to ask the man in charge if the rooster copulated more than once each day. "Dozens of times" was the reply. "Please tell that to the President," Mrs. Coolidge requested. When the President passed the pens and was told about the roosters, he asked "Same hen each time?" "Oh no, a different hen each time." "Please tell that to Mrs. Coolidge," said the President.

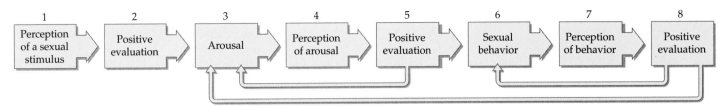

Figure 3.26 Walen–Roth cognitive model of a positive sexual experience. The arrows represent causal links between one cognitive state and another. (After Walen & Roth, 1987.)

chological process. In reality, sex consists mainly of people doing things voluntarily, so an adequate model should explain not just what happens in the genitals, but also how a person passes through the chain of mental states required for sexual behavior.

Some psychologists have attempted to remedy these possible shortcomings. Susan Walen and David Roth, for example, developed a cognitive model of the sexual response cycle that explicitly incorporates mental processes and causal connections (Walen & Roth, 1987) (Figure 3.26). This model begins with perception of a sexual stimulus, which triggers the evaluation of that perception, which in turn (if positive) triggers sexual arousal. The arousal itself is then perceived and evaluated, and a positive evaluation reinforces arousal (a positive feedback loop) and also triggers sexual behavior. That behavior, in turn, is perceived and evaluated, with further feedback effects.

This model has definite merits in terms of its focus on mental events and how they are connected. It might also help explain some sexual dysfunctions. For example, a young woman may be distracted from monitoring her own arousal by other concerns (Is her partner going to withdraw in time? Is her partner being satisfied?). According to the model, this lack of attention to her own arousal breaks the feedback loop and therefore interferes with arousal itself and with resulting positive evaluations and behavior—something that probably does happen (see Chapter 15).

On the other hand, the Walen–Roth model may have shortcomings. For one thing, it has no explicit mechanism for ending sexual arousal or behavior: in the model as shown, they would simply skyrocket out of control. Also, the conscious monitoring of one's own mental states and behaviors may be overemphasized. The minds of academic sexologists may operate this way, but do those of other folks?

All in all, one has to say that our understanding of human sexuality, even as a purely psychobiological phenomenon, lags far behind our understanding of other mental processes, such as vision. We have precise computational models of each stage of visual processing, grounded in detailed anatomical, physiological, and psychometric data. The models may be not right in all details, but they are at least explicit and testable. Little of this yet exists for sex. And when one considers in addition the complex and ever-changing cultural influences on our sexuality, our ignorance is truly humbling. There is only one positive aspect to all this: the field is wide open for young researchers to make great discoveries.

Our Sexual Bodies May Tell Us about Our Evolutionary Past

Several aspects of our sexual anatomy and physiology give us hints about the sexual behavior of men and women during human evolution. For example, we mentioned in Chapter 2 that there is a relationship between testis size in a species and the degree of female promiscuity and sperm competition in that species. We gave chimpanzees and gorillas as examples: sperm competition is much more intense among chimpanzees than among gorillas, and correspondingly, the size of the testes is much greater in chimpanzees.

So how does the size of the human testes compare with those of other species (Figure 3.27)? After allowing for differences in overall body size, the human testes, at 10–14 grams per testis, lie about halfway between the testes of chimpanzees and gorillas, and are in fact about average-sized among primates as a whole (Harcourt et al., 1995). This observation suggests that female promiscuity and sperm competition have been factors in human evolution, but not to any exceptional degree. We will come back to this issue when we deal with promiscuity from a psychosocial perspective (see Chapter 9).

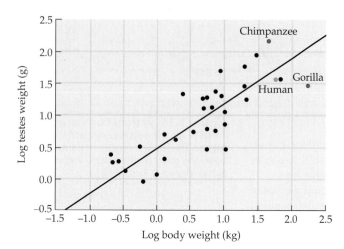

Figure 3.27 Relationship between testis weight and body weight in a variety of primates (note that both axes are logarithmic). The human testis, though larger than that of most primates, is about average-sized in relation to overall body weight. (After Harcourt et al., 1995.)

Another point we made in Chapter 2 was that the sex that invests less in reproduction—usually the male—tends to be subject to sexual selection at the hands of the other sex. Sexual selection may cause the less-investing sex to be larger than the other and to develop extravagant anatomical features such as antlers or vivid coloration.

The evidence of sexual selection on humans is equivocal. Men are certainly larger than females on average, and this difference has no doubt been driven either by direct female choice or by competition among males for mates. On the other hand, men do not have antlers or other striking anatomical features driven by female choice. (Whether they have *psychological* traits driven by female choice is a question we'll discuss in Chapter 6.) Men do have beards, and they have large penises compared with those of most other primates, but women also have anatomical traits that seem to be the products of sexual selection. These traits include the paucity of facial and body hair and prominent breasts.

Thus, it is reasonable to believe that sexual selection has been fairly balanced in its effects on men and women. This conclusion, in turn, suggests that during human evolution both sexes made significant investments in reproduction. Male investment may have taken the form of food provision to women or direct parental care of children. Unfortunately, these ideas will remain speculative unless we can find out more about family structure in our evolutionary past.

Summary

1. A person's sex is usually defined by the appearance of their external genitalia. A man has a penis and scrotum; a woman has a mons, clitoris, labia majora and minora, and a vaginal opening. Sexually ambiguous genitalia do occur, however.

2. A woman's clitoris is a complex erectile organ, only a portion of which is visible externally. Stimulation of the clitoris is a major source of sexual arousal in women.

3. The female reproductive tract includes the vagina, cervix, uterus, and oviducts. All these organs are involved in sperm transport, but they have other functions as well. The vagina is involved in sexual behavior (especially coitus) and (along with the cervix) forms the birth canal. The uterus is the site of implantation and development of the conceptus. The oviducts bring ovum and sperm together for fertilization and transport the resulting conceptus to the uterus. The ovaries are the female gonads; they produce ova and sex hormones.

4. A woman's secondary sexual characteristics include her breasts, which combine sexual functions (being a potential source of sexual arousal to herself and her partner) with a reproductive function (lactation).

5. A man's penis contains three erectile structures and encloses the penile portion of the urethra. Its erotic sensitivity is highest on the glans and frenulum. The foreskin, which covers the glans, is excised in the operation of circumcision. The scrotum contains the testes and has mechanisms for maintaining them below the regular body temperature.

6. A man's internal reproductive structures include the testes, which manufacture sperm and secrete sex hormones; the epididymis, in which sperm mature and become more concentrated; the vas deferens, which stores sperm and transports them to the urethra, and three glands—the prostate gland and the two seminal vesicles—that add the fluid components of semen.

7. Sexual functions are regulated by the nervous and endocrine systems. Erection of the penis and clitoris involves a spinal reflex that starts with stimulation of nerve endings in the genital skin. Drugs that mimic or block neurotransmitters in this pathway can facilitate or impair erection. Similar reflexes control vasocongestion of the walls of the vagina and vaginal lubrication. Inputs from the brain powerfully modulate these reflexes.

8. Seminal emission and ejaculation require the coordinated action of muscles and glands to deliver the various components of semen to the urethra and then to expel

the ejaculate from the urethral meatus. Some women also ejaculate glandular fluid at sexual climax.

9. Orgasm is an intensely pleasurable sensation at sexual climax, accompanied by physiological phenomena such as ejaculation and widespread spasmodic contractions of musculature in the pelvis and elsewhere. The hormone oxytocin is released from the pituitary gland at orgasm and may be involved in making orgasm pleasurable. Brain scanning studies suggest that the prefrontal region of the right cerebral hemisphere is involved in the experience of orgasm.

10. The sexual response cycles of men and women have similarities and differences. Physiologically, the cycle can be divided into four phases in both sexes: excitement, plateau, orgasm, and resolution. Many women are capable of returning to orgasm without leaving the plateau phase (multiple orgasms). Most men experience a refractory period of 30 minutes or more after orgasm, during which they cannot experience another orgasm. A full accounting of the sexual response cycle will have to unify mental processes with the physiological events.

11. The anatomical characteristics of men and women offer clues about the sexual history of the human species. Compared with some other mammals, it appears that the action of sexual selection on the two sexes has been fairly balanced, perhaps because men have made significant investments in reproduction. Anatomical features such as testis size suggest that sperm competition and female promiscuity have existed during human evolution, but not at particularly high levels.

Discussion Questions

1. What criteria do you think should be used to decide whether someone is a man or a woman? Will your criteria categorize all persons, or will some be left "undecided"? (You may want to revise your views after reading later chapters.)

2. Do you think circumcision of newborn boys should be permitted or banned, and why? What about circumcision (or genital mutilation) of prepubertal girls? Do you think that the United States should attempt to eliminate female circumcision in other countries?

3. Do you think that learning about the biological mechanisms of sex enhances sexual satisfaction or, conversely, does it diminish the "magic" of sex?

Web Resources

Gray, H., *Anatomy of the Human Body* www.bartleby.com/107

University of Delaware Histology (microscopic anatomy) site:
female reproductive system:
www.udel.edu/Biology/Wags/histopage/colorpage/cfr/cfr.htm
male reproductive system:
www.udel.edu/Biology/Wags/histopage/colorpage/cmr/cmr.htm

National Organization of Circumcision Information Resource Centers (NOCIRC)
www.nocirc.org

Recommended Reading

Angier, N. (1999). *Woman: An intimate geography.* Boston: Houghton Mifflin Company.

Federation of Feminist Women's Health Centers (1981). *A new view of a woman's body.* New York: Feminist Health Press.

Morgentaler, A. (1993). *The male body: A physician's guide to what every man should know about his sexual health.* New York: Fireside Books.

Wizemann, T. M., and Pardue, M.-L. (Eds.). (2001). *Exploring the biological contributions to human health: Does sex matter?* Washington, D.C.: National Academy Press.

chapter 4

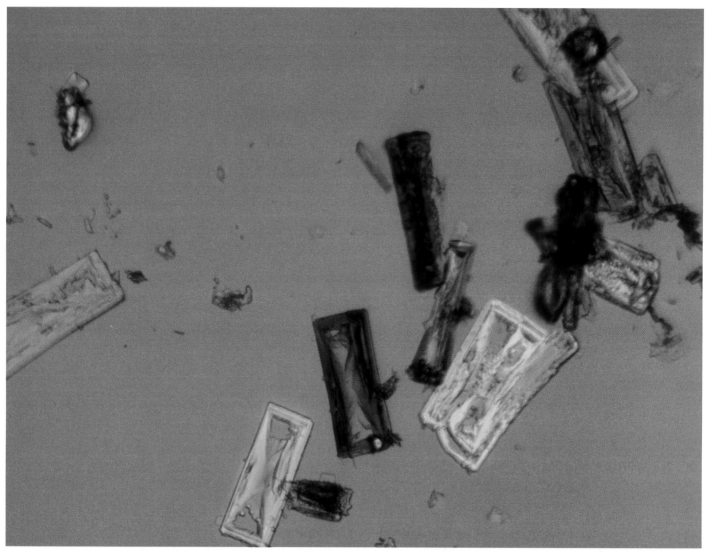

Crystals of estradiol (a natural steroid hormone) and norethindrone (a synthetic hormone used in some contraceptive pills).

Sex Hormones and the Menstrual Cycle

*T*he endocrine system—the system of glands that secrete hormones into the bloodstream—shares with the nervous system the task of regulating sexual development, sexual functions, and sexual behavior. To produce the full range of sexual functions and behaviors, these two systems must interact in the most intimate and subtle ways. Hormones strongly influence activity patterns within the brain, and thus have a major say in whether sexual behavior takes place or not. Conversely, the brain controls the secretion of key hormones that regulate ovarian and testicular function.

In this chapter, we will see numerous examples of interactions between the nervous and endocrine systems. None is more striking, however, than the intricate dance of hormonal and neural signals that orchestrate a woman's menstrual cycle—the very core of her sexual physiology.

There Are Three Classes of Sex Steroids

Most hormones active in sexual and reproductive physiology are either **steroids** (e.g., testosterone), or **proteins** or **peptides** (e.g., oxytocin). A lesser but still significant role is played by two other classes of hormone-like molecules: **prostaglandins** (e.g., prostaglandin $F_{2\alpha}$) and **monoamines** (e.g., dopamine).

Steroids are lipid (fatty) molecules derived from **cholesterol.** That doesn't mean that a person on a low-cholesterol diet or taking cholesterol-lowering medication is in danger of running low on steroids. In spite of its evil reputation, cholesterol is a vital and abundant molecule in every cell of the body and is readily manufactured from acetic acid. What limits and regulates steroid production is not the availability of cholesterol, but the presence or absence of a suite of enzymes that transform it into the various classes of steroids. Only certain cells manufacture (or "express") these enzymes, so only those cells produce steroids.

There are three classes of sex steroids: **progestins** (also called **progestagens**), **estrogens,** and **androgens.** (A fourth class of steroids—corticosteroids—is not directly involved in sexual physiology.) Within each class are several individual steroids, but we will discuss only the four key players: the progestin **progesterone,** the estrogen **estradiol-17β** (or just **estradiol**), and two androgens, **testosterone** and **5α-dihydrotestosterone** (or **DHT**). The discovery and manufacture of sex steroids was a century-long scientific saga that had major consequences for society, especially for women (Box 4.1).

The chemical structures of these four steroids, and their synthesis from cholesterol, are illustrated in Figure 4.1. A specific enzyme catalyzes each step in the pathway, but two enzymes are of particular importance: **aromatase,** which converts testosterone to estradiol, and **5α-reductase,** which converts testosterone to 5α-dihydrotestosterone. The congenital absence of any one of these enzymes can play havoc with a person's sexual development. If a chromosomally male fetus lacks 5α-reductase, for example, it will be born with the outward appearance of a female, but will change its apparent sex back to male at puberty. These rare individuals help us understand how hormones regulate the sexual differentiation of the body, as we'll see in Chapter 5. In addition, they cast an intriguing light on an even deeper question—how we develop an internal sense of ourselves as male or female. We take up this question of gender identity development in Chapter 6.

Testosterone Is a Sex Hormone in Both Men and Women

Testosterone is secreted by the **gonads** and by the **adrenal cortex** (the outer portion of the adrenal gland, whose main function is the secretion of corticosteroids). In men, by far the larger portion of the testosterone circulating in the bloodstream comes from the testes, which turn out between 4 and 10 milligrams of the hormone per day. In the testis, testosterone is produced by the Leydig cells—the cells that occupy the spaces between the seminiferous tubules (see Figure 3.13). In women, the ovaries and the adrenal cortex share about equally in the production of testosterone. In the ovary, it is synthesized by the thecal cells that surround the developing ovarian follicle.

Testosterone levels vary cyclically The secretion of testosterone is not constant over time (Figure 4.2). In a man's blood, its concentration varies according to two different cycles. The shorter (and deeper) cycle is about 2–4 hours in duration. Testosterone levels may fluctuate by three- or fourfold over the course of this cycle—between about 5 and 20 nanograms of testosterone per milliliter of blood (ng/ml). (Techniques for measuring testosterone vary greatly, so you may see wildly diverging statements about

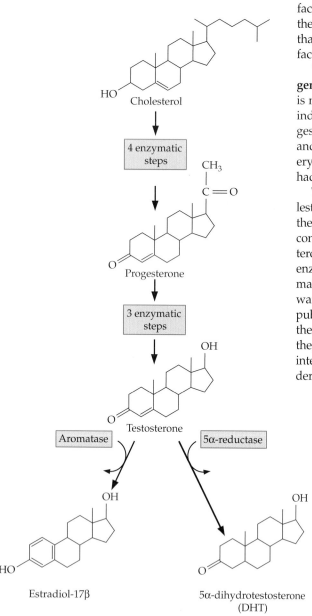

Figure 4.1 Structures and synthetic pathways for the four main sex steroids discussed in this book. The molecular diagrams show the carbon skeletons of each steroid. Single lines are single bonds; double lines are double bonds. Most hydrogen atoms are omitted. Four enzymatic steps convert cholesterol to progesterone. Another three steps convert progesterone to testosterone. Testosterone can be converted either to estradiol or to DHT by the specific enzymes shown.

Box 4.1 Biology of Sex

The Discovery of Sex Steroids

Edward Doisy (1893–1986, Nobel Prize 1943)

In the 1840s a German zoologist, A. A. Berthold, conducted a set of experiments on roosters that suggested the existence of a male sex hormone. He excised the testes from young roosters and observed that their secondary sexual characteristics (such as their bright red combs) and their sexual behavior were diminished. If he excised the testes and reimplanted them in a bird's abdomen, on the other hand, the bird looked and behaved like a normal male. Berthold suggested that the testes manufacture a substance that enters the bloodstream and promotes male development. Analogous experiments done in the 1890s suggested the existence of female hormones.

In the 1880s, the elderly French endocrinologist Charles-Édouard Brown-Séquard announced that he had managed to renew his own sexual vigor and general health by injecting himself with extracts of animal testicles. Thus began a craze for rejuvenation remedies involving sex hormones. In the United States, Dr. John "Goat Gland" Brinkley performed innumerable surgical transplants of goat testicles through the 1920s and 1930s. (For women, he offered the "royal jelly" of honeybees.) We now know, of course, that transplanted animal tissues are quickly rejected by the immune system.

The German chemist Adolf Butenandt isolated and purified the first sex hormone (the estrogen estrone) from urine in 1929 and showed that it was a steroid. For this work, he was awarded the 1939 Nobel Prize in chemistry, but he declined to accept it for political reasons. In 1935 a Dutch group led by Ernst Laquer purified testosterone from bulls' testicles. The American biochemist Edward Doisy purified estradiol from sows' ovaries. He too was awarded a Nobel Prize, but for a different discovery: the structure of vitamin K.

Because these early researchers lacked the techniques—mass spectroscopy, radioimmunoassay, and the like—that modern biochemists take for granted, their work was extraordinarily laborious. Each step of the purification procedure had to be checked by means of bioassays—testing to see, for example, which of the various fractions caused a rooster's comb to grow larger. The process was mind-numbingly inefficient. Doisy started with the ovaries of 80,000 sows and ended up with 12 milligrams of estradiol. Laquer's group started with nearly a ton of bulls' testicles and obtained about 300 milligrams of testosterone.

After the sex steroids were identified, the next step was to synthesize them. In 1936 the Yugoslav-born chemist Leopold Ružička synthesized testosterone, a feat that won him a share of the 1939 chemistry prize with Butenandt (Ružička did accept his prize). By the early 1940s most of the important sex steroids were being produced by pharmaceutical companies, but their prices were so high as to inhibit their use in research or medicine.

During the 1930s a maverick American chemist, Russell Marker of Pennsylvania State College, became convinced that useful starting materials for manufacturing steroid hormones were to be found in a variety of plants. In 1940, Marker collected 40,000 kilograms of plant material in the United States and Mexico. Eventually he determined that the best source was the *cabeza de negro,* a wild yam growing in the mountains near Veracruz, Mexico. In 1943, with the aid of a mule and a spade and with some assistance from local Indians, he filled many sacks with the plant, brought them back to Mexico City, and turned them into nearly 3 kilograms of progesterone—which was then worth a steep $8.00 a gram. Marker co-founded a Mexican pharmaceutical company, Syntex, to produce the various steroids. Syntex's operations drove down the price of steroids, making them readily available as medicines and research drugs. In 1951 Carl Djerassi, an Austrian-born chemist working at Syntex, produced a form of progesterone that could be taken orally. This discovery quickly paved the way for the introduction of the oral contraceptive pill.

Source: Bullough, 1994.

---

what constitutes "normal" testosterone levels.) Because of this variation, a single blood sample is a very untrustworthy indicator of average testosterone levels. The longer cycle is a daily one: mean testosterone levels are somewhat higher in the morning (midnight to noon) than in the evening (noon to midnight) (Winters et al., 2001). (There is inconclusive evidence for a third, annual cycle: some reports suggest that testosterone

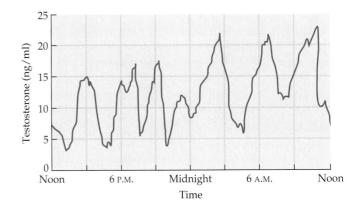

Figure 4.2 Testosterone cycles. Testosterone levels in the blood peak every 2 to 4 hours. Mean levels are higher during the night and morning than during the afternoon and evening.

levels are higher in the fall than in the spring.) These cycles reflect cyclical variations in the production of testosterone by the testis. However, the testis does not generate these cycles by itself—how could it know the time of day, after all? Rather, other hormones impose the cycles on it, as we'll see shortly.

In women, blood concentrations of testosterone also vary over time, though more subtly. Testosterone concentrations vary between about 0.2 and 0.4 ng/ml over the course of the menstrual cycle, with the highest concentrations occurring around the time of ovulation. Even the peak level of about 0.4 ng/ml is less than one-tenth of the average testosterone level in men. In spite of these seemingly low levels, testosterone does play an important role in women's sex lives, as we'll see.

Some tissues convert testosterone to DHT   The Leydig and thecal cells do not express the enzyme 5α-reductase, so they cannot convert testosterone to the more potent androgen 5α-dihydrotestosterone (DHT). Other cells in the body do express that enzyme, however. Among them are the Sertoli cells (the cells lining the seminiferous tubules that nurture the developing sperm). The Sertoli cells pick up testosterone that has diffused the short distance from the Leydig cells, convert a portion of it to DHT, and secrete this hormone into the fluid within the seminiferous tubules, where it influences the maturation of sperm.

Many cells in the tissues of the external genitalia also express 5α-reductase. These cells take up testosterone from the blood and convert it to DHT. This local production of the more potent androgen is vital for the normal development of the male genitalia during fetal life, as we'll see in Chapter 5. DHT acts locally and does not circulate in the blood in significant amounts.

Estradiol Is Synthesized from Testosterone in Both Sexes

The estrogen estradiol, as mentioned above, is synthesized from testosterone by the action of the enzyme aromatase. In both sexes, aromatase is expressed at low levels in the same gonadal cells that synthesize testosterone: the Leydig cells in the testis and the thecal cells in the ovary. Thus, these two cell types secrete low levels of estradiol. In addition, however, other gonadal cells express aromatase at much higher levels: the Sertoli cells in the testis and the granulosa cells in the ovary (the cells within the ovarian follicles that nurture the developing ova). Although not capable of synthesizing androgens themselves, the Sertoli and granulosa cells pick up testosterone and other androgens that have been released by the nearby Leydig or thecal cells and convert them to estradiol. In men, this pathway operates mainly during fetal life and childhood; after that, the Leydig cells are the main sources of estradiol.

In women, on the other hand, this "cooperative venture" of the two follicular cell types is the main route by which estradiol is synthesized and secreted into the bloodstream (Figure 4.3). Because the ovarian follicles undergo a process of maturation linked to the menstrual cycle, the concentration of estradiol in the blood varies greatly with that cycle. It reaches a major peak (of about 0.3 ng/ml) just before ovulation. A second, broader peak is seen during the postovulatory, or luteal, phase of the cycle.

Cells in at least one other tissue—the brain—also express the enzyme aromatase and are therefore capable of converting testosterone to estradiol. This conversion is believed to play a significant role in the sexual differentiation of the brain during prenatal life (see Chapter 5).

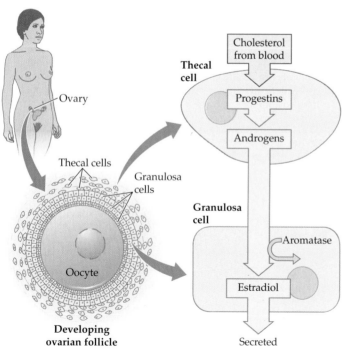

Figure 4.3 Estrogen factory. In an ovarian follicle, the thecal and granulosa cells cooperate to produce estradiol.

Progesterone Is a Female Hormone

Unlike testosterone and estradiol, which have important functions in both sexes, the progestin progesterone is essentially a female hormone. It is not present in significant amounts in men, except as an intermediate metabolite in the synthesis of androgens, and it has no known hormonal function in that sex. In women who are undergoing menstrual cycles, progesterone is present in the blood at high levels during the luteal phase of the cycle. It is also present—at even higher levels—during pregnancy. The source of progesterone is the same set of cells that secrete estradiol: the follicular granulosa cells. After ovulation, however, the ruptured follicle transforms itself into a new secretory structure, the **corpus luteum.** The granulosa cells change their appearance and metabolism and are now called **large lutein cells.** It is in this new guise that they secrete progesterone into the blood. The role of progesterone is to bring the lining of the uterus— the endometrium—into a condition suitable for implantation and pregnancy and to maintain it in that state if pregnancy occurs.

Sex Steroids Act by Activating Specific Receptor Molecules

Just as only certain cells synthesize sex steroids, only certain **target cells** are sensitive to them. What makes a cell sensitive to sex steroids is its possession of specific **receptor** molecules. A hormone fits into its receptor like a key into its lock, and when the two molecules make contact, a sequence of further cellular processes is triggered, which we'll get to momentarily. There are three different kinds of sex steroid receptor molecules, named the **androgen receptor, estrogen receptor,** and **progestin receptor.** Some cells express one kind of receptor, some cells express more than one, and some cells express none and are therefore insensitive to sex steroids.

In cells that do express sex steroid receptors, the level of expression is regulated by numerous factors and can therefore vary over time. A cell that is exquisitely sensitive to a steroid at one time may be nearly insensitive to that same steroid hours or days later. Later in this chapter, we will see how the regulation of receptor expression contributes to sexual functions.

What characterizes individual steroids as androgens, estrogens, or progestins is their ability to bind to and activate androgen, estrogen, or progestin receptors, respectively. But different steroids within a class activate their receptor with different efficacy. Both testosterone and DHT activate androgen receptors, for example, but DHT is twice as potent as testosterone. (In other words, it has the same activating effect at one-half the concentration.)

Because steroids are lipids, they do not dissolve readily in aqueous fluids. Thus, of the testosterone circulating in the bloodstream, only a tiny fraction (about 1 percent) is present as the free steroid. Of the remainder, about two-thirds is bound to a specific carrier molecule known as **sex steroid–binding globulin,** and one-third is bound to the major blood serum protein, albumin. Still, it is primarily the free steroid that acts on receptors. This means that measurements of the total concentration of a steroid in the blood have limited usefulness. Researchers often prefer to measure the level of testosterone (and other steroids) in saliva, which is in equilibrium with free testosterone in serum and is not influenced by bound testosterone.

Once secreted into the bloodstream, a steroid molecule has a **half-life** of 2–3 minutes, meaning that it has a 50 percent chance of being removed within that time. The main site of removal is the liver, which breaks down steroids into inactive metabolites. While it might seem wasteful to break down the hormones so quickly, this process allows blood levels of steroids to change quickly, and thus to reflect the current rate of hormone secretion. This rapid variation, in turn, allows changes in secretory rates to have an effect on target tissues within a few minutes or so.

Steroid Receptors Control Gene Expression

Most steroid receptors are located inside cells. Steroids, being lipids, can easily pass through the fatty outer membrane (plasma membrane) of a target cell and enter its cyto-

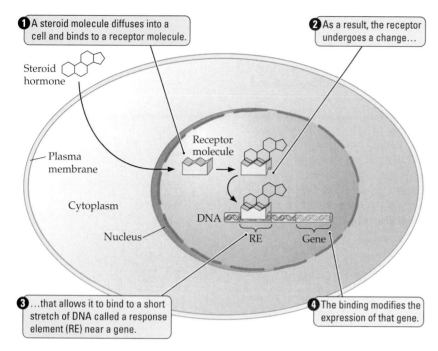

1 A steroid molecule diffuses into a cell and binds to a receptor molecule.

2 As a result, the receptor undergoes a change...

Steroid hormone

Plasma membrane

Cytoplasm

Nucleus

Receptor molecule

DNA

RE   Gene

3 ...that allows it to bind to a short stretch of DNA called a response element (RE) near a gene.

4 The binding modifies the expression of that gene.

Figure 4.4 Steroids influence gene expression.

plasm. This ability makes them very different from the highly water-soluble hormones, such as proteins and monoamines, which cannot enter cells and must therefore bind to receptors located on the outside of the target cell's plasma membrane. When a steroid molecule binds to its receptor, the receptor undergoes a change in shape that allows it to bind to DNA within the cell nucleus, but only to specific DNA sequences called **response elements** (Figure 4.4). A particular gene may possess a response element that recognizes the estrogen receptor, for example, while another gene may possess a response element that recognizes the androgen receptor. The entry of a steroid hormone into a cell (in sufficient concentrations) activates the collection of genes that carry response elements for that hormone's receptors. The activity of these genes, in turn, modifies the cell's structure or function in some way.

From this description, you might conclude that a hormone such as testosterone would have the same effect on all cells that possess androgen receptors, since all cells in the body contain the same genes. However, each cell type in the body has its own control mechanisms that determine which genes, out of the entire suite of genes that possess a steroid response element, are able to respond to the presence of the steroid. In part, these mechanisms involve yet another class of molecules known as **coactivators** that regulate the interaction between steroid receptors and response elements (Molenda et al., 2002). Thus different tissues respond to steroids in different ways: cells in genital tissue may be stimulated to grow faster, cells in the brain may be stimulated to be more electrically active, and endocrine cells may be stimulated to secrete more hormones. In other words, sex steroids modify the behavior of a tissue within the range of options available to that particular tissue.

We should also mention that steroid hormones can affect target cells by other means than binding to the "classic" steroid receptors that control gene expression. They can also affect cellular processes more directly by binding to receptors in the plasma membranes of cells; these receptors influence metabolic processes directly, without involving gene expression. We will have something to say about this process in Chapter 5.

Proteins and Peptide Hormones Are Gene Products

Before we discuss the actions of sex steroids, we need to describe the other major class of hormones that regulate sexual functions: proteins and peptides. Both proteins and peptides are polymers of amino acids linked by peptide bonds (Figure 4.5). The word "peptide" is generally used to refer to relatively short polymers. The peptide **oxytocin,** for example, whose role in orgasm we discussed in Chapter 3, consists of only nine amino acids. The word "protein" refers to much longer polymers, with a hundred or more amino acids. In fact, many protein molecules contain multiple polypeptide chains wound together in a random-looking but actually very precise three-dimensional arrangement. Protein hormones often possess some nonprotein components, such as carbohydrate side chains, that influence their properties or life spans.

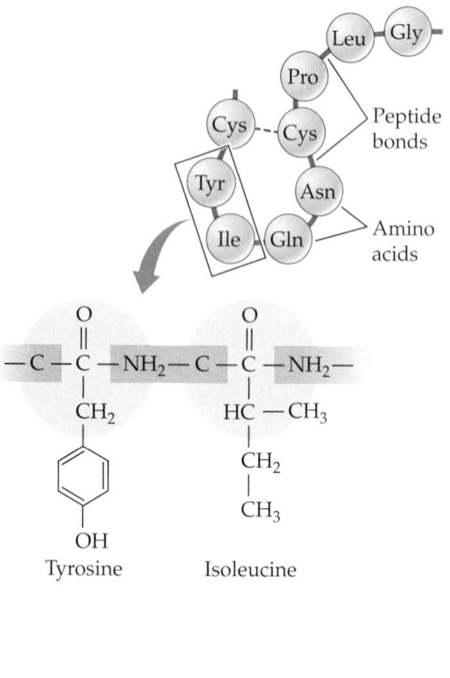

Figure 4.5 Peptide and protein hormones are strings of amino acids joined by peptide bonds (indicated in red). This figure shows oxytocin, a small peptide that consists of nine amino acids (Cys = cysteine; Tyr = tyrosine; Ile = isoleucine; Gln = glutamine; Asn = asparagine; Pro = proline; Leu = leucine; Gly = glycine). A bond between the two cysteines (dotted line) draws the molecule into a ring shape.

Protein and peptide hormones are manufactured by the same process: a gene encoding the protein or peptide is transcribed into messenger RNA, which is then translated into protein on ribosomes. Sometimes, especially in the case of short peptides, the initial gene product is a longer polypeptide chain that is cut to the appropriate length by cytoplasmic enzymes. The trimmed-off portion may have a function too; in the case of oxytocin, for example, it acts as a carrier for the hormone prior to secretion. In other cases, the trimmed-off portion may be a hormone in its own right.

Oxytocin Is Secreted by Neuroendocrine Cells of the Hypothalamus

As we mentioned in Chapter 3, oxytocin is synthesized in the hypothalamus, principally in the cell bodies of two clusters of large neurons named the supraoptic and paraventricular nuclei (Figure 4.6). The hormone is transported down the axons of these cells to the posterior lobe of the **pituitary gland.** It is stored in the axon terminals there, and is released into the bloodstream when a barrage of nerve impulses comes down those same axons. In other words, these **neuroendocrine** cells both manufacture the hormone and (by means of their neuronal activity) control its release.

Oxytocin also seems to act as a neurotransmitter within parts of the brain, and in addition, it is synthesized in the ovary and testis. The function of these other sources of oxytocin is only partially understood. In the testis, oxytocin secreted by the Leydig cells stimulates the contraction of smooth muscle cells surrounding the seminiferous tubules and the tubules of the epididymis, thus moving the contents of the tubules forward. Oxytocin probably has other, still unknown functions in the sexual domain.

Oxytocin is present in the blood at low levels most of the time, but it reaches much higher levels under three circumstances: orgasm (see Chapter 3), childbirth, and breast-feeding (see Chapter 10). It causes the contraction of smooth muscle. In the breast tissue this contraction causes milk letdown, while in the uterus it helps expel the fetus. As discussed in Chapter 3, oxytocin may also have effects within the brain, helping to give orgasm its pleasurable quality.

Oxytocin has a sister hormone, named **vasopressin,** which differs by only one amino acid out of the nine. Vasopressin is synthesized by a second set of neuroendocrine cells in the same two hypothalamic nuclei, and like oxytocin, it is shipped to the posterior lobe of the pituitary gland and released into the bloodstream there. Vasopressin's main function is a nonsexual one: the control of blood volume. Still, both oxytocin and vasopressin play a role in social bonding between sex partners, in rodents at least (see Chapter 9).

GnRH Stimulates the Release of Pituitary Sex Hormones

Another short peptide with an important sexual function is **gonadotropin-releasing hormone (GnRH).** This hormone has ten amino acids and, like oxytocin, is formed by the cutting of a longer precursor molecule. GnRH is produced by another set of neuroendocrine cells in the hypothalamus (Figure 4.7). The axons of these cells do not travel to the pituitary gland, however. Rather, they end

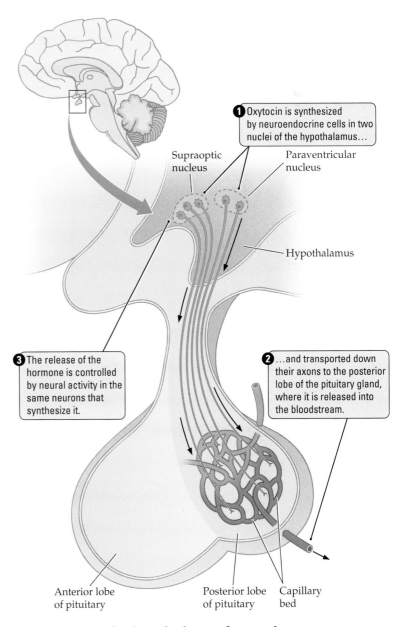

1 Oxytocin is synthesized by neuroendocrine cells in two nuclei of the hypothalamus…

Supraoptic nucleus

Paraventricular nucleus

Hypothalamus

3 The release of the hormone is controlled by neural activity in the same neurons that synthesize it.

2 …and transported down their axons to the posterior lobe of the pituitary gland, where it is released into the bloodstream.

Anterior lobe of pituitary

Posterior lobe of pituitary

Capillary bed

Figure 4.6 Synthesis and release of oxytocin.

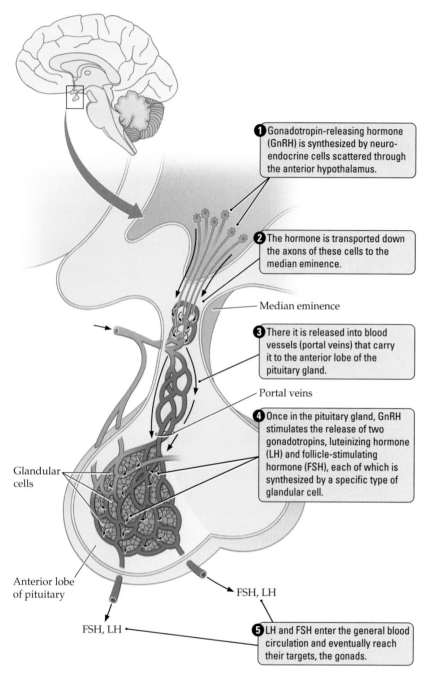

❶ Gonadotropin-releasing hormone (GnRH) is synthesized by neuro-endocrine cells scattered through the anterior hypothalamus.

❷ The hormone is transported down the axons of these cells to the median eminence.

Median eminence

❸ There it is released into blood vessels (portal veins) that carry it to the anterior lobe of the pituitary gland.

Portal veins

❹ Once in the pituitary gland, GnRH stimulates the release of two gonadotropins, luteinizing hormone (LH) and follicle-stimulating hormone (FSH), each of which is synthesized by a specific type of glandular cell.

Glandular cells

Anterior lobe of pituitary

FSH, LH

FSH, LH

❺ LH and FSH enter the general blood circulation and eventually reach their targets, the gonads.

Figure 4.7 Pathway for control of gonadotropin secretion by GnRH.

at the base of the brain, just above the pituitary gland, in a structure called the **median eminence.** Here the axon terminals secrete GnRH into a special set of blood vessels ("portal veins") that carry the hormone the short distance to the anterior lobe of the pituitary gland. The function of GnRH is solely to stimulate the release of two further hormones from glandular cells in the anterior pituitary. The concentration of GnRH in the general circulation is negligible, and it has no systemic effects.

The Pituitary Gonadotropins Are Luteinizing Hormone (LH) and Follicle-Stimulating Hormone (FSH)

The anterior lobe of the pituitary contains several different types of glandular cells, each producing a specific hormone. Many of these hormones have little or nothing to do with sexuality. The two anterior pituitary hormones whose release is triggered by GnRH, however, are crucially involved in sexual functions. These hormones are **follicle-stimulating hormone (FSH)** and **luteinizing hormone (LH).** The names of these two hormones refer to their actions in women; however, they play a vital role in regulating the functions of the gonads in both sexes, as we'll see shortly. These two hormones are therefore known collectively as **gonadotropins.** (The suffix "–tropin" indicates an agent that influences something else—in this case, the gonads.)

FSH and LH are sizable proteins, each composed of two polypeptide chains containing a total of over two hundred amino acids, along with four carbohydrate side chains. One of the two polypeptide chains is the same in FSH and LH; the other is unique to the one or the other hormone.

What makes FSH- and LH-secreting cells sensitive to GnRH is the fact that they express receptors for it. Because GnRH cannot pass through plasma membranes, these receptors have to be on the plasma membranes of the GnRH-sensitive cells, rather than in their cytoplasm or nuclei, as in the case of steroid receptors. When contacted by GnRH, these receptors activate a **second messenger** system—that is, a cascade of internal chemical signals that culminate in the secretion of FSH or LH into the bloodstream (Figure 4.8). This mechanism of action is typical of protein, peptide, and other non-fat-soluble hormones.

The secretion of GnRH into the portal blood vessels is cyclical, with a peak of secretion about every 1 to 2 hours. This cycle is generated by a "clock" in the hypothalamus whose nature is not fully understood. Each pulse of GnRH may trigger a pulse of FSH and LH release, but not all pulses do; thus FSH and LH are secreted in pulses that are somewhat less frequent than the GnRH pulses. A continuous high level of GnRH does *not* cause a sustained release of FSH and LH; rather, release of the two gonadotropins gradually declines to zero. Apparently, if GnRH occupies its receptors for long periods of time, the second messenger system no longer responds, so the effect is the same as if GnRH were absent. This fact can be important clinically: if a person's sexual functions are disrupted due to a deficiency in GnRH secretion, synthetic GnRH can be supplied by intravenous infusion, but it has to be infused as a series of pulses mimicking the natural time course of release from the median eminence.

Other Pituitary Hormones Include Prolactin and Growth Hormone

Two other hormones released from the anterior pituitary—both of them proteins—have sex-related functions. **Prolactin,** as its name suggests, plays an important role in preparing the breasts for lactation (see Chapter 10), but also seems to play a general role in potentiating the effects of other hormones. In addition, it may have behavioral effects. As with FSH and LH, the release of prolactin is controlled by a hormone released from the median eminence. That hormone is **dopamine,** a compound that also functions in the brain as a neurotransmitter (see below). Interestingly, the control dopamine exerts is negative; that is, the less dopamine is secreted into the portal veins, the more prolactin is secreted by the anterior pituitary gland. Thus dopamine functions as a prolactin **inhibitory factor.**

The last anterior pituitary hormone that we'll mention is **growth hormone.** It is also a protein hormone and, in fact, has an amino acid sequence very similar to that of prolactin. As its name implies, it stimulates growth throughout the body. Its main connection with sex is that it plays an important role at puberty (see Chapter 5). Like prolactin, it also plays a role in breast development.

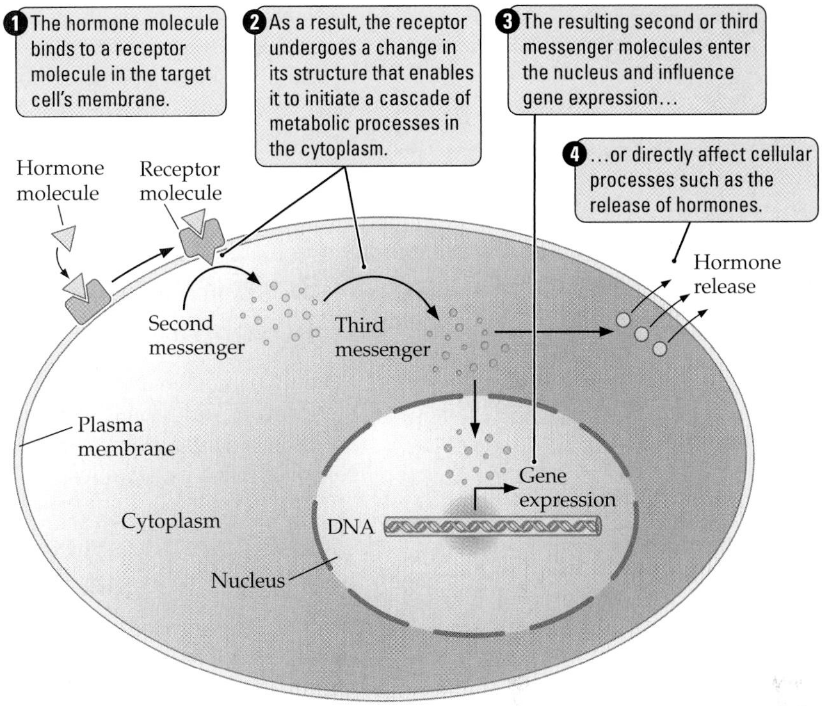

Figure 4.8 Mode of action of protein and peptide hormones such as GnRH.

Protein Hormones Are Secreted by Other Tissues

We need to mention several protein hormones that are not produced by the brain. **Human chorionic gonadotropin (hCG),** as its name suggests, influences the gonads in the same fashion as do FSH and LH; in fact, it is closely related to those hormones in structure. It is synthesized by the conceptus and, later in pregnancy, by the placenta. Because it is synthesized only during pregnancy, it is a useful indicator that a woman is in fact pregnant: pregnancy tests often depend on the detection of this hormone in a woman's blood or urine (see Chapter 10).

Inhibin is a protein that falls into the class of substances known as **cytokines.** These proteins are somewhat less specific than classic hormones: they are made in many different cell types and in turn influence many cell types. Often, they act locally on nearby cells. Inhibin plays a role in regulating ovarian and testicular function. However, it also acts as a classic hormone: it is secreted by the gonads into the bloodstream and acts on the pituitary gland, as we'll see later.

One last protein to be mentioned is **anti-Müllerian hormone.** This protein is also a cytokine, belonging to the same family as inhibin. It is produced by the testis during fetal life and plays an important role in preventing the development of the female reproductive tract in males (see Chapter 5).

Prostaglandins and Monoamines Also Influence Sexual Functions

Prostaglandins are lipids formed from a polyunsaturated fatty acid, arachidonic acid. They are somewhat like cytokines in that they generally act locally. Among other functions, prostaglandins play a role in preparing the uterus and cervix for childbirth (see Chapter 10).

Monoamines are small molecules that include dopamine, norepinephrine (also called noradrenaline), epinephrine (adrenaline), melatonin, and serotonin. **Serotonin** plays a role in sexual function as a neurotransmitter in the central nervous system, as described in Chapter 3, but it is not a hormone. Dopamine, besides acting as a neurotransmitter, does act as a hormone in the hypothalamic–pituitary control system, as described above. **Melatonin,** a hormone secreted by the pineal gland, regulates sexual behavior in animals that have a restricted mating season, but a role for this hormone in human sexuality is uncertain.

A Brain–Pituitary–Testis Loop Controls Gonadal Function in Men

Now that we have introduced the key players, we can look at how they interact to regulate sexual and reproductive functions. First, we'll examine the relatively simple hormonal mechanisms that control gonadal function in men. Then we'll turn to the more complex control system responsible for a woman's menstrual cycle.

The Regulation of Testosterone Levels and Spermatogenesis Is Coupled

The two major gonadotropins, luteinizing hormone and follicle-stimulating hormone, stimulate the two major functions of the testis: hormone secretion and spermatogenesis (Figure 4.9). There is clear experimental evidence for these functions: if the pituitary gland is removed in male experimental animals, or is damaged by injury or disease in men, both testosterone production and spermatogenesis cease, but they recover fully if the animal or man is treated with a combination of synthetic LH and FSH.

You might imagine that LH and FSH would each be independently responsible for activating one of the two testicular functions, hormone secretion or spermatogenesis. But that assumption would ignore the purpose of the entire system. From a reproductive standpoint, hormone secretion and spermatogenesis should be *coupled.* There is no point having the testes secrete high levels of testosterone, with all the consequences for a man's physical and psychological state that we'll describe later, unless he is producing sperm—and vice versa.

To achieve this coupling, LH and FSH interact at the level of the testicular Leydig and Sertoli cells (see Figure 4.9). Leydig cells express LH receptors, and they secrete testosterone (and estrogen) when stimulated by LH. Sertoli cells, on the other hand, express receptors for both FSH and androgens, and each hormone stimulates the Sertoli cell to increase the expression of receptors for the *other* hormone. (In other words, testosterone stimulates the expression of FSH receptors, and FSH stimulates the expression of androgen receptors.) This arrangement results in **synergism,** or cooperative action, between the two hormones, so that Sertoli cells activate high levels of sperm production only when *both* androgens *and* FSH are present.

Testosterone and Inhibin Exert Negative Feedback on Gonadotropin Release

We have described how GnRH from the hypothalamus stimulates the secretion of LH by the pituitary gland, and how LH, in turn, stimulates the secretion

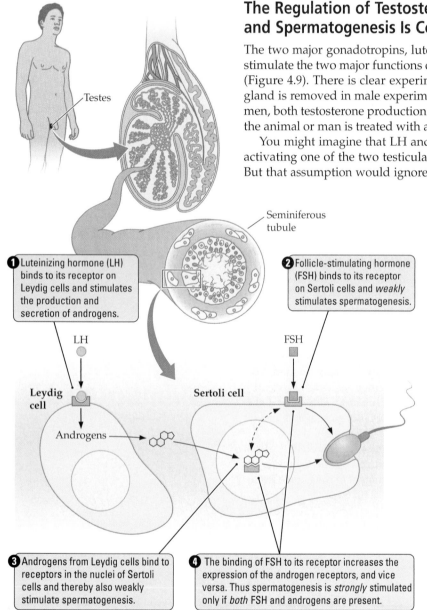

Testes

Seminiferous tubule

❶ Luteinizing hormone (LH) binds to its receptor on Leydig cells and stimulates the production and secretion of androgens.

❷ Follicle-stimulating hormone (FSH) binds to its receptor on Sertoli cells and *weakly* stimulates spermatogenesis.

LH

FSH

Leydig cell

Sertoli cell

Androgens

❸ Androgens from Leydig cells bind to receptors in the nuclei of Sertoli cells and thereby also weakly stimulate spermatogenesis.

❹ The binding of FSH to its receptor increases the expression of the androgen receptors, and vice versa. Thus spermatogenesis is *strongly* stimulated only if *both* FSH and androgens are present.

Figure 4.9 Influence of gonadotropins on the testis.

of testosterone by the testis. The final element in this control system is the **negative feed-back** effect of testosterone on the secretion of LH: the *higher* the concentration of testosterone in the blood, the *less* LH is secreted by the pituitary (Figure 4.10). This negative feedback occurs via two routes. The first is a direct effect of testosterone on the LH-secreting cells in the anterior lobe of the pituitary, depressing their response to the GnRH pulses coming from the hypothalamus. The second is an effect of testosterone on the hypothalamus, decreasing the frequency of GnRH pulses.

The entire hypothalamic-pituitary-testicular control circuit—the positive effects of GnRH on LH secretion, the positive effects of LH secretion on testosterone secretion, and the negative effects of testosterone on GnRH and LH secretion—functions to control testosterone levels and to keep them within a normal range. So, for example, if a man loses one testis (perhaps as a result of surgery for testicular cancer), the resulting drop in testosterone levels will allow LH levels to rise, and this rise, in turn, will stimulate the remaining testis to increase its testosterone production.

What about the regulation of spermatogenesis? Is there an equivalent signal that feeds back to the pituitary or hypothalamus and regulates the secretion of FSH? In part, such a signal is provided by testosterone: because testosterone controls the secretion of GnRH, and because GnRH stimulates both LH and FSH secretion by the pituitary gland, increasing testosterone levels tend to have a negative feedback effect on FSH as well as LH. However, the Sertoli cells also send a signal back to the pituitary gland that is more directly related to spermatogenesis, in the form of inhibin. In a fashion that is not well understood, the level of inhibin secretion by Sertoli cells reflects the rate at which sperm are being produced. The secreted inhibin travels in the bloodstream to the pituitary gland, where it directly depresses the secretion of FSH. Thus there is a second, partially independent control circuit that maintains sperm production at normal levels.

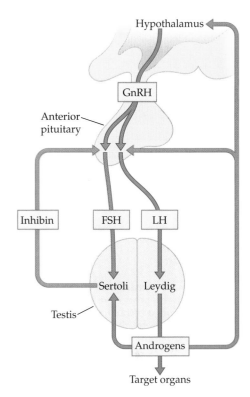

Figure 4.10 Hormonal interactions in the hypothalamic–pituitary–testicular control system. Stimulatory influences are shown in blue, inhibitory influences in red.

Testosterone Has Multiple Functions in Men

Testosterone has an important role in male development, both during fetal life and at puberty. However, we will postpone discussion of these developmental effects of the hormone until Chapter 5. Here, we cover its effects in adult men.

We've already mentioned two effects of testosterone in men: the facilitation (in combination with FSH) of spermatogenesis and the negative feedback regulation of LH secretion. Besides these two functions, testosterone has many others—some structural, some metabolic, and some behavioral. What links these effects is that they all contribute, directly or indirectly, to male sexual function.

Testosterone supports genital tissues   Most of a man's internal and external genital structures require the presence of testosterone for normal functioning. If an adult man is castrated (that is, both his testes are removed, as may sometimes be necessary to treat testicular cancer or prostate cancer), his prostate gland and seminal vesicles cease to produce their secretions and revert to an anatomically less mature state ("involute"). Administration of testosterone causes them to return to a normal functioning state. Not surprisingly, these glands and other genital structures are rich in androgen receptors.

While this kind of involution and recovery occurs only in quite abnormal circumstances in humans, it is a normal and repetitive experience for male animals that are seasonal breeders. Circannual (year-round) variations in the level of testosterone, orchestrated by the hormone melatonin, ensure that the reproductive system of such animals is primed to do its job only during the brief breeding season.

Testosterone also influences the erectile capacity of the penis. In healthy men, penile erections occur during REM sleep. These nocturnal erections cease some weeks after castration and return with testosterone treatment. Erections caused by exposure to erotic stimuli (e.g., a sexually explicit video) are only partially impaired after castration, however (Zverina et al., 1990). Thus, if a man complains that he is having difficulty getting an erection during sex, but still gets nocturnal erections, low testosterone is probably not the cause, and testosterone treatment will probably not help him (see Chapter 15).

Testosterone influences sexual behavior   In addition to its influence on genital structures, testosterone influences the central nervous system, facilitating sexual behav-

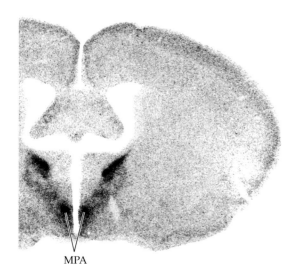

MPA

Figure 4.11 Androgen receptors in the brain of a rat. The receptors have been visualized by in situ hybridization, a technique that detects the messenger RNA that codes for the receptor protein. The receptor is expressed in the medial preoptic area of the hypothalamus (MPA), as well as some other brain regions. (Courtesy of Richard Simerly, Oregon Regional Primate Research Center.)

ior and influencing a variety of other mental processes. This function has been studied in greatest detail in rats (Meisel & Sachs, 1994). If a male rat is castrated and repeatedly tested with receptive females, he continues to mount them, but he performs intromission (vaginal penetration) and ejaculation less and less often over a period of a few weeks. Eventually, he even ceases mounting. Normal behavior can be restored by injection of minute quantities of testosterone into the hypothalamus—quantities that do not raise blood levels significantly. The most sensitive area for restoration of sexual function is a zone toward the front of the hypothalamus known as the **medial preoptic area.** This area is very rich in androgen receptors (Figure 4.11), but such receptors are found at lower levels in many brain regions besides the hypothalamus, suggesting that testosterone has more widespread effects.

It should be borne in mind that circulating testosterone has a half-life of only a few minutes, so testosterone drops to very low levels soon after castration. Why, then, does it take weeks for a rat's sexual behavior to cease? Evidently, testosterone does not regulate sexual behavior on a minute-to-minute basis. Rather, it influences some fairly durable feature of brain organization, such as synaptic circuitry, that is necessary for sexual behavior. We don't know the details of this regulatory process in adult rats. In developing rats, however, testosterone strongly influences the formation of neural structures and synaptic circuitry involved in sexual behavior—a topic that we'll cover in Chapter 5. It probably does something similar, but at a more subtle level, in adults.

Role of conversion to estradiol   Further experiments on rats have clarified how testosterone acts on the brain. If estradiol is injected into the hypothalamus of a castrated male rat instead of testosterone, it works just as well in restoring normal sexual behavior. However, if DHT—a very potent androgen that cannot be converted to estradiol—is injected, no recovery is seen. These findings suggest that when testosterone enters the hypothalamus, it is converted to estradiol (by the enzyme aromatase), and estradiol then facilitates sexual behavior (Baum, 2002). Consistent with this interpretation, both the enzyme aromatase and estrogen receptors are present in the hypothalamus. Furthermore, the administration of drugs that block the action of aromatase interferes with the behavioral effects of testosterone (Clancy et al., 1995; Vagell & McGinnis, 1997). Thus, we can conclude that the conversion (or "aromatization") of testosterone to estradiol is necessary for male sexual behavior in rats. So much for the notion that estrogen is a purely "female" hormone.

Testosterone also influences sexual behavior in humans. Most men who have been castrated experience a profound decline in sexual thoughts and sexual behavior. This decline is variable among individuals and can take many months or even years to show itself. Some castrated men continue to experience sexual desires and to have erections in response to erotic visual stimuli, even without any testosterone replacement therapy (Greenstein et al., 1995). In part, this may be because castration does not completely eliminate testosterone and other androgens from the blood: they are still secreted at low levels by the adrenal gland. However, anti-androgen drugs, which should work against androgens of any origin, also have less than complete effects in extinguishing sexual desire and behavior (see Chapter 14).

The persistence of sexual thoughts and behavior in some castrated and anti-androgen-treated men suggests that humans are less enslaved to hormones than are animals such as rats. It may be that the relevant mental structures are set up under the influence of sex hormones during development (see Chapter 5), but once established, take on a life of their own, reinforcing themselves through a variety of psychological and cultural mechanisms.

There is also some uncertainty about the importance of the aromatization process (the conversion of testosterone to estradiol in the brain) for human sexuality. There have been suggestions that testosterone acts directly on the brain in primates and does not require conversion to estradiol. Aromatization clearly does play some role, however. Aromatase-blocking drugs interfere with sexual activity in male monkeys (Zumpe et al., 1993), and men who are congenitally deficient in the aromatase enzyme have a low sex drive, which can be increased by the administration of estradiol (Carani et al., 1999). It seems most likely that the effects of testosterone on men's sexuality are partly direct (via androgen receptors) and partly indirect (via aromatization and estrogen receptors) (Figure 4.12), but the differences between these two kinds of effects remain to be worked out.

Testosterone has anabolic effects Testosterone and other androgens have a broad influence on body systems, tending to promote tissue growth. These **anabolic** effects are easiest to see in the musculature: androgens are the main reason why men tend to be more muscular than women after puberty. But androgens also promote the formation of red blood cells, increasing the oxygen-carrying capacity of the blood, and they increase the mass of the liver and kidneys.

The use of androgens as drugs is common among bodybuilders; their use among other athletes is generally banned by the governing bodies of their sports. Still, illicit use (by both men and women) probably still occurs, and not all androgens are banned in all sports. Baseball slugger Mark McGwire used the androgen androstenedione (the immediate metabolic precursor of testosterone) legally during the 1998 season, when he hit a record-breaking 70 home runs. According to a controlled study, however, androstenedione supplements do not increase muscle mass or strength in men with normal testosterone levels (King et al., 1999).

Androgen use may have significant ill effects, including sterility (see Chapter 11), liver disease, and pathological aggressiveness ("'roid rage") (Choi & Pope, 1994). In women it can cause **hirsutism** (excess hair growth), acne, voice changes, and reproductive problems. Perhaps the most systematic abuse of androgens occurred in the former German Democratic Republic (East Germany), where thousands of athletes of both sexes (including minors) were given androgens and other drugs as part of a government-sanctioned program. This program brought numerous world records and Olympic medals to the GDR in the period between 1966 and the collapse of the state in 1990, but the health effects for the athletes, especially the women, were ruinous (Franke & Berendonk, 1997). After the reunification of Germany, 107 trainers and officials, including the East German sports minister Manfred Ewald, were convicted of crimes related to the drug program.

Estradiol Has Wide-Ranging Effects in Men's Bodies

Besides being produced locally in the brain from testosterone, estradiol is also secreted by the testes, as we mentioned earlier. This estradiol has several important effects (Sharpe, 1997):

- It facilitates the maturation and concentration of sperm in the epididymis (Hess et al., 1997).
- It is responsible for terminating the growth of the limb bones at the conclusion of puberty (see Chapter 5). Therefore, those rare individuals who congenitally lack estrogen receptors keep on growing after puberty, reaching a height of 7 feet or more.
- It maintains the normal density of bone. Low estrogen levels are associated with bone demineralization (osteoporosis). You may know that osteoporosis sometimes occurs as a consequence of estrogen deficiency in postmenopausal women (see Chapter 12), but in fact estradiol is required to maintain normal bone density in both sexes throughout adult life.

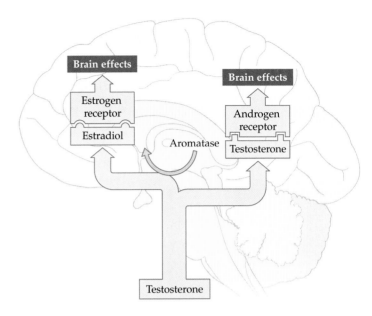

Figure 4.12 Testosterone acts on the brain through two mechanisms: direct binding to androgen receptors (right), and conversion to estradiol followed by binding to estrogen receptors (left).

Androgens promote muscular development in both sexes.

Estrogen receptors are found widely throughout the body—in the skin, gut, and heart, for example—so there are probably other actions of estrogens that remain to be discovered.

Menstruation Is a Biological Process with Cultural and Practical Aspects

The menstrual cycle has one obvious external sign: the vaginal discharge of endometrial tissue and blood that women experience at roughly monthly intervals during their fertile years, except when they are pregnant or nursing an infant. Like the hourly tolling of a bell, this simple outward event is brought about by a complex internal mechanism—wheels within wheels that turn silently within a woman's body, ensuring her readiness to conceive and to carry a fetus. These processes involve the ovaries, the brain, the pituitary gland, and the uterus.

Before looking at the biological processes underlying the menstrual cycle, let's first acknowledge that menstruation itself has important psychological, cultural, and practical aspects (Box 4.2). Most women can remember their first menstrual period—an event that heralds their passage into womanhood more clearly than any other. And while menstruation is at best inconvenient, and in some women is associated with real problems—pain, mood disorders, and even serious ill health—it is also often experienced as a validation of a woman's core identity. In 1999, when the Brazilian gynecologist Elsimar Coutinho published a book titled *Is Menstruation Obsolete?* and suggested ways in which women could abolish the entire phenomenon, many women wondered whether this was the ultimate sexist assault—the "perfecting" of women's bodies by making them more like men's. (We will consider Coutinho's ideas when we take up the subject of contraception in Chapter 11.)

The **menstrual period** (also called **menses**) lasts somewhere between 2 and 6 days (most commonly 4–5 days) and involves a total loss of 30–60 milliliters of coagulated blood, plus other fluids and endometrial tissue, amounting to a total volume of 50–200 milliliters (2–6 ounces) discharged through the vagina. The amount of blood lost is not great—a blood donation is typically 500 milliliters. Still, heavy discharges are a reason to seek medical attention.

Besides the vaginal discharge, a roughly comparable amount of blood and endometrial tissue is discharged internally via the oviducts into the abdominal cavity, where it is reabsorbed. This internal discharge usually creates no problems, and it has the health benefit of conserving the iron and other nutritive components of blood that would be lost by vaginal discharge. Occasionally, however, the internal discharge can carry living endometrial cells to sites outside the uterus, where they may become implanted and survive, causing a condition called **endometriosis.** We discuss this condition in Chapter 17.

Most American women who menstruate use sanitary napkins ("pads"), panty liners, or tampons to absorb their menstrual flow. Pads and panty liners are worn on the outside of the body: the main difference between them is that panty liners are thinner. Tampons—absorbent cylinders made of cotton or synthetic fiber—are placed inside the vagina.

Although tampons are extremely convenient—even allowing such activities as swimming during a woman's period—their use has been linked to a rare but dangerous condition known as **menstrual toxic shock syndrome** (Hanrahan, 1994). This condition, caused by certain strains of the bacterium *Staphylococcus aureus,* is marked by high fever, vomiting, diarrhea, rash, and other symptoms, and can be fatal in up to 10 percent of affected women. The connection between toxic shock syndrome and tampon use was discovered in 1980. Of the 344 women who developed the syndrome in that year (28 of whom died), 70 percent had used one particular type of extra-absorbent tampon—Proctor and Gamble's Rely brand. This brand was withdrawn from the market, and menstrual toxic shock syndrome has become much less common since then: in 1997 there were only 5 reported cases, none of them fatal.

A woman who uses tampons is advised to use the least absorbent tampon compatible with satisfactory function (U.S. Food and Drug Administration, 1999). Tampons should be changed after 4 to 8 hours of use. If the tampon is not saturated after that time (i.e., it still has white cotton showing), it is recommended that the woman switch to a less absorbent tampon. It's a good idea to have varying grades of tampons available to deal with the varying flow over the course of the period: the flow usually lessens toward

Box 4.2	*Society, Values, and the Law*

Attitudes Toward Menstruation

Across many cultures and historical periods, men have often viewed menstruating woman with distaste, fear, or moral concern. The Roman naturalist Pliny the Elder declared that menstrual blood was a dangerous poison. If a man had sex with a menstruating woman, Pliny wrote, he risked serious harm or even death—especially if the sex act coincided with a total solar eclipse!

According to Judeo-Christian Scripture, a menstruating woman is unclean, as is any person who touches her bedding (Leviticus 15:19–21). In the Orthodox Judaic tradition of *niddut,* a woman must sleep apart from her husband for several days during and after her period and must undergo a ritual cleansing bath (*mikvah*) before returning to him. The Christian theologian St. Augustine taught that sex with a menstruating women was sinful. The Qur'an (the holy book of Islam, verse 2:222) likewise prohibits sex with a menstruating woman, and (in some interpretations) prohibits a menstruating woman from praying, fasting, or entering a mosque.

Some cultures have even required women to sleep away from the household altogether during their periods. For example, among the Dogon, a traditional cliff-dwelling people in Mali, Africa, menstruating women have to sleep in a "menstrual hut" for about five nights (see figure). During that time they may work in the fields but may not sleep with or cook for their husbands. A violation of this taboo, it is believed, will bring famine or sickness. The taboo is imposed by the Dogon men, and its ultimate motive, according to anthropologist Beverly Strassmann of the University of Michigan, is that it gives men precise information about the timing of women's menstruation (Strassmann, 1992, 1996). Why is this information important? In a culture such as that of the Dogon, women experience menstrual cycles (and therefore are able to become pregnant) for only quite

short stretches of time: the rest of time they are either pregnant or they are intensively breastfeeding their babies, a practice that suppresses the menstrual cycle (Chapter 10). Knowledge of the occurrence of menstruation helps men identify the limited time when a woman can become pregnant. If she has been adulterous around the time of onset of pregnancy, the father and all of his fellow patrilineage members (persons related to each other by the male line of descent) will reject the child as an imposter. Even if the husband wishes to accept paternity, the other members of his lineage, who own land jointly, have the right to overrule his claims. All male patrilineage members have a common interest in guarding against mistaken paternity attributions, so each patrilineage has its own menstrual hut.

In contemporary Western culture, attitudes toward menstruation vary, but the belief that women should avoid vaginal intercourse during their periods is still widespread. A sizable majority (70–80 percent) of men and women do in fact avoid this practice (Barnhart et al., 1995; Tanfer & Aral, 1996). Among some women, this avoidance is bolstered by the idea that sex during menstruation threatens their own health. Many Latina immigrants to Southern California, for example, believe that sex during menstruation causes cervical cancer (Hubbell et al., 1996). (There is no medical evidence to support this particular notion, but one study has suggested that sex during menstruation

may facilitate the transfer of sexually transmitted diseases [Tanfer & Aral, 1996].)

Other men and women may avoid sex during menstruation out of a distaste for the practice, for religious reasons, or because the woman has symptoms associated with menstruation that make her uninterested in sex. A further possible reason may be the low testosterone levels at the menstrual phase of a woman's cycle, which may reduce her interest in sex.

Still, about 20 percent of women in the United States do engage in vaginal sex during menstruation. These women tend to be white and well educated (Tanfer & Aral, 1996). Some women use a diaphragm (see Chapter 11) or menstrual cup to block the menstrual discharge during sex. Others may simply place a dark-colored towel over their sheets to prevent staining. Alternatively, many couples engage in other forms of lovemaking that do not involve coitus.

the end of the period. It is also a good idea to use a sanitary napkin rather than a tampon for some portion of the menstrual period. Any woman who develops a high fever (38.9°C, 102°F) while using a tampon should remove it and seek medical attention immediately. Although toxic shock syndrome is a serious matter, it is hardly a reason for not using tampons: many millions of women in the United States use them, but only a handful of cases of menstrual toxic shock syndrome are reported per year.

As an alternative to pads and tampons, there are also two "menstrual cups"—called **The Keeper** and **Instead**—that are worn inside the vagina. They dam the menstrual flow rather than absorbing it. As its name suggests, The Keeper is a reusable device—it is made of gum rubber—and it is therefore cheaper over time (and more environmentally friendly) than tampons or pads. It is placed just a little way into the vagina, so coitus is not possible while wearing it. The Instead device is made of soft thermoplastic and is for one-time use. It is placed deep within the vagina against the cervix, and it therefore permits coitus while it is worn. It does not function as a contraceptive, however.

The Menstrual Cycle Involves the Ovaries, Brain, Pituitary, and Uterus

Now let's return to the biology of the menstrual cycle. The first thing to understand is that the active players in the cycle are the ovaries, the hypothalamus, and the pituitary gland. The uterus is influenced in a dramatic way by the hormones produced during the cycle, but it is an entirely passive player, as far as we know. Thus, if the uterus is surgically removed in a premenopausal woman (and the ovaries are left in place), menstruation ceases, but the hormonal fluctuations of the menstrual cycle continue as before.

The Cycle Is of Variable Length

The length of the menstrual cycle varies greatly between women, and can also vary from one cycle to the next in the same woman. Most women have cycles lasting between 24 and 32 days, but cycles as short as 20 days or as long as 36 days are not unusual. Cycle length tends to be irregular when the cycles begin at puberty (see Chapter 5) and at the approach of menopause (see Chapter 12). Women who are markedly underweight, who undergo rigorous athletic training, or who are ill or otherwise stressed may have irregular cycles or may cease to menstruate altogether (**amenorrhea**). Finally, of course, menstrual cycles cease during pregnancy and to a less predictable degree during the time when a mother is breast-feeding her infant (see Chapter 10). It has been claimed that the menstrual cycles of women who live together tend to synchronize, but the reality of "menstrual synchrony" has been contested (Box 4.3).

The Cycle Consists of Menstrual, Follicular, and Luteal Phases

Although menstruation is the obvious outward sign of the menstrual cycle, its most significant internal event is ovulation, the release of an ovum from one or the other ovary about midway between one menstrual period and the next. Some women feel abdominal pain (called **Mittelschmerz**, or "middle pain" in German) at the time of ovulation, and may even be able to tell from the location of the pain whether the ovum was released from the left or right ovary.

The portion of the menstrual cycle between menstruation and ovulation is called the **follicular** or **preovulatory phase** because it is marked by the maturation of follicles in the ovaries. The portion of the cycle between ovulation and menstruation is called the **luteal** or **postovulatory phase** because it is marked by the presence of a corpus luteum, a vital hormone-secreting structure formed from the single follicle that ruptured at ovulation. (Yet another pair of names for these two phases—**proliferative phase** and **secretory phase**—refer to processes that take place in the uterus, which we will examine later.)

A typical 28-day cycle is divided up roughly as follows: the menstrual phase occupies days 1 through 5, the follicular phase occupies days 6 through 14, and the luteal phase occupies days 15 through 28 (Figure 4.13). Of these three phases, the luteal phase is the most constant—it usually lasts within 2 days of 14 days. Most of the variation in total cycle length is accounted for by variation in the other two phases.

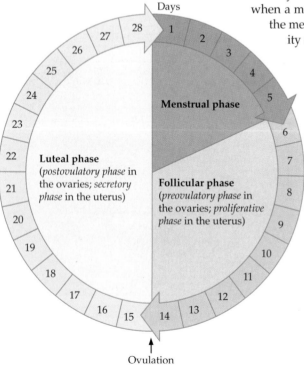

Figure 4.13 A 28-day menstrual cycle. When cycles are markedly longer or shorter than 28 days, it is because of differences in the lengths of the menstrual or follicular phases; the luteal phase is nearly always close to 14 days long, as shown here.

The Menstrual Phase Is Triggered by a Drop in Progesterone Levels

During the menstrual phase, much of the inner lining of the uterus—the endometrium—sloughs off, thus beginning the process of preparing the uterus for the transport of sperm. The sloughing-off process is triggered primarily by a drop in the circulating level of the hormone progesterone, which is secreted by the corpus luteum (Johnson & Everitt, 2000). Blood levels of estrogens also drop at this time. These and other processes are represented diagrammatically in Figure 4.14.

The sloughing off and discharge of endometrial tissue is aided by contractions of the outer muscular layer of the uterus (the myometrium) in a fashion somewhat similar to the process of childbirth. These contractions take place under the influence of prostaglandins secreted by the uterus itself. These uterine contractions are the main cause of pain or cramping during menstruation (**dysmenorrhea**) (Deligeoroglou, 2000). Dysmenorrhea is especially common among young women who have not had children.

There is a negative feedback relationship between estrogen levels and the secretion of the gonadotropins (LH and FSH) by the pituitary gland. This relationship is quite similar to the one we have already described between testosterone and gonadotropin secretion, though with an important extra wrinkle that we'll get to shortly. The negative feedback effect of estrogen is exerted both on the pituitary gland (reducing the sensitivity of the gonadotropin-secreting cells to GnRH) and on the hypothalamus (decreasing the secretion of GnRH). Thus, as estrogen levels fall at the beginning of the menstrual phase, the negative feedback effect diminishes, allowing circulating LH and FSH levels to rise. These increased gonadotropin levels—in particular, the increase in FSH—promote the development of follicles in the ovaries.

The Follicular Phase Is Marked by the Maturation of Ovarian Follicles

As mentioned in Chapter 3, a newborn girl's ovaries contain all the egg cells she will ever possess—about 2 million of them. These cells, called **primary oocytes,** are arrested in the first of their two meiotic divisions. (Recall that meiosis reduces the number of chromosomes by half and also confers genetic heterogeneity on the gametes.) The majority of these cells die during childhood, so by the age of puberty a woman is down to about 400,000 oocytes.

Each oocyte is surrounded by a thin layer of granulosa cells, forming a **primordial follicle** (Figure 4.15). The ovary consists largely of primordial follicles, separated by interstitial tissue that includes the thecal cells. As mentioned earlier, the thecal cells are the ovarian cells that are capable of synthesizing androgens, and thus are equivalent to the Leydig cells of the testis. The granulosa cells are equivalent to the sperm-nourishing Sertoli cells of the testis.

Initial stages of follicular development During a woman's fertile adult life, a constant trickle of primordial follicles—several per day—leave their long-term "frozen" state and enter a process of renewed maturation. In the first stage, which takes about 3 months, the primary oocyte expands in size from about 0.02 millimeter to about 0.1 millimeter in diameter—its final size. The layer of granulosa cells also thickens and attracts an outer layer of thecal cells, so that the whole follicle is now about 0.3 millimeter in diameter and easily visible to the naked

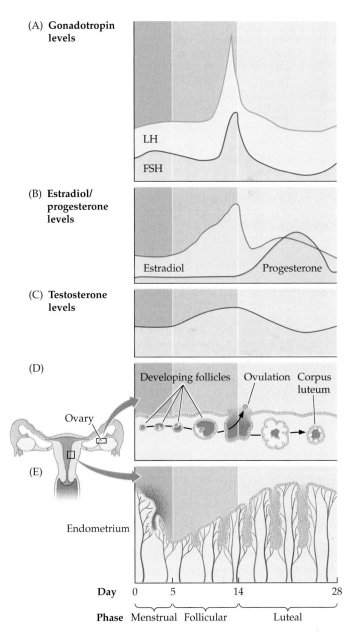

(A) Gonadotropin levels

LH

FSH

(B) Estradiol/ progesterone levels

Estradiol   Progesterone

(C) Testosterone levels

(D)

Developing follicles   Ovulation Corpus luteum

Ovary

(E)

Endometrium

Day   0   5   14   28

Phase Menstrual Follicular   Luteal

Figure 4.14 Main processes of the menstrual cycle. Panels A–C show changes in the circulating levels of the major hormones involved in the cycle. Panel D shows the development of an ovarian follicle, the release of the ovum at ovulation, and the conversion of the follicle to a corpus luteum. Panel E shows the breakdown of the endometrium during the menstrual phase, followed by its regrowth during the follicular and early luteal phases.

Biology of Sex

Menstrual Synchrony: Reality or Myth?

Do women who live together get their periods at the same time? Anecdotal accounts have long suggested that they do, but scientific evidence was lacking until 1970. In that year Martha McClintock, then a graduate student at Wellesley College, decided to investigate the matter. Her results ignited a scientific controversy that still rages today, and which could have significant implications for the future of birth control and other aspects of women's lives.

McClintock kept records of the menstrual periods of the students in her dormitory, and found that, over the course of a semester, the periods of women who spent a lot of time together occurred closer and closer in time. Her analysis, published in the prestigious journal *Nature* (McClintock, 1971), appeared to give "menstrual synchrony" scientific grounding.

What's more, her findings resonated with the spirit of 1970s feminism. Here was a biological expression of solidarity among women—a kinship that men knew nothing about and could never join. McClintock's work was mentioned in many books about women's lives. Before long, menstrual synchrony became common knowledge—something that most people had heard about and probably believed.

In 1998, McClintock, now a psychologist at the University of Chicago, published another paper in *Nature* (Stern & McClintock, 1998). She and colleague Kathleen Stern performed a set of experiments that purported to show *how* menstrual synchrony comes about—namely, by means of pheromones. McClintock and Stern put cotton pads under the armpits of women at two different stages of their menstrual cycles: the follicular phase or the early luteal phase. After a few hours the pads were removed, and volatile compounds were extracted from them and stored. These compounds were then swabbed daily onto the upper lips of a second group of "recipient" women. The next menstrual period in these women occurred either 1–2 days earlier or later than it would have otherwise, depending on what stage of the menstrual cycle the "donor" women were in when their armpits were sampled (see figure; the control cycles varied in length, but are shown here as a standard 28 days for simplicity). McClintock and Stern concluded that women secrete at least two different pheromones at different stages of the menstrual cycle, and that these pheromones have the power to lengthen or shorten the cycles of other women who smell them, thus leading to menstrual synchrony.

Yet the existence of menstrual synchrony, as well as the belief that pheromones are its mechanism, remains highly controversial. Although some studies seem to support McClintock's claims, at least in part (Weller & Weller, 1997; Weller et al., 1995), other researchers have failed to detect synchrony, even in circumstances very similar to those of her original study, or have found methodological problems in the studies that do claim to find synchrony (Schank, 2000). Two groups of researchers failed to find any menstrual synchrony between cohabiting lesbian couples, whom one might imagine would be the *most* likely to synchronize (Trevathan et al., 1993; Weller & Weller, 1998).

One of the most vocal critics of McClintock's work is anthropologist Beverly Strassmann of the University of Michigan. Strassmann studied the Dogon, the traditional West African people who have the standard 28 days for simplicity). McClintock custom of sending menstruating women to a "menstrual hut" (see Box 4.2). Because of this practice, it was easy for Strassmann to keep track of the menstrual periods of all the women in the community. She never observed synchronization of cycles, even between women who were sisters or close friends (Strassmann, 1997). (She also failed to find any relationship between menstrual periods and the phases of the moon, a notion that has even wider currency than menstrual synchrony.)

In 1999 Strassmann published a blistering critique of McClintock's work (Strassmann, 1999). She pointed out (as have others) a variety of potential errors in the studies that have claimed to find menstrual synchrony. As for the pheromone study, Strassmann suggested that inappropriate statistical tests were used, that the claimed statistical significance of the results was marginal, and that McClintock and Stern may have excluded women whose data went against their hypothesis. "Skepticism is warranted," Strassmann concluded.

Another critic of the synchronization theory is psychologist Madelynne Arden of Britain's Leeds University. Arden reanalyzed a 1997 Israeli study that claimed to find "definitive" evidence of menstrual syn-

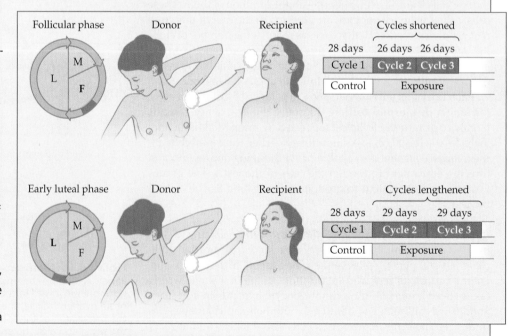

chrony among Bedouin women (Weller & Weller, 1997). She concluded that the Israelis' statistical methods would have found synchrony under any circumstances—even if the timing of the women's periods had been completely random (Arden & Dye, 1998). Yet Arden still thinks that menstrual synchrony may sometimes occur, perhaps among women who have lived together for a long time.

McClintock herself remains adamant that the phenomenon of menstrual synchrony exists, but she is willing to admit that it may be a lot more complicated than she originally thought. Sometimes women synchronize, she says, sometimes they *desynchronize*, and sometimes they just remain random (McClintock, 1999).

Quite a few women believe that they have experienced menstrual synchrony, but they may not have done the arithmetic to see how frequently menstrual periods overlap on a purely random basis. If two randomly chosen women have 28-day cycles and periods lasting 5 days, there is a 1-in-3 chance that their periods will overlap for at least 1 day. Such an overlap may be interpreted by the women as evidence of synchrony, but careful statistical analysis is required to distinguish chance coincidence from a real biological phenomenon.

In spite of this uncertainty, the topic deserves further study. After all, if menstrual synchrony and its pheromonal mechanism turn out to be real, there could be a big payoff for women. One can envisage bottled pheromones that would allow women to schedule their periods at will, or that might even act as contraceptives. The added level of control would certainly help make monthly menstruation a more easily regulated aspect of a woman's life.

eye. At this stage it is called a **preantral follicle,** meaning a follicle that does not yet have a cavity (antrum). At any one time, the two ovaries contain several hundred preantral follicles.

In the next phase (see Figure 4.15), a fluid-filled cavity, or **antrum,** forms within the mass of granulosa cells surrounding the oocyte. The entire follicle—now called an **antral follicle**—swells as the fluid accumulates. When it reaches a diameter of about 2 millimeters, a critical event occurs: the follicular cells begin to express gonadotropin receptors. Specifically, the thecal cells begin to express LH receptors and the granulosa cells begin to express FSH receptors. From then on, the follicle is dependent on circulating gonadotropins for its survival and further development.

Gonadotropin-dependent development The process of follicular development up to this point has occurred independently of hormones and is therefore oblivious to the menstrual cycles going on at the time. Thus, a particular antral follicle may become gonadotropin-dependent at any point in a cycle, or even while the woman is pregnant. Only follicles that happen to become gonadotropin-dependent during the follicular phase of the cycle, when LH and FSH levels are high, will be "rescued" by those hormones and allowed to develop further; all others will die.

(A)

(B)

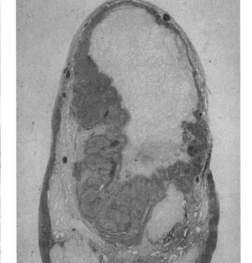

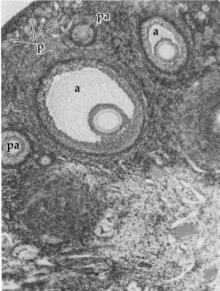

Figure 4.15 Stages of follicular development. (A) Numerous primordial follicles (p) cluster against the outer margin of the ovary. Some have developed into preantral follicles (pa), and a few into antral follicles (a), characterized by their central cavity, or antrum. (B) The single follicle that ovulates transforms subsequently into a corpus luteum, which synthesizes and secretes all three classes of sex steroids: among these, progesterone is vital for the establishment of pregnancy. The corpus luteum is visible here as the oval structure (comprised of dark and light regions) that occupies most of this cross-section of the ovary. The light region consists of large lutein cells, derived from follicular granulosa cells; the darker rim consists of small lutein cells, derived from thecal cells. The two pink structures near the bottom of the image are involuted corpora lutea from previous menstrual cycles.

Figure 4.16 Hormonal loops controlling the menstrual cycle during the follicular phase (A) and during the luteal phase (B).

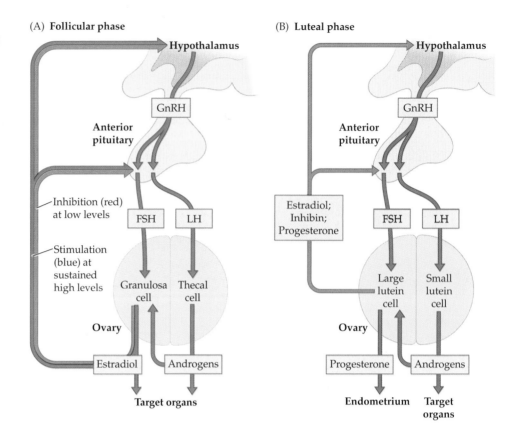

The lucky follicles—about 15–20 of them in a given cycle—continue to enlarge under the influence of gonadotropins during the follicular phase of the cycle. They now begin to synthesize and secrete significant amounts of sex steroids. The thecal cells synthesize androgens, including testosterone; the granulosa cells pick up some of these androgens and convert them to estrogens. A runaway process begins in which the presence of estrogens promotes the proliferation of the granulosa cells, which synthesize more estrogens, and so on. The antral follicles that happen to be most advanced in their development therefore secrete rapidly increasing amounts of estrogens, especially estradiol, into the bloodstream: estradiol levels rise from about 0.1 to about 0.3 ng/ml. At about the same time, one of the 15–20 antral follicles becomes dominant over the others. How this happens is not clear, but this one follicle grows faster than the others and begins to express LH receptors on its granulosa cells. (Recall that, up to this point, only the thecal cells expressed LH receptors.)

High estrogen levels trigger an LH surge   One might think that the rise in estradiol, which happens late in the follicular phase of the cycle, would shut down the

Figure 4.17 Meiosis in the development of human oocytes. The process is similar to the generic scheme for meiosis shown in Box 2.1, with two peculiarities. First, there are two halts in the meiotic process: one long halt during meiosis I (from fetal life to adulthood), and a second, shorter halt during meiosis II (from ovulation to fertilization). Second, the cell division at the end of meiosis I is unequal: a single "secondary oocyte" receives most of the cytoplasm, and the other daughter cell is discarded as a bag of chromosomes—the first polar body. (The remainder of meiosis II will be described in the context of fertilization; see Figure 5.3.)

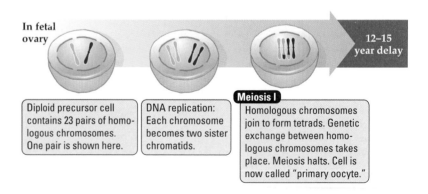

In fetal ovary

12–15 year delay

Meiosis I

Diploid precursor cell contains 23 pairs of homologous chromosomes. One pair is shown here.

DNA replication: Each chromosome becomes two sister chromatids.

Homologous chromosomes join to form tetrads. Genetic exchange between homologous chromosomes takes place. Meiosis halts. Cell is now called "primary oocyte."

secretion of gonadotropins by the pituitary gland, by virtue of the negative feedback effect. It turns out, however, that if high blood levels of estradiol are sustained for 48 hours or so, estradiol now has a *positive* feedback effect, *increasing* the secretion of LH and, to a lesser extent, of FSH (Figure 4.16A). Therefore, a surge of LH enters the bloodstream, raising LH levels far above what they reach at any other time of the cycle. This surge, a critical event in the cycle, begins about 36 hours before ovulation, and it drives the final development of the dominant or **preovulatory follicle** (see Figure 4.15), culminating in ovulation.

The reversal of the effect of estradiol on LH secretion, from negative feedback at low blood concentrations to positive feedback at high concentrations, is mediated by processes both in the pituitary gland and within the hypothalamus. High, sustained levels of estrogen cause the LH-secreting pituitary cells to express more GnRH receptors, and therefore to secrete more LH for a given pulse of GnRH. In addition, the high estradiol levels act directly on the hypothalamus to cause the GnRH cells to release more of their hormone into the portal vessels. The mechanism of this effect is not well understood.

In some animals, such as rats, only females are capable of showing a positive LH response to estrogens. One cannot turn a male rat into an "endocrinological female" by castrating it and implanting ovaries; it won't show an LH surge and therefore won't ovulate or cycle normally. It appears that the brains of female rats are imprinted during fetal life with the capacity to sustain the ovarian cycle, whereas the brains of male rats are not.

In primates, on the other hand, there seems not to be any sex difference of this kind. A castrated male monkey shows the same LH surge in response to sustained high estrogen levels as a female monkey. And if ovarian tissue is transplanted into a castrated male monkey, the animal's hormones will cycle very much like those of a normal female (Norman & Spies, 1986). In humans, too, the LH response to estrogen seems to be similar in both sexes (Gooren, 1986). Thus, with respect to this particular aspect of sexuality, the brains of men and women seem to be undifferentiated. (Later in this book, we'll encounter other aspects of brain organization that are indeed different between men and women).

Maturation of the dominant follicle   The preovulatory surge of LH drives the dominant follicle toward ovulation. The reason that only the dominant follicle responds is that it alone possesses LH receptors both on its thecal cells and on its granulosa cells. The first step in its final maturation is the completion of the long-arrested first meiotic division (Figure 4.17). Unlike most cell divisions, this one is asymmetrical: nearly the entire cytoplasm is bequeathed to a single daughter cell, now called a **secondary oocyte.** The other daughter cell is nothing more than a tiny bag of discarded chromosomes—the so-called **first polar body.** The secondary oocyte immediately enters its second meiotic division, but again the process of division is arrested in midcourse, though for a much shorter time in this case. The completion of these chromosomal rearrangements will be described in Chapter 5.

During this same period, right after the beginning of the LH surge, the follicle undergoes a major endocrinological shift. Under the influence of LH, it shuts down most of its

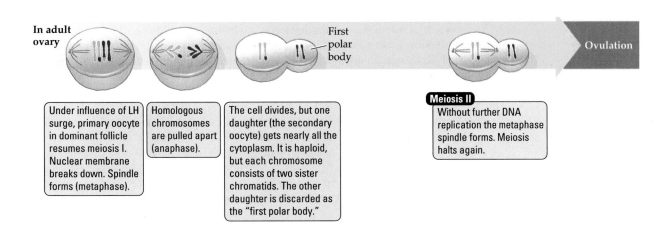

In adult ovary   First polar body   Ovulation

			Meiosis II
Under influence of LH surge, primary oocyte in dominant follicle resumes meiosis I. Nuclear membrane breaks down. Spindle forms (metaphase).	Homologous chromosomes are pulled apart (anaphase).	The cell divides, but one daughter (the secondary oocyte) gets nearly all the cytoplasm. It is haploid, but each chromosome consists of two sister chromatids. The other daughter is discarded as the "first polar body."	Without further DNA replication the metaphase spindle forms. Meiosis halts again.

production of estrogens and begins to produce progesterone, the major sex steroid of the luteal phase. Progesterone is synthesized by the granulosa cells, the same cells that had previously been converting testosterone into estradiol.

Ovulation The dominant follicle enlarges even further during the LH surge, reaching a diameter of 25 millimeters or so and creating a bulge in the wall of the ovary. Finally, **ovulation** occurs: the follicle ruptures, and the secondary oocyte is released into the peritoneal cavity, along with a wrapping of granulosa cells, now called **cumulus cells.** The secondary oocyte is usually called an **ovum** at this stage. This name is not quite correct because the oocyte has still not completed the second meiotic division, so technically it is still the parent cell of an ovum, rather than an ovum itself. Be that as it may, the ovum or secondary oocyte is swept up by the fimbria of the oviduct and passes into the ampulla, where it lingers and may be fertilized if sperm are present.

You may hear reference to an ovulatory "phase" of the menstrual cycle—a period of several days during which ovulation occurs. We see no particular reason for such terminology. Although the time of ovulation may be uncertain, it is in itself a very rapid event taking less than a day. We prefer to think of ovulation as the event that marks the end of the follicular phase and the beginning of the luteal phase, not as a phase in itself.

Growth of endometrium Before continuing with the next phase of the cycle, we need to take a look at what has been happening in the uterus (see Figure 4.14E). At the end of the menstrual phase the endometrium is at its thinnest, but during the follicular phase it gradually thickens again under the influence of the rising levels of estrogens secreted by the developing ovarian follicles. The epithelial cells of the endometrium proliferate (hence the term "proliferative phase" as an alternative to "follicular phase") and form numerous glandular invaginations, which secrete a watery fluid. The thickening endometrium is nourished by newly growing **spiral arteries.** The circulating estrogens also cause the uterine tissue to begin to express progestin receptors.

Changes in cervical mucus The cervix also undergoes changes with the menstrual cycle. The cervix secretes mucus at all times during the menstrual cycle, but during the follicular phase, circulating estrogens promote the secretion of a mucus whose physical and chemical properties favor the passage of spermatozoa. A sample of cervical mucus can be readily collected from the vagina and tested. The best test is to smear some mucus on a microscope slide, add some sperm, and watch how readily the sperm swim through it. If the mucus is collected late in the follicular phase, they should do so readily. A simpler test that requires neither a microscope nor a male helpmate is to stretch a small amount of the mucus between thumb and forefinger: during the late follicular phase, the mucus stretches easily, like egg white. This is an indication that the mucus is in a condition to transport sperm. We will come back to this test in the context of methods for avoiding pregnancy (see Chapter 11).

During the Luteal Phase the Uterus Is Prepared for Pregnancy

After ovulation, the ovum may be fertilized by a sperm—a process described in Chapter 5. Alternatively (and more commonly), it simply dies after a day or two in the oviduct. The woman's body has no immediate way of "knowing" which of these outcomes has actually taken place, so it must work on the assumption that fertilization has indeed occurred. Therefore, for about 2 weeks after ovulation, both the uterus and the endometrium undergo changes that favor the establishment and continuation of pregnancy, regardless of whether fertilization has occurred or not.

The corpus luteum After the dominant ovarian follicle has released its ovum at ovulation, it undergoes a further transformation, becoming a corpus luteum (see Figure 4.15). No longer concerned with producing an ovum, the corpus luteum devotes itself entirely to the secretion of sex hormones (see Figure 4.16B). These hormones—primarily progesterone and estrogen—are important for the luteal phase of the cycle or, if fertilization occurs, for sustaining pregnancy.

The two cell types in the follicle—the granulosa and thecal cells—transform themselves into two new cell types, the large and small lutein cells, respectively. The large lutein cells secrete increasing amounts of progesterone, as we saw above, so the blood levels of this hormone increase early in the luteal phase. They also secrete the peptide hormone inhibin.

The **small lutein cells** continue to synthesize testosterone. Some of this testosterone enters the general circulation—its blood levels peak around the time of ovulation—while another portion of it is taken up by the large lutein cells and converted into estrogens. Thus, although estrogen levels fall shortly before ovulation, they rise again in the latter part of the luteal phase, reaching a peak that may be as high as the preovulatory peak.

The preovulatory surge of LH and FSH is quickly terminated, in part because of the fall in estrogen levels, which removes the positive feedback effect. Both progesterone and inhibin, secreted by the large lutein cells, act to depress the secretion of the two gonadotropins from the pituitary during the entire luteal phase, and they prevent a second LH surge in response to the estrogen peak late in the luteal phase. Still, a low level of LH *is* secreted throughout the luteal phase, and in fact this LH is necessary for the maintenance of the corpus luteum.

Changes in the endometrium and cervix

During the luteal phase, the endometrium of the uterus thickens further under the influence of progesterone (Figure 4.18) and produces a dense, protein-rich secretion. The spiral arteries reach their fullest extent, and the myometrium also thickens. The properties of the cervical mucus change: it takes on a thicker, cloudy appearance, and it can no longer be stretched more than a short distance between thumb and forefinger. Most significantly, sperm penetrate the mucus poorly at this time. Thus, the uterus is least able to transport sperm during the luteal phase, but is in good shape to nourish the conceptus and to allow for its implantation into the endometrium, if fertilization has occurred.

What happens after fertilization (including the completion of the oocyte's meiosis) is the subject of Chapter 5. Here, we are concerned with what happens if fertilization does *not* occur and the menstrual cycle continues.

Toward the end of the luteal phase, the corpus luteum begins to degenerate, and so the blood levels of progesterone and estrogen drop. Why the corpus luteum degenerates is not entirely clear. In many species, the uterus secretes a hormonal signal (a prostaglandin) that triggers the process, but this is not the case in primates. Most probably, LH levels are too low during the late luteal phase to sustain its continued functioning. In any event, the resulting drop in progesterone and estrogen levels means that there is no longer any endocrine support for the luteal phase endometrium. The endometrium therefore breaks down and, along with blood from the disrupted spiral arteries, forms the menstrual flow.

Length of the luteal phase

Why has nature chosen 14 days (give or take a couple of days) as the length of the luteal phase? Basically, this is about the soonest that a woman's body can "know" whether or not pregnancy has been established during that particular menstrual cycle. The signal that pregnancy has begun is the secretion of human chorionic gonado-

(A)

(B)

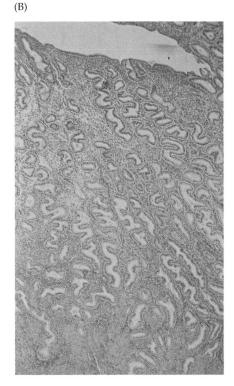

Figure 4.18 The endometrium (A) during the follicular phase and (B) the luteal phase. In the luteal phase the endometrium reaches its maximal thickness, most of which is due to the development of glandular infoldings.

tropin by the conceptus after it becomes implanted in the uterine wall. This hormone replaces LH and keeps the corpus luteum functioning, so that menstruation does not occur and the endometrium can continue to support the pregnancy (see Chapter 10).

Although fertilization generally occurs within 24 hours of ovulation, it takes several more days for the conceptus to reach the uterus and implant, so hCG doesn't reach sufficient levels in the blood to support the corpus luteum until about 10–12 days after ovulation. Thus, if the luteal phase were much shorter than 14 days, menstruation would occur even if the woman were already pregnant, and the conceptus would be lost. If the luteal phase were much longer than 14 days, the extra days would be so much wasted time before the woman's body embarked on another effort to become pregnant.

Sex Steroids Have Effects on Other Systems in Women Besides the Reproductive Tract

Although the main function of sex hormones in women is to regulate the functional state of the uterus and other parts of the reproductive tract during the menstrual cycle, they do have effects on other body systems.

Estrogens Promote Healthy Skeletal and Cardiovascular Systems

Estrogens maintain bone density, protecting a woman from osteoporosis. They also protect against thrombotic disease (pathological blood clotting), including coronary thrombosis (heart attacks). This latter protective effect comes about in part because estrogens lower the level of free cholesterol in the blood.

Premenstrual syndrome is often portrayed as something worse than it is.

Progesterone Influences Brain and Kidney Function

Progesterone has three effects that are of some relevance to women's lives. First, it acts on neural centers in the hypothalamus that control body temperature. Thus a woman's body temperature rises slightly after ovulation, when progesterone levels rise. By keeping track of the timing of this temperature rise, a woman can obtain information about her cycle that is useful in the "rhythm method" of contraception (see Chapter 11).

Premenstrual syndrome (PMS) Progesterone also influences mood: it is an anxiety-reducing agent. Women may not notice any particular reduction in anxiety as progesterone levels rise, but they do sometimes notice an *increase* in anxiety and irritability when progesterone levels *fall,* as they do toward the end of the luteal phase. This **premenstrual tension** is a part of a broader collection of symptoms that can occur together during the few days before menstruation and that often extend into the menstrual phase: the **premenstrual syndrome (PMS)**.

Finally, progesterone (probably in combination with estrogens) causes a decrease in the excretion of sodium by the kidneys, via a complex mechanism that involves the corticosteroid hormone aldosterone. Because sodium is retained in the body, water, too, is retained by osmotic action. This fluid retention increases body weight and may lead to a sense of bloating and to breast enlargement and tenderness. These are also symptoms of PMS. Other symptoms can include headache, nausea, and insomnia.

Premenstrual syndrome is highly variable. About half of all women don't experience PMS at all, 30 to 50 percent experience mild or moderate symptoms, and no more than about 15 percent experience severe symptoms (Woods, 1987). Some studies indicate that only 3 to 5 percent of women experience symptoms meeting a strict definition of

PMS (Kessel, 2000). Women differ in the extent to which they experience PMS not so much because their sex hormone levels differ, but because their bodies respond to sex hormones in different ways (Schmidt et al., 1998).

The psychological effects of PMS may involve an action of progesterone on serotonin systems in the brain. Antidepressants that increase serotonin levels at synapses, such as Prozac (fluoxetine), are often effective in alleviating the symptoms of severe PMS (Freeman et al., 1999). However, a broad range of steps to encourage a healthy lifestyle may be helpful to many women (Daugherty, 1998). Also, it is worth pointing out that PMS is not usually the monster that it is often portrayed to be in popular literature. Most women experience no significant changes in intellectual or physical performance around the menstrual cycle (Walsh et al., 1981; Lebrun, 1994). Even women with severe PMS do not experience significant impairment of cognitive function (Resnick et al., 1998). PMS doesn't disqualify the women who suffer from it from any field of human activity.

Females of Many Species Exhibit Sexual Behavior Only Near Ovulation

In many species of animals, the sexual behavior of females is closely tied to the ovarian cycle. A female rat, for example, shows proceptive and receptive sexual behavior only near the time of ovulation, when coitus can lead to pregnancy. The increase in the female's sexual activity near ovulation is called **estrus** or **heat,** and the whole ovarian cycle is referred to as the **estrous cycle** rather than the menstrual cycle. (Only a few nonhuman animals menstruate; in most, the endometrium is reabsorbed without external bleeding.)

In animals that have an estrous cycle, estrogens and progestins control female sexual behavior by their actions on the brain—in particular, on a region of the hypothalamus known as the **ventromedial nucleus.** The details vary from species to species—sometimes estrogens alone are sufficient, sometimes estrogens and progestins are required together or in a certain temporal sequence—but the net result is an almost robotic connection between the ovarian cycle and sexual behavior (McEwen et al., 1987). Of course, this connection reinforces the function of sexual behavior in most animals: reproduction.

Women's Sexuality Is Not Strictly Tied to the Menstrual Cycle

If women's sexual behavior had reproduction as its sole goal, women would engage in coitus only on the 6 days before and including the day of ovulation, for nearly all pregnancies result from sex on those days. In fact, however, women are capable of desiring, initiating, and engaging in sex at any time of the menstrual cycle, as well as during pregnancy and after menopause, when fertilization is an impossibility. Thus, the most important point to make about women's sexuality is that it is *not* strictly regulated by the hormonal fluctuations of the menstrual cycle.

This emancipation from day-to-day hormonal control, which is also seen among our close nonhuman relatives such as the bonobos (see Chapter 2), illustrates the fact that sexual behavior has acquired functions not directly connected with reproduction. These functions presumably include the interpersonal bonding that the pleasure of sex helps to generate.

Steroid Hormones Impose Some Cyclicity on Women's Sexual Feelings and Behavior

Still, women's sexual feelings and behaviors are not completely constant around the menstrual cycle. We've already discussed cultural forces that tend to diminish sexual activity during a woman's menstrual period (see Box 4.2). There are also some variations in sexual feelings and behavior through the rest of the cycle. There is reason to believe that changes in the circulating levels of steroid hormones, including both estrogens and androgens, are largely responsible for these variations.

Several studies have reported that women's interest in sex, and actual sexual behavior, is higher during the follicular phase and around the time of ovulation than during

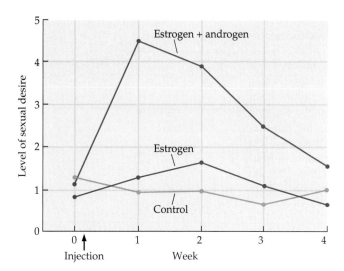

Figure 4.19 Evidence that androgens contribute to female sexual desire. Women whose ovaries had been removed were given depot injections of estrogens alone, estrogens plus androgens, or no injections (control). Only the combined estrogen–androgen injections caused a significant increase in the women's subjectively assessed sexual desire. (After Sherwin and Gelfand, 1987.)

other parts of the menstrual cycle (Harvey, 1987; Hedricks et al., 1987; Dennerstein et al., 1994). Sexual interest and behavior are relatively low during the luteal phase, but some studies report a secondary peak in the premenstrual period.

The increased interest in sex at and before ovulation is facilitated by the high levels of circulating estrogens and androgens at that time. The importance of androgens for women's sexual desire is suggested by a set of observations on women who had had their ovaries and uterus removed some years previously (Sherwin & Gelfand, 1987) (Figure 4.19). Of these women, one group had been receiving no hormone replacement therapy since their surgeries, one group had been receiving monthly injections of estradiol (in a long-lasting "depot" form), and one group had been receiving monthly injections of estradiol plus an androgen. The women who received no treatment or estradiol alone showed low levels of sexual desire, sexual fantasies, and sexual arousal, and these levels changed little around each month. The women who received estradiol plus an androgen, on the other hand, experienced greatly increased levels of desire, fantasies, and arousal compared with the other groups, and these levels closely followed the rise and fall of circulating androgens over the course of each month. (Unfortunately, this was not an ideal study since the women were not randomly assigned to the different groups and were not "blinded" as to the treatment they received.)

Women who have had both their ovaries and their adrenal glands removed, thus eliminating both of their bodies' sources of androgens, experience an even more profound decrease in sexual interest. Again, their sexual interest can be restored by the administration of estrogens plus androgens. (As discussed further in Chapter 15, the use of testosterone to restore sex drive in women may incur some undesired side effects.)

There is still some uncertainty about the relative roles of estrogens and androgens in the normal regulation of sexual desire in women. Some researchers believe that estrogens are the key hormones behind this effect and that androgens play a role only when administered in artificially high doses, or that they exert their effects only by improving women's general sense of well-being, rather than by any specific effect on the sex drive (Wallen & Lovejoy, 1993). We will return to this issue when we discuss the treatment of low sexual desire in women in Chapter 15.

Testosterone Acts on the Anterior Hypothalamus in Both Males and Females

It is believed that testosterone acts on cell groups in the anterior hypothalamus, and possibly elsewhere in the brain, to stimulate sexual interest and behavior in women, just as it does in men. The best evidence for this comes from experiments on nonhuman primates. If a female monkey's ovaries and adrenal glands are removed, she ceases to show proceptive behavior. (That is, she ceases to solicit males for sex, but is still receptive to solicitations *from* males.) Proceptive behavior can be restored to normal levels by tiny depot injections of androgens into the anterior hypothalamus, but not by injections into other nearby regions. Furthermore, the destruction of small regions of the anterior hypothalamus in otherwise normal female monkeys eliminates proceptive behavior, but leaves receptive sexual behavior unaffected (Kendrick & Dixson, 1986). It seems likely that testosterone acts on the anterior hypothalamus of women, too, to increase their interest in sex.

There's a possible additional wrinkle to this story, however. Female rhesus monkeys engage in more frequent sex with males when they are near the time of ovulation, but this is due in part to the fact that they receive more solicitations from males at that time. Why are females more attractive to males when they are ovulating? It turns out that, near the time of ovulation, a female rhesus monkey's vaginal secretions contain pheromones to which males respond with more frequent solicitations (Michael & Keverne,

1970). We will postpone until Chapter 7 the question of whether a similar pheromonal mechanism operates in humans.

Drugs Related to Sex Hormones Are Medically Important

The identification of sex hormones and their role in sexual physiology and behavior has led to the development of several classes of drugs. These drugs exert their effects by mimicking or blocking the actions of sex hormones, or by preventing their synthesis (Figure 4.20).

Receptor Agonists Mimic Hormones

Drugs that mimic the actions of sex hormones generally do so by binding to and activating the receptors that are the normal targets of hormone action. Such drugs are called **receptor agonists** (see Figure 4.20B). The natural agonists for a given receptor—the androgen receptor, for example—are, of course, the hormones that normally activate that receptor in the human body—such as testosterone and DHT. In some cases, these natural hormones (or exact synthetic copies of them) are used in clinical medicine; examples are the use of oxytocin to induce labor and of FSH (made by recombinant DNA technology) to treat infertility.

Often, however, natural hormones are unsuitable for use as drugs. They may not be well absorbed from the gut, or their life spans in the body may be too short. Numerous artificial receptor agonists have been developed that overcome these problems. Examples include the synthetic estrogens and progestins that are the active ingredients in oral contraceptive pills (see Chapter 11).

Receptor Antagonists Block Hormone Effects

Drugs that bind to hormone receptors but fail to activate them are called **receptor antagonists** (see Figure 4.20C). These drugs work by preventing the natural hormones from gaining access to their receptors. An example is the drug **cyproterone,** an antagonist of the androgen receptor that interferes with the action of testosterone and other androgens. It is used to treat androgen-dependent cancers, such as cancer of the prostate, and is also sometimes used to reduce the sex drive of sex offenders ("chemical castration": see Chapter 14). Another example is the progestin receptor antagonist **mifepristone** or **RU-486.** This drug prevents progesterone from playing its usual role in sustaining pregnancy; thus mifepristone is used to induce abortion (see Chapter 11).

Some Drugs Have Mixed Effects

The distinction between receptor agonists and receptor antagonists is often blurred. Take the drug **leuprolide (Lupron),** a synthetic analog of the hormone GnRH. Technically, leuprolide is a GnRH agonist: like GnRH, it binds to GnRH receptors on LH- and FSH-secreting cells in the anterior lobe of the pituitary gland, causing them to secrete their hormones. Given that one of the actions of LH in men is to induce the Leydig cells to secrete more testosterone, you might think that the effect of leuprolide treatment would be to increase the levels of testosterone in the blood. In fact, however, it has this effect only briefly; after a week or so of leuprolide treatment, testosterone levels fall far *below* normal. Thus leuprolide, like cyproterone, is used in the treatment of prostate cancer. The reason for this paradoxical effect is that, as mentioned earlier, the GnRH receptors are attuned to the normal *pulsatile* secretion of GnRH. When leuprolide is present *continuously,* the GnRH receptors are decoupled from the second messenger systems within the LH-secreting cells, and LH secretion drops. This phenomenon is called a **desensitization response.**

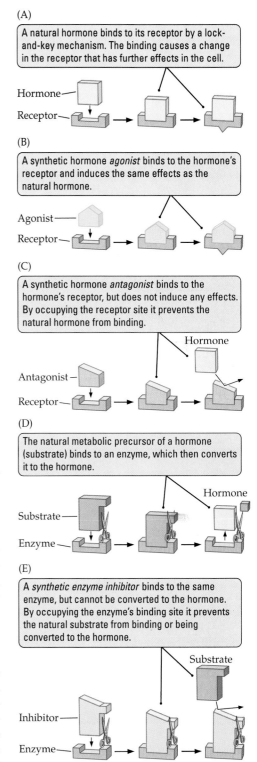

(A) A natural hormone binds to its receptor by a lock-and-key mechanism. The binding causes a change in the receptor that has further effects in the cell.

Hormone
Receptor

(B) A synthetic hormone *agonist* binds to the hormone's receptor and induces the same effects as the natural hormone.

Agonist
Receptor

(C) A synthetic hormone *antagonist* binds to the hormone's receptor, but does not induce any effects. By occupying the receptor site it prevents the natural hormone from binding.

Hormone
Antagonist
Receptor

(D) The natural metabolic precursor of a hormone (substrate) binds to an enzyme, which then converts it to the hormone.

Hormone
Substrate
Enzyme

(E) A *synthetic enzyme inhibitor* binds to the same enzyme, but cannot be converted to the hormone. By occupying the enzyme's binding site it prevents the natural substrate from binding or being converted to the hormone.

Substrate
Inhibitor
Enzyme

Figure 4.20 How drugs interact with hormones.

Mixed agonist–antagonist effects are commonly seen with drugs that bind to the estrogen receptor. Part of the reason for this is that the estrogen "receptor" is, in reality, two slightly different molecules, which are present in different proportions in different tissues. Also, another class of molecules, called **coactivators,** is involved in cellular responses to estrogens and other steroid hormones, and the nature of these molecules may vary from tissue to tissue.

To see the practical importance of these mixed effects, consider two drugs that act on estrogen receptors, **tamoxifen** and **raloxifene.** Both of these drugs are estrogen receptor agonists in some tissues and antagonists in other tissues. Tamoxifen is an antagonist in breast tissue, and is therefore an important drug in the treatment and prevention of breast cancer, but it is an agonist in the uterus, so it *increases* the risk of endometrial cancer (see Chapter 17). Raloxifene is an agonist in bone, so it helps prevent osteoporosis, but it is an antagonist in the breast and uterus, and it is being investigated for use in the prevention of cancers of both those tissues. Drugs such as tamoxifen and raloxifene are known as **selective estrogen receptor modulators,** or **SERMs.** The development of new SERMs that exhibit the desired actions of estrogens, but not the undesired ones, is an area of intense research.

There is concern about the possible health effects of hormones or hormone-like compounds that exist as pollutants in the environment, or that are administered to livestock. This matter is discussed in Box 4.4.

Enzyme Inhibitors Block the Production of Hormones

Drugs that block the synthesis of sex hormones do so by binding to the enzymes that catalyze the production of the hormones, thus inhibiting their action (see Figure 4.20E). An example is the class of drugs known as **aromatase inhibitors,** which prevent the synthesis of estrogens from androgens. We have already mentioned the use of these drugs in a research context to block the conversion of testosterone to estradiol in the brains of experimental animals. Aromatase inhibitors are coming to play an increasing role in the treatment of breast cancer, especially for advanced or recurrent disease (see Chapter 17). By cutting off the supply of estrogens at the source, aromatase inhibitors can have therapeutic effects that are as good as or better than those of receptor modulators such as tamoxifen. **Letrozole** (Femara) and **anastrozole** (Arimidex) are examples of aromatase inhibitors that have been approved for this use. Of course, by depleting estrogen levels throughout the body, these drugs may have undesired side effects. Furthermore, breast cancer cells often cease to express estrogen receptors at some point in the disease. If this happens, all estrogen-related drugs lose their efficacy.

Another example of a medically important enzyme inhibitor is **finasteride** (Proscar). This drug inhibits the enzyme 5α-reductase and thereby decreases the conversion of testosterone to DHT. It is used to treat enlargement of the prostate gland, a common problem in older men (see Chapter 17).

Some Dietary Supplements Contain Hormone-like Compounds

Compounds with steroid-like or steroid-blocking actions also occur naturally in a variety of foods of plant origin. **Isoflavones** are a class of estrogen-like compounds present in legumes and beans, especially soybeans, that have mixed estrogenic and anti-estrogenic effects. A soy-rich diet may decrease the risk of breast cancer and alleviate symptoms related to menopause, although the current data are not conclusive (Vincent & Fitzpatrick, 2000) (see also Chapter 12). The saw palmetto plant contains a variety of bioactive compounds, including anti-androgens. Preparations of saw palmetto, sold as dietary supplements, are widely used for the treatment of benign enlargement of the prostate gland, a common problem in older men. Unfortunately, dietary supplements are poorly regulated in the United States, and as a result their content, efficacy, and safety are uncertain. Saw palmetto is currently the subject of large-scale, placebo-controlled testing (Gerber, 2000).

Box 4.4 Biology of Sex

Sex Hormones in the Environment

In the 1950s and 1960s, crop dusters spread **DDT**—an organochlorine pesticide—far and wide across the United States and other countries. Eventually, the crop-duster pilots were found to have abnormally low sperm counts and a variety of other ailments. It turns out that DDT, and its breakdown product DDE, have potent estrogenic activity. Although DDT was banned in the United States in 1972, it still lingers in the environment. One hundred tons of DDT, dumped into the sewers of Torrance, California, by the Montrose Chemical Corporation, lie on the seafloor off Los Angeles. This deposit—one of the nation's worst Superfund sites—has had catastrophic effects on wildlife and has necessitated the banning of commercial fishing in the area.

Besides DDT, numerous other artificial chemicals mimic or block the effects of estrogens or other sex steroids. Because we inadvertently ingest or inhale small quantities of these **endocrine disruptors** in the process of daily living, there is concern about whether they pose a significant hazard to our health. Much depends on the concentrations at which they act. In 1997, for example, a group at the University of Missouri reported that bisphenol A, a common ingredient in plastics, has estrogenic activity, and that it causes enlargement of the prostate gland in mouse fetuses when fed to pregnant animals at parts-per-billion levels (Nagel et al., 1997). These levels correspond to the amounts that humans ingest from plastic food containers and the like.

Although the University of Missouri study has had its detractors, a panel convened by the U.S. Environmental Protection Agency has cautiously confirmed its validity (Kaiser, 2000). More broadly, there has been concern that endocrine disruptors might be responsible for the broad decline in sperm counts that has been reported in many industrialized countries. We review this topic in Chapter 9.

There has also been some concern about hormones that people might ingest by eating meat from hormone-treated livestock. In North America, beef cattle are commonly treated with steroids, especially estrogens and androgens—either the natural hormones or longer-lived synthetic versions. The hormones, which are usually administered via ear patches, promote growth and are therefore of considerable economic significance. The position of the U.S. and Canadian governments, the World Health Organization, and the World Trade Organization, is that the amounts of these hormones consumed in meat from treated animals are too small to be of any concern (Balter, 1999). However, some researchers, especially in Europe, have expressed a more cautious position, claim-ing that health effects (especially the possibility that meat-derived hormones promote cancer and premature puberty) have not been ruled out (Andersson & Skakkebaek, 1999). Unfortunately, this scientific issue has been used as ammunition in a trade war between the countries of the European Union, where hormone use is banned, and the United States and Canada, where it is permitted. As a result, almost all scientists doing research in the area find themselves being accused of bias in one direction or the other.

Summary

1. Sex hormones may be steroids, proteins and peptides, prostaglandins, or monoamines. The sex steroids are synthesized from cholesterol and fall into three groups: progestins (e.g., progesterone), estrogens (e.g., estradiol), and androgens (e.g., testosterone and 5α-dihydrotestosterone or DHT). A set of enzymes carries out the synthesis and interconversion of the steroids. The enzyme aromatase converts testosterone to estradiol, and the enzyme 5α-reductase converts testosterone to DHT.

2. Testosterone is secreted by Leydig cells in the testis and by thecal cells in the ovary, as well as by the adrenal cortex. In men, its concentration in the blood fluctuates in 2–4-hour cycles, and is higher in the evening than the morning. In women, testosterone levels fluctuate with the menstrual cycle, being highest near the time of ovulation. Some tissues convert testosterone to the more potent androgen DHT. Other tissues, including the testis, ovary, and brain, convert testosterone to estradiol. In women,

the main source of estradiol is the ovarian follicles, and the blood levels of estradiol fluctuate with the menstrual cycle. Progesterone is a female hormone, secreted by the corpus luteum—the reorganized remnants of the follicle that ruptures at ovulation.

3. Sex steroids have a short lifetime in the body. They act by binding to steroid receptors within cells, which in turn activate the expression of certain groups of genes. Steroids activate different genes in different tissues.

4. Peptide and protein hormones are gene products. Peptides are short polymers of amino acids that are usually cut from longer precursors. The peptide sex hormones include two hormones synthesized by neuroendocrine cells in the hypothalamus: oxytocin and gonadotropin-releasing hormone (GnRH). Oxytocin is released into the general circulation from the posterior lobe of the pituitary gland during orgasm, breast-feeding, and childbirth. GnRH is secreted into portal vessels that carry it to the anterior pituitary gland, where it stimulates the release of the gonadotropins into the general circulation.

5. Protein hormones are large amino acid polymers. The protein sex hormones include the two gonad-stimulating hormones (gonadotropins) secreted by the anterior lobe of the pituitary gland: luteinizing hormone (LH) and follicle-stimulating hormone (FSH). Inhibins are protein hormones that are secreted by the gonads and influence the pituitary gland.

6. Prostaglandins are lipid hormones that help prepare the uterus and cervix for childbirth. The monoamine dopamine is a hypothalamic hormone that regulates the release of prolactin from the pituitary gland.

7. In men, a negative feedback loop involving the release of GnRH from the hypothalamus, the gonadotropins LH and FSH from the pituitary, and testosterone and inhibin from the testes acts to regulate testosterone levels and spermatogenesis.

8. Testosterone supports the normal structure and function of male genital tissues, has a broad anabolic (tissue-building) effect, guides development in a male direction, and stimulates sexual feelings and behavior. This last effect is seen in both sexes.

9. Menstruation—the sloughing off of the uterine lining (endometrium)—is the outward manifestation of the menstrual cycle. Menstruation usually lasts 4–5 days, and the entire cycle usually lasts between 24 and 32 days. A variety of factors can disrupt the cycle.

10. The menstrual cycle involves hormonal interactions between the ovaries, the hypothalamus, and the pituitary gland. The resulting cyclical changes in hormone levels regulate the development of ovarian follicles and the state of the endometrium.

11. The menstrual cycle has three phases: the menstrual phase, the follicular phase, and the luteal phase. During the menstrual phase, progesterone and estrogen levels are low, allowing much of the endometrium to be shed as menstrual flow. This change prepares the uterus for its role in sperm transport. LH and FSH levels rise during this phase.

12. During the follicular phase, LH and FSH promote the development of a set of follicles, of which one becomes dominant. The follicles secrete estrogens. Near the end of the follicular phase, rising estrogen levels trigger a surge of LH and FSH secretion, which drives the dominant follicle toward ovulation. In the late follicular phase the uterus is in optimal condition for sperm transport, and the cervical mucus has a highly elastic quality. Nearly all conceptions result from coitus during the 6 days before and during ovulation.

13. Ovulation is the release of an ovum from one ovary. The ovum enters the oviduct, where, if sperm are present, it may be fertilized.

14. During the luteal phase, the remains of the dominant follicle are transformed into a corpus luteum, which secretes progesterone and (later in the phase) estrogens. Progesterone causes the endometrium to thicken and prepare itself for implantation of a conceptus. If implantation does not occur by about 14 days after ovulation, the corpus luteum regresses and menstruation begins.

15. Estrogens have other effects on the body, such as promotion of bone mineralization and protection from cardiovascular disease. Progesterone influences body temperature, mood, and fluid balance. The fall in progesterone levels toward the end of the luteal phase causes physical and psychological symptoms (premenstrual syndrome) in some women.

16. Women experience sexual feelings and engage in sexual behavior at all phases of the menstrual cycle, but there is a tendency for their interest in sex to peak in the late follicular phase, when testosterone levels are high.

17. Many medically significant drugs interact with sex hormones. These drugs may activate hormone receptors (receptor agonists), block hormone receptors (receptor antagonists), or have mixed effects. Other drugs may block the enzymes responsible for hormone synthesis. Hormone-related drugs are used as contraceptives, for prevention of menopausal symptoms, for cancer therapy, and for restoration or suppression of sex drive.

Discussion Questions

1. Make a list of anything you have heard about menstruation. Identify the myths and old wives' tales. Compare and contrast these misconceptions with the material in the text and, if you wish, with your own experience or observations.

2. Discuss how a woman's interest in and desire for sex changes in relation to the menstrual cycle and why this occurs.

3. If you recall the famous story of Lizzie Borden, who murdered her parents with an ax, you may also know that her defense was based on the idea that her hormones and menstrual cycle made her crazy and caused her behavior. Discuss whether you agree with this idea, and why or why not.

Web Resources

King, M. W., The Medical Biochemistry Page www.indstate.edu/thcme/ mwking/home.html

McGill Medicine—Menstrual Cycle Home Page sprojects.mmi.mcgill.ca/ menstrualcycle/home.html

Recommended Reading

Becker, J. B., Breedlove, S. M., Crews, D., and McCarthy, M. M. (Eds.) (2002). *Behavioral endocrinology* (2nd ed.). Cambridge, MA: MIT Press.

Djerassi, C. (2001). *This man's pill: Reflections on the 50th birthday of the pill.* Oxford: Oxford University Press.

Nelson, R. J. (2000). *An introduction to behavioral endocrinology* (2nd ed.). Sunderland, MA: Sinauer Associates.

chapter 5

These adolescent girls of the Ndbele tribe in South Africa are taking part in a ceremony to mark puberty.

Sexual Development

*I*n Chapter 2 we discussed a number of central questions about sexuality—why are there two sexes? why do males and females differ in anatomy and behavior?—from an evolutionary standpoint. In this chapter we begin a discussion of these same questions from a developmental point of view. What are the actual processes that turn a barely visible blob of protoplasm—a fertilized egg—into an adult human being, complete with her or his unique physical appearance, character, and sexuality? Few questions have so perplexed philosophers and scientists over the centuries, and even today our answers are very incomplete.

In this chapter we focus primarily on the development of physical differences between the sexes. In the process, we will see that many individuals, including some who would not hesitate to define themselves as "man" or "woman," deviate to some degree from the male and female stereotypes that are described in textbooks. In later chapters we will ask about the origin of sex differences in personality, feelings, and behavior—attributes that are often lumped under the category of "gender." There we will find that these distinctions between the two sexes are even fuzzier than the bodily differences.

Development Is the Interaction of Genes and Their Environment, Along with a Sprinkling of Chaos

You were endowed at conception with a hybrid genome: a blend of one-half of your mother's genes and one-half of your father's. Unless you happen to be an identical twin, your genome is unique: nothing exactly like it has ever existed on Earth, or ever will. This genetic uniqueness is one reason why you are a unique individual, distinct in significant ways from all other humans who have ever lived.

Yet genes are just strings of DNA, mere chemicals that do nothing unless they are read and acted on—"expressed," in the language of molecular biology. The expression of genes takes places in an environment that also differs from one individual to the next. The interaction between genes and their environment is infinitely subtle.

From the point of view of a particular gene, "environment" means many things. It includes the other genes in the same genome, and their products; the physical conditions, nutrients, hormones, toxins, and disease agents present during fetal life; and the life experiences to which the gene's owner is exposed after birth.

Let's look at some concrete examples of interactions between genes and their environment:

- There is a gene on the X chromosome whose function is to direct part of the embryo to become an ovary. We all have at least one X chromosome, but only about half of us have ovaries. Why? Because that gene exerts its effects only in the absence of another gene, which is located on the Y chromosome. (We'll have more to say about these particular genes shortly.)
- Genes are part of the reason why people differ in intelligence. But if a particular fetus is exposed to sufficient alcohol (ingested by its mother), it may end up with a far lower intelligence than it would have achieved otherwise.
- Genes are part of the reason why people differ in sexual orientation. But monozygotic (identical) twins, who have the same genomes, may end up with different sexual orientations.
- Genetic sex usually determines anatomical sex. But people who choose to embark on hormone treatment and sex reassignment surgery can change their anatomical sex.

Oftentimes, we simply don't know when or how genes and their environment interact to produce a given end result. In the case of monozygotic twins with different sexual orientations, for example, one might be tempted to rule out any factors operating during fetal life, because the two twins shared the same fetal environment. On the other hand, the childhood experiences of monozygotic twins are usually very similar too. In fact, the life experiences of monozygotic twins don't usually differ greatly until an age when they are already aware of their sexual orientation. So what does that leave in terms of possible causative factors?

We have to be aware that there is a fair amount of randomness in developmental processes. Even during life in the uterus, which is largely protected from environmental fluctuations, there is significant variation. In rodents, for example, seemingly insignificant factors, such as a fetus's position in the uterus with respect to other fetuses, can influence its sexual behavior in adulthood (Meisel & Ward, 1981). A rat's position in the uterus is a matter of chance, so we can conclude that a rat's sexual behavior is influenced by chance developmental processes. The more we probe the details of complex processes such as the development of human sexuality, the more we are likely to find evidence that chaotic or random-seeming processes contribute significantly to developmental outcomes.

It's not possible to give an account of human development without drawing a distinction between its usual course and the various ways in which it can deviate from that course. The main text of this chapter describes *typical* sexual development; *atypical* development is described in Boxes 5.2–5.9. Whether these unusual developmental pathways should be described as "abnormalities" is a difficult question, however, since the use of this term may involve value judgments concerning the relative desirability of the various developmental outcomes (Box 5.1).

Box 5.1 *Society, Values, and the Law*

The Meaning of "Normal"

Even the use of relatively neutral labels such as "typical" and "atypical" to denote developmental pathways (as in the titles of Boxes 5.2–5.9) may create the impression that we are identifying a single developmental history as being the normal or desirable one for each sex and any other histories as being unhealthy, abnormal, or undesirable. In reality, however, we don't claim the right or the wisdom to make such judgments.

There has been considerable debate over the years as to what doctors and scientists mean when they use terms such as "normal" and "abnormal," or "health" and "disease." Sometimes these judgments are based simply on frequency of occurrence. If the values of a trait are distributed according to the bell-shaped probability curve (the "normal distribution"), doctors often use a simple rule of thumb: the approximately 95 percent of individuals who fall within two standard deviations of the mean value are "normal," while the 5 percent who lie beyond those limits are "abnormal" and have a medical condition. Such rules of thumb have been used for defining conditions such as precocious or delayed puberty (see Box 5.9). The trouble with such simple probabilistic definitions, though, is that they don't necessarily say anything about what effect the condition has on a person or on society. You can probably think of several undesirable or harmful conditions that are very common, as well as some rare ones that are beneficial or highly valued.

An alternative approach has been to call a condition abnormal (or a disease or defect) if it negates the self-evident function of some body part or process (Boorse, 1981). Thus, we may say that the function of the ear is to hear, and that a person whose ears don't allow them to hear has the disease or defect of "deafness." Similarly, we may say that the function of the penis is to void urine and semen, so that a penis in which the urethra does not open at the tip has the developmental defect of

"hypospadias" (see Box 5.7). Or, we may say that the function of sex is reproduction, so that a proclivity for masturbation or for gay or lesbian sex is a psychological disturbance.

Teleological (purpose-oriented) thinking of this kind is convenient, and perhaps indispensable, in the day-to-day practice of biology and medicine, but it lacks a sound logical foundation because there is no scientific evidence that purpose or conscious design has played any role in the evolution of our species. One can reframe this kind of thinking in a nonteleological way—by saying, for example, that ears evolved because individuals who could hear survived and reproduced better; therefore, functioning ears were adaptive. But to say that something was adaptive during our evolutionary history doesn't necessarily mean that it's a good thing today. In fact, on our overcrowded planet, one can ask whether physical or mental traits that increase people's reproductive success are in fact desirable traits at all.

The dominant view today is that words such as "health," "disease," "normal," and "abnormal" are assigned not purely on the basis of intrinsic properties of the states they describe, but by reference to standards or values held by the user of the words. According to this **normative** view, a state becomes a disease or defect when it is undesired by the person who has the condition, or by the doctor who treats that person, or by society in general (Merskey, 1986). Thus, one person's disease or defect may be another person's glowing good health. In the case of deafness, for example, congenitally deaf persons may be judged to have a defect by hearing people, but not by the deaf individuals themselves. In the sexual realm, states that may (or may not) affect reproduction, such as intersexuality, homosexuality, and transexuality, may be judged unhealthy by people for whom reproduction is an important personal goal, but not by intersexual, homosexual, or transexual people themselves. In the normative view,

there are no empirical means to resolve such disagreements.

There are complications, however. For one thing, society is often able to influence a person's judgment about the worth of their particular state. Thus, a man with a 7-centimeter penis may be made to feel defective, and in fact *made* defective, by the opinion of others, when otherwise he might have been capable of perfectly satisfying sexual interactions. College textbooks are one channel by which society "inscribes" people with identities such as "homosexual" and loads those identities with values, negative or otherwise (Foucault, 1978). However lightly textbook authors attempt to tread, it is inevitable that their writings will transmit some part of their own values—values that are not necessarily better than anyone else's.

Another problem is that no one's sexual life exists in isolation. Parents may have to make decisions on behalf of their children—as to whether or not an intersexed child should undergo genital surgery, for example, and if so, which sex it should be made into (see Chapter 13). Sexual behaviors such as rape and child molestation affect others in the most extreme way. But even simply being an out-of-the-closet lesbian has social repercussions. Thus it may not always be enough just to say "Let people make their own judgments of what is normal and I'll go along with it." It may seem appropriate to criticize and restrict, or conversely, to praise and encourage, other people's actions in the sphere of sex.

As you read this and the following chapters, we urge you to keep an open mind about what is healthy or unhealthy, permissible or impermissible. You may find yourself changing your mind about some things as you learn more. But we also urge you to consider the core values you cherish, to use those values in forming your opinions, and to express those opinions by your actions and by your participation in the marketplace of ideas.

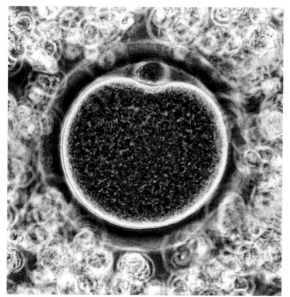

Figure 5.1 An unfertilized hamster ovum. The outer wrapping is the zona pellucida. The larger of the two inner structures is the oocyte halted in meiosis II. The smaller structure is the first polar body—the discarded set of chromosomes from meiosis I. (Micrograph courtesy of R. Yanagimachi.)

Development Passes through Distinct Stages

We'll start with a brief general outline of human development before we focus specifically on sex. Two principles govern development and distinguish the process from, say, the manufacture of automobiles. First, prenatal development proceeds largely by self-assembly: the mother provides the necessary environment and nutrients, of course, but she does not direct development in any way beyond her initial contribution of genes. Second, development is not merely "becoming," but is also "being"—every stage of development must represent a coherent, living organism. In manufacturing a car, it might be convenient to install the engine after the remainder of the vehicle has been assembled; in the development of a fetus, on the other hand, the heart and other organ systems are installed and functioning extremely early in development, when the entire organism is just a few millimeters in size.

Fertilization Is the Fusion of One Sperm with One Ovum

In the previous chapter, we described how a secondary oocyte (or unfertilized ovum: Figure 5.1) is released from an ovarian follicle at ovulation and transported to the ampulla of the oviduct. Sperm also travel to the oviducts from their site of deposition in the vagina. If sperm are present within about 24 hours of ovulation, **fertilization** may occur—that is, a single sperm enters the ovum, producing a **zygote.** If fertilization does not occur, the ovum dies, and the luteal phase continues to menstruation.

Before fertilization can take place, the sperm must undergo two important processes known as capacitation and the acrosome reaction (Figure 5.2). **Capacitation** means the removal of masking proteins on the outer surface of the sperm by enzymes present in the uterus and oviducts. Capacitated sperm swim more forcefully and are capable of responding to the presence of the ovum. Once capacitated, sperm can live only a few hours, so they must find an ovum or die. The **acrosome reaction** occurs when sperm actually reach the **zona pellucida**—the protective membrane that surrounds the ovum. The sperm's acrosome (see Chapter 3) fuses with its outer membrane, exposing receptors that bind to the zona pellucida as well as protein-digesting enzymes that clear a path through it so that the sperm can reach the ovum's plasma membrane.

Once a sperm actually fuses with the plasma membrane, an invisible but vital event takes place: the concentration of free calcium ions (Ca^{2+}) within the ovum increases

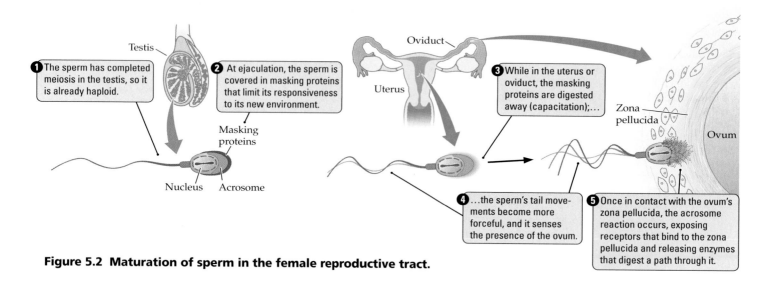

Figure 5.2 Maturation of sperm in the female reproductive tract.

① The sperm has completed meiosis in the testis, so it is already haploid.

② At ejaculation, the sperm is covered in masking proteins that limit its responsiveness to its new environment.

③ While in the uterus or oviduct, the masking proteins are digested away (capacitation);…

④ …the sperm's tail movements become more forceful, and it senses the presence of the ovum.

⑤ Once in contact with the ovum's zona pellucida, the acrosome reaction occurs, exposing receptors that bind to the zona pellucida and releasing enzymes that digest a path through it.

Testis

Nucleus   Acrosome

Masking proteins

Oviduct

Uterus

Zona pellucida

Ovum

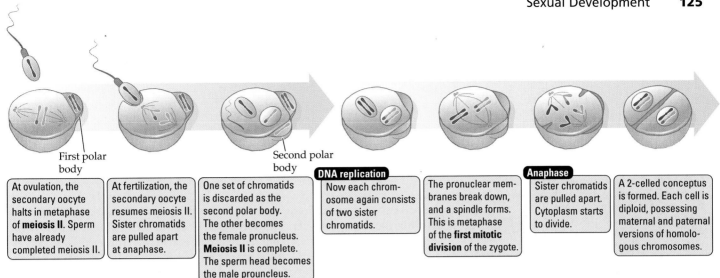

| At ovulation, the secondary oocyte halts in metaphase of **meiosis II**. Sperm have already completed meiosis II. | At fertilization, the secondary oocyte resumes meiosis II. Sister chromatids are pulled apart at anaphase. | One set of chromatids is discarded as the second polar body. The other becomes the female pronucleus. **Meiosis II** is complete. The sperm head becomes the male prounucleus. | **DNA replication** Now each chromosome again consists of two sister chromatids. | The pronuclear membranes break down, and a spindle forms. This is metaphase of the **first mitotic division** of the zygote. | **Anaphase** Sister chromatids are pulled apart. Cytoplasm starts to divide. | A 2-celled conceptus is formed. Each cell is diploid, possessing maternal and paternal versions of homologous chromosomes. |

Figure 5.3 Fertilization and production of the conceptus. This process is a continuation of the process of oocyte maturation described in Chapter 4 (see Figure 4.17).

briefly. This increase, in turn, triggers the release of enzymes from the ovum that change the physical properties of the zona pellucida, making it impossible for any other sperm to pass through. If a second sperm did penetrate the ovum, the resulting zygote would possess too many chromosomes and would probably die early in development.

Within the next few minutes, another important event takes place: the ovum completes its second meiotic division (Figure 5.3). As with the first division, one daughter cell is just a tiny bag of discarded chromosomes, the **second polar body;** the other daughter cell inherits most of the cytoplasm. The ovum now contains two **pronuclei:** a pronucleus derived from the unfertilized ovum, containing a haploid set of maternal chromosomes, and a pronucleus derived from the sperm, containing a haploid set of paternal chromosomes.

You might think that the sensible thing to happen next would be for the two pronuclei to fuse, producing a regular diploid cell with a single nucleus. Instead, however, the two pronuclei undergo a round of DNA replication, so that each chromosome now consists of two identical chromatids. The pronuclear membranes break down, a mitotic spindle forms, and the cell divides. This is the first mitotic cell division of the new organism. Each daughter cell inherits one set of chromosomes from each of the two pronuclei, so these cells, and all their descendants, are diploid.

The term **conception** has the same meaning as fertilization. "Conception" is often used when speaking of the age of an embryo or fetus ("3 weeks after conception"). Less commonly (and never in this book) "conception" is used to mean implantation (see below) or the secure establishment of pregnancy

The Conceptus Implants in the Uterine Wall

The resulting two-celled organism is called a **conceptus.** This term refers to the entire collection of cells derived from the fertilized ovum, regardless of whether or not they contribute to the tissues of the future fetus. The term "embryo" is not really appropriate at the 2-cell stage or for some time afterward, for reasons that we'll see shortly. Nevertheless, the term "embryo" is commonly used—even in scientific articles—to refer to a conceptus from the 2-cell stage onward.

The conceptus remains in the oviduct for about 3 days after ovulation, during which time it undergoes a few more rounds of cell division (Figure 5.4). The conceptus does not get any bigger, however: it remains confined within the original zona pellucida. The cytoplasm of the original ovum simply divides into smaller and smaller packets as the cells multiply. At the 4- or 8-cell stage, the conceptus's genes begin to be expressed for the first time. At about the 16-cell stage, the conceptus becomes a compact mass of cells known as a **morula.** Sometime around the fourth day, the conceptus is swept into the uterus by the action of the cilia lining the oviduct (see Chapter 3).

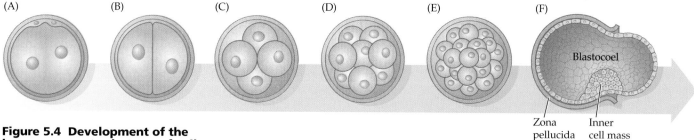

(A) (B) (C) (D) (E) (F)

Blastocoel

Zona   Inner
pellucida   cell mass

Figure 5.4 Development of the human conceptus between fertilization and implantation. Development of the human conceptus between fertilization and implantation. (A) Fertilized ovum showing male and female pronuclei, and polar bodies at top. (B) 2-cell stage. (C) 4-cell stage. (D) 8–16 cell stage. (E) Morula stage (16–32 cells). (F) Blastocyst stage. A central cavity (blastocoel) has formed. The inner cell mass contains the cells that will form the embryo and its membranes. The blastocyst is in the process of "hatching" from the zona pellucida.

The conceptus—now containing about 32 cells—develops a central fluid-filled cavity called a **blastocoel,** and the conceptus as a whole is now referred to as a **blastocyst.** On about the sixth day of development the blastocyst "hatches" from the zona pellucida and implants itself in the wall of the uterus (Figure 5.5). The implantation process requires the presence of both progesterone and estrogens, which are being secreted at this time by the corpus luteum in the mother's ovary. As implantation progresses, the conceptus begins to secrete the hormone **human chorionic gonadotropin (hCG).** This protein hormone is structurally very similar to luteinizing hormone, and it activates LH receptors on the cells of the maternal corpus luteum. By doing so, it "rescues" the corpus luteum from its normal regression at the end of the luteal phase. Thus, hCG is the signal to the mother's body that implantation has occurred.

Many conceptuses never implant, and these die within a few days. Failure of implantation can happen for a variety of reasons, including abnormalities in the conceptus (such as an incorrect number of chromosomes) or in the reproductive tract. In such cases, there would be nothing to tell the mother that fertilization had ever occurred, and a woman who loses a conceptus prior to implantation is not considered to have been pregnant at all. **Pregnancy** is usually taken to begin after successful implantation and the hormonal rescue of the corpus luteum, rather than at fertilization. (The fact that many conceptuses die prior to implantation may influence judgments about the morality of creating, experimenting on, or discarding human conceptuses, as we'll see in Chapter 10.)

The cells of the implanting blastocyst keep dividing, but as yet none of the cells is fated to give rise exclusively to fetal tissues. The cells that line the outer rim of the blastocyst concern themselves with the process of implantation. A small cluster of cells called the **inner cell mass** gives rise to the protective membranes that will enwrap the fetus, most notably the sac called the **amnion.** The amnion contains **amniotic fluid**—the fetus's watery environment for the duration of pregnancy.

During Embryonic Life, the Body Plan and Organ Systems Develop

Finally, by about 2 weeks after conception, the precursors of the various nonfetal tissues have been established. There remains a small plate of tissue derived from the inner cell mass: the **embryo.** This is the tissue that will give rise to the fetus and ultimately to an independent human being. The embryo at this time consists of three stacked layers of different kinds of cells: ectoderm, mesoderm, and endoderm. The **ectoderm** will give rise to the skin, the nervous system, and a few other structures. The **endoderm** will give rise to the lining of the gut and its associated glands, as well as the lungs. The intervening layer, the **mesoderm,** will give rise to most other structures between the gut and the skin, such as the cardiovascular and musculoskeletal systems. In addition, small regions of mesoderm and endoderm will develop into the fetal side of the **placenta**—the vascular organ by which the fetus and its mother exchange gases, nutrients, and hormones—and the **umbilical cord.** The maternal side of the placenta develops from the endometrium.

The embryonic phase of development begins about 15 days after conception and lasts until about 7 weeks after conception. During this relatively brief period the embryo transforms itself from a tiny plate of cells into a semblance of a human being, only 2–3 centimeters long but already in possession of all its major organ systems. A busy 5 weeks indeed!

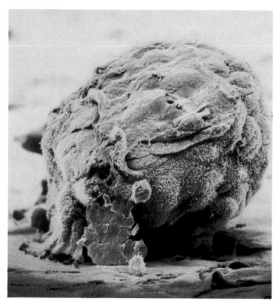

Figure 5.5 Blastocyst in the process of implanting itself in the wall of the uterus (the endometrium) as seen in a colorized scanning electron micrograph.

It is beyond the scope of this book to give a detailed account of embryonic development, but we should briefly mention some important themes here.

Large numbers of **developmental genes** orchestrate body layout and organ and tissue development. The prime movers are the **Hox genes,** four sets of genes that are expressed very early in development and which control the basic body plan. Individual Hox genes are expressed in restricted, though overlapping, territories within the early embryo. The products of Hox genes are transcription factors. Within each territory, these transcription factors switch on further sets of genes that control the development of a particular body part, such as a head or a leg.

Organs often form by means of **morphogenetic movements,** in which sheets or masses of cells invaginate, evaginate, or otherwise deform to produce a new structure. An example is the formation of the central nervous system from the ectoderm (Figure 5.6): the ectoderm invaginates along the midline of the embryo, forming a groove; the groove pinches off, forming a tube; and the tube then gives rise to the spinal cord and brain. Similarly, the lungs develop by evagination from the developing gut, and the retinas by evagination from the developing brain. Morphogenetic movements are instigated by chemical cues; for example, the invagination of the ectoderm to form the neural tube is triggered by a chemical released from a portion of the underlying mesoderm known as the notochord.

Cell migration—the passage of individual cells through preexisting tissue—also contributes to organ development. For example, some ectodermal cells ("neural crest cells") migrate a long distance through the body, giving rise to a variety of tissues, including some glandular, neural, and connective tissue structures. Similarly, the entire cerebral cortex is formed from cells that migrate from the lining of the ventricles, deep within the brain.

Cell death plays an important role in development. We have already seen an example at the very beginning of development in the formation of the first and second polar bodies: cells labeled for destruction from the moment they were formed. During embryonic life, cell death occurs on a massive scale, helping to sculpt structures such as the fingers. (If cells don't die in sufficient numbers, the fingers remain "webbed.") Cell death also occurs in the brain, eliminating many neurons that have made wrong connections.

During development, there is a **progressive restriction of cell fate.** Before the formation of the blastocyst, all cells are **totipotent:** that is, they can become any tissue in the embryo or in the extraembryonic structures such as the amnion. Some cells in the inner cell mass of the blastocyst are **pluripotent:** they can give rise to any embryonic tissue, but not to extraembryonic structures. These cells—referred to as **embryonic stem cells**—have been isolated from human blastocysts (Thomson et al., 1998). (Embryonic stem cells may have important medical applications, but ethical concerns have delayed research in this area.) Later in embryonic development, groups of cells become restricted to forming certain tissues; these cells are called neural stem cells, muscle stem cells, and so on. The progressive restriction of cell fate involves the switching

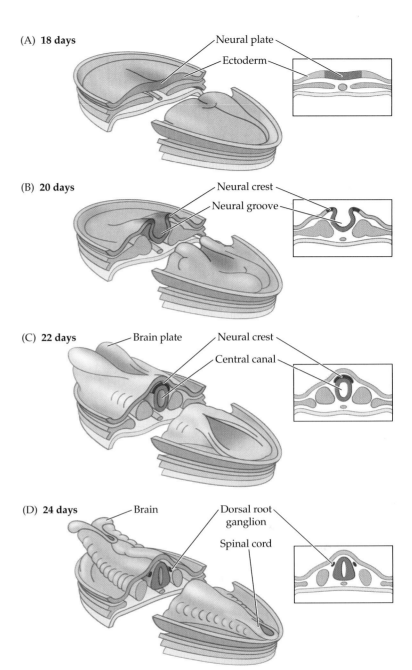

(A) **18 days** — Neural plate, Ectoderm

(B) **20 days** — Neural crest, Neural groove

(C) **22 days** — Brain plate, Neural crest, Central canal

(D) **24 days** — Brain, Dorsal root ganglion, Spinal cord

Figure 5.6 Invagination of the midline ectoderm forms the neural tube—the precursor of the spinal cord and brain. When this process fails to take place normally—as may occur when the mother is severely deficient in folic acid during early pregnancy—severe neurological conditions such as spina bifida or anencephaly (absence of most of the brain) may result.

(A)

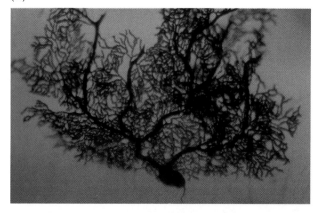

(B)

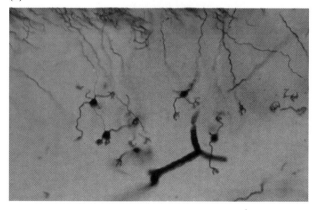

Figure 5.7 Cell differentiation is most obvious in the brain, where developing neurons adopt a bewildering variety of shapes. (A) A cerebellar Purkinje cell; (B) cerebellar granule cells. The large object at the bottom is a blood vessel. (Micrographs by Simon LeVay.)

on of genes needed for given tissues and the inactivation of genes needed for other tissues. This process is regulated by a variety of chemical factors, such as cytokines. (It has proved possible to reverse and redirect cell fate in the laboratory under some circumstances, so it may eventually be possible to obtain, say, new nerve cells from skin cells.)

Cell differentiation is the process by which cells that have adopted a certain fate actually turn into the functional cell types they are supposed to be. This process can involve dramatic changes in cell morphology (generating the intricately shaped cells of the nervous system, for example: Figure 5.7) and metabolism (such as developing the ability to synthesize a particular hormone). Cell differentiation involves an interaction between the genes expressed in a particular cell and the local environment to which that cell is exposed.

Fetal Life Involves Growth and Functional Maturation

The embryonic phase of development is complete by about 7 weeks after conception, at which point the embryo is referred to as a **fetus.** Subsequent fetal development involves mainly an increase in size (**growth**) and the **functional maturation** of body systems (Figure 5.8).

In several respects, the fetus takes control of its mother. For example, it secretes increasing levels of progesterone and estrogens. (More specifically, progesterone is secreted by the fetal side of the placenta, and androgens are secreted by the fetal adrenal gland and converted to estrogens by the placenta.) As a consequence, progesterone and estrogen levels in the mother's blood rise to higher levels than at any other time in a woman's life. These hormones ensure the maintenance of the uterus in a state conducive to pregnancy. Even though the corpus luteum in the mother's ovary normally functions throughout pregnancy, its presence is not necessary after the fetus begins to secrete steroid hormones; pregnancy can continue after surgical removal of both ovaries.

Another way in which these fetal hormones influence the mother to the fetus's benefit is by promoting development of her breasts. Thus, by the fourth month of pregnancy, the breasts are capable of secreting milk. These same fetal hormones prevent the actual secretion of milk, however—the fetus does not want the mother to spend her precious resources on some other child!

The fetus is not just smaller than a child, but is different from one—especially in terms of its adaptation to life in the uterus. Its cardiovascular system, in particular, is organized quite differently: the left and right ventricles pump the blood in parallel, rather than in series as they do after birth, and the lungs are largely bypassed. The fetus's hemoglo-

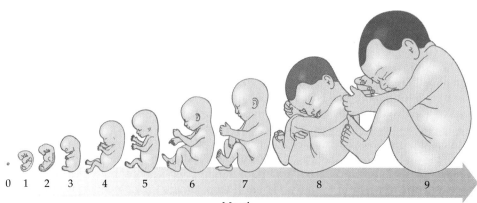

Figure 5.8 Stages of fetal development.

0 1 2 3 4 5 6 7 8 9

Months

bin—the oxygen-carrying molecule in its blood—is different from adult hemoglobin and is designed to operate at lower oxygen levels.

Yet the fetus also does many things that are surprisingly like the actions of an already-born child. It moves, of course—as a mother first notices around weeks 14–16 of pregnancy. Its kicks are what are most noticeable, but the fetus may also make more controlled movements, such as placing its thumb in its mouth. It responds to stimuli such as loud sounds with an increase in heart rate. It drinks copious amounts of amniotic fluid and voids a dilute urine back into the fluid. It wakes and sleeps, and during sleep it has episodes of rapid eye movement (REM sleep—the phase that in children and adults is associated with vivid dreaming). During REM sleep the fetus "practices" breathing by contracting its diaphragm; these movements are essential for normal lung development.

The fetus is not yet a child, however. In particular, the development of the cerebral cortex, and of its connections to other parts of the nervous system, is very incomplete even at birth. It is conceivable—though by no means documented—that a fetus can consciously experience pain, but it cannot establish durable memories. It also seems unlikely that a fetus can make any kind of fine discrimination, such as preferring one musical composer over another, in spite of some mothers' assertions.

Pregnancy and childbirth are described from the parents' perspective in Chapter 10. Birth, which occurs about 9 months after conception, echoes the emergence of our ancestral species from the ocean 350 million years ago. But newborn humans are much better equipped for life out of the water; in particular, they are able to reorganize the circulatory system to the adult pattern within a few minutes by closing three vascular shunts that operate during fetal life. Subsequently, the output of the right ventricle goes entirely to the lungs.

Birth, of course, is not the end of development. The phase that marks the onset of reproductive maturity is puberty, which we will discuss in some detail toward the end of this chapter.

Genetic Sex Is Determined at Fertilization

Our understanding of sex determination is founded on a classic series of studies conducted by the French embryologist Alfred Jost in the 1940s (Jost, 1953). Jost removed the gonadal tissue from fetal rabbits very early in development (Figure 5.9). He found that, regardless of their genetic sex, these rabbits developed as females, albeit without ovaries. Jost concluded that male development involves a gene or genes that trigger the development of testes, which in turn release hormonal signals that masculinize the rest of the body. Female development, Jost correctly reasoned, is a "default" pathway—one that goes forward in the absence of specific genetic instructions to the contrary.

Sex Is Usually Determined by the Presence or Absence of the Y-Linked Gene *SRY*

During the 1950s, the chromosomal basis of sex was worked out. As already mentioned in Chapter 2, males were found to include individuals with certain complements of sex chromosomes: XY (the usual pattern), plus unusual patterns such as XXY, XXXY, and XYY. Females were found to include individuals with certain other patterns: XX (the usual pattern), plus unusual patterns such as X and XXX. (The developmental consequences of these anomalous patterns are described in Box 5.2.) In other words, *any embryo that possesses at least one Y chromosome develops as a male*; all others develop as females. (We mention some unusual exceptions to this rule below.) These findings mean that the father's genetic contribution to the conceptus

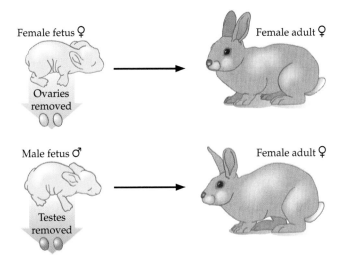

Figure 5.9 Alfred Jost's experiments on rabbits showed that male development requires the presence of a testis. Female development does not require the presence of any gonads.

Box 5.2 Biology of Sex

Atypical Development: Chromosomal Anomalies

The standard sets of sex chromosomes are XX (female) and XY (male). When nonstandard sets occur, they generally arise during one of the two meiotic cell divisions that give rise to male or female gametes. The anomalies described below are some of the most common.

Turner's Syndrome

Persons with Turner's syndrome have either a single X chromosome ("XO") or a single X chromosome plus a truncated portion of a second X chromosome. In either case, they lack a Y chromosome and therefore develop as females. Turner's syndrome occurs in approximately 1 in 4000 live births, and in an even higher fraction of all conceptions. (Many XO conceptuses die early in development.)

Girls with Turner's syndrome usually lack normal ovaries. That's because the germ cells that migrate into the embryonic ovaries require two X chromosomes for their survival and development as oocytes, so in XO embryos they die. This, in turn, causes the ovaries to regress, leaving noth-

ing but connective tissue ("streak ovaries"). Therefore, many girls with Turner's syndrome lack gonadal hormones, do not enter puberty, and are infertile. They usually have short stature, and they may have a variety of other physical traits, such as an unusually broad chest and loose skin around the neck ("neck webbing") (Figure A). Cardiovascular and renal defects are not uncommon. Individuals with Turner's syndrome are not mentally retarded, but they tend to have a characteristic array of cognitive deficits, including problems with visuospatial tasks, memory, and attention (Ross et al., 2000). These cognitive deficits are thought to result in part from the brain's lack of exposure to gonadal steroids.

Turner's syndrome can be treated with growth hormone and androgens to increase childhood growth, and with estrogens to induce the development of breasts and other secondary sexual characteristics. Appropriate regimens of estrogens and progesterone can lead to regular menstruation, and women with Turner's syndrome can sustain pregnancy with the aid of egg donation and hormonal support.

Klinefelter's Syndrome

Persons with Klinefelter's syndrome have a single Y chromosome and two or more X chromosomes (XXY, XXXY). They are male because they possess the *SRY* gene on the Y chromosome, which trumps any number of the feminizing, X-linked *DAX-1* genes so long as each of those genes is on a different X chromosome. The XXY pattern is quite common, affecting about 1 in 1000 live births.

XXY boys are physically unremarkable but tend to exhibit some degree of learning disability, especially with respect to language skills (Rovet et al., 1996). On the other hand, some XXY men do well at the college level and beyond. The full Klinefelter's syndrome becomes apparent at puberty. It is marked to a variable degree by the following traits: tallness, small testes, gynecomastia (breast development in men), feminine body contours, and sparse facial and body hair (Figure B). Endocrinologically, men with Klinefelter's syndrome have low testosterone levels and, in consequence, high levels of LH. Their sperm counts are usually too low for nor-

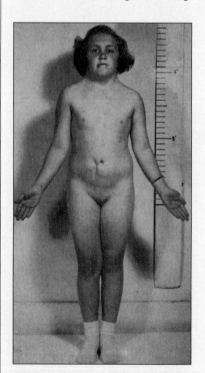

(A) A girl with Turner's syndrome

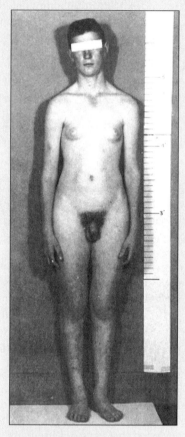

(B) A man with Klinefelter's syndrome

mal fertility because the germ cells that migrate into the testes must have no more than one X chromosome in order to successfully pass through meiosis and become sperm. Men with Klinefelter's also tend to have a low sex drive. Nevertheless, these men may be able to become biological fathers by means of special in vitro techniques (see Chapter 10). Some aspects of Klinefelter's syndrome can be alleviated by long-term treatment with testosterone injections or implants.

XYY Syndrome

Persons with one X and two Y chromosomes develop as males, but may have genital anomalies and low fertility, and tend to have low intelligence. This syndrome is nearly as common as Klinefelter's (about 1 in 1500 live births).

Early studies suggested that XYY men are characterized by an increased likelihood of engaging in criminal behavior. Those studies were marred by ascertainment problems (i.e., by the selection of men who were institutionalized or whose XYY status was discovered subsequent to an arrest or conviction). A recent study of XYY men identified by routine chromosomal analysis at birth did confirm a significantly increased rate of criminal convictions and antisocial behavior compared with XY males in the same birth cohort. Most of this increase could be accounted for by the XYY men's lower intelligence, however, rather than being an independent consequence of the chromosomal anomaly (Gotz et al., 1999).

Triple-X Syndrome

Triple-X syndrome is a mild disorder affecting about 1 in 2000 births. The affected individuals have the XXX pattern and develop as females. There are some cognitive deficits, especially in verbal skills (Rovet & Netley, 1983), and fertility is low, but many XXX women are unremarkable and remain undiagnosed.

There are rare individuals who have standard chromosomes but are of the "wrong" sex (XY females and XX males). A possible reason for this is that *SRY* is missing from the Y chromosome or conversely, is present anomalously on an X chromosome. These individuals, as well as mice with the analogous syndrome, have been of great importance in the elucidation of the mechanisms of sex determination (see text). (Photographs by Earl Plunkett; from Valentine, 1986.)

determines its sex, because the fertilizing sperm contributes either an X or a Y chromosome, whereas the ovum always contributes an X chromosome.

When researchers put these chromosomal observations together with Jost's experimental results, it seemed that there should be a Y-linked gene (a gene located on the Y chromosome) that makes an embryo male by triggering the development of a testis, and that the absence of this gene should permit an embryo to develop as a female. The identification of this gene, however, had to wait many years for the development of molecular genetic techniques applicable to the human genome.

In 1990, a British group reported success (Sinclair et al., 1990). They had studied the very rare individuals who disobeyed the chromosomal rules mentioned above: persons with XX chromosomes who nevertheless were male and persons with XY chromosomes who nevertheless were female (Figure 5.10). It turned out that, in some of the XX males, a tiny fragment of a Y chromosome had "jumped" onto an X chromosome. (This **translocation** must have happened during the development of the sperm that gave rise to these individuals.) Correspondingly, some of the XY females were missing the same tiny fragment from their Y chromosome. The British researchers identified a gene in this small region of the Y chromosome and named it **SRY** (for "sex-determining region of the Y chromosome"). They also identified an equivalent gene in mice. Using genetic engineering techniques, they put the mouse equivalent of *SRY* into the genomes of female mouse zygotes, and found that the mice developed as males. Thus, *SRY* is the gene that makes a fetus male, and fetuses lacking *SRY* develop as females.

Normal
female

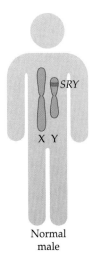
Normal
male

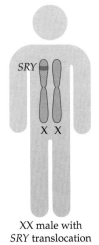
XX male with
SRY translocation

XY female with
SRY missing

Figure 5.10 The genetic basis of sex determination. The presence or absence of the *SRY* gene determines whether a fetus will become male or female.

SRY and Other Genes Direct the Development of the Gonads

It seems likely, then, that *SRY* somehow instructs the embryo to develop a testis. How does that happen? Both the testes and the ovaries develop from common, undifferentiated precursor structures called the **genital ridges,** which are clusters of mesodermal cells on either side of the aorta, in what will become the lumbar region of the fetus. To the side of each genital ridge is a transitory kidney-like structure, the **mesonephros,** that ends up donating tissue to the gonads.

The genital ridges develop at about 4 weeks post-conception. A week or so later, cells within the genital ridges of male embryos begin to express the *SRY* gene. Presumably what happens is that some higher-level gene, present in both sexes, attempts to turn on the *SRY* gene, but this instruction is obeyed only in males because only males have an *SRY* to turn on.

The product of the *SRY* gene is a transcription factor whose job it is to bind to and regulate the expression of other genes. It is believed that *SRY* works within the lineage of cells that can become either Sertoli cells or granulosa cells—the gamete-nurturing cells of the testes and ovaries, respectively (see Chapter 3). When *SRY* is present, these cells develop as Sertoli cells, and the Sertoli cells, in turn, cause the gonads to develop as testes. When *SRY* is absent (i.e., in females), these same cells develop as granulosa cells, and the granulosa cells cause the gonads to develop as ovaries. (Sometimes both ovarian and testicular tissue are present in an individual; this atypical development is discussed in Box 5.3.) These actions involve many lower-order genes, some of which have been identified; the manner in which these genes interact is a topic of current research (Swain & Lovell-Badge, 1999).

Another important gene concerned with sexual differentiation, ***DAX-1,*** is located on the X chromosome. *DAX-1* is expressed in the genital ridges at about the same time that *SRY* is expressed, but in both sexes rather than just in males (since both sexes have at least one X chromosome). Although the details are not yet completely clear, it appears that *SRY* and *DAX-1* work in opposition to each other (Figure 5.11). The action of *DAX-1* seems to be to prevent development of testes and instead promote development of ovaries and their key cells, the granulosa cells. In XX embryos, *DAX-1* operates unhindered by

Figure 5.11 Molecular genetics of gonad development. The genital ridge develops at the back of the abdomen between the aorta and the mesonephros. It can become either a testis or an ovary.

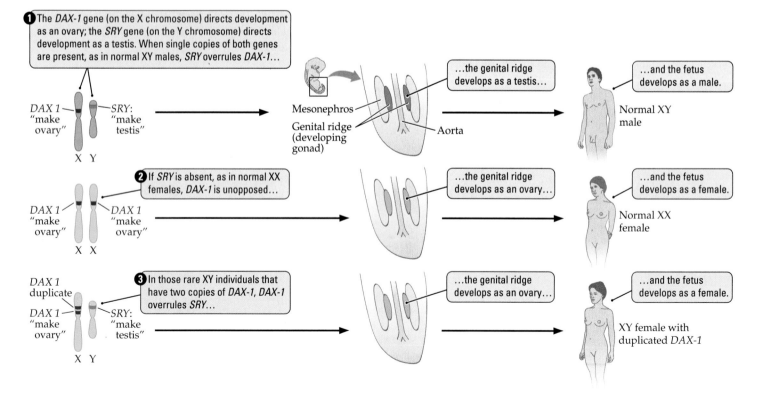

Biology of Sex

Atypical Development: Gonadal Intersexuality ("True Hermaphroditism")

Intersexuality is a broad term encompassing a variety of conditions marked by ambiguous or incomplete sexual differentiation. **Gonadal intersexuality** refers to a rare kind of intersexuality in which a single individual possesses both testicular and ovarian tissue.

Another, more frequently used term for this condition is **true hermaphroditism**.

Hermaphrodite, in Greek mythology, was a male–female figure parented by the gods Hermes and Aphrodite. As mentioned in Chapter 2, hermaphrodites are common or even the rule in some nonmammalian species. The addition of the modifier "true" distinguishes this condition from pseudo-hermaphroditism or nongonadal intersexuality (see Boxes 5.4 and 5.6), in which the gonads are entirely of one sex but nongonadal structures are sexually ambiguous (Figure A). (The life experiences of gonadal and nongonadal intersexes are discussed in Chapter 13.)

We dislike the term "true hermaphrodite" for two reasons. First, the word "true" reflects an outdated notion that the gonads are the only "true" arbiters of a person's sex. Second, the term "hermaphrodite" wrongly suggests that gonadal intersexes resemble hermaphroditic animals—that is, that they are capable of taking both the maternal and the paternal roles in reproduction, or even of producing offspring without engaging in sex at all. They cannot do so—in fact, the majority are infertile. Thus we prefer and in this text will use the term "gonadal intersexuality."

Gonadal intersexes may possess one ovary and one testis; more commonly, one or both gonads contain both ovarian and testicular tissue (ovotestes; Figure B) (Krob et al., 1994). Generally, the testicular tissue is poorly developed, whereas the ovarian tissue appears normal. The internal reproductive tracts and external genitalia are highly variable, but female structures usually predominate, and gonadal intersexes tend to look like and identify as women. Several gonadal intersexes have become pregnant and successful-ly delivered children, but only one instance of a gonadal intersex fathering a child has been reported.

How does gonadal intersexuality arise? The majority of affected individuals have two XX chromosomes—the normal female pattern—and the reason why they develop testicular tissue is not known. In some of these cases it may be that one X chromosome carries an *SRY* gene that has been translocated from a Y chromosome; testicular tissue could then arise in parts of the embryo where that X chromosome is activated.

A substantial minority of gonadal intersexes are chromosomal chimeras, possessing some cells or tissue with the XY (male) pattern and some with the XX (female) pattern. Such chimerism can occur if two separate conceptuses of differing chromosomal sex fuse early in development. Alternatively, two sperm (one X, one Y) may penetrate a single ovum, one fertilizing the ovum itself and the other fertilizing one of the polar bodies, which then fails to degenerate and therefore contributes its progeny to the conceptus.

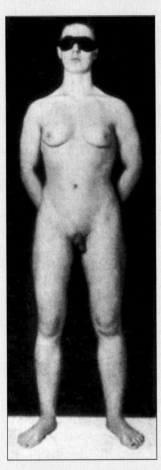

(A) An individual with gonadal intersexuality. (Photograph from Overzier, 1963.)

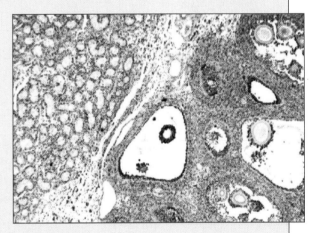

(B) An ovotestis from a dog, showing ovarian tissue on the right and testicular tissue on the left.

SRY, and therefore the genital ridges develop into ovaries and the embryo becomes a female. In most XY embryos, the *SRY* gene overrules the *DAX-1* gene, and therefore the genital ridges develop into testes and the embryo becomes a male. In rare cases, however, an XY embryo carries duplicated copies of the *DAX-1* gene, in which case the two *DAX-1* genes operating in tandem are able to overrule *SRY* and cause the embryo to develop as an XY female. (This, then, is a different developmental origin for XY females than the *SRY* translocation mentioned above.) The findings on *DAX-1* demonstrate that, even though sex is normally determined by the presence or absence of a male-determining gene, the process of female differentiation still involves active gene expression from the very beginning.

Primordial Germ Cells Migrate into the Developing Gonads

Although the gonads develop from the genital ridges under the influence of genes such as *SRY* and *DAX-1*, the gametes themselves—the sperm and the ova—do not originate in the gonads at all. Rather, they are the descendants of a group of cells generated in a transitory extraembryonic region of the conceptus known as the **yolk sac** (Figure 5.12). About 4 weeks after conception, these **primordial germ cells** migrate into the embryo and home in on the developing genital ridges. It appears that they are attracted by some chemical signal put out by the cells of the ridges, for if the ridges are transplanted to some other part of the embryo's body, the primordial germ cells will migrate to that site instead.

Once they have integrated themselves into the gonads, the primordial germ cells or their descendants develop either into primary oocytes (if they are in an ovary) or into the stem cells that will give rise to sperm (if they are in a testis). Apparently the granulosa cells (in females) and the Sertoli cells (in males) play a key role in guiding the developmental pathway of the germ cells. They also trigger the development of thecal cells (in females) and Leydig cells (in males).

X Inactivation Preserves Balanced Gene Expression in the Two Sexes

The fact that males have one X chromosome and females have two creates a problem. The X chromosome contains a large number of genes—probably over a thousand. Most of these genes have nothing to do with sex; they code for blood-clotting factors, visual pigments, and all kinds of other proteins. If nothing were done to compensate for the sex difference in the number of X chromosomes, women would produce twice as much

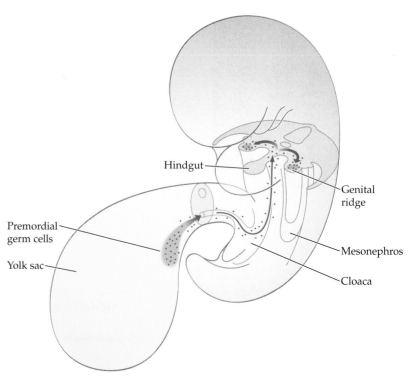

Figure 5.12 Migrating germ cells. The cells that will give rise to the embryo's gametes are generated outside the embryo—in the yolk sac—and migrate from there to the genital ridges.

Figure 5.13 X inactivation.

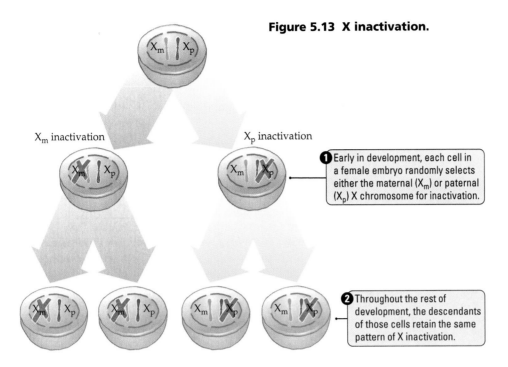

① Early in development, each cell in a female embryo randomly selects either the maternal (X_m) or paternal (X_p) X chromosome for inactivation.

② Throughout the rest of development, the descendants of those cells retain the same pattern of X inactivation.

X_m inactivation

X_p inactivation

blood-clotting factor (and all the other X-lined gene products) as men do. This would cause metabolic havoc.

To prevent this from happening, most of the genes on one of a female's two X chromosomes are inactivated very early in development. As a result, both females and males have the same number of functional copies of most X-linked genes: one.

Each cell present in the female conceptus at the time of X inactivation picks one of its two X chromosomes at random to inactivate: either the one that was inherited from the mother or the one that was inherited from the father. These cells then multiply during embryonic and fetal life, so that each cell gives rise to a clone of cells in the newborn individual, all of whom have inactivated the same X chromosome (Figure 5.13). The cells of a clone may stay near one another, forming a small patch. Normally these patches of cells are not visible. If the two X chromosomes happen to carry different versions of a gene specifying some visible trait, however, the patches can be seen. Such is the case with the orange and black patches of fur in tortoiseshell and calico cats. Some women carry a mutant gene on one X chromosome that causes the absence of sweat glands (**sex-linked anhydrotic ectodermal dysplasia**). In that case, the patches are visible as areas of skin that do and do not sweat. The only way a male could show such a patchy pattern would be if he had the unusual chromosomal pattern XXY (see Box 5.2), in which case one of the X chromosomes would be randomly inactivated, as in females.

The X chromosome whose genes are inactivated remains in the nucleus of every cell, but in an unusually condensed form. It is therefore visible as a dense spot, called a **Barr body,** when cells from a woman or female mammal are stained with appropriate dyes and viewed under a microscope. The presence or absence of Barr bodies in cells scraped from the inside of the mouth offers a simple method of determining a person's chromosomal sex.

Male and Female Reproductive Tracts Develop from Different Precursors

At about 6 weeks post-conception, when the gonads are beginning to differentiate as ovaries or testes, two ducts run from the region of each gonad to the exterior of the embryonic body at the site of the future external genitalia. One of these, the **Wolffian duct,** is the excretory duct for the mesonephros. Because the mesonephros ends up contributing its tissue to the gonads, the Wolffian duct is closely apposed to the gonad. The other duct, the **Müllerian duct,** runs next to the gonad, but does not actually contact it. The

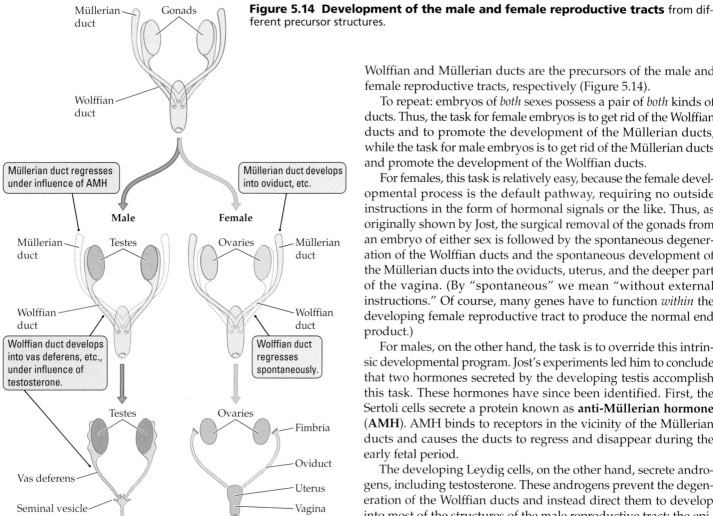

Figure 5.14 Development of the male and female reproductive tracts from different precursor structures.

Wolffian and Müllerian ducts are the precursors of the male and female reproductive tracts, respectively (Figure 5.14).

To repeat: embryos of *both* sexes possess a pair of *both* kinds of ducts. Thus, the task for female embryos is to get rid of the Wolffian ducts and to promote the development of the Müllerian ducts, while the task for male embryos is to get rid of the Müllerian ducts and promote the development of the Wolffian ducts.

For females, this task is relatively easy, because the female developmental process is the default pathway, requiring no outside instructions in the form of hormonal signals or the like. Thus, as originally shown by Jost, the surgical removal of the gonads from an embryo of either sex is followed by the spontaneous degeneration of the Wolffian ducts and the spontaneous development of the Müllerian ducts into the oviducts, uterus, and the deeper part of the vagina. (By "spontaneous" we mean "without external instructions." Of course, many genes have to function *within* the developing female reproductive tract to produce the normal end product.)

For males, on the other hand, the task is to override this intrinsic developmental program. Jost's experiments led him to conclude that two hormones secreted by the developing testis accomplish this task. These hormones have since been identified. First, the Sertoli cells secrete a protein known as **anti-Müllerian hormone** (**AMH**). AMH binds to receptors in the vicinity of the Müllerian ducts and causes the ducts to regress and disappear during the early fetal period.

The developing Leydig cells, on the other hand, secrete androgens, including testosterone. These androgens prevent the degeneration of the Wolffian ducts and instead direct them to develop into most of the structures of the male reproductive tract: the epididymis, vas deferens, ejaculatory ducts, and seminal vesicles. (The prostate gland also develops under the influence of androgens, but it is not derived from the Wolffian ducts.) The development of these structures proceeds throughout the fetal period.

A mutation in the gene for the androgen receptor may result in androgen insensitivity syndrome, a condition that produces nongonadal intersexuality (Box 5.4).

Male and Female External Genitalia Develop from the Same Precursors

In contrast to the development of the internal reproductive tracts, a single set of structures gives rise to both the female and the male external genitalia (Figure 5.15). Thus, the male and female external genitalia are comprised of **homologous** structures. ("Homologous" means having a common developmental or evolutionary origin.)

At about 4 weeks post-conception, the embryo's anogenital region consists of a slit known as the **cloaca.** The cloaca is closed by a membrane. It is flanked by two **urethral folds** and, to the side of the folds, a raised region named the **genital swelling.** At the front end of the cloaca is a small midline promontory called the **genital tubercle.** By 2 weeks later, the urethral folds have fused with each other near their posterior (rear) end. The portion behind the fusion point is called the **anal fold,** and eventually becomes the anus. The region of the fusion itself becomes the perineum. (Even in adults, the line of fusion is visible as a midline ridge or scar known as the **raphe,** which is seen most easily with the help of a hand mirror.)

Box 5.4 Biology of Sex

Atypical Development: Androgen Insensitivity Syndrome

Intersexuality involving nongonadal structures (often called **pseudohermaphroditism**) is much more common than gonadal intersexuality. One example of a condition resulting in nongonadal intersexuality is **androgen insensitivity syndrome** (**AIS**, also called **testicular feminization**), which is caused by a mutation in the gene for the androgen receptor. The mutation either prevents androgens from binding to the receptor or prevents the receptor from binding to its DNA targets. This renders the person's body insensitive to testosterone and other androgens. About 1 in 10,000 live-born children have **complete AIS.** There are also many individuals with **partial AIS,** in whom sensitivity to androgens is reduced, but not absent (Quigley et al., 1995).

Persons with AIS nearly always have the XY complement of sex chromosomes and would have developed as unambiguous males if they did not have the mutation. The reason AIS does not affect XX individuals is twofold. First, androgens play only a limited role in female development. Second, and more significantly, the androgen receptor gene is on the X chromosome, so a mutant gene on one X chromosome will be at least partially compensated by a normal gene on the other. However, an XX woman who is an AIS "carrier" has a 1 in 4 chance of giving birth to an AIS-affected child with each pregnancy.

In XY embryos affected by AIS, testes develop under the influence of *SRY* and secrete their normal hormones: anti-Müllerian hormone (AMH) and testosterone. AMH exerts its normal effects, causing the Müllerian ducts to regress and thus preventing development of the structures that derive from them—the oviducts, the uterus, and the inner portion of the vagina. The secreted testosterone, on the other hand, has no effect. The Wolffian ducts therefore fail to develop into the male reproductive tract, and the precursors of the external genitalia follow the "default" pathway, becoming the typical female structures—the clitoris, labia, and outer portion of the vagina. Even though testosterone is converted into the more potent hormone DHT in these target tissues, DHT is also without effect because it, too, normally binds to androgen receptors.

Newborn children may be diagnosed as having AIS because of a shallow vagina or because the testes are palpable as lumps in the groin. (They cannot descend farther because of the absent scrotum.) Many complete AIS babies are not diagnosed, however, and are simply accepted as normal girls.

Even if girls with AIS are not diagnosed at birth or during childhood, the anomaly will be recognized at puberty or soon after. Girls with complete AIS do not menstruate (since they lack a uterus), do not grow pubic or axillary hair (because such hair growth is androgen-dependent), and are infertile. They do generally develop breasts, however, because the testes and adrenals secrete some estrogens.

Adults with complete AIS tend to be taller than unaffected XX women (Marcus et al., 2000), possibly on account of the growth-promoting genes on the Y chromosome. Nevertheless, complete AIS adults look like women (see figure) and generally identify as such, although their intersexed condition may also be an important part of their identity (see Chapter 13).

Medical treatment of AIS may include gonadectomy (removal of the testes, which, like all undescended testes, carry an increased risk of cancer after puberty) and estrogen replacement (to prevent osteoporosis). Women with AIS may elect to have surgical revision of the vagina to make it adequate for coitus. Another possibility is to deepen and widen the vagina with dilators (see Figure 15.10B). As with most intersexed conditions, however, the medical problems of AIS are often perceived as trivial compared with the psychological trauma that may arise from deception by parents and doctors, stigmatization, and inappropriate treatment (see Chapter 13).

Complete AIS can be mimicked by other genetic conditions in which sensitivity to testosterone is unimpaired but the levels of this hormone are abnormally low during development. These conditions include insensitivity to luteinizing hormone, which is caused by an absence of the LH receptor; this deprives the Leydig cells of their signal to secrete testosterone. A similar condition is caused by a deficiency in one of the hormones involved in the synthesis of testosterone. Unlike persons with complete AIS,

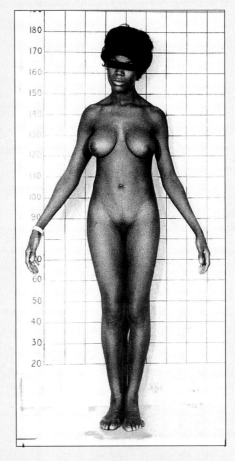

persons with these other conditions will respond to exogenous testosterone with masculinization—which is an undesirable effect, of course, if the person identifies as female.

Children with partial AIS vary greatly in appearance, depending on how complete the insensitivity to androgens is. Some children with partial AIS have normal or near-normal male genitalia and are reared as boys. Some degree of breast development is likely to occur at puberty, however, and infertility in adulthood is a possibility. Others have ambiguous or near-normal female genitalia; most of these children are reared as girls. The genital appearance in partial AIS is mimicked by several other conditions including congenital adrenal hyperplasia (see Box 5.5). (Photograph from Zourlas and Jones, 1965.)

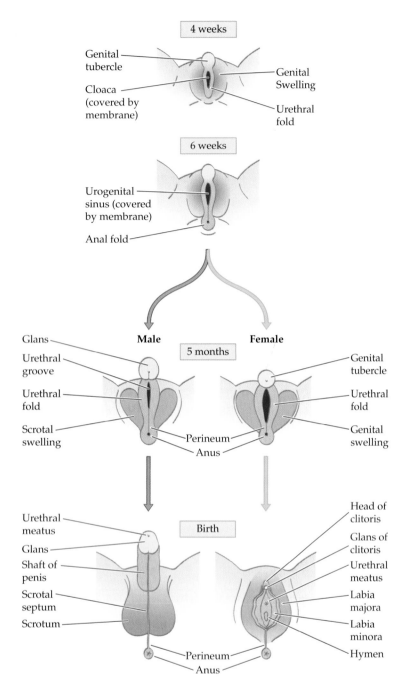

Figure 5.15 Development of the male and female external genitalia from common precursor structures. In males, the urethral folds fuse at the midline to form the penile shaft and enclose the urethra. In females, they remain separate, forming the labia minora.

During the fetal period, the region in front of the fusion point, which includes the opening of the **urogenital sinus,** gives rise to the external genital structures in both sexes. As with the internal reproductive tracts, the female external genitalia develop by default; that is, in the absence of hormonal or other external instructions. Removal of the ovaries, for example, does not affect the process (however, the process *can* be affected by a genetic defect in one of the enzymes involved in the synthesis of corticosteroids; this condition is called congenital adrenal hyperplasia [Box 5.5]). The genital swellings develop into the labia majora. The urethral folds develop into the labia minora, the outer one-third or so of the vagina, and the crura (deep erectile structures) of the clitoris (see Chapter 3). The genital tubercle develops into the glans of the clitoris. Remnants of the cloacal membrane persist as the hymen.

The development of the vagina from two different sources is reflected in its anatomical differences in adult women, already alluded to in Chapter 3. The outer portion of the vagina, which develops from the urethral folds, is more muscular and more richly innervated than the inner portion, which develops from the Müllerian ducts.

In male fetuses, the presence of circulating testosterone, secreted by the testes, is required for the normal development of the genitalia. The tissue of the urethral folds, genital swellings, and genital tubercle express androgen receptors. In addition, they express the enzyme **5α-reductase,** which catalyzes the conversion of testosterone to a more potent androgen, **5α-dihydrotestosterone** or **DHT** (see Chapter 3). (Box 5.6 examines the atypical development that occurs as a result of 5α-reductase deficiency.) DHT binds to the androgen receptors and triggers several processes. The urethral folds fuse at the midline, forming the shaft of the penis and enclosing the urethra (hypospadias—a condition that results when the urethra is not enclosed by the urethral folds—is discussed in Box 5.7). The genital swellings also fuse at the midline, forming the scrotum. The genital tubercle expands to form the glans of the penis. The prostate gland, and probably the homologous paraurethral glands in females (see Chapter 3), develop from the walls of the urogenital sinus, beneath the urethral folds.

Thus we can define the following homologies: the male scrotum is homologous to the female labia majora, the shaft of the penis is homologous to the labia minora, and the glans of the penis is homologous to the glans of the clitoris. These homologies are approximate; some tissue from the urethral folds probably contributes to the deeper clitoral structures in women, for example.

The Gonads Descend during Development

In fetuses of both sexes, the gonads move downward from their site of origin in the upper lumbar region of the embryo. By about 10 weeks post-conception, they are positioned at the rim of the pelvis. In females, the ovaries remain in this position for the remainder of fetal life, but after birth they descend in the pelvis and end up on either side of the uterus.

In males, the movement of the testes is even greater. At 6–7 months post-conception they descend into the pelvis, and shortly before birth they enter the scrotum. Key to this

Box 5.5 Biology of Sex

Atypical Development: Congenital Adrenal Hyperplasia

Congenital adrenal hyperplasia (CAH) involves a genetic defect in one of the enzymes—most commonly **steroid 21-hydroxylase**—that are involved in the synthesis of corticosteroid hormones in the adrenal cortex. (Corticosteroids have functions other than sex, but they are made from the same precursor molecules that give rise to the sex steroid hormones.) Because of this defect, the production of corticosteroids is greatly reduced. The brain and pituitary gland sense this deficit and try to stimulate the adrenal cortex into increased production. The result is excessive growth (hyperplasia) of the adrenal cortex and an overproduction of the precursor steroids, which are then converted into a variety of androgens. The clinical syndrome results both from the lack of corticosteroids—which causes serious metabolic problems in either sex—and from the excess of androgens. The effects of the androgens show themselves in XX individuals (chromosomal females) as partial **masculinization** during fetal and postnatal development. In spite of this partial masculinization, the great majority of XX CAH children are raised as girls.

The steroid 21-hydroxylase gene is located on chromosome 6, one of the **autosomes** (chromosomes other than the two sex chromosomes). Autosomes are present in matched pairs, with one member inherited from each parent; the gene must be defective on *both* members of the pair in order for CAH to result. In other words, CAH is a **recessive trait**. If both parents carry a single defective copy of the gene, each of their children (of either sex) has a 1 in 4 chance of inheriting two defective copies and therefore of developing CAH. About 1 in 16,000 live-born children have the classic form of CAH (Carlson et al., 1999), but a larger number have milder forms of the condition. Among Ashkenazic (Central European) Jews, for example, 1 in 27 children have a mild form of the condition (New & Wilson, 1999).

The adrenal cortex begins secreting corticosteroids at about 6 weeks after conception. In CAH-affected fetuses, the excess secretion of androgens begins at some variable time after that. If the fetus is a chromosomal male (XY), the extra androgens are of little significance because large amounts of androgens are secreted by the testes in any case, and the male differentiation of the genitalia proceeds normally. (After birth, when androgen levels normally drop, the excess androgens in CAH boys may cause too rapid growth and early puberty.)

If the fetus is a chromosomal female (XX), however, problems arise during fetal life. Since AMH is absent, the Müllerian ducts develop in the usual way, so all XX AIS children have a female internal reproductive tract. If the androgen excess occurs early enough in development, it may rescue the Wolffian ducts, which then persist along with the Müllerian duct structures. More commonly, the effects of the excess androgens are seen slightly later in fetal development, during the differentiation of the external genitalia. Although the outcome is variable, the newborn baby's genitalia typically look like female genitalia that have been shifted in the male direction (masculinized). In particular, high levels of prenatal androgens may cause enlargement of the clitoris, and the labia may be partially fused at the midline to form a scrotum-like structure (see figure). If the condition is untreated, further masculinization may occur at puberty.

Usually, however, the condition is recognized at birth and is treated by lifelong administration of corticosteroids. The treatment supplies the missing hormones and, by doing so, stops the compensatory overproduction of androgens. The masculinized genitalia are often "corrected" surgically by, for example, removing, shortening, or "recessing" the large clitoris early in life. This policy has recently been challenged by some persons with CAH and by advocates for the intersexed. We take up this topic in more detail in Chapter 13.

It has recently become possible to treat CAH prenatally. At-risk fetuses can be diagnosed as early as 9 weeks after conception by means of chorionic villus sampling (see Chapter 10). If treatment with a synthetic corticosteroid (**dexamethasone**) is started by 10 weeks, masculinization of the external genitalia can be greatly reduced or prevented entirely (Carlson et al., 1999).

One of the most interesting aspects of CAH from a scientific standpoint concerns the possible effects of the prenatal androgen exposure on the fetus's brain and its later psychosexual development. CAH could be thought of as an "experiment of nature," somewhat analogous to the testosterone treatment of fetal monkeys done by Robert Goy and his colleagues (described below). We discuss CAH from this perspective in Chapter 6. (Photograph courtesy of John Money.)

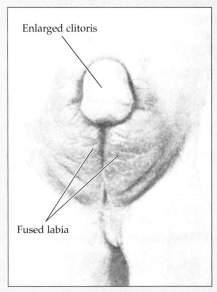
Enlarged clitoris

Fused labia

Partial masculinization of genitalia in a CAH girl.

process are paired structures called **gubernacula:** each gubernaculum is a fibrous band that attaches at one end to the testis and at the other to the abdominal wall near the developing pubic bone. Because the gubernacula do not lengthen as the fetal body grows, they pull the testes farther and farther downward during fetal life. The formation of the gubernacula, and their connection to the testes, is influenced by androgens and by a

Biology of Sex

Atypical Development: 5α-Reductase Deficiency

The enzyme **5α-reductase,** which is normally expressed in some androgen target tissues, such as the external genitalia, skin, and prostate gland, converts testosterone to the more potent androgen 5α-dihydrotestosterone, or DHT. Like congenital adrenal hyperplasia, 5α-reductase deficiency is an autosomal recessive trait that causes a form of intersexuality. For the most part it is very rare, but the condition tends to crop up in clusters in genetically isolated communities. The first and most thoroughly studied of these clusters is in the village of Salinas in the Dominican Republic. In 1974, Julianne Imperato-McGinley of Cornell University Medical College, along with several colleagues, reported that 24 XY individuals in the village had an intersexual condition caused by 5α-reductase deficiency (Imperato-McGinley et al., 1974).

Since the affected individuals are chromosomal males (XY), they develop testes. The testicular hormones, AMH and testosterone, as well as the receptors for these hormones, function normally. Therefore, the affected fetuses develop the internal reproductive structures of males, and the female (Müllerian duct) structures regress. But the external genitalia do not fully develop in the male direction without the presence of DHT. Often they consist of labia-like structures instead of a scrotum, a urogenital sinus into which a blind vaginal pouch and the urethra open, and a phallus that resembles a clitoris more than a penis (Figure A). The testicles may be in the labia

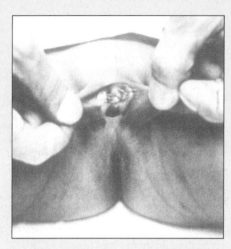

(A) External genitalia of affected child at birth

or in the inguinal canal. The prostate gland is present but small.

The affected individuals are raised as girls or, in communities that are familiar with the syndrome, as intersexes. The increase in testosterone levels at puberty, however, is able to accomplish much of what was left undone earlier: the skin of the scrotum becomes pigmented and corrugated, the testes descend if they were in the inguinal canal, and the phallus enlarges to resemble a penis (Figure B). The rest of the body also changes in the male direction: there is a great increase in muscularity, the

voice deepens, and there is no breast development. In effect, girls seem to grow into men. Only a few traits are completely DHT-dependent and therefore do not appear in 5α-reductase-deficient individuals; these traits include acne and a receding hairline. Facial hair is sparse.

One of the most interesting and controversial aspects of the 5α-reductase story is how the affected individuals respond to their apparent change of sex at puberty. We will postpone our discussion of this matter, however, until Chapter 6. (Photographs courtesy of Julianne Imperato-McGinley.)

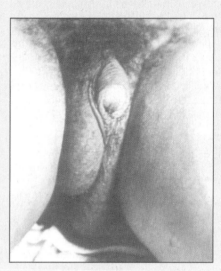

(B) Masculine appearance after puberty

cytokine called **relaxin-like factor** (**RLF**; also known as insulin-like factor-3) that is secreted by Leydig cells in the developing testis. In mice genetically deficient in RLF, the testes fail to descend (Nef & Parada, 1999). (Gubernacula also exist in females, where they attach to the ovaries and likewise cause them to move downward, but this movement is limited by the attachment of the ovaries to the uterus.)

As the testes enter the scrotum, they draw various structures with them: the vasa deferentia, blood vessels, and nerves, as well as a portion of the peritoneal lining of the abdominal cavity (Figure 5.16). Collectively, these structures contribute to the spermatic cord. Although the testes sit in saclike spaces that are developmentally part of the abdominal cavity, the connection between these spaces and the pelvic cavity is usually sealed off after the testes descend. Thus, even though the cremaster muscle (see Chapter 3) can pull the testes upward in the scrotal sac, the testes cannot move all the way back into the pelvis.

Because the Wolffian ducts are attached to the developing testes before the descent begins, the vasa deferentia (which form from the Wolffian ducts) are drawn out along the

Box 5.7 # Biology of Sex

Atypical Development: Hypospadias

Hypospadias is a condition seen in males when the urethral folds fail to fully enclose the urethra. The urethra then opens on the ventral surface of the glans, close to the normal position (see figure); on the shaft of the penis; at the base of the penis; on the front of the scrotum; or even on the perineum behind the scrotum. The abnormal opening may be in addition to the regular opening at the tip of the penis or may replace it. Hypospadias is common: as many as 1 in 350 boys have hypospadias severe enough to require surgical repair (Aho et al., 2000), and far greater numbers have milder forms of the condition. In fact, urologists at the University of Mainz, Germany, examined the location of the urethral meatus in 500 "normal" men and found that only 55 percent of them had a meatus in the supposedly "normal" position at the very tip of the glans. In the other 45 percent, the meatus was located slightly behind the tip on the ventral surface of the glans, or at the level of the corona. Such positioning of the meatus did not impair the men's ability to discharge a single

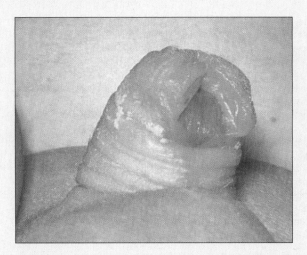

stream of urine, to engage in coitus, or to father children (Fichtner et al., 1995). These men would doubtless be surprised to hear themselves called "intersexes," even though the condition does represent a failure of stereotypical male development.

The cause of hypospadias in individual cases is not usually known. The condition is thought to result from a variety of endocrinological factors, such as deficits in testosterone synthesis or in the conversion of testosterone to DHT, or from exposure of the mother to steroidal drugs, especially progestins. An apparent increase in the incidence of hypospadias over the last 50 years has led to speculation concerning the possible contributory role of hormone-like pollutants in the environment (see Box 4.4), but there is some uncertainty as to how real this increase is.

A variety of techniques are employed to repair severe hypospadias, which are comparable to those used in female-to-male sex reassignment surgery (see Chapter 13). Noting the benign effect of the mild forms of hypospadias, the German urologists questioned whether surgical repair is warranted when these forms are seen in newborns.

course of the descent. That is why the vasa deferentia of adult men take a route that seems unnecessarily circuitous, arching upward over the ureters before they turn downward and medially toward the prostate gland. The kidneys, by moving upward during development, contribute to this circuitous route. (The failure of one or both testes to descend normally, a condition known as cryptorchidism, is covered in Box 5.8.)

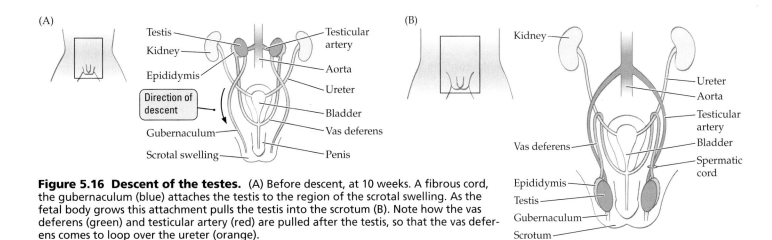

Figure 5.16 Descent of the testes. (A) Before descent, at 10 weeks. A fibrous cord, the gubernaculum (blue) attaches the testis to the region of the scrotal swelling. As the fetal body grows this attachment pulls the testis into the scrotum (B). Note how the vas deferens (green) and testicular artery (red) are pulled after the testis, so that the vas deferens comes to loop over the ureter (orange).

Box 5.8 Biology of Sex

Atypical Development: Undescended Testicles

In 2–5 percent of full-term newborn boys, one or both testicles have not yet arrived in the scrotum. In many of these boys, the tardy testicles will arrive within a few weeks after birth, but if they are still no-shows at 3 months, the condition is considered pathological and is named **cryptorchidism** (Toppari & Kaleva, 1999). About 1–2 percent of boys have this condition.

Where are the missing testicles? On rare occasions they may be completely absent, or present at some erratic location, but usually they are held up somewhere along the path of their fetal descent. They may be on the back wall of the abdomen or pelvis, or they may be lodged in the inguinal canal or even in the upper part of the scrotal sac.

The cause of cryptorchidism is not known for certain. Because the cytokine relaxin-like factor (RLF or Insl3) plays a key role in the normal descent of the testicles, it is suspected that it may also be involved in cryptorchidism. Boys with undescended testicles do not have genetic abnormalities in the RLF gene, but the expression of the gene in the fetal testis may be impaired by estrogens. Thus, fetal exposure to the synthetic estrogen DES increases the risk of cryptorchidism and also impairs RLF expression (Emmen et al., 2000). There is evidence that the placentas of newborns with cryptorchidism may produce unusually high levels of estrogens (Hadziselimovic et al., 2000).

Cryptorchidism is associated with lowered fertility and with an increased risk of testicular cancer after puberty. Undescended testicles can often be surgically moved into the scrotum (**orchiopexy**); this procedure is usually performed at 6–12 months of age. If the testicles are near their goal, they may be induced to complete their descent by treatment with gonadotropins or with GnRH. Correction of cryptorchidism improves the prospects for fertility, but does not eliminate the increased risk of cancer. Once they are in the scrotum, however, the testes can be monitored by regular self-examination (see Chapter 17), thus increasing the likelihood that any cancer that does develop will be caught at an early stage.

Hormones Influence the Sexual Differentiation of the Central Nervous System

Like male and female bodies, male and female brains differ from each other. Though more subtle than the bodily differences, and of course hidden from view, sex differences in the brain may have a greater impact on our lives than sex differences in the body. We therefore turn our attention to the brains of males and females and ask how sex differences in brain organization arise.

The CNS Contains Sexually Dimorphic Structures

We already mentioned in Chapter 3 that parts of the central nervous system (CNS) differ in structure between the two sexes. The example we cited was Onuf's nucleus in the sacral level of the spinal cord. Onuf's nucleus contains the cell bodies of the motor neurons that innervate some of the striated muscles of the pelvic floor, including those associated with the root of the penis. It is larger, and contains more neurons, in men than in women.

The brain also contains sexually dimorphic cell groups. The most extensively studied of these is a cell group in the **medial preoptic area,** the frontmost portion of the hypothalamus. The medial preoptic area is involved (at least in laboratory animals) in the generation of sexual behavior typically shown by males ("male-typical" sexual behavior), such as mounting, intromission, and ejaculation, and it may be involved in higher-level traits, such as partner choice, as well. It may also be involved in the suppression of female-typical behavior. In some species, damage to this area in male animals results in the appearance of female-typical behavior patterns that the animal did not previously show. The role of this region is human sexuality, however, is very uncertain.

Within the medial preoptic area is a cell group that is larger (on average, at least) in males than in females. In rats this cell group is known simply as the **sexually dimorphic nucleus of the preoptic area,** or **SDN-POA.** It was first described by Roger Gorski and his colleagues at UCLA in 1978 (Gorski et al., 1978). In 1989 the same research group, led by Gorski's student Laura Allen, described what may be a human equivalent: a cell group that they named the **third interstitial nucleus of the anterior hypothalamus,** or **INAH3**

(A)

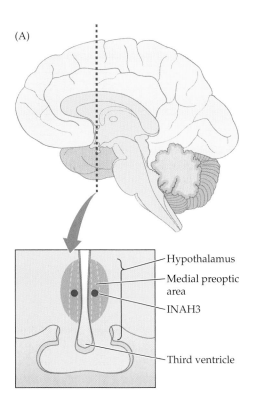

Hypothalamus

Medial preoptic area

INAH3

Third ventricle

Figure 5.17   The third interstitial nucleus of the anterior hypothalamus (INAH3) is larger, on average, in men than in women. (A) INAH3 lies within the medial preoptic area of the hypothalamus, a region concerned with male-typical sexual behavior. The midline slit (III) is the third ventricle of the brain. (B) Micrograph of INAH3 in a man; the nucleus is the oval shaped cluster of darkly stained cell bodies at the center of the micrograph.

(B)

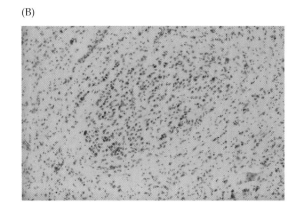

(Allen et al., 1989) (Figure 5.17). Based on the location, morphology, and chemical make-up of SDN-POA and INAH3, it appears that the two structures are homologous—that is, that they have a common evolutionary origin (Byne, 1998).

INAH3 is not the only sexually dimorphic structure in the brain. In fact, INAH3 may be part of a chain of nuclei in the base of the brain that are larger in males than in females (Allen & Gorski, 1990). In addition, there may be some nuclei that are dimorphic in the opposite direction. In the rat, for example, a small group of cells at the very front tip of the hypothalamus, called the **anteroventral periventricular nucleus (AVPV),** is larger in females than in males. AVPV is involved in the neuroendocrine regulation of the ovarian cycle.

Surprisingly, the hypothalamic cell group that is most closely involved in the production of female-typical sexual behavior—the **ventromedial nucleus (VMN),** is not larger in females than in males. This may be because VMN helps regulate other functions as well as sexuality, such as the control of body weight.

Size differences in brain structures are, of course, relatively crude indicators of functional differentiation. There are probably many more subtle differences between the sexes in the nervous system, such as in synaptic connections, neurotransmitter content, gene expression, and neural activity patterns, but currently only a few of these have been documented in humans.

Sexual Dimorphism Can Arise as an Indirect Effect of Hormonal Actions outside the CNS

How do sex differences in the structure of the CNS arise during development? The best-documented cause is the same as the main cause of sex differences in the rest of the body; that is, the higher levels of circulating androgens in males than in females during development. This difference in androgen levels can affect neuronal organization either directly or indirectly.

Let's look first at an example of an **indirect effect.** Marc Breedlove and his colleagues (then at the University of California, Berkeley) studied the development of the rat's equivalent of Onuf's nucleus—called the **spinal nucleus of the bulbocavernosus** (or **SNB**) because its motor neurons innervate the bulbocavernosus muscle (the muscle we are calling the bulbospongiosus muscle; see Chapter 3), as well as other muscles of the rat's genital area (Breedlove et al., 1999).

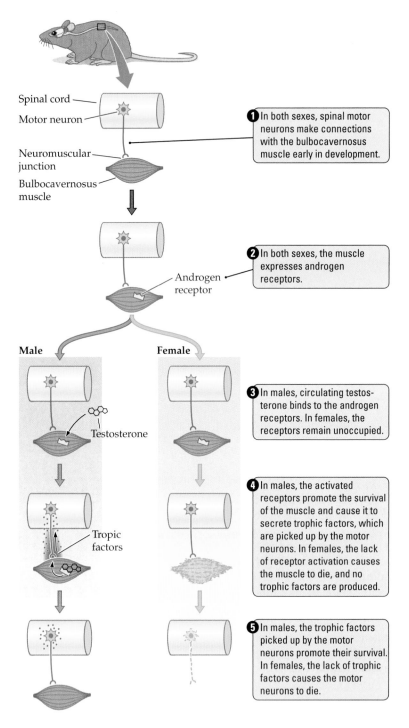

1 In both sexes, spinal motor neurons make connections with the bulbocavernosus muscle early in development.

2 In both sexes, the muscle expresses androgen receptors.

3 In males, circulating testosterone binds to the androgen receptors. In females, the receptors remain unoccupied.

4 In males, the activated receptors promote the survival of the muscle and cause it to secrete trophic factors, which are picked up by the motor neurons. In females, the lack of receptor activation causes the muscle to die, and no trophic factors are produced.

5 In males, the trophic factors picked up by the motor neurons promote their survival. In females, the lack of trophic factors causes the motor neurons to die.

Figure 5.18 Development of sexual dimorphism of the rat spinal nucleus of the bulbocavernosus.

To understand Breedlove's research, you have to know that during fetal development, an excess of motor neurons is generated throughout the spinal cord. Cell death subsequently eliminates those motor neurons that fail to establish connections with muscles. This pruning process is mediated by **trophic factors** secreted by muscles: if the axonal endings of the motor neurons fail to pick up these trophic factors, they die.

Breedlove found that during early fetal development, both male and female rats possess a bulbocavernosus muscle, but in female fetuses the muscle subsequently dies (Figure 5.18). That's because the muscle requires the presence of androgens, which are not present at sufficient levels in female fetuses. Deprived of their target muscle and the trophic factors it produces, the motor neurons in the female rat's SNB also die. Thus the sexual dimorphism in the rat's SNB is an indirect consequence of the sexual dimorphism in the genital musculature.

The situation in humans is somewhat different because women do have a bulbospongiosus muscle—it forms a sling around the clitoral shaft and the vaginal introitus (see Chapter 3). Nevertheless, the total amount of genital musculature innervated by Onuf's nucleus is less in women than in men. Therefore, fewer motor neurons survive in the Onuf's nucleus of women.

Sexual Dimorphism Can Arise as a Direct Effect of Hormones during a Sensitive Period

In the case of the sexually dimorphic nucleus in the medial preoptic area of the hypothalamus (INAH3 or its homologue in the rat, SDN-POA), it appears that the sexual dimorphism is a **direct effect** of differences in circulating androgen levels during development. Roger Gorski and his colleagues studied the effects of manipulating androgen levels in developing rats on the size of the SND-POA (Davis et al., 1995). They found that female rats could be induced to develop a male-sized SDN-POA by administration of testosterone, and that male rats could be induced to develop a small, female-sized SDN-POA by castration—that is, by removal of the rat's own supply of testosterone. In either case, however, the manipulation had to be done during a restricted **sensitive period** of development (Figure 5.19). In rats, this period begins a few days before birth and ends soon after birth. By a week after birth, testosterone treatments come too late to "rescue" the SDN-POA in females. In males, on the other hand, castration still shrinks the nucleus as late as 30 days after birth. Comparable treatments in older pups or in adult rats have little or no effect on the size of the nucleus.

Gorski's group found that about the same numbers of SDN-POA neurons are generated in both sexes. Thus, testosterone does not influence this initial step in the development of the nucleus. Rather, it influences the *survival* of SDN-POA neurons. Soon after they have started to form the nucleus, SDN-POA neurons express androgen receptors, and in fact become dependent on the presence of testosterone for their survival. Thus, the majority of SDN-POA neurons die in females, whereas they continue to develop in males. Furthermore, the SDN-POA neurons can be "rescued" not merely by systemic

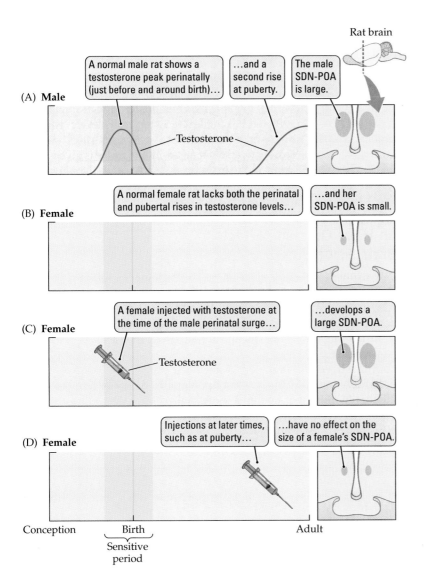

Figure 5.19 Sexual differentiation in the hypothalamus. The presence of testosterone during an early "sensitive period" is necessary for the development of a male-sized SDN-POA in rats.

administration of testosterone, but also by local injections of miniscule quantities of testosterone into the medial preoptic area itself. This finding supports the notion that androgens act directly on the SDN-POA neurons, or at least on targets in their immediate vicinity, to promote their survival and development.

We mentioned in Chapter 4 that the effects of testosterone on the brains of adult rats depend in considerable part on the conversion of testosterone to estradiol within the target tissue by the enzyme aromatase. The same is true during development. If the conversion is blocked by administration of an aromatase inhibitor during the sensitive period, male rats will develop a small SDN-POA in the size range typical of females (Houtsmuller et al., 1994). Thus, the hormone that actually does the work of masculinizing the hypothalamus in male rats is estradiol, formed from circulating testosterone.

We have no direct evidence as to whether similar processes guide the sexual differentiation of INAH3 in humans. If they do, it's likely that the sensitive period is well before birth, rather than around the time of birth, as with rats. That's because humans, with their longer period of development in utero (9 months versus 3 weeks for rats), are born at a much later stage of brain development. Another point to stress is that the sexual dimorphism of INAH3 is not as distinct as that of the rat's SDN-POA: although there is a two- or threefold average difference in the size of INAH3 between men and women, there is considerable variation among individuals of the same sex and some overlap between the sexes. We will have more to say about this when we discuss the development of sexual orientation in Chapter 7.

Some Dimorphisms Depend on Continued Hormonal Effects in Adult Life

Although the concept of a sensitive period is probably valid for a number of sexually dimorphic structures in the CNS, it is not universally applicable. The size of at least one sexually dimorphic nucleus in rats—a cell group called the **posterodorsal nucleus of the medial amygdala** (**MePD**)—is regulated by circulating testosterone levels *both* during development *and* in adult life. Thus, if an adult male rat is castrated, MePD shrinks to the female-typical size within 4 weeks; conversely if an adult female rat is given injections of testosterone, her MePD will grow to the male-typical size within the same period (Cooke et al., 1999). Thus, we cannot automatically assume that a difference between the sexes in the size of a brain structure results from early developmental processes alone.

Androgens Can Have Opposite Effects on Different Brain Structures

What about the AVPV, the hypothalamic cell group that is larger in females than in males? You might think that female hormones, such as estrogens, would play the key role here. It turns out, however, that testosterone is the controlling hormone once again—only the direction of the effect is different. If testosterone levels are *low* during the first few days of postnatal life, the AVPV later develops to the full female size; if they are *high,* the AVPV develops much less (Davis et al., 1996).

How can one hormone have essentially opposite effects on the development of two different nuclei, SDN-POA and AVPV? We don't have a detailed answer to that question, but we should bear in mind that, within a target cell, a steroid hormone activates only a subset of all the genes that possess response elements for that hormone (see Chapter 4). Developmental processes intrinsic to the cell determine which subset of genes that is. Therefore, testosterone might activate genes that accelerate development in one cell type and genes that retard development, or even cause cell death, in another.

Early Hormonal Exposure Influences Later Sexual Behavior

Hormone levels during development not only guide the development of anatomical differences between male and female brains, but also influence an animal's or person's sexual *behavior* in adulthood. Of course, the evidence for this statement comes mostly from animal experiments, which we will discuss first. It is impossible, both for ethical reasons and because of the prolonged time course of human development, to do the equivalent experiments on humans. Still, as we'll see later in this chapter and in subsequent chapters, there are enough clues from a variety of sources to conclude that the animal results are at least partially applicable to humans.

Experiments on Rodents Show Organizational and Activational Effects of Androgens

The key observations of animal sexual behavior were made by a group at the University of Texas, led by William Young, in the 1950s and 1960s (Phoenix et al., 1959). Young's group studied **mounting** and **lordosis,** the stereotypical mating behaviors shown by male and female rodents, respectively. Mounting is just what it sounds like; lordosis is the response to mounting shown by a receptive female. She bends her back into a U-shape and deflects her tail, thus raising and exposing her vulva for intromission by the male (Figure 5.20). Female rodents rarely mount other animals, and male rodents rarely display lordosis in response to being mounted.

It is not possible to reverse these behaviors by manipulating an animal's hormone levels in adulthood. For example, castrating an adult male and giving him estrogens, thus replicating the hormonal environment in which female rodents normally exhibit lordosis behavior, may induce some lordosis behavior, but at nothing like the frequency shown by females.

Figure 5.20 Copulating rats. Mounting and lordosis are the stereotypical sexual behaviors of male and female rodents. The female rat (below) is showing lordosis—an inverse arching of her back that exposes her vulva—in response to being mounted by the male.

The researchers found that they *could* greatly influence an adult guinea pig or rat's tendency to display mounting or lordosis by manipulating the levels of testosterone to which it was exposed *during development.* Thus, if a female animal was exposed to male-like levels of testosterone prenatally and allowed to grow up, she would seldom or never display lordosis when mounted by a male. And furthermore, if this animal was given male-like levels of testosterone in adulthood, she would actually mount other females (Figure 5.21). Pretty much the converse observations were made in male rodents: a male castrated early in development showed little mounting behavior in adulthood, whatever hormones he was given then; if given estrogens, he would display lordosis behavior when mounted by another male.

The experiments just described were focused on the motor patterns shown by rodents during sex. In other studies, the animal had to choose between a male and a female partner. This, then, was a test of what we might call "sexual orientation" in humans (see Chapter 7). Here again, early hormone levels play an important role: female rats exposed to high levels of testosterone early in development are shifted in their partner preference toward females (de Jonge et al., 1988), and males in which the synthesis or action of testosterone is blocked are shifted toward preferring males (Bakker et al., 1993). Similar effects have been described in a variety of other species.

Young's group postulated that hormones have two distinct actions in the regulation of sexual behavior in rodents. First, they help **organize** the formation of sex-differentiated brain circuitry during the early period when the brain is developing. Second, they **activate** the established circuitry in adulthood. The organizational effects depend largely on the presence or absence of sufficient circulating levels of androgens during a sensitive period of development. The activational effects, in contrast, may involve either androgens or estrogens. We will see later in this chapter how estrogens come into play at the time of puberty.

In the years since Young's studies, we have gained some insight into what the organizational and activational processes might involve. With regard to organizational effects, it is striking that the sensitive periods for the organization of sexual *behaviors* tend to coincide with the sensitive periods for the development of sexually dimorphic *structures* such as SDN-POA. Thus, at least in part, early hormone exposure probably organizes later behaviors by helping set up the brain systems that mediate these behaviors. At the most obvious level, these organizational effects would include the formation of nuclei such as SDN-POA, but they probably also include more subtle effects—on a neuron's synaptic connections and neurotransmitter synthesis, for example.

How do hormones *activate* sex-specific behaviors in adulthood? The best-studied animal model is the lordosis reflex, which has been the focus of a research group at Rockefeller University led by Donald Pfaff (Kow & Pfaff, 1998). Female rats exhibit lordosis during only one night of their 4- or 5-day ovarian cycle. The capacity to show the reflex is turned on by two hormones acting in combination: rising estrogen levels during the early part of the cycle, followed by a surge of progesterone near the time of ovulation. These hormones act on the ventromedial nucleus of the hypothalamus (VMN) to facilitate the reflex.

The effect of these hormones on the VMN involves two types of actions. In the first type, the hormones bind to the "classic" steroid receptors and thus regulate gene expression. For example, the binding of estrogen to its receptor causes an increase in the expression of the gene for the progestin receptor, so the neurons of the VMN become more sensitive to progesterone. Other genes turned on by estrogen probably include genes concerned with cell growth, because the dendrites of the VMN neurons (the cytoplasmic extensions that receive synaptic inputs—see Chapter 3) lengthen significantly during the 2 days of the cycle when the cells are exposed to estrogens (Meisel & Luttrell, 1990).

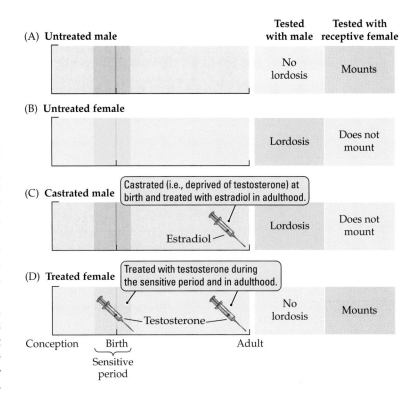

Figure 5.21 Hormones and sexual behavior in rats. Sexual behavior depends on the hormonal environment during a sensitive period early in development and in adulthood. (A) Untreated male. (B) Untreated female. (C) Male castrated (i.e., deprived of testosterone) at birth and treated with estradiol in adulthood. (D) Female treated with testosterone during the sensitive period and in adulthood.

In the second type of action, the hormones bind to "non-classic" steroid receptors in the plasma membranes of the VMN neurons. Some of these receptors are closely associated with synapses and may directly modulate the responsiveness of the VMN neurons to incoming signals, such as the sensory signals generated when the female rat is mounted by a male. Other membrane receptors activate an internal cascade of second messengers, which in turn affect the cells' responsiveness by a variety of means (Kow & Pfaff, 1998). The net effect of all these processes is to ensure that the female rat will respond to mounting by showing lordosis behavior, but only during the narrow window in her estrous cycle when insemination by a male can lead to fertilization.

Primates Have Multiple Sensitive Periods

How relevant is all this to human sexuality? One way of approaching this question is by extending the rodent research to primates. A group at the University of Wisconsin, Madison, led by Robert Goy, conducted a multi-year study of female macaque monkeys that had been treated with testosterone during fetal life. Goy's group obtained results quite comparable to what had been observed in rats and guinea pigs. Even before puberty, the effects of the prenatal testosterone exposure were obvious. Prepubertal monkeys engage in a lot of "play-sex," in which one monkey mounts but does not penetrate another. Males take the mounting role more commonly than do females. Goy's prenatally treated females also commonly took the mounting role in play-sex. This "masculinization" affected other traits besides play-sex behavior. For example, male prepubertal monkeys typically engage in more "play-fighting" or "rough-and-tumble play" than do females, but prenatal treatment with testosterone increased young female monkeys' engagement in this activity (Goy et al., 1988; Wallen, 1996).

After the treated females reached puberty, Goy's group tested their adult sexual behavior (Pomerantz et al., 1986). They first removed the ovaries from the monkeys and gave them a series of testosterone injections, thus simulating the hormonal environment of a normal adult *male* monkey. The females who had been exposed to testosterone prenatally responded to this endocrinological sex reversal by showing male-typical sexual behavior, especially a style of mounting called the "double-footclasp mount," in which the mounting animal raises itself on the hind legs of the other animal. Such behavior was not shown by a comparison group of female monkeys that experienced normal prenatal development, even though they were subjected to the same endocrinological manipulation (ovary removal and testosterone treatment) in adulthood. Thus, it was the *prenatal* exposure to testosterone, in combination with the testosterone treatment in adulthood, that caused Goy's females to perform adult-style mounting.

Goy and his colleagues found that monkeys have not just a single "sensitive period," but several. For example, testosterone treatment of females early in fetal life was most effective in promoting mounting behavior, but treatment later in fetal life was most effective in promoting rough-and-tumble play (Goy et al., 1988). It thus appears that the brain circuits mediating different kinds of sex-differentiated behaviors mature at different times and become sensitive to testosterone levels at different times. It is therefore possible, by precise timing of testosterone treatments, not merely to dissociate a monkey's behavior from its anatomy (in other words, producing a monkey with female genitalia but male-like sexual behavior), but also to dissociate one kind of sex-typical behavior from another (producing a female that participates in rough-and-tumble play but not in male-like play-sex behavior, for example).

We will defer our main discussion of the development of *human* sexual behavior until Chapter 7. There we will make the case that the observations on rodents and primates that we have just described are relevant to human sexual development.

Estrogens seem to play little role in prenatal sexual development, except in the brain, where estradiol (produced by the local aromatization of androgens) helps to masculinize brain circuitry, as described earlier. The ovaries do not produce significant quantities of sex steroids prenatally. Estrogens are present in embryos and fetuses of both sexes—in particular, they reach the fetus from the mother's cir-

When monkeys copulate, the male often grasps the female's feet or legs with his own feet. Juvenile females who have been exposed to androgens before birth will take the male role in this "footclasp" mount during play-sex, but untreated females will not.

culation, and they are also manufactured by the placenta from androgens secreted by the testes (in males) or the adrenal gland (in both sexes). That these estrogens can influence fetal development to some degree is illustrated by the fact that some newborn infants have visible breast development and may even secrete milk (so-called "witch's milk"). In general, however, it seems that the fetus, and particularly its brain, is protected from the effects of external estrogens. These protective mechanisms include the chemical alteration of estrogens as they enter the fetal circulation and the existence of binding proteins that lower the levels of the free steroids. Furthermore, laboratory animals and humans that are insensitive to estrogens because of a congenital absence of estrogen receptors experience no obvious abnormalities of prenatal development (Korach et al., 1996). This stands in marked contrast to the situation of genetic males who lack *androgen* receptors, whose fetal development is radically affected (see Box 5.4).

Other Y-Linked Genes besides SRY Influence Development

So far, we have attributed prenatal sexual differentiation almost entirely to the secretions of the developing testis—AMH and androgens—in males, and to the lack or low levels of comparable hormones in females. Because testis development is controlled by the gene *SRY*, this model places the responsibility for sexual differentiation on the presence (in males) or the absence (in females) of *SRY*, in line with the original hypothesis spelled out by Alfred Jost in the 1940s. But this model is probably incomplete. In particular, there are other genes on the Y chromosome besides *SRY* that influence sexual development. Several Y-linked genes are involved in spermatogenesis (Affara & Mitchell, 2000). An XX male who is male by virtue of having a translocation of *SRY* onto the X chromosome, as described earlier, has defective spermatogenesis and is sterile because he lacks these other Y-linked genes.

There is also at least one gene on the Y chromosome that increases stature, and a part of the reason that men are, on average, taller than women is the fact that they possess this gene (Salo et al., 1995). In fact, it has been reported that male conceptuses grow faster than female conceptuses even before implantation (and therefore long before the testis has started to secrete hormones). Again, this difference is due to a gene on the Y chromosome that is different from *SRY* (Burgoyne et al., 1995).

Finally, studies on sex-reversed mice indicate that some behavioral differences between male and female mice are influenced by genetic mechanisms that do not involve the *SRY*–testis–hormone cascade (Stavnezer et al., 2000). Thus the "classical" mechanism postulated by Jost, while unquestionably of central importance in sexual differentiation, is not the entire story. The nonclassical mechanisms remain to be elucidated.

External Factors Influence Prenatal Sexual Development

There is increasing evidence from animal studies that environmental factors operating during pregnancy can affect the sexual development of fetuses. In rats, for example, subjecting a pregnant female to stress (such as forced immobilization or bright lights) or administering alcohol to her affects the later sexual behavior of her male offspring. In general, these males are partially "demasculinized" in their sexual behavior: they are less ready to approach and mount receptive females, and ejaculate less often, than untreated male rats (Ward et al., 1994). There are also anatomical and chemical changes in the brains of these prenatally stressed rats that are consistent with demasculinization: the volume of the SDN-POA is reduced, and the levels of some neurotransmitters and related compounds are more similar to those typically found in females than in males (Anderson et al., 1986; Reznikov et al., 1999).

Stressing pregnant rats affects their fetuses via the **stress hormones,** which are **glucocorticoids.** Glucocorticoids are one type of **corticosteroid,** a class of steroid hormones secreted by the adrenal glands. The key stress hormones are **corticosterone** (in rats) and **cortisol** (in humans). The brain controls the secretion of stress hormones by a hormonal cascade very similar to the one described in Chapter 4 for sex steroids. A hypothalamic releasing factor called **corticotropin-releasing factor (CRF)** triggers the release of **adrenocorticotropic hormone (ACTH)** from the anterior lobe of the pituitary gland, and ACTH, in turn, triggers the secretion of corticosterone or cortisol from the cortex of the adrenal gland.

When a pregnant female rat is stressed, this hormonal cascade is activated, and corticosterone levels rise both in the mother and in her fetuses. The effect of this rise in corticosterone is to decrease testosterone levels in male fetuses during the sensitive period for the sexual differentiation of the brain. This decrease in testosterone levels causes the partial demasculinization of the brain in prenatally stressed male rats (Ward & Weisz, 1984).

While alcohol and stress can affect fetal development in humans, too (see Chapter 10), there is little evidence pointing to specific effects on sexual development. There has been a controversial suggestion that prenatal stress might predispose men to homosexuality (Dorner et al., 1980), but the evidence to support this suggestion is weak. We discuss this topic further in Chapter 7.

One external factor that can indubitably affect human sexual development is the administration of sex hormones or related drugs to pregnant women. Between 1938 and 1971, several million pregnant women in the United States were given the drug **diethylstilbestrol (DES)**, a synthetic estrogen agonist. It was prescribed for women who were at risk for miscarriage, although, as we now know, it is not effective for that purpose and may in fact promote miscarriage. Administration of the drug to pregnant women was halted when it was found that it caused serious health problems for some of the female children born to those women. About one in a thousand of these girls, when they reached young adulthood, developed a cancer of the cervix or vagina (clear cell adenocarcinoma) that is normally very rare in that age range (Herbst, 1999). Women exposed to DES in utero may also have an increased risk of breast cancer later in life (Sanderson et al., 1998). Others have had fertility problems, and some have anatomical abnormalities of the reproductive tract. There also seems to be an influence, though a subtle one, on the affected women's sexual orientation (discussed in Chapter 7). The DES experience highlighted the dangers of administering hormone-related drugs to pregnant women.

Biological and Social Factors Interact Postnatally

One of the commonest misconceptions about genes and development is that genes run the whole show before birth and the environment takes over after birth. We've just seen how the environment (meaning, in this case, the mother, as well as factors external to her) can influence prenatal development. Conversely, genes continue to play a major role in postnatal development. Still, it is true that there are far more opportunities for the environment to influence development once a fetus has left the protective cocoon of its mother's uterus.

We will have much more to say about postnatal sexual development in later chapters, but we should mention here a couple of examples of ways in which environmental factors interact with biological processes during the period between birth and puberty. One such example concerns social isolation. Breedlove's group compared the effects of housing rats one to a cage and in groups from the time of weaning through adulthood (Cooke et al., 2000). They found that male rats raised in isolation were less likely to respond to the presence of an estrous female with a penile erection, or to achieve intromission with a female, than group-raised rats. Furthermore, the hypothalamic nucleus MePD (whose size is dependent on circulating testosterone levels in adulthood) was smaller in the isolated rats. The nucleus SDN-POA, though not smaller as an entire nucleus, contained neurons that were individually smaller in the isolated rats. Exactly how these behavioral and anatomical differences come about is not certain, but one possibility is that isolated rats have lower circulating testosterone levels than those reared in groups.

A group at Emory University, led by Kim Wallen, has conducted a multi-year study of the interaction of hormonal and social factors in the sexual development of rhesus monkeys and other nonhuman primates (Wallen, 1996). One example of their findings: monkeys reared in same-sex peer groups show different sexual behavior (during their juvenile life at least) than do monkeys raised in mixed-sex peer groups. In either type of rearing environment, males display more mounting behavior than do females—this difference results from their different prenatal hormonal exposure. But the sex difference in mounting behavior is much less marked among monkeys raised in same-sex groups than among those raised in mixed-sex groups. Apparently, exposure to female peers increases the propensity of male juveniles to mount other animals (of either sex), whereas exposure to male peers diminishes the propensity of female juveniles to mount other animals. Thus, prenatal hormone exposure does not rigidly predestine animals' sexual behavior, but generates a predisposition that can be modified by social circumstances.

Puberty Marks Sexual Maturation

During early infancy, the levels of circulating gonadotropins (LH and FSH) are high in both sexes. In girls, the presence of these hormones does not have major or consistent effects on the secretion of hormones by the ovaries, which remains very low throughout childhood. In infant boys, on the other hand, the gonadotropins spur the secretion of enough testosterone by the testes to bring circulating testosterone to adult-like levels (Andersson et al., 1998). The function, if any, of this brief postnatal testosterone surge is not known. By about 6–9 months of age, testosterone sinks back to very low levels, and remains low until **puberty:** the transition to sexual maturity.

Although there are no marked differences in sex hormone levels between girls and boys throughout most of childhood, there *are* sex differences in personality and behavior. In part, these differences reflect the different androgen levels to which girls and boys were exposed during fetal life. We will discuss this topic further in Chapter 6.

The Pubertal Growth Spurt Occurs about 2 Years Earlier in Girls than in Boys

The most obvious biological process during childhood is growth (Figure 5.22). The rate of growth decreases over time: at the age of 1 year a child is growing in height at 15–20 centimeters per year, but by shortly before puberty growth has slowed to about 5 centimeters per year. Then comes the **pubertal** (puberty-associated) **growth spurt,** in which the growth rate rises briefly to a peak of about 10 centimeters per year. (It is also referred to as the **adolescent growth spurt,** but we prefer to reserve the term **adolescence** for the psychosocial processes that accompany and follow puberty—a topic covered in Chapter 12.)

The pubertal growth spurt results in a height gain of about 28 centimeters for boys and 25 centimeters for girls. About 2 years after the beginning of the growth spurt, however, growth in height finally ceases, as the **epiphyses**—the cartilaginous growth zones in the long bones—cease to function and close (that is, they become solid bone).

There is considerable individual variation in the timing of the pubertal growth spurt, but in the contemporary U.S. population it starts at an average age of about 11 (for girls) or 13 (for boys). The age difference allows for about 2 years of additional childhood growth in boys, and this is the principal reason for the 10-centimeter difference in average height between adult men and women.

The spurt in height is not the only change in growth during puberty. There are changes in skeletal structure, with girls developing wider hips and boys developing wider shoulders. Body composition also changes: by adulthood, men have 50 percent more bone and muscle mass than women, and women have twice as much body fat as men. Of course, these are very much statements about averages—there are plenty of muscular women and fat men. Genes influence variations in body composition among individuals of the same sex, and factors such as food availability and athletic training can greatly modify the effects of biological predispositions.

Puberty Is Marked by Visible and Invisible Changes in the Body

More directly relevant to sexuality are pubertal changes in the external genitalia, secondary sexual characteristics, internal reproductive tracts, and gonads. In girls, the most noticeable change in the external genitalia is the growth of **pubic hair** (Figure 5.23), but in addition, the labia majora and minora become more prominent, the vagina deepens, and the vaginal wall thickens. **Axillary** (armpit) **hair** appears a little later than pubic hair.

Figure 5.22 Growth velocity curves for boys and girls. The pubertal growth spurt begins 1.5 to 2 years later in boys than in girls. It is this extra period of childhood growth in males that largely accounts for the sex difference in adult height.

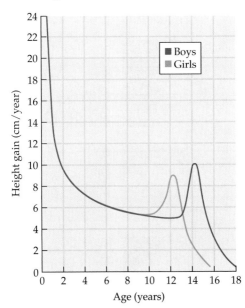

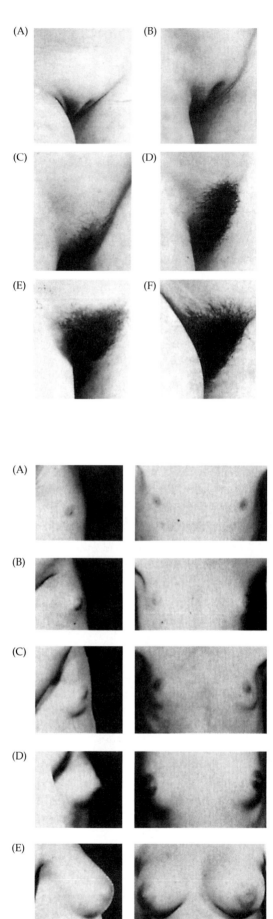

(A)

Figure 5.23 Typical development of pubic hair in girls at puberty.
(A) Pre-pubertal state: no hair is visible. (B) Sparse, long, downy hair grows along labia. This stage occurs at about 8.8 years in African-Americans and 10.5 years in White Americans, but with considerable variability. (C) Coarser, curly hair grows along labia. (D) Hair covers labia. (E) Hair spreads over mons veneris but not to the adult extent or density. (F) Hair forms adult-like "inverse triangle" and extends to inner surface of thighs; this final pattern varies considerably among women. (From van Wieringen et al., 1971.)

The most important secondary female sexual characteristic to appear at puberty is the **breasts.** Breast development goes through several stages (Figure 5.24). The breast first shows itself as a small mound—the **breast bud**—centered on the nipple. As breast development continues, both the nipple and the surrounding areola come to project forward from the breast, and the areola enlarges. With the completion of breast development, the areola lies flush with the breast once more, and only the nipple projects.

Inside a girl's body, puberty is marked by a spurt of growth in the ovaries, uterus, and oviducts. The oviducts, which before puberty have a somewhat contorted course, become straighter. The cervix begins to produce the characteristic secretions of adult life. And in the ovaries, the recruitment of primordial follicles into the process of follicular maturation begins.

The most dramatic event in a girl's puberty is the onset of menstruation: **menarche.** (Pronunciations vary—MEN-ark is as good as any.) Because menarche is an event rather than a process, and a highly memorable one at that, it is commonly used to date female puberty. In the contemporary U.S. population, the average age at menarche is 12–13 years, but the range of 11 to 17, or even 10 to 18, is considered normal. There are also ethnic differences within the U.S. population—the average age at menarche is 12.2 for African-American girls and 12.9 for white girls (Herman-Giddens et al., 1997).

There has been a historical trend toward earlier menarche in a number of Western countries (Figure 5.25). In mid-nineteenth-century Europe, the average age at menarche may have been as high as 16 to 17, although there is some uncertainty about the accuracy of these records. According to historian Vern Bullough, 15 is a more likely age (Bullough, 1981). In the United States at the beginning of the twentieth century, it was about 14. Thus, average age at menarche decreased at an average rate of over 1 month per decade during the twentieth century.

The average timetable for the visible events of female puberty in the U.S. white population is roughly as follows: breast development begins at 10, pubic hair appears at 10.5, and menarche occurs at 12.9. In the African-American population, pubic hair appears at an average age of 8.8, breast development begins at 8.9, and menarche is at 12.2 (Herman-Giddens et al., 1997). In both populations, the pubertal growth spurt peaks about 1 year before menarche.

Menstruation may be irregular for the first year or two after menarche. Furthermore, the initial menstrual cycles tend to be anovulatory. For this reason, a young woman may not be capable of becoming pregnant for a year or two after menarche. However, there is much variation in this respect, and the fact that a young woman has only recently begun to menstruate should not lead her to believe that she is incapable of conceiving.

For boys (Figure 5.26), an early sign of puberty is the enlargement of the testes and scrotum, which begins at the age of 10 to 13. Between 11 and 15, the penis grows in length and then in girth, and pubic hair appears. During the same period, the larynx (voice box) grows and the vocal cords thicken, leading to a deep-

Figure 5.24 Typical development of breasts in girls at puberty seen in side and frontal views. (A) Pre-pubertal appearance. (B) Breast bud stage: nipple, areola, and nearby breast tissue form a small mound at about 8.9 years (for African-Americans) or 10 years (for White Americans). (C) Further enlargement of areola and breast. (D) Nipple and areola project out from breast. (E) Adult-like stage: areola is now flush with the breast; only the nipple projects forward. (From van Wieringen et al., 1971.)

Figure 5.25 Puberty is starting earlier. During the nineteenth and twentieth centuries, girls in Western countries reached menarche at progressively younger ages. The reliability of the nineteenth-century data is uncertain.

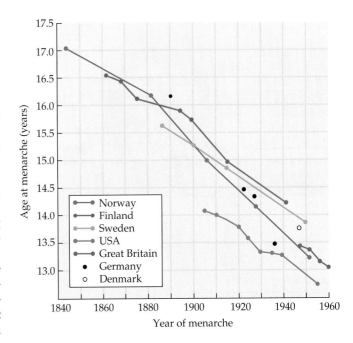

ening of the voice (**change of voice**). The pubertal growth spurt peaks at about 14.

First **ejaculation,** which occurs at about age 13, may occur with **masturbation** (see Chapter 8) or during sleep (a **nocturnal emission**). Initially, the semen lacks mature spermatozoa; in fact, a male can be infertile for a year or two after his first ejaculation. As with girls soon after menarche, however, there is no guarantee on this point.

Many boys experience temporary growth of the breasts during the latter part of puberty. The enlarged breasts nearly always disappear without treatment.

Facial and axillary hair begins to appear about 2 years after the growth of pubic hair. Body hair may appear soon thereafter, especially on the chest, but its appearance is highly variable among individuals and among ethnic groups. Recession of the scalp hairline at the temples may occur soon after the other events of puberty and does not necessarily presage male-pattern baldness.

One pubertal trait that afflicts many teens, especially boys, is **acne**. The key feature of acne is the blockage of **sebaceous** (oil-producing) **glands** associated with hair follicles—most commonly on the face, neck, or back. The blockage is caused by an excess production and shedding of **keratinocytes** (epidermal skin cells) within the glands. The blocked glands become a breeding ground for a common skin bacterium, *Propionibacterium acnes.* The blocked gland is called a whitehead if is below the skin, a blackhead if it reaches the surface, and a pustule or pimple if it becomes inflamed. Severe acne can lead to permanent scarring. The condition can be treated with topical (local) medications containing benzoyl peroxide, salicylic acid, or sulfur. Severe cases may be treated effectively with an oral drug, isotretinoin (Accutane), but this drug can have serious side effects, including fetal defects if taken by pregnant women.

What Drives Puberty?

So far, we have simply described the major phenomena associated with puberty. But what triggers and orchestrates them? Let's start by looking at the proximate (immediate) causes, then track back to the earlier events that get puberty under way.

The proximate causes of most of the phenomena of puberty are, of course, hormones—in particular, androgens and estrogens, along with growth hormone. Although estrogen effects predominate in girls and androgen effects in boys, both androgens and estrogens are needed in both sexes for normal completion of puberty.

Androgen levels rise steadily in both sexes during puberty, but reach much higher final levels in men than in women (see Chapter 4). Androgens are responsible for muscle development, voice deepening, and spermatogenesis (in combination with FSH), as well as the

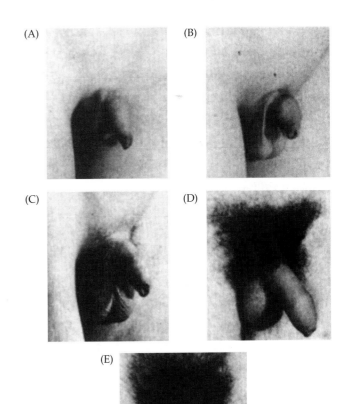

Figure 5.26 Typical development of male external genitalia at puberty. (A) Prepubertal appearance. (B) Enlargement of scrotum and testes. This stage usually occurs between 11 and 13 years. (C) Increase in length of penis and further enlargement of scrotum. (D) Increase in size of penis, especially the glans. Pubic hair appears. (E) Adult appearance. (From van Wieringen et al., 1971.)

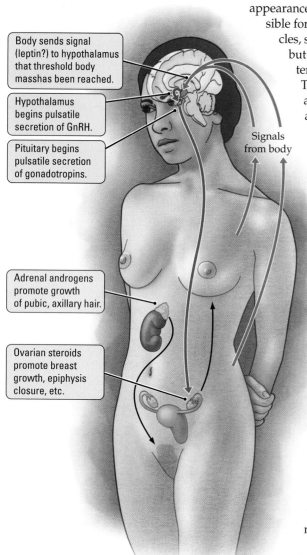

Body sends signal (leptin?) to hypothalamus that threshold body masshas been reached.

Hypothalamus begins pulsatile secretion of GnRH.

Pituitary begins pulsatile secretion of gonadotropins.

Signals from body

Adrenal androgens promote growth of pubic, axillary hair.

Ovarian steroids promote breast growth, epiphysis closure, etc.

Figure 5.27 Hormonal control of puberty. This figure shows the chain of events that drives puberty in girls. The factors that trigger the increase in androgens by the adrenal gland are uncertain, but may include a direct signal from body fat stores. The regulation of puberty in boys is similar, except that the principal gonadal steroids are androgens, especially testosterone.

appearance of pubic and axillary hair in both sexes. In men, androgens are also responsible for the pubertal development of the external genitalia, prostate, seminal vesicles, sebaceous glands, and facial and body hair (and for male-pattern baldness), but full development of these characteristics requires the conversion of testosterone to the more potent androgen DHT in the target tissues (see Chapter 4). Testosterone also acts on the brain to promote the psychosexual development associated with puberty in both sexes; this effect may depend in part on aromatization of testosterone to estradiol in the brain.

Estrogens (in combination with growth hormone and progesterone) promote development of the breasts. Estrogens and progesterone (in combination with FSH and LH) trigger menarche. In males, estrogens are required for the normal functioning of the epididymis in concentrating sperm and are therefore necessary for male fertility (see Chapter 10). In both sexes, estrogens are responsible for an increase in bone density at puberty, as well as for the closure of the epiphyses of the long bones at the end of the pubertal growth spurt. Thus, individuals who cannot manufacture estrogens because they lack the enzyme aromatase, or who lack estrogen receptors, fail to stop growing at the end of puberty, and may reach a height of nearly 7 feet (213 centimeters) (Sharpe, 1997).

What drives the increase in circulating sex steroids during puberty? The initial rise in androgen levels, which triggers the appearance of pubic and axillary hair in both sexes, is due to an increase in androgen secretion by the adrenal glands. The subsequent main increase in sex steroids during puberty, however, is due to their secretion by the gonads. This gonadal secretion is driven by an increase in the release of the gonadotropins LH and FSH by the anterior lobe of the pituitary gland.

Gonadotropin secretion is triggered, in turn, by an increase in the pulsatile secretion of GnRH by the hypothalamus (see Chapter 4). This increase is a key event in puberty (Figure 5.27). The rest of the body seems to be primed from early childhood to heed the call of GnRH (Box 5.9); only the lack of GnRH prevents puberty from taking place at 2 or 3 years of age. Thus, we would like to know why GnRH secretion increases when it does, rather than earlier or later.

The Body May Signal Its Readiness for Puberty to the Brain

One theoretical possibility is that the hypothalamus possesses an internal clock that counts off the years since birth. That seems not to be the case, however. Instead, it has been suggested that GnRH secretion increases when the body has reached a certain critical weight, weight-to-height ratio, or body fat ratio (the proportion of body weight that is due to fat). The timing of puberty correlates better with body weight than with chronological age. In girls, the pubertal growth spurt begins at an average weight of 30 kg (66 lbs). In boys, puberty seems to be triggered at a higher body weight than in girls: about 55 kg (121 lbs).

Menarche occurs at an average weight of 47 kg (103 lbs) in Western countries, but at a significantly lower weight in some developing countries, such as India (Rao et al., 1998). In any given culture, somewhat obese girls tend to experience menarche earlier than thin girls, and very thin girls may not experience menarche at all (**primary amenorrhea**). Furthermore, if women lose most of their body fat after puberty—as can happen during famines, as a consequence of eating disorders such as **anorexia nervosa,** or even as a result of extreme athletic activity—their menstrual cycles may cease (**secondary amenorrhea**).

How might the brain know when the body has reached a certain weight or composition? One hypothesis involves the hormone **leptin,** a peptide hormone that is secreted by fat cells (Kiess et al., 2000). In general, leptin levels in the blood provide an indication of how much fat the body has accumulated. It would make sense if a puberty-inducing signal were derived from fat cells, especially in girls, because a girl should not become

Box 5.9 Biology of Sex

Atypical Development: Precocious and Delayed Puberty

Puberty has generally been considered **precocious** if the appearance of pubic hair or breasts, or enlargement of the testicles, begins before age 8 (in girls) or age 9 (in boys) (Blondell et al., 1999). These criteria may no longer be realistic, for girls in the United States at least, since 7 percent of white girls and 27 percent of African-American girls now have breasts or pubic hair at age 7 (Herman-Giddens et al., 1997). Recent guidelines have suggested that girls should be evaluated for precocious puberty if they have pubic hair or breast development before age 7 (white girls) or before age 6 (African-American girls) (Kaplowitz & Oberfield, 1999). Older girls (e.g., age 8) should be evaluated only if special circumstances apply, such as an unduly rapid progression through the stages of puberty. Criteria for measuring the onset of precocious puberty for other ethnic groups have yet to be developed.

Most cases of precocious puberty are **central** (meaning that puberty is driven by the hypothalamus and pituitary gland in the normal endocrinological manner) and **idiopathic** (meaning that the condition is not caused by some other identifiable disease or defect). Some cases, however, are caused by tumors at or near the base of the brain. Puberty may also be triggered by disorders affecting the gonads.

Besides potentially causing psychological and social problems, precocious puberty can adversely affect a child's final height. Affected children may initially grow faster than normal, but once the pubertal growth spurt ends, they are likely to be overtaken and left behind by their peers. The earlier puberty begins, the shorter the individual is likely to be in adulthood. Girls who enter puberty at the low end of the normal range (say, at 7 or 8) suffer little, if any, loss of adult height because their early entry into puberty is partially compensated by an increased duration of the pubertal growth spurt (Shangold et al., 1989). This is partly why the recent guidelines exclude these girls.

Idiopathic central precocious puberty can be treated with a GnRH analog such as leuprolide (Lupron). You might think that this would be exactly the wrong drug to give, since GnRH normally *triggers* puberty. Recall, however, that GnRH's normal action depends on its *pulsatile* secretion. If a GnRH analog is administered in the form of monthly depot injections, which maintain constant high levels in the blood, it suppresses the secretion of pituitary gonadotropins and hence the secretion of the gonadal steroids. Growth hormone is sometimes also administered. Although the use of these drugs has been somewhat controversial, they now appear to be quite safe and effective.

Puberty is considered **delayed** if the early signs of puberty do not appear by age 13 (sometimes 14) in girls or by age 14 in boys. Delayed puberty is commoner in boys than in girls; it is usually idiopathic, and in this case puberty usually eventually starts spontaneously. It is sometimes possible to kick-start the process with a short course of testosterone treatment. Brain tumors can also cause delayed puberty.

A rare but fascinating cause of delayed puberty is **Kallmann's syndrome.** In this congenital syndrome, delayed puberty is coupled with the inability to smell (**anosmia**), and sometimes with other developmental anomalies. This coupling is a clue to an odd developmental history. It turns out that the GnRH neurons of the hypothalamus are not generated in the brain at all; instead, they are generated in a region of the ectoderm that gives rise to the olfactory mucosa. These neurons migrate into the brain during embryonic life, following the course of the olfactory nerves. In Kallmann's syndrome, the ingrowth of the olfactory nerves is prevented, and so the GnRH neurons remain stuck in the olfactory mucosa, where they are unable to participate in neuroendocrine regulation. This syndrome, like idiopathic delayed puberty, is usually treated with testosterone replacement, which may need to be continued for life.

---

reproductively mature until she has accumulated the energy stores necessary to sustain pregnancy.

Supporting the idea that leptin triggers puberty is the finding that children suffering from a mutation in the gene for the leptin receptor do not enter puberty (Clement et al., 1998). In boys, a rapid rise in leptin levels occurs just before the initial pubertal rise in circulating testosterone (Mantzoros et al., 1997). This finding is also consistent with a role for leptin in triggering puberty. The fact that leptin levels undergo a surge, however, rather than simply tracking total body fat in a linear fashion, suggests that further, as yet unknown regulatory mechanisms are at work.

Dietary Changes May Be the Reason Puberty Is Beginning Earlier

With these insights into the mechanisms that trigger puberty, can we understand why puberty has been occurring at ever younger ages over the last century or so, as described above? The leading hypothesis is that a progressive *change in diet* over this period has allowed children to reach a body weight that triggers puberty at earlier and earlier ages. In particular, the introduction of cheap, calorie-dense manufactured foods has allowed children not merely to grow faster but also, often, to become moderately or severely obese. These changes could be a large part of the reason for the changing age of puberty, but they may not be the entire reason; for one thing, body weight, though a better indicator than chronological age, is still far from being a precise predictor of the time of puberty. Also, even children of average weight seem to be entering puberty earlier than their predecessors.

Another hypothesis is that **endocrine disruptors** (hormone-like pollutants in the environment; see Box 4.4) are causing children to enter puberty early. In one study, a group of children whose prenatal exposure to DDE (an estrogenic breakdown product of the pesticide DDT) and PCBs had been measured was followed until puberty (Gladen et al., 2000). The children with high prenatal exposure did not enter puberty earlier than the others. In contrast to this negative result, a group at the University of Puerto Rico found that girls diagnosed with precocious puberty on that island (where the condition is unusually prevalent) had much greater levels of phthalates (industrial plasticizers) in their blood than girls who entered puberty later (Colon et al., 2000). The hypothesis of a role for endocrine disruptors in the decreasing age at puberty is a topic of continuing study, but is far from established.

A third possibility, and one that has received almost no attention, is that *genes* favoring early puberty are spreading in the population. It is known that genetic differences among individuals influence the age at which they enter puberty (Meyer et al., 1991). In the past, the spread of genes favoring early puberty might have been held in check by the poor survival of children who were born to very young parents. Better medical care and nutrition has changed that pattern. Whether the improved survival of these children has had any significant effect on the distribution of genes favoring early puberty, however, is an open question.

Summary

1. Human development involves the interaction of genes with each other, with the fetal environment, with postnatal life experiences, and with a certain amount of randomness.

2. A fertilized ovum immediately begins a series of cell divisions, becoming a conceptus. At the blastocyst stage, when the conceptus has developed a central cavity, it implants in the wall of the uterus and secretes human chorionic gonadotropin to prevent regression of the maternal corpus luteum. Pregnancy is established at this point. After forming the extraembryonic membranes, the remaining tissue of the conceptus gives rise to the embryo. Embryonic development involves developmental genes, morphogenetic movements, cell migration, cell death, progressive restriction of cell fate, and cell differentiation.

3. By about 7 weeks after conception the embryo has developed its body plan and most of its major organs, and is known as a fetus. Further fetal development involves growth and the gradual onset of function in the various organ systems. The fetus's cardiovascular system is adapted to fetal life and is quickly reorganized at birth.

4. Sex is usually determined by the sex chromosomes: the XX pattern causes female development and the XY pattern causes male development. The key player in male development is the gene *SRY*, on the Y chromosome, which induces the embryo's genital ridges to become testes. In female embryos, which lack *SRY*, the X-linked gene *DAX-1* directs the genital ridges to become ovaries. Anomalous sex chromosome patterns include XXY, which causes Klinefelter's syndrome, and XO, which causes Turner's syndrome.

5. The male and female internal reproductive tracts develop from different precursors, the Wolffian and Müllerian ducts. In nearly all XY embryos, the testes secrete anti-Müllerian hormone (AMH), which causes the Müllerian ducts to regress, and androgens, which cause the Wolffian ducts to develop further and produce the male internal anatomy. In XY embryos lacking functional androgen receptors (androgen insensitivity syndrome), neither the male nor the female reproductive tract develops. In XX embryos (normal females), the lack of AMH allows the Müllerian ducts to develop further, and the lack of androgens allows the Wolffian duct to regress, producing the female internal anatomy.

6. The external genitalia of the two sexes develop from common precursors. The urethral folds give rise to the labia minora in females and to the shaft of the penis in males. The genital swellings give rise to the labia majora in females and the scrotum in males. The genital tubercle forms the external portion of the clitoris in females and the glans of the penis in males. Male-typical development of the external genitalia requires the presence of testosterone and its conversion to 5α-dihydrotestosterone

(DHT). In female fetuses that are exposed to high levels of androgens (as in congenital adrenal hyperplasia), and in male fetuses that lack androgen receptors (androgen insensitivity syndrome) or that cannot convert testosterone to DHT (5α-reductase deficiency), the external genitalia will be sex-atypical or sex-reversed.

7. Both ovaries and testes descend from their original lumbar position during fetal life. The ovaries descend into the pelvis, on either side of the uterus. The testes descend into the pelvis and then through the developing inguinal canal into the scrotum. If the testes fail to descend by soon after birth, spermatogenesis may be impaired; there is also an increased risk of testicular cancer after puberty.

8. Exposure to sex hormones during fetal life is directly or indirectly responsible for the sexual differentiation of the central nervous system. These hormones cause the development of sexually dimorphic structures and circuits, and by doing so (at least in experimental animals), influence the kinds of sexual behaviors that are exhibited in adulthood. The effects of hormones on behavior are thought to occur in two main phases: organizational effects during prenatal brain development, and activational (triggering) effects in adulthood. In some brain systems, however, hormones may influence neural structure even in adulthood.

9. External factors also influence prenatal sexual development. These factors may include drugs, such as synthetic sex hormones and alcohol, as well as maternal stress. After birth, social factors influence the development of the brain and adult sexual behavior, in animal studies at least.

10. Puberty is the transition from childhood to sexual maturity. It is marked by further development of the reproductive tracts and external genitalia, the appearance of secondary sexual characteristics (e.g., breasts, facial hair), signs of functional sexual maturity (onset of menstruation, ejaculation), and a growth spurt followed by cessation of growth. In the United States, puberty begins earlier in girls than in boys, and earlier in African-American than in white girls. Precocious and delayed puberty can usually be treated medically, if necessary.

11. Puberty is caused by a rise in the circulating levels of adrenal and gonadal sex steroids and growth hormone. Gonadal secretion is triggered by a rise in pituitary gonadotropins, which, in turn, is triggered by the onset of pulsatile secretion of gonadotropin-releasing hormone (GnRH) from the hypothalamus. It is thought that the prime trigger for puberty is the attainment of a critical body weight, weight-to-height ratio, or body fat index. The body may communicate this information to the hypothalamus by means of the hormone leptin.

12. In Western countries, puberty has been starting at progressively younger ages over the last 150 years. The most likely reason is a progressive change in nutritional practices, which have led to more rapid weight gain during childhood. Environmental pollutants or genetic changes in the population could be playing a contributory role.

Discussion Questions

1. Imagine that you have just become the proud parent of a newborn baby. Everything went perfectly until the nurse-midwife and pediatrician told you that the baby does not have complete and normal genitalia. The baby is intersexed—it has some genital characteristics of females and some of males. Would this child be stigmatized and disadvantaged? How? Consider what you and your partner would do and why.

2. If you or your partner were pregnant and learned that you would have a baby with Turner's or Klinefelter's syndrome, what would you decide to do about it? What would be the disadvantages of such abnormalities for your child? Argue the reasons for your choice.

3. Puberty is occurring earlier than in the past. Do you think that this creates a social problem? What age of entry into puberty do you think should be considered unacceptably early and in need of treatment? Do you think it would be a good idea to try to increase the average age of puberty by, for example, restricting children's diets?

Web Resources

National Institute of Child Health and Human Development—Turner Syndrome
turners.nichd.nih.gov

The University of New South Wales embryology site
http://anatomy.med.unsw.edu.au/cbl/embryo/embryo.htm

National Institute of Child Health and Human Development—Understanding Klinefelter
Syndrome www.nichd.nih.gov/publications/pubs/klinefelter.htm

Bodies Like Ours (support and information for people with ambiguous genitalia)
www.bodieslikeours.org

Recommended Reading

Larsen, W. J. (1998). *Essentials of human embryology.* Churchill Livingstone.
Pinsky, L., Erickson, R. P., & Schimke, R. N. (1999). *Genetic disorders of human sexual development.* Oxford University Press.

chapter 6

Many gender differences, including boys' preference for rough-and-tumble play, emerge early in childhood.

Gender

*I*n the previous chapters, we discussed sex differences in bodily structure and function and how they develop. We now turn to a topic that is at once more interesting and more controversial: that of sex differences in mental life. Do men and women differ in their cognitive skills, sexual strategies, personalities, behaviors, goals, or values? And if so, how do such differences develop? Are they the products of biological processes, such as the differing hormonal environments that males and females experience before birth? Or do they result from the way our parents treat us in infancy and childhood, or from our own efforts to make sense of the world? Do they perhaps result from a delicate interplay of many factors? And, are they fixed or malleable—over the history of the human race, across cultures, or over the course of a single life span? The answers to such questions are not merely of theoretical interest. They are also deeply relevant to social policy, affecting how we educate our children, how we treat wrongdoers, and how we attempt to develop a more just society.

What Is Gender?

The word **gender,** which derives from the Old French word *gendre* ("kind"), was originally used almost exclusively in a grammatical context: it referred to the two or three classes of nouns ("masculine," "feminine," "neuter") that complicate the learning of German, Spanish, and other languages. In the 1960s, feminists and sexologists borrowed the term to refer to the subjective aspects of male–female differences—aspects that were not well described by the term "sex."

Since then, the word "gender" has gained a wide currency (see Figure 1.1), but its usage varies. In one popular usage, it refers to the male–female difference; in other words, it is used simply as a euphemism for "sex." Academics prefer to maintain a distinction between "sex" and "gender," but they don't always agree on what that distinction is. Some use "sex" to refer to male–female differences that result from biological processes and "gender" to refer to those that result from social or cultural processes (Gentile, 1993). The problem with this approach is that it presupposes that we *know* the causes of male–female differences before we even study them.

A more common practice, and the one we adopt in this book, is to use "sex" to refer to the demographic categories of male and female—categories that are based ultimately on genital anatomy. "Gender" is used to mean the entire constellation of mental and behavioral traits that, to a greater or lesser degree, differ between males and females—*regardless* of how those differences arise. Thus, gender is whatever we can say *about* the sexes, having defined the sexes anatomically.

Note the phrase "to a greater or lesser degree." Some traits are "highly gendered," meaning that the differences between the sexes in those traits are very marked. An example is a person's subjective sense of maleness or femaleness, a trait called **gender identity.** The great majority of males have a secure identity as males, and the great majority of females have a secure identity as females. There are exceptions—transexual and transgendered persons—but they form a very small percentage of the population.

An example of a trait that is highly gendered, but less so than gender identity, is **sexual orientation**—the direction of an individual's sexual attractions. The majority of men are predominantly attracted to women, and the majority of women are predominantly attracted to men, but exceptions are common, numbering several percent of the population.

An example of a trait that is much more weakly gendered is mathematical reasoning. On average, boys outperform girls on tests of this cognitive skill, but it takes the testing of large numbers of children, and the application of statistical tests to the results, to demonstrate a difference; presented with the test score of some randomly chosen child, a psychologist could not tell whether that child was a girl or a boy.

Also, a trait may be highly gendered in one society, or at one historical period , and much less so, or not at all, in another society or at another historical period. Modes of dress provide obvious examples: In nineteenth-century America, dress codes for men and women were strictly enforced by custom and by the law. Now, unisex clothing is widely accepted, at least in informal circumstances. The occupations and incomes of men and women are other examples. But even more basic behavioral traits, such as the positions taken by men and women during coitus, have varied greatly across time and across cultures.

Thus, in discussing gendered traits, we will try wherever possible to give some idea of how markedly they differ between the sexes and how variable or invariable those differences are between cultures. Without such information, one risks becoming mired in trivia, because almost any aspect of mental life will show *some* degree of gender difference if one studies it in sufficient detail. Gender permeates every aspect of our lives, but it *rules* some aspects and merely *colors* others.

Gender Research Has Emerged from a History of Sexism and Stereotypes

In considering differences between the sexes, it would be foolish to ignore certain historical realities: the concentration of economic and political power in the hands of men, and the long tradition of prejudice against women. In 1792, when Mary Wollstonecraft published her *Vindication of the Rights of Women*, it was almost universally accepted that men alone had the intellect, personality, and moral qualities required for public life. Women's qualities, it was agreed, suited them only for nurturing and sustaining roles within the family.

Tremendous changes have overtaken Western countries since Wollstonecraft's time. Considering the opportunities that are open to American women today, we may be tempted to view smugly or judgmentally the way women are still treated in some more traditional regions of the world. But a moment's reflection should show us that there is unfinished business here at home. A nation that cannot agree on the premise that "equality of rights under the law shall not be denied or abridged…on account of sex" (the Equal Rights Amendment to the U.S. Constitution, which was left unratified in 1982), that pays men and women unequally, and that places few women in positions of power or influence is hardly a paragon of gender equity. For these reasons, we should suspect that **stereotypes**—false or overgeneralized beliefs about classes of people—still contaminate views of gender, even within the academic community.

In reaction to this history of prejudice, some researchers and feminists have tended to deny the reality of gender differences altogether, or have attributed them entirely to cultural forces rather than to any underlying biological predispositions. For example, the anthropologist Margaret Mead (1901–1978) wrote an influential book titled *Sex and Temperament in Three Primitive Societies* (Mead, 1935), in which she described three societies in New Guinea. Among the Mundugumor, Mead reported, both men and women were "masculine" by Western standards. Among the Arapesh, both men and women were "feminine." And among the Tchambuli, gender was actually reversed from what Western societies are familiar with: women were "masculine" and men were "feminine." Gender, Mead was saying, varies radically from one society to another, and therefore must be determined by culture.

Similarly, during the ferment of feminist thought and culture in the 1970s, many writers emphasized the role of culture or socialization in the molding of gender, to the exclusion of other factors. Germaine Greer, for example, in her 1971 book *The Female Eunuch*, stated categorically that there were no differences between the brains of men and women (Greer, 1971).

Today, most gender researchers consider such views extreme. Mead's research methods, and the interpretations placed on her research by later feminist authors, have been criticized (Freeman, 1983; Goldberg, 1991). Greer's assertion about the identity of male and female brains has been shown to be incorrect (see Chapters 2 and 4). It may be that Mead, Greer, and some other feminist thinkers felt so strongly the need to undermine traditional notions of "biological inevitability" that they were driven to an extreme antibiological position that the evidence did not warrant.

Yet "biology" is far from "inevitability." In fact, several Nobel Prize–winning scientists have elucidated how life experiences modify the nervous system: Harvard neuroscientists David Hubel and Torsten Wiesel, who shared the 1981 prize, discovered that visual experience modifies anatomical connections in the visual regions of the cerebral cortex, and Columbia University physiologist Eric Kandel won the prize in 2000 for his studies of how learning is encoded by changes at synapses. The evidence that we discuss here suggests that multiple factors, including both innate predispositions and life experiences, interact in the development of gender-related traits, as they do with most aspects of our mental development.

Mary Wollstonecraft (1759–1797) was an Anglo-Irish radical thinker who demanded full political and social equality for women, derided marriage as "legalized prostitution," and (in a posthumously published novel, *Maria*) spoke up for women's right to sexual and romantic feelings. She did eventually marry, but died of puerperal fever (see Chapter 10) a few days after the birth of her daughter Mary (who later married the poet Shelley and wrote *Frankenstein*).

Gender Identity Lies at the Core of Our Personhood

In its simplest conception, a person's gender identity is his or her response to "Do you feel as if you are a man or a woman?" or some similar question. More than 99.9 percent of people will give an answer that is consistent with their genital anatomy. Gender identity is so central to our sense of ourselves, so securely established, and (for most of us) so concordant with our anatomy that it is hard for us to think about it as a mental trait at all. It seems indistinguishable from simply announcing what kind of genitals we have.

Yet there are rare individuals—perhaps one in 12,000 adult males and one in 30,000 adult females (van Kesteren et al., 1996)—who give a discordant answer to that question:

anatomical men who say they feel like women and anatomical women who say they feel like men. Such **transexual** (or transsexual—see Glossary) individuals make us realize that there must be something more to gender identity than just reporting on one's genitals.

For the great majority of you who are not transexual, the separateness of gender identity from anatomical sex can be understood by imagining yourself waking up one morning in a body of the other sex. Very likely you would be horrified, and would move heaven and earth to get back into your "right" body. That is the kind of mental experience transexuals deal with throughout their lives, unless and until they undergo sex reassignment surgery. The unhappiness caused by discordance between anatomical sex and gender identity is called **gender dysphoria.**

Gender May Not Be an "Either/Or" Phenomenon

In many non-Western cultures, the existence of individuals who are neither traditionally masculine nor traditionally feminine has long been recognized and accepted, and such **gender-variant individuals** may be given a specific name and accorded a distinct role in society (Figure 6.1). We will have much more to say about them in our discussion of sexual minorities (Chapter 13). What is interesting about these individuals for our purposes here is that many of them adopt behaviors that are not entirely typical either of males or of females. Their clothing, for example, may be a mixture of men's and women's attire. This observation suggests that gender, when given free expression, may be more of a continuum than a dichotomy, and that not all gender-variant persons are out-and-out transexuals.

Assessment of gender   A similar conclusion has been reached by cognitive scientists in the United States. Sandra Bem, for example, developed a **sex role inventory**—a set of adjectives that describe gender-related personality traits (Bem, 1974) (Figure 6.2). When she administered this inventory to a large number of people, Bem found that their scores did not fall into two completely separate categories, but instead were distributed across a continuum. Furthermore, rather than conceptualizing gender as a unidimensional continuum (from masculine to feminine), Bem preferred to think of gender in two dimensions. One dimension is masculinity–unmasculinity, and includes the assessment of stereotypically "masculine" traits, such as assertiveness. The other is femininity–unfemininity, and includes stereotypically "feminine" traits such as sensitivity. Thus, a particular individual could be high on masculinity and low on femininity ("masculine"), high on femininity and low on masculinity ("feminine"), low on both masculinity and femininity ("undifferentiated"), or high on both masculinity and femininity ("psychologically androgynous"). The Bem inventory has been criticized on a number of grounds—for collapsing what may be multifactorial aspects of gender into two dimensions, for example (Spence & Helmreich, 1978; Twenge, 1999)—but it is still one of the main tests used in studies of gender.

Psychologically androgynous persons can be of either anatomical sex. Some studies suggest that, because of their combination of qualities such as assertiveness and nurturance, these individuals have greater flexibility, social competence, and self-esteem than people who are distinctly masculine or feminine (Katz & Ksansnak, 1994; Kirchmeyer, 1996; Shimonaka et al., 1997). Other studies, however, suggest that masculinity (in either anatomical sex) is more closely associated with overall emotional adjustment and self-esteem than is psychological androgyny

Figure 6.1 Zuni We'wha. In this photograph of a Zuni Indian group, taken around 1890, the women and girls are on the left and the men and boys are on the right. Between them stands the imposing figure of We'wha, dressed in a mixture of male and female attire. We'wha, though anatomically male, was a "two-spirit person," so called because s/he manifested elements of both masculinity and femininity.

1. Self-reliant____	16. Strong personality____	31. Makes decisions easily____	46. Aggressive____
2. Yielding____	17. Loyal____	32. Compassionate____	47. Gullible____
3. Helpful____	18. Unpredictable____	33. Sincere____	48. Inefficient____
4. Defends beliefs____	19. Forceful____	34. Self-sufficient____	49. Acts as a leader____
5. Cheerful____	20. Feminine____	35. Eager to soothe hurt feelings____	50. Childlike____
6. Moody____	21. Reliable____	36. Conceited____	51. Adaptable____
7. Independent____	22. Analytical____	37. Dominant____	52. Individualistic____
8. Shy____	23. Sympathetic____	38. Soft-spoken____	53. Doesn't use harsh language____
9. Conscientious____	24. Jealous____	39. Likable____	54. Unsystematic____
10. Athletic____	25. Has leadership ability____	40. Masculine____	55. Competitive____
11. Affectionate____	26. Sensitive to other's needs____	41. Warm____	56. Loves children____
12. Theatrical____	27. Truthful____	42. Solemn____	57. Tactful____
13. Assertive____	28. Willing to take risks____	43. Willing to take a stand____	58. Ambitious____
14. Flatterable____	29. Understanding____	44. Tender____	59. Gentle____
15. Happy____	30. Secretive____	45. Friendly____	60. Conventional____

Figure 6.2 Bem Sex Role Inventory. For each of the following items, rate yourself on how much the characteristic describes you. Use a scale from 1 (never or almost never true) to 7 (always or nearly always true). See the instructions for scoring in Discussion Question 2 (page 187).

(Jones et al., 1978; Olds & Shaver, 1980). The latter finding is hardly surprising, given the generally higher valuation of masculine than feminine traits in our society and many others.

Trend toward gender diversity   There are also social trends in the United States that make it clear that gender identity is not an either/or affair (either "normal" or "transexual"). In the past, almost all transexuals subscribed to the notion that they had to be either masculine or feminine. Typically, they would live initially in the role of their anatomical sex, then change sexes and live as the other sex. Once the change was accomplished, they would often go to great lengths to conceal their history, especially if it was possible for them to "pass" in their new sex. In part, this process may have been imposed by society's rigid sense of gender classification. Now, especially in sexually liberal communities such as San Francisco, gender-atypical people exhibit quite a range of appearances and life histories. Some may seek hormone treatment and sex reassignment surgery, some may not; some may try hard to "pass" as the other sex, others may be quite unabashed about not passing; some may be consistent in their gender role, others may have one gender role for the office and another for a night on the town. Although numbers are hard to come by, the prevalence of this more broadly defined gender atypicality must be considerably higher than the 1-in-12,000 or 1-in-30,000 figures mentioned above. To encompass this diversity, and to get away from an exclusively medical model of gender atypicality, the term **transgender** is becoming increasingly popular. We will have more to say about this in Chapter 13.

Transexuals Vary in Sexual Orientation

Returning to the medical model, however, two main developmental histories of transexuality have been described. In one kind of transexuality, a cluster of atypical gender traits is evident from childhood. In the other, transexuality is not linked to other gender-variant traits. The two kinds of transexuality often differ in sexual orientation, and they may have different causal mechanisms.

In Alain Berliner's 1997 film *Ma Vie en Rose*, an 8-year-old boy struggles to express his self-perceived identity as a girl. While some such children become transexual adults, more become homosexual adults who identify with their anatomical sex.

Classical transexuality   If we consider a **male-to-female** (or "**M2F**") transexual of this type, he is noticeably feminine from early childhood. He wishes to dress in girls' clothes, to wear his hair long, and to associate with girls, and he expresses the belief that he *is* a girl, or at least that he desires strongly to become one. At puberty, he is distressed by the emergence of male secondary sexual characteristics such as a beard, low voice, and muscular build, and may attempt to conceal them. He is sexually attracted to men, and desires to become a woman in part so as to be able to engage in heterosexual relationships with men. The converse applies to a **female-to-male** ("**F2M**") transexual of this type: as a young girl, she attempts to adopt the appearance and activities of a boy and feels that she is a boy, or wants to become one; at puberty she dislikes her breasts and other female characteristics, is sexually attracted to women, and desires to become a man in part so as to be able to engage in heterosexual relationships with women.

Such individuals have been referred to as **classical, type 1,** or **homosexual** transexuals. The use of the word "homosexual" in this context is somewhat confusing, however. It refers to the fact that these transexuals are sexually attracted to persons of the same anatomical sex as themselves, just as homosexual men and women are. The problem with the use of this term is twofold. First, transexual individuals do not *feel* as if they are homosexual and often resent being described as such. Rather, they feel like a heterosexual person of the other sex. Second, it means that if they undergo sex reassignment surgery, they experience a change in sexual orientation from homosexual to heterosexual—by definition—even though there is usually no actual change in the direction of their sexual attractions. Thus it is often clearer and more acceptable to describe a transexual's sexual orientation with the terms **androphilic** (attracted to males) or **gynephilic** (attracted to females).

Non-classical transexuals   For many years, classical transexuals were believed to be the *only* genuine transexuals, and gender reassignment clinics would not offer sex reassignment surgery unless the patient described a strongly cross-gendered history of the kind just described. Undoubtedly, this led to a degree of deception by patients who were anxious to have a sex change operation but who did not fit entirely into the classical transexual mold, and thus to an overestimate of how many transexuals fit that mold.

Non-classical transexuals are probably quite diverse, but many of them are **heterosexual** with respect to their anatomy at birth—in other words, they are gynephilic males and androphilic females. Quite often, these individuals do not have a markedly cross-gendered childhood. According to sexologist Ray Blanchard of the Clarke Institute of Psychiatry in Toronto, most gynephilic males who seek sex reassignment surgery do so because they are sexually aroused by the idea of themselves in a woman's body, including the possession of a vulva. Blanchard has named this condition **autogynephilia** (Blanchard, 1991, 1993). Autogynephilia, in Blanchard's conception, is a kind of **paraphilia**—sexual arousal by unusual objects or practices (see Chapter 14). It can be thought of as an extreme version of male **heterosexual transvestism**—sexual arousal by the wearing of women's clothes. Some gynephilic M2F transexuals, such as physician and sexologist Anne Lawrence (Lawrence, 1998), have spoken up in support of Blanchard's ideas; others have been critical, or fear that the concept of autogynephilia will make it harder for non-classical M2F transexuals to receive sex reassignment surgery. An F2M version of autogynephilia has not been described; this in itself would fit with the concept of autogynephilia as a paraphilia, since paraphilias are seen almost exclusively in men (see Chapter 14).

Sexual Orientation Should Be Viewed as an Aspect of Gender

Sexual orientation is usually defined as the direction of an individual's sexual attractions. A person may be disposed to experience sexual attraction to people of the other sex (**heterosexuality**), to both sexes (**bisexuality**), or to the same sex (**homosexuality**). In common speech, the terms **straight, bi,** and **gay** or **lesbian** are used in the same sense, though with slightly different connotations (see Chapter 13). Alternatively, as mentioned above, sexual orientation may be categorized as the disposition to be attracted to men (androphilia), to both sexes (bisexuality), or to women (gynephilia). Because sexual orientation is an aspect of sexual attraction, we will defer our main discussion of this trait until the next chapter, which is devoted to attraction.

At this point, we merely want to clarify the relationship between sexual orientation and gender. This relationship may be hard to see for a couple of reasons. First, the commonly used "heterosexual/homosexual" terminology implies that men and women do not differ greatly in sexual orientation: the majority of both men and women are heterosexual, and minorities are bisexual or homosexual. Thus, sexual orientation is not an obvious aspect of gender, since it doesn't differ between the sexes.

The heterosexual/homosexual terminology is grounded more in social attitudes than in scientific reality, however. Heterosexual women and heterosexual men have been grouped together largely because they are in the majority and because their sexual orientations are socially approved, but they do not resemble each other in the key attribute that defines their sexual orientation: heterosexual women are attracted to *men,* and heterosexual men are attracted to *women.* Similarly, homosexual women and men have been grouped together largely because they are in the minority and because their sexual orientation has been socially stigmatized, but they, too, are different from each other: homosexual women are attracted to women and homosexual men are attracted to men.

When we use the androphilic/gynephilic terminology, the gendered nature of sexual orientation becomes much more obvious: most men are gynephilic and most women are androphilic. In this conception, sexual orientation is a highly gendered trait, although not so highly gendered as gender identity.

Historical trends in the conceptualization of sexual orientation have also confused the relationship between sexual orientation and gender. At least until the end of the nineteenth century, homosexuality was thought of as a **gender inversion,** not very different from what we now call transexuality. In other words, homosexual men were thought of as resembling women in most psychological traits, and even in physical appearance. Conversely, lesbians were thought of as resembling men. Then, over the course of the twentieth century, a reaction to this view set in, driven in large part by gays and lesbians themselves. The distinction between homosexuality and transexuality was clarified, and the existence of gender-atypical traits in gay people (aside from their homosexuality) was minimized or completely denied.

In the next chapter we will make the case that the truth lies somewhere between these two extremes: gay people are certainly not transexuals or gender "inverts," but they do tend to have a variety of traits that are gender-atypical to some degree, including the traits of masculinity and femininity as assessed by Bem's sex role inventory. We see this argument as helping to make a broader case: that the various attributes that make up "gender" are partially correlated with one another, rather than varying independently or randomly. Thus, as mentioned above, M2F transexual men are much more likely to be androphilic than are non-transexual men, and gay men are much more likely to show some feminine traits than are heterosexual men, suggesting a correlation (though an incomplete one) between the traits of gender identity, sexual orientation, and other aspects of gender. Theories of gender should account for this correlation, as well as for the fact that the correlation is less than complete.

Men and Women Differ in a Variety of Cognitive and Personality Traits

Over the last three decades, more than 40,000 scientific studies have been devoted to mental differences (or the lack of them) between men and women (Collaer & Hines, 1995). The huge number of these studies, and the fact that they sometimes reported contradictory results, led to a situation in which it was possible to bolster almost any point of view by the selective citation of studies supporting that view. To escape from this situation, researchers applied the technique of **meta-analysis** (Rosenthal, 1991). In that technique, the data from all studies on a given topic are statistically combined. The results of such analyses are inherently more reliable than the individual studies on which they are based (Box 6.1).

Research Highlights

Measuring Sex Differences

Let's say we're investigating possible sex differences in verbal fluency. We administer a quantitative test of verbal fluency to a large number of men and women who, ideally, are drawn at random from the entire population of men and women, or from some defined subpopulation, such as college students. The distribution of results for each sex will approximately follow a bell-shaped curve (the **normal distribution**), but the **means** for the two distributions may differ (Figure A).

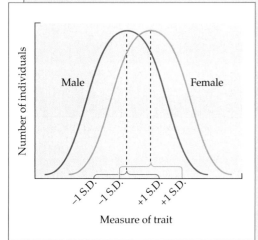

(A) Difference in means. These distributions show the values for some trait in which females tend to score higher than males. In this example, the difference between the means (the vertical lines) is about 80 percent of one standard deviation, giving an effect size, *d*, of about 0.8.

How meaningful is this difference in the means? Traditional statistical tests measure the **statistical significance** of the difference—that is, the probability that the difference is a chance result of sampling rather than reflecting a real difference in the entire population. But even tiny differences may be statistically significant if the number of subjects is very large. If the two distributions overlap greatly, such tiny differences are not very meaningful in any practical sense.

We therefore need a measure that relates the size of the difference in the means to the degree of dispersion within the two groups. A common measure of dispersion is the **standard deviation.** (Technically, this is the square root of the **variance,** which is the mean squared deviation of the individual values from the sample mean.) In a normally distributed population, about 68 percent of the individual values will fall within one standard deviation of the mean, and about 96 percent will fall within two standard deviations of the mean. The difference between the means of the two samples, divided by the pooled standard deviation, is called the **effect size (*d*)**. Thus, if *d* = 0.35, the pooled standard deviation is 35 percent of the difference between the means of the male and female samples.

An effect size of 0.1 or less is considered a trivial or nonexistent difference. An effect size of 0.2 is considered small. An effect size of 0.5 is considered moderate—it corresponds, for example, to a physical difference that is quite evident to the naked eye, such as the difference in height between 14-year-old and 18-year-old girls. An effect size of 0.8 or greater is considered large.

To combine the results of all published studies on sex differences in verbal fluency, researchers would assign a weight to the *d* value for each study that reflects the statistical properties of that study (such as the number of subjects), and then calculate the mean for the weighted *d* values of all the studies. This process is called **meta-analysis**.

If you inspect the curves in Figure A, you will see that the ratio of females to males becomes increasingly unbalanced toward either end of the combined distribution: most of the extreme values at one end are female and most of the extreme values at the other end are male. Thus, even when the *d* value is only moderate, processes that select individuals with extreme characteristics may turn up highly unbalanced numbers of males and females. In real life, such selection processes could include the hiring of people with outstanding abilities in a particular field, the imposition of the death penalty on extremely aggressive individuals, and the like.

Marked sex differences at the extremes of a distribution can also occur *without* any difference in the mean values for males and females, if the values for one sex are more dispersed than for the other (Figure B). In fact, some studies report that the variance in scores on a variety of traits is slightly greater for men than for women, meaning that both very high-scoring and very low-scoring individuals are more likely to be male than female (Hedges & Nowell, 1995).

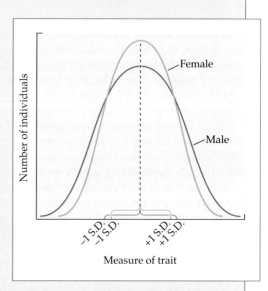

(B) Difference in dispersion. If the data for males are slightly more dispersed than for females, males will predominate at both ends of the distribution.

A second aspect of the study of sex differences that can be aided by statistical analysis is the search for common cognitive or psychological structures underlying data from a variety of different tests. Let's say that you have tested men and women on measures of mathematical reasoning, rapid calculation, visuospatial problem solving, number recall, verbal reasoning, verbal fluency, and word recall. Do these seven tests tap into seven independent psychological traits, or into a smaller number of underlying structures? And if the latter, what are they?

Such questions can be tackled by means of **factor analysis,** of which there are several different varieties. Briefly, your computer looks at all possible pairs of the tests (mathematical reasoning vs. rapid calculation, mathematical reasoning vs. number recall, etc.). For each pair, it measures the **correlation** between the scores on the two tests—that is, the extent to which an individual's score on one test predicts their score on the other. It thereby generates a **matrix** of correlations for all the pairs. From the matrix, the computer derives a number of independent (uncorrelated) factors, each of which accounts for part of the total interpair correlation. If there are indeed common underlying structures, there will be fewer factors than tests, and each factor will derive most of its **loading** (that is, its dependence on the interpair correlations) from some subset of the tests.

Taking the seven tests mentioned, it might be that one factor derives most of its loading from "mathematical reasoning,"

"rapid calculation," and "number recall." One might call this factor "general mathematical ability." A second factor might be "general verbal ability," and a third might be "general visuospatial ability." Alternatively, one factor might derive most of its loading from "mathematical reasoning," "verbal reasoning," and "visuospatial reasoning." One might call this factor "general reasoning ability." In this case, a second factor might be "general fluency" and a third might be "general memory ability."

The value of this approach is that it gets away from presuppositions about how mental skills are grouped, and instead allows the groupings to emerge from the data themselves. Once the factors have been identified, it is possible to calculate sex differences and effect sizes for the underlying factors rather than for the individual tests. Another benefit of factor analysis is that it facilitates the design of future test batteries so as to provide the greatest possible information about the underlying factors.

Cognitive Sex Differences Are Seen in Spatial Sense, Problem Solving, Language Skills, and Memory

Some reported sex differences are seen in aspects of mental life having to do with perception, motor performance, reasoning, judgments, knowledge, and memory—collectively referred to as **cognitive traits**. Others have to do with feelings, behavior (including sexual behavior), attitudes, goals, and values—traits that loosely cluster under the term **personality.**

Within the cognitive domain, men outperform women in some **visuospatial skills**. An example of such a skill is the mental rotation of three-dimensional objects (Figure 6.3), for which substantial effect sizes ($d = 0.6$; see Box 6.1 for an explanation of effect size) have been reported (Voyer et al., 1995). Other visuospatial tasks at which men do well include throwing accuracy ($d > 1.0$; Watson & Kimura, 1991) and navigation or route finding, especially where route finding requires reference to compass directions, distant landmarks, or maps (Beatty & Troster, 1987; Ward et al., 1986; Galea & Kimura, 1993) (Figure 6.4). (Of course, men's superior navigational skills may be counterbalanced by their legendary inability to stop and ask for directions!)

Women navigate as well as or better than men when the route-finding task requires reference to nearby landmarks. This difference may reflect a general female superiority in memorization of the location of objects; for example, women do better than men at a card game in which players have to memorize the locations of like pairs within an array of facedown cards (McBurney et al., 1997). They also outperform men at tasks in which the object is to identify objects whose positions have been switched from one presentation to the next (Silverman & Eals, 1992) (Figure 6.5A,B).

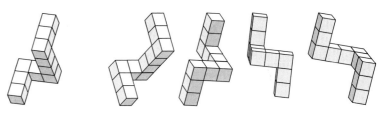

Figure 6.3 Mental rotation task. From the four images at right, the subject is asked to pick the two depicted objects that could be rotated in space to match the object shown at left. Men generally outperform women in this kind of task.

Answer: The first and third images.

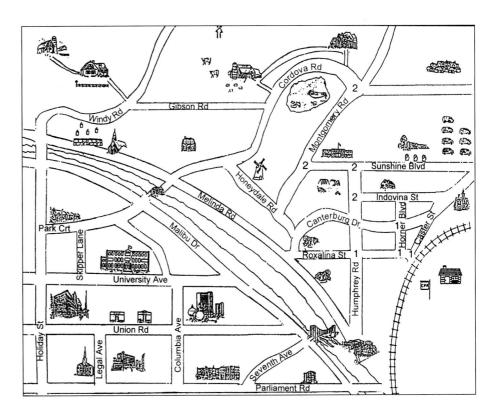

Figure 6.4 Route learning. A reduced-size representation of a tabletop map used by Galea and Kimura to test route-learning ability. Men learned routes on this map faster than women, but women recalled more of the landmarks and street names. (From Galea and Kimura, 1993.)

Figure 6.5A Test of object location memory. Study this picture for 1 minute and try to impress the position of every item on your memory. Then look at Figure 6.5B on page 172. (From Silverman and Eals, 1992.)

Another kind of visuospatial task at which women outperform men involves the rapid and fine manipulation of objects, such as picking up washers (the hardware gizmos, not laundry machines!) and placing them over pegs in as short a time as possible (Nicholson & Kimura, 1996). This difference may be part of a generally better control of the hand and finger musculature in women than in men.

Males (both adult men and boys) outperform females in some aspects of **mathematical ability**, especially mathematical reasoning or problem solving. Thus, scores on the math component of the Scholastic Aptitude Test (SAT) consistently favor males ($d = 0.5$), with little or no change over the years (Reisberg, 1998). This difference is probably due largely to the problem-solving aspects of the SAT, because tests focusing specifically on mathematical problem solving also favor males, while tests focusing on calculating skill favor females, at least among children (Hyde et al., 1990).

Females outperform males in some aspects of **verbal skills**. These aspects include verbal fluency (e.g., rapidly naming many articles of furniture, or words beginning with "b"), spelling, grammar, and verbal memory (Halpern, 1992; Hedges & Nowell, 1995). The differences are small to moderate ($d = 0.1$–0.4), being highest for verbal memory. Women do not have a higher general "verbal intelligence" than men (Hyde & Linn, 1988).

Are there underlying cognitive structures that contribute to the reported sex differences in the performance of the cognitive tasks just listed? Researchers at the University of Western Ontario and at Johns Hopkins University used **factor analysis** (see Box 6.1) to look for underlying structures in the test scores of 187,000 German medical school applicants (Stumpf & Jackson, 1994). They reported finding three factors, which they interpreted as "reasoning," "perceptual speed," and "memory." The reasoning factor favored men ($d = 0.56$), the memory factor favored women ($d = 0.5$), and the perceptual speed factor did not differ between the sexes.

Studies of this kind, which focus on high-achieving individuals, do not necessarily generalize to the entire population of men and women. For example, the apparent male superiority in reasoning could reflect a larger *variability* in reasoning skill in men than in women, rather than a difference in *mean* ability (see Box 6.1). In fact, studies that have searched for underlying factors are not in complete agreement about the nature of those factors or the degree of the sex differences in those factors. Still, it appears that there *are* underlying structures that influence sex differences in a broad way, and that they do not correspond to "math ability" "spatial ability," and "verbal ability" as one might have imagined, but instead cut across those skills.

Is there a difference in **general intelligence** between women and men? There have been claims for a slight difference favoring men, perhaps in the range of four IQ points in standardized tests such as the Wechsler Adult Intelligence Scale (Alexopoulos, 1996; Lynn, 1994). It should be noted that, even if this is true, such differences are minute in terms of effect sizes. Also, the battery of subtests in standard IQ tests is chosen in such a way as to *minimize* sex differences: if one wanted, one could select these subtests so as to produce sizable IQ differences favoring *either* sex. It is probably more useful to think of "intelligence" as a collection of factors, some better developed in women and some in men, rather than as a single general factor.

Personality Differences Include Aggressiveness, Self-Esteem, Emotional Communication, and Values

In the realm of personality, the trait that has received the most attention is **aggressiveness.** Men score higher than women on written tests of aggressiveness, show more verbal and physical aggressiveness in real-life situations, and are more likely to commit violent crimes, both in the United States and across most cultures (Buss & Perry, 1992; Eagly & Steffen, 1986; Ellis, 1988; Hyde, 1986). In the United States, women constitute only 12 percent of persons arrested for murder, and less than 1 percent of persons subjected to capital punishment (Streib, 2001). Aggressiveness shades into other traits, such as assertiveness and competitiveness, which are also more developed in men than in women (Feingold, 1994; Gladue & Bailey, 1995). Effect sizes for aggression-related traits are usually moderate, in the range of 0.4–0.5.

Another set of traits in which men score higher than women are those of **self-esteem,** self-evaluation, and sense of well-being (Kling et al., 1999). Conversely, women are more likely than men to be anxious, to show depressive symptoms, or to be clinically depressed; this tendency is seen worldwide (Weissman & Olfson, 1995). Although well documented, sex differences in these traits tend to be quite small, with effect sizes in the area of 0.2–0.3. Also, it's possible that men feel compelled to put a better face on things that do women, thus giving researchers the impression that they have higher self-esteem, while inwardly they may have performance anxiety and other problems associated with male–male competition. In other words, the reliability of self-report data in this area is uncertain.

Women appear to have greater **emotional sensitivity** than men. They are better at decoding other people's emotions from facial expressions or voice quality, are more expressive of their own emotions, and are more likely than men to take another person's perspective (Eisenberg et al., 1996). Based on self-descriptions, women are more sympathetic than men, but this may not translate into more behavioral expressions of sympathy among women (Eisenberg & Lennon, 1983). Thus, it is possible that women's and men's self-descriptions are influenced by gender stereotypes.

There may be differences in the **moral sense** of men and women. According to Harvard psychologist Carol Gilligan, author of an influential 1982 book, *In a Difference Voice* (Gilligan, 1982), women's moral universe is based on caring, whereas men's is based more on justice and rules. Gilligan cites Portia's famous speech in Shakespeare's *Merchant of Venice* ("The quality of mercy is not strained...") as epitomizing the moral perspective of women.

Some scientific support for Gilligan's point of view comes from studies in which women's and men's values are surveyed by means of written questionnaires. Thus, when women and men are asked to rate the desirability of a variety of traits, the traits rated higher by women include "sensitive," "kind," "understanding," "affectionate," "helpful," and "sincere." When asked to choose the more desirable of two traits, such as "cooperative vs. competitive," "patience vs. determination," "helping vs. being in charge," women tend to choose the more caring alternative. This sex difference has been observed both in the United States and in several Asian countries (Stimpson et al., 1991). A recent

Wanton violence is a predominantly male activity. Here, English and Turkish soccer hooligans do battle in the streets of Copenhagen.

Figure 6.5B Test of object location memory. Having memorized Figure 6.5A as best you can, look at this picture and identify all the pairs of objects that have swapped places. Women typically do better than men at this task. (However, there's plenty of overlap, so if you and an other-sex friend fail to conform to the pattern, you needn't worry!) (From Silverman and Eals, 1992.)

meta-analysis suggests that sex differences in moral reasoning exist, but are small in magnitude ($d = 0.2$–0.3), much smaller than the differences in moral reasoning that exist between cultures (Jaffee & Hyde, 2000). Studies of moral development in children have found little evidence for gender differences (Walker, 1989).

When it comes to contentious moral issues of practical significance, such as abortion, sex differences are small: a 2000 poll found that roughly similar proportions of U.S. men and women are pro-life and pro-choice (Gallup Organization, 2000). Men do support

Anger

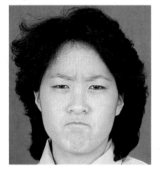

Sadness

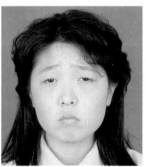

Happiness

Fear

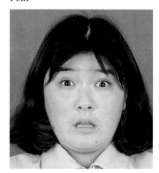

Disgust

Surprise

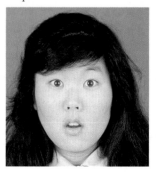

Contempt

These seven expressions, plus an eighth (embarrassment), are interpreted in a consistent way across cultures, but women interpret them more accurately than men. (Courtesy of David Matsumoto.)

the death penalty more than women, consistent with a male justice-based morality (Dillin, 2000). Currently, U.S. women are slightly more likely than men to vote Democratic (Feminist Majority Foundation, 2001)—perhaps consistent with a female caring-based morality—but across history and national boundaries women have voted both to the left and to the right of men.

Differences in Sexuality Include Attitudes toward Casual Sex, Jealousy, and Frequency of Masturbation

Some of the most marked sex differences lie in the area of **sexuality** itself. We will be taking up these issues in later chapters; here we will simply mention some areas in which men and women differ. Men express far more permissive attitudes than women toward casual sex ($d = .81$), as well as toward premarital and extramarital sex (Oliver & Hyde, 1993). Men are also more desirous of engaging in casual sex, and make more attempts to do so (Buss & Schmitt, 1993) (see Chapter 9). Conversely, women are much more likely than men to agree with the statement "I would have sex only if I was in love," and to view sex as a prelude to, or part of, a long-term relationship (Mahay et al., 2000). One area in which women are less restrictive than men, however, relates to their attitudes toward gay or lesbian sex: white women, especially younger white women, are significantly more likely to consider homosexual behavior acceptable than are white men. Other ethnic groups do not show a sex difference.

Women and men tend to seek different things in their sex partners. Women are attracted to older partners, men to younger ones ($d = 0.9$); men are more concerned than women with their partners' physical attractiveness ($d = 0.6$); women are more concerned than men with their partners' status or wealth ($d = 0.5$). Men are more interested in visual sexual stimuli generally, including pornography; this is one of the most marked of all sex differences ($d = 1.3$). Of course, there are any number of exceptions to these generalizations—men who adore powerful older women, and women who are drawn to penniless but handsome youths. But in a statistical sense, these sex differences hold up very consistently (Bailey et al., 1994).

Men and women are both liable to experience **jealousy**, but they experience different *kinds* of jealousy, according to David Buss of the University of Texas. Women, says Buss, are predisposed to experience *emotional* jealousy—that is, to fear that their male partners may commit themselves emotionally to a different woman. Men, on the other hand, tend to experience *sexual* jealousy—to fear, in other words, that their female partners are being physically unfaithful to them (Buss, 2000). We take up the issue of jealousy again in Chapter 9.

Concerning actual sexual behavior, far and away the largest difference is that males masturbate more than females, starting at puberty ($d = 0.96$; Oliver & Hyde, 1993). Males also report more frequent sexual intercourse, a younger age at first intercourse, and a larger number of total sex partners that do females, but these differences are in the small to moderate range ($d = 0.25$–0.4).

Of course, heterosexual sex partners should balance between the sexes: men and women should have the same mean number of different partners of the other sex, for example. The apparent sex difference in this measure has a number of potential explanations (Baumeister & Tice, 2000):

- Dishonest reporting (i.e., inflation by males, concealment by females)
- Different definitions of "sex partners" (i.e., use of a more inclusive definition by men)
- Different methods of estimation by men and women (e.g., counting versus rough guessing)
- Sampling problems (e.g., a failure to sample a wide enough age range, or a failure to sample women with many sex partners, such as prostitutes)

We mentioned earlier that sexual orientation differs greatly by sex, if one defines it in terms of androphilia and gynephilia. Even if one sticks to the traditional homosexual–heterosexual terminology, there are still measurable differences between the sexes: the prevalence of homosexuality is higher in men than in women, and the prevalence of bisexuality is higher in women than in men. We will return to this topic in Chapter 7.

Many Gender Differences Arise Early in Life

Children develop some understanding of differences between the sexes at a young age. Although it might seem difficult to assess a prelingual child's knowledge of the sexes, it can be assessed by **habituation tests.** These tests rely on the fact that young children are interested in novel stimuli (such as pictures of new objects), and they lose interest in, or habituate to, repeated stimuli that are identical or similar. For example, an infant might be presented with a picture of a female face, then another female face, and so on. As more and more faces are presented, the infant will spend less and less time looking at them. But if an image of a *male* face is presented, the infant's interest may increase again, in which case he or she will spend more time looking at the picture. In that case, we can conclude that habituation to the *category* of female faces has occurred, rather than to individual faces or to all faces. This means that the infant recognizes the difference between the faces of males and females. About 75 percent of children display such sex-specific habituation by 1 year of age. They generally rely on simple criteria for determining sex, however, such as hair length and clothing (Leinbach & Fagot, 1993). Infants also discriminate between male and female voices by about the same age (Miller et al., 1982).

Although 1-year-old children may distinguish between the sexes, they probably do not understand that sex is a fixed attribute of individuals. Before about 3 years of age, a child is likely to think that a man who puts on a long-haired wig has become a woman (Kohlberg, 1966). **Gender constancy**—the realization that the sex categories are permanent, and that a man in a wig is still "really a man"—appears by about 3–4 years of age (Bem, 1989) (Figure 6.6).

What about children's sense of their own sex? It appears that most children can identify their own sex and categorize themselves with other same-sex children by 2–3 years of age (Fagot, 1985). This is usually before the age of gender constancy, so children apparently go through a 1–2-year period in which they know their own sex, but do not know that they are unable to change it.

Boys and girls show quite marked differences in behavior from a young age. Even before birth, male fetuses are more active than females, and this difference in activity level persists throughout childhood (Eaton & Enns, 1986). Newborn boys are more wake-

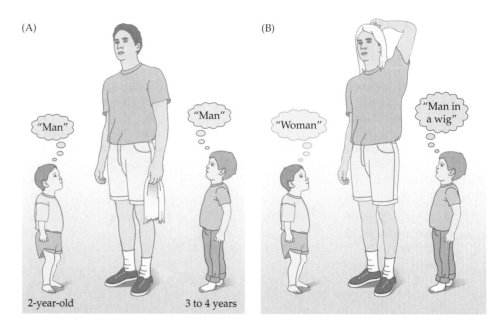

(A)   (B)

"Man"   "Man"   "Woman"   "Man in a wig"

2-year-old   3 to 4 years

6.6 Gender constancy. (A) A 2-year-old child may think that a man who puts on a long-haired wig has become a woman. (B) By 3 to 4 years of age, the child knows that a person's sex is a fixed attribute.

ful than girls, and they cry more readily in response to a painful stimulus (Owens & Todt, 1984; Phillips et al., 1978). Other differences emerge at about 2 years of age. Toy preferences diverge markedly: boys prefer toy vehicles, toy weapons, and construction toys, while girls prefer dolls and toy kitchen implements (Berenbaum & Snyder, 1995; Maccoby & Jacklin, 1987) (Figure 6.7). Boys engage in more play-fighting ("rough-and-tumble play") and aggression than do girls ($d = 0.5$; Maccoby & Jacklin, 1987).

By 2 to 3 years of age, most girls come to prefer other girls as playmates, and boys come to prefer boys (Serbin et al., 1994). Different styles of interaction develop within these same-sex groups: girls tend to cooperate with one another, while boys are more competitive and rough, as if they are contesting dominance (Maccoby, 1990). This segregation by sex increases with age and is virtually universal across cultures (Archer, 1992).

With respect to motor skills, boys show greater throwing accuracy, and girls show finer control of hand musculature, by 2 to 3 years of age (Kimura, 1999). By elementary school age, differences in other cognitive traits begin to emerge; at this age, girls are slightly better at calculating than boys ($d = 0.2$). Boys' superiority in mental visuospatial tasks, such as mental rotation, appears by the age of 9–12 (Kerns & Berenbaum, 1991), and in problem-solving tasks by about 14 (Hyde et al., 1990). This male superiority in visuospatial and problem-solving skills does not translate into better classroom performance, however: girls tend to get better grades than boys in most subjects and across most age levels.

The sex difference in self-esteem and sense of well-being, favoring males, does not emerge in a major way until the mid-teens (Kling et al., 1999). The change seems to be due to a decline in the self-esteem of girls that begins at puberty—a trend that has been noted both in the United States and in China (American Association of University Women, 1992; Watkins et al., 1997).

Figure 6.7 Toy preference test. A child is placed within a circle of toys and its play behavior is videotaped. Later, observers measure the amount of time the child spends playing with toys preferred by girls and those preferred by boys. Examples of data from this kind of study are shown in Figure 6.9. (Courtesy of Sheri Berenbaum.)

There Are Diverse Approaches to the Origin of Gender Differences

So far, we have attempted to describe gender differences without drawing any conclusions about how these differences arise. We now turn to the topic of causes. It turns out that researchers have taken a wide variety of approaches to this topic and have seen gender through the lenses of several different disciplines. We can only touch on the complexity and controversial nature of gender theory in this chapter.

Evolutionary Psychologists Seek Ultimate Explanations

The field of **evolutionary psychology** is dedicated to the proposition that men's and women's personalities and behavior today have been molded by a long period of human and prehuman evolution. During this period, sexual selection (see Chapter 2) has favored the spread of genes that predispose individuals to certain sex-specific traits and behavior patterns. Evolutionary psychologists do not usually concern themselves with the question of what these genes are or how they work, but with the ultimate evolutionary rationale for their existence.

Because evolutionary psychological theories are genetic theories, evolutionary psychologists are working under the assumption that mental and behavioral traits are at least partially heritable. In general, this assumption seems to be a good one. One set of genes that clearly play a role are the genes that determine sex itself (see Chapter 5), although the routes by which they influence gender traits may be very indirect and may be highly dependent on social context. Other genes also influence mental traits. Many lines of research, such as the study of identical twins reared separately, suggest that a wide variety of cognitive and personality traits are moderately to strongly heritable, with something like 25–75 percent of the variability in these traits within a population being accounted for by genetic differences between individuals (Bailey, 1997; Plomin et al., 2001).

One reason for being open to the evolutionary psychological approach is the realization that genes do influence the behavior of males and females in a wide variety of nonhuman species, as we described in Chapter 2. Males of many species compete more strongly with one another for sex partners than do females, for example, and therefore tend to display greater levels of aggressiveness. Thus, it is reasonable to suspect that some common developmental mechanism, such as a differential effect of sex hormones on the developing brain, might contribute to this sex difference in humans and in animals.

Here are some examples of how evolutionary psychology attempts to explain some aspects of men and women's sexual strategies.

Jealousy   Women have always been certain of the identity of their children: any child to whom a woman gave birth was necessarily her genetic offspring. Men, on the other hand, could not be certain which children were theirs: even in a socially monogamous relationship, there was always the risk of being cuckolded, and hence of helping to rear a child fathered by someone else. According David Buss, this difference between the sexes, persisting over countless generations, led to the spread of genes promoting the different styles of jealousy in women and men mentioned above. Men's sexual jealousy served to reduce the likelihood of rearing someone else's child; women's emotional jealousy served to reduce the likelihood that their male partners would abandon them and leave them without resources to rear their children (Buss, 2000).

Interest in casual sex   Men's greater interest in casual sex is readily explained in terms of evolutionary theory. Over the course of human evolution, casual sex involved so little investment of men's resources that the chance of having extra offspring thereby made it well worth the effort. Women, on the other hand, did well to limit their sexual interactions to males who committed themselves to a long-term relationship and child support. Therefore, one can argue, genes promoting male interest in casual sex, and genes reducing female interest, spread widely in human populations.

On the face of it, casual sex offers women little evolutionary benefit. Nevertheless, as discussed in Chapter 2, it is possible that sex outside of a regular pair bond offers women the prospect of conferring better genes on their offspring. We will revisit this question when we discuss the topics of promiscuity and infidelity in Chapter 9.

Cognitive skills   Evolutionary psychologists also believe that cognitive differences between the sexes have developed from a long-standing division of labor between men and women. Because of their greater physical strength, it is argued, men have always taken a leading role in hunting, warfare, and exploration, while women, because of their biologically mandated role in reproduction and breast-feeding, have taken a leading role in activities near the home site. How universal this division of labor may have been during human evolution is open to debate; some critics of evolutionary psychological theory have suggested that early humans may have been primarily foragers rather than hunters, which would have required less marked specialization of gender roles (Gailey, 1987). Still, present-day anthropology suggests that gender specialization is very widespread. Even the "gender-reversed" Tchambuli studied by Margaret Mead fit this pattern: the "feminine" men went off on periodic head-hunting expeditions, while the "masculine" women looked after the children.

Over many generations, such a division of labor might well have favored the spread of genes for different cognitive skills in the two sexes, such as the greater throwing and navigating skills of men and the greater manipulation skills of women. At the same time, one has to be aware of other possibilities—for example, that young boys develop better throwing and route-finding skills than do girls because, in our society, they are given more opportunity and encouragement to practice those skills.

The evolutionary psychological approach does not—or should not—lead to a philosophy of "genetic determinism" (Waage & Gowaty, 1997), in which men and women are seen as genetically programmed robots, and their contrasting traits and sexual behaviors as inevitable and therefore in some sense "right and proper." If there is one trait that evolution has most definitely endowed us with, it is adaptability, not stereotypical behavior.

The Biological Approach Is Conceptually Precise but Faces Practical Difficulties

Biologists assume that mental differences between men and women are the manifestation of sex-differentiated brain systems, and that the development of these systems is open to investigation with the tools of neuroscience, endocrinology, and genetics.

The biological approach has been remarkably successful in elucidating the basis of sex-specific behavior in animals, as we have seen in Chapter 5. One can trace at least the outline of an entire developmental pathway leading to the different sexual behaviors of male and female rats. This pathway starts with the sex-determining genes and progresses through the development of male and female gonads, the differing levels of androgens in males and females during development, the influence of these differing levels on the organization of the brain systems that generate sexual behavior, and the differential activation of these systems by circulating hormones in adulthood.

Some sex-differentiated behaviors are seen very widely among mammals. The male young of many species engage in more rough-and-tumble play than do females, just as happens with humans. It makes sense to suppose that a common developmental mechanism underlies this commonality of behavior. Given the limited opportunities for socialization and cognitive processes in many species, it seems most likely that such a common developmental mechanism would lie in the sphere of hormones and brain development. Still, we have to be cautious in making such assumptions, because even rat pups are subject to different parental treatment according to their sex, and this differential treatment can influence their anatomical and behavioral development (Moore, 1992).

There are two basic problems with applying the biological approach to human sexuality. One is simply the greater size and intricacy of the human brain and the complexity of human sexual behavior compared with what is seen in most other animals (Figure 6.8). A behavior such as lordosis in rats is stereotypical and predictable, and involves the function of a small number of highly specialized brain regions, such as the ventromedial nucleus of the hypothalamus. What about the human traits of emotional and sexual jealousy, mentioned above? Are there brain "centers" for these two forms of jealousy that one might be able to recognize, measure, and compare in men and women? Most likely not. The predisposition to experience these two forms of jealousy, though based in some way on neural systems, is almost certainly buried in the highly elaborate, multipurpose synaptic networks that encompass large regions of the human brain, making them resistant to any kind of simple functional dissection.

Similarly, even though genes contribute substantially to human sexuality, it does not necessarily follow that it will be easy to identify individual genes that strongly influence specific traits—apart from the genes that are involved in sex determination, of course (see Chapter 5). There has been one claim of discovery of a gene that influences men's sexual orientation in a major way, as we will see in the next chapter. In most cases, however, it is likely that genetic influences on psychosexual traits are exerted by large numbers of genes, and that the influence of each of these genes is small and dependent on a complex interplay with the environment. Still, even these so-called **quantitative trait loci** can be identified with the help of modern techniques of genomic analysis. ("Quantitative" means that the trait is continuously graded rather than being an either-or phenomenon; a "locus" is a location on a chromosome identified by genetic or molecular genetic mapping.)

The other problem with the biological approach is the difficulty of conducting experiments. It would be grossly unethical to attempt to replicate the monkey experiments described in the previous chapter in humans—that is, to deliberately manipulate the hormone levels of male and female human fetuses with the idea of studying their sexuality and gender characteristics in adulthood. Thus, researchers are thrown back on "experiments of nature" that may offer parallels to animal studies.

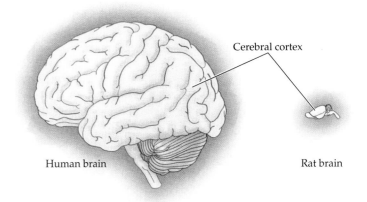

Cerebral cortex

Human brain

Rat brain

Figure 6.8 Brain gain. The great development of the cerebral cortex in humans, compared with what is seen in rats, should make us cautious in attributing sexual behavior to similar neural mechanisms in the two species.

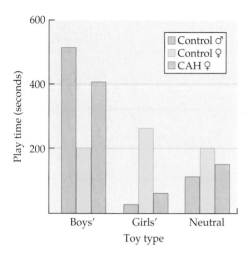

Figure 6.9 Hormones and play.
Exposure to androgens during fetal life influences choice of toys during childhood. Normal girls ("Control ♀"), normal boys ("Control ♂"), and girls with congenital adrenal hyperplasia ("CAH ♀") were observed while playing with toys. The toys available included those generally preferred by boys (e.g., trucks) and those generally preferred by girls (e.g., dolls), as well as gender-neutral toys. The toy preferences of the CAH girls were more like those of boys than of normal girls. (After Berenbaum and Snyder, 1995.)

CAH and gender traits The condition of **congenital adrenal hyperplasia (CAH)**, described in Box 5.5, is one example of such an "experiment of nature." CAH girls are exposed to unusually high levels of androgens prenatally; therefore, researchers have studied them intensively to see whether their gender-related characteristics differ, on average, from those of unaffected control girls (Berenbaum, 1999; Collaer & Hines, 1995; Zucker et al., 1996). They do differ in many respects. In general, CAH girls play more with boy's toys and less with girls' toys than do comparable unaffected girls (Figure 6.9); they are more active, engage more in rough-and-tumble play, and are more likely to be considered tomboys; and they are less sure that they want to be girls. As they mature, they have greater interest in male-typical activities and careers than do unaffected controls, and have less interest in female-typical activities, including the prospect of having children. They are more likely to experience sexual attraction to women than control females, although they are usually closer to a heterosexual than a homosexual orientation. Some CAH women are gender-dysphoric in adulthood, and may even seek sex reassignment surgery, but most identify as women and wish to remain so. CAH women are also atypical in some cognitive traits; for example, they score higher than unaffected women on some tests of visuospatial skills, such as mental rotation.

These observations suggest that the high androgen levels experienced by female CAH fetuses influence the sexual differentiation of the brain, promoting a somewhat more male-typical development than is usual for females. By extension, they suggest that the different androgen levels experienced by normal male and female fetuses contribute to the development of gendered traits in postnatal life. Still, this conclusion has not gone uncontested. It has been argued, for example, that the atypical mental characteristics seen in CAH girls are an indirect effect, perhaps caused by the recognition by the girls or their families that their genitalia are not entirely normal (Mulaikal et al., 1987).

Quite a number of other endocrinological conditions affect gender, including 5α-reductase deficiency (Box 6.2) and androgen insensitivity syndrome (see Chapter 5). Observations of individuals with these conditions are consistent with an influence of prenatal sex hormone levels on gender characteristics. Not all the data support a simple "high fetal androgens = masculine, low fetal androgens = feminine" model, however. In some cases, intermediate, rather than very high or low androgen levels may be optimal for establishing masculine characteristics. In addition, we can infer from animal studies that the *timing* of fetal androgen exposure is probably of great importance, but "experiments of nature" rarely allow for detailed analysis of this variable.

Within-sex variability Biologists would like to know whether prenatal hormone levels, besides helping to set up mental differences between the sexes, also influence variations in gendered characteristics among individuals of the same sex. One group of researchers found suggestive evidence for such an influence by sampling the umbilical blood of newborn children, then studying the children's emotional states over the following 2 years (Marcus et al., 1985). They first observed a basic sex difference; namely, that 1- to 2-year-old boys spend relatively more time in a "happy" or "excited" mood, while girls spend more time in a "quiet" or "peaceful" mood. Among the boys, however, there was a correlation of emotional states with androgen levels in the neonatal blood samples: boys with higher androgen levels spent significantly more time "happy" or "excited" than boys with lower levels. This result suggests that hormones help sculpt personality differences on a finer scale than simply "masculine vs. feminine."

Ideally, of course, one would obtain blood samples during fetal life rather than at birth, and one would follow the children through to adulthood rather than just for a year or two. Because such methods are generally not practicable, researchers have looked for markers in adulthood that might reflect hormone levels during fetal life—the human equivalent of the ice cores that climatologists use to decipher atmospheric conditions in the distant past. In the next chapter, we will describe the use of this approach in the study of sexual orientation.

Transexuality Biologically minded sex researchers would like to identify a genetic or hormonal basis for transexuality. There have been reports of transexuality clustering in families, which is consistent with a genetic influence (Freund, 1985; Green,

Box 6.2 Biology of Sex

Switch Sex, Switch Gender?

An experiment of nature that has been of great interest from the standpoint of gender theory is the syndrome of **5α-reductase deficiency.** As already described in Box 5.6, chromosomally male individuals affected by this syndrome cannot convert testosterone to the more potent androgen dihydrotestosterone. As a consequence, their genitalia at birth look female, at least to casual inspection, and they are usually reared as girls. At puberty, however, the greatly increased levels of circulating testosterone trigger enlargement of the phallus and scrotum, lowering of the voice, and the development of a male body build, so that these children seem to change from girls into men.

In a cluster of cases of this syndrome in the Dominican Republic, studied by Julianne Imperato-McGinley and her colleagues, the great majority of affected individuals shifted from a female to a male gender identity at or soon after puberty (Imperato-McGinley et al., 1979). The transition typically took place over a period of several years—subjects felt that they passed through stages of "not feeling like girls," then "feeling like men," and finally being convinced that they were men.

How should this finding be interpreted? Just giving a normal prepubertal girl large doses of testosterone to induce male secondary development would not make her feel like a man. Therefore, it was not just the increased testosterone levels at puberty that induced a male gender identity in the 5α-reductase-deficient children studied by Imperato-McGinley. Rather, in her interpretation, it was the combination of prenatal testosterone exposure, which had its typical organizing effect on the brain, with the pubertal rise in testosterone, which had an activating effect. Together, these hormonal effects nearly always overrode any effects of being reared as a female.

Imperato-McGinley's conclusions have been criticized for a number of reasons. It was suggested, for example, that the children she studied were not really reared as female, but as a kind of intersex. It is true that, as the syndrome became well known in the area, infants who had the syndrome were recognized by careful inspection of the genitalia at birth, and some of these children were given the slang name "*guevedoces*," meaning "eggs (balls) at twelve," to indicate their special status and the expectation that they would change sex. But Imperato-McGinley also reported on 18 children who were raised in the full belief that they were, and would always remain, girls. Of these children, 17 developed a male gender identity during puberty (and were sexually attracted to women), and 16 completely changed their public gender role to male.

Gender barriers were fairly lax in the communities that Imperato-McGinley studied. Therefore, it has been suggested, the children might have transitioned from one sex to the other even without any influence from prenatal hormones. Partly in response to this criticism, Imperato-McGinley went on to study another cluster of cases in Papua New Guinea, a society with very rigid gender barriers. Here, too, most infants who were raised unambiguously as girls transitioned to a male gender identity and gender role around the age of puberty, albeit with more turmoil than in the Dominican Republic (Imperato-McGinley et al., 1991). Later, as in the Dominican Republic, the condition was recognized by the local communities and given a special name.

The observations on 5α-reductase deficiency leave many loose ends. What were the gender characteristics of the affected individuals during childhood? What would have happened if the children's brains were flooded with testosterone at puberty, but their bodies for some reason had remained female—would they have accepted their continued female identity, or would they still have transitioned to a male identity, becoming in essence transexuals? And what if the whole syndrome were sex-reversed: what if it was a matter of *boys* developing *women's* bodies at puberty? Would they be as accepting of membership in the socially disadvantaged female sex as the 5α-reductase-deficient girls were of membership in the advantaged male sex? The 5α-reductase deficiency syndrome does not provide all the answers to these questions, but it does support the general notion that sex hormones, both before birth and at puberty, powerfully influence a person's gender.

2000). Interestingly, in nearly all cases in which two male-to-female transexuals are found in the same family, they are either both androphilic or both gynephilic. This finding suggests that the two kinds of transexuality have different origins. There have also been reports of an endocrinological disorder related to CAH in transexuals (Bosinski et al., 1997), as well as of anomalies in sexually dimorphic brain structures (Kruijver et al., 2000). These reports are consistent with a role for genes or prenatal hormones in the development of transexuality, and hence perhaps in the development of gender identity in general. Because of the rarity of transexuality, however, the reported findings are based on small numbers of individuals and need to be replicated by independent researchers.

Socialization Theory Attributes Gender to Learning

The dominant idea about gender in the latter part of the twentieth century was that gender-related traits are inculcated into children by parents, teachers, siblings, peers, and society in general. This idea, which is the basis of what is known today as **socialization theory,** can be traced back at least to the eighteenth-century Enlightenment period. Thus the British philosopher John Locke, in his *Essay Concerning Human Understanding* (1790), rejected traditional notions of "innate knowledge," and instead proposed that the newborn child's mind is like a blank slate ("tabula rasa") that is written on by experience.

Influence of behaviorism   In the early part of the twentieth century, learning theory was formalized by **behaviorists**—the followers of the Russian physiologist Ivan Pavlov (1849–1946) and the American psychologist John Watson (1878–1958). In Pavlov's famous experiment, a dog that heard a bell rung every time food was presented to it learned to salivate at the sound of the bell alone. It is easy to imagine how such **classical conditioning** might be responsible for some aspects of sexuality, including gender differences in sexual arousal. Heterosexual men, for example, would gradually come to be aroused, not just by attractive women, but by all kinds of things associated with women, such as women's clothing, women's voice quality, women's behavior, and so on. Conversely, heterosexual women would come to be aroused by objects and behaviors associated with men. Conditioning could also lead to **fetishism**—a condition in which clothing and other items become sex objects in their own right (Figure 6.10). One just has to assume that the fetishist saw these items worn by attractive people at some time in the past. Still, there is no direct evidence that this is how fetishes develop (see Chapter 14).

The Harvard behavioral psychologist B. F. Skinner (1904–1990) developed the theory of **instrumental conditioning,** according to which behavior is molded by judiciously timed rewards and punishments ("positive and negative reinforcement"). Skinner saw behavior as a set of input–output functions, and was not greatly interested in the mind's inner workings, let alone its biological underpinnings. His approach was enormously popular in the study of animal behavior: countless millions of food pellets have been earned by rats running through mazes and by pigeons pecking at buttons in "Skinner boxes."

The researcher most closely associated with the application of behaviorist ideas to gender is sexologist John Money of Johns Hopkins Medical School. During the 1950s

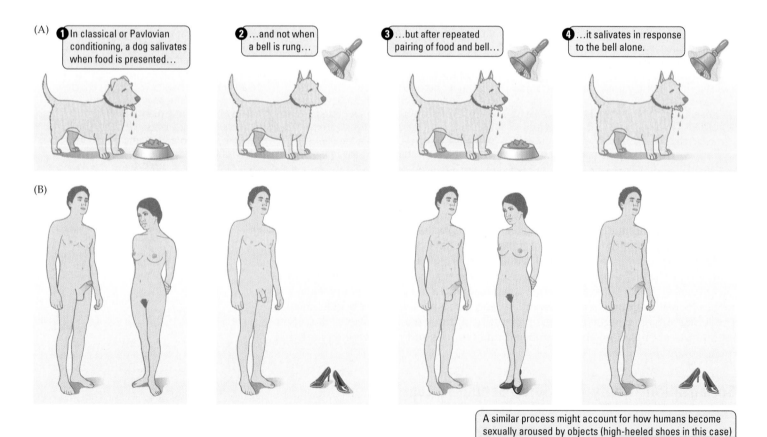

(A)

❶ In classical or Pavlovian conditioning, a dog salivates when food is presented…

❷ …and not when a bell is rung…

❸ …but after repeated pairing of food and bell…

❹ …it salivates in response to the bell alone.

(B)

A similar process might account for how humans become sexually aroused by objects (high-heeled shoes in this case) that are repeatedly associated with an attractive person.

Figure 6.10 Conditioned arousal.

Money, along with colleagues Joan and John Hampson, studied a series of children born with ambiguous genitalia (Money et al., 1955). They reported that such children developed a male or female gender identity and other gender characteristics according to whether they were reared as girls or boys. These observations led Money to the general conclusion that children are born without any predisposition to a particular gender, and learn their gender as a consequence of the countless rewards and punishments that parents consciously or unconsciously deal out to their children.

Intersexed children are not necessarily typical of children in general, of course. Money therefore placed a great deal of weight on the case of one particular child, who was born as a normal boy but who was surgically reassigned as a girl and raised as such, apparently with complete success. Years later, however, the outcome of this "experiment" turned out to be the very opposite of what Money had claimed. The extraordinary denouement of this story injured both Money's reputation and the notion that gender is entirely a matter of socialization (Box 6.3).

In parallel with Money's work, psychologist Walter Mischel of Columbia University proposed a general social learning theory of gender, in which rewards and punishments molded the behavior of boys and girls (Mischel, 1966). Mischel added the nonbehaviorist idea that gender-typical behavior might be molded by **imitation** of individuals perceived as authoritative or protective, such as parents or older siblings, and not just by direct rewards and punishments.

According to these ideas, the presence or absence of role models influences gender development. In one recent study, a group led by John Rust of Goldsmiths College in London tested this notion by examining the gender-related behaviors and interests of over 5,000 3-year-old children, some of whom had older siblings of the same or the other sex (Rust et al., 2000) (Figure 6.11). Those children who had an older sibling of the same sex were more gender-typical than were children who had no siblings (singletons). Conversely, children who had an older sibling of the other sex were *less* gender-typical than the singletons. The effect sizes were moderate ($d = 0.55-0.65$). These data suggest that role models such as older siblings do mold children's gender characteristics to an appreciable degree. Still, as can be seen in the figure, a child's own biological sex is a much stronger predictor of its gender-related traits than is the sex of its older siblings: girls with older brothers, for example, are far more feminine than any boys, even boys with older sisters.

Influence of feminism Beginning in the 1960s, **feminists** laid a great deal of emphasis on social learning theories of gender, and often denigrated biological ideas in the process (Fausto-Sterling, 1992). A corollary of this view was that traditional gender differences could be modified—perhaps abolished altogether—if parents and others would only change the way they treated children. In consequence, many parents made a conscious effort to treat their children in a nonstereotyping fashion—by offering them a choice of traditional boys' and girls' toys, for example.

This strategy has not been uniformly successful—some parents have been surprised by how rigidly their children stick to stereotypical toy preferences. Still, the effect of the new style of child rearing is showing itself in, for example, a far greater participation by girls and young women in school and college sports than was typical a generation ago. (This trend has been aided by Title IX, a 1972 federal law that banned gender discrimination in schools.) Some researchers have suggested that changes in socialization practices have led to a broad reduction in cognitive differences between boys and girls since the 1960s (Hyde & Linn, 1986), but others disagree, attributing apparent changes in gender-related traits to changes in analytical procedures (Knight et al., 1996).

(A)

(B)

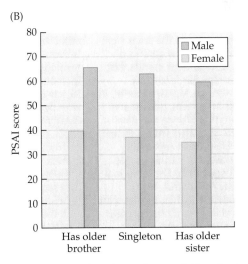

Figure 6.11 Gender role modeling between siblings. (A) Older siblings act as gender role models. (B) This figure shows the Pre-School Activities Inventory (PSAI) score—a measure of gender-typical activities and interests in which male-typical traits score higher and female-typical traits score lower—for 5542 British 3-year-olds, broken down according to whether they are singletons or have an older brother or sister. The children's gender traits are slightly shifted in the direction of the sex of their older sibling. (After Rust et al., 2000.)

Box 6.3 *Personal Points of View*

The Boy Who Was Raised as a Girl

Bruce and Brian Reimer were monozygotic twins, born in Winnipeg, Canada, in 1965. When the twins were 7 months old they developed phimosis, a common condition in which the foreskin of the penis becomes constricted (see Chapter 5). The parents were advised to have the twins circumcised, but during Bruce's operation, an accident with the electrocautery machine led to the complete destruction of his penis.

The parents were understandably devastated and at a loss as to what to do. Eventually they brought Bruce to sexologist John Money at Johns Hopkins Medical School. Since it would not be possible to refashion a normal penis for Bruce, Money recommended that he be surgically transformed into, and reared as, a girl. He told the parents that as long as they treated the child unambiguously as a girl, the child would develop as a girl and become a feminine, heterosexual woman.

The parents followed Money's advice. They immediately renamed Bruce to Brenda and dressed and treated her as a girl. When Brenda was 2 years old, her sex reassignment was completed: her testicles were removed and a rudimentary vagina was constructed from the scrotal skin. Her parents dedicated themselves to rearing Brenda and Brian as sister and brother. Money saw the parents and the twins from time to time, and advised the parents on the appropriate ways to treat Brenda that would best encourage her femininity.

As the years went by, Money reported in detail on the case in lectures, papers, and books. He claimed that Brenda was developing as a normal girl, apart from a certain tomboyishness. While Brian copied his father, Brenda copied her mother, wrote Money (and colleague Anke Ehrhardt) in a 1972 book (Money & Ehrhardt, 1971): "Regarding domestic activities, such as work in the kitchen and house traditionally seen as part of the female's role, the mother reported that her daughter copies her in

trying to help her tidying and cleaning up the kitchen, while the boy could not care less about it." Brenda chose dolls as presents, while Brian chose model cars.

The case became widely cited, both in the popular press and in academic circles, as evidence for the malleability of gender. "This dramatic case provides strong support for a major contention of women's liberationists: that conventional patterns of masculine and feminine behavior can be altered," reported *Time* in 1973. "It also casts doubt on the theory that major sexual differences, psychological as well as anatomical, are immutably set by the genes at conception." "The normality of [Brenda's] development can be viewed as a substantial indication of the plasticity of human gender identity and the relative importance of social learning and conditioning in this process," stated the influential *Textbook of Sexual Medicine* (Kolodny et al., 1979). The case "…illustrated the overriding role of life experiences in molding human sexuality," according to the 1985 edition of the neurobiology textbook *Principles of Neural Science* (Kandel & Schwartz, 1985).

Eventually, Money reported that he had lost contact with the Reimer family. It took detective work by University of Hawaii sexologist Milton Diamond (Diamond & Sigmundson, 1997), and later by journalist John Colapinto (Colapinto, 2000), to discover what had happened to Brenda. It seems that she was never successfully socialized into a feminine gender identity in the way that Money had claimed. Rather, she rebelled

against it at every stage. Although a female puberty was induced by means of treatment with estrogen, Brenda loathed her developing breasts. By the age of 15 she had changed her name to David and was dressing as a boy. David had a double mastectomy, testosterone treatments, and a phalloplasty (reconstruction of a penis). He was always sexually attracted to women, and he eventually married, engaged in coitus with the aid of a prosthesis, and adopted children. He is now a well-adjusted man, husband, and father, albeit with more than his fair share of painful memories (see figure).

If anything, the case of Bruce, then Brenda, then David Reimer suggests the very opposite conclusion to the one drawn by John Money: that prenatal development dictates gender identity and sexual orientation even when rearing conditions, genital anatomy, and pubertal hormones all conspire to produce the opposite result. To draw such an extreme conclusion, however, risks making a mistake similar to that made by Money: the investment of too much significance in a single case history.

Observing socialization   The ideal way to study gender socialization is to observe the process while it is happening. In one study of this kind, psychologist Robert Fagot and his colleagues at the University of Oregon studied interactions between parents and their 18-month-old infants, then followed the infants for about a year afterward. They found that the infants whose parents reacted to their behavior in the traditional fashion (approving of gender-typical behavior and disapproving of gender-atypical behavior) learned to make gender distinctions earlier than other infants and exhibited more traditional gender-specific behavior (Fagot et al., 1992). Studies of this kind support the notion that gender-related traits are inculcated, at least to some degree.

In a rather different kind of study conducted in the 1970s, a group at the University of British Columbia focused on a small Canadian town with the fictitious name of "Notel." This town received television broadcasts for the first time in 1974. The researchers wanted to know what the effect of television would be on the town's children. From our perspective, the interesting part of the study, carried out by psychologist Meredith Kimball, was that devoted to gender issues (Kimball, 1986). Before the broadcasts began, Kimball found that Notel's children had gender-related attitudes that were significantly more flexible than those of children in two comparable towns that already had television. By two years after the beginning of television transmissions, the attitudes of Notel's children had become much more stereotypical and comparable to those of children in the other towns. The girls had particularly marked changes in their attitudes toward peer relationships, while the boys showed marked changes concerning future occupations—in the direction of greater gender rigidity. All in all, the Notel study demonstrated a powerful effect of television in promoting stereotypical gender attitudes. (For good measure, the study also found that Notel's children became more aggressive and less creative after the introduction of television.)

The general weight of evidence supports the popular belief that socialization does influence gender development. On the other hand, the resistance of some children (such as the child studied by John Money) to rearing effects is remarkable. Furthermore, socialization theory has been unable to explain the most flagrant violation of conventional gender: transexuality. There is simply no evidence that children who become transexual are encouraged, trained, or influenced in any way to reject their sex of origin—quite the contrary. It therefore seems unlikely that a complete account of gender development can be made in terms of socialization.

Cognitive Developmental Models Focus on Thought Processes

In contrast to socialization theory, **cognitive developmental models** assert that the key process in gender development is the sequence of ideas and understandings that a child has concerning gender. In some ways, this approach echoes a tradition begun by Sigmund Freud (1859–1939), the founder of **psychoanalysis.** For example, Freud proposed that young children go through certain thought processes when they first observe the anatomical differences between boys and girls: girls suspect that their own penis has been cut off, and they become envious of males who still possess one. Boys, on the other hand, fear that their penises may be cut off in the future, most likely by their fathers. These ideas may exist below the level of consciousness, Freud believed, but they powerfully influence the psychosexual development of boys and girls.

Gender constancy   Today, the details of Freud's theories are considered fanciful by all but a core of diehard Freudian psychoanalysts. Still, the notion that one has to understand the progression of children's ideas to get a handle on gender development is widely accepted. One influential thinker in this area has been Harvard psychologist Lawrence Kohlberg, who is well known for his studies on the moral development of children. Kohlberg laid great weight on the concept of gender constancy, discussed earlier in this chapter—the realization by young children that "male" and "female" are fixed attributes of individuals (Kohlberg, 1966).

This realization of gender constancy becomes an organizing principle that motivates the child to develop stereotypical ideas about the characteristics of males and females—such as that males are strong but cruel and that females are fearful but affectionate (Cowan & Hoffman, 1986)—and to make his or her own behavior correspond to those stereotypes. Behavioral traits such as aggressiveness in boys may result from the boy's desire to demonstrate his gender attributes, according to this school of thought (Ullian, 1981). One problem with this approach, however, is that at least some gender-differentiated traits emerge *before* children realize the constancy of gender.

Gender schemas   An offshoot of cognitive developmental theory that incorporates the concept of socialization is the **gender schema** theory developed by Sandra Bem of

Cornell University (Bem, 1981). A gender schema is a framework of ideas about gender that influences perceptions, judgments, and memories. Under the influence of socialization, most children develop highly polarized schemata of masculinity and femininity, so that perception becomes categorical—that is, a matter of "either masculine or feminine but nothing in between."

A variety of studies support the idea that children's gender schemata influence their perceptions and memories. In one study (Figure 6.12), children were shown pictures of boys and girls performing tasks that were either consistent with gender stereotypes (e.g., girls cooking) or inconsistent with those stereotypes (e.g., girls sawing wood). When tested a week later on their recollection of the pictures, children tended to make mistakes that eliminated conflicts with stereotypes—they might recall that they saw boys, rather than girls, sawing wood, for example (Martin & Halverson, 1983). In another study, students were tested on their ability to recall sentences such as "Jane is a good nurse," "Jane is a bad nurse," "John is a good nurse," or "John is a bad nurse." The students recalled the statements that fit gender stereotypes ("Jane is a good nurse," "John is a bad nurse") better than those that conflicted with stereotypes (Cann, 1993). Results such as these suggest that perceptions related to gender do encounter a filter resembling Bem's gender schema.

Sexual scripts   Another variation on cognitive developmental models is the **sexual script theory** of John Gagnon and William Simon (Simon & Gagnon, 1986). As the word "script" suggests, this theory asserts that sexual behavior is a form of role playing. To take a nonsexual example of a script, shopping in a supermarket involves all kinds of assumptions about the roles that will be played by the shopper, the clerk at the deli counter, the cashier, the bagger, and so on. These roles are not innate attributes of the participants, but have been tacitly negotiated over time to permit smooth and mutually beneficial interactions.

According to Gagnon and Simon, many sexual interactions follow similar scripts, and because they do so, they can change over time under the influence of culture. According to sexual script theory, humans are endowed with few or no biological instincts as to how to behave sexually. Early in the twentieth century, for example, oral sex was something that men largely received from prostitutes and in transient relationships, but it has now become a common and acceptable sexual practice between young adults who are dating, and both males and females take the oral role (Gagnon & Simon, 1987). Thus, both men and women read different meanings into oral sex now than their parents did.

Scripts, according to Gagnon and Simon, influence not only sexual dealings among people, but also the psychosexual development of individuals. They noted that postpubertal boys masturbate a great deal more than do girls, as we mentioned above, while girls' early sexual experiences tend to be with partners. As a consequence, script theory suggests, the meaning of sex for males becomes embedded in the notion of the male's own sexual pleasure, whereas for females it becomes embedded in the notion of relationships.

The interpersonal aspects of script theory shade into the ideas of postmodernist thinkers, such as philosopher Michel Foucault (Foucault, 1978) and "queer theorist" Eve Kosofsky Sedgwick, who is an English professor at the City University of New York (Sedgwick, 1990). In postmodernist thought, the cultural aspects of sex—especially the influences of powerful social structures such as religion, medicine, and the law—become paramount.

Not all students of culture see it as dictating the sexuality of individuals, however. The controversial cultural critic Camille Paglia of the University of the Arts in Philadelphia, for example, has devoted much of her energy to ridiculing postmodernist thought—especially that of Foucault—as it relates to sexuality. Instead, Paglia

(A) (B) (C) (D)

Figure 6.12 Influence of gender stereotypes on children's memories. Children recall images of gender-typical activities (A, B) accurately, but their memory of images showing gender-atypical activities (C, D) may be distorted to make them fit gender stereotypes. (After Martin and Halverson, 1983.)

that individuals, even within the same sex, fall into sexual types, or "personae," that recur across many cultures (Paglia, 1990). She believes in differences between the sexes that transcend culture and that could be more easily be explained in terms of evolutionary psychology. For example, she proposes that men go to extremes, whereas women tend to hold to a safe middle ground—an echo of the evolutionary viewpoint that reproduction is a riskier undertaking for males than for females. A single sentence of Paglia's encapsulating this idea—"There is no female Mozart because there is no female Jack the Ripper"—probably earned her more enemies within academic feminism than any other.

Some neuroscientists are critical of purely cognitive models of mental development. That's because consciousness doesn't necessarily have access to the neural circuitry that underlies our feelings and motivations, or to the processes that modify that circuitry in face of our life experiences. In a recent book, neuroscientist Joseph LeDoux of New York University stresses the importance of delineating the invisible inner workings of the brain as a basis for understanding mental development, and emphasizes that "the self consists of more than what self-aware organisms are consciously aware of." (LeDoux, 2002).

Gender Probably Involves Complex Developmental Interactions

Gender researchers, like researchers in most other areas, tend to invest themselves in certain approaches to their subject, perhaps on account of the training they have received. Some are interested in biological theories, some in socialization, and so on. Yet it is very unlikely that something as complex as human gender could be fully explained by any single approach, and most theorists believe that there must be some confluence of different developmental influences to create gender-related traits.

Take a childhood trait such as toy preference. The observations of atypical toy preference in CAH girls strongly suggest that prenatal hormone exposure contributes to the sex difference in this trait. On the other hand, many parents give boys and girls gender-specific toys *before* the age at which gender-specific play emerges—sometimes as early as 9 months (Pomerleau et al., 1990). Furthermore, children whose parents give them gender-specific toys are more likely to prefer and play with such toys than children who are given a mix of toys (Eisenberg et al., 1985; Katz & Boswell, 1986). Thus, it seems probable that there is an **additive effect** of biological predisposition and socialization on the development of toy preference. In fact, such additive (or subtractive) effects are likely to be the rule, especially for traits that have a large social impact, such as aggressiveness.

The interaction of such factors could be more complex than simple addition, however. The segregation of boys and girls during childhood play, for example, could result from a process of the following kind (Maccoby, 1990). First, a biological predisposition causes boys to enjoy rough-and-tumble play more than girls do. Then, girls learn that mixing with boys exposes them to rough-and-tumble play, so they stay away from boys. According to this model, biological factors and socialization affect different traits (rough-and-tumble play and sex segregation, respectively), and their interaction is not additive, but *conditional*: girls experience no socialization to avoid boys until and unless they get roughhoused by them. (In reality, there is probably far more to sex segregation than this.)

Obviously, one could construct long chains of such interactive effects, particularly as a child grows older. Here's one example of a theory that invokes such a chain to explain a particular gender trait: sexual orientation. Daryl Bem of Cornell University (husband of Sandra, mentioned above) proposed that the first two steps toward sexual orientation are the two just mentioned: boys and girls have a biological predisposition to prefer different activities, and so they are socialized to prefer the company of their own sex. This experience breeds familiarity with the same sex, whereas individuals of the other sex remain strange, scary, "yucky," or otherwise exotic throughout childhood. These strong feelings aroused by members of the other sex are later transformed (by some innate process) into sexual attraction, so that most women become sexually attracted to men and most men to women. A minority of individuals who start off with biologically atypical play preferences will be socialized to play with *opposite*-sex playmates, which ultimately causes them to be sexually attracted to persons of the *same* sex (Bem, 1996).

While there may not be any particular merit in this theory, compared with other theories of sexual orientation (see Chapter 7), it does illustrate the potential complexity of gender developmental pathways. Unfortunately, complexities of this kind are very difficult to study in any meaningful way, so ideas such as Bem's "exotic becomes erotic" theory tend to remain in the arena of speculation.

All in all, gender remains a fascinating and mysterious aspect of human identity. It is so much a part of our innermost nature that we often fail to notice how it affects our thinking and behavior on a day-to-day basis. Yet the pervasiveness of gender was illustrated in an amusing way by a "100 percent accurate gender test" developed by an online magazine, *The Spark* (www.thespark.com) in 2001. The test guessed a person's sex on the basis of their answers to 50 seemingly irrelevant questions, including the following:

- Would you rather be deaf or blind?
- Do you ever think about the beginning of time and wish you could've been there?
- Which word is grosser—"moist" or "used?"
- Which is a better way to ship things—in a truck, or on a boat?
- Please choose one—french fries/onion rings.
- Are clams alive?

The test used a learning algorithm to weight the answers to the questions on the basis of the answers given by prior subjects (who were asked to reveal their true sex at the end of the test). The test never reached the claimed 100 percent accuracy, but it guessed most people's sex correctly, including that of the two authors of this book. It seems, then, that our status as male or female subtly influences almost everything we say or do.

Summary

1. The term "gender," as used in this book, refers to the entire collection of mental traits that differ between men and women, regardless of how those differences arise. Some traits are highly gendered, meaning that the sex difference is glaringly obvious. Other differences are subtle and require statistical demonstration.

2. Research into gender takes place in a historical context dominated by sexism (the traditional devaluation of women) and by feminism (the social and intellectual revolt against that tradition).

3. Gender identity is a person's core sense of being a man or a woman, and is probably the most gendered of all mental traits. While gender identity is generally congruent with anatomical sex, some transgender or transexual individuals feel as if they really belong to the other sex or do not identify closely with either sex. In classic transexuality, the feeling of belonging to the other sex is associated with a lifelong history of gender dysphoria and sex-atypical traits and behaviors, and is usually accompanied by sexual attraction to persons of the same anatomical sex. Some nonclassical male-to-female transexuals are sexually aroused by the thought of themselves in a woman's body (autogynephilia).

4. Sexual orientation is the direction of a person's sexual attractions: toward individuals of the other sex (heterosexuality), both sexes (bisexuality), or the same sex (homosexuality). Alternatively, sexual orientation may be characterized as attraction to men (androphilia), to both sexes (bisexuality), or to women (gynephilia). The latter conception makes clear that sexual orientation is a highly gendered trait.

5. Men and women differ in a variety of cognitive traits. Men outperform women in some visuospatial skills, mathematical reasoning, and problem solving. Women outperform men in fine movements, verbal fluency, and some aspects of memory. The differences are generally moderate in degree, with substantial overlap between the sexes.

6. In the realm of personality, men are more aggressive than women, while women are better at decoding and expressing emotions. Some studies suggest that men and women's moral perspectives differ, being dominated by notions of justice and caring, respectively.

7. In the area of sexuality, men and women differ in frequency of masturbation (men more frequent), attitudes toward casual sex (men more approving), and styles of jealousy (women experience emotional jealousy, men experience sexual jealousy).

8. Many gender differences arise early in life. Most children distinguish perceptually between males and females by 1 year of age, can identify their own sex by 2–3 years, and understand the immutability of sex by 3–4 years. Males are more active than females beginning in fetal life. Boys are more aggressive than girls. Boys and girls prefer different toys, and both prefer to associate with children of the same sex. Sex-specific interaction styles develop within these same-sex groups. Differences in other cognitive traits emerge gradually during childhood. A difference in self-esteem, favoring males, emerges during the teen years.

9. There have been a variety of approaches to understanding the origins of gender-related traits. Evolutionary psychologists propose that sex differences have evolved in response to differences in reproductive investment by males and females and the allocation of different tasks to men and women during early human evolution, as well as to the fact that women, but not men, can be certain who their children are.

10. The biological approach focuses on the influence of genes and hormones on the differentiation of the brain systems that mediate gendered traits. Biologists tend to emphasize the commonality of developmental mechanisms in humans and nonhuman animals. Useful in this regard are "experiments of nature," such as congenital adrenal hyperplasia (CAH), a syndrome in which female fetuses are exposed to high levels of androgens. CAH girls develop a wide variety of gender-atypical traits, suggesting that prenatal androgens influence sex-differentiated traits in humans, as they do in rats and nonhuman primates.

11. Socialization theory sees the development of gender as a learning process in which children's behaviors, cognitive skills, and personalities are molded by rewards and punishments handed out by parents, peers, and society in general. The influence of socialization has been documented by the study of children who have been exposed to different styles of parenting, different degrees of television exposure, and the like. On the other hand, children can be remarkably resistant to rearing effects, and socialization theory has failed to explain the most extreme violation of gender norms: transexuality.

12. The cognitive developmental approach sees gender development in terms of the emerging thought processes of children, the key event being a child's realization that he or she is immutably male or female. One cognitive theory invokes the notion of a gender schema, a framework of ideas about gender that makes perceptions fit categorical stereotypes. According to another cognitive theory, negotiated "scripts" guide sexual interactions and give them meaning.

13. The development of gender characteristics is probably multifactorial, and all the approaches just listed may be necessary for a full understanding of the process. Different factors probably interact, either in a simple additive way or via more complex chains of effects.

Discussion Questions

1. Do you think that this chapter presents a balanced account of psychological differences between the sexes, and of research into their origins? If not, why not? Did anything you read surprise you or cause you to reconsider your beliefs in this area?

2. To score the Bem Sex Role Inventory test (Figure 6.2), add the numbers you assigned to characteristics according to the color of the box in which they appear. Divide your total for each color by 20. The resulting number for the purple boxes is your masculinity score. The number for the green boxes is your femininity score, and that for the orange boxes is irrelevant. A person who scores above 4.9 (the approximate median score) on both masculinity and femininity scales is considered "androgynous." A person who scores 4.9 or below on both the masculinity and femininity scales is considered "undifferentiated." Did the results conform to what you imagined about yourself? Psychologists have varied opinions about how insightful the test is; what do you think?

3. Does society place too much emphasis on gender distinctions, or is this emphasis simply an acknowledgment of reality? What kinds of benefit or harm might this emphasis cause?

4. If there is some biological predisposition toward different traits or abilities in males and females, should that influence public policy in areas such as education and employment? For example, should it affect whether girls and boys are taught together or separately, or what criteria we use to judge whether equal-opportunity programs are working?

Web Resources

Harry Benjamin International Gender Dysphoria Association www.hbigda.org

Gramstad, T.: Androgyny and gender dialectics (a site devoted to the "deconstruction" of gender) www.math.uio.no/~thomas/gnd/androgyny.html

Gender Inn (a bibliographic source for books, articles, and Web sites concerning gender) www.uni-koeln.de/phil-fak/englisch/datenbank/e_index.htm

Recommended Reading

Colapinto, J. (2000). *As nature made him.* New York: HarperCollins.

Deaux, K., & LaFrance, M. (1998). Gender. In D. T. Gilbert, S. T. Fiske, and G. Lindzey (Eds.), *Handbook of social psychology* (4th ed.): Vol. 1. New York: McGraw-Hill.

Fausto-Sterling, A. (2000). *Sexing the body: Gender politics and the construction of sexuality.* New York: Basic Books.

Kimura, D. (1999). *Sex and cognition.* Cambridge, MA: MIT Press.

Mealey, L. (2000). *Sex differences: Developmental and evolutionary strategies.* San Diego: Academic Press.

Ruble, D. N., & Martin, C. L. (1997). Gender development. In Eisenberg, N. (Ed.), *Handbook of child psychology* (5th ed.): Vol. 3. New York: Wiley.

chapter 7

Both external and internal factors affect our attraction to others.

Sexual Attraction and Arousal

*T*he motivation to engage in sexual behavior has twin roots: in the external world and within ourselves. The external factors that influence sexual motivation include the attractiveness or unattractiveness of people that we meet, the way they behave toward us, and a host of other circumstances that modify or channel our sexual arousal. The internal factors include durable aspects of our individual identity (such as our sexual orientation) as well as internal states that change over time (such as being less interested in sex right after having engaged in it). It is this tension between our inner sexuality and the outer world of sexual interactions and behaviors that gives sex its unpredictability and its endless fascination.

Beauty Is Not Entirely in the Eye of the Beholder

Let's start by looking at one aspect of attractiveness: facial appearance. We don't mean to imply that this is the only, or even the main, source of sexual attraction. The remainder of the body is obviously important too, as are a person's psychological attributes, behavior, and so on. As we'll see later, men are somewhat more liable to judge potential sex partners by physical features such as facial appearance, while women are somewhat more liable to judge potential partners by nonphysical features, such the size of their bank accounts. (We leave you to judge which sex is shallower in that regard.)

Still, facial beauty is something that both men and women have celebrated throughout human history, from the "face that launched a thousand ships" (Helen of Troy) to the visage of the latest Hollywood leading man. So facial appearance is clearly one important trigger for sexual interest and arousal.

Here's a thought experiment. You collect photographs of the faces of a hundred men and women and show them to a large number of subjects from around the world. You ask the subjects to rate the faces in order of attractiveness. Would all the subjects place the faces in a similar order, reflecting some absolute scale of attractiveness that all humans use to judge faces? Or would each subject rank the faces in some completely idiosyncratic order, reflecting the total subjectivity of sexual attraction?

The answer, as you probably guessed, lies somewhere between those extremes. People do differ considerably in their judgments of attractiveness; these differences are caused by cultural factors such as the racial group or cultural milieu that a person happens to grow up in, by a person's sex and sexual orientation, or simply by quirky preferences for certain types of faces. But in spite of all these differences, there are also consistencies: some faces strike most people as very beautiful, some as "average-looking," and some as positively unattractive. To a certain extent, beauty is not in the eye of the beholder, but in the face of the beholdee.

Human faces offer astonishing diversity, and no two people would place them in the same order of attractiveness. Yet there do seem to be some universals that affect people's judgments.

A Few Principles Govern Facial Attractiveness

While many aspects of facial appearance may influence attractiveness, three have been the subject of particular study by cognitive psychologists. These are left–right symmetry, "averageness," and masculinity–femininity.

Symmetry   We have already mentioned in Chapter 2 that animals look for symmetry in their mates. So do humans. The more symmetrical a person's face, the more attractive, sexier, and healthier that person seems to others (Grammer & Thornhill, 1994) (Box 7.1). Symmetry raises the attractiveness of the remainder of the body, too.

Facial and bodily symmetry is associated with other kinds of attractiveness. For example, a group at the University of California, Davis, found that symmetrical faces were rated as more attractive—even when the raters were only shown *one side* of the face, so that symmetry itself could not be directly assessed (Scheib et al., 1999). In another study, men's assessment of the attractiveness of women's body odor was correlated with the women's facial symmetry (Rikowski & Grammer, 1999). These findings suggest that

Box 7.1 Research Highlights

Twins, Symmetry, and Attractiveness

(A) Symmetry and attractiveness. Unmanipulated photographs of monozygotic twins 1 and 2. Which do you find more attractive?

(B) "Double-left" and "double-right" composite images of twin 1 (above) and twin 2 (below). Which of the pairs are more similar to each other?

Psychologist Linda Mealey (now at the College of St. Benedict in St. Joseph, Minnesota) and her colleagues studied the relative attractiveness and facial symmetry of monozygotic twins (Mealey et al., 1999). If you want to "play along," first answer the questions under the photographs, then read further.

Monozygotic ("identical") twins share the same genes, but the vicissitudes of development ensure that they do not end up looking perfectly identical. Mealey gathered photographs of 34 pairs of monozygotic twins, and had a large number of college students pick the more attractive member of each pair. In the example shown in Figure A, most students rated twin 2 as more attractive than twin 1.

To compare the visible symmetry of the two faces, Mealey used a computer to make two composites of each face. In each composite, one half of the image—say, the left—was the real image of the left side of the person's face, while the other half was a mirror-reversed version of that same left half—we'll call this the "double-left" image. The other composite was the "double-right" image. Obviously, the more symmetrical the original face, the more similar the double-left and double-right composites of that face would look.

Mealey asked another set of students to look at these composites and judge whether the composites for twin A or for twin B were more alike. This was a judgment as to which twin's face was more symmetrical. Consistently, the twin who was judged more symmetrical by this test was also judged more attractive, even though the two kinds of judgments were made by different raters. In the examples shown here (Figure B), the lower pair of images, made from the more attractive twin 2, were judged more similar to each other than the upper pair of images, made from the less attractive twin 1. Because twins 1 and 2 started out with the same genes, it appears that environmental factors or random processes triggered asymmetrical development in twin 1, with a corresponding reduction in attractiveness.

symmetry and other cues provide information about some common underlying variable, such as health, in the person being observed.

In Chapter 2, we discussed a possible evolutionary explanation for why asymmetry is unattractive (Thornhill & Gangestad, 1999). (We are referring here to random or **fluctuating asymmetry,** not the planned asymmetry of, say, the heart within the thorax.) Because the same genetic instructions guide the development of the two sides of the body, a high degree of fluctuating asymmetry can occur only if the genetic program is derailed in some way. Either the person's genes were of poor quality, or they ran into some kind of interference (such as an infection) during development. Indeed, humans with a high degree of fluctuating asymmetry are more likely to suffer from a variety of disorders—including extremely premature birth, certain forms of mental retardation, schizophrenia, and psychological and physiological distress—than are more symmetrical persons (Shackelford & Larsen, 1997). Thus, it is plausible that evolution would favor the spread of genes conferring the means to assess symmetry and the motivation to prefer it.

There is another, more cognitive interpretation of this preference, which is not necessarily inconsistent with the one just given. Symmetrical structures may be more attractive than asymmetrical structures because less information is required to mentally process and memorize them. One only has to process one side of the structure and then add the fact that the other side is its mirror image. Consistent with this interpretation, we find symmetry attractive in animals, snowflakes, poetry, and musical compositions, and not just in our potential sex partners.

Averageness A more controversial aspect of facial attractiveness is **averageness.** In common parlance, "average-looking" is hardly a compliment. Nevertheless, artificial faces generated by computer averaging of many real faces of the same sex (let's call them "Average Joe" and "Average Jane") are rated as more attractive than the real faces used to generate the composites (Langlois et al., 1994). It is possible that Average Joe and Average Jane are attractive because they resemble internal **prototypes** of the male and female face—hypothetical mental representations that we may use as a basis for assessing attractiveness, and which could correspond to our "ideals" of male and female beauty.

More recent studies, however, have shown that Average Joe and Average Jane are not the most attractive of all possible faces. A group at the University of St. Andrews in Scotland, led by David Perrett, reported that it was possible to generate an even more attractive computer-averaged female face, simply by starting with a collection of real female faces that were rated as more attractive than most (Perrett et al., 1994) (Figure 7.1). We'll call this image "Super-Jane." This finding makes clear that simple averageness is not the only key to attractiveness.

The Scottish group went one step further. They instructed their computer to measure the differences between Average Jane and Super-Jane, and then to generate a new image

Figure 7.1 Average Jane, Super-Jane, and Ultra-Jane. Average Jane (left) was generated by computer-averaging the faces of 60 U.K. Caucasian women aged 20–30. Super-Jane (center) was generated by computer-averaging the 15 faces rated as the most attractive of the 60; she was rated more attractive than Average Jane. Ultra-Jane (right) was generated by exaggerating the differences between Average Jane and Super-Jane; she was rated as more attractive than Super-Jane. (From Perrett et al., 1994.)

(we'll call her "Ultra-Jane") in which the facial features went beyond those of Super-Jane, in a direction away from Average Jane. So if Super-Jane's chin was smaller than Average Jane's, for example, the computer made Ultra-Jane's chin even smaller than Super-Jane's. Ultra-Jane, which was now very remote from an average female face, was rated as even more attractive than Super-Jane.

It may be that the main aspect of Average Joe and Jane that is attractive is their facial symmetry—computer-averaged faces are necessarily very symmetrical. While Average Joe and Average Jane may indeed resemble our internal prototypes of male and female faces, these prototypes do not seem to correspond to our ideals of male and female beauty, aside from their symmetry.

Masculinity–femininity   What, then, is so attractive about Ultra-Jane? Most likely, it is that she is very *feminine*. It is possible to computer-generate a face that "morphs" continuously from a "hyper-masculine" face through an androgynous face to a "hyper-feminine" face (Figure 7.2). Nearly everyone finds faces near the extremes of this range to be the most attractive, according to psychologist Victor Johnston of New Mexico State University. This finding suggests that masculinity–femininity is an important aspect of attractiveness (Johnston et al., 2001).

The actual cues to facial masculinity–femininity are things such as jaw width (wider in males), mouth and nose width (wider in males), chin size (larger in males), lip fullness (fuller in females), eyebrow bushiness (bushier in males), and eye size (larger in females). Such differences are largely generated under the influence of androgens (male traits) and estrogens (female traits) at puberty. Thus, faces seem to become more attractive the more sexually differentiated they are. (We will see later that factors intrinsic to the observer, such as the phase of a woman's menstrual cycle, also influence judgments of attractiveness.)

Why are these sexually differentiated traits attractive, in an evolutionary sense? In part, they simply announce that the person has undergone a sex-typical puberty and is therefore likely to be fertile. In addition, the traits may be advantageous in themselves. Victor Johnston, for example, has suggested that the extreme masculine face represents the "healthy hunter," who would be well adapted for survival in early human evolution: the wide mouth and nose facilitate a high respiration rate during strenuous exercise, for example, while the prominent brow ridge and eyebrows keep sunlight and sweat out the eyes.

On the other hand, some attractive traits could be nonadaptive or even maladaptive. In Chapter 2 we discussed evidence that sexual selection can lead to traits that are actual handicaps, such as antlers that get caught in trees or long tails that hamper birds' flight. Whether humans have any such traits is unclear, but one could interpret women's small jaws in that way—they might have made eating difficult in the days before cooked or processed food. Women's large breasts could also be a handicap. Such ideas are entirely speculative, but they do offer a potential reason why every person is not perfectly beautiful: early in our species' history, there may have been a trade-off between extreme attractiveness and the ability to survive.

Figure 7.2 The face that changes sex. Seven frames from a movie of a face that gradually morphs from hyper-masculine (left) through androgynous (center) to hyper-feminine (right). The faces at the two extremes are generally rated the most attractive. (The complete movie can be seen at http://www.psych.nmsu.edu.) (From Johnston et al., 2001.)

The Attractiveness of Bodies May Be Related to Reproductive Success

Men's and women's bodies are more distinct than are men's and women's faces. Like facial attractiveness, bodily attractiveness is often a matter of being near one or the other extreme of the masculine–feminine continuum. Thus body parts that differ relatively little between the sexes, such as the hands and feet, also contribute relatively little to judgments of attractiveness. In general, then, it is likely that the attractiveness of a body signals information about its sexual differentiation under the influence of sex hormones, and hence about its fertility, strength, health, and other traits important for reproduction.

Devendra Singh of the University of Texas, Austin, has produced evidence that one simple variable, the **waist-to-hip ratio,** has an important influence on attractiveness (Singh, 1994a, 1994b, 1995). After puberty, women store much of their fat in the area of the hips, buttocks, and thighs. Men tend to accumulate their fat higher in the body, at the waist and above. Thus, the ratio of the body circumference at the waist to the body circumference at the hip is lower for women than for men, and this holds across a wide range of body sizes, from leanness to obesity (Figure 7.3).

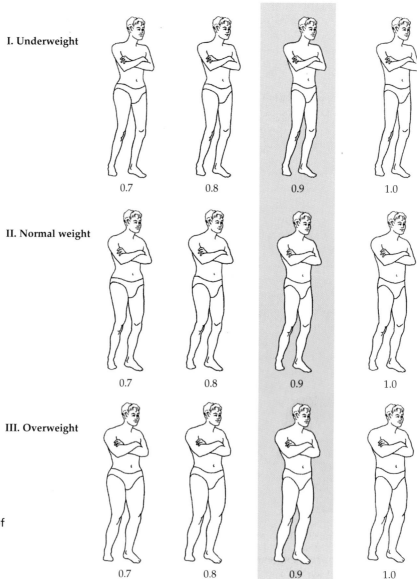

Figure 7.3 Waist-to-hip ratio and attractiveness. Women are most attracted to men with a waist-to-hip ratio (WHR) of 0.9 (shaded row); this is true whether men are underweight (row I), normal weight (row II), or overweight (row III). Men are most attracted to women with a WHR of 0.7–0.8.

Women judge men to be most attractive if they have a waist-to-hip ratio of 0.9, while men judge women to be most attractive if they have a waist-to-hip ratio of 0.7–0.8. These preferences hold up across diverse cultures. According to Singh, both men and women perceive variations in waist-to-hip ratio as indicating a person's healthiness, and there is some evidence that this perception is well grounded: men and women with ratios far from the "optimum" for their sex are at increased risk for a variety of diseases.

Although the waist-to-hip ratio may be a universal indicator of attractiveness, absolute body fatness is not. In contemporary U.S. culture, thin women are generally considered more attractive than those who are of average weight or obese, at least to judge by the appearance of successful female models and film stars. In some non-Western cultures, on the other hand, obese women may be strongly preferred, as we discussed in Chapter 1 (see Box 1.2).

What's the explanation for such a radical difference in standards of beauty? Most likely it has to do with food availability. In societies where calorie-rich food is scarce and most people are thin, obesity demonstrates that a woman has exceptional access to resources. Obesity also indicates that a woman has energy reserves to successfully carry a pregnancy, even if future food supplies should dwindle. In the contemporary United States, on the other hand, most of us can get enough food to become obese, and future shortages are unlikely. Obesity has therefore lost its value as a measure of attractiveness. Why extreme thinness should be held up as the ideal of female beauty, on the other hand, remains something of a mystery. Perhaps it is simply the fact that thinness, in our society, is difficult to achieve.

Female **breasts** are obviously sexually attractive to many men, but the issue of breast *size* is less clear. Any student of contemporary American culture might conclude that the attractiveness of breasts increases without limit as they become larger, so that only the crippling burden of carrying around several liters of silicone could bring the "rack race" to a halt. Psychological research has produced more equivocal findings. One study found that increasing breast size had *no* effect on the perceived attractiveness of women to men, and actually decreased their attractiveness to other women (Horvath, 1981). A more recent study found that men did prefer breasts of larger-than-average size, but not nearly as large as women *thought* men liked (Thompson & Tantleff, 1992).

In terms of men's bodies, the two just-mentioned studies found that the width of the shoulders and the size of the pectoral muscles ("pecs") influenced women's ratings of male attractiveness, presumably by increasing their perceived strength (Figure 7.4A). Men have used clothing and adornment to increase their apparent shoulder width since time immemorial. Interestingly, women with a need to assert strength (such as historical female monarchs and contemporary women in the male-dominated business world) have followed the same strategy (Figure 7.4B).

Are these various cues to attractiveness hard-wired into our brains, perhaps as a result of our genetic endowment, or are they a matter of learning and culture? One way this question has been addressed is by making comparisons across cultures (Bernstein et al., 1982). In the case of female breasts, some human cultures place little emphasis on them as sexually attractive features and do not require women to cover them. This is the case in the traditional culture of Mali (West Africa), for example (Dettwyler, 1994). In non-Western cultures that do consider the breasts sexually attractive, the preferred appearance may range from small and upright to long and pendulous (Ford & Beach, 1951).

An offbeat theory to explain the evolution of large human breasts was proposed by Desmond Morris in his book *The Naked Ape* (Morris, 1967). Morris suggested that women's breasts evolved to mimic buttocks, which, he argues, were important cues for rear-entry coitus in our prehuman ancestors. By developing breasts that looked like buttocks, women encouraged men to "come around to the front"—with important consequences in terms of pair bonding. This theory would seem to fall into the category of wild ideas that are almost certainly wrong, but that will never be proved one way or the other. It is important to point out that our close relatives, the bonobos, practice a great deal of front-to-front sex (see Chapter 2), even though bonobo breasts are small and have no apparent sexual significance.

Can breasts be too big? This is porn actress Pandora Peaks with porn movie director Russ Meyer.

(A)

(B)

Figure 7.4 Shouldering the male role. Broad, muscular shoulders are generally considered attractive in men (A). Women who wish to project authority in a male-dominated field may use shoulder pads to give a similar appearance (B).

Figure 7.5 Improving on nature. A stretched lower lip, produced by insertion of progressively larger plugs or plates, is considered attractive in parts of Chad and Ethiopia. This woman is Ethiopian.

People generally find faces of individuals from their own ethnic group more attractive than faces from other groups—a finding that almost certainly reflects an influence of early experience. However, individuals in different cultures rely on similar cues to attractiveness. Furthermore, people make consistent judgments of faces from other cultures. The way that Caucasians rank the attractiveness of Japanese faces, for example, is similar to the way that Japanese rank those same faces (Perrett et al., 1994). It appears that there are more similarities than differences in the way people from different cultures assess attractiveness.

Of course, styles of adornment considered attractive vary greatly between cultures. U.S. readers may not find the woman illustrated in Figure 7.5 particularly attractive, for example. Even here, though, there is some suggestion of universality, because the particular trait that you may find unattractive in this woman—her enormously stretched lower lip—is an exaggeration of a feminine trait that is also perceived as attractive in Western culture: full lips. Full lips result in part from the action of estrogens and thus, like full breasts, offer clues about a woman's fertility.

If there is some universality to attractiveness, one may wonder whether very young children are sensitive to it. It seems that they are. When infants as young as 4 months are presented with pairs of images of faces, one of which has been rated by adults as more attractive than the other, the infants spend more time looking at the more attractive face (Samuels et al., 1994).

From the general appearance of a person's face and body, we can assess their age, which is an important criterion for attractiveness in women, at least according to men. When judging women solely by physical appearance, men find women decreasingly attractive from the late teen years onward (Mathes et al., 1985). A preference for women of youthful appearance is found in men of all ages, but is most marked for younger men. This preference is hardly surprising from the point of view of evolutionary psychology, since younger women are at the height of their fertility and can expect enough healthy years ahead to nurture children to adulthood (Kenrick et al., 1996). Women's judgments of men's physical attractiveness do not vary nearly so much with the men's age, consistent with the fact that a man's reproductive potential declines less rapidly with age.

Everyone knows that the odor of a person's body can have a strong influence on their attractiveness. Some researchers, however, have gone farther, claiming that there are specific sex pheromones in men and women that influence sexual arousal through unconscious mechanisms. This topic is highly controversial, however (Box 7.2).

Attractiveness Is Strongly Modulated by Sexual Orientation

So far, we have largely focused on objective aspects of attractiveness, with some reference to the fact that men and women tend to find different traits attractive. Next we focus on aspects of sexual attraction that are intrinsic to the person who is experiencing the attraction. The most important variable in this area is **sexual orientation.** As already spelled out in the previous chapter, sexual orientation defines how a person's disposition to experience sexual attraction varies with the sex of their potential sex partners. In the usual **heterosexual/bisexual/homosexual** categorization, the

Box 7.2 Biology of Sex

Human Sex Pheromones: Are They Real?

An ever-increasing number of products are available for sale that claim to contain human sex pheromones—skin-borne effusions that are purported to turn people on at a single sniff. Just a few years ago, the Erox Corporation, with its Realm Men and Realm Women, was the only player in this field, but now a quick Web search identifies dozens of competitors. Unfortunately for scientific romantics, just as human sex pheromones have hit a public relations high point, the scientific community has turned increasingly skeptical about their existence.

Sex pheromones were first identified in insects, in which they function as powerful come-hither signals, luring prospective mates from blocks away. Many nonhuman mammals also release sex-specific odorants, which are detected by a special sense organ in the nose, called the **vomeronasal organ** or **VNO** (Keverne, 1999). The cells in the VNO of rodents possess a special suite of receptor molecules not found in the regular olfactory mucosa, and nerves run from this organ to parts of the brain that are known to be involved in sexual behavior. When a rodent's VNO is blocked, its sex life is seriously disrupted. And when male mice are genetically modified to lack a key protein in the VNO, they fail to distinguish males from females and engage in sexual behavior with both. Surprisingly, however, this seems to be because they fail to detect pheromones from males that normally block male–male sexual behavior (Stowers et al., 2002).

The main proponents of the idea that humans have a sex pheromone system have been entrepreneur David Berliner (founder of the Erox Corporation) and neurophysiologist Luis Monti-Bloch of the University of Utah (seen examining a volunteer's nose in the figure) (Monti-Bloch et al., 1998). In a series of well-publicized studies in the early 1990s, Monti-Bloch claimed to find a VNO in the human nose and identified two chemicals in human sweat that triggered specific electrical activity in the VNO: one that worked on men, the other on women. Monti-Bloch and Berliner reported that these chemicals, metabolic precursors or derivatives of sex hormones, induced a sense of well-being in those who smelled them. These chemicals became the active ingredients in Berliner's Realm perfumes.

More recently, however, a slew of studies have cast doubt on the very existence of the VNO system in humans. Three groups of researchers (at the University of Texas, at the Walter Reed Medical Center in Washington, and at the École Pratique des Hautes Études in Paris) searched for a VNO in the noses of a large number of living persons. The two U.S. groups (Won et al., 2000; Zbar et al., 2000) found evidence for a VNO in only a minority of people. The French group did estimate that as much as 73 percent of the population might have some trace of a VNO, but when they examined histological specimens of the structure under the microscope, they found no receptor cells and no nerve fibers connecting it to the brain (Trotier et al., 2000). This finding is consistent with anatomical studies suggesting that the VNO is a vestigial structure in humans—a relic of our evolutionary past that forms during embryonic life, but then atrophies, leaving a nonfunctional remnant (Smith & Bhatnagar, 2000).

Genetic studies support this conclusion. Rodents have three groups of genes, named *V1R*, *V2R*, and *V3R*, that code for the receptor molecules in the VNO. Two groups of researchers (one at the Institut de Genetique Humaine in Montpellier, France, and the other at Caltech) have searched for the corresponding human genes, but all they have found are "pseudogenes"—nonfunctional relics of what used to be working genes in our long-ago evolutionary past (Giorgi et al., 2000; Kouros-Mehr et al., 2001). These findings are inconsistent with the notion that humans have a working VNO similar to that of rodents.

Richard Doty, director of the Smell and Taste Center at the University of Pennsylvania Medical Center is now very skeptical of the pro-VNO results of the Monti-Bloch group. He suggested that technical problems, such as failure to prevent test odors from spreading to the regular olfactory mucosa, could account for their findings. According to Doty, human sex pheromones probably don't exist. Even in rodents, he added, "pheromones" are not very pheromone-like, because they don't elicit automatic responses, as they do in insects (Doty, personal communication). There is a possibility that human sex pheromones exist, but are sensed by the regular olfactory system, not the VNO. And, of course, consciously perceived odors affect sexual attraction. There are those who still believe that the olfactory system plays a central role in human sexuality, perhaps even influencing traits such as sexual orientation (Kohl & Francouer, 1995).

All in all, things don't look good for human sex pheromones—although you wouldn't know it from the marketing of those Love Potions #10. But basic principles of economics mean that with the influx of so many new products, the prices have come down: an $80 bottle of Realm was once the only option, but you can now get pheromone products for as little as $7.95. A cheap date indeed.

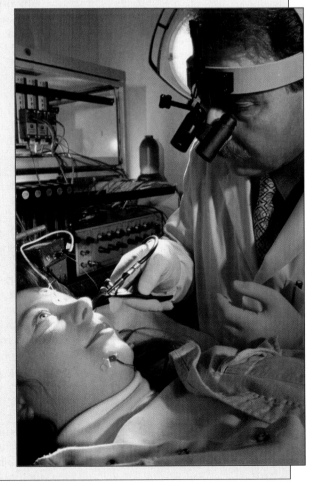

sex of the desired partners is defined relative to the sex of the viewer (i.e., attraction to persons of the opposite sex, of both sexes, or of the same sex). In the alternative **androphilic/bisexual/gynephilic** categorization, the sex of the desired partners is defined absolutely (i.e., attraction to males, to both sexes, or to females).

Not all cultures conceptualize sexual orientation in the same way (see Chapter 13), and one can argue that it is arbitrary to focus on sexual orientation, as just defined, as if it has some kind of natural primacy over other dimensions of sexual desire. To some extent, we focus on sexual orientation here for nonscientific reasons, especially because, in our culture, homosexuality has historically been viewed as a moral, legal, or medical deviance that needs to be prevented or corrected. Still, given that men and women do form the most basic divisions of the human race, attraction to men or to women (or to both) can reasonably be considered a basic classification of individuals' sexuality.

Somewhere between 0.5 and 4 Percent of Men and Women Are Homosexual

Of course, heterosexuality is the preponderant sexual orientation in the United States, and probably has been in all human societies. The first person to make a large-scale, systematic study of the distribution of sexual orientation was sexologist Alfred Kinsey of Indiana University, whom we met in Chapter 1. During the 1940s, Kinsey and his colleagues interviewed tens of thousands of men and women about many aspects of their sex lives. They published the results in two famous books, one focusing on men and the other on women (Kinsey et al., 1948; Kinsey et al., 1953).

Kinsey classified individuals' sexual orientation on a 7-point ranked scale, whereby "group 0" referred to individuals who were sexually attracted exclusively to persons of the other sex (heterosexual), "group 6" referred to individuals who were attracted exclusively to persons of the same sex (homosexual), and the intervening groups 1–5 referred to individuals who were attracted in varying degrees to both sexes. This "Kinsey scale," or variations on it, has been used by many subsequent researchers. It is not perfect; in particular, it suggests incorrectly that people have a fixed amount of sexual energy that they divide up in some characteristic way between male and female partners. But it has the merit of being simple and familiar.

When Kinsey published his findings, Americans were shocked by the apparent high prevalence of homosexual or bisexual attraction and behavior. One particular data point became engrained in the public consciousness: Kinsey reported that 10 percent of white U.S. males fall into group 6 or 5 (exclusively or nearly exclusively homosexual) for a period of at least 3 years between the ages of 16 and 55. This finding rapidly became simplified as "one in ten people are gay."

Important pioneer though Kinsey was, his sampling methods were haphazard by modern standards, and he very likely oversampled gay people. The significance of his figures is therefore not worth detailed discussion. Among recent U.S. studies that have used modern sampling techniques, the most important is the **National Health and Social Life Survey** (**NHSLS**), a survey of about 3400 men and women that was already mentioned in Chapter 1 (Laumann et al., 1994; Laumann & Michael, 2000). We will be referring to NHSLS frequently throughout the remainder of this book, as well as to a comparable but far larger British study (19,000 subjects) called the **National Survey of Sexual Attitudes and Lifestyles** (**NSSAL**) (Wellings et al., 1994). Both studies were spurred by the ravages of the AIDS epidemic. Both were initially planned as governmentally funded projects, both were axed by sex-shy politicians, and both were finally completed with private funding.

Concerning sexual orientation, NHSLS (which used a 5-point rather than a 7-point scale) obtained much lower figures for the prevalence of homosexuality than did Kinsey: only 6.3 percent of U.S. men and 4.4 percent of women said that they currently experienced *any* sexual attraction to persons of their own sex, and only 2.4 percent of men and 0.3 percent of women were attracted *exclusively* to persons of the same sex (Figure 7.6). NSSAL obtained roughly similar figures.

Interestingly, the shape of the sexual orientation histograms in Figure 7.6 is different for men and for women. For men, the distribution is clearly bimodal, with most individuals lying at or near one or other end of the distribution. For women, on the other hand, the distribution is unimodal—that is, there is no peak at the homosexual end of the distribution. This finding suggests that the homosexual–heterosexual nomenclature describes objective categories of men, whereas in women it is no more than an arbitrary way of dividing up a continuum.

The authors of both these studies were careful to emphasize that the percentages of persons who experience same-sex attraction should be considered minimal estimates, because their subjects may have been reluctant to admit to a stigmatized orientation. The true prevalence of exclusive homosexuality could be as high as 4 percent, according to some estimates (Taylor, 1993). We may never get an accurate estimate of the prevalence of homosexuality, however, until that orientation is as socially accepted as heterosexuality—at which point most people will have lost interest in the topic.

Estimates of the prevalence of homosexuality across different cultures or historical periods are even less certain. Sociologist Fred Whitam of Arizona State University has concluded that homosexual men constitute about 5 percent of the male population of large cities in many different countries (Whitam, 1983). The NHSLS and NSSAL both find that homosexuality is much less prevalent in rural than in metropolitan areas; this is probably because gay people migrate to cities. Thus, Whitam's 5 percent is not an estimate of the global prevalence of homosexuality.

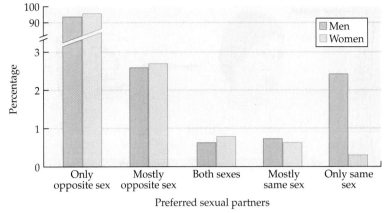

Figure 7.6 Sexual orientation data for U.S. men and women aged 18–59. (Data from NHSLS.)

The Prevalence of Bisexuality Depends on Definitions

The NHSLS and NSSAL studies suggest that bisexuality—when defined as any degree of sexual attraction to both men and women—is more prevalent than exclusive homosexuality in both sexes. The majority of bisexuals defined in this fashion, however, are much more attracted to the other sex than to the same sex (Kinsey group 1, or the "mostly opposite sex" column in the histograms of Figure 7.6). If bisexuality is defined as a roughly equal attraction to the two sexes, it is far less common, especially in men.

Indeed, some sexologists have contested the notion that true bisexuality exists in men at all. Kurt Freund, for example, studied sexual orientation by measuring men's physiological arousal (penile tumescence) while they viewed erotic photographs of men and women; he claimed never to have encountered a man who was aroused both by adult men and adult women (Freund, 1974). It is also true that "bisexual" is commonly used as a self-identifier by young men who are on their way to **coming out of the closet** (openly identifying as gay); as many as 40 percent of self-identified gay men say that they described themselves as "bisexual" at some point during early adulthood, according to one magazine survey (Lever, 1994). Thus, many self-identified "bisexual" men can be expected to come out as gay within a few years (Stokes et al., 1997). Still, bisexual organizations with plenty of male members do exist, and there is little reason to doubt the validity of these men's self-identification. No one doubts the reality of bisexuality in women, even if the numbers are uncertain. We take up the topic of bisexuality again in Chapter 13.

The Categorical Perception of Sex May Influence Sexual Orientation

How does sexual orientation "work"? According to the simplest model (Figure 7.7A), one could imagine that people respond differentially to male-typical and female-typical features in the faces, bodies, and behaviors of the people they meet, and that these differential responses constitute their sexual orientation. Thus, a straight man is straight because he finds small chins, narrow jaws, large eyes, and breasts, as well as female mannerisms and personality traits, attractive and (in the right circumstances) sexually arousing; a gay man is gay because he is attracted by wide jaws, large chins, smaller eyes, muscular chests, and male mannerisms and personality traits. In other words, a person's sexual orientation emerges directly from the way they process and evaluate raw sensory data. The problem with this model is that there is not enough perceptual information

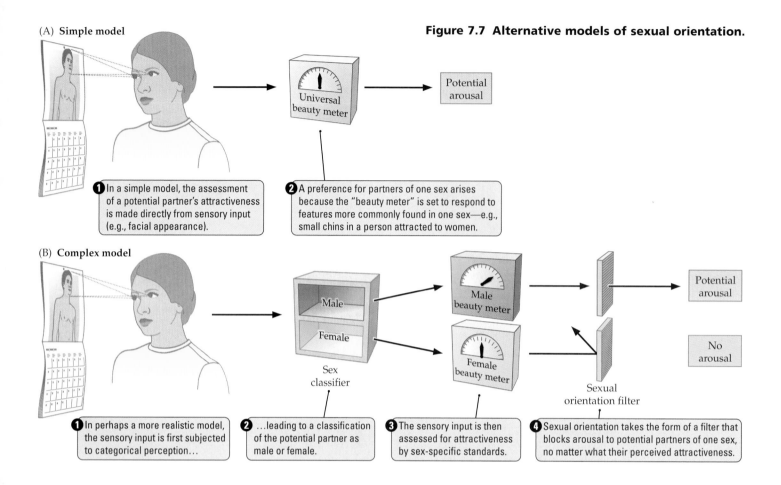

(A) Simple model

Universal beauty meter

Potential arousal

1 In a simple model, the assessment of a potential partner's attractiveness is made directly from sensory input (e.g., facial appearance).

2 A preference for partners of one sex arises because the "beauty meter" is set to respond to features more commonly found in one sex—e.g., small chins in a person attracted to women.

(B) Complex model

Male

Female

Sex classifier

Male beauty meter

Female beauty meter

Sexual orientation filter

Potential arousal

No arousal

1 In perhaps a more realistic model, the sensory input is first subjected to categorical perception…

2 …leading to a classification of the potential partner as male or female.

3 The sensory input is then assessed for attractiveness by sex-specific standards.

4 Sexual orientation takes the form of a filter that blocks arousal to potential partners of one sex, no matter what their perceived attractiveness.

Figure 7.7 Alternative models of sexual orientation.

in, say, faces, to support exclusive heterosexuality or homosexuality; many faces cannot be reliably discerned as male or female. With multiple cues the identification of a person's sex becomes highly reliable, of course, but sexual attraction is often experienced when sensory cues are limited.

According to a more complex model (Figure 7.7B), one could imagine that when presented with, say, a face, people first make an unconscious and nearly instantaneous classification of that face as male or female, based on the visual cues available. Such a process is called **categorical perception**. There is evidence to support the idea that the sex of faces is indeed perceived categorically (O'Toole et al., 1998). This judgment of a face's sex (which is likely to be correct, but could be wrong) powerfully influences the assessment of its attractiveness (Meerdink et al., 1990). If a straight woman perceives a face to be male, for example, she assesses the attractiveness of the face by reference to her standards of male attractiveness (such as those we have discussed above), and a face judged attractive may trigger sexual arousal. If she perceives a face as female, she may assess the attractiveness of the face (heterosexual women can make judgments of female beauty, after all), but whatever the result, it does not lead to sexual arousal.

This model helps explain how sexual orientation can be exclusive even though faces, bodies, and behaviors do not necessarily provide unambiguous cues to a person's sex. It also helps explain how an exclusively heterosexual or homosexual person can be sexually attracted to and aroused by a person of the "wrong" sex, and even have a sustained relationship with that person: so long as the person is *perceived* as being a member of the preferred sex, attraction and arousal are possible. Once the illusion is shattered, however, that person becomes nonarousing and even positively unattractive (because his or her attractiveness is now assessed with reference to standards for the other sex). These moments of shocked revelation have long been a staple of late-night television. The model can also account for why bisexual persons may be aroused by entirely different "looks" in men and in women.

Sexual Orientation Is Not an Isolated Trait

In the previous chapter we mentioned that lesbians and gay men have traditionally been thought of as having many characteristics of the other sex. Words such as "effeminate" have been applied to gay men, and "mannish" to lesbians, usually with derogatory implications. In reaction to such stereotyping, gays and lesbians themselves have tended to emphasize how similar they are to other people of the same sex, with the single exception of their sexual attractions.

You probably know at least one or two gay people. If you happen to be gay yourself, you may have scores of gay friends and acquaintances. Either way, you can hardly have avoided noticing that lesbians and gay men are a very mixed bunch. Some are the picture of orthodoxy for their sex, some are a trifle nonconformist, and some are flagrant gender rebels. Straight people are not always "straight-acting," either.

Psychologists have approached this issue by studying gender-related traits in large numbers of gay and straight people. All too often, unfortunately, these studies have focused on the differences in the mean results for the gay and straight groups, and have ignored the diversity *within* the two populations—let alone studying what traits bisexual men or women might exhibit.

Gays and Lesbians May Be Gender-Nonconformist during Childhood

Probably the single clearest finding has to do with the *childhood* of gay men and lesbians. As a group, children who become gay adults (we'll call them "pre-gay children") conform less strictly to gender norms than children who become straight adults (Bailey & Zucker, 1995). Pre-gay boys tend to engage less in rough-and-tumble play, aggressive behavior, and athletics, to be less focused on typical boys' toys and boys' activities, to enjoy interacting with girls, to have a social reputation as a "sissy," and to have less stereotypically male career plans. For pre-lesbian girls, the opposite is true: such girls tend to be very active physically, to be considered a tomboy, to have male-typical career plans, and so on. The differences are considerably more marked for males than for females—in large part because girls are generally more diverse than boys in terms of their adherence to gender norms. Nevertheless, the overall effect sizes (*d*) are large: 1.3 for males and 1.0 for females. Furthermore, the relationship between childhood gender nonconformity and adult homosexuality appears to hold for males and females in several different cultures (Whitam, 1980; Whitam & Mathy, 1991).

For the most part, these findings are based on interviews in which gay and straight adults are asked to recall their childhoods. One could argue that this approach invites distortions, caused perhaps by people's desire to fulfill stereotypes. (One example: Radclyffe Hall, who wrote the 1928 lesbian classic, *The Well of Loneliness*, is said to have had her childhood photographs retouched to eliminate her long hair.) In the case of men, however, the findings of these retrospective studies are bolstered by two prospective (forward-looking) studies, one of which is described in Box 7.3. Unfortunately, no comparable prospective study of females has been performed.

It is important to emphasize that, even though the connection between childhood gender nonconformity and adult homosexuality is very strong, it is not strong enough that one can predict a child's future sexual orientation with confidence. The majority of gay men have mildly gender-nonconformist childhoods, as do quite a few straight men. Similarly, just being a tomboy does not mean that a girl will become lesbian or bisexual. Far from it: the odds are still quite strongly in favor of her becoming heterosexual.

Gay Adults Show a Mixture of Gender-Typical and Gender-Atypical Traits

Numerous studies have compared the cognitive traits, personalities, and behaviors of gay and straight adults. Gay men seem to be *gender-atypical* in some of these traits. For example, several studies have found that gay men are less aggressive than straight men, perform less well on tests of visuospatial skill (such as mental rotation and targeting accuracy; Figure 7.8), and perform better on some tests of verbal fluency (Ellis et al., 1990; Gladue & Bailey,

(A)

(B)

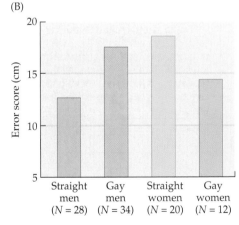

Figure 7.8 Targeting accuracy is a visuospatial skill that varies with both sex and sexual orientation. (A) Subjects threw a ball underhanded toward the center of a target; results for both hands were averaged together. (B) Heterosexual men were more accurate (made smaller errors) than heterosexual women. Gay men performed worse, and lesbians performed better, than their heterosexual counterparts. (After Hall and Kimura, 1995.)

Box 7.3 Research Highlights

Boys Will Be Girls

There has long been "folk wisdom" to the effect that feminine boys have a high chance of becoming homosexual when they grow up. In the late 1960s, psychiatrist Richard Green of UCLA initiated an ambitious prospective study to test the truth of this notion (Green, 1987). He recruited 66 families in which there was a son (aged 4 to 10) who was markedly feminine. These were not just slightly unmasculine boys. Here's an excerpt from one interview Green had with a 5-year-old boy, "Richard," whose parents brought him to Green because of his persistent cross-dressing, role-playing as a girl, and avoidance of male playmates:

> Green: Have you ever wished you'd been born a girl?
> Richard: Yes.
> Green: Why did you wish that?
> Richard: Girls, they don't have to have a penis.
> Green: They don't have to have a penis?
> Richard: They can have babies. And—because they—it doesn't tickle when you tickle them here.
> Green: It doesn't tickle when you tickle them here? Where your penis is?
> Richard: Yeah. 'Cause they don't have a penis. I wish I was a girl.
> Green: You wish you were a girl?
> Richard: You know what? I might be a girl.

Green also recruited 56 boys as matched controls; these boys were chosen without regard to their gender characteristics. He interviewed the boys and their parents repeatedly during their childhood, adolescence, and (in many cases) young adulthood.

The central finding of the study could hardly be more striking. The control boys who Green was able to follow through to adolescence or adulthood became, with one slight exception, totally heterosexual (see figure). Of the feminine boys he was able to follow, the majority became bisexual or homosexual. Since some of these boys were only in their mid-teens at their last interview, there is every reason to imagine that some of them moved further toward exclusive homosexuality as they entered adulthood. Interestingly, although many of the feminine boys had wished they were girls, most of them actually became fairly conventional gay men without markedly feminine traits, and only one expressed an interest in sex reassignment surgery.

In spite of the marked difference in outcomes for the two groups, we should make a couple of cautionary points. First, some of the feminine boys were entirely heterosexual at their last interview (in fact, "Richard" was one of these). Thus, childhood characteristics are not entirely predictive of adult orientation, even for these extreme gender-nonconformist kids. Second, most gay men do not have a history of such radical gender nonconformity during their childhood; in fact, some recall a very conventionally masculine childhood.

Green himself went through a striking evolution during the course of the study. At the outset, he believed that socialization and parental treatment were the main determinants of gender. (He trained with

John Money, whose socialization theory was discussed in Chapter 6.) Green tried to help parents steer their feminine sons toward masculinity, and he referred some of them to a UCLA psychologist named George Rekers, who instituted efforts to make the

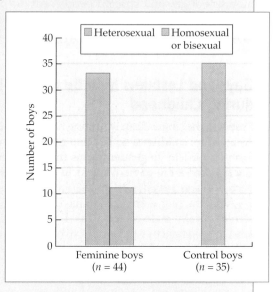

boys more masculine by means of behavioral therapy. Later Green became very "gay-friendly" and increasingly accepted biological theories of gender and sexual orientation. He now runs the gender identity clinic at the Charing Cross Hospital in London, where he studies biological markers that may be associated with homosexuality and transexuality.

1995; Hall & Kimura, 1995; Wegesin, 1998). There have also been some negative reports in these same areas, however (Gladue & Bailey, 1995). For the most part, these and other studies have failed to find comparable differences between lesbian and heterosexual women.

Generally, gay men describe themselves as less masculine in a range of traits than do straight men, and lesbians describe themselves as less feminine than do straight women (Lippa, 2000). Gays and lesbians also tend to disregard gender norms in their choice of occupations and recreational interests (Lippa, 2002). Some occupational choices of gay men, such as their strong representation in the arts, theater, and professional dance (Bailey & Oberschneider, 1997), are not easily explicable either in terms of gender conformity *or* gender nonconformity (see also Chapter 13).

In the area of sexuality, gay people have some gender-typical and some gender-atypical traits (Bailey et al., 1994). The most striking gender-*typical* trait concerns interest in uncommitted sex. Like straight men, gay men have a strong interest in casual sex and multiple partners. Because those partners are men, gay men are in a far better position to satisfy this interest than are straight men, who are restricted by women's lower interest in uncommitted sex. For lesbians, it's the opposite: like heterosexual women, they tend to have a low interest in casual sex and to have few partners. In some cultures and time periods, this behavioral difference between gay men and lesbians has reached remarkable proportions. In San Francisco in the pre-AIDS era, for example, almost one-half of the white gay men, and one-third of the black gay men, reported that they had had at least 500 different male sex partners, whereas most of the lesbians had had fewer than 10 female partners (Bell & Weinberg, 1978). More recent national studies have come up with much less dramatic findings, but still confirm that men who have sex with men tend to have more total partners than any other group. In the NHSLS study, for example, men who had had at least one male sex partner in the previous 5 years reported (on average) a total of 17 partners in that period, compared with 5 for men who had no same-sex partners.

The gender-*atypical* sexual traits include the following. Lesbians are significantly more interested than straight women in visual sexual stimuli, though they do not match gay or straight men in this regard. Lesbians are less concerned than straight women with their partners' social status. Gay men are less prone than straight men to sexual jealousy. They are also somewhat less focused on their partners' youth as a criterion for attractiveness (Bailey et al., 1994).

In short, there is a partial correlation between sexual orientation and other aspects of gender. Gays and lesbians are not gender "inverts," but they are distinctly atypical in some gender-related traits. The differences between gay and straight people are generally more marked for men than for women. There is also much variation *within* the categories of lesbians and gay men—terms such as "butch/femme" and "top/bottom" are often used within those communities to categorize gay people in terms of gender roles or preferred sexual behaviors. So far, this kind of variation has been the subject of very little scientific study, but we shall have more to say about it in Chapter 13.

Diverse Theories Attempt to Explain Sexual Orientation

What causes a person to become heterosexual, bisexual, or homosexual? This is a question that has aroused a great deal of interest and controversy over the years, both among the general public and among doctors and academics. In popular discourse, the question has often been phrased in such forms as "What makes people gay?"—as if heterosexuality didn't require any explanation. In reality, of course, heterosexuality, homosexuality, and bisexuality all need some kind of explanation (even if the last of these three has been largely ignored or lumped together with homosexuality).

Most theories of sexual orientation could be described as either psychodynamic or biological. **Psychodynamic theories** attempt to explain the development of a person's sexual orientation in terms of internal mental process, especially as they are affected by interaction with others, rewards and punishments, and so on. Examples include psychoanalytic theory and socialization theory. **Biological theories** attempt to explain sexual orientation in terms of phenomena such as brain circuitry, hormones, genes, and evolution. The conflict between proponents of these two classes of ideas has been going on for at least a century (see Box 1.1). It is unlikely that either class of theory, by itself, can provide a complete understanding of sexual orientation.

Freud Put Forward Elaborate Developmental Theories to Explain Both Heterosexuality and Homosexuality

Throughout most of the twentieth century, thinking about sexual orientation centered on the psychoanalytic theories of Sigmund Freud (see Box 1.1). Freud saw heterosexuality as the end stage of a number of phases of psychosexual development (Freud, 1975) (Figure 7.9). Initially, Freud proposed, a child's sex drive (**libido**) is directed toward himself or herself, and receives satisfaction through stimulation of the mouth ("oral phase"), the anus ("anal phase," in which sexual pleasure is derived from defecation or from the retention of feces), and finally of the phallus (penis or clitoris—"phallic phase"). Young boys become so focused on their genitalia, Freud said, that their libido becomes attached

Figure 7.9 Freud's theory of male homosexuality. Freud interpreted male homosexuality as resulting from a blockage of normal psychosexual development. In addition, he proposed that the preference of some homosexual men for receptive anal sex results from a failure of the transition from the anal phase to the phallic phase at about 2 years of age.

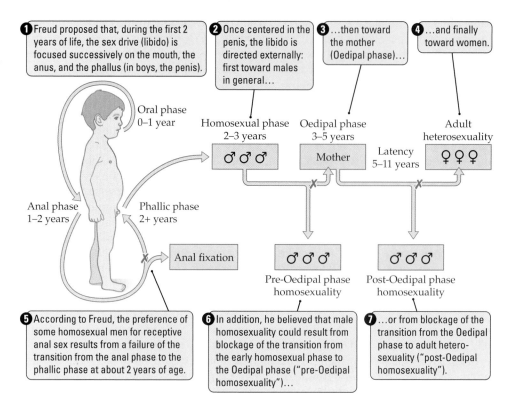

❶ Freud proposed that, during the first 2 years of life, the sex drive (libido) is focused successively on the mouth, the anus, and the phallus (in boys, the penis).

❷ Once centered in the penis, the libido is directed externally: first toward males in general…

❸ …then toward the mother (Oedipal phase)…

❹ …and finally toward women.

Oral phase 0–1 year

Homosexual phase 2–3 years

Oedipal phase 3–5 years

Adult heterosexuality

Latency 5–11 years

Mother

Anal phase 1–2 years

Phallic phase 2+ years

Anal fixation

Pre-Oedipal phase homosexuality

Post-Oedipal phase homosexuality

❺ According to Freud, the preference of some homosexual men for receptive anal sex results from a failure of the transition from the anal phase to the phallic phase at about 2 years of age.

❻ In addition, he believed that male homosexuality could result from blockage of the transition from the early homosexual phase to the Oedipal phase ("pre-Oedipal homosexuality")…

❼ …or from blockage of the transition from the Oedipal phase to adult hetero-sexuality ("post-Oedipal homosexuality").

to all persons with male genitalia. This "homosexual phase" occurs at around the age of 2. It is not consciously remembered later, but evidence of its existence can supposedly be uncovered through psychoanalysis. A year or two later, the boy's libido becomes strongly directed toward his mother (the "Oedipal phase"). As childhood ends, the boy breaks off this "sexual" relationship with his mother as part of the process of becoming an autonomous human being. His libido is then free to be directed toward other females, and he becomes a heterosexual adult.

Male homosexuality, Freud suggested, can develop by one of two routes. In the first route ("pre-Oedipal homosexuality"), it is a leftover from the early homosexual phase that all boys supposedly go through. In the second route ("Oedipal homosexuality"), on which Freud and his followers placed more emphasis, homosexuality results from the growing boy's failure to break the Oedipal bond—often as a result of a too-close-binding mother or, conversely, a distant or hostile father. In adulthood, such a man seeks to reenact that intense sexual bond with his mother. You might think that that desire would make him heterosexual, since his mother was, after all, a woman. But by one of those sleights-of-hand for which Freud was famous, he proposed that the boy goes through an identity reversal: he actually takes his *mother's* role, and seeks male sex partners because they represent *himself* (Freud, 1955a).

Freud suggested that girls' libido comes to be directed toward their fathers in a fashion analogous to a boy's Oedipal relationship with his mother. A girl could become lesbian, he said, through such events as the birth of a younger sibling. To her, this event might be seen as unwelcome confirmation that her adored father was intimate with her (unconsciously) hated rival—her own mother. The realization of her father's "infidelity" might embitter the girl and turn her permanently away from men (Freud, 1955b). Extreme penis envy could have the same effect. It is perplexing that such unsubstantiated notions dominated all discourse on the topic of sexual orientation for the better part of a century, and are still taken seriously by some Freudian analysts.

Of greater concern is the effect that Freudian theories have had on gay people. Freud himself spoke quite positively about homosexuals and did not think that they could readily be "converted" to heterosexuality. Many of Freud's followers in the United States, however, thought otherwise. Until recent times, when homosexuality became more socially accepted, many gay men who wished to become straight underwent long, expensive, and traumatic courses of psychoanalysis. The hope was that by uncovering and working through the childhood events and relationships that were thought to be responsible for their "condition," these men could attain the "normal" end point of psychosexual development: heterosexuality. Successful transformations occurred rarely, if ever, however, and many gay men were severely traumatized by this kind of therapy (Duberman, 1991). Freudian theory also traumatized the parents of gays and lesbians by making them feel responsible for their children's homosexuality. Still, some contemporary psychoanalysts have reworked Freudian theory in a more gay-positive vein (Isay, 1989).

Sexual Orientation Has Been Widely Attributed to Socialization

In Chapter 6 we mentioned the work of John Money, who proposed that parents guide their children's developing gender and sexual orientation by innumerable tiny rewards and punishments. We described how Bruce Reimer, the boy who was reared as a girl, became Money's poster child for this theory, but later became Money's nemesis when he changed sex back to male and demonstrated a thoroughgoing heterosexuality (see Box 6.3).

We also mentioned in Box 7.3 how Money's trainee Richard Green initially shared Money's beliefs. He thought that the mothers of feminine boys might be responsible for encouraging their gender-nonconformist traits. "You've got to get these mothers out of the way," he told the parents of one such child. "Feminine kids don't need their mothers around" (Green, 1987). He later became skeptical of these ideas, and he demonstrated that behavioral therapy aimed at eliminating feminine behavior in boys did nothing to avert the boys' emerging homosexuality.

One potentially very powerful form of socialization consists of sexual interactions. In this vein, it has often been suggested that both male and female homosexuality result from molestation during childhood, from rape during young adulthood, from consensual same-sex experiences in boarding schools, or from other early sexual experiences. Actual surveys that ask heterosexual and homosexual men and women about experiences of this kind have yielded some positive results. In the NHSLS, for example, men and women who reported having been touched sexually by an adult during their childhood had a greater likelihood of identifying as homosexual or bisexual than did men or women who had no such childhood experience (Figure 7.10).

Not too much should be read into these figures, however. For one thing, it is possible that heterosexual and non-heterosexual adults differ in how they recall or define childhood molestation. Also, the adults who reported molestation were far more active sexually in many ways: they were more likely to participate in group sex, they had more experience with oral and anal sex, and so on (the possible reasons for this are discussed in Chapter 12). A degree of bisexuality, at least, could be seen as part of this global elevation of sexual interest and activity. Finally, most homosexual and bisexual adults do not recall any history of childhood molestation or rape; in fact, many become aware of same-sex attraction before engaging in sexual interactions of any kind.

Consensual same-sex experiences in boarding schools do not seem to influence adult sexual orientation. According to the NSSAL, boys and girls who attend single-sex boarding schools do engage in much more homosexual behavior than children who attend coeducational schools, but are no more likely to become gay in adulthood.

Socialization effects could, of course, be much subtler than those just mentioned, and could include important cognitive aspects. Women, in particular, whose sexual feelings are more strongly modulated by considerations of love and intimacy than are those of men, may for that reason be more responsive to the vagaries of individual life history and to culturally based identities and **sexual scripts** (see Chapter 6), which might give their sexual orientation greater fluidity than that of men (Peplau & Garnets, 2000; Peplau et al., 1999). At the height of the feminist movement in the 1970s, for example, quite a few women expressed their sense of solidarity with the community of women by entering into lesbian relationships, and later returned to relationships with men (Whisman, 1996). Also, some women become aware of attraction to other women after having raised a family in a heterosexual partnership. One could argue that such women feel "permitted" to experience same-sex attraction because they have accomplished a major socially sanctioned goal of heterosexuality: reproduction and child rearing. Men may also

Figure 7.10 Adult–child sexual contacts and sexual orientation. Persons who report having been touched sexually by an adult during their childhood are more likely to identify as homosexual or bisexual than persons who do not report such contact. (Data from NHSLS.)

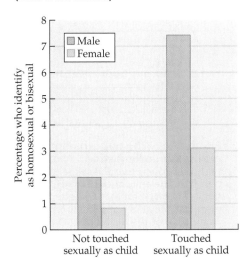

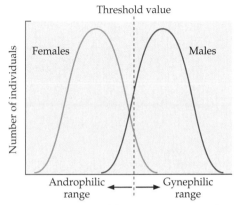

Figure 7.11 The prenatal hormonal theory of sexual orientation. In its simplest form, this theory proposes that adult sexual orientation depends on the level of androgens to which the brain is exposed during a sensitive developmental period. Most males and a few females exceed some threshold of androgen exposure and therefore become attracted to females. Most females and a few males fall below that threshold level and therefore become attracted to males. In the figure, the threshold has been arbitrarily set at a value that would produce more homosexual males than females, corresponding to what has been observed in most studies.

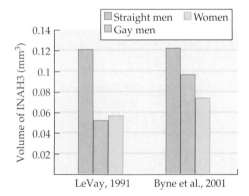

Figure 7.12 The hypothalamus and sexual orientation. Two autopsy studies found that the sexually dimorphic hypothalamic nucleus INAH3 is smaller in gay men than in heterosexual men, but they did not agree on the magnitude of the difference. (Data from LeVay, 1991; Byne et al., 2001.)

come out as gay later in life, but most such men report that they were aware of same-sex attraction throughout their earlier "heterosexual" period.

Biological Theories Focus on Prenatal Hormones and Genes

The leading biological theory of sexual orientation proposes that sexual orientation, like other aspects of gender, reflects the sexual differentiation of the brain under the influence of prenatal sex hormones. In the simplest conception of this theory (Figure 7.11), everything depends on androgen levels during a sensitive period of prenatal development. Fetuses whose brains are exposed to high levels of androgens during this period (mostly males, but a few females) will be sexually attracted to women (gynephilic) in adult life; fetuses whose brains are exposed to low levels of androgens (mostly females, but some males) will be sexually attracted to men (androphilic) in adult life. Alternatively, it might not be the hormone levels themselves, but the brain's sensitivity to hormones, that differs between "pre-gay" and "pre-straight" fetuses.

The prenatal hormonal theory has a solid basis in animal research: as we described in Chapter 5, the sexual orientation of animals can be modified by manipulation of their early hormonal experience. Of course, it is not ethically possible to do comparable experiments in humans. As we mentioned in Chapter 6, however, experiments of nature, such as congenital adrenal hyperplasia (CAH), lend some support to the prenatal hormone theory: CAH women are more likely to experience same-sex attraction than are unaffected women.

Neuroanatomical markers Researchers have also looked for biological "markers": anatomical, physiological, or endocrinological traits that might distinguish gay and straight people. For example, one of the authors of this book (S. L., then at the Salk Institute in San Diego) compared the size of INAH3, a sexually dimorphic nucleus in the human hypothalamus (see Chapter 5), in autopsy tissue from gay and straight men. He reported that INAH3 in the gay men was significantly smaller than in the straight men, and not significantly different from its size in women (LeVay, 1991). A recent replication study found a difference of the same kind, but smaller in degree, and the statistical significance of the difference between the gay and straight men was borderline (Byne et al., 2001) (Figure 7.12). Why the two studies obtained somewhat different results is not known. Neither research group was able to obtain autopsy tissue from women known to have been lesbian, so the question of a size difference related to sexual orientation in women remains unexplored.

Laura Allen and her colleagues at UCLA, who first described the sex dimorphism in INAH3, have described another neuroanatomical sex difference of the opposite kind (Allen & Gorski, 1992). A structure called the **anterior commissure,** which is a band of fibers connecting the left and right hemispheres of the cerebral cortex, is larger, on average, in women than in men. Allen's group reported that, in gay men, the anterior commissure is *larger* than in straight men; thus, as with INAH3, it is sex-atypical in gay men. Unlike INAH3, the anterior commissure plays no obvious role in sexuality, and the meaning of the reported size difference remains unclear.

Other anatomical differences There have also been reports of bodily differences related to sexual orientation. Jeff Hall and Doreen Kimura (then at the University of Western Ontario) reported in 1994 on the **fingerprints** of gay and straight men (Hall & Kimura, 1994). Fingerprint patterns, as you know, do not change over time; in fact, their layout is finalized by 16 weeks after conception. Thus they offer a particularly stable developmental marker.

In general, people tend to have more ridges on the fingers of their right hand than their left hand, and this asymmetry is more marked in men than in women. Hall and Kimura found that a significantly larger proportion of gay than straight men have the minority, leftward asymmetry. A recent replication study failed to confirm Hall and Kimura's findings, however (Mustanski et al., 2002), so the issue of a connection between sexual orientation and fingerprints must be considered unresolved.

Marc Breedlove's group reported on another marker related to the fingers (Williams et al., 2000). They compared the length of the fingers in heterosexual and homosexual men

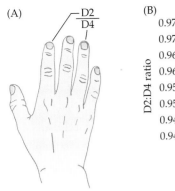
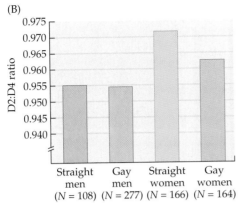

Figure 7.13 Finger length ratios and sexual orientation in women as reported by Marc Breedlove and colleagues. (A) The D2:D4 ratio is the length of the index finger divided by the length of the ring finger. (B) The D2:D4 ratio for the right hand was lower in heterosexual men than in heterosexual women, probably as a result of higher androgen exposure during male fetal development. The D2:D4 ratio was also reported to be lower in lesbians than in heterosexual women—a finding that was taken as evidence that lesbians were exposed to atypically high fetal androgen levels. (After Williams et al., 2000.)

and women (Figure 7.13). Here again, there is a basic sex difference: in women, the index finger (or second digit—D2) is nearly as long as the ring finger (or fourth digit—D4), but in men the index finger is usually significantly shorter than the ring finger, especially on the right hand. In other words, the D2:D4 ratio is usually lower in men. Breedlove's group reported that the D2:D4 ratio is also lower (on average) in lesbians than in heterosexual women, though not as low as in heterosexual men. In a follow-up study (Brown et al., 2002), they reported that the D2:D4 ratio is lower in self-described "butch" lesbians (lesbians who are more masculine in gender role) than in "femme" lesbians (lesbians who are more feminine in gender role). Breedlove's group did not find a difference between gay and straight men. Again, there have been some conflicting findings, so Breedlove's study may not be the last word on the topic. Furthermore, because the basic sex differences in fingerprints and digit length ratios are quite small, these traits may not be ideal for studying aspects of gender such as sexual orientation.

Differences in the auditory system   A group at the University of Texas, Austin, led by experimental psychologist Dennis McFadden, has reported on subtle differences between the hearing of homosexual and heterosexual women (McFadden & Pasanen, 1998, 1999). The ear actually emits very weak sounds, called **otoacoustic emissions,** that are generated as a by-product of the sensory processes in the inner ear (Figure 7.14). These emissions can be monitored with a microphone placed in the ear canal. They occur both spontaneously and in response to sounds presented to the ear, such as clicks. In general, women generate stronger and more numerous otoacoustic emissions than men, and this sex difference exists as early as infancy. Its functional significance is unclear, but it is thought to arise as a consequence of different degrees of androgen exposure prenatally (McFadden, 2002). McFadden's group found that the strength and number of otoacoustic emissions in lesbian and bisexual women were intermediate between those typical of men and of women.

McFadden's group went on to examine the function of the auditory system at higher levels. They did so by monitoring **evoked potentials** in the brain with electrodes placed on the scalp as clicks were presented to one or the other ear. Again, they found basic sex differences in these patterns of brain activity: the evoked potentials in lesbian and bisexual women were intermediate between those of heterosexual men and heterosexual women (McFadden & Champlin, 2000). This functional difference was not simply a secondary consequence of the differences in ear function just described, but reflected differences in the organization of the central auditory pathways. So far, no other research group has attempted to replicate McFadden's findings.

(A)

(B)

Figure 7.14 Hearing and sexual orientation. Functional properties of the ear differ between the sexes and between women of differing sexual orientations, according to a University of Texas research group. (A) Recording of otoacoustic emissions (OAEs). (B) Number of spontaneous OAEs (for right ear only) in straight, bisexual, and gay men and women. Women in general produced more spontaneous OAEs than did men, but homosexual and bisexual women produced significantly fewer spontaneous OAEs than did heterosexual women. (Photograph courtesy of Dennis McFadden; B after McFadden and Pasanen, 1999.)

Limitations of the prenatal hormonal theory All these findings, as well as the cognitive differences mentioned above, can be neatly explained in terms of the prenatal hormonal theory. One simply has to assume that homosexual (and possibly bisexual) individuals were exposed to atypical androgen levels during a sensitive period of development, and that these atypical androgen levels influenced not only sexual orientation, but also some other cognitive traits, finger length ratios, otoacoustic emissions, and the like—whatever traits happened to be differentiating at the time.

Even though this hypothesis is simple and potentially explains a lot of findings, there are some important caveats and limitations to point out:

- Most of the findings are consistent with a *predisposing* influence of prenatal hormones on sexual orientation, rather than a *determining* influence.
- Some findings are inconsistent with the hypothesis: there are some prenatally organized traits that differ between the sexes, but do not differ between gay and straight people, or do so in the opposite direction from the one predicted by the hypothesis. For example, when McFadden's group examined the auditory evoked potentials of gay and bisexual men, they found that they differed from those of straight men, but in a direction *away from* those typical of straight women, rather than being intermediate between the sexes (McFadden & Champlin, 2000).
- Some of the findings have potential alternative explanations. It is conceivable, for example, that the size of INAH3 can be modified in adult life, perhaps even as a consequence of a person's sexual feelings or behavior, rather than simply reflecting fetal hormone levels.

Several of the findings mentioned above have yet to be replicated in independent laboratories; hence, their conclusions must be considered provisional. Past experience suggests that not all the findings will be replicated. Statistically significant results can turn out to be wrong for a number of reasons: for example, the subjects may not have been randomly selected from the entire population under study (a very difficult criterion to fulfill in human studies). Negative results can also be wrong—because of poor measurement techniques, for example. It may take many years for the truth to emerge, especially in an understudied field such as human sexuality.

Factors influencing prenatal hormone levels The prenatal hormone theory is not an ultimate explanation of sexual orientation because it does not explain *why* androgen levels (or sensitivity to androgens) should differ between "pre-gay" and "pre-straight" fetuses. It is possible that a variety of different ultimate causes, including both endogenous and environmental processes, could modulate fetal hormone levels or hormone responsiveness, and hence ultimately influence sexual orientation.

One example of a potential *environmental mechanism* is prenatal stress. We mentioned in Chapter 5 that **stress** on pregnant rats causes their male offspring to show sex-atypical sexual behavior in adult life, and also affects the size of the sexually dimorphic nucleus (SDN-POA) in the rat's hypothalamus. The German endocrinologist Günter Dörner proposed that male homosexuality in humans is caused by extremely stressful events affecting the mother during her pregnancy—rape, death of the father, destruction of the home, and the like (Dörner et al., 1980). A detailed study of the pregnancy histories of women who had gay and straight sons, however, found that stressful events were no more common or more severe during the "gay" pregnancies than during the "straight" pregnancies (Bailey et al., 1991). This finding seems to have put the stress theory of homosexuality to rest. Of course, one could imagine a variety of other environmental factors that might affect fetal hormone levels, such as alcohol or drug use. At present, however, there is no evidence that any environmental factors operating during pregnancy affect the ultimate sexual orientation of the fetus.

Another possibility is that prenatal hormone levels can fluctuate as a basically *random* consequence of the complexity of developmental processes (see Chapter 5), producing bell-shaped distributions like those sketched in Figure 7.11. In that case, it might not be possible to define any antecedent causes.

A third possibility is that a fetus's *genes* affect prenatal hormone levels or sensitivity to hormones. One research group studied a plausible candidate gene—the gene for the androgen receptor—in gay and straight men (Macke et al., 1993). The thought was that subtle differences in that gene might affect how the developing brain responded to testosterone, thus leading to the organization of circuits for androphilic or for gynephilic attraction. In fact, however, the researchers drew a blank: they found no differences in the gene between the two groups of men.

Genetic influences on sexual orientation   More generally, researchers have studied the question of whether genes influence sexual orientation at all, regardless of which genes or which developmental pathway might be involved. The findings here have been positive. For one thing, homosexuality runs in families. (So does heterosexuality, but that is not news!) If you are a man and you have a gay brother, for example, that increases your own chances of being gay by about fivefold; and similarly if you are a women with a lesbian sister (Bailey et al., 1999; Pattatucci & Hamer, 1995). Gay people sometimes crop up across several generations of a single family (Figure 7.15). This raises the likelihood that the family clustering is due to genes, rather than to the parenting styles of particular couples.

One way to focus more directly on genetic influences on sexual orientation is to study twins. It turns out that monozygotic twins, who have all their genes in common, are considerably more likely to have the same sexual orientation than are dizygotic twins, who share about half their genes (Bailey & Pillard, 1995; Kendler et al., 2000). There are even cases in which monozygotic twins reared separately from birth have both turned out to be gay (Box 7.4). In general, the twin data are consistent with the idea that sexual orientation is moderately heritable. By some estimates, as much as 50 percent of the total variability in sexual orientation in the population is controlled by genes. Nevertheless, monozygotic twins can also have differing sexual orientations, so genes are clearly not the whole story. Some studies suggest that the heritability of sexual orientation may be much lower in women than in men.

In 1993 a team led by molecular geneticist Dean Hamer of the National Cancer Institute reported identifying a chromosomal location where a gene influencing men's sexual orientation seemed to be

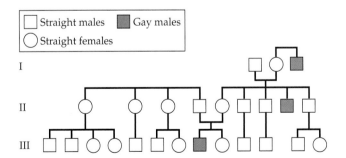

Figure 7.15 Male homosexuality can run in families. This family tree (circles = females; squares = males) illustrates the occurrence of gay men (solid symbols) in three successive generations of a family. Note that, if the homosexuality of these men was caused by genes, those genes were passed to generations II and III by the gay men's heterosexual sisters, not by the gay men themselves, who had no children. (After Hamer et al., 1993.)

Box 7.4 *Personal Points of View*

Gay Twins

Sometime around 1980, a 24-year-old man walked into a gay bar in a Western city some distance from his home. To his puzzlement, total strangers seemed to recognize him, but greeted him with a name that wasn't his. Eventually the reason for their confusion became apparent: though he never knew it, this man had an identical twin from whom he had been separated at birth. He took steps to meet his twin, and when they met, they realized that they had far more in common than just their looks: both had had a speech impediment during childhood, both had emotionally labile personalities, and both became aware that they were gay at about the age of 14. After they met, the two men became lovers.

These two men formed part of a long-running study of twins reared apart, run by Thomas Bouchard Jr. of the University of Minnesota (Eckert et al., 1986). The study followed six pairs of monozygotic twins (two male, four female) in which at least one twin was gay or bisexual. In the second male pair, both twins had been involved in both same-sex and opposite-sex relationships, but they currently identified differently (one gay, one straight). One might say that these twins were concordant for some degree of bisexuality. In each of the four female pairs, on the other hand, the co-twin of the lesbian twin was unambiguously heterosexual.

Although the number of such twins available for study is necessarily tiny, Bouchard's data are consistent with other kinds of studies suggesting that sexual orientation is moderately heritable, and that it may be more heritable in men than in women.

A contrasting story concerns a pair of male monozygotic twins reared *together* who nevertheless underwent very different psychosexual development. The twins, "Frank" and "Paul," grew up in Los Angeles. Although genetically identical, they already looked different in infancy: Paul was the prettier baby, and he was frequently mistaken for a girl, even though his parents didn't dress or treat him as such.

By the age of 4 or 5, Frank (who was named after his father and spent a great deal of time with him) showed many masculine traits, such as an interest in outdoor sports. Paul had a childhood illness that prevented him from spending much time with his father. He hated sports and liked dressing up in women's clothes, using makeup, playing with dolls, and participating in kitchen activities. These traits developed to the point that, when the twins were 8, the parents enrolled Paul in Richard Green's study of gender-nonconformist boys (see Box 7.3). Green interviewed both boys at irregular intervals until they were in their mid-20s (Green, 1987).

Throughout their teens and early 20s, Frank self-identified as exclusively heterosexual and had a succession of girlfriends. Nevertheless, he worked for a time as a prostitute servicing men, and eventually entered into a lasting sexual relationship with a man, which he claimed was for practical reasons only. In this relationship, Frank always took the insertive role in anal and oral sex—a role that he saw as preserving his masculinity. He continued to see a girlfriend, but had sex with her less and less often. "I think I'm pretty straight," he told Green. "You can't really think you are straight when you are doing these kinds of things, you know. I think in my own head that I'm still straight, just for my own ego."

Paul became much more gender-conformist in his teens. "I admit I have feminine ways," he told Green, "but I try my hardest not to flaunt it in public." He entered into sexual relationships with both males and females, but was predominantly attracted to males. "I like to see pretty ladies," he said, "but I turn on more with guys." (Quotations from Green, 1987)

Green suggested the twins shared some genetic predisposition to homosexuality, but that their different childhood experiences induced different gender traits, and these in turn influenced how Paul and Frank felt about and acted on their homosexual feelings.

---

situated (Hamer et al., 1993). By comparing the DNA of pairs of gay brothers, Hamer concluded that a "gay gene" was located on the X chromosome, at a particular location known as Xq28 near one end of the chromosome. Because men inherit their X chromosome from their mothers, an X-linked trait in men must be inherited from the mother's side of the family. Hamer reported finding evidence for that kind of inheritance from the study of family trees (the family tree shown in Figure 7.15 supports this model). Nevertheless, Hamer's results have not been independently confirmed, and in fact, a Canadian research group has reported a failure to replicate them (Rice et al., 1999).

An evolutionary puzzle The idea that genes predisposing people to homosexuality could exist and, apparently, be perpetuated across generations is counterintuitive. After all, exclusively homosexual behavior is a guarantee of nonreproduction, and the genes of people who don't reproduce die with them rather than being handed on.

Several hypotheses have been put forward to explain this paradox (Hamer & Copeland, 1994; Ruse, 1988; Trivers, 1974; Weinrich, 1987):

- It's possible that, throughout most of human evolution, cultural forces compelled homosexual persons to enter heterosexual relationships and have children in spite of their lack of heterosexual feelings. Even today, many lesbians and gay men do have children (see Chapter 13).

- It's possible that "gay genes" confer some reproductive benefit that we don't know about, and that this benefit outweighs the deleterious reproductive effect of homosexuality itself.

- Some genes have harmful effects on reproductive success when present on both chromosomes of a homologous pair (the homozygous state), but beneficial effects when present on a single chromosome (the heterozygous state). An example is the gene for sickle-cell anemia, which causes a serious blood disorder in persons who are homozygous for the gene, but confers resistance to malaria in persons who are heterozygous. Because the heterozygous state is much more common than the homozygous state, the benefit to heterozygous persons outweighs the harm to homozygous persons, so the gene persists in the population. A "gay gene" could likewise predispose homozygous persons to homosexuality, but confer some unknown benefit on persons who are heterozygous.

- A gene for homosexuality in one sex might be a gene for heterosexuality (or "*hyper*-heterosexuality") in the other sex. For example, a gene might promote attraction to men (androphilia) in both sexes. Such a gene would have a deleterious effect on reproductive success in men, but this might be outweighed by its beneficial effect on reproductive success in women. If this theory were right, one would expect the female relatives of gay men to have increased reproductive success— something that hasn't been reported.

- The persistence of "gay genes" might be explicable in terms of the theory of kin selection (see Chapter 2). That is, homosexual people may act altruistically toward close relatives such as siblings, helping them rear extra offspring successfully. This benefit could compensate for their own lower reproductive success. Childless lesbians and gay men often do act benevolently toward their nephews and nieces, though not as single-mindedly as this hypothesis would lead us to expect. It is also possible that, earlier in human evolution, persons carrying "gay genes" achieved powerful positions in society that allowed them to direct resources toward their relatives.

- "Gay genes" might have an entirely deleterious effect on reproductive success, but they could conceivably still be maintained in the population by the occurrence of new mutations. Thus newly appearing "gay genes" could compensate for those that are lost by nonreproduction. For this mechanism to work, the genes would have to be located in a chromosomal region that is subject to an unusually high mutation rate. Such regions do exist and are responsible for the persistence of some genetic traits that are deleterious to reproduction, including one form of mental retardation.

None of these theories is particularly persuasive. It is possible that, if and when "gay genes" are actually identified and their mode of action clarified, the reasons for their persistence will become apparent.

All in all, the routes by which people become straight, bisexual, or gay are still fairly mysterious. Currently, biological theories are attracting more attention than others. Given the variety of biological findings presented here, it would be surprising if it turned out that sexual orientation was entirely a matter of socialization. But different processes may operate in different people, and significant interactions between biological processes and environmental factors could also occur. In Chapter 6, we briefly mentioned one "interactive" theory of sexual orientation: the "exotic becomes erotic" theory of Daryl Bem. There are many other possibilities waiting to be explored.

Familiarity Both Increases and Decreases Attraction

How attractive we find people (and things in general) is strongly influenced by our prior experience, but this influence can work in either direction, making them more attractive or less attractive. In general, **mere exposure** to any stimulus—whether it be the music of a particular composer, a particular kind of food, or a particular face—makes us like that stimulus better when we encounter it again, even if we don't remember having experienced it before, and even if we don't recognize who or what it is (Moreland & Zajonc, 1977). (This is not true for stimuli that are intrinsically aversive, however, such as foods that make us sick.)

The extreme example of a mere exposure effect is the **imprinting** of newly hatched ducklings on the first moving thing they see—usually their mother, but occasionally some other creature (such as a behavioral scientist). Once imprinted on that creature, the ducklings will follow it to the ends of the Earth, even without being rewarded for doing so.

Human relationships are not so simple, alas, but prior exposure still counts for something. We mentioned earlier, for example, that people judge faces of their own race or ethnicity more attractive than faces of other ethnicities—simply because they have had more exposure to their own. Such ethnic preferences may go out the window in a multiracial society like our own, however, in which the dominant white ideals of beauty have become so familiar and pervasive as to affect or even supplant the standards of some minority groups.

Probably related to the mere exposure effect is the fact that we tend to be attracted to people who are similar to ourselves—in attitudes, age, race, educational level, and so on (Byrne et al., 1968). This tendency is called **homophily** (not to be confused with "homophile," which is an obsolete term for "gay"). There is only one flagrant exception to the homophily rule: most people are sexually attracted to persons of the other sex, not the same sex as themselves. The fact that sexual orientation flies in the face of homophily bolsters the notion that it is a uniquely important aspect of sexual attraction that has its own developmental mechanisms.

Homophily is usually assessed by comparing the characteristics of couples who are in sexual partnerships. Two major factors prevent people from entering into partnerships with persons they might find optimally attractive, however. The first is the existence of a sexual "marketplace": people have finite resources (in terms of good looks, personality, income potential, etc.) with which to "buy" a partner, so they usually have to settle for a less attractive partner (in a broad sense) than they would choose if they had unlimited resources. They tend to be satisfied with a relationship in which they feel they have gotten their "money's worth" (Hatfield et al., 1978; Lawrence & Byers, 1995), and this usually means a relationship between rather similar persons.

The second factor is the socially circumscribed milieu in which the formation of sexual partnerships usually takes place. In the United States, people commonly meet their partners at school or work. In some cultures, the choice of partners may be strongly constrained by social customs (for example, marriages may be "arranged," or interracial dating may be stigmatized). All of these factors are likely to cause sexual partners to resemble each other more than would be expected on a chance basis, even if people have little intrinsic preference for similar sex partners.

Conversely, there are ways in which familiarity breeds—not contempt, necessarily, but a lowered attraction. Take the fact that adult siblings are very rarely tempted to embark on an incestuous relationship with each other. You may think that the reason for this goes without saying—we know that such relationships are immoral, so we never embark on them. In the world of sex, however, knowing that something is immoral has never been much of a guarantee that it won't happen. So why don't brothers and sisters become sexual partners more often than they do, particularly in this age of loosened sexual standards?

The answer seems to be that children who are very close in childhood—not just siblings, but also unrelated children who grow up together in communes (Shepher, 1971)—tend not to find each other sexually attractive in adulthood. Consistent with this idea, siblings who did *not* spend their childhood together may indeed find each other attractive, fall in love, and desire to have a sexual relationship. (The gay male twins described in

Box 7.4 are an example of this phenomenon.) According to the pioneering Finnish sociologist Edward Westermarck (1862–1939), this relationship between familiarity during childhood and sexual nonattraction in adulthood is a fundamental mechanism by which the human species reduces the prevalence of incest, with its negative genetic consequences.

Sexual familiarity may also reduce attractiveness. In Chapter 3, we mentioned the Coolidge effect—the observation that male animals that have just mated will mate again more promptly if presented with a novel female. Humans who engage in sex, of course, do not usually have alternative mates standing by waiting to test their arousability. Still, on a longer time scale, something analogous to the Coolidge effect seems to operate in humans. People, especially men, tend to find their steady sex partners less sexually attractive over time—even if other factors actually increase the intimacy of the pair bond (see Chapter 9). No wonder women's magazines run so many articles on "how to revive your partner's love interest" and the like. Men's magazines should do the same.

Perceived Attractiveness Varies around the Menstrual Cycle

Another way in which attractiveness is affected by factors intrinsic to the viewer has to do with the menstrual cycle. Two research groups have found that women prefer men with more masculine faces near the time of ovulation, when they are most likely to conceive, and prefer less masculine faces at other times (Johnston et al., 2001; Penton-Voak & Perrett, 2000). Other researchers have reported related findings. Earlier in this chapter we mentioned an association between the attractiveness of body odor and facial symmetry: the odors of more symmetrical persons are rated more attractive. When Steve Gangestad and Randy Thornhill carried out such tests on women at different stages of their menstrual cycle, they found that the women showed a preference for the odors of symmetrical men only at or near the time of ovulation (Gangestad & Thornhill, 1998).

These changes in perception of male attractiveness around the menstrual cycle have a tempting explanation in terms of evolutionary psychology: women may be primed to look for "good genes" when good genes are most useful—during their fertile period. During the rest of their cycle they may be drawn to other males, such as their regular partner (who, by the law of supply and demand, is not likely to be the most genetically favored male out there).

Does this mean that partnered women are more likely to engage in sex outside the partnership during the fertile days of their cycle? It seems that they are (Gangestad & Thornhill, 1998). We are not suggesting that partnered women consciously set out to have babies by that "tall, dark stranger." Indeed, a tall, dark baby might be hard to explain to the rest of the family. To the extent that women engage in extra-pair sex at all, they often take care *not* to get pregnant. But their evolutionary history, mediated by the ebb and flow of sex hormones around the menstrual cycle, does seem to influence their sexual desires.

Sexual Arousal Has Multiple Roots

Sexual arousal may be caused by the appearance of a sexually attractive person or by some particular aspect of that person, such as their sexually suggestive behavior or their nudity. On the other hand, arousal may come entirely from within, apparently triggered by nothing.

Sexual Arousal May Occur during Sleep

One form of sexual arousal that comes from within occurs during sleep. Most people experience erotically charged dreams from time to time. The content of those dreams may be worrisome to some people—if, for example, they involve sex with a person other than the dreamer's regular partner. There is no reason to think that the content of sexual dreams is informative or predictive about the dreamer's waking sex life, however. As with dreams

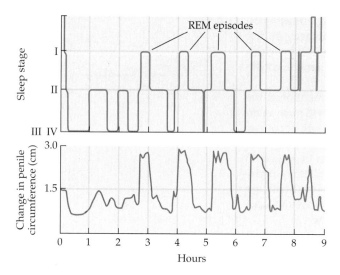

Figure 7.16 Penile erections accompany REM sleep. The graph shows an entire night's sleep (9 hours) for a normal young man. The upper trace indicates the stages of sleep as determined by electroencephalography (EEG): stage I is light sleep, stages III and IV are both deep, delta-wave sleep. There are 5 REM episodes, shown here as being stage I, although they are actually a distinct kind of sleep characterized by rapid eye movements. The lower trace shows changes in penile circumference (3.0 = maximal erection). Note that the erections occur during the REM episodes. (After Brain Information Service, UCLA School of Medicine.)

in general, we do not know why sexual dreams occur or what they mean, if anything—so we might as well just enjoy them.*

Penile erection occurs as a frequent accompaniment to **rapid-eye-movement (REM) sleep** in men (Figure 7.16). REM sleep is the phase of sleep during which vivid dreams are experienced, but the dreams do not have to be erotic in nature for erection to occur. If a man has erectile difficulties in waking life, it is of interest to determine whether he has normal erections during sleep; if so, his problems may have to do with anxiety or other psychological factors, rather than with the mechanics of erection itself (see Chapter 15).

About 90 percent of men and at least 37 percent of women experience **nocturnal orgasms** (Kinsey et al., 1948; Wells, 1986). These may occur as the climax of erotic dreams, and they may then be called **wet dreams.** Sometimes men see the evidence of a seminal emission on waking without recalling any erotic dream or orgasm. Alternatively, a person may wake at the height of an erotic dream in a state of physiological arousal, but without having reached orgasm.

Fantasy Is a Common Mode of Sexual Arousal

Sexual **fantasy**—imagined sexual experiences during waking hours—is another route by which internal mental processes promote sexual arousal. The great majority of men and women engage in sexual fantasy. It may occur when no actual sexual behavior is possible—mentally undressing attractive classmates during a boring lecture would fall into this category. Or it may accompany masturbation or sex with a partner. In either of these cases, it may add a great deal of arousal, and may even be necessary to reach orgasm.

Men engage in sexual fantasy quite a bit more than women, both in the regular course of the day and during masturbation or sex with a partner (Leitenberg & Henning, 1995). In one study, heterosexual male and female college students were asked to keep written records of all their sexual fantasies as they had them. The men averaged 7.2 fantasies per day, as compared with 4.5 for the women (Jones & Barlow, 1990). In another study, over 4000 men and women were asked whether they had thought about sex within the previous 5 minutes. Among 14–25-year-olds, the sex difference was not great: 52 percent of the men and 39 percent of the women said "yes." Among 26–55-year-olds, the total amount of sexual thought decreased, and the sex difference increased: 26 percent of the men and only 14 percent of the women said "yes" (Cameron & Biber, 1973).

The content of sexual fantasies varies a great deal, but the common items are fairly similar to the kinds of behaviors people actually engage in. According to one study of heterosexual college students (Hsu et al., 1994), over half of both males and females reported that they had recently fantasized the following activities: touching and being touched sensually, oral–genital sex, naked caressing, watching a partner undress, seducing a partner, having intercourse in unusual positions, walking hand in hand, being seduced, and having sex in an unusual location.

There are some gender differences in the content of fantasies (Figure 7.17). In the study just mentioned, men were much more likely than women to fantasize masturbating their partner, having more than one partner simultaneously, having sex with a virgin, watching a partner undress, making love with the possibility of being discovered, having sex with a famous person, engaging in anal sex, and forcing a partner to submit. The only behavior that women fantasized significantly more often than men was getting married. In general, the men were more adventurous in their fantasies: women nearly always fantasized about sexual behaviors that they had at some time actually engaged in, while

---

*Sigmund Freud proposed that many seemingly nonsexual dreams (such as a dream of riding on horseback) represent the symbolic fulfillment of erotic desires that have been repressed from consciousness. The interpretation of such dreams became a centerpiece of psychoanalytic therapy (Freud, 1900). Like so many of Freud's ideas, this one has resisted any kind of empirical investigation, but has nonetheless established itself in popular culture.

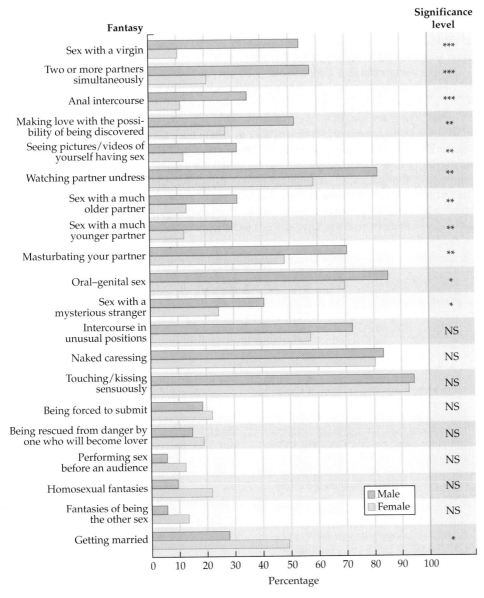

Figure 7.17 Selected recent sexual fantasies reported by 160 heterosexual college students, arranged in approximate order from the most male-biased to the most female-biased. (Data from Hsu et al., 1994.)

*** p < 0.001; ** p < 0.01; * p < 0.05; NS: not significant.

men frequently fantasized about sexual behaviors that they had never engaged in, such as whipping a partner or being whipped.

The fantasies of lesbians and gay men are similar to those of straight men and women, aside from the sex of their imagined partners (Price et al., 1985). Questions about fantasies are often used to assess sexual orientation, under the assumption that the sex of a person's fantasy partners should give a more truthful indication of what they find arousing than asking them directly about their attraction to men and to women. This assumption, however, is debatable. In the Hsu et al. study, for example, 19 percent of the men and 33 percent of the women (all of whom identified as heterosexual) reported having had at least one recent fantasy of engaging in sex with a same-sex partner. Does that mean all these people were actually sexually attracted to same-sex partners in real life? Probably not.

To some extent, the sexual fantasies of men and women differ in a way that is consistent with stereotypes about male and female sexuality: men are more likely to focus almost exclusively on the visualization of explicit sexual behavior, and their fantasies often involve taking a dominant role in sex acts. Women's fantasies, on the other hand, tend to include more romance, affection, and indications of committed relationships (such as the marriage fantasy mentioned above), and may involve taking a more passive role in sex acts (Ellis & Symons, 1990; Leitenberg & Henning, 1995). To what extent these sex differences arise from some deep biological difference between men and women, or whether they simply represent the sexual scripts that men and women have been acculturated to accept, is hard to say.

People sometimes feel guilty about their sexual fantasies, especially if the fantasies involve behaviors that they wouldn't want to engage in in real life. Yet persons who can enjoy a range of sexual fantasies without experiencing guilt seem to have a generally more satisfying sex life (Box 7.5).

Women quite commonly have fantasies in which they are sexually coerced, raped, or otherwise subjected to force by a partner (Knafo & Jaffe, 1984). Is it healthy or unhealthy for women to have such fantasies? In one study (Strassberg & Lockerd, 1998), women who reported engaging in force fantasies (more than half the total number of women in the sample) were, if anything, better adjusted sexually than those who did not—they suffered from less guilt about sex, for example. They also engaged in more sexual fantasies generally than other women. They did not differ from other women in terms of their actu-

Box 7.5 *Society, Values, and the Law*

Lust in the Heart

During the 1976 presidential election campaign, Jimmy Carter held an 18–20-point lead in the polls over incumbent Gerald Ford, until he gave an ill-advised interview to *Playboy* magazine. During a portion of the interview that Carter thought was not being recorded, the conversation turned to the moral status of adultery. Carter, a Baptist minister, admitted that he had "lusted in his heart" for many women. (Later, he explained that he was referring to the period before his marriage.) When it appeared in *Playboy,* Carter's admission triggered a major drop in his popularity, and he briefly trailed Ford before recovering to win the election.

Considering that most people have experienced similar fantasies, Carter's admission hardly seems like a cause for deep moral concern. Yet the Christian religion—which condemns adultery—has traditionally held that imagining a sinful deed such as adultery is itself sinful. As Jimmy Carter reminded *Playboy,* "Christ said, 'I tell you that anyone who looks on a woman with lust has in his heart already committed adultery.'" Partly because of this teaching, many people feel guilty about having sexual fantasies that would offend against their own moral beliefs if acted out in real life.

Scientific research cannot by itself decide moral questions, but it can sometimes provide information that is useful in making moral judgments. Suzana Cado and Harold Leitenberg (Cado & Leitenberg, 1990) studied two groups of people who experienced sexual fantasies during sexual intercourse (which might include fantasies of having sex with some other person). One group of subjects consisted of men and women who felt guilty about their fantasies; the people in the other group did not. Cado and Leitenberg reported that the "guilty" men and women had more sexual dissatisfaction and more sexual dysfunction than the other group.

This finding could mean that guilt about sexual fantasies causes sexual dysfunction. Alternatively, both the guilt and the dysfunction might be part of a broader problem with sexual expression, caused perhaps by attitudes learned in the home or during religious education. At any event, therapists generally attempt to reassure patients about the harmlessness, and possible benefits, of sexual fantasies—even those that involve "deviant" acts.

More of a problem may arise if a person has a strong desire to actually engage in potentially harmful sexual behavior. An example might be a pedophile who has a strong desire to have sex with children, but is trying not to act on that desire out of moral concern or fear of punishment. Very likely, such a person would experience fantasies of sexual contact with children. Should a therapist encourage him to suppress these fantasies or change their content (thus keeping the potential crimes as far from his mind as possible), or should he be encouraged to give his fantasies free rein (thus allowing him to vent his desires in a harmless way)? Most researchers have concluded that it is beneficial to steer the pedophile's fantasies away from their preferred subject (Johnston et al., 1992), on the assumption that such fantasies are a link in the chain that leads to actual child molestation (McKibben et al., 1994). Still, more research is needed to test this assumption (Leitenberg & Henning, 1995).

Jimmy Carter

al experience of sexual coercion or molestation. It may be that rape fantasies are, in a sense, fantasies of sexual power—the woman having the fantasy imagines herself as being so attractive that the other person loses all self-control (Hariton, 1973).

Sexual Arousal Is Influenced by Other Forms of Arousal

A number of scientific studies suggest that emotional arousal of any kind—whether it consists of fear, anger, hilarity, or some other emotion—can promote sexual arousal. In one well-known study by Donald Dutton and Arthur Aron (Dutton & Aron, 1974), a female interviewer approached men who had just crossed one of two footbridges in British Columbia, Canada. One bridge was fear-inspiring: it was a rickety, narrow, 70-meter-high footbridge that spanned a rock-strewn gorge. The other was a solid, wide bridge that crossed a small rivulet at a height of only 3 meters. The interviewer asked the men to write a story based on a picture they were shown. They were also offered the interviewer's phone number. The men who crossed the fear-inducing bridge included significantly more sexual content in their stories than did the men who crossed the safe bridge, and more of them called the woman (50 percent versus 12.5 percent).

In another study (White et al., 1981), one set of men were put in a state of arousal by one of several means—by physical exertion, by hearing a taped comedy routine, or by hearing a description of a gruesome murder. Another, control set of men were not exposed to any arousing stimulus. Subsequently, both sets of men were shown a videotape of an attractive or of an unattractive woman. At the conclusion of the tape, the viewers were asked about their impression of the woman's sexiness and their interest in dating or kissing her. The men who were exposed to any of the three forms of arousal were more sexually interested in the attractive woman than were the nonaroused men. Conversely, the aroused men were *less* sexually interested in the unattractive woman than were the nonaroused men. Thus, it appears that nonsexual arousal does not translate directly into sexual arousal, but interacts in some way with sexual attraction to modulate sexual arousal. It might do this by increasing attention, for example. However, the theoretical basis for this general effect, which is called **misattribution of arousal,** is unclear.

Hormones Influence Sexual Arousability

Are there biological correlates of sexual arousal? The first thing one thinks of in this context is testosterone. A popular misconception is that this hormone influences sexual arousal—particularly in men—on a minute-by-minute or hour-by-hour basis. A man who is feeling "horny" (that is, who is experiencing an unfocused sense of sexual arousal and is motivated to find some way of satisfying it) might comment that he "can feel the testosterone flowing," or the like.

In reality, testosterone does not seem to have any short-term influence on the sexual feelings of either men or women. For example, a research group at Georgia State University (Dabbs & Mohammed, 1992) wondered whether heterosexual couples would be more likely to have sex on evenings when the testosterone level of one or both partners was high. They recruited a number of couples and had them take saliva samples early and late in the evening over many nights. Salivary testosterone levels (which correlate well with the level of free testosterone in the blood) were no higher early on the "sex" evenings than on the "no sex" evenings, in either the men or the women. Testosterone levels *were* higher *late* on the "sex" evenings—after sex had occurred—than late on the "no sex" evenings. This finding suggests that sexual activity triggers a rise in testosterone, but that high testosterone does not trigger a desire for sexual activity.

There is evidence, however, that testosterone has a longer-term influence on our capacity to experience sexual arousal. The clearest connection between testosterone levels and sexual **arousability** is found in boys around the time of puberty. In one study of boys in grades 8, 9, and 10 of a public school system, those boys who were experiencing the rise in testosterone levels associated with puberty were much more likely to experience sexual

Nonsexual arousal, such as that caused by riding a roller coaster, can facilitate subsequent sexual arousal.

feelings and engage in sexual behavior than boys of the same age whose testosterone levels had not yet risen (Udry et al., 1985). This finding is consistent with animal research suggesting that testosterone activates brain circuits involved in male-typical sexual behavior (see Chapter 5). One might imagine an alternative interpretation: that the rise in testosterone at puberty only stimulates physical maturation, and that psychosexual development occurs as an indirect effect involving learning or social forces. The researchers rejected this idea, however, because the boys' sexual motivation was less closely related to their degree of physical maturation than it was to their testosterone levels. More recent longitudinal studies by the same research group have supported a role for testosterone in the onset of sexual feelings and behavior—in both boys and girls (Halpern et al., 1997, 1998).

Still, a temporal correlation is hardly a definitive demonstration of causality, especially in the complex field of endocrinology. An ideal experiment would be to vary testosterone levels in children artificially and then study the effects on their sexuality. Normally such an experiment would be unethical, but a group of pediatricians at Pennsylvania State University College of Medicine took advantage of the fact that boys with delayed puberty (see Chapter 5) receive testosterone as part of their treatment (Finkelstein et al., 1998). A group of such boys agreed to participate in a study in which their testosterone treatments were alternated with placebo treatments in a double-blind design (that is, neither the patients nor their doctors knew who was receiving the real hormone). The researchers then studied the boys' sexual ideation and behavior over a period of 21 months. The treated boys did think more about sex, and they engaged in more sexual touching and "necking." Still, the effects were relatively weak, and the researchers concluded that social effects must also play an important role in determining when adolescent boys begin to engage in sexual behavior. We will discuss the social side of this matter in Chapter 12.

Testosterone levels do influence sexual arousability in adult men: men who have a profound reduction in testosterone levels for any reason ("hypogonadal" men) suffer a decline in sexual desire and activity, and this decline can be reversed by testosterone replacement therapy (Wang et al., 2000). Most men seem to have levels of testosterone that are well above the "ceiling" for its effect on arousability, however. In other words, variation in the testosterone levels of healthy men does not account for variation in their sexual feelings and behavior, or does so only to a small degree (see also Chapter 15).

The situation in women is more complex because at least two groups of hormones are involved—androgens, including testosterone, and estrogens—and their levels vary around the menstrual cycle. Testosterone levels in women are quite low compared with those in men (see Chapter 4), so there is more potential for changes in testosterone levels to modulate sexual arousability.

The Pennsylvania State University study of children with delayed puberty, mentioned above, included girls as well as boys. The girls were treated with oral estrogens, which had almost no effect on the girls' sexual thoughts or behaviors. In general, it appears that testosterone is more important than estrogens in influencing female sexual arousability, both in adolescent girls and in adult women, and may contribute to changes in women's sex drive around the menstrual cycle (Davis, 2000; Morris et al., 1987; Udry & Talbert, 1988; Van Goozen et al., 1997). Estrogens may have important indirect effects on sex, however: a reduction in estrogen levels, such as the decline that occurs at menopause, may lead to vaginal dryness and hence to painful intercourse (dyspareunia—see Chapter 15), which in turn may cause a decline of interest in sex.

Sexual Arousal Is Mediated by Specific Brain Systems

Two research groups (Rauch et al., 1999; Redouté et al., 2000) have used the technique of **positron emission tomography**, or **PET** (Figure 7.18A), to map the regions of the brain that are active during sexual arousal. In the PET technique, a person lies with his head within a ring of gamma ray detectors. He then receives an intravenous infusion of a chemical tracer labeled with a positron-emitting radioisotope (for example, H_2O labeled with ^{15}O). Because the brain shunts blood preferentially to those regions that are more active, the tracer reaches a higher concentration in those regions. The gamma radiation emitted by the radioisotope is detected by the scanner and displayed as a set of color-coded slices through the brain.

(A)

(B)

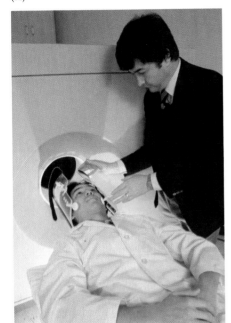

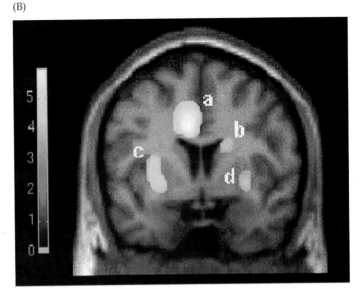

Figure 7.18 The brain and sexual arousal. (A) Person undergoing a PET scan. The standing man is Michael Phelps, co-inventor of the PET technology. (B) Brain activity specific to sexual arousal in men. This image shows the difference between scans during sexual arousal and scans in non-sexually aroused states. The anterior cingulate area of the left hemisphere (a) is one of the regions that is most active during sexual arousal. The other active regions visible in this slice are components of the basal ganglia. (B from Redouté et al., 2000; courtesy of Jerome Redouté.)

Typically, researchers compare the scan obtained while a volunteer is in the condition of interest (sexual arousal in this case) with one or more "control" scans. In one study by a French research group (Redouté et al., 2000), the volunteers (who were men) viewed three kinds of film clips: sexually arousing, humorous, and emotionally neutral. By digitally subtracting one scan from another, the researchers obtained "difference scans," which represented the brain activity due specifically to sexual arousal rather than to, say, simply viewing a film clip. In another study, by a group at Massachusetts General Hospital (Rauch et al., 1999), sexual arousal was elicited by directing the volunteer's imagination with a script; this state was compared with another kind of pleasant arousal (arousal by a desire to compete) generated in the same way, as well as with the nonaroused state.

Both research groups found that sexual arousal caused increases in brain activity at a number of sites, both within the cerebral cortex and in several subcortical structures, as well as some decreases in brain activity at other sites. Only some of the sites were common to the two studies, however. One of these was the left anterior cingulate cortex, a large region of cortex on the medial surface of the left cerebral hemisphere, toward the front of the brain (Figure 7.18B). This cortical region seems to play a major role in the processing of happy states; it is also active (along with some other regions) in men or women who are in love when they view photographs of their beloveds (see Chapter 9).

The PET technique has very limited temporal resolution; it cannot track changes in brain activity over time periods of less than a few minutes, whereas important brain processes occur on a time scale of milliseconds. PET also has poor spatial resolution; it cannot visualize the tiny cell groups in the hypothalamus, for example. But researchers have succeeded in studying the activity of these cell groups in nonhuman primates with the aid of microelectrodes inserted directly into the brain. It turns out that many neurons in the medial preoptic area, the ventromedial nucleus, and nearby—regions that are known to be involved in sexual functions (see Chapter 4)—are highly active during sexual arousal as well as during sexual behavior (Oomura et al., 1988).

Cultural Factors Regulate Sexual Arousal

Much more than we commonly recognize, our ability to experience sexual arousal is shaped by the society in which we live. This fact has been made abundantly clear by studies of diverse cultures that value sex differently or that have different expectations for women's and men's sexual roles (Suggs & Miracle, 1999).

(A)

(B)

Figure 7.19 Religious attitudes toward the body. (A) Classical Greek sculpture celebrated the beauty of nude or near-nude individuals, including gods, as shown here in this statue of the sea-god Poseidon. (B) In early Christian times, religious figures (except for Jesus on the Cross) were shrouded in all-concealing clothing, as in this Byzantine-influenced Italian relief from the eighth century.

One way that societies regulate sexual arousal is by prohibiting public display of the genitalia. In societies in which women wear clothing of any kind, they are required to cover the vulva while in public places. Even in societies in which women traditionally went without clothing, as among the Kwoma people of New Guinea, men were required to look aside when approached by a woman (Ford & Beach, 1951). Men are nearly always required to cover their genitals, too.

The sight of a woman's vulva is sexually arousing to heterosexual men, as has been shown by controlled experiments conducted in strip clubs (Linz et al., 2000). Thus, social prohibitions against female nudity have the effect of reducing men's arousal, especially in public. Prohibitions against male nudity may have a similar effect on heterosexual women, even if they are not as "visual" as men when it comes to sexual arousal.

In Victorian Britain, ladies had to be transported to the water inside horse-drawn "bathing machines."

It therefore seems likely that prohibitions against public nudity serve the social function of reducing sexual arousal, especially in a public context. This, in turn, may have the effect of reducing sexual coercion and disputes over potential sex partners, thus facilitating general social cooperation. One only has to watch the incessant squabbles over sex partners that characterize many nonhuman species to conclude that they might do well to put some clothes on, too.

Social rules about exposure of the body serve as indicators of general attitudes toward sexuality. In ancient Greece, male athletes competed without clothing, and the nude or near-nude body was celebrated in sculpture (Figure 7.19A). In early Christian art, on the other hand, clothing served to desexualize the body—or indeed, to de-emphasize the body as a whole—as part of an emphasis on humanity's spiritual nature (Figure 7.19B).

The nineteenth century was another period when Europeans went to extraordinary lengths to conceal the body. When bathing at the seaside, for example, gentlemen wore garments so all-covering as to hamper their ability to swim, while ladies of any social position had to take to the waters in "bathing machines" that hid them from public view entirely. These practices were part of a general belief that sexual arousal was dangerous to health, morals, and social order.

Our current U.S. society is far freer in its attitudes toward exposure of the body, and far more sex-positive, than were our Victorian forebears, but we are certainly not the most liberal of contemporary societies in these respects. We consider it unacceptable for women to bare their breasts in public, for example, and even men may not bare their upper bodies in a wide range of ordinary circumstances, such as at the office or in a classroom. Art depicting nudity may be censored. Correspondingly, anti-sex attitudes are still quite widespread in our society.

In American society, boys and girls receive different messages about the appropriateness of being sexually aroused, of arousing others, and of engaging in sexual behavior. There has long existed a **double standard,** whereby similar patterns of sexual thought and sexual behavior are judged differently in males and females. Girls have been taught the virtues of **sexual modesty,** meaning a reluctance to become sexually aroused, to actively solicit sex partners, or to respond positively to solicitations. Boys have been taught that sexual arousal and the active pursuit of sex partners are permissible, or even praiseworthy. Even though there may well be biological predispositions for girls and boys to think and act differently with regard to sex, these predispositions have been greatly amplified by cultural norms.

Since the 1960s, the double standard has greatly eroded in the United States, under the influence of the **sexual revolution** and the **women's movement**. Nevertheless, it still has an important influence, especially among some immigrant minorities. Even in mainstream American culture, one can see the influence of the double standard in such realms as the television situation comedy. In sitcoms, women's sexual arousal and their pursuit of men are often portrayed as comical in themselves, whereas men generally have to do something way out of line—such as mistakenly come on to another man—to make their sexual activities humorous.

Nudity in art still displeases some conservatives. In early 2002, U.S. Attorney General John Ashcroft spent $8000 of taxpayers' money on curtains that conceal two partially nude statues in the Great Hall of the Department of Justice, where he holds formal events (National Coalition Against Censorship, 2002). This photograph shows Ashcroft in front of one of the statues before the changes were made.

Summary

1. Sexual attraction is a response to another person that is influenced by objective attributes of that person, as well as by both durable and temporally varying characteristics of the person experiencing the attraction.

2. One objective attribute that increases a person's attractiveness is facial and bodily symmetry. One reason we may find symmetry attractive is because it indicates that genetic programs of development have gone forward unimpeded.

3. The "masculinity" and "femininity" of faces is an important part of their attractiveness. Most people find very masculine or very feminine faces most attractive. Strongly sex-differentiated faces may be a cue to fertility.

4. The attractiveness of bodies is also often a matter of their masculinity or femininity. The waist-to-hip ratio differs between the sexes and is an important determinant of attractiveness across many cultures.

5. Youthful appearance—another cue to fertility—is an important criterion of physical attractiveness in women, but less so in men.

6. Sexual orientation defines how a person's disposition to experience sexual attraction varies with the sex of their potential partners. Somewhere between 0.5 and 4 percent of the population is homosexual. The percentage that is bisexual depends greatly on the definition used, but is always higher in women than in men. In judging the attractiveness of potential sex partners, we see them through two mental lenses: our perception of their sex, and our own sexual orientation.

7. Lesbians and gay men, although very diverse, tend to be sex-atypical in some other traits besides their sexual orientation, both during childhood and in adult life.

8. A variety of theories have been put forward to explain how a person develops his or her sexual orientation. According to Freudian psychoanalytic theory, heterosexuality emerges from a complex sequence of stages of psychosexual development; the disruption of several of these stages may lead to homosexuality. According to socialization theory, a child's ultimate sexual orientation is molded by innumerable rewards and punishments handed out by parents and others.

9. According to biological theories, sexual orientation is affected by factors such as prenatal hormone levels, which are thought to influence the organization of brain systems responsible for sexual attraction. Genes play a significant, but not a decisive, role in determining the sexual orientation of men; a role for genes in women's sexual orientation is less clear.

10. Other factors modulating sexual attraction include familiarity and, in women, the phase of the menstrual cycle.

11. Sexual arousal may be triggered internally or by external factors. Internal processes include erotic dreams and daytime sexual fantasies. Fantasies are a healthy part of most people's sex lives.

12. External events that cause emotional arousal of any kind—such as fear—can modulate sexual arousal.

13. Testosterone plays an important role in conferring the capacity for sexual arousal in males, especially at puberty. Testosterone does not play a minute-by-minute role in sexual arousal, however. Both testosterone and estrogens may contribute to sexual arousability in women; testosterone is probably the more important of the two.

14. Sexual arousal is accompanied by activity in specific regions of the cerebral cortex, as well as in neurons in the hypothalamus and elsewhere.

15. Cultural factors regulate sexual arousa—for example, by discouraging nudity. A cultural double standard has traditionally restricted the sexual arousal and sexual behavior of women while encouraging those of men.

Discussion Questions

1. Cultural influences shape sexual arousal and attractiveness. Identify the culture of your ancestors, and identify the attributes that your culture finds sexually attractive (e.g., are skinny women or those with "curves" and "meat on their bones" more attractive?).

2. In some cultures, such as those in many Islamic countries, women's bodies are expected to be almost totally covered in public; elsewhere, such as on nude beaches in the south of France, almost the entire body may be exposed. Which is more attractive? Compare this perspective on sexual attractiveness with that of your fellow students.

3. Consider your reaction as you walk around campus or other areas and see people holding hands, kissing, lying on the grass in a passionate embrace, or almost having sex. What are your reactions to seeing such displays of sexual arousal? How does your reaction differ if the couple are homosexual or heterosexual? Do you think we should have rules or limits on the extent of public displays of sexual arousal? If so, what do you think these should be?

4. Compare and contrast your own views on what influences sexual arousal and attractiveness with those of the text and your class. What are the influences of hormones, alcohol, and other factors?

5. Should sexual partners discuss what is arousing for each person? What are the costs and benefits of this type of communication? What are your attitudes toward talking with an intimate partner about what is arousing and what is not? Imagine for a moment that your partner had a fascination with your feet and wanted to kiss and touch them—and this tickled. How would your attitudes encourage or discourage this discussion?

6. As a class, make a list of words or phrases (e.g., common expressions, slang, words in other languages) that are used for (a) a woman who has sex; (b) a woman who doesn't; (c) a man who has sex; and (d) a man who doesn't. After the list is complete, discuss the attitudes and values it illustrates about men and women who have sex. Do you think that a double standard exists?

Web Resources

MIT Encyclopedia of Cognitive Science, Evolutionary Psychology of Sexual Attraction
cognet.mit.edu/MITECS/Entry/thornhill

Finn, R. *A long tradition: The biological basis of sexual orientation is a research area that is coming out of the closet* www.the-scientist.com/yr1996/jan/biodef_960108.html

Recommended Reading

Buss, D. (1994). *The evolution of desire: Strategies of human mating.* New York: Basic Books.
Langlois, J. H., Kalakanis, L., et al. (2000). Maxims or myths of beauty? A meta-analytic and theoretical review. *Psychological Bulletin, 126,* 390–423.
LeVay, S. (1996). *Queer science: The use and abuse of research into homosexuality.* Cambridge, MA: MIT Press.

chapter 8

Sexual behavior in humans is nearly endless in variety.

Sexual Behavior

*W*hich human behaviors do you consider sexual? Which of these, if any, do you engage in or find enjoyable? Which do you consider morally acceptable, and which strike you as repugnant? Probably no two people would give precisely the same answers to these questions. There are likely to be as many varieties of sexual expression as there are human beings on this planet. In this chapter, we survey common forms of sexual behavior, with a central emphasis on sexual practices in the contemporary United States and other Westernized countries. We defer a discussion of unusual sexual practices to Chapter 14.

Everyone has to make important decisions about their sex lives. Do I want to have sex at all, and if so, under what circumstances, and in what kind of a relationship? Do I want to have children, and if not, how should I prevent pregnancy? How can I best reduce the likelihood of acquiring or transmitting diseases in the course of sexual encounters? These important questions are discussed in later chapters. For the moment, we deal with sexual behavior as if these larger issues did not exist.

When President Bill Clinton denied having sex with White House intern Monica Lewinsky, it focused national attention on what "having sex" means.

People Have Differing Ideas about What Constitutes Sexual Behavior

"I did not have sexual relations with that woman, Miss Lewinsky." History will probably record these words as the most famous utterance of the forty-first president of the United States, William Jefferson Clinton. It turned out that Clinton and White House intern Monica Lewinsky had engaged in oral sex (specifically, mouth–penis contact, or *fellatio*) to the point of ejaculation. Was that "having sex"? Not according to Clinton—and there are plenty of people who agree with him: 59 percent of college students surveyed in 1991 stated that oral–genital contact did not constitute "having sex" (Sanders & Reinisch, 1999). There is a wide perception, especially among men, that "real" sex is one thing and one thing only: a man inserting his penis into a woman's vagina and keeping it there until he ejaculates.

For the purposes of this book, we take a more inclusive view: we consider any behavior sexual if it is accompanied or followed by physiological signs of sexual arousal, such as penile erection or vaginal lubrication, whether or not ejaculation or orgasm occurs. Even behaviors that are not accompanied by physiological arousal should probably be considered sexual if they are perceived to be such by the participants. And "sex," by our definition, can involve a single person, two or more persons of any sex, or even a human and an animal (a topic covered in Chapter 14). Of course, the boundaries of sexual behavior are difficult to define precisely: hugging or kissing, for example, may be sexual in some contexts and not in others. But it's probably better to be overinclusive here than to omit behaviors that are significant modes of sexual expression for some people.

Masturbation Is a Very Common Form of Sexual Expression

We have already discussed one way in which people can arouse themselves sexually: through sexual fantasy (see Chapter 7). Fantasy is not a behavior, because it doesn't involve *doing* anything in the external world. But people also have the capacity to arouse themselves sexually through physical stimulation of their own bodies—**masturbation.**

The term "masturbation" is sometimes used to indicate any kind of manual stimulation of the genitals, including those of a partner. Most commonly, though, the term is reserved for **autoerotic** (self-arousing) behavior, whether by use of the hand or by other means, and we use it in that sense here.

Negative Attitudes toward Masturbation Are Still Prevalent

If you felt a certain tension or anxiety when you realized the topic of this section, be assured that you are not alone. In this age of relative openness about sexuality, masturbation is the one common form of sexual expression that still triggers a great deal of embarrassment, guilt, or denial—not just for people who practice it, but also for people who talk about it. During the planning of the NHSLS survey (see Chapter 7), federal administrators demanded that questions about masturbation be removed from the interview protocols. Then, after the project became privately funded, the interviewers themselves balked at the idea of asking about the topic. In the end, questions about masturbation had to be placed on a special form that subjects could fill out by themselves. In the NSSAL (the equivalent British survey), masturbation fared even worse: reactions to the topic were so negative that it had to be dropped from the survey.

It's not just sex surveys that have problems with masturbation. Although "masturbation" is not one of the "seven forbidden words" that have been banned from the airwaves by the Federal Communications Commission (those words, for the record, are "shit," "piss," fuck," cunt," "cocksucker," "motherfucker," and "tits"), it might just as well be on the list, considering the rarity with which it is spoken. What's more, it's not just the word, but the entire concept, that is largely excluded from public discourse (Box 8.1).

Part of the reason for the difficulty people have in discussing masturbation is historical. In Victorian times, masturbation was considered disgusting, sinful, and unhealthy

Box 8.1   *Society, Values, and the Law*

The Dreaded M Word

Joycelyn Elders, pediatrician and director of the Arkansas Department of Health, was appointed U.S. Surgeon General by President Bill Clinton in 1993. Elders had (and still has) a passionate interest in reducing sexually transmitted diseases and unwanted pregnancies, and she felt that simply preaching abstinence was not an effective strategy for accomplishing these goals. Her support for programs that encouraged contraception led conservatives to call her the "Condom Queen." (This nickname had racial overtones, since it was a riff on the Reagan-era phrase "welfare queen"—always conceptualized as a black woman.)

In December 1994, Elders gave a speech at a United Nations-sponsored conference on AIDS. Afterward, she was asked about masturbation as a form of safe sex. Masturbation, she replied, "is a part of human sexuality, and it's a part of something that perhaps should be taught." Specifically, she recommended that information about mastur-

bation be included in a comprehensive program of sex education in schools.

When Clinton learned of her statement, and learned that it was going to be published in *U.S. News and World Report,* he fired her. Her dismissal was one of the few Clinton actions that had the enthusiastic support of Republican House Speaker Newt Gingrich.

Dr. Elders was unrepentant. "Masturbation," she later wrote in an on-line column, "is not a four-letter word, but the President fired me for saying it. In this so-called 'communications age,' it remains a sexual taboo of monumental proportions to discuss the safe and universal practice of self-pleasure. No doubt, future generations will be amused at our peculiar taboo, laughing in sociology classes at our backwardness, yet also puzzled by it given our high rates of [sexually transmitted] disease and premature pregnancy. We will look foolish in the light of history" (Elders, 1997).

Joycelyn Elders

and was referred to by terms such as "self-pollution." According to many authorities of the time, masturbation led to "degeneracy," a condition of physical, mental, and moral decay that affected not just the masturbator, but also any offspring that he or she might have (Hare, 1962). In that period, it was believed that the consumption of rich or highly flavored foods provoked masturbation, and that bland foods discouraged it. Two bland foods that are still popular today, the graham cracker and Kellogg's Corn Flakes, were specifically introduced with the hope of reducing the prevalence of masturbation and sexual arousal. (Sylvester Graham was a minister and moral campaigner; John Harvey Kellogg was a doctor and eugenics enthusiast.) Health manuals recommended a variety of methods for discouraging masturbation, and one could even purchase mechanical devices that made masturbation impossible. (Actually, such devices are still for sale, though they now seem to be used as bondage toys more than as aids to abstinence.)

Few people are campaigning against the evils of masturbation in the United States today, but children may still inherit negative attitudes about it from their parents. Furthermore, the Roman Catholic Church still holds that masturbation (along with many other forms of sexual expression) is sinful, so some Catholics may not masturbate, or may feel guilty about masturbating, for that reason.

Another reason for masturbation's bad reputation is the belief that it is an activity practiced only by people who cannot get access to "real" sex. The derogatory terms "jerk" (whose meaning has been influenced by the phrase "jerking off," slang for male masturbation) and its British equivalent "wanker" mean something like "loser"— a person who is so unattractive or socially inept that they are driven to have sex with the one person who cannot turn them down: themselves.

Unsweetened corn flakes were introduced at the Battle Creek Sanitarium in Michigan by anti-masturbation crusader John Harvey Kellogg. His brother Will added sugar to the flakes and successfully marketed them as a breakfast cereal.

Thus, several factors combine to make people feel bad about masturbation. In the NHSLS survey, about half of all the respondents who stated that they masturbated also stated that they felt guilty after they did so. The youngest age group interviewed (18–24) reported the highest levels of guilt.

Several Demographic Factors Influence Masturbation

What is the reality of masturbation? In the NHSLS survey (Figure 8.1), about half the interviewees stated that they had masturbated at least once during the previous 12 months. The frequency with which these people masturbated, however, was strongly influenced by their sex (men masturbated more than women), age (older people masturbated less often than younger people), ethnicity (African-Americans masturbated less than other groups), religion (nonreligious and non-Christian people masturbated more than Christians), educational level (higher educational attainment was associated with more frequent masturbation), and marital status (unmarried people masturbated more than married people). Of course, one has to bear in mind the possibility that these differences were due in part to differences in the truthfulness of the interviewees in the different groups.

While the data in Figure 8.1 illustrate two potential biological influences on the frequency of masturbation (sex and age), they also show how strongly cultural factors influence the practice. The strong association between edu-

Figure 8.1 Biological and cultural factors influence whether people masturbate. These histograms show the percentages of various groups who acknowledge having masturbated at least once in the previous 12 months, as categorized by (counter-clockwise from top left): age, marital status, education, religion, and race/ethnicity. (Data from NHSLS.)

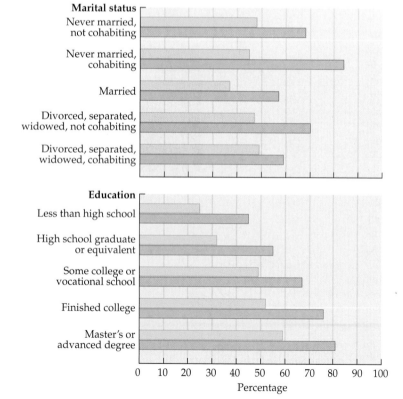

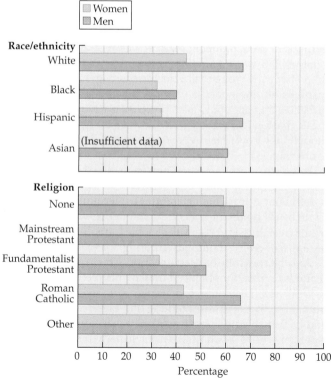

cational level and frequency of masturbation is particularly interesting. Highly educated people are less religious than other groups, and they also tend to believe that pleasure is one of the main reasons for engaging in sex. Both these factors might make highly educated people less inhibited about engaging in masturbation (or reporting that they masturbate).

Men experience orgasm during masturbation more frequently than women do. In the NHSLS survey, 82 percent of the men but only 61 percent of the women stated that they always or usually had an orgasm when masturbating. This sex difference is not unique to masturbation: women are less likely than men to have an orgasm during sex with a partner, too. In fact, the average woman is more likely to experience orgasm when masturbating than when engaged in sex with a partner (Hite, 1977).

Asked *why* they masturbated, the men and women in the NHSLS survey gave similar answers: they did it to relieve sexual tension, for the physical pleasure, and/or because a partner was not available.

The NHSLS data lend only limited support to the notion that partner unavailability is the major reason for masturbation. Married people did masturbate less than unmarried people, but that could have been in large part because the married interviewees were older than the unmarried ones, and the frequency of masturbation declines with age. More telling is the comparison between unmarried people who were and were not cohabiting with a partner. Those who had a partner masturbated as often as or more often than those who did not have a partner. Thus, it doesn't seem that people have a certain fixed endowment of sexual energy that they can allot either to partnered or to unpartnered sex. Many people who masturbate simply add it to their other sexual activities.

Women Use More Diverse Techniques of Masturbation than Men

Most of what is known about how people masturbate comes from the work of Masters and Johnson (see Chapter 3), who observed several hundred men and women masturbating as part of their overall studies of sexual behavior (Masters & Johnson, 1966). Women use quite diverse methods of masturbation (Figure 8.2). One common technique involves manually stimulating the area of the clitoris with a circular or to-and-fro motion of the fingers. Alternatively, pulling on the labia minora causes the clitoral hood to move to and fro on the clitoral glans, thus stimulating the clitoris indirectly. Another way of stimulating the clitoris is for a woman to cross her legs and squeeze them together rhythmically. Yet another technique is to rub or press the genital area against some object, such as a bed or pillow. Women sometimes use electric vibrators, either to stimulate the genitalia directly, or attached to the back of the hand so as to give the fingers an extra vibratory motion.

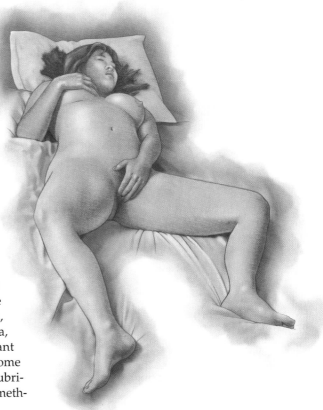

Figure 8.2 Female masturbation.

Many men imagine that women masturbate by thrusting their fingers or an object deeply into the vagina, thus simulating coitus. Some women do this, but it is quite a bit less common than clitoral stimulation. Some women can give themselves a different kind of orgasm by deep pressure in the region of the G spot (see Chapter 3).

While manually stimulating the genitals, many women stimulate the nipples or breasts with their free hand. In fact, some women can bring themselves to orgasm by breast stimulation alone. A small number of women can experience orgasm by fantasy alone, without any kind of physical stimulation of the body (Whipple et al., 1992).

Men's techniques of masturbation tend to be a bit more stereotyped than women's (Figure 8.3). The usual method is to grasp the shaft of the erect penis with one hand and move the hand rhythmically up and down, thus stimulating the most sensitive areas of the penis: the glans, corona, and frenulum (see Chapter 3). The penis does not produce a significant amount of lubrication (and neither does the hand!). For that reason, some men like to use saliva, oil, soapsuds, or a water- or oil-based sexual lubricant—whatever feels good and does not irritate the penis. Alternative meth-

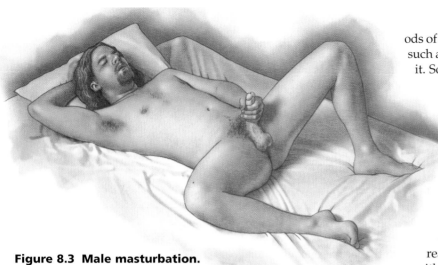

Figure 8.3 Male masturbation.

ods of masturbation include lying in contact with an object such as a pillow or the edge of a bed and thrusting against it. Some men like to stimulate the nipples or anus with their free hand while masturbating with the other, but few can reach orgasm without direct stimulation of the penis.

Most men take about 2 to 3 minutes from the beginning of masturbation to the point of orgasm, compared with about 4 minutes for women (Kinsey et al., 1948; Kinsey et al., 1953). Some men and women like to draw out the experience over a period of many minutes, perhaps approaching orgasm several times and then easing off before finally climaxing; others like to reach orgasm as quickly as possible and have done with it.

Gay People Masturbate More Than Heterosexuals

Intuitively, one might imagine that gay men and lesbians would enjoy masturbation more than heterosexual men and women, and might masturbate more frequently. Gay people's own bodies, after all, are of the sex that they find sexually attractive, so autoerotic behavior might be more arousing for them than for straight people. According to the NHSLS survey, gays and lesbians (or persons with recent homosexual experience) do masturbate far more frequently than do heterosexual men and women (Figure 8.4).

This difference was confirmed in a survey of male German college students: the gay students not only masturbated more frequently (regardless of whether they were partnered or not), but also derived greater pleasure from masturbation (Schmidt, 2000). Furthermore, the gay male students were far more likely than the straight male students to masturbate in front of a mirror—48 percent of the gay students had done so in the previous 12 months, versus only 18 percent of the straight students (Schmidt, G., personal communication). Comparable data for women are not available.

These findings suggest that gay people's relatively greater interest in masturbation may result from a greater erotic response to their own bodies, although other explanations are possible. This is not meant to imply that gay people are, in general, erotically focused on themselves. Both lesbians and gay men are as "other-directed" in their sex lives as heterosexual men and women (see Chapter 13).

Different Cultures Have Different Attitudes toward Masturbation

Masturbation is poorly thought of in many cultures besides our own. Some cultures have taboos against male masturbation on account of beliefs about semen: that it is contaminating or, conversely, that it is so valuable that its loss will cause ill health or even death. Anthropologists studying non-Western societies have generally reported that masturbation is rare and is mainly practiced by children or adolescents.

Some societies approve of masturbation by women more than by men. Hortense Powdermaker, an American anthropologist who spent a decade living in a Melanesian village in New Ireland (part of Papua New Guinea) during the 1920s, wrote as follows:

A woman will masturbate if she is sexually excited and there is no man to satisfy her. A couple may be having intercourse in the same house, or near enough for her to see them, and she may thus become aroused. She then sits down and bends her right leg so that her heel presses against her genitalia. Even young girls of about six years may do this quite casually as they sit on the ground. The women and men talk about it freely, and there is no shame attached to it. It is a customary position for women to take, and they learn it in childhood. They never use

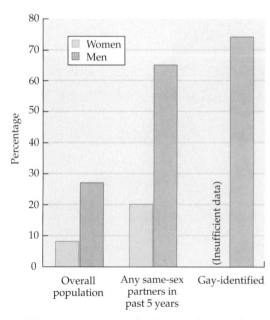

Figure 8.4 Masturbation and sexual orientation. Homosexual behavior or identity is associated with a high frequency of masturbation. These histograms show the percentages of men and women who masturbate at least once per week. (Data from NHSLS.)

their hands for manipulation [of their genitals]. (Powdermaker, 1933, cited in Ford & Beach, 1951)

Does evolutionary psychology have anything to say about masturbation—a behavior that seems disadvantageous from the point of view of reproductive success? It is possible that male masturbation is an adaptive behavior because it gets rid of "aged" sperm that have been stored for some time and that are no longer in optimal condition for fertilizing ova (Baker & Bellis, 1993). Alternatively, masturbation in both sexes may simply be a by-product of selection for other behavioral traits that increase reproductive success, such as a high sex drive.

In Chapter 6 we mentioned Gagnon and Simon's idea that the high rate of masturbation by pubertal boys plays a role in focusing male sexuality on the physical pleasure of sex. Conversely, it has been suggested that the relatively low frequency of masturbation by girls might hinder their development of the ability to experience sexual pleasure and orgasm in partnered sex. Some therapies aimed at overcoming sexual problems in women, especially the inability to experience orgasm, therefore involve instruction in masturbation. We discuss this issue further in Chapter 15.

The Kiss Represents True Love—Sometimes

We could have titled this section "Osculatory Behavior," but that would miss out on what is the most important thing about the kiss for many people: its romance. To anyone familiar with the poetry and music that depicts the kisses of dying lovers—Shakespeare's Romeo and Juliet and Wagner's Tristan and Isolde, among many others—or who remembers the great screen kisses of Clark Gable and Vivien Leigh (in *Gone with the Wind*) or Ingrid Bergman and Cary Grant (in *Notorious*), to name just two, the kiss signifies one thing and one thing only: a passionate love that transcends life itself.

The Kiss, completed in 1898 by Auguste Rodin, was originally intended to represent Paolo and Francesca, the doomed lovers in Dante's *Inferno*.

In reality, of course, kisses come in many different degrees and flavors, from the no-contact "air kiss" and the perfunctory cheek peck to the wildest oral adventures that tongue, lips, and teeth are capable of. A kiss may mean nothing, it may be a way of saying that "real sex" is on the way, or it may solemnify the union of two souls "till death do us part."

Surprisingly, kissing is not as ubiquitous a custom as we Westerners might imagine. Anthropologists Clellan Ford and Frank Beach listed eight non-Western societies in which kissing of any kind was unknown (Ford & Beach, 1951). One of these societies was that of the Thonga, who live in the southern lowlands of Mozambique. "When the Thonga first saw Europeans kissing," wrote Ford and Beach, "they laughed, expressing this sentiment: 'Look at them—they eat each other's saliva and dirt.'" It's difficult to know, however, whether this was an accurate portrayal of the attitudes of the Thonga at the time, or just a traveler's anecdote.

Even in the United States, attitudes toward kissing vary. In the Kinsey studies of the 1940s, well-educated men and women were much more likely than less educated people to report engaging in **deep** ("French") **kissing**—another example of the association between education and more liberal attitudes toward sexual practices. It is likely that deep kissing has become more broadly accepted today than it was in Kinsey's time, although rising concern about AIDS and other sexually transmitted diseases may discourage deep kissing in a casual context.

Of course, mouths can roam farther than a partner's mouth. Almost every body part is licked, sucked, bitten, or chewed on in the heat of somebody's passion. Breasts are a perennial favorite. Oral–genital contacts are discussed below. Even the sucking of toes ("shrimping") can be highly arousing to both partners, and would probably be practiced more often if it didn't seem faintly humorous.*

---

*Britain's Queen Elizabeth was not amused, however, when she opened the *Daily Mirror* one morning in 1992 and saw a photograph of her daughter-in-law, the Duchess of York (better known as "Fergie"), having her toes sucked by her "financial advisor" at a villa in the south of France. Fergie and Prince Andrew divorced in 1996.

"Petting" and "Fondling" Refer to a Variety of Noncoital Behaviors

People engage in all kinds of hand-to-body and body-to-body contacts, sometimes as **foreplay** (behavior designed to increase pleasure and arousal prior to some "main event," such as coitus), and sometimes as the "main event" in itself. "Necking," "petting," and "heavy petting" are words traditionally used to describe some of this behavior: **necking** means kissing and touching confined to the head and neck; **petting** means touching naked skin below the neck, but not the breasts or genitalia; **heavy petting** usually means touching the breasts or genitalia. **Fondling** is a broader term that could include any of these behaviors. Sometimes "petting" is used to describe anything short of coitus or anal penetration, in which case it would include oral–genital contact. Some kinds of petting may be accompanied by orgasm, but the participants are not "having sex" by many young people's way of thinking (see above).

Figure 8.5 Tribadism.

General body-to-body contact, accompanied by rubbing or thrusting motions of the pelvis that stimulate the clitoris or penis, is a common part of sexual activity for many people, and may readily lead to orgasm. When two women engage in this activity, rubbing their vulvas against each other's bodies with pelvic thrusting motions, it is called **tribadism,** or "dry humping" (Figure 8.5).

Oral Sex Has Become Increasingly Popular

Oral contact with the genitals is a behavior that some people find disgusting. Others, however, find it an extremely arousing and intimate form of sex, which may be either the "main event" or a part of foreplay.

Oral sex has become an increasingly prevalent activity among younger people over the last few decades, both in the United States and Britain. Thus, paradoxically, younger people are more likely than older people to have engaged in oral sex at some point during their lifetime. In the NSSAL (British) study, for example, only 50 percent of women in the 45–59 age bracket said that they had ever participated in any kind of oral sex, but 83 percent of women in the 25–34 age bracket had done so. The corresponding figures for men were 62 percent and 88 percent. Of course, there are always alternative explanations of such data, such as that older people forget some of the things they did in their wilder years. The Kinsey surveys of the 1940s reported much lower rates of oral sex than the recent NSSAL and NHSLS surveys, however, suggesting that the increase over time is real.

Oral–genital contacts are of three main kinds: mouth–penis contact (fellatio, also known as a "blow job," "sucking off," "going down on," or "giving head"), mouth–vulva contact (cunnilingus, "eating," or "going down on"), and mouth–anus contact (anilingus or analingus, "rimming").

Fellatio Is Oral Stimulation of the Penis

In the case of **fellatio** (Figure 8.6A), the terminology can get a bit confusing. Although you may see the phrases "active partner" and "passive partner" used to refer to the owner of the penis and the mouth, respectively, these terms are unclear, because either partner can do the active "work" of fellatio. The man whose penis is being fellated may just lie there and let his partner do everything, or he may position himself on top of his partner and actively thrust into his partner's mouth. Another commonly used pair of terms is "insertive partner" and "receptive partner." Unfortunately, "receptive" is also confusing, because one can also speak of a man who is being fellated as "receiving" oral sex. We therefore reluctantly use the unromantic terms **insertor** and **insertee** to refer to the partners in fellatio and other kinds of penetrative sexual behavior.

Figure 8.6 Oral sex. (A) Fellatio is sexual contact between a man's penis and his partner's mouth. The partner can be either a woman or (as here) another man. (B) Cunnilingus is sexual contact between a woman's vulva and her partner's mouth. The partner can be a man (as here) or another woman.

(A)

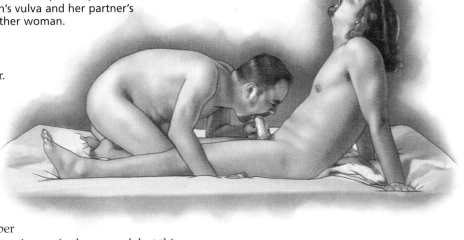

Fellatio, like most sex, is a pretty simple matter. The insertee (who can be of either sex) takes the insertor's penis into the mouth, and usually runs the lips rhythmically up and down the shaft of the penis, keeping them fairly tight so as to provide optimal stimulation. The insertee may also use the tongue to stimulate the most sensitive portions of the penis, the corona and frenulum. As a variation, the insertee may lick the scrotum or take one or both testicles into the mouth.

The insertor often wants his penis to go deeper and deeper into his partner's mouth as he becomes increasingly aroused, but this may cause gagging, depending on the length of the man's penis and his partner's experience. As with every aspect of two-person sex, good communication is key.

(B)

Fellatio can be continued to the point that the insertor ejaculates. Here again, however, communication is important. Some people don't like the experience of receiving the ejaculate in the mouth, or have concerns about disease transmission (a topic discussed in Chapter 16). As to swallowing the ejaculate, the perennial question is, how many calories does it contain? The answer seems to be around 15 calories, or less than one-tenth of a candy bar. And, although we realize that 99.9 percent of you do not need to be told this, there is no chance of becoming pregnant by swallowing semen.

In heterosexual contexts, men enjoy fellatio more than women do (Figure 8.7). Thus, it seems that women engage in fellatio to give their male partners pleasure more than as a directly pleasurable experience for themselves. The NHSLS study also found cultural differences: African-American men and women were less likely to enjoy fellatio than other groups, and more educated people tended to enjoy it more than less educated people.

Not a great deal is known about fellatio in non-Western cultures. One well-studied exception is the Sambia, a tiny Melanesian ethnic group (about 2000 individuals) living in the Eastern Highlands of New Guinea. The Sambia believe that boys can become men only by ingesting semen, which they say triggers puberty and confers the qualities of manhood (Herdt, 1981). Before puberty, boys are removed from their families, and for about 10 years they are housed collectively. During this period they engage in daily ritualized fellatio, first as insertees and then, as they mature physically, as insertors. At the end of this period, the boys leave the male group and take wives. Similar beliefs and customs occur widely throughout Melanesia, but sometimes the transfer of semen is accomplished by anal sex rather than by fellatio. Besides their ritual significance, these activities provide a sexual outlet for the older youths, who have no access to women.

Cunnilingus Is Oral Stimulation of the Vulva

In **cunnilingus** (Figure 8.6B), a woman's partner explores her vulva with lips and tongue. The tongue provides very effective sexual stimulation for many women because it is soft, wet, warm, and highly mobile. Thus it is much easier to stimulate the clitoris and

Figure 8.7 Popularity of oral sex. The graph shows the percentages of men and women who find fellatio and cunnilingus "very appealing." (Data from NHSLS.)

Figure 8.8 Mutual oral sex may be called "69" or "soixante-neuf." Though shown here between two women, any sex combination can perform this activity.

labia minora in an uninhibited way with the tongue than with, say, the fingers, which may provide too-harsh stimulation to the most sensitive areas, such as the glans of the clitoris. For some women, cunnilingus is the only way by which they regularly achieve orgasm (Hite, 1977).

Considering that men enjoy fellatio more than women, you might expect that women would enjoy cunnilingus more than men. In the NHSLS study, however, slightly more men than women said that they found cunnilingus "very appealing" (see Figure 8.7). Again, there were cultural differences: cunnilingus was more popular among more educated men and women than among the less educated, and less popular among African-Americans than among other groups.

If a couple arrange themselves in head-to-tail fashion, they can engage in mutual oral sex (Figure 8.8). This practice is often called "69" or "soixante-neuf" (the French for 69). While sixty-nining can be very exciting, it has two possible drawbacks. The first is that each partner may be distracted from enjoying what is going on at one location by the need to attend to the other location. Also, when fellatio is performed in the 69 position, the tongue of the insertee is located on the upper, less sensitive surface of the penis and cannot easily reach the area of the frenulum.

There is little information about the prevalence of **anilingus** (oral–anal contact). This practice can be very arousing because the skin around the anus is erotically sensitive. Sometimes anilingus is performed as a prelude to anal penetration. Many people avoid anilingus, however, because of negative associations with defecation or because of health concerns, which are to some extent justified (see Chapter 16).

Anal Sex May Be a Part of Either Heterosexual or Male Homosexual Behavior

By **anal sex** (Figure 8.9), we mean penetration of the anus by the penis ("butt-fucking"). Anal sex should be distinguished from rear-entry coitus (see below and Figure 8.14), in which the penis penetrates the vagina from behind. Anal sex is illegal in some states (Box 8.2).

Although anal sex is often though of in connection with sex between men, it is not particularly rare in heterosexual sex. Heterosexual couples may engage in anal sex in order to avoid pregnancy, to avoid "having sex" in the narrow sense of the phrase, because the greater tightness of the anus (compared with the vagina) may be stimulating to the man, because anal stimulation is arousing to the woman, or simply for the sake of variety. In the 1991 National Survey of Men, 20 percent of men (aged 20–39) had engaged in anal sex at least once in their lives (Billy et al., 1993). In the NHSLS survey, 10 percent of men and 9 percent of women said they had engaged in anal sex with an opposite-sex partner within the previous 12 months. Again, there is a cultural difference: Hispanic men are more likely to engage in anal sex than are men of other ethnic groups.

The mechanics of anal sex deserve some discussion. The anus is normally kept tightly closed by a **sphincter** muscle, and the sphincter may go into even stronger contraction as the penis begins to make entry. Anxiety on the part of the insertee may also promote spasm of the sphincter. For anal penetration to take place without causing discomfort to the insertee, it is usually necessary for the insertor to start very slowly, or to hold a finger or the tip of the penis against the orifice for 15 to 30 seconds or until the sphincter relaxes. People who have some experience of receptive anal sex learn how to relax the sphincter during penetration and tend to enjoy the experience more than first-timers. Because the anus has no natural lubrication, it is usually necessary to employ some lubricant, such as K-Y, during anal sex.

As it passes through the anal orifice, the penis enters the **rectum,** the lowermost portion of the intestinal tract. Repeated thrusting is likely to bring the insertor to orgasm by direct stimulation of the penis. The insertee is stimulated by friction against the anal skin and possibly by the massage of deep structures (especially the prostate gland, if the insertee is male). Only a minority of insertees can be brought to orgasm by anal sex alone, but they may reach orgasm if they accompany the anal penetration with masturbation.

There are three general positions that couples can adopt for anal sex. In one, the insertor approaches the insertee from the rear; the insertee may be standing or lying prone, but is usually most comfortable with hips flexed. This can be accomplished by lying on one side with knees up, by leaning over an object such as a bed, or by adopting a crouching posture. In a second position, the insertee lies on her or his back, with legs raised and perhaps draped over the shoulders of the insertor, who approaches from the front. In a third approach, the insertor lies supine and the insertee sits atop him, facing forward or backward. In this case, the insertee must do most of the thrusting.

The anus can also be penetrated with objects other than the penis, such as a dildo (see below), a finger, or even the entire hand and forearm ("fisting"). Some objects may go into the rectum more easily than they come out, however, triggering an embarrassing trip to the emergency room and, conceivably, surgery to remove the foreign body. The medical literature records the extraction of all kinds of objects from the rectum—usually of men—including plastic and glass bottles, cucumbers, carrots and other root vegetables, tools, cigar containers, a curtain rod, and even a baseball. The rectum is also sometimes used for nonsexual "body packing"— as in smuggling narcotics. The insertion of any large, hard, or sharp object into the rectum risks a potentially fatal perforation of the bowel wall. Noncoercive penetration by the penis does not harm the anus or rectum, however, even when practiced repeatedly over many years (Chun et al., 1997).

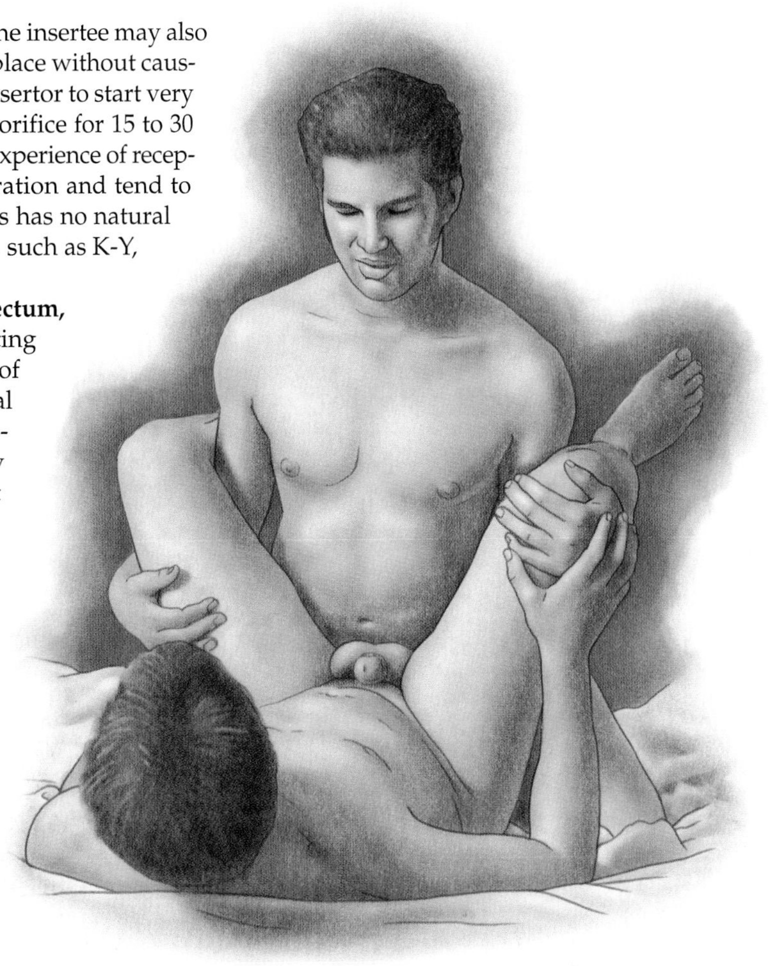

Figure 8.9 Anal penetration may be performed by a man on a woman or on another man (as here).

Most Sexual Encounters Culminate in Coitus

Penetration of the vagina by the penis is called **coitus** ("sexual intercourse," or "fucking," in plain English). Coitus is central to many people's sex lives. Ninety-five percent of sexual encounters between opposite-sex adults include coitus, according to the NHSLS study, and it is usually the final behavior in an encounter. Still, same-sex couples have equally satisfying sex lives without the option of coitus. Furthermore, many sexually active adolescents (who were not interviewed in the NHSLS study) engage primarily in noncoital behaviors, such as oral sex (see Chapter 12).

Coitus Can Be Performed in Many Different Positions

Perhaps the most striking thing about human coitus, compared with coitus in animals, is the wide variety of positions that a couple may adopt to perform it. Among animals, only our close relative the bonobo exhibits any significant degree of flexibility in this

Box 8.2 *Society, Values, and the Law*

The Crime of Sodomy

It may surprise you to learn that state governments can and do regulate the kinds of sexual behavior that American adults engage in, even in the privacy of their own homes. This legal tradition dates back to the colonial period and is ultimately based in Judeo-Christian doctrines. A 1671 statute of Plymouth Colony (Massachusetts), for example, cites the exact words of the Old Testament (Katz, 1993):

> If any Man lyeth with Mankind, as he lyeth with a Woman, both of them have committed Abomination; they both shall surely be put to Death, unless the one party were forced, or be under fourteen years of Age: And all other Sodomitical filthiness, shall surely be punished according to the nature of it. (The words from "If . . . Death" are from Leviticus 20:13.)

In a legal context, anal sex is referred to by the otherwise obsolete term **sodomy**. (This word also has a religious origin: the citizens of Sodom engaged in anal sex with angels, according to one interpretation of Genesis 19.) In quite a few states, such as Virginia and Texas, sodomy also includes oral sex. Currently it is against the law for anyone to engage in sodomy in ten states (mostly in the "Bible Belt"). In three other states (Kansas, Oklahoma, and Texas) sodomy is illegal only when performed between two persons of the same sex. In an important 1986 decision (*Bowers v. Hardwick*), the U.S. Supreme Court ruled by a narrow majority that state sodomy statutes are constitutional, rejecting a challenge based on the constitutional right to privacy. Some state courts have ruled differently. In striking down Arkansas's sodomy statute, for example, the Supreme Court of that state ruled in 2002 that ". . . the fundamental right to privacy implicit in our law protects all private, consensual, noncommercial acts of sexual intimacy between adults" (Supreme Court of Arkansas, 2002).

Although the police may not spend a whole lot of time checking up on people's bedrooms, the sodomy statutes are not entirely dead letters, as the following case illustrates. In September of 1998, deputies responded to a false report of an armed intruder at an apartment in Houston, Texas. On entering the apartment, they saw two men engaged in sex. The men, John Lawrence and Tyron Garner, were arrested, jailed for over 24 hours, and convicted of a Class C misdemeanor. In April 2001, a Texas Court of Appeals upheld the convictions and the constitutionality of the sodomy statute.

Sodomy statutes can also affect women. In 1993, a lesbian living in Virginia, Sharon Bottoms, was denied custody of her 2-year-old son because she admitted to engaging in cunnilingus with her female partner—sodomy, according to the Virginia statute. The decision was reversed on appeal, but then reinstated by the Virginia Supreme Court.

regard: bonobos engage in both front-to-front and rear-entry coitus (see Chapter 2). But humans can and do attempt an almost unlimited number of different positions, a few of which are sketched in Figure 8.10.

If you actually tried a large range of positions such as those shown in the figure, you would probably find that each provided a somewhat different physical and emotional experience, and thus might be preferable in some particular situation. Some positions, for example, allow the man to make thrusting motions of his pelvis, but restrict the woman's mobility. Some allow the reverse, while yet others allow both partners some degree of freedom. Thus, there may be positions that are appropriate when one or the other partner is in an aggressive, take-control mood or, conversely, desires to play a submissive or passive role. In some positions, the hands of one or both partners are free to explore and stimulate erogenous zones; in others, the arms and hands may be occupied in supporting the weight of the body. Some positions require strenuous exertion and cannot be maintained for long periods of time, while others are more relaxed and may be suitable for couples who want to engage in prolonged, leisurely sex, or for obese or frail persons. Yet others may be suitable if the woman is advanced in pregnancy. Some positions allow for eye contact between the man and the woman; this may be crucial for a head-over-heels-in-love couple, but less so, perhaps, during commercial sex. Some positions provide more erotic stimulation to the man, and others provide more stimulation to the woman; such considerations may be relevant if the couple is trying to reach orgasm simultaneously. Some positions provide the woman with more clitoral stimulation, and some stimulate the area of the G spot, which may affect the quality of the woman's orgasm or whether she experiences one at all (see Chapter 3). In short, there seems to be every reason for couples to experiment and to communicate, not just for variety's sake, but so as to suit their sexual behavior to their needs.

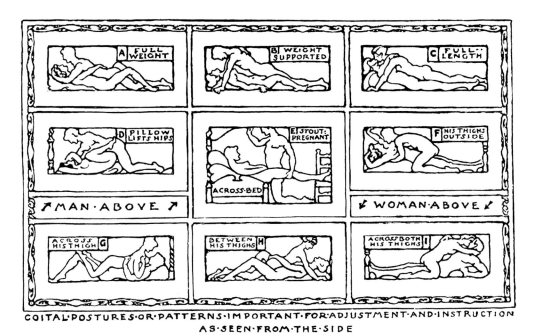

Figure 8.10 Coitus (penile–vaginal penetration) can be performed in numerous positions. These illustrations are from a 1940s manual used by physicians in marriage counseling.

The Man-Above Position Is the Traditional Favorite of Americans

In spite of the possible advantages of experimentation, Americans tend to stick to one tried-and-true position for coitus, in which the woman lies on her back with her legs parted and the man places himself above her, supporting his upper body with his hands or elbows (Figure 8.11). This **man-above position** is also referred to derisively as the "missionary position," presumably with the thought that missionaries might teach or practice sexual behaviors that offer little erotic excitement. At the time of his surveys in the 1940s, Kinsey estimated that 75 percent of Americans had never tried any other position for coitus.

With coitus in the man-above position, one partner guides the man's penis into the woman's vagina. If the woman does this, it may give her a sense of control that otherwise is lacking in the "subordinate" position. Because the man is above, he has to do most of the "work" of coitus (i.e, the pelvic thrusting); the woman's freedom of movement is

Figure 8.11 The man-above position for coitus is also called the "missionary position."

restricted by the man's body, especially if he is much larger than she is. This position has the advantage of allowing eye contact during sex, but the disadvantage that the man's hands are not free to roam over the woman's body.

The man-above position generally provides good erotic stimulation for the man. For the woman, it is more variable. Some women are well stimulated by coitus in this position; for others, there is insufficient stimulation, especially of the G spot, since the penis is directed toward the rear wall of the vagina (Box 8.3).

The Women's Movement Encouraged Alternative Positions

Since Kinsey's time, the sexual revolution and the women's movement have spurred Americans to try other positions besides the man-above position. The connection between the women's movement and changes in coital position was well illustrated in 1979, when students at Radcliffe College celebrated their school's centennial with T-shirts proclaiming "A Century of Women on Top."

Simple variations on the missionary position include the woman's achieving more hip flexion by curling her legs around the man's back or even draping them over his shoulders, as described for anal sex. Such positions allow the man's penis to extend more deeply into the vagina than when the woman's legs are straight or only slightly bent at the knees.

A more drastic change is for the couple to adopt the **woman-above position** (Figure 8.12). Although NHSLS and NSSAL did not ask about coital positions, other, less formal studies have done so, and it is clear that the woman-above position has become increasingly popular since Kinsey's day. In one 1974 survey, 75 percent of married people employed the woman-above position at least on occasion (Hunt, 1974).

In the woman-above position the man lies on his back, and the woman either lies on top of him in a face-to-face arrangement (which allows full body contact) or sits upright. The woman-above position gives the woman greater control, since she generates much of the thrusting motion. In general, the woman-above position may give the man somewhat less erotic stimulation than the man-above position, and the woman may receive somewhat more stimulation. Furthermore, especially when the woman adopts a sitting position, it is relatively easy for her or the man to manually caress her breasts or her clitoris, thus increasing her erotic stimulation further. Because men tend to reach orgasm faster than women, these features of woman-above coitus may be helpful to couples who want to reach orgasm at about the same time.

Another alternative is the **side-to-side position** (Figure 8.13), in which the man and the woman face each other, but each lies with one side directly on the bed (or floor, or grass!). Coitus in this position tends to be relatively relaxed, since neither partner's thrusting is aided by gravity and penetration tends to be shallow. This may be desirable if the intention is to prolong the sexual encounter, or if health concerns restrict one or both partners' ability to expend energy. One problem with side-by-side coitus, however, is that limbs tend to get trapped under bodies and may go numb in the midst of the proceedings.

In **rear-entry coitus** (Figure 8.14), the man faces the woman's back. As with anal sex (with which it should not be confused), there are a number of ways of accomplishing rear-entry coitus: the couple may lie side by side with the woman

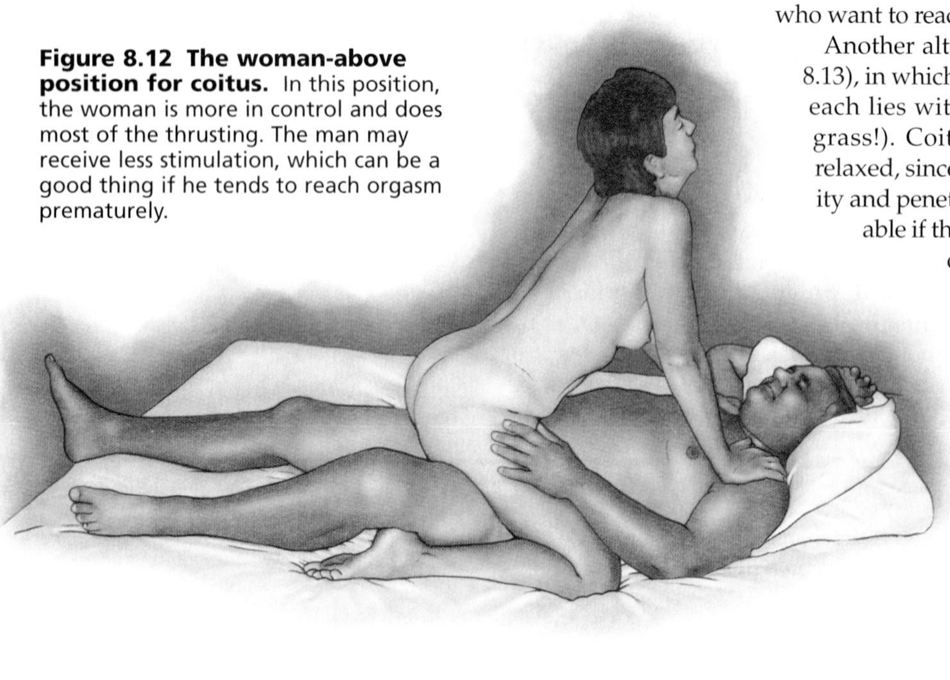

Figure 8.12 The woman-above position for coitus. In this position, the woman is more in control and does most of the thrusting. The man may receive less stimulation, which can be a good thing if he tends to reach orgasm prematurely.

Box 8.3 Research Highlights

Progress in Coitus Research

Leonardo da Vinci was the ultimate "Renaissance man," whose inquiring mind led him to study almost every aspect of the world and human experience. In 1492, Leonardo made an anatomical drawing titled *Coitus of a Hemisected Man and Woman*, in which a copulating couple are represented as if they have been sliced down the middle (Figure A). Of course, Leonardo didn't really cut people in half; he just imagined it, and as a result, the anatomical details are highly suspect.

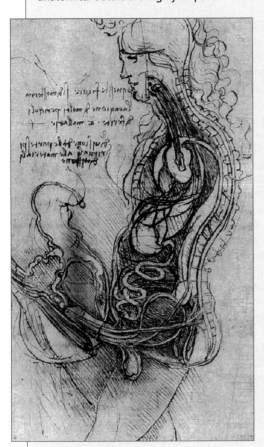

(A) *Coitus of a Hemisected Man and Woman* (ca. 1492), by Leonardo da Vinci

Leonardo showed the man's penis sticking straight out from his body like a flagstaff. He also had some odd ideas about internal anatomy: What is that tube that runs from the woman's uterus to her breast? The scientific value of Leonardo's study, however,

lay not so much its veracity, or lack thereof, as in its implied message: that sex was a suitable subject for study.

Half a millennium later, gynecologist Willibrord Schultz and his colleagues at the University Hospital in Groningen, Holland, decided to check on Leonardo's conception of coitus by means of magnetic resonance imaging (MRI) (Schultz et al., 1999). It wasn't easy. First, there was the question of space. If you have ever been inside an MRI machine, you'll know that it's a tight fit: the tube you lie in is only 20 inches in diameter. Imagine having someone else in there with you, and then going through the contortions required even for missionary-position sex. The researchers had to select smallish volunteers, and in fact, the first couple that succeeded in achieving penetration in the MRI machine were amateur acrobats.

The researchers had an even more serious problem, however: the male volunteers' penises did not stand up well to the study's high-stress conditions. It took nearly a minute to acquire a single MRI image, and the men just couldn't keep their penises stationary and erect inside the women's vaginas for that length of time.

Five years after the start of the study, however, two unexpected breakthroughs occurred. The researchers obtained a new MRI machine that could generate an image in a mere 12 seconds, and sildenafil (Viagra) came onto the market (see Chapter 15). By swallowing a pill an hour before entering the machine, the men were able to maintain an erection as long as necessary. At last the researchers obtained sharp pictures of the man's fully erect penis deep within the woman's vagina (Figure B).

In these pictures, the penis is not straight, as depicted by Leonardo, but bent upward, with the hinge point near the abdomen. Thus, the entire penis (including the root of the penis within the man's body) has the shape of a boomerang.

In the images, the sensitive lower surface of the penis presses against the back wall of the woman's vagina, an arrangement that may be highly stimulating to the man. Yet the penis makes little contact with the front wall of the vagina, which is the location of the controversial G spot. (The particular women who participated in the study said they did not have G spots.) These

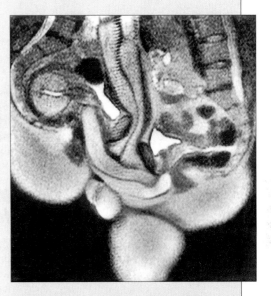

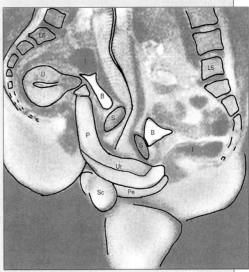

(B) MRI image of coitus (top) with explanatory drawing (bottom). P = penis; Ur = urethra; Pe = perineum; U = uterus; S = symphysis; B = bladder; I = intestine; L5 = lumbar 5; Sc = scrotum. (From Schultz et al., 1999.)

findings support the notion that positions other than the missionary position would provide better stimulation to the female partner, especially if she desires stimulation of the G spot.

Figure 8.13 The side-to-side position for coitus. Because both partners are lying directly on a flat surface, it is a less tiring position and thus can be sustained for longer periods of time.

Figure 8.14 Rear-entry coitus. This position leaves the woman's breasts and clitoris free for manual stimulation by either partner.

turned away from the man, or the woman may be lying prone or in a crouched position, or standing and leaning over some object. Because the penis enters the vagina from the rear, it comes into strongest contact with the vagina's front wall, and penetration tends to be fairly shallow.

As indicated by its slang name, "doggy-style," rear-entry coitus is a reminder of our kinship with the animal world. It has a number of potential advantages and disadvantages. The man may find contact with the woman's back and buttocks arousing, and the fact that the woman's front is free makes it easy for either partner to stimulate her breasts and clitoris during coitus. Rear-entry coitus in the side-by-side position may be the most comfortable position for a woman in the later stages of pregnancy. In rear-entry coitus, the angle of penetration of the vagina is ideal for women who like stimulation of the G spot, but there is no direct stimulation of the clitoris. And because of the angle, the penis may tend to slip out of the vagina. Another possible disadvantage is that eye contact is limited.

Men and Women May Have Different Preferences for Sexual Encounters

People vary considerably in their preferred scenarios for a sexual encounter. Coitus is the preferred culmination of a sexual encounter for most people. Some like to precede coitus with extended foreplay, while others like to engage in coitus as soon as both the man and woman are physiologically aroused (i.e., erect and lubricating, respectively). In general, women are more interested in extended foreplay and "afterplay" (sexual activity after coitus) than are men, who tend to be very focused on coitus (Denney et al., 1984).

Men usually lose their erection soon after ejaculating, and often their psychological arousal with it. (For a tale about an erection that did not go down, see Box 8.4.) Thus, men who wish their female partners to feel sexually fulfilled by an encounter may need to delay their own orgasm until their partner is satisfied, whether that satisfaction means orgasm, more than one orgasm, or a certain length or intensity of nonorgasmic sex. A man can delay his ejaculation by any of a number of methods, such as simply thrusting slowly, pausing, using positions in which he is less strongly stimulated, using a condom, or mentally detaching himself from the erotic stimulation he is receiving. He can also use techniques taught by therapists specifically to treat **premature ejaculation** (see Chapter 15).

That women often prefer sex on a more relaxed schedule than men is made obvious when two women get together. According to a nonrandom survey by *The Advocate,* a gay and lesbian magazine, 96 percent of lesbians spend more than 15 minutes on a love-making session, and 39 percent spend more than an hour (Lever, 1995). Besides taking longer than a typical heterosexual encounter, woman–woman sex is marked by a greater variety of behaviors and by an emphasis on general body contact in addition to specific genital contacts (Hite, 1977).

While on the topic of same-sex encounters, it's worth pointing out that same-sex couples have one advantage over opposite-sex couples: they are dealing with partners whose basic anatomy, physiology, and psychology are intimately familiar to them even before their first sexual experience. Furthermore, people's upbringing often allows them to communicate more effectively with persons of their own sex than with persons of the other sex. Thus, gay and lesbian couples may find it easier to express their sexual desires and needs with-

Box 8.4 *Sex in History*

Penis Captivus: The Origin of a Medical Myth

When dogs mate, ejaculation occurs within seconds, but the two animals are sometimes unable to separate for many minutes thereafter. This happens because the male's penis is constricted by the muscular wall of the female's vagina and has difficulty losing its erection. Accounts of a comparable phenomenon in humans are a part of many cultures, but its entry into the medical literature as **penis captivus** ("captured penis") originates with a hoax by Sir William Osler, a celebrated Canadian physician and medical teacher (Nation, 1973).

In 1884, the *Philadelphia Medical News* published an article by one of its editors,

William Osler (1849–1919)

Theophilus Parvin, on the topic of **vaginismus,** a painful spastic contraction of the vaginal musculature (see Chapter 15). Parvin speculated that vaginismus might be responsible for the phenomenon of penis captivus, which had previously been considered fictitious. Osler, who was an editor of the same journal and considered Parvin a pompous prig, wrote a letter to the journal under the assumed name of Egerton Y. Davis and had it mailed from Montreal. After effusive praise of Parvin's article, "Davis" went on to describe an actual case of penis captivus that he had treated. Davis said that he was summoned by a gentleman late one night:

> At bedtime, when going to the back kitchen to see if the house was shut up, a noise in the coachman's room attracted his attention, and, going in, he discovered to his horror that the man was in bed with one of the maids. She screamed, he struggled, and they rolled out of bed together and made frantic efforts to get apart, but without success. He was a big, burly man, over six feet, and she was a small woman, weighing not more than ninety pounds. She was moaning and screaming, and seemed in great agony, so that after several fruitless attempts to get them apart, he sent for me. When I arrived I found the man standing up and supporting the woman in his arms, and it was quite evident that his penis was tightly locked in her vagina, and any attempt to dislodge it

was accompanied by much pain on the part of both. It was, indeed, a case 'De cohesione in coitu.' I applied water, and then ice, but ineffectually, and at last sent for chloroform, a few whiffs of which sent the woman to sleep, relaxed the spasm, and released the captive penis, which was swollen, livid, and in a state of semi-erection, which did not go down for several hours, and for days the organ was extremely sore. The woman recovered rapidly and seemed none the worse.

Delighted to find his hypothesis vindicated, Parvin had the letter published in the *Medical News,* and it was frequently cited thereafter as the medical authority for the condition of penis captivus.

There have been sporadic but poorly documented reports of penis captivus since Osler's time (e.g., Musgrave, 1980). Whether penis captivus ever really happens or not, the widespread belief in the phenomenon reflects men's anxiety about coitus, female genitalia, and female sexuality in general. Another expression of this anxiety is the notion that the vagina has teeth that can injure or devour the penis (**vagina dentata**). This idea has cropped up in many cultures (Beit-Hallahmi, 1985; Walker, 1983); for example, it is an integral part of the creation myth of the Yanomamo, a native people of the Amazon basin. The meaning of the vagina dentata myth has been debated by psychoanalysts since the time of Freud (Otero, 1996).

out talking past each other. This very familiarity may also create problems, however, by lessening the sense of mystery and tension that energizes durable sexual relationships. We revisit this issue in Chapter 9.

Vibrators and Dildos Are Used to Enhance Sexual Pleasure

Innumerable natural and artificial objects have been recruited for sexual use at one time or another. Some serve minority sexual interests (see Chapter 13) or fetishisms (see Chapter 14), or are designed to alleviate sexual dysfunctions (see Chapter 15). Here we discuss the two commonest kinds of sexual aids, vibrators and dildos.

Vibrators (sometimes referred to as "personal massagers") are electrical devices that use either a plug-in connection or batteries. Their function is exactly what their name implies: to provide vibratory stimulation. Typically, a vibrator consists of a handle and a vibrating head, whose shape may be designed to stimulate a specific target: clitoris, vagi-

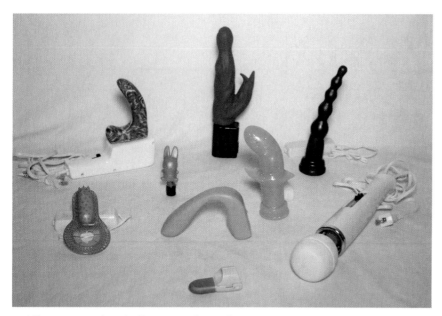

Vibrators are electrically powered sexual stimulators. Photo © 2002 Janice Cripe, courtesy of Blowfish (www.blowfish.com).

na, the entire vulva, penis, or anus. Plug-in vibrators generally provide stronger stimulation and a greater range of speeds, whereas battery-powered devices are more portable, safer from electric shock hazards, and often less expensive (though perhaps not when the cost of battery replacement is factored in).

Vibrators are most often thought of as an aid to women when masturbating, and indeed, they are quite commonly used for that purpose. Many women need prolonged, continuous clitoral stimulation to reach orgasm, and a vibrator may be the most effective way to provide it.

Women may also use a vibrator during partnered sex. A woman engaged in coitus or oral sex, for example, may simultaneously stimulate her clitoris with a vibrator. If her partner is a man, he may be unfamiliar with vibrators, or may feel that a woman who uses one is telling him that he is an inadequate lover. As always, communication is key.

Men may also use vibrators—either the same models used by women or models specifically designed for stimulation of the penis (these may have a vibrating sleeve or ring). Although only a minority of men actually need a vibrator to reach orgasm, its use may enhance sexual pleasure. A vibrator may be used to stimulate the scrotum, perineum, or anus while the penis is stimulated by masturbation or partnered sex.

Dildos are sex toys designed for penetration of the vagina or anus. They are not electrically powered; in fact, they predate the discovery of electricity by thousands of years. They may be realistic imitations of a penis (sometimes complete with scrotum), but they also come in a wide variety of other shapes and sizes, some designed to stimulate the clitoris at the same time the shaft of the dildo penetrates the vagina. The back end of the dildo may be flared to prevent its getting lost in the rectum, in which case it may be called a "butt plug." Alternatively, it may be double-ended, allowing two people to use the same dildo simultaneously.

Another kind of dildo is made to fit into a strap that a woman can wear around her hips or around one thigh. Strap-on dildos are mostly used in sex between women. These devices also have a long history: Ford and Beach (1951) reported that women of the Azande people of eastern Sudan traditionally used a banana, manioc, or sweet potato tied around the waist to engage in vaginal penetration with female partners. Strap-on dildos can also be used by a woman to anally penetrate a man.

Dildos are made from a range of materials, but silicone rubber is generally preferred for its flexibility, smooth surface, and ease of cleaning. (Cleanliness is an important issue, as dildos can transmit STDs and other infections.) Dildos usually have to be used with a lubricant, not just for anal penetration but for vaginal penetration as well. They need to be used gently and with respect for anatomy—that is, they should be moved in the natural direction of the rectum or vaginal canal. It is also best to use small sizes, at least to begin with. (Some health issues connected with the use of sex toys are mentioned in Chapter 16.)

Dildos are designed for penetration of the vagina or anus. Photo © 2002 Janice Cripe, courtesy of Blowfish (www.blowfish.com).

Some Cultures Have Discussed Sexual Behavior More Openly Than Others

American culture seems to be in a state of transition with regard to the discussion of sexual practices. On the one hand, one can walk into a chain bookstore and purchase books that cover not only mainstream sex, but any number of minority interests, from fisting to sex with animals. On the other hand, sex education in schools is still a very controversial topic, reflecting a conflict between traditional negative attitudes toward sex and an increasing desire for openness and realism, especially in the areas of masturbation, homosexuality, contraception, and disease prevention.

The *Kama Sutra* Is the Classic Work on How to Make Love

Because attitudes in the United States have been changing so rapidly over the past few decades, open discussion of sexual behavior seems like a modern American phenomenon. In reality, however, some other societies have been more open in the way they deal with sexuality than we are. Nothing illustrates this better than the *Kama Sutra of Vatsyayana,* which was written in India no later than the fifth century C.E. ("C.E.," or "common era," is the nonreligious designation for the era you probably know better as "A.D.").

Kama sutra means "love guide." In Hindu teaching, *kama* (love) is one of the four goals of life (*puruṣarthas*). Unlike the selfless love that is celebrated in Judeo-Christian tradition, however, *kama* includes a hefty dose of erotic pleasure, and this is a central topic of Vatsyayana's book.

Western readers will see little of spiritual significance in the *Kama Sutra.* In fact, some of it seems downright Machiavellian, as, for example, when Vatsyayana gives advice to a woman who suspects that her lover is about to dump her (dump him first and take all his money), or when he suggests to a king's sex-starved wives how to smuggle a strange man into the harem (dress him as a woman and distract the guards). Hinduism is a holistic religion that values all aspects of human life, however, rather than being purely ascetic or transcendental, as Westerners sometimes imagine. Furthermore, Vatsyayana emphasizes that *kama* is subservient to other *puruṣarthas*, especially to *dharma* (right conduct).

To give some idea of Vatsyayana's practical approach, he begins the chapter on sexual intercourse with a discussion of genital size. Unlike current textbooks such as this one, which tend to downplay the significance of size variations, Vatsyayana considers it a major problem if a man's and woman's genitals are mismatched—particularly if the man is a "hare" (i.e., has a small penis) and the woman is a "female elephant" (i.e., has a large, deep vagina).

In such a case, Vatsyayana recommends penis enlargement, which is to be accomplished by repeated application of the bristles of certain tree-living insects, followed by rubbing the penis with oil for 10 nights and sleeping with the penis hanging down through a hole in the bed. ("He should take away all the pain from the swelling by using cool concoctions.") If this does not provide the woman with satisfaction, the man can use *apadravyas*, which are metal or ivory sleeves studded with "pleasure bumps" on the outside. They fit over the penis in a modular fashion, increasing its girth and length as much as desired. In an extreme case, the man should forget about his penis altogether and simply tie the tubular stalk of a bottle gourd around his waist with string—another variation on the strap-on dildo.

The *Kama Sutra* is best known for its detailed description of coital positions, which include all the ones we have discussed plus more exotic

Erotic sculptures at the temple of Kandariya Mahadeva, Khajuharo, India, dating from the 11th century C.E.

This sexual position, from the *Kama Sutra*, is said to "require practice."

ones that "require practice." There are also several chapters on foreplay, with detailed instructions for embracing, kissing, touching, slapping, scratching with the nails, and biting. Every kind of foreplay escalates by precise gradations, so as to slowly increase the degree of passion. Thus, if a man gives a woman a "line of points" (a mark caused by a niplike bite by several teeth), she should respond with a "broken cloud" (a circular arrangement of marks caused by biting down on a large chunk of skin). He, in turn, may respond with the "biting of the boar," and so on.

Vatsyayana covers fellatio in considerable detail, and cunnilingus briefly, but he barely mentions anal sex. (According to Indian tradition, the Moslems introduced anal sex in the eleventh century.) Vatsyayana describes sex between women, but he sees it as a choice of last resort (e.g., in the king's harem when no man can be smuggled in). Sex between men is chiefly a matter of eunuchs (castrated men) performing fellatio on other men in connection with bodily services such as massage. There is no notion of homosexuality as a durable orientation.

Vatsyayana is far more mindful of women's interests than are other ancient texts on sexuality, such as Ovid's *Art of Love* (a poem from the decadent period of Roman literature, which is basically a man's guide to seduction). Many of Vatsyayana's observations on how men and women interact seem right on target today. But his understanding of women's bodies is rudimentary: he seems not to know of the clitoris, for example.

Whether the open and positive attitude toward sex seen in the *Kama Sutra* was generally typical of Vatsyayana's time is difficult to know. For one thing, the book was written for and about the idle rich. The sex lives of the great majority of Indian people in the fifth century are lost to history.

The Spirit of the *Kama Sutra* Is Absent in Contemporary India

The United States is not the only society in which attitudes toward sexual behavior have changed over time. Sexual behavior in contemporary India is very different from that described in the *Kama Sutra*. Although Westernization is liberalizing the sexual attitudes and practices of some Indians, large segments of Indian society have negative attitudes toward sex. These attitudes derive from repressive Hindu teachings that have developed since Vatsyayana's time, from Moslem influences, and from Victorian thinking absorbed from the British during the colonial period. A generally low valuation of women has compounded the problem. Sex is little spoken of, and communication between partners is often poor. Here is how Indian sexologists Jayaji Krishna Nath and Vishwarath Nayar describe marital sex:

According to Hindu tradition, a husband should only approach his wife sexually during her *ritu* (season), a period of 16 days within the menstrual cycle. But intercourse is forbidden on 6 of these 16 days, the first four days and the eleventh and thirteenth. This leaves only 10 days for conjugal relations, but since the all-important sons are [thought to be] conceived only on even nights and daughters on uneven nights, the days for conjugal relations shrink to five. Then there are the *parvas*, the moonless nights and those of the full moon when sexual relations lead either to the birth of atheist sons (*Brahma Purana*) or the "hell of feces and urine" (*Vishnu Purana*). Add to these taboos the many festival days for gods and ancestors when erotic pleasures are forbidden. Sex is also beyond the pale during the day.

Sex is a particularly unhappy experience for women of the lowest caste ("untouchables") living in cities:

Most of these women portrayed their experience with sexual intercourse as a furtive act in a cramped and crowded room, lasting barely a few minutes and with a marked absence of physical or emotional caressing. It was a duty, an experience to be submitted to, often from a fear of beating. None of the women removed their clothes during intercourse since it is considered shameful to do so. (Nath & Nayar, 1997)

Mangaia Exemplifies a Sex-Positive Society

Among contemporary or near-contemporary societies with relatively open attitudes toward sexual behavior are a number of Polynesian cultures. Mangaia, the southernmost of the Cook Islands, is a case in point (Figure 8.15). Anthropologist Donald Marshall visited Mangaia in the 1950s. He described a culture where children grow up with a broad knowledge of sexuality and of what is expected of men and women (Marshall, 1971). In part, this is because families sleep together in large rooms, so children get to witness the sexual behavior of adults. (This would probably be considered child abuse in our own society.) In addition, children are freely permitted to engage in sex play and masturbation, and they learn the sexual anatomy of both sexes, including three different names for the clitoris. (Compare this with traditional Indian society, in which women may have no word to refer to their genitalia at all.)

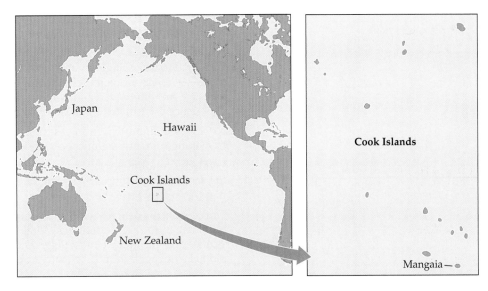

Figure 8.15   Mangaia is the southernmost of the Cook Islands in the South Pacific.

At puberty, boys undergo the superincision ritual (see Chapter 3). The older man who performs the superincision also instructs the boy in heterosexual behavior, including foreplay and oral sex. In particular, he is told to make sure that his partner experiences several orgasms before he reaches orgasm himself. A few weeks later the boy has sex with an older woman who helps him practice various sexual positions and shows him how to hold back his arousal so that he and his partner can experience orgasm simultaneously. Conversely, girls receive instruction from older women and sexual initiation from an older man, usually a relative (another no-no by Western standards).

Mangaians attach no value to virginity, and adolescent boys and girls engage in frequent sexual encounters with each other. These encounters may occur in some out-of-the-way spot. In addition, however, boys may go "sleep-crawling"—meaning that they visit their girlfriends' homes at night. Mothers may pretend to be asleep but actually listen in to make sure that their daughters are having an appropriate experience, including orgasm. One of the functions of these teenage encounters is to identify marriage partners who will be sexually compatible.

With all this sex-positive thinking, you might imagine that the Mangaians' slogan would be "make love, not war." In fact, however, the Mangaians are said to have fought 54 wars with neighboring islands simply over the right to call their own island "Mangaia," which means "great power." It may be that sexual permissiveness, which encourages a high birth rate, balances the attrition of the population caused by these inter-island conflicts.

Summary

1. Sexual behavior is difficult to define precisely, but it includes much more than coitus (sexual intercourse). Any behavior that is accompanied by physiological signs of sexual arousal, or that is perceived as sexual by the participants, should be included.

2. Attitudes toward masturbation or autoerotic behavior have traditionally been very negative. These attitudes derive from moral teachings, from the notion that masturbation is unhealthy, and from a sense that people who masturbate are those who can't find a sex partner. Even today, many people feel guilty about masturbating.

3. According to the NHSLS survey, about half of U.S. adults masturbate at least once per year. Factors associated with higher rates of masturbation include male sex, a younger age, and a higher educational level. Factors associated with lower rates of masturbation include being married, having religious beliefs, and being African-

American. Gay people masturbate more than heterosexuals and derive more enjoyment from it. Masturbation does not seem to be simply a substitute for sex with partners.

4. Men tend to use a single technique for masturbation—direct manual stroking of the penis—whereas women use a greater variety of techniques, such as manual stimulation of the clitoris, labia, or vagina, or rubbing of the vulva against objects. Men experience orgasm during masturbation more frequently than do women.

5. Kissing is an important form of sexual expression in the United States, where it often has strong romantic significance, but it is not practiced in all human cultures.

6. Petting or fondling includes a variety of behaviors short of penetrative sex, including sensuous touching and kissing of the body. It may be a prelude to coitus (foreplay), or it may form the entire sexual encounter, especially among adolescents.

7. Oral sex means contact between the mouth and the penis (fellatio), the vulva (cunnilingus), or the anus (anilingus). Oral sex has become increasingly popular among younger people in the United States and Britain, where 80–90 percent of young people have engaged in it. Like many noncoital sexual behaviors, it is more common among well-educated people.

8. About half of U.S. men, but fewer women, find fellatio very appealing. Cunnilingus is enjoyed about equally by men and women; about a third of the U.S. population finds it very appealing. Oral sex may be performed mutually in a head-to-tail arrangement; this behavior is called sixty-nining, or soixante-neuf.

9. Anal sex (penetration of the anus by the penis) is practiced in both male–male and female–male encounters. About 10 percent of Americans engage in heterosexual anal sex at least once a year. Anal sex can be performed in a variety of positions and does not damage the anus or rectum.

10. Most adult heterosexual couples include coitus (vaginal penetration by the penis) as the culmination of a sexual encounter. The most popular and traditional position for coitus in the United States is with the man above ("missionary position"), which requires the man to do most of the pelvic thrusting. The women's movement of the 1970s encouraged the exploration of other positions, such as the woman-above position and rear-entry coitus. Each position may have particular advantages and disadvantages for certain couples or in certain situations.

11. Some couples like to make coitus almost the entirety of a sexual encounter, while others include much foreplay and afterplay, or even dispense with coitus altogether. In general, women prefer more protracted lovemaking, and do not place as much emphasis on coitus as do men. Thus sexual encounters between women tend to be considerably longer than heterosexual encounters. Women generally take longer to reach orgasm that do men, so men may have to learn to postpone their own orgasms in heterosexual encounters if the man and woman wish to experience orgasm simultaneously.

12. Vibrators are electrically powered devices that deliver erotically arousing vibratory stimulation. They may be used by men or women, but they are particularly associated with use for masturbation by women and to help women reach orgasm in partnered sex. Dildos are unpowered, sometimes penis-shaped objects used for vaginal or anal penetration, either in partnered or in solo sex.

13. Different cultures have varied greatly in the openness with which they discuss sexual behavior. The classic how-to manual on sexual behavior is the *Kama Sutra* (India, fifth century or earlier). This book demonstrates that explicit discussion of sex is not the sole prerogative of modern Western society. Contemporary India, on the other hand, is dominated by negative attitudes toward sex.

14. Some cultures are more sex-positive than others. In many Pacific Island cultures, such as Mangaia, children receive instruction and initiation into sexual practices at puberty. An important aim of this instruction is to encourage sexual pleasure and to ensure that men help their partners experience multiple orgasms.

Discussion Questions

1. Why do you think that college graduates engage in a greater variety of sexual behaviors than do people who did not go to college?

2. Do you agree with Joycelyn Elders (see Box 8.1) that teaching about masturbation would help reduce unwanted pregnancies and sexually transmitted diseases?

3. Are there any sexual behaviors described in this chapter that you think people in general should not engage in? Is your view based on your moral beliefs, on practical (e.g., health) considerations, or some other reason?

4. Would it be a good or a bad thing if Mangaian attitudes toward sex became the rule in the United States today? How would it change our society?

5. Masturbation is often a stigmatized topic. Make a list of all the things you have ever heard about masturbation on a piece of paper; don't add your name. After a list of all these items from your class is put on the board, compare and contrast your views of these myths and misconceptions. Discuss how these misconceptions arose throughout history and have influenced our behavior.

6. Imagine you were a parent in Victorian times and you found your baby playing with his genitalia, as all babies do. The Victorians believed that masturbation was bad, unhealthy, and led to disease. Imagine what you as a parent might do to prevent this terrible fate from befalling your baby. What might you do to prevent the baby's hands from touching his genitalia?

7. Former President Bill Clinton and a significant percentage of society think that "oral sex" is not really sex. Do you agree or disagree? Discuss what behaviors are included in your view of "having sex."

8. Consider your attitudes and beliefs about whether the government should regulate the kinds of sex acts that American adults engage in (see Box 8.2). Should oral or anal sex be prohibited? Imagine that you are testifying before a Senate committee, and argue what should or should not be permitted or prohibited.

Web Resources

Sexual Health InfoCenter, Better Sex   www.sexhealth.org/bettersex/

Society for Human Sexuality   www.sexuality.org

Nerve.com, an online magazine devoted to sex and culture   www.nerve.com

Recommended Reading

Comfort, A., and Park, C. (1998). *The new joy of sex and more joy of sex.* New York: Pocket Books.

Stengers, J., and Van Neck, A. (2001). *Masturbation: The history of a great terror* (K. A. Hoffmann, Trans.). New York: Palgrave.

Dodson, B. (1987). *Sex for one: The joy of self-loving.* New York: Harmony Books.

Gregersen, E. (1983). *Sexual practices: The story of human sexuality.* New York: Franklin Watts.

Loulan, J. (1984) *Lesbian sex.* San Francisco: Spinsters Ink/Aunt Lute.

Silverstein, C., and Picano, F. (1992). *The new joy of gay sex.* New York: HarperCollins.

Vatsyayana (1991). *The Kama Sutra of Vatsyayana* (R. F. Burton, Trans.) New York: Arkana.

chapter 9

Many sexual relationships are culturally sanctioned through marriage. Here ministers of Reverend Sun Myung Moon's Unification Church perform a mass wedding ceremony for over 20,000 couples.

Sexual Relationships

*I*n previous chapters we discussed sexual attraction, sexual arousal, and sexual behavior. Now we step back and take a look at the interpersonal frameworks within which partnered sex may occur—in other words, sexual relationships.

Of course, we have to interpret the word "relationship" broadly if we are to encompass the full expression of human sexuality. In common discourse, a "one-night stand"—or an even briefer sexual encounter between strangers—may not constitute a relationship, but for our purposes it does. So does a partnership that lasts a lifetime. So do sexual encounters that involve coercion or payment, although we defer discussion of those two topics to later chapters. What interests us here is the dynamic that brings people together as potential sex partners, keeps them together for minutes or decades, and ultimately separates them.

Sexual Relationships Are Motivated by Many Factors

Why do people enter into sexual relationships? According to the contemporary Western ideal, they do so for two leading reasons: they are physically attracted to each other, or they are romantically in love with each other—preferably both.

Certainly, sexual attraction and romantic love are powerful forces that propel many people into sexual encounters or enduring relationships. But they may be mingled with, or entirely replaced by, a wide variety of other motives. These motives include nonspecific sexual arousal; rage; the desire for status, security, or profit; the desire to please others, to conform, or to follow moral beliefs; or, alternatively, the desire to rebel and to demonstrate disobedience or nonconformity; and finally, of course, the desire to bear and rear children. Most sexual relationships are probably fueled by some combination of these forces.

Let's take a look at some of these motives. The term **nonspecific sexual arousal** refers to the fact that people can be sexually aroused without having a particular partner in mind. This is true of both sexes, but it is particularly true of men, who might describe themselves as "horny" under those circumstances. This kind of arousal is what sends men actively looking for a casual sex partner, whether it be in a bar, a red-light district, or a gay "cruising zone." Because men are often not able to obtain sex with partners they are attracted to, they may settle for sex with persons they are not attracted to—perhaps even with persons of the "wrong" sex. Thus, nonspecific sexual arousal can function independently of sexual attraction as a motivator for engaging in a sexual relationship.

The desire for status or security is often mingled with more explicitly sexual motives for sexual relationships. Simply having a boyfriend or girlfriend confers status, especially among teens. A girl whose boyfriend is older or has high status by the criteria of teen society will see her own status elevated. A boy whose girlfriend is considered desirable also becomes desirable. Of course, the famous **double standard** is still in effect, at least to some degree: if a girl is known to have multiple sex partners, her status may be reduced to that of a "slut," but if a boy has multiple sex partners, his status may be raised even above that of a boy who just has a steady girlfriend—at least within his own circle of peers.

Such status seeking was exemplified in 1993 by members of the "Spur Posse," a gang of boys at Lakewood High School, near Los Angeles, who made sex into a competitive sport, the aim being to see who could have sex with the most girls. Some gang members tallied more than 60 "conquests"—including girls as young as 10 years old. What was shocking to many about the Spur Posse's exploits—besides the young age of the girls they victimized—was the explicit way in which the desire for status among peers was made into the prime instigator for sexual activity. Yet, in reality, status seeking and male–male competition are very commonly significant influences on sexuality, especially among adolescents. There is little question that a connection between male–male competition and sexual activity is part of our evolutionary heritage, as we saw in Chapter 2.

As a factor promoting entry into sexual relationships, the desire for security probably has significant evolutionary roots. For both sexes, but for women especially, single life would have been extremely difficult throughout most of human evolution. And if this long evolutionary history has failed to engrave a desire for security sufficiently on our genes, our culture has amply reinforced it. Until a generation or two ago, a woman who failed to marry (an "old maid," as she was once called) was guaranteed a lifetime of poverty or dependence; in many cultures, she still is. Only in the mid-nineteenth century did it become possible for some American women to lead a financially and socially independent life as a single person or in partnership with another woman. Things have changed radically since then, but a combination of genetic and cultural history still influences women to consider material factors such as wealth and power in choosing mates (Buss, 1989; Waynforth & Dunbar, 1995). In fact, these traits are part and parcel of sexual attractiveness itself.

Rage and the profit motive, as factors motivating sexual relationships, will be discussed in Chapters 18 and 19. What about the desire to conform—or to rebel? The desire to conform—to the wishes of parents or of society in general, or to moral or religious teachings—may be the most important factor of all. Heterosexual partnership, especially in the framework of marriage, is an overwhelmingly powerful social structure—a bedrock concept that shapes people's ideas, plans, and actions from early childhood. That's most clear in the case of **arranged marriages**—still the norm for millions of people around the world—in which the husband and wife may not see each other until their wedding day, or shortly before. They may hope for (and ultimately obtain) love and sexual pleasure, but these factors do not trigger the actual choice of a partner. Even in more individualistic societies, heterosexual marriage sweeps many people into relationships for reasons that have nothing to do with love or sexual desire. Many gays and lesbians get married, for example, even though they may have little prospect of a passionate or erotically satisfying relationship with an opposite-sex spouse (see Chapter 13).

Ironically, the desire to rebel may an equally strong instigator of sexual relationships. One of the main tasks of adolescence is cutting parental bonds; often, embarking on a sexual relationship is seen as a means to do this. No wonder teens so often establish sexual partnerships that seem calculated to earn their parents' disapproval—they may in fact be so intended, consciously or unconsciously. We will have more to say on this score in Chapter 12.

Finally, there is the desire to have children. For some, procreation is the only moral justification for sex. For many, the desire for children is a major reason for entering into a marriage or other form of heterosexual partnership. Sometimes, a woman will enter into a brief sexual relationship with a man with the sole intention of becoming pregnant; she may want to rear a child as a single woman, in partnership with another woman, or with a husband or male partner who is infertile or who carries some harmful hereditary trait. Of course, there are other ways to accomplish this end, such as adoption, artificial insemination, or in vitro fertilization (see Chapter 10), but good old-fashioned sex is still the cheapest, simplest, and most popular method of having a baby, inside or outside of a long-term relationship.

Many Indian Hindu couples have only one brief meeting before their wedding.

Religion and the Law Influence Sexual Morality

A major thread in Western thought is the idea that sexuality is morally suspect, an inferior state of being, or a threat to the integrity of society. Of course, successful societies have had to permit, or even encourage, enough sex to allow for reproduction, but some have hedged sexuality with numerous restrictions. This has often been done through religious teachings.

The traditional function of sexual relationships was the production of large families. This nineteenth-century family was typical of the period.

Ancient Jewish Doctrines Forbade Many Sexual Behaviors

The restrictions laid down by the religious leaders of ancient Israel and incorporated into the Book of Leviticus (part of the Jewish Torah and the Christian Old Testament) have been fundamental to Western moral tradition. According to Leviticus, God gave Moses a list of prohibited sexual behaviors, along with appropriate punishments for transgression (often death by stoning or burning). The forbidden behaviors included adultery, incest (including sex with relatives by blood and by marriage), sex during menstruation, sex between men, and sex with animals.

Leviticus did not prohibit marital sex, and numerous passages in the Old Testament attest to the positive moral status of the marriage bond and of sex within that bond. Nor did Leviticus prohibit sex between an unmarried man and an unmarried woman. Other biblical passages, however, made clear that a woman who was not a virgin when she married could be executed (Deuteronomy 22). No equivalent punishment was laid down for men, showing that the double standard was already well in place in early Jewish society.

Christianity Began with Negative Views of Sexual Expression

Early Christian thinkers thought poorly of *any* kind of sexual behavior or sexual desire. This attitude was influenced by several factors: the belief that Jesus himself had been **celibate** (unmarried and sexually inactive), a reaction to the sexual excesses of the Roman Empire, an ascetic trend in Greek philosophy, and the personalities of two particular men who helped mold the ethical structure of early Christianity, St. Paul (died ca. 64 C.E.) and St. Augustine (354–430 C.E.). Both of these men had conversion experiences that led them to condemn worldly desires (Box 9.1).

Virginity, or at least celibacy, thus became the most virtuous of states for Christian men and women. Certainly, most Christians did have sex and get married, but in doing so they ceded the high moral ground to the faith's ascetic monks, nuns, friars, and hermits. Since the twelfth century, all Roman Catholic clergy (but not the clergy of the Eastern Catholic and Orthodox churches) have been required to be celibate.

In the thirteenth century St. Thomas Aquinas (1225–1274) restored a measure of moral legitimacy to procreative sex within marriage. He based his argument on "natural law," holding that the natural purpose of sex, intended by God, was procreation. Aquinas used that same argument to condemn any kind of nonmarital, extramarital, or nonprocreative sex, including some kinds that were not specifically mentioned in Leviticus. These included sex between unmarried persons (called **fornication** in Christian tradition), masturbation, and even nocturnal emissions. Though marital sex was permitted, the Church applied all kinds of restrictions, analogous to the traditional Hindu restrictions mentioned in Chapter 8. These rules forbade sex during and after menstruation and pregnancy as well as on Fridays, holy days, Lent, and so forth.

Aquinas's teachings remain at the core of modern Roman Catholic teachings about sex (John Paul II, 1981). The Vatican has slightly liberalized its doctrines in recent years, however. It has acknowledged that sex, besides its direct procreative function, supports procreation indirectly by helping to cement the marital bond. Concordant with that view, it has sanctioned the timing of marital sex so as to avoid pregnancy—the "rhythm method" of contraception (see Chapter 11). Such a practice would have shocked Aquinas.

Other conservative churches, such as the Eastern Orthodox churches, the Southern Baptist Church, and the Church of Jesus Christ of Latter-Day Saints (Mormons), agree fully with the Roman Catholic position in condemning all sexual relationships outside of marriage. Because these churches incline to moral absolutism, they often attempt to influence government policies in ways that impose their moral views on the entirety of society—by opposing legislation that extends protections to unmarried or same-sex couples, for example.

Many mainstream Protestant denominations in America are divided on issues of sexual ethics. For this reason, and also because of the emphasis these denominations place on the role of individual conscience, they tend to come out with nondogmatic or ambiguous position statements on these issues. Here are two examples:

> Although all persons are sexual beings whether or not they are married, sexual relations are only clearly affirmed in the marriage bond. (United Methodist Church, 2000)

> We believe it is best to postpone intercourse until marriage. If a teenage couple decides to have a sexual relationship, they have the responsibility to use effective contraception. (Presbyterian Church [U.S.A.], 1998)

The most liberal denominations, such as the Religious Society of Friends (Quakers) and the Unitarian Universalist Association (which incorporates traditions from other religions besides Christianity), are nonhierarchical and therefore do not attempt to lay down specific rules of sexual conduct. In general, Quaker and Unitarian Universalist congregations look favorably on all loving relationships, including sexual relationships between two men or two women, and they are more concerned with issues of social justice than with what people do in their bedrooms.

Box 9.1 # *Sex in History*

Sex and *The City of God*

After the Bible, no book has influenced Western ideas of morality more than *The City of God,* written by St. Augustine (Figure A), who served as Bishop of Hippo in

(A) A fifteenth-century depiction of St. Augustine

Roman North Africa between 412 and 427 C.E. Augustine was brought up as a Christian, but left the faith and spent his teen years in Carthage, where he had two mistresses and fathered a son. As he recounts in his *Confessions,* he was torn by guilt, and prayed to God: "Give me chastity and continence, but not yet." ("Continence," in this context, means sexual self-restraint.) After some years in Italy, at the age of 33 he reconverted to Christianity, became a celibate hermit, and then a bishop.

Augustine began *The City of God* soon after Rome was sacked by the Visigoths. During that event, many pious virgins were raped. Some people held that these women had sinned, and that they should have committed suicide rather than yield to the conquerors. Augustine, in contrast, held that they retained their virtue because chastity is lost by intention, not by the mere act of intercourse.

This idea of sinfulness being in the individual mind is an important theme in *The City of God.* To Augustine, the doctrine of the Fall of Man meant that all humans are born in a state of sin (Figure B). As told in Genesis, Adam and Eve's sexual awareness arose directly from their sin of eating the forbidden fruit. As a result, they covered their genitals with fig leaves. Sexual desire, Augustine wrote, is part of our punishment for Adam and Eve's sin. It is a sin in itself, even when not expressed in sexual behavior. The fact that couples desire privacy during sex shows that they are aware that sex is wrong.

The sinfulness of sex, according to Augustine, lies in the fact that it is driven by passion (lust) rather than by the will. Thus, if Adam had not sinned, a man's penis would have been like other parts of his body—under voluntary control—and a couple could have had sex with no more passion than during any other activity of life. As it is, he wrote, sexual arousal is a physiological necessity if intercourse is to take place, and this means that sex is not consistent with virtue. Nevertheless, a husband and wife can lessen the sinfulness of sex by concentrating on the intention to procreate and minimizing their sexual arousal.

Augustine's views on sex were shared by some of his contemporaries, such as St. Jerome. Although there was also a sex-positive tradition within the early Church, the sinfulness of sexual arousal became a major theme of Christianity through the Middle Ages. The most popular medieval manual of moral doctrine, written by the French friar Vincent of Beauvais (ca. 1190–ca. 1264), stated that "a man who loves his wife very

much is an adulterer. . . An upright man should love his wife with his judgment, not his affections" (Boswell, 1980).

Some Christian sects have gone so far as to require universal celibacy, even though this requirement imperiled the sects' continued existence. One example was the Harmonist sect, a group of German immigrants who established themselves in Pennsylvania in 1804. Like many members of the early Church, they renounced sex in expectation of the imminent Second Coming of Christ. Although they adopted

(B) Albrecht Dürer's etching (1504) of Adam and Eve's expulsion from the Garden of Eden

some children and also gained some adult converts, by 1876 they were mostly elderly, and the last member of the sect died around 1920. The Roman Catholic Church, in contrast, abandoned St. Augustine's doctrine of the sinfulness of sex in marriage, forbade contraception and abortion, and now has about a billion adherents worldwide.

Some Religions Are More Permissive than Christianity

Contemporary Judaism has two main branches, Orthodox and Reform Judaism. Orthodox Jews follow scriptural teachings (the Torah) as literally as possible and tend to be quite restrictive in sexual matters. Reform Judaism, the numerically preponderant branch in North America, is much more liberal in sexual matters, as may be exemplified by its actions relating to homosexuality and gay people. Already in 1977 the Central Conference of American Rabbis (the main voice of Reform Judaism) called for the decriminalization of homosexual behavior and for an end to discrimination against gay people. During the 1980s rabbinical schools began accepting openly gay or lesbian students. In 1996 the CCAR called for the legalization of same-sex civil marriage, and in 2000 it resolved to permit rabbis to officiate at same-sex weddings (Central Conference of American Rabbis, 2000).

Islam's founder, Mohammed (died 632 c.e.), was very different from Jesus: he was a civil ruler, a successful general, and a sexually active man with many wives. He condemned homosexuality but encouraged most other forms of sexual expression, especially within the context of marriage. As Islam spread, some ascetic movements developed within it, such as the monastic Sufis of Persia, but by and large Islam remained a sex-positive religion. Recently, however, Islamic fundamentalism has led to severe restrictions on sexual expression in some countries. In 2001, for example, a young Nigerian Muslim woman was sentenced to a hundred lashes for engaging in nonmarital sex (Reuters News Service, 2001b). Since the rise of Islamic fundamentalism in Iran there have been numerous reports of executions for adultery and other sexual offenses in that country; these executions are alleged to have been carried out by stoning. Such punishments are not consistent with the teachings of Islam's sacred book, the Qur'an.

The founder of Buddhism, Siddhartha Gautama or Buddha (died ca. 483 b.c.e.), renounced earthly pleasures at the age of 29, and his religion emphasizes self-denial as the way to escape suffering. Many Buddhist men lead ascetic, celibate lives as monks, but some branch-es of Buddhism, as in pre-Western Japan, permitted and even

Reform Jewish rabbis are permitted to officiate at same-sex weddings, such as this wedding between two men.

praised homosexual relationships within the monasteries. The general Buddhist populations, however, have always been expected to participate fully in life, including sexual relationships.

One particular branch of Buddhism known as Vajrayana or **Tantric Buddhism** empha-sizes the control of physical and mental functions, including sexual activity, as a means to enlightenment. Rather than simply condemning erotic desire, Tantric Buddhism seeks to rechannel it. Tantric sex—which is part of a larger framework of **yoga** practices—may involve prolonged sexual encounters combined with meditation, concentration, and breath control. During Tantric sex, little thrusting or other movement occurs. The man may postpone his orgasm or avoid it altogether, or he may learn to ejaculate retrogradely (into the bladder), a mode of release that is accompanied by a less exciting orgasm.

U.S. Law Respects Sexual Privacy—To a Point

Some of the early American colonists, such as the Pilgrim Fathers at Plymouth Colony, attempted to set up societies governed by the edicts of the Old Testament. (We mentioned in Chapter 8 that they copied the words of Leviticus directly into their sodomy statute.) As the American population grew and became more diverse, however, it became clear that religious beliefs, if given the power of law, might tear society apart. Influenced by humanists such as Thomas Paine (1737–1809), the framers of the Declaration of Independence and the U.S. Constitution rooted government in the concept of natural human rights, separat-ed the powers of churches and the state, and protected individual liberties.

One constitutional right that has been particularly important in the sexual domain is the **right of privacy.** This right was not made explicit in the U.S. Constitution or the Bill of Rights, but the U.S. Supreme Court has held that its existence is implied by several amendments, especially by the due process clause of the Fourteenth Amendment. In a 1965 decision (*Griswold v. Connecticut*), the Supreme Court used the right of privacy to

Box 9.2 *Society, Values, and the Law*

Miscegenation Statutes

It may surprise you to learn that, within your parents' lifetime, marriage across racial lines (**miscegenation**) was a crime in some states. Virginians Mildred Jeter and Richard Loving (see photo) found this out in 1958. They married out of state and then returned to Virginia to live. Because Mildred was African-American and Richard was white, they were convicted of violating Virginia's 1924 Racial Integrity Act, which forbade marriages between whites and nonwhites.

In his sentencing opinion, the state judge declared that "Almighty God created the races white, black, yellow, malay and red, and he placed them on separate continents. And but for the interference with his arrangement there would be no cause for such marriages. The fact that he separated the races shows he did not intend for the races to mix." The Lovings were sentenced to a year in prison, but the sentence was suspended provided that they left the state and did not return for 25 years. They moved to Washington, D.C., where they appealed the case. In its 1967 *Loving v. Virginia* decision, the U.S. Supreme Court struck down the

Virginia statute and affirmed the right to marry across racial lines. The justices based their ruling on the due process clause of the Fourteenth Amendment to the Constitution.

Although the *Loving* decision struck down all miscegenation statutes, some states were slow to remove them from their statute books. At the end of the twentieth century, one state, Alabama, still had an anti-miscegenation clause in its state constitution. It read: "The Legislature shall never pass any law to authorize or legalize any marriage between any white person and a Negro, or descendant of a Negro." The clause was removed by a popular ballot measure in 2000. Still, 40 percent of voters opposed the measure, reflecting a continuing antipathy to interracial marriage among Alabama's white population.

Among the more than 8000 interracial married couples now living in Virginia are U.S. Supreme Court Justice Clarence Thomas and his wife Virginia.

affirm the right to use contraceptives, which had been forbidden by a Connecticut state law. In 1967 the Supreme Court, in *Loving v. Virginia,* affirmed the right to marry across racial lines (Box 9.2). The most famous right-of-privacy case was the controversial 1973 *Roe v. Wade* case, in which the Court affirmed a woman's right to have an abortion (see Chapter 11). In Chapter 8 we mentioned another right-of-privacy case, *Bowers v. Hardwick* (1985), in which the Court ruled that the right of privacy did not cover the right to engage in anal or oral sex ("sodomy"), at least between a same-sex couple.

Some people would draw a sharp distinction between the law and morality. "You can't legislate morality" is a commonly heard view. In reality, however, the law is influenced by the moral views of the population, and it, in turn, influences individuals' sense of what is right or wrong. Thus, in the *Bowers v. Hardwick* case, the majority opinion stated that "the law . . . is constantly based on notions of morality, and if all laws representing essentially moral choices are to be invalidated under the Due Process Clause, the courts will be very busy indeed." Conversely, the general reluctance of American governments to police people's sexual relationships or behavior has helped establish a climate in which nonmarital, extramarital, and homosexual relationships are seen as much less serious moral offenses than they were a few generations ago.

People's Moral Judgments about Sex Depend on Its Context

In a series of studies begun in the 1960s, sociologist Ira Reiss (then at the University of Minnesota) showed that people judge the morality of heterosexual behavior by the relationship within which it occurs: the more affectionate, intimate, or committed the rela-

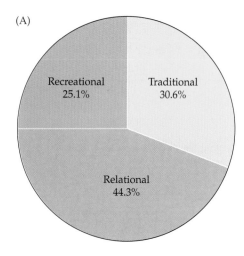

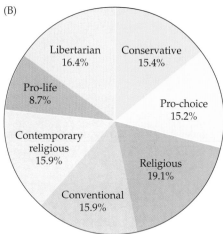

Figure 9.1 Moral perspectives on sexuality. (A) Americans can be grouped into three moral perspectives. (B) These three perspectives can be broken down into seven clusters of moral stances. (Data from NHSLS.)

tionship, the more likely people are to consider sexual acts morally acceptable (Reiss & Miller, 1979). Some nonheterosexual behaviors, on the other hand, may be judged without regard to the relationship within which they occur.

Moral Judgments Are Linked to Beliefs about the Purpose of Sex

As to how committed a heterosexual relationship need be for sex to be morally acceptable, people's views on this question are influenced by their beliefs about what sex is for (DeLamater, 1987). People who believe that the main purpose of sex is procreation tend to be the most restrictive, disapproving of nonmarital sex or of sex acts that cannot lead to pregnancy. People who believe that sex has a major purpose in cementing relationships tend to approve of sex between unmarried persons if the relationship is a committed one, but to disapprove of extramarital or casual sex. People who believe that the purpose of sex is primarily recreational, or to give pleasure, tend to consider any type of consensual heterosexual sex morally acceptable. We may call these three moral perspectives the **traditional, relational,** and **recreational** perspectives (Figure 9.1A). About 31 percent of the U.S. population have a traditional perspective, about 44 percent have a relational perspective, and about 25 percent have a recreational perspective, according to the National Health and Social Life Survey (NHSLS).

The Diversity of Attitudes Is Multidimensional

The three moral perspectives just mentioned do not simply represent three positions on a single conservative-to-liberal continuum, as became clear when the NHSLS researchers studied the interviewees' responses to a battery of nine statements that probed moral attitudes. Factor analysis of the data (see Box 6.1) suggested that the population could be broken down into seven "clusters." The "traditional" group comprised two clusters, named "conservative" and "pro-choice." The "relational" group comprised three clusters ("religious," "conventional," and "contemporary religious"). The "recreational" group comprised two clusters ("pro-life" and "libertarian") (Figure 9.1B).

The moral positions of the people in these seven clusters can be seen by looking at their responses to the nine statements (Figure 9.2). The two clusters in the traditional group ("conservative" and "pro-choice") share many views that reflect traditional morality, such as the view that "premarital sex" (what we call nonmarital sex) among teenagers, as well as same-gender sex and sex unaccompanied by love, are wrong. Religious teachings are important to both these clusters. The major dividing point between them is a radical difference of opinion on abortion, with the "pro-choice" cluster being adamantly in favor of a woman's right to choose. It is surprising that such a large pro-choice bloc exists within the "traditional" perspective.

The three clusters in the "relational" group share the belief that sex should take place only in the context of a loving relationship, but need not necessarily be confined to marriage; they all reject the notion that premarital sex is necessarily wrong. Of the three clusters in this group, two are strongly influenced by religion. One of these (the "religious" cluster) thinks that homosexual relationships and abortion are wrong, while the other ("contemporary religious") takes a liberal view on both these topics. The third group within the "relational" group—the "conventional" cluster—is not influenced by religious beliefs and is pro-choice on abortion, but is largely opposed to extramarital and homosexual relationships.

The two clusters in the "recreational" group share the belief that sex outside a loving relationship may be morally acceptable. Neither group is much influenced by religion. However, one cluster ("pro-life") is strongly opposed to premarital sex among teenagers, homosexual relationships, and abortion, while the other group ("libertarian") takes a permissive stance on these behaviors.

This study reveals a far more complex set of moral stances than is captured by the usual conservative-to-liberal spectrum. So who are the people that make up the various clusters? It turns out that a person's likelihood of belonging to a particular cluster is strongly affected by a variety of demographic and other factors:

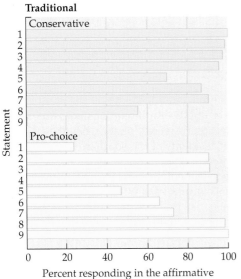

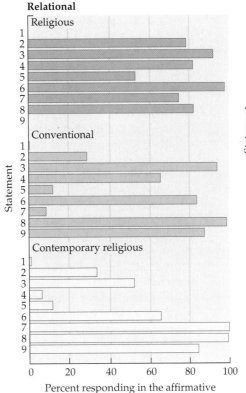

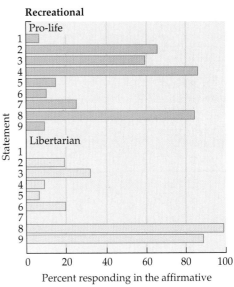

Statements
1. Premarital sex is always wrong.
2. Premarital sex among teenagers is always wrong.
3. Extramarital sex is always wrong.
4. Same-gender sex is always wrong.
5. There should be laws against the sale of pornography to adults.
6. I would not have sex with someone unless I was in love with them.
7. My religious beliefs have guided my sexual behavior.
8. A woman should be able to obtain a legal abortion if she was raped.
9. A woman should be able to obtain a legal abortion if she wants it for any reason.

Figure 9.2 Moral stances on sexual issues. Responses to nine sex-related statements can be grouped into seven clusters. The histograms show the percentage of individuals who agree with the statements.

- **Sex.** Women are more likely than men to belong to one of the two traditional clusters, while men are more likely than women to belong to one of the two recreational clusters. This observation goes along with a wide body of research indicating that women take a more relationship-oriented view of sex than do men (see Chapter 6). Within the relational group, women are overrepresented in the "religious" and "contemporary religious" clusters, reflecting a greater influence of religion on women's views than on men's.

- **Age.** Older people are overrepresented in the two traditional clusters. This reflects the fact that older people grew up when social attitudes were more conservative than they are now, and that older people are more likely to be married and to have children, both of which tend to make people's views more conservative. Young people are overrepresented in the "conventional" cluster within the relational group; in fact, this cluster includes a quarter of all adults under the age of 30. This observation suggests that the sexual morality of many young people is founded on humanistic rather than religious principles.

- **Education.** Increasing educational level is associated with a decreased likelihood of belonging to either of the traditional clusters or to the "pro-life" recreational cluster and an increased likelihood of belonging to the "libertarian" recreational cluster. This observation goes along

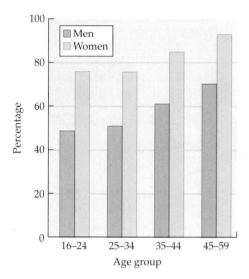

Figure 9.3 Sex and age strongly influence sexual attitudes. The percentages of NSSAL interviewees who stated that "one-night stands" are always or mostly wrong varied with their sex and age.

with a large body of evidence that educational attainment is associated with relatively permissive attitudes toward sexuality. Within the relational group, highly educated people are overrepresented in the "contemporary religious" cluster. This largely reflects the tendency of educated people to approve of homosexual relationships, regardless of their religious affiliation.

- **Region.** People living in the northeastern United States or on the West Coast are far less likely to belong to one of the traditional clusters, and far *more* likely to belong to the "libertarian" recreational cluster, than the U.S. population as a whole. For residents of the southern states, it's the reverse. Although these differences are largely explained by differences among these regions in educational level and religious affiliation, there seem also to be "regional cultures" that influence people's sexual morality (Klassen et al., 1989).

- **Race/ethnicity.** Race or ethnicity is not strongly predictive of sexual attitudes. African-Americans and Hispanics tend to be less approving of homosexuality and abortion than whites, however, and are less likely to fall into the "libertarian" cluster.

- **Sexual orientation.** Not surprisingly, people who have engaged in homosexual sex are found predominantly in the two clusters that are characterized by approval of this behavior: the "contemporary religious" cluster within the relational group and the "libertarian" cluster within the recreational group. As with any correlational finding, however, it is difficult to tell cause from effect. That is, we can't tell whether having a moral stance that approves of gay sex promotes participation in this kind of behavior, or whether the experience of being gay causes people to move toward a permissive moral stance on this issue. Most likely, both trends are operative.

- **Religion.** Conservative Protestants, such as Baptists, are greatly overrepresented in the "conservative" traditional cluster and underrepresented in the "libertarian" recreational cluster. For people without any religious affiliation, it's exactly the reverse. Mainstream Protestants are broadly distributed across all seven clusters. Although Catholics are most strongly represented in the "religious" relational cluster, reflecting Catholic opposition to abortion and homosexuality, they are quite well represented in other clusters, including the "pro-choice" traditional cluster and even the "libertarian" recreational cluster. This observation confirms many surveys showing that American Catholics tend to disagree with the Vatican on issues of sexual ethics.

The combined influence of just two demographic traits, sex and age, on sexual attitudes is very strong. Figure 9.3, based on data from the British National Survey of Sexual Attitudes and Lifestyles (NSSAL), shows the percentage of interviewees who disapproved of "one-night stands." Less than half of young men disapproved of this behavior, but over 90 percent of women in the oldest age bracket did so.

Although the survey data imply that people's sexual attitudes can be predicted to a considerable extent from their demographic characteristics, we don't mean to downplay the individual aspects of moral reasoning. People may be influenced by all kinds of life experiences to rethink their beliefs—by facing the reality of an unwanted pregnancy, by having a daughter or son come out as gay, and so on. You may feel that your own attitudes are permanent and the only correct ones, but if you write them down and check again in 20 years, you may be surprised by how much they have changed.

Americans' Attitudes Have Changed over Time

While on the topic of changing attitudes, let's take a look at how the moral stances of Americans on sexual topics have changed over the last few decades. The **General Social Survey (GSS)**—a project of the National Opinion Research Center at the University of Chicago—has asked Americans a standard set of questions on a variety of topics since

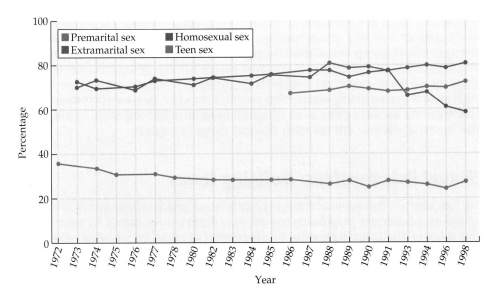

Figure 9.4 Changing attitudes. This graph shows changes in the percentage of the U.S. population that considered premarital sex, extramarital sex, homosexual sex, and teen sex "always wrong," from 1972 to 1998. The question about teen sex (which was first asked in 1986) specified 14–16-year-olds. (Data from National Opinion Research Center, 2002.)

the early 1970s (National Opinion Research Center, 2002) (Figure 9.4). The GSS has found a steady though modest decline in the percentage of the population who consider sex before marriage "always wrong," and a corresponding rise in the percentage who consider it "not wrong at all." When interviewees are asked specifically about sex between 14–16-year olds, however—a question that was first asked in 1986—opinions are far more negative, and have not changed significantly over the period that the question has been asked.

With regard to extramarital sex, public opinion has actually become more negative. Between 1973 and 1998, the percentage of people who believe that extramarital sex is "always wrong" increased from 70 percent to 81 percent.

With regard to sex between two adults of the same sex, opinion has changed in a more complicated way. During the 1980s, when public concern about AIDS was at its height and the disease was largely blamed on gay men, disapproval of homosexual behavior increased. During the 1990s, on the other hand, there was a marked liberalizing trend, so that by 1998 fewer people disapproved of homosexual behavior than in 1973. Still, a majority of the U.S. population considers gay sex "always wrong."

Attitudes in Other Countries Differ from Those in the United States

How does American opinion on sexual morality compare with opinion in other countries? In 1997 the Gallup Organization conducted a survey of moral issues in 16 countries (Gallup Organization, 1997) (Figure 9.5). One of the questions asked whether it was wrong for a couple to have a child out of wedlock. Nearly half of Americans thought that this was wrong, placing the United States pretty much in the middle of the spectrum of world opinion. The residents of some countries, such as India and Singapore, were much less permissive on this question, whereas those in other countries, especially in Europe, were much more permissive. That the United States should fall somewhere in the middle of world opinion is perhaps to be expected, given the wide mix of ancestries and cultures its people represent.

In spite of the diversity of attitudes toward the morality of sex, it's worth emphasizing a belief that represents a common moral ground for many people—the idea that it's not the sex act itself, but its context, that has moral significance. In particular, sexual behavior that may endanger established relationships is very broadly disapproved of. Whereas only about one out of five Americans thinks that nonmarital sex is always

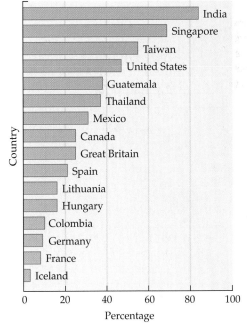

Figure 9.5 Moral stances on having a child out of wedlock vary greatly around the world. This graph shows the percentage of persons in 16 countries who believe that it is morally wrong for a couple to have a baby if they are not married. The true figures for India, Mexico, and Colombia are probably higher than given here, because rural areas, which are usually more conservative, were not sampled in these countries. (Data from Gallup Organization, 1997.)

wrong, four out of five think that *extra*marital sex is always wrong. The British NSSAL study came up with very similar findings, but in addition found that cohabitations and even *non*-cohabitational sexual relationships are viewed as morally protected, albeit not to the same degree that marriages are: most people felt that persons in such relationships should not engage in sex outside the relationship. Evidently, most people place a high moral value on lasting sexual relationships, even when they are not formalized by marriage, and see monogamy as an important factor in preserving them. In that sense, the "sexual revolution" has not really changed things very much.

Sexual Relationships: Defining Terms

We turn now to a discussion of different kinds of sexual relationships, starting with brief sexual encounters and progressing toward more durable associations. To some extent, this order of discussion represents the progression of sexual relationships within the course of a typical life span, but we defer an explicit consideration of how sexual expression changes over the life span until Chapter 12.

The terms used to refer to sexual relationships are sometimes ambiguous, or carry unstated implications. Here is how we use some key terms in this book:

- **Heterosexual relationship:** A sexual relationship between a male and a female, regardless of their sexual orientation. We say "male" and "female" rather than "man" and "woman" so as to include relationships involving minors.
- **Homosexual relationship:** A sexual relationship between two males or two females, regardless of their sexual orientation.
- **Marriage:** A legally sanctioned union. With rare exceptions involving sex reassignment surgery (see Chapter 13), all current marriages in the United States are between one male and one female.
- **Cohabitation:** A sexual relationship between two persons who live together, but are not currently married to each other. If the two persons are a man and a woman, and neither is married to anyone else, the relationship may be legally recognized as a **common-law marriage.** Cohabitation of two persons of any sex may be legally registered as a **domestic partnership** in some jurisdictions.
- **Single:** Neither married nor cohabiting (but elsewhere, often used to mean unmarried).
- **Extramarital relationship:** A sexual relationship between two persons, at least one of whom is currently married to someone else. Also called **adultery,** a term that may carry an implication of sinfulness.
- **Extra-pair relationship:** A sexual relationship between two persons, at least one of whom is currently paired with someone else, whether married, cohabiting, or dating. A broader concept than extramarital relationship.
- **Nonmarital relationship:** A sexual relationship between two persons, neither of whom is currently married to anyone.
- **Premarital relationship:** A sexual relationship between two persons who are known to have subsequently married (not necessarily each other). We do not use this phrase very often, and never in reference to current relationships, except when we are citing other people's usage (questions in surveys and opinion polls, for example). Outside of this book, you will often see the term "premarital relationship" or "premarital sex" used loosely to mean relationships between young people who may be expected to get married (not necessarily to each other) at some later time.
- **Monogamy:** Formally, "monogamy" means being married to just one person. We use the word here in its popular sense of being in a sexual relationship with just one person.

Casual Sex Has More Appeal to Men than to Women

By **casual sex,** we mean sexual encounters that the participants do not view as part of a durable sexual relationship. It includes sex between people who have known each other only very briefly, as well as those who have known each other for some time but do not intend the encounter to be the beginning of a longer sexual relationship.

We mentioned above that men and women differ in their attitudes toward casual sex, with men far more likely than women to consider "one-night stands" morally acceptable. Does this difference in moral stance translate into differences in behavior? Psychologists Russell Clark and Elaine Hatfield performed a rather sneaky "real-life test" of this question (Clark & Hatfield, 1989). They recruited attractive male and female college students as confederates and had them approach unwitting students of the other sex somewhere on the campus (Figure 9.6). They were told to say "I have been noticing you around campus and I find you to be very attractive." Then they asked one of three questions: "Would you go out with me tonight?" "Would you come over to my apartment tonight?" or "Would you go to bed with me tonight?"

The male and female "victims" were about equally willing to go out with the confederate—about half assented to this request. When the request was phrased in ways that referred more explicitly to the desire for casual sex, however, women's responses rapidly fell off—in fact, not a single woman agreed to go to bed with the male confederate. Men's responses, on the other hand, became more positive: 69 percent of the men agreed to go to the female confederate's apartment, and 75 percent agreed to go to bed with her. In other words, reducing a casual date to its sexual essentials robbed the date of its appeal to women, but actually *enhanced* its appeal to men! When you consider that some of the men must have been in ongoing relationships, some must have been gay, and some must have been otherwise engaged that evening, a 75 percent rate of assent to having sex is fairly astonishing. Of course, we don't know whether men and women in other age ranges, or who are not college students, would respond in the same way, but it seems likely that the sex difference would be the same.

On the basis of these data, you might think that a straight man's quest for casual sex would be a fruitless one, and that his only recourse would be to go to a prostitute. This may be the case in some cultures, and may have been the case historically in our own culture, but the current reality is different. Some women *do* agree to casual sex, and may even initiate it.

There are several possible reasons why women are more willing to engage in casual sex or brief relationships today than they were in earlier generations. The availability of reliable contraception and, if necessary, legal abortion are probably the most important. In addition, a woman who is known to have engaged in premarital sex, even casual sex, suffers much less damage to her reputation than her mother or grandmother would have done—let alone a woman from the time of Leviticus. By and large, men no longer expect their brides or cohabiting partners to be virgins. Still, the fear of disease and the fear of violence are two very real concerns that limit women's willingness to embark on casual sexual relationships.

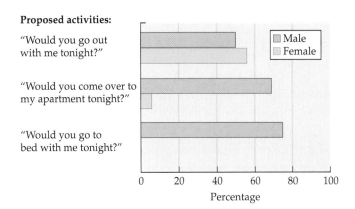

Proposed activities:

"Would you go out with me tonight?"

"Would you come over to my apartment tonight?"

"Would you go to bed with me tonight?"

Figure 9.6 Sex differences in willingness to engage in casual sex. The figure shows the percentage of male and female college students who agreed to three activities proposed by an attractive but unfamiliar student of the other sex. (After Clark and Hatfield, 1989.)

Singles bars used to be prime locations for finding casual dates.

Stereotyped Behaviors Mediate Sexual Approaches

The classic locale for men and women to meet with casual sex in mind is the singles bar, but there are any number of other possible meeting places, including health clubs, the common areas of apartment complexes, and the like. Travel makes both men and women more open to casual sex, probably by removing the constraints associated with their home environment, or by making it less likely that their escapades will become known. When travel is accompanied by partying and binge drinking, as commonly happens during those infamous spring break trips, casual sex becomes pretty much universal. Evidently, some women are just as interested in casual sex as are men, once their moral reservations or socially imposed controls are overcome.

Back in the 1980s, when singles bars were the uncontested focus of the singles scene, independent sex researcher Timothy Perper used them to study how men and women negotiate a casual sexual encounter (Perper, 1985). Perper found that men and women use rather stereotyped behaviors, analogous to the stereotyped courtship behaviors shown by animals. Contrary to what one might imagine, women often take the first step in the interaction. This **proceptive** behavior includes looking at, approaching, and talking to the man. A process of escalation then occurs, which involves the progressive turning of the man and woman toward each other, and the synchronization of body movements. Synchronization starts with apparently coincidental synchronization of hand or head movements, such as reaching for a drink, and may progress to complete synchronization of body movements, such as swaying in time to music. At each step, one partner may validate the other's escalation or may break the process by failing to synchronize, thus allowing the process to cool off or terminate. At some point, the man typically takes a more controlling role in which he makes the sexual nature of the interaction more explicit.

Psychologist Monica Moore, of Webster University at St. Louis, has studied women's proceptive behavior—essentially, **flirting** (Moore, 1998). Like Perper, she finds that women's body language is crucial in the early stages of sexual interactions. Behaviors that serve as solicitations include smiling, short darting glances, prolonged eye contact, lip licking, nodding, tossing the hair back, playing with the hair, touching the neck, raising the skirt slightly, and walking by a man with hips swinging and breasts pushed forward. In a social situation such as a singles bar, Moore found that the likelihood of a man approaching a woman was very strongly correlated with the number of such solicitations that she performed. In other words, flirting works. Some women—and men too—are natural flirts, while others may need some education to increase their flirting skills (Box 9.3).

In studies such as those just mentioned, it is not possible to say whether the observed encounters actually led to casual sex or not. Although the described behaviors are definitely proceptive—that is, they are sexual solicitations—that doesn't mean that either party intends to, or is obliged to, follow through. On the contrary, women in particular may use flirtatious behavior simply as a way to get to know men, with sex as a later option. A man may believe that a woman who flirts with him has essentially committed herself, and may see that as justification for using pressure to get sex. Yet, even if a woman is flirtatious, accepts drinks, goes to a man's residence, gets undressed, and even starts to engage in sex, she is still morally and legally entitled to back out. A man who uses force in such circumstances is committing rape and faces severe penalties (see Chapter 18).

Gay bars are still important for gay male dating, but they are no longer the only place where gay men can meet.

Casual Sex Is More Accepted in the Gay Male Community

Casual sex is more prevalent among gay men than in the heterosexual population. The reasons for this are threefold: gay men are not restrained by women's reluctance to engage in casual sex; pregnancy is not an issue; and gay men, being already stigmatized by society for their sexual orientation, are less likely to pay attention to public opinion on the topic of casual sex.

Besides gay bars, which are an important feature of gay male life in many U.S. cities, there are other institutions that offer the opportunity for sexual encounters on an even more casual or totally anonymous basis. These encounters include those in bathhouses, public toilets, and outdoor cruising locations such as parks and freeway rest areas, as well as encounters mediated by personal ads or the Internet. While casual sex carries little stigma in gay male communities (see Chapter 13), that does not

Box 9.3 Society, Values, and the Law

The Flirting Academy

For £250 ($380)—travel and accommodations not included—men and women who need to hone their flirting skills can take an intensive weekend course at London's Flirting Academy, run by self-improvement guru Peta Heskell, author of *Flirt Coach* (Heskell, 2001).

"Flirting isn't just about getting sex," Heskell told London's *Sunday Times*. "Being a good flirt means you're confident and good at putting people at ease with themselves. That's enriching for business, for those in committed relationships and for those looking to meet a partner." Heskell believes that people are born with flirting skills, but often learn to repress them. She faults an increasingly intolerant culture that has imposed anti-flirting rules in the workplace, on college campuses, and elsewhere.

The course begins with a brainstorming session on the meaning of the word "flirt," followed by discussions of the participants'

flirting techniques. During the lunch break, participants go out in the streets and practice their charms on unsuspecting Londoners. That's to teach them how to deal with failure, Heskell says. "One woman saw [pop icon] Bob Geldof and beamed at him. She came back quite disheartened because he looked straight through her. I said, 'For all you know, he might be having the worst day of his life. Just because he didn't respond to you doesn't mean you have to take it personally. Let it go and move on. Eventually, if you smile at enough of the right people, one will smile back at you!'"

Besides teaching the tricks of body language described by Monica Moore, Heskell emphasizes listening and reciprocating, and echoing the "flirtee's" speech patterns and vocabulary. "It's not about what you say," says Heskell, "it's the tone, pace, facial expression and body language of how you say it that makes that initial impression."

The weekend includes movement and dance sessions, as well as discussions about how to feel positive about oneself. "Body language is important," Heskell says, "but before you can hold eye contact with a stranger you need to be in a confident, trusting state."

For men who want to cut to the chase, another option is to take a seminar or home study course in "Speed Seduction" with Ross Jeffries, author of *How to Get the Women You Desire into Bed* (Jeffries, 1992). Jeffries says he was a total loser with women until he applied the principles of Neuro-Linguistic Programming (a New Age self-improvement philosophy that emphasizes mental exercises and self-hypnosis) to the mating game, whereupon he says he became a modern-day Casanova—a claim that may be worthy of some skepticism.

Source: Marlin, 1999.

---

mean that all gay men engage in it. Some limit their sexual activity because of the risk of acquiring AIDS or other diseases. Some live in rural areas where potential partners are scarce. And most importantly, many gay men are involved in monogamous relationships and have no desire to engage in casual sex.

Although we have cited some statistics about the very high numbers of sex partners reported by gay men in San Francisco in the pre-AIDS era (see Chapter 6), more recent numbers for the entire U.S. population are much more moderate. In the NHSLS study, men who identified as homosexual or bisexual reported an average of 3.1 sex partners in the previous 12 months. That is more than the 1.8 partners reported by men who identified as heterosexual, but far fewer than one might imagine based on some widely held stereotypes about gay men.

There do exist bars and other locations where lesbians can meet, but little is known about casual sex between women. The NHSLS survey interviewed too few lesbians for the data to be meaningful. The much larger NSSAL survey identified 175 women who had had at least one sexual encounter with another woman in their lifetime. Of these women, only one had had more than 10 female partners, and none had had more than 20. Although the nature of the encounters was not investigated, the low numbers suggest that casual sex between women is uncommon. This is not just a matter of lack of opportunity: lesbians express the same low interest in casual sex and multiple sex partners as do heterosexual women (Bailey et al., 1994).

Dating Relationships Are Usually Short-Lived and Fluid

Nonmarital, non-cohabitational sexual relationships (often called **dating** relationships) have become extremely common in Western countries. Sometimes a relationship of this kind leads to cohabitation or marriage. Sometimes it is a brief romance that breaks up when the pair find themselves incompatible, find better partners, or get separated by external circumstances such as the end of a school year. Sometimes it is a durable relationship between two people who for some reason don't want to or are unable to live together. Although we think of dating relationships as being the hallmark of the teenage years or young adulthood, there are plenty of older people—unmarried, divorced, or widowed—who also engage in them.

Because of the informality of these relationships, there is no clear terminology to describe them, though phrases such as "girlfriend/boyfriend," "hooking up," "seeing each other," "going together," "they're an item," or "they're dating" are clear enough. Except among the most traditionally minded couples, relationships of this kind usually include some degree of physical intimacy, but not necessarily coitus or other genital contact. Some men and women engage in sex outside the dating relationship, but more commonly dating relationships are sexually exclusive, so that a person who dates several partners over a period of time is usually engaging in **serial monogamy**—a very common lifestyle, especially among adolescents and young adults.

First Dates Follow a Script

A dating relationship begins, of course, with a **first date.** On a first date, both partners often feel considerable uncertainty about what is going to happen, even if they have known each other for some time in a nonsexual way. On a heterosexual first date, the man typically has greater expectations for a sexual interaction than does the woman (Mongeau et al., 1998).

First dates are usually heavily "scripted."

Because of the uncertainty associated with a first date, the participants often follow socially established rituals, which researchers call **scripts** (see Chapter 1). The ritualization of the first date is particularly marked when the two persons are complete strangers to each other, as you may observe by watching a few episodes of the TV reality show *Blind Date.* With a heterosexual date between college students, the script demands that the man take the leading, active role: he picks up the woman, does the driving, plans and pays for the activities, initiates any sexual intimacy, and takes her home. The woman takes the reactive role, accepting or rejecting the date, the activities, and the sex (Rose & Frieze, 1993). This pattern conforms to a more general social expectation that men will be the ones who initiate sexual interactions and women the ones who say "yes" or "no," thus setting limits (Metts & Cupach, 1989).

Violations of this script do occur quite frequently, of course. It's not especially uncommon for the woman to initiate the date, for example. If she does so, however, the subsequent script changes. Most significantly, the man usually has a greatly increased expectation that sexual intimacy will occur (Mongeau & Carey, 1996). In reality, heterosexual first dates that are initiated by women tend to include relatively little sexual intimacy, so men's expectations in this regard are often disappointed (Mongeau & Johnson, 1995). This is a potential source of conflict and may be a factor in predisposing some men to commit date rape (Muehlenhard et al., 1985) (see Chapter 18).

The "man initiates, woman chooses" script may remind you of the common patterns of sexual interaction seen in many nonhuman species, as described in Chapter 2. Before concluding that evolutionary forces are at work, however, bear in mind that the script just described relates primarily to contemporary American college students. In the nineteenth century, "dating" was very different: single young women of the middle or upper classes met men in their own homes in the presence of their parents or a female companion (**chaperone**), and little physical intimacy occurred until the couple was engaged to be married. In many contemporary cultures in which women are secluded, dating is virtually unknown. In the world of dating, "universals" remain to be identified, if they exist at all.

As a dating relationship continues, the social scripts that organized the first date are gradually replaced by **interpersonal scripts**—sets of rules and expectations that are generated by the dating couple themselves (Metts & Cupach, 1989). These scripts allow for increasing self-disclosure, intimacy, and nonverbal communication. Also, the sex difference in the expectation of sexual intimacy diminishes. That's because women become more willing to engage in sex as the relationship becomes more committed, in line with evolutionary theory (Buss, 1995).

Same-Sex Dates May Be Scriptless

Same-sex dating has not been the subject of a great deal of study, but it's worth raising a few speculative points. First, in many environments (such as high school, college, or work) there is a presumption of heterosexuality, whereas homosexuality or bisexuality is seen as transgressive (see Chapter 13). Thus, for a same-sex date to happen, there has to be an initial recognition or mutual disclosure that the two persons are open to a same-sex relationship. This disclosure, once achieved, may promote a more rapid development of the relationship than would be typical for an opposite-sex couple—a sort of conspiratorial or us-against-the-world intimacy, as it were. Conversely, some same-sex couples may have difficulty achieving intimacy because of inculcated negative feelings about homosexuality (internalized homophobia: see Chapter 13).

For women especially, sexual exploration and the development of a homosexual or bisexual identity may occur in the context of a preexisting and intense same-sex friendship (Peplau et al., 1999). In such cases, the two persons may essentially be in love before the question of sexual attraction and sexual behavior comes into play at all. Dating under these circumstances has a very different meaning than it does in dates between most opposite-sex or male–male couples, in which the two persons are typically not very emotionally intimate on their first date, but may be very conscious of sexual attraction and the possibility of sexual behavior.

Cultural scripts are probably less important for same-sex dating than for heterosexual dating. Social customs do not dictate which participant in a same-sex date should make the arrangements and pay for them, who should initiate sexual intimacy, or who should set limits—except possibly that the older person in an age-disparate relationship might be expected to take the initiative. Therefore, extemporization and interpersonal scripts may be more important right from the beginning. Also, since both persons are of the same sex, a gender-based mismatch concerning expectations of sexual intimacy is less likely (Bailey et al., 1994).

Dating Relationships Evolve Rapidly

Non-cohabitational relationships are often very dynamic—they are processes, rather than states. The process may be one of growing love, leading to cohabitation or marriage, or of gradual realization by one or both partners that "this was not meant to be," with a resulting breakup. Often this dynamic process is viewed as being entirely intrinsic to the relationship—in other words, as an exploration of mutual attraction and compatibility. But there is also an external process that involves a sexual "marketplace." In this process, each person consciously or unconsciously assesses whether they have the best possible partner, given their own "worth" and the range of other options available (Lawrence & Byers, 1995). For this reason, and because dating relationships are not morally "protected" to the same degree that live-in relationships are, jealousy tends to be a more active force in dating relationships than it is in cohabitations or marriages. This jealousy sometimes leads to controlling behavior and to emotional or physical abuse (Thorne-Finch, 1991).

Given that there is a virtually limitless universe of potential alternative partners out there, it may seem odd that dating couples become committed to each other at all. There appears, however, to be a tendency to idealize the partner that helps stabilize the relationship (Murray & Holmes, 1999). This idealization does not mean blindness to a partner's shortcomings, but a minimization of their importance, as well as a tendency to construct mental representations in which the partner's perceived faults are tied to virtues and thus balanced by them ("Yes, he drinks too much, but only socially, and that's part of his outgoing personality that I like so much.").

Cohabitation Is an Increasingly Prevalent Lifestyle

Most men and women hope to enter into a durable, live-in sexual relationship—a cohabitation or marriage—eventually. Often, a desire for children comes into play here, but even people who don't want children commonly want to be part of a long-term, loving relationship.

Married or cohabiting? These days, it's hard to tell the difference.

Cohabitation is the word we use to describe the relationship of two people who live together in a sexual relationship without being legally married. A wide range of other expressions may be used to describe these relationships, from moralizing phrases such as "living in sin" to more neutral terms such as "de facto unions," "domestic partnerships," or "common-law unions." Cohabitations include both opposite-sex and same-sex couples.

Cohabitation has become an increasingly prevalent form of relationship over the past few decades, both in the United States and in other Western countries. For nearly all men and women born before 1940, the first live-in sexual relationship was marriage. Among men and women born after 1953, on the other hand, about half made cohabitation their first live-in relationship, and today the majority of young people enter into a cohabitation before marriage, if they marry at all. The number of U.S. households consisting of cohabiting couples increased by 72 percent during the 1990s, and the increase was even higher in the seven states (Florida, Michigan, Mississippi, North Carolina, North Dakota, Virginia, and West Virginia) where cohabitation is still technically illegal (Fields, 2001).

What factors influence the choice of marriage or cohabitation as a first live-in relationship? According to the NHSLS, younger people, as well as people whose parents separated while they were children, are more likely to cohabit; members of conservative Protestant denominations, as well as people who put off their first sexual experience until after the age of 18, are more likely to marry. City dwellers are more likely to cohabit, country folk to marry.

Although so many people now make their first live-in relationship a cohabitation, only a small fraction of the U.S. population (about 7 percent of men and women aged 18–59) is cohabiting at any given time. That's because cohabitations are typically short-lived: according to the NHSLS data, about half of all cohabiting couples married or split up within a year of moving in together. Roughly equal numbers of cohabitations ended in marriage and in separation. (A smaller number ended in the death of one partner.)

Cohabitation signals a withdrawal from the sexual marketplace and has the flavor of a "trial marriage." In that vein, one might expect that couples who cohabit and then marry would have unusually durable marriages because the incompatible couples would have been weeded out during the period of cohabitation. In fact, according to the NHSLS data, the reverse is true: marriages that are preceded by cohabitation end more quickly than those that are not (Bumpass & Sweet, 1989). The reason for this is not entirely clear. In part, it may be because couples who cohabit have less traditional views about marriage in general and show this by divorcing more readily. Also, if it is characteristic of live-in relationships to run out of steam after a certain period of time, cohabitors will have used up some of that time on their cohabitation, so the ensuing marriage will be that much shorter.

Some cohabitations differ from trial marriages in significant ways. About 40 percent of cohabiting couples have children, for example (including children of the couple and children from prior relationships). Some cohabitations

Lesbian-rights pioneers Del Martin and Phyllis Lyon of San Francisco have been cohabiting since 1953. (Photograph by Jane Cleland.)

are lengthy; about 20 percent last over 5 years. Some are between elderly people—widowed or divorced—who see no particular need to marry because they will not have children, or who prefer not to marry in order not to disturb inheritance arrangements. Some are same-sex couples, for whom legal marriage is not an option in the United States.

Many cohabiting couples appreciate the informality of their relationship. They may be less burdened by social expectations and less constrained by traditional roles than if they were married. It may be easier to preserve financial independence, if that is desired. And breaking up, if it comes to that, is less of a public embarrassment. On the down side, cohabiting couples are often denied many rights provided automatically to married couples. Therefore, cohabitation can bring bureaucratic hassles, especially if there are children. Cohabiting couples—particularly same-sex couples—have to draw up wills, durable powers of attorney, and other documents if they want their wishes to be respected in case of death or incapacitation.

Marriage Is Still the First Choice of Americans

At any given time, somewhere between 50 and 60 percent of adult Americans are married and living with their spouses. Because marriage is such a central aspect of most Americans' sexual lives, we will discuss it in more detail when we look at sexuality across the life span in Chapter 12. Here we take a snapshot view of marriage.

Most, if not all, human cultures have formalized heterosexual unions in some way, but the manner in which this has been done has varied greatly. In ancient Israel, one way for a couple to marry was simply to let it be known that they had had intercourse (Biale, 1984). In India, a wedding is an elaborate ceremony that takes up the best part of a week and involves lengthy rituals and enormous expense, particularly on the part of the bride's parents. In the United States, getting married can mean anything from a quick visit to a government office to a multimillion-dollar union of dynasties.

The Formalization of Sexual Unions Has Social and Personal Functions

Formalizing sexual unions by marriage has a variety of purposes. In many cultures, women have been viewed as men's property; in such cultures, marriage was a transaction marking the transfer of a woman from her father to her husband. More positively, marriage has functioned in several ways to create an environment favorable for child rearing. First, marriage was traditionally a means to identify the man responsible for the support of a woman and her children. Even today, husbands are usually required to contribute to the support of all children their wives bear during their marriage, no matter who fathered them. Second, by publicly identifying two persons as a couple, marriage places an obligation on others to respect the sexual exclusivity of their relationship, thus reducing social friction. Third, marriage may bring the couple's extended families together; this was an important function of marriage in traditional societies, in which marriages were often used to end vendettas or to create social alliances. Finally, by making it difficult for a man and woman to separate, marriage is intended to stabilize their union and ensure that they stay together long enough to rear their children. Some Americans think that this function has been undermined by the ease with which people can now get divorced (Box 9.4).

The Institution of Marriage Is Changing

Marriages have changed tremendously over the years. Young people are marrying later, they are more likely to divorce, and they are more likely to marry a second or third time. A marriage is now no more than an episode in many people's lives.

Married couples form much more isolated units than in the past. Before industrialization and the shift of the population to cities, a married couple typically formed part of a large extended family that dwelt together under one roof. Although some Americans, especially Hispanics, still maintain that pattern to some degree, the mean household size in the United States is now less than three persons; most married couples live alone or accompanied only by their children, and the number of children has fallen dramatically.

Box 9.4 | *Society, Values, and the Law*

Covenant Marriages

Traditionally, a couple's wedding vows included the promise to stay together "until death do us part," and nearly everyone did. Divorce gradually became more common in the nineteenth and early twentieth centuries, and the practice was given another boost by the introduction of **no-fault divorce** in the 1970s. In a no-fault divorce, either partner may unilaterally end the marriage without having to prove wrongdoing by the other. Currently, about half of all American marriages end in divorce (see Chapter 12). Some wedding ceremonies acknowledge this lowered expectation of permanence by changing the phrase "until death do us part" to "until love's death do us part," or something similar.

Believing that the breakup of marriages is a major cause of personal distress and social harm, some Americans (mostly conservative Protestants) have advocated a return to **covenant marriages,** in which the couple commit themselves to a lifelong monogamous relationship. A typical covenant marriage includes a vow such as the following: "Believing that marriage is a covenant intended by God to be a lifelong relationship between a man and a woman, we vow to God, each other, our families, and our community to remain steadfast in unconditional love, reconciliation, and sexual purity, while purposefully growing in our covenant marriage relationship."

To give covenant marriages some "teeth," three states (Louisiana, Arizona, and Arkansas) have made these marriages into legal alternatives to conventional marriages, and several other states have debated whether to do the same. In a legal covenant marriage, the couple is required to undergo premarital counseling. Once married, the couple may not receive a no-fault divorce. Divorce may be legally granted only if one party proves that the other party has committed adultery or a felony or has permanently abandoned the marriage, or if the couple has been separated for 2 years. So far, only very small numbers of couples have chosen the covenant marriage option.

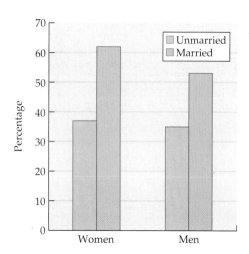

Figure 9.7 Happily married. The graph shows the percentage of married and unmarried women and men who call themselves "very happy" (when given a choice of "very happy," "fairly happy" and "not too happy"). (Data from Gallup Organization, 2000c.)

Several factors—the improved status of women, their entry into the labor market, the pervasive presence of labor-saving devices in the home, and the fact that women are pregnant less often—have decreased (though not abolished) the differences between the roles of husband and wife in marriage. Thus, husbands and wives have become all-purpose companions: they are expected to be romantic partners, friends, economic collaborators, fellow workers in the home, and colleagues in parenting. And they are expected to sustain all these relationships with far less support from relatives or neighbors than was customary a generation or two ago. It is no small challenge, but for many it works: married people are significantly happier than the unmarried (Figure 9.7).

Many Societies Have Permitted Polygamy

Nearly all Americans think of a marriage as involving just two people, and the law reinforces this attitude: anyone who marries someone while still married to someone else is committing the crime of **bigamy.** Thus, you might be tempted to think that *Homo sapiens* is a naturally monogamous (or at least socially monogamous) species, comparable to many songbirds (see Chapter 2).

Anthropological studies suggest the reverse: **polygamy** is commonplace. Of the 185 human societies surveyed by Ford and Beach (Ford & Beach, 1951), 155 (84 percent) have traditionally permitted men to have more than one female mate (**polygyny**), and in most of those societies polygynous unions are legally recognized. Anthropologist Helen Fisher (now at Rutgers University) carried out an even more extensive study, with a similar result: out of 853 preindustrial societies, 84 percent permitted polygyny (Fisher, 1989). Thus our own culture is one of a small minority of cultures that do not permit the practice.

The exact arrangements in polygynous societies vary. Often, the first mate has some kind of official status as "principal wife." In a smaller number of societies polygynous relationships are permitted, but not legally formalized. In such cases, the later mates may be **concubines** whose attachment to the household is impermanent and whose children have no inheritance rights.

Given that there are roughly equal numbers of men and women in most societies, not every man in a polygynous society can have multiple wives. In fact, most men in such societies have just one wife at best; it is the wealthy and powerful who have many. The extreme cases were the **harems** associated with Oriental rulers. According to Jewish legend, King Solomon had a harem of a thousand wives, each of whom prepared a banquet every evening in the faint hope that he would dine with her. Harems were traditionally attended by **eunuchs** (castrated men).

A marked excess of women can occur in societies whose menfolk have been decimated by warfare. In fact, a close reading of the passage in the Qur'an that authorizes polygamy suggests that the institution was intended to help the numerous war widows of early Islamic society, as well as their fatherless children (Hasan, 1996).

Polygamy is connected to the idea that women are men's property—if a rich man has many cattle, why shouldn't he have many wives, too? Thus the Christian prohibition of polygamy, which distinguishes it from many other religions such as Islam, can be viewed as an attempt to assure some equity in marriage. Still, shades of polygamy still persist in Western culture: plenty of rich men support mistresses, and a polygamous culture persists among some traditionalist Mormons (Box 9.5).

Societies in which one woman takes more than one husband or mate (**polyandry**) have been very uncommon. They have tended to be societies in which resources are so limited that a man cannot maintain a wife and children on his own. That has been true for high-altitude communities in Tibet and other parts of the Himalayas (Samal et al., 1997). In these communities, two or more brothers typically share a wife. Usually the oldest brother fathers most of the children, and younger brothers eventually obtain their own wives or become monks. Less formal arrangements of the same kind tend to crop up in parts of the world, such as southern Africa, where low-income male migrant workers live together in communal groups. These groups often share a common girlfriend—an arrangement that has been disastrous in terms of HIV transmission. Female prostitution (see Chapter 19) can also be viewed as a kind of polyandry.

Somewhat related to polygamy is **polyamory**. This recently coined term refers to a movement of people who practice and advocate a variety of loving but nonmonogamous relationships. Polyamory has roots in the free love, commune, and wife-swapping movements of the 1960s and 1970s, and some polyamorists could be aptly described as "aging hippies." What distinguishes polyamory from those earlier movements, however, is that it involves little, if any, casual sex.

Polyamorists are linked in small groups, such as "triads," "quads," and "pentacles," who may live together as a family. Within a group, not everyone necessarily has sex with everyone else (Figure 9.8). Within triad A, B, and C, for example, A may have sex with B and C, but B and C may not have sex with each other. This arrangement is called a "vee." Alternatively, A, B, and C may have sex in all combinations or as a simultaneous threesome. This kind of triad is called a "triangle." Bisexuality is common among polyamorists, especially among the women, but it is not universal.

Polyamorists adopt a wide variety of rules to regulate their sexual relations. Usually they don't engage in casual sex outside their group. While polyamory presents an interesting alternative to standard monogamous relationships, its appeal is limited by the problem of jealousy (see below).

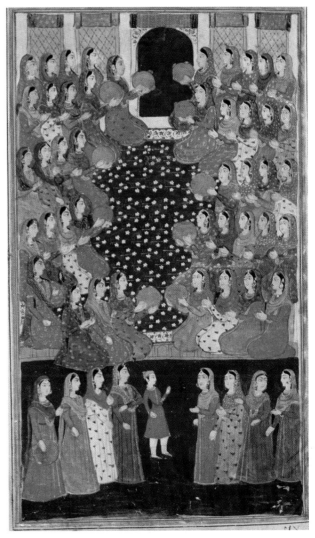

Harem of an early caliph (successor of Muhammad).

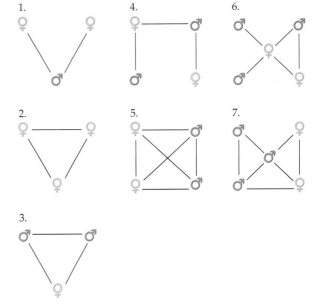

Figure 9.8 Polyamory. Polyamorists are small groups of people linked by sexual bonds. "Poly" relationships are highly diverse. They may consist of three (1–3), four (4,5), five (6,7), or more persons. All the members of a group may have sexual interactions with one another (2,3,5), or they may have sex only in certain combinations (1,4,6,7). The sexual interactions may be all heterosexual (1,4), all homosexual (2), or both heterosexual and homosexual (3,5,6,7).

CULTURAL DIVERSITY

Mormon Polygamy

Mormon leader Brigham Young (1801–1877), who led the Mormon migration to Utah, is believed to have had 27 wives. He made polygamy part of the doctrine of the Church of Jesus Christ of Latter-Day Saints, asserting it was a necessary path to the highest salvation. Many early Mormons followed his teaching on this matter. The practice drew the Mormons into conflict with the U.S. government, which passed anti-polygamy laws and refused to grant Utah its statehood. In 1890 the Church disavowed polygamy, and when Utah finally became a state in 1896, its constitution banned the practice. Still, the ban was never written into specific statutes.

In spite of the official end of Mormon polygamy, "fundamentalist" Mormons in isolated areas continued the practice. There may be as many as 30,000 polygamists living in Utah and nearby states today. They have been excommunicated by the Church.

In the 1950s, when Utah police raided polygamists' homes and attempted to break up their families, public opinion was so outraged that the matter was dropped. After that, polygamists kept a low profile, and the state ignored them.

The matter came up again in the late 1990s when one polygamist, 50-year-old telemarketer Tom Green, began doing the rounds of national talk shows along with his five wives (see figure). All of his wives, including "head wife" Linda Kunz, declared their happiness with their marital arrangement. Green, his wives, and their 25 children lived in a collection of trailers in a remote valley in southwestern Utah, where they subsisted largely on welfare payments.

As is typical for Mormon polygamists, Green married each of his wives when she was 14 or 15 years old. Although Green believed that he and his wives were united before God, he denied that he had broken any laws. That was because he divorced each of his wives in Nevada before marrying the next. Thus, he claimed, the women were wives in spirit, but more like mistresses in law—and any number of mistresses is legal.

Green's activities were a great embarrassment to the state of Utah, which was trying to reposition itself as a modern state attractive to high-tech industries. In 2001 Juab County prosecutor David Leavitt—himself a descendant of polygamists and the brother of Utah's governor—brought Green to trial on four counts of bigamy. Leavitt argued that even though Green had divorced his earlier wives, their continued cohabitation amounted to common-law marriage, and that multiple common-law marriages constituted bigamy. The jury bought the argument and found Green guilty. He was sentenced to 5 years' imprisonment.

Green's troubles were compounded in 2002, when he faced trial for child rape. The charge arose from the fact that Linda Kunz bore their first child when she was only 13 years old. Green argued that the court had no jurisdiction because the sexual episode that led to Kunz's pregnancy occurred outside of the United States. Nevertheless he was convicted and received 5 years to life in prison, the lightest possible sentence.

The legal grounds for Green's bigamy conviction run counter to the recent trend toward greater permissiveness in sexual arrangements. Technically, anyone living with two girlfriends or two boyfriends could face legal action under Leavitt's definition of bigamy. On the other hand, law enforcement and child welfare officials cite many social ills that are associated with Mormon polygamy: incest, physical and sexual abuse of children, poverty, welfare and tax fraud, criminal nonsupport of children, and diminished educational opportunities and health care (Cart, 2001).

Love Cements Many Sexual Relationships

Love, in some form or another, is the glue that holds couples in sexual relationships. Long celebrated by poets (Box 9.6), love has recently come under the scrutiny of psychologists and even brain scientists, though no consensus has been reached on what exactly love is, or what causes it.

There Are Different Kinds of Love

One thing that is clear is that there are several aspects to love, or several kinds of love. Some kinds, such as the nurturing care that a mother gives her child, the liking that forms the basis of friendships, or the charitable feelings that Jesus instructed his followers to direct toward all fellow humans, are not sexual. Even within the context of sexual rela-

Box 9.6

Sex in History

Love in Literature

We've mentioned that men tend to be more oriented toward physical attraction and women toward commitment. Here are two poems about love that flout that association. First, a surviving fragment of a 2500-year-old love poem by the Greek lyric poet Sappho (in prose translation by H. T. Wharton) that expresses the overwhelming physical immediacy of her love:

> That man seems to me peer of gods, who sits in thy presence, and hears close to him thy sweet speech and lovely laughter; that indeed makes my heart flutter in my bosom. For when I see thee but a little, I have no utterance left, my tongue is broken down, and straightway a subtle fire has run under my skin, with my eyes I have no sight, my ears ring, sweat pours down, and a trembling seizes all my body; I am paler than grass, and seem in my madness little better than one dead. But I must dare all, since one so poor . . .

In contrast, this sonnet by William Shakespeare (1564–1616) focuses on love as an enduring commitment:

> Let me not to the marriage of true minds

> Admit impediments; love is not love
> Which alters when it alteration finds,
> Or bends with the remover to remove.
> O, no, it is an ever-fixèd mark
> That looks on tempests and is never shaken;
> It is the star to every wand'ring bark,
> Whose worth's unknown, although his height be taken.
> Love's not Time's fool, though rosy lips and cheeks
> Within his bending sickle's compass come;
> Love alters not with his brief hours and weeks,
> But bears it out even to the edge of doom.
> If this be error and upon me proved,
> I never writ, nor no man ever loved.

And here are two literary observations on falling *out of* love:

> To think that I've wasted years of my life, that I've longed to die, that I've experienced my greatest love, for a woman who didn't appeal to me, who wasn't even my type!

(*Swann's Way,* by Marcel Proust, translated by Scott Moncrieff and Terence Kilmartin)

William Shakespeare (1564–1616)

> Methought I was enamored of an ass…
> O, how mine eyes do loathe his visage now!

(Titania in Shakespeare's *Midsummer Night's Dream*)

---

tionships, different aspects of love are apparent. Most strikingly, the quality of love tends to change over the duration of a relationship, starting with passion and developing over time into a calmer but deeper bond (Hatfield & Walster, 1978). The early kind of love is called romantic love, passionate love, or limerence (Tennov, 1979), and popularly, "falling in love" or "being head-over-heels in love." The later kind of love is called companionate, realistic, or mature love.

Here's how one teenager explained the difference (Montgomery & Sorell, 1998): "Being in love with someone and loving someone are two different things; when you're *in love* with someone, you think they're just wonderful and everything they do is perfect and they have no faults. When you *love* someone you know about their faults and you realize that they may not be exactly as you want them to be, but you love them in spite of it."

Romantic Love May Be a Human Universal

Romantic love—being *in love*—is an intense and erotic attraction that involves the idealization of the loved person. It does not require familiarity with the loved person, nor need it be reciprocated. In fact, familiarity and reciprocation may hasten the end of romantic love by helping to transform it into companionate love.

Some anthropologists and historians have maintained that romantic love is a product of Western industrial society, or that in preindustrial societies it was experienced only by the leisured elite classes (Aries, 1965; Stone, 1988). To test this notion, William Jankowiak (of the University of Nevada) and Edward Fischer (of Tulane University) combed through anthropological sources that described courtship, marriage, and family relations in 166 cultures (Jankowiak & Fischer, 1992). They found clear evidence for the existence of romantic love in 147, or 86 percent, of these cultures. For most of the remaining cultures there was no clear evidence one way or the other. Jankowiak and Fischer concluded that the capacity for romantic love is a human universal or near-universal.

Here are a couple of items cited by Jankowiak and Fischer that document the existence of romantic love in cultures very different from our own. Nisa, a woman of the hunter-gatherer !Kung people of the Kalahari Desert of southern Africa, when interviewed by an anthropologist, drew a distinction between a husband and a lover. A relationship with a husband is "rich, warm and secure," she said, while that with a lover is "passionate and exciting, although often fleeting and undependable." She added that "when two people come together their hearts are on fire and their passion is very great. After a while, the fire cools and that's how it stays" (Shostak, 2000).

In *The Jade Goddess,* a tale from the Chinese Sung Dynasty (928–1233 C.E.), a man by the name of Chang Po falls in love with a woman who is already engaged to someone else. He sinks into prolonged despair, but when he finally expresses his feelings to her, she reveals that she feels the same way about him, and they elope. They suffer from poverty and isolation, and eventually decide to return home. On the eve of their return Chang Po draws his beloved into his arms and says, "Since heaven and earth were created you were made for me and I will not let you go. It cannot be wrong to love you" (Lin, 1961). The story is strikingly similar to the romances that were celebrated during the same period by the wandering minstrels (troubadours and minnesinger) of Europe (see Chapter 1), although there was little contact between the European and Chinese cultures.

Even if the capacity for romantic love is universal, modern Western culture is probably unusual in the emphasis it places on romantic love as a prerequisite for marriage. In many cultures, including our own until a century or so ago, choices of marriage partners were generally made by parents or decided by a variety of economic or other practical considerations in which love played little role. If a young man and woman were in love and wanted to marry, elopement was often a necessity.

Being in Love May Be the Justification for Marriage or for Sex

"Love and marriage," crooned Frank Sinatra in 1955, "go together like a horse and carriage." (The lyrics were by Sammy Cahn and Jimmy Van Heusen.) Yet as late as the 1960s, only 30 percent of women said that being in love was a necessary condition for marriage. The corresponding figure for men was over 60 percent. By 1984, these figures had risen to over 80 percent for both sexes (Simpson, 1986). Presumably, women's increasing economic independence has allowed them to reject the notion of marrying for nonromantic reasons such as economic security or social status. By the 1990s, less that 4 percent of Americans said they would marry someone they didn't love, compared with 50 percent of Indians and Pakistanis—in whose countries arranged marriages are still common (Hatfield, 1994).

Falling in love also seems to give people permission—women especially—to engage in sexual intercourse for the first time. In the NSSAL study, 58 percent of women mentioned "being in love" as a reason why they first had intercourse. Only 30 percent of men mentioned this factor, however; a much more frequently cited reason was "I was curious about what it would be like."

People Fall in Love with Attractive Persons Who Show Some Interest in Them

What actually causes person A to fall in love with person B? If we knew the answer to that question and it could be bottled, we would not be slaving over a college textbook! In a general way, however, we can point to several factors that are likely to be involved. First, person A is likely to be lonely or "looking for love." In fact, the best protection against falling in love is to be in love already. Second, person B should be *attractive* to person A by the kind of criteria we discussed in Chapter 7. Third, B should display some interest in A. The degree of interest may be very small, and may have no sexual content in B's mind, but it may still be enough to trigger A's passion. In other words, falling in love is often a reciprocation of the expression of positive feelings by the beloved (Curtis & Miller, 1997).

Is it possible to fall in love "at first sight"? About half of the U.S. population thinks that it is; in fact, 44 percent of men and 36 percent of women say that it has happened to them (Gallup Organization, 2001). Since there is no objective test for "being in love," it is hard to confirm or refute their claims. But the fact that many people say that they have experienced love at first sight highlights the fact that familiarity is not a necessary ingredient for romantic love.

Researchers Are Probing the Biological Basis of Love

Speaking of objective tests, there has been some research aimed at finding a biological basis for love. One interesting line of animal research focuses on voles. As we mentioned in Chapter 2, two closely related species of these small mammals differ in their sexual and social behavior. The mountain vole (*Microtus montanus*) is sexually promiscuous and does not form durable attachments. The prairie vole (*M. ochrogaster*), on the other hand, forms lifelong pair bonds that are established at first mating (Figure 9.9A) (Carter & Getz, 1993). Detailed comparisons of the brains and endocrine systems of these two vole species suggest that pair bonding in prairie voles is mediated by several hormones or neurotransmitters, including the two peptides released by the posterior lobe of the pituitary gland, oxytocin and vasopressin (Carter, 1998) (see Chapter 4). A research group at Emory University (Thomas Insel, Zuoxin Wang, and colleagues) have facilitated pair bond formation in prairie voles by injecting these hormones directly into the brain (vasopressin into males, oxytocin into females). Conversely, injection of antagonists to these two hormones prevents pair bond formation when it would otherwise have occurred. A key difference between prairie and mountain voles seems to lie in the DNA sequences of the genes that code for the oxytocin and vasopressin receptors. These genetic differences cause the receptors to have different distributions within the brain in the two species (Figure 9.9B), thus affecting the ability of the hormones to influence brain function (Insel et al., 1998). When the researchers created a strain of genetically modified mice that possessed the gene for the prairie vole's vasopressin receptor, these mice showed greater affection for each other than do ordinary mice (Young et al., 1999).

These findings do not necessarily mean that oxytocin and vasopressin play a role in triggering romantic attachments between humans, but such attachments do probably have *some* kind of neurochemical basis. There has been speculation that neurotransmitters of the catecholamine family, such as dopamine, norepinephrine, and a related compound called phenylethylamine, might be important for sexual attraction and love in humans (Walsh, 1991). An Italian research group reported finding neurochemical changes in persons who had recently fallen in love resembling those seen in obsessive-compul-

Figure 9.9 Prairie home companions. (A) After mating, male and female prairie voles tend to stay together in a monogamous partnership until one of them dies. The male and female share parental duties. This behavior contrasts with that of the closely related mountain vole, which does not form pair bonds. (B) Receptors for the hormone vasopressin (indicated here by red, orange, and yellow) are distributed differently in the brains of the monogamous prairie vole (left) and the nonmonogamous mountain vole (right). This difference probably contributes to the behavioral differences between the two species. (Courtesy of Zuoxin Wang and Thomas Curtis.)

(A)

(B)

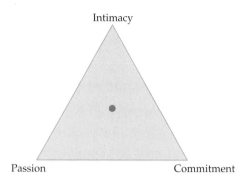

Intimacy

Passion   Commitment

Figure 9.10 Sternberg's love triangle. Robert Sternberg proposed that love consists of three elements—passion, intimacy, and commitment—that can be represented as a triangle. (Note that this use of the term "triangle" has nothing to do with the common use of "love triangle" to describe a love relationship involving three people.)

sive disorders (Marazziti et al., 1999). There have also been efforts to delineate the brain circuitry involved in romantic love by means of imaging techniques (Box 9.7).

One Theory Proposes that Love Has Three Components

Psychologist Robert Sternberg of Yale University has proposed that love comprises three elements: passion, intimacy, and commitment. These elements can be represented as the three vertices of a triangle (Sternberg, 1986) (Figure 9.10). When each of the three elements is present in the same degree, they form an equilateral triangle, whose size is proportionate to the degree of love. When the three elements are present to an unequal degree, they form an isosceles or scalene (unequal-sided) triangle.

The **passion** element in Sternberg's triangular model is the motivational component. It is strongest in the initial heat of romantic love. It is the "urge to merge," in both the physical and psychological senses. **Intimacy** is the emotional component: it refers to the feelings of closeness and connectedness in a relationship. It is expressed in the desire to promote the well-being of the beloved, in self-disclosure to the beloved, and in valuing the beloved in one's life. **Commitment** is the cognitive component. It refers, in the short term, to the decision that one loves the beloved. In the longer term, it refers to the commitment to maintain the loving relationship—as expressed in the marriage vows, for example. It is the element over which one has the greatest conscious control.

Just as the three primary colors can be combined in different proportions to create a variety of hues, the three elements of Sternberg's love triangle can be combined in different ways, producing different kinds of love, which can be represented by triangles of differing shapes (Figure 9.11). Sternberg names these kinds of love as follows:

- **Liking** is the kind of love in which intimacy is high but passion and commitment are low. It corresponds to what we usually call friendship.
- **Infatuation** is the kind of love in which passion is high but intimacy and commitment are low. It corresponds to "love at first sight," when one loves a person without knowing them well or thinking much about the matter.
- **Empty love** is the kind of love in which commitment is high but passion and intimacy are low. It could be the final, stagnant stage of a romantic relationship in which passion and emotional involvement have waned, but the person is still consciously committed to keeping the relationship going. But it could also be the first stage of an arranged marriage, leading to more complete love. Thus "empty love" may be a poor choice of terms that undermines Sternberg's assertion that commitment is a valid constituent of love.
- **Romantic love** is the kind of love in which both intimacy and passion are high, but commitment is low. Sternberg mentions the love of Romeo and Juliet, and of Tristan and Isolde, as being examples of romantic love in this sense.
- **Companionate love** is the kind of love in which intimacy and commitment are high, but passion is low. As mentioned earlier, it frequently occurs in marriage and cohabitations after physical attraction has abated.
- **Fatuous love** is the kind of love in which passion and commitment are high, but intimacy is low. According to Sternberg, it is seen in whirlwind romances in which two lovers rush off to get married and set up a home together without ever getting to know each other very well. These are high-risk relationships, although there is always the possibility that intimacy will develop.
- **Consummate love** is the kind of love in which all three elements are present in full. It represents the kind of love that most of us strive for and, having achieved, try to maintain—with variable success.

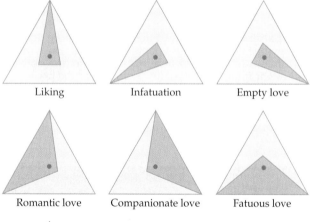

Liking   Infatuation   Empty love

Romantic love   Companionate love   Fatuous love

Consummate love

Figure 9.11 Sternberg's seven types of love combine passion, intimacy, and commitment in different proportions.

Box 9.7 Research Highlights

This Is Your Brain in Love

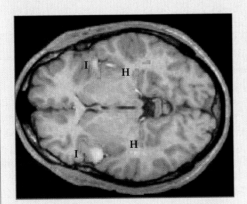

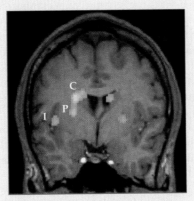

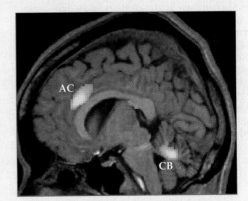

(A) A horizontal slice (front to the left, left side at top), showing activity in an infolded region of the cerebral cortex called the insula (I) and the hippocampus (H).

(B) A frontal slice, showing activity in the insula and in two regions of the basal ganglia, the caudate nucleus (C) and the putamen (P).

(C) A near-sagittal (midline) slice (front to the left), showing activity in the anterior cingulate cortex (AC) and the cerebellum (CB).

Neuroscientist Semir Zeki, of University College, London, along with his Swiss graduate student Andreas Bartels, wanted to find out what brain regions might underlie the experience of romantic love (Bartels & Zeki, 2000). They put up posters around London that advertised for men and women who were "truly, deeply and madly in love." Seventy women and men responded. The subjects had had a relationship with their beloveds for an average of about 2 years—thus, they were not in the first flush of falling in love.

The subjects filled out a "passionate love questionnaire" (Hatfield & Sprecher, 1986), which asked them to rate their agreement with statements such as "For me, X is the perfect romantic partner," "I will love X forever," and "I eagerly look for signs indicating X's desire for me." Seventeen subjects (11 women and 6 men—all heterosexual) who scored highly on the questionnaire were rolled into a **functional magnetic resonance imaging (fMRI)** scanner (see Chapter 8). This high-tech mind-reader constructs an image of the brain in which changes in blood flow (induced by brain activity) are represented as color-coded pixels. It produces images comparable to those produced by positron emission tomography, discussed in Chapter 7, but with somewhat better spatial resolution.

To allow the subjects to experience the emotion of romantic love while lying in the unromantic bowels of the fMRI scanner, Bartels and Zeki gave each subject a photograph of their beloved to gaze at. Of course, a whole lot goes on in the brain when you look at a picture, most of which has nothing to do with the emotion of love. To get rid of the irrelevant information, the researchers alternated the picture of each subject's beloved with pictures of several other friends with whom the subject was not in love. They then digitally subtracted the scans taken while the subjects viewed the "friend" pictures from those taken while they viewed the "beloved" pictures, creating images that represent the brain regions that became more or less active when a subject viewed their beloved's picture. These images, the researchers argue, show the brain regions involved when a person experiences the emotion of romantic love.

One of the regions that becomes more active is a deeply infolded zone of the cerebral cortex named the *insula* (Figures A and B). The insular cortex has been known to play a role in emotions—both negative and positive ones—for some time. Interestingly, the insula in the left hemisphere was far more active than the corresponding region in the right hemisphere. So much for the popular notion that the left and right hemispheres are the homes of reason and emotion, respectively.

Another region that became more active was the anterior cingulate cortex—a region that also becomes active when people view sexually arousing material without being in love (Figure C) (see Chapter 7). This observation makes sense, since we expect erotic arousal to be a component of romantic love.

Among the regions whose activity *decreased* during the experience of love were zones previously implicated in the experience of painful emotions such as sadness, anger, and fear. These regions include the prefrontal cortex of the right hemisphere and a deep (subcortical) structure known as the amygdala. It appears that the brain regions serving positive and negative emotions have a reciprocal, seesaw relationship, such that love diminishes anger, and vice versa.

Most of the regions that were activated during the experience of romantic love have previously been shown to be active while a subject is under the influence of euphoria-inducing drugs such as opiates or cocaine. Apparently, both romantic love and those drugs activate a "blissed-out" circuit in the brain.

Still, this finding raises the usual question one must ask when attempting to measure tough-to-define emotional experiences: Are Bartels and Zeki studying what they think they're studying? All their subjects were in relationships with their beloveds, suggesting that they were *happily* in love. But romantic love is often unrequited, and that is far from a happy experience—it can lead to depression, even suicide. If Bartels and Zeki had tested a bunch of *unhappy*—but definitely "in love"—lovers, they might have found a very different pattern of activity from the one they reported. In other words, it is uncertain whether all the brain centers that lit up in their experiments are truly involved in the experience of love itself, rather than the euphoria that accompanies love when it is reciprocated. (fMRI images from Bartels and Zeki, 2000.)

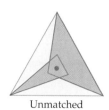

Matching   Unmatched

Figure 9.12 Couples may have matching or unmatched love triangles. The members of the couple on the left (represented by blue and purple) both have triangles approximating Sternberg's "infatuation." In the couple on the right, one member's triangle corresponds to "infatuation" and the other's to "companionate love." According to Sternberg, the couple on the left are more likely to be satisfied with their relationship.

Besides asserting that love is made up of these three elements in various combinations, Sternberg claims that people are most likely to be satisfied with their love relationships when their own and their lovers' triangles match, or nearly match (Figure 9.12) (Sternberg & Barnes, 1985). When a couple's triangles are mismatched, as when one partner is high on commitment but low on passion, while the other is the reverse, both partners are likely to be dissatisfied.

Sternberg's theory has attracted a great deal of attention. One obvious prediction of the theory is that it should be possible to detect the existence of the three distinct components of love—passion, intimacy, and commitment—by giving people questionnaires about their loving relationships and submitting the results to factor analysis or related statistical techniques. Studies of this kind have come up with mixed results, but one study, by Robert Lemieux of Western Maryland College and Jerold Hale of the University of Georgia, did produce a result favoring Sternberg's model (Lemieux & Hale, 1999). The researchers gave 233 unmarried male and female college students a twenty-item questionnaire, in which the subjects were asked to rate their degree of agreement or disagreement with statements such as "My partner is sexually exciting." Factor analysis of the responses revealed three factors corresponding to the three elements of Sternberg's love triangle. Seven of the questions (including the one just cited) contributed primarily to the "passion" factor. Another seven (including "There are things I can tell my partner that I can't tell anyone else") contributed primarily to the "intimacy" factor. The remaining six questions (including "I think of our relationship as a permanent one") contributed mainly to the "commitment" factor.

Lemieux and Hale's study bolstered Sternberg's triangular theory of love. It also found sex differences in two of the three factors: women scored higher on both "intimacy" and "commitment" than did men, whereas both women and men scored about equally on "passion." Thus the "average" loving relationship between a man and a woman is likely to be somewhat unbalanced, with the woman experiencing more intimacy and commitment than her partner. For both men and women, the strength of all three factors contributed to their degree of satisfaction with the relationship, but the strength of the "intimacy" factor was the best predictor of satisfaction. Lemieux and Hale later replicated their study using married men and women. The main difference was that, as one might imagine, the "commitment" factor was now the best predictor of satisfaction (Lemieux & Hale, 2000).

Although Sternberg's theory is more a description of what love *is* than an explanation of how love comes about, it is potentially useful in studying how relationships run into trouble and how broken relationships might be healed. Because each partner's love triangle will change its shape and size over the course of a relationship, mismatches are very likely to develop. Identifying such mismatches may allow a counselor to focus a couple's attention on aspects of their relationship that need work. The simple, graphical nature of Sternberg's theory makes it suitable for use in a therapeutic setting.

The Relationship of Commitment to Love Is Debated

There have been quite a few other efforts to dissect love. To mention just one, Beverley Fehr of the University of Winnipeg has studied the terms that people use when they are asked to freely describe concepts such as "love" and "commitment" (Fehr, 1988). If commitment is one component of love, as Sternberg's model proposes, then all the terms that people use to describe commitment should be contained within a larger list of terms used to describe love. In fact, however, Fehr found that her subjects used two different, though partially overlapping, lists of terms to describe the two concepts (Figure 9.13). Furthermore, some of the terms used to describe commitment were quite negative, such as "feeling trapped."

Thus, to rescue Sternberg's model, one would have to say that it uses special meanings of "love" or "commitment" that are somewhat different from the way most people think of these terms: specifically, a broader meaning of "love" or a narrower meaning of "commitment." Indeed, it is likely that most people are not comfortable with the intellectual aspect of love contained within Sternberg's notion of "commitment."

Happiness

Caring

Perseverance

Wanting to be with the other

Trust

Faithfulness

Understanding

Loyalty

Living up to your word

Love   Commitment

Figure 9.13 Love and commitment. Beverley Fehr found that people use partially overlapping lists of terms to describe "love" and "commitment." Some of the terms are shown here.

Here's the heart of the debate: Can you *decide* to love someone, or is love simply something that *happens* to you? Most Americans think of it as something that happens to you. Yet, as psychoanalyst Erich Fromm (1900–1980) pointed out, the cognitive aspects of love help us understand how arranged marriages not uncommonly grow into successful, loving relationships. "One neglects to see an important factor in erotic love, that of *will*," Fromm wrote. "To love somebody is not just a strong feeling—it is a decision, it is a judgment, it is a promise. If love were only a feeling, there would be no basis for the promise to love each other forever. Hence the idea of a relationship which can be easily dissolved if one is not successful with it is as erroneous as the idea that under no circumstances must the relationship be dissolved" (Fromm, 1956).

Unrequited Love Is Painful for Both Parties

The ultimate in mismatched love triangles is nonreciprocated or **unrequited love,** in which A loves B but B doesn't love A. These ill-starred relationships are very common: already by college age, most men and women have experienced episodes of unrequited love, both as the suitor and as the rejector (Baumeister et al., 1993). Because romantic love is characterized by a longing for union with the beloved, unrequited love can be viewed as the most extreme or purest form of romantic love, in which the desire for union is not diluted by its actual attainment.

Unrequited love can also be thought of as part of the matching process by which people find long-term mates. If, as we have suggested earlier, there is a sexual marketplace in which people find partners of roughly their own "worth," there has to be a trial-and-error process by which people find out what their own worth is. In the old days of arranged marriages, this kind of market negotiation was done by parents. Now, a chain of unrequited or short-lived relationships may achieve the same thing. An adolescent may start by having a crush on a film star or some other figure whose looks, wealth, or social standing places them far above what the adolescent has to offer. Rejection may be followed by pursuit of a somewhat more appropriate partner, and so on, until a good match is found.

This is not to say that in unrequited love affairs, the rejector is always more attractive (in some objective sense) than the unhappy suitor. There is, of course, a hefty dose of idiosyncrasy and quirkiness in love. Sometimes a person will see nothing in a suitor whom everyone else is salivating over. Sometimes a difference in sexual orientation will prevent love from being reciprocated, whatever the suitor's attractiveness. Sometimes the rejector, though idealized to virtual sainthood by the suitor, is really a ne'er-do-well who would ruin the suitor's life if they ever did hook up. But commonly rejectors fail to respond positively to suitors' advances because they rate the suitors as less attractive than they "deserve"—and they may quite often be right.

Rejection in Love Damages Self-Worth

The experience of unrequited love is painful for the suitor, of course. There is not merely the failure to obtain what, for a few desperate weeks at least, seems like the only thing worth having on Earth. There is also the humiliation of rejection—being told, in some way or another, that one is not "good enough." Rejection in love is a crushing, if short-lived, blow to one's self-esteem. Yet the suitor does at least have a "script" to follow. The role of the unrequited lover is utterly familiar to everyone; it is celebrated in one popular song after another. It is a dramatic role with its prescribed times for grief, anger, acceptance, and moving on.

This late nineteenth-century Japanese woodblock print, *Reflected Moonlight,* depicts Lady Ariko, a poet of the medieval Heian court with her lute, preparing to drown herself because of her unrequited love for a lord. Lady Ariko's poem, which appears at the top right of the print, expresses the anguish of the rejected lover: "*How hopeless it is/it would be better for me to sink beneath the waves/perhaps there I could see my man from Moon Capital.*"

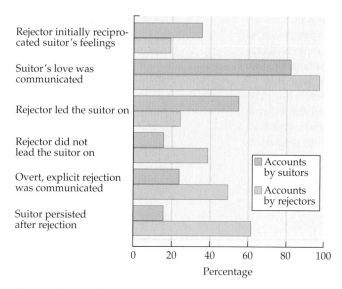

Figure 9.14 Unhappy memories. When college students were asked to recall their experiences of unrequited love—both experiences in which they were rejected and experiences in which they did the rejecting—the two kinds of narratives differed markedly. The figure shows the percentage of "suitor" and "rejector" narratives that included the six listed assertions. (Data from Baumeister et al., 1993.)

Most people can follow this script and emerge unscathed and perhaps the stronger for the experience. For a minority, however, especially those with controlling or manipulative personalities or poor communication skills, it may be difficult to take "no" for a final answer, and a single-minded pursuit of the desired person may ensue. This pattern has been termed **obsessive relational intrusion** (Cupach & Spitzberg, 1998), and can lead eventually to criminal **stalking** (see Chapter 18).

The Rejector Experiences Guilt

As psychologist Roy Baumeister and his colleagues at Case Western Reserve University point out, the experience for the *rejector* is very different, but often equally painful (Baumeister et al., 1993). At the beginning, certainly, the rejector may get a psychological boost from the realization that they are the object of someone's affection, even if not the particular someone they would have liked. Later, however, the rejector is likely to experience considerable guilt. This guilt has three sources: guilt at having led the suitor on, even if unintentionally or to a small degree; guilt at not returning the suitor's affection—a violation of the social norm of reciprocity; and guilt at inflicting humiliation on the suitor by telling them that they are not loved in return. Furthermore, the rejector's role is largely "unscripted": there are few social models for how a rejector is supposed to behave or feel. Thus the rejector may end up failing to communicate the rejection clearly to the suitor, perhaps representing it instead as a matter of unfortunate circumstances that might conceivably be overcome in the future. The rejector may even weasel out of making any explicit rejection at all—by avoiding the suitor, for example. When one considers that the suitor is likely to read the most optimistic interpretation into anything the rejector says or does, the potential for misunderstanding is great.

In fact, by analyzing numerous accounts of unrequited love told from the perspective of suitors and rejectors, Baumeister's group found systematic biases in the way the episodes were recalled (Figure 9.14). Suitors were much more likely than rejectors to recall that the rejector initially reciprocated the suitor's advances, and that the rejector led the suitor on. Rejectors, on the other hand, were more likely than suitors to recall that the rejector gave the suitor an explicit rejection, and that the suitor persisted unreasonably in spite of the rejection. The researchers interpreted these biases as representing efforts by suitors to rebuild their self-esteem and by rejectors to justify themselves and reduce their feelings of guilt. The larger conclusion is that it is neither loving nor being loved that is a positive experience in itself, but only the mutuality of love.

Couples in Relationships Resemble Each Other

One striking fact about couples is how similar their two members commonly are to each other. In Chapter 7 we mentioned the concept of homophily; that is, the fact that people tend to be attracted to others who resemble themselves. It's not surprising, then, that couples should resemble each other to some degree, but the actual extent of that resemblance *is* surprising. According to the NHSLS, couples resemble each other far more than would be expected by chance in race or ethnicity, religion, age, educational level, and socioeconomic status. This is true not just for married and cohabiting couples, but for couples in short-term partnerships as well. (The one exception is that short-term partners are less likely to be matched for religion than are more permanent partners.) This resemblance also extends to height, eye color, physical attractiveness, intelligence, and other personality variables (Caspi & Herbener, 1990; Feingold, 1988). The tendency of sexually partnered couples to resemble each other is called **homogamy.** (Sometimes this term is reserved for married couples.)

To some degree, homogamy is an accident—a consequence of the fact that people naturally tend to find mates among the people they commonly encounter, who are likely to be of the same race, age, religion, and so on. This observation shows that sexual relationships are embedded in larger social structures, but it doesn't say whether homogamy has any *effect* on relationships, for good or bad.

There is some evidence, however, that homogamy does contribute to the success and stability of sexual relationships. Longitudinal studies have found that couples who resemble each other in a variety of respects are more likely to stay together, and express greater satisfaction with their relationships at later times in the relationship, than couples who are less alike (Caspi & Herbener, 1990; Caspi et al., 1992; Hill et al., 1976; Meyer & Pepper, 1977). Similarity between couples may strengthen relationships because companionate love—the hallmark of long-term relationships—is exactly that: a companionship. Like friends, couples who are similar to each other tend to have shared interests and attitudes. Thus they communicate approval to each other, bolster each other's self-esteem, and help stabilize each other's personalities.

In addition, outside forces tend to stabilize relationships between couples whose members are similar. For example, a couple's two birth families are more likely to interact socially, and to actively support the couple's relationship, if the couple are of the same race than if they are of different races. Similarly, people in general tend to be less supportive of couples who differ greatly in age than of age-matched couples, as if there is something not quite legitimate about a relationship between two people who are distinctly different in age.

In spite of these stabilizing influences of homogamy, it also presents hazards. In particular, similarity tends to undermine the mystery and tension associated with romantic love and sexual attraction. One can speculate that similarity between couples contributes to the reduction in sexual activity that often occurs over the duration of a long relationship. With heterosexual couples, of course, there is always the difference of sex: gender-based differences offer an enduring mystery that may help to sustain erotic interest. With same-sex couples, on the other hand, gender-based differences are likely to be less marked, though they are not necessarily entirely absent (see Chapter 13). The similarity of same-sex partners may present a challenge to the maintenance of erotic interest over time. In particular, it may contribute to "lesbian bed death"—the low frequency of sex that has been reported for established lesbian couples (Blumstein & Schwartz, 1983). A similar phenomenon has been described for many long-term gay male relationships (McWhirter & Mattison, 1984).

Communication Is a Key Factor in the Success of Relationships

Another important factor that is thought to influence the success of relationships is **communication.** In fact, many therapists name communication problems as the number one reason for dissatisfaction in marriages and other long-term relationships. According to several longitudinal studies, couples who communicate well before or at the time of marriage are likely to be satisfied with their relationships when interviewed several years later. Couples who communicate poorly early on (even though they may be just as happy at that stage) are likely to be dissatisfied with their marriage later. And couples who communicate via aggression are likely to be separated or divorced a few years later. These correlations are so strong that researchers can predict with 65–90 percent accuracy the state of a marriage 5 years down the road, simply on the basis of communication styles at the outset (Markman, 1981; Rogge & Bradbury, 1999).

Further bolstering the importance of communication in relationships are studies that demonstrate the benefit of interventions to improve communication skills. A research group at the University of Denver's Center for Marital and Family Studies, led by Howard Markman and Scott Stanley, focused on couples who were planning to marry (Markman et al., 1993). Some of the couples participated in a five-session Prevention and Relationship Enhancement Program (PREP), aimed at improving communication and conflict resolution skills. Five years later, the couples who took the PREP course had significantly better communication skills, and lower levels of marital violence, than the control couples. Furthermore, the couples who took the course were more likely to be together after 5 years: only 8 percent of them had divorced or separated, compared with 19 percent of the control couples. At later times, however, the beneficial effects of the early counseling seemed to wane.

The good results reported by PREP and other comparable programs have caused some states to consider making premarital counseling programs mandatory for all marrying couples, with the hope of improving the rather dismal statistics on marriage duration and divorce (see Chapter 12). It is far from certain that a mandatory program would have the same benefits as a voluntary one, however, since motivation tends to be a key factor in self-improvement programs. The idea of governments telling people how to run their marriages is also offensive to some.

Communication May Be Inhibited by Upbringing or by the Gender Barrier

So what constitutes good and poor communication in a marriage or other sexual relationship? It's partly a matter of *what* is communicated, and partly a matter of *how.*

In terms of the *what,* there is first of all the fact that many couples are reluctant to communicate at all about sexual issues. This reluctance results in part from a tradition of silence about sexual matters that is inculcated into young children. Parents tend not to discuss sexual function or genital anatomy with their children, nor do they typically disclose much about their own sex lives or sexual problems. Children quickly learn that sex is a taboo subject. The result is a sense of shame that may profoundly inhibit communication in adulthood.

In heterosexual relationships, the gender barrier may compound communication problems. Boys and young men tend to talk about sexual matters among themselves; so do girls and young women. This leads almost to separate languages: young men, for example, may be perfectly comfortable using words such as "dick" and "pussy" among themselves, but the same words may seem vulgar when used with a female partner. So they are thrown back on words such as "penis" and "vagina," which may put them in an uncomfortable, almost clinical mindset. When this language difficulty is combined with limited knowledge about the other sex's anatomy and physiology, communication may be severely inhibited. Similarly, girls and young women may discuss sexual and relational issues at great length among themselves, but be quite unprepared to bring up these same issues with men.

Couples may also be reluctant to discuss sexual matters for a more subtle reason: they may fear that bringing sexual matters out into the open will destroy the "sacred mystery" of sex, thus reducing it to a humdrum matter on the same level as grocery shopping. There may be some validity to this point of view. If a couple has a satisfying sex life without explicit verbal communication, there is certainly no reason to force it on them. There are many ways to communicate "This is fun" or "I'd rather do it this way" other than in words. Still, not even the most intimate of couples are mind readers, so problems that are not clearly communicated tend to remain unresolved and to multiply.

There are also cultural factors that inhibit communication in certain groups. Asian Americans, especially Asian American women, may find it a very foreign concept to discuss sex or relationship problems, either with a partner or with a therapist (Del Carmen, 1990). Hispanic Americans, too, have a custom of marital silence on sexual issues. This custom derives in part from the traditional expectation that men will exhibit tough, independent masculinity, or **machismo** (Guerrero Pavich, 1986). In addition, some immigrants, such as Latina women from Mexico and Central America, may lack the most basic knowledge about sexual anatomy and physiology, which makes communication even more difficult. Balancing these problems, however, is a sense of teamwork or mutual obligation that many minority and immigrant couples possess,

What went wrong? Many couples find it difficult to discuss sexual problems because they have been socialized to discuss sex only in same-sex groups.

as well as a strong involvement of extended families in the maintenance of marital relationships. These factors contrast with the more individualistic approach to relationships that typifies European-American culture.

What with all these obstacles, quite ordinary acts of communication can seem all but impossible in the domain of sex and intimate relationships. "I wish you'd help me reach orgasm," "Sorry, but I don't feel like sex tonight," "I'd like to have sex more often," "I'm missing the hug you used to give me when I came home," "I feel jealous when you spend so much time with Chris," and any number of other statements and requests may be invested with all kinds of negative overtones. Yet if they do not get said, it only gets harder and harder to say them. Finally, just making such a statement seems so out of line that it carries the unspoken subtext: "And, by the way, our relationship is going down the tubes."

Premarital Programs Teach Communication Skills

Programs such as PREP teach very basic communication skills that are often as relevant to work and general social life as they are to sexual relationships. At the core of all communication, for example, is one person saying something and the other person listening and responding. In premarital counseling programs, couples may practice this interaction in a formalized manner. The couple may be seated facing and looking directly at each other, perhaps touching each other. One partner ("Pat") holds a speaker's token, such as a square of linoleum (representing "the floor"), and makes a statement, such as, "Kim, I find myself feeling hurt when you just breeze in and start chatting with the kids as if I'm not there." Pat then yields the "floor" to Kim, who replies in a fashion that paraphrases what Pat has just said, such as, "You mean, I seem to just take you for granted?" Pat may clarify the initial statement: "Not all the time, just when the kids are around." Then Kim gives a response representing a proposed resolution: "You may be right, Pat—sorry! I can understand how you must feel. However much I love the kids, you're the number-one person in my life and I want to make sure you know it." And so on.

Cheesy though such "active listening" exercises may seem, they do teach two important points: the right of one partner to make a clear statement of a potential problem without interruption, and the obligation of the other to provide some feedback—to acknowledge understanding the statement and to process it in some way so as to bring the interaction to a satisfactory close. In other words, "uh-huh?" may not be a fruitful response to each and every one of your partner's utterances. It's not expected that couples will continue to pass floor tiles to and fro for the rest of their natural lives, but the hope is that notion of ordered, reciprocal communication will persist.

Interactions of this kind do run the risk of confusing sexual relationships with therapeutic relationships. Partners are not therapists—that is, they are not outsiders whose role is simply to empathize, but players *within* the drama. Thus, it doesn't necessarily help to tell your partner how much you understand their point of view unless that understanding is accompanied by action and resolution. Here's how one experienced marriage counselor, John Gottman of the University of Washington, presents the issue:

> Let's say my wife is really angry with me because I repeatedly haven't balanced the checkbook and the checks bounce. ...What would it accomplish if I say 'I hear what you're saying, you're really angry with me, and I can understand why you're angry with me because I'm not balancing the checkbook'? That's not going to make her feel any better—I still haven't balanced the damned checkbook! ... Real empathy comes from feeling your partner's pain in a real way, and then doing something about it. (Wyatt, 2001)

Self-Disclosure Facilitates Trust

An important role of communication is to allow for **self-disclosure.** If a couple wanted to form a physical union, they'd have to open up some skin so that the living tissues could grow together. So it is with psychological unions. It's not possible to form an intimate relationship with the mask that a person presents to the workaday world, but only with the inner person. That requires a voluntary exposure of the rational and irrational thoughts, happy and painful memories, and fears and hopes for the future, that lie hidden within us.

According to Susan and Clyde Hendrick of Texas Tech University (Hendrick, 1981; Hendrick & Hendrick, 1992; Hendrick et al., 1988), self-disclosure proceeds in a stepwise fashion: a disclosure by one partner tends to provoke an equivalent disclosure by the other, so that trust gradually builds between the two. In the Hendricks' studies, the degree of self-disclosure between partners predicted the degree of satisfaction in the relationship and the likelihood that the relationship would endure.

Self-disclosure—in particular, the expression of emotions—is often more difficult for men than for women. Except for the emotion of anger, boys and young men in our culture are typically permitted little freedom of emotional expression, and by adulthood they may be severely deficient in "emotional intelligence." Therapy aimed at reawakening men's ability to communicate their feelings may have a major beneficial influence on their relationships (Levant, 1997).

How Couples Deal with Conflict Affects the Stability of Their Relationship

Conflicts are inevitable in all but the briefest relationships, but how conflicts are handled says a lot about the likelihood that a relationship will last. John Gottman and his colleagues have carried out numerous longitudinal studies of conflict styles in marriage; typically, the researchers videotape conflict-laden interactions between partners early in their relationship, analyze and quantify the communications within the interaction, and then follow the relationship for a period of years.

One of the key findings is that the expression of anger is not necessarily a bad thing (Gottman & Krokoff, 1989). Disagreement and anger do cause unhappiness at the time they are expressed, but couples who express conflicts through disagreement and anger are actually *more* likely to be satisfied with their relationships a few years down the road than couples who use other conflict styles, such as criticism, defensiveness, contempt, whining, stubbornness, withdrawal, and belligerence. Belligerence means, not anger, but challenging the spouse's power and authority with remarks like "What can you do if I *do* go drinking with Dave? What are you gonna do about it?" Belligerence by a husband represents a refusal to accept his wife's influence in the relationship and is one of the most destructive communication patterns in conflict situations (Gottman et al., 1998).

That doesn't mean that couples should just lay into each other—far from it. For one thing, negative communications such as the expression of anger have to be balanced with positive ones. The University of Washington researchers have found that a certain *ratio* of positive to negative interactions in conflict resolution situations—about five times as many positive interactions as negative ones—characterizes stable marriages (Gottman & Levenson, 1999). When negative communications are too frequent, they may come to taint the entire relationship, but when they are too rare, it may be a sign that marital problems are not being processed at all.

A common interactive style involves an initial conflict-laden conversation that breaks off without a resolution, followed by a later, more positive conversation on the same topic. This "rebound" conversation seems to be one of the most crucial processes in marriage. Gottman's group was able to predict, with 92.7 percent accuracy, whether a couple would divorce or not in the following 4 years, simply on the strength of their positive interactions during the rebound conversation (Gottman & Levenson, 1999). This degree of predictability is remarkable when one considers that the likelihood of divorce is also influenced by completely unrelated factors, such as the loss of a job (Lester, 1996). Thus the old advice to "kiss and make up"—and to find a resolution to the problem that triggered the conflict—seems to be right on the mark.

Getting angry does not threaten the stability of a relationship, so long as expressions of anger are balanced by positive interactions.

Love, Jealousy, and Infidelity Are Intertwined

Jealousy is the unpleasant feeling caused by the fear or realization of one's partner's infidelity. Colloquially, "jealous" also means "envious" (desiring what someone else possesses), but that is not how we use the word here.

Jealousy is almost a physical pain, and like pain, it comes in two forms. One is the instant stab of jealousy that we may feel when our beloved shows some unwonted attention to a potential rival. This feeling probably involves a physiological stress response. The second form is the gnawing, suspicious frame of mind that takes over a jealous person and colors all their interactions with their partner—the "green-eyed monster" that settled on Shakespeare's Othello.

As we saw in Chapter 6, men and women are made jealous by the fear of different kinds of infidelity. Men are most jealous when they fear their partners are being physically unfaithful—actually engaging in sex with another person. Women are most jealous when they fear their partners are being emotionally unfaithful—giving affection or signs of commitment to another person.

Evolutionary Theorists Attribute a Positive Function to Jealousy

While some sociologists have discussed jealousy as a purely cultural phenomenon (Reiss, 1986), evolutionary psychologists see the capacity for jealousy as a hardwired adaptation to certain inescapable facts about reproduction. First, as we saw in Chapter 2, female mammals make a much greater biological contribution to reproduction than do males, but in some species, such as ours, this imbalance may be countered by the extra resources (food, protection) that males bring to a partnership. Second, females can be certain that any offspring they bear are their own; males, on the other hand, cannot be certain that their mate's offspring were really fathered by themselves. Thus, during human evolution, the major risk for a woman was that a man would take up with another mate, leaving her with insufficient resources to rear her children alone. The major risk for a man, on the other hand, was that he would unwittingly devote a great deal of time and effort to helping rear children who were actually fathered by another man. According to David Buss of the University of Texas, these differences in risks explain why men and women experience different kinds of jealousy: men are anxious not to be cuckolded, while women are anxious not to be deserted (Buss, 2000).

Because our capacity for jealousy is "built in" by evolution, it is a blind passion, not a rational process. A man doesn't say to himself, "Oh, my wife's on the pill so I'm not worried if she sleeps around." A childless lesbian couple isn't impervious to jealousy simply because there are no children for whom resources are needed. Evolution knows nothing about pills or sexual orientation: it just provides everyone with an emotional mechanism that has been effective in the past for protecting their reproductive interests.

Jealousy is neither a good thing nor a bad thing, but rather a psychological function that can have both positive and negative consequences. The negative consequences can be truly horrendous: about 13 percent of all homicides are spousal murders, most of them triggered by jealousy. Battered women who seek refuge in shelters are commonly there because of spousal jealousy. And many more relationships are poisoned by less extreme expressions of the same emotion.

Jealousy exists because men and women are tempted to cheat on their partners—not all men and women, and not all the time, but often enough to demonstrate that love—the main glue of relationships—is not always strong enough by itself to preserve monogamy. That's where jealousy attempts to take over the job. And that's where jealousy can have a positive value for the person who experiences it, painful though it is.

Jealousy is part of the mechanism that detects and gives salience to cheating by a partner and that motivates action to prevent or end it. As Buss points out, there must have been an evolutionary spiral in which skill at cheating and skill at detecting cheating spurred each other's development. At any event, humans are now extremely good at both if they want to be. And although jealousy is often dismissed as irrational or pathological, it's surprising how often "irrational" jealousy turns out to be well founded, even when the signs of infidelity are subtle indeed.

Jealousy Can Become a High-Stakes Game

The spiral gets even more convoluted, however. Women, in particular, may *intentionally* attempt to provoke their partner's jealousy by mentioning their attraction to another man or by openly flirting with another man. If a woman's flirtation is successful in attracting a response, that raises her attractiveness in the eyes of her partner. That's because people rarely rely entirely on their own estimation of a partner's attractiveness, but also take other people's opinions into account. What's more, the woman closely monitors her partner's response to the flirtation. If he isn't jealous, or stoically hides his jealousy, that's a bad sign: it may reveal a lack of commitment to their relationship. Thus a demonstration of jealousy can be an important confirmation that the relationship is strong.

We mentioned earlier that couples tend to be roughly matched in attractiveness (in the broad meaning of the word). Nevertheless, there are couples who are unmatched in this respect, or who become so in the course of a relationship. In such cases, it is the more attractive partner who is the more likely to be unfaithful. That's partly because the more attractive partners feel that they are not getting their "fair market value" in the relationship (Hatfield et al., 1979), and partly because they are approached more often by third parties. Correspondingly, the less attractive partners in unmatched relationships are more committed to those relationships, and they experience more intense jealousy when confronted with the possibility of infidelity (Hansen, 1985). In other words, the more difficult people think it would be to replace their partner with another of equal value, the more susceptible they are to jealousy.

Several therapists have laid out useful techniques for distinguishing healthy from unhealthy jealousy and for overcoming the unhealthy kind (Barker, 1987; Dryden, 1999). Self-destructive or aggressive jealousy obviously merits therapeutic intervention. Still, one way to deal with jealousy is not to overcome it or ignore it, but to act on it, specifically by making oneself more attractive to one's partner or by going out of one's way to demonstrate love and commitment. "Men who are successful at keeping their partners often step up their displays of love when threatened with a possible partner defection," writes Buss. "Men who fail in these displays tend to be losers in love."

Extra-Pair Relationships Have Many Styles and Motivations

As we've just discussed, jealousy exists because people who are in coupled relationships, whether dating, cohabiting, or married, may also engage in sexual relationships outside their ongoing partnership. We now turn our attention to the forms and motivations of such **extra-pair relationships.**

About the only thing that all extra-pair relationships have in common is that, as mentioned earlier, they tend to incur social disapproval. Monogamy and serial monogamy are considered the ideal forms of sexual relationship, and anything that violates that ideal is stigmatized, though to varying degrees depending on circumstances. Even fantasies about sex with a person outside the partnership are widely considered a form of infidelity, in spite of the fact that most men and about half of all women experience such fantasies (Yarab et al., 1998).

If we discount fantasies, we are still left with a broad range of behaviors that fall into the category of extra-pair relationships. These behaviors include casual flirting, fondling, genital contact and coitus, and falling in love. Extra-pair relationships may be single encounters, brief "flings," longer "affairs," or a succession of such relationships with a variety of different partners. They may take place with or without the knowledge or acquiescence of the person's regular partner, who may be a spouse, cohabitational partner, or girlfriend or boyfriend.

During Evolution, Males and Females Have Derived Different Benefits from Infidelity

Why do people engage in extra-pair relationships? We can approach this question first from an evolutionary perspective. In Chapter 2 we saw that promiscuity is quite common among animals, including quite a few species that form pair bonds ("socially monogamous" species). Male animals probably engage in extra-pair sex because it is a relatively inexpensive way to have more offspring—potentially, many more. Having more offspring is not usually a powerful reason for females to be promiscuous because they are so limited in the total number of offspring they can produce. That's especially true for mammals such as ourselves. More likely reasons for females to engage in extra-pair sex are to acquire the resources provided by the extra-pair male or to give her offspring better genes than those provided by her regular mate.

These motives probably operate in humans, too. Evolution has given men a "wandering eye" because extra-pair sex can be a very cheap way for a man to have offspring. If the woman is already partnered, so much the better (from a purely evolutionary perspective): as long as her partner is deceived, the offspring will have *his* protection and resources as well as their mother's. The only costs to the promiscuous man are the resources he has to devote to securing the woman's favors and the risks of injury or damage to his reputation that he may incur at the hands of the woman he approaches, her partner, or his own partner. Like jealousy, the impulse to be promiscuous is a blind passion, not an intellectual process, so it operates in homosexual as well as heterosexual relationships. And a man may use contraceptives in an adulterous affair, blithely unaware that he is thwarting any advantages of such escapades that may have been favored by evolution.

Are women also spurred into extra-pair sex for evolutionary reasons? According to Steve Gangestad and Randy Thornhill of the University of New Mexico, they are. These researchers have provided evidence that when women have sex outside their marriages or regular partnerships, they go for men who are better endowed genetically than their regular partners. They do this, among other methods, by choosing men who are physically symmetrical—a sign of good genes (see Chapter 7). They also prefer men who are of high social standing. In addition, they tend to engage in extra-pair sex during the portion of their menstrual cycles when they are most likely to conceive (Gangestad & Thornhill, 1997). All in all, the behavior of women who engage in extra-pair relationships seems well designed to endow their offspring with better genes than those offered by their regular partner.

Although evolution may provide the motivation for people to engage in extra-pair sex, it doesn't necessarily explain why particular men and women in our society engage in such relationships while others do not. Many other factors come into play here. Moral beliefs, concern for their partners' feelings, or fear of the consequences restrain many people from engaging in extra-pair sex even though they would like to. Conversely, lack of physical satisfaction or love in the primary relationship, or prolonged absence of the primary partner, can drive some people into affairs. So can the sense that one is not getting one's "money's worth" in the primary relationship because one's partner is less attractive or desirable than oneself. So can the sheer excitement of having a new partner or of falling in love all over again. People may also cultivate secondary relationships to provoke a jealous response on the part of the primary partner, to "get even" with the primary partner if that partner is already having an affair with someone else, or to precipitate an end to the primary relationship. Finally, gay people who are heterosexually married may find their only sexual satisfaction in secondary relationships.

People who are in the early stages of a relationship may cultivate a "back-burner" relationship with another partner, perhaps an "ex." This strategy could be either a form of insurance in case the main relationship doesn't work out, or simply a means to increase sexual enjoyment or attention. Such "back-burner" affairs are less common when primary relationships have lasted for some time and have turned into cohabitations or marriages. These more mature relationships are exposed to another danger, however, related to the transition from romantic to companionate love. This transition reopens the possibility of romantic love—with a different person. It's the stuff of soap operas, but it's often the stuff of real life, too: a man or woman is deeply attached to their regular mate, but is also head over heels in love with someone else.

Extra-Pair Relationships Are Surprisingly Rare

Given all these possible reasons for extra-pair relationships, it's actually somewhat surprising how uncommon these relationships are (Figure 9.15). In the NHSLS, over 90 per-

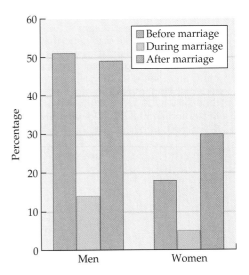

Figure 9.15. Marriage is an interlude of monogamy according to NHSLS data. The graph shows the percentage of men and women born between 1943 and 1952 who said they had more than one sex partner before, during, and after their first marriage.

cent of the women and over 75 percent of the men reported that they had been completely monogamous over the entire duration of a marriage or cohabitation, whereas many of these same people had multiple partners *before* and *after* those long-term relationships.

It's possible, of course, that the interviewees were less than honest about their extramarital relationships. Evolutionary psychologists have argued that the real figures are much higher: David Buss (Buss, 2000) concludes from a survey of numerous studies that 30–50 percent of American men and 20–40 percent of American women have at least one extramarital affair over the course of a marriage. Still, even that conclusion is compatible with the idea that most Americans are monogamous for the greater part of their married lives.

Are Affairs Newsworthy? Americans and Europeans Differ

In the United States, extramarital relationships of public figures—politicians, religious leaders, athletes, and the like—frequently seize the headlines. Sometimes the exposure ends careers or permanently damages reputations. In Europe, people take a bemused view of these American scandals, often perceiving them as self-righteous witch hunts or as holdovers from a more prudish past.

Attitudes are different in Europe for two reasons. First, European society has moved further from traditional notions of sexual morality. For example, only 8 percent of the French think that it's wrong to have a baby out of wedlock, compared with 47 percent of Americans (see Figure 9.5). In fact, the French take more liberal views than do Americans on many sexual topics (Saguy, 2002).

In addition, Europeans have greater respect for the private lives of public figures; they see little connection between people's sex lives and their ability to perform their public functions. France's Socialist Prime Minister François Mitterand is a case in point. When Mitterand died in 1996 at the age of 79, his funeral was attended not only by his wife Danielle and their two sons, but also by his longtime mistress Anne Pingeot and their 21-year-old daughter Mazarine. The French press and public had largely ignored Mitterand and Pingeot's relationship over the years, and Pingeot's presence at the funeral raised few eyebrows. Even Roman Catholic Cardinal Jean-Marie Lustiger, who delivered the eulogy, seemed unconcerned.

Standing at the coffin of French President Francois Mitterand are his wife Danielle (with white scarf) and their children and grandchildren, as well as his mistress Anne Pingeot (standing a step back) and their daughter. Neither the fact that Pingeot was his mistress, nor that she was 30 years younger than Mitterand and had a child with him, drew much public attention.

Summary

1. People enter into sexual relationships for a variety of reasons: sexual attraction and love; nonspecific sexual arousal; desire for status, security, or profit; the desire to conform or to rebel; rage; and the desire to have children.

2. Sexual relationships are influenced by individual and societal attitudes concerning the morality of sex. The Christian religion was very anti-sex in its early days, but current teachings are more diverse. Some other religions have embraced sexuality more warmly. To some degree, U.S. law and public opinion acknowledge that people have a right to freedom of sexual expression.

3. People tend to judge the morality of sexual behavior by its context, being more approving of sex in committed relationships than of casual or extramarital sex. Beliefs about the morality of sex are tied to beliefs about its purpose. Americans can be grouped into several clusters with characteristic attitudes on sexual matters; to a considerable degree, a particular person's beliefs can be predicted by demographic characteristics such as age, sex, religion, and educational level. Americans have become far more accepting of sex between unmarried couples over the past several decades.

4. Casual sex is more appealing to men than to women. In environments where casual sex is socially approved, such as singles bars, women tend to initiate sexual encounters. Flirting behaviors by both sexes are quite stereotyped. Casual sex is more accepted and prevalent in the gay male community than among heterosexuals.

5. Non-cohabitational ("dating") relationships tend to be fluid and short-lived, leading either to a live-in relationship or to separation.

6. Cohabitations (nonmarital live-in relationships) have become increasingly prevalent. About half of all first live-in relationships are now cohabitations. Most cohabitations break up or progress to marriage within a year, but some last longer, such as those between same-sex couples who would like to marry but cannot do so. The informality of cohabitation carries both benefits and risks.

7. Although marriage is declining by some measures, most Americans still get married at least once in their lives. The public formalization of sexual unions by marriage has had a variety of functions in different cultures, including the stabilization of the parenting environment.

8. Marriage is changing: people are marrying later in life (often after cohabitation) and divorcing more frequently. Married couples form more isolated social units than in the past. The roles of husband and wife have become less distinct. Society expects marriage to serve an increasing number of psychological and practical functions.

9. Sexual activity generally declines over the course of a marriage, but married couples are generally happier, and feel more sexually and emotionally fulfilled, than unmarried people.

10. Many cultures and religions have permitted polygamy (usually polygyny—one husband with several wives). A small polygamous culture still exists in the United States among "fundamentalist Mormons." Another nonmonogamous U.S. culture is represented by polyamorists: small, informally cohabiting groups with a variety of sexual arrangements.

11. Love is the glue that holds many sexual relationships together. Typically, romantic or passionate love progresses to companionate love over the course of a long relationship.

12. Romantic love exists in most or all cultures. Certain hormones or neurotransmitters and particular regions of the cerebral cortex may play a specific role in romantic love.

13. One theory of love proposes that it consists of three elements—passion, intimacy, and commitment—whose relative contributions may be represented by a triangle. The shape of a person's "love triangle" changes over the course of a relationship. A couple is most likely to be satisfied with their relationship when their triangles match.

14. Unrequited love is painful to both suitors and rejectors: to suitors because it denies them their love object and diminishes their self-esteem, and to rejectors, because it causes them guilt.

15. Couples in relationships tend to resemble each other in a variety of respects. Homogamy contributes to satisfaction in relationships, but may contribute to the decline in erotic interest between long-term partners.

16. Couples' communication styles predict their satisfaction with and the durability of their relationships. Couples commonly have difficulty communicating about sexual matters, due to a culture of sexual shame as well as to the gender divide. Some premarital counseling programs teach communication skills.

17. Self-disclosure is an incremental and reciprocal process in relationships that builds intimacy and trust.

18. How couples deal with conflict is strongly predictive of how long the relationship will last. Optimal strategies involve not the avoidance of anger, but a balancing of angry with positive interactions, and the follow-up of hostile interactions with positive "rebounds."

19. Jealousy, though a painful experience, has a positive function in protecting relationships against infidelity and in testing the strength of love bonds. Gender differences in jealousy—sexual jealousy in men and emotional jealousy in women—may reflect the different reproductive interests that men and women have had over the course of human evolution.

20. Infidelity also may have different evolutionary explanations in men and in women: it opens the possibility of more offspring for men and of better-quality offspring for women. Many circumstantial factors influence whether people in long-term part-

nerships will engage in sexual relationships outside those partnerships. National surveys suggest that most married Americans are in fact monogamous for most or the entirety of their marriage.

Discussion Questions

1. Compare and contrast your beliefs about what is right or wrong in the sexual domain with your peers' and your parents' beliefs (e.g., extramarital sex, premarital sex, casual sex, promiscuity, age of consent, homosexual behavior, contraception, abortion, and divorce). Identify the attitude cluster where you fit best (see Figure 9.1). Discuss how your attitudes have or have not changed over time.

2. Compare your attitudes toward monogamous, polygamous, polyamorous, and cohabiting relationships with those of your peers.

3. Discuss the preferred characteristics of your ideal marriage partner. In a group discussion, compare your ideal with that of your peers. Are these ideal characteristics the same ones your parents would expect?

4. If you have had an experience with a relationship breakup, describe your reactions to that breakup, how it felt, and what you learned. If you have not had a breakup, imagine the things that would distress you enough to lead to a breakup.

5. Discuss what is important to you in a relationship about communication and conflict negotiation. Are you reluctant to discuss sexual issues? Why? Compare your ability to communicate with those factors discussed in the text that hinder communication.

6. Discuss your experiences with jealousy and compare them with those of your peers.

7. Which method do you think is most effective for selecting a marriage partner—arranged marriage, or falling in love? Why?

Web Resources

The Polyamory Society www.polyamorysociety.org

Association for Couples in Marriage Enrichment www.bettermarriages.org

Beliefnet (interfaith site with considerable discussion of sexual and relationship issues) www.beliefnet.com

Recommended Reading

Baumeister, R. F., & Wotman, S. R. (1992). *Breaking hearts: The two sides of unrequited love.* New York: Guilford Press.

Buss, D. M. (2000). *The dangerous passion: Why jealousy is as necessary as love and sex.* New York: The Free Press.

Gottman, J. M. (1994). *Why marriages succeed or fail: What you can learn from the breakthrough research to make your marriage last.* New York: Simon and Schuster.

Markman, H., & Stanley, S. (1996). *Fighting for your marriage: Positive steps for preventing divorce and preserving a lasting love.* San Francisco: Jossey-Bass.

Parrinder, G. (1996) *Sexual morality in the world's religions.* Oxford: Oneworld Publications.

Wallerstein, J. S., & Blakeslee, S. (1998). *The good marriage: How and why love lasts.* Boston: Houghton Mifflin.

chapter **10**

From conception through delivery, pregnancy brings about many changes in a woman's body.

Fertility, Pregnancy, and Childbirth

*I*n Chapter 5 we described the processes of conception and implantation, as well as the sexual differentiation of the embryo and fetus. We now take a broader look at pregnancy and childbirth from the perspectives of both the fetus and its parents. In this chapter we assume that couples want to become parents—and parents of a healthy child. We will see how a couple can optimize their chances of achieving this goal, and how medical science has improved their odds of doing so. In Chapter 11 we take the opposite tack, looking at strategies to prevent pregnancy and childbirth.

Pregnancy and Childbirth Raise Major Health Concerns

In the past, pregnancy and childbirth were events to which women looked forward with an equal measure of joy and terror. Joy, because producing and rearing children defined the whole purpose of a woman's existence. And terror, not just because of the pain of childbirth, but because of the grave risk that pregnancy would end in the death of mother, baby, or both.

Before the advent of modern medicine, no amount of wealth or power could avert the human cost of reproduction. Remember England's King Henry VIII (1491–1547) and his six wives? Yes, he had a couple of them beheaded, but two of the remaining four— Jane Seymour and Kathryn Parr—died in or soon after childbirth. Of these six women's eleven children, most died in infancy, and only three reached adulthood. Memorials to the millions of women who have died in childbirth are everywhere, from India's fabled Taj Mahal to a humble stone in the pioneers' graveyard at Coloma, California, that records the death of 32-year-old Hannah Seater and her newborn son in 1852.

Early medical efforts to reduce these mortality rates sometimes backfired. Thus, in early-nineteenth-century Europe, poor women gave birth in specialized "lying-in hospitals," but more than one in ten mothers in these hospitals died of an illness known as **puerperal fever** that came on soon after childbirth. Scottish physician Alexander Gordon (1752–1799) proposed that this condition was caused by an infection. He was proved right by Ignaz Semmelweis (1818–1865), a Hungarian physician who directed a lying-in hospital in Vienna. Semmelweis tried the simple experiment of having medical personnel wash their hands after performing autopsies and before attending women in labor. This practice greatly reduced the incidence of the disease. Puerperal fever was caused by **streptococcal bacteria,** as we now know. Although Semmelweis's ideas were widely ridiculed, they eventually led to the general introduction of **antisepsis** in obstetrics—a practice that has saved the lives of millions of women and their babies (Adriaanse et al., 2000).

Today the prospects for pregnant women and their fetuses are far brighter than in the past. If we exclude pregnancies that are terminated by induced abortion, 80 percent of all established pregnancies in the United States culminate in the delivery of a live child. Once a child is born, it has a 99.3 percent chance of surviving infancy. And fewer than one in 10,000 pregnancies now leads to the death of the mother (Centers for Disease Control, 1999a, b; 2000e).

Still, there is always room for improvement, especially because the statistics for some U.S. minorities are worse than those for the general population. And parents want not just a live child, but one who is in the best possible shape to face the rigors of life "on the outside." To achieve this goal, it helps for parents to learn as much as possible about pregnancy and childbirth and about the factors that promote or compromise the health of the mother and her fetus.

In 1847, Ignaz Semmelweis ordered his medical students to wash their hands in a chlorinated solution before attending to women in labor. This practice greatly reduced mortality from puerperal fever, which was caused by streptococcal bacteria. Semmelweis himself died of a streptococcal infection that he acquired during gynecological surgery.

Pregnancy Is Suggested by a Missed Period and Confirmed by Hormonal Tests

As you'll recall from Chapter 5, we say that pregnancy is "established" not at fertilization, but a few days later, when the conceptus implants in the uterine wall and starts to secrete the hormone **human chorionic gonadotropin (hCG).** This hormone blocks the regression of the corpus luteum that normally takes place at the end of the luteal phase of the menstrual cycle. Menstruation therefore does not occur, and a **missed menstrual period** is the usual way that a woman finds out she is pregnant.

Unfortunately, the absence of a period at the expected time is not a totally reliable indicator of pregnancy. Many women have irregular periods anyway, and even in a woman who is normally very regular, a period can be missed or delayed as a result of illness or stress or for some other reason. Conversely, some "spotting" (light bleeding) can occur even when a woman is pregnant.

There are other signs that may help to confirm the pregnancy, including breast tenderness, fatigue, and nausea (the beginnings of the "morning sickness" that plagues some women during the first 3 months of pregnancy; see below). In addition, a woman

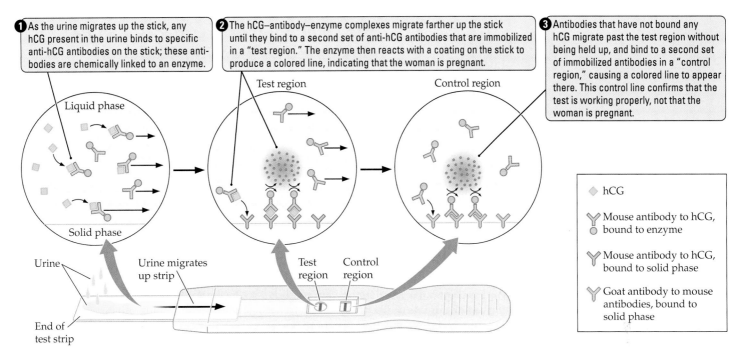

① As the urine migrates up the stick, any hCG present in the urine binds to specific anti-hCG antibodies on the stick; these antibodies are chemically linked to an enzyme.

② The hCG–antibody–enzyme complexes migrate farther up the stick until they bind to a second set of anti-hCG antibodies that are immobilized in a "test region." The enzyme then reacts with a coating on the stick to produce a colored line, indicating that the woman is pregnant.

③ Antibodies that have not bound any hCG migrate past the test region without being held up, and bind to a second set of immobilized antibodies in a "control region," causing a colored line to appear there. This control line confirms that the test is working properly, not that the woman is pregnant.

Test region

Control region

Liquid phase

Solid phase

Urine

Urine migrates up strip

Test region

Control region

End of test strip

◆ hCG

Y Mouse antibody to hCG, bound to enzyme

Y Mouse antibody to hCG, bound to solid phase

Y Goat antibody to mouse antibodies, bound to solid phase

Figure 10.1 How a home pregnancy test works. The user holds one end of the test stick in her urine stream for a few seconds (or dips it in a collected specimen).

who has been monitoring her basal body temperature as a means to determine her "fertile window" (see below) may notice that her temperature stays high, rather than falling as it usually does at the end of the luteal phase. None of these signs is foolproof either, however, and this is why pregnancy tests are important.

Pregnancy tests detect the presence of hCG in the mother's blood or urine. The most sensitive (and expensive) laboratory test is a **radioimmunoassay,** which can detect hCG in the mother's blood almost immediately after implantation—several days *before* a woman would notice a missed period. The more usual laboratory tests, which use enzyme-linked antibodies, detect pregnancy with about 98 percent accuracy at the time of the missed period. To get a laboratory test, a woman must see a health care provider.

Another option is to purchase a home pregnancy test kit. These kits, which also use enzyme-linked antibodies (Figure 10.1), are convenient, inexpensive, and popular—about 19 million kits were sold in 1999. A variety of brands is available, ranging in price from about $7 to $17. These tests are quite sensitive; most can detect pregnancy by the first day after a missed period, and some can do so 3 days *before* a missed period.

Unfortunately, home pregnancy tests are not nearly as reliable as laboratory tests. Although most of the products claim "99 percent accuracy," that figure refers to their use by professionals in unrealistic laboratory conditions. In real-world use, at least 25 percent of home test results are incorrect (Bastian et al., 1998). The main problem is a high rate of false negatives: test results indicating that the woman is not pregnant when in fact she is. False negatives can occur because of too-early testing, too-dilute urine, or failure to follow the instructions exactly. A false negative result can cause a woman to postpone getting prenatal care, and may lead her to continue the consumption of alcohol or drugs that are capable of harming the embryo (see below). Thus it is a good idea to follow up a negative test with a second test a few days later; to facilitate retesting, some test kits are available as two-packs. There is a great need for a more reliable home pregnancy test.

The secretion of hCG is presumptive evidence of pregnancy. There is a slight possibility that it might instead be due to the presence of a tumor that secretes hCG. Definitive clinical evidence of pregnancy can be obtained at 5–6 weeks by means of an **ultrasound** or **ultrasonographic scan.** This technique generates an image using high-frequency sound waves that are reflected off structures within the mother's body. It can determine whether there is one or more embryos, and by 2–3 weeks later it can detect the fetal heartbeat.

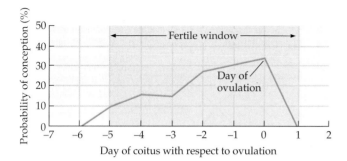

Figure 10.2 The likelihood of conception depends on when coitus occurs with respect to the day of ovulation. (After Wilcox et al., 1995.)

The Likelihood of Pregnancy Can Be Maximized by Tracking Ovulation

For a typical healthy young couple who are having sex several times a week without any form of contraception, there is about a 70 percent chance of pregnancy within the first 6 months. If the woman does not become pregnant within a year, the couple is described as **subfertile.** This doesn't mean that there is no further chance of pregnancy, but rather that an investigation to find out why pregnancy has not occurred is warranted.

There are many steps that a couple can take to increase the chances of pregnancy. The most important concerns the *timing of coitus* with respect to the woman's menstrual cycle. Coitus is most likely to result in pregnancy when it takes place on the same day as ovulation: there is about a 33 percent chance of success on that day (Wilcox et al., 1995) (Figure 10.2). Because sperm survive in the female reproductive tract for several days, pregnancy can also result from coitus up to 5 days prior to ovulation, but there is a lower likelihood of success. At 5 days prior to ovulation, the chance of success drops to 10 percent. It is unlikely, though not impossible, that pregnancy will result from coitus on any other day of the cycle.

To take advantage of this information, a couple needs to know the day of ovulation. If a woman has a very regular cycle that is near 28 days in length, it may be sufficient simply to count the days from the beginning of the previous menstrual period: Assuming that the luteal phase lasts approximately 14 days, the total cycle length minus 14 days gives the approximate interval from the beginning of menstruation to the next ovulation.

A more accurate method of estimating the day of ovulation is to track **basal body temperature.** To use this technique, the woman measures her temperature with a digital thermometer or a special-purpose BBT thermometer every morning before getting up. Typically, a woman's basal body temperature is relatively low during the follicular phase (say, about 97.6°F, or 36.4°C), dips slightly on the day of ovulation, and rises sharply to a level above the follicular phase level (say, to 98.2°F, or 36.7°C) on the day after ovulation, staying high for the remainder of the luteal phase (Figure 10.3). What matters is the *change* in temperature, not the absolute temperature, which may vary from woman to woman and with the measurement technique being used.

Since the main indicator is the rise on the day *after* ovulation, when coitus no longer stands a good chance of leading to conception, it is not helpful for getting pregnant on that particular cycle. Rather, the woman has to follow her temperature over several cycles to determine the usual interval between the onset of menstruation and ovulation. This information can then be used to time coitus during future cycles.

If the basal body temperature does not show the mid-cycle rise, it is possible that ovulation is not occurring. If the rise is not sustained for at least 10–12 days, the luteal phase may not be long enough for pregnancy to be established (see below). These potential problems can be investigated and treated by fertility specialists.

Another way to estimate the time of ovulation is by examining the consistency of the **cervical mucus** present in the vagina. The woman takes a

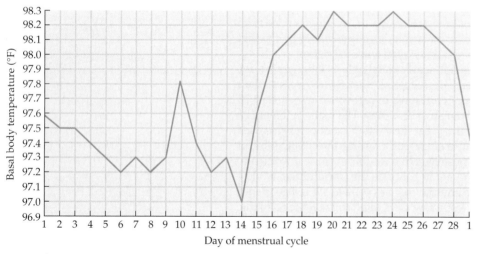

Figure 10.3 A typical basal body temperature chart for one menstrual cycle and the first day of the next cycle. Day 1 is the first day of menstruation. Ovulation (on day 14 in this example) is marked by a slight dip in temperature, followed by a rise of at least 0.4°F over the following 48 hours. The higher temperature is sustained for the duration of the luteal phase. Random spikes, such as the one here on day 10, are common and should be ignored. If the cycle is longer than 28 days, ovulation is likely to occur later than day 14.

sample of the mucus by inserting a finger into her vagina, or even simply by wiping her vulva with a tissue. Then she tests the stretchability of the mucus by touching her mucus-wetted finger to her thumb and gently separating them again. For about 2 days, ending on the day of ovulation or the day before, the mucus is clear and slippery, and it stretches out into a thin thread between finger and thumb, like raw egg white (Figure 10.4). During the rest of the cycle it is white and thick and does not stretch out into a thread, or there is no mucus present at all. With experience, these changes in the property of the mucus can be felt as changes in vaginal sensations, from dry or sticky to slippery and back, even without doing a digital test. The 2 days marked by the most stretchable mucus, and possibly the following day, are the most favorable times for coitus if pregnancy is desired.

Yet a third way to estimate the day of ovulation is to detect the surge in **luteinizing hormone (LH)** that begins about 36 hours before ovulation (see Chapter 4). Home test kits designed to detect the LH surge are available; they work in a similar fashion to home pregnancy tests. In over 90 percent of cycles, ovulation occurs within 2 days of the LH surge as detected by the kit, according to one study (Behre et al., 2000), so sex during those 2 days has a high likelihood of leading to conception.

Besides timing sex to coincide with ovulation, there are other steps that couples can take to improve their chances of pregnancy. The man's ejaculations should not be too frequent, otherwise the total number of sperm deposited during a single ejaculation may be too low; spacing ejaculations at 24-hour or 48-hour intervals may be optimal. Coitus should be in the man-above position; this seems to be the position that nature intended, because gravity helps the ejaculate pool near the cervix, rather than running out of the vagina, as can happen in the woman-above position. The woman should remain lying on her back, preferably with knees raised, for half an hour after coitus. Also, douching before sex should be avoided. (This does *not* mean that frequent ejaculation, the woman-above position, or douching are effective contraceptive techniques—see Chapter 11.)

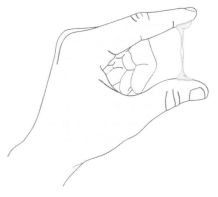

Figure 10.4 Cervical mucus test. For about 2 days prior to ovulation, the cervical mucus can be drawn out into a thread between finger and thumb.

Infertility Can Result from Problems in the Woman or in the Man

Subfertility and **infertility** (total inability to achieve pregnancy) are surprisingly common. About 15 percent of couples have enough difficulty establishing a pregnancy that they seek medical attention. Fertility problems are about equally likely to be caused by a disorder on the man's side or on the woman's side. Occasionally there is a problem on both sides. In about 25 percent of cases the cause cannot be identified.

A Variety of Factors Can Reduce Sperm Counts

The most common group of conditions affecting fertility is characterized by insufficient or poor-quality sperm in the man's semen. Sperm-related problems are the cause of about 25 percent of all couples' difficulties with achieving pregnancy. The usual rule of thumb is that a man is likely to be subfertile (i.e., have difficulty becoming a father) if there are fewer than 20 million sperm per milliliter of semen or if the fraction of the sperm that have normal motility is less than 50 percent.

A recent detailed study (Guzick et al., 2001) found that sperm count, sperm motility, and sperm morphology all affect a man's fertility, but that each parameter has a "gray zone" within which his fertility is difficult to predict (Table 10.1, Figure 10.5). The gray zone is narrowest for sperm morphology, making it the best indicator of fertility; it is widest for sperm count, making it a relatively poor indicator. Nevertheless, sperm counts are easy to perform, so many studies of fertility focus on this parameter.

What causes insufficient or defective sperm? There are actually many possible causes. Undescended testicles, sex chromosome anomalies, infections that cause blockage of the reproductive tract, and intensive chemotherapy can

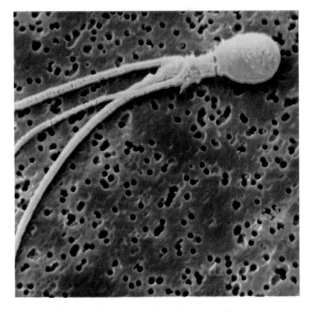

Figure 10.5 Abnormal (multi-tailed) spermatozoon. Up to 88 percent of a man's spermatozoa can have abnormal morphology, as shown in this electron micrograph, without affecting his fertility. Scoring of abnormalities is rather subjective, however, so the same man's semen may get different scores in different clinics.

TABLE 10.1 *Characteristics of semen affecting fertility*

	Subfertile range	"Gray zone"	Fertile range
Ejaculate volume (ml)	<1	1–2	>2
Sperm count ($\times 10^6$/ml)	<13.5	13.5–48	>48
Sperm with normal morphology (%)	<9	9–12	>12
Sperm with normal motility (%)	<32	32–63	>63

Source: Data for sperm count, morphology, and motility are from Guzick et al., 2001; data for ejaculate volume are from Johnson & Everitt, 2000.

all cause irreversible reduction or failure of spermatogenesis. Heating of the testes, as can occur with too-tight clothing or with strenuous exercise, causes a lowered sperm count that is usually reversible. Environmental toxins can also cause lowered sperm counts, and they are suspected to have contributed to a general reduction in sperm counts in the population of the United States and other countries over the last several decades (Box 10.1).

Various steps can be taken to achieve pregnancy in cases of problems with sperm quality. If sperm numbers are too low, semen can be collected over a period of time and frozen. Then the entire collected amount can be placed in the woman's vagina or directly into her uterus at a time coinciding with ovulation. This procedure is usually called **artificial insemination by the husband (AIH),** although the man could equally be the woman's cohabitational partner. Men with normal sperm counts may also sometimes store their own sperm for future AIH use. They may do this in advance of medical procedures that could affect their fertility, such as chemotherapy, radiation treatments, or surgery on the testes or reproductive tract (including sterilization: see Chapter 11).

In Vitro Fertilization Can Circumvent Many Sperm Problems

Some sperm quality problems may require the use of **in vitro fertilization (IVF),** a technology introduced by British researchers in 1978. "In vitro" means "in glass"—in a petri dish, in fact. In the standard IVF procedure (Figure 10.6), the woman is given hormones to promote the development of a batch of follicles on a precisely timed schedule. When the follicles are nearly ready to ovulate, a fine needle is passed into each one under ultrasound control, and the oocyte is flushed out. As many as two dozen oocytes can be harvested in a single procedure. The collected oocytes are placed in a petri dish, and the man's sperm are then added. Only a small number of sperm are needed because no long-distance migration is involved. This procedure costs about $8000 for a single cycle.

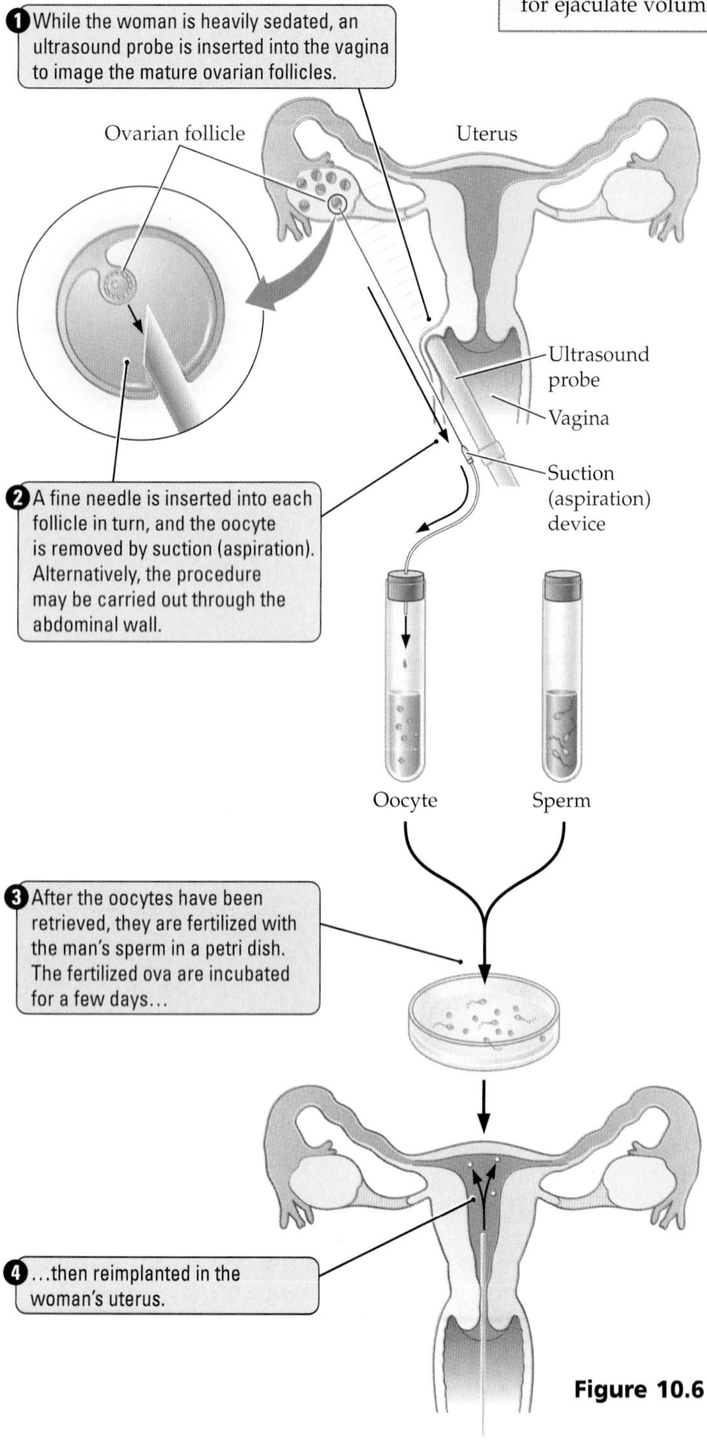

1 While the woman is heavily sedated, an ultrasound probe is inserted into the vagina to image the mature ovarian follicles.

Ovarian follicle

Uterus

Ultrasound probe

Vagina

Suction (aspiration) device

2 A fine needle is inserted into each follicle in turn, and the oocyte is removed by suction (aspiration). Alternatively, the procedure may be carried out through the abdominal wall.

Oocyte

Sperm

3 After the oocytes have been retrieved, they are fertilized with the man's sperm in a petri dish. The fertilized ova are incubated for a few days...

4 ...then reimplanted in the woman's uterus.

Figure 10.6 Standard in vitro fertilization procedure.

Box 10.1 Research Highlights

Are Sperm Counts Declining?

In 1992 a Danish research group published some disturbing news about male fertility (Carlsen et al., 1992). According to their meta-analysis of about 61 prior studies that employed standardized sperm-counting techniques (Figure A), average sperm counts in several Western countries dropped by nearly one-half between 1940 and 1990—from 113 to 66 million sperm per milliliter of semen (ml). This drop was accompanied by a drop in ejaculate volume (from 3.4 to 2.75 ml) and by an increase in the prevalence of certain male reproductive disorders, such as undescended testicles (cryptorchidism) and testicular cancer. A continuation of this trend in the future would significantly reduce male fertility within a few decades.

The Danish findings have been contested. In 1999, for example, a group at Columbia University in New York argued that the apparent fall in sperm counts in the United States was an illusion caused by variations in where the sampling was done (Saidi et al., 1999). Specifically, many of the early U.S. studies were done in New York, where (according to the New York researchers, at least) sperm counts are higher than in the rest of the country. (You are free to speculate on the reasons for this finding.) The later studies were done in other cities, such as Los Angeles, where sperm counts are said to be lower.

Another, even more extensive meta-analysis was published in 2000 by a group led by Shanna Swan of the University of Missouri (Swan et al., 2000). This study basically confirmed the original Danish claim (Figure B) and presented new evidence that the decline has continued at least through 1996. Another Danish study reported that the median sperm count in unselected young Danish men is now only 41 million per ml (Andersen et al., 2000). This level is already in the "gray zone" within which fertility may be affected (see Table 10.1). Furthermore, a French group found that sperm counts measured at a single sperm bank in Paris declined markedly between 1973 and 1992, belying the Columbia group's geographic explanation (Auger et al., 1995). Thus the decline in sperm counts appears to be real, although further research to verify the phenomenon is certainly warranted.

If the decline is real, what is causing it? One trivial explanation—more frequent ejaculation—has been ruled out by studies that control for the length of abstinence prior to specimen donation. Lifestyle changes such as the increased popularity of tight-fitting pants and underwear, which keep the testes too warm, are a possible cause. Most attention, however, has been

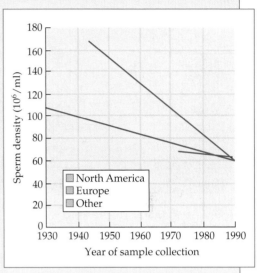

(B) Sperm counts have declined fastest in Europe, more moderately in North America, and barely at all in other parts of the world, according to a reanalysis of 101 prior studies by Swan et al. (2000). The reliability of this conclusion depends on a variety of assumptions, such as that the measurement techniques have remained constant over time. Some researchers have contested these findings. (After Swan et al., 2000.)

focused on the possibility that the decline is caused by environmental pollutants, especially by "endocrine disruptors"—agricultural pesticides and other industrial chemicals that mimic or antagonize sex hormones (see Box 4.4). Agricultural workers do suffer a decline in sperm counts that is related to their degree of pesticide exposure (Abell et al., 2000). Whether endocrine disruptors are responsible for the decline in the general population is less certain (Juberg, 2000). However, the steep declines in agricultural countries such as Denmark, where pesticide use is intense, suggest this possibility.

(A) Sperm are counted in a precisely calibrated chamber called a hemocytometer. In spite of the standardization of methods, slight variations in counting procedures could result in a false impression of changing sperm counts over time.

If the man's sperm are not capable of performing even this simplified task, further variations on IVF are available. A hole can be drilled through the zona pellucida to allow direct access to the oocyte (**zonal drilling**). One or several spermatozoa can be injected into the space between the zona and the oocyte (**subzonal insemination**). Or a single spermatozoon

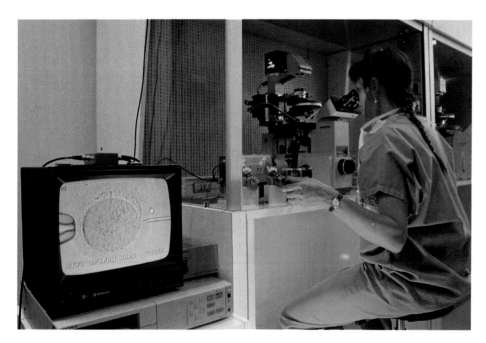

Figure 10.7 Intracytoplasmic sperm injection. The technician uses a stereomicroscope and micromanipulators to perform the procedure. As may be seen on the video monitor, the oocyte (in the center of the screen) is immobilized by gentle suction from a flat-tipped pipette (at left). A sharp, fine-tipped pipette (at right) is then inserted through the zona pellucida and a single spermatozoon (not visible) is injected into the oocyte's cytoplasm.

can be injected via a micropipette directly into the cytoplasm of the oocyte (**intracytoplasmic sperm injection** or **ICSI**) (Figure 10.7). With this technique, introduced by Belgian researchers in 1991, even nonmotile or otherwise defective sperm can be used. In fact, even a man who produces no mature sperm at all may be able to father a child: haploid precursor cells can be harvested by needle aspiration of the man's testis and used instead. ICSI has greatly increased the number of infertile men who can become fathers, but there remains some concern that the oocyte could be damaged by the procedure (Hewitson et al., 1999).

Regardless of the exact IVF procedure used, the artificially fertilized oocytes are usually kept in tissue culture for several days, during which time they divide several times (Figure 10.8). It is possible at this stage to remove a cell or two from the conceptuses without harming them; the sex and genetic makeup of the removed cells can then be determined. This **preimplantation genetic screening** procedure is useful if one of the parents carries a disease-causing gene and the couple wants to ensure that their child does not inherit it.

A number of conceptuses—usually about four—are then placed in the woman's uterus simultaneously, in order to maximize the chances that at least one of them will implant. If several implant, the woman is offered the opportunity to have the number reduced by abortion (often euphemized as "fetal reduction"), but this practice presents ethical problems for some women. Most of the high-number multiple births that have attracted headlines over the past few years involve mothers who have undergone IVF or other assisted reproduction procedures (see below) and have declined abortion. High-number multiple pregnancies are associated with all kinds of serious risks to the fetuses and the mother; only a few have the happy outcomes that the media like to focus on. Thus, in one study of 11 high-number multiple pregnancies (mostly quadruplets), 9 of the 48 fetuses were stillborn, and at least 9 of the remainder suffered disabilities that were still evident at the age of 2 years (Lipitz et al., 1990).

A more common problem, however, is not multiple fetuses, but zero fetuses. Nearly four out of five IVF attempts do not lead to a successful pregnancy, so couples may have to repeat the procedure several times, at mounting expense, and with no guarantee of ultimate success. The prospects are particularly poor for women over 40, only about 8 percent of whom will achieve a successful pregnancy after a single IVF attempt (Centers for Disease Control, 2001a). Still, over 45,000 babies have been born by IVF in the United States since the technique was introduced here in 1981.

Another set of ethical issues revolves around surplus conceptuses that are not placed in the uterus. These conceptuses may be discarded or stored in a frozen state for later use, but some have become the subject of legal battles when couples split up. In addition, medical researchers would like to use the unwanted conceptuses to obtain **embryonic stem cells,** which are believed to have many potential medical uses. Political and ethical considerations have hindered this use, even though conceptuses that are not used will simply be thrown away.

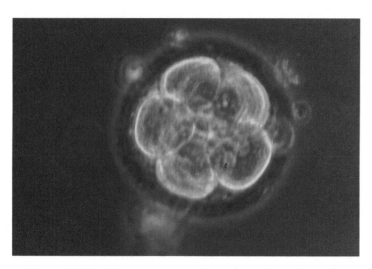

Figure 10.8 A human conceptus, 3 days after in vitro fertilization. At this stage, the conceptus consists of about 8 cells. Note that the cells are still confined within the original zona pellucida. The conceptus can be reimplanted at this stage, allowed to mature further in vitro, or frozen for future use.

In an alternative procedure that does not leave any surplus conceptuses, oocytes are harvested from the woman as before, but they are placed directly in the woman's **oviducts** (fallopian tubes), along with sperm from the man. Fertilization then takes place in the oviduct. This procedure is called **gamete intrafallopian transfer** (**GIFT**).

There remain some questions about the safety of IVF and related procedures (collectively known as **assisted reproductive technology,** or **ART**). Some studies have reported that babies born as a result of ART have an increased likelihood of suffering from neurological abnormalities, other major congenital abnormalities, or low birth weight (Schultz and Williams, 2002). If further studies repeat these findings, ART techniques need to be refined to reduce these risks.

Sperm Can Be Donated

Sometimes the male partner is completely sterile, or the couple does not want to use his sperm, as, for example, when he carries a gene for a serious disorder. Some single women also want to become pregnant, as do some women who are partnered with other women. In all such cases, women can use **artificial insemination by donor** (**AID**). In this procedure, sperm from a third party are placed in the woman's vagina or uterus. **Sperm banks** provide suitable semen at fairly low cost. Sperm donors are usually college students who are paid a small fee to donate semen (by masturbation). The donors are screened for heritable medical problems (in themselves or their families) and for infections such as human immunodeficiency virus (HIV) that might be transmitted to the recipient woman. Information about potential donors' physical appearance, field of work or study, and other interests is usually available to potential recipients.

Some women, especially lesbians, may arrange the whole matter themselves with the help of a male friend and a turkey baster. Although this option is simple and inexpensive (99¢ for the baster), it is probably a bad idea for both medical and legal reasons. The donor may not be adequately screened for genetic problems or communicable diseases, and there may be future disagreements about the donor's rights or obligations vis-à-vis any child who is produced.

Abnormalities of the Female Reproductive Tract Frequently Reduce Fertility

The second most common group of conditions affecting fertility is characterized by abnormalities of the woman's reproductive tract. Such conditions are responsible for about 20 percent of infertility cases. The commonest site of abnormalities is the oviducts. They can become scarred, obstructed, or denuded of cilia as a consequence of **pelvic inflammatory disease**—a general term for infections of the uterus or oviducts, usually caused by sexually transmitted organisms such as chlamydia or gonorrhea (see Chapter 16). Another condition that can interfere with fertility is **endometriosis,** in which endometrial tissue grows at unusual locations, such as on the oviducts or ovaries (see Chapter 17). Although surgery can sometimes restore fertility in such conditions, it often fails to do so. In such cases it is possible to take the oviducts out of the equation by performing IVF and placing the resulting conceptuses directly in the uterus.

Failure to Ovulate Can Be Dealt with by Drugs or by Oocyte Donation

Another 20 percent or so of infertility cases are caused by problems with ovulation. We discussed the failure to begin menstrual cycles at puberty—**primary amenorrhea**—in Chapter 5. A postpubertal (but premenopausal) woman may also stop cycling (**secondary amenorrhea**) or cycle irregularly (**oligomenorrhea**). These conditions can be caused by weight loss, athletic training, stress, certain drugs, a pituitary tumor, or reduced ovarian sensitivity to gonadotropins (**idiopathic anovulation**). Sometimes, failure to ovulate can occur in a woman who is experiencing normal menstrual periods. This condition can be diagnosed on the basis of a low level of progesterone during the luteal phase. Most ovulatory problems can be reversed by lifestyle changes, psychotherapy (if the cause is an eating disorder, for example), or drug treatment.

One drug commonly used to treat ovulatory problems is **clomiphene** (Clomid, Serophene, or generic versions). This drug is an estrogen antagonist; by binding to estrogen receptors in the hypothalamus, it blocks estrogen's negative feedback effect on FSH secretion (see Chapter 4), so FSH levels rise and promote the maturation of ovarian follicles. Another estrogen antagonist, tamoxifen, may be used for the same purpose. Sometimes these drugs work too well: 5–10 percent of clomiphene-induced pregnancies are twins (compared with about 1 percent of normal pregnancies), and up to 1 percent are higher-number multiple pregnancies, which normally occur very rarely.

If the woman's oocytes cannot be used, oocytes can be obtained from donors. Obtaining oocytes from female donors is more complex and expensive than sperm donation, however, because the donor must undergo hormone treatment followed by oocyte aspiration, as described above for IVF. There are certain risks for the donor, including the risk of injury or infection associated with the procedure itself, the risk of unwanted pregnancy (because the donor cannot use oral contraceptives during the period before the donation), the risk of psychological trauma, and a possible negative effect on future fertility (Healy, 1998). Still, over 7000 donated oocyte transfers were performed in the United States in 1998. The donors—who are often college students—are typically paid a few thousand dollars. For both sperm and oocyte donations, there is a market for donors who are perceived to be genetically superior, and higher fees may be paid in such cases, especially for oocytes (Box 10.2).

Surrogate Mothers Bear a Child for Someone Else

If the woman cannot sustain a pregnancy at all—say, because her uterus is malformed or has been removed, or because her general medical condition makes pregnancy inadvisable—an option is to use a **surrogate mother.** Gay male couples who wish to have children may also resort to this option. In **traditional surrogacy** the surrogate agrees to be artificially inseminated with semen from the man, and she then carries any resulting fetus or fetuses to term. If the woman who cannot sustain a pregnancy can nevertheless produce oocytes, those oocytes can be fertilized with the man's sperm by IVF and then implanted in the surrogate. This procedure is called **gestational surrogacy.** In a further wrinkle on gestational surrogacy, the oocytes used for IVF may be taken from neither the infertile woman nor the surrogate, but from a third woman whose genes are considered preferable to those of the surrogate.

Either way, when the child (or children) is born, the surrogate gives it up for adoption by the couple. The surrogate is paid a large sum—usually about $18,000 plus expenses—and the total cost to the couple is about $60,000. Although detailed contracts spell out the various parties' obligations, surrogacy can be a psychological and legal minefield, and there is some question about the propriety of a rich couple using a (usually) poor woman's body to carry their child.

As an example of the problems that can arise, a California couple, attorneys Charles Wheeler and Martha Berman, used the Internet to search for a woman who would be willing to carry a fetus for them (Reuters News Service, 2001a). The woman was to be implanted with oocytes that were donated by a third woman and fertilized in vitro with Wheeler's sperm. Helen Beasley, a British legal secretary and single mother, agreed to carry the fetus for about $19,000. A verbally agreed-upon condition was that, if it turned out that she was carrying more than one fetus, Beasley would have any excess fetuses aborted before 12 weeks of pregnancy. The implantation succeeded, but when she was 8 weeks pregnant, she told the couple that she was carrying twins. According to Beasley, the couple did nothing for several weeks, but when she was 13 weeks pregnant, they told her to abort one of the fetuses.

Beasley refused, claiming that it was too late for a safe abortion, and the couple therefore washed their hands of the matter, saying that they would not take the twins. Beasley moved to San Diego to give birth there. In August of 2001 she filed a breach-of-contract and fraud suit against Wheeler and Berman, demanding that they take the twins and pay her unspecified damages. The case, which has not yet come to trial, highlights a difficult legal and ethical question: Who is the responsible parent, the person who initiates the surrogacy and pays all the expenses, or the woman who actually bears the fetus (or fetuses)?

Box 10.2 *Society, Values, and the Law*

Designer Gametes

Most women who donate oocytes for IVF are motivated principally by the desire to help infertile couples have a baby, and are paid quite modestly—about $2000 to $3000 per procedure. But some wealthy couples are willing to lay out much larger sums for donors who they think will produce oocytes of exceptional genetic quality. Their hope, of course, is to have unusually gifted or attractive children. This desire has led to the development of a cutthroat market for "über-eggs." Ads in college newspapers (Figure A) now mention payments of $50,000, $80,000, or even $100,000 for suitable donors. Few, if any, women have actually received payments at these levels, which are largely advertising hype, but payments of $20,000 or so are not uncommon. At this level, a young woman can pay her way through college with a few donations.

- **Are you a healthy woman between the ages of 19–30?**
- **Would you like to give childless couples the chance to have a family of their own?**
- **Do you want to earn up to $25,000 toward your college tuition?**

If you answered yes to these questions, contact Collegiate Fertility Services, Inc. You must be willing to take medication and to undergo minor surgical procedures.

(A) Ads seeking oocyte donors often highlight the generous financial remuneration involved.

What does it take to be a high-end donor? Beauty, brains, athletic achievement, and social skills, probably in that order. The ads demand SAT scores at the 1300+ level or even higher, and it helps if the woman is an accomplished cellist and track star, won the Intel Science Talent Search, and is fluent in Norwegian and Japanese. The "beauty" part is fuzzier, but probably more important; there may be an advertised height and race requirement, but everything depends on the reactions of the couple when they meet the potential donor. "You look even more gorgeous than the pictures," was one couple's reaction to meeting Rachel, a tall, strawberry blonde graduate student with a creamy complexion and blue-green eyes. Rachel earned about $18,000 for that "donation," and has done others at a higher price since (Weiss, 2001).

The American Society for Reproductive Medicine has serious reservations about the commercialization of oocyte donation. The society's ethics committee has laid out several concerns (American Society for Reproductive Medicine, 2000). High payments may be essentially coercive, causing women to ignore their own psychological reservations or the possible risks of the procedure. This may be particularly true for women of limited means or with high expenses, such as students at the Ivy League colleges where much of the recruitment is done. Women facing such large inducements may conceal negative aspects of their medical or family history. Another concern is that the payments devalue human life by turning human tissues into commodities; payment for organ donations is widely prohibited for this reason. Furthermore, paying high prices for "genetically favored" gametes may imply that all humans do not have equal intrinsic worth, contrary to the values that many Americans hold dear. And last, high prices may ultimately restrict oocyte transfers to the very rich.

For all these reasons, the Society recommends that compensation be limited to $5000 unless special circumstances justify a higher amount, and that no payment should be above $10,000. It is clear, however, that some agencies are ignoring these limits. And while greed no doubt plays a role in this, one can make the countervailing ethical argument that high payments increase the total number of donors, to everyone's benefit.

There is also a market for "superior" sperm—usually from men with high intellectual attainment. For many years the focus of this activity was the Repository for Germinal Choice in Escondido, California. The Repository—a nonprofit organization—was founded in 1980 by Bausch and Lomb executive Robert Graham, who invented the shatterproof plastic eyeglass lens. It distributed sperm from Nobel Prize winners, including William Shockley, co-inventor of the transistor (Figure B) and other high achievers. Shockley, who was widely reviled as a white supremacist, thought that the future of our society was threatened by the low rate of reproduction by people of high intelligence; sperm donation was his way of countering that trend.

The Repository has since gone out of business, but another outfit, Heredity Choice, continues to offer semen from prominent scientists and others. For four of the eight donors in one of the lists from this company, it is stated that the donor's offspring "resemble their mothers [in physical appearance]."

(B) Seen a younger version of this man—Nobelist William Shockley (1910–1989)—in your neighborhood? Maybe it's one of the tireless sperm donor's offspring.

This is, of course, what couples want—a child who can pass as their own but who has the intellect of the genetic father. Unfortunately, there is little reason to believe that certain men's sperm confer their father's mental qualities while allowing the mother's looks to dominate. If it turns out the other way around, will the couple love their child as much, or will they feel resentful? Another problem with using sperm from high-achieving men is that such men tend to be relatively old—several of Heredity Choice's donors are in their fifties. Sperm quality decreases with age, and the American Society for Reproductive Medicine's guidelines state that donors should be under 40.

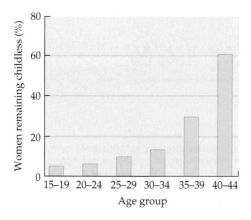

Figure 10.9 Age and infertility. The graph shows the percentage of women who remain childless after first marriage in spite of continued efforts to produce a child, grouped by age at marriage. Note that the likelihood of infertility rises rapidly in the mid-thirties. (After Johnson and Everitt, 2000.)

Adoption Is Limited by the Supply of Healthy Infants

Adoption is a low-tech but often very successful way for infertile couples to have children. The main problem with adoption from the perspective of would-be parents is a severe shortage of the preferred adoptees—that is, healthy infants of the same race or ethnicity as themselves. Excluding adoptions between relatives, the number of adoptions in the United States has decreased greatly over the last 30 years, and is now only about 50,000 per year (Stolley, 1993). The main reason for the decline is the greater willingness of unmarried mothers to keep their babies, but legalized abortion and better access to contraception may also have played a role. Older or "special-needs" children (i.e., children with disabilities or other medical or psychological problems) are much more readily available; so are sets of siblings who want to be adopted together. Sixty percent of children awaiting adoption in the United States are from racial or ethnic minorities. Given the shortage of the preferred adoptees, many American couples adopt children from abroad, even though this usually involves 1–3-year waiting periods. The cost of adoption varies from zero (for special-needs children) to $15,000–20,000 for an adoption from abroad.

Fertility Declines Steadily with Age

A major factor affecting fertility is age. You might imagine that couples stay completely fertile until the woman's menopause, whereupon fertility drops to zero. In reality, fertility drops off steadily starting in young adulthood, as shown in Figure 10.9. Already by their mid-thirties about one in four couples is infertile. This decline in fertility has several causes, including more frequent failure of ovulation, decreasing sperm counts and sperm quality, and an increased likelihood of spontaneous abortion early in pregnancy.

Children who are born to older parents, especially older mothers, also stand a greater risk of having chromosomal abnormalities. One of these is **Down's syndrome,** caused by an extra copy of chromosome 21 (i.e., three copies instead of two). (The syndrome is named for John Down, the nineteenth-century British physician who first described it.) It usually includes mild or moderate mental retardation and a characteristic facial appearance including a flat facial profile, a depressed nasal bridge, and a small nose (Figure 10.10). It affects 1 in 885 births at a maternal age of 30, but the rate gradually increases

(A)

(B)

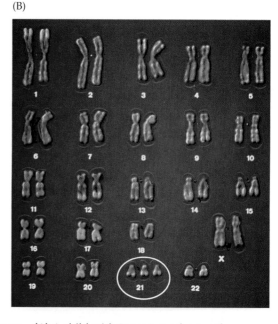

Figure 10.10 Down's syndrome. (A) A child with Down's syndrome; the syndrome is marked by a characteristic facial appearance and sometimes by other physical anomalies. (B) Chromosomes in a person with Down's syndrome, showing the three copies (circled) of chromosome 21 (trisomy 21).

to 1 in 25 births at a maternal age of 45 and older. There are about 350,000 people with Down's syndrome in the United States. Screening for Down's syndrome is recommended when the mother is 35 or older. Because the great majority of babies are born to younger women, however, and because these women are typically not screened during pregnancy, 4 out of 5 children with Down's syndrome are born to women *under* 35.

Chromosomal abnormalities increase with maternal age because the mother's oocytes remain "frozen" in their first meiotic division from early in her fetal life (see Chapters 2 and 4). As the decades roll by, the meiotic apparatus loses its integrity, and the chromosomes may therefore be misapportioned when cell division is finally completed. Down's syndrome usually occurs when a copy of chromosome 21 that should have been jettisoned into a polar body remains in the secondary oocyte, so that the mother contributes two copies and the father contributes one.

Increasing paternal age also raises the chances that a child will have certain medical problems. These problems include dwarfism, Marfan's syndrome (a connective tissue disorder), neurofibromatosis (abnormal growth of nerve tissue), and prostate cancer. A recent study from Israel added schizophrenia to the list (Malaspina et al., 2001). Genetic anomalies in a man's sperm increase over his lifetime because the sperm precursor cells are constantly dividing to produce new sperm. Thus, an older man's sperm are the product of a greater total number of cell divisions, and each round of DNA replication carries some finite risk of introducing a harmful mutation. Nevertheless, most children of older fathers are healthy.

While we are on the topic of birth defects, the question often comes up as to whether a parent with a birth defect is likely to pass that defect on to his or her children. A Norwegian study of 8000 women with birth defects found that their children were between 5 and 82 times more likely than control children to have the same defect as their mother, but no more likely to have other defects. The association was clearest for cleft palate, cleft lip, clubfoot, and limb defects (Skjaerven et al., 1999). Nevertheless, 96 percent of the children of these mothers were free of any defects. The effects of birth defects in fathers have not been well studied.

Women's menstrual cycles may become irregular in their early or mid-forties. This is the onset of the **climacteric,** the period of transition from fertility to infertility, which may last as long as 10 years. The final termination of menstrual cycles, or **menopause,** occurs at an average age of 51 or 52 in the United States. We will have more to say about the physiological and psychological changes associated with menopause in Chapter 12.

A postmenopausal women can become pregnant with the aid of reproductive technology: donated oocytes can be fertilized in vitro (usually with her husband's sperm) and the conceptuses placed in her uterus. The pregnancy must be supported with hormone treatments. The oldest woman known to have become a mother by this procedure was Arceli Keh, who gave birth to a healthy daughter at Loma Linda University Medical Center in 1996, when she was 63 years old (Paulson et al., 1997). She had lied to her doctors about her age, representing herself as 10 years younger.

Many Conceptuses, Especially Those with Abnormalities, Do Not Survive

Nature has not completely mastered the difficult task of creating a normal embryo. Some large fraction—perhaps more than 50 percent—of all human conceptuses are genetically abnormal and have little or no chance of giving rise to a viable child. The commonest of these abnormalities are three or four entire sets of chromosomes instead of two (triploidy or tetraploidy), three copies of a particular chromosome instead of two, as in Down's syndrome (trisomy), or one copy of a particular chromosome instead of two (monosomy). Trisomies and monosomies may affect either the autosomes or the sex chromosomes. (Sex chromosome anomalies were discussed in Chapter 5.)

Most of these defects occur at the very earliest stages of development. Triploidy, for example, results from fertilization of the oocyte by more than one sperm or from complete failure of a polar body to form. In some cases, environmental factors such as alcohol consumption, general anesthesia, or X-ray exposure around the time of ovulation may trigger chromosomal abnormalities.

The great majority of abnormal conceptuses are lost at some point in their development. Many fail to implant, and the mother is never aware of their existence. Others implant briefly, causing a transient release of hCG and a slight prolongation of the luteal phase, but then die, so that menstruation ensues. Of pregnancies that proceed far enough to be detected clinically, about 20 percent are subsequently lost by spontaneous abortion, usually during the first 3 months. At least half of all spontaneously aborted embryos and fetuses have chromosomal abnormalities, whereas only 0.5 percent of live-born babies have them.

What about the spontaneous abortions that have no obvious genetic cause? Some of these may be caused by more subtle genetic defects in the fetus. There are also a variety of maternal problems that can lead to fetal loss, however. Malformations of the reproductive tract constitute one such group of problems. Also, women with immunological disorders such as **systemic lupus erythematosus** have a high risk of spontaneous abortion.

Rhesus Incompatibility Can Threaten Second Pregnancies

One major immunological cause of fetal loss is blood group incompatibility, especially when the fetus possesses the blood group antigen known as **Rh (rhesus factor)** and the mother does not. Rh, like other blood group antigens, is a molecule on the surface of red blood cells. In cases of **Rh incompatibility** the fetus will have inherited the factor from its father. The combination of Rh-negative mother and Rh-positive father is common—it is the case for about 10 percent of all couples in the United States—but only a minority of their pregnancies are marked by problems. These problems arise when the mother develops antibodies against Rh and those antibodies cross the placenta and attack the fetus. This does not happen routinely because the fetus is immunologically isolated from the mother. Nevertheless, the mother may develop anti-Rh antibodies at childbirth if the fetus bleeds into the maternal circulation during delivery. These antibodies develop too late to affect that child, but they may attack a subsequent fetus, destroying its red blood cells and rendering it severely anemic (**fetal erythroblastosis**). Such an attack can kill the fetus or newborn child, or it can leave the child mentally retarded.

Luckily, the initial immune response to a mother's first Rh-positive fetus can be blocked by administration of a Rh-specific immunoglobulin, either soon after delivery or during the pregnancy itself. By binding to Rh, the immunoglobulin hides it from the maternal immune system. If fetal erythroblastosis does occur in a subsequent pregnancy, the fetus or the newborn child may have to undergo a blood transfusion.

Ectopic Pregnancy Can Endanger the Mother's Life

Another serious condition that causes fetal loss is implantation of the fetus at a location other than the uterus (**ectopic pregnancy**) (Tay et al., 2000) (Figure 10.11). This happens in about 1 percent of all pregnancies. The most common sites of ectopic pregnancy are the oviducts ("tubal pregnancy"), but other possible sites include the cervix, the ovary, or elsewhere within the abdominal cavity.

Ectopic pregnancies can be caused by congenital malformations of the oviducts or uterus, by damage to the oviducts resulting from pelvic inflammatory disease or appendicitis, or by treatment with certain sex steroids and contraceptives that interfere with the normal movement of the conceptus into the uterus. The cause of most cases is not known, however. The rate of ectopic pregnancy is increasing, and the main culprit is the increasing prevalence of pelvic inflammatory disease due to chlamydia infections (see Chapter 16).

Ectopic pregnancy commonly leads to early spontaneous abortion. Alternatively, as the embryo grows, it may cause internal hemorrhage or rupture of an oviduct, both of which are emergencies that threaten the mother's life. Recognition of the condition is hampered by the fact that the woman may not know she is pregnant—the symptoms can appear within 3 weeks of the beginning of pregnancy. Therefore, if a woman is of childbearing age and has engaged in coitus recently, and she experiences abdominal pain (often severe and one-sided), shoulder pain (caused by irritation of the diaphragm), pain on defecation or urination, abnormal vaginal bleeding (e.g., a watery but dark discharge), or signs of shock (faintness, nausea, rapid pulse, feelings of dread), she should see a doctor right away.

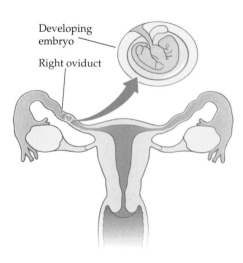

Developing embryo

Right oviduct

Figure 10.11 Ectopic pregnancy can occur in the oviduct (as shown here), on the ovary or cervix, or elsewhere.

Ectopic pregnancy can usually be diagnosed by an ultrasound scan, or by monitoring the levels of pregnancy hormones in the blood. If these hormones rise more slowly than in a normal pregnancy, an ectopic pregnancy is suspected. The condition is treated surgically or with a drug (methotrexate) to induce abortion. Whatever the woman's views on abortion, she should bear in mind that an ectopically implanted embryo cannot survive under any circumstances, so her only choice is whether or not to safeguard her own health. Even if one oviduct has to be removed, which is often the case, the woman can still become pregnant via the other one. She has an elevated risk of experiencing another ectopic pregnancy, and therefore needs to be monitored closely, but 90 percent of subsequent pregnancies are located normally in the uterus.

Pregnancy Is Conventionally Divided into Three Trimesters

Let's return to the happier topic of normal pregnancy. First of all, how long does a normal pregnancy last? The figure usually given is 266 days from ovulation to birth, but this seems to be an underestimate, at least for white women under private medical care in the United States. For women in this category who have not given birth previously (**primiparous** women), the median duration of pregnancy is 274 days, which is 9 calendar months. For women who have given birth previously (**multiparous** women), it is 269 days (Mittendorf et al., 1990).

Usually, a woman does not know the precise date of the ovulation that led to her pregnancy, but only the date of onset of her last menstrual period. This takes place about 14 days before ovulation, so a primiparous woman's "due date" is about 288 days—or 9 calendar months plus 2 weeks—after the onset of her last menstrual period. This is a week later than the date given by the often-cited **Naegele's rule,** which says that a woman's due date is 9 calendar months plus 1 week after the onset of her last menstrual period. For multiparous women, the due date is 9 calendar months plus 9 days from the onset of the last period, which is close to Naegele's rule. Eighty percent of natural births occur within 2 weeks before or after the due date; only births occurring outside those limits are considered "premature" or "delayed."

The fact that two different starting dates can be used to "time" pregnancy leads to some confusion. A fetus's age can be given either as a **gestational age** (i.e., timed from ovulation) or as a **menstrual age** (timed from the last menstrual period) (Figure 10.12). We use gestational ages here, but you will see menstrual age used quite often, especially in materials prepared for expectant mothers.

Women do not always recall the date of their last menstrual period. If not, the age of the fetus can be determined within 2 or 3 days by measurement of its size with an ultrasound scan during its early period of rapid growth.

In Chapter 5 we divided prenatal life into three phases of unequal duration, in which the developing organism is referred to first as a conceptus, then as an embryo, and finally as a fetus. In the context of prenatal care, however, pregnancy is usually divided into three **trimesters,** each of them three calendar months long. These time periods do not correspond to any particular biologically significant milestones, but are simply convenient ways to refer to early, middle, and late pregnancy. The growth and appearance of the fetus over the first half of pregnancy is shown in Figure 10.13.

The Fetus Secretes Sex Hormones to Sustain Pregnancy

As we saw in Chapter 5, the fetus takes control of its mother's body in many respects. It is true that the mother's ovarian hormones—especially progesterone and estrogens—are initially required to bring the uterine lining (endometrium) into a state that can sustain implantation. However, the conceptus usurps this system, first by secreting hCG, which prevents the corpus luteum from regressing and therefore keeps progesterone levels high, and later by secreting its own supply of estrogens and progesterone.

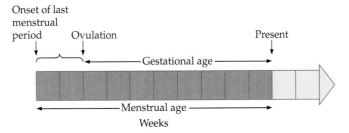

Figure 10.12 Gestational and menstrual age. A fetus's gestational age is about 2 weeks less than its menstrual age.

Figure 10.13 Embryonic and fetal growth and changes in appearance through the fifteenth week of pregnancy.

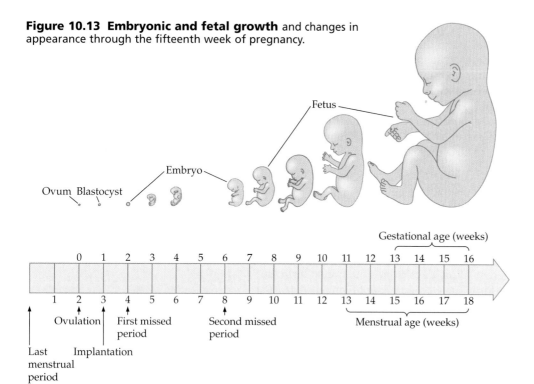

These hormones enter the mother's circulation, eventually rising to levels not experienced at any other time of her life. Their main role is to sustain the endometrium, but they also prepare the uterine musculature for childbirth and the breasts for lactation. Estrogens are secreted by the fetus's adrenal glands, and progesterone is secreted by the fetal side of the placenta. Thus, by less than 2 months into a pregnancy, the mother's ovaries can be removed and the pregnancy will continue normally.

Women May Experience Troublesome Symptoms during Early Pregnancy

The first trimester is in many ways the most significant period of pregnancy. During this time, as described in Chapter 5, the conceptus implants in the uterine wall and sets up a system of hormonal and metabolic communication with the mother. Then, in less than 2 months, it develops from a tiny, featureless plate of cells into a miniature human being with all its organ systems in place. By the end of the first trimester the fetus is about 10 cm in its longest dimension (crown–rump length) and weighs about 50 grams (1.75 ounces). The external genitalia have differentiated as male or female, and most of the fetus's organ systems are functioning in a rudimentary way.

The first trimester is an important period for the mother as well. She learns that she is pregnant, a piece of news that may bring delight or anxiety. She has to decide, perhaps in discussions with her partner, whether to continue the pregnancy or not. Assuming that she goes ahead with it, she is likely to experience some of the early symptoms of pregnancy, especially breast tenderness and morning sickness.

Breast tenderness is a sign that the breasts are already preparing for suckling the infant, even though it will be months before they are actually brought into service. Recall from Chapter 5 that the female breasts undergo a burst of development at puberty under the influence of rising estrogen levels. The rise of estrogen and progesterone levels during pregnancy, as well as the secretion of a prolactin-like hormone by the placenta, causes further growth of the alveoli, the tiny sacs that are lined with secretory cells. By the fourth month of pregnancy the alveoli contain small amounts of secreted material. By this time the breasts and nipples are noticeably larger and the areolae have often become wider and more deeply pigmented.

Morning sickness affects about half of pregnant women, but it varies in degree, from mild nausea upon awakening to persistent and even life-threatening vomiting. It is often associated with aversions to certain foods, especially strong-tasting foods and animal products (meats, eggs, and fish). Several studies have reported that women who experience vomiting are less likely to have a miscarriage than women who do not, suggesting that morning sickness has some positive value. It has been proposed that morning sickness evolved as a mechanism to protect the fetus from potentially toxic compounds in food during the critical first few weeks when its organ systems are developing (Flaxman & Sherman, 2000). Eating bland food does tend to alleviate the condition, which usually disappears by the end of the first trimester.

Other symptoms experienced by many women during the first trimester include frequent urination, tiredness, sleeping difficulties, backaches, mood swings, and sometimes depression. The woman's male partner may develop analogous symptoms, and may even gain weight faster than the pregnant woman. The phenomenon of pregnancy-like symptoms in men is known as **couvade.** (The average woman gains only about 1–2 kilograms [2–4 pounds] during the first trimester, and less than 50 grams of that is the fetus itself.)

Prenatal Care Provides Health Screening, Education, and Support

When a woman finds out that she is pregnant (if not before), she can take many practical steps to safeguard her own and her fetus's health. These steps include seeking out prenatal care, ensuring good nutrition, avoiding harmful substances, and learning about exercise and sex during pregnancy.

Numerous studies have shown that **prenatal care** benefits almost every aspect of pregnancy: it decreases the likelihood of maternal, fetal, or neonatal death, and fetal prematurity and low birth weight (Centers for Disease Control, 2001k). Unfortunately, prenatal care is not as universally accessible in the United States as it is in European countries. In 1999, 17 percent of pregnant American women received no prenatal care during the critical first trimester, and 4 percent received little or no care throughout their pregnancies. In spite of considerable improvements over the last decade, African-American and Hispanic women still tend to receive less prenatal care than white women, and suffer correspondingly high rates of adverse events during or following pregnancy. Teenage, unmarried, poor, and uneducated women are particularly likely to miss out on first-trimester care (Centers for Disease Control, 2001b).

What does prenatal care accomplish? Even before she becomes pregnant, a woman can be tested for her immunity to German measles (**rubella**). If a woman is not immune to this disease and contracts it during pregnancy, the fetus can suffer serious developmental defects, such as deafness and mental retardation. Therefore it is a good idea for a non-immune woman to be vaccinated before pregnancy begins. She can also be tested for HIV; this is important because the virus can infect the fetus during pregnancy or at birth, and antiretroviral therapy can diminish the risk that this will happen.

The first post-conception health care visit typically takes place soon after the first missed period. At this point the health care provider takes a history and does a general examination, a Pap smear, a cervical culture (to test for gonorrhea and other conditions), a rubella test if not done previously, and a test for blood type and Rh factor. A clinical pregnancy test may be done, even if the woman has already done a home pregnancy test. The provider advises the woman on nutrition and related matters (see below), answers her questions, and helps her make informed decisions about how to manage her pregnancy and childbirth.

On one or more occasions during the first trimester, the provider conducts a pelvic exam. This exam, which includes a visual check of the external genitalia and vagina as well as a digital palpation of the pelvic organs, should also be done annually when a woman is not pregnant, and we describe it in more detail in Chapter 17. In addition to the pelvic exam, many providers perform an ultrasound exam at some point during the first trimester, especially if there is some indication of a problem, such as bleeding. This exam permits determination of fetal age, the number of fetuses, and abnormalities such as ectopic pregnancy. It is not usually possible to discern the fetus's sex by ultrasound during the first trimester.

Adequate Nutrition Is Vital to a Successful Pregnancy

Producing a baby is an expensive proposition, metabolically speaking: it takes about 75,000 kilocalories (kcal; the "Calories" of common dietary usage), which averages out at about 250–300 kcal per day above what the mother needs to support herself. Most of that energy (65,000 kcal) goes toward fetal development; the remainder goes toward fat accumulation by the mother. At term (just before childbirth), a woman typically weighs 9–15 kilograms, or 20–35 pounds, above her pre-pregnancy

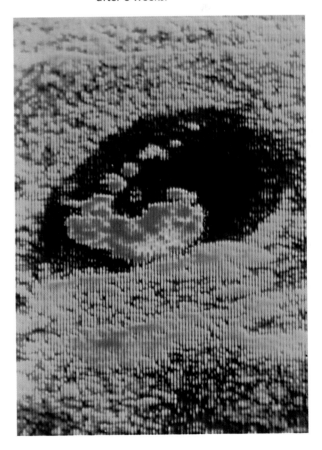

False-color ultrasound image of a fetus after 8 weeks.

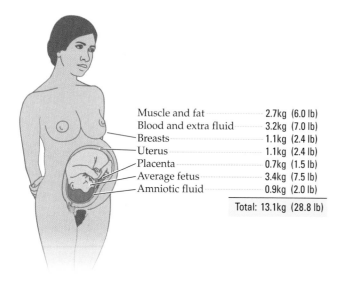

Muscle and fat	2.7kg	(6.0 lb)
Blood and extra fluid	3.2kg	(7.0 lb)
Breasts	1.1kg	(2.4 lb)
Uterus	1.1kg	(2.4 lb)
Placenta	0.7kg	(1.5 lb)
Average fetus	3.4kg	(7.5 lb)
Amniotic fluid	0.9kg	(2.0 lb)
	Total: 13.1kg	(28.8 lb)

Figure 10.14 Where do those extra pounds go?
The distribution of extra weight for a woman who gains 13.1 kilograms (28.8 pounds) during pregnancy.

weight; this includes the weight of the fetus, placenta, and amniotic fluid, as well as her own increased fat deposits, enlarged breasts, and increased volume of blood and tissue fluids (Figure 10.14). The ideal total weight gain varies with pre-pregnancy weight and height: overweight women should gain the least (7–11 kilograms, or 15–25 pounds) and underweight women the most (13–18 kilograms, or 28–40 pounds).

During the first half of pregnancy, most of the mother's extra energy consumption goes into her own fat deposits. During the second half of pregnancy, when the fetus is gaining weight rapidly, that maternal fat is used to supply the fetus with energy, so the mother herself is effectively in starvation mode (a negative energy balance), even though she continues to eat. Although mothers usually end pregnancy with more body fat than they started with, much of the excess may be consumed in the process of breast feeding (see below).

Women who start pregnancy with a normal weight (i.e., a body mass index* of 20–25) are in the best position to produce a healthy child (Cnattingius et al., 1998). Underweight women risk producing an underweight child, who is more likely to suffer a variety of medical problems. Being either underweight or overweight is associated with an increased likelihood of premature birth, which also may have adverse consequences for the child (see below). Women who are overweight face an increased risk of certain serious disorders during pregnancy, including diabetes and hypertension.

Besides sheer calories, a pregnant woman needs to consume adequate amounts of other nutrients, especially protein, calcium, iron, vitamin A (but see below), and folic acid (or folate). The fetus is adept at taking these nutrients from its mother and does not usually suffer any deficiency, but the mother may do so. Iron deficiency, for example, may cause the mother to become anemic. Severe folate deficiency during the first few weeks of pregnancy increases the likelihood that the fetus will have malformations of the nervous system and spinal column, such as **spina bifida.** Thus, supplements are often recommended for women who are or might become pregnant. Megadoses of vitamins should be avoided, however: excessive consumption of some vitamins, especially vitamins A and D, can cause birth defects or mental retardation.

Tobacco, Alcohol, Drugs, and Radiation Can Harm the Fetus

As well as consuming the right foods, a pregnant woman needs to avoid a number of agents that can harm the fetus (Table 10.2). Alcohol and tobacco head this list. Heavy alcohol consumption increases the likelihood of birth defects and infant mortality, and it is associated with a specific cluster of symptoms known as **fetal alcohol syndrome** (Thackray & Tifft, 2001). Children with this syndrome are small, have a characteristic facial appearance (Figure 10.15), and may be mentally retarded or have behavioral problems. There is some uncertainty as to whether consuming one or two drinks a day is harmful. Some studies have reported that as few as two drinks a day can have ill effects on the fetus, including reduced intelligence (Streissguth et al., 1990). For that reason, most experts recommend complete abstention from alcohol during pregnancy. Heavy alcohol consumption in early pregnancy has one apparent benefit: it halves the likelihood that a woman will give birth to a child with Down's syndrome (Torfs & Christianson, 2000). But that's not because it prevents or cures the syndrome: it merely increases the likelihood that a Down's-syndrome fetus will abort spontaneously.

Figure 10.15 A boy with fetal alcohol syndrome and his adoptive parents. Typical facial features include short eye slits, a flat mid-face, a short nose, an indistinct philtrum (groove between nose and lip), and a thin upper lip.

*The body mass index (BMI) is the woman's weight in kilograms divided by the square of her height in meters. Easy-to-use BMI charts are available on the Internet (for example, at www.niddk.nih.gov/health/nutrit/pubs/unders.htm).

TABLE 10.2	Examples of substances, organisms, and physical agents that can harm the developing fetus

Agent	Possible consequences
Drugs	
Alcohol	Fetal alcohol syndrome
Tobacco	Spontaneous abortion, prematurity, low birth weight, addiction of neonate, sudden infant death
Isotretinoin (Accutane)	Heart, brain malformations; mental retardation
Thalidomide	Limb defects, deafness, blindness
Vitamins A and D (in excessive amounts)	Fetal malformations
Androgens, estrogens	Abnormalities of external genitalia and reproductive tract, especially in females
Diethylstilbestrol (DES)	Reproductive cancers (females); reduced fertility (males)
Aspirin (late in pregnancy)	Interferes with blood clotting, potentially causing hemorrhage in mother, fetus, or neonate
Heroin	Spontaneous abortion, low birth weight, respiratory depression of neonate, addiction of neonate
Cocaine	Neonatal intoxication and addiction
Infections	
Rubella	Damage to ears, eyes, heart
Genital herpes	Spontaneous abortion, premature birth, birth defects
HIV	AIDS in infancy/childhood
Chlamydia	Premature birth, neonatal eye infection
Physical agents	
X rays	Increased risk of childhood cancer
Nuclear radiation	Increased risk of childhood cancer
Cosmic radiation (high-altitude flight)	Possible increased risk of childhood cancer, for very frequent flyers
High body temperature (over 38°C or 100.4°F) in early pregnancy (from fever, excessive exercise, saunas)	Variety of birth defects

Smoking is one of the most harmful practices a woman can engage in during pregnancy. It increases the likelihood of spontaneous abortion, premature birth, low birth weight, and congenital malformations. Its ill effects continue after a child is born: 25 to 40 percent of all cases of sudden infant death syndrome can be attributed to the mother's smoking during pregnancy (Pollack, 2001; Wisborg et al., 2000), and babies whose mothers smoke during pregnancy have a 59 percent higher chance of dying during infancy than those born to nonsmokers (Centers for Disease Control, 2002b). Unfortunately, about one in eight American women smokes during pregnancy; younger white women are especially likely to do so (Centers for Disease Control, 2001l). It is testimony to the addictive power of tobacco that, even though its ill effects on fetal health are widely known, only about 20 percent of female smokers actually quit during pregnancy (Floyd et al., 1993).

Many drugs—including prescription, over-the-counter, and recreational drugs—can harm the fetus (Koren et al., 1998). The most notorious **teratogenic** (malformation-inducing) drug is **thalidomide,** which caused thousands of babies to be born with serious birth defects (mostly in Europe) in the late 1950s and early 1960s. The drug has recently been reintroduced under strict controls to prevent its use by women who are or who may become pregnant, but the possibility of misuse is still a matter of concern (Lary et al., 1999). We described the ill effects of **diethylstilbestrol** (**DES**) in Chapter 5. Another dangerous teratogenic drug is **isotretinoin** (Accutane, Roaccutane), used for the treatment of severe acne. Because teenage girls have high rates of both acne and unintended pregnancy, the possibility of disaster is real, in spite of intensive educational programs (Jones et al., 2001). Isotretinoin is chemically related to vitamin A (see below). **Addictive drugs** such as cocaine, heroin, and nicotine cause the baby to be born in an addicted state, as well as having other harmful effects. A pregnant woman, or one who may become pregnant, should discuss all drugs she is taking with her doctor; often, drugs that are harmful to the fetus or whose safety has not been established can be replaced with safer ones.

Vitamin A, though essential for normal fetal development, can cause malformations in excessive doses (National Institutes of Health, 2001). Of particular concern is "preformed vitamin A," which is present in liver and eggs and is often added to breakfast cereals, nonfat milk, and other foodstuffs (check the ingredient list for "retinyl palmitate," "vitamin A palmitate," or similar compounds). Pregnant women should limit their intake of these substances to 100% of the recommended daily allowance. Beta-carotene, which is present in many vegetables and can be converted to vitamin A in the body, is of minor concern.

Another agent that can harm the fetus is **radiation.** X rays during pregnancy should be avoided if possible, but the chances of ill effects are low, so the medical benefits of the X ray may outweigh the risks in some cases. Medical or occupational exposure to nuclear radiation should also be avoided. Exposure to cosmic radiation may be a significant issue for pregnant women who work as flight crew on commercial airliners, especially on high-altitude flights and polar routes, where the radiation flux is highest (Friedberg et al., 2000). It does not present a hazard to pregnant passengers, except possibly the most frequent business travelers.

The Second Trimester Is the Easiest

The second trimester begins at 13 weeks of gestational age. Most women experience the second trimester as a period of calm and well-being. Morning sickness and most of the other unpleasant symptoms of early pregnancy usually disappear. Only the need for frequent urination persists, and in fact may become worse as the enlarging uterus presses on the bladder. Signs of pregnancy become obvious: the abdomen swells, stretch marks may begin to appear, and the breasts may expel small amounts of colostrum (see below).

Around the middle of the second trimester the mother will begin to feel the fetus's movements. This event, known as **quickening,** has always had great psychological significance—it is a major step in the bonding of the mother (and perhaps other family members) with her child. In early Christian doctrine, quickening marked the entry of the soul into the fetus, so that abortion before quickening was not necessarily a sin. The beginning of fetal movement does not mean that the fetus is now a conscious being, however: the cerebral cortex, which is probably the main locus of consciousness, is still at an extremely rudimentary stage of development at the time of quickening.

Specialized Tests Can Detect Fetal Abnormalities

At prenatal care visits during the second trimester, the health care provider monitors the fetus's growth and well-being. In addition, tests may be done to check for congenital disorders. These tests may include ultrasound scans, amniocentesis, and chorionic villus sampling. These procedures can also be used to determine the fetus's sex (Box 10.3).

An ultrasound scan done at the beginning of the second trimester, or slightly earlier, can come up with evidence suggestive of congenital abnormalities, including Down's syndrome. One particular feature of the fetus—the thickness of the skin fold at the neck—is particularly correlated with the likelihood of Down's syndrome and other anomalies. When the measurement of this skin fold (called a **nuchal translucency test** or **nuchal fold test**) is combined with biochemical tests, about 90 percent of fetuses with Down's syndrome can be identified. Ultrasound tests of this kind, done at about 10–14 weeks of pregnancy, are becoming a common part of prenatal care.

Box 10.3 Society, Values, and the Law

Choosing Children's Sex

As they plan for pregnancy, many couples would prefer their child to be of one particular sex, male or female. Sometimes their preference has specific medical reasons. In particular, if the child is at risk of inheriting a genetic disorder that crops up predominantly in one sex, the couple may want a child of the other sex. This usually means a girl, because most sex-linked disorders affect boys. The explanation for this is that most sex-linked disorders result from defective genes on the X chromosome. Girls have two X chromosomes, so a defective gene on one is usually compensated by a normal version on the other. Boys have only one X chromosome, so defective X-linked genes cannot be compensated and therefore cause disease (see Chapter 5).

More commonly, couples want a child of a particular sex for some social reason. For example, they may have one or more children of one sex and now want to "balance" the family with a child of the other sex, perhaps with the thought that it is good for a brother to have a sister, or vice versa. In such a case, obviously, it might be either a girl or a boy that they want.

Somewhat more troubling is the general social preference for boys in many cultures. Boys are preferred because they will help with farm work, because they will bring money into the family, or because their children will carry on the family name. Girls are less desired in some cultures because marrying them off requires heavy bridal payments or because they may be essentially lost to their birth family after marriage. Some people do prefer girls—often because they are seen as easier to raise—and many have no preference, but boys are preferred over girls in nearly all countries. The figure shows people's preference for a boy or a girl in 16 countries. Interviewees were asked "Suppose you could only have one child. Would you prefer that it be a boy or a girl?" Interviewees that expressed no preference are omitted. The data for India probably understate the preference for boys, because the large rural population, where the traditional preference for boys is strongest, was not sampled. (Data from Gallup Organization, 1997.)

In the past, there have been many superstitions about how to have a child of a particular sex, but only one technique actually worked: killing or abandoning newborn children of the unwanted sex. Female infanticide was common in feudal China and is said to be still practiced in China today, partly as a consequence of that country's strict one-child policy (Jowett, 1990). The practice may have abated recently in response to a partial easing of the policy (Pan, 2002).

Since the 1960s it has been possible to determine the sex of a fetus long before birth. As we already mentioned in Chapter 5, the nuclei of most cells in females contain a dense clump of genetic material called a **Barr body.** Fetuses slough off cells into the surrounding amniotic fluid, and these cells can be sampled by amniocentesis. Sex determination by amniocentesis is somewhat invasive and costly, however, and was usually done only where there was a question of a genetic disorder.

The introduction of obstetric ultrasonography has made it a simple and inexpensive matter to visualize a fetus's genitals and hence to determine its sex. This can be done as early as 12–14 weeks post-conception. As a consequence, sex-selective abortion is now an option, even for poor people in developing countries. In fact, the practice of aborting females has become so prevalent in India and China that the sex ratio of newborn children has become noticeably skewed toward males (Coale & Banister, 1994; Khanna, 1997). In China, for example, about 119 male births are registered for every 100 female births, and in some parts of India the ratio is 126:100 (Dugger, 2001). The natural sex ratio at birth is about 105:100, at least for Western populations. Thus there is a looming shortage of marriageable women in both those countries. The only good thing one can say about this is that the shortage is likely to raise the perceived value of women and thus to hasten the end of discriminatory practices such as bridal payments.

Simply telling pregnant women their fetus's sex late in pregnancy, when abortion is not an option, can cause problems. In a study conducted in Egypt, women who were informed that their fetuses were not of the sex they wanted experienced significantly more medical difficulties during labor than women who remained ignorant of their fetus's sex (Kamel et al., 1999).

Considerable efforts have been devoted to developing techniques for selecting a child's sex before conception. Because the

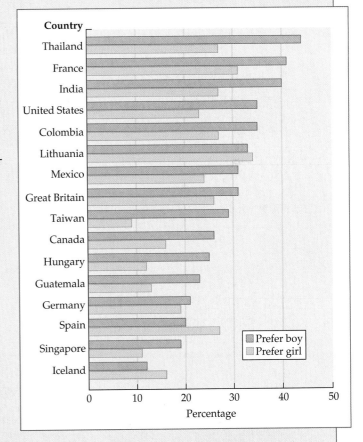

fetus's sex is determined by whether the oocyte is fertilized by an X-bearing or a Y-bearing sperm (see Chapter 5), researchers have attempted to sort out the two kinds of sperm from the roughly equal mixture that exists in semen. This is a difficult task, however, since the X and Y chromosomes, like

Box 10.3 (continued)

all the sperm's chromosomes, are inactivated during spermatogenesis and hence do not produce any antigens or other markers that could be used to identify the sperm that carry them.

For that reason, researchers have focused on the sperm's total DNA content: because X chromosomes are larger than Y chromosomes, X-bearing sperm contain about 2.9 percent more DNA than Y-bearing sperm. This difference can detected, though not with complete accuracy, by a technique called **flow cytometry.** In this technique, sperm are labeled with a fluorescent dye that binds to DNA, then made to flow one by one past a laser detector. Re-

searchers at the Genetics and IVF Institute in Fairfax, Virginia, have achieved partial separation of X- and Y-bearing sperm with this method. They have then used X- or Y-enriched fractions of sperm to inseminate women who desire a girl or a boy, respectively. The researchers claim over 90 percent success with girls; results with boys are only slightly better than chance (Fugger, 1999; Fugger et al., 1998).

A more complex, but more reliable, method of selecting a child's sex is by preimplantation genetic screening. Several conceptuses are produced by in vitro fertilization, and only conceptuses of the preferred sex are implanted in the woman's uterus.

Although this is mostly done to avoid sex-linked diseases, some fertility clinics are said to offer this service for the purpose of "family balancing."

As with so many issues in the area of reproductive technology, the possibility of selecting children's sex triggers strong reactions. Some say that the practice is morally offensive or will have bad social consequences, such as a skewed sex ratio (Fletcher, 1983). Others say that it is a good idea because children will be more like what their parents want, and therefore more loved. Some say the practice should be banned; others believe it should be left up to the mother, or to both parents, to decide (Cowan, 1992).

If the nuchal translucency test is positive, or if there are other reasons to be concerned about fetal abnormalities, such as advanced maternal age or a history of abnormalities in previous pregnancies, more invasive tests may have to be done. In **amniocentesis** (Figure 10.16A), the doctor first determines the precise position of the uterus and the fetus with an ultrasound scan, then passes a thin needle through the front wall of the abdomen into the amniotic sac in which the fetus is floating, avoiding the fetus itself. A sample of the amniotic fluid, containing some free-floating cells derived from the conceptus (i.e., from the fetus or its membranes) is withdrawn. These cells are then grown in tissue culture and examined for chromosomal abnormalities. The fluid itself is tested for a protein called **alpha-fetoprotein,** whose levels are raised if the fetus has a neural tube defect such as spina bifida. Amniocentesis is sometimes done as early as 9 weeks

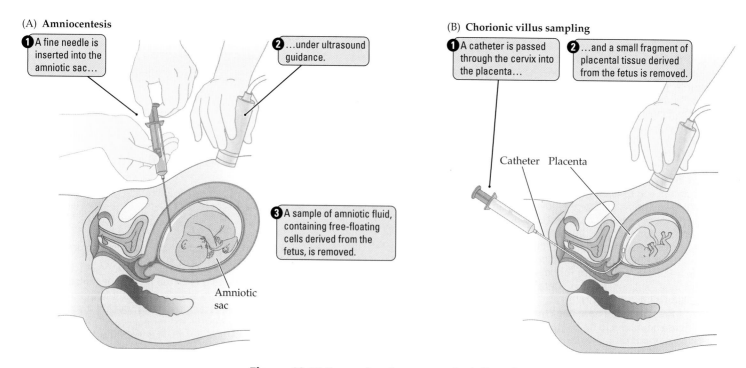

(A) **Amniocentesis**

❶ A fine needle is inserted into the amniotic sac...

❷ ...under ultrasound guidance.

❸ A sample of amniotic fluid, containing free-floating cells derived from the fetus, is removed.

Amniotic sac

(B) **Chorionic villus sampling**

❶ A catheter is passed through the cervix into the placenta...

❷ ...and a small fragment of placental tissue derived from the fetus is removed.

Catheter   Placenta

Figure 10.16 Screening for congenital disorders.

post-conception, but a more usual time is around 15 weeks. The procedure carries a slight risk (about 1 in 300) of causing a miscarriage.

An alternative to amniocentesis is **chorionic villus sampling** (Figure 10.16B). In this procedure, a catheter is passed through the cervix and a sample of tissue is taken from the placenta. The procedure may also be done with a needle passed through the abdominal wall. Chorionic villus sampling can be done a little earlier than amniocentesis, and the sampled cells can be examined directly rather than being placed in tissue culture first. Thus the results are obtained significantly earlier than with amniocentesis, which is an important consideration if the results cause the mother to choose abortion. Unfortunately, chorionic villus sampling carries a slightly higher risk of causing a miscarriage than does amniocentesis.

Some indication of the presence of fetal abnormalities can also be obtained by measuring the levels of various hormones and metabolites in the mother's blood. Such testing is usually done early in the second trimester.

In the great majority of cases, the outcome of these tests is reassurance that the baby is probably healthy. Unfortunately, a few women do receive the devastating news that their fetus has a severe abnormality, and must decide how to respond to that information. In such cases, most women choose to abort the fetus—partly because women who are opposed to abortion under any circumstances tend not to seek prenatal testing in the first place. Most women who have had a fetus diagnosed with an abnormality will have a normal fetus in a subsequent pregnancy, but the risk of having a second abnormal fetus may be raised if the condition is a genetic one. A genetic consultation can clarify this risk.

Sex during Pregnancy Is Healthy

As the second trimester rolls on, the mother will have switched to looser clothing to accommodate her expanding belly, but otherwise the progress of her pregnancy at this time is fairly uneventful. One topic that couples often think about as the mother grows larger is sex: is it a good idea in the latter half of pregnancy? In particular, can it harm the fetus? The answer is that, in a normal pregnancy, the fetus is well protected from anything the couple might do during sex. About the only way that sex can harm the fetus is if the mother acquires a sexually transmitted disease from her partner. Such diseases can be transmitted to the fetus during pregnancy or as the fetus passes through the birth canal.

It has been widely thought that sex late in pregnancy may increase the likelihood of premature childbirth, but in one recent study, women with normal pregnancies who had sex in late pregnancy were significantly *less* likely to have their babies prematurely than women who did not (Sayle et al., 2001). That doesn't mean that sex has a protective effect—it was probably just that the healthier women in the study were both more likely to enjoy sex *and* less likely to go into labor prematurely. In spite of these reassuring findings about normal pregnancy, women who are at high risk for premature labor should probably desist from coitus about 4 weeks before their due date.

Regardless of whether sex in late pregnancy is safe for the fetus, it may be less than satisfactory for the couple. Sexual activity generally drops off markedly during pregnancy. In one prospective study of first pregnancies (Robson et al., 1981), sexual activity dropped off in the first trimester, remained level over the second, and then dropped off again in the third, when only 38 percent of women engaged in one or more acts of coitus per week (Figure 10.17). Marital conflict, depression affecting the mother, a history of previous miscarriages, and the couple's belief that sex could harm the fetus were all linked to a decrease in sexual activity during pregnancy.

Couples who do continue to have sex late in pregnancy can make it more enjoyable by exploring new positions (Figure 10.18). The man-above position generally becomes awkward; the side-by-side position may be preferred (see Chapter 8). If coitus is uncomfortable in any position, manual or oral contacts may be excellent alternative ways to make love.

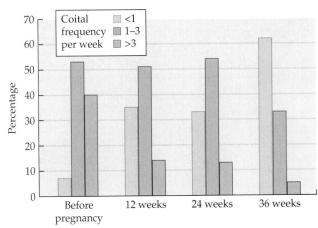

Figure 10.17 Pregnancy puts a damper on sex. The graph shows the percentage of women who engaged in coitus at the stated frequencies before and during their first pregnancies. (Data from Robson et al., 1981.)

Moderate exercise is beneficial for pregnant women. Swimming and brisk walking are recommended.

Moderate Exercise during Pregnancy Is Beneficial

Another issue that concerns some women is exercise. Traditionally, pregnant women were thought of as fragile creatures who needed to be spared any kind of exertion. It's now clear that, except in the case of certain problem pregnancies, exercise has a positive value in maintaining the woman's health and sense of well-being. It is especially useful in counteracting backache, constipation, mood swings, and sleeplessness.

The American College of Obstetricians and Gynecologists (ACOG) recommends that pregnant women engage in moderate, low-impact forms of exercise, such as brisk walking and swimming. ACOG adds two caveats: first, a woman should avoid doing exercises that involve lying on her back after 20 weeks of pregnancy, and second, she should avoid exercises that significantly raise her body temperature, especially during the first trimester or when she has a fever already. That's because high maternal temperatures may increase the likelihood of fetal abnormalities and may also cause dehydration, which can overstress the mother's already hardworking cardiovascular system. If a woman experiences pain, dizziness, excessive shortness of breath, uterine contractions and chest pain, or bleeding or fluid loss from the vagina, she should stop exercising and see her doctor.

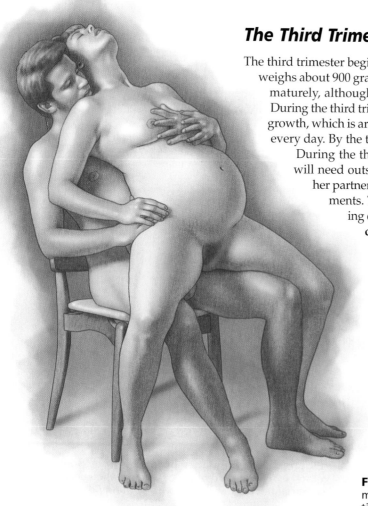

The Third Trimester Is a Time of Preparation

The third trimester begins at 26 weeks of gestational age. At this time, the fetus already weighs about 900 grams (2 pounds) and has a decent chance of surviving if born prematurely, although its survival would require weeks of intensive neonatal care. During the third trimester, the fetus increases rapidly in weight; at the time of fastest growth, which is around 33 weeks, the fetus is putting on about 50 grams (2 ounces) every day. By the time of birth it has reached about 3.2 kilograms (7.1 pounds).

During the third trimester, the fetus practices many of the behaviors that it will need outside its mother, including breathing. The mother, and possibly her partner too, may be awakened frequently at night by its vigorous movements. The mother's uterus also "practices" for childbirth by undergoing occasional, irregularly spaced contractions. These **Braxton-Hicks contractions** (or **false labor**) are normal and do not endanger the fetus. Only if the contractions come at regular intervals and become gradually more frequent, stronger, and longer-lasting need a woman be concerned that true labor is beginning.

Women's experience of the third trimester varies greatly. Some women sail through it serenely, while others are overwhelmed by physical problems (backache, urinary frequency, fatigue, or sleeplessness) or by anxiety about childbirth and motherhood. Couples may find themselves bonding more closely than at any previous time in their relationship, or there may be increasing tension. Depression is not uncommon at this time: about one in eight middle-class women experiences clinical depression during the weeks before she gives birth (**antepartum depression**), as does one in four impoverished

Figure 10.18 Sex during the later stages of pregnancy may be facilitated by a willingness to try new positions or activities other than coitus.

inner-city women (Hobfoll et al., 1995). Understandably, depression is particularly common among women who do not have a partner.

A Hospital Is the Best Location for Childbirth if Problems Are Foreseen

More positively, the third trimester is a time of preparation for birth. By this time, the mother will probably have already decided where to have her baby. If it is her first baby, she and her partner should be taking classes in preparation for the birth.

Concerning where to have the baby, there are three choices: at home, in a hospital, or (in some areas) in a stand-alone facility known as a **birthing center.** Most births in the United States take place in hospitals. The great advantage of this location is the immediate availability of medical expertise and equipment in case anything goes wrong. The disadvantage is that a hospital can be a relatively impersonal and sometimes intimidating environment, and the mother may feel that less attention is paid to her wishes for the birth process than if she were in her own home.

Many hospitals have taken steps to make their childbirth facilities more welcoming and to involve the woman and her partner in decision making. They may have "birthing rooms"—rooms that are more homelike and less clinical than traditional delivery rooms. Hospitals now encourage the presence of the woman's partner at the birth—sometimes even if the baby has to be delivered by cesarean section (see below). Most hospitals also encourage immediate mother–child contact after the birth, so long as there are no serious medical problems that make that impracticable.

A birthing center (if one is available) offers a compromise between hospital and home. However, it may be staffed by midwives rather than by obstetricians (Box 10.4), and it will not have the same equipment as a hospital. Thus it may still be necessary to move the mother to a hospital if complications arise. For that reason, a birthing center that is part of a hospital complex may be preferable to one that is some distance away.

An important consideration influencing the choice of location for a birth is the estimated likelihood of complications. The health care provider will advise the mother to have her child in a hospital if labor begins prematurely, if the fetus is not optimally positioned for birth, if there is more than one fetus, if the mother's pelvis is unusually narrow, or if there exist any other medical conditions that increase the risk of complications. For low-risk pregnancies, there are no good studies comparing the outcome of home and hospital births; research in this area is needed. In the meantime, there is no reason why the mother's (and her partner's) wishes concerning the birth location should not be respected.

Childbirth Classes Prepare Parents for Birth

Many different kinds of childbirth classes are available to parents. Besides providing general education about pregnancy, childbirth, and infant care, many of these classes incorporate the ideas of the French "prepared childbirth" pioneer Fernand Lamaze (Lamaze, 1981). Reacting against the use of general anesthetics during labor, which was widespread in the 1950s and 1960s, Lamaze asserted that women could experience a pain-free childbirth without anesthetics. His followers today do not make such an extreme claim (Lamaze International, 2002). The **Lamaze method** teaches breathing exercises, techniques for relaxing abdominal and perineal muscles, and techniques for focusing attention away from (or reinterpreting) potentially painful sensations during labor. His method takes advantage of the fact that the transmission of painful signals to the brain is "gated" by other sensory inputs and by attentional mechanisms. Thus, a non-painful sensory stimulus, such as the tactile sensation produced by light fingertip massage of the abdomen or thighs (**effleurage**), reduces the perceived intensity of simultaneous painful signals from the uterus or birth canal. Similarly, the woman can cause painful sensations to recede by focusing visual attention on something in the environment, such as a picture on the wall, by listening to words spoken by her partner, or by imagining pleasant scenery or experiences.

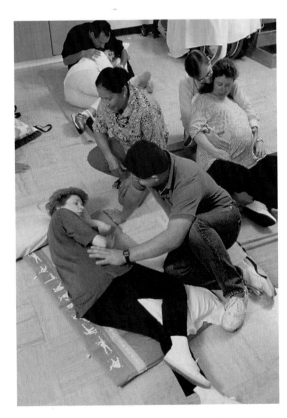

Childbirth classes help expectant mothers and their partners prepare for the physical and psychological demands of labor.

Box 10.4 *Sexual Health*

Childbirth Professionals

A variety of trained professionals provide childbirth care. All M.D.s receive a basic grounding in obstetrics (childbirth medicine), and there are still some family doctors for whom delivering babies is a regular part of their general practice. An **obstetrician,** on the other hand, is a physician who specializes in obstetrics or in the combination of obstetrics and gynecology. Besides being an M.D., she or he is usually board-certified in obstetrics and gynecology, or working toward certification. Most obstetricians work in hospitals, but some work at birthing centers.

A **nurse-midwife** is a registered nurse with specialized training, degrees, and usually certification in midwifery (childbirth care). She may work in a hospital (where she often has sole responsibility for uncomplicated births), at a birthing center, or at the mother's home. A **traditional midwife** does not have formal training, but has learned by apprenticeship to an experienced midwife. In developing countries, over 60 percent of babies are delivered by traditional midwives (Piper, 1997). A **doula** is a woman who is trained to help and emotionally support the mother during and after childbirth, but does not perform the delivery herself (Klaus & Kennell, 1997). The doula's role can also be played by the woman's partner.

Other professionals who may specialize in childbirth include obstetric surgeons, anesthesiologists, and technical personnel who run monitoring equipment.

Lamaze teachers do not oppose anesthesia during labor if it seems necessary, and a fair proportion of women who take Lamaze classes do receive some kind of anesthesia. Another type of childbirth preparation, the **Bradley method,** stresses "natural" childbirth and places a lot of weight on the role of the woman's partner as "birth coach." Although developed by a physician, it is more anti-medical in flavor than the Lamaze method, and women who take classes based on the Bradley method are less likely to accept anesthesia or other medical interventions during labor than women who take Lamaze classes (Monto, 1996).

Most hospital-based childbirth classes do not closely follow either the Lamaze or the Bradley model, but are based on the experience of the people teaching them. They tend to be eclectic, practically oriented, and responsive to the parents' needs, rather than being based on some overarching theory of childbirth management.

One form of childbirth that has gained some popularity recently is water birth. The mother (often with her partner and midwife) sits in a pool or tub of warm water during delivery, and the baby is born underwater. (The baby is smart enough not to take a breath until it is brought above the water surface.) The advantage of this style of childbirth is said to be its gentleness. Some hospitals and birthing centers have birthing tubs available, or they can be rented.

The Fetus Also Makes Preparations for Birth

While the parents are preparing themselves for childbirth, so is the fetus. Although the fetus's growth rate slows dramatically after 33 weeks, its organ systems undergo rapid maturation. Much of this preparation for birth is orchestrated by **corticosteroids** secreted by the fetus's adrenal glands. In response to hormonal instructions from the fetus's hypothalamus and pituitary glands, the adrenals pump out increasing amounts of corticosteroids during the third trimester, and there is a particularly significant surge of these hormones about a month before birth. Among their effects are important changes in the lungs, which synthesize large amounts of **surfactant.** This soapy substance reduces the sur-

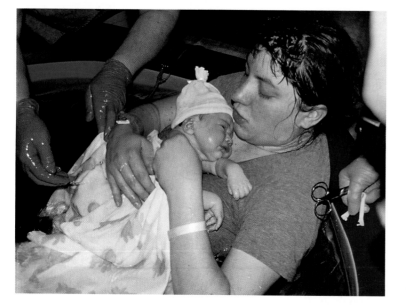

A water birth

face tension of fluids in the lungs, thus facilitating the inflation of the lungs when the newborn takes its first breath of air. Corticosteroids also instruct the fetus's liver to manufacture and store **glycogen,** a polymer of glucose that will be used to supply the brain's critical glucose needs before, during, and just after birth. Rising corticosteroid levels before birth also trigger two changes in blood production: a change in the site of production, from the liver to the bone marrow and spleen, and a switch in the kind of hemoglobin contained in the red blood cells—from fetal hemoglobin, which operates at relatively low oxygen levels (and therefore takes up oxygen from the mother's blood), to adult hemoglobin, which operates at higher levels.

Labor Has Three Stages

The process of childbirth is referred to scientifically as **parturition,** and more commonly as **labor.** During most of pregnancy, parturition is prevented by the inability of the uterine musculature (**myometrium**) to contract in an organized manner, as well as by the cervix, whose thick wall contains a dense network of collagen (connective tissue) fibers that resists expansion. Thus the Braxton-Hicks contractions, mentioned above, put some downward pressure on the fetus, but this pressure is easily resisted by the cervix, so the fetus does not move into the birth canal.

Labor takes place in three stages. The first stage consists of the uterine contractions that open the cervix. The second stage is the actual delivery of the baby. The third stage is the period from the delivery of the baby to the delivery of the placenta.

Animal Studies Suggest that the Fetus Issues the Signal for Parturition

What causes these processes? The immediate causes of parturition are fairly well understood. Cervical softening is triggered by prostaglandins (see Chapter 4) and nitric oxide (see Chapter 3). Both of these substances are produced locally in the uterus and cervix. Uterine contractions are triggered by prostaglandins and by the hormone oxytocin.

Secretion of oxytocin by the mother's pituitary gland is a reflex (Figure 10.19): stimulation of the cervix as the fetus passes through it causes neuronal signals to be sent to the spinal cord and from there to the hypothalamus, where the cell bodies of the oxytocin-secreting neurons are located (see Chapter 4). These neurons then release a surge of oxytocin from their terminals in the posterior lobe of the pituitary, and the oxytocin triggers a contraction of the myometrium.

Of course, there must be higher-order controls that decide *when* these processes should begin. In large animals that have been studied in the laboratory, such as sheep and goats, the ultimate signal derives from the fetus—specifically, from its hypothalamus, which somehow "knows" when it is time to be born. The hypothalamus orders the fetus's adrenal glands to increase their secretion of corticosteroids over and above the already high levels existing in late pregnancy, and these hormones induce an increase in estrogen secretion by the fetal side of the placenta. The estrogens enter the maternal circulation, promote prostaglandin secretion in the uterus, and facilitate the oxytocin reflex.

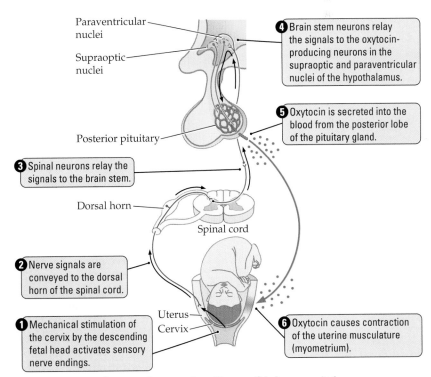

Paraventricular nuclei

Supraoptic nuclei

Posterior pituitary

4 Brain stem neurons relay the signals to the oxytocin-producing neurons in the supraoptic and paraventricular nuclei of the hypothalamus.

5 Oxytocin is secreted into the blood from the posterior lobe of the pituitary gland.

3 Spinal neurons relay the signals to the brain stem.

Dorsal horn

Spinal cord

2 Nerve signals are conveyed to the dorsal horn of the spinal cord.

1 Mechanical stimulation of the cervix by the descending fetal head activates sensory nerve endings.

Uterus

Cervix

6 Oxytocin causes contraction of the uterine musculature (myometrium).

Figure 10.19 The uterine contractions of labor result from a neurosecretory reflex involving oxytocin.

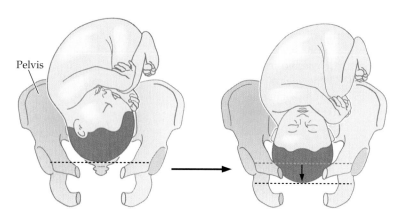

Figure 10.20 Lightening, or engagement, is the sinking of the fetus's head deep into the mother's pelvis.

In women, the signals that initiate parturition are poorly understood. It is possible that the human fetus's brain also sends out a triggering signal, because malformed fetuses that lack brains (**anencephalic** fetuses) are often born late (Mannino, 1988). A high ratio of estrogens to progesterone in the maternal blood may play a role, but even this is uncertain.

Before labor begins, the fetus changes its position in the uterus, as its head sinks deep into the pelvis against the cervix (Figure 10.20). This event, called **engagement** or **lightening,** is often noticed by the mother as a bit of extra space opens up between her breasts and her swollen belly. In first pregnancies, engagement may occur a week or more before birth; in later pregnancies, it occurs shortly before or during labor.

The First Stage of Labor Is Marked by Myometrial Contractions and Cervical Dilation

Labor may be heralded by the discharge of the mucous plug that seals off the cervix during pregnancy. The plug may be tinged red with blood, and this event is therefore traditionally called the "bloody show." The amniotic sac may also rupture early in labor, or it may be ruptured by a health care provider. The rupture produces a gush or leakage of amniotic fluid from the vagina ("water breaking"). In other cases the sac does not rupture until later in labor, and occasionally a baby may be born "in a caul"—that is, in an unruptured amniotic sac. A baby that comes gift-wrapped in this fashion is considered lucky in some cultures.

The first stage of labor can last anywhere from a couple of hours to a full day. The two main processes that permit parturition are the institution of strong, coordinated **contractions** of the myometrium and the elimination of much of the connective tissue in the cervix (**softening** or **ripening**) (Figure 10.21). The effect of the contractions is not to move the fetus downward, but to pull the cervix upward, so that the vagina and cervix together form a single, continuous **birth canal.** At the same time, the cervix softens, so that the upward pull exerted by the myometrium causes the cervix to thin out (**effacement**) and the cervical canal to open up enough to allow passage of the fetal head (**dilation** or **dilatation**).

In a typical hospital birth, the mother is "prepped" for delivery at some point during this process, principally by cleaning her vulva and all nearby skin with an antiseptic solution. Sometimes her pubic hair is shaved, and she may also be given an enema to empty her large bowel, with the idea of preventing any fecal incontinence during the delivery. These two practices are usually unnecessary, however, and are becoming uncommon.

Over the course of the first stage, the frequency and intensity of the contractions increases. The first stage is usually divided into two distinct phases, based on the progress of cervical dilation. In the **early phase,** the cervix dilates from 0 to 4 centimeters. The contractions are mild, spaced 15–20 minutes apart, and last 60–90 seconds. Between contractions, the woman can walk the halls with her partner, take a shower or bath (if her water hasn't yet broken), practice relaxation exercises, or even get some sleep. The early phase generally lasts 6–12 hours, but it can last over 24 hours.

In the **active phase,** the cervix dilates from 4 centimeters to its full width of 10 centimeters. Contractions occur as often as every 3 minutes and last about 45 seconds. There will be some bleeding from the vagina. The active phase usually lasts 4–8 hours. The latter part of the active phase, when the cervix dilates from 8 to 10 centimeters, is sometimes called the **transition;** it is a short period of very intense and frequent contractions. The transition is the part of labor that is most likely to be painful and exhausting, and it is here that the woman can most usefully apply what she has learned in her prenatal classes: relaxing rather than fighting the contractions, and directing her attention to other sensory inputs.

Many forms of **anesthesia** are available for women who are experiencing a great deal of pain during labor. These include intravenous general anesthetics such as barbiturates, opiate analgesics, tranquilizers, spinal anesthetics (that numb much of the lower part of the body), and nerve blocks that numb the area of the vulva. Anesthetics that act systemically (i.e., those administered orally or intravenously) will reach the fetus and have the potential to depress its responsiveness during labor and after birth. Another possible disadvantage of anesthetics is that they may impair the mother's ability to assist the birth process. One technique that minimizes these problems is the injection or continuous infusion of a local anesthetic, possibly in combination with an opiate analgesic, into the back, just outside the membrane (dura mater) than enwraps the spinal cord (**epidural anesthesia**). Still, most anesthesiologists believe that the choice of anesthetic procedure should be based on individual circumstances—there is no single method that is appropriate for all situations (American Society of Anesthesiologists, 1999). Pregnant women do well to discuss the issue of anesthesia and develop a birth plan ahead of time with their health care provider.

There are forms of natural pain relief that may be useful to many women. These include such seemingly simple activities as walking, pelvic rocking, showering, using a Jacuzzi, using a "birth ball," breathing exercises, and guided imagery. Hypnosis may also help some women.

Delivery Is Accomplished by Uterine Contractions Aided by "Bearing Down"

The second stage of labor is the actual movement of the fetus through the birth canal. This movement happens because the cervix is anchored by ligaments and connective tissue sheets to the pelvic floor. Thus, once the first-stage contractions have pulled the cervix up to its maximum extent, further contractions must pull the fundus of the uterus down, toward the birth canal, and this movement inevitably pushes the fetus through the canal.

Although the delivery of the fetus can be accomplished purely by uterine contractions, women usually feel an urge to push, or "bear down"—that is, to assist the birth process by voluntary contraction of the muscles of the abdominal wall and the diaphragm. Bearing down works by increasing the intra-abdominal pressure, which adds to the already high intrauterine pressure produced by the myometrial contractions. The process is quite similar to what happens during defecation, especially when one is constipated: gut peristalsis does most of the work, but "bearing down" helps things along.

Women may experience the urge to bear down during first-stage contractions, but should resist the urge because bearing down accomplishes nothing until the cervix is fully dilated. There may also be times when the health care provider tells the woman not to bear down during the delivery itself. This may be necessary while the provider adjusts the fetus's position in the birth canal, as well as during the final expulsion of the head, when slowing the process may help reduce the risk of vaginal tears.

The second stage of labor is quite variable in duration: it may last just a few minutes or it may take several hours. It is usually lengthier and more stressful for a woman's first delivery than for subsequent deliveries. It is also usually longer if the woman receives anesthesia that interferes with her ability to bear down. The second stage is usually perceived as less painful than the transition phase of the first stage.

Toward the end of the second stage, the baby's head appears at the vaginal opening ("crowning"). At this point, if it seems likely that the delivery of the head will tear the vaginal wall, the provider may make an incision in the perineum to extend the vaginal opening a short distance backward, toward the anus (Figure 10.22). This procedure, called an **episiotomy,** is done under local anesthesia.

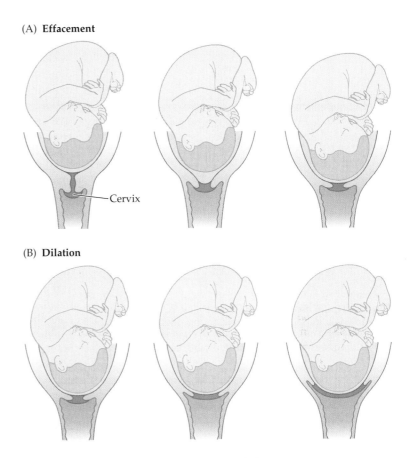

(A) Effacement

Cervix

(B) Dilation

Figure 10.21 Cervical changes during labor. (A) Effacement is the thinning of the cervix. (B) Dilation is the opening of the cervix, from fully closed to a width of 10 centimeters.

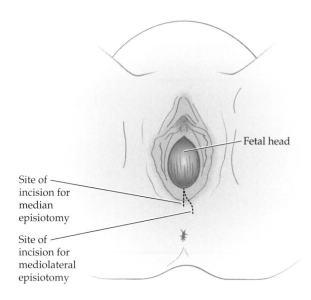

Site of incision for median episiotomy

Site of incision for mediolateral episiotomy

Fetal head

Figure 10.22 Episiotomy is a surgical cut made to extend the vaginal opening, facilitating passage of the fetus's head. The cut may be made in the midline (median) or diagonally to one side (mediolateral).

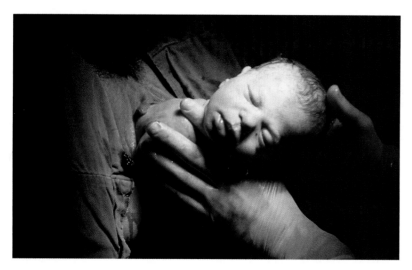

The hard part is over: once the head and shoulders are free, the rest of the fetus emerges easily.

The thought behind doing an episiotomy is that, if the vaginal wall is likely to rupture anyway, it is better to make a clean incision that can be neatly sewn up afterward. Still, many people feel that episiotomies are done too often, mostly to hurry delivery along, even though speedy delivery does not convey any particular medical benefit (Eason & Feldman, 2000). In a 1997 meta-analysis, hospital policies that set restrictive criteria for episiotomy, so that only about one in four women received them, led to better outcomes than did policies that placed no restrictions on the procedure (Piper, 1997). Medical students are now taught not to perform episiotomies routinely. At one large teaching hospital in Philadelphia, the episiotomy rate fell from 70 percent of all deliveries in 1983 to 19 percent in 2000 (Goldberg et al., 2002).

The Newborn Child Adapts Quickly to Life on Land

Once the fetus's head and shoulders have exited the birth canal, the rest of the body follows fairly readily. The compression of the fetus's thorax as it passes through the canal effectively "squeegees" the fluid out of its lungs, thus preparing them for their first breath. With the passage of the entire body through the canal, the second stage of labor is complete.

The fetus at this point is still attached to the placenta by the umbilical cord, so it is still getting its oxygen from its mother's lungs. Very shortly after birth, however, the fetus takes its first breath, probably in response to cold and tactile stimulation. Then, in a beautifully orchestrated feat of physiology, the vascular shunts that sustain the placental circulation (see Chapter 5) close off, replacing it with the definitive pulmonary circulation. The two sides of the heart now work in series, rather than in parallel.

The cessation of pulsation in the umbilical blood vessels can be readily seen. At this point, the cord is clamped and cut (sometimes by the mother's partner), and the baby is finally a free-living organism. The mother is often given the chance to hold and perhaps breast-feed her baby, at least for a short while. In many hospitals the mother has the option of keeping the baby with her, unless the baby has some health problem that necessitates moving it to the nursery.

The Third Stage Is the Expulsion of the Placenta

The third stage of labor consists of further myometrial contractions that separate the placenta from the uterine wall and expel it (along with the other fetal membranes) through the birth canal. This can occur almost immediately after delivery of the fetus, or it can take an hour or more, but it usually takes about 30 minutes. Occasionally there may be serious bleeding during this third stage due to rupture of maternal blood vessels that supply the placenta.

The expelled placenta is called the **afterbirth.** In many cultures, the afterbirth is ritually burned or buried. The females of most mammalian species—even non-carnivorous ones—*eat* the afterbirth (**placentophagia**), for reasons that are not very clear (Kristal, 1980). Several human cultures have explicit taboos *against* eating the afterbirth, suggesting that a placentophagic instinct lurks somewhere in the human psyche.

The fetal blood in the afterbirth and umbilical cord can be donated to a cord-blood bank; it is of potential use in the treatment of leukemia and related diseases. Banking the blood for the baby's own potential use, though a growing trend, doesn't make a whole lot of sense, given the low chance that the baby will need it (American Academy of Pediatrics, 1999b).

Cesarean Sections Can Be Life-Saving, But Are Done Too Frequently

An alternative to normal vaginal delivery is a **cesarean section,** or **C-section,** in which the baby is delivered via a surgical incision in the front of the abdomen and the uterus (Figure 10.23). The procedure is so named because Julius Caesar was supposedly born by this method; "section" means "cutting." References to cesarean sections (on dead mothers) reach back to the seventh century B.C.E., but the first documented cases in which both mother and child survived are from the time of the Renaissance. Such cases remained rarities until the mid-nineteenth century and the introduction of antisepsis. By 1999, 860,000 C-sections—more than one in every five deliveries—were being performed annually in the United States.

Cesarean sections are done when vaginal delivery is deemed inadvisable for a variety of medical reasons (as when the mother's pelvis is too narrow), when labor does not progress after a prolonged period and the mother (or fetus) is becoming exhausted, or when certain complications occur during labor. A cesarean section may also be performed if the fetus's position is unfavorable—that is, it is in some other orientation than head down and cannot be manipulated into the head-down position. Another reason for a cesarean section may be to avoid exposing the baby to an infection present in the birth canal, such as herpes (see Chapter 16).

A much higher proportion of American than European women have C-sections, and while the procedure is often a lifesaver, it appears that many C-sections in the United States are unnecessary. Part of the reason why American physicians perform so many C-sections is that they are poorly trained in the use of instruments (forceps, vacuum devices) to facilitate difficult vaginal deliveries (American Society of Anesthesiologists, 1999).

The fact that a woman has had a C-section does not mean that she must have a C-section in all subsequent pregnancies, but there is an increased risk of one serious complication, rupture of the uterus, in women who attempt vaginal delivery after a prior C-section (Lydon-Rochelle et al., 2001).

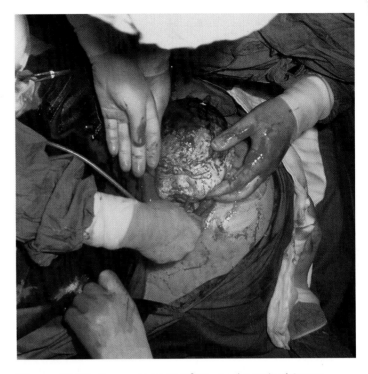

Figure 10.23 A cesarean section. In the United States, this procedure is done more often than is medically necessary.

Premature and Delayed Births Are Hazardous

Labor is considered premature if it begins before 37 weeks of gestational age. In most cases of premature labor the cause is not known, but predisposing factors include multiple fetuses, teen pregnancy, the mother's use of tobacco or drugs, malnutrition, and a variety of illnesses during pregnancy. Premature labor can sometimes be halted with the use of drugs; if not, it leads to **premature** or **pre-term birth.** This happens in about 10 percent of all pregnancies in the United States.

Premature birth is dangerous to the baby's health: about 75 percent of all neonatal deaths (aside from those associated with congenital defects) strike the 10 percent of babies who are born prematurely. Pre-term babies, especially those who are small for their gestational age or who are born very prematurely, also have a much higher likelihood of suffering long-lasting physical and behavioral disabilities than do babies delivered at term (Lopez Bernal & TambyRaja, 2000; Schothorst & van Engeland, 1996). Even so, the majority of "preemies" do fine and, though small at birth, eventually catch up with their peers.

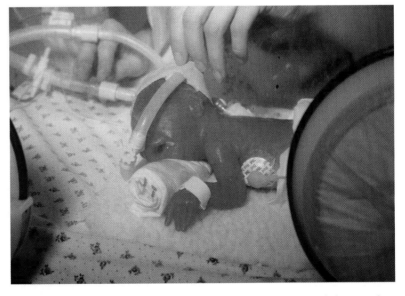

Premature infants have a good chance of surviving, but they require intensive medical care and may end up with some kind of disability.

Labor is considered **delayed** if it occurs more than 2 weeks post-term: about 10 percent of babies are born at least this late. Like premature labor, delayed labor has risks. The fetus may grow too large to pass through the birth canal, and in a minority of cases the placenta may cease to adequately nourish the fetus, so that it is born too small for its gestational age. Post-term babies are about three times more likely to die neonatally than are babies born at term. To avoid these ill effects, labor may be **induced** with drugs such as oxytocin and prostaglandins. This practice itself carries some risk, but it does at least allow for the date of delivery to be planned ahead of time (Box 10.5).

The Period after Birth Places Many Demands on Parents

The weeks after birth are called the **postpartum.** Although there can be medical problems for the mother during this period, including serious ones such as infections acquired during the birth process, its main feature is physical recovery from the stresses of pregnancy and childbirth. A vaginal discharge continues for a few days after parturition, and is then replaced by small volumes of a dark, bloody discharge known as **lochia;** this ceases after a few weeks, but spotty bleeding may continue for 6–8 weeks. The uterus gradually shrinks back to its original dimensions, episiotomy or C-section incisions heal, and the mother's levels of estrogen and progesterone, which drop precipitously at delivery, eventually return to more normal levels.

Psychologically, the postpartum is a highly variable experience. On the plus side, the mother has the relief of putting pregnancy behind her and the joy of a new baby. Over the first few days after parturition these positive feelings tend to dominate. After that, however, the mother faces a great deal of stress. She finds herself back home and devoting a great deal of time and effort to looking after her infant, yet she still needs quite a bit of "mothering" herself. In this situation, the degree of support she receives from her partner or others makes an enormous difference to her psychological well-being.

Postpartum Depression May Be Accompanied by Disordered Thinking

Many women experience variable moods after childbirth, including periods of sadness and crying ("postpartum blues"). In some women this sadness is sufficiently intense and sustained to be diagnosed as **postpartum depression** (Georgiopoulos et al., 2001). Not uncommonly, it is accompanied by some degree of suicidal feelings. Women who were psychologically distressed during late pregnancy, and who lack social support, are especially likely to suffer from postpartum depression (Nielsen Forman et al., 2000).

There is some debate about the prevalence of postpartum depression. One large longitudinal British study found that women were significantly *less* likely to be depressed after childbirth than they were during the prenatal period, especially the third trimester: 13.5 percent of women scored high on tests of depression at 32 weeks of pregnancy, but only 9.1 percent did so at 8 weeks after childbirth (Evans et al., 2001). In general, there seems to be little, if any, difference in the prevalence of depression among women who have recently given birth and women in the general population (O'Hara et al., 1990).

What *is* more prevalent in the postpartum period is depression accompanied by serious disruption of thinking—**depressive psychosis** (Kendell et al., 1976). On rare occasions, this disorder can lead to infanticide or suicide. In a uniquely tragic case in June 2001, a Houston woman with a prior history of severe postpartum depression with psychosis drowned her 6-month-old daughter as well as her four older children. At her 2002 trial, the woman, Andrea Yates, pleaded not guilty of murder by reason of insanity, but she was found guilty and sentenced to life in prison.

Postpartum depression, like depression in general, seems to result from both environmental and endogenous factors. Its relationship to lack of social support, as just mentioned, is evidence of an environmental influence. Endogenous factors have not been identified with certainty, but the hormonal and metabolic changes at parturition, espe-

Sex in History

The Blackout Babies

The New York skyline during the 1965 blackout

On November 9, 1965, electrical power went out over most of the northeastern United States, putting a stop to all business activities for over 24 hours. Television sets flickered and failed, and darkness covered the land. So how did people fill this unexpected void in their lives?

The answer seemed to be forthcoming 9 months later. On Wednesday, August 10, 1966, the *New York Times* ran a front-page story under the headline "Births Up 9 Months After Blackout." The *Times*'s reporters had learned of unusually high numbers of births in several New York City

hospitals on Monday, August 8. Later articles reported that the birth rate declined over the following days and was back to normal by the end of the week. New Yorkers, it seemed, had found a "creative" way to deal with their time off during the power outage.

The only problem with this story was—it didn't happen! Mondays are always busy days in maternity wards anyway. That's because many deliveries are induced, and can therefore be planned ahead of time. These induced deliveries tend to pile up on Mondays because obstetricians don't like to work on weekends any more than the rest of us do. As shown by statisticians Alan Izenman (of Colorado State University) and Sandy Zabell (of Northwestern University), the August 8 birth peak was actually no higher than any other Monday peak in New York City (Izenman & Zabell, 1981). Furthermore, the variability in the length of pregnancy means that, even if there was a city-wide orgy of unprotected sex on November 9, one would not expect a surge in births to occur on a precise day in August of the following year.

The *New York Times* later backpedaled on its report, but to no avail: the "blackout babies" became an unshakable urban legend. Similar stories have appeared in the media on many occasions since then, most recently in early October 2000, 9 months after all those drunken Millennium celebrations.

cially the severe drop in estrogen levels, are good candidates. Estrogen treatments can alleviate some cases of postpartum depression and psychosis (Ahokas et al., 2000), as can regular antidepressants, counseling, and general social support.

Childbirth and Parenthood Affect Sexual Expression and Marital Satisfaction

The postpartum is a period of low or absent sexual activity, especially coitus, for most women. There are plenty of reasons for this: they are exhausted from the travails of pregnancy and childbirth, they are preoccupied with maternal responsibilities, and their genitalia take time to recover from the stresses of parturition, especially if there has been an episiotomy or a spontaneous tear that had to be sewn up. In addition, low postpartum estrogen levels tend to decrease vaginal lubrication, making coitus uncomfortable. Obstetricians often recommend that women wait about 6 weeks before resuming coitus, and most women do wait about that long (Reamy & White, 1987).

Some women may be concerned that pregnancy and parturition have reduced their attractiveness (perhaps on account of weight gain or stretch marks) or their ability to enjoy coitus and satisfy their partner (perhaps because of stretching of the vagina). These fears are ill-founded. Weight gain can be reversed, and it may not reduce attractiveness even if it isn't. Stretch marks fade. The vagina tightens. (This process can be aided by Kegel exercises; see Chapter 17.) Evolution designed women to have sex after childbirth, after all—if that were not so, the human race would have long since become extinct.

Although nearly all couples resume sex within a few months of childbirth, the transition to parenthood has profound and often negative effects on their relationship and their sexuality. These effects have been studied most carefully for married couples. For the "average" couple, marital conflicts increase about ninefold after the birth of the first child, the perceived quality of the marriage drops precipitously, husband and wife fall back into stereotypical gender roles, the husband withdraws into work, and the frequency of marital conversations and sex goes into a steep decline (Gottman & Notarius, 2000). Of course, not every couple is the "average" couple—many marriages and cohabitations blossom after children appear, and counseling can help couples "survive" parenthood (Cowan & Cowan, 1992). And on the converse side, remaining childless is no guarantee of marital bliss. All the same, parenthood is clearly a tremendous challenge to a relationship. We will revisit this topic when we take a broader look at sexuality across the life cycle in Chapter 12.

Breast Feeding Is the Preferred Method of Nourishing the Infant

Breast feeding—the trait that links humans with all other mammals—represents many things: a beautifully orchestrated physiological process, a wellspring of intimacy between mother and child, and a source of physical and psychological health for both. In addition, it is a focus of controversy—between those who promote the virtues of breast feeding and those who see it as something that technology and the demands of modern society have rendered obsolete or excessively burdensome.

Lactation Is Orchestrated by Hormones

Breast feeding cements the bond between mother and infant and provides the infant with the best possible nutrition, but it is time-consuming. The World Health Organization recommends 2 years of breast feeding, but few American mothers breast-feed their babies beyond 6 months.

As mentioned earlier, the breasts are ready to **lactate** (produce milk) by about the fourth month of pregnancy. And the main hormone that triggers lactation—**prolactin**—is released by the mother's pituitary gland in ever greater amounts as pregnancy proceeds. Yet lactation does not take place to any significant degree. That's because the high circulating levels of estrogens and progesterone block prolactin's action on the breasts. Once estrogen and progesterone levels drop, as they do at parturition, prolactin triggers copious lactation, so that the alveoli of the breast become distended with secreted material.

Although prolactin is circulating in the mother's blood before and after parturition, its continued secretion depends on a reflex triggered by the baby's suckling. Sensory signals generated by the act of suckling are transmitted to the mother's spinal cord and thence to the hypothalamus, where they stimulate release of a prolactin-releasing factor. This factor then passes to the anterior lobe of the pituitary gland, as described in Chapter 4, and triggers the release of prolactin into the general circulation.

While prolactin triggers lactation—that is, the production of milk and its accumulation in the breast tissue—another pituitary hormone, oxytocin, is responsible for the actual **ejection** or **letdown** of milk from the breast tissue into the lactiferous ducts and thence into the nipples (see Chapter 3). The milk ejection reflex is similar to the oxytocin reflex involved in triggering uterine contractions during parturition, except that the afferent pathway of the reflex begins in the nipple rather than in the birth canal. The surge of oxytocin induced by suckling stimulates the contraction of smooth muscle cells that surround the alveoli; the contraction of these cells squeezes the contents of the alveoli into the ducts. The release of oxytocin also causes uterine contractions, which help the uterus return to its pre-pregnancy size.

TABLE 10.3	*Main constituents of mature human milk*
Water	Approximately 90 percent
Sugar (lactose)	Approximately 7 percent (by weight)
Fat	3–6 percent (by volume)
Proteins	Lactalbumin and lactoglobulin
Amino acids	Includes all essential amino acids
Vitamins	Includes A, B_1, B_2, B_{12}, C, D, E, K
Energy content	Approximately 650 kcal/liter

The Content of Breast Milk Changes over Time

For the first few days after birth, the material secreted by the breasts is not mature milk, but a thick, yellowish material called **colostrum.** This material is lower in fat (2–3 percent) and sugar than mature milk, but richer in proteins, especially immunoglobulins. These immunoglobulins are antibodies against a wide variety of infectious organisms and other antigens to which the mother has been exposed at some point in her life. By absorbing these antibodies, the baby derives a degree of **passive immunity** against those organisms (passive in the sense that the baby has not manufactured the antibodies itself). Both colostrum and mature milk contain macrophages—scavenging cells of the immune system—which may also contribute to the infant's immune defenses. Because colostrum is not very energy-rich, and is produced in limited amounts (40 ml on the first day, 400 ml at 3 days), a breast-fed baby relies primarily on its own fat and glycogen supplies for energy until the secretion of mature milk begins. Thus, a normal breast-fed baby may lose up to 10 percent of its birth weight while waiting for the mature milk to come in.

Over the first 2 weeks after birth, the breast secretions gradually become mature milk (Table 10.3) and increase greatly in volume. By 3 weeks after birth, a breast-fed baby is drinking a little over a liter of milk per day, which provides it with about 700 kcal of energy (Saint et al., 1984). Most of that energy comes from the fat content of the milk. Lactose, or milk sugar, also provides some energy, but has additional benefits. First, it stimulates the growth of normal intestinal bacteria (specifically, **lactobacilli**). Second, it breaks down into two simpler sugars, glucose and galactose. Glucose is the brain's preferred energy source, and galactose is required for the manufacture of **myelin,** the insulating sheath that surrounds nerve fibers.

Infant Formula Is an Alternative to Breast Milk

Over most of human history, mothers had no choice but to breast-feed their babies. In the nineteenth century, breast feeding began to be seen as burdensome or undignified, and women of means would sometimes pay working-class women who had milk to spare (perhaps because they had lost their own infants) to breast-feed their children. These women were called **wet nurses.** In the twentieth century, breast feeding largely gave way to bottle feeding, and the industrial production of **infant formula** began. Most formula is based on cows' milk; soy-based formula is recommended only for infants who cannot digest cows' milk. The production of infant formula is tightly regulated by the U.S. government.

In the 1950s and 1960s, only about one in five women breast-fed their infants, but starting in the 1970s, their numbers began to rise again. This shift was propelled by medical research, which demonstrated that breast feeding has specific health benefits, and by the women's movement, which rejected the image of breast feeding as demeaning. Breast feeding became a cause, spearheaded by La Leche League International (founded in 1956). Some activists organized boycotts of the infant formula manufacturers, especially Nestlé, to protest their promotion of formula use in nonindustrialized countries. Currently, about 60 percent of American mothers breast-feed their babies initially, but only about one in five still does so at 6 months (Ryan, 1997).

Breast Feeding Has Many Advantages and Some Drawbacks

Breast feeding, as compared with bottle feeding, has many advantages:

- **Health benefits for the baby.** Breast-fed babies are less likely to develop infectious illnesses, such as pneumonia, botulism, bronchitis, bacterial meningitis, staphylococcal infections, influenza, ear infections, rubella, and diarrhea, and are also less prone to asthma. These benefits are experienced primarily during the period of breast feeding; the long-term health of breast-fed and bottle-fed infants is about the same. Some studies indicate that breast feeding aids the infant's cognitive development and slightly increases its intelligence in adulthood (Angelsen et al., 2001; Mortensen et al., 2002).
- **Health benefits for the mother.** By stimulating the release of oxytocin, breast feeding helps shrink the uterus to its pre-pregnancy size and reduces postpartum bleeding. It also helps the mother shed the excess weight she gained during pregnancy (breast feeding is Nature's own liposuction). It also reduces her risk of ovarian cancer and early (premenopausal) breast cancer.
- **Psychological benefits to the mother and infant.** Breast feeding helps establish a close bond between mother and child. Breast feeding is usually pleasurable and relaxing for the mother. It may even be erotically arousing: some women actually experience orgasms during breast feeding.
- **Convenience and expense.** Breast feeding is much less expensive than bottle feeding, even when considering the extra food the mother must consume to support it. Breast feeding is more convenient than bottle feeding in the sense that no preparations are required: the breast milk is always there, perfectly prepared, at the right temperature, and sterile.
- **Contraceptive effect.** Breast feeding suppresses ovarian function by interfering with the pulsatile secretion of GnRH from the hypothalamus (McNeilly, 2001). Normal menstrual cycles do not usually begin until 6 weeks after parturition at the earliest. In some non-Western cultures women nurse their children for several years after birth, and the associated reduction in fertility is a major factor in spacing out their offspring. It takes intensive nursing to achieve a marked contraceptive effect, however, and most American women stand a good chance of becoming pregnant even if they continue to nurse. The first ovulation after parturition may not be preceded by a menstrual period, so nursing women receive no foolproof signal that fertility has returned.

Breast feeding also has several disadvantages:

- **Health problems for the mother.** Women sometimes develop sore nipples from nursing, or their breasts become uncomfortably engorged. About 20 percent of women develop an inflammation or infection of the breast (**mastitis**), often as a consequence of cracked nipples or a blocked lactiferous duct (Kinlay et al., 2001). These conditions can be easily treated, however.
- **Health problems for the baby.** The infant can acquire some infections, including HIV and hepatitis, from the mother via her milk. Many drugs (including contraceptives) can pass from the mother to the child via milk and may harm the child. A mother who plans to breast-feed should discuss all drugs with her physician.
- **Inconvenience.** Although breast milk comes already prepared and heated, the process of feeding it to the baby takes a lot of time—several hours each day. It is a real challenge for working women. One option is for the woman to remove milk with a breast pump and refrigerate it, so that it can be fed to the baby later by bottle, perhaps by the woman's partner.

In many non-Western cultures, the contraceptive effect of prolonged breast feeding plays an important role in spacing out a woman's children.

Organizations such as the National Institutes of Health, the American Academy of Pediatrics, the American College of Obstetricians and Gynecologists, the World Health Organization, and of course La Leche League all would like to see more women breast-feed their babies. Still, if a woman cannot do so for one reason or another, she should not feel that she has failed her child. Formula-fed infants can thrive as well as breast-fed ones.

If a mother does breast-feed her infant, when should she stop? The American Academy of Pediatrics has recommended that babies be exclusively breast-fed for 6 months, with continued partial breast feeding for 1 year or more. The World Health Organization has recommended 2 years of breast feeding. The average for nonindustrial societies is 3–5 years. Very few American mothers continue to breast-feed beyond 1 year, and those that continue to 2 years face strong societal disapproval. Many Americans view the breasts primarily as sex organs, and consider the breast-feeding of a 2-year-old to be sexual child abuse. There have been cases in which children have been legally removed from their mothers on account of too-lengthy breast feeding (Healy, 2001).

Biological Mechanisms May Contribute to Maternal Behavior

We mentioned that breast feeding helps to cement the mother–child bond. This observation brings up the question of whether there's a "chemistry" to mother love—some hormone or neurotransmitter that causes a mother to devote herself so selflessly to her helpless infant. Some people think that there is, and point a finger at the two hormones primarily involved in lactation, prolactin and oxytocin. Both of these hormones are known to play a role in the generation of maternal behavior in animals, including rodents and larger animals such as sheep. During pregnancy, prolactin "primes" certain centers in the brain, especially in the hypothalamus and nearby, changing their synaptic wiring in such a way as to prepare the animal to show maternal behavior. After parturition, prolactin and oxytocin released by suckling, combined with visual and olfactory cues, trigger the actual display of maternal behavior (Rosenblatt, 1994). Thus, by suckling, the offspring not only obtain milk, but also "push their mother's buttons," causing her to groom them, protect them, fetch them if they stray, and so on.

Similar mechanisms may well operate in humans and other primates, too, but the situation is more complex. For one thing, many female primates show "aunting" behavior—that is, they will temporarily mother another female's infant, even if they have never been pregnant themselves. They may even permanently adopt a strange infant—as, of course, humans sometimes do. Indeed, even rodents will often show maternal behavior to strange pups, given enough exposure to them. Thus, the hormonal changes induced by pregnancy, parturition, and lactation may play a role in human maternal behavior, but they can hardly be the whole story.

Summary

1. The onset of pregnancy is marked by a missed menstrual period and other symptoms. It can be confirmed by urine or blood tests that detect the human chorionic gonadotropin (hCG) secreted by the implanted conceptus.

2. To enhance the chances of pregnancy, coitus should be timed to occur at or just before ovulation. The time of ovulation can be estimated by tracking basal body temperature or changes in cervical mucus, or by the use of test kits that detect the surge of luteinizing hormone prior to ovulation.

3. Infertility or subfertility can be caused by problems in the man or in the woman. If it results from a low sperm count or sperm quality, in vitro fertilization may still make pregnancy possible. An alternative is artificial insemination with donated sperm.

4. Abnormalities of the female reproductive tract, resulting from sexually transmitted infections or other causes, can reduce fertility. The oviducts are the commonest site of such problems. They can sometimes be corrected surgically, or else an embryo produced by in vitro fertilization (IVF) can be placed directly in the uterus.

5. Problems with ovulation can often be treated with drugs. An alternative is the use of donated oocytes.

6. If a woman cannot sustain pregnancy at all, surrogate motherhood or adoption are possible solutions.

7. Fertility declines steadily with age in both sexes. Age also raises the likelihood of fetal abnormalities such as Down's syndrome.

8. Many conceptuses do not survive. Many of those that fail to implant or die early in pregnancy are abnormal. Other conditions, such as ectopic pregnancy or rhesus incompatibility, can cause fetal loss or harm the fetus or the mother.

9. Pregnancy (the period from ovulation to birth) lasts about 9 calendar months and is conventionally divided into three trimesters. The first trimester may be marked by troublesome symptoms such as morning sickness. It is a critical period of fetal development during which the main body plan and organ systems are laid out. This process can be impaired by maternal infection or poor nutrition, or by use of alcohol, tobacco, or a variety of drugs. Prenatal care offers important benefits, but many women do not receive such care in early pregnancy.

10. The second trimester is usually easier for the mother. The fetus can be screened for congenital abnormalities and its sex determined at this time. Moderate exercise benefits the mother. The frequency of sexual activity tends to decline during pregnancy, but for most women there is no health reason for abstaining from coitus.

11. In the third trimester both the parents and the fetus make preparations for birth. Childbirth classes teach strategies to facilitate delivery and to minimize pain.

12. Labor has three stages. In the first stage, myometrial contractions and cervical softening prepare the birth canal for the passage of the fetus. In the second stage, the fetus passes through the canal and is delivered. Rapid physiological changes adapt it to an air-breathing existence. In the third stage, the placenta (afterbirth) and fetal membranes are expelled.

13. Difficult births may necessitate surgical widening of the vaginal opening (episiotomy) or delivery via an abdominal incision (Cesarean section). Both of these procedures may be done more commonly than is necessary. Various forms of anesthesia are available if labor is excessively painful. There are also forms of pain relief that do not rely on medications.

14. Premature or delayed labor is associated with increased risks of harm to the fetus.

15. The period after birth (postpartum) is a time of recovery for the mother, but is marked by depression with disordered thinking in some women.

16. The birth of a child, especially a first one, can bring great happiness, but also causes major stresses. Marital satisfaction tends to decline after the transition to parenthood, and the frequency of sexual activity decreases.

17. Hormones prepare the mother's breasts for lactation and mediate the release of milk during suckling. The content of milk changes during the weeks after childbirth. Breast feeding has significant advantages over formula feeding, but formula-fed infants usually thrive.

Discussion Questions

1. Imagine that for some reason you or your partner were not able to become pregnant on your own. Discuss your preference for some alternative method (e.g., adoption, assisted reproductive technology, surrogate motherhood) of becoming parents. Discuss what the pros and cons of each solution would be for you.

2. Imagine that you or your partner were pregnant and learned that the embryo had a genetic defect such as Down's syndrome. Discuss the costs and benefits of the options available to you (e.g., abortion, deliver the child and put it up for adoption, keep and raise the child) and the rationale behind each one.

3. Imagine that you or your partner are happily pregnant and expect a normal delivery. Would you elect to deliver the child at home, in a hospital, or in a birthing center? Would you prefer an M.D. or a certified nurse-midwife to deliver your baby? Why?

4. Your baby is born and is healthy. Discuss the pros and cons of breast feeding versus bottle feeding. Which would you select? Give your reasons.

5. Discuss the ethical issues of in vitro fertilization (IVF). Imagine that you are testifying before a U.S. Senate committee on reproductive technology, and take a position for or against IVF. Give your reasons.

6. Do you think that the capability to select a child's sex prenatally is a good thing or a bad thing, and why? Do you think the practice should be permitted, discouraged, restricted, or banned?

Web Resources

American College of Obstetricians and Gynecologists www.acog.org

American Society for Reproductive Medicine www.asrm.org

Carr, I. *Dying to Have a Baby: The History of Childbirth* www.umanitoba.ca/outreach/manitoba_womens_health/hist1.htm

IFCONLINE—Independent Fertility Counselling Online www.infertility-info.com/

National Down Syndrome Society www.ndss.org

Society for Assisted Reproductive Technology www.sart.org

Recommended Reading

American College of Nurse-Midwifery & Jacobs, S. (1993). *Having your baby with a nurse-midwife: Everything you need to know to make an informed decision.* New York: Hyperion.

American College of Obstetricians and Gynecologists (2000). *Planning your pregnancy and birth* (3rd ed.). Washington, D.C.: ACOG.

Carson, S. A., Casson, P. R., & and Shuman, D. J. (1999). *The American Society of Reproductive Medicine complete guide to fertility.* Lincolnwood, IL: Contemporary Books.

Cunningham, F. G., Gant, N. F., Leveno, K. J., Gilstrap, L. C., Hauth, J. C., & Wenstrom, K. D. (2001). *Williams obstetrics* (21st ed.). New York: McGraw-Hill.

Gotsch, G., & Torgus, J. (1997). *The womanly art of breastfeeding* (6th ed.). Schaumburg, IL: La Leche League International.

Misri, S. (1995). *Shouldn't I be happy? Emotional problems of pregnant and postpartum women.* New York: Free Press.

Varney, H. (1997). *Varney's midwifery* (3rd ed.). Sudbury, MA: Jones and Bartlett.

chapter 11

Condoms are reliable contraceptives when used properly.

Preventing Childbirth

*I*n the previous chapter we spoke of pregnancy as if it were the universally desired consequence of heterosexual sex. Of course, that's not the case. For most men and women, there are substantial periods of life during which they want to engage in sexual relationships, but do not want to produce children. For better or worse, human ingenuity has come up with a wide variety of methods to achieve that end. These methods, especially those that fall into the general categories of contraception and abortion, are the topic of this chapter.

Birth Control Has a Long History

In the ancient Mediterranean world, "birth control" was accomplished largely through the neglect, abandonment, or outright killing of unwanted babies. Various forms of contraception were also used, though probably with limited success. These methods involved placing some substance, such as olive oil, a vinegar-soaked sponge, or even crocodile dung, in the vagina before sex, or douching with wine or vinegar afterward. The withdrawal method of contraception is mentioned in the biblical story of Onan, who "spilled his seed upon the ground" to avoid impregnating his deceased brother's wife (Genesis 38).

Male condoms—sheaths placed over the penis—also have a long history. One person who popularized their use, both as contraceptives and to prevent the transmission of disease, was the Italian adventurer and ladies' man Giacomo Casanova (1725–1798). At that time, most condoms were made from animal intestines, and they were so expensive that they had to be used repeatedly. Mass-produced rubber condoms (hence "rubbers") became available at the end of the nineteenth century, followed by latex condoms in the 1930s.

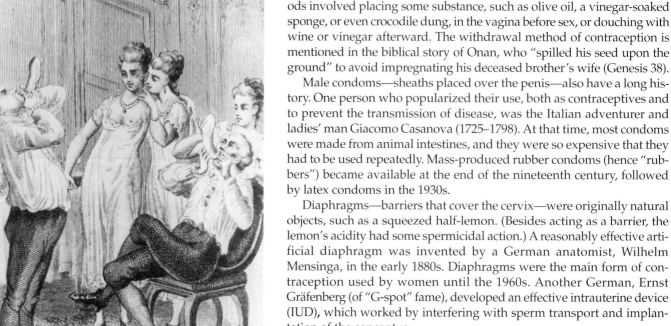

Casanova made the testing of condoms into a social activity.

Diaphragms—barriers that cover the cervix—were originally natural objects, such as a squeezed half-lemon. (Besides acting as a barrier, the lemon's acidity had some spermicidal action.) A reasonably effective artificial diaphragm was invented by a German anatomist, Wilhelm Mensinga, in the early 1880s. Diaphragms were the main form of contraception used by women until the 1960s. Another German, Ernst Gräfenberg (of "G-spot" fame), developed an effective intrauterine device (IUD), which worked by interfering with sperm transport and implantation of the conceptus.

Scientific discoveries about the endocrinological basis of the menstrual cycle led to the introduction of oral contraceptives ("the pill") for women in the 1960s. Oral contraceptives, which contain gonadal steroids, were so effective that they essentially eliminated the fear of unwanted pregnancy for many women, and thus helped spur the "sexual revolution" of that time. Most recent developments in contraceptive technology employ gonadal steroids or related compounds.

Feminists and Eugenicists Led the Campaign to Legalize Contraception

The history of contraception in the United States is not merely a story of technological advances, however, but also one of profound social and intellectual conflicts. At least until the end of the nineteenth century, contraception was viewed by many as morally offensive because it subverted what was thought to be the natural or divinely intended function of sex: procreation. Indeed, that is still the official position of the Roman Catholic Church today. Early proponents of contraception were harassed, fined, or jailed. Massachusetts physician Charles Knowlton was jailed in 1833 for writing a book about contraceptive techniques. His book nevertheless became very influential in both America and Europe.

In 1873 moral crusader Anthony Comstock succeeded in persuading Congress to pass legislation (the "Comstock Law") that banned the dissemination of "obscene" material—which included information about contraception—through the mails. Some states passed their own Comstock laws, some of which even forbade physicians to inform their patients about contraceptive techniques. One birth control advocate, Edward Foote, was fined $3000 in 1876—a huge amount in those days.

Two different groups of people led the struggle to legalize contraception. One group consisted of early **feminists,** most notably Margaret Sanger (Box 11.1), who sought to alleviate the suffering imposed on poor women by the ceaseless cycle of pregnancy and infant care. The other group consisted of **eugenicists,** who believed that society was threatened by the unrestrained reproduction of a genetic underclass. These two groups

Box 11.1 Sex in History

Margaret Sanger and the Birth Control Movement

Margaret Sanger was born in Corning, New York, in 1879. Her mother, Anne Higgins, died at age 50 after bearing eleven children, and Margaret attributed her early death to the burden of too-frequent pregnancy. Margaret trained as a nurse and in 1902 married an architect, William Sanger. The couple had three children, then moved to New York City and became involved in socialist causes. One of the people who influenced Margaret was anarchist Emma Goldman.

Working as a visiting nurse in New York's Lower East Side, Sanger came to realize that unrestricted births were putting a crushing economic and health burden on working-class women. In 1914 Sanger began publishing a radical feminist monthly called *The Woman Rebel*, which included appeals for the right to practice birth control. Sanger was indicted under the Comstock Laws, which forbade the dissemination of information about contraception. She jumped bail and spent a year in Europe. There she met sexologist Havelock Ellis, whose emphasis on the importance of female sexuality influenced her. She also visited a birth control clinic in Holland, where women were being fitted with a new type of diaphragm, and she later imported this diaphragm into the United States.

Sanger returned to the United States in 1915 to face the charges against her, hoping to make her trial into a showcase for the birth control cause. The charges were dropped, however, because of widespread public sympathy for Sanger—especially because her only daughter had died that same year. She therefore went on a national lecture tour to promote birth control and was arrested in several cities.

In October of 1916 Sanger opened the country's first birth control clinic, the Brownsville Clinic in Brooklyn, New York. The police closed it down after just 9 days of operation. Sanger was arrested and, because she refused to pay a fine, spent 30 days in prison. While in prison she taught contraceptive methods to other inmates.

The Brownsville affair drew widespread sympathy and financial support to her cause. Although she lost the appeal of her conviction, the appellate court did rule that physicians could provide contraceptive information for medical reasons. This ruling allowed Sanger's group to open a doctor-staffed birth control clinic, and others followed. In 1917 Sanger began publication of a monthly, the *Birth Control Review*, and in 1921 she founded the American Birth Control League, forerunner of the Planned Parenthood Federation.

Sanger separated from her husband in 1914 and began a series of affairs, including ones with Havelock Ellis and with novelist and socialist H. G. Wells. In 1922 she married a wealthy oil magnate, James Slee, who provided financial backing for the birth control movement.

During the 1920s Sanger broadened her arguments for birth control, including some ideas that were espoused by eugenicists. She advocated the involuntary sterilization of the mentally retarded, as well as measures to decrease the reproduction rate of various social groups that she considered "unfit." Eventually, Sanger was perceived as too radical for the movement she had started. She resigned the presidency of the American Birth Control League in 1928 and thereafter gradually gave up her role as leader of the birth control movement in the United States. After the Second World War, however, she came out of retirement to help found the International Planned Parenthood Federation, and she served as its president from 1952 to 1959.

Sanger was always trying to find improved birth control techniques. After gonadal steroids were synthesized, she arranged for funding to support research into hormone-based contraceptives—research that paid off in 1960 when the Food and Drug Administration approved the first contraceptive pill.

Sanger died in 1965, just a few months after the U.S. Supreme Court, in *Griswold v. Connecticut*, declared that married couples had the right to use birth control. Despite her misguided eugenicist views, Sanger's life and work were important, not just for her achievements in the area of birth control, but because she set an example of nonviolent direct action in the service of social progress—an example that was followed by many other movements later in the twentieth century.

In Britain, Marie Stopes (1880–1958) had a career quite comparable to that of Sanger. Her sex manual, *Married Love*, caused enormous controversy on its publication in 1918. She opened Britain's first birth control clinic in 1921. The organization named for her, Marie Stopes International, now provides reproductive health services in more than 30 countries.

Sources: Margaret Sanger Papers Project, 2000; Planned Parenthood Federation, 2000.

Margaret Sanger (1879–1966)

formed an uneasy alliance until the Nazi period, when the American eugenicist movement faded away.

The birth control movement did not achieve definitive success until the 1960s and 1970s, when two decisions of the U.S. Supreme Court (*Griswold v. Connecticut*, 1965, and *Eisenstadt v. Baird*, 1972) overthrew laws that banned the use or distribution of contra-

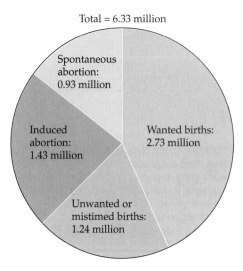

Total = 6.33 million

Spontaneous abortion: 0.93 million

Induced abortion: 1.43 million

Wanted births: 2.73 million

Unwanted or mistimed births: 1.24 million

Figure 11.1 Fewer than half of all U.S. pregnancies lead to the birth of a wanted child. This chart shows the outcome of the 4.3 million pregnancies that are established in the United States per year. (Data from Alan Guttmacher Institute, 2000.)

Figure 11.2 Poor contraceptive coverage. Many medical insurance plans provide no coverage for prescription contraceptives (diaphragms, IUDs, and oral, injectable, or implantable hormone-based contraceptives). (Data from Alan Guttmacher Institute, 2002a.)

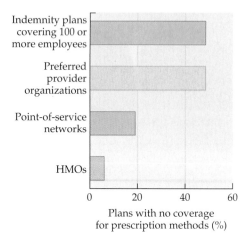

Indemnity plans covering 100 or more employees

Preferred provider organizations

Point-of-service networks

HMOs

Plans with no coverage for prescription methods (%)

ceptives. These rulings were based on a constitutional right of privacy, and in fact helped establish that right.

Following these decisions, federal and state governments began supporting family planning initiatives—for example, through the Medicaid program. The AIDS epidemic, which began around 1980, spurred the social approval of one form of contraception—condoms—because it offered some protection against the transmission of HIV. Currently, 95 percent of American women aged 15–45 who need contraception (that is, who are sexually active and fertile but do not want to become pregnant) are using some contraceptive technique.

Contraception Has Not Yet Solved the Problem of Unwanted Births

On the basis of this high rate of contraceptive usage, you might imagine that almost all pregnancies would be planned and would lead to the birth of wanted babies. Unfortunately, this is far from the truth. As you can see from Figure 11.1, fewer than half of all pregnancies lead to wanted births; the remainder lead to unwanted or mistimed births, or end in induced or spontaneous abortions.

Contraception remains controversial in some quarters even today, especially with regard to its use by teens. Should schools address the problem of teen pregnancy by providing information about contraception, and perhaps by making contraceptives available, or should they emphasize abstinence from sexual activity before marriage? We take up this question in Chapter 12. Because of this controversy, the U.S. government has been much less active in the field of contraception services, education, and research than are governments in many other industrialized countries. Thus, much of the burden of education and service provision has fallen on nongovernmental organizations.

Another practical problem is financial: many medical insurance plans do not cover contraceptive drugs or devices that require a prescription, or do so less generously than for other kinds of drugs and devices (Figure 11.2). Outpatient visits for contraceptive advice and fitting of contraceptive devices are often not covered either, even when the policies cover outpatient medical visits for other purposes (Planned Parenthood Federation, 2002). Health maintenance organizations (HMOs) are usually more generous in this respect than other forms of medical insurance. Federal legislation to mandate equal coverage of contraceptive and noncontraceptive prescription drugs and services has been introduced in Congress on more than one occasion (most recently in 2001), but has not yet been enacted. Providing full contraceptive coverage in employment-based medical plans is estimated to cost no more than about $21 per employee per year (Alan Guttmacher Institute, 2002).

Different Users Need Different Kinds of Contraception

All men and women who are heterosexually active during their fertile years need to give some thought to the regulation of reproduction. Typically, people's interests in this matter vary over the life span, which can be divided into three phases:

- In the early fertile years, from soon after puberty to some point in adulthood, people are very sexually active, but are not in the kind of stable relationship that would be optimal for parenting. Furthermore, the demands of schooling and careers, the pursuit of social activities, and economic constraints all make parenthood an unattractive option at best, and a disaster at worst. Thus, sexually active young people in this phase of life need a form of birth control that is highly reliable and yet reversible.

- If and when couples settle down and wish to start families, they may still not want to have as many children as would result from totally unprotected sex. For such people in the middle of their fertile years, birth control still needs to be reversible, but it need not be highly reliable.

- For people later in their fertile years who have already had as many children as they want, birth control again needs to be highly reliable, but it may not need to be reversible.

Another important factor that varies over the life span is the degree to which men and women have shared interests in birth control. A married or cohabiting couple has typically established a great deal of trust and common purpose, and usually forms a monogamous unit. Thus, it relatively easy for the man and woman to implement a method of birth control that works for them as a couple.

For young singles, this process may be more problematic. Although trust, collaboration, and monogamy may all be desirable traits, they are far from universal in practice. Statements such as "I'm on the pill" or "I'll pull out" may need to be viewed skeptically. Thus, it often comes down to a question of how a man can protect *his* interests and how a woman can protect *her* interests. From these individual perspectives, birth control methods should ideally be either self-reliant or evident in use (as putting on a condom is, for example), so that each partner can be confident that an effective method is being employed.

Here are some issues that people who are choosing a contraceptive technique need to consider. (For convenience, we use "you" language here, but we hope that you will consider the viewpoints of other potential users besides yourself.)

- **Reliability.** How reliable does the method have to be? If becoming a parent would be a disaster for you, and especially if abortion is not acceptable to you as a second line of defense, then your contraceptive method needs to be as close to 100 percent reliable as possible. With some methods, such as oral contraceptives, fewer than 1 percent of users will become pregnant in a single year, provided they practice the method properly. This percentage is called the **perfect-use failure rate** of the method. All humans are fallible, however; for example, a woman may forget to take the pill for a day or two. Thus the **typical-use failure rates** of contraceptive methods tend to be higher—about 6 percent for the pill. Only a few methods have typical-use failure rates below 1 percent; these are methods, such as sterilization, contraceptive implants and injections, and some IUDs, that you can basically forget about once you have taken the initial steps.

- **Reversibility.** Do you want to put a permanent end to your ability to become a parent? If so, sterilization is a good option. Other techniques, such as condoms, are reversible immediately. With some others, such as depot injections, it may take several months for fertility to be restored.

- **Protection against sexually transmitted diseases (STDs).** Are you sure that you are in a monogamous relationship and that both you and your partner are free of STDs? If you are, consider yourself fortunate. If not, the protective value of contraceptive methods should be taken into consideration. Male and female condoms offer the best protection against STDs, including HIV. Condoms can be combined with other techniques, such as oral contraceptives, to add STD protection and increase reliability.

- **Ease of use.** Some methods, such as condoms and diaphragms, demand some time and attention before or during every sexual encounter. Some require taking a pill consistently every day—a seemingly simple task that researchers have found to be quite difficult in practice (see below). Also, bear in mind that some sexually active people have physical or mental disabilities that make certain contraceptive methods especially challenging for them. Some contraceptive methods require a significant investment of time and effort at the beginning (such as going to a clinic for a prescription or an IUD insertion). If you will need contraception only occasionally, these latter methods may be "overkill."

Ideally, dating couples who engage in sex will cooperate to ensure that pregnancy doesn't occur, but a self-reliant method, or one that is evident in use, may allay concerns about partner reliability.

- **Intrusiveness in use.** Some methods, such as condoms, interfere with the "spontaneity" of sex. They may also decrease sensitivity or introduce strange sensations and (especially with female condoms) strange noises. How much of a disadvantage is this to you?
- **Cost.** Can you afford fairly substantial up-front expenses, such as may be involved in seeing a doctor for a prescription, a diaphragm, an IUD, or sterilization? Do you qualify for any kind of financial help? Will your partner split the costs with you? Even if you have to pay yourself, the costs of such methods may even out over time, compared with pay-as-you go methods such as condoms. And the costs of effective contraception are likely to be less than the costs of an unwanted pregnancy, however you deal with it.
- **Safety.** Do you have any risk factors that would make it inadvisable to use certain contraceptive methods? (We will discuss these risk factors below.)
- **Moral considerations.** Do you share the Roman Catholic Church's view that preventing pregnancy by any artificial means is wrong? If so, you may want to consider the "rhythm method" or "natural family planning"; with these methods, the couple reduces the likelihood of pregnancy by abstaining from coitus during the fertile portion of the woman's menstrual cycle. Do you think that preventing conception is acceptable, but that preventing the implantation of an *already fertilized* conceptus is wrong? If so, you may want to select a method that works entirely by preventing conception.
- **Cooperation and trust.** Is your relationship with your partner or partners such that you can collaborate on a contraceptive strategy? Ideally, you will discuss contraception (including the matter of STDs) with your partner and choose an appropriate method before first having coitus. Ideally, you will take joint steps to put it into practice, and you will be able to trust your partner's commitment to making it a success. But if you are less than confident in your partner's reliability, you may want to use a method for which you alone are responsible. If

TABLE 11.1 *Usage and failure rates of the most common contraceptive techniques*

Method	Usage (percentage of all contraceptive users who use this method)	Failure rate (percentage of women using this method who become pregnant in 1 year)	
		With perfect use	With typical use
Physical methods			
Male condom	20.4	3.0	16.0
Diaphragm	1.9	6.0	18.0
IUD	0.8	0.8	4.0
Hormone-based methods			
Pill	26.9	0.1	6.0
Injection	3.0	0.3	0.4
Implant	1.3	0.05	0.05
Behavioral methods			
Rhythm	2.3	9.0	19.0
Withdrawal	3.0	4.0	24.0
Sterilization			
Male	10.9	0.1	0.2
Female	27.7	0.5	0.5

Source: Alan Guttmacher Institute, 2000a.

you're a woman, remember that it's you who will become pregnant if contraception fails, and if you do become pregnant, your partner's ongoing support may not be a sure thing. If you're a man, remember that you cannot force your partner to have an abortion, and that you can be held legally responsible for any child you father, whether you wanted the child or not.

In Table 11.1, we summarize some key information about the most common methods of contraception. As shown in the table, contraceptive pills and the male condom are far and away the most popular contraceptive methods among those that are reversible. Nevertheless, they are far from ideal in terms of their reliability in typical use. As we'll discuss below, some of the less popular methods, such as implants and injections, are well worth considering.

Physical Methods Block Sperm Transport

Most contraceptive techniques work by physically interfering with gamete transport (condoms, diaphragms, intrauterine devices, and male and female sterilization), by suppressing the woman's fertility with hormones (contraceptive pills, implants, and injections), or by timing sex so as to avoid the woman's "fertile window" (rhythm or fertility awareness methods). There are also techniques that rely on a combination of methods, such as certain intrauterine devices. We begin with reversible physical methods, some of which have a long history of safe and successful use.

Male Condoms Are Reliable when Properly Used

The **male condom** (Figure 11.3) is a disposable sheath that is placed over the penis before coitus. It works simply as a barrier to the entry of semen into the vagina. Some condoms are coated with the spermicide nonoxynol-9, which kills sperm chemically, but the amount of spermicide is probably not enough to be effective in the event that the condom breaks. For that reason, couples who want the added protection of a spermicide would do better to use a vaginal spermicidal foam (see below) in conjunction with the condom.

Most condoms are made of latex. Some are made of polyurethane plastic, and some of animal intestinal tissue. Latex condoms are the cheapest: they cost less than 50 cents apiece when bought in multipacks, and there are quite a few programs that distribute them free. When used properly (Box 11.2), they are an effective contraceptive, and they also provide substantial protection against transmission of HIV and other infectious agents. They should be used in conjunction with water-based lubricants only. Oils, fats, lotions, petroleum jellies, and any lubricants containing those substances will weaken the latex and may cause the condom to break.

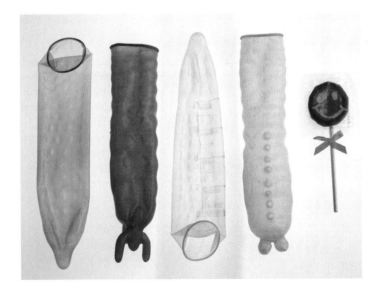

Figure 11.3 Male condoms come in a variety of types, sizes, and even flavors.

Some men and women are allergic to latex. (But if a spermicide-coated latex condom causes an allergic reaction, it may be to the spermicide rather than to the latex, so a non-coated latex condom may be worth trying.) Another potential disadvantage of latex condoms is that they lessen the sensations of coitus to a noticeable degree, especially for the man. However, this may actually be an advantage if it allows the man to engage in coitus for longer before reaching orgasm.

If either of these factors prevent the use of latex condoms, polyurethane or natural-tissue condoms can be tried. Both of these are more than twice as expensive as latex condoms. The polyurethane condom is thinner and slicker than latex, and it is not damaged by oil-based lubricants. It is an effective contraceptive. Its disease-preventing abilities have not been fully researched, but are thought to be good. Natural-tissue condoms are also effective contraceptives, but they are known to

Box 11.2 Sexual Health

How to Use a Condom

Condoms have a 3 percent failure rate (meaning a 3 percent chance of pregnancy per year) with *perfect* use, but a 16 percent failure rate with *typical* use. To turn yourself from a 16-percenter into a 3-percenter, follow these instructions.

Before you even open the condom package, squeeze it to check for the presence of an air bubble, which means that the package is undamaged.

Put the condom on after the penis becomes erect, but before coitus begins. Waiting until the man is near orgasm is a bad idea because it may not be possible to pull out in time. There is also a theoretical possibility of a woman's becoming pregnant from the small number of sperm present in the pre-ejaculate ("pre-cum" or bulbo-urethral gland secretion; see Chapter 3).

Make sure that the condom isn't dried up or brittle, but don't try to test it by, for example, inflating it. Put a small amount of water-based lubricant inside the condom, and place the condom on the tip of the

penis. If the condom has a little pouch at the end to hold the ejaculate, squeeze the pouch closed between your fingers to stop air getting trapped there. If there is no pouch, make a similar space by pinching the tip of the condom between your fingers.

If the penis is uncircumcised, pull the foreskin back before unrolling the condom.

Unroll the condom to the base of the penis, or as far as the condom will go. Squeeze out any air pockets. If the condom won't unroll, you have put it on backwards. Consider it contaminated and start again with a new one.

If the condom is unlubricated or insufficiently lubricated, put some water-based lubricant or contraceptive foam on the outside of the condom.

Engage in coitus! (Most instructions neglect to mention this step.)

After ejaculating, but while the penis is still erect and inside the vagina, grasp the edge of the condom with your fingers and withdraw the penis from the vagina, thus

ensuring that the condom doesn't slip off during withdrawal.

Take the condom off and throw it away in the trash (not the toilet). Wash the penis before bringing it into contact with the woman's vulva again.

A new condom should be used every time you have sex.

If a condom breaks and semen leaks into the vagina during the woman's fertile period, the likelihood of pregnancy resulting is high. Consider using emergency contraception within 72 hours.

Condoms can also be used during anal and oral sex to prevent disease transmission, but very thin-walled condoms may not be strong enough for anal sex. To reduce the likelihood of breakage, always use plenty of lubricant.

Store condoms in a cool, dry place, not in a spot prone to excessive heating, such as an automobile glove compartment. If you carry one around with you, replace it if you haven't used it in a few weeks.

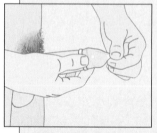

1 Squeeze the tip of the condom while placing it on the penis.

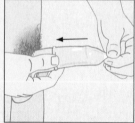

2 Unroll the condom as far as it will go.

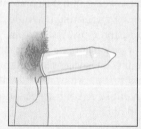

3 The condom is ready for action.

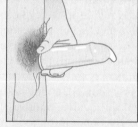

4 After ejaculation, withdraw the penis while holding the base of the condom.

5 Dispose of the condom in the trash, not the toilet.

be *ineffective* in preventing the transmission of HIV and some other STDs. Thus, they should be used only if STDs are not an issue.

Condoms come in quite a variety of sizes, styles, colors, and even flavors. A standard-size condom, which measures about 180 millimeters long by 52 millimeters across when flat, will fit most men after a fashion, but there are smaller ("snugger fit") and larger ("large," "magnum," "magnum XL") condoms available. There are also condoms whose width is greater near the tip, and condoms with various kinds of ribbed or bumpy surfaces. If condoms are going to be a part of your life for the foreseeable future, it may be worth ordering one of the sampler kits that are available on the Internet (at sites such as www.condom.com). These kits contain up to 32 different types of condoms from a variety of different manufacturers. (Testing them all could provide material for an interesting term paper.) Just be wary of natural-membrane or novelty condoms that may not provide adequate contraception or disease protection.

Condoms do sometimes break: the reasons include use of old, defective, or inappropriately sized condoms, insufficient lubrication, use of oil-based lubricants, failure to leave a space at the tip, and unusually vigorous sex. Strategies to prevent breakage include inspection of the condom before and during sex, use of plenty of water-soluble lubricant, changing condoms during prolonged coitus, using thicker condoms, or doubling up two condoms (with lubricant between them).

To get some idea of condom breakage rates under conditions of expert but real-world usage, a group headed by longtime contraceptive expert Robert Hatcher of Emory University interviewed prostitutes in legal brothels in Nevada, where condom usage is legally mandated (Albert et al., 1995). The prostitutes reported breakage rates of about 1 per 1000 usages. When the researchers undertook the noble task of examining the used condoms from 372 sexual encounters at the brothels, they found not a single broken condom. Over a 5-year period, over 20,000 HIV tests (see Chapter 16) were performed on legal Nevada prostitutes, and every single test came back negative. The message is clear: used correctly, condoms are very reliable.

Advantages of the male condom:
- It is cheap and readily accessible.
- It is reliable when properly used.
- It offers significant protection against STDs. This makes it an attractive option for use in conjunction with other methods, such as oral contraceptives.
- It lacks the possible side effects of hormone-based contraceptives.
- It is evident in use.
- It is fully and immediately reversible. In fact, it is the only reversible contraceptive method controlled by men.

Disadvantages of the male condom:
- Putting on a male condom can be intrusive during sex, because it cannot be put on until the man already has an erection. However, the man and woman can cooperate in putting on the condom, thus incorporating the procedure into the lovemaking process. Psychologically, this cooperation can be a valuable aid in building trust and intimacy.
- The man must maintain his erection for as long as the condom is in use. This can be difficult for men with erectile dysfunction. It also means that the man must withdraw promptly after ejaculating.
- Erotic sensation is reduced, especially for the man. This can be an advantage, however, if the man tends to reach orgasm earlier than he desires.
- Reliability is less than ideal in typical use.

Female Condoms Are Relatively Intrusive

The **female condom** (Reality condom, Femidom) is made of polyurethane. It resembles a large, nonelastic male condom, but it is stiffened by rings at each end (Figure 11.4). The ring at the closed end, which is inside, but not attached to, the condom, fits around the cervix rather like a diaphragm (see below). The ring at the open end is larger and stays outside the body. Thus the condom covers the entirety of the vagina and adjacent parts of the vulva. The condom comes with lubricant on the inside.

To insert the condom, the inner ring is first squeezed between the fingers and then pushed into the vagina with a finger until it can't be felt. This draws most of the condom into the vagina, but the free end should remain outside. During coitus, the man's penis should be guided into the inside of the condom. After use, the free end should be twisted to enclose the contents and the condom gently pulled out. This should be done before the woman stands up. As with male condoms, the female condom should be disposed of in the trash, not the toilet.

The Reality condom costs about $2.50 per unit, making it much more expensive than male condoms. Because of its price, some women in developing countries wash, dry, and reuse the female condom, and one laboratory study has

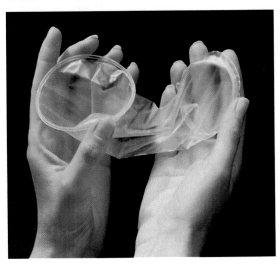

Figure 11.4 The Reality female condom is made of polyurethane. It is an effective contraceptive, but has not won broad consumer acceptance in the United States.

found that it stands up well to 10 cycles of reuse (McIntyre et al., 1998). It is approved only for single use, however, so most women should not reuse it.

Advantages of the female condom:

- The female condom is the only contraceptive controlled by the woman that probably offers substantial protection from STDs. Its disease-preventing action may be even better than that of the male condom because it covers parts of the vulva adjacent to the vagina that may be susceptible to genital warts and other infections (see Chapter 16). However, research into the female condom's actual ability to prevent disease transmission is quite limited (Macaluso et al., 2000).
- It can be inserted ahead of time, thus avoiding any interruption of lovemaking.
- The outer ring may provide extra stimulation of the clitoris during coitus.
- It does not require the man to maintain an erection during use.
- It is free of the side effects of hormone-based contraceptives.
- It is easily and immediately reversible.

Disadvantages of the female condom:

- Many couples find that the female condom reduces erotic sensation and, in fact, generates noneroticsensations and noises. The female condom tends to be less appealing to men than to women; part of the reason for this is that the protruding free end (which covers part of the vulva) is considered unaesthetic (Family Health International, 1999).
- There is the possibility that the man will unwittingly insert his penis into the vagina outside of the condom, thus nullifying its barrier function. This shouldn't happen, however, if both man and woman are alert to the possibility.
- Sometimes the entire condom may be drawn into the vagina during coitus. If this happens the condom should be replaced with another. To prevent this occurrence, it is sometimes necessary to hold the outer portion of the condom.
- Male and female condoms should not be used together because the friction between them may pull one of them out of place.

Most couples prefer the male condom to the female condom (Macaluso et al., 2000), and the female condom has not won substantial consumer acceptance in the United States since its approval by the Food and Drug Administration (FDA) in 1992. Still, its obvious advantages make it well worth a trial. Some couples may find that it is quite acceptable; they may be able to deal with the noise problem by adding extra lubricant, for example. The female condom has wider appeal in developing countries, where women often have a greater need to take charge of their own protection.

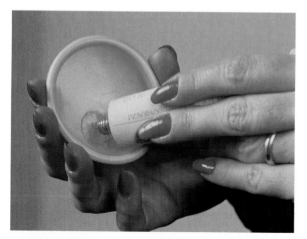

Figure 11.5 Diaphragms have lost popularity in the United States, but are still widely used elsewhere.

Diaphragms and Cervical Caps Are Inconvenient but Have Few Side Effects

The **diaphragm** (Figure 11.5) used to be a very popular form of contraception prior to the development of oral contraceptives, but is now used by fewer than 1 in 50 women. It is a dome-shaped piece of latex or rubber that is stiffened by a rubber-covered metal spring or strip around its perimeter. It fits against the walls of the vagina, covering the cervix. It works by preventing sperm from entering the cervix. However, sperm can migrate around the edges of the diaphragm, and it must therefore be used in conjunction with a spermicidal cream or jelly.

The diaphragm should be inserted before coitus—either immediately before, or sometime earlier (Box 11.3). If inserted more than a couple of hours prior to sex, however, the contraceptive cream may dissipate, reducing its effectiveness. After coitus, the diaphragm should be left in place for at least 6 hours. Repeated coitus can occur without removing or replacing the diaphragm, but more spermicide should be inserted with the aid of an applicator tube.

Box 11.3 *Sexual Health*

How to Use a Diaphragm

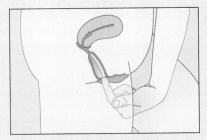

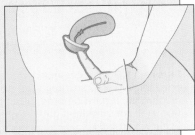

1 Put spermicidal cream or jelly around the rim of the diaphragm and in the center of the hollow side.

2 Fold the diaphragm.

3 Insert the diaphragm, hollow side up, and push it into the vagina.

4 Feel with a finger to make sure that the diaphragm is properly covering the cervix.

The keys to successful use of a diaphragm are selection of the appropriately sized diaphragm (done by a birth-control specialist or other experienced professional), proper timing of insertion and removal, correct use of spermicide, correct placement, and care and regular inspection of the diaphragm.

The diaphragm can be inserted immediately before coitus or up to 2 hours earlier. It must be left in place at least 6 hours after coitus, but no more than 24 hours.

Before insertion, empty your bladder. Place about a teaspoonful of contraceptive cream or jelly in the center of the hollow side of the diaphragm, and spread it around so that it covers that side and also the rim. Do not use Vaseline or any oil-based lubricant: these are ineffective and can damage the diaphragm.

Find a comfortable position for inserting the diaphragm. You can lie on your back with your knees bent, squat, or stand with one leg raised onto a chair. Fold the diaphragm between thumb and fingers, but not so tightly as to squeeze out the spermicide. Push it far up into the vagina so that the upper part of the rim lodges in the hollow beyond the cervix. With your index finger, push the front part of the rim until it sits snugly behind the pubic bone. Use your finger to check that the diaphragm is lying snugly against the cervix.

Between inserting the diaphragm and having sex you can pursue regular activities, go to the toilet, etc., and the diaphragm will stay in place. If you have a bowel movement, wash your hands scrupulously and then recheck that the diaphragm remains properly located.

You can insert extra spermicide into the vagina with an applicator. This is a good idea if you engage in coitus for a second time in a short period. (In that situation, do not remove the diaphragm to add more spermicide inside it.) It may also be a good idea if you know you are at the time of ovulation, when conception is most likely.

Male condoms can be used in conjunction with a diaphragm. This is a good idea while you are still learning how to use the diaphragm. The use of a condom also greatly increases protection from sexually transmitted diseases.

To remove the diaphragm, lift the front rim away from the cervix with your index finger and pull it away, following the direction of the floor of the vagina. It helps to bear down gently while doing so.

Wash the diaphragm with mild soap, rinse thoroughly, dry completely, and check visually for holes or other damage by holding the diaphragm against the light. Dust the diaphragm with cornstarch and put it away in its container in a place that is protected from heat.

Have the fitting rechecked by a professional within a few weeks if you have only recently started having sex. Otherwise, have it rechecked if you have gained or lost a lot of weight or have been pregnant, or in conjunction with an annual health examination.

A diaphragm should not be left in place longer than 24 hours, since doing so may raise the risk of toxic shock syndrome (see Chapter 4). The diaphragm is removed by working a finger under the front rim and breaking its adhesion to the cervix, whereupon it can be pulled out. It is washed with warm water and mild soap, dried, and stored.

Because the diaphragm's efficacy depends on its snug fit, it must be individually sized and prescribed by a clinician. The fit may change after childbirth or substantial gain or loss of weight. The diaphragm also needs to be periodically examined for pinhole leaks; this can be done by holding it up to the light and stretching the rubber slightly.

Advantages of the diaphragm:
- It is somewhat less intrusive than condoms because it can be inserted ahead of time and does not usually affect sensation during sex.
- It lacks the side effects of hormone-based contraceptives.

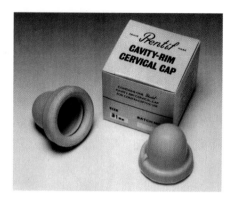

Figure 11.6 The cervical cap holds onto the cervix by suction. Like the diaphragm, it must be used in conjunction with spermicide. (Courtesy of Cervical Cap Ltd.)

- It is relatively cheap. Although it requires a medical visit for initial fitting, the diaphragm itself costs only a few dollars and lasts for a year or two, so the only ongoing expense is for the contraceptive cream.
- Long-term use of the diaphragm is associated with a lowered risk of cervical cancer (Coker et al., 1992), probably because the diaphragm offers some protection against infection of the cervix with human papillomavirus, the virus that causes cervical cancer (see Chapter 17).

Disadvantages of the diaphragm:
- It is inconvenient, both because of the necessity for professional fitting and because of the need for insertion, removal, and cleaning. If the woman wishes to insert the diaphragm ahead of time, she has to have some idea of whether and when coitus is going to take place.
- Its failure rate is significantly greater than that of hormone-based methods and even slightly greater than that of condoms.
- It provides much less disease protection than condoms, although the spermicide has some antimicrobial action.

A new diaphragm, the **Lea Contraceptive** (also called **Lea's Shield**), may be approved by the FDA soon. This silicon device incorporates a one-way valve that lets fluids escape from the cervix into the vagina, but not vice versa. The valve also allows air to be removed from behind the diaphragm, thus improving the suction fit against the cervix. An important feature is that one size fits all, so it does not have to be fit by a clinician and will be sold without prescription, like condoms. Also, it can be worn for longer than a regular diaphragm. Testing so far suggests that Lea's Shield is about as reliable as a regular diaphragm, and may be better for women who have previously had children (Mauck et al., 1996).

The **cervical cap** (Figure 11.6) is smaller and more steeply domed than the diaphragm. It is held in place not by fitting against the walls of the vagina, but by holding like a suction cup onto the cervix itself. Like the diaphragm, it must be prescribed and individually fitted. Spermicide is placed inside the cap, and it is folded and inserted rather like a diaphragm. After insertion, the woman feels with a finger to make sure that it is sitting right on the cervix. Like the diaphragm, the cap can be inserted an hour or two before intercourse, and must be left in place for at least 6 hours afterward. The advantages and disadvantages of the cervical cap are similar to those of the diaphragm, but there are some differences:

Advantage of the cervical cap:
- The cervical cap is an alternative to the diaphragm for women whose vaginal anatomy makes a diaphragm difficult to fit.

Disadvantages of the cervical cap:
- Its failure rate is somewhat higher than that of the diaphragm, especially in women who have had children.
- Even if properly inserted, it can be dislodged from the cervix during coitus.

In general, diaphragms and cervical caps may be good options for women who need to be in charge of their own contraception but cannot or do not want to use hormone-based methods.

Spermicides Are Not Very Reliable when Used Alone

Some women use **spermicides** as their sole method of contraception. Spermicides are sperm-killing chemicals, such as nonoxynol-9, that come in the form of contraceptive foams, jellies, creams, suppositories ("inserts"), sponges, or dissolvable films (Figure 11.7). They are placed deep in the vagina no more than 2 hours prior to coitus (but no less than 10 minutes prior to coitus in the case of suppositories, which need time to dissolve). They must be left in place for at least 6 hours afterward—in other words, the woman should not rinse out her vagina during this time.

Advantages of spermicides:
- They are readily available without a prescription.

- They are inexpensive.
- They have few side effects, except in the case of allergic reactions.

Disadvantages of spermicides:

- Spermicides can hardly be recommended as the sole means of contraception, as their failure rate is quite high—about 25 percent for the foams and possibly higher for the suppositories. They are better suited for use in combination with barrier methods.
- Spermicides, used alone, offer no significant protection against several sexually transmitted diseases, including gonorrhea, chlamydia, and HIV. In fact, frequent use of spermicides can cause genital irritation or lesions, thus *increasing* the likelihood of acquiring or transmitting HIV (Centers for Disease Control, 2002c).

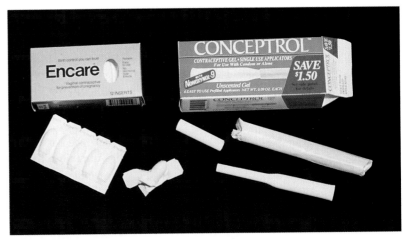

Figure 11.7 Spermicides come in a variety of forms. Both Encare inserts and Conceptrol gel contain the spermicide nonoxynol-9.

Intrauterine Devices Block Sperm Transport and May Prevent Implantation

Intrauterine devices (IUDs) are plastic objects, often in the shape of a T, that are placed in the uterus. They work by causing a low-grade inflammation of the uterus that interferes with sperm transport. They may also interfere with implantation if fertilization should occur. Some IUDs also release progestins; we will discuss the contraceptive action of progestins in the section on hormone-based contraceptives below.

IUDs were once widely used in the United States, but one poorly designed IUD, the Dalkon Shield, caused a number of deaths in the 1970s. The resulting litigation led to most IUDs being withdrawn from the market (Bullough & Bullough, 1997). Currently, only two models of IUDs are available in the United States: the **ParaGard** or **Copper-T** and the recently approved **Mirena**. (A third model, the **Progestasert**, has recently been withdrawn—for economic reasons, not safety concerns.) Fewer than 1 percent of American women use IUDs, but they are much more popular elsewhere: more than 100 million women use them worldwide. They have a unique combination of features that makes them well worth considering.

An IUD must be inserted by a trained health care professional. (Not all gynecologists are familiar with the procedure.) It is passed through the cervix while folded up inside an inserter; once it is in the uterus, the inserter is removed, and the IUD unfolds like a model ship in a bottle (Figure 11.8). A plastic thread is attached to the bottom of the T which is left

Figure 11.8 IUD insertion. (A) The Mirena IUD. (B) Insertion of the ParaGard IUD. The Mirena is inserted in a similar way.

(A)

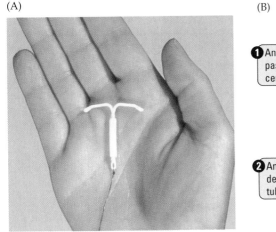

(B)

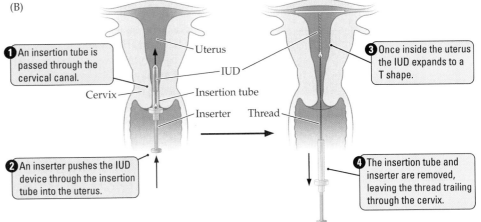

❶ An insertion tube is passed through the cervical canal.

❷ An inserter pushes the IUD device through the insertion tube into the uterus.

Uterus

IUD

Cervix

Insertion tube

Inserter

Thread

❸ Once inside the uterus the IUD expands to a T shape.

❹ The insertion tube and inserter are removed, leaving the thread trailing through the cervix.

trailing through the cervix. Every month after her period the woman or her partner must make sure the thread is in place—meaning that the IUD has not been discharged and is properly positioned. The thread also helps in the removal of the IUD, which must be done by a professional. The insertion and removal can be quite uncomfortable procedures.

The ParaGard can be left in place for up to 10 years. The Mirena, which releases the progestin levonorgestrel, lasts for 5 years. Any IUD should be removed if the woman reaches menopause while using it.

Advantages of the IUD:
- Both the ParaGard and the Mirena IUDs are very effective, with perfect-use failure rates of no more than 1 percent. The typical-use failure rate of 4 percent is actually better than that of contraceptive pills, though not as good as that of contraceptive implants or injections.
- There are few side effects, and no systemic hormonal side effects, even with the hormone-releasing Mirena.
- Once inserted, IUDs are highly convenient and nonintrusive, requiring only the monthly thread check.
- With the Mirena, menstrual cramping and bleeding may be reduced and sometimes abolished altogether.
- IUD contraception is reversible immediately on removal of the device (but see below).

Disadvantages of the IUD:
- The one-time costs are fairly high: $350–400 for the Mirena and $179 for the ParaGard, plus the clinic's fees for insertion and removal, but there are no ongoing costs (unless condoms are added for disease prevention).
- Some cramping and irregular bleeding may occur, but these usually go away after a short period of use. With the ParaGard, menstrual flows may be increased.
- IUDs offer no protection against STDs.

For women who have an STD while an IUD is in place, the IUD may increase the likelihood of pelvic inflammatory disease or worsen preexisting disease. Because pelvic inflammatory disease can damage the oviducts and lead to infertility (see Chapter 10), it may not be quite correct to say that the IUD is a perfectly reversible contraceptive technique. For this reason, some experts are reluctant to recommend IUDs for young women who have not had children and who will want to have them in the future. Still, the likelihood of IUD use leading to infertility is small. In fact, a recent large-scale study conducted in Mexico found no association between the use of copper IUDs and damage to the oviducts (Hubacher et al., 2001). Women who currently have an STD or pelvic inflammatory disease should not receive an IUD, and women who are at increased risk of acquiring STDs because they have multiple sex partners are also advised against using this form of contraception.

IUDs increase the likelihood that any pregnancy that does occur will be ectopic (see Chapter 10). Women who are at increased risk of ectopic pregnancy for any reason should not use an IUD.

Couples who have had children and are thinking about sterilization may want to consider an IUD: it is reversible, less invasive, less expensive, and nearly as effective. IUDs may also be a suitable way to space out pregnancies. Even young women who have not had children may want to consider an IUD. The slightly increased risk of pelvic inflammatory disease may be balanced by the health and psychological benefits of greater contraceptive efficacy compared with barrier methods or oral contraceptives. In short, the IUD is a form of contraception that deserves to be more popular than it currently is.

Hormone-Based Methods Interfere with Ovulation, Sperm Transport, and Implantation

A considerable variety of hormone-based contraceptives are available. They differ in the kinds and amounts of hormones they contain as well as in their form of delivery: pills, implants, or injections. Because oral contraceptives (pills) are so popular—they are the choice of more than one in four women who use any kind of contraception—and because they come in a number of significantly different formulations, we will devote most of our attention to them.

Contraceptive pills (Figure 11.9) contain either a combination of two hormones—an estrogen and a progestin—or just one hormone, a progestin. Both hormones are synthetic: the estrogen is either ethinyl estradiol or another compound, mestranol, that is converted into ethinyl estradiol in the body. The progestin can be any of a number of compounds, including levonorgestrel (the compound released by the Mirena IUD). Synthetic steroids are used because they are broken down in the body much more slowly than the natural hormones, so that the pills need be taken only once a day.

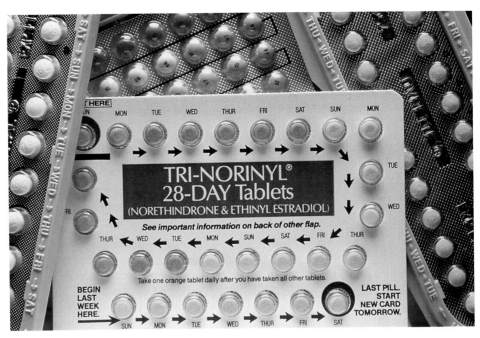

Figure 11.9 A variety of combination contraceptive pills in 28-day dispensers. Note the orange dummy pills for the 7-day drug holiday seen at the bottom of the photograph.

Combination Pills Are Reliable but May Have Side Effects

The most commonly used type of contraceptive pill is the **constant-dose combination pill.** Such pills, of which there are many different brands, as well as generic versions, usually contain between 20 and 50 micrograms (mcg) of estrogen and between 0.1 and 1.0 milligrams (mg) of progestin. (Part of the reason for the varying progestin doses is that progestins vary in potency: 0.1 mg of one may be the functional equivalent of 1.0 mg of another.) Typically, a woman takes one pill a day for 21 days, followed by no pills (or inactive dummy pills) for 7 days. A month's supply can cost as little as $15 for generic products.

A second, more recent kind of combination pill is the **triphasic** (or **multiphasic**) **combination pill** (examples are Triphasil, Ortho-Novum 7/7/7, and Tri-Norinyl). In these pills, the amounts and ratios of estrogen and progestin vary around the cycle. The idea is to minimize the total doses of hormones and decrease side effects. These pills are more expensive than constant-dose pills, costing $25 or more per month. Whether they have practical benefits that justify the increased cost is unclear.

The main site of action of combination pills is the brain—specifically, the hypothalamic–pituitary control system (see Chapter 4). The progestin component of the pill exerts a negative feedback effect on the hypothalamus and pituitary, decreasing the secretion of FSH. The estrogen component potentiates this effect by increasing levels of progestin receptors. It also has an FSH-suppressing effect of its own. Because FSH secretion is suppressed, the FSH-dependent maturation of ovarian follicles does not occur; therefore, there is no ovulation and little secretion of estrogens by the ovaries. This suppression of ovulation is the main route by which the combination pill prevents pregnancy.

A second site of action is the uterus. The hormones cause the cervix to secrete thick mucus that hampers sperm transport. The endometrium develops under the influence of the hormones, but it may not be able to sustain implantation. During the 7-day drug-free portion of the cycle, the endometrium collapses and bleeding occurs. This bleeding simulates a natural menstrual period, although the amount may be less than a woman normally experiences.

During the drug-free period, the pituitary is relieved of its feedback inhibition and secretes FSH, which in turn causes the development of ovarian follicles to begin. The woman is just as well protected from pregnancy during the drug-free days as during the rest of the cycle, however, because the further development of these follicles is suppressed as soon as the next cycle of pills begins. If the woman forgets to begin the next cycle, however, the developing follicles can proceed to ovulation within a couple of days or so, potentially leading to pregnancy.

The reason for the 7-day drug-free interval is mainly to give the woman the sense (one could say "illusion") that she is experiencing normal menstrual cycles. Other than this possible psychological benefit, there is no proven health benefit of the drug-free interval and the withdrawal bleeding it causes. Women do not have to menstruate to remain healthy or to preserve their future fertility (Coutinho & Segal, 1999) (Box 11.4).

Many physicians prefer to prescribe pills containing as little estrogen as possible (i.e., 20 mcg or thereabouts), because it is primarily the estrogen in combination pills that is responsible for the health risks associated with these products (see below). Low-estrogen combination pills are as effective in preventing pregnancy as are higher-estrogen products. They do not always regulate the woman's menstrual cycle as effectively, however, and this can be a reason why some women discontinue low-estrogen combination pills (Thorneycroft & Cariati, 2001).

Advantages of combination pills:
- With perfect use, combination pills are extremely reliable: no more than one in a thousand women will become pregnant per year. Unfortunately, it is easy to forget a pill or two. In fact, one group of researchers who installed electronic spies in women's pill boxes found that about half the women forgot to take three or more pills per cycle (Potter et al., 1996). This compliance problem undermines the pill's reliability. Thus, the typical-use failure rate is about 6 percent—slightly worse than the IUD. Still, even this rate is quite good.
- They are convenient, nonintrusive, and do not interfere with the spontaneity of sex nor diminish the sensations of coitus. It is probably these aspects of the pill that have made it so popular.
- They are easily reversible. Fertility should return to normal levels by 3 months after stopping the combination pill.
- Many women experience lessened menstrual flows and diminished or absent menstrual cramps when on the pill.

Box 11.4 *Sexual Health*

Is Menstruation Obsolete?

Is Menstruation Obsolete? was the provocative title of a 1999 book by Brazilian contraception expert Elsimar Coutinho and reproductive endocrinologist Sheldon Segal of the Population Council (Coutinho & Segal, 1999). The book promotes the notion of suppressing menstruation, based on the following ideas:

- A cycle of regular monthly menstruation is not women's natural state. During most of human evolution, women would have spent almost their entire fertile years pregnant or nursing their offspring, and would have experienced infrequent menses. Regular menstruation is a by-product of the recent Western trend toward earlier menarche, fewer children, and abbreviated breast feeding.
- As recently as the nineteenth century, bloodletting was the medical treatment for almost all ills, and the notion that menstrual bleeding rids the body of impurities is an ingrained medical and popular superstition. Many women are convinced that monthly bleeding is essential for their health, yet no health benefit of regular menstruation has ever been demonstrated.

- Menstruation is associated with a number of serious ill effects, including premenstrual syndrome, menstrual cramps, anemia, and endometriosis.

- Menstruation can be safely reduced or eliminated by the continuous use of combination contraceptive pills, Depo-Provera, certain implants not available in the United States, and the Mirena IUD, as well as by more natural methods such as breast feeding and intensive exercise.

Coutinho and Segal's ideas run counter to a feminist perspective that sees menstruation as central to a woman's identity (Grahn, 1994; Shuttle & Redgrove, 1999). It is possible that the suppression of menstruation by some women would unnecessarily "pathologize" menstruation for all women. Coutinho and Segal's ideas have generated fairly widespread support within the medical community (Thomas & Ellertson, 2000), but some experts question whether the long-term effects of menstrual suppression have been well enough studied to justify its recommendation at this point. In spite of these reservations, it seems that some kind of movement toward more widespread suppression of menstruation may be in the offing. An example is the expected introduction of Seasonale, a new combination pill that is taken continuously for twelve weeks (see text).

- Use of combination pills is associated with a diminished incidence of several conditions: ovarian and endometrial cancer, ovarian cysts, pelvic inflammatory disease (probably because the thicker cervical mucus impedes the entry of microorganisms into the reproductive tract), ectopic pregnancy, noncancerous diseases of the breast, iron deficiency anemia (because of the diminished menstrual bleeding), acne, and possibly colorectal cancer, osteoporosis, and arthritis. Some of these effects are quite marked: the risk of ovarian cancer, for example, is reduced by 80 percent in women who use the combination pill for 10 years. Together, these effects offer a substantial health benefit.

Disadvantages of combination pills:
- They offer no protection against STDs, including AIDS. (However, condoms can be added for disease protection.)
- The woman needs to remember to take the pills regularly—a disadvantage compared with the implant and depot injection methods discussed below.
- The method is not evident to the woman's partner, unless he is present every day when she takes the pill. Thus, he has no objective assurance that effective contraception is being practiced.
- The combination pill can have several side effects, some of them serious or, in rare instances, fatal. Frequently reported side effects include nausea, breast pain, increased breast size, irregular bleeding, abdominal pain, back pain, decreased vaginal lubrication, weight gain, blotchy discoloration of the skin, emotional lability or depression, and decreased or increased interest in sex. In a placebo trial of one triphasic combination pill, however, only breast pain and emotional lability were substantially more frequent in the patients who received the real pill, and even with these two side effects, the differences did not quite reach statistical significance (Redmond et al., 1999). Among the less common but more serious side effects are hypertension (increased blood pressure) and disorders of blood clotting, including coronary thromboses (heart attacks), venous thromboses (clots in large veins), pulmonary embolism (clots that get carried to the lungs), and strokes (clots or bleeds in cerebral arteries). Although these complications are not common, the reality of the increased risk has been well established. The risk for women over 35 who smoke is particularly high, and such women are usually advised not to use combination pills.
- There have been conflicting data on whether the use of oral contraceptives increases the risk of breast cancer. The current view, based on meta-analyses of numerous studies, is that oral contraceptive use *is* associated with a slightly increased risk of breast cancer during the time of contraceptive use, but that the increased risk disappears by 10 years after cessation of use (American Cancer Society, 2000).
- Combination pills should not be used by nursing mothers because the hormones can reach the baby via the milk. Also, the pills reduce the production of milk.

As a 37-year-old smoker, this woman faces a relatively high risk of experiencing serious side effects if she uses combination contraceptive pills.

The possible serious side effects of the combination pill should be kept in perspective. It is safer to take the combination pill than to experience the effects of inadequate contraception: pregnancy, childbirth, or abortion. Furthermore, the major risks pertain mostly to identifiable groups of women who can be counseled to use alternative methods.

Progestin-Only Pills Have Fewer Side Effects but Are Somewhat Less Reliable

The **progestin-only pill** (or "**mini-pill**") contains very low doses of progestins. A brand called Micronor, for example, contains just 0.35 mg of the progestin norethindrone. Compare that with the 1.0 mg of norethindrone, plus an estrogen, in the combination pill Ortho-Novum 1/35 and its generic equivalents (and then ask yourself why Micronor is more than twice as expensive as the generic version of Ortho-Novum!). How can a pill that contains so much less of an active ingredient have a reliable contraceptive effect? And if it does, why don't the combination pills go out of business? The answer is that the progestin-only pill works differently from the combination pill, is somewhat less reliable, requires greater care in use, has some unique side effects—and is more expensive.

The progestin-only pill does not reliably shut down ovulation, although it does do so in some women. It works mainly through its effect on the cervical mucus, making it viscous and hostile to sperm transport. It may also make the endometrium hostile to implantation. These actions of progestin require lower doses than its actions on the hypothalamus and do not require the presence of estrogens.

The effects of each progestin-only pill last a very short time—barely 24 hours. Therefore, a woman who uses this method of contraception must be very careful not to miss a dose, or even to delay a dose by more than an hour or so. There is no 7-day drug holiday every month, as with the combination pill: the progestin-only pill must be taken every single day for as long as contraception is required.

Both the perfect-use and typical-use failure rates are slightly higher for progestin-only pills than for combination pills. The failure rates tend to be higher for younger women, who may lack the regular lifestyle or sense of commitment that is necessary to keep taking the pill on time. Still, the progestin-only pill remains one of the most reliable birth control methods.

Many of the advantages and disadvantages of progestin-only pills are similar to those of combination pills. Here we compare the two kinds of pills.

Advantages of progestin-only pills:
- Progestin-only pills lack the estrogenic side effects of combination pills (although weight gain can still be a problem, as progestins have anabolic actions). They are a good alternative for women who experience serious side effects with the combination pill or who fall in risk groups for which the combination pill is contraindicated.
- Progestin-only pills can be used by mothers who are breast-feeding their infants, starting 6 weeks after birth.

Disadvantages of progestin-only pills:
- Unlike the combination pill, which often turns irregularly cycling women into 28-day menstrual automata, the progestin-only pill has the opposite effect, tending to disrupt the menstrual cycles of women who were previously quite regular. This effect is highly variable from woman to woman, however, and does not have major health consequences so long as total blood loss is not increased. It can be a reason why some women discontinue this form of contraception, however.
- The progestin-only pill is somewhat less reliable than the combination pill in typical use.

Given the wide variety of contraceptive pills available—with more coming on the market all the time—a woman who is considering this form of contraception should consult with a knowledgeable professional who can recommend a pill suited to her needs and who can recommend appropriate changes if side effects crop up. As a woman may be taking the pill for years, it is worth some investment of time and effort to make sure that she is taking the right one for her.

Implants Circumvent the Compliance Problem

We now shift our attention to hormone-based contraceptives that are administered **parenterally**, that is, other than by mouth. We have already mentioned one parenteral hormone-based contraceptive: the progestin-releasing IUD. However, hormones account for only part of the action of that device. The methods we consider now depend entirely on the slow release of progestins.

The first such method is the **contraceptive implant,** of which only one brand, **Norplant,** is currently available in the United States (but see below). Norplant is a set of six matchstick-sized Silastic capsules that are implanted under the skin of the upper arm, where they remain for up to 5 years, slowly releasing the progestin levonorgestrel (Figure 11.10). The capsules release a total of about 0.5 mg of progestin per day initially, but the rate of release declines over time: after 2 years, it is about 0.2 mg per day.

The implantation must be done by a trained professional, who makes a very small incision in the skin under local anesthesia and uses an inserter to place the capsules in the subcutaneous tissue in a fan-shaped arrangement. The implantation is done within a few days of the onset of the woman's menstrual period to ensure that she is not pregnant. The implantation costs $500 to $750, which includes a medical examination, the insertion, and the cost of the capsules. The incision heals over in a few days, but the site may be sore for a longer period.

Removing the capsules can be tricky: the capsules may become embedded in tough connective tissue, or they may migrate slightly under the skin. More than one office visit may be required to get them out. It is important to remove the capsules after they expire, however, because they continue to release low levels of progestin. These may impair fertility to an unpredictable degree, and if pregnancy does occur, it has a greater than usual chance of being ectopic. New capsules can be implanted when the old ones are removed. Removal costs $150 to $200.

Because the release rate of the capsules changes over time, so does their mechanism of action. During the first year or so, the release rate is high enough to block ovulation in many women, especially smaller women, for whom the fixed release rate produces a higher blood concentration of the hormone. If ovulation is blocked, so is menstruation, but there may still be some irregular bleeding or spotting. Later in the implant's life, it works mainly by its effects on cervical mucus and endometrial structure, blocking sperm transport and implantation like a progestin-only pill.

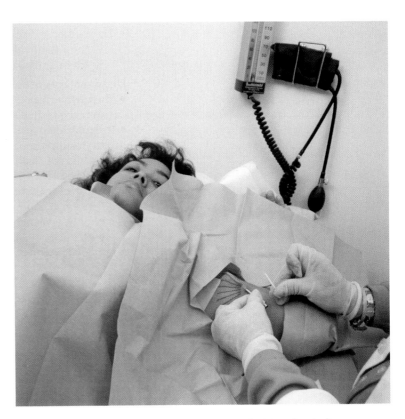

Figure 11.10 Norplant slow-release capsules being inserted. The 6 lines drawn on the woman's arm show where the capsules will be placed.

In 2000 it was discovered that some batches of Norplant were releasing lower than expected amounts of progestin. Women who received Norplant from those batches were advised to use alternative forms of contraception. At this writing, Norplant is not being distributed in the United States, and women can get it only by finding a provider who has implants from unaffected batches available.

Another form of Norplant, Norplant 2, uses just two capsules instead of six, but is not available in the United States.

Another implant, **Implanon,** is used in Europe and may become available in the United States within a year or two. It releases a different progestin, desogestrel, and provides protection for 3 years. It is a single capsule, rather than two or six, as with Norplant, so insertion and removal are easier.

Advantages of contraceptive implants:
- Implants, when properly manufactured, are extremely reliable. During the first year, the perfect-use failure rate of Norplant is 0.05 percent, which is essentially zero. Because the release rate declines over time, Norplant's efficacy also declines, so that the perfect-use failure rate for the fifth year is 1–2 percent. Since Norplant places no demands on the user after the initial office visit, however, there is no compliance problem, and the typical-use failure rate is the same as the perfect-use rate. This makes Norplant one of the most reliable of all reversible contraceptive methods, even over the full 5-year span.
- Aside from the insertion and removal, Norplant is totally convenient and nonintrusive.
- There are no estrogenic side effects.

- The method is fully reversible, although reversal does require an office visit for removal of the implants. Fertility returns almost immediately after removal.

Disadvantages of contraceptive implants:
- The method has a high up-front cost, but is slightly cheaper than pills over the course of 5 years.
- Irregular menstruation can be bothersome, but some women benefit from suppressed menstruation.
- Implants are visible in some women, especially those who are light-skinned. This visibility can be a disadvantage in the sense that it deprives the woman of privacy. On the other hand, it is objective evidence that contraception is in place. Seeing a woman's implants may offer her partner or partners a kind of assurance that is not available with pills.
- Implants provide no protection from STDs.

Progestin Injections May Abolish Menstruation

Progestin can also be administered through intramuscular injection of a **slow-release (depot) form** of the hormone. The only such method currently approved for use in the United States is **Depo-Provera**, which contains the progestin **medroxyprogesterone acetate (MPA)**. An injection of 150 mg of MPA in depot form provides contraception for 3 months. An injection costs about $50, so a year's contraception costs about $200.

Like Norplant, Depo-Provera is usually administered within a few days of the onset of menstruation to ensure that the woman is not pregnant. Repeat injections should not be delayed more than 2 weeks beyond the 3-month approved period, or pregnancy may occur.

Initially, a woman who uses Depo-Provera may experience irregular bleeding. After a year of use, however, at least half of women experience complete cessation of menstruation. Some women consider this a worrisome side effect, while others consider it a convenience. There seem to be few medical problems caused by reducing or eliminating menstruation in this fashion, and some experts believe that doing so offers substantial health benefits (see Box 11.4).

Advantages of progestin injection:
- The injection of progestin is much simpler and cheaper than the implantation of capsules, and no removal is required. These advantages are counterbalanced by the necessity for repeat injections, however.
- The injection site is not visible, so the woman's privacy is preserved. (Again, this could also be a disadvantage, because there is no objective evidence of contraception.)

Disadvantages of progestin injection:
- Progestin injection is slightly less reliable than implants. Still, with a typical-use failure rate of 0.4 percent, it is among the most reliable contraceptive techniques. It is more reliable than contraceptive pills unless the pills are used perfectly, which rarely happens.
- Although contraception with Depo-Provera is fully reversible, it may take as much as a year for a woman to return to full fertility after discontinuing the injections.

Neither Norplant nor Depo-Provera has made major inroads into the U.S. contraceptive market: the combined users of these two methods amount to no more than about 4 percent of all women who use some form of contraception. Considering the combination of efficacy, convenience, nonintrusiveness, and safety that these methods offer, and their popularity in some other countries, this low level of use is surprising. In one study, women were asked why they did not use these methods (Tanfer et al., 2000), and the most common reasons given were ignorance about the methods, satisfaction with currently used methods, and fear of side effects. Nevertheless, considerable numbers of women said that they planned to use Depo-Provera in the future, suggesting that the use of this method will increase.

Once-a-Month Injections of Combination Contraceptives May Improve Compliance

The Pharmacia Corporation, which manufactures Depo-Provera, brought out a new injectable contraceptive, **Lunelle,** in 2000. Lunelle is an estrogen–progestin combination that is injected once a month. The hormones remain active for about 15 days, and most women experience withdrawal bleeding between approximately the eighteenth and twenty-fourth days after the injection. The main advantage of Lunelle over the combination pill is that women are less likely to forget a monthly injection than a daily pill, so this method may have a lower typical-use failure rate. The main disadvantage is the need for a medical visit every month. Compared to Depo-Provera, Lunelle is less convenient (more frequent injections) but it offers the advantages of speedier reversibility and regular withdrawal bleeding (an advantage to women who value menstruation).

New Hormone-Based Methods Are On the Horizon

A variety of new hormone-based contraceptive methods are being researched or tested. Some of them may be available by the time you read this, while others are in early development and may never see the light of day.

Extended-use combination pills   The standard combination pill employs a 7-day drug-free interval every month. Even now, however, some physicians prescribe combination pills in such as way as to provide a drug-free interval only once every 2 months ("bicycling"), once every 3 months ("tricycling"), or never ("continuous use") (Nelson, 2000). Such "off-label" prescribing is done to increase the pill's efficacy and to eliminate withdrawal bleeding and the symptoms associated with it. A new preparation specifically packaged for this use, called **Seasonale,** may appear on the market before long. A woman takes this pill continuously for 12 weeks, followed by a 7-day drug-free interval, and so on. Thus she will experience four menstrual periods per year instead of thirteen ("tricycling"). FDA approval of Seasonale, if it comes, will signify the agency's blessing of planned menstrual suppression in healthy women (see Box 11.4).

Vaginal hormone delivery   Oral contraceptive pills can be placed in the vagina instead of being swallowed. They are said to be effective in that mode, which avoids the potential gastrointestinal side effects of oral delivery (Coutinho & Segal, 1999), but this practice cannot be recommended, given the paucity of studies.

A variation on the same approach is the use of a ring-shaped device that is placed in the vagina around the base of the cervix (Ballagh, 2001). The ring releases hormones, either an estrogen–progestin combination or progestin alone. With the combination-hormone ring, the woman leaves the ring in place for 21 days and removes it for 7 days, as with the combination pill. One combination-hormone ring—the **Nuvaring,** produced by Organon— has given indications of reliability and good acceptance by women who have used it (Roumen et al., 2001). It could well be available by the time you read this.

Contraceptive patches   Contraceptive patches are analogous to the combination pill, but the hormones enter the body through the skin (transdermally). One such patch, the **Ortho Evra** (Figure 11.11), was approved by the FDA in 2001. Some women experience skin reactions to the patches, but compliance is better with the patches than with the pill because it is easier to remember to put on a patch once a week than to take a pill once a day (Audet et al., 2001). Potential side effects are similar to those of the combination pill.

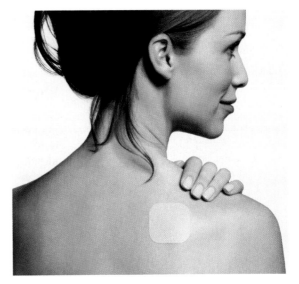

Figure 11.11 The Ortho-Evra patch releases an estrogen–progestin combination that is absorbed through the skin.

GnRH agonists   You will recall from Chapter 4 that the secretion of the pituitary gonadotropins is triggered by the release of gonadotropin-releasing hormone (GnRH) from the hypothalamus, but that this release must be pulsatile to be effective: continuous release of GnRH actually *shuts down* the secretion of gonadotropins. A group of researchers led by Malcolm Pike of the University of Southern California are attempting to take advantage of this phenomenon to develop an entirely new form of female contraception. They plan to use a synthetic GnRH agonist, **deslorelin.** Because it is a peptide, deslorelin has to be delivered by nasal spray, rather than orally. (Taken orally, it would be broken down in the gut.)

Used in this fashion, deslorelin blocks ovulation very effectively. The problem with this approach is that gonadal steroid secretion is reduced to such low levels that serious side effects, comparable to those of menopause, can result. The researchers plan to give women supplemental steroids to avoid these problems. The steroids will be administered in such a way as to provide four periods of withdrawal bleeding per year, comparable to the "tricycling" approach mentioned above. This method is in early stages of development.

Androgen-based contraceptives for men   Currently, men's contraceptive choices are very limited, and no hormone-based methods for men are available. However, it is well known that the administration of testosterone reduces men's fertility. It does so by a negative feedback effect on the release of pituitary gonadotropins, which leads in turn to depressed spermatogenesis. Several research groups are trying to turn this knowledge into an effective male contraceptive.

Testosterone by itself is of questionable usefulness because it has to be given in amounts that cause unacceptable side effects. Therefore, in some studies, periodic injections of smaller amounts of testosterone have been combined with oral progestins, which depress gonadotropin secretion in men just as they do in women. This approach has succeeded in reducing sperm counts to infertile levels, and this reduction is reversible. There are still some side effects, however, including weight gain and disturbances of blood lipid chemistry (Anawalt et al., 2000; Wu et al., 1999). The acceptability of this approach to men is also uncertain.

Behavioral Methods Are Demanding and Have Limited Reliability

For couples who do not want to use "artificial" contraception of any kind, for moral or other reasons, there are contraceptive options that depend simply on the manner or timing of sexual encounters. Although these options are considered by some to be more "natural" than other forms of contraception, and although they are inexpensive and free of the side effects of other methods, they make such demands on their users that their reliability in typical use is far below that of the best artificial methods.

Rhythm Methods Depend on Avoiding the Fertile Window

Nearly all pregnancies result from coitus during a 6-day period ending with the day of ovulation (Wilcox et al., 1995). Therefore, couples who avoid coitus during this fertile window will greatly decrease the likelihood of pregnancy. We discussed methods for identifying the **fertile window** in Chapter 10 in the context of overcoming infertility. The **rhythm methods** of contraception put those methods in reverse. Thus they are sometimes called **fertility awareness methods** or **periodic abstinence methods.**

Unfortunately, very different requirements exist when information about the fertile window is used for contraception than when it is used to achieve pregnancy. When the aim is to achieve pregnancy, it is quite sufficient to identify just the day of ovulation, since this is the day when coitus is most likely to result in pregnancy. This can be done very accurately with an at-home test that detects the LH surge, as described in Chapter 10. The fact that the couple may miss some earlier fertile days is of little consequence. When the aim is to *avoid* pregnancy, however, the earlier fertile days are of great consequence: the couple must start abstaining from coitus at least 5 days *before* ovulation. Thus,

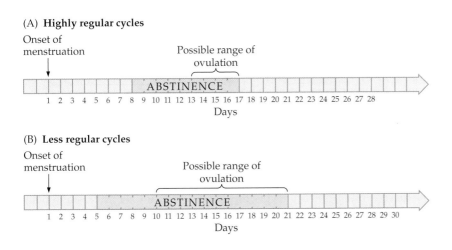

Figure 11.12 The calendar method requires abstinence at the time of ovulation. (A) This method of contraception works best for women with highly regular cycles. (B) For women with less regular cycles, it may be necessary to abstain from coitus for 16 or more days of each cycle. The period of abstinence can be shortened somewhat by using methods that detect the occurrence of ovulation.

detecting ovulation in any given cycle is of no great help in avoiding conception in that cycle—the information comes too late.

The calendar method   In the simplest and least satisfactory rhythm method, called the **calendar method,** the woman simply assumes that ovulation occurs 14 days before the onset of menstruation. If she has a very regular menstrual cycle—say, 28 days—then the presumed day of ovulation will be 28 minus 14 days—that is, day 15 if the onset of menstruation is called day 1—and the fertile window will be from day 10 to day 15. However, she must add some leeway on either side, given that the day of ovulation is not known precisely. Abstinence from coitus from day 8 to day 17 (inclusive) would be reasonable (Figure 11.12A).

This period of abstinence is already a large fraction of the cycle—and an even larger fraction of the non-menstruating part of the cycle, which is when most couples prefer to have intercourse. But things get worse for the many women who are not perfectly regular. These women have to expand the forbidden period to allow for variation in the time of ovulation. Suppose that, after keeping track of her menstrual periods over 6 or 12 months, a woman finds that her shortest cycles are 25 days and her longest cycles are 32 days. This variation in cycle length is due mostly to variation in the length of the interval between the onset of menstruation and ovulation. Thus, to allow for the possibility of a 25-day cycle, the couple should start abstaining from sex 3 days earlier than for a 28-day cycle—that is, on the fifth day after menstruation begins. To allow for the possibility of a 32-day cycle, they should continue abstaining 4 days longer than with a 28-day cycle—that is, until the twenty-first day (Figure 11.12B).

Another often-recommended way of doing the calculation is to subtract 18 days from the length of the woman's shortest cycle (this would give 25 minus 18, or 6, in the example just cited), and to subtract 11 days from the woman's longest cycle (this would give 32 minus 11, or 21, in the example). The period of abstinence is then taken as being the sixth to the twenty-first day after the onset of menstruation.

However the calculation is done, it's clear that the calendar method rules out coitus during most of the non-menstruating part of the cycle (as well as possibly the tail end of the menstrual period) for women with significant variation in cycle length. Thus the method is quite frustrating, and particularly so because the couple will not actually be fertile on most of the forbidden days—they just won't know whether they are fertile or not.

Other methods   More sophisticated rhythm methods involve the detection of the time of ovulation and the use of that information to judge when coitus can safely take place. As mentioned above, ovulation can be detected with a home test kit. Alternatively, it can be detected by following basal body temperature, as described in Chapter 10. Some women even know when they are ovulating because of abdominal pain (*Mittelschmerz;* see Chapter 4). However they detect it, coitus can begin 2 days (or, to be extra safe, 3 days) after ovulation. Unfortunately, that doesn't tell the couple when they have to stop again, so that date would have to be calculated on the basis of the calendar method. Even so, detecting ovulation can add a lot of permissible days for women who have irregular cycles.

Yet another rhythm method tracks changes in the **cervical mucus** around the menstrual cycle. This is sometimes called the **ovulatory method** because it is the only method that can provide advance warning of ovulation in a particular cycle. We described the changes in the properties of the cervical mucus in Chapter 10. Immediately after the end of menstruation there is usually little or no cervical mucus, and coitus is relatively safe at that time. A few days later a thick, whitish mucus appears, followed later by the thin, clear, slippery mucus that can be stretched out between thumb and finger. The days when the thin mucus is present are called the peak days; usually there are 1 or 2 such days. Ovulation occurs within 24 hours of the last peak day. The couple must abstain from coitus from the first day of *any* mucus (not just the thin mucus) until 3 or (to be safe) 4 days after the last peak day.

It is possible to combine the cervical mucus method with the basal body temperature method (or the home test kit method). This combined approach is sometimes called the **sympto-thermal method** and may be more reliable than either method used alone.

Sometimes the term "rhythm method" is used to refer only to the calendar method, and the more sophisticated methods—those that involve the detection of ovulation— are described collectively as **natural family planning.** One could argue about exactly how "natural" these methods are, of course.

Advantages of rhythm methods:
- They are inexpensive or free (but will be more expensive if LH test kits are used).
- They are usable by people who consider other forms of contraception morally wrong.
- They avoid the side effects and health risks of other forms of contraception.
- They are completely and immediately reversible.
- They are not intrusive (at least on the days when sex is permitted).

Disadvantages of rhythm methods:
- Their reliability is poor compared with that of other methods. It is difficult to give accurate figures for the reliability of the various rhythm methods—there are simply too many unknowns involved. The Alan Guttmacher Institute gives a 9 percent failure rate with perfect use and a 19 percent failure rate with typical use (see Table 11.1) for the rhythm methods as a whole, placing them among the least reliable of the methods that have any documented efficacy. Factors such as regular cycles, high motivation, and a flair for precise record keeping will all help couples achieve success.
- A particular problem with the low reliability of the rhythm methods is that the people who use them are often opposed to abortion as a backup method of preventing childbirth. However, a couple who is using rhythm methods to have children less frequently, rather than to avoid having them altogether, may find these methods perfectly adequate.
- Couples may find it psychologically stressful to avoid sex for a substantial portion of each cycle. Recall from Chapter 4 that women's interest in sex tends to peak before and around the time of ovulation— that is, within the period when she is required to abstain from sex using these methods.
- The more accurate rhythm methods (cervical mucus, basal body temperature) are quite demanding of time and attention.
- A woman needs to keep track of her cycles for at least 6 months before even beginning to use the calendar method.
- There is no protection from STDs if condoms are not used during the permissible portion of the woman's cycle.

The Withdrawal Method Is Unreliable and Stressful

In the **withdrawal method** of contraception, the man simply removes his penis from the woman's vagina before he ejaculates. It sounds simple, so why does the method have a 24 percent failure rate with typical use?

Part of the reason is that some sperm may be present in the pre-ejaculatory fluid, or "pre-cum," especially if the man has not urinated since his last ejaculation. However, if this were the only way in which the method could fail, it would probably be one of the most reliable of contraceptive techniques. The real reason why the method is so unreliable, of course, is that the man doesn't always pull out in time. He simply gets carried away, or he ejaculates without sufficient warning. Also, he may spill semen on the labia, from where some hardy spermatozoa may make it all the way into the woman's reproductive tract.

Advantages of withdrawal:
- It requires no advance preparation.
- It is free (aside from the cost of rearing any babies that result).
- There are no medical side effects or health risks.

Disadvantages of withdrawal:
- The failure rate is high. It certainly is not recommended for men who ejaculate prematurely, or for teenagers; both these groups will have great difficulty with compliance.
- It may be psychologically stressful. Both partners may be so concerned about the possibility that the man will ejaculate that they will be unable to focus on enjoying coitus.
- It provides little or no disease protection.

Noncoital Sex Can Be Used as a Means of Avoiding Pregnancy

Knowing that only penile–vaginal intercourse (coitus) can lead to pregnancy, many couples engage in other forms of sexual activity, including everything from kissing and fondling to body-on-body contact, hand stimulation of the genitals, and anal and oral sex. Sometimes these alternative forms of sex are promoted as a way to avoid pregnancy; in that context, they may be referred to as "**outercourse**"—the opposite of intercourse.

Advantages of noncoital sex:
- It is completely reliable if adhered to. (Semen must not be deposited near the vaginal opening, however.)
- It is free and requires no preparation.
- There are none of the side effects that may be associated with other forms of contraception.
- For teens who have not yet engaged in coitus, it may be valued as a way to preserve a kind of virginity.
- There is some STD protection, depending on what kinds of noncoital activities are engaged in.

Disadvantages of noncoital sex:
- It misses out on what many heterosexual men and women consider the most pleasurable and intimate kind of sex.
- It may be difficult to refrain from coitus once noncoital sex is under way, and if coitus does happen, contraception may not be available.
- Some forms of noncoital sex, especially anal and oral sex, have a potential for disease transmission that is as great as that of coitus (see Chapter 16).

There Are Contraceptive Options After Unprotected Coitus

You got carried away. He said he was going to pull out. She said she was on the pill. The condom broke. The diaphragm slipped. Who cares how it happened—it's 11 P.M., ovulation is tomorrow, and a few million spermatozoa are going gangbusters for the cervical canal. Your whole life—as a parent—is passing before your eyes. What next?

A woman's first impulse is to rinse out the contents of her vagina—preferably with something that will kill sperm. Coca-Cola is said to be the traditional favorite of teens. Some women use water, or a commercial douche. Some use spermicidal foam.

None of these methods is to be recommended as a regular form of postcoital contraception. Even the spermicidal foam, which is probably the best of the options just mentioned, is a highly unreliable way to prevent pregnancy when applied after coitus, because some sperm are likely to have gotten beyond the reach of the spermicide before it is ever placed in the vagina. Any of these methods may prevent pregnancy on a one-shot basis—if you're lucky. But the point is, you really can't afford to leave it to luck.

For that reason, a woman in this situation may do better to forget about Coca-Cola or douches or foam and simply assume that sperm have made it to the safety of her cervix. She now has two effective options to prevent pregnancy: taking a high dose of contraceptive pills to prevent implantation of any conceptus that forms, or having an IUD inserted, with the same purpose.

The pill method is sometimes called **emergency contraception** or the **morning-after pill.** Let's be clear: it is not contraception in the strict sense of the word, because the aim is not to prevent conception, but to prevent implantation of an already fertilized conceptus. Nor is it abortion in the usual sense of that word, because it prevents the establishment of pregnancy rather than terminating an already established pregnancy. It falls into a gray area between the two. Some people who are opposed to abortion categorize it as abortion and consider it morally wrong for that reason. Most people, including many who are opposed to abortion, view it as more akin to contraception and find it no more morally troubling than standard precoital contraceptive methods (Goldberg & Elder, 1998).

A woman who needs emergency contraception should consult her health care provider. Emergency contraception involves taking two high doses of oral contraceptives 12 hours apart. The first dose should be taken no later than 72 hours (3 days) after coitus. Thus, it doesn't have to be literally the "morning after," but the sooner the first dose is taken, the greater the probability of success (Figure 11.13).

The oral contraceptives used can be either the estrogen–progestin combination type or the progestin-only type. The pills can be taken from regular contraceptive packs, but the number of pills to be taken varies from brand to brand. With Alesse, for example, the woman takes five pink pills for each of the two doses, so one pack of Alesse contains more than enough pills. With Ovrette, on the other hand, she takes twenty yellow pills for each of the two doses, so two packs need to be available. Planned Parenthood maintains an extensive list of usable pills on its Web site, along with dosages and detailed instructions. (Forgive us if we're insulting your intelligence, but it's important not to use the dummy pills that may be provided for the drug-free week of the cycle!) The same kind of pills should be used for the first and the second doses.

There are also contraceptive pills that are specifically packaged and marketed for postcoital use (Figure 11.14). These include the cutely named **Plan B** (a progestin-only pill containing levonorgestrel; one pill is taken for each dose) and **Preven** (a combination pill containing levonorgestrel and ethinyl estradiol; two pills are taken for each dose). Several organizations are campaigning to have these pills approved for over-the-counter sale, so they may be available without a prescription by the time you read this. If they are not, it makes good sense for a woman to ask her doctor or birth control clinic to prescribe them in advance of need, so that the least possible delay is involved.

Because of the high doses used, the estrogen-containing combination pills can cause vomiting. It is a good idea to take an anti-nausea pill, such as Dramamine, 30 minutes before the contraceptive, because if vomiting does occur, an unknown fraction of the contraceptive dose may be lost. A woman who vomits after the first dose should take an anti-nausea pill before the second dose, or she can insert the pills in her vagina, pushing them as far in as possible with her fingers.

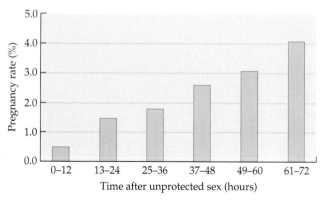

Figure 11.13 Emergency contraception works best when initiated as soon as possible after unprotected sex. (After Piaggio et al., 1999.)

Emergency contraceptives are not totally reliable. The combination pill reduces a woman's likelihood of becoming pregnant by about 75 percent, whereas the progestin-only pill does so by about 85 percent, so progestin-only pills are somewhat more effective. Both methods work best when the first dose is taken within 24 hours of coitus. If emergency contraception fails and a pregnancy is established, the fetus will not have been harmed by the pills.

A woman who doesn't have sex very often might ask herself whether she could rely solely on post-coital pills for her contraceptive needs. The answer is an emphatic no: emergency contraceptive pills are not reliable enough to replace other methods of contraception, and the repeated bouts of nausea might eventually turn you off sex altogether!

The other strategy to prevent implantation is to have an IUD inserted. The ParaGard IUD is used for this purpose. Of course, this is a much more expensive and inconvenient option than taking pills. However, it is virtually 100 percent reliable, and it can be done up to 10 days after coitus, rather than 3 days with the pills. Furthermore, the IUD can be left in place, in which case it will provide very reliable contraception for up to 10 years. Alternatively, it can be removed as soon as the woman has had her next menstrual period.

Figure 11.14 Plan B is a progestin, levonorgestrel, specifically packaged for use as an emergency contraceptive. The woman takes one pill as soon as possible (and no later than 72 hours) after unprotected sex, and the other pill 12 hours later.

Sterilization Is Highly Reliable but Should Be Considered Irreversible

Sterilization is a surgical procedure that puts a permanent end to fertility. There are a variety of procedures that have this effect, including removal of the gonads (orchiectomy in men, ovariectomy in women) or of the uterus (hysterectomy). These operations are done to treat some medical condition, and sterility is a by-product of the procedure. Here, however, we focus on surgical procedures that are used to terminate fertility *electively* in otherwise healthy men and women: **vasectomy** in men and **tubal sterilization** in women. Both methods work by blocking gamete transport.

Sterilization is a serious issue for any individual or couple to face. Although, as we'll see below, sterilization procedures can be successfully reversed in some cases, there is no guarantee of success, so people who choose sterilization should be clear in their minds that they want to lose their fertility for good. They may want this under a number of circumstances:

- They simply don't want children and are certain they will never change their minds. (However, health care providers may be reluctant to sterilize healthy young men or women who don't have children.)
- They have had enough children and are confident that they will want no more, even if they remarry or their children die.
- A medical condition makes pregnancy a serious health hazard.
- They have a significant likelihood of passing on a serious congenital disorder.

Even though sterilization is such a major decision, it is very popular. About 40 percent of all users of contraception rely on sterilization of the male or female partner as their contraceptive technique. The majority of people who choose sterilization are married couples with children.

Although the sterilization procedure is simpler, cheaper, and safer in men than in women, 72 percent of all sterilizations in the United States are done on women. Among black Americans, the female bias is even stronger: 95 percent of sterilized African-Americans are female (Piccinino & Mosher, 1998). At least in part, this sex imbalance reflects an unfounded fear among men that sterilization will affect their masculine self-image, their sexual performance, or their enjoyment of sex. In addition, it may reflect an acknowledgment that relationships are not always sexually exclusive; thus, seen from the narrow perspective of a particular couple, sterilization of the man may be seen as inadequate because the woman could still become pregnant by some other man.

Vasectomy Is a Brief Outpatient Procedure

The vasectomy procedure is very simple and is usually done under local anesthesia (Figure 11.15). The physician locates the vas deferens by palpation of the scrotal sac above one of the testes, makes a small incision, isolates the vas, and cuts out a short segment of it. The free ends are tied, cauterized, or sealed with clips to prevent them from rejoining. The incision is then closed with a couple of stitches and the procedure is repeated on the other side. In an alternative procedure, the scrotal skin is pierced with sharp-tipped forceps rather than being cut with a scalpel. Because the incision is so small, it needs no stitches and heals faster. In either case, the man goes home the same day.

The man should refrain from strenuous exercise for a couple of days after surgery. He can usually resume sexual activity in about a week. He is not yet sterile, however, because sperm remain in the portions of the vasa deferentia distal to the cut. It takes about 15–20 ejaculations to get rid of these sperm. The man's semen must be checked microscopically for absence of sperm before he can engage in unprotected coitus.

Complications of the procedure can include bleeding, infection, and—fairly commonly—the appearance of lumps formed by leaked sperm (sperm granulomas). These usually clear up by themselves, but they can be treated surgically if necessary.

Vasectomy costs between $250 and $1000 for the complete treatment—that is, the medical examination, the procedure, the follow-up, and the semen examination. It is nearly completely reliable; occasional failures result from too-early resumption of unprotected sex or from occasional reconnection of the severed ends of the vas.

About the only way that vasectomy can harm a man's sex life is if he feels psychologically damaged by the procedure. For most men, it's quite the reverse: they and their partners are able to enjoy sex more because they no longer have to worry about contraception or pregnancy. The procedure has no effect on sexual desire, the ability to perform, testosterone levels, or secondary sexual characteristics. Because sperm form such a small component of semen (see Figure 3.14), the volume of the ejaculate is reduced by a negligible amount—no more than 5 percent.

Of course, there are men who for one reason or another end up wanting the procedure reversed. There is an operation called **vasovasostomy** in which the surgeon, using an operating microscope, locates the two cut ends of the vas and sews them together. The procedure is expensive, however, and has no more than about a 50 percent chance of success. Quite aside from the difficulty of getting a functional reconnection, the man may have formed antibodies against his own sperm, which interfere with sperm production. Moreover, the man and his partner may be significantly older at this point, so that they

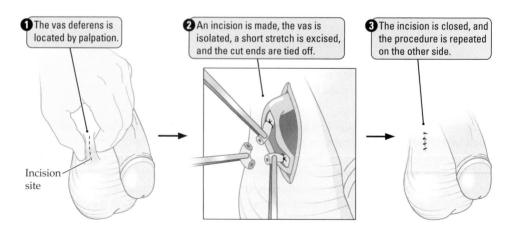

❶ The vas deferens is located by palpation.

Incision site

❷ An incision is made, the vas is isolated, a short stretch is excised, and the cut ends are tied off.

❸ The incision is closed, and the procedure is repeated on the other side.

Figure 11.15 Vasectomy is a relatively simple procedure that can be performed under local anesthesia.

also have to contend with the natural reduction in fertility that comes with aging (see Chapter 10).

Some men deposit a sperm sample in a sperm bank prior to the vasectomy procedure, with the hope that they can become fathers via artificial insemination in case they change their minds. However, there is no assurance that this will be possible, as frozen sperm can deteriorate over time, and there will be only a limited amount available.

Advantages of vasectomy:
- It is almost 100 percent reliable.
- Once accomplished, it is totally convenient, nonintrusive, and free.
- It lacks the side effects and possible health complications of the hormone-based methods.
- Vasectomy is cheaper and safer than tubal sterilization.

Disadvantages of vasectomy:
- Vasectomy is not reliably reversible. Attempts at reversal are very expensive.
- The up-front expenses are considerable.
- There is no STD protection.

Tubal Sterilization Is More Invasive and Expensive

Female sterilization is quite analogous to male sterilization: the oviducts are tied and cut (**tubal ligation**), cauterized, or closed off with clips or other devices (Figure 11.16). The result is that oocytes and sperm cannot meet. Tubal sterilization is a more invasive procedure than vasectomy, however, since it involves entering the abdominal cavity. Many sterilizations are done after childbirth or after an abortion. Female sterilization costs $1000 to $2500, and even more if the procedure requires hospitalization. Insurance or Medicaid coverage may be available, however.

There are three main kinds of female sterilization procedures, called laparoscopy, mini-laparotomy ("mini-lap"), and laparotomy. These procedures differ not so much in what is done to the oviducts, but in the surgical approach. In a **laparoscopy,** no extended incision is made in the abdominal wall. Instead, a viewing instrument (laparoscope) is inserted through one tiny incision, and an instrument to clamp or cut the oviducts is inserted through another tiny incision. Sometimes the two instruments are combined into one and only a single incision is made. The laparoscopic procedure is the least stressful, requires no stitches afterward, and can be done under either local or general anesthesia. Often, the woman can go home the same day.

In a **mini-laparotomy** or "mini-lap," a small scalpel incision (about 3 centimeters long) is made somewhere between the navel and the mons pubis. The oviducts are located

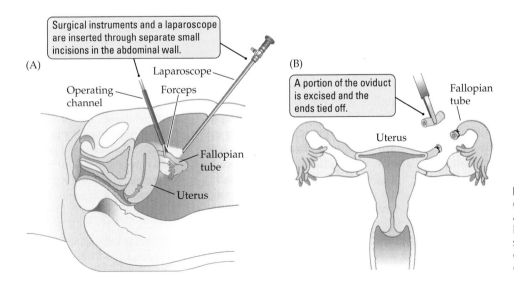

Figure 11.16 Tubal sterilization. (A) Laparoscopic procedure for tubal ligation. (B) A portion of the oviduct may be excised and the ends tied off, as shown here, or the oviduct may be closed off by cauterization or the application of clips.

and pulled to the incision, where they are tied and cut, or closed with clips, and then allowed to fall back into their normal position. The incision is then sewn up. Recovery takes a few days.

A **laparotomy** is a traditional surgical approach to the abdominal cavity, involving an extended incision (about 10 centimeters long) in the midline of the anterior abdominal wall. It is no longer performed as commonly as the laparoscopy or mini-lap, since it requires general or spinal anesthesia, leaves an evident scar, and necessitates a more extended recovery period.

There is another procedure that involves an approach via the rear wall of the vagina (**culposcopy** or **culpotomy**). This approach has the advantage of leaving no visible scars, but the woman has to abstain from coitus for several weeks, and the failure rate is higher with this approach. For those reasons, it is not commonly used.

Tubal sterilization, like any internal surgery, can occasionally cause hemorrhage or infection. General anesthesia, if used, also carries some risk. These or other complications occur in 1 to 4 percent of cases (or somewhat more with the vaginal approach), but they can usually be dealt with effectively. In general, one can say that tubal sterilization is a very safe procedure, but not quite as safe as vasectomy.

Like vasectomy, tubal sterilization has no effect on other aspects of sexual functioning. Menstrual cycles usually continue as before, and a woman's interest in sex and her physiological reactions during sex are undiminished. She may enjoy sex more because she is no longer concerned about pregnancy.

Tubal sterilization can be reversed by microsurgical techniques in some cases, but the operation is very expensive and success is quite unpredictable. A woman would be unwise to bank on the possibility of reversal when opting for sterilization.

The advantages and disadvantages of tubal sterilization are very similar to those of vasectomy, but there are a few important differences between the two.

Advantages of tubal sterilization:
- A woman may find it easier to undergo sterilization herself than to persuade her partner to do so. A married woman does not need her husband's permission in order to be sterilized, although it would certainly be a good idea to get his agreement if possible.
- Choosing to undergo sterilization herself covers the woman for all sexual encounters, not just those with her husband or regular partner.

Disadvantages of tubal sterilization:
- Tubal sterilization is more invasive, somewhat riskier, and more expensive than vasectomy.

In general, sterilization has considerable advantages over reversible forms of contraception. Couples should bear in mind, however, that there are some very good alternatives available. For example, if a couple is in their late thirties, a single insertion of a ParaGard IUD may carry them through to the woman's menopause with little chance of failure or of serious side effects, yet is easily reversible if necessary.

Disabled Persons Have Special Contraceptive Needs

Many men and women with physical and mental disabilities are sexually active, but they may face special problems related to contraception (Best, 1999). If they have a movement disorder, arthritis, multiple sclerosis, or a spinal cord injury, they may not be able to put on a condom, insert a diaphragm, or check an IUD. Oral contraceptives are not advisable for women with reduced mobility because they may raise the risk of blood clots. IUDs are not advisable if the woman does not have normal sensation in the pelvic area. If the disabled person has a nondisabled partner, the couple may agree to leave contraception to that partner. That may not be an option if the disabled person is not in a steady relationship, however.

Contraception is a particularly important issue for mentally retarded female adolescents and young women, who face a heightened risk of sexual abuse and who may not be able to comply with the usual contraceptive regimes (Haefner & Elkins, 1991). Careful counseling, repeated over time and tailored to the particular young woman's needs, is often required. Depot injection methods may be particularly useful for these women; the reduction in menstrual periods associated with these contraceptives may be an advantage in itself, because normal menstrual periods may create hygiene problems for mentally retarded women (Elkins et al., 1986).

A Variety of Safe Abortion Procedures Exist

An **induced abortion** is the intentional termination of a pregnancy. In a **spontaneous abortion,** or **miscarriage,** the embryo or fetus dies of its own accord and is expelled (see Chapter 10). In this chapter, we use "abortion" to refer exclusively to induced abortions (Box 11.5).

An abortion may be induced in order to safeguard the mother's health (**therapeutic abortion**), or because the woman chooses not to carry the fetus to term (**elective abortion**). An elective abortion may be done because the pregnancy was not wanted (contraception failed or was not used, or the pregnancy resulted from rape), because the fetus is known or suspected to suffer from some defect or disease, or even because it is of the nonpreferred sex.

The moral status of abortion, and the degree to which governments should restrict or regulate the practice, are highly contentious issues in contemporary society. In this chapter, we first describe the technology of abortion and then discuss the social conflicts that surround it.

Abortions can be done either by physically removing the fetus and its membranes from the uterus (surgical abortion) or by administering drugs that cause the death and expulsion of the fetus in a manner that resembles a miscarriage (medical abortion). Currently, surgical abortions are done much more commonly than medical abortions.

Vacuum Aspiration Is the Standard First-Trimester Surgical Method

Surgical abortions are done in different ways depending on the age of the fetus. During the first trimester, most surgical abortions are done by **vacuum aspiration** (Figure 11.17).

Box 11.5 *Society, Values, and the Law*

Abortion in the United States: Some Key Statistics

- One in four of all established pregnancies in the United States is terminated by abortion—that's about 1.3 million abortions per year. Forty-three percent of all women have had at least one abortion by the age of 45. However, the abortion rate has declined by more than 20 percent since 1980.

- Young single women are the major recipients of abortion. Two-thirds of all abortions are performed on never-married women. Half of all abortions are performed on women under 25 years old. Twenty percent are performed on teenagers.

- Minority women are disproportionately represented among abortion recipients. Hispanic women are twice as likely as white women to have an abortion, and black women are three times as likely. In spite of Catholic teachings concerning the sinfulness of abortion, American Catholic women are just as likely to have an abortion as are non-Catholics.

- Fifty-eight percent of women who have abortions were using some kind of contraceptive technique when they became pregnant.

- Eighty-eight percent of all abortions are performed within the first 12 weeks of pregnancy. Legal abortion performed by 8 weeks of pregnancy has less than a 1 in 500,000 chance of causing the mother's death. Abortion performed after 21 weeks has a 1 in 6000 chance of causing the mother's death.

- Abortion is legal in all U.S. states. Thirty-one states require minors to notify or obtain consent from their parents (or failing that, from a court).

- A first-trimester abortion costs about $400. Most managed care plans provide some coverage. Fourteen percent of abortions are paid for by state programs. Federal programs do not pay for abortions unless they are medically necessary.

- The clinics of the nonprofit Planned Parenthood Federation perform 20 percent of all abortions in the United States. One of the largest for-profit abortion providers is Family Planning Associates, with 23 clinics in California and Illinois.

Source: Alan Guttmacher Institute, 2000b.

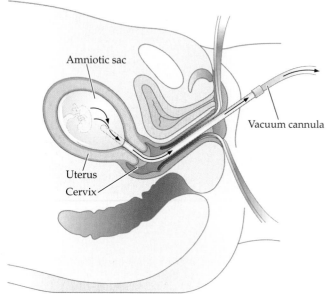

Figure 11.17 Vacuum aspiration is the abortion procedure most commonly used in the first trimester.

This procedure—which accounts for the majority of all abortions done in the United States—is done on an outpatient basis with local anesthesia or no anesthesia. The first step in the procedure is a rinsing of the vagina with an antiseptic solution. Next, the provider dilates the cervix by passing a series of metal rods of increasing diameter through the cervical canal. Alternatively, a stick made from the seaweed *Laminaria digitata* is inserted into the cervical canal the evening before the procedure. The laminaria absorbs fluid and expands, gently opening the cervix.

Once the cervix has been dilated, the provider passes a cannula into the uterus. The other end of the cannula is connected to a pump that applies suction. (With very early abortions, suction may be applied by hand, using a syringe.) The suction breaks up the fetus and its membranes and removes them from the uterus. This process takes less than 5 minutes. The extracted tissue is examined to ensure that the abortion is complete. The provider may insert a curette (a metal loop) to clean the walls of the uterus of any remaining tissue.

The woman remains in the clinic or doctor's office for an hour or so before being allowed to go home. She may experience a certain amount of bleeding and cramping over the following week or two. The woman should refrain from coitus for 3 weeks to allow the cervix to close fully. Complications are rare, but can include heavy bleeding, infection, or perforation of the uterus.

The vacuum aspiration procedure just described is sometimes referred to as a **D and C,** which stands for **dilation and curettage.** More properly, the term "D and C" is used for a once-common abortion procedure in which the removal of the fetus was accomplished entirely by the use of a metal curette, without vacuum aspiration. (This kind of D and C is still commonly done for non-abortion purposes, such as cancer diagnosis; see Chapter 17.)

Dilation and Evacuation Is Used Early in the Second Trimester

Dilation and evacuation, or **D and E,** is the procedure most commonly used early in the second trimester. It is sometimes done at up to 20 weeks of pregnancy or beyond, but most D and Es are done in the period from 13 to 16 weeks.

D and Es are usually done under general anesthesia in a hospital. The procedure is fairly similar to a vacuum aspiration abortion, but the cervix has to be dilated more widely. A suction cannula is used to remove fluid and some tissue, then the remainder is removed with forceps or other instruments. Finally, the lining of the uterus is cleaned with a curette.

The D and E is a very safe procedure, but it has a somewhat greater likelihood of complications, such as excessive bleeding, than vacuum aspiration abortion.

Induced Labor and Hysterotomy Are Done Late in the Second Trimester

Late in the second trimester, the D and E procedure becomes more risky, and other surgical techniques may be used. In one method, the provider simply induces premature labor. This may be done by injecting a strong salt solution into the amniotic sac (**saline-induced abortion**). Alternatively, and more commonly, labor is induced by administration of a **prostaglandin.** The drug is either injected into the amniotic sac or administered by means of a vaginal suppository (in which case this procedure should be considered a medical rather than a surgical abortion). Contractions usually begin within an hour or so, and the fetus is expelled within 48 hours.

If the woman's health is such that labor seems risky, the fetus may be removed by means of a surgical incision in the abdomen and the uterus (**hysterotomy**). This procedure is essentially equivalent to a cesarean section (see Chapter 10), except that the fetus is smaller and nonviable. Both induced labor and hysterotomy are done infrequently—each of them accounts for fewer than 1 percent of all abortions in the United States.

A very infrequent late-term abortion procedure is a variant of the D and E known as **intact dilation and extraction** (**intact D and X**). In this procedure, the provider manipulates the fetus into a breech position, then delivers the fetus's lower body. Before the head is delivered, the provider punctures it and suctions out the brain, thus easing delivery of the head and ensuring that the fetus is not born alive. This procedure is done very rarely, and it is mainly of interest because it has been a major target of abortion opponents, who refer to it as **partial-birth abortion.** The American Medical Association has recommended that this procedure not be used unless alternative methods would expose the mother to greater risk (Epner et al., 1998).

Medical Abortions Are Two-Step Procedures

In a **medical abortion,** the woman receives two different drugs 2 or more days apart. The first drug terminates the pregnancy, while the second causes uterine contractions and the expulsion of the remains of the fetus and its membranes, as with a spontaneous miscarriage. Medical abortions can be performed any time up to 7 to 9 weeks after the start of the last menstrual period.

The drug used to terminate the pregnancy can be either **mifepristone** (also known as **RU-486**) or **methotrexate.** These two drugs work in quite different ways. Mifepristone is a progestin receptor antagonist. Recall that progesterone, secreted by the corpus luteum and later by the placenta, is required to keep the uterus in a state capable of sustaining pregnancy (Figure 11.18). When mifepristone blocks progestin receptors, it is as if progesterone is absent, so the endometrium begins to break down and ceases to support the fetus, which detaches from the endometrium and dies. Methotrexate, on the other hand, is a cancer drug that kills rapidly dividing cells: it has a direct toxic effect on the fetus. Regardless of which drug is used in the first step, the drug used to cause contractions is always the same: the prostaglandin **misoprostol.**

From the perspective of the woman, the two drug combinations are slightly different. Mifepristone is given by mouth; methotrexate is usually given by injection. With mifepristone, some women (about 10 percent) will expel the fetal remains before they even take the misoprostol. For the other 90 percent, bleeding begins within 24 hours of taking misoprostol, and the entire process takes no more than about a week. With methotrexate, on the other hand, the abortion does not begin before the misoprostol is taken, and the entire process can last over 2 weeks—sometimes up to 5 weeks (Creinin & Pymar, 2000). Either way, a follow-up visit to the clinic is required to check that the abortion is complete.

There is also a small difference in reliability: mifepristone works in about 96 percent of cases, and methotrexate works in 90 percent of cases. If either procedure should fail, the woman should have a surgical abortion, because the fetus may well have been seriously damaged.

The use of mifepristone to induce abortion has been approved by the FDA. In contrast, the use of methotrexate for the same purpose has not been approved by the FDA, so

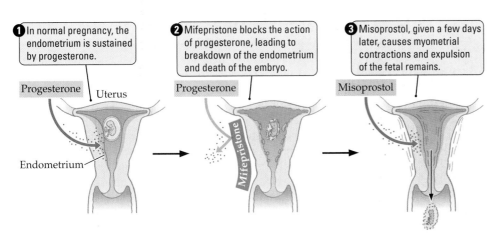

❶ In normal pregnancy, the endometrium is sustained by progesterone.

Progesterone   Uterus

Endometrium

❷ Mifepristone blocks the action of progesterone, leading to breakdown of the endometrium and death of the embryo.

Progesterone

Mifepristone

❸ Misoprostol, given a few days later, causes myometrial contractions and expulsion of the fetal remains.

Misoprostol

Figure 11.18 Medical abortion with mifepristone and misoprostol.

while this use is perfectly legal, it is "off-label," and physicians who prescribe it do not have to fulfill certain training and other requirements, as they do with mifepristone.

There are differences between clinics in which drugs are preferred and how they are administered. With respect to mifepristone, Planned Parenthood clinics follow FDA guidelines to the letter: they limit the procedure to 7 weeks of pregnancy and give three mifepristone pills. Some for-profit clinics, on the other hand, extend the treatment to women who are up to 9 weeks pregnant and give only one mifepristone pill, which they believe is equally effective. This belief is supported by research studies (World Health Organization, 2001b). As each pill costs the clinic $90, the savings are considerable.

Mifepristone was developed in France, and had been widely used in Europe for several years before it was approved by the FDA in 2000. So far, neither mifepristone nor methotrexate has caught on in the United States, however (Gellene, 2001). Despite the many advantages that medical abortion has over surgical abortion, the great majority of all abortions are still surgical. Here are the advantages and disadvantages of medical abortion compared with surgical abortion:

Advantages of medical abortion:
- It requires no invasive surgical procedure.
- It can be performed earlier than surgical abortion—as soon as pregnancy is confirmed.
- Medical abortions can be more readily obtained outside of abortion clinics than can surgical abortions; thus, there may be less chance of harassment by abortion foes.
- The actual abortion happens in the privacy of the woman's home.
- The abortion may seem more like a natural miscarriage.

Disadvantages of medical abortion:
- Medical abortions take longer. A surgical abortion is over within minutes of starting the procedure, whereas a medical abortion takes 1 to 5 weeks.
- Medical abortions are limited to 7 or 9 weeks from the beginning of the last menstrual period. Even the safest kind of surgical abortion can be done until about 14 weeks.
- Medical abortions generally cost $100–300 more than surgical abortions. (Some clinics charge the same for first-trimester abortions by either method.)
- For a teenager who is trying to conceal the abortion from her parents, having the abortion at home is a disadvantage. Another disadvantage of having the abortion at home is the possibility of seeing the fetal remains, which may disturb some women.

The abortion debate is often portrayed as a face-off between extreme pro-life and pro-choice activists, but many Americans hold intermediate positions.

Americans Are Divided on Abortion, but Most Favor Restricted Availability

In its landmark 1973 decision in *Roe v. Wade,* the U.S. Supreme Court ruled that states could not enact outright bans on abortions performed before the age of fetal viability, which was taken to mean before the end of the second trimester of pregnancy. Since that time, Americans have remained divided on the issue of abortion.

The abortion debate is often portrayed as if there are simply two opposing camps: "**pro-life**," meaning people who believe that elective abortion is always wrong and that it should be a criminal offense, and "**pro-choice**," meaning people who believe that women should be allowed to make all abortion decisions for themselves. When Americans are asked, "Do you consider yourself pro-life or pro-choice?" most will identify themselves as one or the other, with

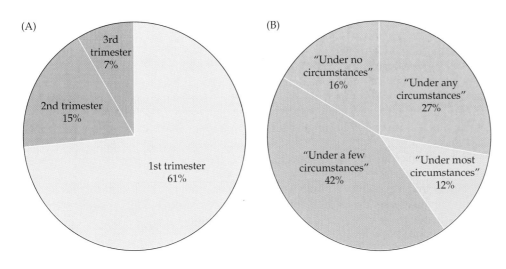

(A)

3rd trimester 7%

2nd trimester 15%

1st trimester 61%

(B)

"Under no circumstances" 16%

"Under any circumstances" 27%

"Under a few circumstances" 42%

"Under most circumstances" 12%

Figure 11.19 Americans' views on abortion are not as simple as "pro-life vs. pro-choice." (A) Abortion is considered more acceptable when it is done early: the graph shows the percentage of U.S. adults who believe abortion should be permitted in each of the three trimesters of pregnancy. (Data from Goldberg and Elder, 1998.) (B) Only minorities of Americans have extreme opinions in response to the question, "Under what circumstances should abortion be legal?" (Data from Gallup Organization, 1999.)

slightly more people calling themselves pro-choice (48 percent) than pro-life (42 percent) (Gallup Organization, 1999).

When polls ask Americans about abortion in more detail, however, it becomes apparent that their views are not strictly polarized. For example, many people believe that abortion should be permissible in the first trimester, but many fewer believe that it should be permissible in the second or third trimesters (Goldberg & Elder, 1998) (Figure 11.19A). In this respect, Americans tend toward a more conservative position than was spelled out in *Roe v. Wade*, which made abortion legal in both the first and second trimesters.

Furthermore, while 60 percent of Americans think that the *Roe v. Wade* decision was a good thing, this does not mean that they agree with the core of the decision, which was that a woman has a right to an early abortion for any reason. Americans generally are very favorable to the notion that a woman should be able to have an abortion if her life is at risk, if the fetus is likely to have a congenital disorder, or if the pregnancy resulted from rape. In contrast, they are very *unfavorable* to the idea that a woman should be allowed to have an abortion for a reason of mere convenience—such as the fact that having the baby would interfere with her career. Seventy percent of Americans believe that abortion under these circumstances should be illegal, contrary to the *Roe v. Wade* ruling.

In other words, when people are asked in detail about their positions, it seems that most people are not fully "pro-life" or "pro-choice," but occupy some kind of intermediate position, in which the timing of, and reasons for, the abortion are critical. Only minorities of Americans believe that abortion should be illegal under all circumstances or legal under all circumstances (Figure 11.19B). The commonest opinion is that abortion should be legal under a limited set of circumstances.

How do views on abortion vary with major demographic variables? First, women and men do not differ in their representation in the pro-choice and pro-life camps, but women hold their opinions more strongly than men. This is hardly surprising, given that abortion affects women more directly than it affects men. Age does not influence views on abortion either.

The three variables that do correlate quite strongly with abortion views are religious beliefs, political affiliation, and educational level. People with strong religious beliefs, or who are Republicans, are more likely to have restrictive views on abortion, while Democrats and people who have high levels of educational attainment are more likely to have permissive views.

Religion, Science, the Law, and Feminism Offer Different Perspectives on Abortion

Let's take a look at some different perspectives on abortion. The extreme *pro-life view* is represented by the official view of the Roman Catholic Church and some conservative Protestant churches, which would like to see abortion banned completely except to prevent the imminent death of the mother. In the case of the Catholic Church, this view is part of a broader stance against nonreproductive sex. The Church has declared that not merely abortion but also sterilization, artificial contraception, nonmarital sex, homosexual sex, and masturbation are all sinful. Although, as mentioned, the effect of these pronouncements on the opinions and behavior of American Catholics is limited, the Church has other means to exert its will—for example, by banning abortion and sterilization procedures at Catholic hospitals, which constitute 11 percent of all hospitals in the United States, and by exerting political pressure on issues related to contraception, gay rights, and so on.

The Catholic Church's motivation for calling abortion sinful goes beyond the belief that sex is morally acceptable only for married people who want children. It also includes the beliefs that it is a sin to willfully take human life and that human life begins at conception. In this sense, the Church's anti-abortion stance is linked to its doctrines in nonsexual areas, such as its stance against capital punishment. This part of Catholic dogma is much more in line with attitudes in America today, and that is why so many Americans oppose abortion but are more permissive toward other aspects of nonprocreational sexual expression.

When *does* human life begin? The answer depends on the exact meaning of "human life." Most *biologists* would agree with the Catholic Church that an individual human being's life begins at conception, because that is when the individual is assigned its unique genetic makeup and begins the process of cell division and differentiation. Birth, on the other hand, is a fairly arbitrary point in life. A human fetus is an organized, reactive, human-like being well *before* birth, and yet it is not a fully independent being until long *after* birth, if ever. Birth is an incremental step on a long journey toward independent personhood.

At the same time, biologists also understand that "human life" is continuous from one generation to the next. A fertilized ovum is formed from the parents' oocyte and sperm, and these are formed from precursor cells that come from the grandparents, and so on back in time to the origins of the human race and even to the origins of life on Earth. Even conception, in that sense, is an arbitrary moment in the grand flow of life.

Furthermore, biologists are aware that Nature "throws away" many conceptuses before they even have a chance to implant in the mother's uterus. For these reasons, biologists may be reluctant to believe that a conceptus suddenly acquires the same morally protected status as an already-born human being. Probably the dominant view among biologists is that the morally protected status of a human life is fairly low until the brain processes that mediate feelings, thoughts, and memories have begun, which would be late in pregnancy at the earliest.

The law takes a different view of human life. In general, no fetus has independent legal status as a human being until it is born. Abortion, even when illegal, is not murder in legal terms, and a fetus (whether living or aborted) cannot be represented in court. One goal of anti-abortion activists is to have fetuses legally recognized as human beings. Efforts in this direction usually center around topics that seemingly have no direct connection to abortion. These include efforts to have "unborn children" given specific rights as victims of violent crimes or made eligible for medical coverage under governmental insurance programs (Pear, 2001).

Feminists generally take an extreme pro-choice stance. The National Organization for Women, for example, is opposed to all laws that criminalize abortion—even the elective abortion of viable late-term fetuses. The ethical underpinning for this view is the belief that women, by virtue of the role they play in nurturing their offspring before and after birth, are in the best position to make judgments about whether to continue a pregnancy or not, and that governmental intrusion would lead to abuses (Cowan, 1992).

The Abortion Debate Focuses on Specific Issues

Because the majority of Americans do not hold extreme views on abortion, pro-life and pro-choice activists generally wage their battles over positions in the center, not over the absolute banning or legalization of abortion. Several questions have been the focus of intense debate:

- Should abortion be restricted by imposing conditions on it, such as mandatory 24-hour waiting periods, mandatory counseling about alternatives to abortion (such as adoption), or—in the case of minors—requirements for parental notification or consent? Abortion foes have been quite successful in these areas. The U.S. Supreme Court has ruled that such restrictions are constitutional (*Planned Parenthood v. Casey,* 1992), and many states have enacted some or all of them. (But parental consent laws must allow for judicial bypass.)

- Should abortions be banned after a certain duration of pregnancy? Abortion foes have been less successful here. *Roe v. Wade* permitted the banning of abortion after the age of fetal viability, and implied that this age was at the end of the second trimester. Later Supreme Court rulings, however, stated that only an individual doctor could decide whether a particular fetus was viable or not, and that viability was not linked to a fixed fetal age.

- Should certain abortion procedures, such as intact D and X ("partial-birth abortion"), be banned? State bans on intact D and X were ruled unconstitutional by the U.S. Supreme Court in 2000 (*Stenberg v. Carhart*). The U.S. Congress passed bans on the procedure in 1996 and 1997, but President Clinton vetoed those bills. If a similar bill is passed and signed under the current administration, it will be subject to Supreme Court review.

- Should indigent women's abortions be paid for by public funds? Currently, states are required to fund such abortions only when pregnancy results from incest or rape or when the mother's life is in danger. Some states voluntarily fund abortions in other circumstances.

- May anti-abortion protesters be kept away from people entering or leaving abortion clinics? This contentious issue has been the subject of several Supreme Court rulings. Currently, fixed "buffer zones" around a clinic entrance are legal, but "floating" buffer zones (meaning that a person entering or leaving a clinic may not be approached, wherever they are physically located) are not (*Schenk v. Pro-Choice Network,* 1997).

- May living cells obtained from aborted fetuses be used for medical purposes? President Clinton approved the use of federal funds to support research in this area, and fetal brain cells were used experimentally to treat Parkinson's disease during his presidency (Freed and LeVay, 2002). President George W. Bush has been under pressure to reverse this policy, and to ban the use of **embryonic stem cells** (cells in the conceptus that can give rise to all fetal tissues) derived from IVF procedures (see Chapter 10). Under current policy, federal funding may be used to support medical research involving already existing stem cell lines, but not research on new cell lines created in the future.

Since so many abortion-related issues have ended up in the lap of the U.S. Supreme Court, and since the court has often decided them by narrow margins, the opinions of future appointees to the court could profoundly influence abortion rights in the United States.

The Availability of Abortion Varies by Location

Partly because of the fierce controversy over abortion, the availability of abortion varies greatly within the United States. In many large metropolitan areas there are plenty of abortion providers. In fact, because of the falling numbers of abortions, there is considerable competition between clinics, and a woman may be able to shop around for a competitively priced procedure. In nonmetropolitan and southern areas, where opposition to abortion is strongest, it may be difficult to locate an abortion provider at all. Thirty-two percent of all American women live in counties where there is not a single abortion provider (Alan Guttmacher Institute, 2000b). Fear of harassment, or even violence (Box 11.6), is part of the reason why so few doctors perform abortions.

Box 11.6 *Society, Values, and the Law*

The Deadly Fringe of the Pro-Life Movement

The great majority of pro-life activists confine themselves to legal forms of expression, but a small number have resorted to violence to terrorize abortion providers and their employees and clients, both in the United States and in Canada. There have been a number of such incidents over the last several years:

- March 10, 1993: Michael Griffin shot and killed abortion provider Dr. David Gunn outside a clinic in Pensacola, Florida. Griffin was convicted of murder and sentenced to life imprisonment.

- July 29, 1994: Paul Hill shot and killed Gunn's successor, Dr. John Britton, along with a guard, James Barrett. Hill was convicted and sentenced to death.

- December 30, 1995: John Salvi III shot seven people, killing two of them, at two abortion clinics in Brookline, Massachusetts. Salvi was convicted and sentenced to life in prison, but died an apparent suicide in 1996.

- January 29, 1998: An off-duty police officer was killed and a nurse was severely injured in a bomb attack on a Birmingham, Alabama, abortion clinic. At this writing, the suspect in that attack, Eric Rudolph, is still at large.

- October 23, 1998: Dr. Barnett Slepian, an abortion provider in Amherst, New York, was shot and killed by a sniper who fired through his kitchen window. The alleged killer, James Kopp, was apprehended, escaped from prison, fled to France, and was rearrested there. In 2002 he was extradited to the United States to face trial.

Many other recent incidents have involved woundings of abortion providers or clinic personnel or bombings of clinics. In the wake of the anthrax mailings in the fall of 2001, hundreds of hoax anthrax letters were sent to abortion clinics, seriously disrupting their operations.

Who are these violent extremists? Some have a religious background—Hill, for example, is an ex-Presbyterian minister. Salvi seems to have been mentally ill. Others, such as Rudolph, may have links to the militia movement. Still others, such as Kopp, may be members or supporters of Operation Save America (previously called Operation Rescue), which organizes protests outside abortion clinics. Operation Save America officially denounces violence, but some of its regional leaders openly support the murder of abortion providers on Web sites such as www.armyofgod.com.

The message on this Chinese billboard from the 1980s reads: "To achieve the four modernizations [modernization of industry, agriculture, the military, and science], a couple should have only one child." The Chinese one-child policy is implemented by a combination of "carrots" for those who comply and "sticks" for those who don't. In rural areas, for example, school fees have been raised to the point that a couple may not be able to afford to send more than one child to school.

One thing that most pro-life and pro-choice activists agree on is that contraception is preferable to abortion as a means of preventing childbirth. Improved access to contraceptive services, better education in contraceptive methods, development of new methods, and changes in religious attitudes toward contraception all have the potential to greatly reduce the numbers of abortions performed in the United States.

Some Countries Use Birth Control to Regulate Population Growth

While we have examined contraception and abortion largely from the point of view of the individual, society as a whole also has an interest in regulating births. Many developing countries see population control as the key to economic development and protection from famine. China, for example, has imposed strict limits on reproduction via its "one-child policy." This policy limits most urban couples to one child; couples in rural areas may have a second child if the first was a daughter. The one-child policy is realized to a considerable extent through abortion: considerable pressure is put on women who have a child to terminate any later pregnancies.

Until recently, India has been less successful in reining in its population growth, but it is now beginning to do so, thanks largely to a state-run sterilization program. The program is voluntary but is backed by strong incentives and peer pressure.

Some developed countries, on the other hand, are economically threatened by declining birth rates and aging populations. This is particularly true of Japan, whose population will decline by at least 14 percent by 2050 (Efron, 2001), but 38 other countries face declining birth rates. The governments of many of these countries are initiating programs to increase the number of births; for example, by making child support payments, providing child care so that mothers can work, and so on.

The population of the United States is expected to grow only slowly over the next few decades. Thus the U.S. government feels no need to actively curb or encourage population growth and generally leaves family planning decisions to individuals. It is generally critical of high-pressure birth control programs in other countries, citing the potential for human rights abuses.

Summary

1. Although various forms of contraception have been known since ancient times, moral repugnance, restrictive laws, and ignorance prevented effective contraception in the United States until the early twentieth century. Margaret Sanger led the struggle to legalize contraception, to educate the public about contraceptive methods, and to introduce improved methods. Contraception was not fully legalized in the United States until 1972.

2. All currently available contraceptive methods have advantages and disadvantages. Different people have different contraceptive needs, and therefore choose different methods. In particular, young people need highly reliable but reversible methods. Couples who are spacing out their children do not need such reliable methods. Those who want no more children may choose irreversible methods—that is, sterilization.

3. Several factors need to be considered when choosing a contraceptive method: How reliable does it need to be? Does it need to be reversible? Does it need to confer protection against sexually transmitted diseases? How convenient does it have to be? How intrusive can it be (in other words, how much can it disrupt the spontaneity of sex or reduce the sensations of sex)? How much money can you spend on it—both up front and over time? Do you or your partner have particular risk factors that make certain methods inadvisable for you? How well can you trust your partner to follow the method correctly?

4. The most popular reversible contraceptive methods are the male condom and contraceptive pills. Among the reversible methods, the most reliable with typical use are hormone implants and injections, followed by pills and intrauterine devices (IUDs). Barrier methods (condoms and diaphragms) can be reasonably reliable with correct use. Behavioral methods (withdrawal and rhythm methods) are relatively unreliable.

5. Male condoms (sheaths that cover the penis) require careful use to prevent failure and are somewhat intrusive, but they are cheap, readily accessible, offer significant protection against STDs, and are free of the side effects of hormone-based methods. They are the only male method that is reversible. Female condoms offer similar benefits, but are even more intrusive than male condoms.

6. Diaphragms and cervical caps are another barrier method of contraception. They are used in conjunction with contraceptive chemicals to prevent the entry of sperm into the cervix. They are less intrusive than condoms, but they provide much less disease protection and are fairly inconvenient to use. They lack the side effects of hormone-based methods, but are also significantly less reliable than those methods.

7. Intrauterine devices render the uterus hostile to sperm transport and implantation. They are very reliable and quite convenient once fitted. They offer no disease protection.

8. Contraceptive pills contain either a combination of estrogen and progestin or progestin only. They work by blocking ovulation and by rendering the uterus hostile to sperm transport and implantation. They are fairly convenient once prescribed, nonintrusive, and very reliable if taken regularly. They offer no STD protection. Estrogen-containing pills may have a number of side effects as well as some long-term health risks (and benefits). Progestin-only pills sometimes cause irregular bleeding.

9. Hormone-based contraceptives may also be administered by subcutaneous implantation (Norplant), by long-term depot injections (Depo-Provera), or by once-a-month injections (Lunelle). They may also be available shortly in the form of contraceptive patches (Ortho-Evra) and vaginal rings (Nuvaring). These non-pill methods have the advantage of greater reliability.

10. Current research is focused both on better hormone delivery methods and on new hormone-based methods, including the use of gonadotropin-releasing hormone agonists for women and androgen-based contraceptives for men.

11. In rhythm methods, couples avoid sex near the time of ovulation, which they can determine by a variety of techniques, including simple calendar calculations, temperature measurements, or examination of cervical mucus. Rhythm methods are the only contraceptive methods approved by the Roman Catholic Church.

12. In the withdrawal method, the man withdraws his penis prior to ejaculation. This method is stressful and unreliable.

13. Noncoital sex ("outercourse") is a reliable form of contraception if adhered to strictly.

14. Emergency contraception involves taking high-dose oral contraceptives to prevent pregnancy after unprotected sex or failure of a barrier contraceptive. This method interferes with the implantation of any conceptus that may have formed. It is less effective than regular contraception and has side effects. Another possible postcoital contraceptive technique is the insertion of an IUD.

15. Sterilization is the cutting and/or tying off of the vasa deferentia (in men) or oviducts (in women). The procedure blocks gamete transport and is nearly completely reliable in preventing pregnancy. The majority of sterilizations are done in women, but the procedure is simpler, safer, and less expensive in men. Although intended to be permanent, sterilization can be reversed in some cases. Sterilization is generally chosen by couples who have all the children they desire.

16. In the United States, 1.3 million abortions are performed every year. Most abortions are done in the first trimester of pregnancy and are performed by the vacuum aspiration method, in which the cervix is dilated and the contents of the uterus suctioned out under local anesthesia. A slightly more complex procedure, dilation and evacuation, is used early in the second trimester.

17. Early abortions may also be induced with drugs. Medical abortion is a two-step procedure involving the administration of a drug that terminates the pregnancy (mifepristone or methotrexate), followed about 2 days later by a drug (misoprostol) that induces contractions and the expulsion of the fetal remains.

18. The moral and legal status of abortion is contentious. The extreme anti-abortion ("pro-life") position is that abortion is always wrong and should be illegal, except perhaps when done to save the mother's life. The extreme opposing ("pro-choice") view is that a woman should have the right to choose abortion under any circumstances. Most Americans describe themselves as pro-life or pro-choice, but actually hold to an intermediate position, believing that abortion should be permitted under certain limited conditions, such as early in pregnancy or when the fetus has a congenital defect.

Discussion Questions

1. Your sister or best friend asks you to help her decide which contraceptive method is best for her. She says she could not take pills, use a diaphragm, or use the rhythm method because she is too forgetful. She does not want to have to contemplate an abortion because it is against her values. Recommend two forms of contraception that would be suitable. Compare their actions and side effects. Compare their rates of effectiveness.

2. A teenager tells you that she has absolutely no risk of getting pregnant because she can tell when her boyfriend is about to ejaculate by the look on his face, and she makes him pull out. Explain to her the facts of this method of contraception, suggest an alternative method, and describe how it works and its advantages and disadvantages.

3. Your best friend sighs with relief and says he almost got his girlfriend pregnant, but she miscarried. He doesn't want to have that happen again. Explain to him the pros and cons of condoms and tell him how they should be used. Identify the problems that can make a condom ineffective and explain how to avoid them.

4. In Russia, condoms are expensive, and teenagers have reused them. Is this a good idea? Why or why not?

5. In your view, in what circumstances should abortion be legal, and why? (Alternatively, give a reasoned presentation of someone else's views, such as those of the Roman Catholic Church.) Has anything you read in this chapter influenced your views?

Web Resources

Planned Parenthood Federation of America www.plannedparenthood.org

Marie Stopes International www.mariestopes.org.uk

Alan Guttmacher Institute www.guttmacher.org

National Abortion Federation www.prochoice.org

National Abortion and Reproductive Rights Action League www.naral.org

National Right to Life Committee www.nrlc.org

Recommended Reading

Chesler, E. (1992). *Woman of valor: Margaret Sanger and the birth control movement in America.* New York: Simon and Schuster.

Hatcher, R. A., et al. (1998). *Contraceptive technology.* 17th edition. New York: Ardent Media.

chapter 12

The role of sexuality in human lives varies across the life span.

Sexuality across the Life Span

No two lives are alike, yet sexuality does unfold in a somewhat predictable manner across the life span. In fact, a person's age is one of the best predictors of their sexual behavior and relationships. Sex researchers tend to focus on a narrow age range within the total life span—from adolescence to midlife—when sexuality has its greatest social relevance. Here we try to expand that view and develop a conception of sexuality as a work that is already in progress at birth and that remains so until death.

Is Childhood a Period of Sexual Innocence?

Given all the taboos that surround the topic of sexuality, it is difficult enough to study the sex lives of adults. When it comes to the question of children's sexuality, however, the difficulties are magnified many times over. Most Americans believe, or would like to believe, that children are sexless—that they lack all sexual feelings, engage in no sexual behavior, and have little or no knowledge about sex. In this conception, children are like Adam and Eve before the Fall—they are sexually "innocent," and this innocence needs to be protected at all costs. Only molestation by an adult makes children aware of sex, according to this theory, and then only in a fashion that inflicts lifelong psychological wounds. Even asking children about their knowledge of sexual matters is often viewed as a form of molestation—a violation of their right to know nothing.

Do young children have a sex life? There are wildly diverging opinions on this question.

A polar opposite perspective was offered by Sigmund Freud (Freud, 1975), as described in Chapter 7. Freud believed that young children, especially infants, have a sex life that is more active, more passionate, and far less restrained than that of adults. According to Freudian theory, the infant's libido, or sex drive, undergoes several dramatic transformations, passing sequentially through oral, anal, and genital phases. At the age of about 3 years, children fall in love with their opposite-sex parent (the **Oedipal phase**). This attachment triggers all kinds of conflicts and anxieties, including castration anxiety in boys and penis envy in girls. Eventually, children deal with these conflicts by banishing them from consciousness. There ensues a period of **latency,** which begins at about the age of 5 or 6 and extends to the time of sexual reawakening at puberty. Memories of the early sexual period do not return to consciousness, but they help shape many aspects of adult sexuality, including sexual orientation.

The Study of Childhood Sexuality Faces Practical Difficulties

Does the truth lie at one of these two extremes, or somewhere in between? There are several possible ways one might try to answer this question. One is to ask adults to recall their sexual feelings and sexual behavior during their childhood. Another is to ask children themselves about their sex lives. Yet another is to observe children's sexual behavior directly, or to obtain such observations secondhand from parents or other caregivers.

None of these approaches is terribly satisfactory. Adults have very limited memories of their childhood and none of their infancy. Those memories that they do have may have been distorted by frequent rehearsal or by the attempt to "use" a memory for some purpose, such as to explain a sexual dysfunction in adult life. Infants cannot be interviewed about their sex lives. Older children can be interviewed, but their understanding may be limited and their replies may be too easily influenced by suggestion. In addition, parents may be reluctant to permit questioning of their children on sexual matters except under unusual circumstances, such as in the case of a suspected sexual assault. Direct observation of children's sexual behavior may be difficult if the behavior is infrequent. There are also likely to be serious questions of interpretation—that is, of the purpose or meaning of the behavior to the child itself—as well as ethical or legal considerations that may limit the use of this approach.

For all these reasons, we cannot expect to reach definitive conclusions about childhood sexuality. Nevertheless, it is a topic that is well worth studying, for two important reasons. First, childhood sexuality, if it exists at all, is presumably the antecedent to adolescent and adult sexuality, and may therefore help us understand how the diversity of adult sexual behavior arises. Second, a knowledge of normal childhood sexuality seems like a precondition for understanding how children are affected by sexual abuse and for developing strategies to help them mend the damage caused by that abuse.

Primates Display Sexual Behavior Early in Life

All of the higher nonhuman primates exhibit a variety of sexual behaviors before puberty. Infant rhesus monkeys, for example, start engaging in presenting and mounting behaviors (copulatory behaviors that are typical of adult females and males, respectively) pretty much as soon as they begin to wander away from their mothers (Wallen, 2000). These behaviors are not accompanied by actual coitus, however. They seem in part to be play behaviors that serve a rehearsal function, but in addition, they are used as a form of aggression or submission. Juvenile males do most of the adultlike ("footclasp") mounting (see the photo on page 148), but presenting is done by both males and females.

Cultures Vary in Their Attitudes toward Childhood Sexuality

Cross-cultural studies indicate that human children also readily engage in sexual behavior, but societies vary in whether they encourage, tolerate, or suppress it (Frayser, 1994). An example of a society that encourages childhood sexuality is the Chewa people of Malawi. Chewan parents encourage their children to play at being husband and wife in little huts situated away from the village. The Lepcha (the aboriginal people of Sikkim in the Himalayas, now part of India) believe that coitus is necessary for girls to mature into women. Similarly, several tribes in New Guinea believe that male-on-male fellatio is necessary for boys to develop into men (Herdt, 1981). Polynesian peoples are generally very tolerant of childhood sexual expression: boys and girls may masturbate in public without punishment or censure (Ford & Beach, 1951, and see Chapter 8). In some cultures, such as that of the Hopi Indians of the American Southwest, adult men manually stimulate the genitals of boys while singing them to sleep. Women of the Siriono people of Bolivia used to engage in sexual relations with the prepubescent brothers of their husbands.

More commonly, however, adults exert some degree of restraint on children's sexual expression. There are usually mild restraints on heterosexual play or masturbation during early childhood, but they may become stronger during later childhood. These restraints tend to be stronger in societies in which sexual restraint is expected of adults; thus, children are essentially being trained to develop the sexual attitudes they will show in adulthood. In societies in which there is a sexual double standard in adulthood (that is, in which women are expected to show more sexual restraint than men), that double standard is inculcated in childhood.

In Contemporary Western Culture, Children Are Insulated from Sex

Western culture has gone through radical changes that have greatly altered the experience of childhood. Indeed, the very concept of children as a distinct group of people entitled to special treatment barely existed before the sixteenth century (Jackson, 1993). Before the nineteenth century, families generally slept together, so young children observed adult sexual behavior. Also, because farming was the commonest occupation, children frequently saw sexual behavior and parturition among animals. Young children frequently went naked, so they were not prevented from exploring their own bodies or investigating the anatomy of their many siblings.

By the end of the nineteenth century, however, the belief that children needed to be kept in a state of sexual innocence was fully engrained. While there have been changes since then, especially in terms of formalized sex education, these educational programs have tended to present sex as something dangerous, marked by three special risks: disease, pregnancy, and sexual deviance.

To some extent, children get a more positive image of sex from television, although many would argue that the representation of sex on TV errs in the opposite direction, too often failing to show the possible negative consequences of sexual interactions. Furthermore, television deals mainly with the romantic aspects of sex and is resolutely uninformative when it comes to the nitty-gritty of sexual anatomy and sexual behaviors. A particularly ludicrous example of this occurred in 2000, when comedian Tom

Nudity allows children to familiarize themselves with anatomical sex differences.

Research Highlights

Children's Sexual Knowledge

In a 1982 book, sexologists Ronald and Juliette Goldman described their studies of the sexual knowledge of children aged 5 to 15 in Australia, Britain, Sweden, and North America (Canada and the United States) (Goldman & Goldman, 1982). One of the questions they asked the children was, "How can anyone know a newborn baby is a boy or a girl?" The Goldmans categorized the children's answers into three groups:

Group 1 included answers that were noninformative (no answer), based on irrelevancies ("If it's bigger it's a boy"), authoritarian ("The doctor puts a name tag on the wrist"), or fanciful ("Boys come out here and girls here").

Group 2 included descriptions of semi-recognized physical differences ("Boys stand up to go to the wee-wee and girls don't," "They're different down there") or physical differences recognized by pseudonyms ("A boy has those things—it's very rude—we call them wallies").

Group 3 included answers that accurately described or named body parts ("It's embarrassing, but the boy doesn't have a slit down the middle but has a round tube," "You can see if the baby has a penis or not—the girl has a vagina").

The distribution of answers to this question given by North American children is plotted in the figure at right. Even at the age of 9, most North American children were unable to give an accurate answer to this question. Children in Sweden, where universal sex education begins in kindergarten, were far better able to answer this and all other sex-related questions (data not shown).

It is possible, of course, that embarrassment, rather than ignorance, prevented some children from giving correct answers. There may also have been some improvement since the time of the Goldmans' study. Still, the level of apparent ignorance is remarkable. Among other things, it casts doubt on the notion that 3- to 5-year-old children experience penis envy or castration anxiety, as Freud claimed, since these feelings were supposed to be triggered by the recognition of anatomical sex differences between girls and boys.

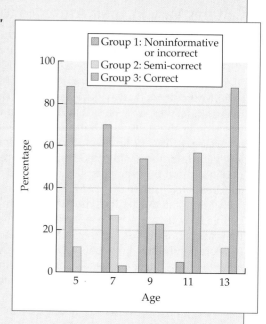

Green—a survivor of testicular cancer—attempted to demonstrate testicular self-examination on his MTV show. The volunteer's genitals were "tiled out," so that viewers could only surmise that something indecent was going on between his knees and his navel. All in all, it seems that children in contemporary Western culture—especially in the United States—are likely to be less knowledgeable about some basic facts of life than are children in many non-Western cultures or children in our own culture a few centuries ago (Box 12.1).

Witnessing Parental Sex Does Not Harm Children

One way that children might acquire sexual knowledge is by observing their parents naked or witnessing their sexual encounters. In some families this may happen by accident, but for families who live in crowded conditions (as do many low-income families) it may be an inevitable part of life.

Many parents do not permit their children to see them naked or to witness their sexual encounters, in part because clinicians and therapists have suggested that these experiences are harmful to children and may even represent a form of sexual abuse (Kritsberg, 1993). Research on this topic has led to reassuring findings, however. In one 18-year longitudinal study—the UCLA Family Lifestyles Project—young children who saw their parents naked or engaging in sex were no more likely to experience psychological problems in later childhood or adolescence than children who did not (Okami et al., 1998). In fact, there was a tendency for them to have *fewer* problems—a result that is in line with another, retrospective study (Lewis & Janda, 1988).

Children Engage in a Variety of Sexual Behaviors

What about children's actual sexual behavior? Newborn babies may already exhibit penile erections or vaginal lubrication (Martinson, 1976; Masters et al., 1982). In fact, erections have been detected in male fetuses several weeks before birth by means of ultrasound imaging. These physiological processes continue to occur through infancy and childhood. They are not necessarily brought about by what we would normally consider *sexual* stimuli, however. According to Kinsey's group (Kinsey et al., 1948), penile erections in young boys are triggered by a wide variety of physical stimuli (the motion of a car, sitting in warm sand) or exciting or fearful events (playing exciting games, being asked to go to the front of the class, punishment, looking over the edge of a building). Thus it seems that erections in young boys are part of a generalized arousal response.

Masturbation is a very common practice among children of both sexes. Infants may touch or fondle their genitals in a fairly casual fashion. By about 6 to 12 months children engage in more purposeful self-stimulation, such as rubbing or thrusting their genitals rhythmically against bedding or a doll. Later, as control of the hands improves, manual masturbation is seen. Some children of both sexes reach a climax of excitement followed by relaxation, very comparable to orgasm in adults—though boys do not ejaculate, of course (Kinsey et al., 1948; Kinsey et al., 1953).

It is also common for young children to show their genitals to adults or to other children and to attempt to view the genitals of others. In adults, such behaviors would be called **exhibitionism** and **voyeurism,** respectively, and would probably be considered pathological (see Chapter 14), but parents and preschool staff report that most—or at least sizable minorities of—normal young children show these behaviors (Davies et al., 2000; Friedrich et al., 1991).

In addition, there may be sexual or quasi-sexual contacts between children. Children often kiss and hug each other. They may also attempt to touch each other's genitals. Sometimes these behaviors are incorporated into games such as "show," "doctor," "house," and the like. In "doctor"—just in case your childhood memories are hazy—one child complains of some pain and another investigates its cause. The genitals are often examined—even if the "pain" is an earache. In the UCLA Family Lifestyles Project, about half the mothers reported that their children had engaged in play-sex of this kind before the age of 6. Children who did so were no more likely to be maladjusted as teenagers than children who did not (Okami et al., 1997).

Children Rarely Engage in Adultlike Sexual Behaviors

In the studies just mentioned, only very small numbers of children engaged in more adultlike sexual behaviors, such as pretended coitus, oral sex, body-on-body rubbing, or inserting a finger or an object into the vagina or anus. At first glance, this might seem surprising, given that coitus-related behaviors (presenting and mounting) are almost universal among the young of nonhuman primates. Bear in mind, however, that children (at least in contemporary American culture) have little opportunity to observe adults engaged in sexual behavior beyond kissing and hugging. If imitation forms the basis of interpersonal sexual behaviors in childhood, one would not expect to see many children attempting coitus or other forms of penetrative sex.

According to parents' reports, children's overt sexual activities are most frequent around the age of 3 or 4; they become gradually less common from then until the age of 12 (Friedrich et al., 1991). It is not clear whether this change represents a real decline in sexual feelings and behaviors, however, or a concealment of them in response to the admonitions of parents and other adults. In studies in which older children or adolescents have been asked directly about their current or earlier sexual behaviors, a different picture emerges; namely, one of increasing sexual interest and activity before and during the onset of puberty. This is particularly true for boys (Rutter, 1971). In terms of play-sex, children may graduate from "doctor" to more adultlike games such as "7 minutes in heaven," in which two children are put in a closet and given that much time to kiss or fondle, while the others giggle outside. In general, unforced sexual encounters between similarly aged children or preadolescents—even between siblings—seem to have no deleterious effects on those children's psychological or sexual adjustment in later life (Greenwald & Leitenberg, 1989; Leitenberg et al., 1989).

Some Children Have Sexual Contacts with Adults

Significant numbers of children have sexual contacts with adults or adolescents. There have been no random-sample surveys of children inquiring about their sexual experiences with adults, but a number of surveys have asked adults to recollect such experiences from their childhood. In these surveys, about 15 percent of women and 7 percent of men report that they had at least one childhood sexual experience involving physical contact with an adult (Gorey & Leslie, 1997). Adults in different age brackets are about equally likely to recall such experiences, suggesting that the frequency of their occurrence has not increased or decreased greatly over the last few decades. If one includes noncontact experiences, such as exposure of a man's genitals to a child, the percentages are higher.

Most Child–Adult Contacts Involve Older Children and Are Single Encounters

According to the NHSLS data, most children who have sexual experiences with adults or adolescents have only one such experience, or if they have multiple experiences, they are all with the same partner. For girls, that partner is most often an adult male, and less often an adolescent male. For boys, it is most commonly an adolescent female, less often an adolescent male, and even less often an adult male. The data also showed that 80–90 percent of adult–child contacts involve the adult touching the genitals of the child. Oral contacts and vaginal or anal penetration are much less common.

How old are children when they have sexual contact with adults or adolescents? The most likely age bracket for a child to have sexual contact with a male is 7–10 years, but about one-third of such contacts occur in the under-7 age bracket. The most likely age bracket for a child (nearly always a boy) to have contact with a female is 11–13 years. Since the females involved are usually adolescents, as mentioned above, we are talking about contacts between two individuals who differ in age by only a few years.

Who are the adults that have sex with children? We will postpone discussion of their psychological characteristics until Chapters 13 and 14, where we consider adult–child sex from the perspective of the adult. Here we consider their relationship to the child. As shown in Table 12.1, only a very small percentage of these adults are strangers to the children with whom they have contact. Most are relatives or family friends. Boys are most likely to have contacts with family friends, while girls are most likely to have contacts with relatives. As the table shows, girls as a group are equally likely to have contacts with fathers and stepfathers. Many more girls live with their fathers than live with stepfathers; thus, a girl who lives with a stepfather has a relatively higher likelihood of experiencing a sexual contact with him.

Some Kinds of Adult–Child Sex Are Much More Harmful than Others

The effects of adult–child sex on children are controversial. In the minds of most members of the public, politicians, and jurists, as well as some therapists, such contacts are always extremely harmful to the child. Adult–child sex is widely referred to as "sexual abuse of children." It is a criminal offense on the part of the adult everywhere in the United States, and people convicted of it ("child molesters") are punished more severely than almost any other criminals. Sentences of 60 or more years of imprisonment may be imposed, even in cases in which the adult does not use force (Tran, 2001). Just writing down a fictitious description of (highly abusive) adult–child sex in his private journal cost one Columbus, Ohio, man a 10-year prison sentence (Doulin, 2001).

On the other hand, cross-cultural studies suggest that adult–child sex may not always have serious harmful consequences. We have mentioned several examples of cultures in which such contacts are or were common, accepted, and without obvious damaging

TABLE 12.1	*Percentage of adult–child sexual contacts involving different relationships of the adult to the child*		
		Child's sex	
Relationship of adult to child		**Girl**	**Boy**
Father		7	1
Stepfather		7	1
Older brother		9	4
Other relative		29	13
Teacher		3	4
Family friend		29	40
Mother's boyfriend		2	1
Older friend of child		1	4
Other person known to child		19	17
Stranger		7	4

Source: Data from NHSLS.
Note: The percentages add up to more than 100 because some children had contacts with more than one adult.

effects. These are often cultures, like that of ancient Greece, in which young unmarried men have little sexual access to women and have sexual contacts with pubertal or prepubertal boys instead. (Of course, we lack detailed information about the mental health of the affected children in this particular case, so we cannot be sure that they were unharmed.)

Many studies have focused on the effects of adult–child sexual contacts in the United States and other contemporary Western cultures. These include studies of children known to have had such contacts as well as surveys of adults who recollect such contacts from their childhood. When children who have had sexual contacts with adults are viewed as a single group, they do experience more negative consequences than control groups of children who have not had such contacts. The harmful consequences include both short-term effects (fearfulness, depression, inhibition of emotions, hostility, and antisocial behaviors) and long-term effects (mood disorders, phobias, panic disorders, antisocial personality, suicidality, substance abuse, poor academic performance, sexual promiscuity, and sexual victimization of others) (Green, 1992; Paolucci et al., 2001).

A somewhat different picture emerges, however, when the details of the adult–child contacts are taken into account. The children who are most likely to experience adverse effects are, not surprisingly, those who were coerced into a sexual contact (Molnar et al., 2001). Sexual contacts that are repeated over a long period of time, that are with a family member (incest), or that involve a very large age difference may also be more likely to cause harm than isolated or nonincestuous contacts or those with a small age difference between the child and the older person. Girls are also more likely to suffer harm than boys. According to meta-analyses and original studies by psychologist Bruce Rind of Temple University and his colleagues, most children who experience sexual contacts with adults suffer no long-term adverse consequences, or only mild ones (Rind, 2001; Rind et al., 1998). Rind's work has ignited a firestorm of political and academic controversy (Box 12.2).

Memory Problems Bedevil Sexual Abuse Cases

The issue of adult–child sex and its consequences is greatly complicated by problems of recall. Ideally, children would give reliable testimony about sexual contacts that they had recently experienced, and adults would have accurate memories of sexual experiences during their childhood. Unfortunately, neither is necessarily the case. Children can be induced to believe and report events that didn't happen, and adults can be induced to "recover" supposedly repressed memories of childhood sexual abuse, even when such memories are demonstrably false (Box 12.3).

Box 12.2   *Society, Values, and the Law*

When Science Meets Politics: The Rind Affair

In 1998, psychologist Bruce Rind, an adjunct professor at Temple University in Philadelphia, published (along with two colleagues) an article on adult–child sex in *Psychological Bulletin,* a journal of the American Psychological Association (Rind et al., 1998). The article was a meta-analysis—a mathematical reworking of data from 49 previous studies that had asked college students about their sexual experiences as children. Rind's group found that college students who reported childhood sexual contacts with adults were, on average, slightly less well adjusted than students who reported no such contacts. On its face, this result suggested that sexual contacts with adults do have long-lasting harmful effects on children, albeit only mild ones. However, Rind found that the students who had experienced sexual contacts with adults as children had also experienced a relatively poor family environment, and that this poor environment accounted for most or all of the difference in adjustment between the two groups of students. Rind's group concluded that adult–child sex does not inevitably inflict long-term harm.

For a while, Rind's study did not attract public attention, but some months later a caller to Laura Schlessinger's radio talk show complained about it. This discussion alerted a number of conservative groups, which began attacking the APA. The paper "gives pedophiles a green flag," said a spokeswoman for the Family Research Council, a fundraising group for conservative causes. This opinion was echoed by Tom DeLay, majority whip of the U.S. House of Representatives, and in July 1999 the House passed a resolution "rejecting the notion that sex between adults and children is positive."

In an attempt to protect itself, the APA did everything short of disowning Rind's paper: it adopted a resolution "opposing child abuse," told its journal editors to be more mindful of the social implications of

controversial studies, and asked the American Association for the Advancement of Science to check Rind's conclusions. (The AAAS declined.) Many academics were dismayed by the APA's reaction; psychologist Edward Katkin of the State University of New York, Stony Brook, called it "groveling and cowardly."

The controversy might have died down at this point, had not psychologist Scott Lilienfeld of Emory University written an analysis of the Rind affair and submitted it to APA's flagship journal, *American Psychologist.* Although Lilienfeld's paper was critical of the APA's behavior, it was accepted for publication. In early 2001, however, the editor of *American Psychologist,* Richard McCarty, got cold feet: he withdrew his acceptance and asked Lilienfeld to write a revised paper without any mention of Rind's study. Outraged, Lilienfeld unleashed a barrage of emails to the psychological and sexological communities, accusing the APA of bending to political pressure. Lilienfeld received so much support that McCarty was obliged to reverse himself and publish the article, although it was accompanied by critical commentaries.

Undaunted, Rind himself continued the same line of research. In 2001 he published a study in which he asked 129 gay and bisexual men about their adolescent sexual contacts with adult men. The men who reported such experiences (at as early as 12 years of age) rated those experiences positively and were just as well adjusted as the men who had no such contacts (Rind, 2001).

Rind believes that the public fails to make important distinctions between, say, the repeated rape of a 5-year-old girl by her father and the willing sexual involvement of an adolescent boy with an adult. The former is likely to be highly traumatic, while the latter, according to Rind, is a violation of social norms with no implication for personal harm. He also acknowledges, howev-

er, that "lack of harmfulness does not imply lack of wrongfulness."

Bruce Rind is not the only person to have gotten into trouble for questioning whether sex between adults and children is inevitably harmful. In 1999, Harris Mirkin, a political scientist at the University of Missouri, published an article characterizing public attitudes toward adult–minor sex as a "moral panic" and advocating respect for minors' rights to choose their sex partners (Mirkin, 1999). The article languished in obscurity until 2002, when the scandal involving Roman Catholic priests grabbed the headlines (see Box 14.4). At that point, Missouri state legislators demanded that Mirkin be fired, and both houses of the legislature voted to reduce the University of Missouri's budget by an amount roughly equal to Harris's salary. The University's chancellor defended Mirkin and vowed to absorb the cut elsewhere.

Another uproar was caused by a book titled *Harmful to Minors: The Perils of Protecting Children from Sex,* by journalist Judith Levine (Levine, 2002). Among other things, Levine contended that sex with an adult can be a positive experience for some teens. She expressed approval of a 1990 Dutch law that legalized consensual sex between adults and minors down to age 12. Even before the book's publication, Minnesota legislators called for the book's publisher, the University of Minnesota Press, to pull it. Criticism also came from academe. "The claim that any sexual relationship between a child and an adult can be consensual is just not possible" was the reported comment of David Spiegel, associate chairman of the Psychiatry Department at Stanford University School of Medicine. Levine was unrepentant, replying, "The hysteria surrounding my book is precisely what my book is about."

Sources: Goode, 1999; Holden, 1999, 2001b, 2001c; Robinson, 2002; Wilgoren, 2002.

Strategies to Prevent Adult–Child Sex Are Quite Effective

None of this should be taken to minimize the fact that some children are indeed traumatized by sexual abuse. These children are at risk of developing **post-traumatic stress disorder,** just as are adult rape victims (see Chapter 18). One aspect of this disorder is **dissociation**—the tendency to "stand outside" the traumatic experience and to fail to experience the normal emotional responses to it. Another common trait shown by sexually

Box 12.3 *Society, Values, and the Law*

Sex and Suggestibility

In 1984, Peggy McMartin Buckey, along with her son Raymond and four others, faced over two hundred counts of child molestation—crimes that were alleged to have taken place at the McMartin Pre-School in Manhattan Beach, California (Figure A). During their trial—the longest in United States history—extraordinary allegations surfaced. These allegations involved not merely sexual abuse of young children, but also underground satanic rituals involving animal sacrifice and pornography. After 7 years (including a retrial for Raymond Buckey), all the defendants were acquitted. Memories of the trial still hang heavy over child care workers, therapists, and prosecutors everywhere. Yet the lessons of the McMartin case still have not been fully learned.

The core issue in the trial was the believ-ability of the 349 children who told social workers and investigators that they had experienced, witnessed, or been told about sexual abuse at the school. It became apparent during the trial that many of these children were inculcated by their interviewers with false memories of events that never happened. We may never know whether there was any kernel of truth to the McMartin allegations, but what is certain is that unscrupulous investigators, overzealous prosecutors, and sensation-seeking media blew the case up into a hysterical witch hunt.

Sadly, the McMartin case was not the last of its kind. In 1989, Robert Kelly, the owner of the Little Rascals day care center in North Carolina, was charged, along with six others, with molesting 29 children at the center. The defense argued that the children's stories were inculcated, but Kelly was convicted and sentenced to 12 life sentences. Dawn Wilson, the center's cook, was also sentenced to life imprisonment. In 1995 their convictions were overturned, and all the charges were later dropped.

In the same year that the North Carolina appeals court reversed Kelly and Wilson's convictions, 43 men and women were arrested in the picturesque apple-growing town of Wenatchee, Washington, and charged with raping and molesting 60 children. Among the defendants were the pastor of the local Pentecostal Church and his wife. The whole case was driven forward by a police detective whose 9-year-old foster daughter accused 90 people of satanic ritual abuse. Again, children were pressured by

(A) Peggy McMartin Buckey and Raymond Buckey

therapists to "remember" episodes of molestation and assault. The pastor and his wife spent 135 days in jail before being acquitted, but some defendants were convicted and are still in prison.

There is a close connection between these cases and the epidemic of "recovered memories" that swept the country in the late 1980s and early 1990s. In 1992, for example, a Missouri women who was in therapy with a church counselor "remembered" that she had been repeatedly raped by her father—a minister—between the ages of 7 and 14, that she became pregnant as a result, and that she was forced to perform an abortion on herself with a coat hanger. When her story was publicized, her father had to resign his post as a minister. Before he could be tried, however, a medical examination revealed that the daughter had never been pregnant and, in fact, was still a virgin. The therapist paid $1 million in settlement of the case.

Numerous studies document that memories can be inculcated. The leading figure in this field of research is Elizabeth Loftus (for many years at the University of Washington, now at the University of California, Irvine), who testified at the McMartin trial and in many similar cases (Loftus & Ketcham, 1996; Loftus, 1997) (Figure B). In her best-known experiment, Loftus instilled her subjects with a false memory of having been lost in a shopping mall as a child, along with various things that happened to the child while lost. Others have instilled "childhood memories" of hospitalization for an ear infection, of the sprinklers going off in a store, of an accident at a wedding reception, and the like.

Nothing distinguishes these false memories from real ones—except that they are false.

Several circumstances that are common in sexual abuse prosecutions promote the inculcation of false memories. One is that the initial account comes from a trusted or authoritative person. Another is that the subject is interviewed repeatedly. Oftentimes, details that the subject denies in initial interviews are gradually incorporated into the false memory of the event. Both these factors operate in many sexual abuse cases, Loftus says. Another dangerous but common practice is for the interviewer to encourage the subject to exercise their unfettered imagination. Loftus quotes one therapist as recommending that interviewers tell the client: "Spend time imagining that you were sexually abused, without worrying about accuracy. . . . Who would have been likely perpetrators?" But, Loftus's research has shown, the mere act of imagining a fictional past event facilitates the process of "remembering" it.

The sexual abuse of children does happen, and when it does it's a tragedy. But there's something about these crimes, or the rumor of them, that often triggers the wholesale abandonment of elementary principles of justice, such as the presumption of innocence.

Sources: Associated Press, 1999; Landsberg, 2000; Lyon, 1998; Rohrlich, 2000; Schneider & Barber, 1998.

(B) Elizabeth Loftus

abused children is self-blame. Therapy may be focused on helping the child to experience the missing emotions and to realize that the adult perpetrator was the sole guilty party.

Many schools have programs intended to teach young children how to avoid sexual encounters with adults by learning to distinguish between "good touch" (e.g., patting, hugging) and "bad touch" (e.g., genital fondling). There has been some concern that such programs might inculcate sex-phobic attitudes, especially considering that U.S. schools do not provide general sex education for young children. A study of college-age women, however, concluded that women who underwent these prevention programs in childhood were as well adjusted sexually as other women, and were much less likely to have experienced adult–child sexual contact subsequent to the instruction (Gibson & Leitenberg, 2000). Thus these programs seem to be quite effective.

Preadolescence May Be Marked by an Increase in Sexual Interest

The period between about 8 and 12–13 years of age is often called **preadolescence.** During this period the biological processes of puberty begin (see Chapter 5). Preadolescence may be marked by some degree of increased sexual feelings and behavior, but this varies greatly from one individual to another.

In the United States, where young children receive little or no sex education, the early preadolescent years (say, around 8 or 9) are the time when most children learn about coitus and other "facts of life." Much information is spread through peer networks, rather than coming from parents or school instruction, so comical misunderstandings are the rule. For example, children may fail to understand the difference between the anus and the vagina, or may think that babies grow in the mother's stomach and emerge via the belly button. Because sex education tends to focus on the reproductive aspects of sex, aspects that are not vital for reproduction, such as the clitoris and female orgasm, get little attention and are often not discovered until after puberty.

Preadolescent Children Segregate by Sex

Preadolescent children spend much of their time in all-male or all-female groups, a phenomenon called **homosociality.** Obviously, this pattern of socialization minimizes their opportunities for heterosexual interactions. Nevertheless, some older preadolescents do engage in sexual behaviors with the other sex. In one study of students in an urban public school system, 30 percent of students entering the sixth grade (approximately 11 years old) stated that they had already engaged in sexual intercourse (Kinsman et al., 1998). The students who had done so differed in a number of respects from those who had not: they were more likely to be male, African-American, from poorer neighborhoods, from single-parent families, and to have engaged in nonsexual risky behaviors. Nationwide, the proportion of preadolescents who have experienced coitus is much lower than 30 percent (Figure 12.1), but varies greatly with ethnicity (Centers for Disease Control, 2000f).

The fact that preadolescent children socialize primarily with peers of the same sex facilitates homosexual behaviors. Boys may engage in pairwise or group masturbation, for example. It's possible that preadolescents who later become homosexual enjoy such behavior somewhat more than those who become heterosexual, but the behavior is certainly not restricted to pre-gay children and is in no way predictive of a child's ultimate sexual orientation.

Strict Gender Norms May Traumatize Pre-Gay Children

Actually, preadolescent children who later become gay or lesbian tend to distinguish themselves not so much by their sexual behavior, but by gender nonconformity in a variety of nonsexual traits (see Chapter 6). A pre-gay boy may be less interested in contact sports than other boys, while a pre-lesbian girl may be *more* interested in such sports. Such gender nonconformity may be apparent in earlier childhood, and it may worry

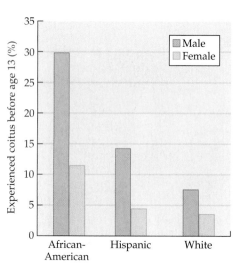

Figure 12.1 Early sexual activity. The graph shows the percentage of males and females who have experienced coitus before age 13. (Data from Centers for Disease Control, 2000f.)

parents or teachers, but young children themselves are usually blind to it, so gender-nonconformist children are not seriously disadvantaged within their peer groups.

During the preadolescent years, however, gender norms become much stricter, both within peer groups and with respect to the expectations of adults. The problems are more severe for gender-nonconformist boys than for girls, because some degree of masculinity in a girl may actually be an advantage. A degree of aggressiveness or competitiveness may help her gain a leadership position in a peer group, for example. Boys who are unmasculine or positively feminine, on the other hand, may find themselves excluded from both their male and female peer groups, and may have to content themselves with the company of other misfits at the fringes of childhood society. Furthermore, epithets such as "faggot" and "dyke" are used with increasingly frequency in the preadolescent years, and hearing these epithets begins the internalization of homophobic attitudes. Of course, the degree to which pre-gay children experience these problems before adolescence varies greatly, depending on how gender-nonconformist they are as well as on the attitudes of parents, the school they attend, and so on.

Adolescence Is a Time of Sexual Exploration

The term **adolescence** is used to mean roughly the teen years (13–18 or 13–20). The beginning of adolescence may correspond to the biological events of puberty, such as menarche and first ejaculation (see Chapter 5). The end of adolescence, however, is arbitrary. In fact, the concept of adolescence could be considered a social construction, designed to accommodate the ever-widening gap between the age of reproductive maturity and the age at which society is willing to grant men and women full adult freedoms and responsibilities.

The beginning of adolescence is usually marked by a great increase in a boy or girl's sexual feelings, and often by an increase in sexual behavior as well. This sexual awakening may in part be a response to the obvious bodily changes that accompany puberty. In addition, however, the rising blood levels of gonadal steroids, especially testosterone, seem to directly activate the brain circuitry underlying sexual responsiveness, as discussed in Chapter 7.

Many Cultures Have Puberty Rites

Puberty, and the consequent increase in sexual feelings and expression, is an important event in a young person's life, and has been marked by special **coming-of-age ceremonies** in many human cultures (Ford & Beach, 1951). In girls, puberty includes a dramatic event—menarche—and girls' puberty rites are usually centered around this event. Common features of girls' rites are seclusion, cleansing, instruction, and body modification. A fairly typical rite is that of the Lenge people of Mozambique. The girl's hymen is opened with a special tool made of horn, and she remains for a month in seclusion in an "initiation school," during which time she receives sexual instruction in the form of magic formulas. At the end of the period she spends an entire day bathing in the sea. She receives fertility medicines and returns home, but remains in seclusion for 2 or more months. In some cultures a girl's puberty is marked by tattooing, ornamental scarring, ear piercing, tooth filing, female circumcision, or stretching of the labia minora. After the ceremonies are complete, the girl dons the clothes of a mature woman.

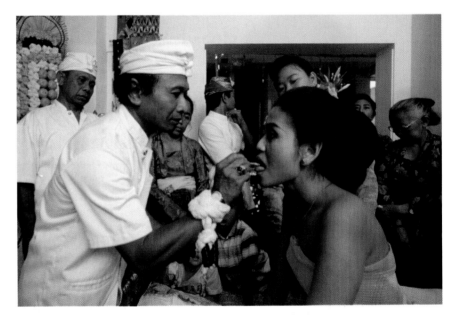

Puberty rites vary around the world. This teenage girl in Bali is having her teeth filed, an important puberty rite that seeks to rid an individual of their "wild" nature. The points of the canine teeth are slightly filed down.

For boys, puberty rites may be simple or complex. On the Truk Islands in the West Pacific, a boy whose pubic and facial hair becomes noticeable simply puts on an adult loincloth and goes to live in the men's dormitory. Among the Keraki of New Guinea, on the other hand, puberty rites take up to a year. The boys undergoing initiation are gathered in a clearing, where they are shown a sacred musical instrument, the bullroarer, and struck a blow on the back with a heavy banana stalk. There follows a parade and a feast. The boys are confined for nearly a year in a special longhouse, during which time they take the receptive role in anal sex with older males. At the end of this period the boys return home and take on the role of adults. Body modification, including circumcision or subincision, is a common feature of male puberty rites around the world.

In the contemporary United States, puberty rituals may be associated with certain religions and ethnic groups. An example is the Jewish **bar mitzvah,** a combination of religious instruction and family celebration. Hispanics have the **quinceañera,** a celebration for girls who reach the age of 15 and (traditionally, at least) have maintained their virginity. It incorporates a Roman Catholic Mass as well as a traditional *vals* (waltz) danced by the girl, her male escort, and 14 *damas* and 14 *chambelanes* ("bridesmaids" and their escorts).

Most Americans, however, do without special puberty rituals. Perhaps this is because parents and society in general devote so much effort to restricting teen sexuality and to keeping adolescents in a subadult state. Advertising a girl or boy's sexual maturity would hardly assist this endeavor.

There Are Strong Social Influences on Teen Sexual Behavior

Although the physiological processes of puberty play a key role in kick-starting adolescents' sex drive, there are also important social influences on teen sexuality, especially with regard to sexual behaviors with partners. We mentioned above that sexual activity tends to start earlier among children at lower socioeconomic levels. This pattern relates to the entire community in which an adolescent lives, not just to the adolescent's individual circumstances (Brewster et al., 1993). Thus, adolescents are likely to initiate sexual activity early if their community has a low average income, few college graduates, a high crime rate, or high unemployment. It is likely that such communities offer adolescents few constructive goals and therefore give them little motivation to avoid sexual behavior, especially risky sexual behavior such as unprotected coitus (Billy et al., 1994).

Sexual behavior starts later among children who are religiously observant and who are of higher intelligence (Halpern et al., 2000; Halpern et al., 1994). The effect of intelligence is a marked one and is seen in sexual behaviors ranging from kissing to coitus. More intelligent youths may be more occupied with educational and other career-related activities and thus have less time for sexual relationships. They may also be more alert to the potential negative consequences of early sexual activity.

Another factor that is associated with the early initiation of sexual activity is having a significantly older boyfriend or girlfriend (VanOss Marin et al., 2000). This is hardly surprising, given that older partners are likely to be more sexually experienced.

Males Masturbate More than Females

One of the commonest sexual behaviors among adolescents is masturbation. Many male adolescents begin masturbating to ejaculation as soon as they are physiologically capable of it, or soon thereafter (Kinsey et al., 1948). They typically masturbate 2–3 times per week, according to one study of Southern California teens (Hass, 1979), but the frequency of masturbation decreases for males who are having sex with partners. Female adolescents are less likely to masturbate at all; only about one in four do so, according to one national survey (Coles & Stokes, 1985). Those that do masturbate do so only about once per month, on average (Hass, 1979).

The Sexual Behavior of American Teens Has Increased and Diversified

Adolescent sexuality in the United States has changed greatly over the last 50 years (Joyner & Laumann, 2001). In the period immediately after the Second World War, most adoles-

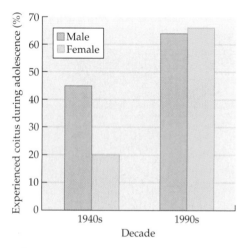

Figure 12.2 Coitus has become more common among teens. The graph shows the percentage of females and males who experienced coitus during adolescence in the 1940s and in the 1990s. The 1940s data refer to coitus by age 19; the 1990s data refer to coitus by twelfth grade. (Data from Kinsey et al., 1948, 1953; Centers for Disease Control, 2000f.)

Figure 12.3 Number of sex partners is increasing. Adolescents, especially females, had progressively more opposite-sex partners during the second half of the twentieth century. The graphs show the percentage of males and females who had the stated number of opposite-sex partners before the age of 18, by birth cohort. (Data from NHSLS.)

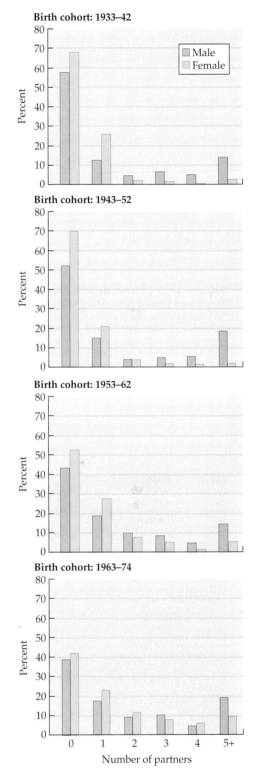

cents' goals were focused on completing schooling, entering the labor force, marrying, and starting a family. Adolescents dated, and this behavior was important for adolescents' social standing and the development of gender-appropriate roles, but dating generally involved sexual behaviors short of coitus. Engaging in coitus endangered the status of adolescent and unmarried young adult females. The status of males was not endangered in the same way (the "double standard"), but males generally found it difficult to persuade females to have intercourse with them. Prostitutes offered one possible outlet.

Many social changes since the 1940s have led to a much more widespread engagement of adolescent males and females in sexual behaviors, including coitus (Centers for Disease Control, 2000f; Kinsey et al., 1948; Kinsey et al., 1953) (Figure 12.2). One was the introduction of oral contraceptives in 1960 (see Chapter 11). Another was the legalization of abortion (extended to the entire United States by the Supreme Court's *Roe v. Wade* decision of 1973). Yet another was the introduction of effective treatments for some sexually transmitted diseases. These factors reduced the "cost" of coitus to women, including adolescents. Another factor was feminism, which resulted in the entry of women into the labor market, increased college attendance by women, and the postponement of marriage. These changes reduced the importance of marriage to women's social and economic status, so that preserving their "marriageability" by refusing to engage in coitus lost much of its value.

These changes have also had "snowball effects" that have further reduced inhibitions on adolescent sexuality. Children—especially African-American children—are increasingly being brought up by single but sexually active mothers. Because parents are important role models, such children (especially daughters) are likely to view nonmarital or non-cohabitational sex as acceptable for themselves. Media portrayals of teen sexual behavior have also become increasingly frequent and graphic, further establishing such behavior as the social norm.

Finally, there has been a general increase in individuals' sense of self-reliance that has distanced them to some degree from family and ethnic traditions and from religious and other moral authorities. This change has allowed individuals, including adolescents, to make sexual choices based primarily on the criterion of "feeling good" rather than "being good."

All in all, these changes have led to a considerable increase in the proportion of adolescents who engage in heterosexual intercourse and in the total number of partners that they have (Figure 12.3).

Noncoital Sex Is Popular among Teens

Oral sex is common among teens because it is a way to have sex to the point of orgasm without loss of "virginity" or risk of pregnancy (Remez, 2000). In many teens' minds, oral sex also carries a lower risk of transmitting STDs—a belief that is only partially true (see Chapter 16). A series of newspaper articles in the late 1990s suggested that oral sex was increasing very rapidly among teens (Lewin, 1997; Stepp, 1999). Because the U.S. government has been reluctant to support surveys of teens' sexual behavior, statistical data on this point are skimpy. What data there are suggest that oral sex has become much more popular recently among African-American teens—the proportion of black male adolescents who had ever engaged in oral sex nearly doubled between 1988 and 1995 (Gates & Sonenstein, 2000)—but not among other groups, who already had fairly high rates of oral sex in the 1980s.

Ethnic differences in teen sexual behavior are well illustrated by a 1995 study of the heterosexual behaviors of adolescent males that intentionally sampled large numbers of Hispanic and black youth (Gates & Sonenstein, 2000) (Figure 12.4). Being masturbated by a female partner and receiving oral sex were about equally common in all three sam-

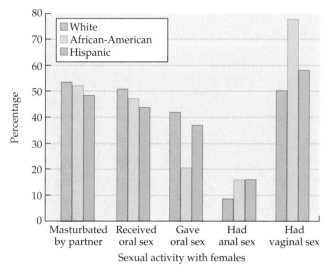

Figure 12.4 Ethnic differences in teen sex practices. The graphs show the percentages of never-married American males aged 15–18 who have ever engaged in the stated sexual activities with females, by race/ethnicity. Asians and Pacific Islanders were not sampled. (Data from Gates and Sonenstein, 2000.)

This teenage mother and her child are likely to face economic hardship.

pled groups (white, black, Hispanic). Giving oral sex to a female partner (cunnilingus), on the other hand, was far less common among blacks than among the other groups, and anal sex was much less common among whites than among the other groups. Black male adolescents were much more likely to have experienced vaginal sex (coitus) than were white or Hispanic males.

This particular survey did not include Asian-American and Pacific Islander (AAPI) adolescents, but other surveys of this heterogeneous group have reported very low rates of sexual behaviors, far below those of whites, blacks, or Hispanics. In one study, only 27 percent of AAPI high school students had ever engaged in vaginal intercourse, compared with 50 percent of whites, 57 percent of Hispanics, and 72 percent of blacks (Schuster et al., 1998). Their experience of other sexual behaviors was also relatively low. All in all, cultural origins seem to influence the amount and kind of sexual behaviors people engage in quite strongly, even during the rebellious teen years.

There Is Controversy about How to Reduce STDs and Pregnancy among Teens

Several factors oppose and limit the trend toward more widespread sexual behavior (especially sexual intercourse) among adolescents. One is the fear of AIDS, which first came to public attention in the early 1980s, and which by 2001 had caused the deaths of 439,000 Americans (see Chapter 16). Another is a social movement, led by conservative Christian groups, aimed at encouraging teenagers to postpone sexual intercourse. The leaders of these groups may be motivated primarily by religious concerns, but they can also point to serious negative practical consequences of teen sex, especially teen pregnancy and sexually transmitted diseases.

Of course, unwanted pregnancy and STDs can result from sex during adulthood, too, but adolescents are particularly at risk because they tend to be less cautious and less knowledgeable about how to prevent these negative consequences of sex. One way that this problem could be rectified would be to provide more extensive sex education and contraceptive services to young people, as is done effectively in many European countries. In Sweden, for example, girls experience their first sexual intercourse about a year earlier than do American girls, but the rate of teen pregnancy is hardly more than a third of what it is here, teen abortions are much less common, and the incidence of AIDS is about one-tenth the U.S. rate (Posner, 1992).

In the view of Christian conservatives, however, such a program would encourage increased sexual behavior and would therefore be self-defeating. Thus, conservatives promote **abstinence-only programs,** which teach adolescents that they should not engage in sexual intercourse until marriage (Box 12.4) (meaning that they should do without this activity for a decade or more; see below). According to the National Campaign to Prevent Teen Pregnancy, however, abstinence-only programs have never been shown to reduce unwanted pregnancy or STDs. What *have* been proved effective are school programs that combine encouragement of abstinence with education about contraception and how to avoid STDs (Kirby, 1997).

Happily, teen birth rates have been declining steadily in all ethnic groups in the United States over the last decade (Figure 12.5), Overall, the teen birth rate fell by 22 percent during the 1990s, and the fall was even more marked for black teens (31 percent) and for younger teens (aged 15–17—a 29 percent drop). The decline has been much slower among Hispanic teenagers than among non-Hispanic whites, however. In 2000, nearly 1 in 10 Hispanic girls in the 15–19-year age bracket delivered babies, with consequent economic and social disadvantages for many of these mothers and their children.

The decline in teen births is due to a decrease in pregnancy rates, not to an increase in abortions (Centers for Disease Control, 2001c). The reason for the decline in pregnancy rates is not entirely clear, but two identifiable factors are the use of more effective contraceptive methods and an increased abstinence rate among female teenagers (Alan Guttmacher Institute, 1999). More generally, improving economic and social conditions in disadvantaged communities probably contributed to the decline in teen births during the 1990s, because high teen birth rates are a feature of impoverished, socially disorganized, and crime-ridden communities (Kirby et al., 2001).

Teen Sexuality Is Central to Identity Development

Although public attention focuses mainly on the possible negative consequences of adolescent sexuality and on ways to prevent its expression, we shouldn't ignore the positive role that sexuality plays in the process of growing up. Adolescence involves the development of an identity and a social role independent of one's parents (Erikson, 1968; Steinberg, 2001). Answering questions about one's sexuality figure centrally in this process. Teens must answer many such questions: What is my gender? What is my sexual orientation? What am I looking for in sexual relationships? How attractive am I? Who can I "afford" as a sexual partner, and what is my best strategy for entering into a partnership? How does my sexuality relate to other aspects of my identity, such as my career goals, my ethnic origins, or my religion?

None of these questions are purely intellectual ones—they cannot be answered simply by reason or introspection. They require social exploration. This exploration takes place chiefly in the milieu where sexual interactions are likely to arise; namely, in one's peer group. Hence the transfer of energy and allegiance from parents to peers that characterizes adolescence.

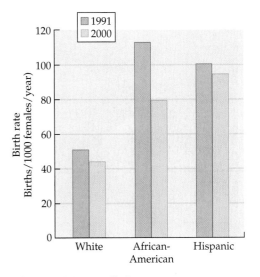

Figure 12.5 Declining teenage birth rates. The graph shows birth rates (births per 1000 females per year) in 1991 and 2000 for females aged 15–19, by ethnicity. (Data from Centers for Disease Control, 2001c.)

Box 12.4 # Research Highlights

Taking the Pledge: Do Teens Keep Their Promise to Remain Virgins?

In the early 1990s the Southern Baptist Church and other conservative religious groups began sponsoring "virginity pledge" programs. In these programs, teens stand up in front of their peers and promise not to have intercourse before they get married. Pledge programs became wildly popular in the mid-1990s, and although they may have tapered off a bit since then, it's estimated that well over 2.5 million teens have taken such vows.

These programs include a lot more than simply taking a pledge. Pledgers interact via Internet sites, rallies, and summer camps and by purchasing merchandise. Although the movement is actually organized by adults, it has been able to cultivate an image of being organized by teens themselves. Partly for that reason, the movement has succeeded to some degree in making virginity "cool."

Do these programs work? According to sociologists Peter Bearman and Hannah Brückner of Columbia University, they do—sort of. Bearman and Brückner analyzed data on over 90,000 students who had been surveyed as part of the NIH-funded National Longitudinal Study of Adolescent Health. They found that, on average, taking a virginity pledge caused a teenager to defer his or her first sexual intercourse by 18 months (Bearman & Brückner, 2001).

Eighteen months may not seem like much—"until marriage" it certainly isn't. But it's a lifetime in the breakneck world of teen culture. If all the nation's teens put off sex for this amount of time, a major drop in teen pregnancy and STDs would surely follow.

At the same time, Bearman and Brückner had to qualify their findings in important ways. The pledges were effective only for younger adolescents, not for those over 17. Pledges lost their effectiveness if too many students in a given school—more than about 40%—took the pledge. And, most disturbing of all, when pledgers *did* finally engage in intercourse, they were significantly less likely than nonpledgers to use contraception.

One potential problem with Bearman and Brückner's result is the possibility that it was caused by what statisticians call a "selection effect." In other words, perhaps the pledgers were already more likely than nonpledgers to remain virgins *before* they took the pledge, in which case the pledge itself may not have had any extra effect. This could explain why increasing the percentage of pledgers in a school decreases the effectiveness of the pledge: the more students who are recruited, the larger will be the fraction of them who are not strongly motivated to remain virgins.

The researchers believe that they ruled out selection effects. The reason why pledge programs work best when only a minority of students in a school take the pledge, they say, is that pledging creates an "identity movement"—a group of individuals who gain identity, purpose, and self-esteem from their group membership. Such identity movements lose their psychological effectiveness when they no longer have minority status. For this reason, the researchers believe that pledge programs can never be effectively expanded to cover the majority of teens.

Teen sexual relationships often have a playful quality.

For many adolescents, sexual exploration involves **serial monogamy,** in which the youth has a series of exclusive relationships with girlfriends or boyfriends (or both). Within such serial relationships adolescents can discover what gives them pleasure and how to interact intimately with another person. Typically, the sexual content of these relationships progresses during the adolescent years from kissing and fondling to noncoital orgasmic contacts, and possibly to coitus.

Teen Sexuality Is Less Focused than That of Adults

Adolescent sexual relationships often have a playful quality that reflects both the participants' temporal proximity to childhood and the exploratory and rehearsal functions of these relationships. Adolescents also direct their affections over a much broader landscape than do adults. "Crushes" on older persons such as teachers, idolization of film and pop music stars, and passionate friendships with same-sex peers are all common. Even animals come into the picture: the intense relationship between some adolescent girls and horses is a well-known example. In other words, teens do not maintain as sharp a boundary between sexual and nonsexual attachments as many adults do.

Teen Social Structures Reflect Evolutionary Roots

Traditionally, American teen society has had two major features: a competition among males to establish a status hierarchy, based on performance in sports, show of wealth, or the like, and a competition among females to attract high-status males, based primarily on looks. These strategies have obvious similarities to the mating games of many other mammals (see Chapter 2), suggesting that evolutionary processes are at work. The main difference is that in humans, *both* sexes are doing the choosing, whereas in most other mammals mate choice is exerted primarily by females.

This difference may have to do with the large investment that human males typically make in parenting, compared with the males of most other mammalian species. If a man has to devote himself more or less monogamously to one female and her offspring in order to give those offspring a decent chance of reaching reproductive age, he has a strong incentive to make sure she is the highest-quality female he can obtain. This is true regardless of whether his choice results from rational thought processes or from instincts instilled by evolution.

Traditional Social Patterns Have Been Modified

This traditional pattern of teen society is still in evidence, but it has been considerably modified by the changing status of women. Adolescent girls no longer have to define their own worth purely by their attractiveness to high-status males or by their prospects in the marriage market. They have their own sports, their own wealth, and their own prospects for educational success and career advancement. Men do not necessarily come into the picture at all—a woman, especially a well-educated woman, can live successfully as a single person or in partnership with another woman.

Of course, most teenage girls are heterosexual and do desire sexual relationships with males, but they are in a much improved negotiating position with respect to those relationships. Their grandmothers had the urgent task of finding a breadwinning husband almost immediately after adolescence, and had to do so without losing their "good name"—that is, without engaging in too much sex. Thus, they had very little opportunity to check out a variety of men, especially at the sexual level.

Nowadays, male and female teens are more equally positioned, and because marriage is so far off (if it is in the picture at all), sexual relations have a more purely recreational and affectional function, divorced from economic considerations. For that reason, girls may increasingly rate male partners on the basis of looks rather than on indicators of economic success. In fact, the increased attention to male physical attrac-

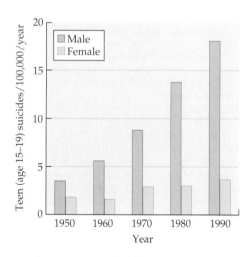

Figure 12.6 Suicide by male teens has increased much faster than for females over the last five decades. (Data from Centers for Disease Control, 1994.)

tiveness (of both face and body) that has been such a notable phenomenon over the last decade or so can probably be traced to the decreased economic value of men to women (Luciano, 2001).

Male Adolescents Face Increased Challenges

The changing balance of sexual power between male and female adolescents has had major effects on males. On the beneficial side, male teens now have a much better chance of achieving sexual relationships (including coitus) with females within their own social groups, rather than having to resort to prostitutes as their grandfathers often had to do. Thus sex is more likely to happen within an ongoing and perhaps loving relationship than it was in the past. On the down side, male teens are now prey to the kinds of anxieties—concerning their attractiveness, especially—that used to be the sole province of females. All in all, social and sexual anxieties have probably increased greatly for male teens, and this has led to definite negative consequences for some male teenagers' mental health. To take an extreme indicator of psychological distress, suicide among male teens has increased dramatically since 1950—much more so than for females (Centers for Disease Control, 1994) (Figure 12.6). How much of this increase is due to problems related to sex and relationships is uncertain.

Gender Norms Are Loosening for Some Teens

With the loosening of traditional attitudes over the last few decades has come an increasing interest among adolescents in issues of gender and sexual orientation. Most teens, whatever their sexual orientation or gender identity, are likely to know of the existence of sexual minorities and the cultures that they have established—if only that there is a gay bar somewhere in town. Many teens are personally acquainted with one or more gay or (less likely) transgendered people. They therefore see a greater range of options open to themselves. This doesn't mean that all is now well for gay, bisexual, or transgendered youth. Far from it—increasing openness has created problems for many of them, as we'll discuss in Chapter 13. Still, adventuresome teenagers may explore gender and sexual orientation issues in ways that were completely off limits to earlier generations. For example, many large cities are host to raves and other events where gay and straight young people mix and any attire is acceptable so long as it violates gender norms. Of course, only a small fraction of older adolescents participate directly in such scenes, and those that do face some associated problems such as drug use. Still, the existence of this subculture helps to break down not only the categories of masculine and feminine, but also those of gay and straight.

Canadian Marc Hall (right) went to court for the right to bring his boyfriend, Jean-Paul Doumond, to his Catholic High School prom in Oshawa, Ontario, in 2002.

In Young Adulthood, Conflicting Demands Moderate Sexual Expression

In Chapter 9 we discussed the kinds of sexual relationships that adults may engage in. We now attempt to describe how those relationships structure individual life courses. We'll start with collective data—data that describe generic Americans, with their off-white skin color, predominantly heterosexual orientation, and 2.1 children.

Most Young Men and Women Have Only a Few Sex Partners

The median age at first marriage in the United States is now about 27 for men and 25 for women, up from 23 and 21 in 1970 (U.S. Census Bureau, 2001). Assuming an age of 13 for puberty, Joe Median can therefore expect a period of 14 years between puberty and marriage, and Jane Median can expect a period of 12 years. By many measures, this period includes Joe and Jane's peak sexual years. It includes the years of most frequent sex-

Young adults typically spend several years dating before they move in with a partner.

ual behavior (including masturbation) (Kinsey et al., 1948; Kinsey et al., 1953), of greatest fertility (see Chapter 10), and of greatest sexual attractiveness (for females, at least—see Chapter 7). Typically, Joe and Jane spend a portion of this period without a sexual relationship, a portion dating (with varying degrees of sexual intimacy), and a portion (usually about a year) cohabiting with the partners they ultimately marry.

Given all one reads and hears about sex among young adults, the actual statistics may be surprising (Figure 12.7). Between age 18 and the time of first marriage or cohabitation—what we might call the young adult dating years—men and women have fairly low numbers of sex partners. The actual numbers vary with sex: men have more partners than women (or say they do, at least). They also vary according to whether the person's first live-in relationship is a legal marriage or a cohabitation. Those who marry without a prior cohabitation (who are in a minority) tend to be more traditionally minded and therefore have fewer dating partners before marriage, while those who enter into a cohabitation before (or instead of) marriage are more liberally minded and therefore have more dating partners prior to the cohabitation. But in all groups, significant numbers of individuals have *no* new sex partners during the dating years (they may have no partners at all, or a continuation of a relationship they began before age 18). In no group does the majority have more than four new partners during the dating years.

Young People Must Allocate Time and Resources between Sex and Other Goals

Why don't young adults have more sex partners than they do? In part, they may simply be satisfied by the relationships that they are in. They may also be restrained by moral beliefs. In addition, the fear of AIDS probably plays a role. The NHSLS data indicate fewer sex partners for young people who came of age during the AIDS era than for those who did so during the decade before the beginning of the epidemic.

More broadly, the decision to seek out new sex partners can been viewed within the context of a larger cost–benefit analysis that young people have to perform (Posner, 1992). Seeking sex partners takes time and resources; it therefore becomes more costly the more valuable the person's time is. In general, time is extremely valuable to young people who are seeking to advance their careers through education or other means, so such people have less time to spend in the sexual marketplace than young people who are unemployed or in dead-end jobs. They will therefore be motivated to delay sexual gratification.

On the other hand, the time it takes to find a new partner varies with attractiveness—an unattractive person needs to devote more time and resources to finding a partner than does an attractive one. Since attractiveness includes not just looks, but also such variables as wealth or prospects for wealth, this means that people with less education may have to spend more time and effort to find sex partners than do well-educated, upwardly mobile young people, and may therefore be less motivated to do so.

We might therefore expect a curvilinear relationship between educational level and number of sex partners, with people at some middle educational level having the most partners. That is in fact what is found, although the differences between the educational groups are not enormous (Figure 12.8).

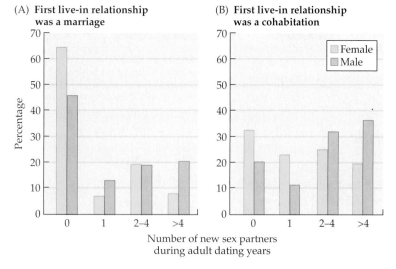

Figure 12.7 Two routes to a live-in relationship. Women and men whose first live-in relationship is a marriage have relatively few sex partners (A) during the dating years compared with people who enter cohabitations (B). The graphs show the percentages of women and men born between born 1963 and 1974 who had the stated numbers of new sex partners between the age of 18 and the time of their first live-in sexual relationship. (Data from NHSLS.)

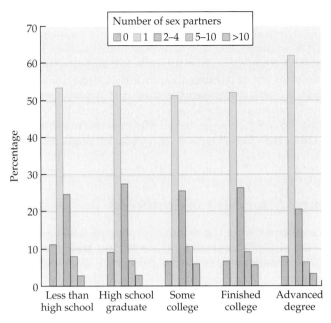

Figure 12.8 Education level and number of sex partners. Both ends of the educational spectrum are associated with lower numbers of sex partners. The graph shows the percentage of persons who had the stated numbers of sex partners in the previous 5 years, by educational level. (Data from NHSLS.)

Finding Same-Sex and Opposite-Sex Partners Involves Different Costs

The cost of acquiring sex partners also varies according to the kind of partner that is sought. If a man is seeking a male partner, for example, he can find one with much less effort than if he is seeking a female partner, at least if he lives in a large city where there is a gay culture. That's because males in general require less persuasion and fewer signs of commitment to enter into sexual relationships than do females (see Chapter 7). Conversely, a woman who is seeking a female partner may have to spend more time than one who is seeking a male partner—not just because lesbians are rarer than heterosexual men, but because, being women, they are less ready to enter a sexual relationship. Other things being equal, we would therefore expect a bisexual man to concentrate on homosexual relations, and a bisexual woman to concentrate on heterosexual relationships, simply on a cost–benefit basis.

All in all, a complex web of factors influences how worthwhile it is for a particular person to seek out sexual relationships. These factors include strength of sex drive, cost of time, availability of partners, attractiveness of self and of partners, risk of pregnancy, costs or benefits of pregnancy, risk of disease, costs of disease, effect of relationship on reputation, and so on. Individuals may not consciously assess these costs and benefits—they do not take out a pocket calculator before deciding whether to head out for a singles bar on Friday night. Rather, they learn by a process of trial and error over a period of years and develop a sexual style matched to their perceived needs.

Personality Differences Influence How Sexual Decisions Are Made

Dimensions of personality such as intelligence and impulsivity greatly affect how these cost–benefit assessments are made. An impulsive person, for example, is likely to assess costs and benefits over a short term. Such a person will be relatively uninfluenced by the long-term costs of sex, such as pregnancy or STDs. Cautious people, on the other hand, may be overinfluenced by long-term costs, thus unnecessarily denying themselves the rewards of sexual intimacy.

It is during the young adult dating years that sexual relationships are most likely to have significant negative consequences for society at large—especially unwanted pregnancy and STDs, including AIDS. In attempting to reduce these consequences, policymakers would do best to take into account the web of causation that guides young people's sexual behavior, rather than simply moralizing about it. For example, in order to prevent the spread of STDs, it is desirable to decrease the number of different sex partners Joe and Jane Median have. To achieve that end, however, it might be better to focus on strengthening and rewarding Joe and Jane's nonmarital relationships, with the hope of increasing their duration, rather than declaring war on nonmarital relationships in general.

Companionate marriage had its origins in ancient Rome. This couple is portrayed in a wall painting from the city of Pompeii.

The Institution of Marriage Is Evolving

To understand the place of cohabitation and marriage in people's lives today, it's important to recall that the institution of marriage has changed greatly over the centuries. In ancient Greece, marriage was not companionate—a wife was not expected to be a social partner to her husband, but was chiefly there to have children (who were then looked after largely by slaves). **Companionate marriage** had its origins in Roman culture, and it got a boost from the banning of polygamy by the early Christian church. It did not reach its heyday, however, until the nineteenth and early twentieth centuries, when the improved education of women gave them increased intellectual parity with men, which therefore led to their being more desirable companions for men.

Companionate Marriage Makes the Availability of Divorce a Necessity

The institution of companionate marriage contains the seeds of its own demise. First, companionate marriage demands intimacy and affection, yet not all couples are capable of sustaining these feelings over a lifetime, so companionate marriage demands the availability of at-will divorce. Indeed, the divorce rate has skyrocketed since Victorian times (see below). Yet the availability of divorce makes marriage a less serious commitment in the first place. Essentially, it converts marriage from a *status* to a *contractual relationship* (Posner, 1992). A sign of the increasingly contractual status of marriage is the appearance of custom-designed legal agreements. These include **prenuptial agreements,** which are used primarily to specify the distribution of wealth in the eventuality of divorce, postnuptial agreements, which are similar agreements made after marriage, and **covenant marriages** (see Chapter 9).

Second, a companionate marriage implies some kind of equivalence between husband and wife. Indeed, past generations would be amazed at the similarity of the roles of men and women in present-day marriages—especially in terms of the distribution of breadwinning, household, and decision-making responsibilities. That's not to say that women earn as much as men (they don't), or that men do their fair share of housework (they don't), but the fact that these activities are shared at all is a major break from the past.

This increasing equivalence has been brought about not only by the education of women and their entry into the labor market, but also by the precipitous decline in the number of children produced by women during marriage. If we visit the home of Joe and Jane Median—who have married each other since we last met them—we will find that *they do not have a single child in their home with them.* In other words, the number of married-couple households with no children under 18 is greater than the number of such households with one or more children, so the median number of children living in a household is zero (U.S. Census Bureau, 2001). This lack or small number of children minimizes the biologically distinct roles of men and women. Yet the more equivalent the roles of men and women in marriage become, the more dispensable husband and wife are to each other. So couples stay together only as long as they agree to, and the externally structured institution of marriage becomes less relevant.

Yet a third reason for the decline in marriage as a formal structure is the end of the distinction between "legitimacy" and "illegitimacy"—that is, between children born to married and to unmarried mothers. Illegitimate children used to be seriously disadvantaged in life, but that is no longer the case, and this fact has removed another rationale for legally structured marriage because it makes marriage and cohabitation more equivalent. One in three U.S. babies is now born to an unmarried mother (Centers for Disease Control, 2001b).

Marriage May Soon Become a Minority Status

So is marriage on the way out? That depends on how you look at the numbers. If you consider an imaginary cohort of American men and women who pass their entire lives in a particular year—say, 2000—you will find that the great majority of them (over 90 percent) will marry at least once. This finding suggests that marriage is still an attractive institution to most people. However, this model disregards the length of time for which people are married, and this time is shrinking (see below). In addition, it predicts the future only if one assumes that the younger generation will mimic the behavior of their elders, which is unlikely.

The percentage of men and women over 15 who are never-married, separated, or divorced at any given time is steadily rising, and the percentage who are currently married is steadily falling. Currently, about 52 percent of all women over 15 are married. If current trends continue, unmarried women will outnumber married women by about 2010 or soon thereafter. So Jane Median will not only have no children living in her household, she won't even be *married* when we come knocking on her door. (Bear in mind that we are talking about a woman's likely status at a given moment in time—Jane will still be married for *some* part of her life.)

That marriage will become a less significant part of people's lives is also suggested by trends in Europe, which seems to be ahead of the United States in this regard. In Britain, for example, the average age at first marriage has risen to 29.6 years for men and 26.4 years for women (Office for National Statistics, 1999). In Denmark, already by 1993, the average age at first marriage for women was 28, and 46 percent of Danish babies were born to unmarried mothers (European Council, 1994).

Cohabitation May Carry Rights and Obligations

For people who want the intimacy of a live-in relationship, long-term cohabitation is an alternative to marriage (and the only option for same-sex couples). Many people like the informality of cohabitation. On the other hand, cohabitation is not completely lacking in formal structure. Cohabiting couples may enter into a legal contract comparable to a prenuptial agreement. Even if they do not, there may be an implied contract, which if breached can form the basis of a **palimony suit** (Box 12.5). (Palimony law varies from state to state.) Also, some states have domestic partnership laws that confer certain rights and obligations on cohabiting partners, and the state of Vermont allows same-sex couples to enter into a civil union that confers a variety of marriage-like rights and obligations, including inheritance rights.

What we are seeing, in effect, is a gradual diversification of live-in relationships from the original two options—permanent legal marriage versus unstructured cohabitation—to a cafeteria-style system in which couples can define the kind of relationship they want. Although disturbing to moral conservatives in the United States, such arrangements are seen even in some conservative cultures around the world. The Shi'ite branch of Islam, for example, has a temporary marriage called **mut'a** (**siqeh** in Iran). The terms of this marriage are specified by the partners in advance. Mut'a may last for as little as 30 minutes if the man and woman just want to have a one-time sexual encounter, or it might last for a year if a man is living away from home for that period of time and wants a temporary wife for the duration. It is a real marriage in the sense that any offspring of the relationship are legitimate. It is open to unmarried women and to married or unmarried men. In some parts of the Islamic world, however, *mut'a* has become a legal cover for prostitution.

In spite of the social changes just described, most Americans still want to be in long-term, two-person, live-in sexual relationships. By the age of 27, according to the NHSLS, more than 70 percent of American men and more than 85 percent of American women have entered such relationships.

Box 12.5 *Society, Values, and the Law*

Cohabitation and Palimony

Two celebrity cases awakened Americans to the notion that sexual relationships between unmarried couples could entail legal obligations. In the mid-1970s, Hollywood actor Lee Marvin (*The Big Heat, The Wild One*) broke up with his longtime girlfriend Michelle Triola. Triola sued and demanded a large portion of Marvin's assets. Although the 1979 judgment denied Triola her main financial objectives, it did recognize the possible contractual nature of the relationship between unmarried couples. The term "palimony" was coined by analogy with *alimony*—legally regulated payments by one divorcing spouse to the other. In fact, however, "Marvin actions" are not closely analogous to divorce suits.

In the same year as the Marvin decision, tennis great Billie Jean King broke up with her "secretary" and live-in lover Marilyn Barnett. After two failed suicide attempts, Barnett threatened to publish love letters from King. King paid Barnett $25,000 to suppress the letters, but Barnett didn't consider that enough and brought a palimony suit, in which she claimed that King had promised to support her for life. The suit forced King to reveal her bisexuality publicly—an admission that cost her millions of dollars in lost commercial endorsements. Barnett's case was thrown out, but mainly because it smacked of extortion rather than because of any legal weakness in the concept of same-sex palimony. The case helped make the public aware that same-sex live-in relationships could generate financial obligations and thus give rise to suits for palimony—or "galimony" as the newspapers called it in the King case.

Many African-American Families Are Headed by a Single Woman

There is an exception to this tendency in the case of African-American women, who are far less likely to enter live-in relationships, including marriage, than other groups. Even when they have children, they are more likely to be unpartnered than are women in other groups (U.S. Census Bureau, 2001) (Figure 12.9). Role modeling may play a role here—that is, if young black women have mothers who are single parents, they may follow the same path. A more important factor, however, is the shortage of young black men (Tucker & Mitchell-Kernan, 1995). Because black men have a much higher death rate than black women, and are much more likely than black women to be incarcerated or partnered with non-blacks, the effective sex ratio in the black community is skewed strongly toward women. This imbalance is worsened by the relatively high unemployment rate among young black men, which makes them less desirable as live-in partners. Thus black women are often single, even though they generally prefer to be partnered (Oropesa & Gorman,

Figure 12.9 Single parenthood. (A) African-American women are much more likely to be single mothers than are women of other groups. (B) The graph shows the percentage of family households that are not headed by a married couple; the great majority of these are single-mother families. (Data from the U.S. Census Bureau, 2001.)

(A)

(B)

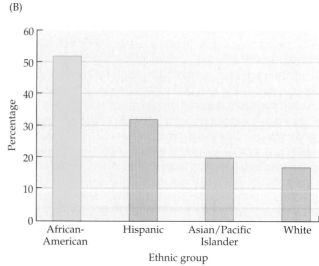

2000). All of these statistics apply largely to African-Americans living in the inner city, however; among those who live in the suburbs, living arrangements are much more like those of other middle-class Americans.

Most Married Couples Are Satisfied with Their Sex Lives

Marriage has many functions, but this book is about sexuality, so our main concern is with marital sex. Here the picture is somewhat paradoxical: married (and cohabiting) couples generally seem happier with their sex lives than they should be, based on the raw statistics on their sexual activities.

NHSLS data illustrating this point are shown in Figure 12.10. The figures show that married women, as a group, are less likely than dating women to have sex more than twice a week. They are also less adventurous sexually, at least in terms of a lesser likelihood of engaging in oral sex (either fellatio or cunnilingus). In addition, women in any long-term relationship, including marriage, are less likely to experience orgasm reliably than are women in short-term dating relationships. Paradoxically, women's physical satisfaction with sex is much greater in long-term relationships than in short-term relationships, and their emotional satisfaction is higher in marriage than in any other class of relationship. Data for men (not shown) are roughly comparable, except that men have a high likelihood of experiencing orgasm regardless of the kind of relationship they are in.

Statistically, marital sex doesn't appear to be all that hot, but married people are generally satisfied with it.

Marriage Makes Sex More Satisfying for Women

What is the cause of this paradox? There could be two kinds of reasons. These results could be an artifact reflecting different demographic characteristics among the various groups studied. Alternatively, it could be that marriage somehow confers satisfaction—especially emotional satisfaction—on the sexual aspects of relationships. The NHSLS researchers carried out a statistical analysis to resolve this question (Waite & Joyner, 2001), and came up with the following answer. For men, the paradox is indeed a demographic artifact—when men are matched for other characteristics, they are about equally likely to be satisfied by sex within marital and nonmarital relationships. For women, on the other hand, the finding is *not* an artifact. In other words, women derive extra emotional satisfaction from sex within a married relationship simply by virtue of that rela-

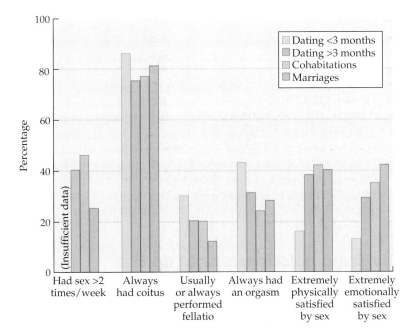

Figure 12.10 The paradox of marital sex. Married women have sex less frequently, engage in less oral sex, and are less likely to experience orgasm, but are more likely to derive physical and emotional satisfaction from sex, than are women in dating relationships. (Data from NHSLS.)

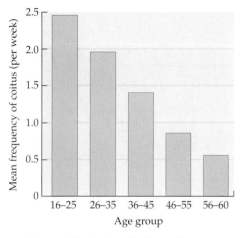

Figure 12.11 Marital sex becomes less frequent with increasing age. The data in this graph are from the Kinsey studies, so they may not be accurate today, but the trend is probably similar.

tionship being a marriage. We may speculate that the reason for the extra satisfaction is the high level of commitment and exclusivity represented by the institution of marriage—traits that are more important to women than to men (see Chapter 6).

The Frequency of Sex Declines during Marriage

Sexual interactions between married partners tend to fall off over time. Several factors are at work here. First, there is a loss of sexual interest associated with increasing familiarity between the partners (**habituation**) and the dimming of passionate love. This factor seems to be responsible for a decline in the frequency of coitus over the first year or two of marriage (Call et al., 1995). There is also a long-lasting decline in sexual interest and frequency of coitus following the birth of children (Fischman et al., 1986). Finally, there is a decline in sexual behavior associated with the process of aging itself. This age-related decline may have a number of components, including a lessening of the physiological processes associated with arousal, a decreasing sex drive due to falling blood levels of gonadal steroids, a general decrease in health and fitness, including an increased likelihood of obesity, and external factors such as the decreasing physical attractiveness of aging partners. Whatever the causes, the frequency of marital coitus declines steadily as the years go by (Figure 12.11).

Women's Marital Satisfaction Declines during Middle Age

Marital satisfaction also falls off over time, although to a highly variable degree; some couples remain highly satisfied with their marriages over a long lifetime. The birth of the first child is associated with a significant drop in marital satisfaction (Tomlinson, 1987), apparently because both husbands and wives tend to see themselves as having to shoulder an unfair share of family responsibilities. Other landmarks, such as the entry of the oldest child into adolescence (Gottman & Levenson, 2000) and retirement (Lee & Shehan, 1989), may also be associated with decreased marital satisfaction.

On the whole, wives are less satisfied with their marriages than are husbands (Schumm et al., 1998). A particularly striking change happens between the ages of 45 and 59. At the commencement of this period, men's and women's emotional satisfaction with their primary sex partners (usually their spouses) is about the same, but during the period men's satisfaction increases substantially, while women's satisfaction falls (Figure 12.12). Thus, by the late fifties, men are more than twice as likely as women to describe themselves as "extremely emotionally satisfied" with their partners. Physical satisfaction follows a very similar trend.

This sex difference in marital satisfaction probably results ultimately from the greater power and income of men. Not uncommonly, men in their late forties and fifties divorce and remarry younger partners. Women are generally less able to do so, both because of their relatively limited resources and because men value youth in their partners more than women do. Thus, if women are still married, it is more likely to be to husbands whom they have had for many years.

In general, people's satisfaction with their marriages or other relationships depends on whether they think they have a "good deal"—that is, whether they think the relationship is beneficial to themselves, or at least equitably balanced (Walster et al., 1978). Thus, if a person comes to view their partner as less attractive, that will increase their sense of being in an inequitable relationship and make them more desirous of breaking up. Unfortunately, the perception of decreased attractiveness can result not from any actual change in the partner, but from a change in the viewer; specifically, from exposure to other, highly attractive people who make the partner seem unattractive by a **contrast effect** (Box 12.6).

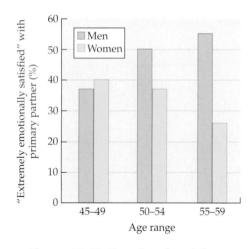

Figure 12.12 Emotional satisfaction changes with age. Between the ages of 45 and 59, men become more emotionally satisfied with their partners (usually their spouses), but women become *less* satisfied. (Data from NHSLS.)

Many Factors Bring Relationships to an End

A large fraction of all marriages end in separation or divorce. (We'll refer to these events as "breakups" or "marital disruption.") In the preceding section, and in Chapter 9, we discussed some of the family circumstances and psychological factors that seem to pro-

Box 12.6 Research Highlights

Contrast Effects and Marital Woes: The Farrah Factor

Thanks to the media, we are now being bombarded with nonstop images of extremely attractive people—something that our great-grandparents were rarely exposed to. Is this why we don't stay married as long as our great-grandparents did? Some researchers think so, and have come up with evidence to back up their belief.

In a 1980 study, psychologists Douglas Kenrick and Sara Gutierres of Arizona State University set a bunch of male college students a fairly untaxing task: they had to watch *Charlie's Angels*—a TV show that featured Farrah Fawcett and other beauties. Another bunch of "control" students didn't watch the show. Then all the students were asked to judge the suitability of an average-looking woman as a blind date. The men who had seen *Charlie's Angels* rated the woman significantly less attractive than did the controls. Evidently, seeing extremely beautiful women had made the average-looking woman less attractive by a contrast effect, just as a gray object looks darker after one has been looking at a white object (Kenrick & Gutierres, 1980).

Can such a contrast effect influence the attractiveness of one's own partner? Apparently so. In 1989, Kenrick's group published a study in which they showed men nude magazine centerfolds. After seeing the pictures, the men rated their own partners less attractive than did men who had seen nonattractive images, and they even

rated their love for their partners as less intense (Kenrick et al., 1989).

The researchers did an equivalent study on women. Women's ratings of the attractiveness of their partners were unaffected by viewing photos of naked men. When women viewed photos of men that were accompanied by descriptions of the men's leadership qualities and achievements, however, there *was* an effect: they rated their

satisfaction with their current partners lower than did women who viewed pictures of men described as unambitious or ineffectual. Of course, this finding fits with other evidence that women's judgments of attractiveness are strongly influenced by nonphysical attributes, such as social position.

Do these contrast effects actually influence the durability of marriages? To find out, sociologists Satoshi Kanazawa (of Indiana University of Pennsylvania) and Mary Still (of Cornell University) tried to think of a profession that involved frequent contact with attractive young people. They chose teaching. They identified 646 male and female teachers (junior high, high school, and college) from data in the General Social Survey and compared them with non-teachers matched for a variety of demographic factors that are known to influence divorce rates. The male teachers—but not the female teachers—were significantly more likely to be divorced or never married than the non-teacher controls. That, Kanazawa and Still surmise, is because male teachers are constantly seeing attractive young women—and the contrast effect makes their own wives seem unattractive (Kanazawa & Still, 2000).

You may well be able to think of alternative explanations for Kanazawa and Still's finding. But just to be safe, you might want to dump that teacher boyfriend before he dumps you.

---

mote or prevent the breakup of marriages. In a broader, demographic sense, the likelihood of marital disruption is linked to three major factors: the passage of time, age at marriage, and ethnicity (Centers for Disease Control, 2001e).

The likelihood of marital disruption is highest during the first few years of marriage, but breakups continue at significant rates thereafter. One in five of all first marriages ends within 5 years, one in three ends within 10 years, and one in two ends within 20 years. Statistically, marriages are not safe from disruption until one of the partners dies.

Marriage during the teen years increases the risk of disruption (Figure 12.13). If the woman is under 18 at marriage, the chances of breakup within 10 years are double what they are for the marriages of women who are over 25 (one in two versus one in four). The reasons for the vulnerability of teen marriages probably include the immaturity of the partners, the economic stresses of early marriage, and the fact that some teen marriages are "shotgun" (forced by pregnancy).

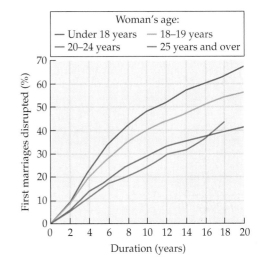

Figure 12.13 Teen marriages are less durable. The percentage of first marriages that have broken up rises faster over time for marriages in which the woman is younger than 18 or aged 18–19 than for marriages at older ages. (Data from Centers for Disease Control, 2001e.)

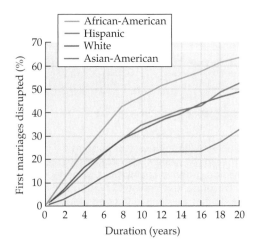

Figure 12.14 Ethnicity influences the durability of marriage. The percentage of first marriages that have broken up rises fastest for marriages in which the wife is African-American and slowest for marriages in which the wife is Asian-American. (Data from Centers for Disease Control, 2001e.)

African-American couples are more likely to break up than whites or Hispanics, and Asian-Americans are less likely to break up (Figure 12.14). This ethnic effect is quite strong: by 10 years after marriage, about one in two black couples, one in three white and Hispanic couples, and only one in five Asian-American couples have broken up.

Dissimilarity Between Husbands and Wives Shortens Marriages

There are other factors associated with a raised likelihood of marital disruption. In Chapter 9 we mentioned the concept of homophily—the idea that people are attracted to others who resemble themselves. Homophily seems to influence marital stability, according to NHSLS data. Thus, married couples that have different religions are more than twice as likely to break up as couples that share the same religion. Couples that differ in ethnicity are 69 percent more likely to break up than couples that do not. Large age differences also increase the chances of a breakup. The reason for these trends is not entirely clear. Besides possible direct effects, such as marital tensions arising from the partners' differences, there are likely to be indirect effects: couples who differ in religion or ethnicity may be more isolated from their extended families than couples who share the same religion or ethnicity, and may be exposed to social prejudice. Thus their marriages may receive less external support.

Statistically, this interracial couple stands a much higher chance of breaking up than do couples of the same ethnicity. Interracial couples may lack the social supports that help sustain marriage.

Virgins Have Longer Marriages

Premarital sexual relationships also have an effect on the length of marriages. As mentioned in Chapter 9, couples who cohabit before marriage are more likely to break up. Furthermore, *any* experience of coitus before marriage (on the part of either partner) is associated with a significantly increased likelihood of marital disruption, even after controlling for other demographic variables (NHSLS data; Kahn & Udry, 1991).

Why does virginity at marriage have this apparent protective effect? One possibility is that men and women who are virgins at marriage have religious or moral convictions that lead them both to value virginity and to avoid marital breakup. Indeed, many studies have shown that religiously observant people have longer-lasting marriages than do nonobservant people (Koenig et al., 2001; Mahoney et al., 2001).

Of course, when individual divorced people are asked about why their marriages ended, they do not refer to demographic variables, but rather to specific problems in their own marriages. These problems include extramarital relationships (see Chapter 9), sexual or psychological incompatibility, money problems, drinking and drug use, and so on (White, 1991). In non-Western societies, infertility is also a major reason for divorce (Betzig, 1989; Inhorn, 1996).

Marital Disruption Can Have Negative and Positive Consequences

In the immediate aftermath of a divorce, negative emotions such as anger, guilt, sadness, or fear for the future often predominate. Yet divorce is a mixed bag in terms of its effects on the man and woman and on any children they may have.

Divorced Men and Women Suffer Physical, Psychological, and Economic Damage

When marriages end, there are all kinds of negative consequences that go far beyond the bitter feelings of the breakup itself (Amato, 2000; Smock, 1993). Divorced people suffer higher rates of psychological and physical ill health (including mortality) than do married people. They are less happy, less sexually active (Stack & Gundlach, 1992), more socially isolated, and more prone to substance abuse. Divorced women—who usually retain custody of children—generally suffer a severe drop in per capita household income. (Divorced men, on the other hand, may see a rise in per capita household income.) The children of divorced parents experience a heightened risk of depression, behavior problems, low academic performance, substance abuse, criminality, and early sexual activity (Amato, 2000).

Of course, not all these consequences can be blamed on divorce per se. People who divorce are generally unhappy in their marriages, and if divorce were not possible, they might become even less happy, and might eventually suffer impairments to their mental and physical health at least as severe as those that affect divorced men and women. What is really desirable is to increase people's marital satisfaction so that they won't want to split up in the first place; we discussed some strategies to accomplish this in Chapter 9.

Divorce May Be the Start of a New Life

Marital disruption can also have positive consequences (Hetherington & Kelly, 2002). In fact, if it didn't, it would be hard to explain why divorce is so popular—there are about 1.2 million divorces in the United States annually, compared with about 2.4 million marriages. The benefits of divorce include escape from an unhappy, possibly abusive relationship and the potential for forming a better one. Divorce is always a challenge, but for some people, women especially, it can be the key that reveals previously untapped sources of talent, energy, and resolve. For married men and women who are homosexual or bisexual—and their numbers are significant—divorce may be an opportunity to "come out of the closet" and develop same-sex relationships.

Most Divorced People Remarry

Most divorced men and women marry again. Men remarry more quickly than women, but even among women, 75 percent remarry within 10 years (Centers for Disease Control, 2001e). The chances of remarrying are influenced by age at divorce (younger women are more likely to remarry) and ethnicity (black women are less likely to remarry). Remarriage brings economic and other benefits, especially to women. It is also associated, not surprisingly, with an increase in sexual activity—clear evidence that the general decline in sexual behavior during marriage is not solely a biological effect of aging.

Stepchildren May Be Disadvantaged

Unfortunately, children of divorce tend to remain disadvantaged when their mothers remarry: the adverse effects that strike children of divorced parents (see above) also strike stepchildren at about the same frequency (Coleman et al., 2000). Stepchildren tend to suffer from low self-esteem (Martin et al., 1999), and they are twice as likely to suffer from behavioral problems as children who live with their biological parents (Bray, 1999).

The problems of stepchildren may be due in part to the long-lasting negative effects of the original divorce. In addition, however, the average stepparents simply don't seem to care for their stepchildren as well as they do for their biological children. Only a minority of stepparents say that they "love" their stepchildren (Duberman, 1975), and stepchildren suffer a disproportionate share of virtually every form of child abuse, ranging from simple neglect all the way to sexual assault or murder by their stepparents (Daly and Wilson, 1998; Emmert and Kohler, 1998). Furthermore, the disproportionate abuse suffered by stepchildren can't be explained by the general economic or social circumstances in which stepfamilies live; rather, it appears to be a direct consequence of the stepparent/stepchild relationship.

This difference between the treatment of stepchildren and biological children can probably be traced to an evolutionary reality: as discussed in Chapter 2, evolution has favored the development of altruistic behavior toward biological kin more than toward biologically unrelated individuals (Wilson & Daly, 1997). Nevertheless, stepfamilies *can* flourish, and strategies exist for avoiding or overcoming problems in the stepparent-stepchild relationship (Bray & Kelly, 1998).

Later Marriages Are Less Durable

Another downside of remarriage is that later marriages are somewhat less durable than first marriages. For example, a woman 25 years old or older who marries for the first time has a one in four chance of breaking up within 10 years, but if she has been married previously, she has a one in three chance of breaking up within the same period. In other words, experience gained from the first marriage doesn't seem to stabilize later marriages. Bear in mind, though, that it's a special subset of people who remarry; namely, those who have already divorced at least once. These people may see less moral or practical value in lasting marriages, or they may have personality traits or economic circumstances that undermine marital stability.

Menopause is an aspect of aging, but it comes at what we now consider midlife.

Menopause Marks Women's Transition to Infertility

Starting in their early or mid-forties, women may find that their menstrual periods become less regular than they have been. This change marks the onset of a gradual transition to infertility—a period called the **climacteric**. The final cessation of menstrual cycles—the **menopause** or **"change of life"**—occurs at an average age of 51 or 52 in U.S. women. There is considerable variation in the age at menopause, however: a few women are still menstruating and capable of becoming pregnant in their late fifties, while some reach menopause in their early forties.

Menopause May Be Caused by Depletion of Oocytes

It's not known exactly what triggers menopause or why women reach menopause at such variable ages. However, women who start menstruating early, who have fewer pregnancies, who have short cycle lengths, who have had one ovary removed, or who don't use oral contraceptives are all likely to experience earlier menopause than other women (Cramer & Xu, 1996). In women who smoke, these effects are accentuated. Heredity also influences the timing of menopause (Cramer et al., 1995).

These findings suggest that women are born with the capacity for a certain number of ovarian cycles, and that the main reason for the transition to infertility may be the depletion of oocytes and the diminishing ability of any remaining oocytes to respond to pituitary hormones. By the time of menopause, the ovaries contain very few follicles (Figure 12.15). Consistent with this view, the secretion of pituitary gonadotropins does not decrease at menopause, but rather *increases*—in response to the decline in blood levels of ovarian steroids (Johnson & Everitt, 2000). Thus, although the brain tells the ovaries when to *start* cycling (at menarche), it apparently doesn't tell them when to *stop* cycling.

Figure 12.15 Depletion of oocytes is the factor most likely responsible for the onset of menopause. This micrograph shows ovarian tissue at the time of menopause. The field shows connective tissue and a corpus albicans—the degenerated remains of a corpus luteum (asterisk)—but no follicles at any stage of development.

Decreased Hormone Levels Affect Women's Sexual Responses

Menopause influences women's sexuality in a number of ways. First, the reduction in circulating ovarian hormones, especially estrogens, has direct effects on the body. These effects include a reduction in vaginal lubrication in response to sexual arousal and a rise in the pH (decrease in acidity) of vaginal fluids. These changes may lead to painful coitus (**dyspareunia**) and vaginal inflammation (**vaginitis**). There is also likely to be a reduction in the size of the breasts and the uterus.

Menopause may be accompanied by a variety of other symptoms that can influence sexual expression indirectly. The reduction in estrogen levels often leads to instability in the control of blood vessels (**vasomotor control**), so that many menopausal women experience **hot flashes or hot flushes** (dilation of blood vessels in the skin, causing reddening and a sensation of warmth), night sweats, headaches, tiredness, and heart palpitations (bouts of accelerated or irregular heartbeats). The extent to which these menopausal symptoms occur, and how bothersome women find them, is highly variable, and there are differences among ethnic groups; for example, African-American women seem to have worse vasomotor symptoms than other groups (Avis et al., 2001).

Lowered estrogen levels may also have long-term heath effects. The most significant of these are a loss of bone density (**osteoporosis**), which carries a risk of fractures and vertebral compression (Figure 12.16), and changes in blood lipid chemistry, which increase the risk of atherosclerosis and heart attacks. In addition, there are noticeable effects on the skin (loss of thickness, elasticity, hydration, and lipid content).

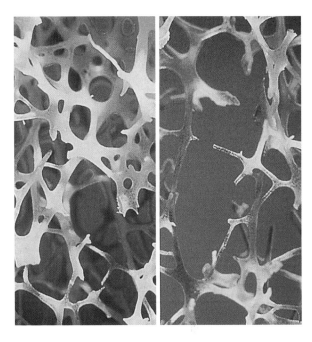

Figure 12.16 Osteoporosis. Low estrogen levels after menopause can lead to thinning of the mineral structure of bone. These are scanning electron micrographs of normal bone (left) and osteoporotic bone (right).

Women Typically Experience Some Decline in Sexual Desire at Menopause

Menopausal women experience a decrease in sexual desire and sexual arousal. This decline probably results mainly from the combined effects of menopause we have just listed. Other factors, such as direct effects of declining gonadal steroid levels on the brain systems that mediate sexual arousal, could also play a role.

Still, the decline in sexual desire associated with menopause is fairly modest in degree. Other factors, such as general health, marital status, and smoking, have larger effects on sexual desire than does menopausal status (Avis et al., 2000). Bear in mind that androgens play a significant role in female sexual desire (see Chapter 4), and although some androgens come from the ovaries, they are also secreted by the adrenal glands. This latter supply continues after menopause and is often sufficient to maintain a high level of sexual interest.

The psychological effects of menopause on sexuality are quite diverse. For women who believe that the main or only purpose of sex is reproduction, the loss of fertility at menopause may lead to a loss of interest in sex. For the larger number of women who see a recreational or emotional significance in sex, on the other hand, menopause may actually be welcome because it removes the fear of unwanted pregnancy. Such women may get increased pleasure from sex for that reason.

Hormone Replacement Therapy Can Reduce Menopausal Symptoms

Menopausal and postmenopausal women have the option of taking gonadal steroids or other drugs to compensate for the loss of their own ovarian hormones. This practice is called **hormone replacement therapy** or **HRT.** The most common HRT regimen is a combination of estrogens and progestins. It is the estrogens that alleviate menopausal symptoms. Progestins are added to protect the woman from one unfortunate side effect of the estrogen treatment, which is an increased risk of endometrial cancer. For a woman whose uterus has been surgically removed, progestins have little benefit, and the therapy may consist of estrogens alone. This regimen is sometimes called **estrogen replacement therapy** or **ERT.** Androgens are sometimes added, primarily for their effect on the sex drive.

Like hormone-based contraceptives, HRT can be administered by a variety of routes, including pills, patches, gels, and injections. The drugs can be administered cyclically; this often causes regular monthly bleeding similar to the withdrawal bleeding seen with oral contraceptives. Alternatively, the drugs can be administered continuously, in which case there may be irregular "spotting." Side effects such as breast tenderness, bloating, and vaginal bleeding are fairly common and cause some women to discontinue treatment, but others appreciate the reduction of menopausal symptoms and the prospects for long-term health benefits.

About one in four postmenopausal women in the 50–55 age bracket uses HRT, but HRT use is much reduced among older postmenopausal women: less than 5 percent of women over 75 use it (Connelly et al., 2000). Lower-income women are also much less likely to use HRT than middle- or upper-income women (Finley et al., 2001).

HRT is somewhat controversial on two levels, philosophical and medical. At the philosophical level, some people argue that the postmenopausal state is natural, not a medical condition in need of treatment. They suggest that the effort to "pathologize" menopause is antifeminist or is being led by drug companies with the purpose of increasing profits (Leysen, 1996; Love & Lindsey, 1998). On the other hand, one can point out that a woman of 52 (the average age at menopause) can now expect to live another 33 years, something that is itself unnatural in terms of human evolution. It may take unnatural measures to ensure a woman's well-being over this period.

The medical controversy has to do with the fact that HRT has both benefits and risks over the long term (Burkman et al., 2001; Seibert, 2000). HRT decreases the risk of osteoporosis, colorectal cancer, and possibly Alzheimer's disease. On the other hand, HRT *increases* the risk of blood clots, just as combination oral contraceptives do (see Chapter 11), and it may increase the risk of heart disease, too. Estrogen-only replacement therapy increases the risk of endometrial cancer, as mentioned above.

There has been a long-running debate about whether HRT increases the risk of breast cancer. Over 50 epidemiological studies have looked at this issue. According to a recent analysis of these studies, estrogen-only replacement therapy does not do so, and the more common combined estrogen–progestin therapy probably does not do so either (Bush et al., 2001). One reputable study suggests that the combined therapy does increase breast cancer risk, but that the increased risk is confined largely to women who take the hormones for more than 5 years and who have a body mass index below 24.4 (Schairer et al., 2000). A recent large-scale study found an increased risk even during the first 5 years of HRT, however (Women's Health Initiative, 2002).

How do the potential benefits and risks of HRT balance out? That is still a largely unanswered question, especially over the longer term. The Women's Health Initiative study just mentioned, however, found that women who used one common estrogen/progestin HRT regimen (Wyeth's Prempro) for 5 years were more likely to experience any of a number of harmful effects than were women who took a placebo. Thus, it appears that the global effect of this form of HRT may be harmful. Nevertheless, only small numbers of women suffered ill-effects and there was no significant difference in mortality between the two groups.

The development of a variety of new drugs, including the selective estrogen receptor modulators (see Chapter 4), may make it possible to provide the long-term beneficial effects of HRT without the harmful ones. Raloxifene, for example, has been approved by the FDA for the prevention of osteoporosis, and it may be less likely to cause endometrial cancer than estrogen alone. HRT is a rapidly evolving field of research, however; women considering it should get up-to-date medical advice tailored to their own circumstances so that they can make an informed decision.

For women who have menopausal symptoms but do not wish to embark on HRT, there may be some benefit to be derived from food supplements. There has been particular interest in **isoflavones,** which are plant-derived molecules with an estrogen-like structure (see Chapter 4). One double-blind study done in Brazil found that women who took 100 milligrams of soy isoflavones daily experienced significantly fewer hot flashes and other symptoms than women who took a placebo (Han et al., 2002). Unfortunately, the researchers did not compare the isoflavone regime with standard HRT. The long-term consequences of isoflavone use are not known.

Men's Fertility Declines Gradually with Age

Men do not experience a sudden or complete cessation of fertility comparable to menopause. Instead, they experience a gradual reduction in fertility and sexual function with aging, evidenced by declining sperm counts and ejaculate volume (see Chapter 10), an increased likelihood of erectile dysfunction (see Chapter 15), and decreased sexual desire and frequency of sex. More general changes associated with aging include loss of muscle bulk and bone density, changes in the skin and hair, and possible cognitive changes such as memory impairment. Some of these changes may be caused by a decline in blood levels of testosterone and other hormones (such as growth hormone) with aging, but there doesn't seem to be any good correlation between testosterone levels and sexual activity among normal older men, any more than there is among younger men (Sadowsky et al., 1993).

Some people refer to this collection of changes as the **male menopause** or **andropause** (Heaton & Morales, 2001), but these terms are misleading if they suggest that the changes are sudden or that there is a total cessation of reproductive function. Although sperm counts decline, some men have fathered children in their eighties.

There has been considerable recent interest in the use of testosterone replacement therapy to treat aging men with low testosterone levels and sexual or other problems (Morley, 2000). At this point, there is little information about the long-term consequences of such treatment. One obvious concern is that it might increase the risk of developing prostate cancer or accelerate the growth of preexisting, undiagnosed cancers.

The Sex Lives of Old People
Have Traditionally Been Ignored

Our knowledge of sexuality in old age is fairly limited. There has been a traditional assumption that old people are asexual, and any indications to the contrary (such as sexual behaviors by the residents of nursing homes) have generally been viewed with embarrassment and disapproval. It didn't help that the two big national surveys we have referred to in this book, the American NHSLS and the British NSSAL, restricted their samples to men and women under 60, as if the sex lives of older people were nonexistent or unimportant. Indeed, the very word "old" has been largely excluded from social discourse, and has been replaced by euphemistic terms such as "senior," "elderly," and the like.

We may speculate that younger people's discomfort with the notion of sexuality in old age originates in a failure of empathy. In other words, when faced with the fact that old people engage in sex, they imagine themselves having sex with an old person—that is to say, with someone they might well find sexually unattractive, so they are repelled. What they *fail* to imagine is being *in the mind* of an old person, whose ideas of attractiveness may be quite different from their own. In particular, judgments of attractiveness are influenced by familiarity and intimacy, so an old person may find their spouse of many years sexually attractive even though few younger people would concur. In a survey commissioned by the American Association of Retired Persons, 53 percent of women over 75, and 63 percent of men over 75, reported strong physical attraction to their partners. These percentages were actually *higher* than for women and men in younger age brackets (American Association of Retired Persons, 1999).

The fact is that nearly everyone continues to have sexual feelings into old age, and many people express these feelings behaviorally in one way or another. In considering sexual expression in old age, it's important not to fall into either of two traps (Meston, 1997). On the one hand, there is the danger of subscribing to folklore about the inevitable decline of sexual intimacy with aging. On the other, there is the temptation to expect or demand patterns of sexual expression similar to those of younger people. Certainly, old

The sexuality of this older couple is important to the well-being of their relationship.

age brings physical changes and illnesses that may affect sexual expression. These problems may necessitate some changes in sexual behavior, but they rarely make sexual behavior impossible or unrewarding to the old person or their partner.

Aging Is Accompanied by Physiological Changes in the Sexual Response

Let's look first at some of the physical changes associated with aging (Gelfand, 2000; Thienhaus, 1988). Old people—and we are being deliberately vague about precise ages, because these changes occur slowly and vary from one person to the next—experience changes in the physiological processes of sexuality. For men, these changes include the following:

- The penis becomes erect more slowly in response to either tactile or mental stimulation. The erect penis is less hard. Some degree of erectile dysfunction is reported by two-thirds of normal older men (Litwin, 1999).
- Ejaculatory volume is smaller, and the ejaculate is discharged less forcefully. (It may flow out slowly or even be discharged retrogradely into the bladder.)
- The erection is lost more rapidly.
- The refractory period (time before another erection and ejaculation are possible) is longer.

Women may experience the following changes:

- There are atrophic changes in the vagina, vulva, and urethra. The walls of the vagina become thinner, and the entire vagina may become shorter and narrower.
- There is decreased vaginal lubrication.
- There are fewer contractions during orgasm.
- There is a more rapid decrease in arousal after orgasm.

Medical Conditions, Drugs, and Social Factors Can Impair the Sexuality of Old People

Sexual performance can also be impaired by medical conditions that become commoner with advancing age. These conditions include arthritis, heart disease, osteoporosis, incontinence, diabetes, emphysema, and obesity. Surgeries such as prostatectomy, colostomy, mastectomy, hysterectomy (removal of the uterus), or heart surgery can affect sexual performance, either directly, or indirectly by causing embarrassment or poor self-image. (A properly performed hysterectomy should not directly interfere with coitus.)

Old people take more prescription drugs than younger people, and many of these drugs can interfere with sexual performance (Mooradian, 1991). Examples include anti-hypertension drugs, diuretics, tranquilizers and antidepressants, cancer chemotherapy, ulcer medicines, and anticoagulants. (Individual drugs vary, as do patients' responses to them; alternative drugs can often be prescribed that do not impair sexual desire or performance.) Excessive alcohol use impairs sexual performance in old people, just as it does in younger people.

Psychological and social factors that can impair sexual expression in old people include depression, poor self-image, performance anxiety, bereavement, lack of an available partner, and the internalization of the negative expectations of others, especially the old person's children and medical professionals.

When old people are asked to express their current concerns about sexual matters, gender differences emerge that are quite in line with what we have learned about younger people. In particular, men mention problems of performance, especially erectile dysfunction, whereas women mention relationship problems, including the lack of a partner (Avis, 2000; Wiley & Bortz, 1996). Both sexes report that their level of sexual activity has declined in the past 10 years, and say that they wish they were more active. The two factors that seem to influence old people's sex lives the most are their health status and their sense of how sexually responsive their partners are (Bortz et al., 1999).

Coping Strategies May Require Flexibility

Concerning the availability of a partner, recall that women not only live longer than men, but also tend to marry men who are older than themselves. This age difference may be even more marked in second or later marriages. The combination of these two factors makes for long widowhoods: a 50-year-old woman whose husband is 5 years older than herself can expect (on average) to become a widow at age 75 and to live for 10 years thereafter.

Single men aged 75 and over are in short supply. Two-thirds of men in that age bracket are married and living with their wives, whereas only 29 percent of women over 75 are married and living with their husbands (U.S. Census Bureau, 2001). Thus, the odds are stacked against a widowed woman in that age bracket being able to remarry.

Of course, there are other possibilities: some widowed or divorced old women form sexual relationships with younger or married men, or with other women. But such choices will strike many old women as inappropriate or immoral. People's attitudes tend to be conditioned by the environment in which they grew up, so today's old people—who came of age before the sexual revolution of the 1960s— are likely to be less open to unconventional sexual relationships. In the AARP survey mentioned above, two-thirds of women over 75 said that it was wrong to engage in sex with anyone but a spouse— a far higher percentage than for women in younger age brackets (American Association of Retired Persons, 1999).

Thanks to sex differences in life expectancy, a single old man may be a hot property.

The same attitudes apply to actual sexual behaviors. For old couples who have difficulty with coitus (because of physiological changes in one or both partners), it might make good sense to practice oral sex instead. However, people born before about 1942 came of age at a time when oral sex was relatively uncommon and was practiced mainly by the better-educated levels of society. This age cohort did not necessarily join the rush to oral sex in the 1960s; in fact, nearly half of them have never had a single experience of fellatio or cunnilingus, according to NHSLS data, and many of them probably consider these behaviors immoral. Obviously, it may be hard for such people to accept or enjoy oral sex now that they are in their retirement years, even if it is suggested to them by health care providers or others.

Some Old People Remain Sexually Active

There are conflicting data about exactly how sexually active old people are. In one study (Brecher, 1984), the majority of married men and women in their sixties and seventies reported that they continued to engage in sexual intercourse, and many masturbated (Table 12.2). Because these data were based on responses to a magazine questionnaire, however, there is some question about their representativeness.

The AARP survey reported that, among women and men over 75 who have a sex partner, only about 25 percent engage in sexual intercourse once a week or more (American Association of Retired Persons, 1999). Among the women over 75, only 13 percent said that sexual activity was important to their quality of life.

According to data from the General Social Survey, which is based on a random sample of the U.S. population, 47 percent of over-60 respondents said that they had had at least one sex partner during the previous year (Butler, 2001). That figure contrasted sharply with the under-60 respondents in the same survey, 88 percent of whom had had at least one sex partner in that time.

Two psychologists at San Francisco State University surveyed 200 healthy men and women aged 80–102 who lived in retirement communities (Bretschneider & McCoy,

	Percentage of respondents who engaged in behavior		
Behavior	**Age 50–59**	**Age 60–69**	**Age 70+**
Women who masturbate	47	37	33
Men who masturbate	66	50	43
Married women who have intercourse with husbands	88	76	65
Married men who have intercourse with wives	87	76	59

TABLE 12.2 *Sexual behavior of respondents to a questionnaire in* **Consumer Reports**

Source: Brecher, 1984.

1988). Most were unmarried. The researchers found that the most common sexual activity among these people was touching and fondling without coitus, followed by masturbation and then coitus. As has been consistently reported in other studies, the frequency with which these old people engaged in most sexual behaviors was predicted by the frequency with which they engaged in the same behaviors earlier in life. In other words, people are creatures of habit, and they don't change their sexual behaviors as they age unless they have to. The one activity whose frequency was not predicted by earlier frequency was coitus. That is probably because of the aging-associated physical problems mentioned above, as well as social factors, such as loss of a spouse.

Sex Has Health Benefits

Although some people believe that sex in middle or old age carries health risks (especially for people with heart disease), there are a number of studies suggesting the opposite; namely, that old people who engage in frequent sex live longer (Box 12.7). Of course, there may be medical circumstances in which exertion of any kind is to be avoided, but the exertion of intercourse is no greater than that of other activities that people regularly engage in, such as climbing stairs.

Opportunities for Sexual Expression by Nursing Home Residents Could Be Improved

For the minority of elderly Americans who are in nursing homes and comparable care-providing institutions, sexual activity tends to be very low. In part, of course, this is because nursing home residents are in poor health. Still, one small-scale survey found that some nursing home residents—men especially—desired sexual interactions (Spector & Fremeth, 1996). This desire was often frustrated, however. Residents cited the lack of privacy as an important barrier to sexual expression. Even masturbation requires some degree of privacy. Nursing homes vary greatly in this area—some could provide much more privacy than they do, thus allowing more opportunity for sexual behavior.

It seems likely that, as baby boomers (people born shortly after the Second World War and who lived through the sexual revolution of the 1960s) enter their retirement years, there will be an increasing focus on sexual activity and sexual satisfaction among old people. Not only are baby boomers more interested in sexual variety and less tied to the notion that sex is only for reproduction, they also have a greater sense of entitlement with regard to personal fulfillment generally. Thus, they will be far less ready to give up sex if physiological or social problems get in their way. The huge demand for Viagra when it came on the market in 1998 was a token of things to come: both men and women are likely to demand effective medical treatments for age-associated sexual dysfunction. They will also make sure that sexual expression by old people is recognized and respected, rather than being pushed into the closet.

Box 12.7 Research Highlights

Sex and Death among Welsh Cheesemakers

The idea that sexual activity is debilitating to health—especially for men, who have to expend precious semen in the sexual act—is widespread in human cultures. To test the truth of this idea, epidemiologist George Davey Smith of the University of Bristol, England, along with two colleagues, descended on the quiet town of Caerphilly, Wales, renowned for its cheese (Davey Smith et al., 1997).

Most of the men in this town are participating in a longitudinal study of factors that affect long-term health. Nine hundred and eighteen of them (aged 45–59, mostly married) answered a question about how often they experienced orgasm. (Before the researchers could survey the entire town, local doctors persuaded them to delete this particular question.)

By 10 years later, 150 of the 918 men had died. The men who had told the researchers that they had a high frequency of orgasm (at least two orgasms per week) were the least likely to have died. Those who had an orgasm between once a week and once a month were 60 percent more likely to have died (after adjustment of the data to allow for age differences). Those who had an orgasm less than once a month

were *twice* as likely to have died. Even when the researchers adjusted for a variety of potentially confounding factors, such as social class, blood pressure, and presence of heart disease, the differences between the groups remained nearly as great.

One can't be certain of the direction of cause and effect in a study like this. It's possible that preexisting health conditions caused some men to be relatively inactive sexually and also shortened their lives. Alternatively, the men who had frequent sex might have had a lower death rate because they were in more loving marriages, rather than more sexually active ones. Still, the findings are consistent with a number of other studies that have reported lower mortality, or a lower incidence of myocardial infarction, in men and women who were more sexually active or who derived more enjoyment from sex (Abramov, 1976; Palmore, 1982; Persson, 1981).

Given the apparent protective effect of orgasms, the researchers commented that a public health campaign, modeled on the "at least five a day" campaign to get people to eat fruits and vegetables, might be in order—with some adjustment of the recommended frequency, of course.

Summary

1. People generally think of childhood as a period of sexual innocence. Sigmund Freud proposed the opposite; namely, that young children are full of sexual desires, which they direct initially at their own bodies and later at their opposite-sex parent. Efforts to finding the truth in this matter face many practical difficulties.

2. Nonhuman primates engage in sexual behaviors long before puberty. Some non-Western societies tolerate or encourage childhood sexual behaviors, while others attempt to restrain it. In the contemporary United States, children are generally prevented from engaging in or learning about sex.

3. Physiological responses suggestive of sexual arousal are seen in infants and young children, but seem to be triggered by a wide range of stimuli, such as strong emotion of any kind. Masturbation is common in young children, and other sexual behaviors, such as the display of genitals or the inspection of other children's genitals, are also seen. Young children rarely engage in adultlike sexual behaviors, however.

4. Some children, usually older ones, have sexual contacts with adults. These contacts are usually one-time events rather than ongoing relationships. Most adults who have sexual contacts with children are relatives or acquaintances of the child, rather than strangers. Coercive or repeated adult–child sexual contacts can cause long-lasting psychological trauma. Noncoercive, sporadic contacts may cause little or no harm.

5. In late childhood (preadolescence), children tend to socialize in same-sex groups and to impose strict gender codes. This practice can be traumatic for gender-noncon-

formist children. Although segregation by sex limits opportunities for heterosexual encounters, some children do engage in coitus before the age of 13.

6. Adolescence is usually defined as the teen years (13–19). In early adolescence, rising gonadal hormone levels trigger increasing interest in sex. Most adolescent males masturbate frequently, but females do so less often. Adolescent heterosexual behavior gradually progresses through kissing and fondling and noncoital sex to coitus. Some characteristics of teen sexual behavior seem to reflect its evolutionary origins, but personal and demographic factors such as intelligence, education, and ethnicity also play an important role. Women's changing expectations, as well as the availability of reliable contraception, have modified teen sexual behavior.

7. The problematic aspects of teen sexuality (such as STDs and unwanted pregnancy) are often emphasized at the expense of its positive aspects. Sexual exploration by adolescents is important for identity development.

8. Young adults typically spend a few years "dating" before they enter their first live-in relationship, but the average number of sex partners during this period is quite low. During the dating years, sexual desires have to compete with other interests, such as career advancement.

9. Western society is moving from a traditional, one-size-fits-all institution of marriage to a greater variety of live-in sexual relationships. Because women have fewer pregnancies than in the past and are more likely to be in the labor market, distinct gender roles in marriage have diminished. People are marrying later and divorcing more readily; marriage may soon become a minority status for American adults. Nevertheless, most people desire to be in some kind of monogamous, long-term live-in relationship. African-American women have difficulty achieving such relationships because of an effective shortage of African-American men, so they commonly head families without live-in male partners.

10. Married men and women tend to have less sex than those who are dating or cohabiting, and they are less adventurous sexually, but their physical and emotional satisfaction with their sex lives is high. For women, simply being married makes sex more satisfying. However, sexual interactions and marital satisfaction tend to fall off over time.

11. One in three marriages breaks up within 10 years. The likelihood of breakup is increased by a number of factors, such as early (teen) marriage, dissimilarity between husband and wife, sexual experience or cohabitation before marriage, and ethnicity.

12. Divorced people suffer a variety of physical and psychological ill effects. Most divorced men and women remarry within 10 years.

13. Menopause—the cessation of menstrual cycles—is the culmination of a gradual transition to infertility in women. The hormonal changes of menopause can impair the physiological processes of sexual arousal and may be accompanied by a decline in sexual interest and activity.

14. Hormone replacement therapy (HRT) can alleviate menopausal symptoms, but may have unpleasant side effects that cause many women to discontinue treatment. Long-term HRT has risks and benefits for women's health.

15. Men experience a gradual decline in fertility, physiological arousal, and sexual interest, rather than a rapid transition to infertility. Some men father children in old age.

16. The sex lives of old people have generally been ignored by the public and researchers alike. Nevertheless, most people continue to experience sexual desire into old age. The physical expression of this desire may be compromised by declining physiological responsiveness (for example, erectile dysfunction and loss of vaginal lubrication) or by a variety of medical conditions, drugs, or social circumstances. Nevertheless, many old women and men continue to engage in sexual behaviors, including masturbation, coitus, and noncoital contacts. Even those in declining health, such as nursing home residents, may desire sexual and affectional contacts; such contacts can be facilitated by ensuring their privacy.

Discussion Questions

1. What are your attitudes and values about what is normal sexuality during childhood? If you were a parent and found your child "playing doctor" with the child next door, how would you respond?

2. Describe your ideal marriage partner or cohabitational partner and their characteristics (e.g., appearance, personality, occupation). What circumstances or conflicts (if any) do you think would lead you to consider a separation or divorce (e.g., infidelity, refusal to have children, disease, cross-dressing?

3. Identify the myths and "what you have heard" about menopause. Contrast these descriptions with the facts. What behaviors are characteristic of menopause? Do men have a "change of life"?

4. Describe the advice you would give to your mother or an older female friend who asks you to explain the pros and cons of hormone replacement therapy. Do you think that the fact that menopause is a natural part of the aging process should discourage women from attempting to counteract its effects with HRT?

5. Think about your grandparents and people who are older than 60. What are your beliefs and thoughts about sex among these people? What do you think are the barriers to enjoying a happy sex life after 60?

6. Think about relatives or friends you know who have been in a nursing home. Should nursing homes encourage residents to enjoy a healthy sex life? What are the pros and cons of, and the barriers to, doing so?

Web Resources

National Campaign to Prevent Teen Pregnancy www.teenpregnancy.org

North American Menopause Society www.menopause.org

American Psychological Association—Aging and human sexuality resource guide
www.apa.org/pi/aging/sexuality.html

Recommended Reading

Butler, R. N., & Lewis, M. I. (2002). *The New Love and Sex After 60*. New York: Ballantine Books.

Bray, J. H., & Kelly, J. (1998). *Stepfamilies: Love, marriage, and parenting in the first decade*. New York: Broadway Books.

Elam, J. (1998). A cross-cultural comparison of puberty rites and ceremonies for females. Located at www.emory.edu/OXFORD/Publications/Review/puberty.html.

Levine, J. (2002). *Harmful to minors: The perils of protecting children from sex*. Minneapolis: University of Minnesota Press.

Martinson, F. M. (1994). *The sexual life of children*. Westport, CT: Bergin and Garvey.

Steinberg, L. (2002). *Adolescence* (6th ed.). Boston: McGraw-Hill.

chapter 13

The rainbow flag symbolizes the diversity of communities that have forged an identity based in part on their distinct sexuality.

Sexual Minorities

Some men and women differ markedly enough in their sexuality from the majority of Americans to establish themselves as members of distinct social minorities with their own history, culture, and political agenda. In this chapter we focus on several such groups: gay men, lesbians, bisexuals, transgendered persons, and intersexes, as well as one group whose status as a "sexual minority" is problematic: pedophiles.

We are not concerned here with what causes people to be gay, lesbian, and so on—we discuss that question in other chapters—but rather with what the personal and social significance of belonging to such a group may be. We will see that, historically, sexual minorities have developed a self-conscious identity in the process of battling societal oppression. To some extent, this history repeats itself in the psychological development of each member of these minorities today.

The Basis for Defining Homosexual People Has Changed over Time

Currently, we think of homosexual or gay people (lesbians and gay men) as people whose sexual feelings are directed predominantly toward persons of the same sex as themselves. Whatever the actual determinants of sexual orientation (a topic discussed in Chapter 7), we think of gay people's sexual desire as a durable attribute that helps define who they are, rather like ethnicity.

It hasn't always been that way. Certainly, there is occasional mention in classical literature (in Plato's *Symposium,* for example) of the notion that particular individuals are either heterosexual or homosexual (Figure 13.1). The more usual concept over the past 2000 years, however, has been that everyone shares roughly the same sexual feelings—a predominant desire for the opposite sex, with some capacity for same-sex attraction. In societies in which women were largely unavailable, as in ancient Greece, many unmarried men had sex with male youths, but this behavior was not usually thought to mark them off as a special kind of person, and was often tolerated or approved of. A very similar cultural pattern existed in Afghanistan under the Taliban, where women were inaccessible and hidden behind their *burkas.* "We can't see the women to see if they are beautiful," one Afghan man told a reporter from the *Los Angeles Times.* "But we can see the boys, and so we can tell which of them is beautiful" (Reynolds, 2002).

Some early Christians, such as St. Paul, strongly disapproved of homosexual behavior by either men or women, but they represented such behavior as a willful violation of a person's true nature as heterosexual, not as a sign of some deep difference between two *kinds* of people. This attitude persisted through most of Western European history. Sexual behavior between men was called **sodomy,** and was thought of as a wicked behavior that anyone might engage in if not restrained by morality or the law. Sexual behavior between women was largely ignored.

Several factors facilitated the development of the concept of a homosexual *identity.* One was the growth of cities, which allowed homosexual men to find each other and form social groups. Already in eighteenth-century London, feminine-acting men called "mollies" were gathering in certain taverns ("molly-houses"), where they might dress in women's clothes and participate in mock marriages to each other (Norton, 1999). By the mid-nineteenth century, most large cities in Europe and the United States had some kind of homosexual male subculture. Still, many sexual relationships between men devel-

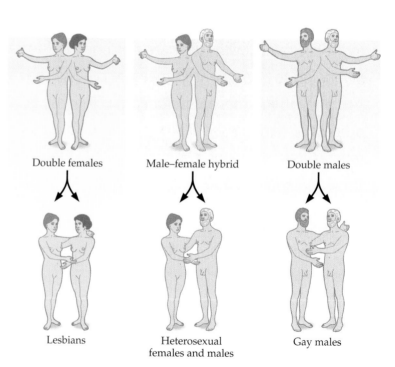

Figure 13.1 Theory of origins. In Plato's *Symposium* (*The Drinking Party*), written in Athens during the fourth century B.C.E., a participant presents an extemporized creation myth to account for the existence of persons of different sexual orientation. All humans, he said, originally consisted of double creatures, each with four arms, four legs, and two sets of genitals. Some were double females (left), some were male-female hybrids (center), and some were double males (right). These creatures were cut in two by an angry god, forming the humans we know today. Sexual desire is the desire to be reunited with one's other ancestral half. Thus, humans descended from the double females are lesbians, humans descended from the hybrids are heterosexual women and men, and humans descended from the double males are homosexual men. This is one of the few instances in classical literature in which a writer makes a clear distinction between gay and straight people and considers how such differences might have arisen.

Double females   Male–female hybrid   Double males

Lesbians   Heterosexual females and males   Gay males

oped without any sense on the part of the men that they had thereby acquired some special sexual identity (Katz, 2001).

There was no equivalent homosexual culture for women, but many educated American women formed **Boston marriages**—same-sex cohabitations that were quite likely sexual, but were not viewed as such by society at large (Faderman, 1981). (The phrase "Boston marriage" has recently developed a somewhat different meaning, referring to lesbian couples who do not have sex with each other.)

Also, some women passed as men, and were thus able to earn men's wages and enjoy male privileges, including forming relationships with (or even marrying) women (San Francisco Lesbian and Gay History Project, 1989). Passing women fought in the Civil War (Box 13.1) and worked as railroad employees. An influential New York politician of the 1880s and 1890s, Murray Hall, married two (conventional) women and pursued many others; Hall was discovered to be a woman at the time of her death. Of course, the very fact that passing women were pretending to be men limited their ability to establish any kind of community.

Another factor promoting the development of a homosexual identity was the development of a new style of marriage that emphasized affection and mutual support between husband and wife. This **companionate marriage** (see Chapter 12) probably reached its highest point in the late nineteenth or early twentieth century. Earlier, when noncompanionate marriage was the rule, married homosexual men and women could pursue their own sexual interests without much disturbance of social norms. With companionate marriage, on the other hand, there was an expectation of durable sexual and social intimacy between husband and wife. Fulfilling this expectation was psychologically difficult for homosexual people, and it also made same-sex affairs more dangerous. Thus there was an increase in the numbers of homosexual men and women who remained unmarried, and who were therefore available to populate a homosexual subculture.

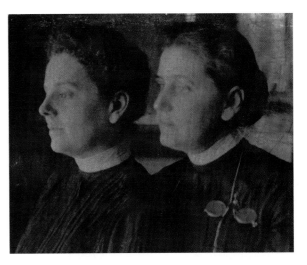

A "Boston marriage" was the cohabitation of two women—often academics—in nineteenth-century New England. In most cases we do not know whether these relationships were sexual or not, though it is likely that some were. This photograph shows social reformer and Nobel Peace Prize winner Jane Addams (right) (1860–1935) with her benefactor and life companion Mary Rozet Smith.

Box 13.1 *Sex in History*

Passing Women in the Civil War

In nineteenth-century America, thousands of women passed as men. Passing women even fought in the Civil War: Philip H. Sheridan, a Union Army general in the Civil War, published the following account in his 1888 memoirs:

> I was informed that there certainly were in the command two females, that in some mysterious manner had attached themselves to the service as soldiers; that one, an East Tennessee woman, was a teamster in the division wagon-train and the other a private soldier in a cavalry company temporarily attached to my headquarters for escort duty. While out on the foraging expedition these Amazons had secured a supply of "apple-jack" by some means, got very drunk, and on the return had fallen into Stone River and been nearly drowned. After they had been fished from the water, in the process of resuscitation their sex was disclosed, though up to this time it appeared to be known only to each other… After some little search the East Tennessee woman was found in camp, somewhat the worse for the experiences of the day before, but awaiting her fate contentedly smoking a cob-pipe. She was brought to me, and put in duress under charge of the division surgeon until her companion could be secured. To the doctor she related that the year before she had "refugeed" from East Tennessee, and on arriving in Louisville assumed men's apparel and sought and obtained employment as a teamster in the quartermaster's department. Her features were very large, and so coarse and masculine was her general appearance that she would readily have passed as a man, and her case the deception was no doubt easily practiced. Next day the "she dragoon" was caught, and proved to be a rather prepossessing young woman, and though necessarily bronzed and hardened by exposure, I doubt if, even with these marks of campaigning, she could have deceived as readily as did her companion. How the two got acquainted I never learned, and though they had joined the army independently of each other, yet an intimacy had sprung up between them long before the mishaps of the foraging expedition. They both were forwarded to army headquarters, and, when provided with clothing suited to their sex, sent back to Nashville, and thence beyond our lines to Louisville.

Source: Katz, 1992.

A third factor was the attention paid to same-sex desire by nineteenth-century doctors. Most prominent among these doctors was the German sexologist Richard von Krafft-Ebing, whose 1886 book *Psychopathia Sexualis* was an instant classic. Krafft-Ebing and other early sexologists portrayed homosexuality as a mental disorder. This might not seem particularly advantageous to gay people—in fact, it led to traumatic attempts to "cure" them. However, it did strengthen the notion that homosexuals were a distinct kind of people, and thus unwittingly contributed to the development of gay and lesbian self-awareness.

Homosexuals Were Thought of as Gender Inverts

Although the concept of homosexual people became established in the nineteenth century, it was tied to a particular idea about homosexuality, which was that homosexual men were like women and homosexual women were like men (Hekma, 1994). Indeed, many descriptions of homosexual men and women from that period read like descriptions of what we would now call transexuals—people whose entire self-identification and social role is at odds with their genital anatomy. Homosexual men were "effeminate" and lesbians were "mannish," the thinking went. If they weren't, they probably were not really homosexual, but were simply engaging in same-sex relationships for some reason of convenience. The "real" homosexuals were "congenital inverts," who not only seemed like persons of the other sex, but also took a gender-atypical role in sex—homosexual men preferred to be penetrated rather than to penetrate, for example.

Novelist Radclyffe Hall (1880–1943) portrayed lesbians, including herself, as gender inverts.

This was not just the view of doctors, but also of society at large, and of many homosexual men and women as well. The very first gay activist, the German lawyer Karl-Heinrich Ulrichs (1825–1895), made gender inversion central to his theory of homosexuality (Kennedy, 1988). The same idea was typified in the masculine character of the heroine of *The Well of Loneliness,* a 1928 novel by British author Radclyffe Hall that became a central document of lesbian culture.

We now know that this is a very one-sided view of gay people: some gay men are quite feminine and some lesbians quite masculine, but others are not. As discussed in Chapter 6, gay men do differ from straight men in some gender-specific traits—on average. Similarly, lesbians do differ from straight women in some traits—on average. But there are plenty of more or less conventionally gendered lesbians and gay men, too.

We may surmise that, in the early days of gay and lesbian culture, it was only the most gender-atypical gay people who came to public and medical attention (the "mollies," for example). They were, in essence, exposed, or **outed,** by their own inability to conform to gender norms, while more conventionally gendered gay people remained largely invisible. Furthermore, the notion of a "congenital invert" was an easy one to grasp: if a gay man is "really" a woman, then it's no surprise that he's attracted to men. In fact, some early sexologists claimed to find all kinds of traits in gay people consistent with that view—that lesbians were taller than straight women, had male-like hormones or chromosomes, and so forth (LeVay, 1996). Although most of these findings have since been shown to be false, there do seem to be some biological markers associated with sexual orientation, as we saw in Chapter 7.

Gay People Were Later Subdivided on the Basis of Gender Characteristics

During the twentieth century, the diversity of gay people became much more apparent (Chauncey, 1994; Faderman, 1991). To accommodate this recognition, a new idea took hold—one that had also been proposed by Ulrichs in his later writings. This idea was that there are two kinds of lesbians and two kinds of gay men. The two kinds of lesbians were called **butch** and **femme:** the butch lesbians looked, dressed, and acted like men and took a dominant role in sex, while the femme lesbians were like heterosexual women and took a submissive role in sex. A lesbian couple would consist of a butch–femme pair. Similarly, gay men were thought to be of two kinds, sometimes referred to as **tops** and **bottoms:** tops were defined by a preference for the insertive role in anal intercourse, and were relatively masculine and dominant generally, while bottoms preferred the receptive role and were more feminine. With this thinking, lesbian and gay male relationships were "regularized": although they were same-sex relationships, they mimicked heterosexual relationships in the sense that they were formed by the union of a more masculine and a more feminine partner.

This general conception of gay sexuality persisted through the 1950s and was very much part of gay and lesbian culture. According to an oral history of mid-twentieth-century lesbian life in Buffalo, New York, young working-class women who entered the lesbian culture had first to figure out whether they were butch or femme. After this fateful decision was made, all their relationships, social roles, and sexual behaviors were governed by their identity as one or the other (Kennedy & Davis, 1983).

During the 1970s, the women's movement strongly affected lesbian culture. To be a femme, or "lipstick lesbian," was now politically suspect because it seemed like pandering to a man's image of women. Most lesbians therefore became butch; they cut their hair short, learned how to repair automobiles, and the like. At the same time, gay male culture moved toward a more aggressively masculine image, especially in cities such as San Francisco, where the "clone look" (short hair, mustache, leather jacket, flannel shirt, tight jeans) predominated. Gay men worked on their bodies in order to become the kind of men they were themselves attracted to, and any kind of femininity was despised, or at best laughed at.

Since those years there has been a relaxation and splintering of gender norms among both lesbians and gay men. Today's gay and lesbian communities are characterized by a kaleidoscopic variety of "types" and a generally more playful attitude toward gender. Butch and femme lesbians have reappeared, minus the strict rules of yesteryear. No one would be surprised to see two butch or two femme lesbians forming a couple, for example—something that would have been unusual in the 1950s. As for "tops" and "bottoms" among gay men, these terms are frequently used as self-descriptions in gay men's personal ads, but actual surveys of gay men's sexual behavior suggest that the majority of gay men who engage in anal sex are "versatile"—that is, they will take the insertive role on one occasion and the receptive role on another (Detels et al., 1989).

In addition, the lesbian/straight and gay/straight dichotomies are themselves under siege, especially among women. While some women remain out-and-out lesbians, others move fluidly between relationships with both men and women. Of course, one might call these women bisexuals (see below), rather than lesbians. However, they may reject any such labels themselves, preferring to define their sexual desires in terms of the specific people they are attracted to, rather than by overall classes of partners. Thus, they challenge the centrality of sexual orientation as we currently define it.

Gay men's personal ads often include references to "top" and "bottom," but in reality many gay men are versatile in their sexual behavior.

(A)

(B)

A woman's privilege is to change her mind, and actress Anne Heche (*Psycho, Wag the Dog*) has certainly done so. For 2 years in the mid-1990s she dated actor Steve Martin. Then she lived for 3 years with lesbian comedian Ellen DeGeneres (A). They planned to have a baby and get "married" in Vermont, but in August 2000 they broke up. (B) A year later Heche married Coleman Laffoon, a cameraman she met while working on a documentary about DeGeneres. How do we label someone like Heche? Is she straight, lesbian, bisexual—or just a trendsetter?

The Struggle for Gay Rights Is a Worldwide Movement

As with some other minorities, gay people's sense of identity developed out of a history of oppression and the struggle against that oppression. Thus, to understand the gay community today it is necessary to have some knowledge of its political history, a history that begins in Europe rather than in the United States.

The Gay Rights Movement Began in Germany

We mentioned Karl-Heinrich Ulrichs as the first gay rights activist. He stood up at the 1867 Congress of German Jurists to demand the abolition of the sodomy statutes, but he was shouted down and was not able to finish his speech. After that, he wrote a series of pamphlets defending homosexuality, and he developed a circle of gay acquaintances. For several decades, he was the Western world's only "out" gay man. His actions cost him his career, but they gave homosexuality a human face (Kennedy, 1988).

The world's first gay rights organization, the Scientific-Humanitarian Committee, was founded in Berlin in 1897. The main figure behind this group was Magnus Hirschfeld (see Box 1.1), a gay Jewish doctor and sexologist who developed a biological theory of sexual orientation and gender (Wolff, 1986). For 30 years, Hirschfeld led the struggle to have the German sodomy statutes overthrown. His organization drew considerable public interest and sympathy, and seemed close to success on several occasions, but it was ultimately broken up by the Nazis, and Hirschfeld was forced to live abroad. Several thousand German homosexuals—nearly all men—were sent to concentration camps, where most of them died. The identifying symbol that homosexuals were forced to wear in the camps—a pink triangle—was later adopted as an icon for the gay rights movement worldwide.

Hirschfeld founded his political campaign on the thesis that homosexuality was a biologically inborn condition. For that reason, he argued, sex between two homosexual men or two homosexual women was natural and normal, and discrimination against people on the basis of their innate desires, or their fulfillment of those desires, was unjust. It was what we would call a civil rights argument, and identifying gay people as a distinct class of people similar to an ethnic group was central to the argument.

Interestingly, Hirschfeld was opposed by another gay rights group, the *Verein der Eigenen* (League of Free Spirits), which took a very different line. The members of the *Verein* were mostly men who were attracted to teenage youths. They claimed that gay men were *not* special, and that *everyone* was capable of same-sex attraction. They defended man–youth love as a noble German tradition, and sought to have the sodomy statutes overthrown on the basis of a perceived right to privacy. The *Verein* also disintegrated during the Nazi period.

In the Postwar Period Gay Rights Organizations Were Founded in the United States

After the Second World War, gay activism moved to the United States (Marcus, 2002). The first durable American gay rights organization, the Mattachine Society, was founded in Los Angeles in 1950 (Figure 13.2). Its founders were inspired in part by the German example, in part by the publication of the first Kinsey Report in 1948, and in part by their own experience of police harassment and social oppression. The first lesbian organization, the Daughters of Bilitis, was founded in San Francisco 5 years later. (The founders of this organization were Del Martin and Phyllis Lyon, who are pictured in Chapter 9.) These organizations functioned largely as support groups for gays and lesbians, who were generally reviled at that time. Witch-hunts of gay people (among others) were initiated by Republican Senator Joseph McCarthy in the early 1950s, and in 1953 President Eisenhower ordered that all homosexuals in federal employment be investigated and dismissed.

The black civil rights movement of the 1960s made a great impression on gay people, some of whom participated in that struggle. One of these was pacifist Bayard Rustin, a close associate of Martin Luther King, Jr., who helped organize the 1963 March on Washington. In the mid-1960s, more politically active gay organizations sprang up on the East Coast and began a series of actions, such as picketing the White House.

Figure 13.2 Early gay activists.
Members of the Washington offshoot of the Mattachine Society and other East Coast groups picketing the White House in 1965.

The Stonewall Rebellion Initiated a More Confrontational Phase

Early in the morning of June 28, 1969, a riot broke out outside the Stonewall Inn, a bar in New York's Greenwich Village that catered to gay men, transvestites, and transexuals (Duberman, 1993). The riot was in response to a police raid—something that gay bars endured frequently in those days. The rioting evolved into street demonstrations that continued for several nights. These demonstrations were followed by the formation of more confrontational gay rights organizations. The "Stonewall Rebellion" is often viewed as the starting point of the modern gay rights movement. In 1999, 30 years after the riots, President Clinton placed the Stonewall Inn on the National Register of Historic Places.

At the time of the Stonewall Rebellion, the status of gay people in the United States was still quite dismal. Homosexuality was officially listed by the American Psychiatric Association as a mental disorder, and many gay people were attempting to be cured of it (Duberman, 1991). Most Americans thought that sex between two men or two women was morally wrong, most states had sodomy statutes, and gay relationships had no status under the law. Gay people had no legal protection from discrimination and were often dismissed from public or private employment on the basis of their sexual orientation. Not a single openly gay person had ever been elected to public office, and there were virtually no gay role models in any occupation. Bars were almost the entirety of gay social life.

The 1970s were a period of rapid change. The first gay rights marches took place in 1970. In 1971, the National Organization for Women officially acknowledged the role of lesbians in that organization. In 1973, homosexuality was deleted from the American Psychiatric Association's list of mental disorders. In 1974, the first openly gay person won elected office—Elaine Noble was elected to the Massachusetts House of Representatives—and others followed (Box 13.2). A few gay people came out of the closet in other fields of life: in 1975, for example, NFL running back David Kopay announced that he was gay.

During the 1970s, urban gay districts such as San Francisco's Castro Street drew thousands of young gay men from around the country and became the center of their sexual, social, and political lives (D'Emilio, 1990). Homosexuality became a topic of considerable public interest, and while many people continued to despise gay people, others became sympathetic. By 1977, about 40 cities had enacted some kind of antidiscrimination ordinances.

In that same year, the passage of an antidiscrimination ordinance in Miami triggered a backlash from conservative Christians, led by singer Anita Bryant. Many antidiscrimination ordinances were repealed around the country, and an initiative to dismiss gays from employment as teachers (the "Briggs Initiative") nearly passed in California. When

Box 13.2 *Sex in History*

Harvey Milk

Harvey Milk (1930–1978) (center), with San Francisco Mayor George Moscone (left)

If the American gay rights movement has a martyr, it is City Supervisor Harvey Milk of San Francisco. Born to a New York Jewish family, Milk was always conscious of Jewish history and thus of the need to struggle actively against oppression. He moved to San Francisco in 1972, and after two failed attempts, won election to the Board of Supervisors in 1977. He was the first openly gay man to be elected to city government in the United States.

During his short tenure as Supervisor, Milk helped lead the successful campaign to reject California Proposition 6, the "Briggs Initiative," which would have forced the state to fire openly gay teachers. He was instrumental in passing San Francisco's first gay rights ordinance. And he encouraged gay activism with a series of public speeches, which often acknowledged the example set by the black civil rights struggle. "The Blacks did not win their rights by sitting quietly in the back of the bus," he declared at the 1978 San Francisco Gay Pride parade. "They got off! Gay people, we will not win our rights by staying quietly in our closets. We are coming out! We are coming out to fight the lies, the myths, the distortions! We are coming out to tell the truth about gays!" Milk was also inspired by the black civil rights movement to call for a gay and lesbian March on Washington.

On November 27, 1978, shortly after Proposition 6 was rejected, Milk and San Francisco Mayor George Moscone were shot dead in their City Hall offices by Dan White, an anti-gay Supervisor and former police officer who represented a conservative blue-collar district of the city. At his trial, a psychiatrist testified that White's addiction to junk food was a sign of mental disorder; this became the infamous "Twinkie defense." White received an extraordinarily light sentence—less than 8 years in prison. When the sentence was announced, gay men rioted, torched police cars, and broke down the doors of City Hall. In retaliation, anti-gay police officers attacked a gay bar and clubbed most of the customers.

White was released after just 5 years, but committed suicide 2 years later. The March on Washington that Milk had called for took place in October of 1979; it was the first of several increasingly effective national demonstrations for gay rights. Milk's life has been commemorated in a biography (Shilts, 1982), plays, music, and the names of many gay organizations.

former Governor Ronald Reagan, former President Gerald Ford, and President Jimmy Carter came out against the Briggs initiative in 1978, it was the first time such prominent politicians had ever expressed a pro-gay position.

The AIDS Epidemic Was a Catastrophe With a Silver Lining

The AIDS epidemic, which began around 1980 and continues today, caused the deaths of huge numbers of gay men and deeply traumatized the survivors. Yet the epidemic has also had quite unexpected and paradoxical effects, helping to advance the recognition and acceptance of gay people in ways that would have seemed unimaginable twenty years ago.

The first cases of AIDS in the United States occurred among gay men in New York, San Francisco, and Los Angeles in 1979 and 1980. The disease was given its name, Acquired Immune Deficiency Syndrome, in 1982, and the causative virus, HIV, was identified in the following year. Because the virus was readily transmitted by anal intercourse, and because many gay men had numerous sex partners and did not use condoms, the infection spread rapidly in gay communities. In addition, because of the long latency between infection and overt disease (see Chapter 16), very large numbers of gay men became infected before the disease came to public attention at all.

Since then, AIDS has made terrible inroads among American gay men: about 350,000 of them have been diagnosed with the disease, of whom about half have died (Centers for Disease Control, 2002a). Many others have been infected with HIV, but have not yet developed AIDS. Among the gay men who have died of AIDS in the United States and Britain are such notables as actor Rock Hudson, dancer Rudolf Nureyev, artist Keith Haring, singer Freddie Mercury, director Derek Jarman, novelist Paul Monette, and AIDS activist Pedro Zamora (of MTV's *Real World*).

How can we say that the AIDS epidemic—which continues today—has had a silver lining? We do so because the response of gays and lesbians, and of Americans in general, to the epidemic forever changed the image and status of gay people in our society—for the better. The initial public and political response to AIDS was to ignore it or dismiss it as a "gay disease" (Shilts, 1987). In reaction, countless thousands of gay men were motivated to involve themselves in AIDS activism and gay activism. Lesbians, who during the 1970s had been involved in feminist causes more than in specifically lesbian or gay ones, joined forces with gay men and founded co-gender organizations. Gays and lesbians came out of the closet in droves. Americans came to *know* gay people—not just the distant famous ones, but also family members, neighbors, and co-workers. The percentage of Americans who said that they personally knew someone who was openly gay rose from 30 percent in 1983 to 73 percent in 2000 (Rubin, 2000).

The collective effect of these disclosures was immense, bringing the most unlikely allies to the gay cause. When arch-conservative Republican Senator Barry Goldwater of Arizona discovered that his grandson Ty Ross was gay, he began to support gay causes, including nondiscrimination statutes and the right of gay people to serve in the military. "I'm an honorary gay by now," the 85-year-old Goldwater said on one occasion (Grove, 1994).

Gay People Are in Transition

Because of this rapid change of attitudes, which is still ongoing, the current status of gays and lesbians in American society is full of paradoxes:

- Most Americans continue to believe that sex between men or between women is wrong, but most also believe that gay people should be protected from discrimination in employment, housing, and so forth (Figure 13.3).

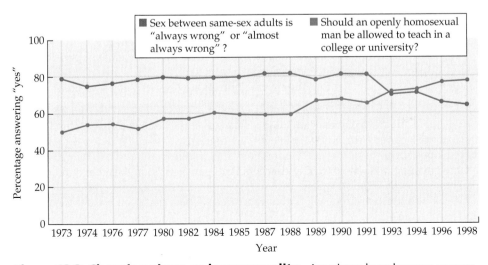

Figure 13.3 Changing views on homosexuality. Americans have become progressively more accepting of gay people over the last 30 years, as exemplified here by their responses to a question about gay men teaching college, but a majority of Americans still think that gay sex is morally wrong. (Data from General Social Survey.)

TABLE 13.1	*Same-sex cohabitations reported to U.S. Census, 1990 and 2000, for selected states*		
State	**1990**	**2000**	**Increase**
California	36,602	92,138	152%
New York	13,748	46,490	238%
Florida	8492	41,048	383%
Kentucky	862	7114	725%
West Virginia	307	2916	850%
Idaho	178	1873	952%
Wyoming	30	807	2590%

Source: Human Rights Campaign, 2001c.

- Many states still have sodomy statutes, but some cities in those same states have gay rights ordinances.
- Gays and lesbians are being discharged from the armed services in increasing numbers (1212 men and women were discharged on account of their homosexual orientation in 2000), but a majority of Americans now think that gays should be able to serve openly in the military, and even within the armed services, opposition to gays serving in uniform has dropped dramatically (Center for the Study of Sexual Minorities in the Military, 2001).
- Rural states have the most anti-gay attitudes, yet the number of cohabiting gay couples has increased much faster in rural states than in the populous coastal states (Table 13.1). In Wyoming—where gay college student Matthew Shepard was brutally murdered in 1998—the number of cohabiting same-sex couples reported to the U.S. census increased 27-fold between 1990 and 2000.
- Lesbians are still a largely invisible minority, yet the percentage of U.S. women who say they recently had sex with other women increased 15-fold from 1988 to 1998—from 0.2 percent to 3 percent of women nationwide, according to data from the General Social Survey (Butler, 2001).
- Reported hate crimes based on sexual orientation have more than tripled since 1991 (Human Rights Campaign, 2001b), yet many gay people say they feel safer and more accepted than ever before.
- Same-sex marriage is not legal anywhere in the United States, and few churches will bless same-sex unions, yet more and more gay couples consider themselves "married," and many raise children.
- Gays claim that they are campaigning for "equal rights," but their opponents say they want "special rights."
- Many gays believe that they were "born that way," but many of their opponents say homosexuality is a "chosen lifestyle."

The rapid advances made by gays and lesbians over the last 20 years have made them the focus of a culture war. Network television programs such as *Ellen* and *Will and Grace* have helped promote a new and "happening" image of lesbians and gay men, especially among young, well-educated city-dwellers. Anti-gay groups, on the other hand, spread their message via religious pronouncements, political campaigning, and the Internet. Anti-gay attitudes are strongest in nonurban areas, where gay people are less common and less visible.

The state of Colorado illustrates the conflicts that arise between these two constituencies. By 1992, three Colorado cities, including Denver, had ordinances that protected gays and lesbians from discrimination in such areas as housing and employment. In that year, however, the voters of the entire state, which is predominantly conservative and rural, passed a constitutional amendment ("Amendment 2") to rescind those cities' ordinances and prohibit any similar ordinances in the future. The affected cities brought a legal action to have Amendment 2 overthrown (because, among other things, it violated gay people's fundamental right to participate in the political process). After a lengthy trial, the amendment was indeed declared unconstitutional, and the U.S. Supreme Court eventually upheld that decision. Nevertheless, the state of Colorado still excludes sexual orientation as a protected classification in its hate crime and nondiscrimination laws.

Gay Rights Are a Global Issue

The status of lesbians and gay men varies greatly around the world. The United States has been a leader in gay people's political struggle over the last several decades—in fact, some other countries, such as Britain, use the word "Stonewall" in the names of their own gay rights organizations, as if to acknowledge the worldwide significance of that 1969 riot. But this does not necessarily mean that gay people have made more advances or lead happier lives here than elsewhere.

Some countries, especially in Western Europe, have a tradition of social tolerance that has allowed their gay citizens to sidestep some of the inequities that their American counterparts have experienced. In France, for example, sex between men has been legal since 1791. Also, the "religious right" is a much less significant political force in most European countries than it is in the United States. Thus, with relatively little effort, gay couples have acquired the full legal rights of marriage in the Netherlands and domestic partnership rights nearly comparable to marriage in several Scandinavian countries (Gay-Civil-Unions.com, 2002). In these and several other European countries, anti-gay discrimination and gay-bashing are less common than in the United States, and gay culture flourishes. The 1950 European Convention on Human Rights has been interpreted to protect the rights of sexual minorities, the Council of Europe has required its member nations to rescind their sodomy statutes, and the European Court of Human Rights has ruled that lesbians and gay men must be allowed to serve openly in member nations' armed forces (Center for the Study of Sexual Minorities in the Military, 2000).

In contrast, there are other parts of the world where lesbians and gay men are still subject to extreme persecution (International Gay and Lesbian Association, 1999). In fact, most countries ban homosexual behavior completely, ban it for one sex, or have a higher age of consent for gay sex than for heterosexual sex. Only five countries in Africa, six in Asia, one in the Middle East (Israel), and seven in the Americas allow the same rights of sexual expression for gay and straight people. Police harassment of gay people is common in many countries, especially in the Balkan nations, Central and South America, and China. Some heads of state, such as Zimbabwe's president Robert Mugabe, have encouraged violence against gay people, claiming that homosexual behavior is unnatural. "If dogs and pigs do not do it," Mugabe said in a 1995 speech, "why must human beings?" (Wright, 2000).

Killings of gay people on account of their sexual orientation happen frequently in Central and South America, but they have also occurred in Britain and, as mentioned above, in the United States. Brazil is one of the worst offenders: an estimated 1600 Brazilians are believed to have been killed on account of their sexual orientation or gender identity between 1980 and 1997, and several leading gay male, lesbian, and transgender activists have been shot dead by police officers or have died after police beatings (International Gay and Lesbian Association, 1999). The ill-treatment of sexual minorities in Central and South America is probably connected to the culture of **machismo,** which values stereotypical masculinity in men and stereotypical femininity and subservience in women.

Resistance to discrimination and harassment has been promoted by the efforts of the International Lesbian and Gay Association (ILGA), the United Nations, and the World Health Organization. These efforts have been opposed by anti-gay factions in the United States, however. In 1994, the U.S. delegation to the United Nations, at the instigation of

Rio de Janeiro's Carnaval makes Brazil look hospitable to every shade of gender diversity. In fact, however, Brazil and other Latin American countries have a high rate of assaults on and murders of gay and transgendered men and women.

Senator Jesse Helms of North Carolina, engineered the expulsion of ILGA from the U.N. Council. Probably more important than international efforts, however, is the work of gay rights activists within many countries. In many cases, these activists can point to indigenous homosexual traditions that have been obscured or repressed as a result of Westernization. The Internet is playing an important role in facilitating these activities in the face of governmental censorship.

Growing Up Gay Is Hard to Do

It's possible that, at some future time, a person's sexual orientation will be of as little significance as, say, their handedness. Right now, however, gay people have to grow up in a largely hostile society, and the experience of this hostility strongly colors gay people's worldview.

We mentioned in Chapter 7 that many gays and lesbians are somewhat gender-nonconformist as children. Of course, there's a lot of variation among individuals. Some pre-gay children act like miniature transexuals, and cannot be cajoled or forced by any means to behave like conventional kids of their own sex. Others fit easily into the conventional mold. The majority are probably somewhere in the middle—not quite conventional boys and girls, but not outrageously unconventional either.

A pre-gay child's position on this gender continuum strongly affects their growing-up process (see Chapter 12). Markedly gender-nonconformist children "out" themselves before they even enter kindergarten. Parents may already suspect—with good reason—that the child is likely to become gay, and they may do everything in their power to prevent it, including punishment and various kinds of "therapy." A "sissy" boy may quickly become the least favorite child in the family—especially in the eyes of his father. For tomboyish girls, it's less predictable—some such girls thrive. In any case, tomboyishness is much less reliable a predictor of future homosexuality in girls than is femininity in boys (Bailey & Zucker, 1995).

Initially, a gay child's experiences in school may be unremarkable, but trouble often crops up in the preadolescent years (age 8–13; see Chapter 12). Because children form same-sex social networks at this age, and rigorously enforce gender norms, a child who is gender-nonconformist to any extent may be excluded from friendship groups and even verbally abused. This can happen even before the child becomes aware of same-sex attraction—in fact, some of these children don't become gay at all. But it's all the same to their peers: terms of abuse such as "faggot" and "dyke" are used commonly in preadolescent and adolescent school society, and unlike racial epithets, they rarely evoke any rebuke from teachers. As the child gets older, things may go from bad to worse as abusive words are supplemented by abusive deeds. Furthermore, many gay and lesbian adolescents are now announcing their homosexuality, either to close friends or to the whole world, but this openness can bring severe retribution (Box 13.3).

Gay adolescents who are more conventional in their gender characteristics have the option of passing as straight, and many do. Quite commonly, such teens go into an "overachiever" mode, in which academic excellence serves to mask their problematic sexuality. Although this course of action may avoid the kind of harassment that more obviously gay teens experience, it inflicts its own wounds; specifically, a hemming in of normal self-expression that interferes with psychological development and with sexual and social relationships in later life.

It's not possible to provide a single image of what it's like to grow up gay. For some youths, like those described in Box 13.3, it can be an unrelenting torment. Some are rejected by their parents or run away from home, perhaps becoming prostitutes in the nearest big city. Some contemplate or attempt suicide (Richardson, 1995), although whether the rate of attempted or completed suicide is higher among gay than straight youth is uncertain (Savin-Williams, 2001b).

Yet, for increasing numbers of today's adolescents, growing up gay can be relatively painless or, indeed, a very positive experience. What has made such a difference for today's gay youth is the existence of role models, the frequent discussion of gay issues on youth-oriented television shows such as the *Ricki Lake Show,* the presence of support organizations such as Gay-Straight Alliances in some schools, the efforts of some teach-

Box 13.3 *Personal Points of View*

Hatred in the Hallways

Human Rights Watch is an international organization that investigates human rights abuses, usually far from our shores. In 2001, however, it published an investigative report on human rights abuses suffered by gay children in public schools right here in the United States (Human Rights Watch, 2001a). Here are two fairly typical stories

"Nikki L.," California

Everyone thinks I have a problem. They blame me, they blame my mom. They want me to be quiet. But I'm a lesbian. I feel like I've always known it. But I didn't get into trouble 'til seventh grade. I told a friend. Next thing I know, everyone seems to know. I got yelled at—on the playground, in gym, in the hall, in classes.

Only one teacher ever did anything. Miss Johnson, my English teacher—I love her—she made them stop it. I felt safe with her. I would go to her room for lunch and recess. She made me feel safe. She liked my poetry—encouraged me to write.

But everywhere else was bad. I tried to defend myself. I'm little but I'm tough. When kids hit me, I hit back. I got suspended twice. Three days each. A group of boys tried to beat me up, but I kicked them. I was just defending myself, but the vice-principal thinks I have a reputation. He calls me a "hard ass." I'm tough. I'm not gonna let anyone just push me around and hit me.

But I got really sick of going to school. I would tell my mom I was feeling sick so I didn't have to go to school. Finally she called the school. The principal said I needed to document three incidents before they would do anything. There were about twenty to thirty kids, mostly boys, who harassed me. My grades dropped.

Then one day I was walking home and some kids threw a brick at me. It hit me in the head. They were calling me a "fucking dyke." I sorta lost consciousness and my head was bleeding. That did it. I decided to never go back to school. I'm too scared.

Now I do independent study. My grades are back up. It's good. I don't have many friends. They are all a lot older than me. But that's okay—I like older people. They don't care if I am a dyke.

"Dylan N.," Nevada

Dylan N. told his family that he was gay when he was 12, but that fact came as no surprise to them. "From a young age, I was set aside as different," he explained when Human Rights Watch interviewed him in December 1999 in Atlanta, Georgia.

During the first semester of his sophomore year, Dylan appeared on a local public access television program as a participant in a discussion about the experiences of lesbian, gay, bisexual, and transgender students in high school. When word spread among his classmates that he was gay, they subjected him to constant harassment because of his sexual orientation. Some of his peers began to taunt him routinely by calling him a "fag," "butt pirate," "fairy," "homo," "queer," "sissy," "ass licker," "AIDS whore," and other derogatory terms. "It was all part of the normal daily routine," said Dylan.

The verbal harassment escalated almost immediately into physical violence. Other students began spitting on him and throwing food at him. One day in the parking lot outside his school, six students surrounded him and threw a lasso around his neck, saying, "Let's tie the faggot to the back of the truck." He escaped from his tormentors and ran inside the school. Finding one of the vice-principals, he tried to tell her what had just happened to him. "I was still hysterical," he said. "I was trying to explain, but I was stumbling over my words. She laughed."

The school took no action to discipline Dylan's harassers. Instead, school officials told him not to discuss his sexual orientation with other students. "Looking back on it, I was so out," he said. "I tried to start GSAs [gay-straight alliances]. Like, I tried to do so much."

After the lasso incident, the harassment and violence intensified. "I was living in the disciplinary office because other harassment was going on. Everyone knew," he said. "It gave permission for a whole new level of physical stuff to occur." To escape the relentless harassment, Dylan asked for a transfer to another school in the district. When the semester ended, the district placed him in an alternative school for students with poor academic records or behavioral problems.

"The principal [at the alternative school] had a real issue with me," Dylan said. "The principal told me he wouldn't have me acting like a faggot at school. After a semester there, I realized that it was not a place where I could get an education."

Dylan was successful in securing a transfer to a traditional school the following year, when he was 15, but school officials again directed him not to discuss his sexual orientation with other students.

Derek Henkle ("Dylan N.")

The gag rule imposed on him by the school did not protect him from his peers, who learned that he was gay from his former classmates at his first school. "It was the same thing all over again," he said. "They'd push me up against the lockers and call me a fag. They'd chase me around campus in their cars, screaming and yelling 'fag' out the windows." Once, he told us, a teacher walked out of the room while some of his classmates were throwing things at him.

On another occasion, a group of students surrounded him outside the school, punching him, shouting that he was a "bitch," and jeering while security officers stood nearby. When the fight ended, he related, "I was completely bloody. I was bleeding from both lips, my nose, behind my ear."

Dylan tried to return to his second school, the alternative school, but school officials turned down his request to be placed there again. "What they did was they put me in the adult education program. Their justification was, I would be around people who were much more accepting. What they didn't tell me was I would have no chance of getting a high school diploma," he said.

("Dylan," whose real name is Derek Henkle, sued his school district for violation of his constitutional rights to free speech and equal protection [Lambda Legal Defense and Education Fund, 2000]. In an August, 2000 settlement, the district agreed to pay Henkle $451,000 and to institute a stringent antiharassment policy [Reich, 2002]. He is now a gay activist working on youth issues.)

ers to confront anti-gay attitudes and bullying, and the greater willingness of some parents to accept and love their gay children. Much depends on the kind of environment in which adolescents find themselves. But given the continuing trend toward tolerance and even positive acceptance of gay people, we may expect that the experience of adolescence will improve even further for the next generation of gay youth.

While growing up gay may have its challenges, gay and lesbian adults are just as well-adjusted and happy with their lives as are straight men and women, according to national survey data from the National Opinion Research Center (Horowitz et al., 2001). Thus, there is a solid basis for reassuring gay teens and their parents that their sexual orientation will not have any long-lasting negative impact on their lives.

The National Coming Out Day logo, created by Keith Haring. National Coming Out Day is an opportunity for closeted gays and lesbians to reveal their sexual orientation.

Coming Out Is a Lifelong Process

Although there are some analogies between gay people and ethnic minorities, there is one major difference: Ethnic minority children are usually brought up by parents of that same minority, whereas most pre-gay children are brought up by straight parents. Thus, whether or not gay people are "born gay" in a *biological* sense (see Chapter 7), they are usually "born straight" in a *social* sense: they are born into a predominantly straight culture, and everyone, including probably themselves, expects them to become heterosexual adults. **Coming out of the closet,** though it may involve a dramatic moment or two, is really a lifelong voyage away from that social expectation of heterosexuality and toward a fully integrated gay identity (Troiden, 1989).

The process of coming out has several stages. The first is coming out to oneself; that is, realizing and consciously accepting that one is gay. Although it is only the first step in the process, it is the hardest step for many gay people, especially those who grow up in a social setting that strongly disapproves of gays and lesbians, or whose religion labels homosexual behavior as immoral. Many gay people live in denial for many years, perhaps even for their entire lives. Particularly if they are fairly conventional in their gender traits, they may stereotype gay people as "swishy" or "dykey" and fail to recognize themselves within those stereotypes. They may actually engage in homosexual behavior for many years without considering same-sex desire to be part of their identity. "I was convinced that I wasn't a homosexual," said former Republican Congressman Robert Bauman, who, though married, led a secret gay life for 20 years. He was exposed by the FBI in 1980, at the age of 43, and was voted out of office a few weeks later. "It took me almost 3 years of religious and psychiatric counseling for me to acknowledge that I was gay," he said later (Marcus, 1992).

The second phase is coming out to others. Of course, that's usually a gradual process: a gay adolescent may come out first to another gay youth, a best friend, a sibling, or a counselor. Parents tend to find out late; gay adolescents fear parental rejection, sometimes with good reason. If parents have anti-gay views, they may react very negatively to their child's disclosure, and this can cost a gay teen a home, a college education, and much more. On the other hand, many parents whose initial reaction was negative go through a rapid change of heart after their child comes out, and may even take an activist role and join pro-gay organizations such as Parents, Families and Friends of Lesbians and Gays (PFLAG). Among minority and immigrant families especially, there is a strong instinct to close ranks around a family member who is perceived to be victimized or stigmatized by society.

Nowadays gay people have the option of coming out in a more public fashion. "I'm on *Oprah,* coming out," said one 19-year-old woman on Oprah Winfrey's TV show, after years of abuse at school. "I think I've come long way." Besides talk shows, another opportunity is offered by National Coming Out Day (October 11), an annual event that for some gay people has the flavor of a coming-of-age rite (Human Rights Campaign, 2001e). Nevertheless, coming out publicly can still be a risky business for some people, especially for those who live in conservative areas or whose jobs might be endangered by disclosure of their sexual orientation.

The third phase of coming out is joining a gay or lesbian community. For some gay men, that means moving to a big city that has a well-developed gay community. An example is West Hollywood, California, an independent city within Los Angeles whose population is about one-third gay men. Lesbians tend to be more scattered, but some smaller cities, such

Box 13.4 *Society, Values, and the Law*

Gay Meccas: West Hollywood and Northampton

Los Angeles has been an important center of gay life and gay activism since the first gay rights organization, the Mattachine Society, was founded there in 1950. During the subsequent decades, gay culture focused on an unincorporated area east of Beverly Hills, where gay bars could not be raided by the Los Angeles Police Department. In 1984 this area incorporated as the City of West Hollywood; it currently has a majority of gay men on the City Council, and about one-third of its residents are gay men.

West Hollywood's gay culture centers on Santa Monica Boulevard, which is lined with gay bars, clubs, and coffeehouses, a gay bookstore, gymnasiums, theaters, design showrooms, clothing stores, hair salons, and galleries, as well as the offices of a gay church (the Metropolitan Community Church, a national gay-focused organization). On weekend evenings, the western end of the boulevard, known as Boystown, is thronged by young gay men of every race and gender who pack into the bars and clubs there, or cruise one another (check out one another sexually) in the street. The boulevard also hosts Los Angeles' annual Gay Pride parade, as well as gay-oriented "Hallowe'en" and Mardi Gras festivities.

The streets behind the boulevard are lined with apartment blocks housing thousands of gay men, many of whom work (or are seeking work) in the entertainment industry. Most of these apartment blocks are arranged around a central courtyard with a pool and are little gay worlds in their own right.

The eastern end of the Boulevard is seedier. The main signs of gay life here are male prostitutes—both hustlers and male-to-female transgenders (see Chapter 19). There is also a gay sex club on the boule-vard just beyond the city limits, where men can engage in group sex in a nearly pitch-dark labyrinth.

The collision of Hollywood, homosexuality, and a warm climate has fostered an obsession with looks, physique, and sexual performance in West Hollywood that is rivaled in the United States only by Miami's South Beach. Alcohol and drug use and sexually transmitted diseases are significant problems in the city, and it has one of the highest rates of HIV infection in the nation.

Lesbians are fairly well represented in West Hollywood, too, but their real strength is in small woman-oriented cities such as Northampton, Massachusetts. Northampton is home to a leading women's college, Smith College. The area can boast a long history of woman-loving women, most notably the poet Emily Dickinson (1830–1886) who lived in nearby Amherst.

Northampton's current mayor, Clare Higgins, is lesbian, but the city is not lesbian-dominated, and there is no lesbian street scene analogous to West Hollywood on a Saturday night. Rather, lesbians blend in fairly intimately with heterosexual and bisexual women, collaborating with them in business and in academic work. There is an annual Gay Pride march and festival at which lesbians predominate (see figure), a lesbian softball league, and other lesbian-oriented sports and cultural events, as well as lesbian-owned bookstores, cafes, and restaurants, but to a casual visitor it may not be obvious who the lesbians are. In fact, there are said to be at least three categories of homosexual women in Northampton: "lesbians," who tend to be politically active lesbian feminists; "gay women," who are often professional women who dress and

act fairly conservatively; and "dykes," who revel in the stereotype that the word "dyke" suggests and are likely to be political radicals.

Smith College is, of course, lesbian-friendly: it is one of the few colleges nation-wide to offer health benefits to students' domestic partners, for example. It offers quite a number of lesbian-oriented courses and has an active lesbian, bisexual, and transgender alliance. The majority of the students are straight, however, and Smith has to combat its image as a "lesbian school" in order not to scare away non-lesbian applicants.

as Northampton, Massachusetts, have become centers of lesbian life. In locations such as West Hollywood and Northampton, gay people can find communities that offer sex partners, acceptance, and a wide range of gay or lesbian cultural institutions (Box 13.4).

Moving to a "gay ghetto" has lost quite a bit of the significance it once had for young gay people, however. That's because many young lesbians and gay men can now find other gay people, be openly gay, and experience some degree of organized gay life in the communities where they grow up. In addition, the Internet, with its gay "megasites" such as PlanetOut.com and its endless opportunities for gay networking, chat, and cyber-sex, has brought the gay community to gay youth in their own homes.

One problem with moving to a gay mecca is that it may also represent a flight from other aspects of a gay person's cultural identity. In becoming openly gay and moving to gay "ghettoes," many young gay people isolate themselves from their ethnic roots, their religion, and their extended families. Here is how one San Francisco Bay Area lesbian leader, Abby Abinate, expressed the matter:

> When I went to Eureka, to my Yurok tribe, I felt as though I was somewhat accepted but they were not always ready for me as a queer, so I had to keep that part hidden a little. It felt easier for me to live in San Francisco than at home. But when I was in San Francisco, in a lesbian group, I felt they couldn't understand the Indian part of me. They're different from what I'm used to: different values, different approaches, a different sense of humor. They didn't know about those families back home I grew up with, the disputes, the importance of questions like 'How's the fishing?' There was no place where all of me was validated. (Faderman, 1991)

Thus, an important fourth stage of coming out for gay people is integrating the gay side of their identity with other aspects of who they are. This may involve returning to their roots, or participating in organizations that straddle the boundary that they have crossed—gay Catholic groups or gay Asian groups or gay Deaf groups. They can also become active politically in their own communities to raise awareness of the fact that gay people are among them. In these ways, they break down the psychological compartments within their own lives and also contribute to an improved understanding of gay people generally.

The Life Experiences of Lesbians and Gay Men Are Different

Although lesbians and gay men are both homosexual, and by that token share the experience of stigmatization and the process of coming out, there are also significant differences between what being gay means for a man and for a woman. All of the following differences, of course, are generalizations that have many exceptions, but they do give lesbian and gay male lives rather different flavors.

Gay men feel alienated from the larger community of heterosexual men, whom they often view as oppressors. Lesbians are not equally alienated from heterosexual women; on the contrary, they have a long history of involvement in the women's movement, so much so as to partially or completely submerge their own lesbian identity.

Gay men are more sexually active, have more sex partners, and have more permissive views on topics such as pornography than lesbians. Gay men often settle down eventually in cohabitational relationships, but only after some period of sexual exploration that is far more adventurous than what most lesbians experience.

Lesbians are more fluid in their sexual orientation than gay men (Peplau & Garnets, 2000). The concept of a "political lesbian"—a woman who partners with women as a political statement—has no male parallel. Poet Adrienne Rich spoke of a "lesbian continuum" that spans the entirety of woman-identified experience; it includes, but is not limited to, same-sex genital desire (Rich, 1986). No equivalent continuum spans gay male experience, at least in contemporary U.S. culture. And some women actually seem to change sexual orientation during their lifetime—usually toward the homosexual end of the spectrum. Men may come out as gay late in life, but most will say that they were previously in the closet, not that they were previously attracted to women.

Gay men have a much greater likelihood of acquiring HIV from gay sex than do lesbians. Lesbians are generally much less likely to contract HIV, and when they do, it is usually through sex with men or intravenous drug use, not through sex with women (see Chapter 16).

Lesbians and gay men tend to espouse different theories of why they are gay. These days, most gay men believe that they were born gay (Lever, 1994). Lesbians are much more diverse in this respect: some think they were born lesbian, but others attribute their orientation to childhood experiences, particular women they met, or even outright choice (Lever, 1995). For a gay man, coming out feels like a process of *admitting* who he is; for a lesbian, it may feel more like *sensing out* or even *creating* who she is, because her lesbian identity often seems to emerge from her relationships with women, rather than resulting from some kind of biological imperative (Diamond, 1998).

Lesbians and Gay Men Are Well Represented in Certain Occupations

Gay people are found in all walks of life, but they seem to gravitate toward certain fields in which they are accepted or feel comfortable or in which their special talents are useful. Accurate numbers are hard to come by, but on the basis of random-sample surveys, we can make some general statements. First, both lesbians and gay men are much more likely to be self-employed than are straight women or men (Yankelovich Partners, 1994). Perhaps the experience of anti-gay prejudice makes gay people prefer to be their own masters. Second, gay men are more likely to be in technical and professional occupations than are straight men, while lesbians are more likely to be in blue-collar employment than are straight women (Badgett, 1995).

Concerning the specific occupations that may attract lesbians and gay men, there is relatively little hard information, but a lot of speculation. Lesbians do seem to be overrepresented, and particularly successful, in professional sports such as golf and tennis, but, of course, only a tiny fraction of all lesbians are in this field.

There has been a long-lived assumption that gay men are overrepresented, and especially successful, in the creative arts. The fact that so many of the prominent gay men who have died of AIDS were creative artists (see the list given earlier for examples) suggests that this assumption is correct—it isn't just that the prominent gay men in other fields are all in the closet. In fact, a survey of one group of male creative artists—professional dancers—came up with the conclusion that one-half or more of the men in this field are gay (Bailey & Oberschneider, 1997). Why there should be a connection between male homosexuality and artistic expression is unclear, but that connection holds up across cultures (Whitam & Dizon, 1979).

Another set of occupations in which gay men seem to be disproportionately represented are those involving personal service or caring; many are nurses, teachers, flight attendants, or waiters. To some extent, such occupational choices can be seen as part of a broader gender nonconformity on the part of gay men (Lippa & Arad, 1997). Occupations that combine artistic creativity and personal service, such as hairstyling, floristry, and interior design, are the most stereotypical of all gay male occupations—these are the occupations in which you are assumed to be gay until proven otherwise.

One point of mentioning these apparent occupational preferences is to highlight the fact that gay people are not simply people who get together to have sex, nor are they simply a community united in political resistance to oppression. They also, to a degree, share common interests and a common sensibility (the "camp" humor of gay men, for example). If and when gay people are fully accepted by mainstream society, it is not likely that they will be completely assimilated and disappear from view, as has happened, for example, to left-handers. More probably, homosexuality will retain a special salience, and gay people will be valued for their unique gifts.

Gay ballet dancer Rudolf Nureyev (1938–1993) (shown here with Denise Jackson) and lesbian tennis star Martina Navratilova typify stereotypical occupations for gay men and lesbians, respectively. These occupations probably do have far more than their share of gay or lesbian practitioners, but most gay people are not in these or other stereotypically gay fields of work.

Gay Sex Has Its Own Style

With the exception of coitus, most sexual behaviors that male–female couples engage in are also practiced by same-sex couples (see Chapter 8). It's worth pointing out some differences, however. First, no one has gay sex in order to make a baby, so physical pleasure and emotional intimacy are the sole reasons for engaging in it. (Actually, making money can be another motivation for either gay or straight sex, as we'll see in Chapter 19.)

Among the sexual behaviors practiced by female couples are kissing, fondling, oral or manual breast stimulation, body-to-body rubbing involving the vulva (tribadism), cunnilingus, rimming (anilingus), manual stimulation of the clitoris, penetration of the vagina or anus with a finger or sex toy, and S/M play. Among behaviors practiced by male couples are kissing, fondling, nipple stimulation, body-to-body rubbing involving the penis, fellatio, anal penetration with a finger or the penis, intercrural (between-the-thighs) intercourse, and S/M play. Many of these behaviors can be either unidirectional or reciprocal (for example, reciprocal fellatio, or "69").

Same-sex couples take their time over sex (Masters & Johnson, 1979). Lesbians may spend a great deal of time on breast and nipple stimulation, for example, before focusing on the genitals, and may extend the entire sexual interaction for well over an hour. Gay men also enjoy nipple stimulation. (In S/M play, nipple clamps may be used to provide more intense and long-lasting stimulation.) Gay men often bring each other close to orgasm and then back off, thus prolonging sexual pleasure and causing a more intense orgasm when it finally arrives.

Although nearly all lesbians and many gay men confine their sexual behavior to paired encounters in the privacy of their own bedrooms, some gay men have sex in other places, including outdoor locations such as public toilets (Box 13.5), parks, and freeway rest areas and indoor semi-public locations such as bathhouses, sex clubs, and "back rooms" attached to gay bars. Some of this sexual activity is in groups rather than pairs.

One reason why gay men have sex in places such as parks and toilets is simply the lack of other options. Gay men who live with their parents, who are heterosexually married, or who live some distance from where they meet their sex partners may not be able to bring their sex partners home. Cohabiting gay men who are seeking extra-pair sex may be in the same situation. But another reason is probably the thrill-seeking aspect of sex in public places—the sense of hunting and being hunted, combined with the possibility of public disclosure. Yet another reason is the opportunity to have sex with a number of different partners in a short time.

These motivations are probably also behind sex in **bathhouses.** Gay bathhouses are facilities where large numbers of men engage in sex in a semi-public environment. A bathhouse may have a pool, but the real action is in a warren of dimly lit corridors, cubicles, and steam rooms, where men engage in brief sexual encounters, most of which do not culminate in orgasm. There are also community rooms (TV rooms, weight rooms) where there may be conversation and social life. Because bathhouses usually operate as private membership facilities, they are usually exempt from police action. Early in the AIDS epidemic bathhouses were closed down in many cities, though this action stirred conflicts within the gay community between sexual libertarians and AIDS activists (Shilts, 1987). Many still operate or have reopened, however, usually under city regulations that attempt to discourage sex or enforce safe sex practices.

Although gay male culture includes and is fairly accepting of outdoor sex, bathhouses, and the like, it's worth reemphasizing that large numbers of gay men live in very ordinary monogamous relationships that, aside from their same-sex aspect, are indistinguishable from the relationships of most heterosexual Americans. These different lifestyles reflect something of a political dichotomy within the gay male community. More conservative gay men are anxious to emphasize the normality and conventionality of gay culture, hoping that this will speed the acceptance of gay people by mainstream society (Bawer, 1993; Sullivan, 1995). More radical gay men see their role as breaking down society's traditional taboos concerning sex and restoring its status as a primitive, creative, and even spiritual life force (Thompson, 1995; Warner, 2000). Something of the same dichotomy exists among lesbians, too, but the sexual revolutionaries are in a smaller minority (Atkins, 1999).

There Are Sexual Subcultures within the Gay Community

We've already mentioned that lesbians and gay men vary in their gender characteristics ("butch" and "femme" lesbians, "top" and "bottom" gay men). Why these differences arise we don't know, but given that there have been historical changes in the prevalence of these types, it seems unlikely that they can be completely inborn traits. More likely, they arise from an interplay between social forces and inborn predispositions.

Box 13.5 Research Highlights

The Tearoom Trade

Gay men have had sex in public toilets since before public toilets existed. A faded manuscript in the Vatican library records the testimony of one Arnaud de Vernoilles, a very gay cleric in fourteenth-century France. The favorite spot for buggery, he told the Inquisition, was the village dung-heap—as close to a public toilet as you could find in medieval times. Luckily, the inquisitors were after heretics, not sodomites, so Arnaud wasn't burnt at the stake (Ladurie, 1979).

Fast-forward six centuries: In his 1970 book *Tearoom Trade* (Aldine Publishing), Episcopal priest-turned-sociologist Laud Humphreys documented, in unblushing detail, the goings-on in a toilet located in a city park somewhere in the Midwest during the mid-1960s. Toilets used for gay sex were commonly called "tearooms."

Humphreys was able to study this illegal behavior because he pretended to be one of the participants. He did not actually engage in physical contact with anyone, but he posed as a person who was aroused by watching others engage in sex—a voyeur (see Chapter 14). He also served as a lookout who warned the participants of the approach of strangers or police officers.

Humphreys found that the commonest kind of sex practiced in the tearoom was fellatio. Younger or more attractive men generally took the insertive role, and older or less attractive men took the receptive role, suggesting that the insertive role was more desirable. Humphreys collected all kinds of numerical data about the length of time spent in the toilet, the men's movements and signals, and even such minor details as what proportion of fellators swallowed the ejaculate (four-fifths).

Humphreys could not find out much about the participants inside the tearoom because the sex was anonymous—in fact, there was an unwritten rule against verbal exchanges of any kind. He did get to know a few of the men well enough to interview them elsewhere. To get a larger interview sample, however, Humphreys traced over 100 participants by their car license plates. He later called at their homes in disguise, posing as a social health researcher, and by this subterfuge obtained detailed informa-

tion about them. He found that about half of the men were married and living with their wives. Although married, many of these men had "role-segregated" marriages that involved relatively little day-to-day interaction between the spouses.

Humphreys concluded that the tearoom participants fell into several types. Some men were basically heterosexual but were not sexually fulfilled in their marriages, and therefore saw the tearoom as providing a quick, cheap, and non-committal sexual outlet. Some men were bisexual. Some were homosexual, but married and deeply closeted. Others were homosexual and connected to gay society, but used the tearoom for an easy outlet when their regular partners were unavailable.

In general, Humphreys drew rather a sad-sack portrait of the toilet's patrons. Whatever their sexual orientation, these men's furtive bouts of fellatio seemed like futile efforts to experience the intimacy and self-realization that had been denied them in the larger world. None of them were having much fun, or at least that's how it struck Humphreys. He suggested that the "tearoom trade" might wither away if the stigmatization and persecution of gay people were ended, because the tearoom participants would feel better about themselves and would more readily form connections to homosexual society.

Humphreys' book won the annual prize of the Society for the Study of Social Problems, but it evoked both positive and negative reactions. The positive reviews noted Humphreys' skill and courage in exploring a little-known corner of society's sexual underworld. People who criticized the study focused on the fact that Humphreys' subjects did not participate vol-

untarily, or even wittingly, in the study—a violation of the norms of sociological research. In later editions of the book, the publishers milked the controversy for all it was worth, putting reviewer comments such as "A disgracefully poor example of social science research" right on the back cover.

Since the 1970s, the explosion of gay culture has made tearooms less necessary than in the past. But that hasn't dimmed some gay men's interest in them. Apparently, present-day gay men seek out partners in public toilets more for thrill-seeking purposes than from necessity. In fact, at least three gay-themed feature films touch on the topic: *Taxi zum Klo* (*Taxi to the Toilet,* 1980, directed by Frank Ripploh), *Prick Up Your Ears* (1987, directed by Stephen Frears), and *Get Real* (1998, directed by Simon Shore).

The high point of gay toilet history came in April 1998, courtesy of pop singer George Michael. The multi-platinum icon was arrested for soliciting sex from an undercover police officer in a public toilet in Beverly Hills, California (see photo). Michael was convicted of lewd conduct and fined $810, but he more than recouped his losses with his music video *Outside,* which reenacted the event with Michael in the role of the policeman. The real police officer, Marcello Rodriguez, responded by suing Michael for $20 million, claiming emotional injury.

There are other subtypes among gay people that form the basis of sexual subcultures (Figure 13.4A). Among gay men, there exists an extensive **leather** or **sadomasochistic** culture. Sadomasochism (S/M) is the practice of deriving erotic excitement from inflict-

(A)

(B)

(C)

Figure 13.4 There are sexual subcultures among homosexual men. These are the covers of three magazines serving different sexual interests.

ing or undergoing pain, punishment, or degradation (see Chapter 14). S/M "tops" or "masters" bind, slap, beat, whip, pierce, or verbally abuse "bottoms" or "slaves," usually in a carefully orchestrated manner that allows for the "bottom" to terminate the session if it gets too intense. People who are into gay S/M consider the practice to have therapeutic or even spiritual significance (Beam, 1994; Thompson, 1991). S/M practitioners generally wear leather, but not all gay men who are into leather are S/M practitioners; in other words, S/M and leather are two partially overlapping subcultures.

S/M practitioners are not necessarily gay, of course, but they are a far more visible and accepted subculture within the gay community than in the heterosexual world. Leather bars are common in gay communities. Gay leather art is widespread: artist Tom of Finland and photographer Robert Mapplethorpe were both well known for their portrayals of the subculture. Some lesbians are also into leather or S/M practices (Samois, 1987). Although psychiatrists may label sadomasochism a mental disorder, most gay people think of it as a normal but minority sexual interest. To get away from the medical connection, some gay men and lesbians construe S/M as standing for "sex magic" or "sensuality and mutuality."

Another gay subculture is that of **bears** (Wright, 1996). A stereotypical "bear" is a big, bearded man with plenty of body hair and a noticeable beer gut (Figure13.4B). It's not really appearance or body type that defines a bear, however, so much as an attitude: specifically, a rejection of the necessity to conform to the "pretty boy" or "muscle boy" images so popular elsewhere in the gay world, combined with a warm, nonjudgmental personality. Bears generally pair up with other bears fairly like themselves, but older bears may also pair up with younger "bear cubs." There are numerous social organizations for bears in most parts of the United States.

Lesbians don't have such prominent sexual subcultures as gay men, although, as just mentioned, some lesbians are into S/M practices. Lesbians do have innumerable *social* subcultures, ranging from literary salons to softball leagues to women's music festivals. The latter are Woodstock-like events, but they combine music with art, crafts, discussion groups, and many other activities. The grandmama of these festivals is held in Michigan in August; it attracts thousands of lesbian, bisexual, and other woman-identified women (Michigan Womyn's Music Festival, 2002).

Some Gay People Are Parents

Because sex between two men or two women is nonprocreative, you may think of lesbians and gay men as being childless. That's not necessarily the case. In one national random-sample survey (Yankelovich Partners, 1994), women who identified as homosexual were almost as likely to be mothers as women who did not (Figure 13.5). Homosexual men were much less likely to be fathers than straight men, but even so, 27 percent of them had at least one child.

Where do these children come from? Most come from opposite-sex relationships, such as marriages—many lesbians and gay men have been in such relationships before coming out as gay, or are still in them. Increasing numbers of lesbians and gay men, however, are making parenting a part of their gay experience; they are producing and rearing children as gay couples or, less commonly, as single gay persons.

Gay couples who wish to become parents can avail themselves of most of the reproductive options described in Chapter 10. Lesbians can simply have sex with a man or use artificial insemination, perhaps utilizing sperm from a male relative or friend. Gay male couples can employ a surrogate mother, who may be artificially inseminated or made pregnant through IVF. (In the latter case, the genetic mother could be a female relative of one of the men.) They can also adopt a child. Either way, having a child is an expensive proposition for gay male couples.

The ultimate wish of gay would-be parents is probably for both partners to be the true genetic parents of their child. Some gay male couples mix their sperm prior to artificial insemination. This practice randomizes and conceals the identity of the genetic father, but it does not produce a genetically blended embryo, of course, since only one spermatozoon actually fertilizes the oocyte. Currently, there is no reproductive technology that would allow for the production of a child whose genetic parents are both of the same sex. Developing such a technology would present a major challenge because of the phenomenon of genomic imprinting, which makes it necessary for a fetus to receive both male- and female-derived genes (see Chapter 2).

The legal status of gay parenting is evolving rapidly and varies greatly from state to state (Human Rights Campaign, 2001a). A known homosexual identity used to be the kiss of death for any adoption proceedings. (It was also grounds for homosexual parents to be denied custody after divorces.) In some states adoption by openly gay parents is still difficult or impossible. Florida has a law banning adoption by gay individuals or couples; that law has been challenged in the courts, but unsuccessfully so far. Some other states, however, have policies that allow for adoption by single gay persons or gay couples, as well as arrangements by which the same-sex partner of a biological parent can be declared an adoptive co-parent. The American Academy of Pediatrics has put itself on the record as supporting same-sex co-parent adoptions (American Academy of Pediatrics, 2002).

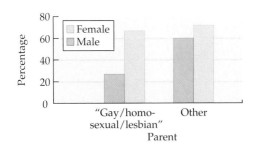

Figure 13.5 Gay parents. The graph shows the percentage of homosexual and non-homosexual U.S. men and women who are parents of at least one child. (Data from Yankelovich Partners, 1994.)

Gay parents John Ross and Don Harrelson with their children Jake and Jennifer.

The Children of Gay Parents Generally Thrive

In the past, people opposed to gay adoptions or gay parenting argued that the children would be exposed to immoral behavior, and that they might become gay themselves as a result of inculcation or even seduction. (Anti-gay activists have often painted gay people as child molesters, and have also claimed that molestation during childhood results in homosexuality in adulthood; see Chapter 14.) With the increasing acceptance of gay people, opponents have switched to potentially more rational arguments, claiming that children need both a male and a female parent for normal development, or that children of gay parents will suffer from taunting and prejudice, especially at school.

What *is* life like for the children of gay parents? First, we should point out that the majority of such children are produced in a heterosexual union prior to their gay parent's coming out. Oftentimes, these children have to deal with their parents' separation. This may well be a traumatic experience, but it is one that countless children of heterosexual parents undergo, too, and usually survive without lifelong wounds. Somewhat moderating the trauma in such cases may be the children's realization that the difference in sexual orientation was the reason for the breakup, rather than years of strife or abuse. In the past, the gay parent often saw little of the children after the breakup, but these days the children may reside with either parent and are likely to see both. Of course, children who reside with the gay parent may acquire another one if that parent takes a same-sex partner.

For children who are produced or adopted by gay couples, the experience is different. For one thing, they are almost certain to be wanted and loved—gay couples don't have children by accident. Also, they will not have to cope with the memory of a marital breakup (though gay parents, too, may break up eventually, of course).

Many gay couples agree with the notion that children need role models of both sexes, or at least that a child needs a role model of its own sex. Thus, gay male couples who are raising a girl, or lesbian couples who are raising a boy, may ensure that a same-sex role model is available in the shape of a close family friend, for example. Other couples dismiss the notion that gender role–modeling is important for healthy development.

Since 1980 there have been no fewer than 21 studies of children brought up by gay (mostly lesbian) parents. According to a recent review of these studies (Stacey & Biblarz, 2001), children of gay parents do not differ significantly from children of heterosexual parents on numerous measures of mental health and social adjustment, or in the quality of their relationships with their parents. There are some differences, however. Daughters of lesbians are more likely to dress and behave in gender-nonconformist fashion than are other girls, and have a greater likelihood of aspiring to careers that are not stereotypically female. They are somewhat more sexually active in their teen and young adult years, are more open to the idea of a same-sex sexual relationship, and are more likely to have actually tried such a relationship.

Sons raised by lesbians are less stereotypically masculine in their childhood behaviors than boys raised by heterosexual parents. They are somewhat *less* sexually active in their teen years than other boys. Like the daughters, they are more open to the idea of a same-sex relationship.

None of the reported differences seem to represent serious negative consequences of gay parenting, and some seem to be quite positive. As to the somewhat higher likelihood of these children engaging in same-sex sexual relationships, this could result from a variety of factors: inheritance of genes predisposing them to same-sex attraction, role modeling, or simply the fact that gay parents do not impose any particular expectations regarding sexual orientation on their children, so that those who happen to experience some degree of same-sex desire will be more likely to act on it.

Children of openly gay parents may suffer a degree of teasing or taunting during preadolescence or adolescence. There is no evidence that this causes long-term harm, however. On the contrary, perhaps as a result of this experience, they become significantly less homophobic, more accepting of social diversity, and more empathetic with disadvantaged groups than do other children (Stacey & Biblarz, 2001).

Homophobia Has Multiple Roots

Antagonistic feelings and behaviors directed toward gay people are very common. They range all the way from the simple belief that all homosexual behavior is morally wrong—an attitude held by 55 percent of all Americans (Butler, 2001)—to the killing of lesbians and gay men by a few hate-filled **gay-bashers.** At least 29 men and women were murdered on account of their sexual orientation or gender identity in the United States in 1999 (National Gay and Lesbian Task Force, 2001).

The word **homophobia** literally means the *fear* of homosexuality, but it has come to be used for the entire spectrum of anti-gay attitudes and behaviors, and that is how we use it here. A variety of different factors probably contributes to homophobia, so it may be difficult to unravel the causes of a particular person's anti-gay attitude or to figure out what sparked a particular hate crime.

Cultural Indoctrination Transmits Homophobia across the Generations

Children and adults learn to dislike homosexuality and gay people by receiving anti-gay messages from parents, teachers, religious authorities, political figures, and so on. The fact that the children of gay parents are more tolerant of homosexuality than are other children (see above) is a simple illustration of that learning process—those children miss out on anti-gay messages from their parents. The messages can be quite vocal and explicit: the Roman Catholic church, for example, labels homosexuality a moral disorder, calls gay sex sinful, and has actively opposed numerous gay rights initiatives in the United States and worldwide. For example, it successfully lobbied the U.N. Fourth World Conference on Women to delete sexual orientation from its anti-discrimination statement (Tempest, 1995).

Anti-gay activist Fred Phelps demonstrates outside the courthouse during the trial of Matthew Shepard's murderers.

Many heterosexual people hold negative beliefs about samesex relationships—that they are less loving and less stable than opposite-sex relationships, for example (Testa et al., 1987). In the past, these attitudes were inculcated by the medical and psychotherapeutic professions. Although it is many years since homosexuality ceased to be listed as a mental disorder, there are still some doctors and therapists who make disparaging statements about gay relationships, perhaps in an effort to drum up support for dubious "conversion therapies" (Nicolosi, 1991; Socarides, 1995).

Silence can also convey an anti-gay message. Examples include the failure of teachers to discourage the use of abusive terms such as "fag" and "dyke," the failure of 24 states to enact hate crime legislation covering sexual orientation, and the failure (until recently) of the media to present positive images of gay men and women.

Although cultural indoctrination is a powerful force, it does not provide an ultimate explanation of homophobia because it does not explain how anti-gay social attitudes arose in the first place. Thus, we have to focus on how individuals may develop or express these attitudes.

A Failure of Empathy May Underlie Homophobia

In Chapter 12 we suggested that the widespread discomfort with the idea of old people having sex arises from a **failure of empathy.** The same process may well occur with gay sex (LeVay, 1996). A heterosexual man, when he thinks about homosexuality, imagines himself engaging in sex with another man. Because he is heterosexual, this idea is a turnoff, and he transfers this aversion to men who actually engage in such behavior. What he fails to do is put himself in the *mind* of a man who is sexually attracted to men.

This model readily explains why homophobic attitudes are directed against gay men much more than against lesbians. Heterosexual men are not turned off by imagining themselves doing what lesbians do, which is to say having sex with a woman. In fact, most heterosexual men are aroused by the idea of two women engaging in sex. Laws have traditionally ignored sex between women rather than punishing it, and hate crimes against lesbians are far less common than those against gay men (Federal Bureau of Investigation, 2001). That's because, until recently, it was heterosexual men who controlled societal attitudes. Of course, there *is* prejudice against lesbians, too, so this prejudice must have other explanations. In part, it probably reflects a belief that lesbians are not subservient to men or dependent on men, and that they therefore threaten men's dominant position in society. In that sense, anti-lesbian prejudice is an aspect of **sexism** (Pharr, 1993). The close involvement of lesbians in the women's movement may have strengthened anti-lesbian prejudice, especially in men who resent the progress women have made toward equal rights.

Homosexuality Is Seen As Transgressive

Another motivation for anti-gay prejudice is the sense that gay people break rules—not just society's rules, but what seems to some heterosexual people to be the natural order of things. Gay people break these rules by engaging in gay sex, but in addition, they may do so by being gender-nonconformist. In fact, the earliest experience of anti-gay prejudice that many pre-gay children experience is really a prejudice against gender transgression. Sometimes this attitude is called **femiphobia** because it is directed most strongly against males who act like females, rather than vice versa. Even some gay men are femiphobic, devaluing other gay men who seem at all feminine. In gay men's personal ads, for example, "masculine" and "straight-acting" are frequently cited as sought-after qualities, while femininity is often dismissed with stock phrases such as "no fats or fems" (Bailey et al., 1997).

People who view lesbians and gay men as transgressors tend to be those who themselves live by very strict rules. They may spend a great deal of psychic energy on controlling the expression of their own emotions. They may see homosexuality as threatening because it invites imitation—not necessarily in the sexual domain, but in the more general sense of "letting go" or "letting it all out." Such individuals are often antagonistic not just to lesbians and gay men, but to a wide range of "transgressive" groups. Thus, what may matter is not the particular hate-inspiring qualities of gay people or other groups, but the psychological structures that imbue some individuals with hatefulness (Young-Bruehl, 1996).

Are Gay-Bashers Gay?

Pursuing this same line of thought, is it possible that people who hate or actually attack lesbians and gay men are themselves homosexual or bisexual? The thinking behind this idea is that a homophobic attitude is part of a defense mechanism that helps these people control, hide from, or mask their own homosexual urges.

One study did come up with experimental evidence in support of this hypothesis. Henry Adams and his colleagues at the University of Georgia recruited two groups of self-described "exclusively heterosexual" men: one group consisted of men who scored very high on an index of homophobic attitudes, while the other group scored low (Adams et al., 1996). The researchers then showed the men videotapes of male–female, female–female, and male–male sex. During the viewing, the men's sexual arousal was monitored by penile plethysmography (measurement of penile erection). When asked, all the men said that they were aroused only by the heterosexual and "lesbian" tapes. According to the plethysmographic data, however, the homophobic men (but not the non-homophobic men) were also aroused by the "gay male" tapes, even though not to the same extent as by the heterosexual tapes (Figure 13.6). The researchers concluded that strongly homophobic attitudes are associated with homosexual feelings that the person denies or is unaware of. More research is needed to reach any definite conclusion on this matter.

Somewhat related to these ideas is the so-called **homosexual panic defense,** a legal strategy that has been used successfully to defend gay-bashers (Green, 1992). This defense is based on the notion that a man with unconscious homosexual urges will react with uncontrollable violence when propositioned for sex by a man (Chuang & Addington, 1988). However, the whole notion of unconscious sexual desires, though promoted by

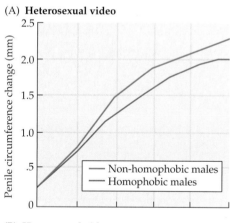

(A) Heterosexual video

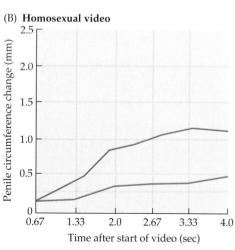

(B) Homosexual video

Figure 13.6 Do homophobic men have homosexual urges? These graphs show the penile responses of homophobic and non-homophobic men, all of whom identified themselves as heterosexual, to heterosexual and homosexual videotapes. Both groups responded to the heterosexual videos, but only the homophobic men responded to the homosexual videos. (After Adams et al., 1996.)

Freud and his followers, has never been clearly documented. Furthermore, the idea that a homosexual panic response is less controllable or voluntary than other forms of violence has little evidence to support it. At the trial of Aaron McKinney, accused of the 1998 gay-bashing murder of Matthew Shepard, McKinney's lawyers attempted to present a homosexual panic defense, but the judge disallowed the defense under Wyoming law.

The Improved Status of Gay People Has Triggered a Homophobic Reaction

Numerous once-stigmatized groups in American society have made progress toward equal opportunity and social acceptance over the last half-century. Very commonly, these advances have provoked backlashes, sometimes violent ones (Avakame, 1999). Some whites see affirmative action as unfairly favoring blacks, some men resent the attention paid to women's issues, and so on. Similarly, some heterosexual people resent the attention that has recently been paid to lesbians and gay men. They may feel that gay people are being given "special rights," or that the television networks are "promoting" homosexuality (Goldberg, 1995).

People who express these ideas most strongly tend to be those who, though belonging to the dominant culture, feel that they have lost out or been unfairly disadvantaged or marginalized. Typically, they have a wide-ranging resentment against many minorities, so that they earn a reputation as "bigots." They may have little specific reason to dislike gay people, but they sense that gay men and lesbians are a relatively vulnerable target.

Overcoming Homophobia Is a Grassroots Enterprise

That homophobia needs to be overcome is, of course, a value judgment that you may or may not agree with. Considerable research has been done on methods to achieve this end, however. Because anti-gay attitudes have such diverse roots, it is unlikely that any one strategy will be successful by itself.

To some extent, the reduction of homophobia can be engineered from above—by the passage of nondiscrimination and hate crime statutes, for example. Twenty-six states now have hate crime statutes that include sexual orientation (National Gay and Lesbian Task Force, 2002). Also, the gay-positive attitudes of prominent people such as former President Bill Clinton doubtless have had a significant effect on public attitudes generally.

Still, homophobic or gay-friendly attitudes are very personal matters that may be difficult to influence by public policy measures alone. Even if this can be done, passing such measures in our democracy requires a considerable degree of popular support. Thus, it is at the level of the individual where the crucial changes must occur.

Social science research suggests that people's attitudes toward gays and lesbians, as in other matters, are most readily influenced by interactions with relatives, friends, co-workers, and other people with whom they have ongoing associations (Sears & Williams, 1997). Recent history supports that view; for example, as mentioned earlier in the chapter, there has been a large increase over the last two decades in the fraction of Americans who know a gay person, and a dramatic easing of anti-gay attitudes over the same period. This, in turn, suggests that further progress will be achieved most readily by a continuation and extension of these interactions, particularly into those parts of America and in those walks of life where they have been sparse up to now. Thus, people who would like to see better acceptance of gays and lesbians (including gay people themselves) have an opportunity to work toward this goal many times a day in the course of their regular lives.

Bisexuals Are Caught between Two Worlds

Bisexual ("bi") men and women are people who experience a significant degree of sexual attraction to both sexes. As we discussed in Chapter 7, bisexual women are abundant—probably more abundant than lesbians. The matter of bisexuality in men is more controversial: some sexologists claim that true male bisexuality is rare, or even nonexistent, and that self-described bisexual men are simply gay men who are only partway out of the closet. As we mentioned, studies suggest that many "bisexual" men do later move toward a more exclusive homosexuality, but there are also men who remain self-identified as bisexual over considerable periods of time. In addition, there are heterosexually identified men who have sex with men or male youths as well as with women; this practice is particularly common in societies where marriage is noncompanionate and women are sequestered. Without more information about these men's feelings, it is hard to know whether they should be considered bisexual or not, but they do not consider themselves to be so.

Another complicating matter is that many self-identified bisexuals are not attracted to men and to women in the same way. For example, a bisexual man may be more emotionally attracted to women, but more physically drawn to men (Matteson, 1991). Alternatively, the strength of a person's attraction to one or the other sex may change over the life span. A unidimensional measure of sexual orientation, such as the Kinsey scale, does little justice to these complexities.

Bisexuals are to be envied in one respect because they are open to a wider universe of sexual experience than are exclusively homosexual or heterosexual persons. On the other hand, they also face significant challenges. Antipathy toward bisexuals (**biphobia**) is quite widespread. For one thing, people generally dichotomize sexual orientation—they tend to believe that bisexuals are really either heterosexual or homosexual (Dworkin, 2001). Indeed, many bisexuals themselves start out with the same belief, and as a consequence spend years of their lives (and sometimes a lot of money on therapy) trying to figure out what they "really" are. For bisexuals, the crucial part of the coming out process is letting go of the notion that they must be either gay or straight (Fox, 1991; Weinberg et al., 1995). Even after they have accomplished this realization themselves, they must constantly deal with other people who have not (Box 13.6).

Another potentially harmful stereotype about bisexual people is that they need to express their sexual attraction to both men and women, and therefore are incapable of being in a durable monogamous relationship (Spalding & Peplau, 1997). Possibly this is true for some individual bisexuals—after all, plenty of heterosexual and homosexual people do not stay in relationships long either. But there are also bisexuals who are in durable and monogamous relationships with a partner of either the same or the other sex (Yoshizaki, 1991).

Other negative views that bisexuals may have to contend with are that they are "oversexed" or that they are responsible for the spread of AIDS. In one study of college students, negative attitudes toward bisexuals (especially bisexual men) were more prevalent than negative attitudes toward lesbians and gay men (Eliason, 1997) (Figure 13.7). Part of the reason for this may simply be the interviewees' unfamiliarity with bisexual people: two-thirds of them said that they had no bisexual friends or acquaintances, and those two-thirds had more negative attitudes toward bisexuals than the remainder of the students.

Bisexuals have lagged behind gays and lesbians in developing a community identity (Highleyman, 2000). The 1970s were a paradoxical time for them. On the one hand, there was a wide enthusiasm for the notion that everyone is (or should be) bisexual and gender-blended. This idea was expressed in any number of ways, including the cult movie classic *The Rocky Horror Picture Show* (directed by Jim Sharman, 1975). On the other hand, bisexual women were accused by lesbian feminists of betraying the feminist cause by sleeping with men. Bisexual men were (and often still are) dismissed by gay men as people incapable of coming to terms with their homosexual feelings.

Perhaps in reaction to these mixed messages, bisexuals began to develop their own sense of community. A Bisexual Center was founded in San Francisco in 1976, and various regional bisexual organizations sprang up. Bisexuals formed their own contingents in gay rights marches starting in the late 1980s, and the 1993 March on Washington for Lesbian, Gay and Bi Equal Rights was the first national event to include "bi" in its name. BiNet, the main national-level bisexual organization, was formed in 1990, and several important books by or about bisexuals appeared in the early 1990s (Hutchins & Kaahumanu, 1991; Weinberg et al., 1995; Weise, 1992).

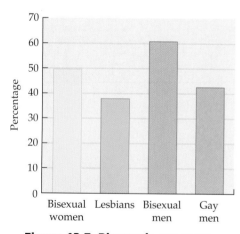

Figure 13.7 Bisexuals are more disliked than homosexuals. The graphs show the percentage of heterosexual college students who rated gay men, bisexual men, lesbians, and bisexual women as either "very" or "somewhat" unacceptable. (Data from Eliason, 1997.)

Box 13.6 *Personal Points of View*

Scenes from Bisexual Life

The following is excerpted from an autobiographical essay by bisexual activist and writer Elizabeth Reba Weise (Weise, 1991):

I came of age in that odd non-time, the 1970s, the decade that felt like a long afternoon nap after the rush and activity of the sixties. So let me begin by explaining how I *didn't* become a bisexual. It wasn't because I have an overactive libido, and it wasn't because it was a hip thing to do in the glitter rock seventies. It did have to do with everything else in the universe, or perhaps nothing.

When I was thirteen I made a list of all the things I wanted to do in my life. Two of the top items were someday having a girlfriend and someday having a boyfriend. I wrote romantic stories about meeting amorous young women over the recorder music files at the library and then falling in love on rainy walks after folk dances. And even in those stories, when the other woman would declare herself to be a lesbian, I'd say, 'And I'm bisexual.' . . .

So I went home to Seattle, bound and determined to finally *be a lesbian*. . . . And before my big chance came again, I fell in love—with a man. We met at a party where the lines of sexual preference were tenuous at best. . . . In that atmosphere your interest and not your persuasion mattered. I remember thinking, 'But he was supposed to be a woman.' However, he *was* clear-thinking and deep-minded and appreciated good science fiction. . . .

That went on for many years. At times we lived together, at times we

Elizabeth Reba Weise

lived apart. During one of those times I went to the lesbian support group at the university the night they talked about bisexuality, and kept going back. One evening a born-again baby dyke, all het up about her newly won status as Oppressed Person, shouted at me, 'You oppress us by sleeping with men! You steal our woman energy!' I stopped going to the support group. . . .

Then, finally, I found a girlfriend. . . . It was a wonderful thing to be young, in love, and a dyke. It was vindication. Walking down the street hand-in-hand just daring anyone to

say anything, I suddenly felt as if everything in my life had fallen into place. I was attracted to a woman. I was in love with a woman. I was a lesbian.

But reality broke through soon enough. There was the fact that I wasn't a 'real' dyke, defined by [lesbian comedian] Kate Clinton as 'penis-pure and proud.' Again, after the honeymoon of acceptance, everyone was waiting for me to renounce my feelings for men. I wasn't part of the family.

My girlfriend and I broke up. I got back together with my boyfriend. I began an existence as a closeted bisexual in the lesbian community. My hair got shorter and shorter. One day I realized that I felt uncomfortable walking down the street hand-in-hand with my lover for fear someone would see us and my cover would be blown.

I moved out again. A friend and I rented a huge old blue farmhouse in the middle of Seattle and by default started a bisexual women's household. . . . We were a feminist bisexual nexus. We held support groups, potlucks, slumber parties, dance parties, and political screaming arguments. It was everything I'd always wanted from the lesbian community, without the fear of being thrown out. Being a part of the Seattle Area Bisexual Women's Network gave me the support to stop worrying about what other people thought about my sexuality and get on with life. We helped each other relearn that it's what you do and not who you sleep with that matters.

Bisexuals debate whether they should ally closely with lesbians and gay men, forge an independent social identity, or act as some kind of bridge between heterosexual and homosexual people. The bisexual community is very much a work in progress.

Transgendered People Cross Society's Deepest Divide

Transgendered women are anatomical females who identify themselves as men or want to become men, and transgendered men are anatomical males who identify themselves as women or want to become women (Denny, 1998). As we saw in Chapter 6, the term "transgender" is employed in a rather broad way to encompass all individuals who feel

Box 13.7 CULTURAL DIVERSITY

Transgenders in Cross-Cultural Perspective

Transgendered men and women have probably existed in all human societies. In fact, they have been recognized and given special names in many societies that have no notion of gay people, even though gay people are (by the criteria of our own society, at least) a lot more common. That is probably because being transgendered is a much more visible and striking departure from social norms than is being homosexual.

In many societies, transgendered people have been accorded a special status in society—often, a spiritual or sacred one. Throughout Polynesia, for example, there existed a class of M2F transgenders known as **mahus**. There was typically one mahu per village. The mahu dressed in female (or a mixture of female and male) attire, engaged in women's activities, and had sex with conventional men. He was attached to the village headman's household and performed sacred dances. He was traditionally accorded high status, and families encouraged or even trained one of their sons to become a mahu. From time to time, a European explorer or trader took a fancy to a mahu and brought "her" to his ship for sex, only to be shocked by the discovery of his male anatomy.

In several Native American cultures, rituals conducted at or before puberty gave a boy the option to choose between the status of a conventional male and that of a transgendered **two-spirit** (male–female) **person,** or **berdache** (Williams, 1986). Among the Tohono O'odham (Papago) Indians of the Sonoran Desert, for example, a boy who seemed to prefer female pursuits was tested by being placed within a brushwood enclosure, along with a man's bow and arrows and a woman's basket. The enclosure was

(A) Amazons battling Greek soldiers

then set on fire. If, in escaping the flames, the boy took with him the bow and arrows, he became a conventional man, but if he took the basket, he became a berdache. The berdaches wore special clothes fashioned from male and female attire, practiced mostly female occupations, and engaged in sexual relationships with conventional men. They were often **shamans** (healers who derived their curative powers from their knowledge of the spirit world), chanters,

dancers, or mediators (see Figure 6.1 for a photograph of the Zuni berdache, We'wha).

The ancient Greek historian Herodotus reported that there were women warriors called **Amazons** among the Scythian tribes north of the Black Sea (Figure A). The Amazons, Herodotus said, cut off one breast in order to use a bow and arrow more effectively. Long thought to be mythical, the existence of Amazons was confirmed by the discovery of female bones,

more comfortable in the identity of the other sex than in that of their own. The term **transexual** is used for the subset of transgendered men and women whose identification with the other sex leads them to request sex change (or **sex reassignment**) surgery. Transgendered and transexual people have existed in most—perhaps all—human societies (Box 13.7).

When transexuals undergo sex reassignment surgery, they do in fact change sex by the usual criterion for "male" and "female," since this criterion depends on genital anatomy. A *female* preoperative transexual becomes a *male* postoperative transexual, and vice versa. Thus the terminology quickly becomes confusing. To keep things straight (though nothing is completely "straight" in the transgender world), people refer to **male-to-female** (M2F) and **female-to-male** (F2M) transexuals. These identifiers remain unchanged after surgery, although many postoperative transexuals like to drop the whole along with weapons, in some Scythian tombs in southern Ukraine (Ascherson, 1996).

A sixteenth-century explorer in northeastern Brazil reported on female warriors among the Tupinamba Indians:

> There are some Indian women who determine to remain chaste: they have no commerce with men in any manner, nor would they consent to it even if refusal meant death. They give up all the duties of women and imitate men, and follow men's pursuits as if they were not women. They wear the hair cut in the same way as the men, and go to war with bows and arrows and pursue game, always in company with men; each has a woman to serve her, to whom she says she is married, and they treat each other and speak with each other as man and wife.

The explorers were so struck by these women that they named the river that ran through the region the "River of the Amazons."

In northern India and Pakistan there exists a large group of M2F transexuals known as **hijras** (Figure B). Indian hijras are devotees of the Hindu goddess Bahuchara Mata, whose temple is at Ahmedabad in the state of Gujarat. Hijras remove their entire external genitalia, dress as women, and earn a living by performing dance ceremonies at marriages and the births of male infants. They engage in receptive anal sex with conventional men, often as prostitutes. The **jogappas** of southern India are very similar to the hijras, except that they do not emasculate themselves.

No persons have suffered more from the global spread of European culture than these transgendered men and women. In Polynesia, the mahus have disappeared or, as in Tahiti, have lost their honored position in society. In India, the British introduced sodomy statutes; these statutes are still a part of the Indian penal code, and are used as justification for police brutality against hijras and other sexual minorities. In the

(B) A hijra performs for a marriage

Americas, the Spanish conquistadors suppressed transgendered people ruthlessly: Vasco Núñez de Balboa, during his famous journey across Panama that led to the discovery of the Pacific Ocean, executed many cross-dressing men by throwing them to his dogs; others were burnt at the stake. In fact, the existence of homosexual and transgender practices among American Indians was presented as evidence of their barbarism and thus as a moral justification for their conquest.

In the United States, berdaches were persecuted by white administrators, often by being forced to return to a conventional male role. On reservations today the Indian words for berdache, such as the Lakota *winkte*, have become terms of abuse analogous to "faggot."

Among the Navajos, berdaches, called *nadle*, were highly respected healers and chanters, but by the 1940s most had died or had been compelled to return to a male role. A tragic reminder that these negative attitudes persist took place in June 2001, when 16-year-old Fred Martinez, Jr., a self-described two-spirit Navajo youth, was bludgeoned to death in a desolate area in Cortez, Colorado. The man convicted of his murder, 18-year-old Shaun Murphy, boasted to friends that he had "beat up a fag," according to a police affidavit. No hate crime charge could be added because the state of Colorado does not include sexual orientation or gender identity in its hate crime statute.

Sources: Nanda, 1990; Quittner, 2001; Williams, 1986.

"transexual" designation and simply get on with their lives as a more or less normal person of their new sex.

In Chapter 6 we also mentioned an important distinction between "classical" or "homosexual" transexuals on the one hand and "heterosexual transexuals" on the other. Homosexual transexuals are M2F transexuals who are sexually attracted to men (**androphilic**) or F2M transexuals who are attracted to women (**gynephilic**): in other words, the designation "homosexual" refers to their sexual orientation with respect to their *preoperative* anatomical sex. Homosexual transexuals often do not feel that they are homosexual or gay, but rather, that they are heterosexual individuals of the sex that they wish to become. Homosexual transexuals usually have a very strong childhood history of gender nonconformity—often, even as young children, they insist that they are of the other sex and refuse to conform to their anatomical sex in clothing, hairstyles, and so on.

Heterosexual transexuals are M2F transexuals who are sexually attracted to women (gynephilic) or F2M transexuals who are sexually attracted to men (androphilic). Heterosexual transexuals often do not have a childhood history of gender nonconformity and may in fact be heterosexually married. In Chapter 6, we mentioned the theory that heterosexual M2F transexuality is a form of fetishism (**autogynephilia**) in which the man is erotically aroused by the idea of himself in a woman's body (Blanchard, 1993). Consistent with this interpretation, many heterosexual M2F transexuals have a history of **fetishistic cross-dressing**—that is, of being erotically aroused by dressing in women's clothes (see Chapter 14). (Homosexual M2Fs may wear women's clothes to feel comfortable or to pass as women, but not for erotic arousal.) Heterosexual transexuals seem to have become more common recently; part of the reason may be that, in earlier years, many of them posed as homosexual in order to meet medical criteria for sex reassignment surgery.

Sex Reassignment Is a Multi-Stage Process

A transexual has what is officially categorized as a mental disorder: **gender identity disorder** (of childhood, adolescence, or adulthood). You might therefore think that the best way to deal with transexuality would be to give the transexual some kind of psychotherapeutic treatment in the hope of bringing their gender identity into congruity with their anatomical sex. Such treatments are rarely, if ever, successful, however. Transexual people generally feel that their gender identity is a central and immutable aspect of their personhood, just as conventionally gendered men and women do. Any attempt to change their gender identity is perceived as a violation of their inner selves. Yet their unhappiness with their situation (**gender dysphoria**) can lead to depression, self-mutilation, or even suicide. Therefore, doctors and therapists have followed a different strategy, helping transexual people to achieve their dream of changing their anatomical sex and their social gender role. Transexuals call this process **transitioning.**

The earliest Americans to receive sex reassignment surgery went abroad for the procedure. A celebrated case was that of George Jorgensen, who had surgery in Denmark in 1952, returned to the United States as Christine Jorgensen, and attracted enormous publicity. The first sex reassignment procedure in the United States was done at Johns Hopkins University Hospital in Baltimore in 1966. By the late 1970s, about 1000 Americans were changing sex every year. The majority of sex change surgeries were in the male-to-female direction, but the proportion that are female-to-male has increased greatly since then.

One way in which a transexual person can change sex is by going to a **gender identity clinic.** These clinics usually follow the standards of care laid out by the Harry Benjamin International Gender Dysphoria Association (Harry Benjamin International Gender Dysphoria Association, 1998). (Benjamin was an American psychiatrist who, in the 1950s, was the first to clearly distinguish transexuality from homosexuality.)

At a gender identity clinic, the sex change process has several distinct stages. First, the client is *evaluated* psychologically and physically. This stage may include psychotherapy, with the goal of probing the client's history, mental health, and motivation, and education about the sex reassignment process and the inevitable limitations of the results.

In the second stage, known as the **real-life experience,** the client lives in the community for a period of time—usually 1–2 years, but sometimes less—as a member of the other sex. The idea is to make sure that the client can function in the desired gender role. This can be a very difficult time for the client because many transexuals cannot pass easily as a person of the other sex without medical treatment (and often not even *after* such treatment). Furthermore, the clinic generally encourages the client to act and dress in a fashion that is very stereotypical for the other sex, which may produce a caricature-like result.

In the third stage, the client is given *hormones* to begin the process of bodily change: estrogens for an M2F or androgens for an F2M transexual. The hormones' effects are not permanent, so hormonal treatment usually continues for life. Sometimes the treatment accompanies or even precedes the real-life experience.

When an intact man is given estrogens, their effects include changes in body fat distribution to a more female pattern, a decrease in the frequency of erections, and possibly a cessation of ejaculations. The breasts may enlarge, sometimes to a degree that makes

In 1952, George Jorgensen created a sensation by having sex reassignment surgery in Denmark and returning as Christine Jorgensen.

later breast augmentation surgery unnecessary. Estrogens do not abolish facial hair or reverse baldness, however. The M2F client often has to undergo a lengthy process of beard removal by **electrolysis**. (In some men, laser treatments may accomplish the same result faster, but experience with this method is still limited.)

When an intact woman is given androgens, a beard appears, though sometimes only a very thin one. The voice deepens, and the body fat distribution changes in a male direction. Because hormones do not remodel the skeleton, however, the general body shape may remain quite similar to that of the client's original sex, so that passing as the new sex may be difficult.

The fourth stage of transitioning is *surgery*. For an M2F transexual, the key procedures are removal of the penis and testicles, construction of a vagina, and breast augmentation (Figure 13.8). Other procedures that may be done include surgery to the vocal cords (to raise the pitch of the voice), reduction of the laryngeal cartilage (Adam's apple), reduction of the nose and some other facial structures, and liposuction to the waist.

For an F2M transexual, surgery can include removal of the breasts, ovaries, oviducts, uterus, and vagina. (The breasts may be removed before the real-life experience if they are large enough to make passing as a man impossible.) In addition, a scrotum and penis may be constructed (**scrotoplasty, phalloplasty**). Removal of the ovaries may have particular significance because, in some U.S. states, it is a requirement for a legal change of sex.

Construction of a penis that looks natural, contains a functioning urethra, and can be made to have an erection (with the aid of a pump/reservoir system or some kind of stiffening device: see Chapter 15) is a very costly multi-stage process, and the results are far from ideal. Frequently, the new urethra develops narrowings (**strictures**) or unwanted openings to the outside (**fistulas**), which necessitate further surgery. Urinary tract infections can occur. Furthermore, there is major scarring in the body region that is used as the source of graft tissue. Because of the expense and the imperfect results, many F2M transexuals forgo a phalloplasty. In some clients, the clitoris can be enlarged by hormonal treatment and surgery (**metoidioplasty**—the spelling varies) to produce a small penis (Figure 13.9) (Hage, 1996). This organ is not generally usable for coitus, but it may be capable of erection and orgasm, and the procedure may also be psychologically and socially beneficial in confirming a male identity. Even with this simpler procedure, however, complications requiring further surgery are common.

The fifth stage of transitioning is surgical, endocrinological, and psychological *follow-up*, which may last for several years. Postoperative transexuals have to make many practical decisions (for example, whether to be open about the sex change or to conceal their past), and they face all kinds of personal and social challenges. Even getting an amended birth certificate may be a struggle.

Establishing sexual and affectional relationships is often extremely difficult. Postoperative transexuals who can pass as members of their new sex have to deal with the problem of whether and when to let their prospective partners know about their history. When a heterosexual man finds out that his female partner was born a man, he may refuse to accept the reality of the sex change, and may therefore reject the woman and possibly even assault her. No wonder so many transexuals choose to make these revelations in the relative safety of the *Jerry Springer Show*. Luckily, there are also people who are willing to accept transexuals as truly belonging to their new sex, or who are even specifically attracted to transexuals. Some transexuals remain in a relationship that existed prior to their transition.

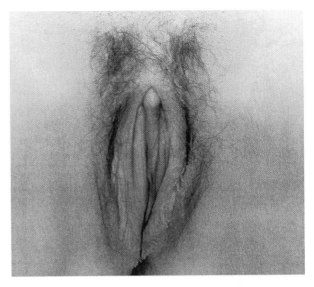

Figure 13.8 The vulva after sex–reassignment surgery. The clitoris is constructed from the top surface of the penis with its nerve supply intact, and may therefore be capable of triggering orgasm. The clitoris and adjacent labial tissue are covered with mucosa derived from the penile urethra, giving them a pink color. The remainder of the penile skin, including the glans, is inverted to form the vagina. Often, additional skin must be grafted from other areas to make the vagina deep enough for coitus. (Courtesy of Eugene A. Schrang, M.D.)

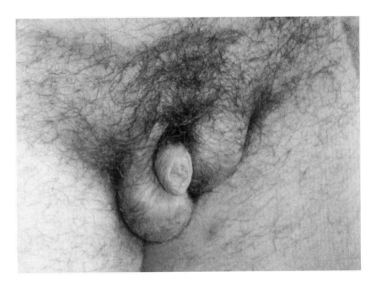

Figure 13.9 Metoidioplasty for F2M sex reassignment. Metoidioplasty is the transformation of the clitoris into a small penis by hormone treatment and surgery. This procedure is a simpler, less invasive, and less expensive alternative to the construction of a large penis usable for penetrative sex (phalloplasty). This F2M transexual also had a scrotum constructed from labial skin, with testicular implants.

These days, most M2F transexuals who seek sex reassignment at gender identity clinics are heterosexual (and probably autogynephilic) transexuals. Homosexual M2F transexuals more often pursue another strategy (Denny & Bolin, 1997): they learn about sex reassignment through peer networks, obtain hormones on the black market, and, when they feel they are ready for surgery, go straight to a private surgeon. Of course, such self-medication carries significant risks.

The long-term outcome of sex reassignment surgery is mixed. Most postoperative transexuals do quite well, while some are dissatisfied, request reversal of the procedure, become depressed, or even commit suicide. Among the factors that correlate with long-term satisfaction are young age at reassignment, good general psychological health, a body build that permits passing as the other sex, good family and social support, and success of the surgical procedures themselves (Eldh et al., 1997). Whether the psychological outcome of sex reassignment surgery is good enough to justify offering the procedure (and for paying for it out of public funds) is still a matter of some debate (Blanchard & Fedoroff, 2000).

Because young age seems to be so important, some centers (especially in Europe) are now treating children at or before puberty. Their strategy is to postpone puberty with drugs such as leuprolide (see Chapter 5), thus preventing the appearance of difficult-to-reverse traits such as a beard or breasts. A few years later, when the child is considered old enough to give informed consent, the definitive hormonal and surgical treatment is undertaken.

One problem that affects most transexuals is the expense of transitioning: sex reassignment can easily cost $30,000 and may run up to $150,000 or more if a multi-stage phalloplasty is involved. Governments and insurance companies provide little or no assistance in most cases. (Medicaid does sometimes pay for sex reassignment surgery, however.) How is a teenager or young adult to raise this kind of money in a hurry? Not uncommonly, the answer is through prostitution (see Chapter 19).

Some Transgenders Do Not Want Surgery

The whole philosophy behind transexuality and sex reassignment surgery is *medical:* the idea is that transexuals have a "problem" that needs to be "treated" in order to make them "well." Not all transgendered people accept this medical model. To some, it is *society* that has a "problem" with gender-variant people, and it is society that needs to be "treated."

Certainly it is true that contemporary U.S. society has what seems like a pathological aversion to transgendered people, who are victimized by abuse and hate crimes at a much higher rate than are lesbians and gay men. Could it be that the desire to undergo sex reassignment surgery represents the internalization of these hostile attitudes? Kate Bornstein, a gender theorist who is herself a postoperative M2F transexual, puts it this way (Bornstein, 1994):

> People think that they have to hate their genitals in order to be transsexual. Well, some transsexuals do hate their genitals, and they act to change them. But I think that transsexuals do not 'naturally' hate their birth-given genitals—I've not seen any evidence of that. We don't hate any part of our bodies that we weren't taught to hate. We're taught to hate parts of our bodies that aren't 'natural'—like a penis on a woman or a vagina on a man.

As Bornstein sees it, the way to "treat" transexuality is to get rid of society's rigid gender norms and the force that she believes maintains them—sexism:

> Doing away with gender is key to doing away with the patriarchy, as well as ending the many injustices perpetrated in the name of gender inequity.... The struggle for women's rights (and to a lesser degree men's rights) is a vital stopgap measure until we can do away with the system whose very nature maintains the imbalance and prohibits any harmony.

Kate Bornstein, an M2F transexual, believes that social pressures force people into impossible-to-live-up-to gender categories.

Many transgendered people do not have sex reassignment surgery, for a wide variety of reasons. They may not have the money, they may be put off by the less than ideal results, or they may be perfectly satisfied with cross-dressing and "passing" as a person of the other sex. This choice also gives them the option of switching between male and female roles. They may even get satisfaction from *not* passing—from being recognizable as a "gender outlaw" rather than trying to deceive everyone. If they move to a city such as San Francisco or West Hollywood, where people are used to all kinds of gender diversity, they will be relatively safe and accepted. Still, a recognizably transgendered person is a potential target for abuse anywhere in the United States.

The debate between those who accept a medical model of transexuality and those who reject it has practical implications. For one thing, it affects the issue of whether medical insurance companies and governments should pay for sex reassignment surgery. It also affects the issue of discrimination against transgendered people. In July 2001, for example, a New Jersey appeals court ruled that transexuality could be considered a "handicap," thus allowing an M2F transexual who was fired from his job to sue his employer under state laws that protect disabled people. Without the medical model, such a recourse would not be available.

Transgenders and Transexuals Struggle for Awareness and Acceptance

Transgendered people have had a difficult struggle to gain recognition as a group distinct from lesbians and gay men. Of course, the introduction of sex reassignment surgery in the 1960s, with all the attendant publicity, did educate the public about the phenomenon of transexuality, but it also caused most people to accept the medical model of transexuality, which, as just mentioned, is rejected by some transgenders.

One factor that has hampered the advancement of transgendered people is that they are relatively few in number. Thus, their political activism has generally taken place under the umbrella of the much larger gay rights movement. Still, like bisexuals, transgenders have fought to clarify their separate identity. In gay rights and gay pride marches and parades, transgendered people form their own contingents, and these events now usually carry names such as "March for Lesbian, Gay, Bisexual, and Transgender Equality."

Legal protections for transgendered people lag behind those for gays and lesbians (Human Rights Campaign, 2001d). Only 4 states (California, Minnesota, Missouri, and Vermont) and the District of Columbia include gender identity in their hate crime statutes, whereas 23 states include sexual orientation. Only 2 states (Minnesota and Rhode Island) plus D.C. have statutes that protect transgenders from discrimination in employment, whereas 11 states protect gays and lesbians from employment discrimination. (Quite a few cities do have nondiscrimination ordinances covering transgendered people, however.)

Intersexuality Raises Complex Social and Ethical Issues

You will recall from Chapter 5 that there are many anomalies of biological development that affect the sexual differentiation of the body or the brain. These conditions include chromosomal anomalies (Turner's syndrome, Klinefelter's syndrome), genetic anomalies affecting sex hormones (androgen insensitivity syndrome, congenital adrenal hyperplasia, 5α-reductase deficiency), and gonadal intersexuality (presence of both ovarian and testicular tissue). In addition to these well-defined conditions, many children are born with anomalous external or internal genitalia whose condition does not fall into any well-characterized syndrome. All these conditions are considered varieties of **intersexuality.** If at some future time a biological basis for transexuality is also documented (right now, there are only hints; see Chapter 6), then transexuality may also come to be considered a kind of intersexuality, but currently it is thought of as a separate condition.

Some intersexes need medical or surgical treatment to save their lives or to correct conditions that greatly interfere with urination, coitus, and the like. They may also request surgical treatment to bring their genital anatomy into a more typical male or female form. However, intersexed people often have nightmarish experiences with the medical profession, starting in early childhood. Often, they become so alienated that they stay clear

Cheryl Chase, founder of the Intersex Society of North America, believes that surgery on intersexed children should, whenever possible, be postponed until the child is old enough to make an informed decision. Here she is addressing the International Gay and Lesbian Human Rights Commission. (Photograph by Donna Aceto.)

of doctors in adulthood, possibly missing out on medical or psychotherapeutic treatments that could benefit them (Box 13.8).

Intersexes are just beginning to build a community and to become socially and politically engaged. The Intersex Society of North America (ISNA) seeks to provide not only support for intersexes but also education and advocacy that will help break down the shame and silence that surrounds them. ISNA's founder, Cheryl (née Charlie) Chase, was born with gonads containing both ovarian and testicular tissue—making her what used to be called a "true hermaphrodite." She also had a small penis, but doctors later reassigned her to be female, whereupon the penis became an excessively large clitoris, and it was cut off. In consequence, Cheryl grew up without the capacity to experience orgasm.

Chase's overriding priority is overcoming the sense of shame associated with intersexuality. This shame is not just psychologically damaging; it is also the main motivation behind the "corrective" surgery done on intersexed children. Most of this surgery is not medically necessary, or could be left until the child is old enough to make decisions for him- or herself, says Chase. It is performed because doctors and parents want above all to get rid of anatomical deviations; they want to "normalize" the child. Yet this cannot be done with any confidence until the child is able to communicate what is "normal" for him or her. Although Chase faces considerable resistance, there is a gradual movement among pediatricians to rethink the traditional notion of early surgical intervention in the treatment of intersexed children.

Despite being an advocate for intersexes, Chase acknowledges the biological and cultural primacy of male and female. "I'm not a radical postmodern theorist who wants to deconstruct sexuality," she says. "I don't think it's realistic or beneficial to encourage parents to bring up children with an intersex identity." What she does want is for doctors to communicate with parents, parents with children, and adult intersexes with the public.

Are Boy-Loving Men a Sexual Minority?

Some men are predominantly attracted to youths or boys who may be under the legal **age of consent.** (Age of consent laws are complex and vary from state to state; in most U.S. states where male–male sex is legal, the age of consent is 16, 17, or 18.) Some of these men are **pedophiles**—defined medically as people who are sexually attracted to prepubertal children (see Chapter 14). A greater number are attracted to pubescent or postpubescent teens.

Men who actually engage in sexual behavior with underage youths risk arrest and lengthy prison sentences. So do men who produce, sell, or buy pornographic or other representations of such behavior or pictures of underage boys or youths that are deemed indecent (see Chapter 19). Thus, the activities of boy-loving men are greatly restricted. However, they are at least theoretically entitled to freedom of thought and political expression. Their main voice is the North American Man–Boy Love Association (NAMBLA), which was founded in Boston in 1978 (see Figure 13.4C).

NAMBLA advocates the abolition of all age of consent laws. It argues that at least some boys are capable of giving meaningful consent to sex, that noncoercive man–boy sexual relationships are harmless and in fact potentially beneficial to the boy, and that other laws offer protection against genuinely abusive adult–child sexual relationships. It also points out that some other cultures have tolerated or even encouraged man–boy relationships, and that some widely admired figures have been sexually attracted to boys or have been accused of engaging in sexual contact with them (Box 13.9). NAMBLA paints age of consent laws

Intersex activists and supporters demonstrate against genital surgery on intersexed children.

Box 13.8 *Personal Points of View*

What It's Like to Be Intersexed

Sherri Groveman, a 42-year-old tax lawyer, lives alone in a ranch-style home in one of the sun-baked suburbs of San Diego. She's a pleasant, forthright, freckle-faced, *womanly* woman. So why, within a few minutes of the start of our interview, did I innocently ask: "And did you enjoy playing with other boys—girls, I mean?"

I blushed and apologized, but Groveman wouldn't let me get away with it. It was a Freudian slip par excellence—evidence that a part of me considered her a male, regardless of all the evidence to the contrary. And the reason? Because I knew that she had been born with testes, and that every cell in her body contained an X and a Y chromosome—usually the biological signature of a male.

Groveman has androgen insensitivity syndrome, which has made her developing body unresponsive to the testosterone secreted by her testes. She was born with the outward appearance of a girl, but lacking the internal reproductive tract of either sex (see Chapter 5).

Sherri's condition was recognized a few weeks after birth when her testes, in the attempt to migrate down into her nonexistent scrotum, became lodged in her groin, where they could be felt as lumps. They were removed surgically, out of concern that they might become cancerous. (This is a legitimate concern in all cases of undescended testicles, but such cancers rarely occur during childhood, so the operation could have been put off for many years.) Sherri was brought up thinking that she had had hernia surgery, but an occasional remark from her mother, to the effect that "not all girls could become mothers," hinted that more might be amiss.

Because Sherri now lacked gonads of any kind, she would need hormone replacement to bring about the bodily changes associated with female puberty. When she was eleven, her mother prepared her for this by telling her something slightly closer to the truth: that she had been born with "twisted ovaries" that had been removed to prevent cancer. (The twisted-ovaries story, says Groveman, is a "lie heard round the world"—a standard cover-up recommended by doctors, intended to protect the growing girl's sense of her own femininity.) Sherri learned that she would not menstruate and could never bear children, but she did not learn the real cause, nor was she told of possible difficulties in her sex life.

After this 10-minute conversation, she did not discuss the matter with either of her parents for the next 28 years.

With puberty, her private shame threatened to become a public one. She developed most of the outer features of a woman, but she did not grow pubic hair, which depends on androgens in both men and women. So she had to conceal her lower body in school showers and locker rooms, and from future boyfriends. Worse, she found that her vagina was too narrow and short. "Everyone was using tampons," she says, "so I bought some and tried putting one in, but it hurt like hell, because of the narrow entry-way." And her vagina was less than 2 inches long—too short for intercourse.

Convinced that she had a dirty secret for which she herself was to blame, Groveman became a "gregarious loner"—outwardly sociable, but shunning intimacy with anyone. The only time her condition was discussed was at her periodic endocrinological checkups. The discussions were not with Groveman herself, though, but among the doctors and medical students who gathered around her crotch. She was told nothing about her condition, and she was asked nothing about her psychological health.

At age 21, Groveman figured out the cause of her condition on her own by rummaging through textbooks in a medical library. She was devastated—not so much at discovering her intersexed status, but at discovering she had been lied to for two decades by parents and doctors. This discovery led to her complete estrangement from the medical profession: she stopped taking estrogens and didn't see a doctor for another 14 years.

"Finding out about myself the way I did really damaged me," she says. "I thought, 'How can I embark on a relationship and not tell my partner? I'd be participating in that same lie that was told to me.' And yet I thought I would *have* to lie. After all, no one told me the information, so I thought it must be so horrible, such a hideous and freakish thing, that if I told anyone else they would bolt."

At the age of 35, however, she did go back to a doctor; she was in a tentative relationship with a man and wanted to know if anything could be done to help her have vaginal intercourse. The doctor confirmed that Groveman had AIS and put her back on estrogens to correct the severe osteoporosis

that had been brought on by the lack of hormones. She also recommended that Groveman use vaginal dilators—plastic tubes that she was to sit on for 15 minutes twice a day. Although these dilators do help some women, Groveman did not like them, and she eventually broke off the relationship with her boyfriend.

In all those years, Groveman had never met anyone resembling herself, and this, she says, was the deepest cause of her loneliness and shame. A few months after the breakup with her boyfriend, however, she came in contact with an AIS support group that was forming in England, and she flew over to attend the inaugural meeting. "There was nothing I would not have given to participate," says Groveman. "I would have cut off my arm—I was that desperate to look into someone else's eyes and have them know what I was experiencing." She has been back for ten subsequent meetings, and she has herself founded a U.S. support group that works closely with its U.K. counterpart (see Web Resources).

The support groups believe that AIS children, like other children, will grow up into sexual adults, but that this development cannot take place properly if the child is sentenced to "solitary confinement," wondering if they are the only person who suffers from a condition so shaming that no one will talk about it. Thus, the groups believe that the best way for parents and affected children to get over their anxieties is to meet and socialize with others who have similar experiences.

Although Groveman identifies as a woman, her identity as an intersex is now just as important to her. Indeed, she is waging a small campaign to have the intersex status more widely recognized: in the "M/F" box on the census form she wrote "I (intersex)", and she is trying (unsuccessfully so far) to have the same designation included on her driver's license. "I want people to acknowledge the reality of intersexes," she says. "I'm not asking for unusual accommodations."

Groveman doesn't attribute her problems solely to victimization by society. "It's going to be horrible no matter what, there's no way around it," says Groveman. "But I was never sorry that I was born intersexed. I wouldn't trade. This is who I was meant to be in this world."

Source: LeVay, 2000.

Box 13.9 *Sex in History*

Boy-Loving Americans?

In winter I take my eel-basket and eel-spear and travel out on foot on the ice—I have a small axe to cut holes in the ice.

Behold me well-clothed going gayly or returning in the afternoon, my brood of tough boys accompanying me,

My brood of grown and part-grown boys, who love to be with no one else so well as they love to be with me,

By day to work with me, and by night to sleep with me.

In *Leaves of Grass,* the collected works of the celebrated American poet Walt Whitman, are many passages like the one above that express Whitman's love of boys or young men. Was this love simply a matter of romantic friendship, or did it include sexual attraction and sexual behavior? We may never know for certain, but Whitman's diaries, the recollections of men who knew him, and other historical sources all suggest that it was sexual (Katz, 1992; Shively, 1986).

Henry David Thoreau, social critic (*Civil Disobedience*) and lover of nature (*Walden*), was captivated by pubescent boys. "Those young buds of manhood in the streets are like buttercups in the meadows," he wrote in his diary. At the age of

Walt Whitman (1819–1892)

22, Thoreau fell in love with an 11-year-old boy, Edmund Sewall. After the two went for a week's sailing vacation together, Thoreau wrote a poem beginning, "Lately, alas, I knew a gentle boy,/Whose features all were cast in Virtue's mould,/As one she had designed for Beauty's toy,/But after manned

him [i.e., subsequently turned him into a male] for her own stronghold" (Katz, 1992).

Pop singer Michael Jackson's love of children has long been public knowledge. In general, there has been no suggestion that this love represents anything other than altruistic benevolence. In 1993, however, Jackson was sued by a 13-year-old boy and his parents: they alleged that Jackson, who befriended the boy when he was 12, engaged in sexual behavior with him during a sleepover at Jackson's Neverland ranch. The matter was settled out of court for an amount that has been reported to be in the $15–20 million range. Jackson has consistently denied any impropriety, and a criminal investigation was dropped.

D. Carleton Gajdusek won the 1976 Nobel Prize in physiology or medicine for his research on infectious brain diseases resembling mad cow disease (transmissible encephalopathies). He adopted dozens of boys and youths from Papua New Guinea, where he did fieldwork. In 1996, at the age of 72 and while he was director of a research unit at the National Institutes of Health, Gajdusek was charged with having repeated sexual relations with one of these youths, starting when the youth was 15. He was convicted and given a 30-year prison sentence, of which all but 1.5 years were suspended.

as violating not just the rights of boy-loving men, but also those of man-loving boys. Its Web site carries numerous testimonials that are stated to have been written by such boys. NAMBLA does not advocate the legalization of coercive sex, nor does it recommend breaking the law. It does provide outreach to incarcerated sex offenders, however.

There are possible rebuttals to most of NAMBLA's arguments. While it does appear that older boys are not necessarily traumatized by consensual relationships with adults (Green, 1992), such relationships may cause them to become prematurely sexually active, which introduces a variety of health and social risks. There is also the question of parents' rights if a man engages in sex with their child without their consent. And the fact that other cultures have condoned man–boy sex does not in itself show that such behavior is morally acceptable for our own culture. After all, allowing small boys to work as chimney sweeps (climbing up chimneys to clean them from the inside) should not be acceptable today simply because it was acceptable in nineteenth-century America.

NAMBLA has attempted to form connections with the gay community, but has often been rebuffed; it has rarely been allowed to form contingents in gay pride and gay rights marches, for example. In general, gay activists have tried to keep boy-loving men at a distance out of concern that their own image will be tarnished by any link. In 1994 the International Gay and Lesbian Association ousted NAMBLA from membership in the association.

In September 2000, the parents of a 10-year-old Massachusetts boy who had been sexually assaulted and murdered by two men brought a $200 million lawsuit against NAMBLA, claiming that the men had been incited to commit the crime by reading NAMBLA's literature and by visiting NAMBLA's Web site. The American Civil Liberties Union has undertaken NAMBLA's defense. "We take the Supreme Court seriously when it says that the First Amendment is there to protect unpopular speech," an ACLU board member said (Terry, 2000).

Summary

1. The idea that same-sex desire defined a specific class of "homosexual" persons first became prevalent in the late nineteenth century, as a result of urbanization, the rise of companionate marriage, and the writings of sexologists. Initially, homosexual men and women were thought of as "congenital inverts"—persons born with many physical and psychological traits of the other sex.

2. In the twentieth century it became apparent that homosexual people were not all of a kind. This led initially to the concept of a "butch/femme" or "top/bottom" duality, but more recently it has become apparent that gay people include a wide variety of "types" that cannot easily be shoehorned into gender categories. Sexual orientation is a more fluid concept than originally conceived, especially for women.

3. The modern gay rights movement began in nineteenth-century Germany and spread to the United States after the Second World War. A key event was the Stonewall Rebellion, a riot in New York City in 1969 that led to the politicization of the gay community. The AIDS epidemic, which began in the late 1970s, devastated gay male communities. It was also the spur to more effective political action and to greater openness on the part of gay people.

4. The rapid advances made by lesbians and gay men have made them the focus of a cultural conflict between conservative and progressive forces in American society. The same conflict is playing itself out worldwide; in some countries, gay people have gained greater acceptance than in the United States, while in others they are more severely stigmatized.

5. Pre-gay children who are gender-nonconformist typically experience taunting, abuse, or efforts to normalize them. For gay people, psychological development is a process of "coming out." This process involves several stages: self-realization and self-acceptance, disclosure to others, joining the gay community, and integrating one's homosexuality with other aspects of one's cultural identity.

6. Gay sex and gay relationships are quite similar to their heterosexual counterparts. Gay men tend to be more sexually adventurous and to have more partners than lesbians or heterosexual people, but monogamous gay relationships are also common.

7. Many lesbians and some gay men become parents, either in earlier heterosexual relationships or as a result of a variety of reproductive strategies that are open to gay couples. The children of gay parents generally thrive: they may experience some taunting in school, but they are as well-adjusted as the children of straight parents, and they tend to be more tolerant and empathetic. They are more open to the idea of entering into homosexual relationships themselves.

8. Anti-gay attitudes and behavior (homophobia) have multiple roots. These roots include cultural indoctrination, an instinctive aversion to the idea of engaging in sex with a same-sex partner, an image of homosexuality as a transgression of social rules, a defense mechanism against one's own real or feared homosexual tendencies, and a backlash against the recent social advances of the gay community. Overcoming homophobia depends primarily on personal interactions at a grassroots level.

9. Bisexual men and women have the advantage of a wider potential range of sexual experience, but they also face social stigma (biphobia). They may be mischaracterized as closeted gay people, as oversexed, as spreaders of AIDS, or as inconstant partners. Bisexuals have attempted to forge a social and political identity that is at least partially separate from that of gay people.

10. Transgendered people identify with or want to become the other sex. Transgenders have existed in most cultures and have often played a respected role in society, but in the contemporary United States they are exposed to widespread abuse.

11. Transexuals are transgendered people who seek sex reassignment. Homosexual and heterosexual male-to-female transexuals differ greatly in their life histories and in their reasons for seeking sex reassignment.

12. The sex reassignment process (transitioning) involves several stages, including evaluation, real-life experience in the gender role of the other sex, hormonal treatment, surgery, and postoperative follow-up and counseling. The results of sex reassignment surgery are far from perfect, but the psychological outcome is usually quite good, even though transexuals face serious challenges in their sexual and social relationships.

13. Some transgendered people do not want sex reassignment surgery. They may simply live full-time or part-time in the role of the other sex, or in a gender-blended role, not "passing" as either male or female. To some, the goal is to break down the social institution of gender.

14. Transgendered people are becoming increasingly active politically and are beginning to receive more understanding and acceptance, along with legal protections in a few jurisdictions.

15. Intersexed people have biological conditions affecting sexual differentiation. Many intersexes become inculcated with a sense of shame and isolation and may experience great difficulties in establishing intimate relationships. Some intersexes have organized to fight against what they consider potentially harmful surgical procedures that are performed on many intersexed children.

16. Boy-loving men are an extremely stigmatized group whose desired sexual relationships are severely punished. The organization that represents these men, NAMBLA, challenges the limits of First-Amendment (free-speech) rights.

Discussion Questions

1. How do your views on homosexuality compare with those of your grandparents, your parents, and your college peers?

2. Imagine you are recently married and about to have your first baby. Everything looks perfect. Then the baby is born, and you learn that the child's genitalia are not clearly male or female. As parents, would you use surgery and/or hormonal treatments to transform the child into something more like a normal male or female? Would you do nothing until the child could choose? What would you choose to do, and why?

3. You and your partner have three children, and one of them is very gender-nonconformist. He is a boy who loves ballet, is very feminine, and wants to play with his sister's dolls and wear her clothes. He says he really should have been a girl. As parents, how would you respond to this? What would your thoughts and actions be?

4. Your very best friend or your close cousin confides in you that they are homosexual and are desperate to have a child. Would you support this choice? Why or why not? What do you think the effect on the child might be?

5. You are a board member of a local school district. This school district proposes to start a program in which openly gay faculty would provide support, information, and role models for students. Would you support or discourage this program? Give a rationale for your answer. What would the effect of the program be on the students?

6. What are your beliefs, attitudes, and values in relation to boy-loving men? If you were asked to testify before a government panel about the rights of this group, what opinion would you give? Would you be concerned if your son were exposed to materials from this group? Why or why not?

7. Imagine that you have always been attracted emotionally and sexually to your own sex, and that your family has rather traditional religious and conservative views. Would you tell your family? If you were to disclose your sexual orientation to your family, how would you do it? What do you think their response would be?

Web Resources

Human Rights Campaign (political and educational organization for the gay, lesbian, bisexual, and transgender communities) www.hrc.org

National Gay and Lesbian Task Force (serves the same communities as the Human Rights Campaign, but with an emphasis on grassroots activism) www.ngltf.org

American Civil Liberties Union—Lesbian and gay rights page
www.aclu.org/issues/gay/hmgl.html

Lambda Legal Defense and Education Fund www.lldef.org

BiNet USA (main national bisexual organization) www.binetusa.org

International Foundation for Gender Education (transgender/transsexual organization)
www.ifge.org

Gender Education and Advocacy www.gender.org

Intersex Society of North America www.isna.org

Androgen Insensitivity Syndrome Support Group www.medhelp.org/www/ais

North American Man/Boy Love Association www.nambla.de

Transsexual Women's Resources (extensive site for M2F transsexuals with detailed coverage of medical and surgical issues) www.annelawrence.com/twr/

FTM International (for F2M transgender/transexuals) www.ftm-intl.org/

Parents, Families and Friends of Lesbians and Gays (PFLAG) www.pflag.org

Recommended Reading

Dreger, A. D., ed. (1999). *Intersex in the age of ethics.* Hagerstown, MD: University Publishing Group.

Faderman, L. (1991). *Odd girls and twilight lovers: A history of lesbian life in twentieth-century America.* New York: Columbia University Press.

Garber, M. (1995). *Vice versa: Bisexuality and the eroticism of everyday life.* New York: Simon and Schuster.

Herek, G. M., ed. (1998). *Stigma and sexual orientation: Understanding prejudice against lesbians, gay men, and bisexuals.* Thousand Oaks, CA: Sage Publications.

Hutchins, L., and Kaahumanu, L. (1991). *Bi any other name: Bisexual people speak out.* Boston: Alyson.

Martin, A. (1993). *The lesbian and gay parenting handbook: Creating and raising our families.* New York: HarperPerennial.

Rust, P. C. R., ed. (2000). *Bisexuality in the United States: A social science reader.* New York: Columbia University Press.

Sandfort, T. G. M., Brongersma, E., and Naerssen, A. X. (1991). *Male intergenerational intimacy: Historical, socio-psychological, and legal perspectives.* New York: Harrington Park Press.

Savin-Williams, R. C. (2001). *Mom, Dad, I'm gay: How families negotiate coming out.* Washington, D. C.: American Psychological Association.

Siegel, L., and Olson, N. L., eds. (2001). *Out of the closet, into our hearts: Celebrating our gay family members.* San Francisco: Leyland.

Townsend, L. (1997). *The leatherman's handbook* (Silver jubilee ed.). New York: Masquerade Books.

Wright, L., ed. (1997). *The bear book: Readings in the history and evolution of a gay male subculture.* New York: Harrington Park Press.

chapter 14

For some, sexuality is inextricably tied to fetish objects or to behaviors outside the sexual norm.

Atypical Sexuality

*M*ost of us, at one time or another, have experienced a bizarre sexual fantasy or have tried out some "kinky" sexual practice. Such thoughts and behaviors may add spice to our sex lives and help maintain our interest in sexual relationships. However, have you ever been sexually aroused by a horse? Have you ever masturbated while holding an item of lingerie? Have you ever enjoyed having your sex partner inflict pain on you during sex? For some people—mostly men—such unusual sexual desires come to dominate their lives. These desires become problematic when they cause distress to the people who experience them, or when they are acted out in behaviors that harm others or run afoul of the law. In this chapter we describe a variety of atypical sexual desires and behaviors, review theories about what causes them, and consider treatment options.

"Paraphilia" Is the Psychiatric Term for Problematic Sexual Desire or Behavior

There is no precise or objective boundary between normal and abnormal sexual feelings and behaviors. Social norms, moral teachings, legal proscriptions, and medical theories all have something to say on the matter, but they do not necessarily agree, nor does what they say remain constant over time. A century ago, homosexuality lay well outside the bounds of "normal" sexuality: psychiatrists called it a disease, nearly everyone considered it immoral, and the law prohibited it. Nothing has changed about homosexuality itself over the intervening years, but it is now no longer labeled a disease, it is either legal or rarely prosecuted, and it is increasingly accepted as a normal aspect of sexual diversity. Clearly, then, social attitudes strongly color what is considered sexually normal and what is considered abnormal, sick, or wrong.

The sexual revolution has encouraged a more tolerant or accepting attitude toward minority sexual interests, and many of these interests now spark curiosity or amusement more than they do moral concern. Yet there is a point at which unusual sexual interests become problematic and call for treatment or for preventive measures. Most obviously, sexual interests whose expression engages other people without their consent, or that actually harms them, require some kind of intervention. Even when no other person is involved, however, treatment may be called for. The person who experiences unusual sexual desires may be deeply troubled by them. He may feel that his desires are morally wrong. He may fear that he will act on his desires in a way that will harm others or land him in trouble. His life may be so disrupted by compulsive sexual thoughts or behaviors that his relationships and his livelihood are put at risk. Thus, even in this age of sexual permissiveness, there is a need for psychiatrists and other therapists to deal with unusual sexual feelings and behaviors as illnesses that need treatment.

The term **paraphilia** is used by psychiatrists to cover any unusual and problematic form of sexual expression, most of which are seen predominantly or almost entirely in men. According to the fourth edition of the American Psychiatric Association's *Diagnostic and Statistical Manual of Mental Disorders* (DSM-IV), paraphilias are "recurrent, intense sexually arousing fantasies, sexual urges, or behaviors involving (1) nonhuman objects, (2) the suffering or humiliation of oneself or one's partner, or (3) children or other nonconsenting persons. . . . The behavior, sexual urges or fantasies cause clinically significant distress in social, occupational, or other important areas of functioning" (American Psychiatric Association, 1994). In a 2000 revision to DSM-IV, however, the APA made clear that many paraphilias can be diagnosed even if the person who has them does not experience any subjective distress or impaired functioning (American Psychiatric Association, 2000). This is quite a significant shift; it emphasizes that psychiatrists may go beyond responding to clients' complaints and may use their expertise for other purposes, such as protecting society from sex crimes.

The DSM-IV lists seven specific paraphilias—fetishism, transvestism, exhibitionism, voyeurism, masochism, sadism, and pedophilia—as well as unspecified "other conditions." Although we will use this nomenclature in this chapter, we are interested in the entire range of these sexual feelings and behaviors, of which only the extremes fit the definition of paraphilias.

The prevalence of paraphilias is unclear because people are generally unwilling to admit to them. (Paraphilic behaviors are often illegal, especially when they involve other persons without their consent.) The paraphilias that come to medical or legal attention most often are those that involve victims (Figure 14.1).

Fetishists Are Aroused by Inanimate Objects, Substances, or Body Parts

Fetishism is a good illustration of the continuum between normal sexuality and mental illness. Most of us find that certain items of clothing or perfumes enhance a partner's sexual attractiveness—whole industries depend on that fact. For many of us, particular body parts—breasts, penises, buttocks, legs, feet—carry a special erotic charge. For some people, though, it may be impossible to reach orgasm, or to be sexually aroused at all,

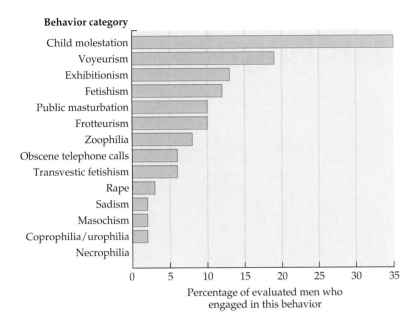

Behavior category

Child molestation
Voyeurism
Exhibitionism
Fetishism
Public masturbation
Frotteurism
Zoophilia
Obscene telephone calls
Transvestic fetishism
Rape
Sadism
Masochism
Coprophilia/urophilia
Necrophilia

0   5   10   15   20   25   30   35

Percentage of evaluated men who
engaged in this behavior

Figure 14.1 The prevalence of paraphilias was evaluated clinically for suspected inappropriate sexual interests. Of course, these behaviors are biased toward those that bring men to medical or legal attention; namely, those that involve victims. (Data from Abel and Osborn, 2000.)

without the presence of those specific items or without focusing on those particular body parts. This condition is called paraphilic fetishism. In moderate paraphilic fetishism, the person still engages in conventional sexual relationships (either heterosexual or homosexual), but attempts to incorporate the fetishistic objects into those relationships. In extreme paraphilic fetishism, the fetishistic items become a replacement for a sex partner: a man may simply masturbate with the preferred objects, or may fondle or lick the preferred body part without engaging in penetrative sex or even treating the partner as an entire person. The latter kind of behavior is sometimes called **partialism.**

Common objects of fetishistic desire are shoes, lingerie, and other items of clothing. Sometimes it is certain materials, such as leather, rubber, or silk, that are arousing. A fetishist may break into a woman's home to obtain items of her clothing. Items such as used jockstraps may be stolen from locker rooms or bought and sold via personal ads in gay magazines.

Besides the body parts mentioned above, a few fetishists are fixated on abnormal anatomical features such as deformed feet or amputation stumps. There are even fetishists who seek to undergo amputations themselves (Box 14.1).

Sometimes fetishists become aroused by certain acts that seemingly have no connection to sex, including such odd things as blowing up balloons or imagining triangles rotating in space (Abel & Osborn, 2000). In short, there seem to be few restrictions on the possible targets of fetishistic desire, but the most common ones are closely associated with women or with sexual activities.

In the pornographic video industry, fetishism is a major growth area: fetish-related videos comprise 25 percent or more of some companies' production. Obviously, only a tiny fraction of the consumers of these videos seek or need psychiatric attention.

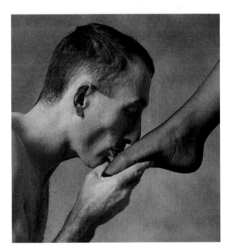

Fetishism is erotic fixation on inanimate objects or, as here, on certain body parts.

People Cross-Dress for a Variety of Reasons

Some people repeatedly or continually wear the clothes of the other sex. Both men and women may **cross-dress,** and they do so with a variety of motives. There may be entirely practical, nonsexual reasons for cross-dressing. Women have often cross-dressed in order to pass as men and thus obtain male employment or other privileges of masculinity. Male attire may be more practical for many activities. In fact, as women have gained increasing parity with men, traditionally masculine attire, such as blue jeans, has become unisex. Men, on the other hand, may dress as women for entertainment purposes ("doing drag"), in which case their clothing, makeup, and hairstyle is likely to be an exaggeration or caricature of femininity (see the photo of a cross-dresser on page 423). None of these practices could be considered a paraphilia.

Box 14.1 Research Highlights

Amputation Fetishes

In early 2000, a Scottish surgeon created a sensation by announcing that he had amputated the legs of two physically healthy men and planned to do the same for a third man. "I have no doubt that what I was doing was the correct thing for those patients," Robert Smith told a news conference. The patients agreed, telling reporters that they were much happier without their legs.

Can the desire to be rid of a limb be a sexual fetish? Yes, according to sexologist John Money of Johns Hopkins University. In 1977, Money and his colleagues described two kinds of individuals: "acrotomophiles," who are sexually fixated on people who have had amputations, and "apotemnophiles," who are aroused by the notion of actually being an amputee (Money et al., 1977). Popularly, these two groups of individuals have become known as "devotees" and "wannabes." Devotees are commoner than wannabes. (Some authors use

"apotemnophile" to refer to either group.) Still other men are "pretenders"—they act as if they have amputations or other disabilities (Bruno, 1997).

Not uncommonly, these three groups overlap. In one case history, a man became aware of an attraction to amputees at the age of 8. Later, he began fantasizing about photographs of amputees, and pretended to be an amputee himself, using crutches or a wheelchair. He eventually sought to have a leg amputated, but could not find a surgeon willing to perform the operation (Everaerd, 1983). Other people have actually cut off their own limbs or penises (Wise & Kalyanam, 2000).

The condition of "wannabes" seems to have a parallel with autogynephilia, a condition in which a man seeks sex reassignment surgery because he is erotically aroused by the concept of himself as a woman (Blanchard, 1993) (see Chapters 6 and 13).

Autogynephilia seems to be an extreme version of heterosexual transvestism. Similarly, someone who is originally a "devotee" may eventually become a "wannabe."

Smith (the Scottish surgeon) disagrees with this interpretation. He thinks that the devotees are indeed fetishists, but that the wannabes have a nonsexual problem with body image, analogous to that suffered by anorexics, who are obsessed by the notion that they are too fat. Given the difficulty of treating apotemnophilia with any form of psychotherapy, Smith feels that is justified to carry out the desired operations, just as sex reassignment surgery is justified for classical (homosexual) male-to-female transexuals because psychotherapy does not usually cure their gender identity disorder. Nevertheless, Smith was ordered by his hospital to stop performing the procedures.

Source: Elliott, 2000.

Men and women may also cross-dress because it gives expression to a cross-gendered or "gender-blended" identity. Even "doing drag" often has this flavor: some gay men are very good at doing drag, and derive special satisfaction from it. By doing so, these gay men may be expressing a gender identity that deviates from the more stereotypical masculinity of other men.

Transexuals, of course, are more completely transgendered than any gay men or lesbians, and for them wearing the clothes of the other sex may be a serious expression of their gender identity. Typically, transexuals attempt to *pass* as the other sex, not to *parody* it, although their behavior may be perceived as a parody if they are unsuccessful. As mentioned in Chapter 13, transexuals often have to live as a member of the other sex for a year or so before they become candidates for sex reassignment surgery, and this obviously involves cross-dressing. Importantly, "classical" or homosexual transexuals do not generally cross-dress for purposes of erotic arousal, but simply because those clothes express who they feel they are. Thus, cross-dressing by homosexual transexuals is *not* a paraphilia.

Another class of cross-dressers, however, comprises heterosexual men who wear women's clothes because they find the practice sexually arousing. This trait *is* usually considered a paraphilia, although the practice is often sporadic and harmless. It is also a kind of fetishism, and is therefore referred to as **transvestic fetishism,** or simply **transvestism.** (You will sometimes see the word "transvestism" used to refer to the non-paraphilic cross-dressing behaviors described above, but DSM-IV restricts its use to cross-dressing done for purposes of fetishistic sexual arousal.)

Some heterosexual transvestites have fantasies of themselves as seductive women when they cross-dress. Most heterosexual transvestites cross-dress in secret, but some venture out in public while cross-dressed, and they may be sexually excited by doing so.

It seems that there is a continuum of traits in which heterosexual men's sexual desires move from their usual target—women—to *representations* of women that can be progressively stripped away, co-opted, and internalized. The first stage in this continuum is regular fetishism, in which a woman's identity is represented by an object, such as a piece of feminine attire, that is separable from the woman and can be completely owned and controlled by the man. In the second stage (transvestic fetishism), the clothing that represents the woman is put on, rather than simply viewed or handled. This practice may lead to fantasies of *being* an alluring woman. In the extreme stage, the man seeks sexual satisfaction in actually being surgically reassigned as a woman—the condition known as **autogynephilia** (see Chapters 6 and 13). Certainly, most fetishists do not progress through this entire series of traits, but autogynephiles often have regular fetishism and transvestic fetishism in their history. A fairly typical case history, which illustrates the blurring of fetishism, transvestism, and borderline autogynephilia, is presented in Box 14.2.

Box 14.2 *Personal Points of View*

Heterosexual Transvestic Fetishism: A Case History

Zucker and Blanchard (1997) presented the case history of "Mario," a transvestic fetishist who was seen at the Adult Gender Identity Clinic of the Clarke Institute of Psychiatry in Toronto, who is fairly typical of men with this condition. The following is an abridgement of that case:

Mario was the third of five children born to immigrant parents. In childhood, he was obese and clumsy. He was teased by other boys on account of his weight problem and became a loner with few close friends of either sex. In prepubescence, he was, by his own description, "somewhat antisocial," and he got into a number of fights. This aggressiveness persisted to some extent into later life, and he was arrested three times in adulthood for getting into fights after drinking.

At the age of 11 or 12, Mario began dressing in his sister's clothes when no one was home. He initially wore lingerie, but later came to include dresses and makeup on occasion. Mario was sexually naive at this point and did not understand the arousal he felt when he put on women's clothes.

Mario's first ejaculation occurred at age 14. He was lying face down on his bed wearing a brassiere and panty hose and examining the lingerie pages of a department store catalog. While studying a photograph of a model with panty hose like those he had on, he began unconsciously to thrust against his mattress, with resulting ejaculation. In later life, he continued to find women in lingerie more attractive than nude women and to be more aroused by lingerie advertisements than by pornography. The young Mario realized that there was something unusual about his sexual behavior and wondered for a time if he were homosexual.

In later adolescence and adulthood, Mario's tranvestic and masturbatory activities were accompanied by fantasies of sexual interaction with women. In one favorite fantasy, Mario would cross-dress with a woman's permission (sometimes at her insistence) and then have sex with her in a quasi-lesbian interaction. In a variant of this fantasy, he would *be* a lesbian and, in the aggressive role, make love to another woman. Mario was also sexually aroused by the sight of himself cross-dressed in the mirror. Although he would feel like a woman when cross-dressed, he never developed any desire for hormonal or surgical feminization, and his only fantasies of sex change were of some temporary metamorphosis with a prompt return to the male role. He never fantasized sex with a man and never had any homosexual experiences. He had a number of heterosexual relationships of short duration.

Mario's cross-dressing was to remain, by and large, a private activity. In later years he did, however, occasionally indulge in the thrill of driving around in his car at night dressed as a woman.

At the age of 28, Mario met Maria, a woman 4 years younger than himself and from the same ethnic background. They married 3 years later. The couple had a very active sex life, with intercourse occurring up to 20 times per week. Mario did, however, tend to indulge in private fantasies during coitus, including the fantasy that he and Maria were two women engaged in a lesbian interaction. Maria was completely ignorant of Mario's transvestic behavior.

Mario first consulted a psychiatrist at the age of 32, complaining of headaches and dizzy spells. He initially denied any marital problems, but finally admitted his cross-dressing after several months in treatment. Mario subsequently decided that if he could bring up the subject with a psychiatrist, he could bring it up with his wife.

Maria reacted very negatively to this information. She initially feared that Mario's cross-dressing had something to do with homosexuality, but later came to realize that this was not the case. On the few occasions when Maria saw Mario in women's attire, she became highly distressed, and she grudgingly tolerated his cross-dressing only in her absence. She told Mario that she believed he was afflicted by the "evil eye," and she wanted his cross-dressing to stop, certainly before they began having children.

Mario had, in fact, throughout his life, repeatedly tried to overcome his transvestism, quite apart from any pressure from Maria. Overwhelmed by guilt and shame, he had, on numerous occasions, thrown away his entire feminine wardrobe, with the resolution never to cross-dress again. Prolonged abstinence, however, made him very nervous, and he always returned to cross-dressing when the tension became unbearable.

Source: Abridged from Zucker & Blanchard, 1997.

The Mirror is the magazine of Tri-Ess, an organization for heterosexual cross-dressers.

Certainly, not all heterosexual cross-dressers go this route. For others, cross-dressing may lose some of its sexual significance over time and become a matter of gender expression more than sexual expression. Such men may join Tri-Ess, a support organization that publishes a magazine and organizes events where heterosexual cross-dressers can socialize in a safe and accepting atmosphere.

Heterosexual transvestites tend to have problems in their sexual relationships. Initially, they may conceal their cross-dressing from their female partners, or they may present it as a nonsexual, recreational behavior that has nothing to do with their relationship. Many heterosexual transvestites are married (Docter & Prince, 1997), and their wives may be accepting of their transvestism, initially at least (Talimini, 1982). In time, however, heterosexual transvestites often seek to bring cross-dressing into their sexual relationships, and this may be disturbing to their partners. Even if the woman is liberally inclined, she may come to perceive that her partner is more erotically invested in his own transvestism than he is in her.

Exhibitionists Are Aroused by Women's Reactions

Exhibitionists, or "flashers," are men who expose their genitals to women in public or semi-public places. Typically, an exhibitionist will station himself in some location where women are present, but which offers little danger of his being identified or arrested. As a woman approaches, the man will step into her line of sight and open his coat to expose his genitals. Alternatively, he may take away a book or newspaper that conceals them. During this action, the man typically fantasizes having a sexual interaction with the woman. He may masturbate and ejaculate while doing so; alternatively, he may flee and masturbate later, using his recollection of the event as an arousing stimulus.

An exhibitionist often misinterprets his victim's reactions—whether of shock, fear, or amusement—as a reciprocation of his sexual interest. Because of this **cognitive distortion** on the exhibitionist's part, the women's emotional reactions tend to reward him and promote a continuation of his behavior. Women who encounter an exhibitionist do best to stay calm and simply walk away, although there is the option of attempting to have the man arrested if circumstances permit.

Exhibitionists tend to engage in a series of many self-exposures over the course of a few days, then desist due to guilt or fear of arrest. The behavioral cycle is likely to recur weeks or months later, however.

Exhibitionism is very common. It accounts for over one-third of all convictions for sex crimes in the United States and other countries (Rooth, 1973). Exhibitionists seen at one clinic admitted to having committed an average of over 500 exhibitionist acts each (Abel et al., 1987). Up to half of all adult women have been the victim of an exhibitionist at least once in their lives (DiVasto et al., 1984).

Gay men may also expose themselves or masturbate publicly, but they usually do so in the context of known gay "cruising areas," such as little-visited sectors of parks (see Chapter 13). The main intent of this activity is to draw other gay men into sexual behavior, but it may have a paraphilic significance in itself. This activity may shock nonparticipants who happen to be in the locality, resulting in complaints to the police and the deployment of plainclothes officers to eradicate it.

Related to exhibitionism is **obscene telephone calling,** in which the perpetrator (almost always a man) calls a known or unknown victim (usually a woman) and makes sexual suggestions or utters obscenities. As with exhibitionism, the obscene telephone caller is sexually aroused by the reaction (real or perceived) of the woman he is exposing himself to, the only difference being that the exposure is auditory rather than visual.

Most exhibitionists and obscene telephone callers are shy men who lack social skills, especially in their interactions with women, and have general feelings of inadequacy (Dwyer, 1988; Matek, 1988). The urge to commit exhibitionist acts usually begins in adolescence and persists for many years, but the behavior becomes less common in men over 40.

Women occasionally engage in exhibitionist behavior, but this behavior is usually part of some broader mental illness, not an isolated paraphilia. Some women have been convicted of obscene telephone calling, but these calls are usually acts of revenge against men who they believe have wronged them, rather than being done for purposes of erotic arousal (Matek, 1988).

Voyeurism Is an Exaggeration of Normal Male Behavior

Voyeurs, or "peeping Toms," are men who are erotically focused on watching people (usually women) while they are undressing, naked, or engaged in sexual behavior. Typically, voyeurs carry out their activities in a discreet fashion, such as by peering through a bedroom window from a dark location. Thus, even though they may masturbate while watching, they are usually safe from arrest and may never come to the attention of the women who are being observed. Some voyeurs may use mirrors to peer under women's clothing, or look through peepholes into dressing rooms or toilets. Occasionally, voyeurs may be emboldened to enter people's homes in order to watch them while they sleep. A recent twist on voyeurism is offered by Internet sites that allow people, for a membership fee, to spy on the homes of young women.

Voyeurism is one of the commonest of all paraphilias (Abel & Osborn, 2000). It is an extension of normal male sexuality, which includes a strong visual component. Many adolescent or adult males might take advantage of an opportunity to watch women who are undressed or engaged in sexual activity, especially if they can do so "guilt-free" because the woman's bedroom is in plain sight from their own window or from the street. The popularity of pornographic movies and pornographic images on the Internet reflects a similarly widespread interest. One could speculate that male interest in voyeuristic activities is increased by the general lack of opportunity for men to see naked women or to watch them engaged in sex. This could give nudity and sexual behavior an extra mystery and allure.

Voyeurism becomes a paraphilia when the man derives most or all of his sexual gratification from the practice, and when his activities invade the privacy of others, disturb his own life or relationships in a significant way, or put him at risk of arrest. As with some other paraphilias, the risk of discovery may add to the sexual excitement of voyeuristic practices.

Frotteurism Involves Surreptitious Physical Contact

A **frotteur,** or "masher," is a man who is sexually fixated on having physical contact with others—usually women—in public places without their knowledge or consent. He seeks out women in places that are sufficiently crowded that physical contact goes unremarked—subway cars, elevators, crowded bars, sporting events, and the like. He rubs his hand, leg, erect penis, or an object such as a newspaper against the woman's thighs, buttocks, vulva, or breasts. In doing so, he imagines that he is in an intimate sexual relationship with the woman, or that the woman is enjoying or aroused by the contact. Because he may ejaculate under his clothes during the behavior, the frotteur may wear a plastic bag or plastic wrap around his penis to prevent any visible staining of his clothes. If he is arrested, evidence of such precautions may be used to prove his criminal intent. In general, however, frotteurs are not noticed or apprehended.

Frotteurs seek out locations where they can make bodily contact with women without arousing suspicion.

Sadomasochism Involves the Infliction or Receipt of Pain or Degradation

In regular discourse, the word **sadist** may be applied to any cruel person, and the word **masochist** to anyone who is a "glutton for punishment." Clinically, however, these words are reserved for individuals who are sexually fixated on inflicting or receiving pain or humiliation.

The terms "sadism" and "masochism" were introduced by the late-nineteenth-century German sexologist Richard von Krafft-Ebing (see Chapter 1). "Sadism" is derived from the name of the Marquis de Sade (1740–1814), a French nobleman who described his own sadistic interests in *The 120 Days of Sodom* (Sade, 1976), a book he wrote while imprisoned in the Bastille. "Masochism" is derived from the name of Leopold von Sacher-Masoch (1836–1895), who described his masochistic interests in *Venus in Furs* (Sacher-Masoch, 2000). The terms "sadism" and "masochism" are often combined into the single

A dominatrix is paid to play the sadist role for masochistic clients.

Jeffrey Dahmer of Milwaukee killed at least 17 boys or youths—and dismembered and possibly ate some of them—for sexual gratification. He was killed in prison in 1994.

term **sadomasochism** (**S/M**) because they often coexist in the same person or involve reciprocal interactions between a sadist and a masochist.

Sadomasochism may involve the infliction of physical pain—by spanking, paddling, whipping, piercing, cutting, burning, nipple clamping, or "cock-and-ball torture." Alternatively (or in addition), the emphasis may be on placing someone in a humiliating position by means of restraints (**bondage**) or verbal abuse. The person may be forced to engage in some degrading activity, such as licking their tormentor's boots, wearing a dog collar and leash and being led around on all fours, or being urinated or defecated on. Dominance and submission seem to be the key erotic elements. Sadomasochistic behavior is often associated with the wearing of leather or military uniforms.

Like other paraphilias, sadomasochism is an extension of normal sexual expression. Many or most people can be aroused to some degree by slapping or biting their sex partner, or by being slapped or bitten. Sadists and masochists go beyond that to focus all their sexual attention on the infliction or receipt of pain or humiliation. The usual physiological manifestations of sex, such as erection, ejaculation, and orgasm, play only a minor role, or may even be dispensed with entirely.

Most people are not willing to participate in S/M activities with the intensity or for the duration that sadists and masochists desire, so sadists and masochists often have to seek out partners willing to satisfy them. You might think that this would be an easy matter: sadists ("tops," "doms") could simply pair off with masochists ("bottoms," "submissives")—perhaps through personal ads or the Internet—and go do their thing together. This does happen, but in general, there is a problem with numbers. Masochists are quite a bit more common than sadists, so "tops" are in short supply. Furthermore, both masochists and sadists are much more likely to be male than female. For gay men, of course, that's not a problem: in fact (as mentioned in Chapter 13) there exists a flourishing gay male S/M subculture, most of whose practitioners would roundly deny that there is anything pathological about their activities. For a heterosexual male masochist, one way to satisfy his paraphilia is to pay for the services of a **dominatrix**—a woman who is paid to inflict pain or humiliation, usually in a theatrical, sexually charged fashion. Such a woman is not usually a sadist in the clinical sense. There does also exist a heterosexual S/M subculture, however, in which considerable numbers of women are involved, either as tops or bottoms. There are also S/M communities in which homosexual and heterosexual men and women freely mingle.

Sadomasochistic sexual activity often has a staged quality. A top who is beating a tied-up bottom will pay no heed if the bottom screams and begs the top to desist, but if the bottom uses a prearranged "safe word" or nonverbal signal, the top will desist immediately. Also, S/M aficionados usually take precautions to avoid HIV transmission—an obvious risk if blood is drawn.

All in all, it is debatable whether the members of the S/M culture are truly paraphiliacs. Some of them probably are, in the sense that they are exclusively fixated on S/M activities as a sexual outlet and are incapable of deriving sexual satisfaction in other ways. Many others are in conventional sexual relationships and simply enjoy S/M as part of a varied sexual diet or because it arouses their partners. S/M practitioners rarely come to the attention of clinicians or law enforcement officials (see Figure 14.1), which suggests that their sexual practices do not generally cause distress to either party. In the 2000 revision of DSM-IV, sadism is defined as a mental disorder only if it involves the infliction of pain or suffering on a *nonconsenting* person (American Psychiatric Association, 2000).

There do exist a very small number of persons who are fixated on torture and even murder as a sexual outlet. Some of the most notorious serial killers, such as Jack the Ripper and Jeffrey Dahmer, may have been sadists in the clinical sense (Jentzen et al., 1994). However, such sexual killers often have a complex pathology, including brain damage, psychosis, and a history of severe childhood abuse (Pincus, 2001). There is evidence to suggest that some rapists are sadists, in the sense that they are sexually aroused by the forcible or nonconsensual nature of rape (see Chapter 18). Rape is not in itself categorized as a paraphilia, however.

Some masochists inflict pain or suffering on themselves without the aid of a partner. A particularly dangerous form of this behavior is **autoerotic asphyxia,** in which a person derives erotic arousal from self-strangulation (Box 14.3).

Box 14.3

Research Highlights

Autoerotic Asphyxia

"When you find my body hanging . . . with a tight noose around my neck, do not look for a murderer. I have executed myself. I say execute rather than suicide because I didn't really intend to hang unto death." This cryptic note was found next to the strung-up, half-naked body of a young Canadian man. Indeed, the cause of his death was not murder, nor was it suicide. It was autoerotic asphyxia—a sexually charged near-death experience that went a step too far.

People who practice autoerotic asphyxia do so in order to increase the intensity of orgasm by constricting the flow of blood to the brain during masturbation. The practitioners of this behavior—nearly all male—may tighten a belt around their necks or suspend themselves by a noose, often using a closet rail, rafter, or tree. The cerebral cortex is partially knocked out by the resulting lack of oxygen, and its normal inhibitory influence on lower centers of the brain is removed. This probably results in the same kind of heightened, woozy orgasm that some people experience with the use of nitrate inhalers or "poppers." But autoerotic asphyxia carries a dire risk of accidental death if the practitioner passes out before he has time to release the constricting ligature.

One of the most famous cases of suspected autoerotic asphyxia was that of Australian rock star Michael Hutchence (lead singer for INXS), who died in 1997. Hutchence hanged himself from a closet rail, using a belt. His death was officially ruled a suicide (Hand, 1998), but numerous details pointed toward autoerotic asphyxia as the cause of death, according to Hutchence's fiancée, Paula Yates (Barrie, 1999).

For many practitioners, autoerotic asphyxia is about more that experiencing a supernormal orgasm. To judge by the death scenes of victims, it is often linked with a complex of paraphilic elements, including bondage, punishment, and execution by hanging. The victim's body may be tied up around the ankles and genitals as well as the neck, and sadomasochistic literature or images are often found in the vicinity. Transvestism can also play a role: one victim was found dressed in women's clothes and surrounded by documents containing passages such as "the law of the land for any man dressed as a woman and found guilty is that he be hanged." Other victims have been found wearing makeup, or with shaved legs.

As with Hutchence, many possible cases of autoerotic asphyxia come to light only when the person has died. But on the basis of a few studies of living practitioners, it seems that the behavior typically begins experimentally, in adolescence. In some men the behavior develops such intensity that it becomes their only possible sexual outlet. A few studies suggest that experience of sexual abuse in childhood may provoke the behavior, but this is far from certain.

Autoerotic asphyxia is not extremely rare as a cause of death among young men. According to a study by Stephen Hucker and Ray Blanchard of the Centre for Addiction and Mental Health in Toronto, about ten known deaths per year result from the practice in the Canadian provinces of Alberta and Ontario. According to a police officer who conducted a detailed study of autoerotic asphyxia after his own brother fell victim to it, 500–1000 young men die in this way in the United States annually, and about 30% of adolescent hanging deaths can be attributed to it (Anonymous, 2001).

As frightening as these numbers are, accurate statistics are difficult to collect, since so many cases of autoerotic asphyxia are misidentified as suicides, either because the family covers up the evidence that the deceased was masturbating or because the authorities make a default assumption that a hanging is a suicide. But even if there are no obvious clues at the scene, such as magazines or bondage gear, an alert pathologist may spot other indications of the true cause of death: the victim may place a thick cloth between the ligature and his neck in order to prevent rope burns, for example, or the closet rail may show wear from repeated use.

Autoerotic asphyxia is an exceptionally dangerous activity. Somewhat less dangerous is the practice of partial suffocation during sex with a partner. This practice may have physiological effects similar to those of self-strangulation, but with less risk of a fatal outcome. Still, depriving your brain of oxygen is *never* a good idea.

Men in whom autoerotic asphyxia has developed into a compulsive behavior should seek psychotherapeutic treatment in an attempt to rechannel their sexual energy. Unlike many paraphilias, this one is simply too dangerous to be a reasonable risk. Unfortunately, the secrecy with which most men practice autoerotic asphyxia usually ensures that medical examiners, not psychiatrists, are the first to find out about it.

Source: Blanchard & Hucker, 1991.

Zoophiles Are Sexually Fixated on Animal Contacts

Sexual contacts between humans and animals (traditionally called **bestiality**) are not particularly rare. In the Kinsey studies, about 8 percent of men stated that they had had at least one sexual contact with an animal (Kinsey et al., 1948). For men raised on farms, the figures are higher: nearly half of such men reported at least one sexual contact with an animal, and about 17 percent reported a contact leading to orgasm. In such contacts, the man may penetrate the animal vaginally or anally or may induce the animal to fellate him.

For women, the numbers are considerably lower: 3.6 percent of the women in the Kinsey studies reported having some kind of sexual contact with an animal—usually a household pet—after adolescence (Kinsey et al., 1953). These contacts usually involved generalized body contact. Only very occasionally was the women brought to orgasm by the contact; those cases generally involved dogs that were induced to lick the woman's vulva. Anyone who visits bestiality-related pornographic Web sites might conclude that sexual interest in animals is an all-female trait; in reality, of course, these sites present images of women because they are intended for heterosexual male consumption.

Most human–animal contacts occur during the preadolescent or adolescent years and constitute only a tiny fraction of the person's total sexual activity. They can hardly be considered signs of a paraphilia. A few people—mostly men—do persist in having sexual contacts with animals throughout their lives, however, largely to the exclusion of human sexual contacts. This condition is called **zoophilia.** In one recent case study, a man was found (by penile plethysmography) to be sexually aroused more strongly by horses than by any other species, including humans (Earls & Lalumière, 2002).

People who engage in persistent sexual contacts with animals often display other kinds of paraphilic behavior. There seems to be a connection between human–animal sex and generalized psychiatric disturbance: in one study, 55 percent of psychiatric inpatients had a history of human–animal sexual contacts or fantasies, compared with 10–15 percent of controls (Alvarez & Freinhar, 1991).

In Necrophilia, Nonresistance of the Partner May Be Arousing

Necrophilia is a sexual fixation on corpses. It is a rare paraphilia, with probably fewer than 200 cases having been reported in the medical literature. Still, there is enough interest in necrophilia to keep some Internet bulletin boards busy. Necrophiliacs may take positions as mortuary workers or other jobs that give them access to dead bodies. (Of course, the overwhelming majority of mortuary workers are not necrophiliacs.)

Necrophiliacs may view or touch a dead body while masturbating or may actually have penetrative sex with it. Apparently, it is the nonresistance and nonrejection by the dead person that is a key motivator for necrophiliac behavior (Rosman & Resnick, 1989). In fact, some men are turned on when their (living) sex partners feign unconsciousness, "play dead," or join them in necrophiliac fantasies. Such activities may not be entirely harmless, because some men have committed murder to satisfy their necrophiliac interests.

Pedophilia and Child Molestation Are Not Identical

The word **pedophile** has been used in a variety of senses. We use it here to denote a person—usually a man—whose sexual interest in prepubescent children exceeds his sexual interest in physically mature adults (Freund, 1981). The DSM-IV attempts to give this definition some extra specificity in terms of age: the pedophile should be at least 16 years old and the individuals to whom he is principally attracted may be up to 13 years old, but are at least 5 years younger than himself. (This definition is intended to exclude sexual attractions among prepubescent or pubescent children of roughly similar age.)

A **child molester** or **sexual offender against children** is any adult who has had sexual contact with a prepubescent child. Whether the child participated willingly or unwillingly in the sexual relationship may be an important variable in terms of the consequences for the child (see Chapter 12), but it does not affect the adult's designation as a sex offender, since children are deemed legally incapable of giving consent to sexual activity with adults.

It's worth noting that, although the legal offense of "child molestation" is broadly defined in most states, most actual child molestation convictions are for nonpenetrative acts, such as touching a child's genitals or buttocks. That's because penetrative sex between an adult and a child is less common, and because it may be prosecuted as rape or aggravated sodomy rather than child molestation.

The terms "pedophile" and "child molester" denote different but overlapping populations (Figure 14.2). Some pedophiles do not actually have sex with prepubescent children because they consider it wrong, are afraid of the consequences to themselves, or are able to derive sufficient sexual satisfaction from relationships with adolescents or adults. Some child molesters, on the other hand, are not principally attracted to prepubescent children; their behavior may result from a variety of other factors, such as the lack

Figure 14.2 Pedophiles and child molesters are distinct but partially overlapping populations.

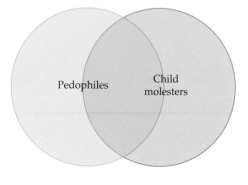

of available older partners, the desire to hurt one of the child's parents (perhaps an ex-girlfriend of the perpetrator), alcohol or drug intoxication, neurological damage, or other factors. Nevertheless, there is a substantial population of individuals who are both pedophiles and child molesters.

Some adults are primarily attracted to postpubescent teenagers—say, in the 13- to 17-year range. These adults do not fit the definition of pedophiles given above. The term **ephebophile** (*ephebe* means "youth") is sometimes used to designate this group. Since many people experience sexual attraction to some youths in this age bracket, the defining feature of ephebophiles is really their lack of sexual attraction to adults.

In lay discourse, the distinction between pedophiles and ephebophiles is often blurred: any men who are attracted to, or have sex with, adolescents below the age of legal consent (which varies from state to state, but may be as high as 18) are commonly referred to as pedophiles or child molesters (Box 14.4).

Some child molesters have sexual interactions with their own children or stepchildren (**intrafamilial child molesters** or **incest offenders**). Others have interactions with children outside their immediate families (**extrafamilial child molesters**). Some studies have suggested that most extrafamilial child molesters are true pedophiles, with a predominant and persistent sexual interest in children, while intrafamilial child molesters do not have a consistent attraction to children and are more like conventional heterosexual adults (Barbaree & Marshall, 1989). More recent studies, however, suggest that most intrafamilial child molesters—even those who molest their own biological daughters—fit a pedophilic profile. That is, when tested in the laboratory, they are more physiologically aroused by images of children, or taped descriptions of sexual interactions with children, than by comparable stimuli depicting older persons (Barsetti et al., 1998; Seto et al., 1999).

There are two real differences between extrafamilial and intrafamilial child molesters, however. First, even without any treatment, intrafamilial molesters who come to the attention of the law are unlikely to repeat their offenses, whereas some extrafamilial molesters do repeat their offenses many times (see below). This finding suggests that at least some extrafamilial child molesters have an engrained paraphilia, whereas intrafamilial offenders do not. Second, the great majority of intrafamilial offenses are against girls (daughters or stepdaughters), whereas extrafamilial offenses are against girls and boys in roughly equal numbers (Quinsey et al., 1995).

This brings us to the question of the relationship between pedophilia and sexual orientation. One possibility is that pedophiles might be attracted to children without regard to the children's sex. Another possibility is that pedophiles might have a sexual orientation like that of nonpedophiles, so that one could designate pedophiles as heterosexual (primarily attracted to girls) or homosexual (primarily attracted to boys). On the basis of laboratory testing as well as offense histories, it appears that the latter possibility is closer to the truth: most pedophiles (and child molesters) have a preference for either female or male children. Heterosexual pedophiles predominate; they outnumber homosexual pedophiles by about 2:1 or 3:1 (Blanchard et al., 1999, 2000). Still, the fraction of pedophiles who are homosexual is considerably higher than the fraction of men in the general population who are homosexual.

There are differences between homosexual and heterosexual pedophiles (Langevin et al., 1978; Freund et al., 1987). Homosexual pedophiles who come to the attention of the law are more likely than heterosexual pedophiles to have had sexual contacts with multiple children. They are more likely to have had contacts with children who were strangers to them or only slightly acquainted with them. They are more likely to reoffend after conviction. Finally, homosexual pedophiles tend to be more emotionally disturbed and to have lower levels of intellectual function.

The studies on which the foregoing statements are based, however, were focused for the most part on offenders against pubescent children and even young adolescents. True pedophiles, who are attracted primarily to prepubescent children, do not distinguish between males and females as sharply as do most male adults, to judge from their physiological responses to images of nude boys and girls (Freund et al., 1991). This finding makes some kind of sense, because prepubescent boys and girls resemble each other much more closely than adult men and women resemble each other.

Box 14.4 *Society, Values, and the Law*

Priests Who Molest Minors

In January 2002, a defrocked Roman Catholic priest, John Geoghan, was convicted by a Massachusetts court of sexually fondling a 10-year-old boy in a swimming pool, and was sentenced to a 9- to 10-year prison term. In addition to that boy, more than 130 people have accused Geoghan of molesting them while they were minors. Seventy of Geoghan's victims, as well as 16 parents, brought an action against the Archdiocese of Boston, which remains unsettled as of this writing.

The Geoghan case was nothing new. Another Massachusetts priest, James Porter, had been convicted in 1992 of abusing 28 children and sentenced to 18–20 years' imprisonment, and similar cases have occurred around the country. What caused a particular outcry in the Geoghan case, however, was the role of Geoghan's superiors. Reporters for the *Boston Globe* discovered that Cardinal Bernard Law (the Archbishop of Boston), as well as other church officials, had known that Geoghan was an incorrigible sex offender. Instead of dismissing him or turning him over to prosecutors, they shuffled him from parish to

parish over a period of 30 years, thus giving him the opportunity to molest new and unsuspecting victims. Furthermore, another 80 priests in Boston alone had been accused of similar offenses and had also been protected by church officials. (Their names have since been given to prosecutors.) Besides moving abusive priests around, church officials used another strategy to keep the abuse quiet: in many cases, they paid large sums of money to victims on condition that the victims remain silent about their experiences.

The 2002 scandal spread like wildfire. Between January and June, at least 218 priests resigned or were removed from ministry on account of known or alleged sex acts with minors. In June 2002, the U.S. Conference of Bishops announced a new policy that mandated the removal from all ministerial duties of any priest known to have had sexual contact with a minor, even if the event occurred in the distant past.

The problem of priestly abuse is not limited to the United States. In Ireland, an overwhelmingly Catholic country, 800 men

John Geoghan

The question of the sexual orientation of pedophiles and child molesters has political significance for gay people. Quite often, anti-gay activists label all gay men "child molesters," probably in an attempt to paint gay men as evil. Conversely, gay activists often claim that the majority of men who molest boys are actually "heterosexual." Neither of these claims is correct. Most gay men are not sexually attracted to children and do not molest them. On the other hand, men who molest boys are usually attracted to boys more than to girls and are indeed homosexual in that limited sense. They may be married to women, but that doesn't say anything about their sexual orientation.

Pedophilia generally begins early—at adolescence—and persists over the lifetime. As a pedophile becomes an adult, it becomes increasingly difficult for him to associate with children without arousing suspicion. He may engage in youth work, child care, or similar activities in order to do so. So long as he does not attempt to engage in sexual relations with the children in his care, such involvement is not problematic. Some pedophiles have doubtless been very beneficial to children or have directed their sexual desires into productive or creative channels (Box 14.5). On the other hand, there always exists the possibility that the pedophile whose occupation involves contact with children will take advantage of that association to initiate sexual contacts.

What are pedophiles like as people? Early studies suggested that they are deficient in social skills, lack empathy, lack self-esteem or self-assertion, are lonely and psychologically distressed, experience cognitive distortions (such as the belief that children benefit from having sex with them), are emotionally disturbed, and have disordered thought processes akin to schizophrenia (Langevin et al., 1978). In contrast, more recent research finds that pedophiles are rather unremarkable people, with few distinguishing characteristics except for a relatively low level of intellectual function (Quinsey & Lalumière, 2001).

and women say they were abused by clergy, and more than 3000 persons have asked to give testimony to a commission investigating the matter. Bishop Brendan Comiskey resigned over allegations that he protected a priest who was accused of sexually abusing 66 boys. (The priest himself committed suicide.) In Poland, Catholic Archbishop Juliusz Paetz resigned after being accused by priests of sexually molesting them while they were in training.

To put these events in perspective, it's worth stressing four points:

First, the recent spate of allegations concerns events that happened over several decades; there is no evidence of a sudden recent increase in the prevalence of abuse by priests.

Second, some allegations are likely to be false. An allegation of childhood abuse made by a woman against Cardinal Roger Mahony of Los Angeles in April 2002, for example, was quickly deemed not credible by police investigators. Also, some persons whose accusations are true may exaggerate the harm caused by the abuse in the hope of maximizing their monetary compensation. Others have suffered real and long-lasting harm, however, including loss of their religious faith.

Third, even with the large numbers of allegations, there is no suggestion that the majority of priests engage in sexual abuse of minors. There are over 42,000 Roman Catholic priests in the United States, so the 218 priests mentioned above make up only 0.5 percent of the total.

Fourth, priests are not the only people who may take advantage of positions of influence to sexually abuse minors. In February 2000, for example, the U.N. High Commissioner for Refugees released a report stating that there was rampant sexual exploitation of minors by aid workers in many West African refugee camps. In the United States, high school teachers, social workers, and youth services providers are charged with sexual offenses against minors from time to time.

The victims of priestly abuse are of both sexes and range in age from prepubescent to adult, but there seems to be a preponderance of teenage males. As we discussed in Chapter 7, teens are sexually attractive to many adults, so many of the abusive priests could be gay men who preferentially target teens for practical reasons, such as accessibility and ease of control, not because they have an unusual proclivity for young partners. Some, however, may be ephebophiles. Only a minority of the abusive priests appear to have a preference for prepubescent children, so most do not fit the definition of pedophiles, even though this term is commonly used in media accounts of the scandals.

Are there an unusually large number of Catholic priests who are gay? Father Donald Cozzens, head of a Catholic seminary in Cleveland, has argued that there are, and that the Catholic priesthood is "primarily a gay culture" (Cozzens, 2000). Possible reasons include the exodus of many heterosexual priests who desire to marry and the attraction of an all-male culture to some gay men. With its requirement for celibacy, the priesthood may seem like a safe haven for young Catholic men who are troubled by homosexual desires. It's also possible that more gay men than straight men have the traits of spirituality and benevolence that suit a person for the priesthood. Most gay Catholic priests, like most straight ones, probably live celibate lives or find sexual outlets that do not involve minors and are not connected with their ministry.

Some observers connect the problem of abusive priests with the Roman Catholic Church's long-standing requirement for priests to be celibate and its ban on the ordination of women. In an editorial in March 2002, the *Pilot* (the newspaper of the Boston Archdiocese) raised the question of whether there would be fewer incidents of abuse if celibacy were optional and women could become priests. The editorial attracted a great deal of attention as a possible voice of dissension from official Vatican policy, but a later statement from the newspaper said that the editorial had been "misinterpreted."

Sources: Goodstein & Dillon, 2002; Graham, 2002; Holley, 2002; Mehren, 2002; Stammer & Lobdell, 2002.

The reason for these discordant results is not entirely clear. However, there seem to be marked differences among different kinds of pedophiles and child molesters. Men who seek sex with boys, men who prefer very young children, men who have a history of very large numbers of sexual contacts with children, and men who use force to obtain sexual contacts all tend to have more personality disturbances and more signs of mental illness than do other pedophiles.

It's also worth emphasizing that nearly all psychological studies of pedophiles are actually studies of apprehended or convicted child molesters. Little is known about the psychological traits of pedophiles who have not had sexual contacts with children or who have had such contacts without being apprehended. Research in this area is inhibited by legal reporting requirements: mental health professionals who learn of actual or threatened incidents of child molestation are compelled to report them to law enforcement authorities, thus undermining the confidentiality that would be a necessary basis for research.

Female pedophiles and child molesters are rare, but they do exist. One Canadian study (Cooper et al., 1990) reported on a 20-year-old woman who exhibited multiple paraphilias, including pedophilia, and who had been both a victim of and a perpetrator of incest. Her pedophilic interests were confirmed by tests of physiological arousal (vaginal photoplethysmography). Incarcerated female child molesters generally have severe psychiatric disturbances (Green & Kaplan, 1994), but the majority of women who have sexual contacts with prepubertal boys are probably never apprehended, because the affected boys tend not to view the contacts as abusive (McConaghy, 1998).

Like other paraphilias, pedophilia is an exaggeration of a sexual interest that exists quite widely in the male population. You may be reluctant to believe that many "normal"

Box 14.5 *Sex in History*

Lewis Carroll: A Victorian Pedophile?

"Lewis Carroll" was the nom de plume of Oxford University mathematician, writer, and photographer Charles Dodgson (1832–1898) (Figure A). He was the author of two immortal children's books, *Alice in Wonderland* and *Through the Looking Glass,* as well as the poem *The Hunting of the Snark* and various mathematical treatises.

Carroll was, to put it mildly, interested in little girls. He wrote the *Alice* books for Alice Liddell, the young daughter of an Oxford dean. He had a succession of close friendships with at least 40 girls—friendships that generally, though not always, faded when the girls reached their teen or adult years. He wrote thousands of letters to young girls, often illustrating them with his own artwork. He photographed innumerable girls (Figure B), many of them nude. He never married.

It is likely that Carroll was a heterosexual pedophile. Carroll's early biographers downplayed that possibility by painting him simply as a socially inept, Peter Pan-like figure who was emotionally stuck in childhood and remained asexual throughout his adult life. A recent biography (Cohen, 1995) concedes that Carroll was a pedophile, but largely evades the issue of his sexual feelings and behavior. Another biographer (Leach, 1999) attempts to "rescue" Carroll: she points out correctly that some of Carroll's "child-friends" were actually teenagers. She also suggests (less plausibly) that Carroll was the adulterous lover of Alice Liddell's mother, Lorina.

"Diagnosing" the sexuality of long-dead figures such as Carroll is fraught with risk and is complicated by conflicting motives—the desire to preserve the sanctity of a beloved children's author versus the desire to read psychopathology into the lives of historical figures. Even if we accept the likelihood that Carroll was a pedophile, it is impossible to know whether his activities were limited to voyeurism (as suggested by his photography) or extended to sexual contacts with children. His diaries still exist, and they suggest that he experienced deep guilt in some part of his life, but for what reason is not made clear. Some possibly key pages of the diary have been excised, and unless they resurface, Carroll's sexuality is likely to remain an enigma.

(A) Lewis Carroll (Charles Dodgson) (1832–1898)

(B) One of Carroll's photographs of young girls

men are sexually aroused by children, but this has been demonstrated by penile plethysmography. Arousal is generally greatest in response to older children and to children of the same sex as the adults whom the subject finds arousing (that is, to girls in heterosexual men and to boys in homosexual men) (Freund et al., 1989).

In a study by researchers at the University of Southern California, substantial numbers of male college students stated that they were sexually attracted to some young children (Briere & Runtz, 1989) (Table 14.1). Interestingly, the USC students who acknowledged these interests differed from the other students in a number of respects. They reported more traumatic early sexual experiences, had more sex partners, used pornography more frequently, acknowledged a greater likelihood of raping a woman, and had attitudes supportive of sexual dominance over women. Of course, few, if any, of these students were likely to go on to molest children (or rape women) in real life. There was no suggestion that any of these men were pedophiles in the sense that their sexual interest in children exceeded their sexual interest in adults. But the findings illustrate that the capacity for sexual arousal by children is widespread.

TABLE 14.1	Percentage of male undergraduate college students (surveyed anonymously) who acknowledged sexual interest in children in various ways	
Type of interest		**Percentage of students**
Experienced sexual attraction to some small children		21
Had sexual fantasies involving children		9
Masturbated to fantasies involving children		5
Might have sex with a child if they could avoid detection		7

Source: Briere & Runtz, 1989.

Sex Offenders Do Not Necessarily Repeat Their Offenses

Sex offenders, especially offenders against children, are widely perceived as incorrigible monsters who will inevitably repeat their offenses if given the chance. This perception has led to draconian measures against convicted sex offenders: very long prison sentences, denial of parole, detainment after the completion of sentences, and compulsory drug treatments (see below). Registration of sex offenders' addresses, and notification of the public when a registered sex offender moves into a locality, is compulsory in a number of states. These requirements are known as "Megan's laws," named for Megan Kanka, a 7-year-old New Jersey girl who was raped and murdered by a known child molester in 1995. The molester had moved into the Kankas' street without their knowledge.

Some sex offenders do indeed repeat their offenses (**recidivism**). On the other hand, sex offenders as a group are *less* likely to repeat their offenses than are people convicted of many other kinds of crimes. In one meta-analysis of 61 follow-up studies involving over 23,000 sex offenders, only 13 percent were convicted of a repeat offense during a follow-up period that averaged 5 years (Hanson & Bussière, 1998). (Some offenders may repeat their offenses at a later date, of course, or reoffend without being apprehended or convicted.) The perception that sex offenders are unusually prone to recidivism is fostered by distorted media coverage, which focuses preferentially on sex offense recidivists and often provides inaccurate information about them (Berlin & Malin, 1991).

Several factors can predict an increased likelihood of recidivism in these offenders (Hanson & Bussière, 1998). The best predictors are measures of antisocial tendencies (such as antisocial personality disorder or a general criminal history) and measures of atypical sexual interests (for example, child molesters who are pedophiles are more likely to reoffend than those who are not). Not surprisingly, a person who has already committed more than one offense, or whose prior offense involved violence, has an increased likelihood of offending again (Firestone et al., 2000; Prentky et al., 1997).

Given our knowledge of these factors, it may be possible to direct prevention strategies toward the subset of sex offenders who are particularly likely to reoffend, and to allow the remainder to rejoin the community. The current practice of forcing sex offenders to move from city to city for years after they have completed their sentences (Box 14.6) does nothing either to prevent recidivism or to protect the public.

There Are Numerous Theories of Paraphilia

Given that paraphilias often inflict considerable suffering on the persons who experience them and may expose other people to unwanted and potentially harmful sexual activities, it would be very useful to understand their cause or causes. Such understanding might help prevent paraphilias or might lead to effective treatments for people who suffer from them.

Before considering the theories that have been put forward, it's worth reviewing what general statements one can make about paraphilias:

Society, Values, and the Law

The "Geographic Cure"

Got a sex offender on your doorstep? How about shipping him out of your community and letting someone else deal with the problem? That's a common strategy for dealing with sex offenders in the United States.

In 2000, twice-convicted child molester Aramis Linares moved in with his sister's family in Monrovia, California. In accordance with state law, Linares notified the Monrovia Police Department of his address. The police, in turn, petitioned the state's Department of Justice to have Linares declared a "high-risk" sex offender. The state did so, and this designation allowed the police to notify the public. They handed out fliers and gave the local media details of Linares' crimes, his address, and his description. Public protests erupted immediately, and Linares eventually had to move out of Monrovia. But the Monrovia police went further: they gave him a one-way ticket to Reno, Nevada, and escorted him to the plane.

A more disturbing case was that of 43-year-old Nathaniel Bar-Jonah. After kidnapping two boys in his home state of Massachusetts, Bar-Jonah spent 12 years in a treatment center for sexually dangerous offenders. While in detention, he confessed to many bizarre sexual fantasies, including cannibalistic urges. In 1991, however, two psychologists testified that he was no longer a threat to society, and he was released. Within a month, he was arrested

in the attempted kidnapping of another boy. Bar-Jonah avoided jail by agreeing to move to Montana—which he did.

Within months of arriving in Great Falls, Bar-Jonah was charged with molesting an 8-year-old boy whom he was babysitting. The charges were dropped after the boy's mother refused to let him testify. But in December 2000, Bar-Jonah was arrested and charged with the 1996 kidnapping and murder of 10-year-old Zachary Ramsey. Authorities claimed that Bar-Jonah had butchered the boy's remains and fed some of them to unsuspecting neighbors. His trial has been scheduled for mid-2002.

According to Connie Isaac, executive director of the Association for the Treatment of Sexual Abusers, located in Beaverton, Oregon, moving a convicted sex offender from state to state "has absolutely nothing to do with the treatment of the offender and has nothing to do with public safety. It's a good way for one jurisdiction to wash their hands of the problem and say 'It won't be my kid and I don't know anyone in Montana.'"

How would you respond if you learned that a sex offend-

er had moved into your neighborhood? How can public safety be balanced against the right of someone who has "served his time" to get on with his life? Are there better strategies than the "geographic cure"? One district judge in Corpus Christi, Texas ordered 15 sex offenders to identify themselves to their community by putting signs in their yards (see photo). Is this an effective approach?

Sources: Dear & Sibley, 2000; Goldberg, 2001.

- Far more men than women develop paraphilias. Any theory that fails to account for this sex difference is either wrong or seriously incomplete.
- Paraphilias begin at an early age—usually around the time of puberty or early adolescence. Some paraphiliacs recall indications of their condition even before puberty. Thus, theories that attempt to explain paraphilias in terms of experiences during adult life, such as rejection by women, are likely to be inadequate.
- Paraphilias are extensions or exaggerations of common sexual desires and behaviors (Figure 14.3). What distinguishes a paraphilia is not that the person experiences these sexual desires, or even that he engages in the behaviors; it is that he devotes a large portion of his time and sexual energy to them and, in the process, brings suffering on himself and/or harm to others.
- Paraphilias tend to become more severe over time, and persons who start out with one kind of paraphilia may eventually exhibit multiple forms. By the time they come to professional attention, 54 percent of paraphiliacs report experiencing more than one paraphilia, and 18 percent report four or more paraphilias (Abel & Osborn, 2000). Thus, theories that offer a specific explanation for why a person develops *one*

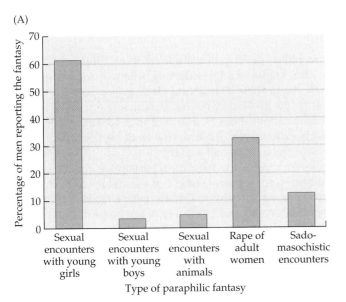

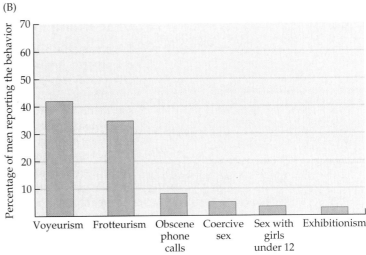

(A)

Percentage of men reporting the fantasy

Type of paraphilic fantasy

Sexual encounters with young girls · Sexual encounters with young boys · Sexual encounters with animals · Rape of adult women · Sado-masochistic encounters

(B)

Percentage of men reporting the behavior

Type of behavior

Voyeurism · Frotteurism · Obscene phone calls · Coercive sex · Sex with girls under 12 · Exhibitionism

Figure 14.3 Atypical fantasies and behaviors in the general male population. (A) Percentage of men who experience paraphilic sexual fantasies during masturbation or intercourse. (After Crepault & Couture, 1980.) (B) Percentage of male college students who admit having engaged in paraphilic or criminal sexual behaviors. (After Templeman & Stinnett, 1991.)

paraphilia are likely to be incomplete. Pedophilia appears to be an exception: few pedophiles or child molesters report having other paraphilias. This finding suggests that pedophilia may be causally distinct from other paraphilias.

- Certain personality traits are common among paraphiliacs—at least among those who are convicted of crimes or come to the attention of medical professionals. These traits include a lack of social skills (especially in dealing with women), a sense of inadequacy, depression, and sometimes a sense of rage against women. More severe or repeat offenders tend to have more severe psychopathology.

- Some paraphiliacs who perform nonconsensual acts with others (such as exhibitionists or child molesters) report that they themselves were exposed to those same acts during childhood. However, recent studies of incarcerated child molesters indicate that they are no more likely to have been molested during their own childhood than are men incarcerated for nonsexual offenses (Abel & Osborn, 2000).

Paraphiliacs commonly have cognitive distortions, believing, for example, that their behaviors are sexually exciting or beneficial to the persons whom they target. Admittedly, the whole notion of "cognitive distortion," which makes self-justification a pathological symptom in its own right, is reminiscent of the mind-control tools used in totalitarian societies. Those who have atypical sexual desires have the right to express their beliefs, as we saw in the case of pedophiles in Chapter 13. Many people who engage in atypical but consensual sexual activities—such as most S/M practitioners—would laugh at the notion that there is anything unhealthy or wrong about their sexuality, possibly with good reason. On the other hand, cognitive distortion really does seem to be at work when, for example, an exhibitionist is convinced that his victim's cries of alarm express sexual excitement and a desire for further intimacy.

There May Be an Inherited Predisposition to Paraphilias

To some extent, paraphilias run in families. In one study, 18.5 percent of paraphiliacs had **first-degree relatives** (parents, siblings, or children) who were also paraphiliac, whereas only 3 percent of persons with other psychiatric conditions had paraphiliacs in their families—a sixfold difference (Gaffney et al., 1984). This finding suggests that a tendency to develop a paraphilia may be inherited. Interestingly, the pedophiles had pedophiles among their relatives, whereas the nonpedophiles had a variety of nonpedophilic paraphiliacs among their relatives. This finding is in line with the theory mentioned above that pedophilia is causally distinct from other paraphilias.

Many Theorists See Paraphilias as a Product of Learning Processes

It is commonly believed that paraphilias develop by some kind of **conditioning** or learning process. According to this idea, a child or adolescent might happen to have a sexually gratifying experience with, say, a shoe. The sexual pleasure—especially that of orgasm—confers attractiveness on the previously neutral stimulus (the shoe). The person therefore continues to fantasize about shoes or uses real shoes during subsequent bouts of masturbation. This practice continually reinforces the erotic significance of shoes until they become an indispensable focus of sexual activity.

The "reward" that is supposed to underlie the learning of paraphilias could be something other than orgasm. For example, some parents might praise and reward sons who dress in girls' clothes, thus providing an initial spur to transvestic fetishism. However, most paraphilias are expressed quite secretly, and in fact may not be expressed behaviorally at all in the initial stages. This observation makes a direct parental role implausible in most cases.

There often seems to be a certain naivete about learning theories of paraphilia, as we will illustrate by focusing on a particular example. Here is one adult male's account of how his shoe fetishism began around the age of puberty:

> I was home alone and saw my uncle's new penny loafers. I went over and started smelling the fresh new leather scent and kissing and licking them. It turned me on so much that I actually ejaculated my first load into my pants and have been turned on ever since. (Weinberg et al., 1994)

This example, and others like it, have been taken as evidence for the learning hypothesis (Hyde & DeLamater, 2000; McGuire et al., 1965). When you think about it, though, how likely is this interpretation? Would a previously normal boy, on seeing a pair of new shoes, just happen to smell and kiss and lick them and thereby become sexually aroused to the point of experiencing his first ejaculation? Isn't it at least as likely that this boy already had a strong predisposition to be attracted by shoes, and that the event he described simply made that attraction apparent to him? All that stories like this one really demonstrate is that fetishism develops early, not that any particular process is responsible for it.

Another problem with this hypothesis is that if the process were really as simple as presented in this story, then we would all have multiple paraphilias. All the details of the environment in which we first experienced orgasm, or the physical characteristics of the person with whom we first had sex, would be engrained and intensified. We would be fixated, for example, on green blouses and bedside lamps and pepperoni pizza and flat feet. But we're not. We may have our sexual preferences, but we tend to respond to whole persons more than to objects or body parts, and we tend to enjoy novelty and variety more than repetition and sameness. Thus, even if learning processes do contribute to the development of particular fetishisms, there must be something else that makes people susceptible to paraphilic development in the first place.

That "something else" could be a style of thinking that drives behavior into deep, repetitive channels. When such thinking interferes with a person's life, it is called an **obsessive–compulsive disorder** (OCD). Most OCDs involve nonsexual behaviors, such as repeated hand washing. Nevertheless, many paraphilias have OCD-like qualities (Travin, 1995). Supporting the notion that paraphilias and OCDs are related is the finding that a single class of drugs is useful in the treatment of both kinds of disorders (see below).

Learning theories could conceivably explain why most paraphiliacs are male. Boys masturbate much more than girls; thus, if masturbation reinforces paraphilic ideation, this reinforcement will occur more often in males.

Some Paraphilias May Represent Disorders of Courtship

The normal process by which a man acquires a sex partner consists of four stages: (1) locating and evaluating a sex partner, (2) initial nontactile interactions, such as smiling, displaying attractive features, and talking with the partner, (3) tactile interactions, such as embracing and fondling, and (4) genital sex. Each of these stages has a paraphilic counterpart: (1) voyeurism, (2) exhibitionism and obscene phone calling, (3) frotteurism, and (4) paraphilic or sadistic rape (that is, rape in which the rapist is sexually aroused by the coercive nature of the act). Two or more of these paraphilias can occur in the same person. Paraphilias have therefore been conceptualized as aspects of a **courtship disorder** (Freund & Blanchard, 1986). The fact that two or more of these paraphilias may occur together in the same person also suggests that they have a common basis. This theory suggests that the causes of paraphilias should be sought in a disruption of the normal development of courtship behavior.

Paraphilias May Represent an Escape Route when Normal Sexual Expression is Blocked

Another, perhaps related, idea is that paraphilias are caused by the blockage of normal avenues of sexual expression. Refusing to be dammed up completely, a person's sex drive finds alternative, abnormal modes of expression.

What could cause the blockage of normal sexual expression? In Freudian theory, this would most likely result from unresolved Oedipal conflicts (see Chapter 7). Such conflicts, Freud proposed, lead either to abnormal forms of sexual expression (what Freud termed "perversions" and we would call paraphilias) or to general emotional or behavioral disturbances that are not explicitly sexual ("neuroses"). The reason that paraphilias are hard to treat, a psychoanalyst would say, is that the paraphilia is "saving" the person from more severe and general mental illness (Stoller, 1977).

A related but more straightforward explanation would be to say that children who happen to be especially timorous, lacking in self-esteem, or socially inept, or who have unattractive looks or personalities, are greatly hampered in their attempts to establish normal sexual relationships and are therefore driven into paraphilic modes of sexual expression as an escape route. After all, most paraphilic behaviors require only rudimentary social skills (pedophilia, exhibitionism) or no social skills at all (object fetishism, voyeurism, zoophilia, necrophilia).

As mentioned above, several studies have reported that paraphiliacs are indeed deficient in social skills and relate poorly to women. It is doubtful that this theory can provide a complete explanation for the development of paraphilias, however, because plenty of socially inept men are not paraphiliacs, and some paraphiliacs have normal social skills (in fact, if we could examine nonapprehended paraphiliacs, it might turn out that most do). One must also keep in mind the possibility that social ineptness and other negative psychological traits might *result* from the paraphilia, rather than being a cause of it. After all, it is difficult to relate gracefully to a woman if one is interested only in her underwear. Still, this kind of theory has some plausibility, and some treatment strategies are based on it (see below).

In the case of transvestic fetishism, Kenneth Zucker and his colleagues at the Centre for Addiction and Mental Health in Toronto have noted that men with this paraphilia are especially likely to have a hostile relationship with their mothers, or to have been separated from their mothers for long periods during childhood or adolescence. These researchers therefore speculate that transvestic fetishism is an unconscious mechanism for maintaining some kind of representational connection with the mother (Zucker & Blanchard, 1997).

Ray Blanchard and other researchers at the Centre for Addiction and Mental Health in Toronto are leading figures in the study of paraphilias.

The Victim–Perpetrator Cycle May Contribute to Paraphilias

There is a widespread belief that people who have been the victims of some form of abusive behavior—especially during childhood—have an increased likelihood of engaging in that same behavior themselves, either soon after the initial experience or years later during adult life. This idea is called the **abused–abuser hypothesis** or the **victim–perpetrator cycle** (Garland and Dougher, 1990).

Why should people behave in this way? One suggestion is that, by incorporating and repeating the abusive behavior, the person attains some kind of psychological mastery over the traumatic experience or revenge for it (Stoller, 1975). Alternatively, the initial abuse might have had pleasurable features for the victim, such as sexual arousal or the receipt of gifts and attention from the abuser; these pleasurable features might foster a desire to engage in that same behavior (as an abuser) in the future. Finally, the initial experience might simply "normalize" the behavior, eliminating the sense that it is something alien or taboo, and therefore making it psychologically easier to practice that behavior in later life.

There is some evidence that children who are sexually abused do have an increased likelihood of sexually abusing other children, but only when they are still children or juveniles (Abel & Osborn, 2000). As mentioned earlier, it does not seem that adult men who have been convicted of child molestation are more likely to have been sexually abused as children than are men convicted of nonsexual offenses.

Anecdotal evidence has been presented to support a role for early abuse in the development of other paraphilias. For example, psychiatrists at the Mayo Clinic in Rochester, Minnesota, interviewed several adolescents who practiced autoerotic asphyxia (Friedrich & Gerber, 1994). The youths said that, during their childhood, they had been sexually or physically abused, and that choking occurred as part of the abuse. This is not quite the typical abused–abuser scenario, because the boys ultimately came to practice the abusive behavior on themselves, rather than on others. The authors' interpretation was that the youths choked themselves because their early choking experiences were combined with erotic arousal.

Back in the days when homosexuality was viewed as a paraphilia, childhood sexual abuse by adult men was often presented as a cause—of both female and male homosexuality. Girls, it was argued, were "turned off" men by abusive experiences, whereas boys were "turned on" to men by the same experiences (McGuire et al., 1965). The problem with this idea, of course, is that it could equally well explain why sexually abused children become *heterosexual:* one would just have to assume that the girls were turned on and the boys turned off by these experiences. When a theory is capable of accounting for diametrically opposite findings, its explanatory power is low.

Organic Disorders May Trigger Paraphilias

There have been quite a few reports of organic disorders in people with paraphilias. According to one survey, 74 percent of paraphiliacs have abnormal hormone levels, 27 percent have signs of neurological disease, 24 percent have chromosomal abnormalities, and smaller numbers have seizure disorders, dyslexia, or mental retardation (Langevin & Watson, 1996). Again, however, there is reason to be cautious in the interpretation of such reports. The natural variation in levels of hormones such as testosterone makes it extremely easy to find abnormalities where none really exist. In addition, hormone levels are readily affected by stressful circumstances, such as arrest or incarceration.

Previously normal men and women can develop abnormal sexual desires and behaviors after damage to certain brain regions caused by strokes, brain infections, or neurodegenerative conditions such as Alzheimer's disease. In the case of **Alzheimer's disease** and other dementias, the deterioration of the cerebral cortex gradually eliminates its "policing" role, so that behaviors that most of us have learned are inappropriate, such as public masturbation or persistent sexual advances, may emerge. Localized damage to the temporal lobes in both cerebral hemispheres, or to the amygdalas, may trigger a strange phenomenon called **Kluver-Bucy syndrome,** which is marked by increased sexual activity, a compulsion to put all kinds of objects in the mouth, and other symptoms. In a study from UCLA, two men who became homosexual pedophiles in later life were shown by positron emission tomography to have damage to the temporal lobes (Mendez et al., 2000). Whether such findings are relevant to the more usual, early-onset paraphilias is uncertain, but they do suggest regions of the brain that deserve to be studied.

No specific genes have been shown to contribute to paraphilias, but the evidence (mentioned earlier) that paraphilias tend to run in families suggests that genetic differences between individuals do play some causative role.

The Causes of Paraphilias Remain Unknown

In spite of the variety of theories just described, the origin of paraphilias remains largely mysterious. Progress in this area is hampered by several factors:

- The long time course of human development, which makes it impractical to follow individuals from their childhood to an age when they may show paraphilic tendencies.
- The rarity of some paraphilias.
- The secrecy and shame that surround paraphilias.
- The problems of extrapolating from convicted sex offenders to the whole population of paraphiliacs.
- The existence of reporting laws that make honest communication between paraphiliacs and mental health professionals difficult.
- The fragmentation of the mental health and judicial systems in the United States, which makes it hard to obtain accurate case histories or statistics. (For this reason, the best studies come from Canada or other countries with national health services and unified legal systems.)

Theories of Causation Have Suggested a Variety of Treatments

Most paraphiliacs do not seek treatment of their own accord. They may be pressured into doing so by spouses, or they may be referred to mental health professionals by the courts. For convicted sex offenders, attending some kind of risk reduction program may be a condition of their sentencing or parole.

The fact that the paraphiliacs themselves are not usually the initiators of their treatment makes that treatment difficult, both practically and ethically. In a practical sense, the paraphiliac may lack the motivation that is a precondition for success in most forms of psychotherapy. Ethically, a therapist working with such a person must walk a fine line between serving the client (responding to his need for help) and serving the state (protecting society from harm) (Laws, 1999). Ideally, those two goals will be brought into alignment; that is, the therapist will help the client accept that treatment to reduce his paraphilic desires or behaviors is in his best interests. Even if he is not convinced that there is anything wrong with his paraphilic desires, he may come to agree that progress in treatment will save his marriage, help him get out of prison, or save him from future legal problems. Of course, a client who is incarcerated may be highly motivated to feign a disappearance of his paraphilic interests, and some reports of treatment successes probably result from uncritical acceptance of such "cures."

Most treatment strategies are based on one or another of the theories of causation outlined above, so we will cover them in roughly the same order.

Behavior Therapy Attempts to Reverse Pathological Learning Processes

If paraphilias result from conditioning or other forms of learning, then it might be possible to treat them by driving the learning process in reverse, or by fostering new learning processes that lead to more normal sexual desires or behaviors. This is the thinking behind a number of treatments that are collectively termed **behavior therapy** or **behavior modification.**

The best-known of these techniques is **aversion therapy.** This technique employs appropriately timed punishments (**negative reinforcement**) to extinguish the pathological feelings or behaviors. Let us say that a man is attracted to prepubescent boys. He is shown pictures of boys, or told to masturbate to fantasies of boys, but these pleasant experiences are interrupted by some unpleasant (aversive) stimulus—usually electric shocks, an unpleasant smell such as ammonia, or a nausea-inducing chemical such as apomorphine. (Ironically, this same chemical, under the trade name Uprima, may soon be approved for the purpose of helping men get erections; see Chapter 15.) Supposedly, the man will gradually lose his sexual interest in young boys as they become more and more strongly associated with the unpleasant experience.

There is a variation of aversion therapy that does away with dangerous shocks and messy chemicals. In this **covert sensitization procedure,** the process is the same, except that the whole thing takes place in the client's mind. He is instructed to fantasize about his paraphilia—fondling a child, for example. But as he approaches the climax of the fantasy, he has to switch to some distasteful imagery, such as discovering that the child is covered with sores. Thus he provides his own negative reinforcement and thereby gradually extinguishes his paraphilic desires—or that is the hope, at least.

In a complementary approach, behavior therapists attempt to treat paraphilic men not by punishing their paraphilic desires, but by rewarding more normal ones. The reward (or **positive reinforcement**) is usually orgasm. In a typical form of this treatment, a pedophile may be told to masturbate to fantasies or images of children, but just before he reaches orgasm, he is told to switch to fantasies or images of adults. As the treatment program goes on, the man is encouraged to use the adult fantasies at an earlier and earlier stage of masturbation, until he has accomplished the entire process with adult fantasies. At this point he has supposedly learned to be sexually aroused by a more normal object of sexual desire—an adult. This procedure is called **orgasmic reconditioning.**

During the 1970s these behavioral approaches were quite popular, and their practitioners claimed success in treating a variety of paraphilias, as well as in converting homosexuals to heterosexuality (Abel et al., 1978; Maletzky, 1974; Maletzky & George, 1973). These methods are still quite widely used in treatment programs for sex offenders (Dougher, 1995), but there is now widespread skepticism about their efficacy (American Medical Association, 1987; Marshall, 1998).

Social Skills Training May Overcome Blockage of Normal Sexual Expression

If the main cause of paraphilias is the blockage of normal sexual feelings and behaviors, then relieving that blockage might allow paraphilic forms of sexual expression to disappear. Psychoanalysts have attempted to do this by uncovering the events of infancy or early childhood that supposedly lead to unresolved Oedipal conflicts or other problems. This approach is extremely time-consuming and expensive. Even if it works, which has never been objectively documented, it is not a practical strategy for treating most paraphiliacs.

Another approach is to strengthen the social skills that are needed for normal sexual expression. Therapists may aim to help their clients improve their self-esteem, assertiveness, empathy, and intimacy. They may help them practice interactions with women, including such basic matters as how to behave on a date as well as how to deal with conflicts and jealousy. This kind of treatment is often conducted in groups.

Relapse prevention. Social worker Karen Swearingen leads a discussion in a sex offender education group at the Circleville Juvenile Detention Center in Ohio.

There are some reports of successes with this kind of approach. One treatment program, for example, was focused on raising the self-esteem of child molesters. It was successful in this aim and, as a by-product, apparently led to a reduction in their pedophilic desires (Marshall, 1997). There was no control group in this study, however.

Related forms of therapy include programs to encourage the correction of cognitive distortions and **relapse prevention programs.** The latter programs include very specific training in how to identify the situations that may trigger a repeat offense and how to avoid or cope with those situations. One controlled study of a relapse prevention program showed little or no beneficial effect (Marques et al., 1994; Marques, 1999).

According to a recent meta-analysis of research into the effectiveness of all kinds of psychotherapy for sex offenders, such treatments do lower recidivism rates, but the effect is a modest one: 12.3 percent of treated offenders reoffend, compared with 16.8 percent of untreated offenders (Hanson et al., 2002).

Drug Treatments Can Be Highly Effective in Reducing Recidivism

Of the various drugs that are used for the treatment of paraphilias (Figure 14.4), the one used most widely in the United States is **medroxyprogesterone acetate,** or **Depo-Provera.** As mentioned in Chapter 11, Depo-Provera is a synthetic injectable progestin that is used as a long-term contraceptive in women. Depo-Provera exerts feedback inhibition on the release of GnRH from the hypothalamus. This leads to a decline in the secretion of gonadotropins by the pituitary, and thus (in men) to a decline in testosterone secretion by the testes (see Chapter 4). Depo-Provera also accelerates the removal of testosterone from the circulation by the liver. The end result is a profound drop in plasma testosterone levels and a concomitant reduction in sexual desires and behaviors. In one study of convicted sex offenders, those treated with Depo-Provera plus psychotherapy were far less likely to reoffend than were control offenders who were treated with psychotherapy only (Meyer et al., 1992). Unfortunately, the study design was imperfect. Offenders were not randomly assigned to the drug treatment or control groups; rather, the control group consisted of men who refused Depo-Provera, and those men might have been less motivated to lose their sexual urges and more likely to reoffend.

Depo-Provera is far from an ideal drug. It can have serious side effects, including liver damage and disorders of blood clotting. Also, it does not "cure" paraphilias in the sense of redirecting the person's libido into normal channels; it simply decreases libido altogether. If the person stops receiving injections, his paraphilic desires and behaviors are likely to return. Some states have mandated Depo-Provera treatment for convicted or recidivist sex offenders. These laws raise ethical and practical problems and are sometimes counterproductive because they restrict treatment options (Stone et al., 2000).

A newer class of drugs that also lowers testosterone levels are the **GnRH agonists,** such as **leuprolide** (Lupron). As described in Chapter 4, the administration of leuprolide initially causes an increase in testosterone levels, but after a week or two, the pituitary becomes desensitized and gonadotropin and testosterone levels fall to below normal levels. We mentioned the use of leuprolide to delay puberty in Chapter 5 (in the context of precocious puberty) and in Chapter 13 (in the context of transexuality). Early studies suggest that leuprolide is very effective in the treatment of paraphilias, although, like Depo-Provera, it can have serious side effects, including a severe reduction in bone density (Krueger & Kaplan, 2001).

An alternative strategy is to block the action of testosterone on its receptors by the means of **androgen receptor antagonists.** The most useful drug in this class seems to be cyproterone acetate, which has been shown (in a double-blind, placebo-controlled study) to reduce sexual fantasies and some sexual behaviors in recidivist sex offenders (Bradford & Pawlak, 1993). Cyproterone is widely used in Canada and Europe, but is not approved in the United States for the treatment of sex offenders.

All the above-mentioned drugs work by interfering with the production or actions of androgens. A different approach is offered by the use of **selective serotonin reuptake inhibitors** (**SSRIs**). These drugs, whose main use is in the treatment of depression, increase the levels of the neurotransmitter serotonin at synapses by preventing its reuptake into presynaptic axon terminals. Several SSRIs, including **sertraline** (Zoloft) and **fluoxetine** (Prozac), have been shown to reduce or eliminate a wide variety of paraphilic desires and behaviors, including exhibitionism, voyeurism, fetishism, and cross-dressing, as well as hypersexuality (see Chapter 15) (Balon, 1998). There is no evidence that SSRIs are effective for the prevention of serious sexual offenses such as child molestation or rape.

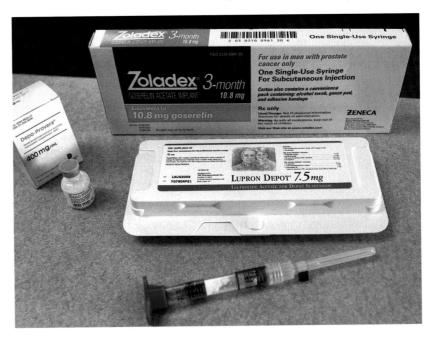

Figure 14.4 Drugs used to treat sex offenders include the injectable progestin Depo-Provera and the GnRH agonists leuprolide (Lupron) and goserelin (Zoladex).

As many people who take SSRIs for depression know, SSRIs can interfere with a person's sex drive or cause erectile difficulties. These "side effects" are probably part of the reason why they relieve paraphilias. However, there also seems to be a specific effect on paraphilic urges: men whose paraphilias are responsive to SSRIs often retain a healthy sex drive, unlike men who are treated with Depo-Provera or the other drugs mentioned earlier. Because SSRIs are also effective in the treatment of obsessive–compulsive disorders, it is suspected that they also relieve the obsessive or compulsive component of paraphilias.

Castration Is a Treatment of Last Resort

Surgical castration (removal of the testicles) removes a man's main source of androgens. The surgery is followed by a rapid drop in circulating androgen levels and a slower, somewhat variable decline in sexual desires and behaviors, including physiological responses such as erection and ejaculation (Zverina et al., 1990). Castration may be more effective than other treatments for the prevention of sexual recidivism (Meyer & Cole, 1997) (Box 14.7). According to one review of studies of castrated sex offenders—most of whom had committed multiple and/or violent offenses prior to surgery—only 1 to 7 percent reoffended, compared with an expected recidivism rate of 50–77 percent (Prentky, 1997).

Castration is a drastic intervention that raises memories of historical abuses. Up until the 1970s, compulsory and widespread sterilization of the mentally retarded, rapists, and some other offenders was carried out in several U.S. states, partly under the influence of the eugenics movement (Reilly & Grob, 1991). One state, Virginia, has recently issued a formal apology for the sterilizations performed in its name (Associated Press, 2002b).

Box 14.7 *Society, Values, and the Law*

Castration: Barbaric Punishment or Ticket to Freedom?

Atascadero State Hospital, near San Luis Obispo in central California, is the end of the road for 400 convicted sex offenders. The men who are incarcerated here have committed at least two sexual assaults against strangers or acquaintances (not against family members). They have served out their sentences in regular prisons, but under California's 1996 "sexual predator law," they can be kept at Atascadero indefinitely. Each inmate is evaluated every 2 years to see if he can be safely let out, but his chances are slim: only one has ever been released. Eventually, the population at Atascadero and other such facilities in California is expected to rise to 1500. And it costs over $100,000 per year to house each inmate.

Brian DeVries wants to change that. DeVries, 42, has molested at least nine boys in four states, and has been held at Atascadero since 1997. He has been given drugs to reduce his paraphilic urges, but he failed his biennial review in 1999 and was looking at spending the rest of his life in the "Gulag," as the inmates refer to Atascadero. So he applied to a court to be

castrated, hoping that the surgery would make him an acceptable candidate for release. In August 2001 Judge Robert Baines agreed to his request, and the surgery was performed a few days later.

Whether the operation will lead to DeVries's eventual release is not yet clear, but there are precedents. Delmar Burrows, 37, was convicted three times of fondling prepubescent boys. Facing life in a state mental hospital, he applied to a judge to be castrated, and the operation was performed in 1997. The same judge later ordered him released. Burrows, who is borderline mentally retarded, now lives quietly in Sacramento. He registers as a sex offender regularly, as required by law, and so far has stayed out of trouble. "I should have done this a long time ago," he told the *Los Angeles Times.* "I feel at peace and as a whole person now. I see those kids, but I don't pay any attention. I used to think bad things."

At least 15 other "sexual predators" in California have requested castration. One of them, William Charles Thiel, has served 30 years in prisons and mental hospitals for

molesting a series of boys. "I want to be able to live any life I've got left with as much freedom as possible," he said. "I'm going on 60 years old. Sex is not a big thing with me anymore. I'd be much happier just to go sit under a tree or listen to the sound of the ocean."

These developments have raised protests from both liberals and conservatives. The ACLU attempted to stop the castration of a sex offender in Arkansas who chose the operation in exchange for a reduced sentence. Ethicists have questioned whether castration under such circumstances can be considered truly voluntary (Hicks, 1993). On the other hand, many members of the public feel that repeat sex offenders should be locked up forever, no matter what treatment they receive. "Even if [castration] does cleanse him of deviant thoughts," said one former neighbor of William Thiel, "he still has to be punished for his crimes. He still hasn't paid his debt to society for what he did to children. That's the worst crime you could ever do."

Sources: Marosi, 2001; Webby, 2001.

The Association for the Treatment of Sexual Abusers (ATSA), which represents the therapists who treat sex offenders, is opposed to castration. The ATSA argues that castration is not necessarily effective, because some castrated men retain sexual desires and behaviors. They also point out that castrated men can obtain testosterone illegally, thus reawakening their libido (Association for the Treatment of Sexual Offenders, 1997). Even so, some states, such as Texas and California, have begun to reintroduce the operation on a voluntary basis, and this has led to the release of some offenders who otherwise would likely have spent the rest of their lives behind bars.

More Research on Paraphilias Is Needed

As you have probably realized while reading this chapter, very little about abnormal forms of sexual expression is well understood or agreed upon. What are the limits of normal sexual experience or acceptable sexual behavior? What makes psychosexual development go awry? How can paraphilias be prevented or cured? Is it possible to treat paraphiliacs humanely and still protect society from sex crimes? Finding the answers to these questions is an enormously challenging and worthwhile goal. Maybe some of you will be motivated to search for them.

Summary

1. The boundary between normal and abnormal sexuality is imprecise and subjective, and is defined socially as well as medically. According to the APA, paraphilias are sexual feelings or behaviors that are targeted at nonhuman objects or nonconsenting persons, or that involve suffering or humiliation, and that cause significant distress or social dysfunction. Many paraphilic behaviors are illegal.

2. In general, paraphilias are extensions or exaggerations of normal sexual feelings or behaviors. Far more men than women have paraphilias. It is quite common for a person to develop multiple paraphilias over time. Paraphiliacs who commit sex offenses often have deficient social skills and other psychological problems. Some have been abused during childhood.

3. Fetishists are sexually fixated on objects, materials, or body parts. Transvestic fetishists are sexually aroused by cross-dressing, but not all cross-dressers are fetishists.

4. Exhibitionists are sexually aroused by exposing their genitals to others (usually women) in public places. Making obscene phone calls is a variety of exhibitionism. Voyeurs spy on women who are undressed or engaged in sex. Frotteurs make body contact with women in crowds.

5. Sadists are sexually aroused by the infliction of pain or psychological degradation, and masochists are aroused by suffering pain or degradation themselves. Most sado-masochistic practitioners interact in controlled settings where no real injury is inflicted, but sadism can extend to real torture and murder.

6. Sexual contacts with animals are quite common, but a paraphilic fixation on animals (zoophilia) is rare, as is a fixation on dead bodies (necrophilia).

7. Pedophiles are sexually attracted to prepubescent children more than to adults. Pedophiles and child molesters are overlapping but nonidentical groups. Most pedophiles are attracted preferentially to children of one sex.

8. Sex offenders repeat their offenses less often than many other kinds of offenders. Certain factors, such as mental retardation, alcohol use, and a history of violence or sexual contact with unrelated children are associated with an increased likelihood of recidivism.

9. A variety of theories attempt to explain paraphilias. Some see them as the result of distorted learning processes, or as the result of a blockage of normal sexual expression. Some categorize paraphilias as forms of obsessive–compulsive disorder. Other theories point to the victim–perpetrator cycle as a cause of sexual offenses, especially against children. There are also biological theories that attribute paraphilias to neurological, endocrinological, or genetic disturbances.

10. The various theories of paraphilia have led to diverse forms of treatment. Behavioral approaches, such as aversion therapy and orgasmic reconditioning, attempt to help paraphiliacs unlearn their paraphilias and relearn normal sexual desires. The efficacy of these approaches is doubtful.

11. Social skills training programs are aimed at overcoming the social and self-esteem problems that act as barriers to normal sexual functioning. Relapse prevention programs help sex offenders identify and avoid situations in which they are likely to reoffend. Programs of this kind often involve group therapy.

12. Drug treatments are aimed at the biological mechanisms that may cause or support paraphilias. Medroxyprogesterone acetate (Depo-Provera) and GnRH agonists reduce testosterone levels, and androgen receptor antagonists block testosterone's effects. These drugs all produce a general decrease in sexual interest and behavior, but they can have serious side effects. They have been found to reduce, but not eliminate, recidivism by sex offenders.

13. Selective serotonin reuptake inhibitors (SSRIs) relieve a variety of mild to moderate paraphilias, perhaps through a reduction of their obsessive–compulsive component.

14. Castration of sex offenders is a drastic but effective method of reducing recidivism. Although there are ethical problems with its use, castration is gradually being reintroduced and has allowed a small number of offenders to reenter the community.

Discussion Questions

1. Do you think society should place any legal restrictions on the expression of non-coercive paraphilias (e.g., as a solo activity or with a consenting partner)? Give a rationale for your point of view.

2. People who engage in paraphilic activities often find it very difficult to give them up. Compare the advantages and disadvantages of various treatments (e.g., psychotherapy, behavior therapy, drug therapy).

3. Entertainers who are strippers, burlesque dancers, or peep show dancers certainly exhibit themselves. Are they exhibitionists?

4. If you were confronted by an exhibitionist who exposed himself, what would you do? Why?

5. A pedophile who has been arrested for molesting a child argues that he has a sexual compulsion that he cannot resist. Do you think treatment should be legally mandated? Which treatments do you think would be best for him, and why?

6. Recently the Catholic Church has faced a major controversy over reports that priests have had sexual contacts with minors (see Box 14.4). In several cases, the priests received counseling and were moved to another parish, where they repeated their behavior. Take a position about what an institution (e.g., religious or educational) should do about reports of child molestation. Should the institution handle the accusation itself or should it turn the matter over to the police? If the reports of molestation are accurate, how should these persons be treated? What should be done to prevent further incidents?

7. Imagine that you're a therapist who is counseling a couple. The woman has caught the man cross-dressing. What questions would you ask him to find out what's really going on and whether he has a paraphilia?

Web Resources

American Professional Society on the Abuse of Children www.apsac.org

Association for the Treatment of Sexual Offenders www.atsa.com

Gray, M. *Sex laws* (tabulates U.S. state and foreign sex laws, with many useful links)
vatavia.net/~vatavian/laws/

Tri-Ess (organization for heterosexual cross-dressers) www.triess-outreach.org

U.S. Department of Health and Human Services (1999). *Child abuse and neglect state statutes elements: Number 35: Sexual offenses* (lists and defines state laws relating to age of consent and sexual offenses against minors)
www.calib.com/nccanch/pubs/stats00/sexual.pdf

Recommended Reading

Bullough, V. L., and Bullough, B. (1993). *Cross-dressing, sex, and gender.* Philadelphia: University of Pennsylvania Press.

Henkin, W. A., and Holiday, S. (1996). *Consensual sadomasochism: How to talk about it and how to do it safely.* San Francisco: Daedalus.

Laws, D. R., and O'Donohue, W. (1997). *Sexual deviance: Theory, assessment, and treatment.* New York: Guilford Press.

Posner, R. A., and Silbaugh, K. B. (1996). *A guide to America's sex laws.* Chicago: University of Chicago Press.

Quinsey, V. L., and Lalumière, M. L. (2001). *Assessment of sex offenders against children* (2nd ed.). Thousand Oaks, CA: Sage Publications.

Weinberg, T. S. (ed.) (1995). *S and M: Studies in dominance and submission.* Buffalo, NY: Prometheus Books.

chapter 15

WARNING: SMOKING CAUSES IMPOTENCE

Smoking greatly increases the risk of erectile dysfunction in men, as shown pointedly in this antismoking poster.

Disorders of Desire and Performance

We turn now from unusual or bizarre forms of sexual expression to more mundane problems that can interfere with even the most conventional of sex lives. There are a number of physiological and psychological conditions that can impair sexual interest or arousal or make sexual interactions painful or unrewarding. Most of these conditions are deficiencies, such as a lack of interest in sex or a difficulty with erection, lubrication, or orgasm. Some, however, represent overexcitable states, such as premature ejaculation and excessive sexual behavior. Either way, these disorders are common. For the most part, they are more readily treatable than the paraphilias discussed in the previous chapter. The major factor impeding their successful treatment is people's reluctance to discuss sexual problems openly with their partners or to seek appropriate professional advice and therapy.

Sexual Disorders Are Common

Large numbers of men and women have problems with some aspect of sexual function. The best survey data on this topic come from the NHSLS, although unfortunately, that survey covers only men and women aged 18–59 (Laumann et al., 1994, 2000). The survey asked about seven kinds of sexual dysfunction: lack of interest in sex, lack of pleasure in sex, pain during sex, problems with erection or lubrication, inability to reach orgasm, climaxing too early, and anxiety about sexual performance. The percentages of the participants who acknowledged having these problems ranged from a low of 3 percent (men who experienced pain during sex) to a high of 33 percent (women who lacked interest in sex).

Although both men and women commonly experience sexual problems, there are marked differences in the kinds of problems they report (Figure 15.1). For women, the leading problems are a lack of interest in sex, a lack of pleasure in sex, and an inability to experience orgasm. For men, climaxing too early (premature ejaculation) is far and away the leading problem, followed by anxiety about performance and a lack of interest in sex.

The prevalence of sexual problems changes over the life span, as is obvious even within the restricted age range surveyed by the NHSLS (Figure 15.2). For women, the prevalence of sexual problems generally decreases with age: women in their fifties are far less likely than women in their twenties to find sex unpleasurable, to experience pain during sex, or to suffer from anxiety about their sexual performance. The only problem for which this trend is reversed is lack of vaginal lubrication, which becomes a more frequent problem after menopause. As men age, they are increasingly likely to lack interest in sex and to have problems with erection.

Presenting these kinds of statistics about the prevalence of sexual problems can be a bit misleading, however, for a couple of reasons. First, most sex is interactive, so the "problem," if there is one, may relate to the relationship between two people, rather than being an attribute of one particular man or woman. A person may be unable to reach orgasm with one partner, for example, but able to do so with another.

Second, a sexual "dysfunction" may not be experienced as a problem by the person who "suffers" from it. In one well-known study, researchers interviewed 100 happily married couples about their sex lives (Frank et al., 1978). More than half of the women and nearly half of the men reported some kind of sexual dysfunction, yet most of these "dysfunctional" women and men were satisfied with their sex lives. Quite a few elderly widows have lost interest in sex, but are not bothered by that fact, and have an active social life otherwise. Is that a problem for these women? Might they not have more of a "problem" if they were somehow persuaded to undergo treatment to restore their sex drive, considering the difficulty they might have in finding sex partners (see Chapter 12)? In other words, there is little reason to consider a sexual dysfunction a problem in need of treatment unless the person or couple experiencing it is distressed by it.

In this chapter we deal first with problems related to physiological arousal: difficulties with erection, lubrication, orgasm, and the like. Then we discuss conditions that cause intercourse to be painful. Finally we cover disorders of desire—too little or too much interest in sex. In contrast to the organization of the previous chapter, we discuss the causes and treatments of these various problems individually. That's because, unlike paraphilias, these conditions tend to have fairly specific causes and treatments.

Nevertheless, we will see interactions among the various conditions: in particular, problems with sexual performance can diminish interest in sex, and conversely, a loss of interest in sex can show itself in performance problems. Thus, clinicians who see women and men with sexual dysfunctions need to inquire about the entirety of their sex lives—both the physical details and the psychological environment—in order to understand what aspect of their sexuality is the root cause of the problem. Oftentimes, specialists with quite varied

Figure 15.1 Sex differences in the prevalence of sexual dysfunctions. These histograms refer only to ages 18–59, the ages that were surveyed. (Data from NHSLS.)

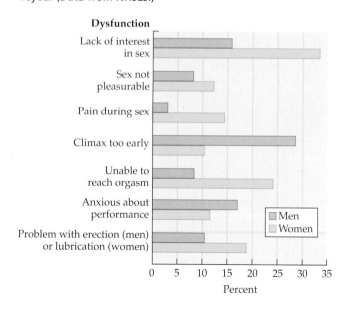

Dysfunction

Lack of interest in sex
Sex not pleasurable
Pain during sex
Climax too early
Unable to reach orgasm
Anxious about performance
Problem with erection (men) or lubrication (women)

Men
Women

0   5   10   15   20   25   30   35
Percent

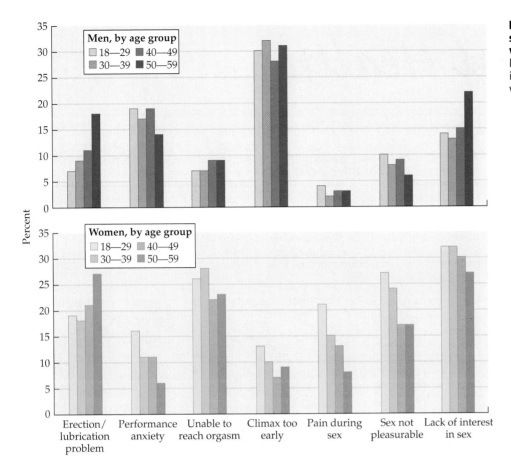

Figure 15.2 The prevalence of sexual dysfunctions changes with age. It is likely that erection and lubrication problems continue to increase after 59, the oldest age surveyed. (Data from NHSLS.)

backgrounds must collaborate in the diagnosis and treatment of sexual dysfunctions (Box 15.1).

Erectile Dysfunction Has Many Causes and Treatments

Erectile dysfunction or **erectile disorder** (once called **impotence**) is a recurrent inability to achieve an adequate penile erection or to maintain it through the course of the desired sexual behavior—if such inability causes distress to the man or difficulty between the man and his partner. The DSM-IV excludes erectile difficulties due to certain causes (such as drug use and general medical conditions) from its definition of erectile dysfunction, but we will include these in our discussion.

There are four basic scenarios of male erectile dysfunction:

- No erection occurs at all.
- Partial erection occurs, but it is not sufficient for the desired activity—usually coitus.
- Full erection occurs, but it is lost before the desired behavior is completed.
- Erection occurs sometimes, but not when the man wants it to.

Erectile dysfunction, like most sexual dysfunctions, can be lifelong (**primary** erectile dysfunction), or it can crop up in someone who has previously had normal erections (**secondary** erectile dysfunction).

Erectile Function Reflects the Balance between Sympathetic and Parasympathetic Inputs to the Penis

Before considering the causes of erectile dysfunction, let's remind ourselves of the normal mechanism of penile erection (described more fully in Chapter 3). Erection occurs when blood enters the sinusoids of the erectile tissue (corpora cavernosa and corpus

Box 15.1 *Sexual Health*

Professionals Who Treat Sexual Dysfunctions

Psychiatrists are medical doctors with specialized training in mental disorders. This combination of medical and mental health training is advantageous in the treatment of sexual dysfunctions because these dysfunctions may have either organic or psychological roots. Because they are M.D.s, psychiatrists can prescribe drugs. Their knowledge of and beliefs about sexual dysfunctions are variable—some psychiatrists are biologically oriented, and some are more psychologically oriented. Most believe that some combination of medical and psychological treatment is appropriate for many kinds of sexual dysfunctions.

Urologists are M.D.s with specialized training in urogenital disorders in men and women. **Gynecologists** are M.D.s with specialized training in women's health, including genital problems. Urologists and gynecologists usually lack specialized mental health training, so they are likely to concentrate on aspects of sexual dysfunction that are biological in origin. Gynecologists are familiar with the sexual dysfunctions that may accompany or follow menopause and can prescribe hormone replacement therapy.

Psychotherapists (or "therapists") are not usually M.D.s; they generally have advanced degrees in clinical or professional psychology. They rely mostly on conversation with their clients for diagnosis and treatment. They know a lot about relationships and often treat couples or groups. Their knowledge of sexual dysfunctions is variable. They do not have specialized training in urogenital disorders and cannot usually prescribe drugs.

Sex therapists are a subgroup of psychotherapists who specialize in sexual dysfunctions. They are usually not M.D.s and cannot prescribe drugs; still, they may know more about the genitals than the average psychiatrist. They often concentrate on the behavioral treatment of sexual dysfunctions, following the tradition established by Masters and Johnson. That is, they discuss the physical details of sex with their clients and recommend techniques such as sensate-focus exercises. If they also address attitudes and belief systems, they may call themselves **cognitive-behavioral therapists.**

Sex surrogates are persons, usually without formal training, who engage in direct sexual interactions with clients under the direction of a sex therapist. The majority are women who deal with male clients. Often, they perform sensate-focus and similar exercises with men who lack a partner of their own. The sexual interactions may or may not include coitus, but this is rarely a major part of the interaction. For a variety of reasons (ethical issues, disease and legal concerns, advances in medical treatments), sex surrogacy has lost popularity and is now available only in a few large metropolitan areas (see Web Resources).

Urologist Jennifer Berman (left) and her sister, psychotherapist Laura Berman, bring complementary skills to the treatment of women with sexual dysfunctions. They run the Female Sexual Medicine Center at UCLA.

---

spongiosum) faster than it leaves. For this to happen, smooth muscle cells in the walls of the arterioles supplying the erectile tissue must relax, allowing the arterioles to dilate and blood flow into the erectile tissue to increase. This relaxation is caused by reciprocal changes in the activity of the autonomic nerves innervating the arterioles. The sympathetic nerve fibers become *less* active, and thus release less of their neurotransmitter, norepinephrine. The parasympathetic nerve fibers become *more* active, and thus release more of their neurotransmitters, acetylcholine, vasoactive intestinal polypeptide (VIP), and nitric oxide. Nitric oxide causes an increase in the levels of cyclic guanosine monophosphate (cGMP) within the smooth muscle cells of the arteriolar walls, and cGMP causes the muscle cells to relax. The changes in neural activity that cause erection can be triggered either by stimulation of the genital area (a spinal reflex) or by erotic thoughts or sights (through pathways that descend from the brain to the spinal cord).

Erectile Dysfunction Can Have Physical or Psychological Causes

A great variety of factors can cause or contribute to erectile dysfunction, ranging from entirely physical factors (such as nerve damage) to entirely psychological ones (such as relationship dissatisfaction). Often, however, there is an interplay of physical and psychological factors, which reinforce each other and need to be disentangled. Here are the major contributing factors:

- **Smoking.** Substances in tobacco smoke damage the lining of arterioles throughout the body, including the penis, preventing them from relaxing normally. Smokers run about twice the risk of erectile dysfunction as non-smokers (McVary et al., 2001). Smoking is particularly harmful in men who have other risk factors for erectile dysfunction.
- **Alcohol.** Everyone knows that alcohol in low or moderate doses increases arousal, reduces inhibition, and acts as a general sexual lubricant. At high doses, however, alcohol depresses sexual functions, including erection. Chronic alcoholics may develop a multiplicity of medical problems that cause erectile difficulties or interfere with sexual desire, even at times when alcohol is not in the body.
- **Obesity.** Men who are obese or who do not exercise regularly are at greatly increased risk of developing erectile dysfunction.
- **Medical conditions.** Many medical conditions can interfere with erection. An especially common cause is diabetes, a condition that can damage both blood vessels and nerves. Forty percent of diabetic men over 60 years old have permanent erectile dysfunction (Chew et al., 2000). Hypertension and other forms of cardiovascular disease are also major culprits. Spinal cord injury can produce complete erectile dysfunction or, if the damage is high in the cord, there may be a specific loss of erections in response to erotic thoughts (**psychogenic erections**). Prostate disease and prostate surgery can cause erectile difficulties by damaging the nerves that run to the penis (see Chapter 17).
- **Trauma.** Injury to the perineal region can damage the blood supply to the penis, leading to erectile dysfunction. Bicycling accidents in which the perineum is struck by the top tube of the bicycle frame are a common cause of such injury. Even without any accidents, prolonged bicycling can damage the perineal vessels and nerves (Sommer et al., 2001). Bicycling enthusiasts should use as wide a seat as practical and take breaks or ride out of the saddle frequently to permit blood to reach the perineal area.
- **Drugs.** The use of many prescription drugs is associated with erectile difficulties. Often, however, it is difficult to tell whether it is the drug itself, or the condition for which the drug is being taken, that is responsible. Drugs commonly prescribed to treat hypertension, for example, are widely thought to cause erectile dysfunction, but a large-scale placebo-controlled study found that they do not do so, or at worst cause only temporary problems (Grimm et al., 1997).

  The only widely prescribed drugs that have been shown unequivocally to contribute to erectile dysfunction are **benzodiazepines** (the "minor tranquilizers" such as diazepam [Valium]), and certain **diuretics** (drugs that increase urine production) (Derby et al., 2001). Among other drugs that probably cause erectile difficulties in some users are certain popular psychiatric drugs such as **selective serotonin reuptake inhibitors (SSRIs)** (e.g., fluoxetine [Prozac]). These drugs appear to interfere with the circuitry within the central nervous system that mediates penile erection (see Chapter 3).
- **Stress.** Any kind of stress can lead to sexual problems, including erectile dysfunction. Examples include relationship difficulties, financial or career problems, illness, bereavement, and so on. Chronic stress may affect sexual function by lowering testosterone levels.

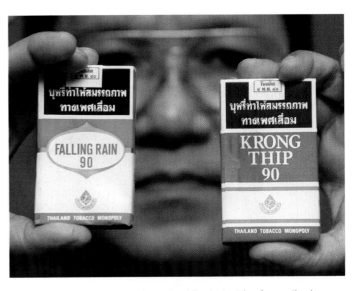

Smokers double their risk of erectile dysfunction. Thailand was the first country in the world to warn of this risk on cigarette packs. These two Thai cigarette packs, held by an official from the Thailand Tobacco Monopoly, contain labels in Thai informing smokers that "cigarette smoking causes sexual impotence."

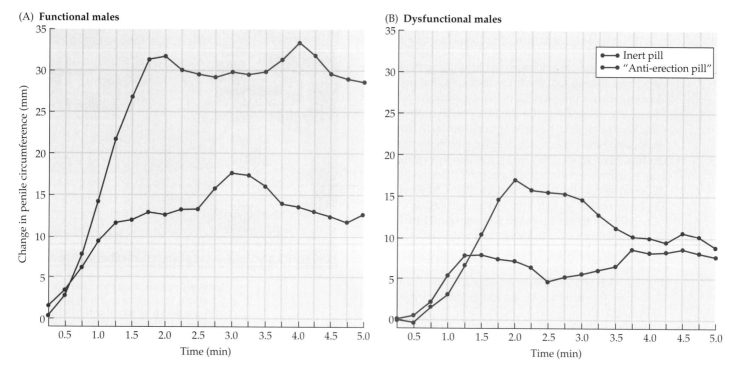

(A) Functional males

(B) Dysfunctional males

Time (min)

Time (min)

Change in penile circumference (mm)

Figure 15.3 Anxiety has opposite effects on arousal in normal men and in men with erectile dysfunction. (A) Normal heterosexual men's penile responses to an erotic video after taking a pill described as an inert placebo or a pill described as lessening erection. The "anti-erection pill" (actually the same inert pill as the placebo) substantially *increased* the men's erectile responses. (B) The same experiment in heterosexual men with erectile dysfunction. The "anti-erection pill" *depressed* the men's erectile responses. (After Cranston-Cuebas et al., 1993.)

- **Anxiety.** According to Masters and Johnson, anxiety about sexual performance is a prime cause of sexual problems such as erectile dysfunction (Masters & Johnson, 1970). Anxiety works either through the emotions it engenders or by setting up thought patterns that distract the person from the direct enjoyment of the sexual experience.

  In more recent studies, David Barlow and his colleagues at the State University of New York at Albany have shown that anxiety has opposite effects in normal men and in men with sexual dysfunctions (Barlow, 1986; Cranston-Cuebas et al., 1993). The researchers showed erotic videos to both normal and sexually dysfunctional men while monitoring their arousal by penile plethysmography. When they increased the men's anxiety (by the threat of electric shocks, or by administering a pill that was described as preventing erection), the penile responses of the dysfunctional men were lessened, but the penile responses of the normal men were actually enhanced (Figure 15.3). In other words, a certain amount of anxiety can actually *increase* arousal in normal men, but it *depresses* the arousal of sexually dysfunctional men.

  These results do not explain how the dysfunctional men came to be dysfunctional in the first place. They might have had biological disturbances that interfered with erection, or they might have developed erectile difficulties as the result of some negative experiences. Once these difficulties begin, however, it seems that a vicious cycle begins in which the erectile dysfunction and the anxiety feed off each other, and this cycle seems to operate more powerfully in sexually dysfunctional men than in normal men. When we bear in mind that anxiety directly affects the activity of the autonomic nervous system, and that the autonomic nervous system in turn controls the constriction and dilation of arterioles in the erectile tissue, it is hardly surprising that anxiety has such marked effects on erectile responses.

- **Depression.** Masters and Johnson also believed that depression is a common cause of erectile dysfunction. These two phenomena are certainly correlated: depressed men are more likely to experience erectile dysfunction that nondepressed men. However, it is equally possible that the erectile dysfunction comes first and makes the men depressed, or that the two phenomena are correlated because they have some causes in common. Current thinking is that erectile dysfunction, depression, and cardiovascular disease all share a number of causes and reinforce each other, triggering a downward spiral of dysfunctionality (Goldstein, 2000).

Urologists and Mental Health Specialists Collaborate

Ideally, erectile dysfunction should be evaluated by both a urologist and a mental health specialist to identify the cause of the dysfunction and to initiate a course of treatment (Rosen et al., 1998). The aim of the evaluation is to determine what the problem is and its likely cause. The mental health specialist will ask detailed questions about the patient's sexual functioning and how long the problem has lasted, and will try to discover whether relationship difficulties or stressful events are contributing to the problem. Contributing factors can range from the trivial (the home offers no privacy for lovemaking) to the profound (the man is married to a woman but is sexually attracted to men). The patient's partner will also be interviewed separately; she or he may communicate important facts (such as a drinking problem) that the patient himself did not divulge.

The urologist will focus on possible biological problems. Does the patient ever have erections on waking in the morning? Most men do quite often have such erections; if the patient does not, there may be an organic cause for the dysfunction. If necessary, it is possible to monitor penile tumescence during sleep, as described in Chapter 7. Erections normally occur during rapid-eye-movement sleep; again, the absence of such erections suggests an organic problem. The urologist can also conduct tests that directly evaluate the erectile capacity of the penis, such as the injection into the penis of drugs that normally cause erection, and can examine the patient for the variety of medical conditions and drug treatments that can cause erectile dysfunction.

Simple Steps May Alleviate the Problem

A clinician will present the findings of the mental health and urological studies to the patient, and perhaps to his partner, and together they will discuss treatment options. Sometimes the cause of the problem can be removed rather simply; for example, if the problem is caused by a prescription drug, it may be possible to substitute another drug that does not have the same effect.

Lifestyle changes such as quitting smoking, reducing alcohol consumption, losing weight (if the patient is obese), and beginning an exercise program may alleviate erectile difficulties. Unfortunately, most of these lifestyle factors do their damage early in adult life; by middle age, changes in lifestyle do little to reduce the risk of erectile dysfunction (Derby et al., 2000). The only exception is exercise, which helps avert erectile dysfunction throughout midlife. (Of course, there are many other well-documented health benefits of making these lifestyle changes in midlife, or even in old age.)

Sometimes all that is required is for the couple to have sex earlier in the day. Also, if the man tends to lose his erection during sex, he may be able to maintain the erection by placing a mildly constricting elastic band ("cock-ring") around the penis after he has achieved erection. The ring diminishes venous outflow from the penis and keeps it erect longer. Such a device should be taken off as soon as it has served its purpose; otherwise, it could cause damage to the penis.

Extended Psychotherapy May Be Necessary

Sometimes more extensive treatment is called for. If the underlying cause is relationship difficulties or performance anxiety, it may take a considerable period of psychotherapy to resolve these problems. One study found that most

Regular exercise is one of the best ways to lower the risk of erectile dysfunction.

Recent advertising for Viagra attempts to associate the drug with relatively young, healthy men.

patients' erectile dysfunction was relieved by psychotherapy, or that the patient and his partner learned to cope with the problem (Hawton et al., 1992). Because there was no control group, however, it is possible that the mere passage of time would have had an equally beneficial effect. Relapses are common in such cases (Hawton et al., 1986).

Sildenafil (Viagra) Has Become the Leading Medical Treatment

Medical treatment of erectile dysfunction centers around the drug **sildenafil** (**Viagra**). Within 3 months of its introduction in the United States in 1999, sildenafil became the nation's most prescribed medication, suggesting that erectile dysfunction is a far more widespread and serious problem than had previously been imagined. As described in Chapter 3, sildenafil acts by blocking the enzyme phosphodiesterase-5, whose job it is to break down cGMP within the smooth muscle cells of the arterioles supplying the erectile tissue. Therefore, in the presence of sildenafil, nitric oxide release by the parasympathetic nerve terminals causes cGMP to reach higher levels and thus to elicit more relaxation of the smooth muscle cells. At the usual doses, sildenafil does not cause erection unless the parasympathetic nerves are active. Thus, simply swallowing a sildenafil tablet does not produce an erection: there has to be some kind of sexual excitation as well.

Sildenafil is not without its problems. It must not be taken in conjunction with nitrate-containing medications or recreational drugs, nor by people who have the eye disease retinitis pigmentosa. It can cause side effects, such as headache and facial flushing. It also sometimes produces blurred vision or changes in color perception. That's because cGMP is used as a signaling molecule by photoreceptor cells in the retina, and the enzyme that breaks down cGMP in the photoreceptors is also inhibited, albeit weakly, by sildenafil.

The introduction of sildenafil triggered a debate about who should pay for it. Facing a cost of $7 per pill (wholesale) and seemingly limitless demand, medical insurance companies, HMOs, and state Medicare administrators saw the potential for financial meltdown. Furthermore, the question arose as to whether helping older men have sex was a legitimate public policy goal or a mere lifestyle enhancement that people should pay for themselves. Some states balked at paying for sildenafil at all, while others set limits on how many pills would be allowed. Utah, for example, initially decided the appropriate number was ten per month, but then reduced the number to five. In 1998 the Clinton administration ordered all states to provide Medicare coverage for sildenafil. This decision provoked objections from some states, and also triggered complaints from some other constituencies (the disabled, women's rights advocates) to the effect that limited financial resources were being misdirected for men's sexual pleasure. In the years since then, however, the controversy has abated: sildenafil is now seen as a more or less conventional medical drug that should be prescribed and paid for by the same criteria as other pharmaceuticals.

Other Oral Drugs Are in Development

Other oral medications for erectile dysfunction may come on the market within the next few years. Some, such as **vardenafil,** are sildenafil look-alikes. More interesting is the drug **phentolamine mesylate** (**Vasomax**). This drug works in a manner complementary to sildenafil: rather than enhancing the action of the parasympathetic nerves on the erectile tissue, it reduces the action of the sympathetic nerves. It does so by blocking the sympathetic neurotransmitter, norepinephrine. Preliminary studies suggest that this drug is quite effective in improving erectile function (Goldstein et al., 2001), but a concern about possible liver toxicity may delay or prevent its approval by the FDA.

A rather different drug under development is **apomorphine** (**Uprima**). This drug improves erectile function not by acting directly on the penis, but by acting on the sex centers of the brain—specifically, the medial preoptic area of the hypothalamus. You may recall from Chapter 14 that apomorphine is used in aversion therapy because it produces

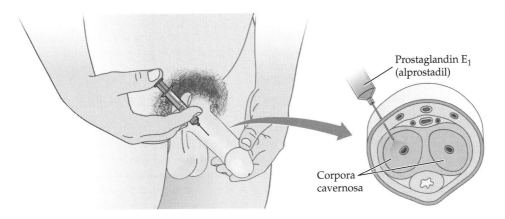

Figure 15.4 Prostaglandin E₁ (alprostadil) produces an erection when injected directly into the corpora cavernosa.

a highly aversive sensation: nausea. When apomorphine is taken for erectile dysfunction, nausea is an unwanted but all too common side effect. Dizziness is another common side effect.

Locally Applied Drugs Require Only That the Erectile Tissue Be Functional

There are also drugs that can be applied locally to produce an erection. One such drug is **prostaglandin E₁ (alprostadil)**, which acts directly on the smooth muscle cells of the arterioles, causing them to relax. The usual proprietary preparations of prostaglandin E₁ (**Edex, Caverject**) have to be injected directly into the corpora cavernosa of the penis, which is quite inconvenient (Figure 15.4). They are also one of the most expensive treatments for erectile dysfunction. In one study, over half the men who tried this technique eventually gave it up (Sexton et al., 1998). Despite its drawbacks, the injection method does provide a very reliable erection within a few minutes.

There is an alternative formulation of prostaglandin E₁ that does not require injection. The formulation, called the MUSE system and developed by the Vivus Corporation, takes the form of a suppository the size of a grain of rice, which is pushed into the urethra with an applicator. Because the drug has to diffuse some distance to reach the erectile tissue, the MUSE system is not as reliable as the injection method. Also, much higher doses have to be used than with the injection method, and in some men these doses cause an aching pain in the penis. There is one other drawback: Because some of the drug comes out in the ejaculate, a man using the MUSE system must not engage in unprotected coitus with a pregnant woman.

Erections produced by prostaglandin administration develop regardless of whether the man is sexually aroused or not; in fact, they work even when the parasympathetic innervation of the penis has been completely destroyed, just so long as the erectile tissue itself is still functional.

Another injectable preparation under development (**aviptadil**) consists of a mixture of phentolamine and the parasympathetic neurotransmitter VIP (Keijzers, 2001). All in all, it seems that there is going to be an increasing range of choices for the pharmaceutical treatment of erectile dysfunction.

Drugs Are Increasingly Being Used for Psychogenic Erectile Dysfunction

All of these erection-producing drugs were originally thought of as treatments for erectile dysfunction that was *organic* in origin, as in the case of diabetics, for example. It turns out, however, that sildenafil also works quite well in cases that are deemed to be psychological in origin, especially when it is used in conjunction with psychotherapy. In fact, it is increasingly believed that the great majority of cases of erectile dysfunction are organic in origin, though psychological factors often play a contributory role (Levine, 2000).

A major limitation of all these drugs, of course, is that they do nothing to *cure* erectile dysfunction; once the drug is discontinued, the erectile dysfunction is likely to recur. Curing erectile dysfunction that is organic in origin would require correcting the underlying condition, and that is rarely possible.

Does sildenafil do anything for men who *don't* have erectile dysfunction? Most medical authorities say that it does not improve the sexual performance of healthy men, but the porn industry says otherwise (Box 15.2).

One class of drugs that do not usually work well in erectile dysfunction is androgens—that is, testosterone and related compounds. Many men with erectile dysfunction have low testosterone levels, but in most cases this is not the cause of the dysfunction, but its consequence. Specifically, the erectile dysfunction prevents the man from engaging in sex, and the sexual inactivity seems to lower testosterone levels. When erectile dysfunction is successfully treated and the man returns to an active sex life, his testosterone levels usually return to normal (Jannini et al., 1999).

Erectile Dysfunction Can Be Treated with Devices and Implants

There are also non-drug methods to help men with erectile dysfunction. One such method is a **vacuum constriction system** (Figure 15.5), versions of which are made by several manufacturers. The man lubricates his penis and places a clear plastic cylinder over it, then draws a partial vacuum inside the tube with the aid of a hand pump. The vacuum draws blood into the erectile tissue. Once an erection has been attained, the man slips a constriction band around the base of the penis to maintain the erection after the cylinder is removed.

The major disadvantage of vacuum systems is that using them interrupts lovemaking in a major way. This almost precludes their use by a man who is engaged in casual dating, but an established couple that takes a light-hearted approach to sex may be able to work the vacuum system into their lovemaking routine. The constriction band often interferes with ejaculation. Another disadvantage is that excessive pumping can pull blood right out of the vessels into the tissue spaces (extravasation). The resulting bruises can take a week or more to heal.

The advantages of vacuum systems are that they are safe (if properly used), effective, and among the least expensive forms of treatment. Also, they do not require that the innervation of the penis be intact. Only about one-third of men who try vacuum systems continue to use them for long periods, however (Dutta & Eid, 1999).

A more invasive and expensive treatment involves the surgical insertion of **penile implants** (Mulcahy, 1999) (Figure 15.6). One kind of implant is a semi-rigid or malleable plastic rod that keeps the penis permanently stiff enough for coitus. It is relatively easy to have inserted surgically, but the permanent erection may be difficult to conceal and therefore

(A)

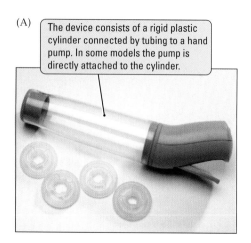

The device consists of a rigid plastic cylinder connected by tubing to a hand pump. In some models the pump is directly attached to the cylinder.

(B)

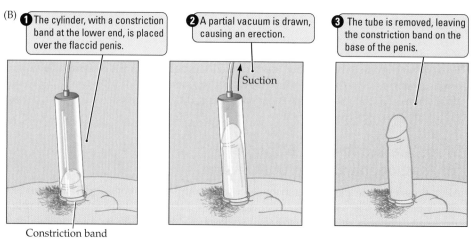

❶ The cylinder, with a constriction band at the lower end, is placed over the flaccid penis.

❷ A partial vacuum is drawn, causing an erection.

Suction

❸ The tube is removed, leaving the constriction band on the base of the penis.

Constriction band

Figure 15.5 Vacuum constriction systems produce an erection by drawing blood into the penis.

(A) **Semi-rigid implant**

The implant occupies both the visible shaft of the penis and the root within the body.

When not being used for sex, the penis, with its implant, is bent downward to be less conspicuous, but there is no change in rigidity.

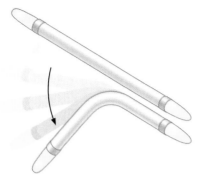

Figure 15.6 Penile implants.

(B) **Inflatable prosthesis**

Two expandable cylinders that can be filled with fluid (saline solution) are placed in the spaces previously occupied by the corpora cavernosa.

A reservoir for the fluid is implanted behind the abdominal wall.

A pump and release valve are implanted in the scrotum.

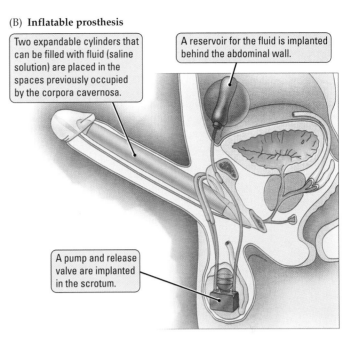

Box 15.2 *Society, Values, and the Law*

Better Porn through Chemistry

Pudgy, hairy, and none too good-looking, Ron Jeremy has nevertheless starred in 1700 pornographic movies over the past 23 years. His secret: being able to get an erection on command and to perform in front of the cameras once, twice, maybe even three times per day. Thanks to some mysterious physiological endowment that marks him off from regular mortals, Jeremy is Mr. Reliable Provider in the world of heterosexual porno movies, an industry that is based in Los Angeles' San Fernando Valley. And that's important, because unlike the feature films that are produced a few miles away in Hollywood, porno movies are made on a tight budget ($10,000–20,000) and an even tighter schedule (usually 3 days' shooting). A single failure to perform may cost a day's delay and spell the difference between profit and loss.

Recently, though, Jeremy has been seeing more competition, thanks to a little blue pill called Viagra. The competition is coming from "pretty boys"—actors who may be easier on the eye than Jeremy but who, until 1999, couldn't hold a candle to him in the performance department. Now they can.

Cheyne Collins, 34, is one of the new breed. "Back then, you could only do one, maybe two scenes a day," he told the *Los Angeles Times.* "Now we're doing five." Collins admits to using Viagra at least some of the time, especially if he's not in the mood "or I'm tired or sick that day." And the production staff love it. "I put Viagra right up there with the polio vaccine, as far as making my job easier," said director Michael McCormick of Metro Productions. Typically, directors give their male actors 30 minutes' warning before their curtain call, so that they can take their pill and be ready for action when the cameras start rolling.

Viagra is widely used as a recreational drug. Porno actors, like anyone else, can readily obtain the pill by answering a few questions on the Internet. The manufacturer, Pfizer, emphasizes that Viagra is for men with erectile dysfunction only, and that the maximum dosage is one pill per day. Still, Pfizer's advertising suggests differently. Initially, the commercials featured old men with bona fide erectile dysfunction, such as prostate cancer survivor and former U.S. Senator Bob Dole. More recently, the ads have featured much younger and more virile-looking men—the kind of men who are less likely to have erectile dysfunction.

Within the porno industry, Viagra has so opened up the field to competition that the established actors are having a difficult time holding onto their turf. Hundreds of men now compete for jobs that previously were assigned to a few trusty stalwarts, and that's causing hard feelings. "No *real* star uses Viagra," claims Ron Jeremy.

Source: Huffstutter & Frammolino, 2001.

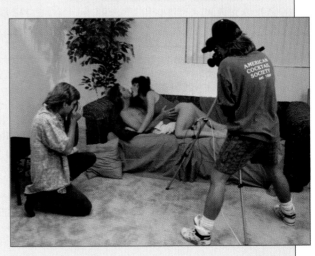

embarrassing in some circumstances. Another kind of implant is inflatable; it is filled from a reservoir that is implanted under the groin muscles. The pump and valves that control the filling and emptying are placed in the scrotum, where they can be accessed manually through the skin. This kind of implant is costlier and more prone to malfunction, and the erect penis is not usually as long as it was originally. On the plus side, the inflatable implant is more discreet and produces a more natural-seeming erection than the semi-rigid implant.

Placing implants in the penis is likely to damage the erectile tissue and reduce or eliminate any natural erectile capacity that the man still has. Therefore, implants should be considered a therapy of last resort, after drugs and other methods have failed.

With the advent of effective drug treatments for erectile dysfunction, implants have lost some of their popularity, but they are still useful for men whose erectile tissue has been damaged by scarring or other processes. Having an implant does not usually interfere with the capacity for orgasm or ejaculation. About 80 percent of men who have penile implants, as well as their partners, are satisfied with them.

Another surgical treatment is **penile artery bypass.** This procedure, which resembles coronary artery bypass surgery, is for men in whom the arteries supplying the penis are damaged or blocked. Only a very few cases of erectile dysfunction meet the criteria for bypass surgery, however; most arterial damage occurs after the arteries break up into numerous fine arterioles within the penis, and these cannot be surgically repaired.

An Erection that Won't Go Down Requires Prompt Medical Attention

Occasionally men have the opposite kind of erectile dysfunction—namely, an erection that won't go away (Pautler & Brock, 2001). This condition is called **priapism,** after the minor Greco-Roman god Priapus, a fertility figure who was always portrayed with an erection. Priapism can result from trauma to the penis or perineum or from the use of some recreational drugs, such as cocaine. It can also result from the use of drugs injected into the penis to cause erections, especially a drug that is no longer commonly used for that purpose, papaverine.

A man who has an erection that won't go down should seek immediate medical attention. If there is a blockage of blood flow through the penis, the erectile tissue may become anoxic, in which case permanent damage can occur within a few hours. Priapism can usually be reversed by administration of drugs that mimic the sympathetic neurotransmitter norepinephrine (alpha-adrenergic agonists). These drugs cause the arterioles supplying the sinusoids to constrict; the reduced input pressure then allows the valves that regulate venous outflow to open, relieving the erection. The drugs may be given orally or may be injected directly into the penis.

Priapism is named for the Greco-Roman fertility god Priapus, who was always portrayed with an erection. In this wall painting from Pompeii, Priapus weighs his penis against a bag of gold—an allusion to the wealth of the family that commissioned the painting. For mere mortals, an erection that won't go down calls for prompt medical attention.

Premature Ejaculation Is Men's Number One Sex Problem

Premature ejaculation (sometimes called **rapid ejaculation**) is ejaculation that occurs directly on intromission or soon thereafter. This definition is certainly imprecise, and it is probably interpreted differently by different investigators (Rowland et al., 2001). According to the World Health Organization's definition, ejaculation must occur within 15 seconds of intromission to be considered "premature" (World Health Organization, 1993), but the APA's DSM-IV simply says that ejaculation is premature if it occurs "before the person wishes." In studies of treatments for premature ejaculation, the untreated patients usually ejaculate about 20–60 seconds after intromission, on average, so the 15-second limit is obviously not widely respected.

The diagnosis of premature ejaculation is not made on the basis of a single episode, of course, since most men have had the experience of ejaculating too soon at one time or another. The problem must persist for 6 months to fit the clinical definition. Like erectile dysfunction, premature ejaculation can be a lifelong (primary) condition, or it can develop in a man who has previously not suffered from it (a secondary condition).

Premature ejaculation is the leading form of sexual dysfunction among men, at least up until age 59 (see Figure 15.1). Thus, it is not simply a problem for hormonally overendowed teenagers, as some people imagine. Its causes are not well understood. According to one theory, it results from early learning. That is, a youth might engage in hasty masturbation or lovemaking, and the reward of orgasm might solidify the habit of haste and make it difficult for him to take his time in the future. Performance anxiety is also commonly blamed, just as it is for erectile dysfunction.

On the other hand, there may be biological causes. Inflammation of the prostate gland (**prostatitis;** see Chapter 17) can cause premature ejaculation; in one Italian study about half of men with premature ejaculation had evidence of chronic prostatitis (Screponi et al., 2001). There has also been speculation that men who ejaculate prematurely might simply have more sensitive penises than other men, but attempts to demonstrate this experimentally have drawn a blank (D. L. Rowland et al., 1993).

Sex Therapy May Help Men to Regulate Excitation

Premature ejaculation is commonly treated by some form of **sex therapy.** This form of therapy is designed to treat a range of sexual dysfunctions by changing learned patterns of arousal or modifying sexual behavior. Sex therapy may be offered to individuals or to couples, either alone or in groups. It may sometimes involve actual sexual behavior in a clinical setting, perhaps with the aid of a sex surrogate (see Box 15.1). Much more commonly, however, the therapist simply describes the techniques and exercises, and the clients or couples practice them as "homework."

One form of sex therapy popularized by Masters and Johnson (1970), the **stop-start procedure,** is intended to treat premature ejaculation. The treatment has several stages:

- Initially, the man masturbates alone, bringing himself to a medium level of excitement. He learns to recognize what this level feels like, then desists from masturbation to allow his state of arousal to decrease. This is repeated a few times, until finally he is allowed to masturbate to orgasm.
- In the next stage, the man and his partner are together, in a position like that shown in Figure 15.7A. She (assuming it's a woman) stimulates his penis by hand or orally, but he tells her to desist before he climaxes. Masters and Johnson recommended that the partner firmly pinch the glans of the man's penis at the time that stimulation ceases (Figure 15.7B).
- The third stage progresses to coitus. The woman simply places the man's penis in her vagina, and the couple lie still for a prolonged period. The idea is that the man gets accustomed to the sensations of coitus without being too excited. Then the woman begins to move somewhat, but the man tells her to stop whenever he approaches orgasm. After several repetitions, the man is allowed to ejaculate. As the exercises proceed, the man should be able to defer his ejaculation for a longer and longer time.

A related technique, called **sensate focus,** consists of touching exercises: the man and his partner take turns exploring each other's bodies, but they avoid erogenous zones, and there is no coitus. In this way, anxiety is reduced by making the experience less of a "performance" than regular sex. Later, the couple graduate to the touching of breasts and genitals, mouth contact, and so on, but always in a relaxed rather than a goal-oriented fashion. (We will have more to say about sensate focus later.)

Figure 15.7 Sex therapy exercises for premature ejaculation. Position of couple for "stop-start" exercises directed at premature ejaculation. (A) The man lies on his back with his legs apart. His partner lies to one side and partly astride him, so that she can manually or orally stimulate his genitals. (B) The "squeeze technique" for premature ejaculation. When the man is close to orgasm, he communicates this fact to his partner with a prearranged signal. The partner then grasps the glans of the man's penis with a thumb on the frenulum and two fingers on the corona, and squeezes firmly for a few seconds. This diminishes the man's urge to ejaculate and possibly causes a partial loss of his erection.

(A)

(B)

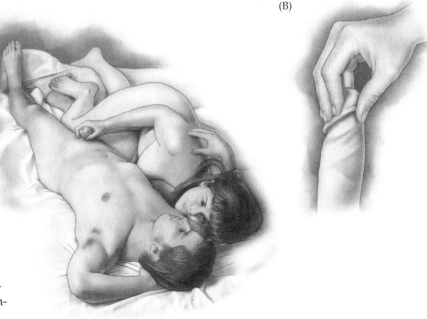

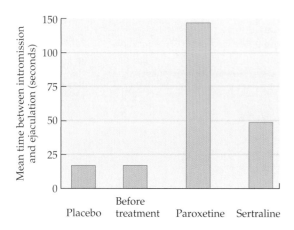

Figure 15.8 Drug treatment for premature ejaculation. Effect of 6 weeks of treatment with a placebo or one of two SSRIs. (Data from Waldinger et al., 2001.)

Exercises of this kind may help men who have been brought up to take "wham, bam, thank-you ma'am" as the governing principle of sex. But how helpful are they generally to men with premature ejaculation? Masters and Johnson claimed success rates of 60 to 95 percent, but more recent studies have come up with much less positive findings (Althof & Schreiner-Engel, 2000). A long-term follow-up study found that men treated with this kind of sex therapy improved temporarily, but relapsed to their pretreatment condition by 3 years after the end of the treatment (De Amicis et al., 1985).

Drug Treatment May Be More Effective

Increasingly, premature ejaculation is being treated with drugs (McMahon & Samali, 1999). Most effective are SSRIs such as paroxetine (Paxil) and sertraline (Zoloft). In one randomized, double-blind study of men with severe premature ejaculation, a 6-week course of paroxetine (20 mg daily) increased the time between intromission and ejaculation sevenfold (Waldinger et al., 2001) (Figure 15.8). The placebo did not increase the time at all. One study found that, after an initial course of the drug, the treatment could be tapered down and discontinued, or simply taken as needed 3–4 hours prior to sex (McMahon & Touma, 1999). In men whose premature ejaculation is caused by prostatitis, treatment of the prostatitis with antibiotics may also correct the premature ejaculation (Brown, 2000).

Delayed Ejaculation Can Be a Side Effect of Several Drugs

Delayed or **absent ejaculation** is the opposite of premature ejaculation: the man can reach the point of ejaculation with difficulty or not at all. This problem is sometimes called **male orgasmic disorder.** There is a slight difference in the meaning of these two terms, however, in that orgasm can sometimes occur without ejaculation ("dry orgasm"). This is commonly the case after surgical removal of the prostate gland, for example (see Chapter 17).

Sometimes delayed ejaculation is specific to a certain kind of sexual behavior, such as coitus or sex with a partner generally; in other cases, the man may not be able to reach orgasm under any circumstances. The condition can be primary or secondary. Either way, it is fairly uncommon.

Delayed ejaculation can have specific causes, such as neurological damage. It can also result from the use of certain drugs, including anti-hypertensive drugs, tranquilizers, and antidepressants. (In some men who are treated for premature ejaculation with SSRIs, the drug works too well, and the men have difficulty ejaculating at all.) In many cases, psychological causes are suspected; this is particularly likely with secondary delayed ejaculation that follows some life event, such as a heart attack or a relationship crisis.

When delayed ejaculation is a side effect of drugs such as antidepressants, it can usually be treated by switching to a different drug or by adding a second drug that counteracts this side effect. Sildenafil and yohimbine (an epinephrine-mimicking drug) are examples of drugs that can be used for this purpose (Rothschild, 2000).

If the cause of delayed ejaculation is not known, it may be treatable by sex therapy. The focus may be on adding stimulation—such as vigorous masturbation, fellatio, or use of a vibrator—either before coitus or instead of coitus. Alternatively, the focus may be on reducing performance anxiety and stress (Apfelbaum, 1989), an approach that is commonly used in treating anorgasmia in women (see below).

Female Sexual Arousal Disorder Involves the Failure of Genital Responses

In women, the three early processes of physiological arousal are vaginal lubrication, engorgement of the vaginal walls, and clitoral erection (see Chapter 3). Failure of any of these processes makes coitus unpleasurable and often downright painful. **Female sexual arousal disorder** is a term used to refer collectively to these problems.

Insufficient lubrication during sex is a common complaint, especially after menopause. In postmenopausal women, the condition may well respond to hormone replacement therapy (HRT; see Chapter 12). If poor lubrication is the woman's only problem, however, hormones are overkill; over-the-counter lubricants do just as good a job, are inexpensive, and have few, if any, side effects.

Erectile dysfunction is usually thought of as an exclusively male problem, but women can experience failure of clitoral erection. Clitoral erectile dysfunction can coexist with *failure of vaginal engorgement;* both can be caused by diseases that compromise the blood vessels supplying the genitalia (Goldstein & Berman, 1998).

The FDA has approved one device for the treatment of problems with physiological arousal (Figure 15.9). Called the Eros Clitoral Therapy Device, it is a miniature version of the vacuum systems used to treat male erectile dysfunction. A soft plastic cup is placed over the clitoris, and a partial vacuum is drawn. The vacuum increases blood flow into the clitoris and into the vaginal walls. There has been one published study of the clinical effects of this device (Billups et al., 2001). Of 15 women with sexual arousal problems (some premenopausal, some postmenopausal), all reported increased sensation, 11 reported more lubrication, 7 reported more orgasms, and 12 reported more satisfaction with sex.

Because sildenafil proved so successful in the treatment of erectile dysfunction in men, it was hoped that it might prove equally useful in women with sexual arousal disorder. Results so far have been less than stellar, however. One study of postmenopausal women with sexual dysfunctions of various kinds found that sildenafil did not provide significant clinical benefit (Kaplan et al., 1999). An Italian study of women in their twenties with sexual arousal disorder obtained somewhat more positive results (Caruso et al., 2001). It may be that sildenafil will turn out to be useful for subgroups of women whose arousal disorder has a well-delineated organic cause. For example, it does seem to be quite effective for arousal disorder caused by medications such as antidepressants (Boyce & Umland, 2001; Nurnberg et al., 1999).

Psychotherapy and sex therapy can play an important role in the treatment of female arousal disorder. We will return to this topic after we have covered other aspects of sexual dysfunction in women.

Figure 15.9 The Eros Clitoral Therapy Device increases blood flow to the clitoris and the surrounding area by drawing a partial vacuum. No constriction band is used.

Painful Intercourse Has a Variety of Organic Causes

Pain during coitus (**dyspareunia**) is much more common among women than among men, and it is especially common among young women (see Figure 15.2). There are many organic conditions that can make coitus painful for women:

- Developmental malformations, intersexed conditions (see Chapter 3), or a persistent unruptured hymen
- Scars from vaginal tearing during parturition or from episiotomy, hysterectomy, sexual assault, or female circumcision
- Vaginal atrophy (a thinning of the vaginal walls that occurs with aging)
- Acute and chronic infections of the vagina and internal reproductive tract, including several STDs and pelvic inflammatory disease (see Chapter 16). These conditions are generally more common among younger women.
- Allergic reactions to foreign substances, such as latex or spermicides
- Failure of physiological arousal, especially vaginal dryness

Organic dyspareunia is treated, where possible, by correction of the underlying condition.

Vaginal Spasm May Make Intercourse Impossible

Dyspareunia can also occur without any obvious physical cause (**nonorganic dyspareunia**). One phenomenon that can occur in association with dyspareunia, especially nonorganic dyspareunia, is **vaginal spasm** (**vaginismus**). In women with this condition, any attempt at vaginal penetration triggers a rapid, strong, and maintained contraction

(A) **Vaginismus**

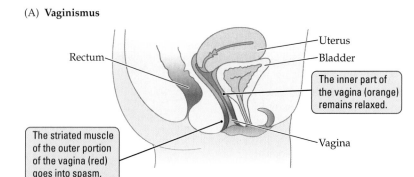

Rectum

Uterus

Bladder

The inner part of the vagina (orange) remains relaxed.

Vagina

The striated muscle of the outer portion of the vagina (red) goes into spasm, preventing coitus.

(B) **Vaginal dilators**

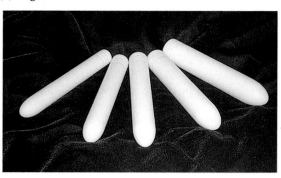

Figure 15.10 Vaginismus. (A) In women with this condition, the striated muscle of the outer portion of the vagina (red) goes into spasm, preventing coitus. The inner part of the vagina (orange) remains relaxed. (B) In one treatment for vaginismus, the woman uses progressively larger dilators in combination with relaxation exercises.

of the striated musculature in the wall of the outer third of the vagina (Figure 15.10A). The spasm may involve the entire musculature of the pelvic floor and even the hip adductor muscles (preventing spreading of the legs). The spasm makes coitus difficult or impossible. The occurrence of vaginismus is not restricted to sexual penetration; it also occurs during insertion of fingers or objects into the vagina. Thus it may prevent the woman from inserting a tampon, or a gynecologist from inserting a speculum.

Vaginismus doesn't necessarily interfere with the capacity for sexual arousal or orgasm. Thus, even when vaginismus makes coitus impossible, a couple may still have an active sex life. Sometimes it is only when a couple want to have children that they seek professional help for the condition. On the other hand, vaginismus can be extremely debilitating for some women, as it can cause physical pain as well as a sense of shame and inadequacy. In severe cases, vaginismus may be associated with panic attacks.

When vaginismus occurs in the absence of any discernible organic condition, it is usually assumed that it results from a conscious or unconscious fear of (or aversion to) coitus. This fear or aversion is thought to stem from early traumatic experiences (such as experiencing or witnessing sexual assault), from the inculcation of very strict religious attitudes toward sex, or even from simple ignorance about sex. By some accounts, women with vaginismus have a characteristic childhood history: they played the good, obedient daughter to a domineering, moralistic, yet seductive father, and vaginismus represents the woman's effort to protect herself from violation (Silverstein, 1989).

Vaginismus is often treated with a combination of psychotherapy and general sex therapy, including sensate focus exercises. A behavioral technique specific to vaginismus is the use of **dilators** (Figure 15.10B): the woman inserts progressively larger-diameter probes into her vagina while doing relaxation exercises. In one study, nearly all the women treated with this form of therapy were able to engage in intercourse after a few sessions (Schnyder et al., 1998). Nevertheless, there is little objective information about the long-term outcome of this or other treatments for vaginismus.

Difficulty in Reaching Orgasm Is Very Common among Women

Very large numbers of women have persistent and recurring difficulty in reaching orgasm (**anorgasmia** or **female orgasmic disorder**). Ten to 15 percent of U.S. women have never experienced orgasm under any circumstances (Althof & Schreiner-Engel, 2000). An estimated two-thirds of all women do not experience orgasm regularly during coitus without other stimulation (Kaplan, 1979). In the NHSLS, 71 percent of women (compared with only 25 percent of men) said that they did not always experience orgasm during sex with their regular partner.

There Has Been a Long Social and Scientific Debate about Female Orgasm

Obviously, these numbers raise the question of what should be considered "normal" orgasmic function in women. Few aspects of human sexuality have been more controversial over the years. In Victorian times, many people thought that anorgasmia was the normal condition and that female orgasm was abnormal, sinful, or dangerous to the woman's health. Freud "normalized" female orgasm, but only in the context of vaginal stimulation; clitoral orgasm, he believed, was a neurotic leftover from infantile sexuality.

Early feminists such as Margaret Sanger (see Chapter 11) stressed women's right to experience sexual pleasure, and in the 1960s and 1970s feminists elevated female orgasm to a universal right. Anthropologists described non-Western cultures in which female orgasm was said to be experienced by all women during all sexual encounters, suggesting that any orgasmic difficulties experienced by American women must be culturally imposed (Marshall, 1971). Meanwhile, sexologists argued over the site of orgasm. Masters and Johnson claimed (in radical opposition to Freud) that orgasm could be triggered *only* by stimulation of the clitoris, while others argued for the existence of an orgasm-triggering location in the vagina—the G spot (see Chapter 3).

Given all this controversy and uncertainty, it's not surprising that the DSM-IV uses vague criteria for female orgasmic disorder: it says that the diagnosis "should be based on the clinician's judgment that the woman's orgasmic capacity is less than would be reasonable for her age, sexual experience, and the adequacy of sexual stimulation she receives." It also emphasizes that the condition is a dysfunction requiring treatment only when it causes "marked distress or interpersonal difficulty."

A Biological Cause for Anorgasmia Cannot Usually Be Identified

Anorgasmia can be caused by drugs, especially by SSRIs, other antidepressants, and anti-hypertensive drugs. Such cases can usually be treated by adjusting dosage, switching drugs, or adding another drug to counteract the effect.

More commonly, anorgasmia does not have any obvious organic cause. In such cases, the clinician or therapist will suggest different strategies depending on the details of the problem. If the woman can experience orgasm with masturbation but not with partnered sex, it may be possible to suggest modifications of partnered sex that will allow orgasm to occur. These modifications could include the addition of clitoral stimulation—by hand or mouth, or with a vibrator (Figure 15.11). This stimulation can be provided by either partner and can take place before, during, after, or instead of coitus. Increasing the duration of sexual activity (for example, by helping a male partner delay his orgasm) or trying different coital positions may also resolve the problem. So many couples are sexually unadventurous or uninformed that these rather simple suggestions may be all that is required.

Encouraging couples to communicate better about their sexual feelings can be very helpful. Men do not automatically know what their female partners find sexually arousing. A man may rush from foreplay to coitus before his partner is sufficiently aroused, in which case coitus may be a turn-off for her, rather than a turn-on. The man may stimulate the woman's nipples or clitoris too strongly—these are tender tissues, after all. A postmenopausal woman may take longer to become aroused than she did earlier in her life. All these things can make it difficult for the woman to experience orgasm. In an environment where the woman feels free to let her partner know whether what he is doing is working or not, these difficulties can often be resolved.

If the woman does not experience orgasm under any circumstances, a somewhat different strategy is called for. Bear in mind that over half of all women say that they never masturbate (NHSLS data; see Chapter 8). Thus, if they are open to trying masturbation, they may be quite easi-

Figure 15.11 Helping a woman experience orgasm during partnered sex. If a woman has difficulty experiencing orgasm during coitus, it may be helpful to adopt a position, as here, that allows either partner to provide clitoral stimulation by hand or with a vibrator.

ly helped to experience orgasm for the first time. Sex therapy for anorgasmia often includes a directed program of self-stimulation, which may begin with general exploration of the naked body and later extend to genital stimulation. Vibrators are particularly useful in these kinds of exercises. Sometimes this directed masturbation program is accompanied by exercises in the use of fantasy or erotic materials. In addition, the woman may be encouraged to perform physical exercises to strengthen her pelvic floor muscles (Kegel exercises; see Chapter 17). Sensate-focus exercises with a partner are often added.

As might be expected, directed masturbation programs are most successful at helping women reach orgasm during masturbation. One study found that 89 percent of women had achieved that goal by the conclusion of the program (Kuriansky et al., 1982). A much smaller fraction of the women (21 percent) were able to reach orgasm during sex with a partner, however, and even fewer (16 percent) could do so during coitus. Some studies suggest that the number of women who reach orgasm during coitus increases after the end of a directed masturbation program (Heiman & Meston, 1997).

Directed masturbation programs work better for women with primary (lifelong) orgasmic disorder than for women who develop the problem after some years of satisfactory orgasmic functioning (Althof & Schreiner-Engel, 2000). In the latter group of women, the problem more usually reflects relationship difficulties or other psychological problems that are not addressed by masturbation training.

Either Too Little or Too Much Interest in Sex Can Cause Problems

We now shift from disorders of sexual performance to disorders characterized by too much or too little sexual desire or sexual behavior. Of course, it is extremely difficult to say what constitutes too much or too little in the sexual domain. Sometimes it the mismatch in sexual interest between the two persons in a relationship that causes one or both of them to seek professional help. In other words, one partner may be frustrated by the other partner's lack of interest in sex, or, alternatively, may be turned off by the partner's too frequent advances. The couple may disagree as to which of them has the "problem." In fact, it may be the relationship that has the problem, rather than either of the two persons involved in it.

On the other hand, there are also cases in which the problem is clearly localized to one person. Sometimes a person's interest in sex is so strong that it takes over their life, interfering with all their other activities and possibly bringing them into conflict with the law. Sometimes a man or woman has a lifelong history of disinterest in sex. If such a person marries, that is very likely to be a problem, no matter who their partner is. Very often, the identity of the partner with the problem is quite obvious to both partners in a relationship and to any clinician with whom they discuss the matter.

Many Organic Conditions Can Cause Hypersexuality

Excessive sexual desire or sexual activity is an extremely controversial issue. There are raging debates among both sexologists and the general public as to what constitutes "excessive" sexuality, how it should be named and conceptualized, what causes it, and whether and how it should be treated.

There is one kind of excessive sexual behavior that everyone agrees is pathological: that which results from a clearly defined medical condition or other organic cause. This kind of behavior is often called **hypersexuality.** Two older terms that you may see used are **satyriasis** (when it occurs in men) and **nymphomania** (in women). Conditions that can trigger hypersexual behavior include dementias, multiple sclerosis, epilepsy, strokes, tumors, and injuries to certain parts of the brain (Absher et al., 2000; Kuhn et al., 1998; Monga et al., 1986; Devinsky & Vazquez, 1993; Gorman & Cummings, 1992; Huws et al., 1991). A few commonly prescribed drugs, such as L-DOPA, which is used to treat Parkinson's disease, cause hypersexuality in a small fraction of the people who take them

(Uitti et al., 1989). Some recreational drugs, as well as alcohol, can have the same effect. Excessive sexual behavior may be also caused by **psychoses**—mental diseases such as schizophrenia that result in severe disorganization of thinking and probably have an organic basis (Krueger & Kaplan, 2000). Hypersexual behavior also sometimes characterizes the hyperactive phase of bipolar (manic–depressive) disorder.

In most of these conditions, the abnormal nature of the person's sexual behavior is obvious because it represents a radical departure from their sexual behavior prior to the onset of the medical condition or before taking drugs. Although the details are not understood, it is a fair guess that these forms of brain pathology disrupt the interactions between the brain regions or circuits that promote sexual behavior and those that restrain it.

Excessive Sexual Behavior Can Be Part of Adolescent "Acting Out"

What about an adolescent girl who goes on a sexual rampage, propositioning strangers in what seem to be totally inappropriate circumstances and having instant sex with anyone who accepts her offers? Is this just risky, rebellious behavior, or does it reflect some kind of serious mental disturbance requiring professional attention? Should we judge it differently if it's a male rather than a female youth?

Obviously there's a blurry line between "normal" adolescent sexual exuberance and what we might consider pathological, but one important consideration is the actual or potential harm (assault, STDs, pregnancy) that can result from this kind of behavior, either to the youth who shows the behavior or to the youth's sex partners. In addition, studies of female and male adolescents who do engage in extreme sexual behaviors have found that they commonly engage in a wide spectrum of antisocial "acting out" behaviors in addition to their sexual activities. They are also likely to have experienced sexual abuse in early childhood (McClellan et al., 1996). Thus, most therapists consider extreme hypersexual behavior in adolescents to be a "cry for help" that requires a serious psychotherapeutic response.

A Person's Sense of Control Helps Distinguish Normal from Excessive Sexual Behavior

The trickiest area to evaluate is "excessive" sexual behavior by adults who do not have organic conditions such as those listed above. Some people—men, for the most part—spend several hours each day engaged in masturbation, reading or viewing pornography, participating in sex-related on-line chat rooms, using commercial phone sex services, seeking casual sex partners in bars, cruising the streets for prostitutes, or having anonymous sex with multiple partners in bathhouses or sex clubs. Sometimes people fall madly in love with completely inaccessible persons, such as movie stars, and for years devote all their energies to writing love letters or scheming some great sacrifice that will prove the sincerity of their love. People who exhibit such behaviors may endanger their marriages, their jobs, and their bank balances. Do these people have a "condition"? Do they need help? Do they just need a stern lecture? Or are they simply part of the diverse spectrum that is human sexuality?

One problem here is that there is no agreement as to what constitutes a normal amount of sex or a desirable number of sex partners. If you ask people this question, men will give you a different answer than women, teenagers than retirees. Community standards vary: you will not hear the same views on Castro Street in San Francisco (a center of that city's gay community) as you will in Colorado Springs, Colorado (home of several religious conservative organizations). To some conservative or religiously minded people, a 10-minute session with your spouse twice a week may represent the upper bounds of normalcy. To some (though certainly not all)

The treatment of "sexual addiction" is a growth industry on the Internet and among therapists.

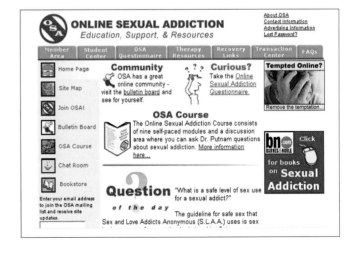

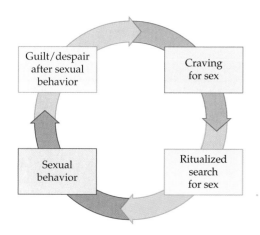

Figure 15.12 Compulsive sexual behavior often takes the form of a four-stage cycle. (After Carnes, 2001.)

gay men, long hours of anonymous group sex on a near-daily basis may seem like a regular part of life.

One relevant issue is the person's sense of control. Do they experience their sexual behavior as something that they voluntarily embark on—something whose pros and cons they have balanced against all the other demands on their time and energy? Or does the behavior feel like something they have very little control over and wish they could be rid of, like a drug addiction?

Is Excessive Sexual Behavior an Addiction or a Compulsion?

There are, in fact, some therapists who have popularized the notion of **sexual addiction.** Notable among these therapists is Patrick Carnes (Carnes, 2001), who has proposed that sex addicts go through a four-stage cycle resembling the cycle experienced by drug addicts (Figure 15.12). The stages are (1) an increasing craving for sex, (2) the ritualized search for sex, such as spending time in on-line chat rooms, (3) sexual behavior itself, which might be masturbation or sex with partners, and (4) a period of guilt or despair after the bout of sexual behavior. While it is fairly clear why craving should lead to search, search to behavior, and behavior to guilt, it is less obvious why guilt should lead to craving. It may be that an underlying craving simply re-emerges when guilt declines sufficiently to allow it to do so. Alternatively, the craving may be a mental structure that helps to master or distract from guilt.

Carnes has suggested that programs like those that treat addictions to substances, such as Alcoholics Anonymous, could be an effective treatment for sexual addiction. A number of such programs (such as Sexaholics Anonymous) have in fact been started, but the efficacy of these programs is uncertain.

The use of the term "addiction" in a sexual context, while it may seem reasonable to laypeople, is controversial among scientists. Addiction, as traditionally defined, is to a *substance* (heroin, for example). It is marked by craving, tolerance (the requirement for ever-increasing doses to produce the same effect), and a characteristic set of symptoms when the addictive substance is withdrawn. Substance addiction also has two characteristic neurochemical features. First, it involves activation of receptors for **endorphins,** the natural brain peptides whose action is mimicked by opiate drugs such as heroin. Drugs that block those receptors, such as **naltrexone,** interfere with the rewarding nature of the addictive drug and diminish craving. Second, the use of an addictive drug causes a characteristic pattern of increased neural activity in regions of the basal forebrain that are concerned with reward and a sense of well-being, as well as the release of the neurotransmitter **dopamine** in those same regions.

Carnes did not address these biological issues in his theory of sexual addiction. For lack of evidence linking hypersexual behaviors to substance addiction, many sexologists have preferred to use the phrase **compulsive sexual behavior** or **obsessive–compulsive sexual disorder** to refer to the condition that Carnes calls sexual addiction (Coleman, 1996). This designation acknowledges a key attribute of the behavior; namely, that it is experienced as being carried out against a person's will and often in a self-destructive fashion. However, it links excessive sexual behavior with other compulsive behaviors, such as compulsive gambling, rather than with substance addiction. It also links excessive sexual behavior with the paraphilias (see Chapter 14), because many paraphilias are experienced as compulsions and often involve behaviors that are not merely atypical in nature, but also excessive in quantity.

The waters have been muddied even further, however, by recent biological findings on compulsive behaviors. It has been reported, for example, that some of the brain regions involved in substance addiction are also involved in compulsive gambling, and that naltrexone reduces compulsive gambling behavior, just as it reduces heroin use (Kim et al., 2001). Some addiction specialists are therefore coming to believe that the same biological processes underlie substance addiction and compulsive behaviors (Holden, 2001a).

So far, analogous studies on sexual behavior are inconclusive. Naltrexone has little, if any, effect on compulsive sexual behavior. On the other hand, viewing sexually attractive faces activates the same "reward" circuitry of the brain that is active during a drug-induced high (Aharon et al., 2001). So does viewing the face of the person with whom one is in love (see Chapter 9). More research is needed to understand whether or not compulsive sexual behavior has the same neurological basis as substance addiction.

Compulsive Sexual Behavior Can Often Be Treated with SSRIs

Regardless of the underlying mechanisms, therapists have to make difficult judgment calls when it comes to treating men who experience sexual compulsions and who want to be rid of them. In some cases, the therapist may feel that the client's sexual behaviors are within a socially accepted "normal" range, and that the client's wish to be rid of them reflects guilt induced by a sex-negative upbringing, not a realistic sense that the behavior is harming himself or others. In such cases, the therapist may encourage the client to explore the roots of his guilty feelings.

Alternatively, the therapist and client may agree that the client's compulsive sexual behavior is harmful and that the treatment goal should be to lessen the craving that triggers it. Psychotherapy to explore the origins of the compulsive behavior may be helpful. In addition, however, drug therapy can be very effective (Bradford, 2001). Selective serotonin reuptake inhibitors are the drugs most commonly used for this purpose. Indeed, the effectiveness of SSRIs in the treatment of many cases of compulsive sexual behavior could be taken as supportive evidence that these behaviors belong to the family of obsessive–compulsive disorders, since SSRIs are known to be helpful in the treatment of those conditions (see Chapter 14). In more serious cases of hypersexuality, especially where there is underlying brain pathology that cannot be corrected, it may be necessary to use drugs that lower testosterone levels or that block testosterone's effects.

Lack of Interest in Sex Is Not Necessarily a Problem

Within the 18–59 age bracket, about one in three women and one in six men say that they lack interest in sex (see Figure 15.1). The number of people who are uninterested in sex probably increases beyond the age of 59. If a person lacks interest in sex, and this lack of interest causes distress or interferes with the person's marriage or relationship, it is considered a clinical condition and is called **hypoactive sexual desire disorder**. It may also be referred to simply as **low libido**. The number of people who have a clinically defined hypoactive sexual desire disorder is much lower than the number of people who say they lack interest in sex; for example, no more than 3 percent of men in the general population are estimated to have the disorder (Simons & Carey, 2001). Many people who lack interest in sex, especially those who are elderly, are not troubled or harmed by this lack of interest and should not be considered as having a problem of any kind.

Note that the diagnosis of hypoactive sexual desire disorder is made on the basis of *desire* rather that *behavior*. Many people are sexually inactive for substantial periods of time even though they have strong sexual desires. They may be waiting for marriage, they may be away from their partner, they may not have access to desirable partners, or they may experience sexual desires that they consider morally wrong to act on. Conversely, some people are sexually active even in the absence of sexual desire—to gratify a partner or to have children, for example.

In the past, the term **frigidity** (literally "coldness") was used in reference to low sexual desire or problems with sexual arousal or performance (such as anorgasmia) in women. It often carried the connotation of blaming the woman for a problem that might equally be due to her partner, to the relationship as a whole, or to social expectations. For that reason most sex researchers and therapists have abandoned the term. If you hear the word "frigid" today, it might have come from a man who is offering an explanation for why a woman has turned down his advances—an explanation that neglects considering any possible deficiencies on his part.

Testosterone Treatment May Restore Sexual Desire in Men

As we saw in Chapter 4, gonadal steroids play a significant role in influencing libido. In men, testosterone is the key player. The role of testosterone was well illustrated in one double-blind, placebo-controlled study conducted at the Seattle V.A. Medical Center

(Bagatell et al., 1994). Healthy male volunteers were given a GnRH antagonist for 6 weeks; the drug lowered their blood testosterone levels to well below normal. By the end of the treatment period the men had a greatly reduced interest in sex, experienced fewer sexual fantasies, and engaged less often in masturbation and sexual intercourse. By contrast, men who received the GnRH antagonist but also received enough testosterone to keep their blood testosterone levels normal did not differ in their sexual responses from the men who received only a placebo.

If hormones, and testosterone in particular, are important regulators of men's sexual desire, one might expect that men with low sexual desire would have lower testosterone levels than men with normal or high desire. Testing this prediction is not easy, however, because testosterone levels fluctuate greatly over short time periods (see Chapter 4). In one study, Raul Schiavi and his colleagues at Mt. Sinai Medical School brought 77 men aged 45–74 into a sleep laboratory and monitored their hormone levels at 20-minute intervals. In this way they were able to obtain meaningful time-averaged measures of testosterone levels (Schiavi et al., 1991). The researchers found that both sexual desire and blood levels of free testosterone decline with age. (Free testosterone means testosterone not bound to carrier molecules and therefore available to exert hormonal effects; see Chapter 4.) Among men of the same age, free testosterone levels were lower in men with low sexual desire than in those with higher desire. Thus, testosterone levels do seem to play a role in determining a man's interest in sex.

Unlike erectile dysfunction, for which testosterone treatment is not very helpful (see above), hypoactive sexual desire disorder in men often does respond to such treatment, especially in men whose testes are secreting lower than normal levels of testosterone (**hypogonadal** men). The common belief is that testosterone treatment has no effect on sexual desire in men whose testes are secreting normal amounts of the hormone (**eugonadal** men). There is one placebo-controlled study, however, in which eugonadal men with hypoactive sexual desire disorder were successfully treated with testosterone (O'Carroll & Bancroft, 1984).

With the availability of transdermal delivery methods (patches), treatment with testosterone and related androgenic steroids has increased in popularity, and may be used for other purposes besides the treatment of low libido (such as muscle building). Androgenic steroid treatment carries significant risks, however: it has the potential to cause or worsen prostate disease (see Chapter 17), liver disease, and heart disease, and it may lower fertility, accelerate balding, and cause mood problems. It is not the "fountain of youth" for normally aging men.

Psychological factors probably play a significant role in hypoactive sexual desire disorder in men—even in men who have demonstrably low testosterone levels. These factors can include inculcated sex-negative attitudes, relationship difficulties, stress, depression, and a feedback effect from erectile dysfunction. Alleviating these difficulties through psychotherapy, relationship counseling, or behavioral sex therapy may be more effective than drug treatment for many men, although objective studies are lacking.

Estrogen or Androgen Treatment May Restore Sexual Desire in Women

The diagnosis and treatment of hypoactive sexual desire in women is more complex than in men. Traditionally, clinicians assessed women's sexual health by asking how often they engaged in intercourse. The answer to this question can give quite an erroneous notion of the state of a woman's libido, however. She may be engaging in intercourse in response to sexual advances by her partner but have little or no interest in sex herself. Conversely, she may have a great interest in sex, but not be able to gratify that interest because of a lack of partner availability or because of her partner's disinterest. To determine whether a particular woman really has a troubling lack of sexual desire requires specific questioning that many clinicians are reluctant to undertake.

As we saw in Chapter 4, women's libido is supported by two classes of steroid hormones, estrogens and androgens, although there is still considerable uncertainty about their relative roles. The levels of these hormones drop when levels of body fat are very low (as a result of starvation, anorexia nervosa, or some athletic training regimens) as well as after menopause. In these circumstances, sexual desire often declines or disappears.

Some women continue to initiate sexual activity long after menopause, however. Their behavior may reflect the importance of cultural factors in sexual desire, or it may be due to the continuing presence of steroids secreted by the adrenal glands.

In premenopausal women who are not menstruating and have low libido (because of low body weight, for example), libido usually reappears when body weight returns to normal and menstruation resumes. In postmenopausal women with low libido, libido may reappear with standard hormone replacement therapy. The positive effect of HRT on sexual desire is probably twofold: part of it is due to the direct effect of estrogens on the brain, and part is due to improved physiological arousal (vaginal lubrication and engorgement and clitoral erection), which makes sex more pleasurable and therefore rekindles an interest in it.

Among premenopausal women who are menstruating but nevertheless have low libido, some have low or undetectable levels of circulating testosterone. The majority of such women respond well to treatment with androgens (Guay, 2001). Similarly, postmenopausal women who are on HRT but nevertheless have low libido often experience a revival of interest in sex after the addition of androgens to the HRT regimen. The superiority of an estrogen-plus-androgen HRT regime over an estrogen-only regime for this purpose has been documented in a double-blind study conducted by endocrinologists at Yale University (Sarrel et al., 1998).

As with men, androgen treatment of women is not to be undertaken lightly. Besides the possible negative side effects already mentioned for men, androgen treatment of women can cause growth of facial and body hair (**hirsutism**), enlargement of the clitoris (**clitoromegaly**), and possibly liver damage and increased cholesterol levels. The American College of Obstetricians and Gynecologists recommends that if androgen therapy is used, the hormones should be taken orally and at a low dosage, and the woman should be carefully monitored for possible side effects (American College of Obstetricians and Gynecologists, 2000).

Sex Therapy May Be Helpful for Low Sexual Desire in Women

Sex therapy is an alternative (or possibly additional) option in the treatment of hypoactive sexual desire in women, as it is in men. As an example of such therapy, let's return briefly to sensate-focus exercises. We initially described the use of these exercises in the treatment of premature ejaculation. Why might the same kind of exercise be beneficial in what seems like the opposite kind of condition—a lack of interest in sex?

During sensate focus exercises, the person who is being touched (the "receiver") is encouraged to concentrate simply on the pleasure of the sensation, and to "let go" of any obligation to reciprocate (Figure 15.13). The only communication that the receiver should provide is to let their partner know if the touching becomes uncomfortable. This can be a valuable exercise for people who have difficulty deriving pleasure from sex because they are too wrapped up in making sure that their partner is being satisfied. These people are being too considerate and too "intellectual" to allow the sheer sensual richness of sex to envelop them. For such people, simply lying back guilt-free and enjoying being pleasured may be an entirely novel experience.

The person who is doing the touching (the "giver") is also learning to enjoy sex in a novel way; namely, through the tactile experience of giving pleasure to a partner, without any direct stimulation of their own erogenous zones. In fact, the giver's fingers may become erogenous zones in themselves. The tactile stimulation received in this way may not lead to physiological arousal, but the very fact that it doesn't may be a good thing. It may allow the giver, like the receiver, to experience sexual pleasure entirely free from the need to perform physiologically.

The efficacy of sex therapy in the treatment of hypoactive sexual desire disorder in women is uncertain, however, as it is in men (Heiman & Meston, 1997).

Figure 15.13 Sex therapy exercise for hypoactive sexual desire in women. In one kind of sensate-focus exercise aimed at treating low libido in women, the woman lies back and is pleasured by her partner while letting go of any responsibility to reciprocate.

The Efficacy of Treatments for Sexual Dysfunctions Needs Further Study

As we have discussed, sexual dysfunctions may be treated with biological methods (drugs, implants), with some form of psychotherapy, or with a combination of approaches. To some extent, the choice of biological or psychotherapeutic treatment reflects the beliefs of health care providers and their clients about the causation of the dysfunctions. In general, there has been a recent trend toward more biologically oriented theories and treatments.

The efficacy of drug treatments has been objectively assessed by means of placebo-controlled trials. It has not been possible to organize comparable trials for psychotherapeutic treatments because the subjects cannot be kept in ignorance of what kind of treatment they are receiving. Nevertheless, there is good evidence that people who seek psychotherapy for a variety of mental health problems are significantly helped by such treatment, regardless of the exact form of psychotherapy they receive (Seligman, 1995). Thus, the question is not whether psychotherapy works in general, but whether it works for specific sexual dysfunctions.

It seems unlikely that psychotherapy could correct an obvious physical problem, such as erectile dysfunction caused by nerve or vascular damage or painful coitus caused by vaginal dryness in a postmenopausal woman. Even in such cases, however, psychotherapy may alleviate the distress caused by these problems—perhaps by facilitating noncoital forms of sexual intimacy.

Where a sexual dysfunction does not have an obvious physical cause, there is no theoretical reason to prefer one form of treatment over another. Studies to compare the efficacy of various treatments in addressing such problems are needed. It may not be feasible to organize a prospective trial in which volunteers are assigned at random to, say, 6 months of psychotherapy or a testosterone patch and followed for 2 years thereafter. It may not be desirable to organize trials in this fashion, however. That's because such trials miss out on important real-world aspects of treatment, such as the selection by clients and their mental health providers of the kind and duration of therapy that seems appropriate to each client. Nonrandomized, even retrospective studies *can* take these real-life factors into account. More studies of this kind are needed to assess the efficacy of current or novel treatments for sexual dysfunctions.

Summary

1. Sexual dysfunctions are common. Among women, the most frequent problems are a lack of interest in sex, difficulty experiencing orgasm, and a lack of vaginal lubrication. Among men, the commonest problems are premature ejaculation, anxiety about performance, and a lack of interest in sex. Over the age span between 18 and 59, the prevalence of sexual problems among women tends to decline, but problems with lubrication increase after menopause. Among men, erectile difficulties and disinterest in sex increase with age. Sexual dysfunctions are clinical problems requiring treatment only if they cause distress or interfere with relationships.

2. Many conditions can lead to problems with penile erection, including smoking, use of alcohol and certain prescription or recreational drugs, diabetes, cardiovascular disease, spinal cord injury, and prostate gland surgery. Among psychological factors that may impair erectile function, performance anxiety is probably the most important. Treatment of erectile dysfunction can include alleviation of the underlying disorder, psychotherapy, or the use of drugs such as sildenafil (Viagra) that improve the response of the erectile tissue to neural input. Among the nondrug treatments available are vacuum devices and penile implants.

3. The causes of premature ejaculation, a very common sexual dysfunction, are poorly understood, but biological factors (such as prostatitis) and psychological factors (such as performance anxiety) are thought to contribute. Men who ejaculate prematurely may be helped by sex therapy, a form of behavioral training. In one form of sex therapy, called sensate-focus exercises, the man and his partner progressively explore each other's bodies while avoiding performance demands. Premature ejaculation can also be treated with selective serotonin reuptake inhibitors (SSRIs).

4. Difficulty in reaching ejaculation or orgasm is fairly uncommon in men, but may be caused by certain drugs, such as SSRIs. It may be treated by changing or adding drugs, or by sensate-focus exercises that increase genital stimulation or decrease performance anxiety.

5. Female sexual arousal disorder refers to difficulties with vaginal lubrication or engorgement or with clitoral erection. Insufficient lubrication is common, especially after menopause; it can be dealt with by the use of lubricants. Hormone replacement often restores physiological arousal in postmenopausal women. So far, sildenafil has not proved as useful in female sexual arousal disorder as it is in male erectile dysfunction. Sex therapy may be helpful.

6. Painful coitus (dyspareunia) can result from a wide variety of biological causes, including developmental malformations, scars, vaginal atrophy, infections, allergies, and failure of lubrication. It can often be treated by correction of the underlying condition. Sometimes dyspareunia is accompanied by spasm of the vaginal musculature during attempted coitus (vaginismus). Vaginismus may result from childhood trauma or sex-phobic upbringing. It is treated by psychotherapy and sex therapy exercises, including the use of dilators.

7. Many women have problems with orgasm. Some have never experienced it, and some do not experience it during partnered sex or during coitus. What is "normal" orgasmic function for women has been long debated. A biological cause for orgasmic dysfunction cannot usually be identified. Sex therapy for anorgasmia may include a program of directed masturbation or sensate-focus exercises. A woman may be helped to experience orgasm during partnered sex or coitus by adding clitoral stimulation, trying different positions, or extending the duration of the sexual interaction. It may also be necessary to address relationship problems.

8. Excessive sexual desire or behavior (hypersexuality) can be caused by neurological damage, various mental illnesses, or certain drugs. In some disturbed or abused adolescents, excessive sexual activity can be a form of "acting out."

9. Excessive sexual behaviors in adults may include frequently repeated and seemingly involuntary involvement in masturbation, partnered sex, pornography use, telephone sex, and the like. Such behaviors may be classed as obsessive–compulsive disorders, and like other such disorders, they often respond well to SSRIs. The use of the term "sexual addiction" to describe these conditions is controversial.

10. Lack of interest in sex (hypoactive sexual desire disorder) is more common among women than among men. Sex hormone levels strongly influence sexual desire. In men, lack of interest in sex often responds to treatment with androgens. In women, it may respond to estrogens, androgens, or a combination of the two. Androgen treatment can cause unwanted or harmful side effects in both sexes, however. Sex therapy may help people with a lack of interest in sex—for example, sensate-focus exercises may help them "let go" of thought patterns that interfere with sexual pleasure, such as a perceived obligation to ensure the partner's satisfaction. The efficacy of sex therapy in the treatment of hypoactive sexual desire disorder needs to be objectively tested.

Discussion Questions

1. "Many people have sexual dysfunctions but are prevented by embarrassment or ignorance from seeking treatment that could help them." "Many people have unrealistic expectations about sex and therefore demand treatments, such as drugs or psychotherapy, when there's really not much wrong with them." Which of these two statements describes contemporary U.S. society more accurately, in your opinion, and why?

2. A married woman friend complains to you that she cannot reach orgasm during intercourse with her husband. If you were a therapist, what questions would you ask her and what recommendations would you give her?

3. An older male friend complains that he has been unhappy with his sexual performance and unable to sustain an erection over the past 2 years. How would you advise him about the various treatment options available?

4. Do you think that anxiety about performance, or excessive attention to one's partner's sexual satisfaction, can interfere with one's own sexual pleasure or performance? If so, what steps could be taken to alleviate the problem?

5. The TV commercials for Viagra have succeeded in bringing erectile dysfunction out of the closet and in prompting many men to seek treatment. If you had funds to run a series of public-service announcements addressing sexual dysfunction in *women*, what would you focus on and what would be the message that you would try to communicate?

Web Resources

Society for Sex Therapy and Research   www.sstarnet.org

International Professional Surrogates Association   members.aol.com/ipsa1/home.html

Sexual Health InfoCenter   www.sexhealth.org

Recommended Reading

Berman, J., Berman, L., and Bumiller, E. (2001). *For women only: A revolutionary guide to overcoming sexual dysfunction and reclaiming your sex life.* New York: Henry Holt.

Heiman, J. R., and LoPiccolo, J. (1988). *Becoming orgasmic: A sexual and personal growth program for women* (rev. ed.). New York: Simon and Schuster.

Kaplan, H. S. (1995). *The sexual desire disorders: Dysfunctional regulation of sexual motivation.* New York: Brunner/Mazel.

Weeks, G. R., and Gambescia, N. (2002). *Hypoactive sexual desire: Integrating sex and couple therapy.* New York: W.W. Norton.

Zilbergeld, B. (1999). *The new male sexuality* (rev. ed.). New York: Bantam.

chapter 16

Human papillomavirus (HPV), seen here in a colorized electron micrograph, can cause genital warts. Some types of HPV cause cervical cancer.

Sexually Transmitted Diseases

The sustained intimacy of sexual contact offers an ideal opportunity for many disease-causing organisms to spread from one person to another. Some of these organisms are highly specialized for transmission by the sexual route, while others can spread either sexually or by other means. The existence of sexually transmitted diseases (STDs) has always added an element of risk to sex, and it has strongly influenced people's sexual behavior and attitudes. The AIDS epidemic, which struck the United States in the late 1970s and continues to cause immense human suffering worldwide, is just the most recent example. Medical research has brought spectacular advances in our knowledge of the causes of STDs, and in many cases has given us the power to prevent or treat them. Yet there are deep social conflicts about how the battle against STDs should be conducted. These conflicts, rooted in moral differences about the nature and purpose of sexuality, have undercut the effectiveness of public health campaigns aimed at eliminating STDs.

Women and men who educate themselves about STDs can greatly reduce their risk of acquiring one. If they do acquire one, they are in a better position to participate in effective treatment and can minimize the risk of passing the disease on to others.

Inca clay figure believed to represent a man with syphilis.

Anti-VD (venereal disease) posters in the mid-twentieth century often blamed prostitutes and promiscuous women for the spread of syphilis and gonorrhea.

Venereal Diseases Were Seen as Punishment for Sexual License

Until recently, sexually transmitted diseases were called **venereal diseases,** after Venus, the Roman goddess of love. The archetypal venereal disease was **syphilis,** the first European cases of which were described in the mid-1490s, a year or two after Christopher Columbus discovered the New World. It is likely that Columbus or his sailors brought the disease from the Americas, where it had been endemic for many centuries (Rothschild et al., 2000). No one made the American connection at the time; rather, the epidemic was thought to have resulted from (or been foretold by) an astrological event: the 1484 conjunction of five planets in Scorpio, the zodiacal sign that rules the genitalia. For centuries, syphilis was essentially untreatable; it spread inexorably and returned to America with the colonists. By 1918, an estimated 1 in 22 Americans were infected (Amstey, 1994).

During the nineteenth century, there was very little sympathy for people with syphilis. They were thought to have brought the disease on themselves by engaging in a sinful behavior—fornication. Except for innocent wives infected by their husbands, syphilitics were denied admission to hospitals for the poor. The facial disfiguration that commonly accompanied late-stage syphilis was taken as proof that the disease was a divine retribution for wrongdoing.

Until the mid-twentieth century, young men commonly used prostitutes as a sexual outlet prior to marriage—a practice that was highly conducive to the spread of syphilis and other venereal diseases. Men preferred to have sex either with very young prostitutes, who might still be free of infection, or with much older prostitutes, who were thought to have reached a noninfectious stage of the disease. Men also used primitive condoms to protect themselves from syphilis and other diseases. Many other men refrained from sex altogether for fear of infection. Thus syphilis and other venereal diseases helped make sex into something frightening and evil.

Syphilis still exists in America, but it may be essentially eliminated within the next few years. This happy prospect has resulted from medical advances, starting with the discovery of the causative bacterium in 1905 and the introduction of the first effective antibiotic, Salvarsan, 4 years later. Also vital to the conquest of syphilis have been grassroots activism and public health campaigns, as well as the decline of prostitution as a social institution.

The history of AIDS has mimicked that of syphilis in many respects: the importation of the disease from another continent (Africa), its rapid spread, the initial lack of any effective treatment, the stigmatization of those who were affected, and the gradually increasing inroads into the epidemic brought about by medical advances, social activism, and public health campaigns. The main difference is that the process has been compressed into a couple of decades rather than half a millennium. Also, syphilis can now be cured; AIDS, so far, can only be held at bay.

A Wide Range of Organisms Can Cause STDs

Currently, 65 million Americans are living with an incurable STD, and 15 million Americans acquire an STD every year (Centers for Disease Control, 2001m). It's important to realize, however, that some STDs occur much more commonly than others. Furthermore, because some STDs are readily treatable while others are incurable, there are enormous differences in the numbers of Americans who are carrying the various STDs at any one time (Table 16.1).

In this chapter we discuss those STDs that are most commonly encountered in the United States. We describe them in a sequence based on the type of organism that causes them, starting with multicellular eukaryotes (insects, to be specific) and progressing to viruses. To an approximation, this also represents a sequence of increasing seriousness: insects are an annoyance, but viruses can be killers.

This kind of organization is not ideal for someone who has, say, a vaginal discharge and wants to know what is causing it and how to treat it. We intend this chapter to be an educational overview of STDs, not a specific source of medical advice for STD sufferers. That's because, for one thing, we are not medical doctors. For another, the infor-

TABLE 16.1	*Estimated incidence and prevalence of some important STDs*	
STD	Incidence (estimated number of new cases per year)	Prevalence (estimated number of people currently infected)
Trichomoniasis	5 million	Not available
Syphilis	70,000	Not available
Gonorrhea	650,000	Not available
Chlamydia	3 million	2 million
Genital herpes	1 million	45 million
Human papillomavirus (HPV)	5.5 million	20 million
Hepatitis B	120,000	417,000
HIV/AIDS[a]	42,000 (reported AIDS diagnoses)	800–900,000

Sources: Cates, 1999; Centers for Disease Control, 2001i.

[a]HIV infections are not all by sexual contact.

mation we provide may not be up to date at the time you read it. Therefore, if you or someone you know has an STD, we urge you to get medical attention. There are also Web sites that carry up-to-date information on STDs and their treatment, such as the site of the Centers for Disease Control (see Web Resources).

Insects Are More of an Annoyance than a Danger

Three species of insects—head lice, pubic lice, and scabies mites—commonly infest human skin. Of these, pubic lice and scabies mites are frequently spread by sexual contact and are therefore discussed here. Louse and mite infestations hardly warrant being called "diseases," since they do not generally lead to serious systemic effects, but they are very bothersome conditions that, luckily, can be quickly and effectively treated.

Pubic Lice Itch, and That's All

Pubic lice (*Phthirus pubis*) are popularly known as "crabs," but they are insects, not crustaceans (Figure 16.1). They are small but visible: a large adult louse may be about a millimeter across and dark or tan-colored, while newly hatched lice are considerably smaller and colorless. Pubic lice are flat, like crabs, so they can lie very close to the skin; this makes them hard to dislodge. In addition, they grab two nearby hairs with their clawlike legs, anchoring themselves in place. Once anchored, they burrow their mouthparts into the skin between the hairs and gorge themselves on their host's blood.

Pubic lice are happiest living among pubic hairs because the spacing between hair shafts in that region is optimal for them, and because the oval cross-section of pubic hairs is matched by the shape of the louse's claws. Pubic lice can also spread to other hairy areas of the skin, however, such as the armpits, eyebrows, and the general body surface of hairy persons. They can even spread to the scalp, especially around the edges. Still, the scalp is the preferred hunting ground of another louse, the head louse.

Pubic lice lay eggs ("nits"), which they glue onto hairs near their base. Each nit can be seen as a tiny dark lump near the base of a hair. It takes about a week for the nits to hatch and start the cycle over. Both the lice and their nits may fall off the body and

Figure 16.1 Scanning electron micrograph of pubic lice. The claws at the ends of the insects' legs are beautifully designed for clamping onto oval-shaped hair shafts.

end up on bedding, underwear, or towels. The lice can survive in these locations for 2 days at the most, but the nits can survive for a week. So it is possible to pick up a louse infestation either by direct contact with an infested person or by using their bedding, clothing, or towels. Most infestations probably happen by direct contact, however. Sleeping with someone is the most favorable situation for transmission: it gives a louse plenty of time to pack its bags, arrange for its mail to be forwarded, and move to its new home.

The "disease" part of a pubic louse infestation is simply the itching that the lice cause—plus any damage done by scratching. The amount of blood lost is trivial, and fortunately, pubic lice don't seem to transmit more dangerous disease agents.

Diagnosing pubic lice is a simple matter of looking for the insects in the region of irritated skin, digging one out, and watching it wave its legs. Pubic lice are probably the one STD that you don't need a medical degree to diagnose.

Pubic lice are treated with insecticidal lotions or shampoos. Medications containing permethrin or pyrethrins (for example, Rid) are available over the counter. The lotion is applied to all hairy areas, left on for 10 minutes, and washed off. All clothes, sheets, and towels that might harbor lice must be washed and dried at high heat. (Items that cannot be washed can simply be left unused for 2 weeks, or dry-cleaned.) As with any STD, all sex partners should be notified.

The over-the-counter medications do not always work well; if they don't, it may be necessary to see a doctor and get a prescription for a more effective insecticide, Lindane. Lindane is left on for only 4 minutes. It should not be used by pregnant or nursing women or young children. Lice and nits may also be removed by close shaving of affected areas.

Scabies May Be Transmitted Sexually or Nonsexually

Scabies is an infestation with a parasitic mite, *Sarcoptes scabiei*. The mites are big enough to see (about 0.4 millimeter across), but they are not usually seen. That's because most of the mites are females, which dig tunnels within the superficial layers of the skin, like moles in garden soil. The tunnels are visible as reddish tracks, or as spots or pustules. If the infested person is sensitive to the scabies mite, there may also be a generalized rash even in places where no mites are located. Unlike lice, the scabies mite does not require hairy skin. In fact, it is commonly found in hairless areas such as the wrists, elbows, between the fingers, and the knees, penis, breasts, or back.

The female mite lives for about 2 months in its tunnels, laying eggs every few days. The eggs hatch after 3–8 days. The young go through a couple of juvenile stages, then return to the skin surface as adults to mate. Impregnated females burrow into the skin again, completing the cycle.

The itching caused by scabies infestations can be severe and may interfere with sleep. Infested persons may scratch themselves to the point of causing sores, which can become infected. Scabies spreads from person to person quite easily, so it is common wherever people live in crowded conditions. Sexual contact is just one of many modes of transmission.

Scabies is best diagnosed by a physician, who may examine skin scrapings under a microscope. The recommended treatment is a topical application of permethrin lotion, which is left on for several hours or overnight before washing off. As with pubic lice, possibly infested items must be washed and dried on a hot cycle or left unused for a week or so. Because the eggs may not all be killed, a repeat treatment 7–10 days later may be necessary.

Trichomoniasis Is Caused by a Protozoan

Trichomoniasis ("trich") is an infection of the vagina or the male urethra and prostate gland with *Trichomonas vaginalis*. This organism is not a bacterium, but rather a single-celled nucleated (protozoan) organism with a bundle of whip-like flagella. In women, trichomoniasis is marked by a malodorous, greenish, or frothy discharge from the vagina. There may be vaginal itching and redness, as well as abdominal discomfort or the urge to urinate frequently. Some women, however, have no symptoms. (Persons who are infected with a disease organism but show no symptoms are referred to as **asymptomatic carriers.**) Women who do have symptoms develop them within 6 months of infection, which usually happens through coitus. (*T. vaginalis* survives poorly outside a human host or even on the outside of the body, so it is not easily picked up from bedding, toilet seats, or casual contact.) An estimated 2 million women in the United States develop trichomoniasis every year, so it is a very common condition. About a fourth of all cases of vaginitis (inflammation of the vagina) are caused by *T. vaginalis.*

In men, *T. vaginalis* infection is usually asymptomatic. Sometimes it is marked by a slight discharge from the urethra, the urge to urinate frequently, and pain during urination.

Trichomoniasis is usually diagnosed by microscopic examination of specimens from the vagina or the urethra. A more sensitive method is to culture (grow) the organism from specimens; this method takes a few days and is more expensive. Trichomoniasis can usually be cured with a single oral dose of metronidazole (Flagyl and its generic equivalents). Some strains of *T. vaginalis* are resistant to metronidazole, however, and the drug should not be used during pregnancy. The infected person's partner should be treated at the same time, whether symptomatic or not; otherwise they may continue to pass the infection back and forth between them.

Bacterial STDs Can Usually Be Treated with Antibiotics

The main sexually transmitted bacterial infections in the United States are syphilis, gonorrhea, and chlamydia. These are serious diseases that can be fatal in themselves (syphilis), impair fertility (gonorrhea, chlamydia), or facilitate HIV infection (all three). Treated promptly, however, they can be readily cured, and complications can be avoided.

Syphilis Is Down but Not Out

Syphilis is caused by infection with a corkscrew-shaped bacterium, or **spirochete,** with the specific name of *Treponema pallidum* (Figure 16.2). It is closely related to the organism that causes a nonvenereal tropical disease, yaws, and may have evolved from the yaws organism somewhere in the Americas in the distant past. Syphilis is spread by direct contact, nearly always sexually. (It can also spread from mother to fetus.)

Untreated, syphilis can last a lifetime and eventually cause death. The disease goes through several stages, starting at the site of infection and eventually affecting many organ systems. In its early stages, a single dose of penicillin eradicates the organism and is followed by a complete cure.

Primary Syphilis Is Marked by a Sore at the Site of Infection

A man or woman acquires syphilis by sexual contact with a person who is in the primary or secondary stage of the disease. Most commonly, infection comes from a primary syphilitic sore, or **chancre** (Figure 16.3), which exudes a fluid containing huge numbers of spirochetes. The chancre is often painless. It may be visible on the penis or labia, or it may be hidden inside the vagina, on the cervix, inside the anus or rectum, or even inside the mouth. Thus it may or may not be possible to tell whether a partner has a chancre.

The spirochetes penetrate the skin and multiply at the site of infection. Between 10 and 90 days (usually about 21 days) after infection, a chancre appears at that same site. The chancre starts as a red bump that then breaks down, becoming a sore or ulcer. The chancre has a hard, rubbery rim and a wet or scabbed-over interior. If left untreated, it will heal by itself within 3–6 weeks.

Because a chancre is a break in the skin, it greatly facilitates the transmission of an even more serious pathogen, HIV (see below). In 1996, an estimated 1000 new cases of

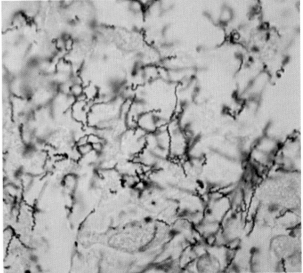

Figure 16.2 *Treponema pallidum,* the bacterium that causes syphilis. The bacteria are the dark, corkscrew-shaped threads. The yellow objects are cells of the host—in this case, an experimentally infected rabbit.

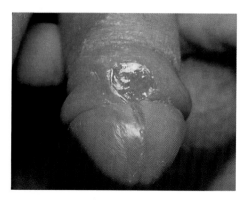

Figure 16.3 Primary syphilitic sores (chancres) on the penis.

HIV infection in the United States were facilitated by the presence of syphilis (Chesson et al., 1999).

Secondary Syphilis Is Marked by a Rash

The second stage of syphilis may begin while the primary chancre is still visible, or it may be delayed for several weeks. The main sign of secondary syphilis is a painless rash, which classically affects the palms and the soles of the feet, but may also occur elsewhere (Figure 16.4). The rash takes the form of red or reddish-brown blotches. It is often accompanied by a fever, swollen lymph nodes, sore throat, and muscle pain. If left untreated, these symptoms generally disappear within a few weeks.

After the Second Stage, the Disease May Remain Latent

In many individuals, the *T. pallidum* spirochetes are not eliminated at the end of the second stage, but continue to multiply in the body, even though the symptoms are gone. After about a year of this latent phase, the person is no longer infectious to sex partners. A pregnant woman can pass the organism to her fetus, however. The fetus may be stillborn, die neonatally, or suffer severe neurological impairment.

During the latent phase, the organism continues to multiply at a slow rate. It may gradually invade the cardiovascular system, the bones, the liver, and the nervous system without initially causing any symptoms.

In Tertiary Syphilis, Many Organ Systems Can Be Affected

Eventually—sometimes decades after infection—syphilis can do serious damage. In this tertiary stage, large ulcers may appear on the skin or internal organs. The disease may attack the heart or the aorta, possibly causing a fatal hemorrhage. It may attack the central nervous system, causing paralysis or mental symptoms. It may attack the skeleton, including the bones of the face, leading to serious disfigurement. Tertiary syphilis is now thankfully rare, but its very rarity, combined with the variety of sites that may be attacked, can make it difficult to diagnose.

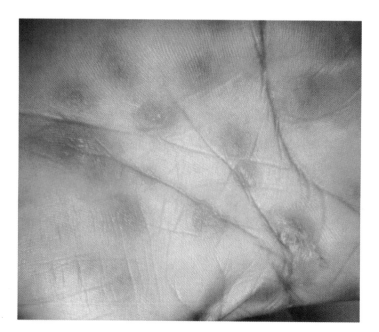

Figure 16.4 Secondary syphilitic rash may appear on the hands, as here, on the soles of the feet, or elsewhere on the body.

Syphilis Is Cured by Penicillin

Syphilis is diagnosed by recognition of the clinical signs and symptoms, by finding *T. pallidum* in the exudate from the primary chancre, or by detecting antibodies to *T. pallidum* in the blood. A single dose of penicillin is curative during the first year after infection; at later times a more prolonged course of the drug may be required. The sex partners of an infected person should be notified and tested. Having had syphilis in the past does not protect a person from getting a new infection.

Syphilis Has Resisted Elimination

The introduction of effective antibiotic treatment, along with other public health measures, has greatly reduced the prevalence of syphilis in the United States from the 1 in 22 rate in 1918, mentioned earlier. In 1998 there were only 2.6 reported new cases of primary or secondary syphilis per 100,000 people—down 86 percent from the level in 1990. This rate of infection is still far above the rate for some other countries, however, such as Canada and Britain, where there is fewer than one new case per 100,000 people per year.

The epidemiology of syphilis in the United States reflects huge social disparities in health status and health care. Syphilis today is largely a black disease: an African-American is 34 times more likely to contract syphilis than is a non-Hispanic white American. (This figure may be somewhat exaggerated due to reporting bias—that is, some private doctors who see white patients may fail to report their cases.) Furthermore, it is not just any blacks, but blacks in the South—most of them poor—who are particularly at risk (Box 16.1). In 1999, half of all cases of syphilis occurred in just 25 of the nation's 3115 counties, most of them located in the South. There have

Box 16.1 *Society, Values, and the Law*

The Tuskegee Syphilis Study

One of the most shameful episodes in the history of American medicine began in 1932, when Public Health Service researchers began a study of the effects of untreated syphilis on several hundred black men living near Tuskegee, Alabama (see figure). The aim of the project was to follow the natural history of the disease, to study whether there were differences between the disease in black and in white persons, and to compare symptoms during life with autopsy findings after death. (The study initially had a treatment element, but this was soon abandoned.)

The researchers, some of whom were based at the Tuskegee Institute (now Tuskegee University, a historically black college), recruited black farmers, renters, and laborers who had latent syphilis. That is, they had progressed beyond the first two stages of the disease but had not yet shown systemic symptoms. Most were poor and poorly educated. Among the incentives that attracted men to the study or kept them in it over the years were medical examinations and blood tests, free trips to Tuskegee, and the promise that burial expenses would be covered. Most of the subjects thought that they were being treated for their condition, but in reality they received only dubious medications such as "tonics."

At the time the study began, a treatment for syphilis existed—the organic arsenical compound Salvarsan—but effective treatment required weekly injections over many months, and serious side effects were common. Some doctors thought that the treatment was worse than the disease for persons in the latent stage. Because of this uncertainty, as well as the expense of treatment and the belief that poor rural blacks were unlikely to cooperate with the treatment regimen, this population often went untreated, so the Tuskegee subjects were not initially singled out to be denied effective medical care.

The study continued for decades, and 13 research papers described the findings. In 1947, a far more effective antibiotic, penicillin, was recognized as the standard of care for syphilis. In the same year, the Nuremberg Code was promulgated in response to the atrocities committed by doctors in Nazi Germany. The code declared that informed consent must be a condition for participation in medical experiments. Nevertheless, the Tuskegee experiment continued, and the subjects were not told that a simple and effective treatment was now available. In fact, the researchers went to considerable lengths to prevent the subjects from receiving treatment at the hands of other doctors. Thus the moral status of the study changed radically.

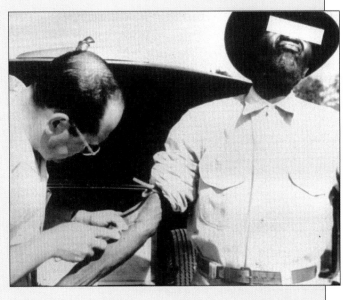

The study did not end until 1972, when a CDC researcher who was opposed to the continuation of the study gave an account of it to an Associated Press reporter. The ensuing publicity led to the rapid termination of the project. By that time, however, dozens of the subjects had died of the disease, and 22 wives, 17 children, and 2 grandchildren had contracted it, probably as a result of the nontreatment of the subjects.

In 1974 a lawsuit brought on behalf of the survivors was settled for $10 million. In May 1997, President Clinton, responding to pressure from civil rights activists and the Black Congressional Caucus, formally apologized to the survivors in a White House ceremony. In response, one of the survivors, Herman Shaw, declared that "it is time to put this horrible nightmare behind us as a nation. . . . We must never allow a tragedy like the Tuskegee study to happen again."

The Tuskegee study was a particularly egregious example of what was once a common phenomenon: the use of poor blacks as research subjects almost as if they were laboratory animals. Not surprisingly, many blacks have developed a deep suspicion of mainstream medicine. Conspiracy theories that may seem outlandish to others, such as the idea that the AIDS virus was manufactured and spread by the federal government with the intent of wiping out black people, find a certain resonance among less-educated blacks.

Research practices have changed greatly since the time the Tuskegee study was begun, and it is unthinkable that such a project could be carried out in the United States today. Even so, much needs to be done to ensure that minority interests are properly addressed in medical research. Furthermore, ethical concerns somewhat similiar to those arising from the Tuskegee study have been raised by the practice of testing drugs and vaccines in developing countries, usually on nonwhite populations. Are these subjects truly informed about the risks and benefits? And after the drugs and vaccines are developed, will they be available or affordable for the populations on whom they were tested?

Sources: Reverby, 1997; Wolinsky, 1997.

also been outbreaks of syphilis in large cities elsewhere; an outbreak among gay men in Los Angeles in 2000 was still continuing in 2002.

The U.S. government has set the goal of eliminating syphilis from the United States by 2005 (Centers for Disease Control, 1999c). "Elimination" in this context does not mean total eradication, since new cases will continue to be imported from overseas, but the termination of any sustained chains of infection within this country. Eliminating the disease would save close to $1 billion annually—mostly by preventing HIV infections caused by the presence of syphilis. Syphilis tends to come and go in the U.S. population in cycles of 7–10 years. We are currently in a trough between cycles, so there is a narrow window of opportunity to achieve the goal of elimination.

Gonorrhea Can Lead to Sterility

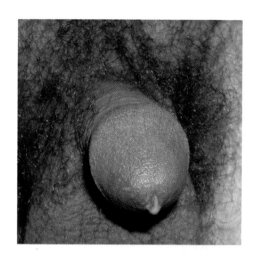

Figure 16.5 Gonorrheal urethritis in men is marked by painful urination and a discharge of pus, or a cloudy fluid that may contain pus, from the penis.

Gonorrhea ("the clap," "the drip") is a common STD caused by infection with the bacterium *Neisseria gonorrhoeae*. Its symptoms develop quickly—within 2 to 10 days of infection in most people. In women, the initial site of infection is usually the cervix. Symptoms include a yellow or bloody vaginal discharge, bleeding during coitus, and a burning sensation when urinating. Quite commonly (perhaps in more than half of cases), however, the initial infection is asymptomatic. In men, the usual site of infection is the urethra, and the symptoms are a discharge of pus from the urethra (Figure 16.5) and pain on urination.

Both men and women can be infected rectally through receptive anal sex. The symptoms of rectal infection include a rectal discharge, anal itching, and sometimes painful bowel movements with fresh (bright red) blood on the surface of the feces. In women, a vaginal infection can spread to the rectum. Infections of the mouth or pharynx can occur as a result of oral sex, especially fellatio, with an infected person.

In women, the infection can spread into the uterus and oviducts, causing **pelvic inflammatory disease (PID)**. In some women, PID symptoms are the first symptoms of gonorrhea to be noticed. These symptoms can include abdominal cramps and continuous pain, vaginal bleeding between menstrual periods, vomiting, and fever. PID may cause scarring of the oviducts, resulting in infertility or subfertility and a heightened risk of ectopic pregnancy (see Chapter 10). In men, the infection can spread to the epididymis, causing pain in the scrotum, or to the prostate gland. **Epididymitis,** like PID, can affect fertility.

Occasionally, *N. gonorrhoeae* spreads to the kidneys. It can also spread through the bloodstream, damaging the nervous system, the joints, or the heart valves. Having gonorrhea increases the likelihood of transmitting or picking up HIV. Babies can become infected—usually in the eyes—during the birth process.

Diagnosis and Treatment of Gonorrhea Are Straightforward—If the Sufferer Seeks Medical Attention

Gonorrhea is diagnosed by identifying the *N. gonorrhoeae* organism. This can be done by direct microscopic inspection of the urethral or vaginal discharge. This test is rather insensitive, however, especially in women; in fact, its results are negative in about half of gonorrhea-infected women. There are more sensitive tests that involve the detection of *N. gonorrhoeae* DNA in the discharge or in urine, either directly or after amplification of the DNA by the **polymerase chain reaction (PCR)**. The organism can also be identified by being grown in culture.

At one time, gonorrhea was readily treatable with standard antibiotics such as penicillin and tetracycline. Unfortunately, the *N. gonorrhoeae* organism has shown a remarkable ability to develop drug resistance (Centers for Disease Control, 2000b). During the 1980s, strains resistant to penicillin and tetracycline became so common that the CDC recommended use of a newer family of antibiotics known as fluoroquinolones, of which ciprofloxacin is the best-known example. By 1999, however, nearly 10 percent of all gonorrhea cases in Hawaii involved fluoroquinolone-resistant strains. In 1999, the first cases that were resistant to another commonly used drug, azithromycin, were reported in Kansas City, Missouri.

One hypothesis is that the appearance of antibiotic-resistant strains has been promoted by the routine prophylactic use of antibiotics by sex workers, especially in Asia. It is certainly true that female sex workers in Asia are very likely to have drug-resistant gonorrhea. Thirty-eight percent of *N. gonorrhoeae* samples isolated from female sex workers in Dhaka, Bangladesh, were resistant to fluoroquinolones (Rahman et al., 2001). In the Philippines, the proportion is even higher—up to 49 percent (Aplasca De Los Reyes et al., 2001).

Luckily, a few expensive antibiotics, such as ceftriaxone, are still effective against all known strains of *N. gonorrhoeae.* The antibiotic sensitivity of the *N. gonorrhoeae* cultured from an infected person can be determined by in vitro tests; these tests allow a doctor to choose the antibiotic most likely to eliminate the infection. Some of the antibiotics recommended for treatment of gonorrhea should not be used by pregnant women or by persons under the age of 18.

The main problem with the diagnosis and treatment of gonorrhea is the fact that an infected woman may have few or no symptoms, at least initially, so that she may not seek medical treatment. Infected men, on the other hand, usually experience severe discomfort and therefore seek medical attention. Because of this disparity, it's important for infected persons to notify their partners so that they, too, may be treated before serious complications develop.

Elimination of Gonorrhea Is Not Yet in Sight

Huge epidemics of gonorrhea swept nations in the early part of the twentieth century, especially during times of war. The introduction of penicillin seemed to promise an end to the disease after World War II, but the sexual revolution, the introduction of oral contraceptives (which, unlike condoms, offer no protection against STDs), and the development of antibiotic resistance allowed gonorrhea to make a comeback. There are now about 650,000 new cases in the United States annually. The incidence of gonorrhea in the United States is 8 times higher than in Canada and 50 times higher than in Sweden (Centers for Disease Control, 2001m).

As with syphilis, the highest incidence rates for gonorrhea are in the South (Figure 16.6A) and among African-Americans (Figure 16.6B). The incidence rate in conservative South Carolina is nearly seven times higher than in swinging California! The disease is found throughout the United States, however; it is particularly common, of course, among people who have sex with multiple partners. Men who have sex with men are also at high risk. ("Men who have sex with men" is a behavioral definition: it includes many gay and bisexual men, of course, but it also covers men who identify themselves as heterosexual but who have sex with men under certain circumstances, such as in prison.) The incidence of gonorrhea among men who have sex with men fell dramatically during the early years of the AIDS epidemic, but then doubled between 1994 and 1999 (Centers for Disease Control, 2001m).

Chlamydia Causes a Common Infection with Serious Complications

Chlamydia is a relatively newly recognized STD. Reported cases in the United States rose from 3 to 207 per 100,000 persons between 1984 and 1997, and chlamydia is now the most common of all reportable infectious diseases (Centers for Disease Control, 2001d). This increase did not represent the explosive spread of a new disease, as with AIDS, however. Rather, the increase was due in part to increased recognition of a condition that had previously been diagnosed as a nonspecific genital infection.

Chlamydia trachomatis is a bacterium, but it is very different from most other bacterial species (Figure 16.7). It is smaller than most bacteria, it has a different type of cell wall, and its genome is so different as to place it (along with some close relatives) in a distinct kingdom. Chlamydia shares with viruses the property of living only inside cells. It depends on the cell it inhabits to do much of its metabolic work, and it exists outside of cells only in the form of inert infective particles. Besides its role in causing an STD, *C. trachomatis* is a leading cause of blindness in tropical countries, where it is transmitted by eye-seeking insects.

Chlamydia is spread by genital contact. Symptoms appear from a few days to 2 weeks after infection. In men, the organism infects the urethra, causing a thin discharge (different

(A)

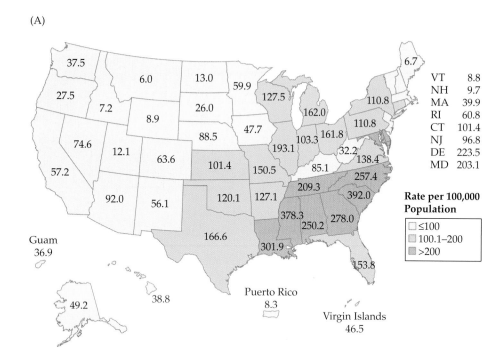

VT	8.8
NH	9.7
MA	39.9
RI	60.8
CT	101.4
NJ	96.8
DE	223.5
MD	203.1

Rate per 100,000 Population

☐ ≤100
▨ 100.1–200
▨ >200

Figure 16.6 Geographic and Racial/Ethnic Distribution of Gonorrhea. (A) Gonorrhea is most prevalent in the southeastern United States. This map shows the number of new cases per 100,000 people in 1999. (Data from CDC, 2001m.) (B) Racial/ethnic differences in the prevalence of gonorrhea. The disease is much more prevalent among African-Americans than among other groups. (Data from CDC, 2001m.)

(B)

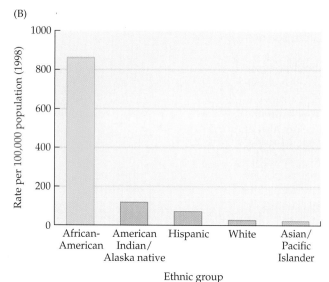

from the thick discharge of gonorrhea) and burning pain during urination. (Urinary tract infections are discussed further in Chapter 17.) Like gonorrhea, the organism can migrate farther up the male reproductive tract and cause epididymitis.

In women, the organism infects the cervix or urethra, causing irritation, a thin vaginal discharge, and painful urination. But 75 percent of infected women (as well as 50 percent of infected men) experience no symptoms. In both men and women, chlamydia infections can also occur in the rectum and in the mouth or throat.

Like gonorrhea, chlamydia can migrate up the female reproductive tract and cause pelvic inflammatory disease (whether the initial infection was symptomatic or not). Up to 40 percent of women with untreated chlamydia infections develop PID; 20 percent of these women with PID will become infertile, and 9 percent of them will have an ectopic pregnancy. About half of all cases of PID are probably caused by chlamydia infections.

As if this wasn't bad enough, chlamydia infection has yet another ill effect: it increases a woman's risk of developing cervical cancer. This increased risk shows up many years after the initial infection and has required large-scale epidemiological studies to verify (Koskela et al., 2000). However, the influence of chlamydia in promoting cervical cancer is not as great as that of another STD, human papillomavirus (see below).

Chlamydia is diagnosed from cell samples obtained from the penis or cervix. (The cervical sampling procedure is different from the Pap test mentioned below.) It can also be diagnosed from urine samples using gene amplification techniques similar to PCR. Chlamydia can be cured with a single dose of the antibiotic azithromycin, or with a week's course of doxycycline.

The demographics of chlamydia are poorly understood because of underreporting and other factors. Reported cases among women outnumber those among men by about 5 to 1, but this is probably due to the fact that there have been extensive campaigns to screen for chlamydia among women (Centers for Disease Control, 2001d). Chlamydia does not seem to be concentrated in the South or among blacks; rather, it is common among young, sexually active men and women across the United States. As many as 1 in 10 of all adolescent girls are infected, and the figures for older adolescents in urban

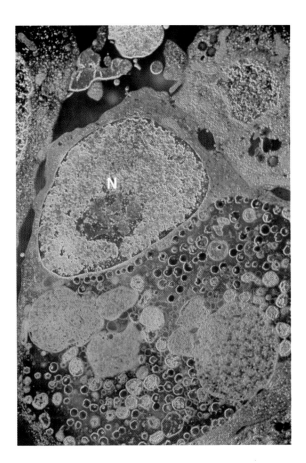

Figure 16.7 Chlamydia organisms, seen in this false-color electron micrograph as small orange–brown spheres, multiply inside an inclusion body within an infected cell (green) whose nucleus (N) is at upper left.

areas may be even higher. By age 30, about half of all sexually active women show evidence of current or prior chlamydia infection.

Screening and treatment campaigns have been quite successful in some states. In the Pacific Northwest states (Oregon, Washington, Idaho, and Alaska) these campaigns brought about a 62 percent decline in infections during the 1990s. The CDC recommends that all sexually active young people who do not use condoms for all sexual encounters be tested for chlamydia once per year. Since the test merely involves giving a urine sample—and taking a single dose of an antibiotic if it is positive—it is a small price to pay for peace of mind.

Viral STDs Can Be Dangerous and Hard to Treat

Viruses are extremely small infectious particles (only a few tens of nanometers in diameter). Like *Chlamydia,* viruses live in and depend on host cells. When not inside a host cell, viruses take the form of inert but infectious packages of genes (**virions**). A virion consists of a core of genetic material (either DNA or RNA) and proteins, surrounded by a **capsid**—a crystal-like array of proteins with associated sugar molecules. In some viruses the capsid is contained within a lipid **envelope** resembling a cell membrane.

A virus's genetic material is extremely limited—it may possess as few as 10 genes, compared with about 1000 genes for a bacterium. Some of these genes code for the proteins of the capsid, which play a vital role in attaching the virus to the plasma membrane of a host cell and injecting its genetic material into the cell. Once inside a host cell, the viral genes take over the cell's metabolic machinery in order to replicate themselves. This replication may occur right away and be followed by the release of new virions. Alternatively, the viral genes may persist in the cell in an inactive form for a long time before ultimately coming out of hiding and generating new virions.

Many viral diseases cure themselves because they trigger an immune response that destroys free virions and any already infected cells. Some viruses have found ways to protect themselves from their host's immune system, however. Finding drugs to cure such viral diseases is difficult for two reasons. First, the virus has only a few genes of its own, so there are only a few metabolic sites of attack that are distinct from the host's own metabolic machinery. Second, some viruses integrate their genes into the host cell's own genome, making them very difficult to detect and remove. Nevertheless, the last 15 years have seen some remarkable advances in the treatment of viral diseases, including viral STDs.

In this section we discuss four classes of viruses: herpes simplex viruses (HSV—the cause of genital and oral herpes), human papillomaviruses (HPV—the cause of genital warts and other conditions), hepatitis viruses (which attack the liver), and the human immunodeficiency virus (HIV), which causes acquired immune deficiency syndrome (AIDS). Roughly speaking, this sequence of viral types reflects the increasing seriousness of the diseases they cause.

Herpes Simplex Virus Infections Often Cause Recurrent Symptoms

The genetic material of herpesviruses is DNA (Figure 16.8). Two herpesviruses, herpes simplex 1 and 2 (HSV-1, HSV-2), may be transmitted sexually. HSV-1 commonly causes **oral herpes,** often in the form of "fever blisters" or "cold sores" on the lips or inside the mouth. If a person with active oral herpes performs oral sex on another person, that other person may acquire a genital HSV-1 infection. A more common cause of **genital herpes,** however,

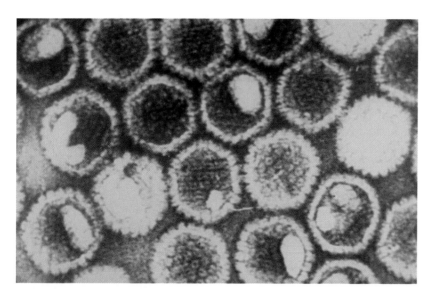

Figure 16.8 Virions of herpes simplex virus 2 (HSV-2), the usual causative agent of genital herpes, are shown in an electron micrograph using negative contrast. (The light-colored structures are the biological elements.) The shell-like structures are viral capsids—arrays of proteins that form cages around the viral DNA. The DNA cores are visible as dense, light-colored clumps within some of the virions. The virions also possess outer membranous envelopes (not visible in this preparation). Each capsid measures about 200 nanometers in diameter.

is HSV-2, which is usually transmitted directly from the anogenital area of one person to that of another.

The symptoms of HSV-2 infection usually occur within 2 weeks after exposure, taking the form of an outbreak of sores at the site of infection. This site is usually somewhere in the genital or anorectal area or on the surrounding skin, but may be elsewhere on the body or around the mouth. The commonest sites are the penis in men and the labia, clitoral hood, or vaginal walls in women. The outbreak may be accompanied by fever and swollen lymph nodes, or rarely by more serious symptoms. The first outbreak is usually worse than any subsequent one. During the first outbreak, the virus can be spread to other parts of the body, including the eyes, by the person's fingers.

Unless the immune system is compromised, the primary infection is quickly mopped up, and the sores disappear within a couple of weeks. The herpesvirus has a trick up its sleeve, however. Some virions bind to the terminals of sensory nerves in the vicinity of the infection site and enter their cytoplasm. Nerve fibers (axons) have an internal transport system that is constantly shuttling material between the neuron's cell body (where the nucleus is located) and the nerve terminals (in the skin, in this case). The virions hop onto this transport system and, over a period of a few days, get a free ride to the cell body. These cell bodies are usually located in the dorsal root ganglia, close to the spinal cord (see Chapter 3). Once the virions have reached a cell body, they may remain inert for weeks, months, or even years. In this location, they are protected from the host's immune system.

At some point, a new round of viral replication occurs, and the new virions hitch a ride in the opposite direction, back to the original infection site or nearby, where they cause another outbreak of sores. Because the host's immune system has already been exposed to the virus, the second and later outbreaks are usually less severe than the first, and during these later outbreaks the virus cannot be spread by the fingers to other parts of the body. Some people infected with herpes have only the initial outbreak, while others may continue to experience outbreaks every few months for the rest of their lives.

A herpes outbreak may begin with tingling or itching at the site where the outbreak is about to occur. Such **prodromal** signs are useful because they can warn the person to desist from sex or use protection (to avoid giving herpes to a sex partner) and to start taking medicine (see below). Shortly after any prodromal signs, a reddish, slightly elevated spot or cluster of spots appears. A day or so later, the spots turn into blisters (Figure 16.9). The blisters then break, leaving sores or ulcers that weep a clear exudate. This exudate contains immense numbers of virions and is highly infectious. After a few more days, the sores crust over, dry up, and gradually heal and disappear.

Herpes outbreaks may be painless or mildly itchy—especially if they occur on a less sensitive patch of skin. Alternatively, they may be quite painful. If they are in a site that is contacted by urine, the act of urination may be extremely painful.

People who have been infected with HSV-2 can be identified by the presence of anti-HSV-2 antibodies in their blood. Many HSV-2-positive individuals deny any history of herpetic outbreaks, which has led to the widespread notion that most HSV-2 infections are asymptomatic. In studies in which HSV-2-positive women have been given careful instructions on how to examine themselves, however, the majority do report an outbreak within a few months (Langenberg et al., 1989; Wald et al., 2000). Presumably many of the remainder would have had outbreaks if they had been monitored for longer periods. Thus, truly asymptomatic HSV-2 infection may not be common among women. The situation among men in this regard is uncertain.

Is There a Stress Connection?

Many people believe that *stress* triggers their herpes outbreaks or increases their frequency, and some scientific studies support this idea (Sainz et al., 2001). However, these

(A)

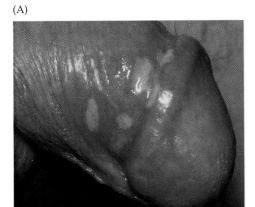

(B)

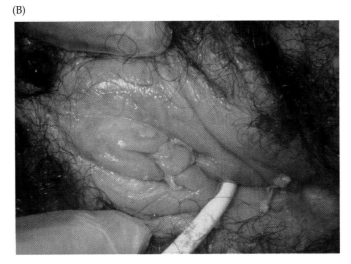

Figure 16.9 Herpes outbreaks commonly occur (A) on the shaft on the penis or (B) on the vulva.

studies have usually failed to allow for **observer bias**—that is, for the fact that stressful events occurring right before outbreaks seem more salient, and are remembered better, simply because they are followed by an outbreak.

To get around this problem, two *prospective* studies required herpes sufferers to keep logs of stressful events and to seal or mail in the logs at regular intervals, even daily (Herpetic Eye Disease Study Group, 2000; Rand et al., 1990). In neither of these studies did statistical analysis reveal any tendency for sufferers to record an increased frequency of stressful events *before* they knew they had an outbreak. In one of these studies, the sufferers had the opportunity to *retrospectively* add mention of earlier stressful events. These people did indeed add many reports of such events for the days before each outbreak—a clear effect of observer bias. Thus there is a real possibility that the stress–herpes connection is fictitious or exaggerated. Further research in this interesting area is certainly warranted, but temporal associations of this kind are notoriously subject to bias—recall our discussion of "menstrual synchrony" in Chapter 4.

Herpes Can Have Serious Effects

Although recurrent herpes outbreaks, even over a lifetime, do not present a serious threat to health, herpes infection can have more serious effects. First and foremost, an infant can be infected during parturition, and that infection can be fatal to the infant or leave it severely impaired. Mother-to-infant transmission can be prevented by delivering the baby via cesarean section.

There has been some evidence for a possible link between herpes infection and cervical cancer, but the most recent studies, including large-scale prospective ones, suggest that this link is marginal or nonexistent (Lehtinen et al., 1992). Finally, some persons experience significant psychological distress on account of their herpes outbreaks, sometimes feeling that they are sexual outcasts who can have sexual relationships only with other herpes sufferers.

Herpes Transmission Can Occur between Recognized Outbreaks

During outbreaks, herpes sufferers can very easily transmit the disease to their sex partners. People with herpes are generally most infectious from the time they experience the first prodromal symptoms to the time that all their sores are dry and crusted over.

What about between outbreaks? Here the evidence is less clear. There have been studies in which women who suffer from periodic genital outbreaks were asked to takes swabs from the affected area at regular intervals—sometimes daily (Koelle et al., 1992; Wald et al., 2000). Material from the swabs was then tested by tissue culture or other techniques for the presence of HSV-2. In about half of the women in these studies, HSV-2 was detected on some days when there was no reported outbreak. About half of these HSV-2-positive days occurred within 7 days of an outbreak (either before or after the outbreak), but others occurred in no proximity to an outbreak. This asymptomatic shedding of HSV-2 was particularly common during the few months after a woman's initial outbreak and became rarer in women who had had herpes for years.

What is unclear is how great the risk of transmitting herpes is during these asymptomatic virus-shedding episodes. One study focused on 144 **sero-opposite** heterosexual couples (that is, couples in which one partner was HSV-2-positive and the other was negative) (Mertz et al., 1992). Over the course of a year, 14 of the initially noninfected partners became infected, and 9 of these acquired their infection at a time when their partners did not report an outbreak. Most of these transmissions occurred in the male-to-female direction. Thus, transmission *can* occur when there is no recognized outbreak, but it is still probably the case that most herpes transmission occurs during outbreaks.

Drug Treatment Can Shorten or Prevent Outbreaks

Genital herpes is usually diagnosed from the patient's history and from clinical observation of the typical herpetic lesions. It is also possible to identify the virus by a variety of techniques. The mainstay of treatment is **acyclovir** (Zovirax and generic equivalents); some related drugs, such as valacyclovir (Valtrex) and famciclovir (Famvir), are also used. There is no difference between the efficacy of acyclovir and the much more expensive valacyclovir (Tyring et al., 1998).

Acyclovir is a synthetic analog of a **nucleoside**—the precursor of a **nucleotide,** or building block of DNA. Once in the body, it is converted into a nucleotide. When the viral DNA-synthesizing enzyme tries to incorporate this nucleotide into its DNA, it gums up the virus's DNA-copying machinery, so that the growing DNA chain terminates. Acyclovir is available as a topical ointment, which is of dubious value, and as oral tablets. If a course of oral acyclovir is started at the first sign of an outbreak, the outbreak is shortened and may never get to the point of producing an exudate. Acyclovir can also be taken continuously to prevent or reduce the frequency of outbreaks (Mindel et al., 1988).

Herpes Is Extremely Common

It's estimated that 45 million Americans aged 12 and over—or 1 in 5 adolescents and adults—are infected with HSV-2 (Cates, 1999). Blacks are significantly more likely to be infected than whites (46 percent vs. 18 percent), but herpes is spreading fast among young whites: over the last 2 decades, the infection rate among white teens increased fivefold (Centers for Disease Control, 2001f). The chances that a sexually active person will encounter an HSV-2-positive partner at some point are very high.

Human Papillomaviruses Can Cause Genital Warts—and Cancer

Human papillomaviruses (**HPV**) (see the opening photo to this chapter) are a group of about 100 DNA viruses, of which about 30 types are sexually transmitted. These viruses infect the cells lining the urogenital tract or the skin near the genitalia. Once inside a host cell, the viral DNA can remain in an inactive form, or it can spur cell division, leading to the appearance of **genital warts** (Figure 16.10) or other skin lesions. The viral DNA of most HPV types remains separate from the host cell's own DNA, but some types, especially type 16 and type 18, can integrate their DNA into the host cell's genome (Jeon & Lambert, 1995), with important consequences (see below).

Genital warts usually appear a few months after infection, but many infected persons have no warts or other symptoms. The warts are benign (noncancerous) tumors that are typically located at the vaginal opening, within the vagina, on the cervix, on the penis, at or within the anus, or even in the mouth. (The common warts that occur elsewhere on the body are caused by a different group of viruses.) They can be single soft, pink bumps or more elaborate, cauliflower-like growths. The medical term for genital warts is **condylomata acuminata.** They are unsightly and highly infectious, but they are usually painless and do not often cause serious health problems.

Visible genital warts are most frequently caused by HPV types 6 and 11. Rarely, these types may later cause cancers of the external genitalia (for example, of the penis, labia, or anus), but this does not happen frequently enough to be a matter of real concern.

HPV types 16 and 18 (the ones that integrate their DNA into the host cell's genome) are not a common cause of raised genital warts. They can cause other kinds of lesions in the genital region, including flat lesions that may be precancerous, but most commonly there are no symptoms. The problem with these HPV types is that, in women, they can eventually promote the development of invasive **cervical cancer.** In fact, HPV infection can probably be considered the principal cause of cervical cancer. A key strategy in preventing the progression from HPV infection to cervical cancer is the **Pap test,** which we'll describe in Chapter 17. For now, be aware that most genital warts do *not* contain the types of HPV that predispose women to cervical cancer.

Some types of HPV, especially certain strains of type 16, can cause **anal cancer** (Da Costa et al., 2002). Men and women who engage in unprotected receptive anal sex are therefore at increased risk for anal cancer, especially if they are HIV-positive. Some specialists therefore recommend regular anal Pap tests for this population (Goldie et al., 2000).

A clinician can remove genital warts by a variety of means, such as by cutting them off, by freezing them with liquid nitrogen, or by the application of podophyllin or other agents. HPV is not usually eliminated from the body by these treatments, however, and the warts sometimes recur. An HPV vaccine is currently in clinical trials (Connett, 2001).

HPV infection is very common: probably 50–75 percent of sexually active men and women acquire an HPV infection at some point in their lives, and an estimated 20 million Americans are currently infected. This estimate is quite uncertain because of the difficulty of knowing whether a person is carrying an asymptomatic infection. Still, over 5 million new infections occur annually—5 times the number of new herpes infections. Thus, the chances of being exposed to HPV are high.

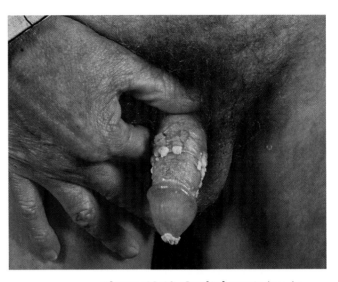

Figure 16.10 Genital warts (condylomata acuminata) on the penis.

Hepatitis Viruses Can Be Sexually Transmitted

Viruses that attack the liver, called **hepatitis viruses,** belong to a number of unrelated types, of which the best known are hepatitis A–E. The most important of these viruses in terms of sexual transmission is hepatitis B, followed by hepatitis A (Figure 16.11).

The **hepatitis B** virus is a small DNA virus. It can be picked up by coitus or by anal or oral sex with an infected partner, as well as by contact with contaminated blood (by sharing needles, for example). The signs and symptoms of hepatitis B include **jaundice** (yellowing of the skin and mucous membranes), fever, general malaise, and tenderness and swelling of the liver (located in the upper right quadrant of the abdomen). The majority of persons with hepatitis B recover uneventfully, but in about 1 in 10 people the infection progresses to a chronic state, which can lead to scarring (cirrhosis) of the liver, liver cancer, and fatal liver failure.

About 120,000 people acquire a hepatitis B infection in the United States each year. The disease is particularly common among gay men, but it is not rare among heterosexual men and women. In one study of heterosexual college students, 14 percent of the students who reported having three or more sex partners in the previous 4 months carried antibodies against hepatitis B in their blood, meaning that they had been infected with hepatitis B at some point.

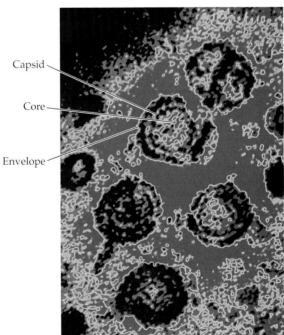

Capsid

Core

Envelope

Figure 16.11 Hepatitis B virions in a negative-contrast, false-color electron micrograph. The capsids, which contain DNA cores, have thin, tightly fitting envelopes.

Chronic hepatitis B can be treated, though not cured, with the drug **lamivudine.** There is also an effective vaccine.

The genetic material of **hepatitis A** is not DNA, but RNA. Unlike the genetic material of HIV (described below), the viral RNA is not transcribed into DNA within the host cell, but is simply copied into more RNA and used directly for the synthesis of proteins. Hepatitis A is transmitted by the fecal–oral route: that is, virions in the feces of an infected person get into the mouth of another. It is often spread by food handlers, but it can also be spread sexually, especially by the practice of mouth-to-anus contact (analingus, rimming) or by anal penetration. The symptoms are similar to those of hepatitis B, but are usually milder, and the disease does not progress to a chronic state. There is no specific treatment, but there is a vaccine.

Gay men are at particular risk of acquiring hepatitis A by the sexual route: in one study conducted in the San Francisco Bay area, 28 percent of gay and bisexual men had anti-hepatitis A antibodies, and 3 percent had evidence of a recent infection (Katz et al., 1997). Those gay men who had practiced insertive anal sex were 6 times more likely to have suffered a recent hepatitis A infection than those who had not—a strong indication that anal sex is an important route of infection.

The **hepatitis C** virus—an important cause of chronic liver disease—is not commonly transmitted via sexual contact.

AIDS Is Caused by the Human Immunodeficiency Virus

Acquired immune deficiency syndrome (AIDS) was first described in 1981. It has since resulted in the deaths of at least 460,000 Americans (Centers for Disease Control, 2002a) and is now a global pandemic (Figure 16.12). It is caused by the **human immunodeficiency virus (HIV)** (Figure 16.13).

To be more precise, there are two forms of HIV, called HIV-1 and HIV-2, but HIV-1 causes almost all cases of AIDS in the United States. HIV-2 exists in some West African countries, along with HIV-1. Here we will use "HIV" to mean "HIV-1."

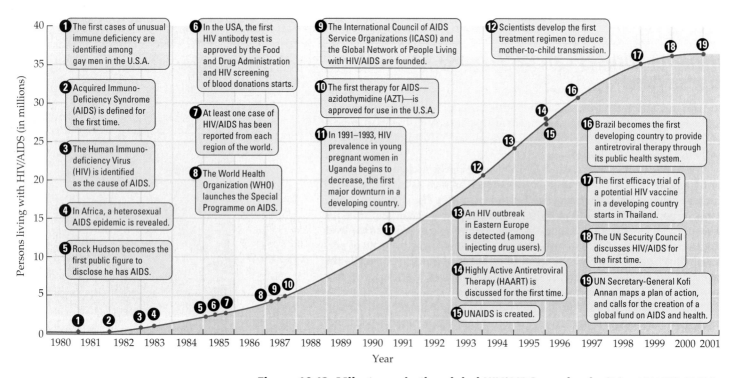

Figure 16.12 Milestones in the global HIV/AIDS pandemic. (After UNAIDS, 2001.)

Both HIV-1 and HIV-2 probably evolved from a similar virus that infects nonhuman primates in central Africa. The virus was able to spread to humans because, in central Africa, monkeys and apes are commonly killed, butchered, and eaten ("bush meat"). For centuries the virus remained isolated in certain regions and was unknown to science. In the second half of the twentieth century, however, urbanization, road building, and jet transportation allowed the virus to spread. Although occasional cases probably occurred in the West before the 1970s, the first major outbreak took place in the mid- to late 1970s among gay men in San Francisco, Los Angeles, and New York. It was this outbreak that drew medical attention and led to the first description of the disease. The virus has since spread by other routes, including contaminated needles, blood transfusions, and heterosexual sex. Even today, however, the majority of new infections in the United States—at least among those cases in which the transmission route is known—result from sex between men (Centers for Disease Control, 2002a) (Figure 16.14). Young gay men are particularly at risk of acquiring and passing on the virus (Box 16.2). (We will discuss the details of HIV transmission shortly.)

Like the hepatitis A virus, HIV is an RNA virus, but the viral RNA, once inside the host cell, is transcribed into DNA and inserted into the host's genome. This makes HIV a **retrovirus**—"retro" because the direction of transcription is opposite from the usual DNA-to-RNA direction. Box 16.3 explains how the virus enters a host cell and uses the host's metabolic machinery to replicate itself.

HIV Can Be Transmitted in Several Ways

There are several nonsexual ways of acquiring an HIV infection, including receiving a contaminated blood transfusion, sharing injection needles or syringes ("works") with an HIV-infected person, and passage of the virus from a woman to her fetus during pregnancy, parturition, or breast feeding. However, we are mainly interested in the sexual modes of transmission, since this is a sexuality textbook, after all.

To understand the risks of transmission, it's important to understand that HIV exists in several body fluids of infected persons—blood, semen, vaginal fluid, breast milk, tears, and saliva—but in very different concentrations. The levels of HIV in tears and saliva are very low—probably insignificant from the standpoint of transmission. Kissing—even deep kissing—an HIV-infected person carries a low risk of transmission. Because of the possibility that there might be blood or open sores in the infected person's mouth, however, the risk is not completely zero. For that reason, the CDC recommends against the practice, but the agency has investigated only one case of possible HIV transmission by this route (Centers for Disease Control, 2001g).

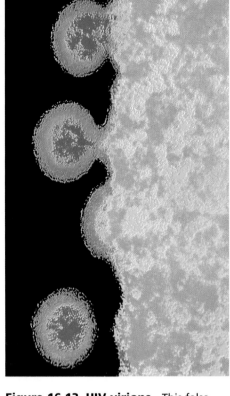

Figure 16.13 HIV virions. This false-color electron micrograph shows virions budding off an infected cell.

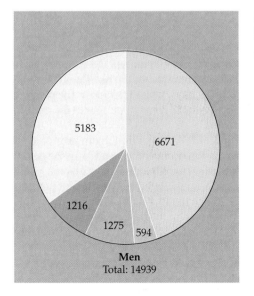

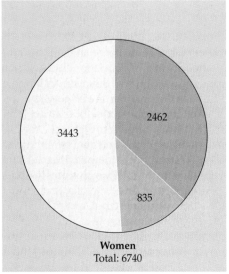

Figure 16.14 Newly reported cases of HIV infection in the U.S. in 2001, broken down by probable route of infection. (Data from CDC, 2002a.)

☐ Men who have sex with men
▨ Men who have sex with men and inject drugs
▨ Injection drug use
■ Heterosexual contact
☐ Risk category not reported

Men
Total: 14939

5183 6671 1216 1275 594

Women
Total: 6740

3443 2462 835

Box 16.2   *Society, Values, and the Law*

AIDS on the Rebound among Young Gay Men?

During the initial outbreak of AIDS in the late 1970s, thousands of gay men became infected with HIV before the disease was even recognized or given a name. Over the ensuing years the general publicity attached to the disease, as well as community-based outreach programs, led to a major decrease in the rate of new infections among gay men. The disease began to move into other communities. Gay men, it seemed, were learning to protect themselves from the disease, chiefly by the use of condoms and by a reduction in the number of their sex partners.

Two decades after AIDS was recognized, however, a whole new generation of young men has entered the gay community, and many of these men—especially those who are African-American or Latino—are acting as if HIV doesn't exist. In a study of 3500 young gay or bisexual men in seven cities, 41 percent said that they had engaged in unprotected (condomless) anal sex in the previous 6 months (Centers for Disease Control, 2001h). Not surprisingly, substantial numbers of these men—especially those who were African-American—were HIV-pos-

itive. The figure shows the percentage of gay or bisexual men aged 23–29 in these cities who tested HIV-positive. Overall, it was estimated that nearly 1 in 20 young gay or bisexual men (and 1 in 7 of those who are black) become HIV-positive every year. Another study conducted among gay men in San Francisco found that the rate of new HIV infections doubled between 1997 and 2000—strong evidence that safer-sex practices are being abandoned (Glionna, 2001).

Among the possible reasons for unsafe sexual practices among young gay men are a youthful sense of invulnerability, a belief that AIDS is no longer as serious a disease as it once was, a glamorization of the HIV-positive status, a high usage of alcohol and illicit drugs—especially crystal methamphetamine—that may cloud judgment, and a lack of suitably targeted public health campaigns.

Young gay men are not the only group who engage in unsafe sex, however. In one study of low-income black women in Atlanta, for example, 45 percent did not use a condom during any sexual encounter during the previous 2 months, and 60 percent

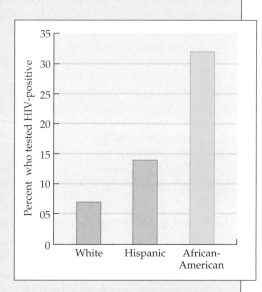

did not know their partners' HIV status (Ornstein, 2001). Low-income black women may not feel empowered to ask about HIV status or to demand condom use, just as is often the case for women in developing countries.

HIV is present at high concentrations in semen and vaginal fluid. Thus, there is at least a theoretical risk of transmission by oral sex; that is, a person who takes the oral role in fellatio or cunnilingus with an HIV-infected partner has a chance of acquiring an infection. Transmission by fellatio has been documented by actual case studies—even apparently in some cases in which the insertive partner did not ejaculate (HIV is present in "pre-cum"). In the case of cunnilingus, there are a very few cases in which transmission probably did occur. Still, according to the CDC, the likelihood of acquiring HIV via fellatio is many times lower than with coitus or anal sex, and the likelihood of acquiring sex via cunnilingus is "extremely low" (Centers for Disease Control, 2000d). Presumably, the likelihood of transmission in the reverse direction, from the mouth of an HIV-infected person to the penis or vagina of their partner, is also very low, unless there is blood or an open sore in the mouth. There is one reported case of oral–anal transmission.

The sexual behaviors that carry the highest risk of HIV transmission are unprotected (condomless) coitus and anal penetration. Transmission occurs more readily in the penis-to-vagina and penis-to-anus directions than in the reverse directions, but reverse transmission does occur. Transmission in either direction is facilitated by the presence of pre-existing STDs, such as syphilis, gonorrhea, herpes, and chlamydia. In Africa, many people have untreated **chancroid,** an STD that causes soft ulcers on the penis or elsewhere. These ulcers greatly enhance transmission in the female-to-male direction and have probably contributed to the rapid heterosexual spread of HIV in Africa.

The risk of acquiring HIV by any kind of sexual contact between women is low (Bevier et al., 1995), but occasional instances have been reported. Of course, bisexual and lesbian women can contract HIV infection from sex with men or from injection drug use.

Box 16.3 Biology of Sex

HIV's Replication Cycle

If you know little and care less about molecular biology, you might want to skip this box. But learning how HIV replicates itself within the cells of an infected person's immune system is central to understanding how the virus causes disease, as well as how anti-HIV drugs work and how better drugs might be designed in the future. So, if you have any interest in these topics, we urge you to read through this account.

The most important target of HIV is a type of immune system cell called the CD4 lymphocyte, a class of "T," or thymus-derived, lymphocytes. It is so called because it carries a particular receptor molecule on its cell membrane, called the CD4 receptor. Some other immune system cells, such as **macrophages** (bacteria-killing cells), also carry CD4 receptors and are also targeted by HIV.

The virus's replication cycle has several stages (see figure; note it is not to scale—the virus is really smaller in relation to the host cell):

1. **Binding.** When a virion meets one of the host's CD4 cells or macrophages, one of the proteins on the viral envelope, called **gp120**, binds to a **CD4 receptor** molecule on the cell's plasma membrane, as well as to a nearby **co-receptor** molecule. The co-receptor can be one of at least three different molecules, known as CCR5, CCR2, and CXCR4. Virions can bind effectively only to cells that carry both the CD4 receptor *and* a co-receptor.

2. **Fusion.** The virus's entry into the cell cytoplasm is accomplished by a second viral envelope protein, called **gp41**, which promotes fusion of the viral envelope with the cell's plasma membrane.

3. **Entry.** As soon as fusion occurs, the viral capsid disintegrates and releases its contents—viral RNA and several enzymes—into the host cell's cytoplasm.

4. **Reverse transcription.** The viral RNA is transcribed into double-stranded DNA, similar to the DNA of our own genes. This step is carried out by a viral enzyme called **reverse transcriptase.**

5. **Nuclear translocation.** The DNA is moved from the cytoplasm of the host cell into the nucleus. A specific viral protein called **Vpr** plays a key role in this step.

6. **Genomic integration.** The viral DNA is inserted into the DNA of one of the host cell's chromosomes. This step is accomplished by another viral enzyme called **integrase.**

7. **Transcription.** The viral genes are now treated like the cell's own genes, and are transcribed into RNA many times over. The host cell's own enzymes carry out the work of transcription. The process is controlled, however, by three viral proteins, called **Tat, Nef,** and **Rev.** Tat is an "amplifier" that makes the cell produce more of the viral RNA than it otherwise would. Rev is a switch that tells the cell when to start producing viral RNA in a form suitable for export. Nef is necessary for the virus to be pathogenic, but its

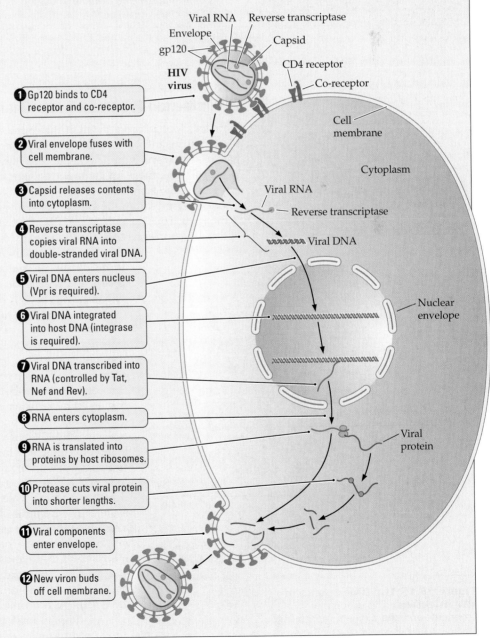

① Gp120 binds to CD4 receptor and co-receptor.

② Viral envelope fuses with cell membrane.

③ Capsid releases contents into cytoplasm.

④ Reverse transcriptase copies viral RNA into double-stranded viral DNA.

⑤ Viral DNA enters nucleus (Vpr is required).

⑥ Viral DNA integrated into host DNA (integrase is required).

⑦ Viral DNA transcribed into RNA (controlled by Tat, Nef and Rev).

⑧ RNA enters cytoplasm.

⑨ RNA is translated into proteins by host ribosomes.

⑩ Protease cuts viral protein into shorter lengths.

⑪ Viral components enter envelope.

⑫ New viron buds off cell membrane.

Viral RNA   Reverse transcriptase
Envelope
gp120   Capsid
    CD4 receptor
    Co-receptor
HIV virus
    Cell membrane
    Cytoplasm
    Viral RNA
    Reverse transcriptase
    Viral DNA
    Nuclear envelope
    Viral protein

exact mode of operation is uncertain. (A few lucky Australian hemophiliacs were transfused with blood containing a mutant HIV lacking Nef—they were all infected, but none got sick.)

8. **Cytoplasmic translocation.** The new viral RNA behaves like the cell's own RNA. First, it moves from the nucleus into the cytoplasm.

9. **Translation.** Once in the cytoplasm, the viral RNA is translated into protein by the host cell's ribosomes. As with tran-scription, a single RNA molecule is translated many times over.

10. **Cutting.** The viral gene products are very long proteins that must be trimmed into shorter lengths to make enzymes and other functional viral proteins. This cutting is accomplished by another viral enzyme, a **protease.**

11. **Assembly.** The viral RNA and proteins move to the vicinity of the plasma membrane, and viral envelope proteins gp120 and gp41 insert themselves into the membrane. The membrane bulges outward, and a new viral capsid assembles within the bulge.

12. **Export.** The bulging section of the plasma membrane (now forming the viral envelope) buds off from the cell. How these last two steps are accomplished is still poorly understood. A cell, though infected with only a handful of virions, may export tens of thousands of new ones.

We will see later how several of these steps have been made the target of attack by specifically designed drugs.

HIV Infection Progresses in a Characteristic Way

Now let's look in more detail at the course of the disease following infection (Figure 16.15). During the weeks after the initial infection, the virus multiplies inside cells in the person's blood and lymph nodes. Its main target is the **CD4 lymphocytes,** a type of white blood cells that make up an important part of the body's immune response. Other cell types may also be infected. During this initial period there are no symptoms, and the infected person's immune system has not yet produced significant levels of antibodies to the virus. Thus the person is "HIV-negative," meaning that the usual HIV blood test, which detects the presence of antibodies to HIV, gives a negative response. Nevertheless, the virus itself is present, and can be detected by PCR. In fact, the virus is often present at extremely high levels during this early phase, and the person can easily infect others. This is the reason why members of high-risk groups are not allowed to donate blood, even if they test HIV-negative.

At some point, usually between 6 weeks and 6 months after infection, the infected person's immune system does mount a response to the virus, antibodies appear in the blood, and the person tests HIV-positive. This change is called **seroconversion.** Seroconversion may be accompanied by an acute flulike illness that is marked by fever, nausea, muscle pain, and sometimes a rash.

The immune response to the virus does succeed in greatly reducing the level of virus in the infected person's blood. The symptoms of acute illness subside, and the person now enters a prolonged **asymptomatic period** that may last 7–10 years or even longer. This period is not a time of quiescence, however, but a long, drawn-out war between HIV and the infected person's immune system. The immune system is initially able to replace the CD4 cells killed by the virus, but this replacement process eventually falls behind, probably because the CD4 progenitor cells in the bone marrow and the thymus gland are themselves affected by the disease process. Thus, the level of CD4 cells in the blood gradually declines from their normal level of about 1000 cells per microliter (cells/μl). By the time CD4 counts have declined to 200–350 cells/μl, there is a risk that symptoms of overt disease—AIDS—will appear. At a level below 100 cells/μl, the risk is substantial.

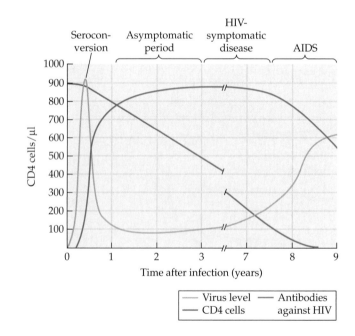

Figure 16.15 The time course of HIV infection. This graph is a schematic and approximate representation of a typical course of infection.

Another method of tracking disease progression is by measuring the amount of the virus in the blood, using sensitive assays such as PCR. Overt disease does not usually appear until viral levels are at least 20,000 copies per milliliter.

The decline in CD4 cells typically takes place at a rate of about 80–100 cells/µl per year in untreated individuals. There is considerable variation in the rate of decline, however, and thus in how quickly a person progresses to AIDS. One factor influencing the rate of progression is genetic diversity among individuals. For example, a very small number of persons completely lack functional CCR5 co-receptors (which HIV uses to bind to the surface of CD4 cells). Most (but not all) such individuals are completely resistant to HIV infection. Other persons have genetic variations in their co-receptors that do not prevent infection but influence the rate of progression to AIDS, either speeding it up or slowing it down by several years (Smith et al., 1997). Genetic variation in the virus itself can also affect the progression rate, as can nonspecific factors such as general health, emotional state, and coping styles (Burack et al., 1993).

An important aspect of HIV biology is that the viral reverse transcriptase (the enzyme that transcribes the viral RNA into DNA) is "sloppy"—it makes many mistakes. Therefore, the virus mutates rapidly. In fact, the virus exists in the body not as a single genetic type, but as a multitude of variants. During the course of the asymptomatic period there are changes in the variants that predominate. At the time of initial infection, most HIV virions are variants that bind to CCR5 co-receptors; these variants attack macrophages (bacteria-killing cells) more than other cell types. At some point during the asymptomatic period, however, variants that bind to other kinds of co-receptors (such as CXCR4) come to predominate. When this switch occurs, a broader range of cell types is exposed to infection by the virus, the level of CD4 cells falls more rapidly, and the onset of symptomatic disease is accelerated.

Some signs and symptoms may appear before the diagnosis of AIDS. These signs include thrush (a fungal infection of the mouth and throat), shingles (a painful rash caused by reactivation of a latent chicken pox infection), unexplained fever, diarrhea, night sweats, and a generalized swelling of lymph nodes. To distinguish these disorders from full-blown AIDS, they are referred to collectively as **HIV-symptomatic disease.** (An outdated term that you may still encounter is "AIDS-related condition," or ARC.)

HIV-positive persons are considered to have AIDS when their CD4 levels drop below 200 cells/µl or when certain illnesses appear. These illnesses include infections that are able to take hold because of the infected person's poorly functioning immune system. Examples of these **opportunistic infections** include an unusual form of pneumonia caused by the protozoan *Pneumocystis carinii*, cryptococcal meningitis, toxoplasmosis, cytomegalovirus disease, disseminated infection with *Mycobacterium avium* complex (MAC), and progressive multifocal leukencephalopathy (a viral infection of the central nervous system). Furthermore, two other infectious diseases that are relatively common in HIV-infected persons—tuberculosis and hepatitis C—take a more serious course when the immune system is compromised. It is beyond the scope of this book to give a detailed description of all these conditions; suffice it to say that they are all potentially fatal.

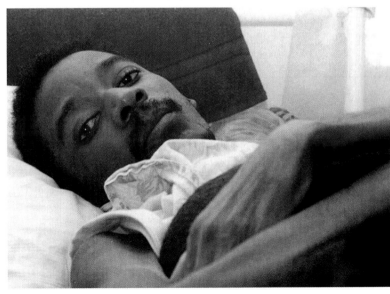

In Zambia, where this man was photographed, nearly 1 in 5 of the adult population is infected with HIV.

Other AIDS-defining illnesses include certain cancers. The best-known among these is **Kaposi's sarcoma,** a cancer of the skin that can also involve internal organs. (Just being HIV-positive isn't enough to cause Kaposi's sarcoma; a second virus—a member of the herpesvirus family known as HHV-8—appears to play a key contributory role [Kennedy et al., 1998].) Lymphoma and cervical cancer are also AIDS-defining conditions in HIV-positive persons. HIV-related cancers occur because of the loss of the usual immune system surveillance that restricts cancer growth. In some cases, HIV itself may make cells cancerous by disrupting their genome during the viral integration step.

Besides these specific illnesses, persons with advanced AIDS often show generalized **wasting**. They may also suffer broad cognitive impairment (**AIDS dementia**). Without any treatment, people diagnosed with AIDS (not just HIV infection) typically survive less than a year before succumbing to one or another of the complications of the disease.

Treatment of AIDS Is Directed at Both the Complications and the Viral Replication Cycle

Before the introduction of effective anti-HIV drug regimens (Figure 16.16), the mainstay of AIDS medicine was the use of drugs to prevent and treat the complications, especially the opportunistic infections. These drugs are still used extensively, especially for persons whose CD4 counts are low in spite of anti-HIV drug treatment. Examples of these drugs are the antibiotic combination trimethoprim-sulfamethoxazole, which is used to prevent *Pneumocystis* pneumonia and toxoplasmosis, and azithromycin, which is used to prevent disseminated MAC infection. Guidelines have been established for the appropriate choice of drugs and the appropriate CD4 levels at which the drugs should be started (U.S. Public Health Service, 2001).

The first drug to specifically target the viral replication cycle was **azidothymidine** (AZT, zidovudine, Retrovir), introduced in 1987. AZT is a synthetic nucleoside that blocks HIV's reverse transcriptase enzyme in rather the same fashion that acyclovir blocks the DNA-synthesizing enzyme of the herpes simplex virus (see above). Used by itself, however, AZT has limited usefulness, because HIV variants that are insensitive to the drug quickly come to predominate in the AZT-treated patient. Thus, AZT treatment by itself added less than a year to the life expectancy of persons with AIDS. Other **reverse transcriptase inhibitors** have been introduced since then; some are nucleosides and some are not.

In 1995 the first of an entirely new class of drugs, **protease inhibitors,** was approved by the FDA. By blocking HIV's protease enzyme, these drugs prevent it from cutting the viral gene products into active viral proteins. Examples are **indinavir** (Crixivan), **saquinavir** (Invirase), and **ritonavir** (Norvir). (Ritonavir has the useful property of boosting the blood levels of other protease inhibitors.) In patients who are treated with only a single protease inhibitor, drug-resistant variants of the virus quickly emerge. Combinations of drugs, on the other hand, are capable of keeping the virus at unde-

Figure 16.16 Anti-AIDS drugs reduce symptoms and improve life expectancy. This man, Scott Russell, has been HIV-positive since 1990.

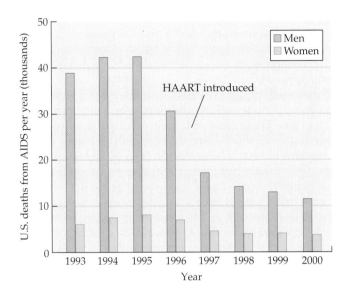

Figure 16.17 U.S. deaths from AIDS per year (in thousands), showing the decline related to the introduction of HAART combination therapy. (Data from Centers for Disease Control, 2002a.)

tectable levels for indefinite periods of time. A typical drug combination for initial therapy might include one protease inhibitor and two nucleoside reverse transcriptase inhibitors. If drug resistance develops and viral levels rise, the treatment can be changed with new drug combinations. If treatment is begun before too much damage has been done, the infected person's immune system can be at least partially reconstituted, and in this case it may be possible to stop administration of the prophylactic drugs intended to ward off opportunistic infections.

This combination therapy (sometime called "highly active anti-retroviral therapy," or **HAART**) has greatly reduced the death rate from AIDS where it is available (Centers for Disease Control, 2002a) (Figure 16.17) and has improved the quality of life for many people with the disease. Still, combination therapy has several shortcomings:

- Combination therapy does not eradicate the virus from the body; viral levels rebound as soon as therapy is stopped.
- Resistance to multiple drugs can eventually develop, making treatment difficult.
- Many of the drugs have serious side effects that limit their usefulness. These effects include gastrointestinal problems, anemia, nerve damage, liver damage, disturbances of fat metabolism, and diabetes.
- Combination therapy is quite burdensome: it may require the patient to take large numbers of pills at precisely timed intervals and to have frequent medical checkups. Noncompliance with the prescribed regimen contributes to the emergence of drug-resistant forms of the virus, with a dramatic reduction in the effectiveness of treatment.
- Combination therapy is expensive. The drugs cost at least $1000 per month, and other medical expenses add another $500–$1500 per month (Valenti, 1998). Although mechanisms to cover these costs exist for many people in the United States, this is not the case for the far more numerous HIV-infected men, women, and children in developing countries.
- Finally, there is considerable uncertainty about when to start combination therapy. The desire to prevent irreversible damage to the immune system is balanced by the possible occurrence of harmful side effects and eventual drug resistance. Current guidelines suggest that therapy should begin when CD4 levels fall below 350 cells/μl or viral levels exceed 55,000 copies per microliter (U.S. Department of Health and Human Services, 2001).

Although combination therapy cannot eradicate an established HIV infection, it may sometimes prevent an infection from taking hold if administered immediately after exposure to the virus. This **post-exposure prophylaxis** has been used with some apparent success in cases of occupational exposure (needle sticks by medical personnel), sexual assaults by HIV-positive men, and sexual encounters between sero-opposite couples (Nwokolo & Hawkins, 2001). It certainly cannot be considered a reliable and safe "morning-after pill" for HIV exposure, however.

Current research is aimed at developing new drugs that attack other points in the virus's replication cycle. These drugs include **fusion inhibitors,** which are intended to block binding of the HIV virion to the CD4 receptor or to the co-receptor, and **integrase inhibitors,** which block the insertion of viral DNA into the host cell's genome.

Intense efforts to develop a **vaccine** against HIV have so far been unsuccessful. Some candidate vaccines are in early clinical trials, but there is so far no indication that they will offer significant protection. No HIV vaccine has so far entered "phase III" (efficacy) trials. It *has* proved possible to protect monkeys against an HIV-like virus, however, using a DNA-based vaccine; this finding suggests that an effective human vaccine may eventually be developed. Current strategies are focused on the development of two-element vaccines: the first shot consists of a harmless DNA virus (canarypox) genetically modified to contain several HIV genes, while the second contains HIV's envelope protein gp120 (Cohen, 2001). Two such vaccines may soon enter phase III trials, but preliminary data indicate that they will not provide complete protection against HIV infection.

There Are Several Ways to Reduce the Likelihood of STD Transmission

In spite of the many medical advances documented in this chapter, STDs remain a major public health problem. They are also a political problem, in the sense that conservatives and liberals often disagree on the best strategies for combating them. Here we consider the main options.

Abstinence Prevents STDs, but Has Drawbacks

Although it may seem too obvious to be worth saying, people who have no sexual contacts with others cannot acquire or transmit any disease by the sexual route. (They can still acquire some "STDs" by nonsexual routes, such as needle sharing, of course.)

Complete **abstinence** from sexual contacts has other potential benefits besides disease prevention. It offers complete protection against unwanted pregnancy without the expense and potential side effects of contraceptive techniques (see Chapter 11). It may allow a person to concentrate their time and energies on nonphysical relationships as well as on nonsexual goals, such as career advancement. Abstinence today may heighten the emotional significance of sexual relationships in the future, such as marriage. For people who have moral qualms about the kinds of sexual contacts they desire (for example, unmarried persons who believe that sex before marriage is wrong, or homosexual persons who believe that gay sex is wrong), abstinence offers the benefit of moral satisfaction.

Sexual abstinence also has costs, however. People who choose it forgo a major source of human pleasure and a significant means of interpersonal bonding. Prolonged abstinence may be experienced as a very painful state, like starvation. While sexual expression is still possible—through masturbation, fantasy, and nonphysical intimacy with others—such expression may heighten rather than reduce the desire for sexual contact. Sexual abstinence is also incompatible with normal procreation and may be perceived as morally wrong, especially in the case of religiously minded married persons. Reluctance to engage in sex may damage intimate relationships over time. Finally, persons who plan to avoid STDs by sexual abstinence may be less prepared to take appropriate precautions if and when they do engage in sexual contacts.

The choice whether or not to be sexually abstinent is a highly personal decision. It is influenced by the strength of a person's sexual desires, their moral beliefs, and their perception of the risks and benefits of sexual relationships. Nevertheless, the choice whether or not to be abstinent may also be influenced by external forces, such as governmental public health campaigns (see below).

Sexually Active Persons Can Reduce Their Risk of STDs by Their Choice of Partners

Persons who do not choose to be abstinent still have options for reducing their risk of acquiring STDs. One way they can do this is to reduce the total number of persons with whom they have sexual contact and to select partners who are unlikely to have an STD. Two virgins who enter into a monogamous relationship have a low risk of passing an STD between them. Even in this situation, however, an STD can be transmitted if one partner has acquired a sexually transmissible infection through nonsexual means. Furthermore, it is difficult to know for certain whether one's prospective partner is really a virgin or whether they engage in sex with others after the supposedly monogamous relationship has begun. People have different understandings of terms such as "having sex" and "being a virgin," as we've seen in earlier chapters. The best one can do is to choose partners with whom one can hope to discuss these matters freely and honestly, and not enter into a sexual relationship until one has done so (Box 16.4).

Different individuals may have quite different likelihoods of acquiring an STD even when their total number of sex partners is the same, thanks to demographic variations in STD prevalence. Statistically, a heterosexual black woman living in the South is at far higher risk of acquiring gonorrhea from a single sexual encounter than is a heterosexual white woman living in the Northwest, simply because her likely partners have a much greater chance of having the disease. Similarly, a gay man in San Francisco has a far greater risk of acquiring HIV from a single sexual encounter than does a straight man in Denver. However, the seriousness of some STDs makes playing the numbers game a risky business: it may be a better strategy simply to assume that one's partners stand a good chance of carrying an STD and act accordingly.

Ideally, both partners would be tested for a variety of STDs, including HIV, before a sexual relationship begins. Traditionally, mandatory premarital testing (usually for syphilis) served this function. As fewer and fewer couples defer sex until marriage, the effectiveness of premarital testing has declined. But couples still have the option of undergoing STD screening before (or during) a sexual relationship. Many public health and family planning clinics will test an unmarried or same-sex couple for a variety of STDs and discuss the results with them as a couple. Undergoing such testing may help lay the foundation for a trusting relationship.

In real life, many men and women enter into sexual relationships without prior STD testing. Even then, some steps can be taken to assess the likelihood of acquiring an STD. First, the couple can discuss each other's sexual histories and whether either partner has an STD or is likely to have been exposed to one. Second, it is a good idea to visually inspect the other partner, especially his or her genitalia. This strategy is particularly useful for women because STDs tend to be more visible in men than they are in women. A visible genital sore, wart, or discharge is a good reason to desist from sexual contact. Unfortunately, the absence of such a visible sign is no guarantee that the person is free of STDs.

HIV testing and counseling are the mainstay of public health campaigns against AIDS.

Some Sexual Behaviors Are Riskier than Others

In terms of STD prevention, the distinction between "abstinence" and "having sex" may be confusing and counterproductive because it suggests that any kind of sexual contact carries the same high risk of disease transmission. In reality, men and women who are sexually active can greatly influence their likelihood of acquiring or transmitting an STD by the choice of sexual behaviors they engage in.

Coitus, anal sex, and anilingus (mouth-to-anus contact) are high-risk sexual behaviors. Most STDs, including HIV, are readily transmitted by unprotected coitus or anal sex. Anilingus has a low likelihood of transmitting HIV, but it is a risky practice because

Box 16.4 *Society, Values, and the Law*

Partner Notification

In late April, 2002, state health officials knocked at the dorm room of Nikko Briteramos, a 6-foot-7 basketball star at tiny Huron University in South Dakota. A few weeks previously, Briteramos had been told that he was HIV-positive—the discovery was made when he attempted to donate blood. Now the officials wanted to interview him about his sex partners in order to notify them of their possible exposure to the virus. But Briteramos didn't let the officials into his room. The reason soon became obvious: he was in bed with his girlfriend. That same day, Briteramos was arrested and charged with five counts of intentionally exposing her to the AIDS virus by having unprotected sex. He was convicted and received a suspended 5-year prison term, and was ordered to spend 120 days in jail. His girlfriend has so far tested HIV-negative, but two other women who had sex with Briteramos have tested positive. Those two women told officials that they, in turn, had recently engaged in sex with 50 other persons (Simon, 2002).

Briteramos's alleged behavior is not uncommon. In a 1998 study led by Michael Stein of Brown University, 40 percent of persons who received primary HIV care at two urban hospitals said that they had not disclosed their HIV status to all their recent sex partners. Among these admitted nondisclosers, 57 percent said that they did not use condoms during all sexual encounters (Stein et al., 1998).

Probably few of you would dispute that it is wrong for people who know they are HIV-positive to engage in unprotected sex without telling their partners of their HIV status. South Dakota is one of 21 states that make such behavior a crime regardless of whether the virus is actually transmitted or not. Even if a condom *is* used, you might question the morality of withholding this information.

A trickier ethical question concerns the role of doctors and health officials in the partner notification process. Generally speaking, doctors' ethical responsibilities are directed toward their patients and include a responsibility to maintain confidentiality. What if a doctor or other medical professional knows that an HIV-positive patient has not notified their sex partners?

The Centers for Disease Control has taken the position that partner notification programs should be voluntary. In other words, officials should notify an HIV-positive person's partners only if that person gives consent. The CDC believes that mandatory notification programs could discourage potentially infected persons from getting tested and are therefore likely to be counterproductive. A similar position has been taken by the ACLU and by AIDS activists (Kaiser Daily Reports, 1998a, 1998b, 2000).

Nevertheless, the majority of states have enacted mandatory partner notification laws (Wasserman & Watson, 2000). Although the details vary from state to state, these programs often require medical personnel or officials to ask HIV-positive persons about their sexual contacts and to inform those partners about their risk of exposure (often without identifying the HIV-positive person). Aside from spouses, however, officials are not likely to be able to identify sex partners if the HIV-positive person declines to name them. In that sense, even "mandatory" programs are voluntary.

of the likelihood of transmission of hepatitis A or B (in the anus-to-mouth direction), as well as other STDs.

Oral sex (fellatio or cunnilingus) is a moderate-risk behavior. Transmission of HIV by oral sex is far less common than by coitus or anal sex, but some other STDs, such as gonorrhea and syphilis, are readily transmitted by this route.

Other sexual behaviors, such as kissing, fondling, hand–genital contact, and general body contact, are low-risk behaviors. They are certainly not free of risk—herpes and syphilis, for example, can both be transmitted by these behaviors—but they are so much safer than the high- and moderate-risk behaviors mentioned above that they offer a sensible alternative for sexually active people when STD transmission is a concern.

Condoms Are the Mainstay of STD Prevention

The lowly condom is the key to STD prevention for sexually active heterosexuals and gay men, especially for those who have multiple or casual partners. The proper use of condoms has already been described in the context of contraception (see Chapter 11). Three points are worth reemphasizing in the context of STD protection:

- Natural-tissue ("lambskin") condoms, although possibly effective as contraceptives, do not provide adequate protection against STDs. Latex condoms are known to be effective for this purpose, and polyurethane condoms are probably effective as well, but studies are limited.

- Anal sex places greater demands on a condom than does vaginal sex. For anal sex, extra-strength condoms are recommended, or two regular condoms can be doubled up. This is particularly important when the insertive partner is known to be HIV-positive.
- Regular latex doesn't taste or smell great, so for oral sex, it's worth investing in chocolate-flavored condoms or whatever other flavor turns you on.

Female condoms are probably at least as effective as male condoms for STD prevention. Unfortunately, female condoms have not achieved widespread consumer acceptance because of the unnatural sensations and sounds associated with their use.

Flat sheets of latex ("dams") are available for the prevention of STD transmission during cunnilingus or anilingus. Some are flavored. Alternatively, a regular condom can be cut lengthwise to produce a flat sheet.

No condom offers complete protection against STDs. With typical use, condoms occasionally break. Furthermore, some STDs, such as syphilis and herpes, can be transmitted to or from skin regions that are not covered by the condom. Still, using condoms or dams is the single most effective step that sexually active men and women can take to reduce STD transmission.

Vaginal douches, spermicidal foams, and the like have not been shown to provide effective STD prevention.

Well-Designed Public Health Campaigns Can Alter Behavior and Reduce STD Prevalence

The U.S. government currently channels $50 million per year in matching grants to the states to support programs that encourage sexual abstinence by unmarried persons. These programs do not usually mention the use of condoms or other contraceptives, or do so only to portray them as ineffective (Sonfield & Gold, 2001). The programs have been designed this way because many legislators believe that nonmarital sex is wrong, or that any positive mention of contraceptive techniques legitimizes and encourages sexual behavior and therefore is likely to cause an increase, rather than a decrease, in STDs and unwanted pregnancies.

Research on abstinence-only programs suggests that they have little or no actual effect on people's sexual behavior (Haignere et al., 1999). What does work? A 1995 study from Jackson State University in Mississippi suggested part of the answer (St. Lawrence et al., 1995). The researchers focused on 246 low-income black adolescents who visited a community health center. The youths were assigned at random to one of two programs. One program consisted of a single session in which the youths were given educational instruction concerning HIV and AIDS. The other was an 8-session program that presented the same education about HIV and AIDS but added training in skills such as correct condom use, risk recognition, assertiveness, how to refuse requests for sex, and self-management. The youths who participated in the skills-training program engaged in more protected intercourse and less unprotected intercourse than did the youths who received the education-only program. The skills-training program did not incite youths to begin sexual activity: of the youths who were sexually abstinent at the start of the skills-training program, only 11.5 percent were sexually active a year later, compared with 31.1 percent of those who took the education-only program. In other words, appropriate skills training, even though it includes training in condom use, seems to help adolescents refrain from sexual activity.

Another effective strategy takes advantage of the fact that people's behavior is readily influenced by individuals regarded as leaders within their peer group or friendship network. In a study from the University of California, San Francisco, researchers identified opinion leaders within the young gay male communities of two West

Safe-sex messages may have more effect when spread by peer networks.

Coast cities (Kegeles et al., 1996). These opinion leaders were asked to deliver messages endorsing safe-sex practices to small gatherings of their friends and acquaintances. These personal contacts were backed up by risk reduction workshops and by distribution of printed materials in places where young gay men gathered. Over the course of the project, the fraction of young gay men in the target cities who engaged in unprotected anal sex with persons other than their primary partners dropped by nearly half. No change occurred over the same period in a control community that was not targeted. A comparable program directed at inner-city black women has also been successful in changing behavior (Lauby et al., 2000).

As advertisers well know, people's behavior can be modified by frequent and prolonged exposure to simple messages, such as TV commercials or public service announcements. In some countries, the mass media approach has been extraordinarily successful in combating STDs. In Thailand, for example, a mass media campaign to promote condom use, along with a condom distribution program and measures to ensure condom use by sex workers, led to a sixfold increase in condom use, an 85 percent decrease in STDs among men, and a decrease in HIV prevalence among pregnant women (Rojanapithayakorn & Hanenberg, 1996).

Unfortunately, political considerations and standards established by the television networks have prevented any equivalent mass media campaign in the United States. In fact, television programming is rife with depictions of sex, or references to sex, but these episodes almost never include any mention of STDs or measures to prevent them. Only the pornographic movie industry has taken some steps in this direction: many of these movies now show condoms in use.

In general, it seems that public health programs can have a substantial impact on STD prevalence, but they need to be based on methods that have been proved effective, and they need to be delivered broadly in time and space, not just for a few months in a few communities.

This 2001 campaign to educate Thai youth about condom use was sponsored by condom manufacturer Durex.

Summary

1. At any one time, over 65 million Americans have one or more sexually transmitted diseases (STDs), and over 15 million new cases occur annually. STDs are caused by insects, protozoans, bacteria, and viruses. In spite of medical advances, STDs remain a major public health problem. They also bolster a perception of sex as something dangerous or immoral.

2. Insect infestations that can be transmitted sexually include pubic lice and scabies. Pubic lice attach themselves to hair shafts, especially in the pubic region. Scabies mites burrow under the surface of the skin. Both infestations can cause severe itching, but do not otherwise threaten health. They can be eliminated with insecticidal lotions or shampoos.

3. Trichomoniasis is an infection of the vagina or urethra with a protozoan. In women, it causes discomfort, a vaginal discharge, and the urge to urinate frequently. In men, the infection is usually asymptomatic. It is generally eliminated by a single oral dose of metronidazole (Flagyl).

4. Syphilis is caused by infection with the bacterium *Treponema pallidum*. The disease has several stages. Primary syphilis is marked by a sore (chancre) at the site of infection. Some weeks later, a rash and fever occur (secondary syphilis). The infection then becomes latent, but may eventually attack a variety of organ systems (tertiary syphilis) and cause death. The disease is readily curable with penicillin in its early stages. The elimination of syphilis in the United States is a realistic public health goal.

5. Gonorrhea is caused by infection with the bacterium *Neisseria gonorrhoeae*. In men, it usually infects the urethra, causing painful urination. In women, it can infect the cervix, causing a vaginal discharge. The infection in women is commonly asympto-

matic, but it can spread to the internal reproductive tract, causing pelvic inflammatory disease and reduced fertility. Rectal infection can occur in either sex. Gonorrhea can be treated with antibiotics, but antibiotic resistance is an increasing problem.

6. Infection with the intracellular bacterium *Chlamydia trachomatis* is extremely common. It can cause a urethral or vaginal discharge and painful urination, but many infected men and women do not have symptoms. Chlamydia is readily treatable with antibiotics. In women, untreated chlamydia infections can lead to pelvic inflammatory disease.

7. Genital herpes is a very common condition caused by infection with the herpes simplex virus type 1 or 2 (HSV-1, HSV-2). It causes an outbreak of sores at the site of infection, which is usually somewhere in the anogenital region. The initial outbreak heals spontaneously, but it may be followed by further outbreaks at the same location that recur for the remainder of the person's life. Herpes infection is incurable, but outbreaks can be limited by antiviral drugs such as acyclovir.

8. Human papillomaviruses (HPV) cause genital warts and other lesions of the genital skin and urogenital tract. Genital warts can be easily removed by a variety of treatments. Some HPV types (not those that cause bulky, raised genital warts) infect the cervix and are the principal cause of cervical cancer.

9. Hepatitis A and B are viral infections of the liver that can be acquired sexually as well as by other routes. Anal penetration and anilingus are the sexual behaviors most likely to transmit hepatitis A. Hepatitis B is transmitted by coitus or oral sex; in a minority of cases it leads to chronic liver disease and liver cancer. No cure exists for either form of hepatitis, but effective vaccines are available.

10. Acquired immune deficiency syndrome (AIDS) is caused by infection with the human immunodeficiency virus (HIV). HIV is a retrovirus, an RNA virus whose genetic material is transcribed into DNA and incorporated into the host cell's genome. The virus originated in central Africa, but a worldwide pandemic began with outbreaks in gay male communities in the United States in the late 1970s. Transmission now occurs by both male–female and male–male sexual contacts (principally by coitus and anal penetration), as well as by exposure to contaminated blood.

11. HIV infection can be marked by an acute illness, followed by a several-year asymptomatic period. Eventually the infection impairs the person's immune system to the point that certain opportunistic infections and cancers may occur. Symptomatic AIDS is a life-threatening condition that cannot be cured, but it may be held in check with a combination of drugs that interfere with various stages of the virus's replication cycle. An effective vaccine is not yet available.

12. There are significant demographic variations in the prevalence of STDs. Several STDs, such as syphilis and gonorrhea, are particularly prevalent among African-Americans, especially those living in the South. AIDS and sexually transmitted hepatitis are particularly prevalent among men who have sex with men, especially men living in metropolitan gay communities. Herpes, HPV, and chlamydia are broadly distributed among sexually active young people nationwide. These demographic variations result from differences in education and health services, as well as differences in sex practices and numbers of sex partners.

13. Women and men can reduce their risk of acquiring STDs by a variety of means. Complete sexual abstinence offers complete protection, but has significant psychological and social costs. Sexually active people can reduce their risk by reducing their total number of different sex partners (ideally, by forming a mutually monogamous relationship), by discussing STDs and sexual history with prospective partners, and by engaging in relatively low-risk sexual behaviors as an alternative to coitus or anal sex. Careful and consistent use of condoms is key to lowering the risk of STDs.

14. Many public health initiatives have attempted to reduce STD prevalence through modification of behavior. Abstinence-only programs are largely ineffective. Programs that teach practical skills, such as how to use condoms and how to refuse sexual invitations, are effective, as are programs that deliver safe-sex messages through peer networks. Mass media campaigns including TV messages have been effective in some countries, but have been difficult to institute in the United States.

Discussion Questions

1. Do you think that there are any circumstances in which it would be acceptable for someone who has an STD not to inform their sex partner? If others in your class have a different opinion, discuss the reasons for your differing views and attempt to reach a consensus.

2. Do you think that legal action should ever be taken to punish someone who transmits a serious STD to a partner (as was described in Box 16.4, for example)? Or do you think that such action is counterproductive? Should everyone simply be held responsible for protecting themselves from STDs?

3. Imagine you are embarking on a sexual relationship with your first partner or a new partner. How would you bring up the matter of STDs and what to do about them? Try to imagine the actual conversation you would have and what the difficulties might be.

4. Imagine you are returning to your high school to give a half-hour presentation about STDs. What age students would you choose to speak to? What would be the main goals you'd like to accomplish? Are there any particular styles of communication that you think would be effective? Is there any way in which you think you could do a better job than an STD specialist from the local health department? Do you think you could communicate equally effectively with boys and girls, and with students of all races or ethnicities?

5. Are there ways in which the United States could contribute more effectively to the battle against AIDS and other STDs in developing countries?

Web Resources

Centers for Disease Control, Division of Sexually Transmitted Diseases
www.cdc.gov/nchstp/dstd/dstdp.html

Centers for Disease Control, Division of HIV/AIDS prevention
www.cdcnpin.org/hiv/start.htm

CDC's 24-hour STD and AIDS hotline www.ashastd.org/NSTD/index.html

National Minority AIDS Council www.nmac.org/

University of California, San Francisco HIV InSite http://hivinsite.ucsf.edu/InSite

AIDS Information Global Education System www.aegis.org

Joint United Nations Program on HIV/AIDS www.unaids.org

Recommended Reading

Jones, J. H. (1993). *Bad blood: The Tuskegee syphilis experiment* (new and expanded ed.). New York: Free Press.
Marr, L. (1998). *Sexually transmitted diseases: A physician tells you what you need to know.* Baltimore: Johns Hopkins University Press.
Shilts, R. (1987). *And the band played on: Politics, people, and the AIDS epidemic.* New York: St. Martin's Press.

chapter 17

Nicole Parsons, who was paralyzed in an auto accident, posed for this ad for a lingerie store under the headline "Every Woman Deserves to Feel Beautiful."

Sex, Illness, and Disability

*I*n previous chapters we have discussed a number of specific topics related to sexual health, including sexually transmitted diseases (Chapter 16) and sexual dysfunction (Chapter 15). We now turn to general health issues that affect sexuality and reproductive function. In this chapter, we discuss medical conditions, including cancers, that involve the genitalia, the reproductive tract, and the breasts. Self-monitoring and frequent medical checkups are crucial in the prevention and treatment of many of these conditions. We also discuss various kinds of disabilities that affect sexual expression. With knowledge, sympathy, and a sense of humor, even severe disabilities can be compatible with a rewarding sex life.

Figure 17.1 Reproductive cancer rates. The graph shows the number of new cases of cancers affecting the reproductive system per year, and deaths per year, in the United States. (Data from American Cancer Society, 2001c.)

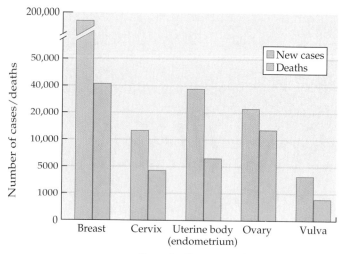

Reproductive cancers in women

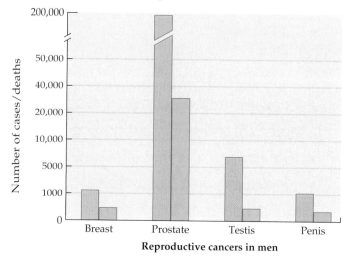

Reproductive cancers in men

Breast Cancer Mortality Can Be Reduced by Early Detection and Treatment

Cancers of the reproductive system strike nearly half a million Americans every year and cause nearly 100,000 deaths, about two-thirds of them among women (American Cancer Society, 2001c) (Figure 17.1). The most common of these diseases among women is breast cancer.

Nearly 200,000 women are diagnosed with invasive breast cancer in the United States each year, and about 40,000 women (as well as about 400 men) die of the disease. It is estimated that 1 in every 8 American women will develop (but not necessarily die of) breast cancer in her lifetime (National Cancer Institute, 2001). Women fear breast cancer not just because it is a potential killer, but also because one treatment for the disease—surgical removal of the affected breast (**mastectomy**)—can do immense damage to a woman's self-image and possibly to her sex life.

Breast Cancer Statistics Must Be Kept in Perspective

We don't wish to downplay the seriousness of breast cancer, but it is worth pointing out that, contrary to many women's belief, breast cancer is far from being the leading killer of women (Centers for Disease Control, 2001j; American Cancer Society, 2001a) (Figure 17.2). Heart disease kills far more women than do all cancers combined. In fact, breast cancer is not even the leading cause of *cancer* deaths among women: lung cancer kills more women in the United States than does breast cancer. Still, breast cancer is a leading cause of death among women in midlife.

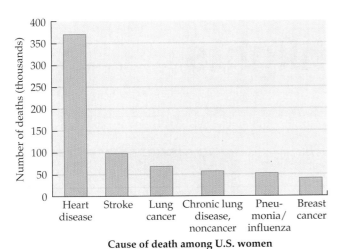

Figure 17.2 Breast cancer is not the leading cause of death among U.S. women. The graph shows the most common causes of death among women in the United States and the number of women who die annually from each of them. (Data from Centers for Disease Control, 2001j; American Cancer Society, 2001a.)

Several Risk Factors Affect a Woman's Chances of Developing Breast Cancer

Although women as a group have a 1 in 8 lifetime chance of developing breast cancer, a number of known risk factors can increase or decrease the risk of breast cancer for a particular woman (Box 17.1).

- *Genes.* Breast cancer tends to run in families (Figure 17.3). A woman who has one first-degree relative with breast cancer faces twice the risk of getting the disease as a woman who does not. Having two first-degree relatives with breast cancer multiplies her risk fivefold. Certain genes normally protect against breast cancer and other cancers; the most important of these are labeled *BRCA1* and *BRCA2*. Women who inherit mutated versions of these genes have a 50–60 percent chance of developing breast cancer by age 70. Mutations in these genes account for only about 10 percent of all breast cancers, however.
- *Age.* Breast cancer is primarily a disease of older women: about 85 percent of newly diagnosed cases are in women over 50.
- *Reproductive history.* Women who had early menarche (before 12) or late menopause (after 55), who had no children, or who had their first child after age 30 have a modestly increased risk of developing breast cancer. Prolonged breast feeding may offer some reduction in risk.
- *Alcohol.* Women who consume two to five alcoholic drinks per day have about a 1.5-fold increase in risk compared with women who consume less than two drinks per day.

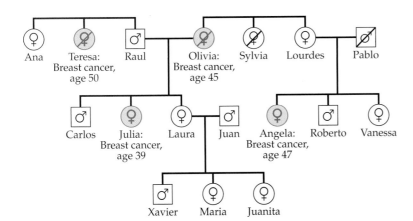

Figure 17.3 A family tree can help to evaluate a woman's risk of breast cancer. With a mother, aunt, cousin, and sister affected by breast cancer, Laura and her daughters face an increased risk of developing the disease. They have the option of being tested for breast cancer genes.

Research Highlights

Lesbians and Breast Cancer

"I am not supposed to exist. I carry death around in my body like a condemnation. But I do live." Poet Audre Lorde wrote these words in her diary in 1979, a year after losing her right breast to cancer. Lorde gave uncompromising public expression to her identity as a person with breast cancer, just as she had expressed her identity as a woman, an African-American, and a lesbian. In her 1980 book *The Cancer Journals,* Lorde suggested that breast prostheses and reconstructive surgeries might harm women with cancer by concealing their suffering and by reinforcing a "normalized" image of femininity. She also stressed the importance of women's networks in helping herself and other women cope with the disease.

Lorde's book helped raise a troubling question: Are lesbians particularly at risk for breast cancer? In 1992, Suzanne Hayes, a researcher at the Office of Women's Health (part of the U.S. Department of Health and Human Services), offered an answer. She suggested that lesbians were 2 to 3 times more likely to develop breast cancer than heterosexual women, based on certain risk factors that she believed were more common among lesbians than among other women. Although never formally published, Hayes's suggestion attracted media attention and eventually became widely accepted, especially in the gay and lesbian communities. Since women as a group have

about a 1 in 8 lifetime risk of developing breast cancer, it was thought that the lifetime risk for lesbians might be as high as 1 in 3.

A more detailed analysis was carried out by a group led by Stephanie Roberts, medical director of Lyon-Martin Women's Health Services in San Francisco (Roberts et al., 1998). The researchers examined the medical records of over 1000 low-income, mostly white women, roughly one-half of whom identified themselves as lesbian and one-half as heterosexual. Three risk factors for breast cancer were indeed more prevalent among the lesbians: a high body mass index, having no children, and having multiple breast biopsies.

It is unlikely that the identified differences would be sufficient to cause a two- or threefold excess of breast cancer among lesbians, but broader studies will be needed to make a reliable estimate. Ideally, one would directly measure the prevalence of breast cancer among lesbians and among heterosexual women, but so far this has not been done in any formal study. One problem is that the sexual orientation of older women—the group in which breast cancer is most common—is not usually mentioned in their medical records.

Even if the risk of breast cancer does not differ greatly between lesbian and heterosexual women, it is quite likely that the *out-*

Audre Lorde (1934–1992)

come of breast cancer is worse for lesbians. That's because lesbians often feel somewhat alienated from the medical profession and may for that reason be less likely to get regular clinical breast examinations. Thus any cancers they do get may be more advanced when diagnosed and therefore less readily treatable.

- *Obesity.* Women who are obese—especially those who become obese during adulthood and those whose body fat is concentrated at the waist—face an increased risk. Some studies suggest that a high-fat diet is a risk factor independent of obesity, but this is uncertain.
- *Medical history.* A history of breast cancer, even when successfully treated, raises the risk of a second, independent cancer in the same or the other breast. A history of having had two or more breast biopsies also increases the risk, even when all the biopsies yielded negative results. The reason for this pattern is not totally clear. It's not that biopsies cause cancer. More likely, multiple biopsies suggest that there is some underlying breast disease that triggered the need for the biopsies and that also increased the likelihood of breast cancer. A history of high-dose radiation treatment that includes the breast raises the risk of breast cancer. (The X-ray doses associated with mammography are believed to be insignificant in this respect.)
- *Hormones.* As mentioned in Chapter 11, the use of oral contraceptives seems to be associated with a slightly increased risk of breast cancer; this increased risk disappears by 10 years after a woman stops using

them (American Cancer Society, 2000). As discussed in Chapter 12, postmenopausal hormone replacement therapy also raises the risk of breast cancer slightly.

Unlike lung cancer, from which a woman can largely protect herself by one simple precaution—not smoking—breast cancer offers rather limited opportunities for prevention through lifestyle changes (mainly weight control and restriction of alcohol intake). Women who are at especially high risk—for example, those who have a cancer-causing mutation of *BRCA2*—have the option of taking the selective estrogen receptor modulator (SERM) **tamoxifen** (see Chapter 4), which provides partial protection against breast cancer (King et al., 2001). Prophylactic removal of the breasts is an effective but drastic preventive measure that is seldom chosen. In general, because of the limited preventive strategies that are currently available, the emphasis is on early diagnosis and treatment rather than on prevention.

Breast Cancers Are Described by Type, Stage, and Grade

Most breast cancers are of one of two *types* that are defined by the tissue of origin. **Ductal carcinomas** originate in the lactiferous ducts, and **lobular carcinomas** originate in the lobules—the collections of alveoli where milk is produced (see Chapters 3 and 10).

The earliest *stage* of breast cancer is confined to its tissue of origin—that is, the ducts or the lobules (**carcinoma in situ,** also called **stage 0**). Caught at this stage, a ductal carcinoma is essentially 100 percent curable. Lobular carcinoma in situ probably does not lead to invasive cancer at all, but a woman diagnosed with this condition does have an increased risk of developing invasive breast cancer at some site in the same or the other breast.

Infiltrating or **invasive** breast cancer is that which has spread into local fatty tissues or beyond. Eighty percent of invasive breast cancers are ductal carcinomas and 10–15 percent are lobular carcinomas. There are four stages of invasive breast cancer: **stage 1** refers to a tumor that has not spread beyond the breast and is no more than 2 centimeters in diameter; **stage 2** refers to a tumor that is more than 2 cm in diameter or that has spread to lymph nodes in the armpit (axilla); **stage 3** refers to a tumor that has invaded the skin or chest wall or that has more extensively involved the lymph nodes; **stage 4** refers to a tumor that has **metastasized,** or spread to distant sites, such as the lungs or bones.

Breast cancers are also *graded* on a three-point scale, based on their appearance under the microscope. In **grade 1** tumors, the cells still retain some semblance of their normal appearance. In **grade 2** tumors they are somewhat less well differentiated, and in **grade 3** tumors they are structurally disorganized and dividing rapidly. Specialized tests can determine whether the cells still carry the estrogen and progestin receptors that are normally found on breast cells. An absence of such receptors represents a more advanced condition and a reduced likelihood that the tumor will respond to hormonal treatment (see below).

Suspicious Lumps Can Be Detected by Breast Self-Examination

Breast tumors are firmer than the surrounding normal breast tissue and can therefore often be felt as lumps in the breast (Box 17.2). This fact is the key to the detection of breast cancer at an early stage, when treatment has a good likelihood of success. It's recommended that women perform **breast self-examination** (BSE) monthly, starting at age 20. Not that a woman in her twenties has a significant likelihood of developing breast cancer—she would have to stay in her twenties for over a thousand years to have even a 50:50 chance of contracting the disease. But by getting to know her breasts early in adult life, she has a much better chance of recognizing changes if and when they occur. Most breast lumps are not cancer, but fluid-filled cysts, areas of fibrosis, or other benign conditions; these lumps tend to stay in place for years, or permanently. What matters are newly appearing or changing lumps: a woman who notices such a lump should seek medical attention, although the chances are still good that the lump is not cancer. She should also seek medical attention if she notices any discharge from the nipple (other than milk).

Box 17.2 *Sexual Health*

Breast Self-Examination

(A)

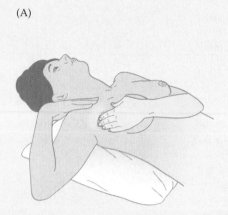

(B)

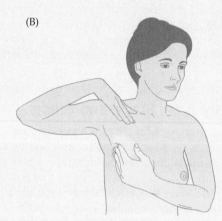

(C)

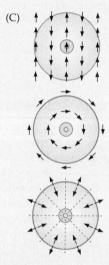

The best time for breast self-examination (BSE) is about a week after your period ends, when your breasts are not tender or swollen. If you are not having regular periods, do BSE on the same day every month.

Lie down with a pillow under your right shoulder and place your right arm behind your head (Figure A).

Use the finger pads of the three middle fingers on your left hand to feel for lumps in the right breast.

Press firmly enough to know how your breast feels. A firm ridge in the lower curve of each breast is normal. (If you're not sure how hard to press, talk with your health care provider.)

Move around the breast in a circular, up-and-down, or wedge pattern. Be sure to do it the same way every time, check the entire breast area, and remember how your breast feels from month to month.

Move the pillow to your left shoulder and repeat the exam on your left breast, using the finger pads of the right hand. Repeat the examination of both breasts while standing, with one arm behind your head (Figure B). The upright position makes it easier to check the upper and outer part of the breasts (toward your armpit), where about half of breast cancers are found. You may want to do the standing part of the BSE while you are in the shower. Some

breast changes can be felt more easily when your skin is wet and soapy.

When examining the breast, follow a regular pattern such as one of these to ensure that every part of the breast is covered (Figure C).

Finally, check your breasts for any dimpling of the skin, changes in the nipple, redness, or swelling while standing in front of a mirror.

If you find any changes, see your doctor right away.

Source: American Cancer Society.

In addition to breast self-examination, it is a good idea for a woman to have a clinical breast examination periodically—say, every 3 years during her twenties and thirties and every year thereafter.

Annual Mammography Is Recommended for Women over 40

Mammography is a breast cancer screening technique that uses low-dose X rays to image the soft tissues of the breast. During a mammographic exam, each breast is compressed between two plastic plates to spread out the breast tissue and make interpretation of the X-ray image easier (Figure 17.4A). The procedure can be uncomfortable, but is very brief. In a recent innovation, the two plates have been replaced by a single cone-shaped probe, which makes for a more comfortable procedure.

The value of mammographic screening has recently become a subject of debate. The American Cancer Society recommends that all women have an annual mammogram from age 40 onward. Mammographic screening programs have not been shown to reduce breast cancer mortality, however, according to one recent analysis (Olsen & Gotzsche, 2001). The value of screening average-risk women in their forties is particularly dubious (Ringash, 2001). Even for women in their fifties, adding annual mammograms to

(A)

(B)

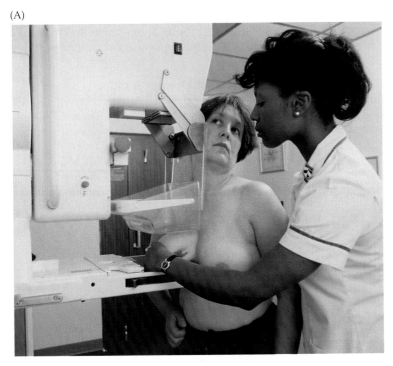
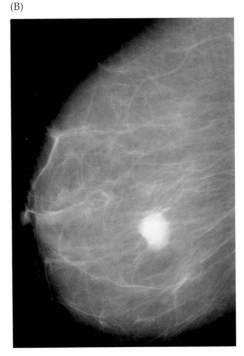

Figure 17.4 Mammography. (A) A low-dose X-ray image is taken while the breast is flattened between two plates. (B) This breast lump, visualized as a white patch on the mammogram, is a ductal carcinoma in situ, the earliest detectable stage and the easiest to cure.

breast self-examination and periodic clinical examination does not reduce breast cancer mortality, according to one large-scale randomized study (Miller et al., 2000). Nevertheless, some groups believe strongly that mammography does save lives (Miettinen et al., 2002). The U.S. Preventive Services Task Force, with the blessing of Health and Human Services Secretary Tommy Thompson, has backed screening for women in their forties and above (Garvey, 2002). In response to recent debate about the usefulness of mammography, 19 major medical and cancer organizations collectively urged women to continue being screened (American College of Obstetricians and Gynecologists, 2002).

If a suspicious lump is seen on the mammogram (Figure 17.4B), further mammography is usually done to establish the lump's position and other characteristics more carefully. Often this more detailed study shows that the lump is not likely to be cancer. If the lump remains suspicious, the next step is a **biopsy:** a sample of the lump is removed with a needle. (Sometimes the entire lump is removed—a more invasive procedure.) Examination of the sample tissue under the microscope allows for a near-definitive determination of whether the lump is cancerous, and if so, of its type and grade. Establishing the stage of the cancer may take further investigations (e.g., lymph node biopsy, whole-body scans). Only about 1 in 5 biopsied lumps turns out to be cancer.

Treatment Depends on the Diagnostic Findings and the Woman's Choice

If the biopsy shows that the lump *is* cancerous, the woman and her doctors must decide on the best course of treatment, based on the diagnostic findings, the woman's age and other circumstances, and the woman's own wishes. Surgical options range from removal of the lump itself plus some surrounding healthy tissue ("lumpectomy") to removal of the entire breast, chest wall musculature, and regional lymph nodes ("radical mastectomy"), with a number of options in between. Most women with stage 1 or stage 2 breast cancer do as well with lumpectomy plus radiation therapy as they do with removal of the entire breast.

The great majority of women diagnosed with invasive breast cancer undergo some kind of surgical treatment. There are several other forms of treatment that they may choose in addition to surgery, either as part of the initial treatment or in the event that the initial treatment fails to eradicate the cancer:

- *Radiation therapy.* Radiation therapy takes the form of X rays at a dose high enough to kill rapidly dividing tumor cells. It may be directed at the affected breast, the chest wall, and regional lymph nodes. The radiation can have unpleasant side effects, such as fatigue and soreness of the skin and the breast itself.
- *Chemotherapy.* Chemotherapy involves the use of drugs such as cyclophosphosphamide, methotrexate, and paclitaxel (Taxol) to kill rapidly dividing tumor cells. It is usually administered as a combination of two or three drugs. The great advantage of chemotherapy is that it works throughout the body, so it kills tumor cells that have spread (metastases) as well as those in the breast and nearby lymph nodes. The potential side effects of chemotherapy are well known: nausea and vomiting, fatigue, hair loss, anemia, infertility, and premature menopause.
- *Hormonal therapy.* The SERM tamoxifen may be used to treat breast cancer if the cancer cells are still expressing estrogen receptors. Synthetic progestins are also sometimes used.
- *Immunotherapy.* A relatively new treatment option—currently used for breast cancer that has not been cured by other treatments—is trastuzumab (Herceptin), an antibody that blocks a growth factor receptor present on the cells of some breast cancers.

If a woman's breast has to be removed, she has several options (Figure 17.5). She can simply live with the loss of the breast. She can use an external **prosthesis** to conceal the absence of the breast in daily life. She can also have **reconstructive surgery,** which can be done either at the time of the mastectomy or later. Reconstructive surgery is not perfect: even when it is well done, it will leave scars, numbness, and a lack of erogenous sensation at the nipple. Still, many women experience a great deal of psychological benefit from the procedure. About 1 in 3 eligible women elect to have reconstructive surgery (National Cancer Institute, 1992).

One type of reconstructive surgery involves the insertion of a silicone gel-filled implant. Any type of breast implant can cause problems at later times, such as capsular contraction (tightening of the connective tissue capsule that forms around the implant, leading to a distortion in its shape). During the 1980s and early 1990s it was widely believed that silicone gel implants were causing crippling autoimmune diseases. This belief led to successful lawsuits against the implants' manufacturer. A recent reanalysis of the data, however, suggests that the implants had no such effect (Tugwell et al., 2001).

(A)

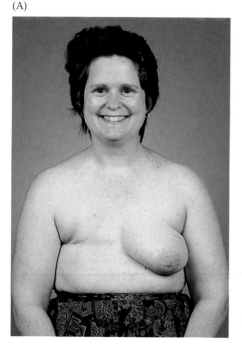

(B)

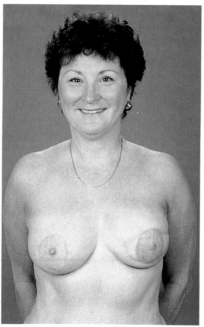

Figure 17.5 Coping with mastectomy. (A) Anita had a modified radical mastectomy without breast reconstruction. She normally wears an external prosthesis. (B) Charlene had her left breast reconstructed immediately after a modified radical mastectomy. These and other breast cancer survivors are featured in the book, *Show Me: A Photo Collection of Brest Cancer Survivors' Lumpectomies, Mastectomies, Breast Reconstructions and Thoughts on Body Image.*

Most Women with Breast Cancer Return to an Active Sex Life

Breast cancer and its treatment can affect a woman's sexuality in a number of ways (Kaplan, 1992). First, the grief, anger, and fear triggered by a cancer diagnosis are likely to put sexual feelings out of mind, at least for a while. Second, the side effects of cancer treatment may be so debilitating as to make sexual feelings and behaviors impossible. Third, some treatments may have hormonal or other effects that decrease physiological arousal or impair libido. Fourth, women who have been through breast cancer treatment, especially if they have had a mastectomy, may fear that they are no longer attractive to their current sex partners, or to potential partners (Box 17.3).

Health care providers who encourage women with breast cancer to discuss these issues are already helping to resolve them (Schain, 1988). Even in the days when radical mastectomy was the standard treatment for breast cancer, most women reported no change in key aspects of their sexuality, such as frequency of sex and overall sexual satisfaction (Morris et al., 1977). Women who have breast-conserving surgeries such as lumpectomy are probably even less likely to report enduring problems with their sex lives (Kiebert et al., 1991). Among women who elect to have breast reconstructive surgery, more than four out of five are very satisfied with the results and report an increase in sexual satisfaction after the reconstruction (J. H. Rowland et al., 1993). Thus, there is every reason for health care providers to convey optimism to women with breast cancer who are concerned about their sex lives.

Notwithstanding the generally good outcome in terms of sexual activity and satisfaction, there are women for whom the prospects are more difficult. Younger women, women who are in an unhappy relationship or not in a relationship at all, and women with a previous history of sexual problems all face more severe challenges to their sexual recovery (Harwood & O'Connor, 1994).

Box 17.3 *Personal Points of View*

Is There Sex after Mastectomy?

Here are some postings from a now-defunct on-line bulletin board for women who have had mastectomies. They illustrate the variety of ways in which mastectomy may affect—or not affect—women's sex lives.

Hi, it has been 3 years since my [reconstructive surgery] and I'm still deathly afraid of dating. Always feeling like that moment will come when sex is a 'should I let him see?' I feel like my body looks like such a mess. Being a woman of color I heal differently—I get keloid [excessive scarring]—so it looks worse on me. I was considering further surgery for correct alignment, but for what? Who looks? I'm a mess. My daughters encourage me to date but I think it's over for me.

It has been 8 years since my mastectomy and I have lost all interest in sex. I am single and I would not want any man to see me the way I look. I am happy to be alive and bird-watch for my pleasure. I am 59 years of age.

I had breast cancer 10 years ago and did not go for the reconstruction surgery. Since then I think I should have. I am a single woman at the age of 55 and when I meet some man and he is told that I had breast cancer it seems to end the relationship. My self-esteem has suffered due to the rejections, as I still would like to have a meaningful relationship with someone some day.

There are men, special men who know what's important, who look past our scars to see who we are. Don't despair, they're out there—don't give up.

I am scheduled for a mastectomy with a reconstruction at the same time. My husband and I have been separated for 2 years, but he has been very supportive and loving during this time. I still feel very sexual even with all this stress and decision making. I often wonder how I am going to feel with a new breast. He says I am still beautiful without my hair and I will be beautiful with a reconstructed breast.

I had a mastectomy and I could not look in a mirror for years without crying, so I know how you feel. I chose tissue expanders, and now I have new perky breasts. Men turn around to look at me now, a 60-year-old with a body like a teenager! My insurance paid for it, and it has changed my life. Do it, you will never regret it.

I had surgery for mastectomy 8 years ago. I have to admit at first it affected my sex life. I would not even undress in front of my husband. But now I have come to terms with it. My husband was very patient with me, he understood what I was going through, and I thank him for this. I would not consider having a reconstruction, as I think this could maybe stir up cancer all over again. [There is no evidence to support this concern.] I am happy to be able to live a full life—nothing has changed.

Urinary and Genital Tract Infections Are Not Necessarily Sexually Transmitted

In Chapter 16 we discussed infectious diseases of the urinary and genital tracts that are transmitted between sex partners. These areas are also vulnerable to infections that are not sexually transmitted. These infections may be triggered or exacerbated by sexual activity, but the causative organism does not actually come from the sex partner.

Urinary Tract Infections Are More Common in Women than in Men

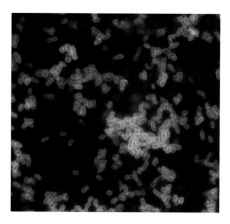

Escherichia coli is a bacterium that normally inhabits the large intestine; it causes symptoms if it spreads to the urinary tract.

Urinary tract infections generally involve the urethra (**urethritis**) and bladder (**cystitis**). If not treated, the infection may spread to the kidneys (**pyelonephritis**). Urinary tract infections are much more common in women than in men. The reason for this sex difference is not entirely clear, but two anatomical factors probably play a role. First, the urethra is much shorter in women than in men, giving microorganisms easier access to the bladder. Second, the urethral opening is closer to the anus in women than in men, making it easier for fecal organisms to be transferred to the urethra. Indeed, the commonest cause of urinary tract infections is *Escherichia coli*, a bacterium that is normally present in feces. Other organisms that can cause urinary tract infections include species of *Mycoplasma* as well as *Chlamydia trachomatis,* which is sexually transmitted (see Chapter 16).

Many conditions predispose people to urinary tract infections, including diabetes, immune system dysfunction, the presence of a urinary catheter, and (in men) disease of the prostate gland. For women, coitus is a major factor: bacteria from the anus, the vagina, or the man's penis can be physically transferred into the urethra by the thrusting motions of coitus. Use of a diaphragm is associated with an increased risk of urinary tract infections compared with the use of other contraceptive techniques. Use of contraceptive foams favors the growth of *E. coli* in the vagina, which may make urinary tract infections more likely.

The symptoms of urinary tract infection include a burning sensation during urination, a need to urinate frequently, discoloration or cloudiness of the urine, and general malaise. The infection can be verified, and the offending organism identified, by culturing a urine sample. The sensitivity of the organism to a range of antibiotics can also be tested in this manner. Most urinary tract infections respond quickly to appropriate antibiotics, but they can be difficult to eliminate in men if the prostate gland is involved (see below).

There are a number of precautions that a woman can take to reduce the likelihood of urinary tract infections (National Institute of Diabetes and Digestive and Kidney Diseases, 2001). It is helpful to drink plenty of fluids, urinate frequently, and acidify the urine by consumption of fruit juices or vitamin C supplements. Urinating before and after sex may reduce the likelihood that bacteria will be able to take up residence in the urethra. After defecation, a woman should wipe herself from front to back, not from back to front. The genitalia of both partners should be washed before sex. Any body part or sex toy that contacts or penetrates the anus during sex should be scrupulously washed before bringing it into contact with the vaginal area. Vaginal sprays and douches should be avoided. Showers are preferable to tub baths.

Bacterial Vaginosis Is a Common Condition

Bacterial vaginosis is a common condition in which the normal vaginal microorganisms (mainly lactobacilli) are replaced by a variety of other, usually anaerobic bacterial species (Schwebke, 2000). The pH of the vaginal secretions rises (they become less acidic), the vagina develops a characteristic fishy (amine-containing) odor, and there may be itching, pain, and a thin, off-white discharge.

Bacterial vaginosis is very common among sexually active women and pregnant women: as many as 16 percent of pregnant women (and 23 percent of pregnant African-American women) have the condition (Centers for Disease Control, 2000a). Vaginal douching, which disturbs the bacterial ecosystem within the vagina, is one of the strongest risk factors for vaginosis (Holzman et al., 2001). It is not clear whether or not sexually transmitted organisms are responsible for bacterial vaginosis, but one organism commonly found in the vaginal secretions of affected women, *Gardnerella vaginalis*, can also infect men. There is some evidence that lesbian couples can transmit the condition to each other (Berger et al., 1995).

In a minority of women bacterial vaginosis may lead to serious complications, such as pelvic inflammatory disease and (in pregnant women) premature delivery. The condition can be treated effectively with antibiotics; metronidazole and clindamycin are commonly used.

Vaginal Candidiasis Is a Fungal Infection

Fungi belonging to the genus *Candida* (mostly *C. albicans*) are normal inhabitants of the vagina, but they can overgrow if the immune system is compromised or the microbial balance is disturbed by use of antibiotics or frequent douching. Medically, this condition is called **candidiasis** or **thrush,** but it is popularly referred to as a "**yeast infection.**" It is marked by inflammation of the vaginal walls and sometimes the labia, severe itching, a yeastlike odor, and sometimes a thick white discharge.

Most women experience at least one episode of vaginal candidiasis in their lifetime. The condition is diagnosed by microscopic examination of the discharge and is treated with antifungal medications (imidazole or other "-azoles") that may be applied locally or taken by mouth. Some of these medications are available without a prescription. It is better to get a medical diagnosis, however, because women tend to use the over-the-counter medications for inappropriate conditions, and this practice can lead to the development of drug-resistant infections (Centers for Disease Control, 2000c).

Conditions Affecting the Uterus Include Cancer and Noncancerous Disorders

The ancient Egyptians and Greeks blamed the uterus for all kinds of physical and mental disorders in women, especially women who did not become pregnant soon after puberty. The uterus, wrote Plato in the *Timaeus*, "is desirous of procreating children, and when remaining unfruitful long beyond its proper time, gets discontented and angry, and wandering in every direction through the body, closes up the passages of the breath, and, by obstructing respiration, drives them to extremity, causing all varieties of disease." We can see a vestige of that belief in the term **hysteria**—used in the nineteenth century to describe an array of mental and psychosomatic symptoms in women—which is derived from the Greek word for uterus.

Doctors no longer automatically ascribe all women's problems to the uterus; nor do they believe that a woman who does not become pregnant is particularly prone to uterine disorders. Still, there are several serious or painful disorders that can affect this organ.

Cervical Cancer: A Success Story

Cancer of the uterine cervix strikes about 13,000 American women annually and causes about 4400 deaths. The reason we call this a "success story" is that the death rate from cervical cancer has dropped by about 75 percent since the 1950s, an improvement that is surpassed only by the survival rates for stomach cancer and some less common cancers.

The majority (85–90 percent) of cervical cancers occur on the outer surface of the cervix, where it protrudes into the vagina. This part of the cervix is lined with flattened epithelial cells called squamous cells, and cancers of this region are called **squamous cell carcinomas.** Lesser numbers of cancers begin in the cervical canal. These cancers usually arise from the glandular cells that line the canal and are called **adenocarcinomas.**

As discussed in Chapter 16, infection with human papillomaviruses (HPV) is the principal factor predisposing women to cervical cancer. The HPV subtypes that increase the risk of cervical cancer, types 16 and 18, are not the types that commonly cause genital warts. These types may cause other kinds of lesions, or they may not cause symptoms at all. Because these viruses are sexually transmitted, having sex with many partners, or with persons who themselves have many sex partners, is a risk factor for cervical cancer. Other, less important risk factors include chlamydia infection (Koskela et al., 2000), smoking, and immune system dysfunction. (Cervical cancer is a common complication of AIDS in women.)

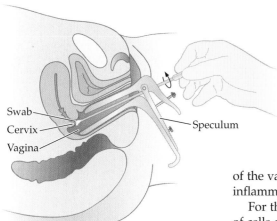

Swab
Cervix
Vagina
Speculum

Figure 17.6 The Pap test. A sample of epithelial cells is taken from the cervix.

The Pap Test Is a Lifesaver

Cervical cancer does not appear out of the blue, but is the end product of a gradual sequence of changes in the cells of the cervical epithelium. Women can monitor this process by having a **Pap test** (or **Pap smear**) regularly. The Pap test is named for the Greek-born pathologist George Papanicolaou (1883–1962), who developed the test in the 1930s at Cornell Medical School. A Pap test is generally done as part of a **pelvic examination,** which women are encouraged to have once a year. In a pelvic exam, the gynecologist or other health care provider first inspects the vulva for external problems, then uses a speculum to hold the walls of the vagina apart so that the vagina and cervix can be visually inspected for lesions, inflammation, or discharges (see Chapter 3).

For the Pap test, a spatula is inserted while the speculum is in place, and a sample of cells and mucus is scraped from the external portion of the cervix (Figure 17.6). To get a sample from the cervical canal, a cotton-tipped swab may be inserted through the cervical os.

The pelvic exam ends with a bimanual vaginal examination. The speculum is removed, and the provider places two fingers of one hand in the vagina while pressing down on the woman's abdominal wall with the other. Using this technique, the provider can palpate most of the pelvic organs. If the exam detects abnormal growths or areas that are unusually tender, they should be investigated further.

The sample taken from the cervix is spread on a slide, chemically fixed, stained, and examined under a microscope. If the cells show precancerous changes, the provider may proceed to a more detailed examination of the cervix using an operating microscope. This procedure is called **colposcopy.** During the colposcopy, the provider may take biopsies or destroy precancerous lesions by freezing or other methods. Follow-up examinations are required to make sure that the lesions do not recur.

If a precancerous lesion escapes detection (most likely because the woman has not had a Pap test for several years, or has never had one), it may progress to true invasive cervical cancer. Symptoms of cervical cancer may include an abnormal, sometimes blood-stained vaginal discharge, pain during intercourse, or bleeding during intercourse. Of course, these symptoms are not specific to cervical cancer, but a woman who experiences them should see a doctor right away to make sure that, if cancer is present, it is caught as soon as possible.

If cancer is present, a battery of examinations and tests are performed in order to "stage" the cancer. Cervical cancer is staged in a fashion analogous to that described earlier for breast cancer, with stage 0 indicating carcinoma in situ and stage 4 indicating spread of the cancer to the bladder, rectum, or distant organs.

Hysterectomy Ends a Woman's Fertility, but Not Her Sexuality

Cervical cancer is usually treated with surgery. The amount of tissue removed depends on the stage of the cancer. Removal of the entire uterus (**hysterectomy**) is the usual treatment for all cervical cancers except stage 0 cancers that have been entirely removed by biopsy. Removal of the oviducts, ovaries, and other pelvic organs may also be necessary. As with breast cancer, chemotherapy or radiotherapy are often used, and the combined use of chemotherapy and radiotherapy is superior to either form of treatment used alone (Green et al., 2001).

Hysterectomy renders a woman infertile, but it should not interfere with her enjoyment of sex or her ability to engage in coitus or experience orgasm. Sometimes the upper part of the vagina may have to be removed, or the vagina may become narrowed as a result of radiotherapy. The latter condition can be treated with dilators.

The battle against cervical cancer could be made even more successful simply by ensuring that all women receive state-of-the-art medical care—meaning annual Pap smears and appropriate treatment when abnormalities are found. It is a sad fact that African-American women are more than twice as likely to die of cervical cancer than other women, simply because of a lack of health education and affordable, culturally sensitive health care.

Most Women Survive Endometrial Cancer

Cancer of the body of the uterus—which nearly always arises in the endometrium—is three times commoner than cervical cancer, but causes only 50 percent more deaths. In other words, the survival rate is better for endometrial cancer: the **5-year relative survival rate** (meaning the percentage of women who are alive 5 years after diagnosis, discounting women who die of other causes) is 84 percent.

You will recall from Chapter 4 that estrogens promote the proliferation of the endometrium. Not surprisingly, then, a high lifetime exposure to estrogens increases the risk of endometrial cancer. This high exposure can come about as a result of early menarche, late menopause, lack of pregnancies or late first pregnancy, obesity (because adipose tissue converts hormonal precursors to estrogens), and estrogen replacement therapy. Combined estrogen–progestin hormone replacement therapy does not increase the risk of endometrial cancer, at least for the first 5–10 years of therapy.

The SERM tamoxifen, even though it is used in the treatment and prevention of breast cancer, actually *increases* the risk of endometrial cancer, at least in women who already have breast cancer: about 1 in 500 women taking tamoxifen as a treatment for breast cancer will develop endometrial cancer. The reason is that tamoxifen is not a pure estrogen receptor antagonist, but has mixed agonist/antagonist actions that vary from tissue to tissue: in the uterus, it seems to work principally as an agonist.

The usual initial symptom of endometrial cancer is abnormal vaginal bleeding or, less commonly, a colorless discharge. A postmenopausal woman who experiences either of these symptoms should seek medical attention, even though they can also be caused by noncancerous conditions. Less common symptoms—usually associated with more advanced disease—are pelvic pain, a palpable mass in the pelvis, and weight loss. The Pap test does not usually detect endometrial cancer.

A diagnosis of endometrial cancer is made on the basis of microscopic examination of cells or tissue removed from the uterus; obtaining this specimen may require a D and C (see Chapter 11). The disease is graded and staged in a fashion similar to breast cancer. Further studies, such as a chest X-ray, may be done to search for metastases.

Endometrial cancer is usually treated by removal of the uterus alone (simple hysterectomy) or in combination with some other pelvic organs, depending on the stage of the disease. Chemotherapy, radiation therapy, and/or progestin treatment may be added.

Other Uterine Conditions Include Fibroids, Endometriosis, Abnormal Bleeding, and Prolapse

Much more common than uterine cancer are several noncancerous conditions that can cause varying degrees of disability: fibroids, endometriosis, abnormal bleeding, and prolapse.

Fibroids (medically called **fibromyomas** or **leiomyomas**) are noncancerous tumors of smooth muscle that grow within or outside the uterus (Figure 17.7). They are very common: 20 to 25 percent of women develop them, usually after the age of 30 but before menopause. They can cause pain and abnormal—sometimes heavy—bleeding, but they are often asymptomatic. When they do cause symptoms, they can be removed surgically. They may be removed by a laparoscopic or a vaginal approach, depending on whether they are growing outside or inside the uterus. They can also be treated by blocking the arteries that nourish them (arterial embolization). Hysterectomy is seldom necessary. Estrogens stimulate the growth of fibroids, so fibroids typically become less of a problem after menopause, when estrogen levels fall.

Endometriosis, which affects an estimated 5 million American women, is the growth of endometrial tissue at abnormal locations. It is usually found within the pelvic cavity but on the outside of pelvic organs, including the uterus, oviducts, and ovaries. It is believed that these ectopic patches of endometrial tissue are derived from cells in the menstrual discharge that pass retrogradely up the oviducts into the pelvic cavity, but other theories of causation have also been proposed.

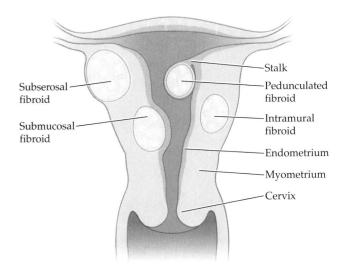

Subserosal fibroid
Submucosal fibroid
Stalk
Pedunculated fibroid
Intramural fibroid
Endometrium
Myometrium
Cervix

Figure 17.7 Fibroids are noncancerous tumors of the uterus. They may be located on the endometrium (submucosal fibroid), within the myometrium (intramural fibroid), or on the outer surface of the uterus (subserosal fibroid). Sometimes they are attached to the inner or outer surface of the uterus by a stalk (pedunculated fibroid).

There is a suspicion, based primarily on animal experiments, that exposure to the industrial pollutant dioxin increases women's risk of developing endometriosis (Koninckx, 1999).

The ectopic endometrial tissue responds to the hormonal changes of the menstrual cycle just as the normal endometrium does. The most common symptom of endometriosis is pelvic pain; this pain may be worse before or during the menstrual period, or at the time of ovulation, or it may be ongoing. Urination and defecation may also be painful during the menstrual period. Endometriosis can cause dyspareunia and, in some cases, infertility.

There is no simple cure for endometriosis. Pain medications are helpful, as are oral contraceptives. Drugs that lower estrogen levels, such as GnRH agonists, keep endometriosis in abeyance, but this kind of therapy cannot usually be maintained for long periods of time. The patches of endometrial tissue can be destroyed by laparoscopic surgery in some cases.

Abnormal endometrial bleeding can be caused by some of the conditions we have already discussed, but it can also occur for a variety of other reasons, or for no apparent reason. The D and C procedure is commonly used to treat such bleeding.

Uterine prolapse is a downward sagging of the uterus. It is caused by weakening of the ligaments that support the uterus and of the muscles of the pelvic floor. Sometimes the front or back wall of the vagina also prolapses, so that the bladder or rectum bulges into the vaginal lumen; these conditions are called **cystocele** and **rectocele** respectively. Sometimes the entire uterus prolapses far enough that the vagina inverts and the cervix extends out of the vaginal introitus (**procidentia**). Uterine prolapse is most often seen in elderly women who have had at least one child because both aging and childbirth weaken the structures that support the uterus. Obesity and smoking* are also risk factors. Uterine prolapse may be treated by a variety of surgical techniques or by insertion of a ring pessary—a plastic ring that keeps the uterus in place. Kegel exercises (Box 17.4) help to prevent uterine prolapse.

Should Hysterectomy Be So Common?

Half a million hysterectomies are performed in the United States annually, and 1 in 3 women have had a hysterectomy by the age of 60. The associated costs exceed $5 billion annually. Are all these operations really necessary or beneficial? One women's advocacy organization argues that they are not (HERS Foundation, 1999).

Hysterectomy does provide significant relief of symptoms related to nonmalignant disorders of the uterus, such as pelvic pain, fatigue, depression, and sexual dysfunctions. Most women who undergo hysterectomy report an improved quality of life a year after the operation, and these improvements are greater than in women treated for these conditions nonsurgically (Carlson et al., 1994a,b).

On the other hand, the chances that a woman will undergo a hysterectomy are influenced by factors such as her race, the region of the country where she lives, and even the sex of her physician (having a male physician increases the likelihood of hysterectomy) (Agency for Healthcare Policy and Research, 1998). Some of these factors may be medically relevant; for example, African-American women are much more likely to develop fibroids than white women, and this increases the likelihood that they will have a hysterectomy. Still, hysterectomy rates are much higher in the United States than in countries with national health services; this disparity raises the suspicion that many hysterectomies in the United States are unnecessary.

Women with noncancerous disorders of the uterus should be aware that there is an increasing range of options for treatment (Bren, 2001). They should not think of hysterectomy as inevitable simply because their mothers had it.

---

*You may be beginning to suspect that we automatically add smoking to the risk factors for any condition, but smoking *does* increase the risk of uterine prolapse. This is because of the chronic coughing (and the resulting raised intra-abdominal pressure) that many smokers experience. To be fair, there are one or two diseases, such as Parkinson's disease, against which smoking may actually have a *protective* effect.

Box 17.4 *Sexual Health*

Kegel Exercises

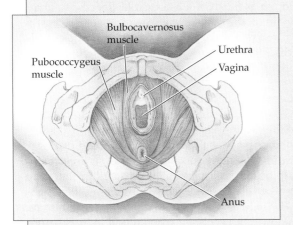

Bulbocavernosus muscle

Pubococcygeus muscle

Urethra

Vagina

Anus

The muscles of the **pelvic floor** help to support the pelvic organs, provide control over urination and defecation, and are active during sexual behavior, especially at orgasm. Unfortunately, women tend to lose tone in these muscles as they age, and childbirth may damage them. Urinary leakage during coughing, sneezing, orgasm, and so on (**stress incontinence**) is a very common problem in women after childbirth and in old age.

Arnold Kegel, a urological surgeon at UCLA, proposed in 1952 that women could avoid the need for surgery to repair their pelvic floor muscles by doing exercises to strengthen them. Since that time, "Kegel exercises" have also been promoted as a way to improve orgasmic function, so they are advocated by sex therapists as well as by urologists. Kegel exercises are also believed to protect against uterine prolapse.

The first step in doing Kegel exercises is to identify the muscles that need to be exercised (National Library of Medicine, 2001). The usual recommendation is for the woman to sit on the toilet with her knees apart, begin to urinate, and then to voluntarily interrupt the flow of urine. The muscles that accomplish this are the **pubococcygeus muscles,** which form a sling around the lower part of the vagina, and possibly other pelvic floor muscles. One problem with this method, however, is that the women who most need to learn the exercises may no longer be capable of interrupting their urine flow. An alternative technique is to place a finger in the vagina and squeeze down on the finger. If a health care provider is teaching the exercises, the provider may place a finger in the woman's vagina and provide verbal feedback on the success of her efforts. Kegel himself used a vaginal pressure transducer to provide biofeedback to his clients, and a variety of transducers are used for this purpose in some clinical settings.

Once the woman has learned how to contract her pelvic floor muscles, she should begin a regular program of exercises. At the beginning it may be difficult to hold a contraction for more than a second or so. But with practice she will soon be able to perform stronger contractions and to hold the contractions for longer. One recommended regimen to aim for is a set of ten 3-second contractions, three times a day.

In one study, healthy women were randomly assigned to practice Kegel exercises or not (Messe & Geer, 1985). At intervals thereafter, the women's capacity for sexual arousal was assessed both subjectively and by measurement of vaginal engorgement. The women who practiced the exercises experienced greater sexual arousal by one week after beginning the exercises than the control group, but did not show further gains thereafter. Kegel exercises are of doubtful value in the treatment of anorgasmia (Trudel & Saint-Laurent, 1983). In one study of women with stress incontinence, Kegel exercises were successful in resolving the problem in about half the patients, and in about two-thirds of these successfully treated women, the benefits persisted for at least 10 years (Cammu et al., 2000).

Although stress incontinence is not as great a problem among men as among women, men can benefit from Kegel exercises. As with women, the muscles can be identified by voluntarily interrupting the urine stream, and once identified, they are exercised by means of progressively longer contractions. The exercises are said to lead to stronger and more pleasurable orgasms. In addition, certain forms of urinary incontinence, including the incontinence that may follow prostate surgery, are helped by the exercises.

Ovarian Cancer Is Usually Diagnosed Too Late to Cure

Ovarian cancer is not particularly common: it strikes about 23,000 American women annually. Unfortunately, the survival rate is worse than that for other reproductive system cancers: only about 1 in 2 women survive 5 years after diagnosis. Ovarian cancer kills about 14,000 women annually, making it the fourth most common cause of cancer deaths among women, after cancer of the lung, breast, and colon. The reason why the survival rate for ovarian cancer is so poor is that 3 out of 4 ovarian cancers have already spread beyond the ovary at the time of initial diagnosis.

Most ovarian cancers are epithelial cancers—they arise in the epithelial covering of the ovary. Risk factors for epithelial ovarian cancer include age (the median age at diagnosis is 65), family history, possession of cancer-promoting genes (these include mutated versions of the breast cancer genes *BRCA1* and *BRCA2*), early menarche, late menopause, not having children, obesity, and prolonged hormone replacement therapy. The use of oral contraceptives for more than 5 years *decreases* the risk of ovarian cancer by about 60 percent.

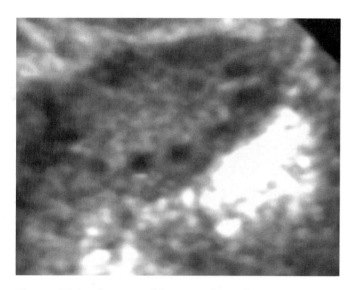

Figure 17.8 Ultrasound image of a polycystic ovary.
The ovary is the dark oval near the top of the image. The dark spots within the ovary are cysts. (Courtesy of Duke University Medical Center, Reproductive Endocrinology and Infertility Unit.)

Early ovarian cancer is usually asymptomatic, and there are no screening tests that have been shown to reduce mortality in average-risk women. Typically, ovarian cancer makes itself known by abdominal swelling (often caused by accumulation of fluid), a constant feeling of a need to urinate or defecate, digestive problems, or pain in the pelvis, back, or leg. Occasionally there is abnormal vaginal bleeding.

Treatment for ovarian cancer typically includes surgery to remove the tumor, or as much of it as possible. Because ovarian cancer usually arises on the surface of the ovary, it spreads easily within the pelvis, and removal of several pelvic organs (especially the uterus, oviducts, and ovaries) may be necessary. Chemotherapy is a standard part of treatment; radiotherapy is less commonly used.

There are a number of other conditions that can affect the ovaries. The most common such condition is the presence of fluid-filled sacs within the ovaries. These **ovarian cysts** may be discovered when they cause pain, or they may be diagnosed during a pelvic exam. In women of reproductive age, the cysts are usually normal ovarian follicles that have not yet ruptured or that may have grown larger than usual (see Chapter 4). These so-called **functional cysts** usually regress without treatment. Cysts can also be a sign of cancer, however, especially when found in girls before puberty or in postmenopausal women.

Polycystic ovary syndrome (Figure 17.8) is a condition characterized by multiple small cysts in the ovaries combined with menstrual irregularity, failure of ovulation, and sometimes hirsutism and acne. The cysts are probably follicles that fail to mature properly. In women with polycystic ovary syndrome there is deficient regulation of gonadotropin secretion by the pituitary gland and of steroid secretion by the ovaries. The cysts do not become cancerous, but the endocrine disruption raises the likelihood of diabetes and heart disease.

Prostatitis Can Be Acute or Chronic

The prostate gland is invisible, and its function (Chapter 3) is not widely understood. (Many people think that semen is produced entirely by the testes.) Thus, the prostate comes to most people's attention only when it malfunctions, which it does all too commonly, especially in old age.

A health care provider can check the condition of the prostate gland by inserting a gloved finger into the anus and palpating the gland through the front surface of the rectum (Figure 17.9). In this way, the provider can assess whether the gland is tender, enlarged, or contains lumps. By massaging the gland, the provider can express a sample of prostatic fluid from the urethra, which can be examined for evidence of prostate disease. A **digital rectal exam** should be part of an annual health checkup, especially for older men.

One prostate disorder that affects men of all ages is **prostatitis**—inflammation of the prostate gland. Prostatitis is probably not a single disease, but rather a collection of disorders, some of which are poorly understood. It can become a chronic and disabling condition that is difficult to treat (Lummus & Thompson, 2001).

The most straightforward, but least common, kind of prostatitis is **acute infectious prostatitis.** It may be caused by infection with *E. coli* or other microorganisms that invade the prostate gland from the urine. Since the urine is normally sterile, a urinary tract infection must precede or coexist with the prostatitis. The symptoms are pain during ejaculation and urination, ongoing pain in the perineum or elsewhere in the pelvic region or lower back, and a fever. The responsible organism may be cultured from the urine, from the urethra, from expressed prostatic fluid, or from the ejaculate. The condition usually responds to antibiotics.

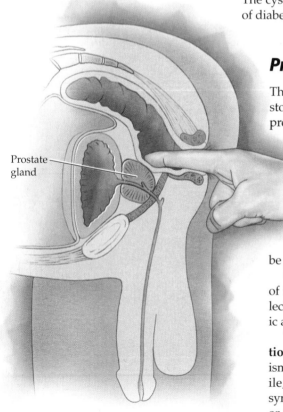

Prostate
gland

Figure 17.9 A digital rectal exam allows the prostate gland to be palpated.

More puzzling is **chronic prostatitis,** a condition marked by roughly similar symptoms, but which continues for months or years. There may be no identified infectious agent, or even if there is one, the condition may not respond to antibiotics. Some researchers believe that this condition is in fact an infection, but that the microorganisms deep within the prostate are not effectively eliminated by antibiotics. A variety of other possible causes have been suggested. In one 1999 study, University of Washington urologists biopsied the prostate glands of 97 men who had been diagnosed with chronic prostatitis. They found that most of the biopsies showed no evidence of inflammation (True et al., 1999). Thus, it is possible that many men diagnosed with chronic prostatitis actually have some other condition. The term **chronic pelvic pain syndrome** is coming into favor as an alternative to "chronic prostatitis," especially where there is no demonstrable infection.

Benign Prostatic Hyperplasia Causes Urinary Difficulties

The prostate gland grows rapidly at puberty, then continues to grow slowly throughout adult life. Because the gland lies within a tight capsule, its growth may eventually constrict the urethra where it passes through the gland (Figure 17.10). The medical term for this condition is **benign prostatic hyperplasia** or **hypertrophy,** or it may simply be called an **enlarged prostate** (National Kidney and Urological Diseases Information Clearinghouse, 1998).

The term "benign" makes it clear that this condition is not cancerous, but it is hardly benign in the popular sense of the word. More than half of all men in their sixties, and as many as 90 percent of men in their seventies and beyond, experience chronic urinary problems as a result of this condition, and it is responsible for 375,000 hospital stays in the United States annually.

As the urethra becomes constricted, the bladder has to work harder to expel urine, and the walls of the bladder become thickened and irritable. The usual symptoms of an enlarged prostate are a weak, discontinuous flow of urine, urgency of urination, leakage, and a need to urinate frequently, including at night.

Benign prostatic hyperplasia does not increase the risk of prostate cancer, but the urinary symptoms often have to be treated. Among the drugs that may be used is **finasteride (Proscar),** which inhibits the conversion of testosterone to dihydrotestosterone, the steroid that is principally responsible for prostate growth. Also useful are the alpha-adrenergic receptor antagonist **tamsulosin (Flomax)** and similar drugs, which relax the smooth muscle of the prostate and the urethra, permitting a greater flow of urine. Alternatively, the urethra may be enlarged by a procedure in which a heated probe is passed into it to destroy part of the prostate.

Eventually, however, many men require surgical removal of a larger portion of the prostate. This operation, which can be done through the urethra (**transurethral resection**), causes sexual dysfunction in some men. The most common such problem is **retrograde ejaculation:** the urethral sphincter at the base of the bladder fails to close at ejaculation (see Chapter 3), so the ejaculate passes backward into the bladder and is later voided in the urine. This renders the man infertile, but does not prevent the pleasurable feelings of orgasm.

Prostate Cancer Is the Commonest Cancer in Men

Aside from the commonest variety of skin cancer (which is not usually life-threatening), prostate cancer is the commonest cancer among American men: nearly 200,000 cases are diagnosed yearly. One in 6 men will be diagnosed with prostate cancer in his lifetime,

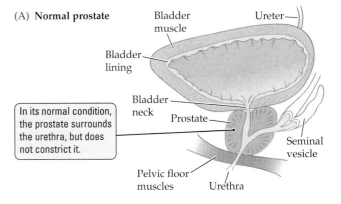

(A) **Normal prostate**

Bladder muscle
Ureter
Bladder lining
Bladder neck
Prostate
Seminal vesicle
Pelvic floor muscles
Urethra

In its normal condition, the prostate surrounds the urethra, but does not constrict it.

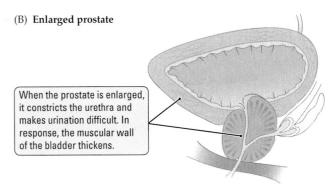

(B) **Enlarged prostate**

When the prostate is enlarged, it constricts the urethra and makes urination difficult. In response, the muscular wall of the bladder thickens.

Figure 17.10 Enlarged prostate.

making this condition more common than breast cancer in women. The disease causes about 31,500 deaths annually, which puts it second only to lung cancer in terms of cancer mortality.

Still, by comparing the number of cases with the number of deaths, you can see that most men who get prostate cancer don't die of it. In 70 percent of men who are newly diagnosed with prostate cancer, the cancer is still confined to the prostate gland, and thanks to effective treatment, almost none of these men will die of the disease.

Prostate cancer is primarily a disease of old men: the average age at diagnosis is 70 years. African-American men are about 70 percent more likely to develop prostate cancer than white men, and twice as likely to die of it. Aside from age and race, no risk factors have been firmly established. Diet may have some influence: high consumption of animal fats or low consumption of fruits and vegetables may raise the risk of the disease.

The early symptoms of prostate cancer are generally similar to those of benign prostatic hypertrophy; namely, problems with urination. There may also be blood in the urine or semen and pain in the lower back, hips, or upper thighs. Prostate cancer may also be detected by a routine digital rectal exam or by the presence of abnormally high levels of a prostate-derived protein, **prostate-specific antigen** (**PSA**), in the blood. None of these symptoms or findings is specific to cancer, however; specialized imaging tests and a biopsy are usually needed to make a firm diagnosis.

Whether periodic digital rectal exams and PSA tests can reduce mortality due to prostate cancer is being addressed by a currently ongoing trial. Because prostate cancer occurs mainly in old men and often grows slowly, and because treatments for prostate cancer can have such negative side effects, some specialists believe that aggressive screening and treatment programs cause more physical and psychological harm than they prevent.

Most prostate cancers are adenocarcinomas; that is, cancers derived from glandular cells. They are graded and staged according to a scheme that is a little more complex than that used for breast cancer (American Cancer Society, 2001d). Suffice it to say that most cases are diagnosed at stage 2, meaning that the tumor is of more than minimal size, but is still confined to the prostate gland.

Treatment Options Range from Watchful Waiting to Surgery and Hormonal Treatment

If the cancer is confined to the prostate gland and appears to be slow-growing, one option for "treatment" is **watchful waiting,** which means not treating the cancer at all, but performing regular checkups to monitor its progression (or lack thereof). The advantage of this approach is that it spares the man all the potential side effects of treatment. The disadvantage is that it may allow the cancer to progress to a stage at which treatment is difficult.

If treatment is undertaken, a common option is **radical prostatectomy,** which means surgical removal of the entire gland plus nearby lymph nodes. Transurethral resection may be done to resolve urinary problems caused by prostate cancer, but it will not generally eliminate the cancer. Radiation therapy can be administered either as an alternative to surgery or as a supplemental treatment. It can be administered externally or in the form of radioactive pellets that are implanted directly into the gland.

Prostate cancer cells are usually androgen-dependent, so hormonal treatments are often used, sometimes to shrink the cancer prior to surgery and sometimes to limit the growth of cancer that has already spread beyond the prostate gland. These treatments can include removal of the testes (castration or **orchiectomy**) or administration of drugs that block androgen receptors (e.g., **flutamide**) or depress androgen secretion by the testes (e.g., the GnRH agonist **leuprolide**). Eventually, hormonal treatments tend to become ineffective; at that point, regular chemotherapy may be used.

Treatments for Prostate Cancer May Result in Sexual Dysfunction

The sexual side effects of treatments for prostate may be very significant. Radical prostatectomy puts a permanent end to ejaculation because most of the volume of the normal ejaculate is the secretion of the prostate gland and the adjacent seminal vesicles, whose ducts run through the prostate gland. It is also likely to cause erectile dysfunction because the autonomic nerves that supply the erectile tissue run through the gland. Some surgical procedures are specifically designed to leave the nerves in place, but nerve-sparing surgery is no guarantee that normal erectile function will be preserved. Although there are news stories almost every year about new ways of destroying the prostate that don't cause erectile dysfunction, the truth is that this side effect is common (at least as a temporary effect) no matter how the procedure is done. Sildenafil (Viagra) can improve erectile performance after prostatectomy, but only if the nerves and blood vessels supplying the penis are spared (Feng et al., 2000).

If hormonal treatment is used, the man will usually experience a loss of libido and an impairment of erectile function, along with other possible side effects. Since hormonal treatment is often continued for as long as it is effective in keeping the cancer in check, a man who elects this form of treatment must pay a heavy price in terms of his sex life.

Testicular Cancer Can Affect Young Men

Testicular cancer is not a particularly common cancer. It strikes about 7400 men in the United States annually, but only about 400 of these men die of the disease. In other words, testicular cancer is usually a curable condition.

Testicular cancer is less biased toward older people than are most cancers. In fact, one common subgroup of testicular cancers usually strike men in their twenties. For that reason, testicular cancers as a group are the commonest form of cancer among men aged between 20 and 34. Some very well known young men, including four-time (and counting) Tour de France winner Lance Armstrong, figure skater Scott Hamilton, and comedian Tom Green have faced the disease. Testicular cancer can strike at any age, however. One celebrity who developed testicular cancer later in life was Hsing-Hsing, the National Zoo's giant panda, who was diagnosed with the disease in 1997, at the ripe old age (for a panda) of 26.

One important risk factor for testicular cancer is a history of undescended testicles. Even if the testicles are surgically relocated to the scrotum early in life, a heightened risk of cancer remains. Men with other developmental abnormalities of the testes, or with Klinefelter's syndrome (see Chapter 5), are also at increased risk of testicular cancer. Testicular self-examination (Box 17.5) is recommended for men in these risk groups and may be beneficial for all men.

Testicular cancer is usually diagnosed when the man himself, or his health care provider, notices a lump or an increase in size in one testicle. There may also be a sudden accumulation of fluid in the scrotum, pain in the testicle, or an ache or heaviness in the lower abdomen, groin, or scrotum.

Cyclist Lance Armstrong has won the Tour de France four times, and fathered three children, since being diagnosed with and treated for testicular cancer that had spread to his lungs and brain.

Orchiectomy Combines Diagnosis and Treatment

There are several diagnostic tests that may strengthen the suspicion that a testicular lump is cancer; these tests include ultrasonographic imaging and blood tests for tumor-related markers such as **alpha-fetoprotein.** The definitive diagnosis is made on the basis of a biopsy, however, which usually involves removing the entire affected testis (orchiectomy) through an incision in the groin.

Microscopic examination of the tumor allows it to be classified. About 30 percent of testicular cancers arise from the stem cells that normally give rise to sperm (see Chapter 3) and are called **seminomas.** These cancers are seen predominantly in middle-aged and old men. The remaining **non-seminoma** cancers are the ones that predominate among young men; they often arise from vestiges of embryonic tissue, and less commonly from the Leydig or Sertoli cells.

Unilateral orchiectomy does not permanently alter testosterone levels because the remaining testis can double its output. (Recall that testosterone secretion is controlled by feedback loops involving the hypothalamus and pituitary gland—see Chapter 4.) The remaining testis should also be able to produce enough sperm for the man to remain fertile. A plastic prosthesis can be inserted in the scrotum to replace the missing testicle.

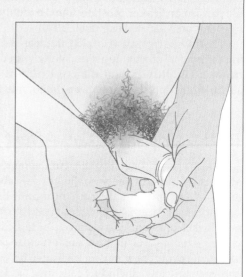

Box 17.5 *Sexual Health*

Testicular Self-Examination

There are no objective data about the value of regular testicular self-examination for men of average risk, and the national cancer organizations neither recommend nor discourage the practice. Still, the exam is simple enough and might possibly be life-saving.

Choose a warm location such as the shower, so that the dartos and cremaster muscles (Chapter 3) are relaxed. Roll each testicle in turn between thumb and fingers. The surface of the testicle is usually fairly smooth, and the epididymis can be felt as a soft, elongated structure behind each testicle. One testicle is normally slightly larger than the other, but it is a matter of concern if one testicle has enlarged from the last time you examined it. Also feel for any lumps, rounded or irregular masses, changes in the consistency of a testis, or tender areas. None of these signs are definitive indicators of cancer—in fact, early testicular cancers are often non-tender—but they merit a visit to your doctor. So does a persistent diffuse aching in the groin or lower abdomen, or a sense of heaviness in one testicle.

While doing a testicular self-examination it is a good idea to examine the remainder of the genital area, especially the penis, for sores, warts, or other lesions that could be caused by a sexually transmitted disease or other condition needing medical attention.

Unfortunately, depending on the stage of the cancer, further treatments may be necessary, and these treatments can interfere with sexual function. The dissection of regional lymph nodes often damages nerves involved in ejaculation, but nerve-sparing procedures may avoid this problem. Radiation therapy and chemotherapy, if required, can both depress sperm production, either temporarily or permanently. Men with testicular cancer who may want to father children in the future have the option of depositing semen samples in a sperm bank before treatment. Lance Armstrong used this method to father three children since his diagnosis.

Most Testicular Problems Are Not Cancer

A variety of noncancerous conditions can affect the testicles and nearby structures:

- **Orchitis** is an inflammation and swelling of a testicle, often as a result of infection with the mumps virus. It is seen most commonly in pre-pubertal boys.

- **Epididymitis** is an inflammation of the epididymis, caused by trauma or by infection with *E. coli* or any of a number of sexually transmitted organisms. It is seen most commonly in sexually active young men. The infection can spread to the testis.

- A **varicocele** is an enlargement of the veins that drain the testicles, causing the spermatic cord to feel like a "bag of worms." The condition is probably caused by a congenital anomaly in the venous valves that direct blood toward the heart. It may impair fertility, but it can be surgically corrected.

- A **hydrocele** is a collection of fluid in the membrane-lined space surrounding one testicle. Hydroceles are not uncommon in newborn babies. They are harmless, but cause discomfort. They can be drained or surgically corrected.

- **Testicular torsion** is a rotation of a testicle in such a way as to cut off its blood supply. It happens in men who have a common congenital deformity of the testicular coverings. Torsion causes sudden and severe pain; it must be treated within a few hours, or the affected testis may die from the lack of blood (**infarction**).

A Few Conditions Affect the Penis

Considering the demands that may be put on it, the penis is a remarkably hardy organ. Aside from erectile dysfunction (see Chapter 15) and sexually transmitted infections (see Chapter 16), it is subject to only a few problems that occur at all frequently:

- **Phimosis** is the inability to retract the foreskin far enough to expose the glans. This is the normal condition in male babies, and it persists in many boys until puberty. There is no need to treat it unless the flow of urine is affected. Phimosis may also be acquired, either as a consequence of poor hygiene or of parents' well-intentioned efforts to retract their son's foreskin for the purpose of cleaning under it.
- **Paraphimosis** is the entrapment of a retracted foreskin behind the corona of the glans. It can occur as a result of efforts to retract a phimotic foreskin. Men who get their penises pierced are also at risk of paraphimosis. It is an emergency condition because it can lead to necrosis of the glans.
- **Peyronie's disease** is an unnatural curvature of the erect penis caused by plaque or scarring within the corpora cavernosa—possibly as a late consequence of trauma. The curvature can be severe enough to prevent penetrative sex. Peyronie's disease can be successfully treated with oral medications, injections, or surgery, but there is a tendency for the condition to recur.

Penile Cancer Is Rare

Penile cancer strikes about 1200 men in the United States per year and causes about 300 deaths. Most penile cancers are skin cancers similar to those found on other parts of the body. Infection with human papillomavirus (HPV) is an important factor predisposing men to penile cancer. As with cervical cancer in women, the HPV subtypes 16 and 18, and some others, are associated with penile cancer. These subtypes do not cause genital warts, but they may cause flat skin lesions, sometimes called flat warts. These lesions should be treated to prevent possible progression to cancer.

Caught early, penile cancer can be treated by fairly minor surgical procedures. If the cancer has invaded the deep structures of the penis, however, part or all of the organ may have to be amputated (penectomy). If only the distal part of the penis is amputated, the man will probably still be able to engage in penetrative sex, experience ejaculation and orgasm, and facilitate his partner's orgasm. If the entire penis is removed, penetrative sex will obviously not be possible. Still, it may surprise you to learn that many men who have had a total penectomy develop the ability to experience orgasm through stimulation of nearby areas of skin. It may be that the sensory nerves that are cut during surgery grow back and reinnervate these adjacent skin regions.

Many Disabled People Have Active Sex Lives

Besides the disorders of the sexual and reproductive organs that we have just listed, many other conditions can have an effect on people's sex lives. Here we briefly focus on two kinds of disabilities—arthritis and spinal cord injuries—that may directly affect sexual behavior, and one—mental retardation—that raises questions of choice and competency.

Probably the main thing to understand about disabilities is that they do not generally interfere with sexual desire, or do so only indirectly in the sense that disabled people may internalize other people's stereotypes of them as sexless beings. Even very severely disabled men and women are likely to experience sexual attraction, to fall in love, to desire intimacy, and to make great efforts to consummate those feelings (Box 17.6). There is every reason to respect and facilitate sexual expression by disabled people.

Box 17.6 *Personal Points of View*

On Seeing a Sex Surrogate

Mark O'Brien was a Berkeley-based writer who, as a consequence of childhood polio, had to spend most of his life inside an iron lung. In a 1990 article for *The Sun*, O'Brien described his efforts to achieve sexual fulfillment. The following is a condensed version of the article, which is available in full on the Web (O'Brien, 1990).

On the phone, Cheryl had explained that she would interview me for the first hour of the session; then, if I agreed, we would do 'body awareness exercises.' I was too scared to ask what this meant, but said I would give it a go.

When March 17 arrived, I felt unbearably nervous. Vera, one of my morning attendants, dressed me, put me in my wheelchair, and pushed me to Marie's cottage. Once inside, Vera put a sheet I had brought with me on the double bed. Then she lowered me onto it. The bed was close to the floor, unlike my iron lung. Since it's difficult for me to turn my head to the left, Vera pushed me over to the left side of the bed, so that Cheryl could lay next to me and I could still see her. Then Vera put

the hose of my portable respirator near my mouth, in case I needed air. I thought it likely because I'd never been outside the iron lung for an hour without using the portable respirator. I was all set.

Oh God, would she ever come? Perhaps she had found out what an ugly, deformed creep I am and was breaking the appointment.

A knock on the door. Cheryl had arrived. I turned my head as far to my left as I could. She greeted me, smiling, and walked to where I could see her better. She doesn't hate me yet, I thought. Marie went out the door with Vera, saying that she would return at 1. Cheryl and I were alone. 'Your fee's on top of the dresser,' I said, unable to think of anything else to say. She put the cash into her wallet, and thanked me.

She wore a black pantsuit, and her dark brown hair was tied behind her head. She had clear skin and large brown eyes and she seemed tall and strong, but then I'm 4' 7" and weigh sixty pounds. As we talked, I decided that she was definitely attractive. Was

she checking out my looks? I was too scared to want to know.

Talking helped me to relax. I began to tell her about my life, my family, my fear of sexuality. I could see that she was accepting me and treating me with respect. I liked her, so when she asked me if I would feel comfortable letting her undress me, I said, 'Sure.' I was bluffing, attempting to hide my fear.

My heart pounded—not with lust, but with pure terror—as she kneeled on the bed and started to unbutton my red shirt. She had trouble undressing me; I felt awkward and wondered if she would change her mind and leave once she saw me naked. She didn't. After she took my clothes off, she got out of bed and undressed quickly. I looked at her full, pale breasts, but was too shy to gaze between her legs.

Whenever I had been naked before—always in front of nurses, doctors, and attendants—I'd pretend I wasn't naked. Now that I was in bed with another naked person, I didn't need to pretend: I was undressed, she

Unfortunately, health care professionals who deal with disabled people often fail to bring up issues of sexual function with them, perhaps out of embarrassment or fear that they will not be able to offer useful advice.

In one large-scale national study of women with and without disabilities, the disabled women were only moderately less active sexually than the nondisabled women (Nosek et al., 1997) (Figure 17.11). The differences that did exist were primarily a consequence of the fact that the women with disabilities were less likely to be in a marriage or cohabitation.

Figure 17.11 Disabilities have only a moderate effect on women's sexual activity. (Data from Nosek et al., 1997.)

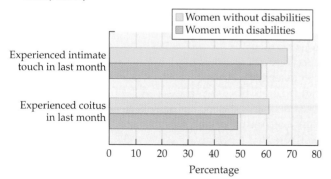

Percentage

Arthritis Is the Number One Disability Affecting Sex

Some disabilities interfere with sexual expression by limiting movement. In this connection, people generally think first of spinal cord injuries, but numerically, the leading villain is **arthritis.** This collection of conditions (chiefly osteoarthritis, rheumatoid arthritis, and systemic lupus erythematosus) affects 15 percent of the U.S. population, with women and the elderly being disproportionately affected.

If arthritis affects the large joints, such as the hips, it may impair the postures or body movements (such as pelvic thrusting) involved in partnered sex. If it involves the small joints of the hands, it may interfere with masturbation, sensual touching, and fiddly tasks such as putting on a condom or inserting a diaphragm.

A certain degree of planning can make lovemaking a much more positive experience for people with arthritis. Sex can be timed for a

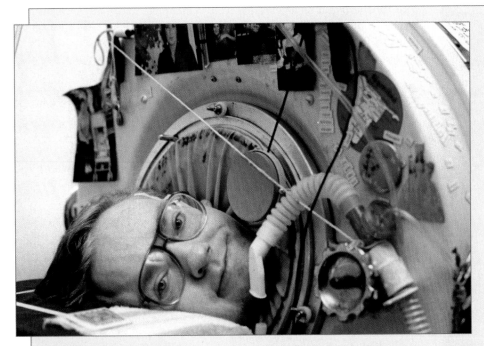

Mark O'Brien (1949–1999)

was undressed, and it seemed normal. How startling!

She stroked my hair and told me how good it felt. This surprised me; I had never thought of my hair, or any other part of me, as feeling or looking good. Having at least one attractive feature helped me to feel more confident. She explained about the body awareness exercises: first, she would run her hand over me, and I could kiss her wherever I wished. I told her I wished that I could caress her, too, but she assured me I could excite her with my mouth and tongue. She rubbed scented oil on her hands, then slowly moved her palms in circles over my chest and arms. She was complimenting me in a soft, steady voice, while I chattered nervously about everything that came to mind. I asked her if I could kiss one of her breasts. She sidled up to me so that I could kiss her left breast. *So soft.*

'Now if you kiss one, you have to kiss the other,' she said. 'That's the rule.'

Amused by her mock seriousness, I moved to her right breast. She told me to lick around the edge of the nipple. She said she liked that. I knew she was helping me to feel more relaxed, but that didn't make her encouragements seem less true.

I was getting aroused. Her hand moved in its slow circles lower and lower as she continued to talk in her reassuring way and I continued my chattering. She lightly touched my cock—as though she liked it, as though it was fine that I was aroused. No one had ever touched me that way, or praised me for my sexuality. Too soon, I came.

After that, we talked a while. I asked Cheryl whether she thought I deserved to be loved sexually. She said she was sure of it. I nearly cried. She didn't hate me. She didn't consider me repulsive.

She got out of bed, went into the bathroom, and dressed. By then it was nearly 1. The door opened. It was Marie and Dixie. They asked me about the experience. I told them it had changed my life. I felt victorious, cleansed, and relieved.

part of the day when the person's arthritis is least bothersome, or medications can be timed to be maximally effective during sex. It may be helpful to precede sexual intercourse with a warm shower, gentle massage, or use of a vibrator to assist arousal.

What about positions for coitus? If the woman has arthritis affecting her hips (one of the commonest conditions), the regular man-above (missionary) position may not be suitable. It may help to modify the man-above position so that the woman keeps her hips together and the man places his legs on the outside of hers. Alternatively, the rear-entry position is often suitable, either with both man and woman lying on their sides, or with both man and woman standing and the woman leaning over and supporting herself on something. If the man's knees or hips are affected, the woman-above position may be the best. If coitus is too painful on a particular occasion, oral or manual stimulation, or use of a vibrator, may be a fine alternative. For some older couples, such techniques are novel, and may be a revelation once tried.

Spinal Cord Injuries Present a Major Challenge to Sexual Expression

There are about 8000 spinal cord injuries in the United States each year. (This number refers to nonfatal injuries that result in significant and permanent neurological deficits.) About 80 percent of the victims are men, and their median age is 26 (Figure 17.12). Most of these injuries result from motor vehicle accidents, violence, sports accidents, or falls. Spinal cord injuries are highly variable in their effects. The major factors influencing the effects are the severity of the injury (i.e., whether there is a complete or only partial disruption of spinal

Figure 17.12 Paraplegia typically strikes young men. Sexual expression is still possible but requires adaptability.

cord function) and its level in the cord. A complete injury at the cervical level results in almost total loss of movement and sensation below the neck (**quadriplegia**), while injuries at lower levels usually affect the legs and the lower portion of the trunk, including the genitalia (**paraplegia**).

One option adopted by many men and women with spinal cord injuries is to make increased use of parts of the body whose movement and sensation is unimpaired. In quadriplegics that may mean primarily the mouth, while for paraplegics it may include the hands and breasts. Many people with spinal cord injuries report that the erotic sensitivity of their unaffected body regions increases over time, so much so that the person may experience orgasm, or highly pleasant sensations comparable to orgasm, from sexual use of those regions. In some cases the sensations may be experienced as if they were coming from the genitalia ("phantom orgasm").

A man with a spinal cord injury may or may not be able to have an erection. If the injury is to the sacral segments of the spinal cord, which provide the parasympathetic outflow to the penis (see Chapter 3), the man is unlikely to be able to have an erection under any circumstances. If the injury is higher in the cord (as in quadriplegics), he probably will be able to have erections in response to sensory stimulation of the genitalia (reflexogenic erections) because the entire reflex loop from the genitalia to the spinal cord and back is unaffected. However, if the injury is complete, the man will not derive any direct sensations from his penis, erect or not. Nor will he have erections in response to erotic sights or fantasies (psychogenic erections) because the long pathways between the brain and the lower spinal cord have been interrupted. Sildenafil has proved helpful for men with spinal cord injuries who have difficulty obtaining or maintaining an erection, but only if at least a partial erection can be obtained without the drug (Schmid et al., 2000).

Ejaculation may be possible for men with lower-level injuries, especially if they are incomplete, but a complete upper-level injury generally makes ejaculation impossible because it cuts off signals from the brain centers that are involved in triggering this process (see Chapter 3). Even if ejaculation is possible, it is not likely to be accompanied by the normal subjective sensations of orgasm. Ejaculation may occur retrogradely (into the bladder) due to the failure of the sphincter at the upper end of the urethra to close.

Men with spinal cord injuries who wish to engage in coitus are usually capable of doing so. If the man is paraplegic, he can take the man-on-top position. He may have to push his flaccid penis into the woman's vagina by hand (the "stuffing" technique); the woman can help this process by actively contracting the muscles of the vaginal walls. The man's penis may then become erect as a result of reflex action as the woman performs thrusting motions. If the man is quadriplegic, the woman does best to kneel astride him and place his penis in her vagina; again, the penis may become erect in response to this stimulation. An additional complication is urinary incontinence. If a urinary catheter is in place, it can be kept in place with the aid of a condom or tape; this, then, will necessitate the use of a lubricant.

Women with spinal cord injuries have deficits roughly comparable to men: besides the loss of movement and sensation (depending on the level and severity of the injury), women may lose vaginal lubrication (necessitating use of a lubricant). With lower-level injuries, engorgement of the vulvar tissues may be lost as well. Coitus is possible in several positions, however, including the man-on-top position, or side by side with either front or rear entry.

In one laboratory-based study (Sipski et al., 2001), somewhat fewer than half of the women with spinal cord injuries were able to reach orgasm, compared with 100 percent of a control group of women. Ability to reach orgasm was lowest with complete injuries affecting the lowest (sacral) region of the spinal cord. Among women who did reach orgasm, the time required to do so was longer than among the control women, but the orgasms themselves were similar in quality.

Paraplegic and quadriplegic women can sustain a pregnancy and deliver a baby vaginally, although there is a somewhat increased risk of complications and of premature birth. Contraception presents some special problems for women with spinal cord injuries (see Chapter 11).

If you are an able-bodied and sexually active young person, you may be wondering whether the sexual options just described are really worth it for spinal-cord-injured men and women or their partners. The answer, however, is often a resounding yes—whether in terms of physical pleasure, intimacy between partners, or the psychological reward of accomplishing such a basic human activity in the face of a major challenge.

Many Mentally Retarded Persons Are Competent to Make Sexual Choices

Traditionally, mentally retarded children and adults were sequestered in institutions. The motive was protection, and they were rarely given the opportunity to make any active decisions for themselves, least of all in the area of sexuality. Often they did not receive any sex education, out of concern that this might encourage sexual behavior. Mentally retarded women (and, to a lesser extent, men) were often sterilized involuntarily, either out of concern that they would not be able to fulfill their parental roles or because of fear that any children they had would themselves be retarded.

Nowadays, mildly and moderately retarded persons often participate in community life and may live in independent or semi-independent settings. There has been an increasing acknowledgment that most mentally retarded persons have sexual feelings—only some profoundly retarded persons seem to lack them. Retarded persons have the same constitutional right as other people (under the right to privacy) to make informed choices about sexual activity, if they are capable of doing so. They also have a right to protection from sexual exploitation, however. Balancing these rights can be difficult.

In general, it is illegal, as well as reprehensible, for anyone to have sexual contact with a mentally retarded person if that person lacks the mental capacity to give informed consent. Mental capacity means knowledge about sex, the intelligence to understand the risks and benefits of sexual activity (including an awareness of the social and moral nature of sexual relations), and the ability to make a decision free of coercion. No one can give consent on behalf of the retarded person (Stavis, 1991). Thus, if a person is judged by psychiatrists or others not to be capable of giving consent, caregivers have a responsibility to protect that person from all sexual contact with others because such contact would be sexual assault or statutory rape. Institutional staff may realize that a retarded person of borderline capacity has the wish to engage in sex and may therefore be motivated to judge that person competent. The downside of doing this is that if the judgment of competence holds up, the retarded person may be sexually exploited by others with little recourse.

Luckily, many retarded persons are well within the bounds of competence, and chiefly need education in such matters as potential sexual behaviors, appropriate partners, privacy, sexual exploitation, STDs, pregnancy prevention, and the like (Lumley & Scotti, 2001). The Arc, a national organization of and for mentally retarded persons, asserts the right of these persons not only to engage in sexual relationships, but also to marry and have children, and if they do have children, to receive assistance in raising them (The Arc, 1996).

Summary

1. One in eight women will develop breast cancer during her lifetime. Risk factors include family history, cancer-causing genes, age, a long reproductive life span, lack of children, high alcohol consumption, obesity, and oral contraceptive use. Regular breast self-examination, clinical examination, and mammograms may save lives by allowing breast cancer to be caught at an early stage.

2. Recommended treatment for breast cancer depends on the stage of the cancer at diagnosis. For women in whom the condition is diagnosed early, there has been a move away from radical mastectomy toward various kinds of breast-conserving surgeries. Chemotherapy, radiotherapy, and hormonal therapy are commonly used in addition to surgery or if the cancer spreads. Although mastectomy is greatly feared by women and is a challenge to their self-image, most women who have had mastectomies return to an active and satisfying sex life.

3. Urinary tract and vaginal infections—with fecal or sexually transmitted bacteria or with fungi—are common in women. These conditions usually respond to antibiotics.

4. Cervical cancer occurs primarily in women who have been infected with certain types of human papillomavirus (HPV). Precancerous changes can be detected by the Pap test. Treatment for all but the least advanced cancers includes hysterectomy (removal of the uterus), an operation that renders the woman infertile, but does not interfere with sexual behavior and pleasure. Mortality from cervical cancer has declined greatly.

5. A risk factor for endometrial cancer is high lifetime exposure to estrogens. Abnormal vaginal bleeding is the symptom that usually brings the condition to the woman's attention. Endometrial cancer is most often treated by hysterectomy, and the survival rate is high. Other common uterine conditions are fibroids, endometriosis, abnormal bleeding, and uterine prolapse.

6. Early ovarian cancer is asymptomatic, and there are no screening tests for this disease. The majority of ovarian cancers have therefore spread beyond the ovaries by the time they are diagnosed, making the disease difficult to treat. Only about 50 percent of affected women survive 5 years. Other ovarian conditions include ovarian cysts and polycystic ovary syndrome.

7. In men, the prostate gland may become inflamed or infected (prostatitis). In many older men, the gland grows too large and causes urinary difficulties (benign prostatic hyperplasia). This condition can be treated with drugs or with surgical procedures. A common surgical treatment called transurethral resection can cause retrograde ejaculation.

8. Prostate cancer is the commonest life-threatening cancer in men. One in 6 men will develop the condition in his lifetime, usually in old age. Screening tests (digital rectal exam and the PSA blood test) can identify men with a high likelihood of having the disease, but the value of screening programs is controversial. Treatment options range from "watchful waiting" to radical prostatectomy, often combined with radiation. Because androgens spur the growth of prostate cancer cells, treatment often includes removal of the testes (orchiectomy) or anti-androgen hormonal treatments. Treatments for prostate cancer may greatly impair sexual function, causing loss of ejaculation, erectile dysfunction, or loss of libido. Sildenafil (Viagra) can improve erectile function in some men after prostatectomy.

9. Testicular cancer—especially the non-seminoma types—affects relatively young men. The condition is usually recognized by a lump or swelling in one testicle. It is treated by orchiectomy. If unilateral, this procedure does not impair sexual function, but farther treatments (lymph node dissection, radiation, chemotherapy) can impair ejaculation and fertility. Other testicular problems include orchitis, epididymitis, varicocele, hydrocele, and testicular torsion.

10. Besides erectile dysfunction, conditions affecting the penis include problems with the foreskin (phimosis, paraphimosis) and abnormal curvature (Peyronie's disease). Penile cancer is rare; HPV plays a causal role in this illness.

11. Some disabilities interfere with sexual behavior by limiting movement or making movement painful. Arthritis is the leading culprit in this respect, with 15 percent of the U.S. population affected. Nevertheless, people with arthritis can usually engage in pleasurable and rewarding sex by advance preparation and by choosing positions for sex that put the least stress on affected joints.

12. Spinal cord injuries can cause a near-complete loss of movement and sensation in the body below the neck (quadriplegia) or in the lower half of the body (paraplegia). Although conscious sensations from the genitalia are often lost, reflex penile erection and vaginal lubrication and engorgement may be preserved, depending on the level and completeness of the injury. Most persons with spinal cord injuries can engage in coitus if they desire it, and women with spinal cord injuries can sustain pregnancy and deliver a baby vaginally.

13. Most mentally retarded persons experience the same sexual feelings and desires as everyone else. They have a right to make informed choices about sexual behavior if they are capable of doing so. Facilitating the exercise of this right must be balanced against the need to protect retarded persons from sexual exploitation. With appro-

priate education, many retarded persons can enjoy active sex lives, and some become parents and raise children.

Discussion Questions

1. You meet another student who you find very attractive, and the feeling is reciprocated. But one of you is able-bodied and the other is paraplegic and confined to a wheelchair. Do you think you could engage in a happy romantic or sexual relationship under these circumstances? What adjustments do you think either of you would have to make? How would you discuss dating and sex?

2. You have a friend whose arthritis makes sexual intercourse very uncomfortable. He fears he may have to give up sex because he can't find a comfortable position. What changes might you suggest to help him find a more comfortable approach?

3. A close friend tells you that she may have breast cancer and that she is going to have a biopsy and further evaluation. She says she would never be able to cope if her breast needed to be removed. Describe the options that may be available to her in terms of treatment. What are the issues that you would like to discuss with her in terms of her concern about mastectomy?

4. The National Cancer Institute spends more than twice as much on breast cancer research as on prostate cancer research. Why do you think that is? Are there differences in the diseases—such as incidence or mortality, age of the affected persons, or the likelihood that research will pay off—that justify this difference in spending? Should "gender parity" be a factor in setting spending levels for sex-specific diseases?

Web Resources

National Women's Health Information Center www.4woman.org

National Breast Cancer Coalition www.natlbcc.org

National Cervical Cancer Coalition www.nccc-online.org

Ovarian Cancer National Alliance www.ovariancancer.org

American Cancer Society www.cancer.org

National Cancer Institute www.nci.nih.gov

Endometriosis Association www.endometriosisassn.org

National Uterine Fibroids Association www.nuff.org

Prostatitis Foundation www.prostatitis.org

Testicular Cancer Resource Center www.acor.org/TCRC

Recommended Reading

American Cancer Society (2001). *A breast cancer journey: Your personal guidebook.* Atlanta, GA: American Cancer Society.

Armstrong L., and Jenkins, S. (2000). *It's not about the bike: My journey back to life.* New York: Putnam.

Bostwick, D. G., MacLennan, G. T., and Larson, T. R. (1999). *Prostate cancer: What every man—and his family—needs to know* (rev. ed.). New York: Villard Books.

Love, S. M., and Lindsey, K. (2000). *Dr. Susan Love's breast book* (3rd rev. ed.). Cambridge, MA: Perseus Books.

Nash, J. (2001). *The Victoria's Secret catalog never stops coming, and other lessons I learned from breast cancer.* New York: Scribner.

Sipski, M. L., and Alexander, C. J. (eds.) (1997). *Sexual function in people with disability and chronic illness: A health professional's guide.* Gaithersburg, MD: Aspen Publications.

chapter _18_

German police officers on a manhunt for a serial rapist and suspected murderer.

Sexual Assault, Harassment, and Partner Violence

This chapter deals with the dark side of sex. Sex is not limited to balanced, happy interactions between loving couples. It can be grossly one-sided, involving sexual desire on one person's part and disinterest, perhaps aversion, on the other's. It can involve physical assault. And intimate sexual relationships can be marred by cruelty and violence. We have touched on these issues earlier: in Chapter 9 we discussed the difficult feelings resulting from unrequited love, as well as the breakup of relationships. In Chapter 14 we described paraphilias, such as exhibitionism and pedophilia, that can lead to the victimization of women and children. Here, we take a broader look at sex as a context for physical and psychological injury.

What Is Rape?

The terms that describe acts of sexual victimization have been given many different definitions. Here we use these terms in ways that correspond approximately to legal usage. **Rape** or **forcible rape** is used to mean penetration of the vagina, anus, or mouth by the penis when performed by force or the threat of force. (Legal definitions vary: sometimes oral penetration is not considered rape, and sometimes vaginal or anal penetration by a finger or an object *is* considered rape.) **Sexual assault** is a broader term that includes any sexual act performed by force or the threat of force. **Statutory rape** means coitus, anal penetration, or oral penetration performed without force, but also without the partner's consent; it is usually applied to cases in which the partner cannot legally give consent on account of young age or mental incapacity. When we use the term "rape" without qualification, we are excluding statutory rape.

Many Women Have Experienced Unwanted Sexual Contacts

Violent sexual offenses are disturbingly common. In the National Violence Against Women (NVAW) Survey, a telephone survey conducted by the U.S. Department of Justice and the Centers for Disease Control in 1995–1996 (U.S. Department of Justice, 1998), 1 in 3 women and 1 in 33 men stated that they had experienced an attempted or completed rape at least once in their lifetime. Most of these events were completed rapes.

According to the National Crime Victimization Survey (NCVS), an annual survey conducted by the U.S. Census and analyzed by the Department of Justice (U.S. Department of Justice, 2000a), the peak age for sexual victimization of women is 16–19 (Figure 18.1). Of women who have been raped, 22 percent were first raped before the age of 12 (U.S. Department of Justice, 1998). Blacks were almost twice as likely to be victimized as whites. One bright spot in these statistics is that rape is becoming less common: between 1993 and 1999, the NCVS reported a 44 percent drop in the rates of rape and attempted rape. This drop is in line with a general decline in personal crimes over the same period.

Most Perpetrators Are Men Known to the Victim

Who are the people who commit rape or sexual assault? Contrary to what one might imagine, more than 2 out of 3 are known to the victim; of these, the majority are friends or acquaintances and the remainder are spouses or other intimate partners (U.S. Department of Justice, 2000b) (Figure 18.2).

Virtually all rape perpetrators are men. It is theoretically possible that a woman could rape a man or another woman, especially in jurisdictions where rape is broadly defined, but sexual violence by women is nearly always treated as sexual assault. The great majority of sexual assaults, too, are committed by men. Of persons incarcerated for sexual assault—typically the more serious offenders—nearly 99 percent are male (Greenfeld, 1997). These men tend to be older than men convicted of other violent offenses.

Of men arrested for rape, 56 percent are white and 42 percent are black. Black men are greatly overrepresented compared with their numbers in the general population (about 12 percent), but at about the same level as in arrests for other crimes of violence (Greenfeld, 1997). Because only a minority of rapes are even reported to the police (see below), let alone lead to an arrest, the racial breakdown of arrestees may not be the same as the racial breakdown of perpetrators.

Why Do Men Rape?

The question of why men rape is an important but highly controversial one (Polaschek et al., 1977). Some researchers attempt to answer it within the context of evolutionary theory: they ask, in other words, why the human mind has evolved in such a way as to induce some

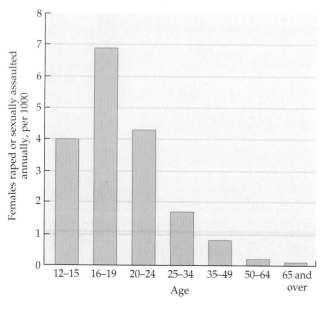

Figure 18.1 Age of rape and sexual assault victims. Young women are most at risk. (Data from U. S. Department of Justice, 2000a.)

men, in some circumstances, to attempt to copulate by force. Others are interested in the social forces within our own culture that may condone or encourage rape, or the life experiences that turn particular men into rapists. There is no agreement as to which of these approaches is the most meaningful, or which leads to the best strategy for eliminating rape behavior.

Rape May Have Evolutionary Roots

As we mentioned in Chapter 2, forced copulation is quite common in the animal world, and the males of a few species—especially the scorpionflies studied by Randy Thornhill—possess anatomical structures that have the specific function of facilitating this behavior. These specializations are clearly *adaptations*—that is, they have evolved because they increase the flies' reproductive success. In particular, forced copulation spares males the cost of acquiring a nuptial gift, which a female normally demands in exchange for sex.

In their 2000 book, *A Natural History of Rape*, Thornhill and Craig Palmer of the University of New Mexico discussed the question of whether the human male's capacity for rape should also be thought of as an evolutionary adaptation. In other words, has the capacity for rape developed because it permits men who rape (in certain circumstances) to have more offspring than they would if they never raped? Or is the trait merely a *by-product* of traits, such as sexual desire and aggressiveness, that have evolved for reasons that have nothing to do with the benefits or costs of rape?

Some aspects of rape do suggest that it might be an evolutionary adaptation. First and foremost, men most commonly rape women who are in their peak reproductive years (see Figure 18.1). The simplest interpretation of this finding is that during human evolution the details of rape behavior, such as the preferred age of victims, have been shaped by rape's reproductive benefits. Another relevant observation is that men rape more commonly when the likely costs of doing so (such as injury or retribution by the victim or the victim's relatives) are low: the high incidence of rape by conquering troops in war is the most striking example of this pattern (Box 18.1). Again, it is as if the behavior has been shaped by the balance of reproductive benefits and costs.

If rape is an evolutionary adaptation, then one would expect men to be more likely to rape if their ability to obtain sex partners through other methods were impaired—just as scorpionflies use this strategy if they don't have a nuptial gift. Consistent with this expectation, rapists and other sexual offenders are predominantly men of low socioeconomic status, and there is some evidence that they typically have a history of frustrated sexual and romantic relationships (Figueredo, 2000). This is not an invariable rule, however: some high-status men with abundant access to women also rape or have the inclination to rape (Lalumière et al., 1996).

What is known so far about rape does not permit a firm conclusion as to whether it is an evolutionary adaptation or not, and Thornhill and Palmer's book leaves the question undecided. It is possible that one could get closer to an answer by means of laboratory studies that measured men's sexual and other responses to rape-related videotapes. By systematically varying the reproductive costs and benefits of the portrayed rape, one could hope to establish whether the men's responses were consistent with the idea that rape is an evolutionarily adaptive behavior.

The discussion of the evolutionary context of rape has aroused a great deal of criticism. Some of the criticism comes from the academic world, and points out apparent shortcomings and inconsistencies in the evolutionary approach—particularly the lack of an explicit, quantitative model in Thornhill and Palmer's book (Ward & Siegert, 2002). One group, led by anthropologist Eric Smith of the University of Washington, has attempted to generate such a model, using data derived from a study of an American Indian people in Paraguay (Smith et al., 2001). The researchers calculated that the reproductive *costs* of rape outweighed its reproductive *benefits* tenfold, suggesting that a predisposition to rape could not be an adaptive trait. In their analysis, the major problem with rape as an adaptive reproductive strategy is that if rape is committed at a random time, the chances that the victim will be near ovulation, and therefore in her "fertile window," are low (see Chapter 10). If men are (or were) able to pick up behavioral, pheromonal, or other indicators of the timing of a woman's ovulation, rape *could* be an adaptive strategy. Thus, the fact that a woman's fertile window is not obvious (as it is in so many

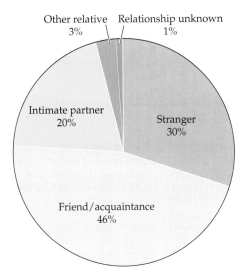

Figure 18.2 Most rapes are not committed by strangers. The graph shows the relationships of perpetrators of rape and sexual assault to their victims. (Data from U.S. Department of Justice, 2000b.)

Box 18.1 *Sex in History*

The "Comfort Women"

Rape by conquering troops has been a part of most wars, but before and during the Second World War, Japan institutionalized the practice. The Japanese took women from the countries they colonized or conquered to serve as sex slaves for their soldiers. An estimated total of 200,000–400,000 women were enslaved; most were Korean, but others were Taiwanese, Chinese, Filipino, Indonesian, or Dutch. The practice was begun in 1932 in Shanghai, but eventually spread to all territories reached by Japanese soldiers. The enslaved women were euphemistically called *jugun ianfu* ("military comfort women").

Here are recent remarks by two former "comfort women":

Yun Doo Ree: When my cuts and bruises had healed slightly, they put me back into the same room. Another officer was waiting for me. They must have warned him about me. He did not wait and did not give me a moment to even think of protesting. He swiftly knocked me down and started pushing his thing inside of me. It happened all so fast. I found myself bleeding. I wasn't even sure where

the blood was coming from. I only felt pain. Something in my body was torn apart. I put my teeth into his cheek. Now we were both bleeding, he from his face and I, somewhere below. . . . I was fifteen.

Ok Seon Lee: I am filled with *han* [unresolved grief]. Nothing—not even the deaths of every Japanese soldier—can bring back my lost life.

Most of these sex slaves died during the Second World War, many at the hands of the Japanese. The Japanese government has declined to offer a formal apology to the survivors or to provide restitution to them out of public funds, despite protests by former comfort women (see figure) and others. It claims that the "comfort women" program was not official Japanese policy. According to historian Hirofumi Hayashi of Kanto-Gakuin University in Yokohama, however, the program "was not only carried out by the total involvement of every section of the military but also by administrative machinery at every level of the Japanese state. [The Emperor] certainly had power to stop it."

Sources: Kang, 2001; Kim-Gibson, 1999.

other animals) may in itself be an adaptation designed to prevent rape by making it less worthwhile for men.

Other critics of the evolutionary approach to rape argue that this approach has the effect of justifying rape by presenting it as something natural or inevitable (Baron, 1985). Evolutionary biologists such as Thornhill and Palmer take the opposite view: they believe that understanding the evolutionary basis of rape is a necessary step toward ending it.

Feminists See Rape as a Learned Form of Male Domination

Social scientists and feminists have generally taken the view that rape is a learned behavior. Here is one fairly typical expression of this point of view by Diana Russell, professor emeritus of sociology at Mills College in Oakland, California:

Males are trained from childhood to separate sexual desire from caring, respecting, liking or loving. One of the consequences of this training is that many men regard women as sexual objects, rather than as full human beings. . . . [This view] predisposes men to rape. Even if women were physically stronger than men, it is doubtful that there would be many instances of female rapes of males: Female sexual socialization encourages females to integrate sex, affection, and love, and to be sensitive to what their partners want. (Russell, 1984)

Closely associated with this point of view is the idea, first put forward by feminists in the early 1970s, that rape is motivated not by sexual desire, but by hostility to women or the desire to exert power over them. Perhaps the most influential expression of this view was the 1975 book *Against Our Will* by Susan Brownmiller. Brownmiller rejected the idea that human rape has parallels in the animal kingdom (but see Chapter 2 for some evidence to the contrary). "No zoologist, so far as I know," she wrote, "has ever observed that animals rape in their natural habitat." She asserted that rape is a deliberately chosen tool of male sociopolitical dominance:

> Man's discovery that his genitalia could serve as a weapon to generate fear must rank as one of the most important discoveries of prehistoric times, along with the use of fire and the first crude stone axe. From prehistoric times to the present, I believe, rape has played a critical function. It is nothing more or less than a conscious process of intimidation by which *all men* keep *all women* in a state of fear. (Brownmiller, 1975; emphasis in original)

Theorists Have Debated whether Rape Is Sexual

Brownmiller's assertion that all men commit or consciously approve of rape as a tool to subjugate women may strike many people today as an extreme example of 1970s male-bashing. But the notion that rape is essentially *nonsexual* is still widespread. Many rape crisis and rape prevention centers carry statements like the following on their Web sites:

MYTH: Rape is sex.

FACT: Rape is not sex. It is a crime motivated by a need to control, humiliate and harm. Rapists use sexual violence as a weapon to hurt and dominate others.

(Sexual Assault Crisis Center of Knoxville, 2001)

Some rape prevention organizations acknowledge that rape can be sexually motivated, but represent this motivation as unusual. Thus, according to one program, "the primary motivation for rape is to dominate, control and humiliate the victim. Rape is rarely for sexual gratification" (Self Defense for Life, 2001).

During the 1970s, psychologists garnered some evidence in support of the feminist position. In one study based on interviews with 133 rapists and 92 rape victims, clinical psychologist Nicholas Groth and his colleagues concluded that sexual motivation was secondary to anger or the desire to dominate in almost every case (Groth et al., 1977).

Let's take a look at some of the arguments and counterarguments used in debating the proposition that rape is not sexual, or not primarily sexual:

Argument: Rapists disregard the normal criteria of sexual attractiveness in selecting their victims; they choose women of any age and any degree of attractiveness, or lack thereof (Brownmiller, 1975).

Counterargument: Rape victims are predominantly in the age range that men find most sexually attractive (see Figure 18.1). There are no published studies comparing the sexual attractiveness of rape victims and same-aged non-victims.

Argument: Rapists choose their victims on the basis of their vulnerability, not their attractiveness (Groth, 1979).

Counterargument: Rapists would be likely to take vulnerability into account whatever their motivation. Yet the weakest females—female children and old women—are *less* commonly raped than are physically stronger young adult women.

Argument: Rapists do more physical harm to their victims than necessary to complete the act of coitus. Therefore, physical harm must be an end in itself (Harding, 1985).

Counterargument: Studies of victims' accounts of rape (Box 18.2) have found that, while some rapes are extremely violent, most are accomplished only by the threat of violence or by the minimal force required to complete coitus (pushing or holding). For example, one large-scale study found that only a minority of victims were slapped (17 percent), beaten (22 percent), or choked (20 percent) (McCahill et al., 1979).

Argument: Victorious soldiers often rape women among the defeated enemy; this shows that hostility is the motivation (Brownmiller, 1975).

Box 18.2   *Personal Points of View*

It Happened to Me

Rape is a horrific experience for the victim, regardless of the exact circumstances of the rape or the level of violence involved. In this box we present three first-person accounts from rape survivors, two by women and one by a man, that give some idea of the range of circumstances in which rape can occur. The first account describes an extremely violent stranger rape.

Maple: I had been out running for about an hour. I was getting close to home when I saw a van parked in a no parking zone, there were 2 men inside looking at a map. When I turned I saw 2 more men standing at the back of the van, I assumed they had gotten out to stretch their legs. I was wrong.

As I walked past them I felt a hand on my shoulder. It was a strong grasp. I tried to pull away, but the grip got stronger, it was then that I knew that I was in trouble. I was pulled into the back of the van. There were 2 more men in there. I was gagged and handcuffed. I was terrified. I don't know how long we drove.

When the van stopped they opened the door and got out. I heard them discussing whether or not they were sure that I wouldn't be heard if I screamed. They were not focused on me and I decided that I should try to get away. I eased myself out of the van and as soon as my feet hit the ground I started to run. I didn't get far when I was tackled from behind. Oh, how it hurt. I was told that it was a stupid thing to do and that I would have to be punished. That was when the knife came out. I remember the searing pain as it cut through the tender skin of my face.

I was picked up and taken inside an old building. Once inside the handcuffs and gag were removed and I was told to scream as much as I wanted, I wouldn't be heard. I didn't scream, but I begged them not to hurt me anymore. The tears that ran down my cheeks stung when they reached the gash opened up by the knife.

I was told to take off my clothes. I couldn't, the knife came out again.

I finally did. I was humiliated already. I was told to lay down, that was the first time that I noticed the mattress on the floor. I couldn't lay down there, I felt that if I did it would mean that I was consenting to what I knew was about to happen. All I could do was say "please NO," the knife came out again and then I was pushed onto the mattress.

They all took off their clothes and stood around the mattress. I was told to open my legs, I couldn't, there came the knife and my legs were pried open. The first was the worst one, it hurt so much. After that I started to go numb and as each one took their turn I felt my body slipping away from me.

The next account describes what is probably a more common form of rape: one that arises out of a party situation where (though not explicitly mentioned in this particular account) alcohol or drugs may have been consumed by the rapist or his victim, or by both.

Steph: The girl invited me to a party that her friends were having. So I went there with her. I met the girls having the party, and they seemed very nice. I started talking to a guy who seemed to be a few years older then me. He was very nice and polite. Maybe I should have seen it coming.

I had a boyfriend at the time, so I just talked to him with only intentions of friendship. To make this story shorter, I ended up in a room with him. I have no idea how. He ended up touching me and removing quite a bit of my clothing. I struggled and I cried the whole time. He took off his pants as well. Then he tried to go inside of me, which he succeeded at. But to be very blunt, it was only a few thrusts of going in and out. It was all so horrible and hurt so much. I ended up getting out from underneath of him. Not quite sure how. He apologized as I ran out of the room very quickly. I wanted to get home, into my house, and into my bed as fast as I could. I never wanted to see this guy again.

Since I was a virgin at the time, I think I lost my virginity to him. How-

ever, it might sound silly, but I do not consider that to be very true. I consider it to be the time with my boyfriend now. In my head I have a definition of losing virginity to involving love. What he did to me did not contain any love."

Male-on-male rape in prison is also common. The trauma of this kind of rape is compounded by the frequent lack of recourse or (as described here) the fear of retribution for "snitching," as well as by the possibility of HIV transmission.

R. D.: While serving my sentence at a former institution, I was severely beaten and gang raped, both orally and anally, by six black inmates. It started by inmate [A] coming by my cell and waking me up at approximately 4:00 A.M. He said he wanted to come in and watch television with me. I didn't think nothing of it because we've had no prior problems before. I did think it was odd though. So he came in and sat on my bed. About 5 to 10 minutes after that, inmate [B], [C], and [D] came into my cell. Then inmate [D] said, 'We want some ass.' I said, 'I don't think so, I don't play that shit.' When he said this, I said to myself, 'Oh no! I'm in trouble!' I looked toward the door for an escape route finding it blocked, I went into myself to prepare for the worst.

Inmate [B] then stood in front of me and pulled out his penis and forced it into my mouth. Inmate [C] then took his turn. Pulling me to my feet, he then took my boxers off, bent me over and forced his penis inside. Inmate [D] laid on the bed, took my head and forced himself inside my mouth. All four of them, plus one more, took turns anally and orally raping me at the same time. Somewhere in the middle of this, inmate [F] entered. During the rape, I believe it was him that said 'Suck this dick, you white bitch.' One said 'If you snitch on us, we'll kill you!!' The other said, 'And if you do and you get transferred, you'll still die.' At that time, I really believed them, and I still think this today.

Sources: (Maple, Steph: Survive-UK, 2001; R.D.: Human Rights Watch, 2001b.)

Counterargument: As mentioned above, this behavior could equally be the result of the low cost of rape in this situation. Also, victorious soldiers preferentially rape *young* women, a pattern that is not explained by the hostility theory.

Argument: Prison rape is clearly motivated by power issues: men rape other men in prison to control newcomers by forcing them to submit to a stronger prisoner (Virginia Commonwealth University, 2001).

Counterargument: Prisoner's accounts indicate a mixture of sexual and power motives. Youth, femininity, and physical attractiveness are attributes that increase a prisoner's chances of being raped, suggesting a role for sexual desire (Human Rights Watch, 2001b).

Argument: Rapists often say that they raped for reasons of power, control, or vengeance, rather than sex (Scully, 1990).

Counterargument: Rapists' accounts of their crimes may describe either nonsexual or sexual motivations. Here are two contrasting examples:

It delighted me that I was defying and trampling upon the white man's law, upon his system of values, and that I was defiling his women . . . I felt I was getting revenge. (Cleaver, 1967)

She stood there in her nightgown, and you could see right through it—you could see her nipples and breasts, and, you know, they were just waiting for me. (Groth, 1979)

The mere fact that men who rape must have an erection to complete the rape suggests that sexual arousal is involved, in completed rapes at least. On the other hand, quite a few men who attempt rape show some kind of sexual dysfunction, such as failure to achieve erection, intromission, or ejaculation (Groth & Burgess, 1977). These dysfunctions could be interpreted as a sign of low sexual arousal.

Although this controversy remains unsolved, it seems likely that sexual desire plays a significant role in most rapes. While some degree of force is associated with all rapes by definition, this does not by itself mean that violence is part of the motivation. Thornhill and Palmer (2000) argue that drawing such a conclusion would be as illogical as concluding that men who visit prostitutes are partially motivated by charity because they give the prostitutes money.

There is one kind of rape that is often accompanied by violence beyond what is necessary to complete the rape: the rape of a wife or cohabitational partner after a breakup (Felson & Krohn, 1990). It seems likely that this kind of rape is motivated in large part by jealousy, anger, or a desire for revenge.

In Chapter 14 we described **sadism,** a paraphilia in which the infliction of pain is a necessary prerequisite for sexual arousal. Is it possible that rapists' motives are sadistic—that is, that they are sexually aroused by the very fact that they are raping rather than engaging in consensual sex? This idea has been tested in a number of studies of incarcerated rapists and nonrapists. In these studies, the men's penile responses were measured while they viewed videotapes of consensual and forcible sex. Some studies found a moderate difference in the direction that one might expect: the nonrapists' responses were lessened by the addition of force imagery, whereas the responses of rapists were not lessened, or were actually enhanced, by the addition of such imagery (Abel et al., 1977; Hall et al., 1993). In one meta-analysis of all studies of this kind, the difference between the responses of rapists and nonrapists was quite substantial (an effect size of about 0.8) (Lalumière & Quinsey, 1994).

Based on accounts given by rapists and rape victims, however, it appears that sadistic impulses motivate only a small percentage of rapes (Groth et al., 1977). Furthermore, some studies of the type just mentioned failed to observe any difference in the penile responses of rapists and nonrapists (Baxter et al., 1986). It is possible that the differences in results relate to the kinds of sexual offenders that were studied, with the more violent offenders being the ones who were sexually aroused by violence, but this remains to be firmly established (Lalumière & Quinsey, 1994). To the extent that there may be differences of this kind, these findings could offer a partial resolution to the sex versus violence debate: rather than being an either/or matter, violence may play a role in contributing to sexual arousal for some, but not all, rapists.

The two classes of ideas just discussed (rape as a product or by-product of evolution, and rape as a learned expression of male domination over women) do not exhaust the possibilities. It has been suggested, for example, that some men rape because of poor parenting, which leaves them deficient in the art of intimacy (Malamuth, 1996; Marshall & Barbaree, 1990). Such men do not necessarily hate or want to dominate women, it is argued, but rape out of distrust or frustration at their inability to form normal romantic attachments. Theories of this kind are not necessarily in conflict with evolutionary psychological ideas: as mentioned above, evolution might equip men with a predisposition to rape if other sexual strategies are blocked.

Rape Laws Have Become More Protective of Victims

As recently as the eighteenth century, women were considered the property of men, and rape of women was considered an offense against men—against the woman's father if she was unmarried and against her husband if she was married (Geddes & Lueck, 2000). A woman who was raped lost value, was shamed, and brought shame on her family. Thus, her kinsfolk might reject her, or even kill her, in addition to seeking vengeance on the rapist. These ideas still persist in some traditional patriarchal societies; for example, many of the countless Bengali women who were raped by Pakistani soldiers during the 1971 war for the independence of Bangladesh were cast out by their families (Asia Pacific Radio Transcripts, 2000).

U.S. law inherited from English law the concept of a "marital exemption" to rape, meaning that it was not rape for a man to force sex on his wife. The thinking was that the wife had given consent to sex by virtue of her marriage vows and could not retract it. Marital rape did not become a crime in all states until 1993.

As an informal extension of the marital exemption, the legal system used to be quite forgiving of rapes that occurred between cohabiting or socially acquainted couples, rapes of dates or pick-ups, or rapes of prostitutes. The women in these circumstances were viewed as having voluntarily placed themselves at the man's disposal. Defendants could often escape severe penalties by arguing that the episode had been inflated as a consequence of domestic discord, or that the victim had signaled her willingness to engage in sex. She might be judged to have done so by dressing or acting provocatively, by voluntarily going to the defendant's home, by entering his bedroom, or by engaging in non-coital sexual behavior.

Simply demonstrating that the victim was of "unchaste character" was often enough to secure an acquittal or to get the charges reduced. Evidence that the victim used contraceptives even though unmarried, that she frequented bars, or that she had a reputation as a promiscuous woman might be introduced for this purpose. In other words, rape laws were used primarily to protect "women of virtue"—women who either were virgins or were married to someone other than the perpetrator.

Before Emancipation it was not considered rape when a white man had forcible sex with a slave. Many slave owners took advantage of this exemption, both for sexual gratification and to produce mixed-race children who could be sold at a high price. Nor was it rape for one slave to have forcible sex with another slave. Slaves were believed to be naturally promiscuous, so a female slave was not considered to have any "virtue" that needed protection.

After the Civil War, white and black Americans were treated entirely differently in the context of rape. During the half-century when rape and attempted rape were capital offenses in South Carolina, for example, that state executed 59 men for those crimes. Yet every one of the victims of those crimes was white, and all but 3 of the executed men were black (O'Shea, 1999). This was in spite of the fact that, today at least, nearly 90 percent of all rapes involve a perpetrator and a victim of the same race (Greenfeld, 1997). Besides these judicial executions, many black men suspected of raping white women were lynched or castrated, whereas few, if

Before emancipation, slave owners had the legal right to engage in sex with their slaves, with or without the slave's consent.

any, white men suffered either fate for raping anyone, white or black. In short, both the law and the mob viewed the rape of a white woman by a black man as more heinous than other, more common types of rape.

Reforms Began in the 1970s

The women's movement brought about many significant changes in the ways in which the legal system and the general public view rape. Starting in the 1970s, **rape shield laws** were introduced. These laws protect rape victims in a number of ways, most notably by preventing the alleged perpetrator from introducing evidence about the victim's prior sexual history. In other words, the defendant can no longer get off by painting the victim as a "slut." The shield laws also often bar the public disclosure of the victim's name.

Laws have also been modified to introduce a range of sexual offenses in addition to rape as traditionally defined. These offenses are called sexual battery, sexual assault, forcible or aggravated sodomy, and the like. The definitions of such offenses vary considerably from state to state. The key point is that it is no longer necessary to prove that coitus occurred, which makes it easier to obtain convictions in many cases. In addition, it is no longer necessary in many states to prove that the victim physically resisted the rape or assault, nor is it necessary to provide corroborating evidence from third parties.

Have the Reforms Gone Far Enough—Or Too Far?

There is some controversy about whether these reforms have gone far enough or, perhaps, too far. According to an analysis by Cassia Spohn and Julie Horney of the University of Nebraska, the reforms have not succeeded in changing the attitudes of jurists and jurors, so the traditional standards are still largely in effect (Spohn & Horney, 1992). There are even still vestiges of the marital exemption. In 33 states, men may have sex with their wives while their wives are unable to give consent (as, for example, when they are unconscious or mentally impaired), whereas it is a crime for men to have sex with other women under the same circumstances (U.S. Department of Justice, 1999b).

On the other hand, critics point to cases in which the alleged perpetrator's defense appears to have been hamstrung by the new laws (Young, 1998). One such case that drew national attention was that of sportscaster Marv Albert. In 1997, Albert was accused of sexually assaulting and biting a woman who later identified herself as Vanessa Perhach. The prosecution was allowed to introduce evidence that Albert had attempted to sexually assault and bite another woman. The defense, however, was not allowed to introduce evidence that supposedly indicated that Perhach had a pattern of falsely accusing men who broke up with her and that biting was part of her sexual repertoire. Albert pleaded guilty to misdemeanor assault (Sandomir, 1997).

Most Sexual Assaults Are Not Reported

One factor that still weights the scales in favor of perpetrators is the reluctance of victims of sexual assaults to report those crimes. Only 20–28 percent of all rapes and sexual assaults are reported to law enforcement officials, compared with 61 percent of robberies (Resnick et al., 2000; U.S. Department of Justice, 2000b). The most common reason cited by victims for reporting an assault is the desire to protect themselves from future assaults by the same perpetrator. The most common reason cited by victims for *not* reporting an assault is that the event was a "personal matter" (Greenfeld, 1997).

The actual reasons for victims' failure to report sexual assaults are probably complex, but may include the following:

- They may not perceive that a crime took place—especially in the context of date rape.
- They may feel that they are partly to blame for the assault if, for example, they voluntarily engaged in fondling before the assault occurred.
- They may be afraid of retribution if they do report the crime.
- They may be afraid of public humiliation or of the trauma of testifying at a trial.

- They may fear that reporting the assault will not lead to a conviction, or that a conviction will not provide them with any practical or emotional restitution.
- If the perpetrator is a partner, they may not want to endanger a relationship that they view as offering important emotional or economic support to themselves or their children.

Most rape prevention organizations encourage a woman (or man) who has been sexually assaulted to report the crime. They believe that doing so can help the victim regain a sense of control and can reduce the likelihood that the perpetrator will offend again. They also acknowledge, however, that this is a deeply personal decision that only victims can make for themselves.

Rape Can Have Severe Ill Effects on the Victim

There are many steps women can take to reduce the likelihood that they will be raped (Box 18.3). If a woman is raped, however, there are many options and services available to help her and aid her recovery.

The first and foremost step toward recovery is getting medical attention. The best place for this is an emergency room or a specialized forensic clinic, where the staff are trained in the appropriate medical and reporting procedures (Patel & Minshall, 2001). A victim can also go to her own doctor, but that option may involve a delay, and the doctor may not have adequate expertise.

All health care providers are required to report rapes and other sexual assaults to the police, but this does not mean that the victim herself is obliged to cooperate or to press charges. In many communities, a woman can have a full forensic (evidence-collecting) examination and still not press charges. Thus she can keep her options open until she is sure whether or not she wants to pursue the matter legally. The desire not to report the crime should not prevent a woman from getting medical attention.

Providers who examine rape victims must assess and treat the physical and psychological injuries that they have sustained (Linden, 1999; McConkey et al., 2001). Careful assessment is important because there may be injuries of which the victim is unaware—particularly if, as is likely, she is in a state of emotional shock. Physical injuries are most commonly found on the face and neck and in the genital region. Genital injury is particularly common among older rape victims: in one large-scale German study, female victims of sexual assault who were older than 55 were at least five times more likely to suffer genital injuries than were women under 35 (Kindermann et al., 1996).

The provider can assess the likelihood of pregnancy or disease transmission and suggest steps to prevent either eventuality. You will recall from Chapter 11 that oral contraceptives can be used within 72 hours after coitus to reduce the likelihood of pregnancy. Prophylaxis against STDs may include antibiotics and, if there seems to be a substantial risk of HIV transmission, a short course of antiretroviral medications (Bamberger et al., 1999).

The effect of rape is likely to extend far beyond the immediate shock or any physical injury that the victim may sustain (Resnick et al., 1997). Rape is the denial of a person's autonomy in the most intimate aspect of their life. Different people react to the immediate experience of rape in different ways—some with an emotional outpouring, some with tightly controlled feelings—but all are at risk of developing a collection of long-term symptoms akin to the **post-traumatic stress disorder** experienced by survivors of other horrific events. In the context of rape or attempted rape, these symptoms have been called **rape trauma syndrome** (Burgess & Holmstrom, 1974). These symptoms may include feelings of numbness or disconnection, alternating with flashbacks and preoccupation with the rape; anxiety, depression, or anger; sleeplessness, inability to concentrate, and physical symptoms such as headaches and digestive disturbances. In the first 2 weeks after being raped, 94 percent of women have symptoms of rape trauma syndrome, and 46 percent still do at 3 months after the event. Even several years later, women who have been raped are at increased risk of depression, anxiety, and substance dependency. The long-term ill effects are particularly severe for persons who were raped at a young age and for those belonging to ethnic groups in which rape victims are highly stigmatized.

Box 18.3 | *Sexual Health*

Reducing the Risk of Rape

Rape and sexual assault are never the fault of the victim. Nevertheless, there are precautions that you can take to reduce the risk of being raped. Rape crisis centers and rape prevention organizations offer the following advice:

General:
- A man who has sexual contact with you against your will is committing a serious crime, no matter what his relationship to you and no matter what the circumstances. By reporting the crime you can help prevent someone else becoming a victim.
- Prepare yourself for "fight or flight:" take self-defense and fitness classes.

Preventing acquaintance rape:
- Until you know a man well, meet him in a group environment where there are other women present, or in a public place.

- Pay for some of the expenses of the date, so that he can't self-justify an assault on the grounds that you "owe him something."
- Avoid drugs and excessive alcohol use, and take the man's use of either, or his attempts to persuade you to use them, as a warning sign. Don't leave your beverage unattended or accept a drink from an opened container that could have been spiked.
- Be explicit if you don't want to have intercourse (or any kind of sex), especially if you are heading for his or your home. Be assertive, not coy. Don't let the man self-justify an assault on the grounds that you "led him on."
  - If the man commences an assault, protest vehemently, threaten to call the police, escape from the situation if possible, use physical force if necessary, or create a loud disturbance.

Preventing stranger rape:
- Make your home secure. Do not open the door to strangers. If you are a woman living alone, do not make that fact obvious.
- Keep your car doors locked whether you are inside or out of the car. Park where it will be safe for you to return—think about what the enviroment will be like after dark. Avoid deserted or ill-lit places. Jog with friends or at times and places where other people jog.

- Never hitchhike or pick up hitchhikers.
- If you find yourself in a threatening situation, run away. If that's not possible, resist forcefully. Fighting or creating a loud disturbance is more effective than pleading or offering no resistance.
- Carry an alarm device such as an air horn. If you carry any kind of weapon, be sure you know how to use it, and what the law is. Generally, a person who is in imminent danger of rape may inflict whatever injury is necessary to prevent it, but no more than that, and only if other means of prevention (such as escape) are not available.

If you become a victim of a sexual assault:
- Whether or not there was a completed rape, call the police or go to an emergency room immediately. Or call 1–800–656-HOPE.
- Do not shower, wash, douche, change your clothes, urinate, eat, drink, or clean up the location of the assault before you go—you may be destroying evidence. Take spare clothes with you.
- If the assailant was a stranger, try to remember his appearance and clothes and any details such as a car license plate number.
- Even if you do not report the assault right after it happens, do so later. The passage of time does not make the crime any less serious.
- Consider contacting a rape crisis center, where you can get expert advice and understanding in a confidential environment. Seeking help is the best way to head off long-lasting trauma.

Not surprisingly, rape trauma syndrome can be marked by severe sexual problems. In one follow-up study of 81 female rape victims, 40 percent of the women said that they did not engage in any sexual contacts for several months after the rape, and almost 75 percent of the women said their frequency of sexual activity was still reduced when they were interviewed 4–6 years after the rape (Burgess & Holmstrom, 1979). The reasons given for the low sexual activity included a loss of interest in sex, difficulty with arousal, painful intercourse, vaginismus, and difficulty experiencing orgasm. Male rape victims have been less intensively studied, but they appear to suffer psychological effects comparable to those reported by women (Groth & Burgess, 1980).

There are many forms of help that can facilitate a rape victim's psychological recovery. Partners, family, and friends can offer practical and emotional support (offering a place to stay, being willing to listen in a loving and nonjudgmental fashion, emphasizing that the rape was not the victim's fault). Counseling or group therapy, which can often be arranged through a **rape crisis center,** may help head off long-term ill effects. Therapy focuses on countering the isolation, self-blame, and disrupted sense of control that rape victims commonly suffer (Regehr et al., 1999), as well as treating any sexual dysfunctions.

For rape victims who do develop long-term psychological symptoms, **exposure therapy** may be more useful than regular counseling (Foa et al., 1991; Foa & Street, 2001). Exposure therapy is a form of cognitive–behavioral therapy in which the person recalls or relives the traumatic event in a controlled, safe environment, usually in combination with relaxation techniques such as breathing exercises.

It's useful to bear two points in mind: First, recovery from rape, as from other traumatic events, does not occur overnight, whatever therapeutic measures are undertaken. On the other hand, most persons who have experienced rape or sexual assault are eventually able to recover, think of themselves as survivors rather than victims, and get on with their lives.

An acquaintance rape–prevention workshop at Hobart College, New York.

Most College Rapes Are Date Rapes

In a 1987 study led by Mary Koss, a professor of public health at the University of Arizona, 28 percent of college women reported at least one sexual experience since the age of 14 that met the legal definition of rape or attempted rape. In addition, 8 percent of college men admitted having engaged in behavior that met the definition of rape (Koss et al., 1987). Not all these events occurred during college years, let alone on a college campus. Still, rapes and sexual assaults at colleges are common. While stranger rape can and does occur on campuses, the majority of these crimes are acquaintance or date rapes. In fact, it was Koss's study that familiarized the public with the term **date rape**.

College Date Rapes Are Common But Underreported

During the latter part of the 1997 school year, a research group led by Bonnie Fisher of the University of Cincinnati (and funded by the U.S. Department of Justice) carried out a large-scale study of college rape. They interviewed a random sample of over 4000 college women about potential rapes or sexual assaults they had experienced during that school year (Fisher et al., 2000). The researchers found that 1.7 percent of the women had experienced a completed rape and 1.1 percent had experienced an attempted rape. (In this survey, "rape" referred to penetration of the vagina or anus by the penis, a finger, or an object, as well as fellatio or cunnilingus, using force or the threat of force. This is a broader definition of rape than those used in some state laws.)

These figures, which covered a portion of a single school year, may not seem particularly high, but they translated into a 20–25 percent risk that a female student would experience an attempted or completed rape during a typical 5-year college career. The survey data also suggested that a college campus with 10,000 female students would see at least 350 attempted or completed rapes per year.

Most of the rapes in the survey occurred after 6:00 P.M. in residences—most commonly the victim's own residence. Most of the victims knew the perpetrator, who was usually a classmate, friend, ex-boyfriend, or acquaintance. About 20 percent of the rapes involved additional injuries, such as bruises and cuts.

About half of the victims who described incidents that the survey categorized as completed rapes did not themselves consider those incidents to be rapes. The reasons for this are unclear. These women may have believed that to be called rape, an encounter must involve coitus or must be accomplished by actual force, rather than by the threat of force. To some critics of this and similar studies, the fact that so many "rape" victims do not categorize the reported incidents as rape suggests that unrealistic criteria are being used to categorize the incidents (Gilbert, 1997). Still, whatever the acts are called, they are clearly serious crimes.

Colleges have become very conscious of the problem of campus rape. Many have introduced policies that are more restrictive than state laws. Most have their own reporting, treatment, and counseling services. At the same time, colleges have to ensure fair treatment for students accused of sexual assaults. The need for balance can create serious difficulties, especially when the case reduces to a "he says/she says" situation. Even in a case in which the entire incident is captured on videotape (Box 18.4), there can be room for differences of opinion about what happened.

An important question is whether students accused of sexual assaults should be dealt with by college disciplinary procedures—in which case suspension or expulsion is the most severe punishment they are likely to experience—or whether they should be turned over to law enforcement officials and processed through the regular judicial system. The National Organization for Women takes the view that colleges are too protective of men accused of sexual assault and rarely fulfill their legal obligation to report criminal offenders to law enforcement (National Organization for Women, 1999).

The Number One "Date Rape Drug" Is Alcohol

In recent years, a lot of media attention has been paid to the use of drugs to facilitate rape. The drug that has received the most attention is **flunitrazepam,** or **Rohypnol** ("roofies"), a benzodiazepine or Valium-type drug (Figure 18.3). Flunitrazepam is not legally available in the United States—it was banned in 1996 on account of its reputation as a date-rape drug—but it is smuggled in from overseas. There have been increasing reports of the use of flunitrazepam to induce stupor in rape victims. The drug may also impair the victim's memory of the event. Another drug that has been used to facilitate rape is **gamma-hydroxybutyrate (GHB)** (Nicholson & Balster, 2001). GHB is a central nervous system depressant that can be lethal when consumed in combination with alcohol or other depressants. Reports indicate that both drugs are given to women surreptitiously, usually by placing them in a drink.

To assess the actual prevalence of the use of Rohypnol in rape, toxicologists analyzed over 1000 urine samples from rape victims who were suspected of being under the influ-

Box 18.4 *Society, Values, and the Law*

Was It Rape?

One of the most notorious and controversial of all campus rapes—if it was a rape—occurred at the Delta Chi fraternity house at the University of Florida at Gainesville during the night of February 26–27, 1999. Two strippers were hired to perform at a fraternity-house party. After the performance, the women left, but one of them, Lisa Gier King, returned to the frat house. A long sequence of sex acts ensued, many of them between King and house member Mike Yahraus. While other fraternity brothers videotaped the proceedings or chanted "We're going to rape a white trash whore," Yarhaus held King's legs apart and penetrated her, ignor-

ing her pleas to "Stop, stop, stop." On the other hand, King also made many remarks that seemed to encourage the action or to express her enjoyment, and she did not make any obvious attempt to escape. Everyone involved, including Yahraus and King, had been drinking heavily.

The next morning, King ran half-naked to another fraternity house. She was taken to a hospital on a stretcher. Yahraus was arrested, but when the police saw the videotape, they dropped the charges, and instead charged King with prostitution and with filing a false police report. These charges were also eventually dropped, but

King pleaded guilty to operating an escort service without a license.

For several months, the National Organization for Women's University of Florida chapter held a weekly protest at the office of the state attorney who handled the case. N.O.W. also organized a petition demanding an inquiry. A documentary film about the incident and its aftermath, titled *Raw Deal*, was shown at the 2001 Sundance film festival (Corben, 2001). The film included extensive excerpts from the videotape of the incident, yet many viewers of the film were left undecided as to whether it portrayed rape or consensual sex.

Figure 18.3 Flunitrazepam (Rohypnol) (A) is called the "date rape drug" but alcohol has better claim to this title, considering how commonly its use is associated with rape—a fact recognized by this poster (B) created by the Los Angeles District Attorney's Office as part of a public awareness campaign to prevent alcohol and other drug-related rapes. (A courtesy of the Orange County Sheriff's Office; B courtesy of the Los Angeles County District Attorney's Office.)

(A)
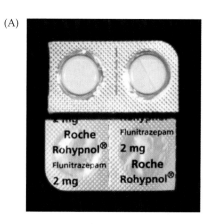

(B)

ence of illicit drugs (ElSohly & Salamone, 1999). Eight percent of these samples did contain benzodiazepines—mostly not flunitrazepam. However, *38 percent* of the samples contained **alcohol.** Of course, merely identifying the presence of these substances in the victim's system says little about how they got there or the role they played in the rape. Evidently, alcohol is still far and away the date rape drug of choice. (We should mention that this study was partially funded by the Hoffman-LaRoche pharmaceutical company—the manufacturer of flunitrazepam.)

Alcohol may cloud a woman's judgment about prudent behavior or about how to extricate herself from a dangerous situation, and it may make her physically incapable of resisting just as effectively as any street drug. Alcohol also promotes rape when consumed by the rapist—by reducing his inhibitions. In one survey of college women, two-thirds of the women who had experienced a sexual assault said that the perpetrator was drinking at the time of the attack (Frintner & Rubinson, 1993). All in all, alcohol is probably the number one "date rape drug," whether consumed by the rapist or his victim.

Who Commits Rape?

A great deal of attention has been focused on men who commit rape. The hope is that the identification of personality traits, childhood experiences, or other factors that may induce some men to rape could lead to the development of more effective strategies for rape prevention.

Rapists Are Ordinary Men

A great deal of research has been devoted to understanding what kinds of men commit rape. There may be some extremely violent rapists who have severe personality disorders or, as suggested earlier, are driven by sadistic impulses. But the majority of rapists, especially those who commit acquaintance or date rape, are fairly unremarkable people. Rapists tend to have a **narcissistic,** or self-centered, personality, but this is true of most serious criminal offenders, so it does not by itself account for a proclivity to rape (Chantry & Craig, 1994).

Indeed, an inclination to rape seems to be very common. In one survey of male college students by Neil Malamuth of UCLA, 37 percent of the men said that there was some likelihood that they would commit rape if they knew that they wouldn't be caught (Malamuth,

1981). One in 12 men admitted to actually having committed acts that would meet the legal definition of rape, although most of these men denied that their acts constituted rape. In another study, 43 percent of college-aged men admitted to having used some kind of coercion, such as ignoring a woman's protests, to have sex (Rapaport & Posey, 1991). With these kinds of numbers, we obviously shouldn't expect men who commit sexual assaults to have rare personality disorders or highly unusual personal histories.

Still, there are some factors that may be associated with an inclination to rape. Malamuth and his colleagues have done extensive studies of male college students to address this issue. They reported that male college students who grew up in a violent home environment, who were abused as children, who became involved in juvenile delinquency, and who had large numbers of sex partners, were interested in impersonal sex, or had dominating or hostile attitudes toward women expressed a greater willingness to engage in coercive sex than did other men. Over a 10-year follow-up period, such men were more likely than other men to engage in aggressive sexual or nonsexual behavior toward women (Malamuth et al., 1995). The researchers also found, however, that men who were capable of empathy were less likely to be aggressive toward women, even when all other factors predisposed them to be so (Dean & Malamuth, 1997).

Malamuth performed one study that directly tested male college students' willingness to hurt women (Malamuth, 1983). In the first part of the study, the men's penile responses to stories of coercive and noncoercive sex were measured, and they were also asked to fill out questionnaires that assessed their agreement or disagreement with statements such as "women actually enjoy being forced to have sex." Then, in the second part of the study, which the students thought was completely unrelated to the earlier tests, they were given the opportunity to "punish" a woman who deliberately annoyed them. This they did by bombarding her with noise whose loudness they were able to control. (The woman was not really exposed to the noise, but the men believed that she was.) Malamuth found that the men who had positive penile responses to coercive sex and who expressed dominating or hostile attitudes toward women delivered more severe punishments to the woman who annoyed them. These findings suggest that men with certain personalities or attitudes—especially "macho" traits or hostility toward women—are in fact more likely to perpetrate violence against women, at least in a nonsexual laboratory situation.

What Happens to Men Who Rape?

Since the majority of rapes are not reported to law enforcement officials, we can assume that the majority of rapists go unpunished. Nevertheless, about 35,000 adults or juveniles are arrested for forcible rape each year (Greenfeld, 1997).

Some rape reports, of course, are judged by law enforcement officials to be unfounded or malicious. In the data analyzed by Greenfeld, these constituted 8 percent of the total. In one study by Eugene Kanin of Purdue University, no fewer than 41 percent of all the reports of completed rape in a small Midwestern city were eventually retracted by the alleged victim (Kanin, 1994). The fact that the allegations were retracted does not necessarily mean that they were false, of course: victims may be motivated to retract true allegations for the same reasons that most victims do not file reports in the first place. But women can also fabricate accusations: according to Kanin, they may be motivated to do so by a desire for revenge, by a wish for sympathy or attention, or to justify some action taken by the accuser. We must always keep in mind the possibility that a man accused of rape has been accused falsely.

Only about 48 percent of men arrested for rape are released on bail—a lower fraction than for any other charge except murder. Of all persons accused of rape, 80 percent face a felony prosecution. About half of all men arrested for rape are convicted (usually of felony rape)—most after a guilty plea. Over two-thirds of convicted defendants received a prison sentence; the average term was 14 years. Another 19 percent of convicted defendants were sentenced to terms in local jails, and 13 percent were placed on probation.

Convicted rapists typically serve about half of their prison terms before release. At any one time, about 230,000 Americans are in prison for rape or sexual assault. Incarcerated rapists differ in some respects from persons incarcerated for other violent offenses (Table 18.1). They are much more likely to be male, to have experienced physical or sexual abuse

	Persons incarcerated for rape	Persons incarcerated for all (or all other) violent offenses
TABLE 18.1 *Characteristics of persons incarcerated for rape and for all (or all other) violent offenses*		
Male (%)	99.6	96.2
White (%)	52.2	48.1
Average age at arrest	31	29
Married (%)	22.1	17.1
Percentage who report being abused during childhood	19	12
Percentage whose victim was female	94.5	44.2
Median age of victim	22	29
Percentage who used a weapon	16.6	45.7
Recidivism (percentage rearrested for any crime within 3 years of release)	52	60

Source: Greenfeld, 1997.

during childhood, to have had a female victim, and to have committed the crime without the use of a weapon. They are slightly older than other offenders, and their victims were younger than victims of other crimes. They were somewhat less likely than other offenders to reoffend after release.

Early Intervention Programs Are of Uncertain Value

We mentioned earlier that the peak age for the sexual victimization of females is 16–19. Thus, many women experience sexual assaults and rapes while they are still in high school. One survey of female students in the ninth through twelfth grades in Massachusetts found that about 10 percent of them had been sexually assaulted at least once by a dating partner (Silverman et al., 2001). The girls who said they had been sexually assaulted exhibited a range of unhealthy behaviors, including substance abuse, unhealthy weight control habits, pregnancy, and suicidality. That is not to say that the sexual assaults necessarily led to those negative consequences; in part, the heightened risk of assault and the unhealthy behaviors may have been different aspects of the same disadvantageous rearing environment.

Given that sexual violence begins early, considerable efforts have been made to develop rape prevention programs aimed at adolescents who are beginning to date. A team led by Vangie Foshee of the University of North Carolina tested the effectiveness of one such program, which they called the Safe Dates Project (Foshee et al., 1996, 1998, 2000). Fourteen schools in a rural, mostly white North Carolina county were randomly assigned to offer the program or not. In the schools that offered the program, eighth- and ninth-grade students were exposed to a ten-session curriculum, a play, and a poster contest. These activities focused on changing norms for dating violence and gender stereotyping, as well as improving conflict management skills and awareness of services. The program also had a community element, involving a crisis line, training of counselors, and a support group.

When students were surveyed a month after completing the program, the results seemed quite promising: the students in the schools where the program had been offered were less likely either to suffer or to inflict violence or psychological abuse in a dating context than were students in the control schools. In 12 months, however, these behavioral differences between the two groups of students had evaporated, although there was still an improved awareness of conflict resolution techniques and of the availability of community services among the students who took the program. Follow-up "booster programs" failed to help students maintain their improvements: students who took a "booster program" 2 years after the initial program did not preserve or recover their initial behavioral benefits (Foshee, 2001).

Evolutionary psychologists Randy Thornhill and Craig Palmer believe that programs of this kind are unlikely to be effective because they make unrealistic assumptions—especially the assumption that sexual coercion by men is the product of gender socialization and is not sexually motivated. They advocate what they consider to be a more realistic educational program: one that would acknowledge men's predisposition to sexual violence and would emphasize the need to control their urges in order to avoid harming other persons or bringing severe punishments on themselves (Thornhill & Palmer, 2000).

Sexual Harassment Occurs in Many Environments

Sexual harassment is unwelcome sexual behavior in the workplace or in other structured environments. Such behavior has probably been going on for as long as organized human societies have existed, but its scale was limited until women began working in factories in the early nineteenth century. This development offered a double incentive for sexual harassment of female workers by men: sexual attraction and resentment against women's invasion of a traditionally male workplace (Jones, 1996). This mix of motives is still operating today.

The concept of sexual harassment did not really come to the attention of the American public until the mid-1970s, when the term began to be widely used by women's rights activists. Two of these activists, Lin Farley and Catherine MacKinnon, published influential books on the topic in the late 1970s (Farley, 1978; MacKinnon, 1979). Farley represented sexual harassment as a tool used by men to control women, just as Susan Brownmiller had done for rape a few years earlier (see above). MacKinnon, a law professor, attempted to convince the legal community that sexual harassment constitutes illegal sex discrimination. She was successful in this aim: In 1980, the U.S. Equal Employment Opportunity Commission (EEOC) declared that sexual harassment in the workplace is a form of sex discrimination that violates the 1964 Civil Rights Act.

The EEOC defines sexual harassment as follows:

> Unwelcome sexual advances, requests for sexual favors, and other verbal or physical conduct of a sexual nature constitutes sexual harassment when submission to or rejection of this conduct explicitly or implicitly affects an individual's employment, unreasonably interferes with an individual's work performance or creates an intimidating, hostile or offensive work environment.

It is ironic that the man who led the EEOC from 1982 to 1990, Clarence Thomas, was himself later accused of sexual harassment (Box 18.5).

Very similar problems can arise in faculty–student relationships at colleges and between doctors, therapists, lawyers, ministers, and other professionals and their patients or clients. Unwelcome sexual behavior in these environments is not always illegal, but it is widely prohibited by college administrations, professional governing bodies, and the like.

There Are Two Kinds of Workplace Sexual Harassment

Sexual harassment in the workplace takes two different forms. The first involves an explicit or implicit "deal": "If you go out with me, I'll see that you get a merit raise," or "If you don't have sex with me, you can kiss your job goodbye." This kind of sexual harassment is called **quid pro quo** ("what for what?") harassment. It is generally considered the more reprehensible kind: if the facts are not in dispute, there can be little doubt about its illegal and damaging nature.

The second kind of sexual harassment, called **hostile-environment** harassment, involves a pattern of unwelcome sexual attention that simply makes life difficult for the

Box 18.5   *Sex in History*

He Says, She Says: The Clarence Thomas Hearings

In 1991, U.S. Supreme Court Justice Thurgood Marshall announced his intention to retire, and President George Bush nominated Judge Clarence Thomas as his replacement. Thomas, like Marshall, was black, but ideologically he was far to the right of Marshall. Thomas's appointment was opposed by many organizations, including the NAACP, who feared he would help roll back affirmative action and other liberal programs.

The U.S. Senate held its confirmation hearings later that year. The hearings became a media circus when Anita Hill, a law professor at the University of Oklahoma, charged that Thomas had sexually harassed her when she worked as his assistant at the Department of Education as well as subsequently when he was chairman of the Equal Employment Opportunity Commission. According to Hill, Thomas had requested dates with her, and after she refused, he harassed her with mentions of sexual topics, including pornographic movies. He repeatedly mentioned that his penis was unusually large and that it gave great pleasure to women who performed oral sex on him. "One of the oddest episodes I remember," said Hill, "was an occasion in which Thomas was drinking a Coke in his office. He got up from the table

at which we were working, went over to his desk to get the Coke, and asked, 'Who has put pubic hair on my Coke?'" Hill said that the harassment caused her physical and emotional suffering and eventually caused her to leave her job. Thomas denied all of Hill's charges, which he considered politically motivated. "A high-tech lynching for uppity blacks" was his memorable description of the proceedings.

The Senate, which at the time included only two women, voted 52–48 to confirm Thomas's appointment. This result could be seen as a defeat for people concerned about sexual harassment. From a wider perspective, however, the Clarence Thomas hearings probably helped aided their cause by focusing public attention on the issue. Between 1991 and 1996, filings with the EEOC increased from about 6000 to about 14,000 per year, and total awards to victims increased from about $8 million to about $28 million. The number of filings has remained level since then, but the total awards to victims have risen to about $55 million by 2000 (U.S. Equal Employment Opportunity Commission, 2001).

Although the U.S. Senate was narrowly divided in its vote on Clarence Thomas, it took unanimous action 3 years later when it censured one of its own members, Senator

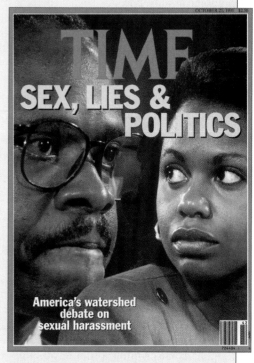

Bob Packwood of Oregon, for sexually harassing female employees and campaign workers. Packwood resigned the day after the vote.

A woman often experiences touching by a man to be unwelcome sexual contact, but the man may be unaware of this unless the woman tells him.

victim. This kind of harassment causes a great deal of suffering, but it is not so easy to characterize and document. For one thing, it depends on the victim's reactions to the perpetrator's actions. Men are less likely to be upset by sexual advances from women than women are by advances from men. Even among women, some will feel more harmed than others. Also, in many cases, it's not obvious how effectively the victim communicated the unwelcomeness of the behavior to the harasser. Thus, it's not always easy to draw the line between acceptable social behavior and sexual harassment. It is hostile-environment cases that have aroused the most criticism from conservatives, including conservative women's groups.

Hostile-environment harassment cases often involve free speech issues. In one important case adjudicated in 1991, a female welder, Lois Robinson, brought an action against her employer, Jacksonville Shipyards, saying that male workers had harassed her by posting nude pinups around the workplace and making sexually suggestive remarks. The shipyard argued that firing the men would constitute an infringement of their First Amendment right to free speech. The court ruled that when an employee's exercise of free speech undermines workplace morale, an employer may fire them without infringing on their right to free speech.

The free speech defense has fared much better on college campuses, partly because they may not count as workplaces if the alleged harassment occurs among students or between students and faculty. In a 1994 case, University of New Hampshire professor Donald Silva got himself into trouble during a technical writing class. In attempting to explain the meaning of the word "simile," Silva quoted the words of belly dancer Little Egypt: "Belly dancing is like Jello on a plate with a vibrator under the plate." Seven women in the class complained of sexual harassment, and Silva was ordered to apologize and undergo counseling. He refused and sued the school, whereupon the school suspended him without pay. Two years later, a federal court ordered Silva reinstated, saying that the school had violated his First Amendment rights by punishing him (Honan, 1994). The school had to pay Silva substantial damages. Thus, in establishing sexual harassment policies, colleges must tread a delicate path between preventing sexual abuses and infringing on free speech.

Sexual Harassment Begins Early

Sexual harassment begins as soon as children enter puberty—if not before. In one national survey of students at 79 public schools, 83 percent of the girls and 60 percent of the boys reported receiving unwanted sexual attention of some kind (American Association of University Women, 1993) (Table 18.2).

It is possible that many sexually colored incidents in schools are of no great significance. A school in Lexington, North Carolina, for example, earned national ridicule in 1996 when it suspended a 6-year-old boy for kissing a female classmate (Nossiter, 1996). But sexual harassment in school can be persistent and traumatic, as was made clear by the 4000 letters received by *Seventeen* magazine in response to an article and poll on the subject (Stein, 1999). Here is one typical letter, from a 12-year-old Mexican-American student in Michigan:

> In my case there were 2 or 3 boys touching me, and trust me they were big boys. And I'd tell them to stop but they wouldn't. This went on for about 6 months until finally I was in one of my classes in the back of the room minding my own business when all of them came back and backed me into a corner and start-

Sexual harassment starts early: The majority of both girls and boys report receiving unwanted sexual attention in school.

TABLE 18.2	**Types of sexual harassment experienced in school by boys and girls in grades 8–11**	
	Boys (%)	**Girls (%)**
Sexual comments, jokes, gestures, or looks	56	76
Touched, grabbed, or pinched in a sexual way	42	65
Intentionally brushed up against in a sexual way	36	57
Flashed or mooned	41	49
Had sexual rumors spread about them	34	42
Had clothing pulled at in a sexual manner	28	38
Shown, given, or left sexual messages or pictures	34	31
Forced to kiss someone	14	23
Called gay or lesbian	23	10

Source: American Association of University Women, 1993.

ed touching me all over. So I went running out of the room and the teacher yelled at me and I had to stay in my seat for the rest of the class.

A common theme of the letters, as in this one, was the lack of concern shown by teachers and school officials: often, the girls felt that they were treated as offenders rather than victims.

Schools are beginning to take sexual harassment more seriously, partly as a result of successful legal actions by students who have been harassed. LaShonda Davis, a fifth-grade student in Forsythe, Georgia, was sexually taunted for months by a male classmate, but the school authorities failed to stop the abuse. LaShonda's mother sued the school board, and the case went all the way to the U.S. Supreme Court. In 1999 the court ruled in her favor, stating that federally funded schools that are willfully indifferent to student-on-student sexual harassment can be held liable.

Students who are lesbian, gay, bisexual, or transgendered, or who are perceived to be so, are at particular risk of sexual harassment, often accompanied by violence (see Chapter 13). One gay high school student, Jamie Nabozny of Ashland, Wisconsin, was subjected to simulated rape as well as to being urinated on and verbally and physically assaulted. School authorities allegedly told him that he was to blame because he was openly gay. The abuse went on for 4 years until he dropped out of school. Nabozny sued for violation of his right to equal protection, and the school district eventually paid him $962,000 in an out-of-court settlement (Stein, 1999).

The Prevalence of Sexual Harassment Varies among Different Occupations

The prevalence of sexual harassment in adulthood is difficult to assess, but it is certainly common. It is probably most prevalent in traditionally male occupations or occupations in which women form a minority. The U.S. armed forces are a case in point. According to a 1995 Pentagon survey, 78 percent of women on active duty, as well as 38 percent of men, had experienced some form of sexual harassment from military personnel or civilian employees during the previous year (U.S. Department of Defense, 1995).

The most notorious incident of sexual harassment involving the U.S. armed forces took place at the 1991 Tailhook convention. This Navy-sponsored annual convention of aviators, held in Las Vegas, was traditionally marked by drinking competitions and general debauchery. During the 1991 convention, intoxicated men formed a gauntlet through which women (including naval officers as well as women who just happened to be in the hotel) were forced to pass, being groped, stripped, assaulted, molested, or verbally abused as they did so. There was a concerted effort by high-ranking officers to cover up the resulting scandal, and two admirals were eventually forced to resign. There can be little doubt that resentment of women's increasing role in the armed forces was a factor in the Tailhook incident and its aftermath: the (male) officer who headed the Navy's inquiry into the incident is said to have told the (female) Assistant Secretary of the Navy that "a lot of female Navy pilots are go-go dancers, topless dancers, or hookers" (Healy & Reza, 1992).

What about the U.S. workplace in general? In a 1994 Louis Harris poll, 32 percent of working women and 7 percent of working men said that they had been sexually harassed at work (Louis Harris Poll, 1994) (Figure 18.4). The women were all harassed by men, the men about equally by men and by women. In 7 of 10 cases, the harasser was a supervisor or other senior employee.

Sexual Harassment Harms Its Victims

The effect of sexual harassment is considerable (Pryor & McKinney, 1995). People who are harassed are likely to feel humiliated, alienated, and vulnerable. They are likely to feel trapped if they have to deal with their harasser on a daily basis. They may experience a variety of psychological and psychosomatic problems, and significant numbers of them quit their jobs. The majority of women who are sexually harassed do not file a complaint, fearing that they will be ignored, ridiculed, denied promotion, or fired if they

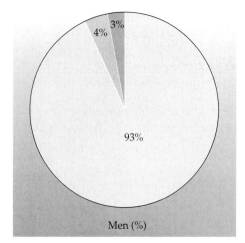

Men (%)

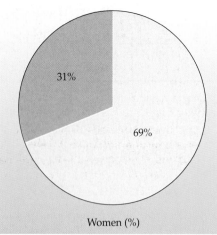

Women (%)

■ Harassed by men
■ Harassed by women
□ Not harassed

Figure 18.4 Who is harassed by whom? (Data from Louis Harris Poll, 1994.)

do. Sexual harassment also reduces productivity, and it costs employers considerable amounts of money in claim settlements or insurance premiums.

Nearly 1 in 4 female college students have avoided classes or dropped courses on account of sexual harassment (Paludi, 1996). In one study, more than 1 in 4 male college professors admitted to having initiated a sexual relationship with a student, but almost none of them believed that they had done anything wrong. (At many colleges, such behavior is permissible so long as the student has no academic relationship with the professor and does not feel harassed by his approaches.)

Victims of Sexual Harassment Can Take Steps to End It

Many organizations, such as the AFL-CIO, the National Partnership for Women and Families, and the Feminist Majority have formulated recommendations for dealing with sexual harassment:

- Know your rights. Consult your organization's written policies concerning sexual harassment.
- Tell your harasser that they are harassing you. Recount what they are doing, explain how it affects you, and demand that they stop. Make sure your tone of voice, facial expression, and body language match the seriousness of your message. Don't accept any excuses the harasser may offer or be sidetracked by diversionary topics. If the harassment is especially severe, so that you might anticipate a violent response to your complaint, do not confront the harasser directly.
- Keep a journal documenting every incident of harassment as it happens, how it affected you, and how you responded. Keep photographs or the originals of any offensive messages or images you receive.
- Tell other people, such as trusted co-workers, about the harassment as it occurs. Ask whether others have experienced sexual harassment from the same person, whether they have witnessed the harassment that you have experienced, and whether they will support you if you take action.
- If the harasser does not stop the offensive behavior, or responds with any vindictive action, complain to your supervisor, your supervisor's boss, your union steward, your personnel department, your principal, or your student advisor, or file an official complaint via the channels established by your organization. Keep records of these actions and their results.
- If you do not get satisfaction through these channels, consider obtaining a lawyer and filing a complaint with the EEOC, your state's Fair Employment Practice agency, or the U.S. Department of Education's Office of Civil Rights. Such complaints must be filed within a certain deadline (within 6 months of the last incident of harassment, in the case of EEOC). These agencies may help you settle the case, or they may give you a "right-to-sue" letter that will facilitate a private lawsuit. If criminal behavior such as sexual assault is involved, you should go directly to the police.

There Are Three Kinds of Stalkers

If rape is the dark side of sex, then **stalking** is the dark side of love. A stalker is emotionally obsessed with a particular victim, and that obsession usually has, or once had, a romantic element. Stalkers put their victims in fear by repeatedly following them, harassing them, lying in wait for them, making phone calls or sending messages to them, vandalizing their property, and the like. Stalking via the Internet (**cyberstalking**) is an increasing problem (U.S. Department of Justice, 1999a).

According to data from the National Violence Against Women (NVAW) survey (Tjaden & Thoennes, 1998), 8 percent of women and 2 percent of men have been put in fear by

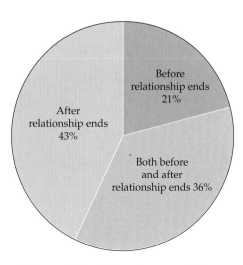

Figure 18.5 When does stalking occur? The graph shows the timing of stalking of women by intimate partners. (Data from Tjaden and Thoennes, 1998.)

a stalker at some time in their lives: about 1 million women and 370,000 men are stalked annually. Eighty-seven percent of stalkers are male, and 78 percent of stalking victims are female. About half of all victims are between 18 and 29 years old.

There are three distinct kinds of stalking. The most common is **intimate partner stalking,** in which the victim is stalked by a current or former spouse, cohabitational partner, boyfriend, girlfriend, or date. Fifty-nine percent of female stalking victims, and 30 percent of male victims, are stalked by intimate partners. It is often assumed that intimate partner stalkers do their stalking after the relationship has broken up, but in actuality, stalking can take place while a relationship is still intact (Tjaden & Thoennes, 1998) (Figure 18.5). Intimate partner stalkers often show a controlling or suspicious attitude toward the victim even before the stalking behavior begins. Anger is a major motivational factor in intimate partner stalking. These stalkers often have a prior psychiatric, criminal, or substance abuse history (Meloy et al., 2000).

According to Brian Spitzberg (of San Diego State University) and William Cupach (of Illinois State University), intimate partner stalking is an extreme example of a common behavior pattern that they call **obsessive relational intrusion** (Cupach & Spitzberg, 1998). A rejected lover will frequently make attempts to continue a relationship, perhaps in an attempt to see whether the rejection is wholehearted or not. Most women and men have experienced this kind of unwanted attention at some time or another, as described in Chapter 9. Certain personality traits in the pursuer, such as a tendency toward manipulativeness, coerciveness, or obsessive thinking, may help turn this behavior into persistent stalking.

In the second kind of stalking, called **delusional stalking,** the stalker has the fixed belief that the victim is in love with him, or could easily be made to fall in love with him, even though there has never been an intimate relationship between the two of them. This kind of delusional thinking is sometimes called **erotomania.** The victim may be an acquaintance—often a person in some kind of authority position or one who has given the stalker some attention, such as a teacher, doctor, or therapist. Alternatively, the victim may be a celebrity whom the stalker has never met. Being stalked is an occupational hazard in the entertainment industry. Delusional stalkers are generally socially inept persons with few intimate relationships. The less the stalker and victim actually know each other, the more likely that the stalker has a serious mental illness.

The third type of stalking is **grudge stalking,** in which the stalker pursues the victim to seek revenge for some actual or imagined injury. This kind of stalking is not usually sexual; common targets are co-workers, employers, administrators, and the like.

Being stalked is an extremely traumatic and stressful experience, and one that may go on for years. Besides having to deal with the constant harassment, the victim is often in fear that the stalking will escalate to violence—and with good reason. In the NVAW survey, 81 percent of women who were stalked by a current or former intimate partner were also physically assaulted by the stalker, and 31 percent were also sexually assaulted. Stalking can culminate in murder.

Celebrities are common victims of delusional stalkers. (A) Actress Rebecca Schaeffer (right; seen here with her television co-star Pam Dawber) was shot dead at her front door by a deranged admirer, Robert Bardo, who got her address from the Department of Motor Vehicles. (B) Talk show host David Letterman was stalked for a decade by a woman, Margaret Ray, who claimed to be his wife. Ray broke into his house and was once caught driving his Porsche. She eventually committed suicide.

(A)

(B)

Doreen Orion, a psychiatrist who was stalked for 8 years by a female client, has suggested an extensive list of precautions that should be taken by stalking victims (Orion, 1998, 2001):

- Tell the stalker "no" once and once only. Thereafter, avoid all contact.
- Keep your address and phone number private. Block your address at the Department of Motor Vehicles and Registrar of Voters. Use a post office box.
- Get a dog. Take self-defense classes. Carry a cell phone at all times. Drive to a police station if your car is being followed.
- Document all stalking incidents and keep all letters and messages received from the stalker.
- Join a stalking victims' support group.
- Consider moving if your case warrants it.
- Consider obtaining a restraining order against your stalker, but bear in mind that most stalkers violate these orders (Tjaden & Thoennes, 1998) and that the police are not going to spend time guarding you.

Stalking is illegal in all 50 states, and stalking across state lines is a federal offense. In some states, however, stalking is only a misdemeanor, in which case the penalties may be minor. Furthermore, it may not be enough just to prove that you were put in fear by the stalker: in some jurisdictions, the stalker must make "credible threats" against you in order to be convicted of a crime.

Intimate Partner Violence Is a Crime with Many Names

The terms have changed over the years—from "wife beating" to "battering" to "spousal abuse" to "domestic violence" to "**intimate partner violence.**" The ugly reality remains the same: violent acts committed within what are supposed to be loving sexual relationships.

The NCVS found that about 1 million violent crimes were committed against intimate partners in 1998, and that 85 percent of these crimes were committed against women. 0.8 percent of women and 0.1 percent of men said they had experienced intimate partner violence during the previous 12 months (Bureau of Justice Statistics, 2000). The NVAW survey came up with somewhat higher figures: 1.5 percent of women and 0.9 percent of men had experienced intimate partner violence during the previous 12 months. Lifetime rates were 25 percent for women and 8 percent for men (U.S. Department of Justice, 1998). The higher numbers in the NVAW survey probably reflect the inclusion of assaults that might not be considered crimes, such as pushing and grabbing. Of course, to the extent that victims may be unwilling to disclose domestic violence to interviewers, all these figures may be underestimates.

Of the criminal acts reported to the NCVS, the majority were simple assaults, meaning assaults that were carried out without a weapon and that caused no injury or minor injury. About 35 percent were aggravated assaults, sexual assaults, robberies, or murders (Table 18.3). About 50 percent of the crimes were reported to the police.

Intimate partner violence represents a significant part of all the violence experienced by women. In 36 percent of cases in which women go to hospital emergency rooms with injuries resulting from violence, an intimate partner was the perpetrator (Bureau of Justice Statistics, 1997). One-third of all murders of women are committed by intimate partners, compared with only 4 percent of murders of men.

Besides being female, risk factors for intimate partner violence include being black, young, divorced or separated, living in a city, and having a low income. The association with poverty is particularly marked: women living in the lowest-income households experience intimate partner violence at 7 times the rate of women in affluent households. (It is possible that this difference is exaggerated if affluent people are less willing to report violence.)

More significant than the physical injuries in most cases are the psychological effects of domestic violence: depression, suicidal thoughts and suicide attempts,

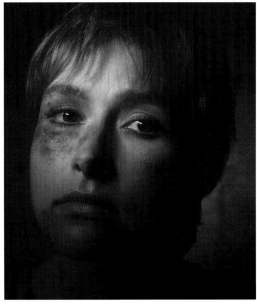

About one-third of all assaults on women are committed by their intimate partners.

TABLE 18.3	Annual rate of violent crimes against intimate partners	
	Crimes against women (per 100,000 women)	**Crimes against men (per 100,000 men)**
Simple assault[a]	498	99
Aggravated assault[b]	123	45
Robbery	89	—
Rape/sexual assault	56	—
Murder	1.2	0.5
Total	767	145

Source: Bureau of Justice Statistics, 2000. Non-lethal crimes are from the National Crime Victimization Survey; murders are from the FBI.

[a]Simple assault is assault without a weapon that results in no or minor injury.

[b]Aggravated assault is assault that causes serious injury or that involves a weapon.

lowered self-esteem, substance abuse, and post-traumatic stress disorder (National Research Council, 1996). The specific variety of post-traumatic stress disorder that occurs in these circumstances is called **battered-woman syndrome;** it is characterized by a sense of inability to escape from the situation and therefore by a cessation of attempts to do so (**learned helplessness**) (Walker, 1999).

Children are present in 43 percent of households where intimate partner violence occurs (NCVS data), and are at risk of being assaulted themselves. The violent atmosphere may profoundly affect the children's social development, increasing the likelihood that they, too, will commit intimate partner violence, abuse children, and have other behavioral problems in adolescence and adulthood (Straus, 1992).

Intimate Partner Violence Is On the Decline

The one bright side to the story is that intimate partner violence has been on the decline. Between 1975 and 1998, spousal murders dropped by 75 percent. Just between 1993 and 1998, the overall rate of intimate partner violence against women dropped by 21 percent, and most of this decline was accounted for by a drop in violence among minorities, according to NCVS data.

Among the factors most likely to have contributed to the decline are a general improvement in economic conditions, a decrease in unemployment among black men, improved awareness of domestic violence and better services for its victims, decreased use of some drugs, and an increased rate of divorce and separation. You may be puzzled by this last item, since we just mentioned that, as a group, persons who are divorced or separated are at *greater* risk of intimate partner violence than those who are not. But people who split up specifically because of domestic abuse probably reduce their risk of future abuse compared with what they would have experienced if they had stayed together. Thus the availability of separation and divorce probably contributes to the prevention of domestic violence.

Intimate Partner Violence Follows an Escalating Cycle

Domestic violence typically occurs as one phase of a three-phase cycle (Walker, 1979):

- *The tension-building phase.* In this phase, the longest of the three, the abuser may be increasingly moody, nit-picking, or sullen. He may threaten the victim or commit minor assaults or property damage. The victim may attempt to stop the progression of the cycle by trying to calm him, by avoiding confrontation, or by satisfying his demands (keeping the children quiet, having food ready on time, etc.).

- *The violent phase.* The actual violent behavior constitutes the shortest phase, typically lasting no more than a day. As many as 9 out of 10 perpetrators are under the influence of alcohol or drugs during the assault, which is often carried out in the presence of children (Brookoff et al., 1997). The victim tries to protect herself, fights back, kicks the abuser out, or flees. The victim, other family members, or neighbors may call the police, who have usually been to this address several times before.
- *The reconciliation phase.* In this phase, the perpetrator is apologetic and tries to make amends by declarations of love. He promises to cease the abusive behavior, to stop drinking, or to seek treatment. He showers the victim with gifts and attention. The victim is relieved and happy, forgives the abuser, and returns to him (or allows him back, if he has left). The victim may retract statements made to the police with the hope of stopping legal proceedings, or may lie to doctors about the cause of her injuries.

Often, the severity of the violence escalates from cycle to cycle, so that it may be more descriptive to refer to a "spiral of violence" rather than a cycle. Some relationships degenerate into a condition of nonstop violence: in a study of cases in which police were called to scenes of domestic violence, 35 percent of the victims said that they were assaulted every day (Brookoff et al., 1997).

Diverse Theories Attempt to Explain Intimate Partner Violence

Evolutionary psychology and feminist theory are in agreement that domestic violence is a method used by men to dominate and control women (Yllö & Bograd, 1988). In evolutionary psychology, the desire to assert control is seen as part of the man's evolutionary inheritance, and it serves (or once served) the function of protecting the man's paternity interests—in other words, it prevents his mate from having sex with other men (Wilson & Daly, 1992). Evolutionary psychologists see sexual jealousy (see Chapter 9) as the main motivator of intimate partner violence.

Most feminist theorists think that men batter women because boys are socialized to be perpetrators of violence and girls are socialized to be victims. This socialization may not be simply a matter of individual training within the family, but also the result of an entire social and political structure that legitimizes this form of violence and, in essence, turn a marriage license into a "license to batter" (Yllö & Bograd, 1988).

A somewhat different theory is the "cycle of violence" theory, which holds that men batter their wives because they saw their fathers battering their mothers, or were abused themselves, during their childhood. Similarly, women may end up as victims of domestic violence because they saw their mothers being beaten or because they themselves were beaten by their fathers. There could be a variety of mechanisms linking these childhood experiences with the adult behavior: it may be that the early experiences "normalize" the behavior, or that the children come to confuse loving and hateful behaviors.

A number of studies have reported a statistical link between witnessing marital violence and engaging in it (Gelles, 1976; Straus et al., 1980). It is possible, however, that this statistical link exists not because of any causal connection, but because children and their parents tend to grow up in similar circumstances and therefore are exposed to many of the same risk factors. Teasing out the various potential causal pathways is a major challenge.

Breaking up Is Hard to Do

Sympathetic outsiders who see a victim—usually a woman—sticking with her abusive mate through escalating cycles of violence often ask, "Why on earth does she stay with that no-good SOB?!" Some of the answers to this question are apparent from first-person narratives written by the victims themselves. One such narrative was published in 1986 by singer Tina Turner (Turner & Loder, 1993). Another (describing a gay male abusive relationship) was written by Olympic diver Greg Louganis (Louganis & Marcus, 1995). Information also comes from research studies (Strube & Barbour, 1983; Walker, 1999).

Victims of intimate partner violence stay with their partners because they are socially isolated, economically dependent, lack self-esteem, or believe that separation and divorce are wrong. Learned helplessness (see above) may leave victims without the will to remove themselves from the abusive situation. Victims often fear that breaking up will bring shame on them and that the perpetrator will pursue and punish them—a fear that is often well justified. Victims may also fear that their children will suffer in a breakup. Perpetrators sense and reinforce all these traits; in particular, they often keep the victim socially isolated and punish her for reaching out to any potential sources of help.

Help Is Available

Services are available to help battered women, whether or not they remain in an abusive relationship:

- Emergency room staff are trained to treat domestic violence injuries and to recognize their cause. When a victim has multiple head and neck injuries at different stages of healing, and there is no other predisposing factor, such as a neurological disorder, domestic violence is likely to be the cause.
- Law enforcement officers and lawyers can assist a domestic violence victim who decides to leave an abusive relationship by arresting the abuser or by helping the victim obtain a restraining order. In some states, such as California, prosecutors will continue domestic violence cases even when the victims retract their accusations ("no-drop policy"). Legal assistance is often available to low-income victims.
- Hotlines, battered women's shelters, women's crisis centers, and city social services can provide practical assistance for women who leave abusive relationships temporarily or permanently.
- Psychotherapists and support groups can help abused women understand the process of victimization and regain the strength and motivation to end it.

Services for male victims, and for victims of same-sex abuse, are less well developed than those for women who are abused by men. Still, most public services for abuse victims are gender-neutral, and the gay and lesbian organizations in many metropolitan areas have domestic violence services. The Los Angeles Gay and Lesbian Center, for example, provides survivors' groups, a batterers' treatment program, crisis counseling, shelter referrals, and educational programs (Los Angeles Gay and Lesbian Center, 2001).

Summary

1. One in 3 women and 1 in 33 men have experienced an attempted or completed rape. Young black women face the highest risk of rape. Two-thirds of rapes and sexual assaults are committed by persons known to the victim (acquaintances or intimate partners). The great majority of perpetrators are male.

2. Conflicting theories attempt to explain rape. Evolutionary psychologists have raised the possibility that it is a behavioral adaptation, meaning that it evolved because it increased the reproductive success of men who committed it. This theory emphasizes the sexual purpose of rape. Feminists, on the other hand, have generally discounted the idea that rape is sexually motivated, and see it as a learned behavior that men employ to dominate women.

3. The law has become increasingly protective of rape victims, but many victims of rape and sexual assault do not report the crimes, perhaps because of shame, a sense of responsibility for the assaults, or a fear of retribution.

4. Besides physical injuries, victims of sexual assaults may suffer a variety of ill effects, including post-traumatic stress disorder. These effects may be countered by counseling and survivors' groups, which help victims regain a sense of control.

5. Most rapes on college campuses are date rapes, in which the assailant is a date or boyfriend of the victim. Alcohol and drug use by either party increases the likelihood of date rape.

6. Rape prevention guidelines emphasize rape awareness, fitness and self-defense, clear communication with dates, caution with alcohol and drugs, avoidance of high-risk situations, and reporting of assaults.

7. Men who rape are usually fairly ordinary people, but they may have grown up in a violent home environment. They tend to have large numbers of sex partners, be interested in impersonal sex, and lack empathy. Of men convicted of rape, most go to prison. The average sentence is 14 years, and the average prison stay is about 7 years. Intervention programs to head off sexual violence in adolescence have had only limited success.

8. Unwelcome sexual attention in the workplace (sexual harassment) is a form of illegal sex discrimination. It can take the form of quid pro quo harassment, in which a demand for sex is accompanied by some inducement or threat, or hostile-environment harassment, in which the sexual attention makes life difficult for the victim. Women in traditionally male workplaces, such as the military, experience a great deal of sexual harassment. Harassment can also occur in other structured environments, such as educational institutions.

9. Sexual harassment causes psychological and psychosomatic problems for its victims and reduces workplace productivity. Victims can take steps to end it by confronting their harasser or by reporting the harassment.

10. Stalking is obsessive following, lying in wait, calling, sending mail or messages, and the like, all directed at a specific victim. In intimate partner stalking, the stalker is a current or former spouse or romantic partner, and the stalking is motivated by sexual jealousy and anger. In delusional stalking, the stalker is mentally disturbed and believes that the victim (often an acquaintance, teacher, therapist, or celebrity) is in love with him or could be made to fall in love with him. In grudge stalking, the stalker is not motivated by sexual interest. Whatever the type of stalking, it can progress to violence. Stalking is illegal, but legal remedies are of limited effectiveness.

11. At least 1 million violent crimes are committed against spouses or intimate partners annually. About 1 in 4 women and 1 in 12 men experience intimate partner violence at least once in their lifetime.

12. Intimate partner violence causes both physical and psychological injuries. Battered women may come to see the violence as inevitable and therefore do little to escape it (learned helplessness). Children often witness parental violence and may themselves be injured. The rate of intimate partner violence has dropped substantially over the past 30 years.

13. Intimate partner violence typically follows a three-phase cycle of tension building, violence, and reconciliation. As the cycle repeats, the violence tends to escalate and may eventually occur without interruption.

14. Victims of intimate partner violence often stay with their partners. The reasons for this may include social isolation, economic dependence, low self-esteem, shame, and fear of retribution. Many services are now available to help victims of intimate partner abuse, whether or not they remain in their abusive relationships.

Discussion Questions

1. Having read some of the conflicting views about rape, what's your opinion: should rape be considered a sexual act or not? And do you think that the answer to this question is relevant to strategies for rape prevention?

2. "On this campus, men still get away with a lot of sexist talk, sexual harassment, and even date rape." "On this campus, political correctness has got to the point that men are scared to show normal friendly behavior to women." Which state-

ment corresponds more closely to your opinion, and why? Do you think your sex influences your opinion?

3. Are you familiar with your college's policies on sexual relationships between students and faculty? If not, find out about them. Would it violate these policies for a professor to express a romantic interest in a student, or to sexually proposition a student, under any circumstances? What about a student propositioning a professor? Do you think the policy is too strict, too lax, insufficiently clear, or quite appropriate?

4. How would you advise a female friend who tells you she is being stalked by a former boyfriend? Would your advice be different if it was a man being stalked by a former girlfriend?

5. Both men and women may sometimes give unclear signals about whether they are willing to engage in sexual contact when on a date. How can a man or woman best make sure that their partner is really willing to engage in sex? What if you or your date have had a few drinks?

6. Not uncommonly, victims recant accusations that their partners beat them. Would you support a "no-drop policy" in your community (i.e., a policy to continue a prosecution in these circumstances)? What kind of evidence could be used to get a conviction if the victim recants?

Web Resources

National Coalition against Domestic Violence—hotline: 1-800-799-SAFE; www.ncadv.org

National Sexual Violence Resource Center www.nsvrc.org

Rape, Abuse, and Incest National Network—hotline: 1–800–656-HOPE; www.rainn.org

Stop Prisoner Rape www.spr.org

Recommended Reading

Brownmiller, S. (1975). *Against our will: Men, women and rape.* New York: Simon and Schuster.
Hicks, G. L. (1995). *The comfort women: Japan's brutal regime of enforced prostitution in the Second World War.* New York: W.W. Norton.
Mullen, P. E., Pathé, M., and Purcell, R. (2000). *Stalkers and their victims.* Cambridge: Cambridge University Press.
Petrocelli, W., and Repa, B. K. (1999). *Sexual harassment on the job: What it is and how to stop it* (4th ed.). Berkeley: Nolo Press.
Schewe, P. A., ed. (2002). *Preventing violence in relationships: Interventions across the lifespan.* Washington, D.C.: American Psychological Association.
Thornhill, R., and Palmer, C. T. (2000). *A natural history of rape: Biological bases of sexual coercion.* Cambridge, MA: MIT Press.
Walker, L. E. A. (2000). *The battered woman syndrome* (2nd ed.). New York: Springer.
Warshaw, R. (1994). *I never called it rape: The Ms. report on recognizing, fighting, and surviving date and acquaintance rape.* New York: Harperperennial.

chapter 19

The marketing of sex has pervaded many human cultures throughout history.

Sex as a Commodity

*L*ike anything that people want, sex has a cash value. Indeed, in one way or another, sex fuels a significant part of the U.S. economy. In this chapter, we focus primarily on the selling of sex itself (prostitution) and the commercial production of sexually arousing materials (pornography). We also take a brief look at the use of sex to market nonsexual products. The selling of sex raises a variety of ethical concerns, and few aspects of sex so sharply divide conservatives and liberals.

Can Money Buy You Love?

A great deal of wealth is transferred between sexual and romantic partners, the bulk of it flowing from men to women. Despite the financial advances of women in western industrialized countries, some social commentators claim that this pattern remains largely intact, and often begins on the first date (Dowd, 2001). Research has shown that men continue to transfer wealth to women throughout courtship and into cohabitation and marriage (Posner, 1989).

Some evolutionary psychologists (e.g., Buss, 1995) assert that men transfer resources to women because, over the course of human evolution, men who did so improved their chances of gaining sexual access to women and had more surviving offspring (see Chapter 2). Women, according to these ideas, tend to enter into sexual relationships with men who provide resources because, in the evolutionary past, they too were more likely to have surviving offspring. In other words, the transfer of resources from men to women equalized their reproductive investments and aligned their motivations, thus making amicable pair bonding possible (again, according to the perspective of evolutionary psychologists).

From this perspective, what we call **prostitution**—engaging in sex for pay—is merely an unvarnished and extreme expression of something that goes on in many or most sexual relationships. What is morally offensive to many people about prostitution is not simply that money is involved, for many women receive their entire financial support from their husbands or boyfriends without bringing their moral status, or that of their partners, into question. Rather it is that the relationship between prostitute and client is brief and loveless, and that the payment is for sex only, not as part of the complex web of commitments, attachments, and dependencies that characterize more durable relationships. Prostitution violates many people's belief—women's especially—that sexual behavior is morally justified only in the context of a loving, committed relationship (see Chapter 9).

Both men and women can be prostitutes, but the majority of prostitutes are women (or girls), and the great majority of the persons who use their services are men. Prostitution may be viewed as a form of **polyandry,** in which one woman has sexual relationships with multiple men. We mentioned in Chapter 9 that polyandrous societies tend to be those in which men have too few resources to be able to support a wife and family on their own. Similarly, the traditional clientele for prostitutes in American society has been single men who lack the resources to marry—often because of their youth.

Although we speak of a person who exchanges sex for money as "being a prostitute," prostitution is often a part-time activity, so the division between prostitutes and non-prostitutes is not always clear. In the days when sailors embarked on months-long voyages, for example, their womenfolk might support themselves for the duration of the voyage by prostitution. Meanwhile, the sailors would be paying for sex with other sailors' spouses in a distant port. Once the voyage was over, the couple would resume their regular marital relationship (Bullough & Bullough, 1987).

Historically, Prostitution Was Viewed as a Necessary Evil

Prostitution is often called "the oldest profession," and with good reason. For millennia, prostitution was about the only way in which unattached women could support themselves. Jewish and Christian scriptures include frequent references to prostitutes (or "harlots"), and Christian tradition holds that one of Jesus' followers, Mary Magdalene, was a reformed prostitute. The Greeks had prostitutes of both sexes (*pornoi,* from which comes our word "pornography"), as well as paid female companions known as *hetairai*. Male youths could accept gifts as inducement to enter into sexual liaisons with adult men, but youths who accepted money were considered prostitutes and risked losing their citizenship (Dover, 1978).

Prostitution, like all sex between unmarried persons, has been condemned as "fornication" throughout the Christian era. Still, moralists such as St. Augustine and St. Thomas Aquinas condoned the social structure of prostitution because they saw it as providing a necessary "safety valve" for the release of male sexual energy. Aquinas compared prostitution to the sewer in a palace: if the sewer was blocked, he said, the palace would fill with pollution (Bullough & Bullough, 1987).

Serious efforts to eradicate prostitution did not begin until the Protestant Reformation of the sixteenth century. They were driven not only by moral concerns, but also by the

St. Mary Magdalene was often portrayed—as in this painting by Titian—in a state of penitence for her sinful past as a prostitute.

problem of sexually transmitted diseases. Prostitution continued to flourish, however. In fact, the heyday of prostitution was probably the late eighteenth and nineteenth centuries, when large numbers of men migrated to cities and women were in short supply. In response to the terrible conditions experienced by prostitutes in London, William Booth founded the Salvation Army in 1865; its first shelter for prostitutes and vagrant girls opened 3 years later. An occasional prostitute did well for herself, however. Laura Bell, originally a poor Irish shopgirl, became known as the "Queen of London Whoredom"; by the time she married Augustus Thistlethwaytes, a bishop's nephew, in 1856, she had accumulated an immense fortune (Simons, 1984). She later became a successful preacher.

In the latter part of the nineteenth century, most U.S. cities saw the development of "red-light districts," (so called because red lights traditionally marked brothels) where prostitution was tolerated or, in a few locations, legal. In the early twentieth century, however, a coalition of reformers, early feminists, and health authorities forced most of these districts out of existence. Epidemics of gonorrhea and other diseases during the First World War triggered a major campaign against prostitution, and the profession went underground.

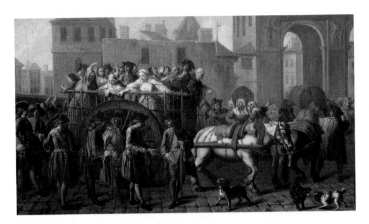

In eighteenth-century cities, prostitutes increased in numbers and were seen as a public nuisance. This painting by Etienne Jeaurat (1699–1789), shows the removal of prostitutes from the streets of Paris.

Prostitution Is on the Decline

By the mid-twentieth century, prostitution was on the decline. Kinsey estimated that men's usage of female prostitutes had dropped by nearly 50 percent over the few decades prior to the time of his survey, and he attributed this decline to a greater willingness of unmarried women to engage in sex with men. College-educated men in particular were no longer visiting prostitutes in great numbers. Still, Kinsey's survey showed that the average unmarried man in his thirties visited a prostitute once every 3 weeks (Kinsey et al., 1948).

A further major decline in prostitution accompanied the sexual revolution of the 1960s and its aftermath. Thanks to oral contraceptives and a sea change in sexual morality, unmarried women became much more willing to have sex with their dates or boyfriends, so the main incentive for men to visit prostitutes disappeared. Whereas 7 percent of men born in 1933–1937 lost their virginity to a prostitute, only 1.5 percent of men born in 1968–1974 did so, according to NHSLS data. During this same period, employment opportunities for many women expanded greatly, so the main incentive for women to work as prostitutes also lost much of its force. Ironically, prostitution declined during a period when opposition to prostitution also declined.

Statistics on the prevalence of prostitution today are hard to come by. One of the best studies of prostitution was conducted in Chicago by the Center for Impact Research (O'Leary & Howard, 2001). According to this study, an estimated minimum of 1800–4000 women and girls work as prostitutes in the Chicago metropolitan area at any one time. (Larger numbers of women exchange sex for drugs, but these transactions do not fit the definition of prostitution we are using here.) Since the Chicago metropolitan area has a female population of about 5 million, this estimate implies that the fraction of all females in that area that are engaged in prostitution could be less than 1 in 1000. The fraction in nonmetropolitan areas is likely to be even lower.

While most prostitutes are female, the proportion of prostitutes who are male or transgendered is significant in some large cities. In San Francisco, for example, an estimated 20–30 percent of prostitutes are male, and 25 percent are male-to-female transgenders (Prostitutes Education Network, 2001b). Most of the transgenders have not undergone sex reassignment surgery, but they may have breast implants or be taking estrogens.

There Is a Hierarchy of Prostitution

Prostitution is difficult to characterize because it takes many different forms. In general there is a hierarchy, ranging from forms that are street-based, cheap, and dangerous, to less visible forms involving large sums of money and greater security for the prostitutes and the prostitutes' clients.

Only a minority of prostitutes solicit customers on the streets, but they form the most visible part of the industry and are exposed to the greatest risks.

Street Prostitution Offers Money and Risks

In the Chicago study just mentioned, 30–35 percent of the prostitutes worked on the streets. **Street prostitution** (or "streetwalking") is the most visible and familiar part of the industry. Streetwalkers are usually picked up by clients ("johns") driving automobiles, but they may also be picked up in bars located near a recognized streetwalking zone. After agreement between prostitute and client about the kind of sex to be engaged in and the fee, sex takes place in the automobile, in a pay-by-the-hour motel, or at some other location.

Street prostitutes occupy the lowest rank of the prostitution hierarchy, and they charge the lowest prices. Many are users of hard drugs. They may be less able or likely to insist on condom use than are other prostitutes, so they face a greater risk of acquiring sexually transmitted diseases and becoming pregnant. For example, one study of women who smoked crack cocaine and exchanged sex for money (or drugs) found that 30 percent had not used a condom in the previous month (Edlin et al., 1994), and in some cities, up to a third of these women were HIV-positive. In another study, which focused on young men who exchanged sex for money (or drugs) in Harlem, New York, 41 percent of the men tested HIV-positive (El-Bassel et al., 2000).

Still, some street prostitutes do use condoms successfully. One method that some prostitutes have perfected is to have a condom concealed in the mouth and unroll it over the client's penis in the course of providing fellatio. The client may never become aware that he is wearing the condom.

Although female, male, and transgendered streetwalkers all service male clients, and all receive about the same payment per client ($40–50 in San Francisco in 1990), their experiences are otherwise quite different (Weinberg et al., 1999) (Table 19.1). Female and transgendered prostitutes tend to be in their late twenties, while male prostitutes (who often describe themselves as **hustlers**) are younger. Prostitution is more of a full-time occupation for women: they service more clients, and earn a larger weekly income from prostitution, than do either transgenders or men. Men spend about twice as much time with each client as do either women or transgenders. In other words, prostitution is a better deal economically for women than for men, which is hardly surprising, given that the majority of potential clients are heterosexual men.

On the other hand, the nonfinancial aspects of prostitution work out better for men. Most significantly, men and transgenders are much less likely to be beaten or raped by a client than are women. Also, men in general have more interest in casual sex and in having multiple sex partners than do women. Accordingly, male prostitutes get more sexual enjoyment, and experience orgasm more often, in the course of their work than do women. (Transgenders quite often get sexual enjoyment, but, because they don't usually use their penis in commercial sex, they rarely experience orgasm.) Not surprisingly, most male prostitutes describe themselves as gay or bisexual, but some (13 percent in the Weinberg study) describe themselves as heterosexual. Most male prostitutes are single and have multiple (mostly male) sex partners outside of their work.

Another difference that traditionally worked to the advantage of male prostitutes was that they tended to be independent agents working only for themselves, whereas women often worked for **pimps.** The women gave the pimps part or all of their earnings, and also commonly had sex with them. In return, the pimps set up the women's living and working arrangements, protected their turf, provided drugs, and paid off mobsters and the police (or, if that didn't work, bailed the women out of jail).

Male-to-female transgendered prostitutes, such as these two in Paris, may deceive their clients about their anatomical sex, but some men specifically seek them out.

TABLE 19.1	Life experiences of female, male-to-female transgendered, and male prostitutes in San Francisco's Tenderloin district			
		Female	**M2F**	**Male**
Mean age		29.3	29.7	23.8
Used hard drugs at least weekly (%)		59	25	26
Income				
Prostitution was only source of income (%)		62	53	32
Mean weekly income in 1990		$1030	$688	$507
Workload				
Mean number of clients per week		26	15	10
Mean time with client (minutes)		24	29	45
Enjoyment				
Ever got sexual pleasure from giving oral sex to client (%)		28	72	64
Usually or always experienced orgasm during sex with client (%)		5	7	45
Negative effects (mean number of occasions in previous year)				
Raped by client		0.41	0.13	0
Beaten by client		0.46	0.23	0.09
Arrested for prostitution		0.63	0.48	0.83
Married or cohabiting (%)		52	19	11
Sexual orientation				
Attracted to men only		65	71	37
Bisexual		35	29	50
Attracted to women only		0	0	13
Mean number of noncommercial sex partners in previous year				
Male partners		1.9	11.0	15.2
Female partners		0.2	0.3	6.9

Source: Weinberg et al., 1999.

Note: These data are not necessarily representative for all cities: arrest rates, for example, may be higher in cities that are less tolerant of prostitution than San Francisco.

The pimping profession seems to have gone into an even steeper decline than prostitution itself, however: in Weinberg's San Francisco study, only 4 percent of the women worked for pimps, and the Chicago study quoted law enforcement officials as saying there were few remaining pimps in that area. To some extent, the pimps' role has been taken over by gang members who control illegal street activity.

A good deal of deception occurs in street prostitution. Prostitutes often con their clients: at least half the prostitutes in the Weinberg study said they had failed to provide promised services or demanded more money than initially agreed to. Transgendered prostitutes frequently deceive their clients about their anatomical sex. They may tape back their penis and refuse to remove their panties, saying that they are having their period. Alternatively, they may use their anus or even their hands to fake coitus.

On the other hand, transgendered prostitutes do not always need to be deceptive, because there are plenty of men who are specifically attracted to transgenders, whom they call "she-males." In the Weinberg study, the transgenders said that an average of 13 men per year were initially deceived but discovered the truth during the course of the sexual encounter. About 15 percent of these men responded violently; of the remainder, about half broke off the encounter, but the others simply carried on, suggesting that the discovery did not affect their enjoyment in a material way.

A rather distinct group of street prostitutes are *homeless* or *runaway youths* (of both sexes). Numerically, these prostitutes form a very small portion of the total prostitute population—or of those who come to the attention of law enforcement, at least. Still, they arouse

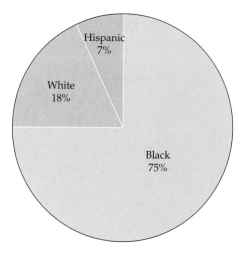

Figure 19.1 Arrests for prostitution in Chicago by race/ethnicity. Because these arrests are sporadic and driven by community complaints, these figures may not be representative of all prostitution in the city. (Data from O'Leary and Howard, 2001.)

a great deal of concern on account of their vulnerability to abuse, violence, and disease. Programs to address youth prostitution have either greatly reduced it or driven it underground in many cities (O'Leary & Howard, 2001). Some runaway youths are "adopted" by men who provide them with shelter and other resources in exchange for a sexual relationship; such arrangements are largely invisible to law enforcement or social services.

Most street prostitutes come from poor and disadvantaged backgrounds, so it is not surprising that minorities, especially African-Americans, are overrepresented in this population (Figure 19.1). For many black prostitutes, alternative employment opportunities are so limited and unrewarding as to make it very difficult to escape from prostitution. Black and other minority prostitutes are more likely to get into trouble with the law than are white prostitutes. That's because they are more likely than white prostitutes to operate on the street, where arrests are most common. In California, many or most transgendered prostitutes are Hispanic immigrants; they come to the United States to escape the abuse they suffer in the macho cultures of Latin America (Leovy, 2001).

Escort Services Are the Main Form of Prostitution in the United States

The organization of **off-street prostitution** is quite fluid, and its terminology is confusing. Some off-street prostitutes work at locations where men can come and select them, such as strip joints, massage parlors, and clubs (see below). Most do not, however, and they therefore need to advertise themselves in some way. They may do this by means of ads in weekly newspapers, adult entertainment magazines, or the Yellow Pages; by cards in telephone booths, bars, and other locations; or by their own Web sites. There are also Internet sites and chat rooms that help guide men to prostitution services or to individual prostitutes who can meet their needs. Word of mouth also plays an important role. However the client identifies the desired prostitute, he contacts them or their manager via pager, telephone, or e-mail, using certain accepted code words to describe what is wanted. ("Massage rates" means that the prostitute will stimulate the client by hand; "full companionship" means coitus, and so on.)

Often, prostitutes who are marketed via advertisements or word of mouth are referred to as **escort service prostitutes** or **escorts.** The older term **call girl** has much the same meaning. *Some* escort service prostitutes do work for escort services—groups of prostitutes whose advertising and appointments are handled by a manager. (If female, the manager may be called a **madam.**) Many others are independent operators, however. It is often difficult to tell which is which simply by looking at the ads. Few escorts do any actual escorting.

Escort service prostitutes may go to the client's residence or hotel room or to a motel room rented for the encounter (**outcall**). Alternatively, the client may come to an apartment rented by the escort or the escort's service (**incall**). Escort service prostitutes are generally expected to be better looking and more presentable than street prostitutes—an obvious drug user would not fare well at this level of the prostitution hierarchy. They also charge more than street prostitutes—$150 an hour and up, plus the cost of the room. If the escort is working for a service, the fee has two parts: an "agency fee," which goes to the service, and a larger "tip," which goes to the escort.

The actual assignation is somewhat ritualized. On the escort's arrival at the client's hotel or other location, there is some discussion to settle what is wanted, the amount of time, and the payment. The client then pays the escort, usually by placing money (or a credit card) on a table rather than giving it to them directly. Assuming that the escort works for a service, they will then call the service to start the clock running. (The call also serves as a security measure.) After that there is conversation, foreplay, putting on of a condom, and whatever sex acts have been agreed on. Some clients offer the prostitute an extra payment to engage in sex without a condom; how often such offers are accepted is uncertain.

Heidi Fleiss was known as the "Hollywood Madam." Her "little black book" supposedly listed many of the most famous names in the entertainment industry. In spite of her threats to reveal these names, she was arrested in 1995. She was convicted of pandering (providing prostitutes), as well as tax evasion and money laundering, and served 3 years in jail (Hubler, 2000). None of the men who used her service were prosecuted, not even actor Charlie Sheen, who admitted paying her $50,000 for her escorts, which cost $2500 a night.

In terms of sexual behavior, the encounter between a client and an escort may be very like a noncommercial sexual encounter. The fact that the client is paying, however, ensures that the focus is on *his* needs. After sex, there may be more conversation. The escort will call the service again at the completion of the assignation, or the service will call when the allotted time expires.

Escort service prostitutes are the most numerous kind of prostitute nowadays. In the Chicago study, they accounted for at least 50 percent of all prostitutes. This form of prostitution is somewhat safer for the prostitute—hygiene and contraception are easier to control, the clients tend to be more predictable (many are traveling businessmen), and arrests are fewer. Also, because there are relatively few public complaints about escorts, the police tend to leave them alone. These "pluses" are all relative to street prostitution, of course; compared with most other jobs, escort service prostitution carries a high risk of injury, disease, and arrest.

While much of this work is anonymous and loveless, some escorts see the same clients over and over again, and their relationships with these "regulars" can become quite intimate and pleasurable to both parties. "Regulars" are also desirable because they are predictable and therefore safer for the prostitute.

At the top of the prostitution hierarchy are the real escorts—beautiful and well-bred young women or men that a client can take to dinner or a show without embarrassment. Such a prostitute might stay with a visiting businessperson for an entire weekend, or even travel abroad to spend time with a well-heeled oil sheik. These top-end escort-service prostitutes often work for madams who have some entry into affluent society.

Even though prostitution is illegal, advertisements for "escorts" and similar services are ubiquitous.

Real escorts are the only kind of prostitute that women use in any significant numbers. Male escorts who are paid by women are called **gigolos.** Gigolos are not particularly common in the United States, but there is a well-accepted gigolo tradition in Europe, where affluent women have long enjoyed more sexual freedom than their American counterparts. One Swiss agency offers a range of personable men at about $70 per hour, plus expenses, with a 3-hour minimum. Clients may specify every detail about the gigolo on-line before the encounter, including the cologne he should wear and the topics of conversation he should be versed in (Gigolos Begleitagentur, 2001).

Massage Parlors and Strip Joints Are Often Fronts for Prostitution

The third kind of prostitute works at or out of a fixed commercial location such as a **massage parlor** or an exotic dance venue (**strip joint**). Massage parlors are often the most readily available locations for prostitution in suburban areas. Services vary, but hand–genital contact (often referred to as "massage" in escort service ads) is the commonest. At strip joints, exotic dancers may provide sex by rubbing their body against the customer's genitalia during a "lap dance." Alternatively, sex may take place in a "VIP room" or off-site after the show. In many communities, massage parlors and strip joints are periodically raided by the police. Not all masseurs and exotic dancers are prostitutes, of course, but ads or word of mouth usually make it clear what services are available at a particular establishment.

The one kind of locale for prostitution that is hard to find in the United States today is an old-fashioned **brothel** or **whorehouse,** whose traditional red lantern, placed in the doorway, gave "red-light districts" their name. Brothels are establishments entirely dedicated to prostitution and lack any cover activity such as massage, drinking, or entertainment. Thus, they have little defense against police raids. Today, durable working brothels can be found chiefly in the rural counties of Nevada, where prostitution is legal, and in remote mining and logging communities, where it may be tolerated. Luckily, a few of the countless

Strip joints and massage parlors are often fronts for prostitution.

Box 19.1

Sex in History

The Best Little Whorehouse in Montana

(A) The Dumas Hotel. The tall windows allowed passers-by a good view of the prostitutes within.

The Dumas Hotel, on Mercury Street in Butte, Montana (Figure A), was built in 1890. In spite of its name, it was designed specifically as a brothel. It functioned as one until 1982, when its last madam, Ruby Garrett, was convicted of tax evasion.

The Dumas was originally built as a high-class "parlor house" brothel, and the upper floor still boasts the luxurious suites that would have been used by the wealthiest men in Butte (Figure B). Later, the basement and first floor were remodeled to serve humbler folk. The basement was subdivided into a warren of "cribs"—tiny cubicles just big enough to accommodate a bed. This is where Butte's miners spent their hard-earned wages on low-paid prostitutes, who worked in three shifts to accommodate the round-the-clock mining schedule. Some of the first-floor cribs opened directly onto the notorious "Venus Alley" behind the brothel, so that prostitutes in the cribs could solicit customers walking in the alley. Several other brothels, as well as gambling dens and saloons, stood on the same street.

In its early years, the brothel's customers could "get lucky" for as little as 50 cents. The prostitutes either rented a crib for a few dollars a day or worked for the owner, who took 60 percent of their earnings. Even at the time of its closing, sex could be had for as little as $20.

The brothel owners bribed the police and the city council to leave them alone. In addition, the city authorities shared St. Thomas Aquinas's view—that prostitution was necessary if women of virtue were to be kept safe from lust-filled men. During the Second World War, however, the police sealed off the Dumas Hotel's basement cribs as part of a national campaign against venereal disease. The upper floors continued to operate, though more discreetly; women no longer paraded in the windows.

The Dumas Hotel was designated a National Historic Landmark in 1973—while it was still operating. It was later slated for demolition, but was then turned into a museum. The property is now for sale. Hopefully it will escape demolition, as it is believed to be the only remaining example of a "parlor house" brothel in the United States.

Source: Giecek, 2000.

(B) One of the upper rooms at the Dumas Hotel

brothels that once flourished in the United States have been preserved as national historic sites (Box 19.1). Legal brothels do exist in quite a few other countries, including the Netherlands (Box 19.2), and in three Australian states, including New South Wales, where the city of Sydney is located.

Good Pay Is the Main Motive for Prostitution

We have already mentioned two traditional motives for prostitution: economic necessity on the part of the prostitutes, and lack of a sex partner on the part of unmarried clients. Today, strict economic necessity is probably the motive for only a minority of prostitutes in the United States—for runaway youths in particular. For other prostitutes, it's not so much that they can't survive by other means, but that they can do so much better by prostitution. Even at the streetwalking level, a single 20-minute "trick" is equivalent to about a day's work at minimum wage. In the Weinberg study, the great majority of the

Box 19.2   CULTURAL DIVERSITY

Prostitution: The Dutch Model

Prostitution has long been legal in Holland. Technically, brothels were illegal, but they have always flourished in the red-light districts of Amsterdam and other communities (especially in towns along the German and Belgian borders, where they serve visitors from those countries). In 2000, brothels were officially legalized, and the law now concerns itself primarily with underage and involuntary prostitution.

In Amsterdam's Burgwallen district, the ground floors of many buildings have been converted in sets of small, narrow rooms, rather like the "cribs" in the Dumas Hotel (see Box 19.1). Each has a tall, doorlike window facing onto the street, and the prostitutes sit on high stools in these windows, advertising themselves to the passers-by (see figure). A man who is interested in a particular prostitute knocks on her window and is admitted, whereupon she draws the blinds. The prostitute may offer basic sex for as little as $20, but extra fees tend to get added on in the course of the assignation—for complete nudity, nonstandard positions, extra time, and the like.

The brothels are licensed, which allows the city some oversight over conditions in them. The prostitutes are not individually licensed, but they are expected to declare their occupation and their earnings on their income tax, and there are medical services provided for them. There is also an active prostitutes' union, De Rode Draad (Red Thread).

While most or all of the window prostitutes are women, both male and female prostitutes can be found in sex clubs, which offer a more convivial atmosphere and a better opportunity to get to know the prostitutes before making a choice. They are more expensive— $80 and up, plus drinks or a substantial cover charge.

There is also a legal zone of street prostitution, on Amsterdam's Theemsweg. It operates from 9 P.M.

until 3 A.M. The zone is fenced in and has a "lounge" provided by the city, where the prostitutes can consult with social workers, medical personnel, and representatives of law enforcement. Free STD examinations and needle exchanges are available (City of Amsterdam, 2001).

streetwalkers said that they would switch to a different job if they could get the same rate of pay. Given their limited education and blank résumés, however, they would not be likely to land such a job, so switching to "square" work would lower their standard of living. At the escort level, the rewards are much higher, even after overheads such as the agency's cut or room rental, so the motivation to stay in prostitution as long as possible is strong.

Two kinds of prostitutes do have special financial needs that make a high income important. One, of course, is prostitutes who are addicted to drugs. The other is transgenders, about half of whom are trying to get the money together for sex reassignment surgery. Based on Weinberg's income data, transgendered street prostitutes who saved half their income could pay for surgery in under 2 years.

Over the years, people have suggested a variety of other, more fanciful motives for prostitution (Bullough & Bullough, 1995). Moralists have claimed that prostitutes have inherited criminal tendencies; psychoanalysts have suggested that they are masochists or are hostile to men. Folk wisdom holds that female prostitutes are especially sensuous women—that they have a high libido, in other words, that can be satisfied only through prostitution. In reality, this seems a more plausible motive for male prostitutes, because many of them do derive sexual pleasure from their work, even at the level of street prostitution, as mentioned above. At the upper end of the escort service spectrum, however, female prostitutes may indeed be rewarded by sexual enjoyment or by the glamour or social climbing that goes with their trade.

One curious theory states that women who prostitute themselves are lesbians who engage in this behavior as a way of concealing their homosexuality from themselves (Caprio & Brenner, 1961). Again, this theory would seem better suited as an explanation for *male* prostitution: hustlers can have any amount of sex with men without ever having to face the question of whether they are gay (recall the "macho" hustler described in Box 7.4).

Men Use Prostitutes for Many Reasons

What about the motives of the men who use prostitutes? We mentioned that the traditional motive—the unavailability of sex partners for unmarried men—has largely disappeared in the United States. Some men do still have difficulty finding unpaid sex partners, however, for a wide variety of reasons. They may be shy, unlikable, or severely disabled (see Box 17.5). They may be away from home or recently separated from a partner. Some men who could get unpaid sex partners prefer to pay in order to avoid the hassles and obligations they perceive to be associated with regular dating. In addition, men who do have regular partners may seek out prostitutes because their partner does not want to have sex as often as they do, or does not want to participate in the particular sex practices that they enjoy. The men may also simply be looking for sexual variety, for someone more attractive than their regular partner, or for the titillation of "forbidden" sex.

Some feminists see men's use of prostitutes as misogynistic. "When men use women in prostitution, they are expressing a pure hatred for the female body," said anti-prostitution and anti-pornography crusader Andrea Dworkin (Dworkin, 1994). Prostitution, according to Dworkin, is "gang rape punctuated by money exchange." Yet some men who are open about their use of prostitutes express a great deal of interest in the women they pay and take great pains to please them. "I have found that escorts are some of the finest and most interesting women you'll ever meet and it's a real treat to get to know them," writes Marc Perkel, author of an on-line guide to escort service prostitution. "I recommend that you prepare for your escort's arrival the same way you would for a date. After all, escorts offer more than just sex. Often you can get good conversation and personal companionship as well. And you get these other services by being as nice to them as to any other woman you date" (Perkel, 2000). In reality, it is likely that the dealings between prostitutes and their clients can range from amiable to abusive.

The Prostitutes' Rights Movement Works for Decriminalization

Margo St. James (right), ex-San Francisco prostitute and founder of the prostitutes' rights group COYOTE, seen here talking with actress Jane Fonda. St. James also instituted the Hookers' Ball, a cultural phenomenon in San Francisco, and nearly won election to the Board of Supervisors in 1996.

In 1973, Margo St. James founded COYOTE (for "Call Off Your Old Tired Ethics") to serve and represent prostitutes working in San Francisco. Within 2 years, COYOTE had several offshoots around the country and boasted over 10,000 members. COYOTE's mission was, and still is, to improve the image and working conditions of prostitutes. COYOTE and other prostitutes' organizations that have emerged subsequently see **decriminalization**—that is, the simple elimination of laws that outlaw prostitution—as the key to their goals. After decriminalization, the thinking goes, prostitution would become just another job, subject to normal labor practices, unionization, and the like.

Initially, the prostitutes' rights movement gained a lot of sympathy because it was seen as part of the sexual revolution of the time. The National Organization for Women endorsed decriminalization in the same year that COYOTE was founded, and Margo St. James was portrayed positively in feminist magazines such as *Ms.* The movement took a major hit from the AIDS epidemic, however: many people saw prostitutes as vectors of the disease, and attitudes toward them became much more conservative.

In the 1980s, some feminists (such as Andrea Dworkin, mentioned above) argued that prostitution was part of the exploitation of women by men. One effect of these feminist views was the redirection of some of the legal persecution of female prostitutes toward the men who were associated with them—that is to say, the pimps and the "johns," their customers. Pimps, as mentioned, have become a less important factor in prostitution. Johns are now arrested in numbers approaching those of prostitutes, and some cities such as St. Paul, Minnesota, publish their names and photographs on the Internet as a form of deterrence (St. Paul Police, 2002). In addition, a new phenomenon, "Schools for Johns," has spread across America. These programs are organized like traffic schools: in exchange for having their arrests expunged from their records, the johns attend a one-day seminar at which they are lectured by feminists, ex-prostitutes, or law enforcement officials about the evils of prostitution.

Although the movement for decriminalization is making little headway today, there is some support for an alternative strategy, **legalization with regulation.** Under this plan, which is modeled on arrangements already existing in some European countries (see Box 19.2), prostitutes would be allowed to work in prescribed locations and under defined conditions. They might be required to be licensed, to take safe-sex classes, or to have periodic examinations for STDs. Proponents argue that this system would reduce the harmful side effects of prostitution, such as disease, unwanted pregnancy, violence, and organized crime.

In the European experience, there has been a negative relationship between the invasiveness of regulations governing prostitution and the extent to which prostitutes follow them. In the Netherlands, for example, prostitutes are not individually licensed or compelled to have medical tests; thus, most Dutch prostitutes are happy to operate within the legal structure, although underaged girls and nonresident aliens do still operate illegally. In Germany, where individual registration and occasional health examinations are required, only an estimated 25 percent of prostitutes operate within the law. In Greece, where prostitutes must register individually and receive mandatory health inspections twice a week, less than 10 percent of prostitutes operate legally; for the remaining 90 percent, health and social services are largely inaccessible (European Intervention Projects AIDS Prevention for Prostitutes, 2001).

Anyone concerned with legal reform of prostitution in the United States needs to bear in mind the reality of this trade-off. It might not be an easy matter to reinvent America's freewheeling system of prostitution as a state-regulated industry. The prostitutes' rights organizations oppose this kind of reform altogether, demanding instead that prostitutes be free to conduct their business how and where they choose (Prostitutes Education Network, 2001a).

A major roadblock to reform is the fact that most Americans, even young ones, still have moral reservations about prostitution (Gallup Organization, 2000a). In a 2000 national poll, 4 out of 5 teens said they considered prostitution a "very serious matter," placing it somewhere between hate crimes and shoplifting on a scale of seriousness (Figure 19.2).

The public discourse on prostitution and prostitutes' rights has led to some changes in terminology. While "prostitute" remains a valid term for anyone who exchanges sex for money, prostitutes themselves have reclaimed and adopted some of the pejorative words from the past, especially "hooker" and "whore." Meanwhile, people who are professionally concerned with prostitutes increasingly use the phrase **sex worker.** This term refers mainly to prostitutes, but it also (to a variable extent) includes people working in related industries, such as phone sex operators, strippers, porno movie actors, and so on. The term **sex trader** is used to specifically include persons who exchange sex for drugs.

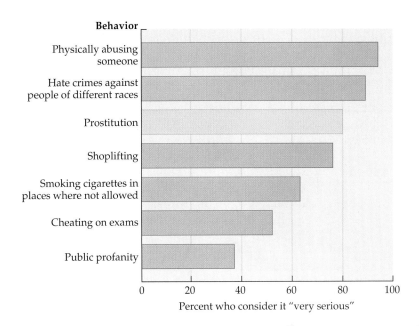

Figure 19.2 How serious is prostitution? Opinions of Americans aged 13–17 about a variety of behaviors. For each behavior the histogram shows the percentage who view that behavior as a "very serious" matter, (versus "somewhat serious," "only a little serious," or "not at all serious"). (Data from Gallup Organization, 2000a.)

The Debate on Prostitution Is Worldwide

Prostitution exists worldwide, of course, and conditions for prostitutes are worse in developing countries than they are in the United States or Europe. In some countries, for example, it is very difficult for prostitutes to demand that their clients use condoms. Still, for many, the ecomomic benefits are real: prostitutes in countries such as Thailand earn an average of about $800 a month, which is significantly higher than the general level of pay for unskilled labor in Southeast Asia. Prostitution and related industries account for 2–14 percent of Southeast Asian economies, and the International Labour Organization, an arm of the United Nations, has urged governments to recognize these industries and treat them like any other (Lim, 1998; Reuters News Service, 1998). In this way, the ILO believes, prostitutes would enjoy better working conditions and governments would receive more tax revenues.

A different line is taken by feminists Janice Raymond and Dorchen Leidholdt, directors of the Coalition against Trafficking in Women. Raymond, of the University of

Juvenile prostitutes are highly visible in some cities around the world, such as here in Bangkok, Thailand.

Massachusetts, echoes Andrea Dworkin when she asserts that prostitution is "rape that's paid for" (Raymond, 1995). The Coalition's goal is to achieve the worldwide criminalization of everyone connected with prostitution—pimps, procurers, johns, and traffickers—except the prostitutes themselves, whom they see only as victims (Coalition against Trafficking in Women, 2001a). The Coalition opposes the use of the phrase "sex workers," favored by many U.N. agencies and officials, because they feel it legitimizes prostitution and makes it morally equivalent to any other form of work (Coalition against Trafficking in Women, 1997).

Underage and Coerced Prostitution Are Global Problems

Three aspects of prostitution that are of particular concern in a global context are prostitution by minors, involuntary prostitution, and transnational trafficking of prostitutes. The numbers of minors involved in prostitution are impossible to estimate, but young prostitutes are very evident in many countries. Although the term **child prostitution** is often used, it may be somewhat misleading, as most prostitution by minors involves adolescents in the 12–18 age bracket.

Most of the demand for underaged prostitutes comes from local men, but visitors from overseas are also an important factor because of their disproportionate wealth. These visitors can be tourists, businessmen, or military personnel. Even the arrival of U.N. peacekeeping forces has spurred the development of underage prostitution in several countries, according to a study by the U.N. itself (ECPAT International, 2001). Many countries, including the United States and Canada, have enacted **extraterritorial legislation,** which makes it a crime for their citizens to have sex with an underaged person in a foreign country, even if the act is legal in that country.

Involuntary prostitution and transnational trafficking of prostitutes are often connected. Women and girls are moved from country to country—usually from poorer to richer countries—to supply the demand for prostitutes (Figure 19.3). For example, many women are transported from Bangladesh to Pakistan and India, from Myanmar (Burma) to Thailand, from Vietnam to China, and from the Philippines and Thailand to Japan (Coalition against Trafficking in Women, 2001b). Women are trafficked to the United

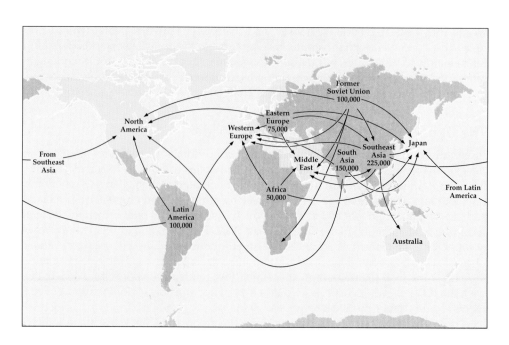

Figure 19.3 Traffic in women and girls for prostitution flows largely from poor to rich countries. (After Terrorism Research Center, 1998.)

States from places all over the world, including Latin America, Southeast Asia, Eastern Europe, and Russia. Western Europe is also a major destination for trafficking.

How voluntary is this movement? In one sense, none of it is: all the women are responding to economic forces that are greater than themselves. But there is clearly a lot of variation in how willingly they participate in the trafficking. Some women know what they are letting themselves in for and see it as a chance for economic betterment. At the other extreme, some women are deceived, enslaved, held prisoner in the host country, and forced to engage in prostitution against their will. Most cases fall into a gray area: the women travel voluntarily and know that they will be working in the sex industry, but experience some degree of deception or coercion. For example, they may have to work longer as prostitutes in the host country to "pay back" their traffickers than they were initially led to believe.

Groups like the Coalition against Trafficking in Women take an unreservedly negative view of this trade, of course. "To say that these women are voluntarily allowing themselves to be trafficked is to ignore the powerful social conditions that push women and girls into that kind of life," says Dorchen Leidholt. "The valuation of women as commodities in the global marketplace is devastating to the rights of all women." Laura Agustín of Connexions for Migrants, an organization that seeks to help migrants avoid exploitation, criticizes the Coalition's stance.

"They call themselves radical feminists, she says, and they say it's impossible to have any kind of voluntary prostitution. It's a theoretical line that says, even if you say you consent because you prefer it to cleaning floors or working in the fields, it can't be that way. It's a motherly stance. It turns women working as prostitutes into children: 'They don't know what they're doing, so we have to save them.' It's not realistic." (Quotations from Gardiner, 2001)

Phone Sex Blends Prostitution and Pornography

Several kinds of sex work straddle the boundary between prostitution and pornography. One is exotic dancing or stripping, which may or may not involve actual sexual contact with customers. Another is **phone sex,** in which a man telephones an operator who engages him in erotic conversation while he masturbates. The customer is charged around $2 per minute, which is billed to his credit card or added to his telephone bill.

Phone sex has a lot of advantages over face-to-face prostitution. It is easier and safer for the operators and allows them to organize their work around their regular lives. It is more convenient and cheaper for the customer. Also, a customer who has a wife or regular partner may feel more comfortable with phone sex than with face-to-face prostitution because (in his judgment, at least) phone sex doesn't cross the boundary into infidelity. And the law is on his side: phone sex doesn't count as prostitution and is legal, so long as both parties are over 18.

Phone sex companies like to create the impression that their operators are motivated by sex, not money, of course. "Missy is a diagnosed nymphomaniac and phone sex is her therapy," announces one Web site. "Most operators will orgasm with the caller," says another. The reality may be slightly different, but doubtless some operators, especially the male ones, do get into the swing of things.

There are phone sex operators for every conceivable taste. Some position themselves as "sex therapists"—no doubt to the annoyance of therapists who have professional training in the subject—or "sex surrogates." Many phone sex outfits have Web sites, where it is possible for the client to view photographs of the operator—or supposedly of the operator—while talking with them.

Phone sex operator "Jade" earns a living in a way that allows her to stay home and take care of her young daughter. This "paperclay" sculpture by Norma Jean Almodovar is one of a series illustrating sex work in America. Almodovar, a retired Beverly Hills call girl, is a leading prostitutes' rights activist. (Courtesy of Norma Jean Almodovar.)

Erotic sculpture from the Sakalawa culture of Madagascar. Such sculptures were traditionally buried with the deceased.

Pornography Has Always Been Part of Human Culture

The word **pornography** (often abbreviated as **porn** or **porno**) refers to depictions of people or behaviors that are intended to be sexually arousing. The depictions can be in any medium, including prose, poetry, painting, the plastic arts, photography, film, or performance. Sometimes the term is restricted to the more down-market products, or products of which the speaker disapproves. More expensive works, or those the speaker considers to have literary or artistic merit, may be called **erotica.** This distinction is too snobbish and subtle for us, however. One catch-all term that is popular with academics and policymakers is **sexually explicit materials.** Even *Gray's Anatomy* is sexually explicit, however, and it hardly fits in the category we are talking about here, because it is not intended to be sexually arousing. So we will stick with the term "pornography."

Pornographic works survive from many ancient cultures. Often, as with the sexually themed ceramics created by pre-Incan and Incan cultures, the intent of the artist remains mysterious—they may have intended the works to have a ceremonial significance, to be sexually arousing, or merely to be humorous. However, some ancient works, such as the sculptures and wall paintings that decorated the brothels of the ancient Roman city of Pompeii, are clearly intended to be sexually arousing.

Pornography Has Battled Censorship

Although early Christian tradition was largely anti-sex, pornography did reemerge in the Italian Renaissance. Early examples include the *Decameron* of Boccaccio (1313–1375), a series of stories that featured some naughty priests and nuns. The Roman Catholic Church banned the book, but relented after the clerical characters were changed into laypeople (Bullough & Bullough, 1995). Later in the Renaissance, pornographic sculptures, such as Michelangelo's *Dying Slave*, appeared. (We are risking a deluge of criticism by calling this great work of art pornographic, but its erotic meaning seems obvious to us, as well as to at least one art critic [Paglia, 1990]).

Developments in communications technology have always affected pornography in important ways. The first book printed with movable type, for example, was Gutenberg's Bible of 1455, but it was quickly followed by an outpouring of less elevated material, such as the *Facetiae* of Poggio Bracciolini (1474), a collection of sexual jokes and stories such as the following:

> A messenger once asked a high-born lady of my acquaintance whether she desired him to take any letters from her to her husband, who was long away from home, as ambassador of the republic. "How can I write him?" she said, "when he has taken his pen away with him and left my inkwell dry?" Which is a clever and honorable reply. (Bracciolini, 1964; cited in Bullough & Bullough, 1995)

Like Boccaccio, English-language pornographers have had to battle the censors. John Cleland's bawdy novel *Fanny Hill, The Memoirs of a Woman of Pleasure,* was a huge success when it was published in 1748 (and is still a delightful read), but Cleland was hauled before the Privy Council and ordered to write no more books of that kind. He actually violated the order with another erotic work, but published it anonymously.

The battle between pornography and censorship heated up in the nineteenth century, when almost anything that was potentially arousing was considered **obscene**—that is, sexually offensive or threatening to public morality. In 1818 an English physician, Thomas Bowdler, decided that Shakespeare himself was too risqué; he produced an expurgated edition of the Bard's work, suitable to be read by "a gentleman in the company of ladies" (Bullough & Bullough, 1995). The word "bowdlerize" thus came to refer to the removal of sexually explicit references from literature. In 1857 the British Parliament passed the Obscene Publications Act, which gave the police wide powers to investigate and eliminate pornography. In the United States, the Comstock Laws (see Chapter 11) restricted the dissemination of sexually explicit material.

Pornographic relief from a brothel in the Roman city of Pompeii.

The effect of these measures was to deepen the divide between mainstream literature and pornography. Some pornographic works, or works that contained pornographic passages, were published and disseminated privately. This was done, for example, with Richard Burton's unexpurgated 1885 translation of *Arabian Nights*, an ancient collection of Persian folk tales that had provided plotlines for Boccaccio, Chaucer, and Shakespeare. Alternatively, erotic material was printed in more tolerant countries and smuggled into England and America. This practice continued well into the twentieth century: James Joyce's avant-garde novel *Ulysses*, for example, was published in Paris in 1922.

Besides works of major literary significance like those just mentioned, large amounts of more ephemeral pornography were printed illegally or smuggled from abroad. Starting in the late nineteenth century, very cheap pornographic materials, such as sexually themed postcards, became available, making pornography available to virtually everyone (Sigel, 2000).

Some writings were banned as obscene or offensive to public morals even though they had no pornographic content. We mentioned in Chapter 11 that writings about contraception were banned under the Comstock Laws. Works that dealt with homosexuality were particularly liable to censorship. The publishers of the 1897 treatise *Sexual Inversion*, by Havelock Ellis and John Addington Symonds, were prosecuted in both Britain and America; the British prosecution led to the book's suppression. The 1928 lesbian novel *The Well of Loneliness* (see Chapter 13) was also the subject of a prosecution in both countries, even though the book did not contain a single sex scene. Again, the British prosecution was successful.

Pornography Increased after the Second World War

Rapid changes happened after the Second World War. D. H. Lawrence's *Lady Chatterley's Lover*, a tale of transgressive love between an aristocratic woman and her husband's gamekeeper, was originally published in Italy in 1928, and was promptly banned in Britain and the United States. In 1959, however, an unexpurgated version was published in the United States by Grove Press, followed by a paperback version in Britain. The fact that the British version appeared in paperback violated an unwritten code, which held that sexually explicit writings should be priced beyond the reach of the average citizen. The publisher, Penguin Books, was prosecuted, but successfully defended itself, basically by presenting a string of experts who testified to the book's literary value. The case drew enormous attention, greatly weakened the anti-pornography forces in Britain, and helped usher in the sexual revolution of the 1960s.

In the 1957 case *Roth v. U.S.*, the U.S. Supreme Court ruled that a work could be ruled obscene only if the "average person, applying contemporary community standards," judged that the work as a whole was designed to cause sexual arousal. This ruling made it somewhat harder to obtain obscenity convictions, but prosecutions continued.

One of the victims of U.S. obscenity laws was publisher Ralph Ginzburg, whose fine art magazine *Eros* got into trouble in 1962. *Eros* was fairly tame in its sexual context, and it was priced high enough to avoid any suspicion of corrupting the masses. Still, it did have transgressive elements, most notably a series of photographs of a naked white woman and black man in intimate bodily contact. (Interracial marriage was still illegal in some states at that time; see Chapter 9.) Ginzburg was prosecuted for distributing obscene material and sentenced to 5 years' imprisonment. The U.S. Supreme Court upheld his conviction in 1966.

The real story of postwar pornography, however, was the increasing acceptance of mass-market products with no literary or fine art pretensions. In 1953, Hugh Hefner founded the magazine *Playboy*; by 1971 it was selling 7 million copies a month. *Playboy* was **soft-core** pornography: it included no images of actual penetrative sex. Still, the magazine waged war on what Hefner considered America's puritanical aversion to sexual pleasure. Hefner's hedonistic empire expanded to include *Playboy* mansions, hotels, resorts, and casinos.

Although *Playboy* has long since been eclipsed by **hard-core** (showing actual coitus) and racier soft-core publications, Hefner has to be considered one of the most influential figures of the sexual revolution. Of course, he represents a mix of sexual liberation and unreconstructed male chauvinism, and he has taken plenty of heat from radical fem-

Michelangelo's *Dying Slave* (1513–1514)

Hugh Hefner with one of *Playboy's* cover girls, Cynthia Maddox, in 1962.

inists. As recently as 2000, when the Chicago City Council named a street "Hugh M. Hefner Way" to mark the location of the original Playboy Club, the local chapter of the National Organization for Women and other feminists protested. They claimed that the city's action violated the United Nations' Convention on Elimination of All Forms of Discrimination Against Women (O'Leary, 2000).

New Technologies Mean New Kinds of Pornography

Perhaps even more important than Hefner in the postwar history of pornography was the Italian film producer Lasse Braun, who began distributing hard-core pornographic movies in the Super-8 format in the mid-1960s. At that time, all pornographic movies were illegal everywhere. Braun's first film, *Golden Butterfly* (1966), was a porno version of Puccini's opera *Madame Butterfly*. By using a long remote control cord held behind his back, Braun was able to play the male lead *and* work the cameras; his girlfriend played the title role. The Super-8 movies were brief—often just 3 minutes—so Braun had to compress the story line and pack in enough sex so that a man could masturbate to climax while watching the film.

In the early 1970s Braun invented the **peep show** format for watching Super-8 porno movies. Based on the fairground peep shows that were popular in Victorian times, Braun's machines allowed a viewer to watch a movie that was projected within a small box or cabinet, thus doing away with the need for a darkened room. Braun manufactured 60,000 machines and distributed them to **adult bookstores** throughout the United States and Europe. These machines, along with the expanding range of pornographic magazines, greatly increased the popularity of these stores. Some stores offered live acts that customers could watch through windows or provided cubicles where men could have sex with prostitutes (or, in the case of gay-oriented stores, with each other).

The popularity of pornographic movies led to their gradual legalization in most European countries and U.S. states during the late 1960s and 1970s. Feature-length movies, shown in dedicated porno movie theaters, became popular in the early 1970s. Films that incorporated humor, such as Gerard Damiano's hits *Deep Throat* (starring Linda Lovelace, 1972) and *The Devil in Miss Jones* (1974), helped to dissipate the furtiveness associated with the genre. These were movies that people could talk about socially and watch as couples, so they won a degree of middle-class acceptance.

The introduction of videocassettes in the late 1970s changed pornography. This medium made the production and distribution of porno movies much easier and cheaper, and a great diversity of movies catering to every taste appeared. By the 1990s, thousands of "adult" videos were being produced annually, and they accounted for a quarter of all video sales. The line between commercial and amateur production became blurred, since anyone could videotape themselves or their friends having sex and sell the resulting product to companies that specialized in such products.

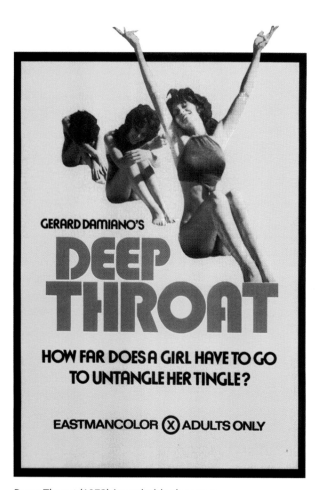

Deep Throat (1972) is probably the most famous pornographic film of all time. It features a woman (played by Linda Lovelace) whose sex life is unexciting until a doctor discovers that her clitoris is located in her throat—a finding that triggers a bonanza of oral sex. The humor in this film broadened its appeal.

As the quantity of video pornography increased, less and less money was spent on producing each video, and the technical quality of the products declined. In addition, the fact that a person could watch X-rated videos on a normal TV set, rather than having to set up a projector in a darkened room or travel to a porno movie theater, reduced the erotic significance of watching them. The introduction of DVD technology, which enables the viewer to interact with the movie by, for example, changing the camera angle with the click of a remote, may change this. DVD production is more expensive because more cameras are required and post-production is more complex, so production is concentrated in fewer hands, and the quality is generally higher.

Computers and the Internet are just the latest of the many technological innovations that have changed pornography. Sexually explicit Web sites, bulletin boards, newsgroups, and chat rooms flourish. Thanks to instant messaging technology, typing speed has become the limiting factor in on-line sex. By facilitating sexual interactions across distance and time, the Internet has blurred the boundary between pornography and regular sex. Currently, most computer users cannot see the person with whom they are interacting, so fantasy, role-playing, and outright deception are common. With the spread of broadband connections and WebCams, however, this is changing: most users will probably be able to interact in real time through video and audio links before long.

Futurists envisage the merging of the Internet with virtual reality technology in a way that will permit realistic sexual interactions between persons at a distance, either in the form of private communication or commercial pornography (Brunker, 2001; Rheingold, 1992). One company, Safesexplus.com, already markets sex toys that can be controlled by a remote partner via the Internet. As its name suggests, the company plays on the fear of sexually transmitted diseases to market the devices. More ambitious is the CyberSuit, which is (or was) under development by Vivid Entertainment, a producer of pornographic videos and DVDs. The CyberSuit is supposed to give the user tactile sensations resembling real sex. As with most robotic and virtual reality projects, however, hype runs far ahead of actual delivered products.

There Is Some Pornography for Women

So far we have described pornography as if all of it caters to men. That is a close approximation to the truth, but a small sector of the industry does provide material for women. In the 1970s, *Playgirl* magazine appeared as a women's counterpart to *Playboy*; it sported centerfolds of ultra-masculine men with semi-erect penises. It was not a huge success with women; in fact, it probably sold better among gay men.

We mentioned in Chapter 7 that women's sexual fantasies include more elements of romance and affection than do those of men. Thus, one might expect that women would prefer erotic materials that contain such elements, and this turns out to be generally the case. In studies in which women and men were shown a variety of erotic photographs and videos, women preferred the materials that contained indicators of affection and psychological intimacy, and were turned off by too graphic depictions of sex acts and by violence (Mosher & MacIan, 1994; Senn & Radtke, 1990). Not surprisingly, then, some commercial pornography directed toward women is soft-core and has a romantic flavor.

Still, hard-core woman-oriented porno movies can be successful. Candida Royalle, a well-known porn star from the 1970s, turned to producing woman- and couple-oriented pornography in the 1980s. Her company, Femme Productions, turns out hard-core videos that present sex from the woman's perspective. Some of the sex scenes in her videos correspond to what one might expect—that is, passionate sex between a woman who is looking for love and a tall dark stranger who just might be Mr. Right. On the other hand, there are also "quickies" with men in elevators. Royalle describes her mission as "giving women permission to enjoy sex" (McElroy, 2001).

A woman-oriented genre that has no close male equivalent is the romance novel. Many of these novels would hardly be considered pornographic because they focus almost exclusively on relationships rather than on sex acts. The ubiquitous Harlequin Romance novels belong to this category. However, Harlequin now publishes more explicitly sexual stories under the Harlequin Temptation imprint, and other publishers have similar imprints. This phenomenon reflects a general trend toward acceptance of more explicit material by women than they were comfortable with in the past.

Lesbians have been pacesetters in women's pornography. Of course, plenty of male-oriented pornography features "lesbian" sex—even *Fanny Hill* has a steamy woman-on-woman sex scene. Little of this material appeals to most lesbians, however, since the actresses, even when they have sex with each other, are usually presented as objects of heterosexual male desire. Thus, lesbians who want pornography have had to generate their own. In 1984, lesbian feminists Nan Kinney and Debbie Sundahl founded *On Our Backs*, a magazine that was far more physical and explicit than anything seen before. Women plied each other with whips, used vulgar language, and gloried in their G-spots. The magazine also launched the career of "sexpert" Susie Bright (Bright, 1999). *On Our Backs* has since been joined by another magazine, *Bad Attitude*, which is even raunchier:

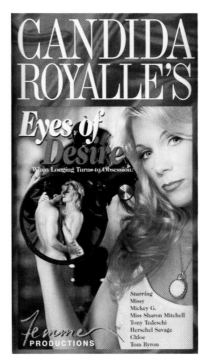

Some hard-core videos are made for women. In Candida Royalle's *Eyes of Desire* (1999), a beautiful photographer experiences a sensual awakening, aided by a high-powered telescope. "Through this new lens of desire, she's drawn into a dangerous game of mystery and lust when she discovers that she, in turn, is being watched by a mysterious stranger from a nearby abandoned estate." (From the film's promotional material.)

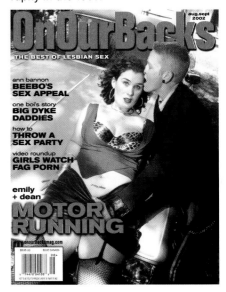

On Our Backs pioneered lesbian pornography in the 1980s.

it revels in politically incorrect images, such as one of a submissive, crouching woman performing fellatio on the strap-on dildo of a leather-clad, standing woman.

There Are Conflicting Perspectives on the Value or Harm of Pornography

Although the pornographers have basically "won" their battle with the censors—only pornography involving minors is still illegal and actively suppressed in the United States—there is still debate about the effects of pornography on society. On the one hand, it can be argued that pornography is victimless: the people who create it do so voluntarily and get paid, and the people who consume it also do so voluntarily and get sexual pleasure. On the other hand, it can be argued that the production and consumption of pornography has deleterious social consequences beyond its effects on the producers and consumers and should therefore be banned or regulated by society in some way.

What might these harmful social consequences be? According to *religious conservatives,* pornography promotes general moral decay and undermines traditional social institutions such as the family. Such allegations are very hard to prove or disprove, and we will not consider them further here.

Anti-porn march through the Times Square area of New York in 1979. The march was led by feminists including Susan Brownmiller, Andrea Dworkin, Gloria Steinem, and Bella Abzug. Dworkin's speech at the closing rally is available online (Dworkin, 1979). The film showing at the theater, *The Possession of Nurse Sherri,* was a hugely successful drive-in slasher movie that, in its original uncut version, contained some lurid sex scenes.

More focused allegations come from the *radical feminist* perspective. The possibility that has provoked the most discussion is that pornography promotes physical or sexual violence or other forms of harm against women. In Chapter 18 we mentioned the feminist idea that men are taught by society to despise women, and that this teaching process is the cause of rape. We cited Diana Russell's arguments in support of this notion. Russell and some other radical feminists, such as Andrea Dworkin and Catherine MacKinnon, believe that pornography is an important part of this teaching process. In fact, Russell defines pornography in a way that incorporates this alleged effect. Heterosexual pornography, she says, is "material created for heterosexual males that combines sex and/or the exposure of genitals with the abuse or degradation of females in a manner that appears to endorse, condone, or encourage such behavior." All other sexually suggestive material, she says, constitutes erotica (Russell, 1994). In 1970s and 1980s, radical feminists declared war on pornographic publishers.

Recent trends in *postfeminist* thought (which stresses diversity among women and a wide spectrum of ideas rather than the battle against male oppression) have led to some different viewpoints on pornography. "Pornography must continue to play a central role in our cultural life," writes Camille Paglia. "Pornography is a pagan area of beauty, vitality, and brutality, of the archaic vigor of nature. It should break every rule, offend all morality" (Paglia, 1994).

The *liberal* perspective generally downplays any harmful effects of pornography, and even sees beneficial effects in terms of encouraging sexual exploration or providing a harmless outlet for fantasies that could be dangerous in real life. Liberals also argue that pornography is protected by the First Amendment, and that exceptions to First Amendment protection cover only forms of expression that put people in immediate danger.

Some writers have combined liberal and postfeminist threads in the defense of pornography. Nadine Strossen, a professor at New York Law School and president of the American Civil Liberties Union (ACLU), argues that the sensual representation of women in pornography is a valid use of free expression and that free expression itself is central to women's equality (Strossen, 1995).

The question of pornography's harmful effects has long been a political football. A commission appointed by President Lyndon Johnson reported in 1970 that there was no evidence linking pornography to sexual crimes. A commission appointed by President Ronald Reagan (the "Meese Commission") came to the opposite conclusion, reporting in 1986 that "substantial exposure to sexually violent materials. . . . bears a causal relationship to antisocial acts of sexual violence" (Meese, 1986).

Research Has Not Resolved the Question of Pornography's Effects

A great deal of research has been done on the question of whether the consumption of pornography by men causes them to harm women. Some studies have been done on "regular" men with no special history of sexual violence. Male college students, for example, may be asked to provide information about their use of pornography and asked questions that assess their likelihood of committing violent acts against women. In more elaborate studies, men are exposed to various kinds of pornographic and nonpornographic materials in a laboratory setting. Then they may be given the opportunity to "harm" a woman by, say, giving her a (fictional) electric shock.

According to a meta-analysis of such studies, most men are not rendered more likely to harm women by exposure to any kind of pornography. Still, a minority of men—about 7 percent or so—do seem to become more likely to harm women after exposure to pornography (Malamuth et al., 2000). These are men with a preexisting hostility toward women or a violence-prone personality, perhaps as a result of childhood experiences. Not surprisingly, exposure to pornographic material that portrays violence (such as sadomasochistic behavior) has a greater effect on these men than do other forms of pornography.

There is some question about the relevance of these findings to the problem of real-world violence against women (Brannigan, 1987). For that reason, studies have been done on men who have been convicted of actual violent crimes against women (along with control groups of men who have not committed such crimes). These studies have basically come up negative: perpetrators of violent crimes against women do not report a greater exposure to pornography—or only a slightly greater exposure—compared with men in the control groups (Allen et al., 2000).

In spite of the large numbers of studies that have been done, the question of whether pornography contributes to violence against women still lacks a definitive answer. If it does do so, it is probably a minority effect—certain kinds of pornography affect certain kinds of men. Still, even such a minority effect could represent a great deal of harm.

Cross-cultural studies suggest that pornography consumption and violence against women do not necessarily go hand in hand. In Japan, for example, pornography—including violent pornography—is produced and consumed in very large quantities, yet sex crimes against women are relatively infrequent. During the period 1972–1995, when the availability and consumption of pornography exploded, the annual number of rapes in Japan fell from 4677 per year to 1500 per year (Diamond & Uchiyama, 1999). In fact, a broad analysis of pornography availability and sex crime rates in numerous countries suggests that the Japanese experience is typical: sex crimes become fewer when pornography consumption increases. This may be because pornography gives potential sex criminals an alternative outlet (Diamond, 1999), or it may be that some underlying social process, such as sexual liberation, causes both an increase in pornography and a decrease in sex crimes.

Such findings suggest that if pornography does promote sexual violence in the United States, there must be specific cultural factors at work here that facilitate the causal link. It might be more useful to study and address those cultural influences than to campaign for restrictions on pornography itself, because it seems unlikely at this point that any major restrictions on adult pornography are likely to be accepted or ruled constitutional.

Underage Pornography Is Widely Condemned, but Common in Some Countries

The situation is different with pornography involving minors. Although it is often called "child pornography" or "kiddie porn," the bulk of this material involves adolescents, so we'll call it **underage pornography.**

In the United States it is illegal to produce, distribute, purchase, download, or possess pornography featuring males or females under the age of 18. Simple nude pictures of minors may be permissible in some circumstances; so may text descriptions, cartoons, or animations of minors engaged in sex. In 1996 the U.S. Congress passed legislation that included provisions making it illegal to produce material that even looked like child pornography, such as computer-generated images. These provisions were struck down by the U.S. Supreme Court in 2002 (Associated Press, 2002a).

Japan has long been the world leader in the production of underage pornography. According to a 1999 estimate by the international law enforcement organization Interpol, 80 percent of the world's commercial underage pornography is produced in that country, mostly using non-Japanese minors, and 40 percent of Japanese pornographic Web sites contain images of minors (Reitman, 2001). Many Japanese men have an unabashed sexual interest in girls between puberty and adulthood; this interest is so well known that it has a name, *rori kon,* which is derived from the English phrase "Lolita complex." (Lolita was the 12-year-old object of a middle-aged man's desire in Vladimir Nabokov's 1955 novel of that name.) In fact, some Japanese schoolgirls make money for expensive purchases by prostituting themselves to adult men; these transactions are arranged by so-called "telephone clubs." Traditionally, the age of consent in some Japanese cities, including Tokyo, was 12, but in 1999 it was raised to 18. At the same time, underage pornography was banned, and there have been some arrests of violators of the new law.

Canada, on the other hand, has slightly eased its restrictions on pornography involving minors. The age of consent in Canada is 14, and in 2001 Canada's Supreme Court ruled that videotapes of lawful sexual activity between minors aged over 14 could legitimately be made and used for personal, unshared consumption (Farley, 2001).

A major concern about underage pornography is the potential for harm to the underaged actors themselves. Even some adult porn actors, such as *Deep Throat* star Linda Lovelace, have portrayed their experience as abusive (Lovelace & McGrady, 1980); the risk that it will be so for minors is much greater. Thus, there is broad agreement in the United States that the ban on the production of pornography that involves real minors should be actively enforced. Even the ACLU supports this ban, although it took a strong position against the 1996 law that banned *simulated* underage pornography (American Civil Liberties Union, 1996a). Adult Sites against Child Pornography (ASACP), an industry watchdog group, attempts to monitor and report Internet Web sites that feature underaged actors.

Legal Regulation of Pornography Is Local and Haphazard

A general problem with the legal regulation of pornography is that local jurisdictions are trying to deal with phenomena that extend far beyond their geographic or economic scope. All over America, towns, cities, and states enact wildly disparate laws based on what those governments believe to be their communities' standards. In 1998, the state of Alabama outlawed the sale of all sex toys, including vibrators, and threatened offenders with a year of prison with hard labor and a $10,000 fine. In 1997 the state of Virginia had a secret panel of citizens judge whether a video titled *Woodburn's Inner City Black Cheerleader Search #10* violated community standards of decency. The panel said "yes." Yet the production and consumption of pornographic videos is a national or international affair: a person who rents such a video in Virginia may consider himself a member of a national community of porn lovers rather than a local community of porn haters. (That particular case was eventually dropped.)

State jurisdictions even try to regulate the Internet. In 1995, Oklahoma outlawed the transmission of material "harmful to minors," and Connecticut banned material intended to "annoy" anyone. In 1996 Georgia criminalized the use of on-line pseudonyms. In 1998 New Mexico banned images of "nudity, sexual intercourse, or any other sexual conduct" (American Civil Liberties Union, 1998). Yet the Internet is global: it is an absurdity to imagine that someone posting material on a Web site at one location could ensure that it complies with the laws of every other location where it might possibly be viewed or downloaded. To the extent that the sexual content of the Internet needs regulation at all, it would require regulation at a planetary level.

Sex Is Part of the Mass Media

Sexually themed content on television and in advertising is rarely as explicit as it is in pornographic videos and the like. On the other hand, television and advertising reaches a much wider audience, including children and people who may not have chosen to see erotic material. Thus even mildly provocative sexual material can elicit a great deal of protest.

There Is Widespread Concern about Sex on Television

Images of the genitalia, anus, and female nipples, hard-core sex, and sexual slang words such as "fuck" are all banned on network TV and many cable channels. Even so, television programming is rife with sexual content—most of it verbal references to sex. And this content has been increasing at a rapid rate. A study by the Parents Television Council (PTC), a group that works to reduce the amount of sex, violence, and foul language on television, found that the number of sexual references or incidents on prime time network television nearly tripled between 1989 and 1999. References to certain sexual topics, such as masturbation, oral sex, "kinky" sex, the genitalia, and homosexuality, increased even faster; references to homosexuality led the field with a 265-fold increase over the decade (Parents Television Council, 2000).

These increases are not necessarily harmful. Increased references to homosexuality, for example, could be seen as long overdue, given that the topic was virtually taboo until the 1980s. Some of the examples that the PTC study cites seem to have more of a consciousness-raising purpose than a salacious one. In one example, a closeted action-movie star tells a film executive that he wants to be open about his sexual orientation: "My life is a living hell. The shame, the hiding. I want to be able to walk down the street with my man and say to the world . . . 'This is the man that I share my bed with'" (*Action*, Fox).

Increasing references to homosexuality on television might have the effect of familiarizing the public with homosexuality and thus decreasing anti-gay discrimination, or it might improve the self-esteem and mental health of gays and lesbians directly. Similarly, increasing references to masturbation might help reduce people's guilt feelings about engaging in that behavior. Even general sexual references might be helpful, given that people's reluctance to discuss sexual matters has often been cited as a cause of relationship problems. Still, it's hard not to conclude that an educational opportunity is being missed. Of the 14,000 sexual references the typical American teenager sees on television each year, only 150 deal with sexual responsibility, abstinence, or contraception (American Academy of Pediatrics, 1995).

In 1996 the U.S. television industry was ordered by Congress to introduce a "voluntary" ratings system that indicates the presence and intensity of sexual content (and violence and foul language) in individual programs. In combination with the V-chip—a device built into all new television sets and available as a set-top box for older sets—this system allows parents to filter out classes of programs they deem unsuitable for their children. The ACLU opposed the system, saying that it amounted to government censorship (American Civil Liberties Union, 1996b). One network—NBC—refused to go along with the full ratings system. It will be several years before V-chip availability and usage increases to a point that the system's usefulness can be judged.

Sex Sells, Sometimes

Sex has been used in advertising for as long as advertising has existed (Figure 19.4). Not surprisingly, people pay attention to and like ads containing images of persons they find sexually attractive. However, there is a downside to the use of sexual content in advertising. People may be turned off by sexual material they don't find attractive; women tend to react neg-

Figure 19.4 Sex in advertising. (A) The first known illustrated advertising poster, a 1491 woodcut used to advertise the book *Histoire de la belle Melusine.* Note the suggestion of auto-erotic activity on the part of the naked mermaid. (B) National Airlines' "Fly Me" and "Take Me" campaigns of the 1970s soon came to be viewed as offensively sexist. (C) Calvin Klein has been a pacesetter in the use of male beauty to sell products.

(A)

(B)

(C)

atively to ads containing female nudity, for example. In addition, sexual content often distracts the viewer from attending to or remembering the name of the product or the advertising message (Jones et al., 1998; Steadman, 1969). Sexual content is most effective when the product itself is related to sex—perfume, for example. Sex does not sell car batteries very well.

Advertisers are constantly trying to extend the limits of acceptability. In 1995, Calvin Klein was forced by public protest to terminate an ad campaign that featured apparently underaged models in sexually suggestive poses (Lippert, 1995). In the following year, all three television networks rejected a Victoria's Secret lingerie ad as too racy (Sloan, 1996).

Advertisers sometimes try to influence sex-related editorial content in the media by using their financial clout. In 1997, for example, the golf ball manufacturer Titleist pulled $1 million in ads from *Sports Illustrated* after the magazine reported that 20,000 lesbian fans attended the Dinah Shore LPGA tournament (Hiestand, 1997). The connection between lesbianism and women's professional golf had long been a taboo subject, and magazines will doubtless think twice about breaching that taboo after *SI*'s experience. When Ellen (played by real-life lesbian Ellen DeGeneres) declared her homosexuality on the television series of the same name, Chrysler, Wendy's, and J.C. Penney all pulled their advertising (Carey & Staimer, 1997). The show continued, but eventually succumbed to declining ratings.

Summary

1. Many relationships involve an exchange of resources for sex. Prostitution—paid sex—is the extreme version of this phenomenon. Prostitutes can be female, male, or transgendered, but nearly all users of prostitutes are male. Prostitution is illegal almost everywhere in the United States, but enforcement varies.

2. Historically, prostitution has been condemned as wrong, but also tolerated as necessary. Concern about STD transmission has been a major factor in anti-prostitution campaigns. Prostitution declined greatly during the twentieth century in the United States, probably because unmarried women became more willing to engage in sexual relations with men.

3. Streetwalkers are the lowest-paid prostitutes. They face a relatively high risk of violence and STDs, and many use drugs. Street prostitutes who are minors may be runaways or homeless; these prostitutes face heightened risks. Among street prostitutes, women do better economically than men, but men enjoy their work more. Female street prostitutes traditionally worked for pimps, but increasing numbers are independent operators or are controlled by gangs.

4. Escorts are off-street prostitutes who obtain clients by advertising or by word of mouth. They may go to the client's location (outcall) or receive clients at a fixed location (incall). Many work for escort services, which arrange their appointments. Escorts are more numerous than street prostitutes; they charge more, and work in somewhat safer conditions.

5. Other prostitutes work at commercial locations such as massage parlors or exotic dance venues. Brothels—establishments that have the sole purpose of prostitution—are rare today, and are legal only in parts of Nevada.

6. Women and men prostitute themselves principally because they can earn much more from prostitution than from other occupations, but sexual pleasure plays some role for high-end escorts and for some male prostitutes. Men use prostitutes for a wide variety of reasons, including difficulty in obtaining unpaid partners, sexual variety, or the excitement of illicit sex. According to some feminists, men use prostitutes to express their hatred of women, but some accounts by men suggest otherwise.

7. Prostitutes' rights organizations campaign for the total decriminalization of prostitution. Feminists have campaigned successfully for increased prosecution and punishment of men who use prostitutes. There is some support for regulated legalization of prostitution, as has happened in some European countries.

8. Conditions for prostitutes in developing countries are poor, but the occupation does offer them an above-average income. Some international agencies believe that pros-

titution should be recognized, governed by fair labor codes, and integrated into regional economies. Some international women's groups believe that activities associated with prostitution, but not prostitutes themselves, should be criminalized.

9. Underage prostitution is a particular concern in an international context. Overseas travelers are important users of underage prostitutes. The United States and many other countries have made it a crime for their citizens to have sex with minors overseas.

10. Many women are trafficked between countries for purposes of prostitution. Some women participate in this traffic voluntarily in search of economic betterment; others are enslaved and prostituted against their will.

11. Pornography consists of depictions of people or behaviors that are intended to be sexually arousing. Pornography has existed throughout history. Developments in communications technology, such as printing, film, videotape, and the Internet, have all led to new forms of pornography. Censorship of pornography increased greatly in Victorian times, but eased after the Second World War. In 1957 the U.S. Supreme Court ruled that the legality of sexually explicit work must be judged by "contemporary community standards."

12. Hugh Hefner's *Playboy* magazine (1953) and the Super-8 porno movie genre pioneered by Lasse Braun in the late 1960s were important in the history of postwar pornography. Feature-length porno movies became popular in the 1970s. The introduction of the videocassette format made production and consumption easier and allowed for greater diversity of content.

13. The Internet has facilitated sexual interactions across time and space. Future developments may allow for audiovisual sexual interactions among live persons in real time. Developments in virtual reality may eventually allow for something resembling real sex between remote persons or between persons and computers.

14. Pornography for women tends to be less sexually graphic than male-oriented pornography and to emphasize intimacy and romance. Still, there is a trend toward more sexually explicit material for women. Lesbians have pioneered a more hard-core approach to pornography.

15. There is debate about the potential harmful effects of pornography. Religious conservatives see pornography as undermining traditional family values. Radical feminists argue that pornography promotes violence against women. Some postfeminist thinkers disagree, saying that pornography plays an important cultural role. Liberals see the restriction of pornography as a violation of free expression.

16. Research studies suggest that most normal men are not made more likely to harm women by viewing any kind of pornography, but pornography that includes violence may make a few men more likely to harm women. Studies of convicted sex offenders indicate that they have not had greater exposure to pornography than other men. Countries with high rates of pornography consumption do not necessarily have high rates of violence against women.

17. Pornography featuring real sexual activity by underaged actors is illegal in the United States and many other countries. A U.S. law banning simulated underage pornography has been overturned.

18. Sexual content on television increased greatly during the 1990s. Responding to public and Congressional concern, the television industry introduced a rating system that warns of sexual (and violent) content. In combination with the "V-chip," it allows parents to filter out material they don't want their children to see.

19. Sex has long been used to sell products. Sexual content draws attention to advertisements, but does not necessarily aid the memorization and recall of product information. Advertisers sometimes attempt to use their financial influence to censor sex-related editorial and program content.

Discussion Questions

1. Do you think that prostitution should be legalized, decriminalized, or remain illegal? Cite your rationale.

2. If prostitution remains illegal, should the emphasis be on prosecuting prostitutes or on prosecuting their customers ("johns")? Should law enforcement devote equal resources to reducing street prostitution and escort service prostitution?

3. Should all depictions of sex involving underaged persons (whether real or simulated) be illegal? Why or why not?

4. Female college students have sometimes been hired as high-priced call girls. What do you think would be the pros and cons of this occupation? If your best friend considered this as a way to pay a tuition bill that was overdue, what would you advise her?

5. Parents are often very upset to find their young sons reading pornographic material. How would you advise parents to respond in that situation?

6. Do you think children should be protected from seeing pornographic material on the Internet? If you do, how would you accomplish this?

Web Resources

Prostitutes' Education Network www.bayswan.org/penet.html

COYOTE Los Angeles www.freedomusa.org/coyotela/coyotela.html

Coalition against Trafficking in Women www.catwinternational.org/

End Child Prostitution in Asian Tourism (ECPAT) www.ecpat.net/eng/index.asp

Adult Sites against Child Pornography www.asacp.org/

Parents Television Council www.parentstv.org/

Recommended Reading

Albert, A. (2001). *Brothel: Mustang Ranch and its women.* New York: Random House.

Bullough, V., and Bullough, B. (1987). *Women and prostitution: A social history.* Buffalo, NY: Prometheus Books.

Delacoste, F., and Alexander, P., eds. (1998). *Sex work: Writings by women in the sex industry* (2nd ed.). San Francisco: Cleis Press.

Dworkin, A. (1981). *Pornography: Men possessing women.* New York: Putnam.

Elias, J. E., Bullough, V. L., Elias, V., and Brewer, G., eds. (1999). *Prostitution: On whores, hustlers, and johns.* Amherst, NY: Prometheus Books.

Elias, J., Elias, V. D., Bullough, V. L., Brewer, G., Douglas, J. J., and Jarvis, W. eds. (1999). *Porn 101: Eroticism, pornography, and the First Amendment.* Amherst, NY: Prometheus Books.

Lane, F. S. (2000). *Obscene profits: The entrepreneurs of pornography in the cyber age.* New York: Routledge.

Strossen, N. (2000). *Defending pornography: Free speech, sex, and the fight for women's rights.* New York: New York University Press.

Afterword

*P*regnant male sea-horses. Anti-Müllerian hormone. Girls who grow up to be men. Love triangles. Episiotomy. Gay parents. Pubic lice. Date rape. Gigolos. We've touched on these and a multitude of other serious, not-so-serious, or downright whimsical topics in the preceding chapters. Amongst all these trees—let alone the ones that died to produce this book—can we discern a forest? Is there an overall take-home message, in other words? Here we suggest a few candidates.

Things Can Be Found out about Sexuality

Is it too obvious a message to state that it is possible to make discoveries about sexuality? We don't think so. All too often, people base their beliefs about sexual matters on traditional authority, gut instincts, introspection, or prejudice. Yet most sexual questions are amenable to rational inquiry, objective description, or experimental analysis. In short, there can be an evidence-based approach to sexuality, and we have endeavored to present the topic in that vein.

Historically, the most influential sex researchers have been those who have set out to scrutinize aspects of sex that previously seemed too personal, too nebulous, or too distasteful to be suitable for objective study. Alfred Kinsey was one such researcher. Although he was not the inventor of the sex survey, he and his colleagues turned this mode of inquiry into an industry, gathering an immense body of data about the sex lives of Americans. Indeed, Kinsey's data files are still being mined for new knowledge today: social psychologist Tony Bogaert of Brock University in Ontario, for example, has used them to study the relationship between numerous variables (such as birth order, handedness, and age at puberty) and sexual orientation or the likelihood of committing sexual offenses (Bogaert and Blanchard, 1996; Bogaert, 1998, 2001). Even more than the actual content of Kinsey's data, however, was the example that he set: the more recent national surveys that we have referred to frequently in this book, especially the NHSLS and NSSAL surveys, represent the continuation of the strategy established by Kinsey, with the addition of modern sampling and statistical techniques.

William Masters and Virginia Johnson were pioneers in the same sense: they made their careers out of directly observing human sexual interactions in the laboratory, and in doing so created and legitimized an entire field of inquiry. By devoting their attention both to healthy men and women and to persons with sexual dysfunctions, Masters and Johnson were able to demonstrate the relevance of directly observing sexual behavior to human health and well-being. Among the more recent studies that have extended their approach, we have mentioned Gary Schubach's catheterization study of female ejaculation (see Chapter 3) and the Dutch study in which couples engaged in coitus inside an MRI scanner (see Chapter 8). Direct observational studies of this kind still raise a few eyebrows, however, and are probably not as well funded as some other fields of sex research.

The biological and medical sciences have long led the way in the objective, quantitative study of human beings. The modern drug trial, with its double-blind, placebo-controlled, crossover design and its rigorous statistical analysis, has become the role model for many other kinds of studies. The usefulness of this approach in sex-related fields is most obvious in the case of drug treatments such as hormone replacement therapy for menopausal women (see Chapter 12). Imaginative researchers have extended this approach to other topics, however. Recall the study described in Chapter 7 (Finkelstein et al., 1998) in which researchers attempted to identify biological factors responsible for the increase in sexual expression at puberty. They gave children with delayed puberty gonadal steroids or a placebo and asked them to report their sexual feelings and behaviors over a period of nearly two years. They were able to document a role for androgens in the emergence of sexual expression in boys, whereas estrogens had little or no comparable effect in girls. Experimental studies of this kind, that *intervene* in a process of interest, are inherently more informative than those that merely *observe* it; the latter, though valuable, tend to establish correlations whose causal structure remains uncertain.

Experimental studies can shed light on purely psychological issues too. In Chapter 7, for example, we described how researchers exposed volunteers to various kinds of nonsexual arousal (such as having them listen to a description of a murder) in order to test the effects of this arousal on their judgments of the sexual attractiveness of faces. In Chapter 12 we described rather similar studies (Kenrick et al., 1989) in which volunteers were exposed to images of highly attractive or less attractive persons to see what effect this exposure had on their views about the attractiveness of their own partners: viewing attractive faces made men rate their partners as less attractive (the "Farrah factor").

Of course, there is something of a trade-off: the more experimental and interventional the design of a study, the more artificial it tends to become, raising questions about its relevance to real-life issues. Thus it is often most useful to combine information from experimental and observational studies, because these tend to balance each others' strengths and weaknesses. Recall, for example, that the "Farrah factor" studies were complemented by an observational study (Kanazawa & Still, 2000) that simply documented that male teachers were unusually likely to get divorced—as if exposure to attractive young people made their own wives seem less desirable.

Many aspects of psychosexual development are resistant to experimental analysis. For one thing, ethical considerations generally bar us from manipulating the lives of children in such a way as to test developmental theories. Still, as recounted in Chapter 7, psychiatrist Richard Green did perform a prospective study of sexual orientation that somewhat resembled a drug trial: he followed gender-nonconformist and conventional boys from childhood through adolescence or adulthood, and reported that most of the gender-nonconformist boys but virtually none of the conventional boys became bisexual or gay. That study included what amounted to a treatment arm: some of the boys were given operant-conditioning treatment to modify their gender-nonconformist behavior. The end-result of this part of the study was negative: the treated boys did alter their behavior but were no less likely to become bisexual or gay than the untreated gender-nonconformist boys. Studies of this kind are extremely arduous and take many years to complete, but they provide the kind of objective information that is difficult to obtain from retrospective studies.

You are exposed to innumerable assertions about human sexuality in the course of daily life—from friends and family, teachers, sex researchers, the media, politicians, ministers, groups that promote or oppose legal protections for sexual minorities, and so on (Figure 1). We hope that, as a result of taking this course, you will be able to take a more critical and informed view of these assertions than you were previously. In particular, we hope that you will ask yourself "How well substantiated is this assertion?" or "How could one design a study that would put this assertion to the test?"

Diversity Is a Key Aspect of Sexuality

As you've learned, people differ greatly in their sexual behaviors, feelings, and attitudes. To some extent, these differences are predictable on the basis of the demographic categories to which people belong. Asian-American teens have less experience of

coitus than African-American teens (see Chapter 12); women and men experience different kinds of jealousy in their sexual relationships (see Chapter 6); old people are less approving of non-marital sex than are young people (see Chapter 9); residents of the Southeastern states are more likely to contract gonorrhea than are other Americans (see Chapter 16), and so on.

Sexual diversity is even greater, of course, when we consider cultures other than our own, or changes that have occurred over history. This book has devoted most of its attention to the contemporary United States and other western countries, since that is the culture in which we and you live. Still, we have given you plenty of examples of cross-cultural and historical diversity. We have described how fat women are considered more attractive than thin women in the traditional cultures of West Africa (see Chapter 1), whereas American women often see *losing* weight as the key to attracting a mate. We mentioned that some of the tribes of New Guinea have institutionalized oral sex between boys and young men (see Chapter 12), and that many Islamic cultures practice (or did once practice) various forms of female circumcision (see Chapter 3) and polygamy (see Chapter 9), whereas all these activities have been criminalized in the United States. We've described major historical changes in sex-related institutions and practices such as dating, marriage, prostitution, pornography, contraception, homosexuality, and nudity, as well as in the particular sexual behaviors that people engage in and that they approve or disapprove of.

Besides the sexual diversity that is demographic or culture-bound, there is also a more individualistic diversity that distinguishes persons who seemingly have no reason to differ from each other. This includes diversity in sexual orientation and gender identity, interest in unusual sex practices or unusual sex objects, engagement in criminal sexual behaviors such as rape and sexual contact with children, and the sexual dysfunctions and the diseases of the sex organs that for poorly understood reasons affect some individuals and not others. Certainly there are plenty of causal pathways that have been proposed to account for this diversity: biological theories of sexual orientation, risk factors that predispose to erectile dysfunction or breast cancer, and socialization processes (including the victim–perpetrator cycle; see below) that may contribute to abusive behavior or sexual violence. Still, by and large we do not understand why certain people exhibit particular feelings, desires, behaviors, dysfunctions, and illnesses, while others do not.

Nature and Nurture Interact in Psychosexual Development

In spite of this uncertainty, it does seem likely that some combination of biological predisposition and life experience contributes to the diversity in sexual outcomes that we see around us—that both "nature" and "nurture" are at work, in other words. Yet the details are still highly controversial. Some people believe that the main effect of nurture is to *reinforce* inborn traits. According to this idea, for example, males may have an inborn predisposition to sexual aggressiveness, but this predisposition is greatly enhanced by the innumerable ways in which society condones or even encourages such behavior. Conversely, there are those who believe that nurture often works *against* nature, so that, in the case of male sexual aggressiveness, the main effect of socialization is to cause men to rein in their aggressive urges. Quite likely, both processes are at work.

As this book neared completion, a study was published that may point the way to a more detailed understanding of the interaction of nature and nurture (Caspi et al., 2002). A team led by clinical psychologists Terrie Moffitt and Avshalom Caspi (both of the Institute of Psychiatry in London and the University of Wisconsin) took advantage of a longitudinal study that has closely followed a representative cohort of 1000 New Zealanders from young childhood to their current age (mid-twenties). Focusing on the white males in the study, the researchers found that the boys who had experienced sexual or physical abuse during childhood were more likely than other boys to commit antisocial acts, including rape and other crimes of violence, in adolescence or adulthood. By itself, this finding merely adds to the evidence for the victim–perpetrator cycle that we discussed in Chapter 14. The researchers went further, however: they examined the men's DNA for genes that might contribute to this behavior. They focused on the gene that codes for monoamine oxidase A, an enzyme that breaks down neurotransmitters such as dopamine and serotonin. This gene (*MAOA*) was already suspected of playing a role in aggressive behavior, because the extremely rare individuals who completely lack a functional *MAOA* gene are known to be prone to violence.

Among the New Zealand subjects, as in other populations, about 1 in 10 carried a version of the *MAOA* gene that is less active than usual, though not completely inactive. Looking at the subjects as a whole, the researchers found no significant tendency for the men with the less-active gene to engage in more antisocial behavior or sexual violence. Thus, whether a man possesses the fully-active or the less-active gene seems, by itself, not to influence his likelihood of committing these acts. The novel finding, though, was this: the men who had been abused during childhood *and* possessed the less-active *MAOA* gene were much more likely to engage in antisocial acts than were the abused men with the fully-active gene. The more severe the childhood abuse, the greater the difference in adult behavior between the men possessing the fully-active and the less-active genes (Figure 2). An astonishing 85 percent of the men who both carried the less-active *MAOA* gene and had suffered severe childhood abuse developed some form of antisocial behavior. In other words, variability in the *MAOA* gene appears to strongly modulate the impact of childhood abuse on sexual and social development, damping the victim–perpetrator cycle when the gene is fully active and exaggerating it when the gene is less active.

Like other findings in behavioral genetics, this study needs to be verified and replicated in other populations. Still, it suggests how nature and nurture can interact in ways that are *conditional* rather than merely additive or subtractive. Thus it may not always be sufficient to compare small groups of subjects who differ in a single variable (such as variation in the activity of a particular gene). Rather, it may be necessary to study much larger populations in which the interactions of two or more variables (such as genetic predisposition and the experience of childhood abuse) can be analyzed. This, of course, would be consistent with our general understanding of human nature, which is that psychological and behavioral traits are the end-products of a complex web of causation, rather than being controlled by simple on/off switches.

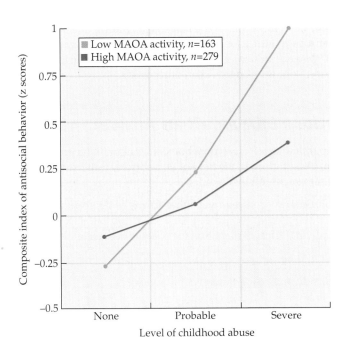

Figure 2 Genes and the victim–perpetrator cycle. This graph plots the antisocial behavior shown in adulthood by males who experienced different levels of abuse during childhood (none, probable, or severe). Men who have a less-active *MAOA* gene (orange) showed a much more pronounced effect of childhood abuse than did those with a fully active gene (green). The y-axis is plotted in units of standard deviation (z score); thus the difference between the severely abused men with low and high *MAOA* activity represents an effect size (*d*) of about 0.6, considered a moderate effect. (After Caspi et al., 2002.)

Understanding and Values Go Hand in Hand

Rational inquiry alone cannot be a sufficient guide to behavior or opinion, whether in sexual matters or in any other field of human experience. There must be guiding ethical principles to provide a framework within which reason operates. We cannot tell you what those principles should be—though we suggest that tolerance, honesty, and a concern for the welfare of our intimate partners could be among them. Although values don't come solely from the intellect, reason and knowledge do help give them expression. If one of your values is to respect the welfare of an intimate partner, for example, knowledge about how to prevent disease transmission and unwanted pregnancy can help you express that value in a practical way.

Just now, when we were listing various kinds of "diversity," we mentioned some traits and behaviors that you may be quite accepting or tolerant of, and others (such as female circumcision and adult–child sex) that you may strongly oppose. Our use of the word "diversity" to cover such a wide spectrum may have grated on you, because "diversity" is one of those words that is commonly used in a purely positive or supportive sense, like "freedom." Yet freedom means the freedom to do both good and evil, and similarly, sexual diversity encompasses feelings that should be fostered and those that should be restrained, behaviors that are admired and those that are detested, and experiences that are considered lucky and those that are considered misfortunes.

We can't tell you which is which, unfortunately, because that would be an attempt (and probably an unsuccessful one) to impose our own value systems on you. But we would suggest that the analysis of consequences can help focus broad moral beliefs onto specific issues. If you believe that an action's benefit or harm to others are the keys factors that decide its moral status, then you will do well to study the benefits and harms that result from the behaviors you are morally concerned with. If you're concerned with whether it's right or wrong for a married man to visit a prostitute, for example, then you'll need to consider the monetary benefit to the prostitute, the risk that he will give the prostitute a disease or conversely that he will acquire a disease from the prostitute and pass it on to his wife, the possible stabilizing or destabilizing effects of the man's action on his marriage, and so on. Particularly when personal judgment passes over into public policy and legislation, this kind of analysis of consequences seems particularly relevant. Research and other forms of intellectual inquiry are necessary to perform such an analysis.

Because of this connection between intellectual inquiry and moral judgments, we wouldn't be surprised if your opinions about the rightness or wrongfulness of certain forms of sexual expression have been modified in the process of reading this book or in discussing the various chapter topics with your classmates. We hope that you will continue to think about your moral stance in sexual matters, and to see scientific inquiry as a useful adjunct to forming moral opinions in this as in other fields.

Many Sexual Questions Still Await an Answer

This book has emphasized—perhaps more than most books of its kind have done—the limits of our knowledge and understanding in the field of sexuality. Here are some examples of important questions that remain unanswered:

- Why exactly has evolution favored sex over other forms of reproduction?
- What is the complete physiological explanation for how we become male or female?
- How does a person come to be gay or straight or bisexual?
- What really goes on inside our heads when we fall in love?
- Why is sex pleasurable?
- How do paraphilias develop?
- What causes men to rape?
- How can we eliminate sexually transmitted diseases?
- What would happen if we legalized prostitution or lowered the age of consent?
- How can we make sex education more effective? And how should we judge that effectiveness?

We have spent quite a bit of time discussing competing ideas on these topics, but—humbling though it is to admit it—we don't have satisfactory or complete answers. The study of human sexuality is still in its infancy; it is still struggling to free itself from a historical tradition of shame and not-so-benign neglect. And because the core of sexuality consists of motivations and feelings—mental phenomena that are less accessible than are sensory experiences or behaviors or rational thought processes—neuroscientists and psychologists have tended to pass the topic by. Hopefully this will change, aided perhaps by some of you who opt for a career in sex research. For no area of inquiry presents more fascinating and challenging questions to a young investigator, or promises greater benefits to humankind.

Glossary

Note on word derivations: The foreign source word, or its meaning, is omitted when it is the same as, or very similar to, the English term or its meaning.

Abortion (Latin *abortio*) The termination of a pregnancy, resulting in the death of the *conceptus;* may be *spontaneous* or *induced*. When unqualified, the term usually refers to an *induced abortion*.

Abused–abuser hypothesis See *victim–perpetrator cycle*.

Acquired immunodeficiency syndrome (AIDS) The disease caused by the *human immunodeficiency virus (HIV);* its onset is defined by the occurrence of any of a number of *opportunistic infections,* or on the basis of blood tests.

Acrosome (Greek *akros*, endmost, *soma*, body) A structure at the front of a *sperm* that contains enzymes and *receptors* required for penetration of the *zona pellucida* of an *ovum*.

Activation The functional maturation in adulthood of the neural circuitry underlying some behavior.

Adaptation A heritable trait that improves an organism's reproductive success in a given environment.

Adenocarcinoma A *carcinoma* arising from glandular epithelial cells.

Adolescence (Latin *adolescere*, grow up) A vaguely delineated period of psychosexual and social maturation that accompanies and follows puberty.

Adrenal gland (Latin *ad*, at, *renes*, kidneys) A gland located near the kidney, whose *cortex* secretes *corticosteroids, androgens,* and other hormones.

Adult bookstore Euphemism for a store dealing in *pornography*.

Afferent Conveying signals toward the *central nervous system*. Contrast *efferent*.

Afterbirth The *placenta,* whose delivery constitutes the final stage of *labor*.

Agonist (Greek *agôn*, contest) A compound, natural or synthetic, that binds to a *receptor* and activates it. Contrast *antagonist*.

AIDS See *Acquired immunodeficiency syndrome*.

AIDS-related condition (ARC) See *HIV-symptomatic disease*.

Alimony Legally mandated financial support of one partner (usually the wife) by the other in a divorce.

Alpha-fetoprotein A *protein* whose presence at elevated levels in the blood of a pregnant woman is suggestive of neural tube defects in the *fetus*. In a man, elevated levels are suggestive of testicular cancer or a variety of other conditions.

Alveolus (plural alveoli) (Latin, little channel) A microscopic cavity, such as the ones in the breasts where milk is produced.

Alzheimer's disease A form of *dementia* associated with aging and marked by specific brain pathology.

Amazon (Greek, supposedly from *a-*, without, *mazos*, breast, but more probably a Persian loanword) A female Scythian warrior; more generally, any tall or powerful woman.

Amenorrhea (Greek *a-*, not, *mên*, month, *rheos*, flow) Absence of *menstruation*.

Amino acids Compounds possessing carboxyl and amino groups that can be linked together to form *peptides* or *proteins*.

Amniocentesis (Greek *kentesis*, tapping into) The sampling of the *amniotic fluid* for purposes of *prenatal* diagnosis.

Amnion or amniotic sac (Greek) The membranous sac containing *amniotic fluid* and the *fetus*.

Amniotic fluid The fluid within which the *fetus* develops.

Ampulla (Latin, flask) The wider section of the *oviduct* near the *ovary;* the usual site of *fertilization*.

Anabolic Tending to increase tissue mass.

Anal sex As used here, penetration of the *anus* by the *penis;* could also include a variety of other behaviors, such as *analingus, fisting,* or anal penetration with a *dildo*.

Anal warts See *genital warts*.

Analingus Sexual contact between the tongue of one person and the *anus* of another.

Androgen (Greek *anêr*, *andr-*, man) Any of a class of *steroids*—the most important being *testosterone*—that promote male sexual development and have a variety of other functions in both sexes.

Androgen insensitivity syndrome (AIS) An *intersexed* condition caused by absent or nonfunctional *androgen receptors;* may be complete or partial. Also known as *testicular feminization*.

Andropause In men, the gradual decline of fertility with age; a hypothetical male equivalent of the female *menopause*.

Androphilic (Greek *anêr*, *andr-*, man, *philia*, love) Sexually attracted to males.

Anencephalic Lacking most of the brain.

Anorgasmia Difficulty experiencing or inability to experience *orgasm*. In women, also called *female orgasmic disorder*.

Anovulation Failure to *ovulate*.

Antagonist A compound, natural or synthetic, that blocks the action of an *agonist*.

Antepartum (Latin) Before birth.

Anterior commissure   A band of *axons* interconnecting portions of the left and right *cerebral hemispheres.* Similar to the *corpus callosum,* but smaller.

Anti-Müllerian hormone (AMH)   A *peptide* hormone secreted by *Sertoli cells* that prevents the development of the female internal *reproductive tract.* Also called Müllerian inhibiting substance (MIS) or Müllerian inhibiting hormone (MIH).

Anus (Latin)   The exit of the gastrointestinal tract.

Apotemnophilia (Greek *apotemnein,* to cut off, *philia,* love)   Sexual arousal by the thought of having a limb amputated, or an *erotic* interest in persons who have amputations.

Areola (plural areolae)   The circular patch of darker skin that surrounds the nipple.

Aromatase   An enzyme that converts *testosterone* to *estradiol,* so called because estradiol is an "aromatic" compound—one containing a benzene ring.

Artificial insemination   An assisted reproduction technique that involves the placement of *semen* in the *vagina* or *uterus* with the aid of a syringe or cannula.

Asexual reproduction   Reproduction in which all the offspring's *genes* are inherited from a single parent.

Autoerotic   Providing sexual stimulation to oneself or being aroused sexually by oneself; related to *masturbation.*

Autoerotic asphyxia   Self-strangulation for purposes of sexual arousal.

Autogynephilia (Greek *autos,* self, *gunê,* woman, *philia,* love)   A form of male-to-female *transexuality* characterized by a man's sexual arousal at the thought of becoming a woman.

Autonomic nervous system   The portion of the nervous system that controls *smooth muscles,* glands, and so forth without our conscious involvement. It has two components, the *sympathetic* and *parasympathetic nervous systems,* that often work in opposition to each other.

Autosome   Any *chromosome* other than a *sex chromosome.*

Aversion therapy   A form of *behavior therapy* that attempts to eliminate unwanted desires or behaviors (such as *paraphilias*) by the use of negative reinforcement; that is, by associating the unwanted thought pattern with an unpleasant experience such as an electric shock.

Axilla (Latin)   The armpit.

Axon (Greek, axle)   The extension of a *neuron* that conveys impulses, usually in a direction away from the *cell body.* Also called *nerve fiber.*

Bacterial vaginosis   A condition in which the normal microorganisms of the *vagina* are replaced by anaerobic species, causing discomfort and a foul-smelling discharge.

Barr body   The condensed, inactivated *X chromosome* visible as a dense spot in the nuclei of female cells.

Bartholin's glands   Glands at the *introitus* that discharge a small amount of fluid during sexual arousal.

Basal body temperature   Body temperature measured in the morning before getting out of bed.

Bathhouse   A facility, usually in the form of a private club, used for casual sex between *gay* men.

Battered-woman syndrome   A version of *post-traumatic stress disorder* affecting women who are victims of *intimate partner violence,* characterized especially by a cessation of attempts to escape from the abusive situation.

Bear   A burly, hirsute *gay* man; more generally, a member of a gay male subculture that rejects many of the prevailing standards of gay male attractiveness and behavior.

Bearing down   Aiding the process of *parturition* by voluntary muscular contractions.

Behavior therapy or behavior modification   Treatment of *paraphilias* or other disorders based on the theories of *behaviorism.*

Behaviorism   The idea that behavior can be understood in terms of a limited set of input–output functions, such as conditioned *reflexes* and *instrumental conditioning.*

Benign   Noncancerous.

Benign prostatic hyperplasia (or hypertrophy)   An enlarged but noncancerous prostate gland.

Berdache (French)   Anthropologist's term for a *two-spirit person.*

Bestiality   Obsolete term for sexual contact between a person and an animal. See *zoophilia.*

Bigamy   The legal offense of marrying someone when already married to someone else.

Binding   The attachment of a hormone, *neurotransmitter,* or *virion* to a *receptor.*

Biopsy (Greek *bios,* life, *opsis,* seeing)   A tissue sample from a living person for diagnostic or (less commonly) for therapeutic purposes.

Biphobia   Prejudice against *bisexuals.*

Birth canal   The canal formed by the *uterus, cervix,* and *vagina,* through which the *fetus* passes during *parturition.*

Birthing center   A facility specializing in childbirth care.

Bisexual   One who is sexually attracted to persons of both sexes.

Blastocyst (Greek *blastos,* a sprout)   A *conceptus* shortly before implantation, when it takes the form of a sphere of cells with a central cavity.

Body mass index (BMI)   A measure of obesity; a person's weight in kilograms divided by the square of their height in meters.

Boston marriage   The *cohabitation* of two women in nineteenth-century New England.

Bottom   Colloquial term for a *gay* man who prefers the receptive role in *anal sex,* or for the person on whom pain is inflicted in a *sadomasochistic* encounter. Contrast *top.*

Bradley method   A method of childbirth instruction that stresses the partner's role as birth coach and which seeks to avoid medical interventions.

Braxton-Hicks contractions   Irregular *myometrial* contractions that occur during the third trimester of pregnancy. Also known as *false labor.*

Breech delivery   The delivery of a baby feet or buttocks first, instead of head first.

Brothel (Old English *brothen,* degenerate)   A house of *prostitution.*

Bulbospongiosus or bulbocavernosus muscle   A muscle that attaches to the base of the *penis* or *clitoris* and assists with *erection* and (in men) *ejaculation.* In women, the internal portion of the muscle surrounds the *introitus:* when contracted, it tightens the introitus and may transfer mechanical stimulation from the introitus to the *clitoris.*

Bulbourethral glands   Small glands near the *root* of the *penis* whose secretions ("pre-cum") may appear at the *urethral meatus* during sexual arousal prior to *ejaculation.* Also known as *Cowper's glands.*

Butch (From the man's name, or from *butcher*)   Colloquial term for a masculine-acting or dominant *lesbian.* Contrast *femme.*

Butt plug   A *dildo* with a flared end, used to penetrate the *anus.*

Calendar method   A simple *rhythm method* of *contraception* based on the timing of *menstrual cycles.*

Call girl   An *escort service prostitute,* especially one who is relatively upscale in terms of clientele and price.

Candidiasis   A fungal infection, for example, of the *vagina.* Commonly called a *yeast infection.*

Capacitation   A chemical change in the surface of a *sperm* within the female *reproductive tract* that allows it to swim more forcefully and to respond to the presence of the *ovum.*

Capsid   An array of *protein* molecules surrounding the core of a *virus.*

Carcinoma   Cancer arising from an epithelium.

Castrate (Latin *castrare*) 1. To remove the *testicles* (usual meaning). 2. In Freudian theory and some other contexts, to remove the *penis* or the entire male *external genitalia*. 3. Uncommonly, to remove the *ovaries*.

Catecholamine Any of a class of molecules derived from the *amino acid* tyrosine that function as *neurotransmitters* or hormones.

Categorical perception A mode of perception that rapidly and automatically assigns stimuli to categories such as male or female.

CD4 lymphocytes A type of lymphocyte that carries the CD4 *receptor;* one of the major targets of *HIV.*

Celibacy (Latin *caelebs*, single) Living under a vow not to marry or (by implication) to engage in sexual relations; complete sexual abstinence.

Cell body The part of a *neuron* where the nucleus is located.

Central nervous system (CNS) The brain and spinal cord.

Cerebral hemispheres (Latin *cerebrum*, brain) The uppermost and, in humans, largest portion of the brain, divided into left and right halves.

Cervical 1. Of or related to the *cervix.* 2. Of or related to the uppermost eight segments of the spinal cord.

Cervical cap A small rubber or plastic cap that adheres by suction to the *cervix,* used as a *contraceptive.*

Cervical mucus Mucus secreted by glands in the *cervix,* whose consistency varies around the *menstrual cycle.*

Cervix (Latin, neck) The lowermost, narrow portion of the *uterus* that connects with the *vagina.*

Cesarean section (C-section) The delivery of a baby through an incision in the abdominal wall and the *uterus.*

Chancre (pronounced SHANK-er) (French) A primary sore on the skin or a mucous membrane in a person infected with *syphilis.*

Chancroid A sexually transmitted disease that causes soft sores on the *penis,* rare in the United States but common in parts of Africa.

Change of life *Menopause.*

Chaperone (French, hood) Traditionally, a female companion who accompanied a woman when meeting men, whose role was to prevent sexual impropriety.

Chemotherapy The use of drugs to treat a medical condition, especially to kill cancer cells.

Child molester An adult who has sexual contact with a *prepubescent* child. Sometimes used more broadly to include adults who have sexual contact with pubescent children or with any person under the legal age of consent.

Chlamydia A sexually transmitted disease caused by infection with the bacterium *Chlamydia trachomatis.*

Chorionic gonadotropin See *human chorionic gonadotropin (hCG).*

Chorionic villus sampling. The sampling of tissue from the *placenta* for purposes of *prenatal* diagnosis.

Chromatid One of the two identical copies of a *chromosome* produced by *DNA* replication.

Chromosomes Rod-shaped nuclear organelles composed of *DNA* and associated *proteins.*

Chronic pelvic pain syndrome A recent alternative term for the condition in men previously labeled chronic *prostatitis.*

Cilium (plural cilia) (Latin, eyelash) A microscopic, hairlike extension of a cell, often capable of a coordinated beating motion.

Circumcision In males, removal of the *foreskin.* In females, the cutting or removal of the *clitoral hood* or a variety of more destructive procedures, sometimes referred to collectively as *female genital mutilation.*

Classical conditioning A learning paradigm studied by Ivan Pavlov, which involves the development of a *reflex* response to some stimulus by its frequent association with another stimulus that already induces that response.

Climacteric (Greek *klimakter*) The transition to infertility at the end of a woman's reproductive life, which consists of a period of several years culminating in *menopause;* more generally, a critical phase of life.

Clitoral hood The female *prepuce;* the loose fold of skin that covers the *clitoris.*

Clitoral reduction Surgery to shorten the *clitoris.*

Clitoridectomy Removal of the entire external portion of the *clitoris.*

Clitoris (Greek) The erectile organ in females, whose external portion is located at the junction of the *labia minora,* just in front of the *vestibule.*

Clitoromegaly A size of the *clitoris* that is deemed excessive, or abnormal growth of the clitoris under the influence of hormones.

Cloaca (Latin, sewer) The common exit of the gastrointestinal and urogenital systems; in humans it is present only in embryonic life.

Closet See *coming out of the closet.*

Cock-ring A band placed around the base of the *penis* to help maintain an *erection.*

Cognitive (Latin *cognoscere*, know) Of or related to the aspects of the mind that process knowledge or information (e.g., perception) as distinct from emotion or personality. There has been a trend toward increasingly broad use of this term.

Cognitive developmental models Theories that ascribe the development of sexual and other traits to a sequence of thought processes, ideas, or beliefs.

Cognitive distortion A distortion of interpretation or judgment, such as might serve to justify or heighten the *erotic* significance of *paraphilic* behavior.

Cohabitation A live-in sexual relationship between an unmarried couple.

Coitus (Latin) Sexual contact involving penetration of the *vagina* by the *penis.* Same as *copulation,* and *sexual intercourse* in usual meaning of term.

Colostrum (Latin) The milk produced during the first few days after birth; it is relatively low in fat but is rich in immunoglobulins that confer *passive immunity* on the baby.

Colposcopy The examination of the *cervix* with the aid of an operating microscope.

Combination pill An *oral contraceptive* pill that contains both an *estrogen* and a *progestin.*

Combination therapy The use of a combination of drugs to treat a medical condition, especially *AIDS.* In the latter case it is also called *highly active anti-retroviral therapy (HAART).*

Coming out of the closet, or coming out Revealing a previously concealed identity, such as being *gay.*

Companionate marriage A form of marriage in which the husband and wife are expected to be emotionally intimate and to engage in social activities together.

Compulsive sexual behavior Sexual behavior perceived subjectively as involuntary and diagnosed as a symptom of an *obsessive–compulsive disorder.*

Conception See *fertilization.*

Conceptus (Latin, conceived) The developing organism from the 2-cell stage onward, including both embryonic and extraembryonic tissues. Used mainly for the early stages of development before the *embryo* has become a distinct entity.

Concubine (Latin *con-*, with, *cubare*, lie down) Historical term for a woman who *cohabits* with a man but is not his wife, especially in *polygamous* cultures.

Conditioning The modification of behavior by simple learning rules such as association and reinforcement. See *classical conditioning, instrumental conditioning.*

Condom (origin unknown) A sheath placed over the *penis* as a *contraceptive* and/or to prevent disease transmission. See also *female condom*.

Condylomata acuminata See *genital warts*.

Congenital adrenal hyperplasia (CAH) An *intersexed* condition caused by a genetic defect in *corticosteroid* synthesis.

Conjugation Contact between two bacteria accompanied by the transfer of a short stretch of *DNA* from one to the other.

Continence 1. (Obsolete) The ability to restrain sexual passion. 2. The ability to prevent involuntary voiding of urine or feces.

Contraception The prevention of *fertilization* and pregnancy.

Contraceptive A device, drug, or practice intended to prevent pregnancy.

Contrast effect A change in the perception of a stimulus induced by prior exposure to a contrasting stimulus.

Coolidge effect The shortening of the *refractory period* caused by the presence of a novel sex partner.

Copulation (Latin *copula*, joining) *Sexual intercourse* or *coitus*, especially in nonhuman animals.

Corona (Latin, crown) The rim of the *glans* of the *penis*.

Corpus callosum (Latin, hardened body) A band of *axons* interconnecting the left and right *cerebral hemispheres*.

Corpus cavernosum (Latin, cavernous body) Either of two elongated erectile structures within the *penis* or *clitoris*, which also extend backward into the pelvic floor.

Corpus luteum (Latin, yellow body) A secretory structure in the *ovary* derived from an ovarian *follicle* after *ovulation*.

Corpus spongiosum An erectile structure than runs along the underside of the *penis* and fills the *glans*. It surrounds the penile *urethra*.

Cortex (Latin, bark) The outer portion of an anatomical structure, as of the *cerebral hemispheres* or the *adrenal gland*.

Corticosteroids A class of *steroids* secreted by the *cortex* of the *adrenal gland*.

Courtship disorder A cluster of *paraphilias*, including *exhibitionism* and *voyeurism*, conceptualized as a disorder of normal courtship behavior.

Couvade (pronounced coo-VAHD) (French) In anthropology, a variety of ritual practices by men during their wives' pregnancies. Medically, pregnancy-like symptoms in the male partners of pregnant women.

Covenant marriage A form of marriage that requires a stronger vow of commitment, and that makes divorce harder to obtain, than a regular marriage.

Covert sensitization A variation of *aversion therapy* in which the negative reinforcement is provided by the subject's own imagination.

Cowper's glands See *bulbourethral glands*.

Cremaster muscle (Greek, suspender) A *striated muscle* that wraps around the *spermatic cord* and the *testis*. Its contraction brings the testis closer to the body.

Cross-dressing Wearing the clothing of the other sex, for any of a variety of reasons. See *transvestism*, *drag*.

Crowning During childbirth, the appearance of the baby's head at the opening of the *vagina*.

Cruising Looking for a sex partner (a colloquial expression used primarily by *gay* men).

Crura (sing. crus) (Latin, legs) Internal extensions of the *clitoris*.

Cryptorchidism (Greek *cruptos*, hidden, *orchis*, testicle) Failure of one or both *testicles* to descend into the *scrotum* by 3 months of postnatal age.

Culposcopy or culpotomy *Tubal sterilization* using an approach through the *vagina*.

Cum 1. Noun: A Colloquial term for ejaculated *semen*. 2. Verb: To *ejaculate* (also *come*).

Cumulus cells (Latin, heap) A layer of cells, derived from the *granulosa cells* of an ovarian *follicle*, that surrounds the *ovum* after *ovulation*.

Cunnilingus (Latin *cunnus*, vulva, *lingua*, tongue) Sexual contact between the tongue or mouth of one person and the *vulva* of another.

Cycle of violence The repeating or escalating cycle of tension building, violence, and reconciliation that characterizes many forms of *intimate partner violence*.

Cystitis Inflammation of the bladder, usually caused by an infection.

Cytokine A type of signaling molecule that may act locally or that may be less specific than a classical hormone in respect to its sites of synthesis and its target tissues.

Dams Flat sheets of latex used to prevent disease transmission during *cunnilingus* or *analingus*.

Dartos (Greek, flayed) A sheet of *smooth muscle* underlying the skin of the *scrotum*, which when contracted throws the skin into wrinkles.

Date rape *Rape* between dating or socially acquainted couples.

Delayed ejaculation Difficulty achieving or inability to achieve *orgasm* or *ejaculation*. Also called *male orgasmic disorder*.

Delayed labor or delayed birth *Labor* or birth that occurs more than 2 weeks after a woman's due date.

Delayed puberty Failure of onset of *puberty* by some criterion age, usually 13 or 14 in girls and 14 in boys.

Delusional stalking *Stalking* motivated by the delusional belief that the victim is in love with, or could be persuaded to fall in love with, the stalker.

Dementia (Latin *mens*, mind) A broad, severe, and usually gradual decline of *cognitive* abilities.

Demography (Greek *demos*, people) The statistical analysis of populations.

Dendrite (Greek *dendron*, tree) The extensions of a *neuron* that receive incoming signals from other neurons.

Depo-Provera An injectable form of medroxyprogesterone acetate, used as a *contraceptive* in women or to decrease the sex drive in male sex offenders.

Desensitization The loss of *receptor* activation caused by prolonged exposure to an *agonist*.

***Diagnostic and Statistical Manual of Mental Disorders* (DSM)** A compilation of diagnostic criteria for mental disorders published by the American Psychiatric Association and updated periodically, the most recent version being a text revision of DSM-IV, published in 2000.

Diaphragm A barrier placed over the *cervix* as a *contraceptive*.

Diethylstilbestrol (DES) A synthetic *estrogen receptor agonist* that was once used as a drug but that caused a variety of serious ill effects.

Dilation and curettage (D and C) A procedure involving the opening of the *cervix* and the scraping out of the contents of the *uterus* with a curette (spoon-like instrument). May be done as an *abortion* procedure or for other purposes. The term is sometimes used to refer to *vacuum aspiration* abortion.

Dilation and evacuation (D and E) An *abortion* procedure that employs *vacuum aspiration* followed by the use of instruments to remove remnants of the *conceptus*.

Dilator See *vaginal dilator*.

Dildo A sex toy, often shaped like a *penis*, used to penetrate the *vagina* or *anus*.

Diploid Possessing the full complement of *chromosomes*, i.e., a *homologous* pair of all *autosomes* and (in humans) two *sex chromosomes*, XX or XY. Usually true of all cells except *gametes*. Contrast *haploid*.

Directed masturbation *Sex therapy* exercises involving *masturbation*, generally with the purpose of treating *anorgasmia*.

Disruptive selection *Natural selection* that divides a population into two distinct types.

Dissociation The distancing of oneself from the emotions evoked by some traumatic experience or memory.

Dizygotic Of or related to twins who develop from separate *zygotes*, and who are therefore no more closely related to each other than non-twin siblings. Also called "fraternal." Contrast *monozygotic*.

DNA (deoxyribonucleic acid) A polymer of *nucleotides* that forms the chemical basis of *genes* in all species except some *viruses*.

DNA polymorphism A specific location within the *genome* where different individuals may have different *DNA* sequences.

Dopamine A *catecholamine* that serves as a *neurotransmitter* and also as a hormone, inhibiting the release of *prolactin* from the anterior lobe of the *pituitary gland*.

Dorsal horn (Latin *dorsum*, back) The portion of the *gray matter* of the spinal cord nearer to the back of the body, where incoming signals are processed. Contrast *ventral horn*.

Double standard The application of different moral standards to males and females, such as the notion that *promiscuity* is more acceptable for men than it is for women.

Douche (French, shower) To rinse the *vagina* out with a liquid; the liquid so used.

Doula (Greek *doulê*, female slave) A woman who supports a mother during *labor*.

Down syndrome A collection of birth defects caused by the presence of an extra copy of *chromosome* 21 (trisomy 21).

Drag The wearing of exaggeratedly feminine clothing by a man, often for entertainment purposes.

Dry orgasm A male *orgasm* not accompanied by *ejaculation*.

Ductal carcinoma Breast cancer arising from the *lactiferous ducts*.

Dyke (origin uncertain) Generally abusive term for a *lesbian*, especially a masculine-acting one.

Dysmenorrhea (Greek *dus-*, badly, *mên*, month, *rheos*, flow) *Menstruation* accompanied by pain.

Dyspareunia (Greek *dus-*, badly, *pareunios*, coupled) Painful *coitus*, especially in women.

Ectopic pregnancy Implantation and resulting pregnancy at any site other than the *uterus*.

Effacement Thinning of the *cervix* in preparation for childbirth.

Effect size (*d*) A measure of the difference between samples from two populations or the same population before and after some treatment; it is the difference between the means divided by the pooled standard deviations.

Efferent Conveying signals away from the *central nervous system*. Contrast *afferent*.

Ejaculation (Latin *e-*, out of, *iaculari*, throw). The forceful expulsion of *semen* from the *urethral meatus*, usually accompanying *orgasm*. See also *female ejaculation*.

Ejaculatory duct Either of the two bilateral ducts formed by the junction of the *vas deferens* and the duct of the *seminal vesicle*. The ejaculatory ducts empty into the *urethra* within the *prostate*.

Embryo (Greek) The portion of the *conceptus* that develops into the *fetus*. Often used loosely for the entire conceptus from the 2-cell stage onward.

Embryonic stem cell A *pluripotent* cell found in the *inner cell mass* of the *blastocyst*.

Emergency contraception See *morning-after pill*.

Emission See *otoacoustic emissions, nocturnal emission, seminal emission*.

Endocrine Of or related to the system of glands that secrete hormones into the bloodstream.

Endocrinology The study of glands and hormones.

Endometriosis The growth of *endometrial* tissue at abnormal locations.

Endometrium (Greek *endo-*, within, *mêtra*, uterus) The internal lining of the *uterus*.

Engagement 1. A commitment to marry. 2. The sinking of a *fetus*'s head into a lower position in the pelvis in preparation for birth. Also called *lightening*.

Engorgement Distension with blood.

Envelope A lipid outer membrane possessed by some *viruses*.

Epididymis (plural epididymides) (Greek *epi*, on, *didumos*, twin) A structure attached to each *testis* through which *sperm* must pass before entering the *vas deferens*.

Epidural anesthesia Anesthesia administered just outside the membrane that surrounds the spinal cord.

Epiphysis (Greek, excrescence) The growth zone near each end of a long bone.

Episiotomy (Greek *epision*, pubic region, *tomê*, a cut) A cut extending the opening of the *vagina* backward into the *perineum*, done by an *obstetrician* with the intention of facilitating childbirth.

Erectile dysfunction or erectile disorder A persistent inability to achieve or maintain an *erection* sufficient to accomplish a desired sexual behavior such as *coitus* to *orgasm*. Earlier known as *impotence*.

Erection The expansion and stiffening of the *penis, clitoris*, or nipples in response to sexual stimulation or ideation.

Erogenous zones Regions of the body whose stimulation can cause sexual arousal.

Erotic (from the Greek love god, Eros) Pertaining to, or eliciting, sexual arousal.

Erotica Sexually themed works, such as books or sculpture, deemed to have literary or artistic merit.

Erotomania The delusional belief that a sexually desired but unattainable person is actually in love with oneself.

Escort Euphemism for a *prostitute* who advertises by print, word of mouth, or the Internet. Contrast *streetwalker*.

Escort service A service that provides *prostitutes*, generally contacted by telephone.

Estradiol The principal *estrogen*.

Estrogen Any of a class of *steroids* , the most important being *estradiol*, that promote the development of female *secondary sexual characteristics* at *puberty*, help regulate the *menstrual cycle*, and have many other functions in both sexes.

Estrogen replacement therapy See *hormone replacement therapy*.

Estrus (Greek *oistros*, gadfly, frenzy) The restricted period within the ovarian cycle when females of some species are sexually receptive; "heat."

Eugenics (Greek *eu*, well, *genos*, race) A movement to improve the human race by restricting the reproduction of persons deemed genetically inferior.

Eugonadal Experiencing normal function of the *testes* or *ovaries*, especially as assessed by levels of *sex steroids*.

Eukaryote (Greek *karyon*, kernel) An organism whose cells contain nuclei.

Eunuch (Greek *eunuchos*, from *eunê*, bed, *echein*, to have [charge of]) A man who has been *castrated*, especially one set in charge of the women in a *harem*.

Evoked potentials Electrical signals that can be detected with electrodes on the scalp, resulting from neural responses to a sensory stimulus.

Excitement phase In Masters and Johnson's four-phase model of sexual response, the initial phase, during which sexual arousal begins and increases.

Exhibitionism A *paraphilia* involving exposure of the *external genitalia* to strangers, sometimes with *masturbation;* also called "flashing."

Exposure therapy A form of psychotherapy for victims of *rape* or abuse in which they are encouraged to recall the traumatic event in a safe environment.

Expression The functional activation of a *gene:* its transcription into *RNA* and, often, the translation of the *RNA* into *protein.*

Expurgate To remove passages deemed offensive, such as sexual references, from a work.

External genitalia The sexual structures on the outside of the body; the *vulva* in females and the *penis* and *scrotum* in males.

External os or os (Latin, mouth) The opening in the *cervix* that connects the *lumen* of the *vagina* with the cervical canal.

Externalities The costs or benefits of an action that are experienced by society as a whole, or by persons other than those directly involved in that action.

Extra-pair relationship A sexual relationship in which at least one of the partners is already partnered with someone else; Includes extramarital affairs.

Extraterritorial legislation Legislation that makes certain activities, such as sex with underage *prostitutes,* illegal even when carried out in a foreign country in which the activity is legal.

Factor analysis A statistical procedure for reducing a large number of variables to a smaller set of underlying "factors."

Faggot (probably from an obsolete abusive term for a woman) Abusive term for a *gay* man.

Failure rate See *perfect-use failure rate, typical-use failure rate.*

Fallopian tube See *oviduct.*

False labor See *Braxton-Hicks contractions.*

False negative A test result that is negative when it should be positive.

False positive A test result that is positive when it should be negative.

Fantasy (Greek *phantazein*, to make visible) An imagined experience, sexual or otherwise.

Fascia (Latin, band) A tough sheet or sheath of connective tissue.

Fellatio (Latin) Sexual contact between the mouth of one person and the *penis* of another.

Female condom A plastic pouch inserted into the *vagina* as a *contraceptive* and/or to prevent disease transmission.

Female ejaculation The discharge of fluid (either urine or the secretions of the *paraurethral glands*) from the *urethral meatus* at sexual climax experienced by some women.

Female genital mutilation A term used to refer to any of several forms of female *circumcision,* with an implication of harmfulness.

Female orgasmic disorder See *anorgasmia.*

Female sexual arousal disorder Insufficient physiological arousal (*lubrication* and engorgement of the *vagina, erection* of the *clitoris*) in women, such as to make sex unpleasurable or painful.

Feminism The movement to secure equality for women; the study of social and psychological issues from women's perspectives.

Femiphobia Prejudice against feminine-acting men or boys.

Femme (French, woman) Colloquial term for a feminine-acting *lesbian.* Contrast *butch.*

Fertile window The period within the *menstrual cycle,* at and just before *ovulation,* when *coitus* has a significant chance of leading to *fertilization.*

Fertilization The entry of a *sperm* into an *ovum,* thus transforming the ovum into a genetically unique *diploid* organism capable of development (*conceptus*). Also called *conception.*

Fetal alcohol syndrome A collection of physical and behavioral symptoms in a child who was exposed to high levels of alcohol as a *fetus.*

Fetal erythroblastosis Anemia, with excessive numbers of immature red blood cells, in a *fetus;* may be caused by *rhesus factor* incompatibility.

Fetishism (French *fétiche*, from Portuguese *feitiço*, religious magic) Sexual arousal by clothing or other inanimate objects.

Fetus (Latin) The developing organism between the time when the main anatomical structures of the body have been established (in humans, taken as 7 weeks after *conception*) and birth.

Fibroids *Benign* tumors arising from *smooth muscle* cells of the *uterus.*

Fimbria (plural fimbriae) (Latin, fringe) One of the fingerlike extensions of the *infundibulum* of the *oviduct.*

Fisting The insertion of the hand or entire forearm into the *rectum* as a sexual act.

5α-dihydrotestosterone (DHT) An *androgen* that plays an important role in the development of the male *external genitalia.*

5α-reductase The enzyme that converts *testosterone* to *5α-dihydrotestosterone* .

Flagellum (Latin, lash) A motile, tail-like extension of a cell such as a *sperm.*

Flasher Colloquial term for an *exhibitionist.*

Fluctuating asymmetry A difference between the left and right sides of the body that results from random perturbations of development, in contrast with consistent asymmetries such as the location of the heart on the left side.

Follicle (Latin *folliculus*, little bag) An *oocyte* with its supporting cells within the *ovary.*

Follicle-stimulating hormone (FSH) One of the two major *gonadotropins* secreted by the *pituitary gland;* regulates the function of the *gonads* in both sexes.

Follicular phase The phase of the *menstrual cycle* when *follicles* are developing under the influence of *gonadotropins.*

Foreplay Sexual behavior engaged in during the early part of a sexual encounter, with the aim of increasing sexual arousal.

Foreskin The male *prepuce:* the loose skin that partially or completely covers the *glans* in males who have not been *circumcised.*

Fornication (Latin *fornicare*, from *fornix*, a vault or brothel) Sex between unmarried persons, considered a sin.

Fourchette (French, little fork) The location where the *labia minora* meet behind the *vestibule.*

French kissing Kissing involving insertion of the tongue into the partner's mouth.

Frenulum (Latin, little bridle) A strip of loose skin on the underside of the *penis,* running between the *glans* and the shaft.

Frigidity An obsolete term for *anorgasmia* or sexual unresponsiveness in women.

Frotteurism (French, *frotter*, rub) A *paraphilia* involving touching or rubbing the clothed *external genitalia* against a stranger without their consent or without their knowledge, as in a crowded public place.

Functional magnetic resonance imaging (fMRI) A form of *magnetic resonance imaging* that maps brain activity by detecting the associated changes in blood flow.

Fundus (Latin, bottom) The end of the *uterus* furthest away from the *cervix.*

Fusion In *HIV* infection, the merging of the *virus's envelope* with the plasma membrane of the target cell.

Gamete (Greek, spouse) A specialized, usually *haploid* germ cell that fuses with another to form a new organism. In humans, the gametes are *ova* and *sperm.*

Gamete intrafallopian transfer (GIFT) An assisted reproduction technique in which *oocytes* and *sperm* are placed together in a woman's *oviducts* without prior *in vitro fertilization.*

Ganglia Collections of *neurons* outside the *central nervous system.*

Gay *Homosexual.* Sometimes used specifically in reference to homosexual men, or to those gay people who are *out* or part of a gay community.

Gay-bashing Hate crimes against *gay* people. Sometimes includes verbal abuse as well as violence.

Gender (Old French, *gendre,* kind) The collection of psychological traits that differ between males and females.

Gender constancy A child's realization that a person's sex is an immutable attribute.

Gender dysphoria (Greek *dus-,* badly, *phoria,* bearing) The unhappiness caused by discordance between a person's anatomical sex and their *gender identity.*

Gender identity A person's subjective sense of being male or female.

Gender identity clinic A clinic that specializes in the treatment of *transexuals* and other *transgendered* adults as well as gender-nonconformist children.

Gender identity disorder (GID) An intense and unshakable sense of belonging to the other *sex.* In *adolescence* or adulthood the condition is often associated with the wish to receive *sex reassignment surgery,* in which case it is equivalent to *transexuality.* GID's status as a mental disorder, particularly in childhood, is controversial.

Gender role A person's social role as male or female.

Gender schema A collection of ideas about *gender* that influences perception and judgment.

Gene A stretch of *DNA* that is transcribed as a unit; a unit of inheritance.

General Social Survey (GSS) A long-running periodic survey of the U.S. population run by the National Opinion Research Center.

Genital end-bulbs Specialized nerve endings found in *erogenous zones,* which probably detect the mechanical stimulation associated with sexual activity.

Genital herpes See *herpes.*

Genital ridge One of two bilateral clusters of cells in the *embryo* that will give rise to the *gonads.*

Genital swellings Regions of the *genitalia* in the *embryo* that will give rise to the *labia majora* (in females) or the *scrotum* (in males).

Genital warts Wartlike growths on or near the *genitalia* or *anus,* caused by infection with *human papillomavirus.* Medically known as *condylomata acuminata.*

Genitalia (Latin) The sexual anatomical structures, including those on the outside of the body (*external genitalia*) and those inside the body (internal genitalia or *reproductive tract*).

Genome An organism's entire complement of *DNA,* including all its *genes.* In some *viruses,* such as *HIV,* the genome is composed of *RNA.*

Genomic imprinting The labeling of *genes* according to whether they are inherited from the mother or the father. For some imprinted genes, only the maternally inherited version is expressed; for others, only the paternal version is expressed.

Geographic cure Ironic expression for moving a sex offender to some distant community.

Gestation (Latin *gestare,* carry) Bearing young in the *uterus;* pregnancy.

Gestational age A *fetus's* age timed from *ovulation.* Contrast *menstrual age.*

Gestational surrogacy An assisted reproduction technique in which a *surrogate* mother is implanted with another woman's *oocytes.*

Gigolo (pronounced JEEG-o-lo) (French, masculinized form of *gigole,* female prostitute) A male *prostitute* who caters to women.

Glans (Latin, acorn) The terminal knob of the *clitoris* or *penis.*

Glycogen A polymer of glucose used for energy storage.

Gonad (Greek *gonê,* generation) An organ that produces *gametes* (a *testis* in males, an *ovary* in females). In humans, the gonads also secrete *sex steroids.*

Gonadotropin or gonadotropic hormone (Greek *tropos,* a turn) A hormone that regulates the function of the *gonads.*

Gonadotropin-releasing hormone (GnRH) A hormone secreted by the *hypothalamus* that stimulates the release of *gonadotropins* from the anterior lobe of the *pituitary gland.*

Gonorrhea (Greek *gonos,* seed, *rheos,* flow, from the misconception that the discharge is semen) A sexually transmitted disease caused by infection with the bacterium *Neisseria gonorrhoeae.*

Gräfenberg spot or G spot A controversial area of increased *erotic* sensitivity on or deep to the front wall of the *vagina.*

Granulosa cells Cells within an ovarian *follicle* that support the *oocyte* and secrete *sex steroids.*

Gray matter A region of the *central nervous system* containing the *cell bodies* of neurons. Contrast *white matter.*

Growth hormone A *peptide* hormone secreted from the *pituitary gland* that promotes growth.

Grudge stalking Nonsexual revenge *stalking.*

Gubernaculum (plural gubernacula) (Latin, steering mechanism, rein) Either of two bilateral fibrous bands that are involved in the descent of the *gonads* in the *fetus.*

Gynephilic (Greek *gunê,* woman, *philia,* love) Sexually attracted to females.

Habituation The decline in a person's response to a psychological stimulus or drug after repeated exposure.

Haploid Possessing half the usual complement of *chromosomes,* i.e., one of each pair of homologous *autosomes* and (in humans) one *sex chromosome,* X or Y. Usually true of *gametes.* Contrast *diploid.*

Hard-core Of or related to explicit *pornography;* includes depictions of body parts or behavior that is excluded by the definition of *soft-core,* especially penetrative sex and *ejaculation.* Contrast *soft-core.*

Harem (Arabic *harim,* forbidden [to enter]) 1. The quarters for wives and *concubines* in a Muslim household. 2. In some species, the group of females who live and mate with a single male.

Hepatitis (Greek *hepar,* liver) Inflammation of the liver; may be caused by any of a number of *viruses.*

Hermaphrodite (Greek *Hermaphroditos,* the legendary son of Hermes and Aphrodite, who fused with the nymph Salmacis into a single person). An organism that combines male and female reproductive functions. For humans, see *true hermaphrodite, pseudohermaphrodite.*

Herpes (Greek, snake) Infection with a *herpesvirus,* especially in the genital area, usually caused by *herpes simplex virus,* type 2.

Herpes simplex virus (HSV) Either of two *viruses* that can be transmitted sexually and that cause recurrent outbreaks of sores near the site of infection.

Herpesvirus One of a large group of *DNA viruses,* including those that cause herpes.

Heterosexual (Greek *hetero-,* other) Sexually attracted to persons of the other sex.

Highly active anti-retroviral therapy (HAART) See *combination therapy.*

Hijra (pronounced HEED-jra) (Gujarati) Member of a class of male-to-female *transexuals* in northern India and Pakistan.

Hirsutism Growth of hair in excessive amounts or in the wrong places, such as on the face in women.

HIV See *human immunodeficiency virus.*

HIV-negative Testing negative for the presence of antibodies to *HIV.* Not a proof of noninfection, as antibodies do not appear until a few weeks or months after an infection.

HIV-positive Testing positive for *HIV* infection, usually determined by the presence of antibodies to the *virus.*

HIV-symptomatic disease Health problems caused by *HIV,* especially those that occur before the criteria for a full-blown *AIDS* diagnosis have been met. Previously known as *AIDS-related condition (ARC).*

Homogamy (Greek *homos*, same, *gamos*, marriage) The tendency of sexually partnered couples, or married couples, to resemble each other in a variety of respects.

Homologous (Greek) Having the same developmental or evolutionary origin.

Homologous chromosomes The two members of a matching pair of *chromosomes* normally present in a *diploid* cell.

Homophily (Greek *homos*, same, *philia*, love) The tendency to be attracted to persons who resemble oneself.

Homophobia Anti-*gay* prejudice.

Homosexual (Greek *homos*, same) Sexually attracted to persons of one's own sex.

Homosociality Socializing within same-sex groups.

Hormone (Greek, stirring up) A compound that is secreted from a gland into the bloodstream and that influences the function of some distant organ or tissue.

Hormone replacement therapy (HRT) The treatment of the symptoms of *menopause* with a combination of *estrogens* and *progestins,* or with estrogens alone. The latter regimen is sometimes called *estrogen replacement therapy.*

Hostile-environment harassment *Sexual harassment* involving a pattern of conduct that creates a hostile or intimidating work environment.

Hot flashes or hot flushes Episodes of reddening and warmth of the skin associated with *menopause.*

Hox genes *Genes* that organize the development of the *embryo's* basic body plan.

Human chorionic gonadotropin (hCG) A *gonadotropin* secreted by the *conceptus* and by the *placenta;* its presence in a woman's blood is an indicator of pregnancy.

Human immunodeficiency virus (HIV) The *retrovirus* that causes *AIDS.*

Human papillomavirus (HPV) Any of a group of *viruses* that can be sexually transmitted and which cause *genital warts* or other lesions; some types predispose infected persons to cancer of the *cervix* and *anus.*

Hustler A male *prostitute.*

Hydrocele A collection of fluid around a *testicle.*

Hymen (Greek, membrane) A membrane, usually perforated or incomplete, that covers the opening of the *vagina.* It may be ruptured by first *coitus* or for other reasons.

Hypersexuality Excessive sexual desire or behavior.

Hypoactive sexual desire disorder Low or absent interest in sex, when this condition causes distress. Also known as low *libido.*

Hypogonadal Suffering from low function of the *testes* or *ovaries,* usually taken to indicate a deficiency of *sex steroids.*

Hypospadias An abnormal location of the *urethral meatus* on the underside of the *glans* or shaft of the *penis* or elsewhere.

Hypothalamus (Greek, below the bridal chamber) A small region at the base of the brain on either side of the third ven-tricle; it contains cell groups involved in sexual responses and other basic functions.

Hysterectomy (Greek *hustera*, uterus) Surgical removal of the *uterus,* sometimes along with the *ovaries* and *oviducts.*

Hysterotomy An *abortion* performed by a surgical incision in the abdominal wall and the *uterus.*

Idiopathic (Greek *idios*, own, *pathos*, suffering) Of or related to a medical condition that occurs for no obvious external cause.

Illegitimate Obsolete term describing a child born out of wedlock; a bastard.

Immunotherapy The use of immunological measures to treat a condition, especially the administration of antibodies to kill cancer cells.

Implantation The attachment and ingrowth of the *conceptus* into the *endometrium* a few days after *fertilization.*

Impotence or impotency *Erectile dysfunction;* this term is obsolete in medical usage.

Imprinting 1. The automatic learning of a behavior on first exposure to a stimulus, such as a chick's following of its mother. 2. *Genomic imprinting.*

In vitro fertilization (IVF) (Latin, in glass) Any of a variety of assisted reproduction techniques in which *fertilization* takes place outside the body.

Incall A form of *escort service prostitution* in which the client and the prostitute engage in sex at a location controlled by the prostitute or the service. Contrast *outcall.*

Incest (Latin *incestum*, non-chastity) Sexual relations between closely related persons, especially when prohibited by law or religious teachings.

Inclusive fitness The likelihood that an individual's *genes* will be represented in future generations, both in direct descendants and in the descendants of close relatives.

Incontinent Unable to prevent spontaneous voiding of urine, or sometime feces.

Induced abortion An *abortion* accomplished intentionally by medical or surgical means.

Induced labor *Labor* triggered artificially by drugs.

Infant formula Manufactured milk substitute.

Infibulation (Latin *fibula*, clasp) The most invasive form of *female circumcision,* involving *clitoridectomy* plus the sewing together of the *labia majora* over the *vestibule.* Also known as *pharaonic circumcision.*

Infidelity The sexual or emotional breach of a supposedly monogamous relationship by the involvement of one of the partners in an extra-pair relationship.

Infundibulum (Latin, funnel) Funnel-shaped opening of the *oviduct* near the *ovary.*

Inguinal canal A short canal passing through the abdominal wall in the region of the groin in males.

Inhibin A *peptide* hormone or *cytokine* involved in the interaction between the *pituitary gland* and the *gonads* as well as in other functions.

Inner cell mass The cluster of cells within the *blastocyst* that give rise to the fetal membranes and the *embryo.*

Insemination See *artificial insemination.*

Instrumental conditioning A learning paradigm studied by B.F. Skinner in which a response to some cue develops when the cue is followed by positive or negative reinforcement (reward or punishment).

Intact dilation and extraction (D and X) A rarely used procedure for late-term *abortion,* in which the *fetus* is destroyed in the process of an intentional *breech delivery.* Sometimes called *partial-birth abortion.*

Integrase A enzyme produced by a *retrovirus* that inserts a *DNA* transcript of the viral *genome* into a host cell's genome.

Intercourse See *sexual intercourse.*

Interneuron A *neuron* interposed between sensory neurons and *motor neurons.*

Intersex A person whose biological sex is ambiguous or intermediate between male and female.

Interstitial cells See *Leydig cells.*

Intimate partner stalking *Stalking* of a current or former spouse or other intimate partner.

Intimate partner violence Violence between sex partners. Also known as wife beating, wife battering, spousal abuse, or domestic violence, but can be perpetrated by and against either sex, and in either a *heterosexual* or *homosexual* relationship.

Intracytoplasmic sperm injection (ICSI) An assisted reproduction technique in which a single *sperm* is injected into the cytoplasm of an *ovum.*

Intrauterine device (IUD) A device placed in the *uterus* as a *contraceptive.*

Introcision An unusual form of *female circumcision* in which the vaginal *introitus* is extended backward into the *perineum.*

Introitus (Latin, entry) The entrance to the *vagina,* usually covered in early life by the *hymen.*

Intromission (Latin *intro,* inward, *missio,* sending) The insertion of the *penis* into the *vagina,* whether or not *ejaculation* occurs. Sometimes used to include insertion of the penis into the *anus* or mouth.

Invasive Of or relating to cancer that spreads to adjacent tissues from its site of origin.

Inversion An obsolete psychiatric term for *homosexuality* seen as a *gender* reversal.

Investment The commitment to or expenditure of resources for a goal, such as reproductive success.

Ischiocavernosus muscle One of the muscles that attaches to the internal portions of the *penis* and *clitoris.* It assists with *erection* and (in men) *ejaculation.*

Isoflavones *Estrogen*-like compounds of plant origin.

Isthmus (Greek) The narrow section of the *oviduct* nearest to the *uterus.*

Jealousy Fear that a partner may be sexually or emotionally unfaithful. Also used loosely to include envy, the desire for something possessed by another person.

Kallmann's syndrome A developmental syndrome characterized by *delayed puberty,* inability to smell, and other problems.

Kaposi's sarcoma A skin cancer that is diagnostic of *AIDS* in *HIV-positive* persons.

Kegel exercises Exercises to strengthen the pelvic floor muscles as a method to treat *stress incontinence* and/or to increase sexual pleasure.

Kin selection The theory that it can be advanageous, in evolutionary terms, to support the reproductive success of close relatives.

Klinefelter's syndrome A developmental syndrome caused by the possession of one or more extra *X chromosomes* in a male (XXY, XXXY).

Kluver-Bucy syndrome A cluster of symptoms, including *hypersexuality,* marked by specific brain pathology.

Labia majora (Latin, greater lips) The outer lips: fleshy skin folds, partially covered in *pubic hair,* that extend from the *mons veneris* downward on either side of the *vulva.*

Labia minora (Latin, lesser lips) The inner lips: hairless, loose folds of skin located between the *labia majora* and immediately flanking the *vestibule.* Their appearance is quite variable from woman to woman.

Labor The process of childbirth.

Lactation (Latin *lac,* milk) The production of milk in the *mammary glands.*

Lactiferous duct One of the ducts that convey milk from the *alveoli* to the *lactiferous sinuses.*

Lactiferous sinus (plural sinuses) One of the storage areas for milk near the nipple.

Lamaze method A method of childbirth instruction that focuses on techniques of relaxation and other natural means of pain prevention.

Laparoscopy Abdominal surgery, such as *tubal sterilization,* performed through a small incision with the aid of a laparoscope (a fiber-optic viewing instrument).

Laparotomy Abdominal surgery, such as *tubal sterilization,* performed through a large incision in the abdominal wall.

Large lutein cells Cells within the *corpus luteum* that secrete *progesterone.*

Latency In Freudian theory, a phase of later childhood when the sex drive has little overt expression.

Latent phase An asymptomatic phase of *syphilis.*

Leather Of or related to a subculture within the *gay* male community, partially overlapping with the *S/M* subculture, that emphasizes leather clothing and masculine appearance.

Legitimate Obsolete term describing a child born to a married couple.

Lek (possibly Swedish *leka,* play) An area used for communal display by males and mate choice by females, especially among some species of birds.

Leptin A hormone secreted by fat cells that may play a role in triggering *puberty.*

Lesbian (from the island of *Lesbos,* home of the ancient Greek lesbian poet Sappho) *Homosexual* (used of women only).

Leuprolide A *GnRH receptor agonist,* used to suppress *gonadotropin* secretion by *receptor desensitization,* for example, in the treatment of *precocious puberty.* Proprietary name is *Lupron.*

Leydig cells Cells located between the *seminiferous tubules* in the *testis* that secrete *steroids,* chiefly *androgens.* Also called *interstitial cells.*

Libido (Latin) The sex drive; sexual interest.

Lightening See *engagement* (2).

Limerence Romantic love.

Lipstick lesbian A *lesbian* who uses makeup; a *femme* lesbian.

Lobular carcinoma Cancer arising from the breast lobules.

Lobule A small subdivision of an organ, such as the breast.

Lochia (Greek) A bloody discharge from the *vagina* that may continue for a few weeks after *parturition.*

Lordosis (Greek) In female rodents, an inverse arching of the back that exposes the *vulva* for *intromission* by a male.

Lubrication The natural appearance of slippery secretions in the *vagina* during sexual arousal, or the use of artificial lubricants to facilitate sexual activity.

Lumen (Latin, light) The cavity of a biological tube.

Lumpectomy Surgical removal of a cancerous breast lump with some surrounding tissue.

Lupron See *leuprolide.*

Luteal phase The phase of the *menstrual cycle* between *ovulation* and the beginning of *menstruation.* A *corpus luteum* is present during this phase.

Luteinizing hormone (LH) One of the two major *gonadotropins* secreted by the *pituitary gland;* regulates the function of the *gonads* in both sexes.

Machismo (Spanish) The traditional Latino culture of manliness, which delineates sharp *gender roles* and gives men certain obligations and privileges.

Macrophage A bacteria-killing leukocyte (white blood cell).

Madam A woman who manages a *brothel* or an *escort service.*

Magnetic resonance imaging (MRI) An imaging technique that maps the distribution of different chemical elements, especially hydrogen, within the body by measuring the radio frequency energy they emit in the presence of an alternating magnetic field.

Mahu A man who took a female *gender role* in Polynesian society and performed ritual dances.

Male orgasmic disorder See *delayed ejaculation.*

Mammary glands (Latin *mamma*, breast) The milk-producing glands within the breasts.

Mammography Radiographic inspection of the breasts.

Marital exemption to rape An outdated legal notion that a man may not be convicted for the *rape* of his wife.

Masochism (from Leopold von Sacher-Masoch) Sexual arousal from being subjected to pain, bondage, or humiliation. Considered a *paraphilia* when the condition causes distress.

Massage parlor An establishment for massage that may also offer the services of *prostitutes.*

Mastitis (Greek *mastos*, breast) Inflammation of the breast.

Masturbation (Latin *masturbari*) Sexual self-stimulation. Sometimes also used to refer to manual stimulation of another person's *genitalia.*

Meatus See *urethral meatus.*

Medial preoptic area A region of the *hypothalamus* involved in the regulation of sexual behaviors typically shown by males.

Median eminence A region of the *hypothalamus* immediately above the *pituitary gland,* where *GnRH* is secreted.

Medical abortion An *abortion* induced with drugs.

Medulla (Latin, marrow) The portion of the brain stem closest to the spinal cord.

Meiosis A pair of cell divisions that produces *gametes.* It features an exchange of genetic material between *homologous chromosomes* and the reduction of chromosome number from *diploid* to *haploid.* Contrast *mitosis.*

Menarche (pronounced MEN-ark, MEN-ar-kee, or men-AR-kee) (Greek *mên*, month, *archê*, beginning) The onset of *menstruation* at *puberty.*

Menopause (Greek *mên*, month, *pausis*, cessation) The final cessation of *menstruation* at the end of a woman's reproductive years.

Menstrual age A *fetus's* age timed from the mother's last *menstrual period.* Contrast *gestational age.*

Menstrual cycle The ovarian cycle in species such as humans in which females *menstruate.*

Menstrual synchrony The synchronization of the *menstrual periods* of women who live or work together.

Menstrual toxic shock syndrome A rare but life-threatening illness caused by a staphylococcal infection and associated with tampon use.

Menstruation, menstrual period, or menses (Latin *mensis*, month) The breakdown of the *endometrium* at approximately monthly intervals, with consequent loss of tissue and blood from the *vagina.*

Mere exposure A phenomenon whereby simply being exposed to some stimulus makes people like it more on a later presentation.

Meta-analysis (Greek *meta*, after) A statistical procedure for combining data from a number of studies on a single topic.

Metoidioplasty (spelling varies) The surgical construction of a small *penis* by enlargement of the *clitoris;* a simpler alternative to a full-scale *phalloplasty.*

Midpiece The portion of the tail of a *sperm* that is closest to the head, containing *mitochondria.*

Midwifery Childbirth care.

Mifepristone A *progestin receptor antagonist* used to induce *abortion.* Also known as *RU-486.*

Milk ejection reflex A hormonally mediated *reflex* that causes movement of milk from the breast *alveoli* to the *lactiferous sinuses.*

Mini-laparotomy or mini-lap Abdominal surgery, such as *tubal sterilization,* performed through a short incision.

Misattribution of arousal The tendency of nonsexual arousal, such as fear, to facilitate sexual arousal.

Miscarriage A spontaneous *abortion.*

Miscegenation (pronounced miss-e-jen-AY-shun) (Latin *miscere*, mix, *genus*, race) Sex between persons of different races, usually when viewed as a sin or a crime.

Mitochondria (Greek *mitos*, thread, *chondra*, granule) Cellular organelles that provide energy by means of oxidative metabolism.

Mitosis Cell division in which the *chromosome* number is preserved. Contrast *meiosis.*

Mittelschmerz (German, middle pain) Pain associated with *ovulation.*

Modesty In the sexual domain, a reluctance to solicit a sex partner or to respond readily to solicitations by others.

Molly (from the woman's name, or directly from the Latin *mollis*, soft) A feminine-acting *homosexual* man in eighteenth-century London.

Monoamines Compounds containing an amine group, including *catecholamines* and *serotonin.*

Monogamy (Greek *monos*, single, *gamos*, marriage) 1. Marriage limited to two persons. 2. A sexual relationship in which neither partner has sexual contact with third parties. Contrast *bigamy, polygamy, promiscuity.*

Monozygotic Of or related to twins who develop from a single *zygote* and who therefore inherit the same *genome.* Often miscalled "identical." Contrast *dizygotic.*

Mons veneris (Latin, mountain of Venus), mons pubis, or mons The frontmost component of the *vulva:* a mound of fatty tissue covering the *pubic symphysis.* At *puberty* it becomes covered by *pubic hair.*

Morning-after pill An *oral contraceptive* pill taken after unprotected sex to prevent implantation and pregnancy. Also called *emergency contraception.*

Morning sickness Nausea, sometimes with vomiting, associated with the early part of pregnancy. It tends to be worse in the morning but can occur at any time.

Morphogenetic movements Movements of tissues within the *embryo* to create new structures.

Morula (Latin *morus*, mulberry) The *conceptus* when it consists of about 16–32 cells arranged in a compact spherical mass.

Motor neuron A *neuron* that excites the contraction of muscle fibers.

Mounting A male-typical sexual behavior: climbing onto the female to reach a position in which *intromission* is possible. (Used mostly for nonhuman animals.)

Mucosa A surface layer of cells (epithelium) that is lubricated by the secretions of mucous glands.

Müllerian duct Either of two bilateral ducts in the *embryo* that give rise to the female *reproductive tract.*

Müllerian inhibiting substance (MIS) See *anti-Müllerian hormone (AMH).*

Multiparous (Latin parere, bring forth) Of or related to a woman who has given birth more than once, or who is pregnant and has given birth at least once previously. Contrast *primiparous.*

Multiple orgasms More than one *orgasm* without an intervening *resolution phase.*

Mut'a (Arabic) A contract to marry for a fixed period of time.

Mutation A change in an organism's *genome.*

Myelin The fatty sheath that surrounds some *axons* and speeds the conduction of nerve impulses.

Myoepithelial cells Cells derived from an epithelium that have contractile properties, such as those that expel milk from the *alveoli* of the breast.

Myometrium (Greek *mus*, muscle, *mêtra*, uterus) The muscular layers of the wall of the *uterus*.

Naegele's rule A traditional rule for the calculation of a pregnant woman's due date: 9 calendar months plus 1 week after the onset of the last *menstrual period*.

National Health and Social Life Survey (NHSLS) A national survey of sexual behavior, relationships, and attitudes in the United States, conducted in the early 1990s.

National Survey of Sexual Attitudes and Lifestyles (NSSAL) A British survey of sexual behavior, relationships, and attitudes conducted in the early 1990s.

Natural selection The survival and reproduction of those individuals that are best adapted to their environment.

Necrophilia (Greek *nekros*, corpse, *philia*, love) A *paraphilia* involving sexual arousal from viewing or having contact with dead bodies.

Nerve fiber See *axon*.

Neuroendocrine Combining neural and *endocrine* functions.

Neuron (Greek, nerve) A single nerve cell with all its extensions.

Neurosis A mental disorder that, according to the theories of *psychoanalysis*, results from unconscious sexual conflicts experienced during childhood.

Neurotransmitter A compound released at a *synapse* that increases or decreases the excitability of an adjacent *neuron*.

No-drop policy A policy on the part of some public prosecutors to continue prosecution of a perpetrator of *intimate partner violence* even if the victim recants the allegations.

Nocturnal emission *Ejaculation* during sleep.

Nocturnal orgasm *Orgasm* during sleep. See also *wet dream*.

Normative With reference to norms or established standards.

Nuchal translucency test or nuchal fold test (Late Latin *nucha*, nape of the neck, from Arabic) The ultrasonographic measurement of the skin fold at the neck of a *fetus*, useful in the *prenatal* diagnosis of *Down syndrome* and other congenital anomalies.

Nucleoside The metabolic precursor of a *nucleotide*.

Nucleotide The monomer or building block from which nucleic acids are formed.

Nurse-midwife A registered nurse with specialized training in *midwifery*.

Nymphomania (Greek *numphê*, nymph, *mania*, madness) Obsolete term for *hypersexuality* in a woman .

Obscene (Latin *obscenus*) Of or related to sexually themed publications, art, films, performances, or behavior deemed offensive to public morals or that violate legal standards of acceptability.

Obsessive–compulsive disorder (OCD) A mental disorder marked by anxiety, repetitive thoughts or urges, and behaviors that temporarily relieve those urges.

Obsessive relational intrusion Obsessive pursuit of a person by a rejected lover.

Obstetrician A physician who specializes in obstetrics (childbirth medicine).

Oedipal phase (from the Greek mythical figure Oedipus, who killed his father and married his mother) In Freudian theory, a phase of psychosexual development in which a child's sex drive is directed toward its opposite-sex parent.

Oligomenorrhea (Greek *oligos*, little, few, *mên*, month, *rheos*, flow). Infrequent or irregular *menstruation*.

Onuf's nucleus A *sexually dimorphic* group of *motor neurons* in the *sacral* segments of the spinal cord that innervates *striated muscles* associate with the *penis* and *clitoris*.

Oocyte (Greek *oion*, egg, *kutos*, vessel) A cell capable of developing into an *ovum*.

Opportunistic infection An infection that occurs because of a weakened immune system.

Oral contraceptive A drug or combination of drugs taken orally to prevent pregnancy; "the pill."

Oral sex Sexual contact between the mouth and the *vulva* (*cunnilingus*), the *penis* (*fellatio*), or the *anus* (*analingus*).

Orchiectomy (pronounced or-kee-EK-te-mee) (Greek *orchis*, testicle) Surgical removal of one or both *testicles*. If both, the same as *castration*.

Orchitis Inflammation of a *testicle*.

Organization The establishment during development of the neural circuitry that underlies some adult behavior. Contrast *activation*.

Orgasm The intense, pleasurable sensations at sexual climax, usually associated with spasmodic contractions of pelvic floor muscles and (in males) *ejaculation*. The third of the four phases of sexual response in the model of Masters and Johnson.

Orgasmic reconditioning A form of *behavior therapy* for *paraphilias* in which the positive reinforcement of *orgasm* is used to strengthen acceptable sexual desires.

Osteoporosis Reduction in the mineral content of bone, predisposing to fractures.

Otoacoustic emissions Faint sounds produced by the inner ear, either spontaneously or in response to auditory stimuli such as clicks.

Out 1. (verb) To expose as homosexual. 2. (preposition, abbreviation for "out of the closet") Openly *gay*.

Outcall A form of *escort service prostitution* in which the client and prostitute engage in sex at a location controlled by the client, such as his hotel room or residence. Contrast *incall*.

Outercourse Sexual activities other than *coitus*, promoted as a means to prevent unwanted pregnancy and avoid sexually transmitted diseases.

Ovarian cysts Cysts within the *ovary* that can arise from a number of different causes.

Ovary (Latin *ovaria*) The female *gonad*; the organ that produces *ova* and secretes *sex steroids*.

Oviduct (Latin *ovum*, egg, *ducere*, conduct) Either of two bilateral tubes that lead from the *uterus* toward the *ovaries*; the usual site of *fertilization*. Also called *fallopian tube*.

Ovulation Release of an *ovum* from the *ovary*.

Ovum (Latin, egg) A mature female *gamete*, prior to or immediately after *fertilization*. Usually taken to include its surrounding *zona pellucida* and *cumulus cells*.

Oxytocin A *peptide* hormone secreted from the posterior lobe of the *pituitary gland*. It plays a role in the *milk ejection reflex* and in the contractions of the *uterus* during *parturition*, as well as possibly in *orgasm* and social bonding.

Palimony (Pal and alimony) Colloquial term for monetary compensation to one partner of a terminated *cohabitation*.

Pap test or Pap smear (named for its inventor George Papanicolaou) The microscopic examination of a sample of epithelial cells taken from the *cervix* or (less commonly) the *anus*.

Paraphilia (Greek *para*, next to, *philia*, love) An unusual form of sexual arousal or behavior that is considered to be a medical problem.

Paraphimosis Entrapment of the retracted *foreskin* behind the *corona*.

Paraplegia (Greek, a stroke on the side) Paralysis affecting the lower half of the body.

Parasympathetic nervous system A division of the *autonomic nervous system*; among many other functions, activity in this system promotes *erection* of the *penis* and *clitoris*. Contrast *sympathetic nervous system*.

Paraurethral glands Glands situated next to the female *urethra*, thought to be homologous to the male *prostate* gland. Their secretions enter the female urethra and may be responsible for some forms of *female ejaculation*. Also known as *Skene's glands*.

Parenteral (Greek *para*, next to, *enteron*, gut) Of or related to the administration of a drug by some other route than orally.

Parthenogenesis (Greek *parthenos*, virgin) *Asexual reproduction* from an unfertilized *ovum*; "virgin birth."

Partial-birth abortion See *intact dilation and extraction*.

Partialism *Fetishism* involving a part of the body.

Parturition (Latin *parturire*, bring forth) Delivery of young, childbirth.

Passive immunity Immunity conferred by immunoglobulins provided medically or by the mother in her milk.

Paternity testing The identification of an individual's father by comparison of *DNA polymorphisms*.

Pedophilia (Greek *pais*, *paid-*, boy, child, *philia*, love) Sexual attraction to *prepubescent* children.

Peeping Tom (from the English folk story of Lady Godiva, who was forced to ride naked through the streets of Coventry; all the citizens averted their eyes except Tom). A *voyeur*.

Pelvic cavity The lowermost portion of the abdominal cavity, where the *reproductive tract*, the bladder, and the *rectum* are located.

Pelvic examination A visual and digital examination of the *vulva* and pelvic organs.

Pelvic inflammatory disease (PID) An infection of the female *reproductive tract*, often caused by sexually transmitted organisms.

Pelvis (Latin, basin) The bowl-shaped skeletal structure that encases the *pelvic cavity*.

Penis (Latin) The erectile, erotically sensitive organ in males that incorporates a portion of the *urethra*. The penis serves sexual functions (sexual arousal of its owner and possibly of his partner, *intromission*, triggering of *orgasm*, and *ejaculation*), and also mediates the voiding of urine.

Penis captivus The inability of a male to withdraw his *penis* from the *vagina* for some time after *ejaculation* due to spasm of the vaginal musculature; it is common in some animals, but accounts of the phenomenon in humans are of doubtful reliability.

Peptide (Greek *peptein*, digest) A polymer of *amino acids*, usually shorter than a *protein*.

Perfect-use failure rate Of a *contraceptive* technique, the percentage of women using the technique correctly who will become pregnant in a year. Contrast *typical-use failure rate*.

Perineum (Latin) 1. As used by *obstetricians*, and in this book, the region of skin between the *anus* and the *scrotum* or *vulva*. 2. As used by anatomists, the entire region that includes the *external genitalia* and *anus* and the space between them, as well as the pelvic tissues deep to these structures.

Perversion An obsolete term for atypical sexual desire or behavior, viewed as a mental disorder. Similar to *paraphilia*, but included *homosexuality*.

Pessary (Latin *pessarium*) A medical device placed in the *vagina*; most commonly a silicone or plastic ring intended to support a *prolapsed uterus*.

Peyronie's disease Pathological curvature of the *penis*.

Phalloplasty (Greek *phallos*, penis, *plassein*, to mold) The surgical construction of a *penis*.

Pharaonic circumcision See *infibulation*.

Pheromone (Greek *pherein*, carry, plus *-mone* by analogy with *hormone*) A volatile compound that is released by one organism and that triggers a specific behavior in another member of the same species.

Phimosis (Greek, muzzling) A tightening of the *foreskin*, preventing its retraction from the *glans*.

Pimp A man who sets up and protects *prostitutes* in exchange for part of their earnings.

Pituitary gland (Latin *pituita*, phlegm) A gland situated below and under the control of the *hypothalamus*; its posterior lobe secretes *oxytocin* and *vasopressin*, and its anterior lobe secretes *gonadotropins* and other hormones.

Placenta (Latin, a flat cake) A vascular organ, partly of fetal and partly of maternal origin, by which gases, nutrients, hormones, and waste products are exchanged between the *fetus* and its mother. When expelled from the uterus, it is called the *afterbirth*.

Plateau phase In Masters and Johnson's four-phase model of sexual response, the second phase, in which sexual arousal is maintained at a fairly high level.

Pluripotent Of or related to cells, such as *embryonic stem cells*, that are able to give rise to differentiated cells of any fetal structures, but not to extraembryonic structures. Contrast *totipotent*.

Polar body The lesser product of an asymmetric cell division during *meiosis*: one of two bags of superfluous *chromosomes* located next to the *ovum* within the *zona pellucida*.

Political lesbian A woman who identifies as a *lesbian* or enters a lesbian relationship as a statement of solidarity with the *women's movement*.

Polyamorists Persons who form nontransient sexual relationships in groups of three or more.

Polyandry (Greek *polus*, much, *anêr*, *andr-*, man) The marriage or mating of one female with more than one male.

Polycystic ovary syndrome A cluster of symptoms including irregular *menstrual periods*, diagnosed by the presence of numerous small *benign ovarian cysts*.

Polygamy (Greek *polus*, much, *gamos*, marriage) Marriage to or (mostly in animals) mating with more than one partner.

Polygyny (Greek *polus*, much, *gunê*, wife) The marriage or mating of one male with more than one female.

Polymastia (Greek *polus*, much, *mastos*, breast) The condition of possessing more than two breasts; supernumerary breasts.

Polymerase chain reaction (PCR) A technique for amplifying *DNA* present in very low amounts.

Polythelia (Greek *polus*, much, *thelê*, nipple) The condition of possessing more than two nipples; supernumerary nipples.

Pornography (Greek *pornê*, prostitute) Material (such as art, writing, photographic images, and film) that is intended to be sexually arousing. Sometimes used specifically for material deemed offensive.

Positron emission tomography (PET) (Greek *tomê*, a cut, *graphein*, write) An imaging technique that maps brain activity by detecting the location of a blood-borne chemical tracer. The tracer is labeled with an isotope that emits positrons (positively charged electrons).

Postmodernism A vaguely defined movement in the arts and humanities dating from the 1980s; among other things, it rejects the objectivity of scientific knowledge in favor of a more fragmented, personal, and function-oriented view.

Postpartum (Latin) The period after birth.

Post-traumatic stress disorder A cluster of physical and psychological symptoms that can affect persons who have experienced severe trauma.

Preadolescence The age range including the beginning of *puberty*, from approximately 8 to 12 or 13.

Precocious puberty *Puberty* that begins early enough to be considered a medical problem.

Pre-cum Colloquial term for the secretions of the *bulbourethral glands* that appear at the *urethral meatus* before *orgasm.*

Premarital Of or related to the period before marriage. Often used loosely to refer to sex between unmarried young persons, on the assumption that they will marry in the future.

Premature ejaculation *Ejaculation* before the man wishes, often within a few seconds of *intromission.* Also called *rapid ejaculation.*

Premature labor or premature birth *Labor* or birth that occurs before 37 weeks of gestational age.

Premenstrual syndrome (PMS) A collection of physical and psychological symptoms that may begin a few days before the *menstrual period* and continue into the period.

Prenatal Of or related to the period before birth.

Prenuptial agreement A contract signed before marriage, spelling out the disposition of wealth in the event of divorce.

Prepubescent Of or related to a child who has not yet undergone *puberty.*

Prepubic fat pad A cushion of fatty tissue in front of the *pubic symphysis.*

Prepuce (Latin *praeputium*) The loose fold of skin that covers the *clitoris* (*clitoral hood*) in females or the *glans* of the penis (*foreskin*) in males.

Priapism (from Priapus, a Greek and Roman fertility god) A persistent, unwanted *erection* caused by injury to the *penis* or by drugs.

Primary amenorrhea Failure to commence *menstruation* at *puberty.* Contrast *secondary amenorrhea.*

Primary sexual characteristics The anatomical characteristics that are generally used to define an individual as male or female: the structures of the *vulva* in females and the *penis* and *scrotum* in males. Contrast *secondary sexual characteristics.*

Primiparous (Latin *parere*, bring forth) Of or related to a pregnant woman who has not given birth previously. Contrast *multiparous.*

Primordial germ cells The cells that will give rise to *oocytes* and to the progenitors of *sperm;* they migrate into the *embryo* from the *yolk sac.*

Proceptive behavior Behavior by females that may elicit sexual advances by males.

Pro-choice Believing that *abortion* should be legal under some or all circumstances.

Prodromal sign (Greek *prodromos*, forerunner) A sign warning of an incipient disease.

Progesterone A steroid hormone secreted by the ovary and the placenta; it is necessary for the establishment of pregnancy.

Progestin or progestagen (Latin *gestare*, carry) Any of a class of *steroids*, the most important natural member being *progesterone*, that cause the *endometrium* to proliferate, help maintain pregnancy, and have other functions. Sometimes the term *progestin* is used specifically to refer to synthetic progestagens.

Prolactin A *peptide* hormone secreted by the anterior lobe of the *pituitary gland* that promotes breast development, among other effects.

Prolapse The slipping out of place of an organ, such as the *uterus.*

Pro-life Opposed to *abortion;* believing that abortion should be illegal under most or all circumstances.

Promiscuity (Latin *miscere*, mix) Engaging in numerous casual or short-lived sexual relationships.

Pronucleus One of two nuclei within a fertilized *ovum*, each containing the *chromosomes* derived from one parent.

Prostaglandins A group of *cytokine*-like lipid molecules that, among many other functions, serve to prepare the *uterus* for *parturition.*

Prostate gland or prostate (Greek) A single gland at the base of the bladder, surrounding the *urethra;* its secretions are a component of *semen.*

Prostate-specific antigen (PSA) An antigen characteristic of cells of the *prostate gland*, whose presence at high levels in the blood is suggestive of, but not diagnostic of, prostate cancer.

Prostatectomy Surgical removal of the *prostate gland.*

Prostatitis Inflammation of the *prostate gland;* may be acute or chronic.

Prostitution (Latin *prostituere*, to put up for sale) The practice of engaging in sex for pay. Sometimes taken to include sex for some nonmonetary compensation.

Protease An enzyme that cuts *proteins* at specific locations.

Protein (Greek *proteios*, primary) A long polymer made up of *amino acids.*

Prototype A mental representation of a class of objects, such as female faces.

Pseudohermaphrodite An *intersex* whose condition involves structures other than the *gonads.* Contrast *true hermaphrodite.*

Psychoanalysis A form of treatment of psychological problems introduced by Sigmund Freud, based on the idea that most such problems result from unresolved sexual conflicts dating from childhood.

Psychogenic Arising in the mind.

Psychologically androgynous (Greek *anêr, andr-*, man, *gunê*, woman) Having psychological traits typical of both males and females.

Psychosis Any mental disorder with severe disruption of thinking.

Puberty (Latin *pubertas*) The transition to sexual and reproductive maturity.

Pubic (Latin *pubes*, downy hair, the genital area) Of or related to the *external genital* area in either sex.

Pubic hair Hair that appears on portions of the *external genitalia* in both sexes at *puberty.*

Pubic lice Insects (*Phthirus pubis*) that preferentially infest the *pubic* region.

Pubic symphysis The junction of the left and right pubic bones, the frontmost elements of the pelvic skeleton.

Pudenda (Latin, things to be ashamed of) Obsolete term for the *external genitalia.*

Pudendal nerves Peripheral nerves supplying the *external genitalia.*

Puerperal fever (Latin *puerpera*, a woman in labor) Obsolete term for a streptococcal infection of the *reproductive tract* occurring at childbirth.

Quadriplegia (Latin *quadri-*, fourfold, Greek *plegê*, stroke) Paralysis affecting almost the entire body below the neck.

Quickening (from the original meaning of quick: alive) The onset of movements by the *fetus* that can be felt by the mother.

Quid pro quo harassment (Latin, what for what) *Sexual harassment* in the form of unwelcome sexual advances, usually made to a worker in a subordinate position, accompanied by the promise of some work-related benefit if the victim is compliant or the threat of some deleterious consequence if the victim is noncompliant.

Radioimmunoassay A technique for measuring low concentrations of a compound by determining its ability to compete with a radioactively labeled version of the same compound for binding to an antibody.

Rape (possibly Latin *rapere*, seize) *Coitus* (and sometimes other penetrative sex acts) accomplished by force or the threat of force. See also *statutory rape.*

Rape crisis center A facility devoted to the support of *rape* victims and to the prevention of rape.

Rape shield laws Laws that protect *rape* victims, for example, by limiting the introduction of evidence about their prior sexual behavior.

Rape trauma syndrome A cluster of persistent physical and psychological symptoms seen in *rape* victims, comparable to *post-traumatic stress disorder.*

Rapid ejaculation See *premature ejaculation.*

Real-life experience A period of 1–2 years when a candidate for *sex reassignment surgery* has to live in the role of the other sex.

Rear-entry coitus A coital position in which the man approaches the woman from the rear. Not to be confused with *anal sex.*

Receptor A molecule or aggregate of molecules to which a hormone or *neurotransmitter* binds. Upon binding, the receptor triggers some specific cellular activity.

Recessive trait An inherited trait that shows itself only when the responsible *gene* is present on both *homologous chromosomes.*

Recidivism (pronounced re-SID-i-vism) (Latin *recidivus,* falling back). The tendency of convicted offenders to reoffend.

Recovered memory A memory—for example, of being sexually abused in childhood—that purportedly was suppressed from consciousness and later recovered in the course of psychotherapy.

Rectum (Latin, straight) The final, straight portion of the large bowel. It connects to the exterior via the *anus.*

Reflex A simple, automatic behavior mediated by a short series of *neurons.*

Refractory period A period of reduced or absent sexual arousability after *orgasm.*

REM sleep The phase of sleep marked by *rapid eye movements* and by vivid dreaming.

Reproductive tract The internal anatomical structures in either sex that form the pathway taken by *gametes* or the *conceptus.*

Resolution phase In Masters and Johnson's four-phase model of sexual response, the final phase, during which sexual excitement subsides.

Rete testis (Latin, net) A network of spaces between the *testis* and *epididymis,* through which *sperm* must pass.

Retrograde ejaculation *Ejaculation* into the bladder, caused by non-closure of the urethral *sphincter.*

Retrovirus An *RNA virus* whose *genome* is translated into *DNA* within the host cell.

Reverse transcriptase An enzyme produced by a *retrovirus* that transcribes viral *RNA* into *DNA.*

Rhesus factor (Rh) An antigen on the surface of red blood cells that, when present in a *fetus* but not in its mother, may trigger an immune response by the mother resulting in *fetal erythroblastosis.*

Rhythm methods *Contraceptive* techniques that rely on avoiding *coitus* during the woman's *fertile window.* Also called fertility awareness methods, periodic abstinence methods, or natural family planning. Sometimes used to mean specifically the *calendar method.*

RNA (ribonucleic acid) A polymer of *nucleotides* that is transcribed from *DNA.* It also forms the genetic material of some *viruses.*

Romantic love Strong sexual attraction combined with single-minded attention to and idealization of the loved person; being "in love."

Root The portion of the *penis* that lies within the body.

RU-486 See *mifepristone.*

Rubella (Latin, reddish, pink) German measles, a viral infection that can cause developmental defects in *fetuses* whose mothers contract the disease during pregnancy.

Rugae (Latin) Circumferential wrinkles in the inner surface of the *vagina.*

Sacral (Latin *sacer,* sacred) Of or related to the lowermost five segments of the spinal cord, whose nerves exit the spinal canal at the level of the sacrum.

Sadism (from the Marquis de Sade) Sexual arousal by the infliction of pain, bondage, or humiliation on others. Such behavior is considered a *paraphilia* when the partner is nonconsenting.

Sadomasochism or S/M The infliction and acceptance of pain or humiliation as a means of sexual arousal. It contains elements of *sadism* and *masochism,* but is not defined as a *paraphilia* so long as the activity is consensual.

Satyriasis (Greek *saturos,* a lecherous forest spirit) Obsolete term for *hypersexuality* in a man.

Scabies Infestation with a mite (*Sarcoptes scabiei*) that burrows within the skin.

Schema See *gender schema.*

Script theory The analysis of sexual and other behaviors as the enactment of socially inculcated roles.

Scrotum (Latin) The sac behind the *penis* that contains the *testicles.*

Secondary amenorrhea Absence of *menstruation* in a woman who has previously menstruated normally. Contrast *primary amenorrhea.*

Secondary sexual characteristics Anatomical characteristics, such as breasts and facial hair, that generally differ between the sexes but are not used to define an individual's sex. Contrast *primary sexual characteristics.*

Selective estrogen receptor modulators (SERMs) Drugs that are *estrogen receptor agonists* in some tissues and *antagonists* in other tissues.

Selective serotonin reuptake inhibitors (SSRIs) A class of drugs, including antidepressants such as fluoxetine (Prozac), that increase the availability of *serotonin* at *synapses.*

Semen (Latin, seed) The fluid, containing *sperm* and a variety of chemical compounds, that is discharged from the *penis* (*ejaculated*) at the male sexual climax. It is formed from the combined secretions of the *testes, prostate gland,* and *seminal vesicles.*

Seminal emission The loading of the constituents of *semen* into the posterior *urethra* immediately prior to *ejaculation.*

Seminal plasma The noncellular constituents of *semen.*

Seminal vesicles Glands situated to either side of the *prostate;* their secretions are a component of *semen.*

Seminiferous tubules Convoluted microscopic tubes within the *testis;* the site of *spermatogenesis.*

Seminoma Testicular cancer arising from the cells that normally produce *sperm.*

Sensate focus A form of *sex therapy* that involves graduated touching exercises.

Sensitive period A period of development when the survival or growth of a biological system depends on the presence of some factor, such as a hormone.

Serial monogamy Engagement in a series of *monogamous* relationships.

Seroconversion The change from negative to positive on an antibody test, such as occurs a few weeks or months after *HIV* infection.

Serotonin A *monoamine* derived from the *amino acid* tryptophan that functions as a *neurotransmitter.*

Sertoli cell A type of cell within the *seminiferous tubules* that nurtures developing *sperm* and secretes hormones.

Sex 1. The category of male or female. 2. Sexual feelings and behavior.

Sex chromosome Either of a pair of *chromosomes* that differ between the sexes. In mammals, the sex chromosomes are named *X* and *Y:* females have two X's, males have one X and one Y.

Sex determination The biological mechanism that determines whether an organism will develop as a male or a female.

Sex pheromones *Pheromones* that elicit or modify sexual behavior.

Sex reassignment surgery Surgery to change a person's *sex*.

Sex steroid Any of the steroid hormones that are active in sexual and reproductive physiology, including *androgens, estrogens,* and *progestins.*

Sex steroid–binding globulin A *protein* in the blood to which *sex steroids* bind.

Sex therapy The treatment of sexual dysfunctions, usually by recommending behavioral changes and sexual exercises such as *sensate focus.*

Sex trader A person who exchanges sex for money, drugs, or other benefits; a broader term than *prostitute.*

Sex worker A person who engages in *prostitution, pornography,* or other sex-related occupations.

Sexism Prejudice on the basis of a person's sex, usually when directed by men against women.

Sexual addiction The idea that a person may be addicted to certain forms of sexual behavior by a mechanism similar to that of addiction to substances.

Sexual assault Coercive or nonconsensual sexual contact, not necessarily including penetrative sex; a broader category of behaviors than *rape.*

Sexual dimorphism An anatomical difference between the sexes.

Sexual dysfunction A difficulty with sexual performance, or too much or too little interest in sex, when perceived as a problem by the affected person.

Sexual harassment Unwanted sexual advances or other intimidating sexual behavior, usually in the workplace. See *quid pro quo harassment* and *hostile-environment harassment.*

Sexual intercourse Sexual contact, usually understood to involve penetration of the *vagina* by the *penis.*

Sexual orientation The direction of a person's sexual feelings: sexual attraction toward persons of the opposite sex (*heterosexual*), the same sex (*homosexual*), or both sexes (*bisexual*). See also *gynephilic, androphilic.*

Sexual predator A person who, on account of having been convicted of more than one sexual assault against nonrelatives, may be confined indefinitely in a hospital for the criminally insane, according to laws enacted in California and other states.

Sexual reproduction Reproduction in which the offspring inherit *genes* from two parents.

Sexual revolution A dramatic increase in sexual permissiveness, particularly associated with the 1960s.

Sexual selection The evolution of traits under the pressure of competition for mates or of choice by mates.

Sexually explicit materials A nonjudgmental phrase denoting *pornography.*

Shaman (Russian) A ritual healer or magician.

She-male Colloquial term for a male-to-female *transgender,* often in the context of *prostitution* or *pornography.*

Shield laws See *rape shield laws.*

Single Neither married nor *cohabiting.* Sometimes used only to mean unmarried.

Single-photon emission computed tomography (SPECT) An imaging technique that detects gamma rays emitted by radioactively labeled tracers.

Sinusoid A vascular space, such as within erectile tissue, capable of being expanded by filling with blood.

Sixty-nine or 69 (from the appearance of the digits) The practice of engaging in reciprocal oral sex. Also called *soixante-neuf.*

Skene's glands See *paraurethral glands.*

Smegma (Greek, soap) A whitish, greasy secretion that builds up under the *prepuce* of the *penis* or *clitoris.*

Smooth muscle Muscular tissue that has no microscopic striations. Its contraction is usually involuntary and under the control of the *autonomic nervous system.* Contrast *striated muscle.*

Socialization The effect of social influences such as family, education, peer groups, and the media on the development of psychological or behavioral traits.

Sodomy Obsolete term for *anal sex,* or for any *homosexual* contact. It is still used as a legal term to refer to prohibited sex acts; its meaning varies between jurisdictions, but commonly includes anal and oral penetration.

Soft-core Of or related to relatively nonexplicit *pornography.* Though vaguely defined, it is generally taken to refer to images that do not show contact between the *genitalia* and any body part, penetrative sex, *ejaculation,* or *semen* or urine. Sometimes, especially on Internet sites, it also excludes the depiction of erect *penises* or engorged *vulvas.* Contrast *hard-core.*

Soixante-neuf (French, sixty-nine) See *sixty-nine.*

Speculum (Latin, mirror) An instrument that permits visual inspection of the *vagina* and *cervix.*

Sperm or spermatozoon (plural sperm, spermatozoa) (Greek sperma, seed, zôion, animal) A male *gamete,* produced in the *testis.*

Sperm bank A facility that collects, stores, and provides *semen* for *artificial insemination.*

Spermatic cord Either of two bilateral bundles of structures, including the *vas deferens,* blood vessels, and the *cremaster muscle,* that pass through the *inguinal canal* to the *testis.*

Spermatogenesis The production of *sperm.*

Spermicide A chemical that kills *sperm,* available as a *contraceptive* in a variety of forms, such as foams, creams, and suppositories.

Sphincter (Greek) A circular muscle around an orifice whose contraction closes the orifice.

Spina bifida A class of congenital malformations caused by incomplete closure of the neural tube.

Spinal reflex A *reflex* mediated by *neurons* in the spinal cord, requiring no participation by the brain.

Spirochete Any of a class of corkscrew-shaped bacteria, including the agents that cause *syphilis* and yaws.

Spontaneous abortion A naturally occurring *abortion;* a miscarriage.

Squamous cells (Latin squama, scale) Flattened, multilayered epithelial cells, such as those covering the *cervix.*

SRY (Sex-determining Region of the Y chromosome) A *gene* located on the *Y chromosome* that usually causes the embryo to develop as a male.

Stalking Obsessive pursuit of a previous, current, or desired sex partner in such a way as to put that person in a state of fear. See *intimate partner stalking, delusional stalking.*

Statutory rape Penetrative sex when a partner is legally unable to give consent on account of young age, mental retardation, or unconsciousness.

Stem cell A progenitor cell that gives rise by *mitosis* to cells characteristic of a particular tissue. See also *embryonic stem cell.*

Stereotype A false or overgeneralized belief about an entire class of people.

Sterilization A surgical procedure to eliminate fertility in either sex. See *vasectomy, tubal sterilization.*

Steroids (Greek stereos, solid) Hormones derived from cholesterol. They include *sex steroids* and *corticosteroids.*

Stop-start procedure A *sex therapy* technique for the treatment of *premature ejaculation* that involves a graded increase in the level of sexual stimulation.

Straight *Heterosexual.*

Streetwalker A *prostitute* who advertises by walking the streets. Contrast *escort.*

Stress incontinence. Urinary *incontinence* during moments of increased intra-abdominal pressure, such as coughing.

Striated muscle Muscular tissue with microscopic striations. Its contraction is usually voluntary and controlled by spinal (or cranial) *motor neurons.* Contrast *smooth muscle.*

Subfertility Difficulty in establishing a pregnancy; arbitrarily defined as the absence of pregnancy after a couple has had frequent unprotected sex for 12 months.

Subincision A form of male *circumcision* in which a cut is made along the underside of the *penis,* exposing the *urethra.*

Subzonal insemination An assisted reproduction technique in which *sperm* are injected into the space between the *zona pellucida* and the plasma membrane of an *ovum* to facilitate *fertilization.*

Suitor Someone who tries to establish a sexual relationship with, or proposes marriage to, another person.

Sunnah (Arabic, religious obligation) *Female circumcision* limited to incision or removal of the *clitoral hood.*

Superincision An unusual form of male *circumcision* in which the upper part of the *foreskin* is incised but not removed.

Supernumerary breasts See *polymastia.*

Supernumerary nipples See *polythelia.*

Surfactant A material produced by the lungs that reduces surface tension.

Surgical abortion An *abortion* induced by a surgical procedure.

Surrogate A person who stands in for another; for example, as a sex partner or as the bearer of a child.

Suspensory ligament A ligament that connects the *root* of the penis to the *pubic symphysis.*

Sympathetic nervous system A division of the *autonomic nervous system;* among many other functions, activity in this system inhibits penile *erection* but helps trigger *ejaculation.*

Sympto-thermal method A *rhythm method* of *contraception* that uses the measurement of *basal body temperature* and the testing of *cervical mucus* to determine the time of *ovulation* and the *fertile window.*

Synapse (Greek, junction) A junction where signals are transmitted between *neurons* or from neurons to muscle fibers.

Synergism or synergy (Greek *sun,* together, *ergos,* work) Cooperativity between two processes, such that their combined effect is greater than the sum of their separate effects.

Syphilis (from the title of a sixteenth-century Italian poem about the supposed first victim of the disease) A sexually transmitted disease caused by a *spirochete, Treponema pallidum.*

Tearoom Obsolete colloquial expression for a public toilet used for casual sex between men.

Testicle See *testis.*

Testicular feminization See *androgen insensitivity syndrome.*

Testis (plural testes) (possibly Latin, witness) The male *gonad:* one of the two glands within the *scrotum* that produce *sperm* and secrete *sex steroids. Testicle* denotes the same organ, but is used mainly when considering the testis as an anatomical object rather than as a functional gland.

Testosterone The principal *androgen,* synthesized in the *testes* and, in lesser amounts, in the *ovaries* and *adrenal glands.*

Thecal cells (Greek *thekê,* case) Cells located on the periphery of an ovarian *follicle* that synthesize *sex steroids.*

Top Colloquial term for a *gay* man who prefers the insertive role in *anal sex,* for a masculine-acting gay man, or for the person who inflicts pain in a *sadomasochistic* encounter. Contrast *bottom.*

Totipotent Of or related to cells, such as certain cells of the very early *conceptus,* that are able to develop into any embryonic or extraembryonic tissue. Contrast *pluripotent.*

Toxic shock syndrome See *menstrual toxic shock syndrome.*

Transexual or transsexual (The spelling with one *s* is preferable, as the Latin prefix *trans-,* across, shortens to *tran-* before a word beginning with *s-,* as in *transect.*) A person who identifies with the other sex and who usually seeks to *transition* to the other sex by means of hormone treatment and *sex reassignment surgery.* Transexuals can be male-to-female (M2F) or female-to-male (F2M), *homosexual* or *heterosexual.*

Transgender A person who identifies with the other sex. A broader term than *transexual,* it includes persons who do not seek *sex reassignment surgery* as well as those who do.

Transition 1. The process of changing sex, including both *sex reassignment surgery* and lifestyle changes. 2. The final phase of dilation of the *cervix* during *labor.*

Transvestism (Latin *trans,* across, *vestis,* garment) Wearing clothes of the other sex for purposes of sexual arousal. Sometimes applied to *cross-dressing* for any reason.

Tribadism (Greek *tribein,* rub) Sexual behavior between two women, who lie front-to-front and stimulate each other's *clitoris* with thrusting motions.

Trichomoniasis or "trich." Infection with the protozoan *Trichomonas vaginalis.*

Trimester (Latin *trimestris,* three-monthly) One of three 3-month divisions of pregnancy.

Triphasic combination pill An *oral contraceptive* regimen that varies the dose of *estrogens* and *progestins* around the *menstrual cycle.*

Trophic factor A signaling molecule that instructs a cell or tissue to grow or survive.

True hermaphrodite An individual possessing both testicular and ovarian tissue—a gonadal *intersex.* Contrast *pseudohermaphroditism.*

Tubal Of or related to the *oviducts.*

Tubal sterilization or tubal ligation A female *sterilization* technique that involves cutting, cauterization, or tying off of the *oviducts.*

Tunica albuginea (Latin, white coat) The capsule that encloses the *testis.*

Tunica vaginalis (Latin, sheathlike coat) A membranous sac enclosing both *testes;* it permits the testes to move freely within the *scrotum.*

Turner's syndrome A developmental syndrome caused by the partial or complete absence of one of the two *X chromosomes* normally present in a female.

Two-spirit person In Native American cultures, a person with the spirit of a man and a woman, roughly corresponding to our conception of a *transgendered* person, but with a more accepted and integrated social role. Also called *berdache.*

Typical-use failure rate Of a *contraceptive* technique, the percentage of women using the technique with a typical degree of care who will become pregnant in a year. Contrast *perfect-use failure rate.*

Ultrasound or ultrasonographic scan An imaging procedure that depends on the reflection of ultrasonic waves from density boundaries within the body.

Umbilical cord The vascular cord that runs from the umbilicus (navel) of the *fetus* to the *placenta.*

Undescended testicles *Testicles* that have not completed their normal developmental migration into the *scrotum; cryptorchidism.*

Unrequited love Love that is not reciprocated.

Urethra (Greek) The canal that conveys urine from the bladder to the *urethral meatus.* It also serves for the discharge of *semen* or female ejaculatory fluids.

Urethral folds Folds of ectodermal tissue in the *embryo* that give rise to the *labia minora* (in females) or the shaft of the *penis* (in males).

Urethral meatus (Latin, passage) The opening of the *urethra* at the tip of the *penis* (in males) or in front of the *vagina* (in females).

Urethritis Inflammation of the *urethra,* usually caused by an infection.

Urogenital sinus The common opening of the urinary and genital systems in the *embryo.*

Urologist A physician who specializes in disorders of the urogenital system.

Uterus (Latin) The womb; a pear-shaped region of the female *reproductive tract* through which *sperm* are transported and where the *conceptus* implants and develops.

Vacuum aspiration An *abortion* procedure in which the *conceptus* is destroyed and removed by suction.

Vacuum constriction system A device for treating *erectile dysfunction* that creates a partial vacuum around the *penis,* thus drawing blood into the erectile tissue.

Vagina (Latin, sheath) A muscular tube extending 8–10 cm from the *vestibule* to the uterine *cervix.* It accommodates the *penis* during *coitus* and expands to permit passage of the *fetus* during *parturition.*

Vaginal code A phenomenon whereby, in some species, *coitus* repeated at a certain frequency facilitates the establishment of pregnancy.

Vaginal dilator A plastic cylinder used to enlarge the *vagina* or to counteract *vaginismus.*

Vaginismus Painful spasm of the musculature of the *vagina* that prevents *intromission.*

Vaginitis Inflammation of the *vagina.*

Varicocele Enlargement of the veins that drain the *testis.*

Vas deferens (plural vasa deferentia) (Latin, vessel leading down) Either of the two bilateral ducts that convey *sperm* from the *epididymis* to the *ejaculatory duct.*

Vasectomy A male *sterilization* technique that involves cutting or tying off of the *vasa deferentia.*

Vasopressin A peptide hormone synthesized by neurons in the hypothalamus and secreted by their axon terminals in the posterior lobe of the pituitary gland; it raises blood pressure and reduces urine volume.

Vasovasostomy Surgery to reverse a vasectomy.

V-chip A device built into television sets that permits the filtering of programs rated as containing sex, violence, or foul language.

Venereal disease (from Venus, the Roman goddess of love) Obsolete term for a sexually transmitted disease.

Ventral horn (Latin *venter,* belly) The portion of the *gray matter* of the spinal cord nearer to the front of the body, where *motor neurons* are located. Contrast *dorsal horn.*

Ventromedial nucleus A cell group in the *hypothalamus* concerned with the regulation of sexual behaviors typically shown by females, such as *lordosis* in rats.

Vestibular bulbs Erectile structures deep to the *labia minora,* on either side of the *vestibule.*

Vestibule The potential space between the left and right *labia minora.*

Vibrator An electrically powered vibrating device used to provide sexual stimulation.

Victim–perpetrator cycle The idea that being victimized in some way, such as by sexual abuse during childhood, predisposes an individual to victimize others in the same way. Also called the *abused–abuser hypothesis.*

Virginity Sexual inexperience, commonly defined as never having engaged in *coitus.*

Virilization (Latin *virilis,* manly) A process that makes a female body, especially the *genitalia,* come to partially resemble those of a male.

Virion A *virus* particle, especially when in an inert form outside its host cell.

Virus (Latin, poison) A very small infectious agent consisting of a core containing *DNA* or *RNA,* a *capsid,* and sometimes a lipid *envelope.*

Vomeronasal organ (VNO) A sense organ in the nose of some animals, but probably vestigial and nonfunctional in humans, that detects *sex pheromones.*

Voyeurism (French *voyeur,* viewer) A *paraphilia* involving spying on persons while they are undressing, naked, or engaged in sex.

Vulva (Latin, wrapping, womb) The female *external genitalia.*

Wet dream An *erotic* dream that culminates in *orgasm* and that may be accompanied by *nocturnal emission* in males.

White matter A region of the *central nervous system* that contains bundles of *axons* but no neuronal *cell bodies.* Contrast *gray matter.*

Withdrawal method A method of *contraception* in which the man withdraws his *penis* from the *vagina* prior to *ejaculation.*

Wolffian duct Either of two bilateral ducts in the *embryo* that give rise to the male *reproductive tract.*

Women's movement The movement for women's rights and social equality, one important phase of which took place during the 1970s.

X chromosome In mammals, one of the two *sex chromosomes.* Females possess two X chromosomes; males possess one X chromosome and one *Y chromosome.*

X inactivation The inactivation of one of the two *X chromosomes* in the cells of female *embryos,* a process that leaves male and female cells with the same number of functional X chromosomes—one.

Y chromosome In mammals, one of the two *sex chromosomes.* It is present only in males and carries the **SRY** *gene,* which usually causes an embryo to develop as a male.

Yeast infection See *candidiasis.*

Yolk sac A transient, early extraembryonic structure; the source of *primordial germ cells.* In the human *conceptus* it never contains yolk.

Zona pellucida (Latin, transparent belt) The capsule surrounding an *ovum* that must be penetrated by the fertilizing *sperm.*

Zonal drilling An assisted reproduction technique in which a hole is drilled through the *zona pellucida* of an *ovum* to facilitate *fertilization.*

Zoophilia (Greek *zoon,* animal, *philia,* love) A persistent preference for sexual contacts with animals, considered a *paraphilia.*

Zygote (ZY-gote) (Greek *zugon,* yoke) A cell formed by the fusion of *gametes:* a fertilized *ovum.*

Illustration Credits

References

Abel, G. G., Barlow, D. H., Blanchard, E. B., & Guild, D. (1977). The components of rapists' sexual arousal. *Archives of General Psychiatry, 34,* 395–403.

Abel, G. G., Becker, J. V., Mittelman, M. S., Cunningham-Rathner, J., Rouleau, J. L., & Murphy, W. D. (1987). Self-reported sex crimes of nonincarcerated paraphiliacs. *Journal of Interpersonal Violence, 2,* 3–25.

Abel, G. G., Blanchard, E. B., & Becker, J. V. (1978). An integrated treatment program for rapists. In R. T. Rada (Ed.), *Clinical aspects of the rapist.* Grune and Stratton.

Abel, G. G., & Osborn, C. A. (2000). The paraphilias. In M. G. Gelder, J. J. López-Ibor, & N. Andreasen (Eds.), *New Oxford textbook of psychiatry.* Oxford University Press.

Abell, A., Ernst, E., & Bonde, J. P. (2000). Semen quality and sexual hormones in greenhouse workers. *Scandinavian Journal of Work and Environmental Health, 26,* 492–500.

Abramov, L. A. (1976). Sexual life and sexual frigidity among women developing acute myocardial infarction. *Psychosomatic Medicine, 38,* 418–425.

Absher, J. R., Vogt, B. A., Clark, D. G., Flowers, D. L., Gorman, D. G., Keyes, J. W., & Wood, F. B. (2000). Hypersexuality and hemiballism due to subthalamic infarction. *Neuropsychiatry, Neuropsychology, and Behavioral Neurology, 13,* 220–229.

Adams, H. E., Wright, L. W., Jr., & Lohr, B. A. (1996). Is homophobia associated with homosexual arousal? *Journal of Abnormal Psychology, 105,* 440–445.

Adham, M. N., Teimourian, B., & Mosca, P. (2000). Buried penis release in adults with suction lipectomy and abdominoplasty. *Plastic and Reconstructive Surgery, 106,* 840–844.

Adler, N. T., & Toner, J. P., Jr. (1986). The effects of copulatory behavior on sperm transport and fertility in rats. *Annals of the New York Academy of Sciences, 474,* 21–32.

Adriaanse, A. H., Pel, M., & Bleker, O. P. (2000). Semmelweis: The combat against puerperal fever. *European Journal of Obstetrics, Gynecology, and Reproductive Biology, 90,* 153–158.

Affara, N. A., & Mitchell, M. J. (2000). The role of human and mouse Y chromosome genes in male infertility. *Journal of Endocrinological Investigation, 23,* 630–645.

Agency for Healthcare Policy and Research. (1998). *Health services research on hysterectomy and alternatives.* Located at http://www.ahcpr.gov/research/hysterec.htm.

Aharon, I., Etcoff, N., Ariely, D., Chabris, C. F., O'Connor, E., & Breiter, H. C. (2001). Beautiful faces have variable reward value: fMRI and behavioral evidence. *Neuron, 32,* 537–551.

Aho, M., Koivisto, A. M., Tammela, T. L., & Auvinen, A. (2000). Is the incidence of hypospadias increasing? Analysis of Finnish hospital discharge data 1970–1994. *Environmental Health Perspectives, 108,* 463–465.

Ahokas, A., Aito, M., & Rimon, R. (2000). Positive treatment effect of estradiol in postpartum psychosis: A pilot study. *Journal of Clinical Psychiatry, 61,* 166–169.

Alan Guttmacher Institute. (1999). *Why is teenage pregnancy declining? The role of abstinence, sexual activity and contraceptive use.* Located at http://www.guttmacher.org/pubs/or_teen_preg_decline.html.

Alan Guttmacher Institute. (2000a). *Contraceptive use.* Located at http://www.guttmacher.org/pubs/fb_contr_use.html.

Alan Guttmacher Institute. (2000b). *Induced abortion.* Located at http://www.guttmacher.org/pubs/fb_induced_abortion.html.

Alan Guttmacher Institute. (2002). *U.S. policy can reduce cost barriers to contraception.* Located at http://www.guttmacher.org/pubs/ib_0799.html.

Albert, A. E. (2001). *Brothel: Mustang Ranch and its women.* Random House.

Albert, A. E., Warner, D. L., Hatcher, R. A., Trussell, J., & Bennett, C. (1995). Condom use among female commercial sex workers in Nevada's legal brothels. *American Journal of Public Health, 85,* 1514–1520.

Alexander, C. J., Sipski, M. L., & Findley, T. W. (1993). Sexual activities, desire, and satisfaction in males pre- and post-spinal cord injury. *Archives of Sexual Behavior, 22,* 217–228.

Alexopoulos, D. S. (1996). Sex differences and IQ. *Personality and Individual Differences, 20,* 445–450.

Allen, L. S., & Gorski, R. A. (1990). Sex difference in the bed nucleus of the stria terminalis of the human brain. *Journal of Comparative Neurology, 302,* 697–706.

Allen, L. S., & Gorski, R. A. (1992). Sexual orientation and the size of the anterior commissure in the human brain. *Proceedings of the National Academy of Sciences of the United States of America, 89,* 7199–7202.

Allen, L. S., Hines, M., Shryne, J. E., & Gorski, R. A. (1989). Two sexually dimorphic cell groups in the human brain. *Journal of Neuroscience, 9,* 497–506.

Allen, M., D'Alessio, D., & Emmers-Sommer, T. M. (2000). Reactions of criminal sexual offenders to pornography: A meta-analytic summary. In M. Roloff (Ed.), *Communication Yearbook 22.* Sage Publications.

Althof, S. E., & Schreiner-Engel, P. (2000). The sexual dysfunctions. In M. G. Gelder, J. J. López-Ibor, & N. Andreasen (Eds.), *New Oxford textbook of psychiatry.* Oxford University Press.

Alvarez, W. A., & Freinhar, J. P. (1991). A prevalence study of bestiality (zoophilia) in psychiatric in-patients, medical in-patients, and psychiatric staff. *International Journal of Psychosomatics, 38,* 45–47.

Amato, P. R. (2000). The consequences of divorce for adults and children. *Journal of Marriage and the Family, 62,* 1269–1287.

American Academy of Pediatrics. (1995). Sexuality, contraception, and the media. *Pediatrics, 95,* 298–300.

American Academy of Pediatrics. (1999a). Circumcision policy statement. *Pediatrics, 103,* 686–693.

American Academy of Pediatrics. (1999b). Cord blood banking for potential future transplantation. *Pediatrics, 104,* 166–118.

American Academy of Pediatrics. (2002). Coparent or second-parent adoptions by same-sex parents. *Pediatrics, 109,* 339–340.

American Association of Retired Persons. (1999). *AARP/Modern Maturity sexuality survey.* Located at http://research.aarp.org/health/mmsexsurvey_1.html.

American Association of University Women. (1992). *How schools shortchange girls.* AAUW Educational Foundation.

American Association of University Women. (1993). *Hostile hallways: The AAUW survey on sexual harassment in America's schools.* American Association of University Women.

American Cancer Society. (2000). *Breast cancer: Prevention and risk factors.* Located at http://www3.cancer.org/cancerinfo/load_cont.asp?st=pr&ct=5&language=english.

American Cancer Society. (2001a). *All about breast cancer.* Located at http://www.cancer.org/eprise/main/docroot/CRI/CRI_2x?sitearea=LRN&dt=5.

American Cancer Society. (2001b). *A breast cancer journey: Your personal guidebook.* American Cancer Society.

American Cancer Society. (2001c). *Cancer facts and figures 2001.* Located at http://www.cancer.org/downloads/STT/F&F2001.pdf.

American Cancer Society. (2001d). *How is prostate cancer staged?* Located at http://www.cancer.org/eprise/main/docroot/CRI/content/CRI_2_4_3X_How_is_prostate_cancer_staged_36?sitearea=CRI.

American Civil Liberties Union. (1996a). *Thought police recruited in new child porn law.* Located at http://www.aclu.org/news/w100396a.html.

American Civil Liberties Union. (1996b). *Violence chip.* Located at http://www.aclu.org/library/aavchip.html.

American Civil Liberties Union. (1998). *Online censorship in the states.* Located at http://www.aclu.org/issues/cyber/censor/stbills.html.

American College of Nurse-Midwifery & Jacobs, S. (1993). *Having your baby with a nurse-midwife: Everything you need to know to make an informed decision.* Hyperion.

American College of Obstetricians and Gynecologists. (2000a). *Androgen replacement no panacea for women's libido.* Located at www.acog.org/from_home/publications/press_releases/nr10–31–00–1.htm.

American College of Obstetricians and Gynecologists. (2000b). *Planning your pregnancy and birth* (3rd ed.). ACOG.

American College of Obstetricians and Gynecologists. (2002). *Medical experts still recommend mammography.* Located at http://www.acog.org/from_home/publications/press_releases/nr02–03–02.htm.

American Medical Association. (1987). Aversion therapy. *JAMA, 258,* 2562–2566.

American Psychiatric Association. (1994). *Diagnostic and statistical manual of mental disorders* (4th ed.) (*DSM-IV*). American Psychiatric Association.

American Psychiatric Association. (2000). *Diagnostic and statistical manual of mental disorders* (4th ed., text revision) (*DSM-IV-TR 2000*). American Psychiatric Association.

American Society for Reproductive Medicine. (2000). Financial incentives in recruitment of oocyte donors. *Fertility and Sterility, 74,* 216–220.

American Society of Anesthesiologists. (1999). *Practice guidelines for obstetrical anesthesia.* Located at http://www.asahq.org/practice/ob/obguide.html.

Amstey, M. S. (1994). The political history of syphilis and its application to the AIDS epidemic. *Women's Health Issues, 4,* 16–19.

Anawalt, B. D., Herbst, K. L., Matsumoto, A. M., Mulders, T. M., Coelingh-Bennink, H. J., & Bremner, W. J. (2000). Desogestrel plus testosterone effectively suppresses spermatogenesis but also causes modest weight gain and high-density lipoprotein suppression. *Fertility and Sterility, 74,* 707–714.

Andersen, A. G., Jensen, T. K., Carlsen, E., Jorgensen, N., Andersson, A. M., Krarup, T., Keiding, N., & Skakkebaek, N. E. (2000). High frequency of sub-optimal semen quality in an unselected population of young men. *Human Reproduction, 15,* 366–372.

Anderson, R. H., Fleming, D. E., Rhees, R. W., & Kinghorn, E. (1986). Relationships between sexual activity, plasma testosterone, and the volume of the sexually dimorphic nucleus of the preoptic area in prenatally stressed and non-stressed rats. *Brain Research, 370,* 1–10.

Andersson, A. M., & Skakkebaek, N. E. (1999). Exposure to exogenous estrogens in food: Possible impact on human development and health. *European Journal of Endocrinology, 140,* 477–485.

Andersson, A. M., Toppari, J., Haavisto, A. M., Petersen, J. H., Simell, T., Simell, O., & Skakkebaek, N. E. (1998). Longitudinal reproductive hormone profiles in infants: Peak of inhibin B levels in infant boys exceeds levels in adult men. *Journal of Clinical Endocrinology and Metabolism, 83,* 675–681.

Angelsen, N. K., Jacobsen, G., & Bakketeig, L. S. (2001). Breast feeding and cognitive development at age 1 and 5 years. *Archives of Disease in Childhood, 85,* 183–188.

Anonymous. (2001). *The autoerotic asphyxiation syndrome in adolescent and young adult males.* Located at http://www.silentvictims.org/.

Apfelbaum, B. (1989). Retarded ejaculation: A much misunderstood syndrome. In S. Leiblum & R. Rosen (Eds.), *Principles and practice of sex therapy: Update for the 1990s.* Guilford Press.

Aplasca De Los Reyes, M. R., Pato-Mesola, V., Klausner, J. D., Manalastas, R., Wi, T., Tuazon, C. U., Dallabetta, G., Whittington, W. L., & Holmes, K. K. (2001). A randomized trial of ciprofloxacin versus cefixime for treatment of gonorrhea after rapid emergence of gonococcal ciprofloxacin resistance in The Philippines. *Clinical Infectious Diseases, 32,* 1313–1318.

The Arc. (1996). *Sexuality: Position paper no. 9.* Located at http://www.thearc.org/posits/sex.html.

Archer, J. (1992). Childhood gender roles: Social context and organization. In H. McGurk (Ed.), *Childhood Social Development: Contemporary Perspectives.* Lawrence Erlbaum Associates.

Arden, M. A., & Dye, L. (1998). The assessment of menstrual synchrony: Comment on Weller and Weller (1997). *Journal of Comparative Psychology, 112,* 323–324; discussion 325–326.

Aries, P. (1965). *Centuries of childhood: A social history of family life.* Random House.

Armstrong, L., & Jenkins, S. (2000). *It's not about the bike: My journey back to life.* Putnam.

Ascherson, B. (1996). *Black Sea: The birthplace of civilization and barbarism.* Vintage.

Asia Pacific Radio Transcripts. (2000). *Bangladesh liberation war rape victims demand justice from Pakistan*. Located at http://www.abc.net.au/ra/asiapac/archive/2000/dec/raap-21dec2000–1.htm.

Associated Press. (1999). Sex abuse charges against former day-care operator dismissed. *News-Times* (Danbury, CT), September 23. Retrieved from (http://www.newstimes.com/archive99/sep2399/naa.htm).

Associated Press. (2002a). Supreme Court strikes down ban on virtual child pornography. *New York Times*, April 16.

Associated Press. (2002b). Virginia governor apologizes for law that forced sterilizations. *Los Angeles Times*, May 3.

Association for the Treatment of Sexual Offenders. (1997). *Anti-androgen therapy and surgical castration*. Located at http://www.atsa.com/ppantiandro.html.

Atkins, D. (Ed.) (1999). *Lesbian sex scandals: Sexual practices, identities, and politics*. Haworth Press.

Audet, M. C., Moreau, M., Koltun, W. D., Waldbaum, A. S., Shangold, G., Fisher, A. C., & Creasy, G. W. (2001). Evaluation of contraceptive efficacy and cycle control of a transdermal contraceptive patch vs. an oral contraceptive: A randomized controlled trial. *JAMA, 285*, 2347–2354.

Auger, J., Kunstmann, J. M., Czyglik, F., & Jouannet, P. (1995). Decline in semen quality among fertile men in Paris during the past 20 years. *New England Journal of Medicine, 332*, 281–285.

Avakame, E. (1999). Females' labor force participation and rape: An empirical test of the backlash hypothesis. *Violence Against Women, 5*, 926–949.

Avis, N. E. (2000). Sexual function and aging in men and women: Community and population-based studies. *Journal of Gender-Specific Medicine, 3*, 37–41.

Avis, N. E., Stellato, R., Crawford, S., Bromberger, J., Ganz, P., Cain, V., & Kagawa-Singer, M. (2001). Is there a menopausal syndrome? Menopausal status and symptoms across racial/ethnic groups. *Social Science and Medicine, 52*, 345–356.

Avis, N. E., Stellato, R., Crawford, S., Johannes, C., & Longcope, C. (2000). Is there an association between menopause status and sexual functioning? *Menopause, 7*, 297–309.

Badgett, M. V. L. (1995). The wage effects of sexual orientation discrimination. *Industrial and Labor Relations Review, 48*, 726–739.

Bagatell, C. J., Heiman, J. R., Rivier, J. E., & Bremner, W. J. (1994). Effects of endogenous testosterone and estradiol on sexual behavior in normal young men. *Journal of Clinical Endocrinology and Metabolism, 78*, 711–716.

Bailey, J. M. (1997). Can behavior genetics contribute to evolutionary behavioral science? In C. Crawford & D. L. Krebs (Eds.), *Handbook of Evolutionary Psychology: Ideas, Issues, and Applications*. Lawrence Erlbaum Associates.

Bailey, J. M., Gaulin, S., Agyei, Y., & Gladue, B. A. (1994). Effects of gender and sexual orientation on evolutionarily relevant aspects of human mating psychology. *Journal of Personality and Social Psychology, 66*, 1081–1093.

Bailey, J. M., Kim, P. Y., Hills, A., & Linsenmeier, J. A. (1997). Butch, femme, or straight acting? Partner preferences of gay men and lesbians. *Journal of Personality and Social Psychology, 73*, 960–973.

Bailey, J. M., & Oberschneider, M. (1997). Sexual orientation and professional dance. *Archives of Sexual Behavior, 26*, 433–444.

Bailey, J. M., & Pillard, R. C. (1995). Genetics of human sexual orientation. *Annual Review of Sex Research, 6*, 126–150.

Bailey, J. M., Pillard, R. C., Dawood, K., Miller, M. B., Farrer, L. A., Trivedi, S., & Murphy, R. L. (1999). A family history study of male sexual orientation using three independent samples. *Behavior Genetics, 29*, 79–86.

Bailey, J. M., Willerman, L., & Parks, C. (1991). A test of the maternal stress theory of human male homosexuality. *Archives of Sexual Behavior, 20*, 277–293.

Bailey, J. M., & Zucker, K. J. (1995). Childhood sex-typed behavior and sexual orientation: A conceptual analysis and quantitative review. *Developmental Psychology, 31*, 43–55.

Baker, R. R., & Bellis, M. A. (1993). Human sperm competition: Adjustment by males and the function of masturbation. *Animal Behaviour, 46*, 861–885.

Baker, R. R., & Bellis, M. (1995). *Human sperm competition: Copulation, masturbation, and infidelity*. Chapman and Hall.

Bakker, J., Brand, T., van Ophemert, J., & Slob, A. K. (1993). Hormonal regulation of adult partner preference behavior in neonatally ATD-treated male rats. *Behavioral Neuroscience, 107*, 480–487.

Ballagh, S. A. (2001). Vaginal ring hormone delivery systems in contraception and menopause. *Clinical Obstetrics and Gynecology, 44*, 106–113.

Balon, R. (1998). Pharmacological treatment of paraphilias with a focus on antidepressants. *Journal of Sex and Marital Therapy, 24*, 241–254.

Balter, M. (1999). Scientific cross-claims fly in continuing beef war. *Science, 284*, 1453–1455.

Bamberger, J. D., Waldo, C. R., Gerberding, J. L., & Katz, M. H. (1999). Postexposure prophylaxis for human immunodeficiency virus (HIV) infection following sexual assault. *American Journal of Medicine, 106*, 323–326.

Barbaree, H. E., & Marshall, W. L. (1989). Erectile responses among heterosexual child molesters, father-daughter incest offenders, and matched non-offenders: Five distinct-age preference profiles. *Canadian Journal of Behavioral Science, 21*, 70–82.

Barker, R. (1987). *The green-eyed marriage: Surviving jealous relationships*. Free Press.

Barlow, D. H. (1986). Causes of sexual dysfunction: The role of anxiety and cognitive interference. *Journal of Consulting and Clinical Psychology, 54*, 140–148.

Barnhart, K., Furman, I., & Devoto, L. (1995). Attitudes and practice of couples regarding sexual relations during the menses and spotting. *Contraception, 51*, 93–98.

Baron, L. (1985). Does rape contribute to reproductive success? Evaluations of sociobiological views of rape. *International Journal of Women's Studies, 8*, 266–277.

Barrie, D. (director). (1999). In excess: The death of Michael Hutchence (documentary film, Channel Four, U.K., August 17).

Barsetti, I., Earls, C. M., Lalumière, M. L., & Bélanger, N. (1998). The differentiation of intrafamilial and extrafamilial heterosexual child molesters. *Journal of Interpersonal Violence, 13*, 275–286.

Bartels, A., & Zeki, S. (2000). The neural basis of romantic love. *Neuroreport, 11*, 3829–3834.

Bastian, L. A., Nanda, K., Hasselblad, V., & Simel, D. L. (1998). Diagnostic efficiency of home pregnancy test kits: A meta-analysis. *Archives of Family Medicine, 7*, 465–469.

Bateman, A. J. (1948). Intra-sexual selection in *Drosophila*. *Heredity, 2*, 349–368.

Baum, M. J. (2002). Neuroendocrinology of sexual behavior in the male. In J. B. Becker, S. M. Breedlove, D. Crews, & M. M. McCarthy (Eds.), *Behavioral endocrinology* (2nd ed.). MIT Press.

Baumeister, R. F., & Tice, D. M. (2000). *The social dimension of sex*. Allyn and Bacon.

Baumeister, R. F., & Wotman, S. R. (1992). *Breaking hearts: The two sides of unrequited love*. Guilford Press.

Baumeister, R. F., Wotman, S. R., & Stillwell, A. M. (1993). Unrequited love: On heartbreak, anger, guilt, scriptlessness, and humiliation. *Journal of Personality and Social Psychology, 64*, 377–394.

Bawer, B. (1993). *A place at the table: The gay individual in American society*. Poseidon.

Baxter, D. J., Barbaree, H. E., & Marshall, W. L. (1986). Sexual responses to consenting and forced sex in a large sample of rapists and nonrapists. *Behaviour Research and Therapy, 24*, 513–520.

Bayer, R. (1981). *Homosexuality and American psychiatry: The politics of diagnosis*. Princeton University Press.

Beam, J. W. (1994). *Leathersex: A guide for the curious outsider and the serious player*. Daedalus Publishing.

Bearman, P. S., & Brückner, H. (2001). Promising the future: Virginity pledges as they affect transition to first intercourse. *American Journal of Sociology, 106*, 859–912.

Beatty, W. W., & Troster, A. I. (1987). Gender differences in geographical knowledge. *Sex Roles, 16*, 565–590.

Bedford, J. M. (1977). Evolution of the scrotum: The epididymis as the prime mover. In J. H. Calaby & C. H. Tyndale-Biscoe (Eds.), *Reproduction and evolution*. Australian Academy of Sciences.

Behre, H. M., Kuhlage, J., Gassner, C., Sonntag, B., Schem, C., Schneider, H. P., & Nieschlag, E. (2000). Prediction of ovulation by urinary hormone measurements with the home use ClearPlan Fertility Monitor: Comparison with transvaginal ultrasound scans and serum hormone measurements. *Human Reproduction, 15*, 2478–2482.

Beit-Hallahmi, B. (1985). Dangers of the vagina. *British Journal of Medical Psychology, 58*, 351–356.

Bell, A. P., & Weinberg, M. S. (1978). *Homosexualities: A study of diversity in men and women*. Simon and Schuster.

Belzer, E., Whipple, B., & Moger, W. (1984). A female ejaculation. *Journal of Sex Research, 20*, 403–406.

Bem, D. J. (1996). Exotic becomes erotic: A developmental theory of sexual orientation. *Psychological Review, 103*, 320–335.

Bem, S. L. (1974). The measurement of psychological androgyny. *Journal of Consulting and Clinical Psychology, 42*, 151–162.

Bem, S. L. (1981). Gender schema theory: A cognitive account of sex typing. *Psychological Review, 103*, 320–335.

Bem, S. L. (1989). Genital knowledge and gender constancy in preschool children. *Child Development, 60*, 649–662.

Berenbaum, S. A. (1999). Effects of early androgens on sex-typed activities and interests in adolescents with congenital adrenal hyperplasia. *Hormones and Behavior, 35*, 102–110.

Berenbaum, S. A., & Snyder, E. (1995). Early hormonal influences on childhood sex-typed activity and playmate preferences: Implications for the development of sexual orientation. *Developmental Psychology, 31*, 31–42.

Berger, B. J., Kolton, S., Zenilman, J. M., Cummings, M. C., Feldman, J., & McCormack, W. M. (1995). Bacterial vaginosis in lesbians: A sexually transmitted disease. *Clinical Infectious Diseases, 21*, 1402–1405.

Berlin, F. S., & Malin, H. M. (1991). Media distortion of the public's perception of recidivism and psychiatric rehabilitation. *American Journal of Psychiatry, 148*, 1572–1576.

Berman, J., Berman, L., & Bumiller, E. (2001). *For women only: A revolutionary guide to overcoming sexual dysfunction and reclaiming your sex life*. Henry Holt.

Bernstein, I. H., Lin, T. D., & McClellan, P. (1982). Cross- vs. within-racial judgments of attractiveness. *Perception and Psychophysics, 32*, 495–503.

Best, K. (1999). *Disabled have many needs for contraception*. Located at http://www.fhi.org/en/fp/fppubs/network/v19-2/nt1924.html.

Betzig, L. (1989). Causes of conjugal dissolution: A cross-cultural study. *Current Anthropology, 30*, 654–676.

Bevier, P. J., Chiasson, M. A., Heffernan, R. T., & Castro, K. G. (1995). Women at a sexually transmitted disease clinic who reported same-sex contact: Their HIV seroprevalence and risk behaviors. *American Journal of Public Health, 85*, 1366–1371.

Biale, R. (1984). *Women and Jewish law: An exploration of women's issues in Halakhic sources*. Schocken Books.

Billups, K. L., Berman, L., Berman, J., Metz, M. E., Glennon, M. E., & Goldstein, I. (2001). A new non-pharmacological vacuum therapy for female sexual dysfunction. *Journal of Sex and Marital Therapy, 27*, 435–441.

Billy, J. O. G., Brewster, K. L., & Grady, W. R. (1994). Contextual effects on the sexual behavior of adolescent women. *Journal of Marriage and the Family, 56*, 387–404.

Billy, J. O. G., Tanfer, K., Grady, W. R., & Klepinger, D. H. (1993). The sexual behavior of men in the United States. *Family Planning Perspectives, 25*, 52–60.

Birkhead, T. R. (1998). Sperm competition in birds: Mechanisms and functions. In T. R. Birkhead & A. P. Møller (Eds.), *Sperm competition and sexual selection*. Academic Press.

Birkhead, T. R. (2000). *Promiscuity: An evolutionary history of sperm competition*. Harvard University Press.

Blanchard, R. (1991). Clinical observations and systematic studies of autogynephilia. *Journal of Sex and Marital Therapy, 17*, 235–251.

Blanchard, R. (1993). Varieties of autogynephilia and their relationship to gender dysphoria. *Archives of Sexual Behavior, 22*, 241–251.

Blanchard, R., Barbaree, H. E., Bogaert, A. F., Dickey, R., Klassen, P., Kuban, M. E., & Zucker, K. J. (2000). Fraternal birth order and sexual orientation in pedophiles. *Archives of Sexual Behavior, 29*, 463–478.

Blanchard, R., & Fedoroff, J. P. (2000). The case for and against publicly funded transsexual surgery. *Psychiatry Rounds, 4*.

Blanchard, R., & Hucker, S. J. (1991). Age, transvestism, bondage, and concurrent paraphilic activities in 117 fatal cases of autoerotic asphyxia. *British Journal of Psychiatry, 159*, 371–377.

Blanchard, R., Watson, M. S., Choy, A., Dickey, R., Klassen, P., Kuban, M., & Ferren, D. J. (1999). Pedophiles: Mental retardation, maternal age, and sexual orientation. *Archives of Sexual Behavior, 28*, 111–127.

Blondell, R. D., Foster, M. B., & Dave, K. C. (1999). Disorders of puberty. *American Family Physician, 60*, 209–218, 223–204.

Blumstein, P., & Schwartz, P. (1983). *American couples: Money, work, sex*. Morrow.

Bogaert, A. F. (1998). Birth order and sibling sex ratio in homosexual and heterosexual non-white men. *Archives of Sexual Behavior, 27*, 467–473.

Bogaert, A. F. (2001). Handedness, criminality, and sexual offending. *Neuropsychologia, 39*, 465–469.

Bogaert, A. F., & Blanchard, R. (1996). Handedness in homosexual and heterosexual men in the Kinsey interview data. *Archives of Sexual Behavior, 25*, 373–378.

Bohlen, D., Hugonnet, C. L., Mills, R. D., Weise, E. S., & Schmid, H. P. (2000). Five meters of H_2O: The pressure at the urinary bladder neck during human ejaculation. *Prostate, 44*, 339–341.

Boorse, C. (1981). On the distinction between disease and illness. In A. L. Caplan, H. T. Engelhardt, & J. J. McCartney (Eds.), *Concepts of health and disease: Interdisciplinary perspectives*. Addison-Wesley.

Bornstein, K. (1994). *Gender outlaw: On men, women, and the rest of us*. Routledge.

Bortz, W. M., II, Wallace, D. H., & Wiley, D. (1999). Sexual function in 1,202 aging males: Differentiating aspects. *Journals of Gerontology. Series A, Biological Sciences and Medical Sciences, 54*, M237–241.

Bosinski, H. A., Peter, M., Bonatz, G., Arndt, R., Heidenreich, M., Sippell, W. G., & Wille, R. (1997). A higher rate of hyperandrogenic disorders in female-to-male transsexuals. *Psychoneuroendocrinology, 22*, 361–380.

Bostwick, D. G., MacLennan, G. T., & Larson, T. R. (1999). *Prostate cancer: What every man—and his family—needs to know* (Rev. ed.). Villard Books.

Boswell, J. (1980). *Christianity, social tolerance, and homosexuality.* University of Chicago Press.

Boyce, E. G., & Umland, E. M. (2001). Sildenafil citrate: A therapeutic update. *Clinical Therapeutics, 23,* 2–23.

Bracciolini, P. (1964). *Facetiae.* Valhalla Books.

Bradford, J. M. (2001). The neurobiology, neuropharmacology, and pharmacological treatment of the paraphilias and compulsive sexual behaviour. *Canadian Journal of Psychiatry. Revue Canadienne de Psychiatrie, 46,* 26–34.

Bradford, J. M., & Pawlak, A. (1993). Double-blind placebo crossover study of cyproterone acetate in the treatment of the paraphilias. *Archives of Sexual Behavior, 22,* 383–402.

Brannigan, A. (1987). Sex and aggression in the lab: Implications for public policy? *Canadian Journal of Law and Society, 2,* 177–185.

Bray, J. H. (1999). From marriage to remarriage and beyond: Finding from the Developmental Issues in Stepfamilies research project. In E. M. Hetherington (Ed.), *Coping with divorce, single parenting, and remarriage.* Lawrence Erlbaum Associates.

Bray, J. H., & Kelly, J. (1998). *Stepfamilies: Love, marriage, and parenting in the first decade.* Broadway Books.

Brecher, E. M. (1984). *Love, sex, and aging.* Little, Brown.

Breedlove, S. M., Cooke, B. M., & Jordan, C. L. (1999). The orthodox view of brain sexual differentiation. *Brain, Behavior and Evolution, 54,* 8–14.

Bren, L. (2001). *Alternatives to hysterectomy: New technologies, more options.* Located at http://www.fda.gov/fdac/features/2001/601_tech.html.

Bretschneider, J. G., & McCoy, N. L. (1988). Sexual interest and behavior in healthy 80- to 102-year-olds. *Archives of Sexual Behavior, 17,* 109–129.

Brewster, K. L., Billy, J. O. G., & Grady, W. R. (1993). Social context and adolescent behavior: The impact of community on the transition to sexual activity. *Social Forces, 71,* 713–740.

Briere, J., & Runtz, M. (1989). University males' sexual interest in children: Predicting potential indices of "pedophilia" in a nonforensic sample. *Child Abuse and Neglect, 13,* 65–75.

Bright, S. (1999). *Susie Sexpert's lesbian sex world* (Rev. ed.). Cleis Press.

Brink, P. J. (1989). The fattening room among the Annang of Nigeria. *Medical Anthropology, 12,* 131–143.

Brookoff, D., O'Brien, K. K., Cook, C. S., Thompson, T. D., & Williams, C. (1997). Characteristics of participants in domestic violence: Assessment at the scene of domestic assault. *JAMA, 277,* 1369–1373.

Brooten, B. (1996). *Love between women: Early Christian responses to female homoeroticism.* University of Chicago Press.

Brooten, B. (2002). *Feminist sexual ethics: Creating debate on how to respect the full human dignity of all persons.* Located at http://www.brandeis.edu/departments/nejs/fse/Pages/project1.html.

Brown, A. J. (2000). Ciprofloxacin as cure of premature ejaculation. *Journal of Sex and Marital Therapy, 26,* 351–352.

Brown, W. M., Finn, C. J., Cooke, B. M., & Breedlove, S. M. (2002). Differences in finger length ratios between self-identified "butch" and "femme" lesbians. *Archives of Sexual Behavior, 31,* 123–127.

Brownmiller, S. (1975). *Against our will: Men, women and rape.* Simon and Schuster.

Brunker, M. (2001). *Sex toys blaze tactile trail on net.* Located at http://www.msnbc.com/News/318124.asp.

Bruno, R. L. (1997). Devotees, pretenders and wannabes: Two cases of factitious disability disorder. *Journal of Sexuality and Disability, 15,* 243–260.

Bullough, V. L. (1981). Age at menarche: A misunderstanding. *Science, 213,* 365–366.

Bullough, V. L. (1994). *Science in the bedroom: A history of sex research.* Basic Books.

Bullough, V. L., & Bullough, B. (1987). *Women and prostitution: A social history.* Prometheus Books.

Bullough, V. L., & Bullough, B. (1993). *Cross-dressing, sex, and gender.* University of Pennsylvania Press.

Bullough, V. L., & Bullough, B. (1995). *Sexual attitudes: Myths and realities.* Prometheus Books.

Bullough, V. L., & Bullough, B. (1997). *Contraception: A guide to birth control methods.* Prometheus Books.

Bumpass, L., & Sweet, J. (1989). National estimates of cohabitation. *Demography, 26,* 615–625.

Burack, J. H., Barrett, D. C., Stall, R. D., Chesney, M. A., Ekstrand, M. L., & Coates, T. J. (1993). Depressive symptoms and CD4 lymphocyte decline among HIV-infected men. *JAMA, 270,* 2568–2573.

Bureau of Justice Statistics. (1997). *Violence-related injuries treated in hospital emergency departments.* Located at http://www.ojp.usdoj.gov/bjs/pub/pdf/vrithed.pdf.

Bureau of Justice Statistics. (2000). *Intimate partner violence.* Located at http://www.ojp.usdoj.gov/bjs/pub/pdf/ipv.pdf.

Burgess, A. W., & Holmstrom, L. L. (1974). Rape trauma syndrome. *American Journal of Psychiatry, 131,* 981–986.

Burgess, A. W., & Holmstrom, L. L. (1979). Rape: Sexual disruption and recovery. *American Journal of Orthopsychiatry, 49,* 648–657.

Burgoyne, P. S., Thornhill, A. R., Kalmus Boudreau, S., Darling, S. M., Bishop, C. E., & Evans, E. P. (1995). The genetic basis of XX-XY differences present before gonadal sex differentiation in the mouse. *Philosophical Transactions of the Royal Society of London. Series B: Biological Sciences, 350,* 253–260; discussion 260–251.

Burkman, R. T., Collins, J. A., & Greene, R. A. (2001). Current perspectives on benefits and risks of hormone replacement therapy. *American Journal of Obstetrics and Gynecology, 185,* S13–23.

Bush, T. L., Whiteman, M., & Flaws, J. A. (2001). Hormone replacement therapy and breast cancer: A qualitative review. *Obstetrics and Gynecology, 98,* 498–508.

Buss, A. H., & Perry, M. (1992). The aggression questionnaire. *Journal of Personality and Social Psychology, 63,* 452–459.

Buss, D. M. (1989). Sex differences in human mate preference: Evolutionary hypothesis tested in 37 cultures. Behavioral and Brain Sciences, 12, 1–149.

Buss, D. M. (1994). *The evolution of desire: Strategies of human mating.* Basic Books.

Buss, D. M. (2000). *The dangerous passion: Why jealousy is as necessary as love and sex.* Free Press.

Buss, D. M., & Schmitt, D. P. (1993). Sexual strategies theory: A contextual evolutionary analysis of human mating. *Psychological Review, 100,* 204–232.

Butler, A. C. (2001). Trends in same-gender sexual partnering, 1988–1998. *Journal of Sex Research, 37,* 333–343.

Butler, R. N., & Lewis, M. I. (2002). *The new love and sex after 60.* Ballantine Books.

Byne, W. (1998). The medial preoptic and anterior hypothalamic regions of the rhesus monkey: Cytoarchitectonic comparison with the human and evidence for sexual dimorphism. *Brain Research, 793,* 346–350.

Byne, W., Tobet, S., Mattiace, L. A., Lasco, M. S., Kemether, E., Edgar, M. A., Morgello, S., Buchsbaum, M. S., & Jones, L. B. (2001). The interstitial nuclei of the human anterior hypothalamus: An investigation of variation with sex, sexual orientation, and HIV status. *Hormones and Behavior, 40,* 86–92.

Byrne, D., London, O., & Reeves, K. (1968). The effects of physical attractiveness, sex, and attitude similarity on interpersonal attraction. *Journal of Personality, 36,* 259–271.

Cado, S., & Leitenberg, H. (1990). Guilt reactions to sexual fantasies during intercourse. *Archives of Sexual Behavior, 19*, 49–63.

Call, V., Sprecher, S., & Schwartz, P. (1995). The incidence and frequency of marital sex in a national sample. *Journal of Marriage and the Family, 57*, 639–652.

Cameron, P., & Biber, H. (1973). Sexual thought throughout the lifespan. *Gerontologist, 13*, 144–147.

Cammu, H., Van Nylen, M., & Amy, J. J. (2000). A 10-year follow-up after Kegel pelvic floor muscle exercises for genuine stress incontinence. *BJU International, 85*, 655–658.

Cann, A. (1993). Evaluative expectations and the gender schema: Is failed inconsistency better? *Sex Roles, 28*, 667–678.

Caprio, F., & Brenner, D. (1961). *Sexual behavior: Psycho-legal aspects*. Citadel Press.

Carani, C., Rochira, V., Faustini-Fustini, M., Balestrieri, A., & Granata, A. R. (1999). Role of oestrogen in male sexual behaviour: Insights from the natural model of aromatase deficiency. *Clinical Endocrinology, 51*, 517–524.

Carey, A. R., & Staimer, M. (1997). Effects of pulling "Ellen" ads. *USA Today*, April 29.

Carlsen, E., Giwercman, A., Keiding, N., & Skakkebaek, N. E. (1992). Evidence for decreasing quality of semen during past 50 years. *BMJ, 305*, 609–613.

Carlson, A. D., Obeid, J. S., Kanellopoulou, N., Wilson, R. C., & New, M. I. (1999). Congenital adrenal hyperplasia: Update on prenatal diagnosis and treatment. *Journal of Steroid Biochemistry and Molecular Biology, 69*, 19–29.

Carlson, K. J., Miller, B. A., & Fowler, F. J., Jr. (1994a). The Maine Women's Health Study: I. Outcomes of hysterectomy. *Obstetrics and Gynecology, 83*, 556–565.

Carlson, K. J., Miller, B. A., & Fowler, F. J., Jr. (1994b). The Maine Women's Health Study: II. Outcomes of nonsurgical management of leiomyomas, abnormal bleeding, and chronic pelvic pain. *Obstetrics and Gynecology, 83*, 566–572.

Carmichael, M. S., Warburton, V. L., Dixen, J., & Davidson, J. M. (1994). Relationships among cardiovascular, muscular, and oxytocin responses during human sexual activity. *Archives of Sexual Behavior, 23*, 59–79.

Carnes, P. (2001). *Out of the shadows: Understanding sexual addiction* (3rd ed.). Hazelden.

Carson, S. A., Casson, P. R., & and Shuman, D. J. (1999). *The American Society of Reproductive Medicine complete guide to fertility*. Contemporary Books.

Cart, J. (2001). Utah paying a high price for polygamy. *Los Angeles Times*, September 9.

Carter, C. S. (1998). Neuroendocrine perspectives on social attachment and love. *Psychoneuroendocrinology, 23*, 779–818.

Carter, C. S., & Getz, L. L. (1993). Monogamy and the prairie vole. *Scientific American, 268* (6), 100–106.

Caruso, S., Intelisano, G., Lupo, L., & Agnello, C. (2001). Premenopausal women affected by sexual arousal disorder treated with sildenafil: A double-blind, cross-over, placebo-controlled study. *BJOG: An International Journal of Obstetrics and Gynaecology, 108*, 623–628.

Caspi, A., & Herbener, E. S. (1990). Continuity and change: Assortative marriage and the consistency of personality in adulthood. *Journal of Personality and Social Psychology, 58*, 250–258.

Caspi, A., Herbener, E. S., & Ozer, D. J. (1992). Shared experiences and the similarity of personalities: A longitudinal study of married couples. *Journal of Personality and Social Psychology, 62*, 281–291.

Caspi, A., McClay, J., Moffitt, T. E., Mill, J., Martin, J., Craig, I. W., Taylor, A., & Poulton, R. (2002). Role of genotype in the cycle of violence in maltreated children. *Science, 297*, 851–854.

Castellsague, X., Bosch, F. X., Munoz, N., Meijer, C. J., Shah, K. V., de Sanjose, S., Eluf-Neto, J., Ngelangel, C. A., Chichareon, S., Smith, J. S., Herrero, R., Moreno, V., & Franceschi, S. (2002). Male circumcision, penile human papillomavirus infection, and cervical cancer in female partners. *New England Journal of Medicine, 346*, 1105–1112.

Cates, W., Jr. (1999). Estimates of the incidence and prevalence of sexually transmitted diseases in the United States. American Social Health Association Panel. *Sexually Transmitted Diseases, 26*, S2–7.

Center for the Study of Sexual Minorities in the Military. (2000). *The effects of including gay and lesbian soldiers in the British armed forces: Appraising the evidence*. Located at http://www.gaymilitary.ucsb.edu/Publications/british_pub1.htm.

Center for the Study of Sexual Minorities in the Military. (2001). *Poll shows reduction of soldiers' opposition to gays*. Located at http://www.gaymilitary.ucsb.edu/.

Centers for Disease Control. (1994). *Programs for the prevention of suicide among adolescents and young adults*. Located at ftp://ftp.cdc.gov/pub/Publications/mmwr/rr/rr4306.pdf.

Centers for Disease Control. (1999a). *Deaths: Final data for 1997*. Located at http://www.cdc.gov/nchs/data/nvsr/nvsr47/nvs47_19.pdf.

Centers for Disease Control. (1999b). *Infant mortality statistics from the 1997 period linked birth/infant death data set*. Located at http://www.cdc.gov/nchs/data/nvs47_23.pdf.

Centers for Disease Control. (1999c). *The national plan to eliminate syphilis from the United States*. Located at http://www.cdc.gov/stopsyphilis/Plan.pdf.

Centers for Disease Control. (2000a). *Bacterial vaginosis*. Located at http://www.cdc.gov/nchstp/dstd/Fact_Sheets/FactsBV.htm.

Centers for Disease Control. (2000b). *Facts about drug-resistant gonorrhea*. Located at http://www.cdc.gov/od/oc/media/pressrel/fs2k0922a.htm.

Centers for Disease Control. (2000c). *Genital candidiasis*. Located at http://www.cdc.gov/ncidod/dbmd/diseaseinfo/candidiasis_gen_g.htm.

Centers for Disease Control. (2000d). *Preventing the sexual transmission of HIV, the virus that causes AIDS*. Located at ftp://ftp.cdcnpin.org/Updates/oralsex.pdf.

Centers for Disease Control. (2000e). *Trends in pregnancies and pregnancy rates by outcome: Estimates for the United States, 1976–96*. Located at http://www.cdc.gov/nchs/data/series/sr_21/sr21_56.pdf.

Centers for Disease Control. (2000f). *Youth risk behavior surveillance: United States, 1999*. Located at http://www.cdc.gov/mmwr/preview/mmwrhtml/ss4905a1.htm.

Centers for Disease Control. (2001a). *1988 assisted reproductive technology success rates*. Located at http://apps.nccd.cdc.gov/art98/nation98.asp.

Centers for Disease Control. (2001b). *Births: Final data for 1999*. Located at http://www.cdc.gov/nchs/data/nvsr/nvsr49/nvsr49_01.pdf.

Centers for Disease Control. (2001c). *Births: Preliminary data for 2000*. Located at http://www.cdc.gov/nchs/data/nvsr/nvsr49/nvsr49_05.pdf.

Centers for Disease Control. (2001d). *Chlamydia in the United States*. Located at http://www.cdc.gov/nchstp/dstd/Fact_Sheets/chlamydia_facts.htm.

Centers for Disease Control. (2001e). *First marriage dissolution, divorce, and remarriage*. Located at http://www.cdc.gov/nchs/data/ad/ad323.pdf.

Centers for Disease Control. (2001f). *Genital herpes*. Located at http://www.cdc.gov/nchstp/dstd/Fact_Sheets/facts_Genital_Herpes.htm.

Centers for Disease Control. (2001g). *HIV and its transmission.* Located at http://www.cdc.gov/hiv/pubs/facts/transmission.htm.

Centers for Disease Control. (2001h). *HIV incidence among young men who have sex with men: Seven U.S. cities, 1994–2000.* Located at http://www.cdc.gov/mmwr/preview/mmwrhtml/mm5021a4.htm.

Centers for Disease Control. (2001i). *HIV/AIDS surveillance report.* Located at http://www.cdc.gov/hiv/stats/hasr1202.htm.

Centers for Disease Control. (2001j). *Leading causes of death.* Located at http://www.cdc.gov/nchs/fastats/lcod.htm.

Centers for Disease Control. (2001k). *Prenatal care.* Located at http://www.cdc.gov/nccdphp/drh/datoact/pdf/rhow8.pdf.

Centers for Disease Control. (2001l). *Smoking during pregnancy in the 1990s.* Located at http://www.cdc.gov/nchs/data/nvsr/nvsr49/nvsr49_07.pdf.

Centers for Disease Control. (2001m). *Tracking the hidden epidemics: Trends in STDs in the United States, 2000.* Located at http://www.cdc.gov/nchstp/dstd/Stats_Trends/Trends2000.pdf.

Centers for Disease Control. (2002a). *HIV/AIDS surveillance report.* Located at http://www.cdc.gov/hiv/stats/hasr1301.htm.

Centers for Disease Control. (2002b). *Infant mortality statistics from the 1999 period.* Located at http://www.cdc.gov/nchs/data/nvsr/nvsr50/nvsr50_04.pdf.

Centers for Disease Control. (2002c). *Sexually transmitted diseases treatment guidelines.* Located at http://www.cdc.gov/mmwr/preview/mmwrhtml/rr5106a1.htm.

Chahnazarian, A. (1991). Determinants of the sex ratio at birth: Review of the recent literature. *Social Biology, 35,* 214–235.

Chantry, K., & Craig, R. J. (1994). Psychological screening of sexually violent offenders with the MCMI. *Journal of Clinical Psychology, 50,* 430–435.

Chauncey, G. (1994). *Gay New York: Gender, urban culture and the making of the gay male world.* Basic Books.

Chen, K. K., Chan, S. H., Chang, L. S., & Chan, J. Y. (1997). Participation of paraventricular nucleus of hypothalamus in central regulation of penile erection in the rat. *Journal of Urology, 158,* 238–244.

Cheng, S.-T. (1997). Epidemic genital retraction syndrome: Environmental and personal risk factors in southern China. *Journal of Psychology and Human Sexuality, 9,* 57–70.

Chesler, E. (1992). *Woman of valor: Margaret Sanger and the birth control movement in America.* Simon and Schuster.

Chesson, H. W., Pinkerton, S. D., Irwin, K. L., Rein, D., & Kassler, W. J. (1999). New HIV cases attributable to syphilis in the USA: Estimates from a simplified transmission model. *AIDS, 13,* 1387–1396.

Chew, K. K., Earle, C. M., Stuckey, B. G., Jamrozik, K., & Keogh, E. J. (2000). Erectile dysfunction in general medicine practice: Prevalence and clinical correlates. *International Journal of Impotence Research, 12,* 41–45.

Choi, P. Y., & Pope, H. G., Jr. (1994). Violence toward women and illicit androgenic-anabolic steroid use. *Annals of Clinical Psychiatry, 6,* 21–25.

Chuang, H. T., & Addington, D. (1988). Homosexual panic: A review of its concept. *Canadian Journal of Psychiatry. Revue Canadienne de Psychiatrie, 33,* 613–617.

Chun, A. B., Rose, S., Mitrani, C., Silvestre, A. J., & Wald, A. (1997). Anal sphincter structure and function in homosexual males engaging in anoreceptive intercourse. *American Journal of Gastroenterology, 92,* 465–468.

City of Amsterdam. (2001). *Public order and safety.* Located at http://www.amsterdam.nl/e_citygovernment/policy/safety.html.

Clancy, A. N., Zumpe, D., & Michael, R. P. (1995). Intracerebral infusion of an aromatase inhibitor, sexual behavior and brain estrogen receptor-like immunoreactivity in intact male rats. *Neuroendocrinology, 61,* 98–111.

Clark, R. D., & Hatfield, E. (1989). Gender differences in receptivity to sexual offers. *Journal of Psychology and Human Sexuality, 2,* 39–55.

Cleaver, E. (1967). *Soul on ice.* McGraw-Hill.

Clement, K., Vaisse, C., Lahlou, N., Cabrol, S., Pelloux, V., Cassuto, D., Gourmelen, M., Dina, C., Chambaz, J., Lacorte, J. M., Basdevant, A., Bougneres, P., Lebouc, Y., Froguel, P., & Guy-Grand, B. (1998). A mutation in the human leptin receptor gene causes obesity and pituitary dysfunction. *Nature, 392,* 398–401.

Cnattingius, S., Bergstrom, R., Lipworth, L., & Kramer, M. S. (1998). Prepregnancy weight and the risk of adverse pregnancy outcomes. *New England Journal of Medicine, 338,* 147–152.

Coale, A. J., & Banister, J. (1994). Five decades of missing females in China. *Demography, 31,* 459–479.

Coalition against Trafficking in Women. (1997). *On the issue of prostitution as "sex work."* Located at http://www.catwinternational.org/sexwork.htm.

Coalition against Trafficking in Women. (2001a). *Philosophy of the Coalition against Trafficking in Women.* Located at http://www.catwinternational.org/philos.htm.

Coalition against Trafficking in Women. (2001b). *Trafficking in women and prostitution in the Asia Pacific.* Located at http://www.catwinternational.org/apmap.htm.

Cohen, J. (2001). Debate begins over new vaccine trials. *Science, 293,* 1973.

Cohen, M. N. (1995). *Lewis Carroll: A biography.* Macmillan.

Coker, A. L., Hulka, B. S., McCann, M. F., & Walton, L. A. (1992). Barrier methods of contraception and cervical intraepithelial neoplasia. *Contraception, 45,* 1–10.

Colapinto, J. (2000). *As nature made him: The boy who was raised as a girl.* HarperCollins.

Coleman, E. (1996). *What sexual scientists know about compulsive sexual behavior.* Located at http://www.ssc.wisc.edu/ssss/wssk_csb.htm.

Coleman, M., Ganong, L., & Fine, M. (2000). Reinvestigating marriage: Another decade of progress. *Journal of Marriage and the Family, 62,* 1288–1307.

Coles, R., & Stokes, G. (1985). *Sex and the American teenager.* Harper and Row.

Collaer, M. L., & Hines, M. (1995). Human behavioral sex differences: A role for gonadal hormones during early development? *Psychological Bulletin, 118,* 55–107.

Colon, I., Caro, D., Bourdony, C. J., & Rosario, O. (2000). Identification of phthalate esters in the serum of young Puerto Rican girls with premature breast development. *Environmental Health Perspectives, 108,* 895–900.

Comfort, A., & Park, C. (1998). *The new joy of sex and more joy of sex.* Pocket Books.

Connelly, M. T., Richardson, M., & Platt, R. (2000). Prevalence and duration of postmenopausal hormone replacement therapy use in a managed care organization, 1990–1995. *Journal of General Internal Medicine, 15,* 542–550.

Connett, H. (2001). HPV vaccine moves into late stage trials. *Nature Medicine, 7,* 388.

Cooke, B. M., Chowanadisai, W., & Breedlove, S. M. (2000). Post-weaning social isolation of male rats reduces the volume of the medial amygdala and leads to deficits in adult sexual behavior. *Behavioural Brain Research, 117,* 107–113.

Cooke, B. M., Tabibnia, G., & Breedlove, S. M. (1999). A brain sexual dimorphism controlled by adult circulating androgens. *Proceedings of the National Academy of Sciences of the United States of America, 96,* 7538–7540.

Cooper, A. J., Swaminath, S., Baxter, D., & Poulin, C. (1990). A female sex offender with multiple paraphilias: A psychologic, physiologic (laboratory sexual arousal) and endocrine case study. *Canadian Journal of Psychiatry. Revue Canadienne de Psychiatrie, 35*, 334–337.

Cooperman, A., & Sun, L. H. (2002). Hundreds of priests removed since '60s. *Washington Post*, June 9.

Corben, B. (director) (2001). *Raw deal: A question of consent*. 105 min. Miami Film Enterprises, Inc.

Coutinho, E. M., & Segal, S. J. (1999). *Is menstruation obsolete? How suppressing menstruation can help women who suffer from anemia, endometriosis, or PMS*. Oxford University Press.

Cowan, C. P., & Cowan, P. (1992). *When partners become parents: The big life change for couples*. Basic Books.

Cowan, G., & Hoffman, C. D. (1986). Gender stereotyping in young children: Evidence to support a concept-learning approach. *Sex Roles, 14*, 211–224.

Cowan, R. S. (1992). Genetic technology and reproductive choice: An ethics for autonomy. In D. J. Kevles & L. Hood (Eds.), *The code of codes: Scientific and social issues in the human genome project*. Harvard University Press.

Cozzens, D. B. (2000). *The changing face of the priesthood: A reflection on the priest's crisis of soul*. Liturgical Press.

Cramer, D. W., & Xu, H. (1996). Predicting age at menopause. *Maturitas, 23*, 319–326.

Cramer, D. W., Xu, H., & Harlow, B. L. (1995). Family history as a predictor of early menopause. *Fertility and Sterility, 64*, 740–745.

Cranston-Cuebas, M. A., Barlow, D. H., Mitchell, W., & Athanasiou, R. (1993). Differential effects of a misattribution manipulation on sexually functional and dysfunctional men. *Journal of Abnormal Psychology, 102*, 525–533.

Creinin, M. D., & Pymar, H. C. (2000). Medical abortion alternatives to mifepristone. *Journal of the American Medical Women's Association, 55*, 127–132, 150.

Crepault, C., & Couture, M. (1980). Men's erotic fantasies. *Archives of Sexual Behavior, 9*, 565–581.

Crews, D., Grassman, M., & Lindzey, J. (1986). Behavioral facilitation of reproduction in sexual and unisexual whiptail lizards. *Proceedings of the National Academy of Sciences of the United States of America, 83*, 9547–9550.

Cunningham, F. G., Gant, N. F., Leveno, K. J., Gilstrap, L. C., Hauth, J. C., & Wenstrom, K. D. (2001). *Williams obstetrics* (21st ed.). McGraw-Hill.

Cupach, W. R., & Spitzberg, B. H. (1998). Obsessive relational intrusion and stalking. In B. H. Spitzberg, & W. R. Cupach (Eds.), *The dark side of close relationships*. Lawrence Erlbaum Associates.

Curtis, R., & Miller, K. (1997). Believing another likes or dislikes you: Behavior making the beliefs come true. *Journal of Personality and Social Psychology, 51*, 284–290.

Da Costa, M. M., Hogeboom, C. J., Holly, E. A., & Palefsky, J. M. (2002). Increased risk of high-grade anal neoplasia associated with a human papillomavirus type 16 e6 sequence variant. *Journal of Infectious Diseases, 185*, 1229–1237.

Dabbs, J. M., Jr., & Mohammed, S. (1992). Male and female salivary testosterone concentrations before and after sexual activity. *Physiology and Behavior, 52*, 195–197.

Daly, M., & Wilson, M. (1988). Evolutionary social psychology and family homicide. *Science, 242*, 519–524.

Darling, C. A., Davidson, J. K., Sr., & Conway-Welch, C. (1990). Female ejaculation: Perceived origins, the Grafenberg spot/area, and sexual responsiveness. *Archives of Sexual Behavior, 19*, 29–47.

Darling, C. A., Davidson, J. K., Sr., & Jennings, D. A. (1991). The female sexual response revisited: Understanding the multiorgasmic experience in women. *Archives of Sexual Behavior, 20*, 527–540.

Darwin, C. (1859). *On the origin of species by means of natural selection, or the preservation of favoured races in the struggle for life*. John Murray.

Daugherty, J. E. (1998). Treatment strategies for premenstrual syndrome. *American Family Physician, 58*, 183–192, 197–188.

Davey Smith, G., Frankel, S., & Yarnell, J. (1997). Sex and death: Are they related? Findings from the Caerphilly Cohort Study. *BMJ, 315*, 1641–1644.

Davies, S. L., Glaser, D., & Kossoff, R. (2000). Children's sexual play and behavior in pre-school settings: Staff's perceptions, reports, and responses. *Child Abuse and Neglect, 24*, 1329–1343.

Davis, A. J. (1998). Female genital mutilation: Some ethical questions. *Medicine and Law, 17*, 143–148.

Davis, D. L. (1996). Cultural sensitivity and the sexual disorders of DSM-IV. In J. E. Mezzich, A. Kleinman, H. Fabrega, & D. L. Parson (Eds.), *Culture and psychiatric diagnosis*. American Psychiatric Association.

Davis, E. C., Shryne, J. E., & Gorski, R. A. (1995). A revised critical period for the sexual differentiation of the sexually dimorphic nucleus of the preoptic area in the rat. *Neuroendocrinology, 62*, 579–585.

Davis, E. C., Shryne, J. E., & Gorski, R. A. (1996). Structural sexual dimorphisms in the anteroventral periventricular nucleus of the rat hypothalamus are sensitive to gonadal steroids perinatally, but develop peripubertally. *Neuroendocrinology, 63*, 142–148.

Davis, S. R. (2000). Androgens and female sexuality. *Journal of Gender-Specific Medicine, 3*, 36–40.

De Amicis, L. A., Goldberg, D. C., LoPiccolo, J., Friedman, J., & Davies, L. (1985). Clinical follow-up of couples treated for sexual dysfunction. *Archives of Sexual Behavior, 14*, 467–489.

Dean, K. E., & Malamuth, N. M. (1997). Characteristics of men who aggress sexually and of men who imagine aggressing: Risk and moderating variables. *Journal of Personality and Social Psychology, 72*, 449–455.

Dear, M., & Sibley, D. (2000). The one-way strategy for sex offenders makes nobody safe. *Los Angeles Times*, October 1.

Deaux, K., & LaFrance, M. (1998). Gender. In D. T. Gilbert, S. T. Fiske, & G. Lindzey (Eds.), *Handbook of social psychology: Vol. 1* (4th ed.). McGraw-Hill.

Deaver, J. B., & McFarland, J. (1917). *The breast: Its anomalies, its diseases, and their treatment*. P. Blakiston's Son.

de Jonge, F. H., Muntjewerff, J. W., Louwerse, A. L., & van de Poll, N. E. (1988). Sexual behavior and sexual orientation of the female rat after hormonal treatment during various stages of development. *Hormones and Behavior, 22*, 100–115.

Delacoste, F., & Alexander, P. (Eds.). (1998). *Sex work: Writings by women in the sex industry* (2nd ed.). Cleis Press.

Del Carmen, R. (1990). Assessment of Asian-Americans for family therapy. In F. Serafica, A. Schwebel, R. Russell, P. Isaac, & L. Myers (Eds.), *Mental health of ethnic minorities*. Praeger.

DeLamater, J. (1987). A sociological approach. In J. H. Geer & W. T. O'Donohue (Eds.), *Theories of human sexuality*. Plenum.

Deligeoroglou, E. (2000). Dysmenorrhea. *Annals of the New York Academy of Sciences, 900*, 237–244.

D'Emilio, J. (1990). Gay politics and community in San Francisco since World War II. In M. Duberman, M. Vicinus, & G. Chauncey, Jr. (Eds.), *Hidden from history: Reclaiming the gay and lesbian past*. Meridian Books.

Dennerstein, L., Gotts, G., Brown, J. B., Morse, C. A., Farley, T. M., & Pinol, A. (1994). The relationship between the menstrual cycle and female sexual interest in women with PMS complaints and volunteers. *Psychoneuroendocrinology, 19*, 293–304.

Denney, N. W., Field, J. K., & Quadagno, D. (1984). Sex differences in sexual needs and desires. *Archives of Sexual Behavior, 13*, 233–245.

Denny, D. (Ed.) (1998). *Current concepts in transgender identity.* Garland Publishing.

Denny, D., & Bolin, A. (1997). *And now for something completely different: An outcome study with surprising results and important implications.* Located at http://www.symposion.com/ijt/hbigda/vancouver/denny2.htm.

Derby, C. A., Barbour, M. M., Hume, A. L., & McKinlay, J. B. (2001). Drug therapy and prevalence of erectile dysfunction in the Massachusetts Male Aging Study cohort. *Pharmacotherapy, 21*, 676–683.

Derby, C. A., Mohr, B. A., Goldstein, I., Feldman, H. A., Johannes, C. B., & McKinlay, J. B. (2000). Modifiable risk factors and erectile dysfunction: Can lifestyle changes modify risk? *Urology, 56*, 302–306.

Detels, R., English, P., Visscher, B. R., Jacobson, L., Kingsley, L. A., Chmiel, J. S., Dudley, J. P., Eldred, L. J., & Ginzburg, H. M. (1989). Seroconversion, sexual activity, and condom use among 2915 HIV seronegative men followed for up to 2 years. *Journal of Acquired Immune Deficiency Syndromes, 2*, 77–83.

Dettwyler, K. A. (1994). *Dancing skeletons: Life and death in West Africa.* Waveland Press.

Devinsky, O., & Vazquez, B. (1993). Behavioral changes associated with epilepsy. *Neurologic Clinics, 11*, 127–149.

de Waal, F. B. M. (1995). Bonobo sex and society. *Scientific American, 272* (3), 1995.

Diamond, L. M. (1998). Development of sexual orientation among adolescent and young adult women. *Developmental Psychology, 34*, 1085–1095.

Diamond, M. (1999). The effects of pornography: An international perspective. In J. Elias, V. D. Elias, V. L. Bullough, G. Brewer, J. J. Douglas, & W. Jarvis (Eds.), *Pornography 101: Eroticism, pornography, and the First Amendment.* Prometheus Press.

Diamond, M., & Sigmundson, H. K. (1997). Sex reassignment at birth: Long-term review and clinical implications. *Archives of Pediatrics and Adolescent Medicine, 151*, 298–304.

Diamond, M., & Uchiyama, A. (1999). Pornography, rape, and sex crimes in Japan. *International Journal of Law and Psychiatry, 22*, 1–22.

Dillin, J. (2000). For voters, High Court is a priority. *Christian Science Monitor,* November 7. Retrieved from http://www.csmonitor.com/durable/2000/11/07/fp2s1-csm.shtml.

DiVasto, P. V., Kaufman, A., Rosner, L., Jackson, R., Christy, J., Pearson, S., & Burgett, T. (1984). The prevalence of sexually stressful events among females in the general population. *Archives of Sexual Behavior, 13*, 59–67.

Docter, R. F., & Prince, V. (1997). Transvestism: A survey of 1032 cross-dressers. *Archives of Sexual Behavior, 26*, 589–605.

Dodson, B. (1987). *Sex for one: The joy of self-loving.* Harmony Books

Domb, L. G., & Pagel, M. (2001). Sexual swellings advertise female quality in wild baboons. *Nature, 410*, 204–206.

Dorner, G., Geier, T., Ahrens, L., Krell, L., Munx, G., Sieler, H., Kittner, E., & Muller, H. (1980). Prenatal stress as possible aetiogenetic factor of homosexuality in human males. *Endokrinologie, 75*, 365–368.

Doty, R. L. (2001). Olfaction. *Annual Review of Psychology, 52*, 423–452.

Dougher, M. J. (1995). Behavioral techniques to alter sexual arousal. In B. K. Schwartz & H. R. Cellini (Eds.), *The sex offender: Corrections, treatment and legal practice.* Civic Research Institute.

Doulin, T. (2001). Man's journal ruled obscene. *Columbus Dispatch,* July 4.

Dover, K. J. (1978). *Greek homosexuality.* Harvard University Press.

Dowd, M. (2001). Liberties—The manolo moochers. *New York Times,* August 29.

Dreger, A. D. (Ed.). (1999). *Intersex in the age of ethics.* University Publishing Group.

Dryden, W. (1999). *Overcoming jealousy.* Sheldon Press.

Duberman, L. (1975). *The reconstituted family: A study of remarried couples and their children.* Nelson-Hall.

Duberman, M. (1991). *Cures: A gay man's odyssey.* Dutton.

Duberman, M. (1993). *Stonewall.* Dutton.

Dugger, C. W. (2001). Abortion in India is tipping scales sharply against girls. *New York Times,* April 22.

Dunn, M. E., & Trost, J. E. (1989). Male multiple orgasms: A descriptive study. *Archives of Sexual Behavior, 18*, 377–387.

Dutta, T. C., & Eid, J. F. (1999). Vacuum constriction devices for erectile dysfunction: A long-term, prospective study of patients with mild, moderate, and severe dysfunction. *Urology, 54*, 891–893.

Dutton, D. G., & Aron, A. P. (1974). Some evidence for heightened sexual attraction under conditions of high anxiety. *Journal of Personality and Social Psychology, 30*, 510–517.

Dworkin, A. (1979). *The lie.* Located at http://www.nostatusquo.com/ACLU/dworkin/WarZoneChaptIa.html.

Dworkin, A. (1981). *Pornography: Men possessing women.* ' Putnam.

Dworkin, A. (1994). *Prostitution and male supremacy.* Located at http://www.igc.org/Womensnet/dworkin/MichLawJournalI.html.

Dworkin, S. H. (2001). Treating the bisexual client. *Journal of Clinical Psychology, 57*, 671–680.

Dwyer, M. (1988). Exhibitionism/voyeurism. *Journal of Social Work and Human Sexuality, 7*, 101–112.

Eagly, A. H., & Steffen, V. J. (1986). Gender and aggressive behavior: A meta-analytic review of the social psychological literature. *Psychological Bulletin, 100*, 309–330.

Earls, C. M., & Lalumière, M. L. (2002). A case study of preferential bestiality (zoophilia). *Sexual Abuse, 14*, 83–88.

Eason, E., & Feldman, P. (2000). Much ado about a little cut: Is episiotomy worthwhile? *Obstetrics and Gynecology, 95*, 616–618.

Eaton, W. O., & Enns, R. (1986). Sex differences in human motor activity level. *Psychological Bulletin, 100*, 19–28.

Eckert, E. D., Bouchard, T. J., Bohlen, J., & Heston, L. L. (1986). Homosexuality in monozygotic twins reared apart. *British Journal of Psychiatry, 148*, 421–425.

ECPAT International. (2001). *Child prostitution.* Located at http://www.ecpat.net/eng/CSEC/faq/faq2.asp.

Edlin, B. R., Irwin, K. L., Faruque, S., McCoy, C. B., Word, C., Serrano, Y., Inciardi, J. A., Bowser, B. P., Schilling, R. F., & Holmberg, S. D. (1994). Intersecting epidemics—crack cocaine use and HIV infection among inner-city young adults. Multicenter Crack Cocaine and HIV Infection Study Team. *New England Journal of Medicine, 331*, 1422–1427.

Efron, S. (2001). Baby bust has Japan fearing for its future. *Los Angeles Times,* June 24.

Eisenberg, N., & Lennon, R. (1983). Sex differences in empathy and related capacities. *Psychological Bulletin, 94*, 100–131.

Eisenberg, N., Martin, C. L., & Fabes, R. A. (1996). Gender development and gender effects. In D. C. Berliner & R. C. Calfee (Eds.), *The Handbook of Educational Psychology.* Simon and Schuster.

Eisenberg, N., Wolchik, S. A., Hernandez, R., & Pasternak, J. (1985). Parental socialization of young children's play: A short-term longitudinal study. *Child Development, 56*, 1506–1513.

Elam, J. (1998). *A cross-cultural comparison of puberty rites and ceremonies for females.* Located at http://www.emory.edu/OXFORD/Publications/Review/puberty.html.

El-Bassel, N., Schilling, R. F., Gilbert, L., Faruque, S., Irwin, K. L., & Edlin, B. R. (2000). Sex trading and psychological distress in a street-based sample of low-income urban men. *Journal of Psychoactive Drugs, 32,* 259–267.

Elders, M. J. (1997). *The dreaded "M" word.* Located at http://www.nerve.com/Dispatches/Elders/mword/.

Eldh, J., Berg, A., & Gustafsson, M. (1997). Long-term follow up after sex reassignment surgery. *Scandinavian Journal of Plastic and Reconstructive Surgery and Hand Surgery, 31,* 39–45.

Elias, J. E., Bullough, V. L., Elias, V., & Brewer, G. (Eds.). (1999). *Prostitution: On whores, hustlers, and johns.* Prometheus Books.

Elias, J., Elias, V. D., Bullough, V. L., Brewer, G., Douglas, J. J., & Jarvis, W. (Eds.). (1999). *Porn 101: Eroticism, pornography, and the First Amendment.* Prometheus Books.

Eliason, M. J. (1997). The prevalence and nature of biphobia in heterosexual undergraduate students. *Archives of Sexual Behavior, 26,* 317–326.

Elkins, T. E., Gafford, L. S., Wilks, C. S., Muram, D., & Golden, G. (1986). A model clinic approach to the reproductive health concerns of the mentally handicapped. *Obstetrics and Gynecology, 68,* 185–188.

Elliott, C. (2000). A new way to be mad. *Atlantic Monthly,* December.

Ellis, B. J., & Symons, D. (1990). Sex differences in sexual fantasy: An evolutionary psychological approach. *Journal of Sex Research, 27,* 527–555.

Ellis, L. (1988). The victimful-victimless distinction, and seven universal demographic correlates of victimful criminal behavior. *Personality and Individual Differences, 9.*

Ellis, L., Hoffman, H., & Burke, D. M. (1990). Sex, sexual orientation and criminal and violent behavior. *Personality and Individual Differences, 11,* 1207–1211.

ElSohly, M. A., & Salamone, S. J. (1999). Prevalence of drugs used in cases of alleged sexual assault. *Journal of Analytical Toxicology, 23,* 141–146.

Emmen, J. M., McLuskey, A., Adham, I. M., Engel, W., Verhoef-Post, M., Themmen, A. P., Grootegoed, J. A., & Brinkmann, A. O. (2000). Involvement of insulin-like factor 3 (Insl3) in diethylstilbestrol-induced cryptorchidism. *Endocrinology, 141,* 846–849.

Emmert, C., & Kohler, U. (1998). Data about 154 children and adolescents reporting sexual assault. *Archives of Gynecology and Obstetrics, 261,* 61–70.

Epner, J. E., Jonas, H. S., & Seckinger, D. L. (1998). Late-term abortion. *JAMA, 280,* 724–729.

Erikson, E. H. (1968). *Identity: Youth and crisis.* Norton.

Erskine, M. S. (1989). Solicitation behavior in the estrous female rat: A review. *Hormones and Behavior, 23,* 473–502.

European Council. (1994). *Recent demographic tendencies in Europe, 1993.* European Council.

European Intervention Projects AIDS Prevention for Prostitutes. (2001). *General conclusions and recommendations.* Located at http://allserv.rug.ac.be/~rmak/europap/summary.html.

Evans, J., Heron, J., Francomb, H., Oke, S., & Golding, J. (2001). Cohort study of depressed mood during pregnancy and after childbirth. *British Medical Journal, 323,* 257–260.

Everaerd, W. (1983). A case of apotemnophilia: A handicap as sexual preference. *American Journal of Psychotherapy, 37,* 285–293.

Faderman, L. (1981). *Surpassing the love of men: Romantic friendship and love between women from the Renaissance to the present.* William Morrow.

Faderman, L. (1991). *Odd girls and twilight lovers: A history of lesbian life in twentieth-century America.* Columbia University Press.

Fagot, B. I. (1985). Changes in thinking about early sex role development. *Developmental Review, 5,* 83–98.

Fagot, B. I., Leinbach, M. D., & O'Boyle, C. (1992). Gender labeling, gender stereotyping, and parenting behaviors. *Developmental Psychology, 28,* 440–443.

Family Health International. (1999). *The female condom: What do we know?* Located at http://www.ama-assn.org/special/contra/support/educate/fpfaq22.htm.

Farley, L. (1978). *Sexual shakedown: The sexual harassment of women on the job.* McGraw-Hill.

Farley, M. (2001). Canada's high court allows some possession of child pornography. *Los Angeles Times,* January 27.

Fausto-Sterling, A. (1992). *Myths of Gender: Biological Theories about Women and Men.* Basic Books.

Fausto-Sterling, A. (2000). *Sexing the body: Gender politics and the construction of sexuality.* Basic Books.

Federal Bureau of Investigation. (2001). *Hate crime statistics, 2000.* Located at http://www.fbi.gov/ucr/cius_00/hate00.pdf.

Fehr, B. (1988). Prototype analysis of the concepts of love and commitment. *Journal of Personality and Social Psychology, 55,* 557–579.

Feingold, A. (1988). Matching for attractiveness in romantic partners and same-sex friends: A metanalysis and theoretical critique. *Journal of Personality and Social Psychology, 59,* 981–993.

Feingold, A. (1994). Gender differences in personality: A meta-analysis. *Psychological Bulletin, 116,* 429–456.

Felson, R. B., & Krohn, M. (1990). Motives for rape. *Journal of Research in Crime and Delinquency, 27,* 222–242.

Feminist Majority Foundation. (2001). *How the gender gap shaped Election 2000.* Located at http://www.feminist.org/research/ggap2000.pdf.

Feng, M. I., Huang, S., Kaptein, J., Kaswick, J., & Aboseif, S. (2000). Effect of sildenafil citrate on post-radical prostatectomy erectile dysfunction. *Journal of Urology, 164,* 1935–1938.

Fernald, R. D. (1993). Cichlids in love. *The Sciences, 33,* 27–31.

Fichtner, J., Filipas, D., Mottrie, A. M., Voges, G. E., & Hohenfellner, R. (1995). Analysis of meatal location in 500 men: Wide variation questions need for meatal advancement in all pediatric anterior hypospadias cases. *Journal of Urology, 154,* 833–834.

Fields, R. (2001). 7 states still classify cohabitation as illegal. *Los Angeles Times,* August 20.

Figueredo, A. J. (2000). A Brunswikian evolutionary-developmental theory of adolescent sex offending. *Behavioral Sciences and the Law, 18,* 309–329.

Finkelstein, J. W., Susman, E. J., Chinchilli, V. M., D'Arcangelo, M. R., Kunselman, S. J., Schwab, J., Demers, L. M., Liben, L. S., & Kulin, H. E. (1998). Effects of estrogen or testosterone on self-reported sexual responses and behaviors in hypogonadal adolescents. *Journal of Clinical Endocrinology and Metabolism, 83,* 2281–2285.

Finley, C., Gregg, E. W., Solomon, L. J., & Gay, E. (2001). Disparities in hormone replacement therapy use by socioeconomic status in a primary care population. *Journal of Community Health, 26,* 39–50.

Finney, A., Fukuda, A., Breuel, K. F., & Thatcher, S. S. (1992). Coagulation and liquefaction of seminal plasma. *Assisted Reproduction Reviews, 2,* 164–169.

Firestone, P., Bradford, J. M., McCoy, M., Greenberg, D. M., Curry, S., & Larose, M. R. (2000). Prediction of recidivism in extrafamilial child molesters based on court-related assessments. *Sexual Abuse, 12,* 203–221.

Fischman, S. H., Rankin, E. A., Soeken, K. L., & Lenz, E. R. (1986). Changes in sexual relationships in postpartum couples. *Journal of Obstetric, Gynecologic, and Neonatal Nursing, 15,* 58–63.

Fisher, B. S., Cullen, F. T., & Turner, M. G. (2000). *The sexual victimization of college women.* Located at http://www.ncjrs.org/pdffiles1/nij/182369.pdf.

Fisher, H. E. (1989). Evolution of human sexual pair-bonding. *American Journal of Physical Anthropology, 78,* 331–354.

Flaxman, S. M., & Sherman, P. W. (2000). Morning sickness: A mechanism for protecting mother and embryo. *Quarterly Review of Biology, 75,* 113–148.

Fletcher, J. C. (1983). Is sex selection ethical? In K. Berg & K. E. Tranoy (Eds.), *Research ethics.* Alan R. Liss.

Floyd, R. L., Rimer, B. K., Giovino, G. A., Mullen, P. D., & Sullivan, S. E. (1993). A review of smoking in pregnancy: Effects on pregnancy outcomes and cessation efforts. *Annual Review of Public Health, 14,* 379–411.

Foa, E. B., Rothbaum, B. O., Riggs, D. S., & Murdock, T. B. (1991). Treatment of posttraumatic stress disorder in rape victims: A comparison between cognitive-behavioral procedures and counseling. *Journal of Consulting and Clinical Psychology, 59,* 715–723.

Foa, E. B., & Street, G. P. (2001). Women and traumatic events. *Journal of Clinical Psychiatry, 62,* 29–34.

Ford, C. S., & Beach, F. A. (1951). *Patterns of sexual behavior.* Harper.

Forger, N. G., & Breedlove, S. M. (1986). Sexual dimorphism in human and canine spinal cord: Role of early androgen. *Proceedings of the National Academy of Sciences of the United States of America, 83,* 7527–7531.

Foshee, V. A., Bauman, K. E., Arriaga, X. B., Helms, R. W., Koch, G. G., & Linder, G. F. (1998). An evaluation of Safe Dates, an adolescent dating violence prevention program. *American Journal of Public Health, 88,* 45–50.

Foshee, V. A., Bauman, K. E., Greene, W. F., Koch, G. G., Linder, G. F., & MacDougall, J. E. (2000). The Safe Dates program: 1-year follow-up results. *American Journal of Public Health, 90,* 1619–1622.

Foshee, V. A., Linder, G. F., Bauman, K. E., Langwick, S. A., Arriaga, X. B., Heath, J. L., McMahon, P. M., & Bangdiwala, S. (1996). The Safe Dates Project: Theoretical basis, evaluation design, and selected baseline findings. *American Journal of Preventive Medicine, 12,* 39–47.

Foucault, M. (1978). *The history of sexuality: Vol. 1.* Pantheon.

Fox, A. (1991). Development of a bisexual identity. In L. Hutchins & L. Kaahumanu (Eds.), *Bi any other name: Bisexual people speak out.* Alyson.

Frank, E., Anderson, C., & Rubinstein, D. (1978). Frequency of sexual dysfunction in normal couples. *New England Journal of Medicine, 299,* 111–115.

Franke, W. W., & Berendonk, B. (1997). Hormonal doping and androgenization of athletes: A secret program of the German Democratic Republic government. *Clinical Chemistry, 43,* 1262–1279.

Frayser, S. G. (1994). Defining normal childhood sexuality: An anthropological approach. *Annual Review of Sex Research, 4,* 173–217.

Freed, C., & LeVay, S. (2002). *Healing the brain: A doctor's controversial quest for a cure for Parkinson's disease.* Times Books.

Freeman, D. (1983). *Margaret Mead and Samoa: The Making and unmaking of an anthropological myth.* Harvard University Press.

Freeman, E. W., Rickels, K., Arredondo, F., Kao, L. C., Pollack, S. E., & Sondheimer, S. J. (1999). Full- or half-cycle treatment of severe premenstrual syndrome with a serotonergic antidepressant. *Journal of Clinical Psychopharmacology, 19,* 3–8.

Freud, S. (1900). The interpretation of dreams. In J. Strachey (Ed.), *Standard edition of the complete works of Sigmund Freud.* Hogarth.

Freud, S. (1955a). Group psychology and the analysis of the ego. In J. Strachey (Ed.), *The standard edition of the complete works of Sigmund Freud.* Hogarth.

Freud, S. (1955b). The psychogenesis of a case of homosexuality in a woman. In J. Strachey (Ed.), *The standard edition of the complete works of Sigmund Freud.* Hogarth.

Freud, S. (1975). *Three essays on the theory of sexuality.* Basic Books.

Freund, K. (1974). Male homosexuality: An analysis of the pattern. In J. A. Lorraine (Ed.), *Understanding homosexuality: Its biological and psychological bases.* Elsevier.

Freund, K. (1981). Assessment of pedophilia. In M. Cook & K. Howells (Eds.), *Adult sexual interest in children.* Academic Press.

Freund, K. (1985). Cross-gender identity in a broader context. In B. Steiner (Ed.), *Gender dysphoria: Development, research, management.* Plenum.

Freund, K., & Blanchard, R. (1986). The concept of courtship disorder. *Journal of Sex and Marital Therapy, 12,* 79–92.

Freund, K., Watson, R., Dickey, R., & Rienzo, D. (1991). Erotic gender differentiation in pedophilia. *Archives of Sexual Behavior, 20,* 555–566.

Freund, K., Watson, R., & Rienzo, D. (1987). A comparison of sex offenders against female and male minors. *Journal of Sex and Marital Therapy, 13,* 260–264.

Freund, K., Watson, R., & Rienzo, D. (1989). Heterosexuality, homosexuality, and erotic age preference. *Journal of Sex Research, 26,* 107–117.

Friedberg, W., Copeland, K., Duke, F. E., O'Brien, K., III, & Darden, E. B., Jr. (2000). Radiation exposure during air travel: Guidance provided by the Federal Aviation Administration for air carrier crews. *Health Physics, 79,* 591–595.

Friedrich, W. N., & Gerber, P. N. (1994). Autoerotic asphyxia: The development of a paraphilia. *Journal of the American Academy of Child and Adolescent Psychiatry, 33,* 970–974.

Friedrich, W. N., Grambsch, P., Broughton, D., Kuiper, J., & Beilke, R. L. (1991). Normative sexual behavior in children. *Pediatrics, 88,* 456–464.

Frintner, M. P., & Rubinson, L. (1993). Acquaintance rape: The influence of alcohol, fraternity membership, and sports team membership. *Journal of Sex Education and Therapy, 19,* 272–284.

Fromm, E. (1956). *The art of loving.* Harper and Row.

Fugger, E. F. (1999). Clinical experience with flow cytometric separation of human X- and Y-chromosome bearing sperm. *Theriogenology, 52,* 1435–1440.

Fugger, E. F., Black, S. H., Keyvanfar, K., & Schulman, J. D. (1998). Births of normal daughters after MicroSort sperm separation and intrauterine insemination, in-vitro fertilization, or intracytoplasmic sperm injection. *Human Reproduction, 13,* 2367–2370.

Gaffney, G. R., Lurie, S. F., & Berlin, F. S. (1984). Is there familial transmission of pedophilia? *Journal of Nervous and Mental Disease, 172,* 546–548.

Gagneux, P., Woodruff, D. S., & Boesch, C. (1997). Furtive mating in female chimpanzees. *Nature, 387,* 358–359.

Gagnon, J. H., & Simon, W. (1987). The sexual scripting of oral genital contacts. *Archives of Sexual Behavior, 16,* 1–25.

Gailey, C. W. (1987). Evolutionary perspectives on gender hierarchy. In B. B. Hess & M. M. Ferree (Eds.), *Analyzing Gender.* Sage.

Galea, L. A. M., & Kimura, D. (1993). Sex differences in route learning. *Personality and Individual Differences, 14,* 53–65.

Gallup Organization. (1997). *Family values differ sharply around the world.* Located at http://www.gallup.com/poll/releases/pr971107.asp.

Gallup Organization. (1999). *Americans divided over abortion debate.* Located at http://www.gallup.com/poll/releases/pr990518.asp.

Gallup Organization. (2000a). *American teens say they get along well with their parents.* Located at http://www.gallup.com/poll/releases/pr000811b.asp.

Gallup Organization. (2000b). *Public opinion about abortion: An in-depth review.* Located at http://www.gallup.com/poll/specialReports/pollSummaries/sr020122viii.asp.

Gallup Organization. (2000c). *Americans are overwhelmingly happy and optimistic about the future of the United States.* Located at http://www.gallup.com/poll/releases/pr001013.asp.

Gallup Organization. (2001). *Over half of Americans believe in love at first sight.* Located at http://www.gallup.com/poll/releases/pr010214d.asp.

Gangestad, S. W., & Thornhill, R. (1997). The evolutionary psychology of extrapair sex: The role of fluctuating asymmetry. *Evolution and Human Behavior, 18,* 69–88.

Gangestad, S. W., & Thornhill, R. (1998). Menstrual cycle variation in women's preferences for the scent of symmetrical men. *Proceedings of the Royal Society of London. Series B: Biological Sciences, 265,* 927–933.

Garber, M. (1995). *Vice versa: Bisexuality and the eroticism of everyday life.* Simon and Schuster.

Gardiner, S. (2001). The grey area of prostitution: Can it be an opportunity or is it always exploitive? *New York Newsday,* March 15. Retrieved from http://www.newsday.com/news/local/newyork/ny-smuggled-grayarea.story.

Garland, R. J., & Dougher, M. J. (1990). The abused/abuser hypothesis of child sexual abuse: A critical review of theory and research. In J. R. Feierman (Ed.), *Pedophilia: Biosocial dimensions,* Springer.

Garvey, M. (2002). U.S. says mammograms help, and that's final. *Los Angeles Times,* February 22.

Gates, G. J., & Sonenstein, F. L. (2000). Heterosexual genital sexual activity among adolescent males: 1988 and 1995. *Family Planning Perspectives, 32,* 295–297, 304.

Gay-Civil-Unions.com. (2002). *International status of same-sex unions.* Located at http://www.gay-civil-unions.com/HTML/International.htm.

Geddes, R., & Lueck, D. *The gains from self-ownership and the expansion of women's rights.* Located at http://lawschool.stanford.edu/olin/workingpapers/WP181GEDDES.pdf.

Gelfand, M. M. (2000). Sexuality among older women. *Journal of Women's Health and Gender Based Medicine, 9,* S15–20.

Gellene, D. (2001). RU-486 abortion pill hasn't caught on in U.S. *Los Angeles Times,* May 31.

Gelles, R. J. (1976). Abused wives: Why do they stay? *Journal of Marriage and the Family, 38,* 659–668.

Gentile, D. A. (1993). Just what are sex and gender, anyway? A call for a new terminological standard. *Psychological Science, 4,* 120–122.

Georgiopoulos, A. M., Bryan, T. L., Wollan, P., & Yawn, B. P. (2001). Routine screening for postpartum depression. *Journal of Family Practice, 50,* 117–122.

Gerber, G. S. (2000). Saw palmetto for the treatment of men with lower urinary tract symptoms. *Journal of Urology, 163,* 1408–1412.

Gerstenberg, T. C., Levin, R. J., & Wagner, G. (1990). Erection and ejaculation in man. Assessment of the electromyographic activity of the bulbocavernosus and ischiocavernosus muscles. *British Journal of Urology, 65,* 395–402.

Gibson, L. E., & Leitenberg, H. (2000). Child sexual abuse prevention programs: Do they decrease the occurrence of child sexual abuse? *Child Abuse and Neglect, 24,* 1115–1125.

Giecek, R. (2000). *The Dumas brothel.* Located at http://www.thedumasbrothel.com/.

Gigolos Begleitagentur. (2001). *Gigolos: What women want.* Located at http://www.gigolos.ch/flash.html.

Gilbert, N. (1997). Advocacy research and social policy. In M. Tonry (Ed.), *Crime and justice: A review of research.* University of Chicago Press.

Gilligan, C. (1982). *In a different voice: Psychological theory and women's development.* Harvard University Press.

Giorgi, D., Friedman, C., Trask, B. J., & Rouquier, S. (2000). Characterization of nonfunctional V1R-like pheromone receptor sequences in human. *Genome Research, 10,* 1979–1985.

Gladen, B. C., Ragan, N. B., & Rogan, W. J. (2000). Pubertal growth and development and prenatal and lactational exposure to polychlorinated biphenyls and dichlorodiphenyl dichloroethene. *Journal of Pediatrics, 136,* 490–496.

Gladue, B. A., & Bailey, J. M. (1995a). Aggressiveness, competitiveness, and human sexual orientation. *Psychoneuroendocrinology, 20,* 475–485.

Gladue, B. A., & Bailey, J. M. (1995b). Spatial ability, handedness, and human sexual orientation. *Psychoneuroendocrinology, 20,* 487–497.

Glionna, J. M. (2001). HIV rate rising among gay men in S.F. *Los Angeles Times,* January 25.

Godfray, H. C. J., & Werren, J. H. (1996). Recent developments in sex ratio studies. *Trends in Ecology and Evolution, 11,* 59–63.

Goldberg, C. (2001). System stands accused in a Montana man's case. *New York Times,* January 23.

Goldberg, C., & Elder, J. (1998). Public still backs abortion, but wants limits, poll says. *New York Times,* January 16.

Goldberg, J., Holtz, D., Hyslop, T., & Tolosa, J. E. (2002). Has the use of routine episiotomy decreased? Examination of episiotomy rates from 1983 to 2000. *Obstetrics and Gynecology, 99,* 395–400.

Goldberg, S. (1991). Feminism against science. *National Review, 43,* 30.

Goldberg, S. B. (1995). *Civil rights, "special rights," and our rights.* Located at http://www.publiceye.org/eyes/our_rit.html.

Goldie, S. J., Kuntz, K. M., Weinstein, M. C., Freedberg, K. A., & Palefsky, J. M. (2000). Cost-effectiveness of screening for anal squamous intraepithelial lesions and anal cancer in human immunodeficiency virus-negative homosexual and bisexual men. *American Journal of Medicine, 108,* 634–641.

Goldman, R., & Goldman, J. (1982). *Children's sexual thinking: A comparative study of children aged 5 to 15 years in Australia, North America, Britain and Sweden.* Routledge and Kegan Paul.

Goldstein, I. (2000). The mutually reinforcing triad of depressive symptoms, cardiovascular disease, and erectile dysfunction. *American Journal of Cardiology, 86,* 41F–45F.

Goldstein, I., & Berman, J. R. (1998). Vasculogenic female sexual dysfunction: Vaginal engorgement and clitoral erectile insufficiency syndromes. *International Journal of Impotence Research, 10* (Suppl. 2), S84–90; discussion S98–101.

Goldstein, I., Carson, C., Rosen, R., & Islam, A. (2001). Vasomax for the treatment of male erectile dysfunction. *World Journal of Urology, 19,* 51–56.

Goode, E. (1999). Study on child sex abuse provokes a political furor. *New York Times,* June 13.

Goodstein, L., & Dillon, S. (2002). Bishops set policy to remove priests in sex abuse cases. *New York Times,* June 15.

Gooren, L. (1986). The neuroendocrine response of luteinizing hormone to estrogen administration in the human is not sex specific but dependent on the hormonal environment. *Journal of Clinical Endocrinology and Metabolism, 63,* 589–593.

Gorey, K. M., & Leslie, D. R. (1997). The prevalence of child sexual abuse: Integrative review adjustment for potential response and measurement biases. *Child Abuse and Neglect, 21,* 391–398.

Gorman, D. G., & Cummings, J. L. (1992). Hypersexuality following septal injury. *Archives of Neurology, 49,* 308–310.

Gorski, R. A., Gordon, J. H., Shryne, J. E., & Southam, A. M. (1978). Evidence for a morphological sex difference within the medial preoptic area of the rat brain. *Brain Research, 148,* 333–346.

Gotsch, G., & Torgus, J. (1997). *The womanly art of breastfeeding* (6th ed.). La Leche League International.

Gottman, J. M. (1994). *Why marriages succeed or fail: What you can learn from the breakthrough research to make your marriage last.* Simon and Schuster.

Gottman, J. M., Coan, J., Carrere, S., & Swanson, C. (1998). Predicting marital happiness and stability from newlywed interactions. *Journal of Marriage and the Family, 60,* 5–22.

Gottman, J. M., & Krokoff, L. J. (1989). Marital interaction and satisfaction: A longitudinal view. *Journal of Consulting and Clinical Psychology, 57,* 47–52.

Gottman, J. M., & Levenson, R. W. (1999). What predicts change in marital interaction over time? A study of alternative models. *Family Process, 38,* 143–158.

Gottman, J. M., & Levenson, R. W. (2000). The timing of divorce: Predicting when a couple will divorce over a 14-year period. *Journal of Marriage and the Family, 62,* 737–745.

Gottman, J. M., & Notarius, C. I. (2000). Decade review: Observing marital interaction. *Journal of Marriage and the Family, 62,* 927–947.\

Gotz, M. J., Johnstone, E. C., & Ratcliffe, S. G. (1999). Criminality and antisocial behaviour in unselected men with sex chromosome abnormalities. *Psychological Medicine, 29,* 953–962.

Goy, R. W., Bercovitch, F. B., & McBrair, M. C. (1988). Behavioral masculinization is independent of genital masculinization in prenatally androgenized female rhesus macaques. *Hormones and Behavior, 22,* 552–571.

Grafenberg, E. (1950). The role of the urethra in female orgasm. *International Journal of Sexology, 3,* 145–148.

Graham, W. (2002). Priest scandals a deep betrayal for many Irish. *Los Angeles Times,* April 14.

Grahn, J. (1994). *Blood, bread, and roses: How menstruation created the world.* Beacon Press.

Grammer, K., & Thornhill, R. (1994). Human (*Homo sapiens*) facial attractiveness and sexual selection: The role of symmetry and averageness. *Journal of Comparative Psychology, 108,* 233–242.

Green, A. H., & Kaplan, M. S. (1994). Psychiatric impairment and childhood victimization experiences in female child molesters. *Journal of the American Academy of Child and Adolescent Psychiatry, 33,* 954–961.

Green, J. A., Kirwan, J. M., Tierney, J. F., Symonds, P., Fresco, L., Collingwood, M., & Williams, C. J. (2001). Survival and recurrence after concomitant chemotherapy and radiotherapy for cancer of the uterine cervix: A systematic review and meta-analysis. *Lancet, 358,* 781–786.

Green, R. (1987). *The "sissy-boy syndrome" and the development of homosexuality.* Yale University Press.

Green, R. (1992). *Sexual science and the law.* Harvard University Press.

Green, R. (2000). Family cooccurrence of "gender dysphoria": Ten sibling or parent-child pairs. *Archives of Sexual Behavior, 29,* 499–507.

Greenfeld, L. A. (1997). *Sex offenses and offenders: An analysis of data on rape and sexual assault.* Located at http://www.vaw.umn.edu/FinalDocuments/sexoff.asp.

Greenstein, A., Plymate, S. R., & Katz, P. G. (1995). Visually stimulated erection in castrated men. *Journal of Urology, 153,* 650–652.

Greenwald, E., & Leitenberg, H. (1989). Long-term effects of sexual experiences with siblings and nonsiblings during childhood. *Archives of Sexual Behavior, 18,* 389–399.

Greer, G. (1971). *The female eunuch.* McGraw-Hill.

Gregersen, E. (1983). *Sexual practices: The story of human sexuality.* Franklin Watts.

Grimm, R. H., Jr., Grandits, G. A., Prineas, R. J., McDonald, R. H., Lewis, C. E., Flack, J. M., Yunis, C., Svendsen, K., Liebson, P. R., & Elmer, P. J. (1997). Long-term effects on sexual function of five antihypertensive drugs and nutritional hygienic treatment in hypertensive men and women. Treatment of Mild Hypertension Study (TOMHS). *Hypertension, 29,* 8–14.

Grossl, N. A. (2000). Supernumerary breast tissue: Historical perspectives and clinical features. *Southern Medical Journal, 93,* 29–32.

Groth, A. N. (1979). *Men who rape: The psychology of the offender.* Plenum.

Groth, A. N., & Burgess, A. W. (1977). Sexual dysfunction during rape. *New England Journal of Medicine, 297,* 764–766.

Groth, A. N., & Burgess, A. W. (1980). Male rape: Offenders and victims. *American Journal of Psychiatry, 137,* 806–810.

Groth, A. N., Burgess, A. W., & Holmstrom, L. L. (1977). Rape: Power, anger, and sexuality. *American Journal of Psychiatry, 134,* 1239–1243.

Grove, L. (1994). Barry Goldwater's left turn. *Washington Post,* July 28. (http://www.washingtonpost.com/wp-srv/politics/daily/may98/goldwater072894.htm).

Guay, A. T. (2001). Decreased testosterone in regularly menstruating women with decreased libido: A clinical observation. *Journal of Sex and Marital Therapy, 27,* 513–519.

Guerrero Pavich, E. (1986). A Chicano perspective on Mexican culture and sexuality. In L. Lister (Ed.), *Human sexuality, ethno-culture, and social work.* Haworth Press.

Guzick, D. S., Overstreet, J. W., Factor-Litvak, P., Brazil, C. K., Nakajima, S. T., Coutifaris, C., Carson, S. A., Cisneros, P., Steinkampf, M. P., Hill, J. A., Xu, D., & Vogel, D. L. (2001). Sperm morphology, motility, and concentration in fertile and infertile men. *New England Journal of Medicine, 345,* 1388–1393.

Hadziselimovic, F., Geneto, R., & Emmons, L. R. (2000). Elevated placental estradiol: A possible etiological factor of human cryptorchidism. *Journal of Urology, 164,* 1694–1695.

Haefner, H. K., & Elkins, T. E. (1991). Contraceptive management for female adolescents with mental retardation and handicapping disabilities. *Current Opinion in Obstetrics and Gynecology, 3,* 820–824.

Hage, J. J. (1996). Metaidoioplasty: An alternative phalloplasty technique in transsexuals. *Plastic and Reconstructive Surgery, 97,* 161–167.

Haig, D. (2000). Of sex and gender. *Nature Genetics, 25,* 373.

Haignere, C. S., Gold, R., & McDanel, H. J. (1999). Adolescent abstinence and condom use: Are we sure we are really teaching what is safe? *Health Education and Behavior, 26,* 43–54.

Halata, Z., & Munger, B. L. (1986). The neuroanatomical basis for the protopathic sensibility of the human glans penis. *Brain Research, 371,* 205–230.

Hall, G. C., Shondrick, D. D., & Hirschman, R. (1993). The role of sexual arousal in sexually aggressive behavior: A meta-analysis. *Journal of Consulting and Clinical Psychology, 61,* 1091–1095.

Hall, J. A., & Kimura, D. (1994). Dermatoglyphic asymmetry and sexual orientation in men. *Behavioral Neuroscience, 108,* 1203–1206.

Hall, J. A. Y., & Kimura, D. (1995). Sexual orientation and performance on sexually dimorphic motor tasks. *Archives of Sexual Behavior, 24,* 395–407.

Halpern, C. T., Joyner, K., Udry, J. R., & Suchindran, C. (2000). Smart teens don't have sex (or kiss much either). *Journal of Adolescent Health, 26,* 213–225.

Halpern, C. T., Udry, J. R., Campbell, B., Suchindran, C., & Mason, G. A. (1994). Testosterone and religiosity as predictors of sexual attitudes and activity among adolescent males: A biosocial model. *Journal of Biosocial Science, 26,* 217–234.

Halpern, C. T., Udry, J. R., & Suchindran, C. (1997). Testosterone predicts initiation of coitus in adolescent females. *Psychosomatic Medicine, 59,* 161–171.

Halpern, C. T., Udry, J. R., & Suchindran, C. (1998). Monthly measures of salivary testosterone predict sexual activity in adolescent males. *Archives of Sexual Behavior, 27,* 445–465.

Halpern, D. F. (1992). *Sex differences in cognitive abilities.* Lawrence Erlbaum Associates.

Hamer, D., & Copeland, P. (1994). *The science of desire: The search for the gay gene and the biology of behavior.* Simon and Schuster.

Hamer, D. H., Hu, S., Magnuson, V. L., Hu, N., & Pattatucci, A. M. (1993). A linkage between DNA markers on the X chromosome and male sexual orientation. *Science, 261,* 321–327.

Hamilton, W. D. (1964). The genetical evolution of social behavior. *Journal of Theoretical Biology, 7,* 1–52.

Hamilton, W. D., Henderson, P. A., & Moran, N. A. (1981). Fluctuation of environment and coevolved antagonistic polymorphisms as factors in the maintenance of sex. In R. D. Alexander & D. W. Tinkle (Eds.), *Natural selection and social behavior.* Chiron Press.

Han, K. K., Soares, J. M., Jr., Haidar, M. A., de Lima, G. R., & Baracat, E. C. (2002). Benefits of soy isoflavone therapeutic regimen on menopausal symptoms. *Obstetrics and Gynecology, 99,* 389–394.

Hand, D. (1998). *Inquest into the death of Michael Kelland Hutchence.* Located at http://www.thei.aust.com/music98/hutchcor.html.

Hanrahan, S. N. (1994). Historical review of menstrual toxic shock syndrome. *Women and Health, 21,* 141–165.

Hansen, G. L. (1985). Perceived threats and marital jealousy. *Social Psychology Quarterly, 48,* 262–268.

Hanson, R. K., & Bussière, M. T. (1998). Predicting relapse: A meta-analysis of sexual offender recidivism studies. *Journal of Consulting and Clinical Psychology, 66,* 348–362.

Hanson, R. K., Gordon, A., Harris, A. J., Marques, J. K., Murphy, W., Quinsey, V. L., & Seto, M. C. (2002). First report of the collaborative outcome data project on the effectiveness of psychological treatment for sex offenders. *Sexual Abuse, 14,* 169–194; discussion 195–167.

Harcourt, A. H., Purvis, A., & Liles, L. (1995). Sperm competition: Mating system, not breeding season, affects testis size of primates. *Functional Ecology, 9,* 468–476.

Harding, C. F. (1985). Sociobiological hypotheses about rape: A critical look at the data behind the hypotheses. In S. Sunday & E. Tobach (Eds.), *Violence against women: A critique of the sociobiology of rape.* Gordian Press.

Hare, E. H. (1962). Masturbatory insanity: The history of an idea. *Journal of Mental Science, 108,* 1–25.

Hariton, E. B. (1973). The sexual fantasies of women. *Psychology Today,* March.

Harry Benjamin International Gender Dysphoria Association. (1998). The standards of care for gender identity disorders. *International Journal of Transgenderism,* April–June. Retrieved from http://www.symposion.com/ijt/ijtc0405.htm.

Hartman, W., & Fithian, M. (1984). *Any man can: The multiple orgasmic technique for every loving man.* St. Martin's Press.

Harvey, S. M. (1987). Female sexual behavior: Fluctuations during the menstrual cycle. *Journal of Psychosomatic Research, 31,* 101–110.

Harwood, K. V., & O'Connor, A. P. (1994). Sexuality and breast cancer: Overview of issues. *Innovations in Oncology Nursing, 10.*

Hasan, Z. (1996). *Polygamy, slavery and Qur'anic sexual ethics.* Located at http://www.shobak.org/islam/polygamy.html.

Hass, A. (1979). *Teenage sexuality.* Macmillan.

Hatcher, R. A., et al. (1998). *Contraceptive technology.* Ardent Media.

Hatfield, E. (1994). Passionate love and sexual desire: A cross-cultural perspective. Annual Meeting, Society for the Scientific Study of Sexuality.

Hatfield, E., & Sprecher, S. (1986). Measuring passionate love in intimate relationships. *Journal of Adolescence, 9,* 383–410.

Hatfield, E., Traupmann, J., & Walster, G. W. (1979). Equity and extramarital sex. In M. Cook & G. Wilson (Eds.), *Love and attraction.* Pergamon.

Hatfield, E., & Walster, G. W. (1978). *A new look at love.* Addison-Wesley.

Hatfield, E., Walster, G. W., & Berscheid, E. (1978). *Equity theory and research.* Allyn and Bacon.

Hawton, K., Catalan, J., & Fagg, J. (1992). Sex therapy for erectile dysfunction: Characteristics of couples, treatment outcome, and prognostic factors. *Archives of Sexual Behavior, 21,* 161–175.

Hawton, K., Catalan, J., Martin, P., & Fagg, J. (1986). Long-term outcome of sex therapy. *Behaviour Research and Therapy, 24,* 665–675.

Healy, D. L. (1998). Ovarian cancer, infertility and infertility therapy. In R. D. Kempers, J. Cohen, A. F. Haney, & J. B. Younger (Eds.), *Fertility and reproductive medicine.* Elsevier.

Healy, M. (2001). Breast-feeding beyond babyhood. *Los Angeles Times,* February 5.

Healy, M., & Reza, H. (1992). Pentagon blasts Navy's Tailhook Investigation. *Los Angeles Times,* September 25. Retrieved from http://www-tech.mit.edu/V112/N44/tailhook.44w.html.

Heaton, J. P., & Morales, A. (2001). Andropause: A multisystem disease. *Canadian Journal of Urology, 8,* 1213–1222.

Hedges, L. V., & Nowell, A. (1995). Sex differences in mental test scores, variability, and numbers of high-scoring individuals. *Science, 269,* 41–45.

Hedlund, P., Ny, L., Alm, P., & Andersson, K. E. (2000). Cholinergic nerves in human corpus cavernosum and spongiosum contain nitric oxide synthase and heme oxygenase. *Journal of Urology, 164,* 868–875.

Hedricks, C., Piccinino, L. J., Udry, J. R., & Chimbira, T. H. (1987). Peak coital rate coincides with onset of luteinizing hormone surge. *Fertility and Sterility, 48,* 234–238.

Heiman, J. R., & LoPiccolo, J. (1988). *Becoming orgasmic: A sexual and personal growth program for women* (Rev. ed.). Simon and Schuster.

Heiman, J. R., & Meston, C. M. (1997). Empirically validated treatment for sexual dysfunction. *Annual Review of Sex Research, 8,* 148–194.

Hekma, G. (1994). "A female soul in a male body": Sexual inversion in nineteenth-century sexology. In G. Herdt (Ed.), *Third sex, third gender: Beyond sexual dimorphism in culture and history.* Zone Books.

Hendrick, S. (1981). Self-disclosure and marital satisfaction. *Journal of Personality and Social Psychology, 40,* 1150–1159.

Hendrick, S., & Hendrick, C. (1992). *Liking, loving, and relating.* Brooks/Cole.

Hendrick, S. S., Hendrick, C., & Adler, N. L. (1988). Romantic relationships: Love, satisfaction, and staying together. *Journal of Personality and Social Psychology, 54,* 980–988.

Henkin, W. A., & Holiday, S. (1996). *Consensual sadomasochism: How to talk about it and how to do it safely.* Daedalus.

Herbst, A. L. (1999). Diethylstilbestrol and adenocarcinoma of the vagina. *American Journal of Obstetrics and Gynecology, 181,* 1576–1578.

Herdt, G. H. (1981). *Guardians of the flutes: Idioms of masculinity.* McGraw-Hill.

Herek, G. M. (Ed.). (1998). *Stigma and sexual orientation: Understanding prejudice against lesbians, gay men, and bisexuals.* Sage Publications.

Herman-Giddens, M. E., Slora, E. J., Wasserman, R. C., Bourdony, C. J., Bhapkar, M. V., Koch, G. G., & Hasemeier, C. M. (1997). Secondary sexual characteristics and menses in young girls seen in office practice: A study from the Pediatric Research in Office Settings network. *Pediatrics, 99,* 505–512.

Herpetic Eye Disease Study Group. (2000). Psychological stress and other potential triggers for recurrences of herpes simplex virus eye infections. *Archives of Ophthalmology, 118,* 1617–1625.

HERS Foundation. (1999). *Hysterectomy educational resources and services.* Located at http://www.ccon.com/hers/index.htm.

Herzog, L. W. (1989). Urinary tract infections and circumcision: A case-control study. *American Journal of Diseases of Children, 143,* 348–350.

Heskell, P. (2001). *Flirt coach.* Thorson Publications.

Hess, R. A., Bunick, D., Lee, K. H., Bahr, J., Taylor, J. A., Korach, K. S., & Lubahn, D. B. (1997). A role for oestrogens in the male reproductive system. *Nature, 390,* 509–512.

Hetherington, E. M., & Kelly, J. (2002). *For better or for worse: Divorce reconsidered.* W.W. Norton.

Hewitson, L., Dominko, T., Takahashi, D., Martinovich, C., Ramalho-Santos, J., Sutovsky, P., Fanton, J., Jacob, D., Monteith, D., Neuringer, M., Battaglia, D., Simerly, C., & Schatten, G. (1999). Unique checkpoints during the first cell cycle of fertilization after intracytoplasmic sperm injection in rhesus monkeys. *Nature Medicine, 5,* 431–433.

Hicks, G. L. (1995). *The comfort women: Japan's brutal regime of enforced prostitution in the Second World War.* W.W. Norton.

Hicks, P. K. (1993). Castration of sexual offenders: Legal and ethical issues. *Journal of Legal Medicine, 14,* 641–667.

Hiestand, M. (1997). Titleist pulls ads from "SI." *USA Today,* April 29.

Highleyman, L. A. (2000). *A brief history of the bisexual movement.* Located at http://www.biresource.org/history.html.

Hill, C., Rubin, Z., & Peplau, L. A. (1976). Break-ups before marriage: The end of 103 affairs. *Journal of Social Issues, 32,* 147–168.

Hines, T. M. (2001). The G-spot: A modern gynecological myth. *American Journal of Obstetrics and Gynecology, 185,* 359–362.

Hite, S. (1977). *The Hite report: A nationwide study of female sexuality.* Dell.

Hobfoll, S. E., Ritter, C., Lavin, J., Hulsizer, M. R., & Cameron, R. P. (1995). Depression prevalence and incidence among inner-city pregnant and postpartum women. *Journal of Consulting and Clinical Psychology, 63,* 445–453.

Holden, C. (1999). Psychologists seek to quell sex furor. *Science, 285,* 521.

Holden, C. (2001a). "Behavioral" addictions: Do they exist? *Science, 294,* 980–982.

Holden, C. (2001b). Psychologists cry foul. *Science, 292,* 1643.

Holden, C. (2001c). Psychology furor resolved. *Science, 292,* 1999.

Holley, D. (2002). Polish archbishop resigns as rumors swirl. *Los Angeles Times,* March 29.

Holzman, C., Leventhal, J. M., Qiu, H., Jones, N. M., & Wang, J. (2001). Factors linked to bacterial vaginosis in nonpregnant women. *American Journal of Public Health, 91,* 1664–1670.

Honan, W. H. (1994). Professor ousted for lecture gets job back. *New York Times,* September 17.

Horowitz, S. M., Weis, D. L., & Laflin, M. T. (2001). Differences between sexual orientation behavior groups and social background, quality of life, and health behaviors. *Journal of Sex Research, 38,* 205–218.

Horvath, T. (1981). Physical attractiveness: The influence of selected torso parameters. *Archives of Sexual Behavior, 10,* 21–24.

Houtsmuller, E. J., Brand, T., de Jonge, F. H., Joosten, R. N., van de Poll, N. E., & Slob, A. K. (1994). SDN-POA volume, sexual behavior, and partner preference of male rats affected by perinatal treatment with ATD. *Physiology and Behavior, 56,* 535–541.

Hrdy, S. B. (1977). *The langurs of Abu: Female and male strategies of reproduction.* Harvard University Press.

Hsu, B., Kling, A., Kessler, C., Knapke, K., Diefenbach, P., & Elias, J. E. (1994). Gender differences in sexual fantasy and behavior in a college population: A ten-year replication. *Journal of Sex and Marital Therapy, 20,* 103–118.

Hubacher, D., Lara-Ricalde, R., Taylor, D. J., Guerra-Infante, F., & Guzman-Rodriguez, R. (2001). Use of copper intrauterine devices and the risk of tubal infertility among nulligravid women. *New England Journal of Medicine, 345,* 561–567.

Hubbell, F. A., Chavez, L. R., Mishra, S. I., & Valdez, R. B. (1996). Beliefs about sexual behavior and other predictors of Papanicolaou smear screening among Latinas and Anglo women. *Archives of Internal Medicine, 156,* 2353–2358.

Hubler, S. (2000). Heidi Fleiss faces post-prison life with a new face. *Los Angeles Times,* August 31.

Huffstutter, P. J., & Frammolino, R. (2001). Lights! Camera! Viagra! When the show must go on, sometimes a little chemistry helps. *Los Angeles Times,* July 6.

Human Rights Campaign. (2001a). *Adoption laws in your state.* Located at http://www.hrc.org/familynet/business/adoption_laws.asp?chapter=17.

Human Rights Campaign. (2001b). *Apparent anti-gay hate crime in Alaska.* Located at http://www.hrc.org/newsreleases/2001/010810alaska.asp.

Human Rights Campaign. (2001c). *Increase in households of same-sex partners.* Located at http://www.hrc.org/familynet/chapter.asp?article=335.

Human Rights Campaign. (2001d). *The law and LGBT workers.* Located at http://www.hrc.org/worknet/law/.

Human Rights Campaign. (2001e). *October 11 is National Coming Out Day.* Located at http://www.hrc.org/ncop/guide/whatis.asp.

Human Rights Watch. (2001a). *Hatred in the hallways: Violence and discrimination against lesbian, gay, bisexual, and transgender students in U.S. schools.* Located at http://www.hrw.org/reports/2001/uslgbt/.

Human Rights Watch. (2001b). *No escape: Male rape in U.S. prisons.* Located at http://www.hrw.org/reports/2001/prison/voices.html.

Humphreys, L. (1970). *Tearoom trade: Impersonal sex in public places.* Aldine Publishing.

Hunt, G. L., Jr., & Warner Hunt, M. (1977). Female-female pairing in western gulls (*Larus occidentalis*) in Southern California. *Science, 196.*

Hunt, M. (1974). *Sexual behavior in the 1970s.* Playboy Press.

Hutchins, L., & Kaahumanu, L. (1991). *Bi any other name: Bisexual people speak out.* Alyson.

Huws, R., Shubsachs, A. P., & Taylor, P. J. (1991). Hypersexuality, fetishism and multiple sclerosis. *British Journal of Psychiatry, 158,* 280–281.

Hyde, J. S. (1986). Gender differences in aggression. In J. S. Hyde & M. C. Linn (Eds.), *The psychology of gender.* Johns Hopkins University Press.

Hyde, J. S., & DeLamater, J. D. (2000). *Understanding human sexuality* (7th ed.) McGraw Hill.

Hyde, J. S., Fennema, E., & Lamon, S. J. (1990). Gender differences in mathematics performance: A meta-analysis. *Psychological Bulletin, 107,* 139–155.

Hyde, J. S., & Linn, M. C. (Eds.) (1986). *The psychology of gender: Advances through meta-analysis.* Johns Hopkins University Press.

Hyde, J. S., & Linn, M. C. (1988). Gender differences in verbal ability: A meta-analysis. *Psychological Bulletin, 104,* 53–69.

Imperato-McGinley, J., Guerrero, L., Gautier, T., & Peterson, R. E. (1974). Steroid 5-alpha-reductase deficiency in man: An inherited form of male pseudohermaphroditism. *Science, 186,* 1213–1215.

Imperato-McGinley, J., Miller, M., Wilson, J. D., Peterson, R. E., Shackleton, C., & Gajdusek, D. C. (1991). A cluster of male pseudohermaphrodites with 5-alpha-reductase deficiency in Papua New Guinea. *Clinical Endocrinology, 34,* 293–298.

Imperato-McGinley, J., Peterson, R. E., Gautier, T., & Sturla, E. (1979). Androgens and the evolution of male-gender identity among male pseudohermaphrodites with 5-alpha-reductase deficiency. *New England Journal of Medicine, 300,* 1233–1237.

Inhorn, M. C. (1996). *Infertility and patriarchy: The cultural politics of gender and family life in Egypt.* Philadelphia: University of Pennsylvania Press.

Insel, T. R., Winslow, J. T., Wang, Z., & Young, L. J. (1998). Oxytocin, vasopressin, and the neuroendocrine basis of pair bond formation. *Advances in Experimental Medicine and Biology, 449,* 215–224.

International Gay and Lesbian Association. (1999). *World legal survey.* Located at http://www.ilga.org/Information/legal_survey/Summary%20information/age_of_consent.htm.

Isay, R. A. (1989). *Being homosexual: Gay men and their development.* Farrar, Straus and Giroux.

Izenman, A. J., & Zabell, S. L. (1981). Babies and the blackout: The genesis of a misconception. *Social Science Research, 10,* 282–299.

Jackson, S. (1993). Childhood and sexuality in historical perspective. In A. Yates (Ed.), *Child and adolescent psychiatric clinics of North America: Sexual and gender disorders: Vol. 2.* W. B. Saunders.

Jaffee, S., & Hyde, J. S. (2000). Gender differences in moral orientation: A meta-analysis. *Psychological Bulletin, 126,* 703–726.

James, S. A. (1994). Reconciling international human rights and cultural relativism: The case of female circumcision. *Bioethics,8,* 1–26.

Jankowiak, W. R., & Fischer, E. F. (1992). A cross-cultural perspective on romantic love. *Ethnology, 31,* 149–155.

Jannini, E. A., Screponi, E., Carosa, E., Pepe, M., Lo Giudice, F., Trimarchi, F., & Benvenga, S. (1999). Lack of sexual activity from erectile dysfunction is associated with a reversible reduction in serum testosterone. *International Journal of Andrology, 22,* 385–392.

Jeffries, R. (1992). *How to get the women you desire into bed.* Straight Forward Publications.

Jentzen, J., Palermo, G., Johnson, L. T., Ho, K. C., Stormo, K. A., & Teggatz, J. (1994). Destructive hostility: The Jeffrey Dahmer case. A psychiatric and forensic study of a serial killer. *American Journal of Forensic Medicine and Pathology, 15,* 283–294.

Jeon, S., & Lambert, P. F. (1995). Integration of human papillomavirus type 16 DNA into the human genome leads to increased stability of E6 and E7 mRNAs: Implications for cervical carcinogenesis. *Proceedings of the National Academy of Sciences of the United States of America, 92,* 1654–1658.

John Paul II. (1981). Apostolic exhortation "Familiaris consortio." Located at http://www.vatican.va/holy_father/john_paul_ii/apost_exhortations/documents/hf_jp-ii_exh_19811122_familiaris-consortio_en.html.

Johnson, M. H., & Everitt, B. J. (2000). *Essential reproduction* (5th ed.). Blackwell.

Johnston, P., Hudson, S. M., & Marshall, W. L. (1992). The effects of masturbatory reconditioning with nonfamilial child molesters. *Behaviour Research and Therapy, 30,* 559–561.

Johnston, V. S., Hagel, R., Franklin, M., Fink, B., & Grammer, K. (2001). Male facial attractiveness: Evidence for hormone mediated adaptive design. *Evolution and Human Behavior, 22,* 251–267.

Jones, C. (1996). *Sexual harassment.* Facts on File.

Jones, J. C., & Barlow, D. H. (1990). Self-reported frequency of sexual urges, fantasies, and masturbatory fantasies in heterosexual males and females. *Archives of Sexual Behavior, 19,* 269–279.

Jones, J. H. (1993). *Bad blood: The Tuskegee syphilis experiment* (New and expanded ed.). Free Press.

Jones, K. L., Adams, J., Chambers, C. D., Erickson, J. D., Lammer, E., & Polifka, J. (2001). Isotretinoin and pregnancy. *JAMA, 285,* 2079–2081.

Jones, M. Y., Stanaland, A. J. S., & Gelb, B. D. (1998). Beefcake and cheesecake: Insights for advertisers. *Journal of Advertising, 27,* 33–52.

Jones, W., Chernovetz, M., & Hansson, R. (1978). The enigma of androgyny: Differential implications for males and females. *Journal of Consulting and Clinical Psychology, 46,* 298–313.

Jost, A. (1953). Problems of fetal endocrinology: The gonadal and hypophyseal hormones. *Recent Progress in Hormone Research, 8,* 379–418.

Jowett, J. (1990). People: Demographic patterns and policies. In T. Cannon & A. Jenkins (Eds.), *The geography of contemporary China: The impact of Deng Xiaoping's decade.* Routledge.

Joyner, K., & Laumann, E. O. (2001). Teenage sex and the sexual revolution. In E. O. Laumann & R. T. Michael (Eds.), *Sex, love, and health in America: Private choices and public policies.* University of Chicago Press.

Juberg, D. R. (2000). An evaluation of endocrine modulators: Implications for human health. *Ecotoxicology and Environmental Safety, 45,* 93–105.

Kahn, J. R., & Udry, J. R. (1991). Premarital sex and the risk of divorce. *Journal of Marriage and the Family, 53,* 845–855.

Kaiser Daily Reports. (1998a). *Names-based reporting: Congressional hearing held on proposed legislation.* Located at http://www.kaisernetwork.org/aids/1998/09/kh980930.1.html.

Kaiser Daily Reports. (1998b). *Partner notification: Coercive measures are counterproductive, ACLU says.* Located at http://www.kaisernetwork.org/aids/1998/09/kh980914.6.html.

Kaiser Daily Reports. (2000). *New York: Activists blast HIV reporting, partner notification law.* Located at http://www.kaisernetwork.org/aids/2000/04/kh000411.3.htm.

Kaiser, J. (2000). Endocrine disruptors: Panel cautiously confirms low-dose effects. *Science, 290,* 695–697.

Kamel, H. S., Ahmed, H. N., Eissa, M. A., & al Abol-Oyoun , S. M. (1999). Psychological and obstetrical responses of mothers following antenatal fetal sex identification. *Journal of Obstetrics and Gynaecology Research, 25,* 43–50.

Kanazawa, S., & Still, M. C. (2000). Teaching may be hazardous to your marriage. *Evolution and Human Behavior, 21,* 185–190.

Kandel, E. R., & Schwartz, J. H. (Eds.) (1985). *Principles of neural science.* Elsevier.

Kang, K. C. (2001). Japanese government knew about sex slaves, researchers say. *Los Angeles Times,* November 30.

Kanin, E. J. (1994). False rape allegations. *Archives of Sexual Behavior, 23,* 81–92.

Kano, T. (1992). *The last ape: Pygmy chimpanzee behavior and ecology.* Stanford University Press.

Kaplan, H. S. (1979). *Disorders of sexual desire.* Simon and Schuster.

Kaplan, H. S. (1992). A neglected issue: The sexual side effects of current treatments for breast cancer. *Journal of Sex and Marital Therapy, 18,* 3–19.

Kaplan, H. S. (1995). *The sexual desire disorders: Dysfunctional regulation of sexual motivation.* Brunner/Mazel.

Kaplan, S. A., Reis, R. B., Kohn, I. J., Ikeguchi, E. F., Laor, E., Te, A. E., & Martins, A. C. (1999). Safety and efficacy of sildenafil in postmenopausal women with sexual dysfunction. *Urology, 53,* 481–486.

Kaplowitz, P. B., & Oberfield, S. E. (1999). Reexamination of the age limit for defining when puberty is precocious in girls in the United States: Implications for evaluation and treatment. Drug and Therapeutics and Executive Committees of the Lawson Wilkins Pediatric Endocrine Society. *Pediatrics, 104,* 936–941.

Katz, J. N. (1992). *Gay American history: Lesbians and gay men in the U.S.A.* (Rev. ed.). Meridian Books.

Katz, J. N. (1993). Plymouth Colony sodomy statutes and cases. In W. B. Rubenstein (Ed.), *Lesbians, gay men and the law.* New Press.

Katz, J. N. (2001). *Love stories: Sex between men before homosexuality.* University of Chicago Press.

Katz, M. H., Hsu, L., Wong, E., Liska, S., Anderson, L., & Janssen, R. S. (1997). Seroprevalence of and risk factors for hepatitis A infection among young homosexual and bisexual men. *Journal of Infectious Diseases, 175,* 1225–1229.

Katz, P. A., & Boswell, S. (1986). Flexibility and traditionality in children's gender roles. *Genetic, Social, and General Psychology Monographs, 112,* 103–147.

Katz, P. A., & Ksansnak, K. R. (1994). Developmental aspects of gender role flexibility and traditionality in middle childhood and adolescence. *Developmental Psychology, 30,* 271–282.

Kegeles, S. M., Hays, R. B., & Coates, T. J. (1996). The Mpowerment Project: A community-level HIV prevention intervention for young gay men. *American Journal of Public Health, 86,* 1129–1136.

Keightley, P. D., & Eyre-Walker, A. (2000). Deleterious mutations and the evolution of sex. *Science, 290,* 331–333.

Keijzers, G. B. (2001). Aviptadil (Senatek). *Current Opinions in Investigative Drugs, 2,* 545–549.

Kendell, R. E., Wainwright, S., Hailey, A., & Shannon, B. (1976). The influence of childbirth on psychiatric morbidity. *Psychological Medicine, 6,* 297–302.

Kendler, K. S., Thornton, L. M., Gilman, S. E., & Kessler, R. C. (2000). Sexual orientation in a U.S. national sample of twin and nontwin sibling pairs. *American Journal of Psychiatry, 157,* 1843–1846.

Kendrick, K. M., & Dixson, A. F. (1986). Anteromedial hypothalamic lesions block proceptivity but not receptivity in the female common marmoset (*Callithrix jacchus*). *Brain Research, 375,* 221–229.

Kennedy, E. L., & Davis, M. D. (1983). *Boots of leather, slippers of gold: The history of a lesbian community.* Routledge.

Kennedy, H. (1988). *Ulrichs: The life and work of Karl Heinrich Ulrichs, pioneer of the modern gay movement.* Alyson Publications.

Kennedy, M. M., Cooper, K., Howells, D. D., Picton, S., Biddolph, S., Lucas, S. B., McGee, J. O., & O'Leary, J. J. (1998). Identification of HHV8 in early Kaposi's sarcoma: Implications for Kaposi's sarcoma pathogenesis. *Molecular Pathology, 51,* 14–20.

Kenrick, D. T., Gabrielidis, C., Keefe, R. C., & Cornelius, J. S. (1996). Adolescents' age preferences for dating partners: Support for an evolutionary model of life-history strategies. *Child Development, 67,* 1499–1511.

Kenrick, D. T., & Gutierres, S. E. (1980). Contrast effects and judgements of physical attractiveness: When beauty becomes a social problem. *Journal of Personality and Social Psychology, 38,* 131–140.

Kenrick, D. T., Gutierres, S. E., & Goldberg, S. E. (1989). Influence of erotica on ratings of strangers and mates. *Journal of Personality and Social Psychology, 25,* 159–167.

Kerns, K. A., & Berenbaum, S. A. (1991). Sex differences in spatial ability in children. *Behavior Genetics, 21,* 383–396.

Kessel, B. (2000). Premenstrual syndrome: Advances in diagnosis and treatment. *Obstetrical and Gynecological Clinics of North America, 27,* 625–639.

Keverne, E. B. (1999). The vomeronasal organ. *Science, 286,* 716–720.

Khanna, S. K. (1997). Traditions and reproductive technology in an urbanizing north Indian village. *Social Science and Medicine, 44,* 171–180.

Kiebert, G. M., de Haes, J. C., & van de Velde, C. J. (1991). The impact of breast-conserving treatment and mastectomy on the quality of life of early-stage breast cancer patients: A review. *Journal of Clinical Oncology, 9,* 1059–1070.

Kiess, W., Muller, G., Galler, A., Reich, A., Deutscher, J., Klammt, J., & Kratzsch, J. (2000). Body fat mass, leptin and puberty. *Journal of Pediatric Endocrinology and Metabolism, 13* (Suppl. 1,) 717–722.

Kim, S. W., Grant, J. E., Adson, D. E., & Shin, Y. C. (2001). Double-blind naltrexone and placebo comparison study in the treatment of pathological gambling. *Biological Psychiatry, 49,* 914–921.

Kimball, M. M. (1986). Television and sex-role attitudes. In T. M. Williams (Ed.), *The impact of television: A natural experiment in three communities.* Academic Press.

Kim-Gibson, D. S. (1999). *Silence broken: The Korean comfort women.* Mid-Prairie Books.

Kimura, D. (1994). Body asymmetry and intellectual pattern. *Personality and Individual Differences, 17,* 53–60.

Kimura, D. (1999). *Sex and cognition.* MIT Press.

Kindermann, G., Carsten, P. M., & Maassen, V. (1996). Ano-genital injuries in female victims of sexual assault. *Swiss Surgery, 1,* 10–13.

King, D. S., Sharp, R. L., Vukovich, M. D., Brown, G. A., Reifenrath, T. A., Uhl, N. L., & Parsons, K. A. (1999). Effect of oral androstenedione on serum testosterone and adaptations to resistance training in young men: A randomized controlled trial. *JAMA, 281,* 2020–2028.

King, M. C., Wieand, S., Hale, K., Lee, M., Walsh, T., Owens, K., Tait, J., Ford, L., Dunn, B. K., Costantino, J., Wickerham, L., Wolmark, N., & Fisher, B. (2001). Tamoxifen and breast cancer incidence among women with inherited mutations in BRCA1 and BRCA2: National Surgical Adjuvant Breast and Bowel Project (NSABP-P1) Breast Cancer Prevention Trial. *JAMA, 286,* 2251–2256.

Kinlay, J. R., O'Connell, D. L., & Kinlay, S. (2001). Risk factors for mastitis in breastfeeding women: Results of a prospective cohort study. *Australian and New Zealand Journal of Public Health, 25,* 115–120.

Kinsey, A. C., Pomeroy, W. B., & Martin, C. E. (1948). *Sexual behavior in the human male.* Saunders.

Kinsey, A. C., Pomeroy, W. B., Martin, C. E., & Gebhard, P. H. (1953). *Sexual behavior in the human female.* Saunders.

Kinsman, S. B., Romer, D., Furstenberg, F. F., & Schwarz, D. F. (1998). Early sexual initiation: The role of peer norms. *Pediatrics, 102,* 1185–1192.

Kirby, D. (1997). *No easy answers: Research findings on programs to reduce teen pregnancy.* National Campaign to Prevent Teen Pregnancy.

Kirby, D., Coyle, K., & Gould, J. B. (2001). Manifestations of poverty and birthrates among young teenagers in California zip code areas. *Family Planning Perspectives, 33*, 63–69.

Kirchmeyer, C. (1996). Gender roles in decision-making in demographically diverse groups: A case for reviving androgyny. *Sex Roles, 34*, 649–663.

Klassen, A. D., Williams, C. J., & Levitt, E. E. (1989). *Sex and morality in the U.S.: An empirical enquiry under the auspices of the Kinsey Institute.* Wesleyan University Press.

Klaus, M. H., & Kennell, J. H. (1997). The doula: An essential ingredient of childbirth rediscovered. *Acta Paediatrica, 86*, 1034–1036.

Klein, R. (1999). *Penile augmentation surgery.* Located at http://www.ejhs.org/volume2/klein/penis10.htm.

Kling, K. C., Hyde, J. S., Showers, C. J., & Buswell, B. N. (1999). Gender differences in self-esteem: A meta-analysis. *Psychological Bulletin, 125*, 470–500.

Knafo, D., & Jaffe, Y. (1984). Sexual fantasizing in males and females. *Journal of Research in Personality, 18*, 451–467.

Knight, G. P., Fabes, R. A., & Higgins, D. A. (1996). Concerns about drawing causal inferences from meta-analyses: An example in the study of gender differences in aggression. *Psychological Bulletin, 119*, 410–421.

Koelle, D. M., Benedetti, J., Langenberg, A., & Corey, L. (1992). Asymptomatic reactivation of herpes simplex virus in women after the first episode of genital herpes. *Annals of Internal Medicine, 116*, 433–437.

Koenig, H. G., McCullough, M. E., & Larson, D. B. (2001). *Handbook of religion and health.* Oxford University Press.

Kohl, J. V., & Francouer, R. T. (1995). *The scent of Eros: Mysteries of odor in human sexuality.* Continuum.

Kohlberg, L. A. (1966). A cognitive-developmental analysis of children's sex role concepts and attitudes. In E. E. Maccoby (Ed.), *The development of sex differences.* Stanford University Press.

Kolodny, R., Masters, W. H., & Johnson, V. (1979). *Textbook of sexual medicine.* Little, Brown.

Kondrashov, A. S. (1988). Deleterious mutations and the evolution of sexual reproduction. *Nature, 336*, 435–440.

Koninckx, P. R. (1999). The physiopathology of endometriosis: Pollution and dioxin. *Gynecologic and Obstetric Investigation, 47*, 47–49.

Korach, K. S., Couse, J. F., Curtis, S. W., Washburn, T. F., Lindzey, J., Kimbro, K. S., Eddy, E. M., Migliaccio, S., Snedeker, S. M., Lubahn, D. B., Schomberg, D. W., & Smith, E. P. (1996). Estrogen receptor gene disruption: Molecular characterization and experimental and clinical phenotypes. *Recent Progress in Hormone Research, 51*, 159–186.

Koren, G., Pastuszak, A., & Ito, S. (1998). Drugs in pregnancy. *New England Journal of Medicine, 338*, 1128–1137.

Koskela, P., Anttila, T., Bjorge, T., Brunsvig, A., Dillner, J., Hakama, M., Hakulinen, T., Jellum, E., Lehtinen, M., Lenner, P., Luostarinen, T., Pukkala, E., Saikku, P., Thoresen, S., Youngman, L., & Paavonen, J. (2000). *Chlamydia trachomatis* infection as a risk factor for invasive cervical cancer. *International Journal of Cancer, 85*, 35–39.

Koss, M. P., Gidycz, K. A., & Wisniewski, N. (1987). The scope of rape: Incidence and prevalence of sexual aggression and victimization in a national sample of higher education students. *Journal of Consulting and Clinical Psychology, 55*, 162–170.

Kouros-Mehr, H., Pintchovski, S., Melnyk, J., Chen, Y. J., Friedman, C., Trask, B., & Shizuya, H. (2001). Identification of non-functional human VNO receptor genes provides evidence for vestigiality of the human VNO. *Chemical Senses, 26*, 1167–1174.

Kow, L. M., & Pfaff, D. W. (1998). Mapping of neural and signal transduction pathways for lordosis in the search for estrogen actions on the central nervous system. *Behavioural Brain Research, 92*, 169–180.

Krafft-Ebing, Richard von. (1886, 1999). *Psychopathia sexualis: With especial reference to contrary sexual instinct: A clinical-forensic study.* Translated by Brian King. Bloat.

Kristal, M. B. (1980). Placentophagia: A biobehavioral enigma (or De gustibus non disputandum est). *Neuroscience and Biobehavioral Reviews, 4*, 141–150.

Kritsberg, W. (1993). *The invisible wound: A new approach to healing childhood sexual trauma.* Bantam.

Krob, G., Braun, A., & Kuhnle, U. (1994). True hermaphroditism: Geographical distribution, clinical findings, chromosomes and gonadal histology. *European Journal of Pediatrics, 153*, 2–10.

Krueger, R. B., & Kaplan, M. S. (2000). Disorders of sexual impulse control in neuropsychiatric conditions. *Seminars in Clinical Neuropsychiatry, 5*, 266–274.

Krueger, R. B., & Kaplan, M. S. (2001). Depot-leuprolide acetate for treatment of paraphilias: A report of twelve cases. *Archives of Sexual Behavior, 30*, 409–422.

Kruijver, F. P., Zhou, J. N., Pool, C. W., Hofman, M. A., Gooren, L. J., & Swaab, D. F. (2000). Male-to-female transsexuals have female neuron numbers in a limbic nucleus. *Journal of Clinical Endocrinology and Metabolism, 85*, 2034–2041.

Kuhn, D. R., Greiner, D., & Arseneau, L. (1998). Addressing hypersexuality in Alzheimer's disease. *Journal of Gerontological Nursing, 24*, 44–50.

Kuriansky, J. B., Sharpe, L., & O'Connor, D. (1982). The treatment of anorgasmia: Long-term effectiveness of a short-term behavioral group therapy. *Journal of Sex and Marital Therapy, 8*, 29–43.

Kynard, B. E. (1978). Breeding behavior of a lacustrine population of threespine sticklebacks (*Gasterosteus aculeatus* L.). *Behavior, 67*, 178–202.

Ladas, A. K., Whipple, B., & Perry, J. D. (1982). *The G spot and other recent discoveries about human sexuality.* Holt, Rinehart and Winston.

Ladurie, E. L. R. (1979). *Montaillou: The promised land of error.* Vintage.

Lalumière, M. L., Chalmers, L., Quinsey, V. L., & Seto, M. C. (1996). A test of the mate deprivation hypothesis of sexual coercion. *Ethology and Sociobiology, 17*, 299–318.

Lalumière, M. L., & Quinsey, V. L. (1994). The discriminability of rapists from non-sex offenders using phallometric measures: A meta-analysis. *Criminal Justice and Behavior, 21*, 150–175.

Lamaze, F. (1981). *Painless childbirth.* Simon and Schuster.

Lamaze International. (2002). *Myths about Lamaze.* Located at http://www.lamaze.org/2000/myth.html.

Lambda Legal Defense and Education Fund. (2000). *Lambda to sue Reno school officials for failing to protect gay student.* Located at http://www.lambdalegal.org/cgi-bin/pages/documents/record?record=560.

Landry, D. J., Kaeser, L., & Richards, C. L. (1999). Abstinence promotion and the provision of information about contraception in public school district sexuality education policies. *Family Planning Perspectives, 31*, 280–286.

Landsberg, M. (2000). McMartin defendant who "lost everything" in abuse case dies at 74. *Los Angeles Times*, December 17.

Lane, F. S. (2000). *Obscene profits: The entrepreneurs of pornography in the cyber age.* Routledge.

Langenberg, A., Benedetti, J., Jenkins, J., Ashley, R., Winter, C., & Corey, L. (1989). Development of clinically recognizable genital lesions among women previously identified as having "asymptomatic" herpes simplex virus type 2 infection. *Annals of Internal Medicine, 110*, 882–887.

Langevin, R., Paitich, D., Freeman, R., Mann, K., & Handy, L. (1978). Personality characteristics and sexual anomalies in males. *Canadian Journal of Behavioural Sciences, 10*, 222–226.

Langevin, R., & Watson, R. J. (1996). Major factors in the assessment of paraphiliacs and sex offenders. *Journal of Offender Rehabilitation, 23*, 39–70.

Langlois, J. H., Kalakanis, L., Rubenstein, A. J., Larson, A., Hallam, M. & Smoot, M. (2000). Maxims or myths of beauty? A meta-analytic and theoretical review. *Psychological Bulletin* 126: 390–423.

Langlois, J. H., Roggman, L. A., & Musselman, L. (1994). What is average and what is not average about attractive faces? *Psychological Science, 5*, 214–220.

Larsen, W. J. (1998). *Essentials of human embryology.* Churchill Livingstone.

Lary, J. M., Daniel, K. L., Erickson, J. D., Roberts, H. E., & Moore, C. A. (1999). The return of thalidomide: Can birth defects be prevented? *Drug Safety, 21*, 161–169.

Lauby, J. L., Smith, P. J., Stark, M., Person, B., & Adams, J. (2000). A community-level HIV prevention intervention for inner-city women: Results of the women and infants demonstration projects. *American Journal of Public Health, 90*, 216–222.

Laumann, E. O., Gagnon, J. H., Michael, R. T., & Michaels, S. (1994). *The social organization of sexuality: Sexual practices in the United States.* University of Chicago Press.

Laumann, E. O., Masi, C. M., & Zuckerman, E. W. (1997). Circumcision in the United States: Prevalence, prophylactic effects, and sexual practice. *JAMA, 277*, 1052–1057.

Laumann, E. O., & Michael, R. T. (Eds.) (2000). *Sex, love, and health in America: Private choices and public policies.* University of Chicago Press.

Laumann, E. O., Paik, A., & Rosen, R. C. (2000). Sexual dysfunction in the United States: Prevalence and predictors. In E. O. Laumann & R. T. Michael (Eds.), *Sex, love, and health in America: Private choices and public policies.* University of Chicago Press.

Lawrence, A. A. (1998). Men trapped in men's bodies: An introduction to the concept of autogynephilia. *Transgender Tapestry, 85* (Winter), 65–68.

Lawrence, K.-A., & Byers, E. S. (1995). Sexual satisfaction in long-term heterosexual relationships: The interpersonal exchange model of sexual satisfaction. *Personal Relationships, 2*, 267–285.

Laws, D. R. (1999). Harm reduction or harm facilitation? A reply to Maletzky. *Sexual Abuse, 11*, 233–241.

Laws, D. R., & O'Donohue, W. (1997). *Sexual deviance: Theory, assessment, and treatment.* Guilford Press.

Leach, K. (1999). *In the shadow of the dream-child: A new understanding of Lewis Carroll.* Peter Owen.

Lebrun, C. M. (1994). The effect of the phase of the menstrual cycle and the birth control pill on athletic performance. *Clinics in Sports Medicine, 13*, 419–441.

LeDoux, J. (2002). *Synaptic self: How our brains become who we are.* Viking.

Lee, G. R., & Shehan, C. L. (1989). Retirement and marital satisfaction. *Journal of Gerontology, 44*, S226–230.

Lehtinen, M., Hakama, M., Aaran, R. K., Aromaa, A., Knekt, P., Leinikki, P., Maatela, J., Peto, R., & Teppo, L. (1992). Herpes simplex virus type 2 infection and cervical cancer: A prospective study of 12 years of follow-up in Finland. *Cancer Causes and Control, 3*, 333–338.

Leinbach, M. D., & Fagot, B. I. (1993). Categorical habituation to male and female faces: Gender schematic processing in infancy. *Infant Behavior and Development, 16*, 317–332.

Leitenberg, H., Greenwald, E., & Tarran, M. J. (1989). The relation between sexual activity among children during preadolescence and/or early adolescence and sexual behavior and sexual adjustment in young adulthood. *Archives of Sexual Behavior, 18*, 299–313.

Leitenberg, H., & Henning, K. (1995). Sexual fantasy. *Psychological Bulletin, 117*, 469–496.

Lemieux, R., & Hale, J. L. (1999). Intimacy, passion, and commitment in young romantic relationships: Successfully measuring the triangular theory of love. *Psychological Reports, 85*, 497–503.

Lemieux, R., & Hale, J. L. (2000). Intimacy, passion, and commitment among married individuals: Further testing of the triangular theory of love. *Psychological Reports, 87*, 941–948.

Leovy, J. (2001). Transgenders, police face cultural chasm on Hollywood streets. *Los Angeles Times*, December 15.

Lester, D. (1996). The impact of unemployment on marriage and divorce. *Journal of Divorce and Remarriage, 25*, 151–153.

Levant, R. (1997). *Men and emotions: A psychoeducational approach.* Newbridge Communications.

LeVay, S. (1991). A difference in hypothalamic structure between heterosexual and homosexual men. *Science, 253*, 1034–1037.

LeVay, S. (1996). *Queer science: The use and abuse of research into homosexuality.* MIT Press.

LeVay, S. (2000). *Male, female, other.* Located at http://www.nerve.com/dispatches/levay/intersex/.

Lever, J. (1994). Sexual revelations: The 1994 *Advocate* survey of sexuality and relationships: The men. *The Advocate*, August 23.

Lever, J. (1995). Lesbian sex survey. *Advocate*, August 22.

Levine, J. (2002). *Harmful to minors: The perils of protecting children from sex.* University of Minnesota Press.

Levine, L. A. (2000). Diagnosis and treatment of erectile dysfunction. *American Journal of Medicine, 109* (Suppl. 9A), 3S–12S.

Lewin, T. (1997). Teen-agers alter sexual practices, thinking risks will be avoided. *New York Times*, April 5.

Lewis, R. J., & Janda, L. H. (1988). The relationship between adult sexual adjustment and childhood experiences regarding exposure to nudity, sleeping in the parental bed, and parental attitudes toward sexuality. *Archives of Sexual Behavior, 17*, 349–362.

Lewontin, R. C. (1995). Sex, lies, and social science. *New York Review of Books*, April 20.

Leysen, B. (1996). Medicalization of menopause: From "feminine forever" to "healthy forever." In N. Lykke & R. Braidotti (Eds.), *Between monsters, goddesses and cyborgs: Feminist confrontations with science, medicine and cyberspace.* Zed Books.

Lim, L. L. (Ed.). (1998). *The sex sector: The economic and social bases of prostitution in Southeast Asia*, International Labour Office.

Lin, Y.-H. (1961). *The Lolo of Liang Shan.* HRAF Press.

Linden, J. A. (1999). Sexual assault. *Emergency Medicine Clinics of North America, 17*, 685–697, vii.

Linz, D., Blumenthal, E., Donnerstein, E., Kunkel, D., Shafer, B. J., & Lichtenstein, A. (2000). Testing legal assumptions regarding the effects of dancer nudity and proximity to patron on erotic expression. *Law and Human Behavior, 24*, 507–533.

Lipitz, S., Frenkel, Y., Watts, C., Ben-Rafael, Z., Barkai, G., & Reichman, B. (1990). High-order multifetal gestation—management and outcome. *Obstetrics and Gynecology, 76*, 215–218.

Lippa, R. A. (2000). Gender-related traits in gay men, lesbian women, and heterosexual men and women: The virtual identity of homosexual-heterosexual diagnosticity and gender diagnosticity. *Journal of Personality, 68*, 899–925.

Lippa, R. A. (2002). Gender-related traits of heterosexual and homosexual men and women. *Archives of Sexual Behavior, 31*, 83–98.

Lippa, R. A., & Arad, S. (1997). The structure of sexual orientation and its relation to masculinity, femininity, and gender diagnosticity: Different for men and women. *Sex Roles, 37*, 187–208.

Lippert, B. (1995). The naked untruth. *Adweek*, September 18.

Litwin, M. S. (1999). Health related quality of life in older men without prostate cancer. *Journal of Urology, 161*, 1180–1184.

Loftus, E. F. (1997). Creating false memories. *Scientific American, 277* (3), 70–75.

Loftus, E. F., & Ketcham, K. (1996). *The myth of repressed memory: False memories and allegations of sexual abuse.* St. Martin's Press.

Lopez Bernal, A., & TambyRaja, R. L. (2000). Preterm labour. *Baillieres Best Practice and Research in Clinical and Obstetrics and Gynecology, 14,* 133–153.

Lorde, A. (1980). *The cancer journals.* Aunt Lute Books.

Los Angeles Gay and Lesbian Center. (2001). *STOP Domestic Violence Program.* Located at http://www.laglc.org/section05/S0512.htm.

Louganis, G., & Marcus, E. (1995). *Breaking the surface.* Random House.

Louis Harris Poll. (1994). *Sexual harassment.* Located at http://www.icasa.org/uploads/sexual_harassment.pdf.

Loulan, J. (1984) *Lesbian sex.* Spinsters Ink/Aunt Lute.

Love, S. M., & Lindsey, K. (1998). *Dr. Susan Love's hormone book: Making informed choices about menopause.* Random House.

Love, S. M., & Lindsey, K. (2000). *Dr. Susan Love's breast book* (3rd rev. ed.). Perseus Books.

Lovelace, L., & McGrady, M. (1980). *Ordeal.* Carol Publishing Group.

Luciano, L. (2001). *Looking good: Male body image in modern America.* Hill and Wang.

Lumley, V. A., & Scotti, J. R. (2001). Supporting the sexuality of adults with mental retardation. *Journal of Positive Behavior Interventions, 3,* 109–119.

Lummus, W. E., & Thompson, I. (2001). Prostatitis. *Emergency Medicine Clinics of North America, 19,* 691–707.

Lydon-Rochelle, M., Holt, V. L., Easterling, T. R., & Martin, D. P. (2001). Risk of uterine rupture during labor among women with a prior cesarean delivery. *New England Journal of Medicine, 345,* 3–8.

Lynch, M., Blanchard, J., Houle, D., Kibota, T., Schultz, S., Vassilieva, L., & Willis, J. (1999). Spontaneous deleterious mutation. *Evolution, 53,* 645–663.

Lynn, R. (1994). Sex differences in intelligence and brain size: A paradox resolved. *Personality and Individual Differences, 17,* 257–271.

Lyon, K. (1998). *Witch hunt: A true story of social hysteria and abused justice.* Avon Books.

Macaluso, M., Demand, M., Artz, L., Fleenor, M., Robey, L., Kelaghan, J., Cabral, R., & Hook, E. W., III. (2000). Female condom use among women at high risk of sexually transmitted disease. *Family Planning Perspectives, 32,* 138–144.

Maccoby, E. E. (1990). Gender and relationships: A developmental account. *American Psychologist, 45,* 513–520.

Maccoby, E. E., & Jacklin, C. N. (1987). Gender segregation in childhood. In H. W. Reese (Ed.), *Advances in child development and behavior.* Academic Press.

Macke, J. P., Hu, N., Hu, S., Bailey, M., King, V. L., Brown, T., Hamer, D., & Nathans, J. (1993). Sequence variation in the androgen receptor gene is not a common determinant of male sexual orientation. *American Journal of Human Genetics, 53,* 844–852.

MacKinnon, C. (1979). *Sexual harassment of working women: A case of discrimination.* Yale University Press.

Mahay, J., Laumann, E. O., & Michaels, S. (2000). Race, gender, and class in sexual scripts. In E. O. Laumann & R. T. Michael (Eds.), *Sex, love, and health in America: Private choices and public policies.* University of Chicago Press.

Mahoney, A., Pargament, K. I., Tarakeshwar, N., & Swank, A. B. (2001). Religion in the home in the 1980s and 1990s: A meta-analytic review and conceptual analysis of links between religion, marriage, and parenting. *Journal of Family Psychology, 15,* 559–596.

Malamuth, N. M. (1981). Rape proclivity among males. *Journal of Social Issues, 37,* 138–157.

Malamuth, N. M. (1983). Factors associated with rape as predictors of laboratory aggression against women. *Journal of Personality and Social Psychology, 45,* 432–442.

Malamuth, N. M. (1996). The confluence model of sexual aggression: Feminist and evolutionary perspectives. In D. M. Buss & N. M. Malamuth (Eds.), *Sex, power, conflict: Evolutionary and feminist perspectives.* Oxford University Press.

Malamuth, N. M., Addison, T., & Koss, M. (2000). Pornography and sexual aggression: Are there reliable effects and can we understand them? *Annual Review of Sex Research, 11,* 26–91.

Malamuth, N. M., Linz, D., Heavey, C. L., Barnes, G., & Acker, M. (1995). Using the confluence model of sexual aggression to predict men's conflict with women: A 10-year follow-up study. *Journal of Personality and Social Psychology, 69,* 353–369.

Malaspina, D., Harlap, S., Fennig, S., Heiman, D., Nahon, D., Feldman, D., & Susser, E. S. (2001). Advancing paternal age and the risk of schizophrenia. *Archives of General Psychiatry, 58,* 361–367.

Maletzky, B. M. (1974). "Assisted" covert sensitization in the treatment of exhibitionism. *Journal of Consulting and Clinical Psychology, 42,* 34–40.

Maletzky, B. M., & George, F. S. (1973). The treatment of homosexuality by "assisted" covert sensitization. *Behaviour Research and Therapy, 11,* 655–657.

Manning, J. T., & Chamberlain, A. T. (1994). Fluctuating asymmetry in gorilla canines: A sensitive indicator of environmental stress. *Proceedings of the Royal Society of London. Series B: Biological Sciences, 255,* 189–193.

Mannino, F. (1988). Neonatal complications of postterm gestation. *Journal of Reproductive Medicine, 33,* 271–276.

Mantzoros, C. S., Flier, J. S., & Rogol, A. D. (1997). A longitudinal assessment of hormonal and physical alterations during normal puberty in boys. V. Rising leptin levels may signal the onset of puberty. *Journal of Clinical Endocrinology and Metabolism, 82,* 1066–1070.

Marazziti, D., Akiskal, H. S., Rossi, A., & Cassano, G. B. (1999). Alteration of the platelet serotonin transporter in romantic love. *Psychological Medicine, 29,* 741–745.

Marcus, E. (1992). *Making history: The struggle for gay and lesbian equal rights.* HarperCollins.

Marcus, E. (2002). *Making gay history: The half-century fight for lesbian and gay equal rights.* HarperPerennial.

Marcus, J., Maccoby, E. E., Jacklin, C. N., & Doering, C. H. (1985). Individual differences in mood in early childhood: Their relation to gender and neonatal sex steroids. *Developmental Psychobiology, 18,* 327–340.

Marcus, R., Leary, D., Schneider, D. L., Shane, E., Favus, M., & Quigley, C. A. (2000). The contribution of testosterone to skeletal development and maintenance: Lessons from the androgen insensitivity syndrome. *Journal of Clinical Endocrinology and Metabolism, 85,* 1032–1037.

Margaret Sanger Papers Project. (2000). *Margaret Sanger: Biographical sketch.* Located at http://www.nyu.edu/projects/sanger/ms-bio.htm.

Mark Welch, D. M., & Meselson, M. (2000). Evidence for the evolution of bdelloid rotifers without sexual reproduction or genetic exchange. *Science, 288,* 1211–1215.

Markman, H. J. (1981). Prediction of marital distress: A 5-year follow-up. *Journal of Consulting and Clinical Psychology, 49,* 760–762.

Markman, H. J., Renick, M. J., Floyd, F. J., Stanley, S. M., & Clements, M. (1993). Preventing marital distress through communication and conflict management training: A 4- and 5-year follow-up. *Journal of Consulting and Clinical Psychology, 61,* 70–77.

Markman, H. J., & Stanley, S. (1996). *Fighting for your marriage: Positive steps for preventing divorce and preserving a lasting love.* Jossey-Bass.

Marlin, E. (1999). First for flirting: UK's only flirting academy. *Sunday Times* (London), December 26.

Marosi, R. (2001). Some sex offenders seeking castration in bid for freedom. *Los Angeles Times*, March 2.

Marques, J. K. (1999). How to answer the question "Does sex offender treatment work?" *Journal of Interpersonal Violence, 14,* 437–451.

Marques, J. K., Nelson, C., West, M. A., & Day, D. M. (1994). The relationship between treatment goals and recidivism among child molesters. *Behaviour Research and Therapy, 32,* 577–588.

Marr, L. (1998). *Sexually transmitted diseases: A physician tells you what you need to know.* Johns Hopkins University Press.

Marshall, D. S. (1971). Sexual behavior on Mangaia. In D. S. Marshall & D. N. Suggs (Eds.), *Human sexual behavior.* Basic Books.

Marshall, W. L. (1997). The relationship between self-esteem and deviant sexual arousal in nonfamilial child molesters. *Behavior Modification, 21,* 86–96.

Marshall, W. L. (1998). Adult sexual offenders. In N. N. Singh (Ed.), *Comprehensive clinical psychology: Vol. 9. Applications in diverse populations.* Elsevier.

Marshall, W. L., & Barbaree, H. E. (1990). An integrated theory of the etiology of sexual offending. In W. L. Marshall, D. R. Laws, & H. E. Barbaree (Eds.), *Handbook of sexual assault: Issues, theories, and treatment of the offender.* Plenum.

Martin, A. (1993). *The lesbian and gay parenting handbook: Creating and raising our families.* HarperPerennial.

Martin, C. L., & Halverson, C. F. (1983). The effects of sex-typing schemas on young children's memories. *Child Development, 54,* 563–574.

Martin, M. M., Anderson, C. M., & Mottet, T. P. (1999). Perceived understanding and self-disclosure in the stepparent-stepchild relationship. *Journal of Psychology, 133,* 281–290.

Martinson, F. M. (1976). Eroticism in infancy and childhood. *Journal of Sex Research, 2,* 251–262.

Martinson, F. M. (1994). *The sexual life of children.* Bergin and Garvey.

Masonjones, H. D. (2001). The effect of social context and reproductive status on the metabolic rates of dwarf seahorses (*Hippocampus zosterae*). *Comparative Biochemistry and Physiology. Part A, Molecular and Integrative Physiology, 129,* 541–555.

Masters, W. H., & Johnson, V. E. (1966). *Human sexual response.* Little, Brown.

Masters, W. H., & Johnson, V. E. (1970). *Human sexual inadequacy.* Little, Brown.

Masters, W. H., & Johnson, V. E. (1979). *Homosexuality in perspective.* Little, Brown.

Masters, W. H., Johnson, V. E., & Kolodny, R. C. (1982). *Human sexuality.* Little, Brown.

Matek, O. (1988). Obscene phone callers. *Journal of Social Work and Human Sexuality, 7,* 113–130.

Mathes, E. W., Brennan, S. M., Haugen, P. M., & Rice, H. B. (1985). Ratings of physical attractiveness as a function of age. *Journal of Social Psychology, 125,* 157–168.

Matteson, D. (1991). Bisexual feminist man. In L. Hutchins & L. Kaahumanu (Eds.), *Bi any other name: Bisexual people speak out.* Alyson.

Mauck, C., Glover, L. H., Miller, E., Allen, S., Archer, D. F., Blumenthal, P., Rosenzweig, A., Dominik, R., Sturgen, K., Cooper, J., Fingerhut, F., Peacock, L., & Gabelnick, H. L. (1996). Lea's Shield: A study of the safety and efficacy of a new vaginal barrier contraceptive used with and without spermicide. *Contraception, 53,* 329–335.

McBurney, D. H., Gaulin, S. J. C., Devineni, T., & Adams, C. (1997). Superior spatial memory of women: Stronger evidence for the gathering hypothesis. *Evolution and Human Behavior, 18,* 165–174.

McCahill, T. W., Meyer, L. C., & Fischman, A. M. (1979). *The aftermath of rape.* Lexington Books.

McClellan, J., McCurry, C., Ronnei, M., Adams, J., Eisner, A., & Storck, M. (1996). Age of onset of sexual abuse: Relationship to sexually inappropriate behaviors. *Journal of the American Academy of Child and Adolescent Psychiatry, 35,* 1375–1383.

McClintock, M. K. (1971). Menstrual synchrony and suppression. *Nature, 229,* 244–245.

McClintock, M. K. (1984). Group mating in the domestic rat as context for sexual selection: Consequences for the analysis of sexual behavior and neuroendocrine responses. *Advances in the Study of Behavior, 14,* 1–50.

McClintock, M. K. (1999). Reproductive biology: Pheromones and regulation of ovulation. *Nature, 401,* 232–233.

McConaghy, N. (1998). Paedophilia: A review of the evidence. *Australian and New Zealand Journal of Psychiatry, 32,* 252–265.

McConkey, T. E., Sole, M. L., & Holcomb, L. (2001). Assessing the female sexual assault survivor. *Nurse Practitioner, 26,* 28–41.

McElroy, W. (2001). *An evening with Candida Royalle.* Located at http://www.interlog.com/~mushroom/royalle.html.

McEwen, B. S., Jones, K. J., & Pfaff, D. W. (1987). Hormonal control of sexual behavior in the female rat: Molecular, cellular and neurochemical studies. *Biology of Reproduction, 36,* 37–45.

McFadden, D. (2002). Masculinization effects in the auditory system. *Archives of Sexual Behavior, 31,* 99–111.

McFadden, D., & Champlin, C. A. (2000). Comparison of auditory evoked potentials in heterosexual, homosexual, and bisexual males and females. *Journal of the Association for Research in Otolaryngology, 1,* 89–99.

McFadden, D., & Pasanen, E. G. (1998). Comparison of the auditory systems of heterosexuals and homosexuals: Click-evoked otoacoustic emissions. *Proceedings of the National Academy of Sciences of the United States of America, 95,* 2709–2713.

McFadden, D., & Pasanen, E. G. (1999). Spontaneous otoacoustic emissions in heterosexuals, homosexuals, and bisexuals. *Journal of the Acoustical Society of America, 105,* 2403–2413.

McGuire, R. J., Carlisle, J. M., & Young, B. G. (1965). Sexual deviations as conditioned behavior: A hypothesis. *Behavioral Research and Therapy, 2,* 185–190.

McIntyre, J., Pettifor, A., & Rees, V. H. (1998). Female condom re-use: Assessing structural integrity after multiple wash, dry and re-lubrication cycles. 12th World Conference on AIDS.

McKibben, A., Proulx, J., & Lusignan, R. (1994). Relationships between conflict, affect and deviant sexual behaviors in rapists and pedophiles. *Behaviour Research and Therapy, 32,* 571–575.

McMahon, C. G., & Samali, R. (1999). Pharmacological treatment of premature ejaculation. *Current Opinion in Urology, 9,* 553–561.

McMahon, C. G., & Touma, K. (1999). Treatment of premature ejaculation with paroxetine hydrochloride. *International Journal of Impotence Research, 11,* 241–245; discussion 246.

McNeilly, A. S. (2001). Lactational control of reproduction. *Reproduction, Fertility, and Development, 13,* 583–590.

McVary, K. T., Carrier, S., & Wessells, H. (2001). Smoking and erectile dysfunction: Evidence based analysis. *Journal of Urology, 166,* 1624–1632.

McWhirter, D. P., & Mattison, A. M. (1984). *The male couple.* Prentice-Hall.

Mead, M. (1928). *Coming of age in Samoa: A psychological study of primitive youth for Western civilization.* Morrow.

Mead, M. (1935). *Sex and temperament in three primitive societies.* Morrow.

Mealey, L. (2000). *Sex differences: Developmental and evolutionary strategies*. Academic Press.

Mealey, L., Bridgstock, R., & Townsend, G. C. (1999). Symmetry and perceived facial attractiveness: A monozygotic co-twin comparison. *Journal of Personality and Social Psychology, 76*, 151–158.

Meerdink, J. E., Garbin, C. P., & Leger, D. W. (1990). Cross-gender perceptions of facial attributes and their relation to attractiveness: Do we see them differently than they see us? *Perception and Psychophysics, 48*, 227–233.

Meese, E. (1986). *Attorney general (Edwin Meese) commission report.* U.S. Government Printing Office.

Mehren, E. (2002). Scandal shaking Catholicism to the core. *Los Angeles Times*, March 13.

Meisel, R. L., & Luttrell, V. R. (1990). Estradiol increases the dendritic length of ventromedial hypothalamic neurons in female Syrian hamsters. *Brain Research Bulletin, 25*, 165–168.

Meisel, R. L., & Sachs, B. D. (1994). The physiology of male sexual behavior. In E. Knobil & J. D. Neill (Eds.), *The physiology of reproduction: Vol. 1* (2nd. ed.). Raven.

Meisel, R. L., & Ward, I. L. (1981). Fetal female rats are masculinized by male littermates located caudally in the uterus. *Science, 213*, 239–242.

Meloy, J. R., Rivers, L., Siegel, L., Gothard, S., Naimark, D., & Nicolini, J. R. (2000). A replication study of obsessional followers and offenders with mental disorders. *Journal of Forensic Sciences, 45*, 147–152.

Mendez, M. F., Chow, T., Ringman, J., Twitchell, G., & Hinkin, C. H. (2000). Pedophilia and temporal lobe disturbances. *Journal of Neuropsychiatry and Clinical Neurosciences, 12*, 71–76.

Merskey, H. (1986). Variable meanings for the definitions of disease. *Journal of Medicine and Philosophy, 11*, 215–232.

Mertz, G. J., Benedetti, J., Ashley, R., Selke, S. A., & Corey, L. (1992). Risk factors for the sexual transmission of genital herpes. *Annals of Internal Medicine, 116*, 197–202.

Messe, M. R., & Geer, J. H. (1985). Voluntary vaginal musculature contractions as an enhancer of sexual arousal. *Archives of Sexual Behavior, 14*, 13–28.

Meston, C. M. (1997). Aging and sexuality. *Western Journal of Medicine, 167*, 285–290.

Metts, S., & Cupach, W. R. (1989). The role of communication in human sexuality. In K. McKinney & S. Sprecher (Eds.), *Human sexuality: The societal and interpersonal context*. Ablex.

Meyer, J. M., Eaves, L. J., Heath, A. C., & Martin, N. G. (1991). Estimating genetic influences on the age-at-menarche: A survival analysis approach. *American Journal of Medical Genetics, 39*, 148–154.

Meyer, J. P., & Pepper, S. (1977). Need compatibility and marital adjustment in young married couples. *Journal of Personality and Social Psychology, 35*, 331–342.

Meyer, W. J., & Cole, C. M. (1997). Physical and chemical castration of sex offenders: A review. *Journal of Offender Rehabilitation, 25*, 1–18.

Meyer, W. J., Cole, C. M., & Emory, E. (1992). Depo-Provera treatment for sex offending behavior: An evaluation of outcome. *Bulletin of the American Academy of Psychiatry and the Law, 20*, 249–259.

Michael, R. P., & Keverne, E. B. (1970). A male sex-attractant pheromone in rhesus monkey vaginal secretions. *Journal of Endocrinology, 46*, xx–xxi.

Michigan Womyn's Music Festival. (2002). *General festival information*. Located at http://www.michfest.com/General/general.htm.

Miettinen, O. S., Henschke, C. I., Pasmantier, M. W., Smith, J. P., Libby, D. M., & Yankelevitz, D. F. (2002). Mammographic screening: No reliable supporting evidence? *Lancet, 359*, 404–405.

Miller, A. B., To, T., Baines, C. J., & Wall, C. (2000). Canadian National Breast Screening Study-2: 13-year results of a randomized trial in women aged 50–59 years. *Journal of the National Cancer Institute, 92*, 1490–1499.

Miller, C. L., Younger, B. A., & Morse, P. A. (1982). The categorization of male and female voices in infancy. *Infant Behavior and Development, 5*, 143–159.

Mindel, A., Faherty, A., Carney, O., Patou, G., Freris, M., & Williams, P. (1988). Dosage and safety of long-term suppressive acyclovir therapy for recurrent genital herpes. *Lancet, 1*, 926–928.

Mirkin, H. (1999). The pattern of sexual politics: Feminism, homosexuality, and pedophilia. *Journal of Homosexuality, 37*, 1–24.

Mischel, W. (1966). A social-learning view of sex differences in behavior. In E. E. Maccoby (Ed.), *The development of sex differences*. Stanford University Press.

Misri, S. (1995). *Shouldn't I be happy? Emotional problems of pregnant and postpartum women*. Free Press.

Mittendorf, R., Williams, M. A., Berkey, C. S., & Cotter, P. F. (1990). The length of uncomplicated human gestation. *Obstetrics and Gynecology, 75*, 929–932.

Mittwoch, U. (1996). Sex-determining mechanisms in animals. *Trends in Ecology and Evolution, 11*, 63–67.

Molenda, H. A., Griffin, A. L., Auger, A. P., McCarthy, M. M., & Tetel, M. J. (2002). Nuclear receptor coactivators modulate hormone-dependent gene expression in brain and female reproductive behavior in rats. *Endocrinology, 143*, 436–444.

Møller, A. P. (1992). Female swallow preference for symmetrical male sexual ornaments. *Nature, 357*, 238–240.

Molnar, B. E., Buka, S. L., & Kessler, R. C. (2001). Child sexual abuse and subsequent psychopathology: Results from the National Comorbidity Survey. *American Journal of Public Health, 91*, 753–760.

Money, J., & Ehrhardt, A. E. (1971). *Man and woman, boy and girl: The differentiation and dimorphism of gender identity from conception to maturity*. Johns Hopkins University Press.

Money, J., Hampson, J. G., & Hampson, J. L. (1955). An examination of some basic sexual concepts: The evidence of human hermaphroditism. *Bulletin of The Johns Hopkins Hospital, 97*, 301–319.

Money, J., Hampson, J. G., & Hampson, J. L. (1957). Imprinting and the establishment of gender role. *Archives of Neurology and Psychiatry, 77*, 333–336.

Money, J., Jobaris, R., & Furth, G. (1977). Two cases of self-demand amputation as a paraphilia. *Journal of Sex Research, 13*, 115–125.

Monga, T. N., Monga, M., Raina, M. S., & Hardjasudarma, M. (1986). Hypersexuality in stroke. *Archives of Physical Medicine and Rehabilitation, 67*, 415–417.

Mongeau, P. A., & Carey, C. M. (1996). Who's wooing whom? II: An experimental investigation of date initiation and expectancy violation. *Western Journal of Communication, 60*, 195–213.

Mongeau, P. A., Carey, C. M., & Williams, M. L. M. (1998). First date initiation and enactment: An expectancy violation perspective. In C. M. Canary & K. Dindia (Eds.), *Sex differences and similarities in communication*. Lawrence Erlbaum Associates.

Mongeau, P. A., & Johnson, K. L. (1995). Predicting cross-sex first-date sexual expectations and involvement: Contextual and individual difference factors. *Personal Relationships, 2*, 310–312.

Montgomery, M. J., & Sorell, G. T. (1998). Love and dating experience in early and middle adolescence: Grade and gender comparisons. *Journal of Adolescence, 21*, 677–689.

Monti-Bloch, L., Jennings-White, C., & Berliner, D. L. (1998). The human vomeronasal system: A review. *Annals of the New York Academy of Sciences, 855*, 373–389.

Monto, M. A. (1996). Lamaze and Bradley childbirth classes: Contrasting perspectives toward the medical model of birth. *Birth, 23*, 193–201.

Mooradian, A. D. (1991). Geriatric sexuality and chronic diseases. *Clinics in Geriatric Medicine, 7*, 113–131.

Moore, C. L. (1992). Variation in maternal care and individual differences in play, exploration, and grooming of juvenile Norway rat offspring. *Developmental Psychobiology, 25*, 165–182.

Moore, M. (1998). The science of sexual signalling: Context and consequences. In G. G. Brannigan, E. R. Allgeier, & A. R. Allgeier (Eds.), *The sex scientists.* Longman.

Moore, T., & Haig, D. (1991). Genomic imprinting in mammalian development: A parental tug-of-war. *Genetics, 144*, 1283–1295.

Moran, J. P. (2000). *Teaching sex: The shaping of adolescence in the 20th century.* Harvard University Press.

More, E. (2001). "She was a queen": Mary Steichen Calderone and the politics of sexuality. *Radcliffe Quarterly*, Winter.

Moreland, R. L., & Zajonc, R. B. (1977). Is stimulus recognition a necessary condition for the occurrence of exposure effects? *Journal of Personality and Social Psychology, 35*, 191–199.

Morgentaler, A. (1993). *The male body: A physician's guide to what every man should know about his sexual health.* Fireside Books.

Morley, J. E. (2000). Andropause, testosterone therapy, and quality of life in aging men. *Cleveland Clinic Journal of Medicine, 67*, 880–882.

Morris, D. (1967). *The naked ape.* Jonathan Cape.

Morris, N. M., Udry, J. R., Khan-Dawood, F., & Dawood, M. Y. (1987). Marital sex frequency and midcycle female testosterone. *Archives of Sexual Behavior, 16*, 27–37.

Morris, T., Greer, H. S., & White, P. (1977). Psychological and social adjustment to mastectomy: A two-year follow-up study. *Cancer, 40*, 2381–2387.

Mortensen, E. L., Michaelsen, K. F., Sanders, S. A., & Reinisch, J. M. (2002). The association between duration of breastfeeding and adult intelligence. *JAMA, 287*, 2365–2371.

Moses, S., Bailey, R. C., & Ronald, A. R. (1998). Male circumcision: Assessment of health benefits and risks. *Sexually Transmitted Infections, 74*, 368–373.

Mosher, D. L., & MacIan, P. (1994). College men and women respond to X-rated videos intended for male or female audiences: Gender and sexual scripts. *Journal of Sex Research, 31*, 99–118.

Muehlenhard, C. L., Friedman, D. E., & Thomas, C. M. (1985). Is date rape justifiable? The effects of dating activity, who initiated, who paid, and men's attitudes toward women. *Psychology of Women Quarterly, 9*, 297–310.

Mulaikal, R. M., Migeon, C. J., & Rock, J. A. (1987). Fertility rates in female patients with congenital adrenal hyperplasia due to 21-hydroxylase deficiency. *New England Journal of Medicine, 316*, 178–182.

Mulcahy, J. J. (1999). Penile prostheses in the sildenafil era. *Molecular Urology, 3*, 141–146.

Mullen, P. E., Pathé, M., & Purcell, R. (2000). *Stalkers and their victims.* Cambridge University Press.

Murphy, M. R., Checkley, S. A., Seckl, J. R., & Lightman, S. L. (1990). Naloxone inhibits oxytocin release at orgasm in man. *Journal of Clinical Endocrinology and Metabolism, 71*, 1056–1058.

Murray, S. L., & Holmes, J. G. (1999). The (mental) ties that bind: Cognitive structures that predict relationship resilience. *Journal of Personality and Social Psychology, 77*, 1228–1244.

Musgrave, B. (1980). Penis captivus has occurred. *British Medical Journal, 280*, 51.

Mustanski, B. S., Bailey, J. M., & Kaspar, S. (2002). Dermatoglyphics, handedness, sex, and sexual orientation. *Archives of Sexual Behavior, 31*, 113–132.

Nagel, S. C., vom Saal, F. S., Thayer, K. A., Dhar, M. G., Boechler, M., & Welshons, W. V. (1997). Relative binding affinity-serum modified access (RBA-SMA) assay predicts the relative in vivo bioactivity of the xenoestrogens bisphenol A and octylphenol. *Environmental Health Perspectives, 105*, 70–76.

Nanda, S. (1990). *Neither man nor woman: The hijras of India.* Wadsworth.

Nath, J. K., & Nayar, V. R. (1997). India. In R. T. Francoeur (Ed.), *The international encyclopedia of sexuality.* Continuum.

Nation, E. F. (1973). William Osler on penis captivus and other urologic topics. *Urology, 2*, 468–470.

National Cancer Institute. (1992). *Cancer statistics review, 1973–1989.* National Institutes of Health (publication no. 92–2789).

National Cancer Institute. (2001). *Lifetime probability of breast cancer in American women.* Located at http://cis.nci.nih.gov/fact/5_6.htm.

National Coalition against Censorship. (2002). *U.S. Dept. of Justice: Semi-nude statues draped.* Located at http://www.ncac.org/action/alerts.html#DOJ.

National Gay and Lesbian Task Force. (2001). *FBI hate crime data woefully underreports crimes against GLBT people.* Located at http://www.ngltf.org/news/release.cfm?releaseID=368.

National Gay and Lesbian Task Force. (2002). *Hawaii makes 26! For the first time, most states will have hate crime laws covering sexual orientation.* Located at http://www.ngltf.org/news/release.cfm?releaseID=387.

National Institute of Diabetes and Digestive and Kidney Diseases. (2001). *Urinary tract infection in adults.* Located at http://www.niddk.nih.gov/health/urolog/pubs/utiadult/utiadult.htm.

National Institutes of Health. (2001). *Vitamin A and carotenoids.* Located at http://www.cc.nih.gov/ccc/supplements/vita.html.

National Kidney and Urological Diseases Information Clearinghouse. (1998). *Prostate enlargement: Benign prostatic hyperplasia.* Located at http://www.niddk.nih.gov/health/urolog/pubs/prostate/index.htm.

National Library of Medicine. (2001). *Kegel exercises.* Located at http://www.nlm.nih.gov/medlineplus/ency/article/003975.htm.

National Opinion Research Center. (2002). *General social survey.* Located at http://www.icpsr.umich.edu/GSS/.

National Research Council. (1996). *Understanding violence against women.* National Academy Press.

Nef, S., & Parada, L. F. (1999). Cryptorchidism in mice mutant for Insl3. *Nature Genetics, 22*, 295–299.

Nelson, A. (2000). Contraceptive update Y2K: Need for contraception and new contraceptive options. *Clinical Cornerstone, 3*, 48–62.

New, M. I., & Wilson, R. C. (1999). Steroid disorders in children: Congenital adrenal hyperplasia and apparent mineralocorticoid excess. *Proceedings of the National Academy of Sciences of the United States of America, 96*, 12790–12797.

Nicholson, K. G., & Kimura, D. (1996). Sex differences for speech and manual skill. *Perceptual and Motor Skills, 82*, 3–13.

Nicholson, K. L., & Balster, R. L. (2001). GHB: A new and novel drug of abuse. *Drug and Alcohol Dependence, 63*, 1–22.

Nicolosi, J. (1991). *Reparative therapy of male homosexuality: A new clinical approach.* Jason Aronson.

Nielsen Forman, D., Videbech, P., Hedegaard, M., Dalby Salvig, J., & Secher, N. J. (2000). Postpartum depression: Identification of women at risk. *Bjog, 107*, 1210–1217.

Norman, R. L., & Spies, H. G. (1986). Cyclic ovarian function in a male macaque: Additional evidence for a lack of sexual differentiation in the physiological mechanisms that regulate the cyclic release of gonadotropins in primates. *Endocrinology, 118*, 2608–2610.

Norton, R. (1999). *Mother Clap's molly house: The gay subculture in England, 1700–1830*. Heretic Books.

Nosek, M. A., Howland, C. A., Rintala, D. H., Young, M. E., & Chanpong, G. F. (1997). *National study of women with physical disabilities: Final report*. Located at http://www.bcm.tmc.edu/crowd/national_study/national_study.html.

Nossiter, A. (1996). 6-year-old's sex crime: Innocent peck on cheek. *New York Times*, September 27.

Nurnberg, H. G., Hensley, P. L., Lauriello, J., Parker, L. M., & Keith, S. J. (1999). Sildenafil for women patients with antidepressant-induced sexual dysfunction. *Psychiatric Services, 50*, 1076–1078.

Nwokolo, N. C., & Hawkins, D. A. (2001). Postexposure prophylaxis for HIV infection. *The AIDS Reader, 11*, 402–412.

O'Brien, M. (1990). On seeing a sex surrogate. *The Sun*, May. Retrieved from http://www.pacificnews.org/marko/sex-surrogate.html.

O'Carroll, R., & Bancroft, J. (1984). Testosterone therapy for low sexual interest and erectile dysfunction in men: A controlled study. *British Journal of Psychiatry, 145*, 146–151.

O'Connell, H. E., Hutson, J. M., Anderson, C. R., & Plenter, R. J. (1998). Anatomical relationship between urethra and clitoris. *Journal of Urology, 159*, 1892–1897.

Office for National Statistics. (1999). *Marriage and divorce in England and Wales, 1997; Adoptions, 1998*. Located at http://www.statistics.gov.uk/pdfdir/mar1099.pdf.

Office of the Attorney General. (2001). *Registrable sex offenses*. Located at http://caag.state.ca.us/registration/soffenses.htm.

O'Hara, M. W., Zekowski, E. M., Phillips, L. H., & Wright, E. J. (1990). Controlled prospective study of postpartum mood disorders: Comparison of childbearing and non-childbearing women. *Journal of Abnormal Psychology, 99*, 3–15.

Okami, P., Olmstead, R., & Abramson, P. R. (1997). Sexual experiences in early childhood: 18-year longitudinal data from the UCLA Family Lifestyles Project. *Journal of Sex Research, 34*, 339–347.

Okami, P., Olmstead, R., Abramson, P. R., & Pendleton, L. (1998). Early childhood exposure to parental nudity and scenes of parental sexuality ("primal scenes"): An 18-year longitudinal study of outcome. *Archives of Sexual Behavior, 27*, 361–384.

Olds, D. E., & Shaver, P. (1980). Masculinity, femininity, academic performance, and health: Further evidence concerning the androgyny controversy. *Journal of Personality, 48*, 323–341.

O'Leary, C. (2000). *Chicago city council honors Hefner*. Located at http://www.saidit.org/archives/may00/article2.html.

O'Leary, C., & Howard, O. (2001). *The prostitution of women and girls in metropolitan Chicago: A preliminary prevalence report*. Located at http://www.impactresearch.org/documents/39.pdf.

Oliver, M. B., & Hyde, J. S. (1993). Gender differences in sexuality: A meta-analysis. *Psychological Bulletin, 114*, 29–51.

Olsen, O., & Gotzsche, P. C. (2001). Cochrane review on screening for breast cancer with mammography. *Lancet, 358*, 1340–1342.

Oomura, Y., Aou, S., Koyama, Y., Fujita, I., & Yoshimatsu, H. (1988). Central control of sexual behavior. *Brain Research Bulletin, 20*, 863–870.

Orion, D. (1998). *I know you really love me: A psychiatrist's account of stalking and obsessive love*. Dell.

Orion, D. (2001). *The anti-stalking website*. Located at http://www.antistalking.com/Default.htm.

Ornstein, C. (2001). Sharp drops in AIDS may be over. *Los Angeles Times*, August 14.

Oropesa, R. S., & Gorman, B. K. (2000). Ethnicity, immigration, and beliefs about marriage as a "tie that binds." In I. J. Waite, C. Bachrach, M. Hindin, E. Thomson, & A. Thornton (Eds.), *The tie that binds: Perspectives on marriage and cohabitation*. Aldine de Gruyter.

O'Shea, M. N. (1999). Race plays into death penalty use. *Augusta [Georgia] Chronicle*, November 14. Retrieved from http://www.augustachronicle.com/stories/111499/met_201-7827.000.shtml.

Otero, S. (1996). "Fearing our mothers": An overview of the psychoanalytic theories concerning the vagina dentata motif. *American Journal of Psychoanalysis, 56*, 269–288.

O'Toole, A. J., Deffenbacher, K. A., Valentin, D., McKee, K., Huff, D., & Abdi, H. (1998). The perception of face gender: The role of stimulus structure in recognition and classification. *Memory and Cognition, 26*, 146–160.

Ottesen, B., Pedersen, B., Nielsen, J., Dalgaard, D., Wagner, G., & Fahrenkrug, J. (1987). Vasoactive intestinal polypeptide (VIP) provokes vaginal lubrication in normal women. *Peptides, 8*, 797–800.

Owens, M. E., & Todt, E. H. (1984). Pain in infancy: Neonatal reaction to a heel lance. *Pain, 20*, 77–86.

Paglia, C. (1990). *Sexual personae: Art and decadence from Nefertiti to Emily Dickinson*. Yale University Press.

Paglia, C. (1994). *Vamps and tramps: New essays*. Vintage Books.

Palmore, E. B. (1982). Predictors of the longevity difference: A 25-year follow-up. *Gerontologist, 22*, 513–518.

Paludi, M. A. (1996). *Sexual harassment on college campuses: Abusing the ivory power* (Rev. ed.). State University of New York Press.

Pan, P. P. (2002). China's one-child policy now a double standard. *Washington Post*, August 20.

Paolucci, E. O., Genuis, M. L., & Violato, C. (2001). A meta-analysis of the published research on the effects of child sexual abuse. *Journal of Psychology, 135*, 17–36.

Parents Television Council. (2000). *What a difference a decade makes: A comparison of prime-time sex, language, and violence in 1989 and '99*. Located at http://www.parentstv.org/publications/reports/Decadestudy/decadestudy.html.

Parish, A. R., & de Waal, F. B. (2000). The other "closest living relative": How bonobos (*Pan paniscus*) challenge traditional assumptions about females, dominance, intra- and intersexual interactions, and hominid evolution. *Annals of the New York Academy of Sciences, 907*, 97–113.

Parrinder, G. (1996) *Sexual morality in the world's religions*. Oneworld Publications.

Patel, M., & Minshall, L. (2001). Management of sexual assault. *Emergency Medicine Clinics of North America, 19*, 817–831.

Pattatucci, A. M., & Hamer, D. H. (1995). Development and familiality of sexual orientation in females. *Behavior Genetics, 25*, 407–420.

Paulson, R. J., Thornton, M. H., Francis, M. M., & Salvador, H. S. (1997). Successful pregnancy in a 63-year-old woman. *Fertility and Sterility, 67*, 949–951.

Pautler, S. E., & Brock, G. B. (2001). Priapism: From Priapus to the present time. *Urologic Clinics of North America, 28*, 391–403.

Pear, R. (2001). Bush plan allows States to give "unborn child" medical coverage. *New York Times*, July 6. Retrieved from http://www.nytimes.com/2001/07/06/politics/06FETU.html?searchpv=day04.

Penton-Voak, I. S., & Perrett, D. I. (2000). Female preference for male faces change cyclically: Further evidence. *Evolution and Human Behavior, 21*, 39–48.

Peplau, L. A., & Garnets, L. D. (2000). A new paradigm for understanding women's sexuality and sexual orientation. *Journal of Social Issues, 56*, 329–350.

Peplau, L. A., Spalding, L. R., Conley, T. D., & Veniegas, R. C. (1999). The development of sexual orientation in women. *Annual Review of Sex Research, 10,* 70–99.

Perkel, M. (2000). *How to use escort services: A men's guide.* Located at http://sex.perkel.com/escort/index.htm.

Perkins, A., Fitzgerald, J. A., & Moss, G. E. (1995). A comparison of LH secretion and brain estradiol receptors in heterosexual and homosexual rams and female sheep. *Hormones and Behavior, 29,* 31–41.

Perper, T. (1985). *Sex signals: The biology of love.* ISI Press.

Perrett, D. I., May, K. A., & Yoshikawa, S. (1994). Facial shape and judgements of female attractiveness. *Nature, 368,* 239–242.

Persson, G. (1981). Five-year mortality in a 70-year-old urban population in relation to psychiatric diagnosis, personality, sexuality and early parental death. *Acta Psychiatrica Scandinavica, 64,* 244–253.

Petrocelli, W., & Repa, B. K. (1999). *Sexual harassment on the job: What it is and how to stop it* (4th ed.). Nolo Press.

Pfaff, D. W., Vasudevan, N., Kia, H. K., Zhu, Y. S., Chan, J., Garey, J., Morgan, M., & Ogawa, S. (2000). Estrogens, brain and behavior: Studies in fundamental neurobiology and observations related to women's health. *Journal of Steroid Biochemistry and Molecular Biology, 74,* 365–373.

Pfeifer, K. (2000). Mechanisms of genomic imprinting. *American Journal of Human Genetics, 67,* 777–787.

Pharr, S. (1993). Homophobia: A weapon of sexism. *SIECUS Report,* February/March 1993. Retrieved from http://www.cyfc.umn.edu/Diversity/Gay/siecus.html.

Phillips, S., King, S., & DuBois, L. (1978). Spontaneous activities of female versus male newborns. *Child Development, 49,* 590–597.

Phoenix, C. H., Goy, R. W., Gerall, A. A., & Young, W. C. (1959). Organizing action of prenatally administered testosterone propionate on the tissues mediating mating behavior in the female guinea pig. *Endocrinology, 65,* 369–382.

Piaggio, G., von Hertzen, H., Grimes, D. A., & Van Look, P. F. (1999). Timing of emergency contraception with levonorgestrel or the Yuzpe regimen. Task Force on Postovulatory Methods of Fertility Regulation. *Lancet, 353,* 721.

Piccinino, L. J., & Mosher, W. D. (1998). Trends in contraceptive use in the United States: 1982–1995. *Family Planning Perspectives, 30,* 4–10, 46.

Pincus, J. H. (2001). *Base instincts: What makes killers kill?* W.W. Norton.

Pinsky, L., Erickson, R. P., & Schimke, R. N. (1999). *Genetic disorders of human sexual development.* Oxford: Oxford University Press.

Piper, C. J. (1997). Is there a place for traditional midwives in the provision of community-health services? *Annals of Tropical Medicine and Parasitology, 91,* 237–245.

Planned Parenthood Federation. (2000). *Margaret Sanger.* Located at http://www.plannedparenthood.com/about/thisispp/sanger.html.

Planned Parenthood Federation. (2002). *The Equity in Prescription Insurance and Contraceptive Coverage Act.* Located at http://www.plannedparenthood.org/LIBRARY/BIRTHCONTROL/equity.html.

Plomin, R., DeFries, J., McClearn, G. E., & McGuffin, P. (Eds.) (2001). *Behavioral Genetics.* Freeman.

Plous, S. (2002). *Social psychology network.* Located at http://www.socialpsychology.org/.

Polak, M., & Trivers, R. (1994). The science of symmetry in biology. *Trends in Ecology and Evolution, 9,* 122–124.

Polaschek, D. L., Ward, T., & Hudson, S. M. (1997). Rape and rapists: Theory and treatment. *Clinical Psychology Review, 17,* 117–144.

Pollack, H. A. (2001). Sudden infant death syndrome, maternal smoking during pregnancy, and the cost-effectiveness of smoking cessation intervention. *American Journal of Public Health, 91,* 432–436.

Pomerantz, S. M., Goy, R. W., & Roy, M. M. (1986). Expression of male-typical behavior in adult female pseudohermaphroditic rhesus: Comparisons with normal males and neonatally gonadectomized males and females. *Hormones and Behavior, 20,* 483–500.

Pomerleau, A., Bolduc, D., Malcuit, G., & Cossette, L. (1990). Pink or blue: Environmental gender stereotypes in the first two years of life. *Sex Roles, 22,* 359–367.

Posner, R. A. (1989). An economic analysis of sex discrimination laws. *University of Chicago Law Review, 65,* 1311–1335.

Posner, R. A. (1992). *Sex and reason.* Harvard University Press.

Posner, R. A. (1998). *Economic analysis of law* (5th ed.). Aspen Publishers.

Posner, R. A., & Silbaugh, K. B. (1996). *A guide to America's sex laws.* University of Chicago Press.

Potter, L., Oakley, D., de Leon-Wong, E., & Canamar, R. (1996). Measuring compliance among oral contraceptive users. *Family Planning Perspectives, 28,* 154–158.

Powdermaker, H. (1933). *Life in Lesu: The study of a Melanesian society in New Ireland.* Norton.

Prentky, R. A. (1997). Arousal reduction in sexual offenders: A review of antiandrogen interventions. *Sexual Abuse, 9,* 335–348.

Prentky, R. A., Knight, R. A., & Lee, A. F. (1997). Risk factors associated with recidivism among extrafamilial child molesters. *Journal of Consulting and Clinical Psychology, 65,* 141–149.

Presbyterian Church (U.S.A.). (1998). *Older youth guide.* Presbyterian Distribution Service.

Price, J. H., Allensworth, D. D., & Hillman, K. S. (1985). Comparison of sexual fantasies of homosexuals and of heterosexuals. *Psychological Reports, 57,* 871–877.

Prostitutes Education Network. (2001a). *International committee for prostitutes' rights: World charter for prostitutes' rights.* Located at http://www.bayswan.org/ICPRChart.html.

Prostitutes Education Network. (2001b). *Prostitution in the United States: The statistics.* Located at http://www.bayswan.org/stats.html.

Pryor, J. B., & McKinney, K. (Eds.) (1995). *Research advances in sexual harassment.* Lawrence Erlbaum Associates.

Quigley, C. A., De Bellis, A., Marschke, K. B., el-Awady, M. K., Wilson, E. M., & French, F. S. (1995). Androgen receptor defects: Historical, clinical, and molecular perspectives. *Endocrine Reviews, 16,* 271–321.

Quinsey, V. L., & Lalumière, M. L. (2001). *Assessment of sex offenders against children* (2nd ed.). Sage Publications.

Quinsey, V. L., Lalumière, M. L., Rice, M. E., & Harris, G. T. (1995). Predicting sexual offenses. In J. C. Campbell (Ed.), *Assessing dangerousness: Violence by sexual offenders, batterers, and child abusers.* Sage.

Quittner, J. (2001). Death of a two spirit. *Advocate,* August 28.

Rahman, M., Alam, A., Nessa, K., Nahar, S., Dutta, D. K., Yasmin, L., Monira, S., Sultan, Z., Khan, S. A., & Albert, M. J. (2001). Treatment failure with the use of ciprofloxacin for gonorrhea correlates with the prevalence of fluoroquinolone-resistant *Neisseria gonorrhoeae* strains in Bangladesh. *Clinical Infectious Diseases, 32,* 884–889.

Rand, K. H., Hoon, E. F., Massey, J. K., & Johnson, J. H. (1990). Daily stress and recurrence of genital herpes simplex. *Archives of Internal Medicine, 150,* 1889–1893.

Rao, S., Joshi, S., & Kanade, A. (1998). Height velocity, body fat and menarcheal age of Indian girls. *Indian Pediatrics, 35,* 619–628.

Rapaport, K. R., & Posey, C. D. (1991). Sexually coercive college males. In A. Parrot (Ed.), *Acquaintance rape: The hidden crime.* Wiley.

Rauch, S. L., Shin, L. M., Dougherty, D. D., Alpert, N. M., Orr, S. P., Lasko, M., Macklin, M. L., Fischman, A. J., & Pitman, R. K. (1999). Neural activation during sexual and competitive arousal in healthy men. *Psychiatry Research, 91,* 1–10.

Raymond, J. G. (1995). Prostitution is rape that's paid for. *New York Times,* December 11.

Reamy, K. J., & White, S. E. (1987). Sexuality in the puerperium: A review. *Archives of Sexual Behavior, 16,* 165–186.

Redmond, G., Godwin, A. J., Olson, W., & Lippman, J. S. (1999). Use of placebo controls in an oral contraceptive trial: Methodological issues and adverse event incidence. *Contraception, 60,* 81–85.

Redouté, J., Stoleru, S., Gregoire, M. C., Costes, N., Cinotti, L., Lavenne, F., Le Bars, D., Forest, M. G., & Pujol, J. F. (2000). Brain processing of visual sexual stimuli in human males. *Human Brain Mapping, 11,* 162–177.

Regan, M. M., Emond, S. K., Attardo, M. J., Parker, R. A., & Greenspan, S. L. (2001). Why do older women discontinue hormone replacement therapy? *Journal of Women's Health and Gender Based Medicine, 10,* 343–350.

Regehr, C., Cadell, S., & Jansen, K. (1999). Perceptions of control and long-term recovery from rape. *American Journal of Orthopsychiatry, 69,* 110–115.

Reilly, P. R., & Grob, G. N. (1991). *The surgical solution: A history of involuntary sterilization in the United States.* Johns Hopkins University Press.

Reisberg, L. (1998). Disparities grow in SAT scores of ethnic and racial groups. *The Chronicle of Higher Education,* 11 September.

Reiss, I. L. (1986). *Journey into sexuality: An exploratory voyage.* Prentice-Hall.

Reiss, I. L., & Miller, B. C. (1979). Heterosexual permissiveness: A theoretical analysis. *Journal of Marriage and the Family, 42,* 395–410.

Reitman, V. (2001). Officer held as Japan moves to stem child pornography. *Los Angeles Times,* January 25.

Remez, L. (2000). Oral sex among adolescents: Is it sex or is it abstinence? *Family Planning Perspectives, 32.*

Resnick, A., Perry, W., Parry, B., Mostofi, N., & Udell, C. (1998). Neuropsychological performance across the menstrual cycle in women with and without Premenstrual Dysphoric Disorder. *Psychiatry Research, 77,* 147–158.

Resnick, H. S., Acierno, R., & Kilpatrick, D. G. (1997). Health impact of interpersonal violence: 2. Medical and mental health outcomes. *Behavioral Medicine, 23,* 65–78.

Resnick, H. S., Holmes, M. M., Kilpatrick, D. G., Clum, G., Acierno, R., Best, C. L., & Saunders, B. E. (2000). Predictors of post-rape medical care in a national sample of women. *American Journal of Preventive Medicine, 19,* 214–219.

Reuters News Service. (1998). *U.N. body urges governments to recognize sex trade.* Located at http://www.whoreact.net/undecrim.html.

Reuters News Service. (2001a). British surrogate mom sues in abortion dispute. Located at http://www.eclj.org/news/euro_news_010813_british.asp.

Reuters News Service. (2001b). Nigerian woman lashed for premarital sex. *New York Times,* January 23.

Reverby, S. M. (1997). History of an apology: From Tuskegee to the White House. *Research Practitioner,* July/August. Retrieved from http://www.researchpractice.com/archive/apology.shtml.

Reynolds, M. (2002). Kandahar's lightly veiled homosexual habits. *Los Angeles Times,* April 3.

Reznikov, A. G., Nosenko, N. D., & Tarasenko, L. V. (1999). Prenatal stress and glucocorticoid effects on the developing gender-related brain. *Journal of Steroid Biochemistry and Molecular Biology, 69,* 109–115.

Rheingold, H. (1992). *Virtual reality.* Touchstone Books.

Rice, G., Anderson, C., Risch, N., & Ebers, G. (1999). Male homosexuality: Absence of linkage to microsatellite markers at Xq28. *Science, 284,* 665–667.

Rich, A. (1986). *Blood, bread, and poetry: Selected prose, 1979–1985.* W.W. Norton.

Richardson, J. (1995). The science and politics of gay teen suicide. *Harvard Review of Psychiatry, 3,* 107–110.

Rikowski, A., & Grammer, K. (1999). Human body odour, symmetry and attractiveness. *Proceedings of the Royal Society of London. Series B: Biological Sciences, 266,* 869–874.

Rind, B. (2001). Gay and bisexual adolescent boys' sexual experiences with men: An empirical examination of psychological correlates in a nonclinical sample. *Archives of Sexual Behavior, 30,* 345–368.

Rind, B., Tromovitch, P., & Bauserman, R. (1998). A meta-analytic examination of assumed properties of child sexual abuse using college samples. *Psychological Bulletin, 124,* 22–53.

Ringash, J. (2001). Preventive health care, 2001 update: Screening mammography among women aged 40–49 years at average risk of breast cancer. *CMAJ, 164,* 469–476.

Roberts, S. A., Dibble, S. L., Scanlon, J. L., Paul, S. M., & Davids, H. (1998). Differences in risk factors for breast cancer: Lesbian and heterosexual women. *Journal of the Gay and Lesbian Medical Association, 2,* 93–102.

Robinson, B. (2002). *A harmful message? New book on child sex sparks uproar.* Located at http://abcnews.go.com/sections/us/DailyNews/childsex_book020405.html.

Robson, K. M., Brant, H. A., & Kumar, R. (1981). Maternal sexuality during first pregnancy and after childbirth. *British Journal of Obstetrics and Gynaecology, 88,* 882–889.

Rogge, R. D., & Bradbury, T. N. (1999). Till violence does us part: The differing roles of communication and aggression in predicting adverse marital outcomes. *Journal of Consulting and Clinical Psychology, 67,* 340–351.

Rohrlich, T. (2000). McMartin case's legal, social legacies linger. *Los Angeles Times,* December 18.

Rojanapithayakorn, W., & Hanenberg, R. (1996). The 100% condom program in Thailand. *AIDS, 10,* 1–7.

Rooth, F. G. (1973). Exhibitionism outside Europe and America. *Archives of Sexual Behavior, 2,* 351–163.

Rose, S., & Frieze, I. H. (1993). Young singles' contemporary dating scripts. *Sex Roles, 28,* 499–509.

Rosen, R., Goldstein, I., & Padma-Nathan, H. (Eds.) (1998). *A process of care model: Evaluation and treatment of erectile dysfunction.* UMDNJ-Robert Wood Johnson Medical School.

Rosenblatt, J. S. (1994). Psychobiology of maternal behavior: Contribution to the clinical understanding of maternal behavior among humans. *Acta Paediatrica* (Supplement), *397,* 3–8.

Rosenthal, R. (1991). *Meta-analytic procedures for social research.* Sage.

Rosing, M. T. (1999). 13C-depleted carbon microparticles in >3700-Ma sea-floor sedimentary rocks from west Greenland. *Science, 283,* 674–676.

Rosman, J. P., & Resnick, P. J. (1989). Sexual attraction to corpses: A psychiatric review of necrophilia. *Bulletin of the American Academy of Psychiatry and the Law, 17,* 153–163.

Ross, J., Zinn, A., & McCauley, E. (2000). Neurodevelopmental and psychosocial aspects of Turner syndrome. *Mental Retardation and Developmental Disabilities Research Reviews, 6,* 135–141.

Rothschild, A. J. (2000). New directions in the treatment of antidepressant-induced sexual dysfunction. *Clinical Therapeutics, 22,* A42–57.

Rothschild, B. M., Calderon, F. L., Coppa, A., & Rothschild, C. (2000). First European exposure to syphilis: The Dominican Republic at the time of Columbian contact. *Clinical Infectious Diseases, 31,* 936–941.

Roumen, F. J., Apter, D., Mulders, T. M., & Dieben, T. O. (2001). Efficacy, tolerability and acceptability of a novel contraceptive vaginal ring releasing etonogestrel and ethinyl oestradiol. *Human Reproduction, 16,* 469–475.

Rovet, J., & Netley, C. (1983). The triple X chromosome syndrome in childhood: Recent empirical findings. *Child Development, 54,* 831–845.

Rovet, J., Netley, C., Keenan, M., Bailey, J., & Stewart, D. (1996). The psychoeducational profile of boys with Klinefelter syndrome. *Journal of Learning Disabilities, 29,* 180–196.

Rowland, D. L., Cooper, S. E., & Schneider, M. (2001). Defining premature ejaculation for experimental and clinical investigations. *Archives of Sexual Behavior, 30,* 235–253.

Rowland, D. L., Haensel, S. M., Blom, J. H., & Slob, A. K. (1993). Penile sensitivity in men with premature ejaculation and erectile dysfunction. *Journal of Sex and Marital Therapy, 19,* 189–197.

Rowland, J. H., Holland, J. C., Chaglassian, T., & Kinne, D. (1993). Psychological response to breast reconstruction: Expectations for and impact on postmastectomy functioning. *Psychosomatics, 34,* 241–250.

Rubin, A. J. (2000). Public more accepting of gays, poll finds. *Los Angeles Times,* June 18.

Ruble, D. N., & Martin, C. L. (1997). Gender development. In Eisenberg, N. (Ed.), *Handbook of child psychology: Vol. 3* (5th ed.). Wiley.

Ruse, M. (1988). *Homosexuality: A philosophical inquiry.* Blackwell.

Russell, D. E. H. (1984). *Sexual exploitation: Rape, child sexual abuse, and workplace harassment.* Sage.

Russell, D. E. H. (1994). *Against pornography: The evidence of harm.* Russell Publications.

Rust, J., Golombok, S., Hines, M., Johnston, K., & Golding, J. (2000). The role of brothers and sisters in the gender development of preschool children. *Journal of Experimental Child Psychology, 77,* 292–303.

Rust, P. C. R. (ed.). (2000). *Bisexuality in the United States: A social science reader.* Columbia University Press.

Rutter, M. (1971). Normal psychosexual development. *Journal of Child Psychology and Psychiatry, 11,* 259–283.

Ryan, A. S. (1997). The resurgence of breastfeeding in the United States. *Pediatrics, 99,* E12.

Sacher-Masoch, L. von. (2000). *Venus in furs.* Viking Penguin.

Sade, Marquis de. (1976). *The 120 days of Sodom, and other writings.* Grove/Atlantic.

Sadowsky, M., Antonovsky, H., Sobel, R., & Maoz, B. (1993). Sexual activity and sex hormone levels in aging men. *International Psychogeriatrics, 5,* 181–186.

Saguy, A. C. (2002). *Puritanism and promiscuity: Sexual attitudes in France and the United States.* Located at http://www.princeton.edu/~sociolog/pdf/asmith1.pdf.

Saidi, J. A., Chang, D. T., Goluboff, E. T., Bagiella, E., Olsen, G., & Fisch, H. (1999). Declining sperm counts in the United States? A critical review. *Journal of Urology, 161,* 460–462.

Saint, L., Smith, M., & Hartmann, P. E. (1984). The yield and nutrient content of colostrum and milk of women from giving birth to 1 month post-partum. *British Journal of Nutrition, 52,* 87–95.

Sainz, B., Loutsch, J. M., Marquart, M. E., & Hill, J. M. (2001). Stress-associated immunomodulation and herpes simplex virus infections. *Medical Hypotheses, 56,* 348–356.

Salo, P., Kaariainen, H., Page, D. C., & de la Chapelle, A. (1995). Deletion mapping of stature determinants on the long arm of the Y chromosome. *Human Genetics, 95,* 283–286.

Samal, P. K., Farber, C., Farooque, N. A., & Rawat, D. S. (1997). Polyandry in a central Himalayan community: An eco-cultural analysis. *Man in India, 76,* 51–56.

Samois (Ed.) (1987). *Coming to power: Writings and graphics on lesbian S/M* (3rd ed.). Alyson.

Samuels, C. A., Butterworth, G., Roberts, T., Graupner, L., & Hole, G. (1994). Facial aesthetics: Babies prefer attractiveness to symmetry. *Perception, 23,* 823–831.

San Francisco Lesbian and Gay History Project. (1989). "She even chewed tobacco": A pictorial narrative of passing women in America. In M. Duberman, M. Vicinus, & G. Chauncey, Jr. (Eds.), *Hidden from history: Reclaiming the gay and lesbian past.* Meridian Books.

Sanders, S. A., & Reinisch, J. M. (1999). Would you say you "had sex" if … ? *JAMA, 281,* 275–277.

Sanderson, M., Williams, M. A., Daling, J. R., Holt, V. L., Malone, K. E., Self, S. G., & Moore, D. E. (1998). Maternal factors and breast cancer risk among young women. *Paediatric and Perinatal Epidemiology, 12,* 397–407.

Sandfort, T. G. M., Brongersma, E., & Naerssen, A. X. (1991). *Male intergenerational intimacy: Historical, socio-psychological, and legal perspectives.* Harrington Park Press.

Sandomir, R. (1997). Judge gives Marv Albert option to avoid jail. *New York Times,* October 25.

Sarrel, P., Dobay, B., & Wiita, B. (1998). Estrogen and estrogen-androgen replacement in postmenopausal women dissatisfied with estrogen-only therapy: Sexual behavior and neuroendocrine responses. *Journal of Reproductive Medicine, 43,* 847–856.

Savin-Williams, R. C. (2001a). *Mom, Dad, I'm gay: How families negotiate coming out.* American Psychological Association.

Savin-Williams, R. C. (2001b). Suicide attempts among sexual-minority youths: Population and measurement issues. *Journal of Consulting and Clinical Psychology, 69,* 983–991.

Sayle, A. E., Savitz, D. A., Thorp, J. M., Jr., Hertz-Picciotto, I., & Wilcox, A. J. (2001). Sexual activity during late pregnancy and risk of preterm delivery. *Obstetrics and Gynecology, 97,* 283–289.

Schain, W. S. (1988). The sexual and intimate consequences of breast cancer treatment. *CA: A Cancer Journal for Clinicians, 38,* 154–161.

Schairer, C., Lubin, J., Troisi, R., Sturgeon, S., Brinton, L., & Hoover, R. (2000). Menopausal estrogen and estrogen-progestin replacement therapy and breast cancer risk. *JAMA, 283,* 485–491.

Schank, J. C. (2000). Menstrual-cycle variability and measurement: Further cause for doubt. *Psychoneuroendocrinology, 25,* 837–847.

Scheib, J. E., Gangestad, S. W., & Thornhill, R. (1999). Facial attractiveness, symmetry and cues of good genes. *Proceedings of the Royal Society of London. Series B, 266,* 1913–1917.

Schewe, P. A. (ed.). (2002). *Preventing violence in relationships: Interventions across the lifespan.* American Psychological Association.

Schiavi, R. C., Schreiner-Engel, P., White, D., & Mandeli, J. (1991). The relationship between pituitary-gonadal function and sexual behavior in healthy aging men. *Psychosomatic Medicine, 53,* 363–374.

Schmid, D. M., Schurch, B., & Hauri, D. (2000). Sildenafil in the treatment of sexual dysfunction in spinal cord-injured male patients. *European Urology, 38,* 184–193.

Schmidt, G. (Ed.) (2000). *Kinder der sexuellen Revolution.* Psychosozial-Verlag.

Schmidt, H. (1998). Supernumerary nipples: Prevalence, size, sex and side predilection: A prospective clinical study. *European Journal of Pediatrics, 157,* 821–823.

Schmidt, P. J., Nieman, L. K., Danaceau, M. A., Adams, L. F., & Rubinow, D. R. (1998). Differential behavioral effects of gonadal steroids in women with and in those without premenstrual syndrome. *New England Journal of Medicine, 338,* 209–216.

Schneider, A., & Barber, M. (1998). Lives ruined because lessons ignored. *Seattle Post-Intelligencer,* February 27. Retrieved from http://seattlep-i.nwsource.com/powertoharm/context.html.

Schnyder, U., Schnyder-Luthi, C., Ballinari, P., & Blaser, A. (1998). Therapy for vaginismus: In vivo versus in vitro desensitization. *Canadian Journal of Psychiatry. Revue Canadienne de Psychiatrie, 43,* 941–944.

Schothorst, P. F., & van Engeland, H. (1996). Long-term behavioral sequelae of prematurity. *Journal of the American Academy of Child and Adolescent Psychiatry, 35,* 175–183.

Schubach, G. (1996). *Urethral expulsions during sensual arousal and bladder catheterization in seven human females.* Ed.D. thesis, Institute for Advanced Study of Human Sexuality.

Schultz, W. W., van Andel, P., Sabelis, I., & Mooyaart, E. (1999). Magnetic resonance imaging of male and female genitals during coitus and female sexual arousal. *BMJ, 319,* 1596–1600.

Schumm, W. R., Webb, F. J., & Bollman, S. R. (1998). Gender and marital satisfaction: Data from the National Survey of Families and Households. *Psychological Reports, 83,* 319–327.

Schuster, M. A., Bell, R. M., Nakajima, G. A., & Kanouse, D. E. (1998). The sexual practices of Asian and Pacific Islander high school students. *Journal of Adolescent Health, 23,* 221–231.

Schwebke, J. R. (2000). Bacterial vaginosis. *Current Infectious Disease Reports, 2,* 14–17.

Schweder, R. A. (2000). What about "female genital mutilation"? And why understanding culture matters in the first place. *Daedalus,* Fall.

Screponi, E., Carosa, E., Di Stasi, S. M., Pepe, M., Carruba, G., & Jannini, E. A. (2001). Prevalence of chronic prostatitis in men with premature ejaculation. *Urology, 58,* 198–202.

Scully, D. (1990). *Understanding sexual violence: A study of convicted rapists.* Unwin Hyman.

Sears, J. T., & Williams, W. L. (Eds.) (1997). *Overcoming heterosexism and homophobia: Strategies that work.* Columbia University Press.

Sedgwick, E. K. (1990). *Epistemology of the closet.* University of California Press.

Seibert, D. C. (2000). Hormone replacement therapy. *Nurse Practitioner Forum, 11,* 225–237.

Self Defense for Life. (2001). *Physical education program outline.* Located at http://www.selfdefenseforlife.com/program%20outline.htm.

Seligman, M. E. P. (1995). The effectiveness of psychotherapy: The *Consumer Reports* study. *American Psychologist, 50,* 965–974.

Senn, C. Y., & Radtke, H. L. (1990). Women's evaluations of and affective reactions to mainstream violent pornography, nonviolent pornography, and erotica. *Violence and Victims, 5,* 143–155.

Serbin, L. A., Moller, L. C., Gulko, J., Powlishta, K. K., & Colburne, K. A. (1994). The emergence of gender segregation in toddler playgroups. *New Directions for Child Development,* 7–17.

Seto, M. C., Lalumière, M. L., & Kuban, M. (1999). The sexual preferences of incest offenders. *Journal of Abnormal Psychology, 108,* 267–272.

Sexton, W. J., Benedict, J. F., & Jarow, J. P. (1998). Comparison of long-term outcomes of penile prostheses and intracavernosal injection therapy. *Journal of Urology, 159,* 811–815.

Sexual Assault Crisis Center of Knoxville. (2001). *What is sexual assault?* Located at http://www.cs.utk.edu/~bartley/sacc/whatIsSA.html.

Shackelford, T. K., & Larsen, R. J. (1997). Facial asymmetry as an indicator of psychological, emotional, and physiological distress. *Journal of Personality and Social Psychology, 72,* 456–466.

Shafik, A. (1998). The mechanism of ejaculation: The glans-vasal and urethromuscular reflexes. *Archives of Andrology, 41,* 71–78.

Shangold, M. M., Kelly, M., Berkeley, A. S., Freedman, K. S., & Groshen, S. (1989). Relationship between menarcheal age and adult height. *Southern Medical Journal, 82,* 443–445.

Sharpe, R. M. (1997). Do males rely on female hormones? *Nature, 390,* 447–448.

Shell-Duncan, B., & Hernlund, Y. (Eds.) (2000). *Female "circumcision" in Africa: Culture, controversy, and change.* Lynne Rienner.

Shepher, J. (1971). Mate selection among second generation kibbutz adolescents and adults: Incest avoidance and negative imprinting. *Archives of Sexual Behavior, 1,* 293–307.

Sherwin, B. B., & Gelfand, M. M. (1987). The role of androgen in the maintenance of sexual functioning in oophorectomized women. *Psychosomatic Medicine, 49,* 397–409.

Shilts, R. (1982). *The mayor of Castro Street: The life and times of Harvey Milk.* St. Martin's Press.

Shilts, R. (1987). *And the band played on: Politics, people, and the AIDS epidemic.* St. Martin's Press.

Shimonaka, Y., Nakazato, K., Kawaai, C., & Sato, S. (1997). Androgyny and successful adaptation across the life span among Japanese adults. *Journal of Genetic Psychology, 158,* 389–400.

Shively, C. (1986). Walt Whitman and Bill Duckett: Man/boy lovers. *NAMBLA Bulletin,* May. Retrieved from http://www.nambla.de/whitman.htm.

Shostak, M. (2000). *Nisa: The life and words of a !Kung woman.* Harvard University Press.

Shuttle, P., & Redgrove, P. (1999). *The wise wound: Menstruation and everywoman.* Marion Boyars.

Siegel, L., & Olson, N. L. (Eds.) (2001). *Out of the closet, into our hearts: Celebrating our gay family members.* Leyland.

Sigel, L. Z. (2000). Filth in the wrong people's hands: Postcards and the expansion of pornography in Britain and the Atlantic world, 1880–1914. *Journal of Social History, 33,* 859–885.

Silverman, I., & Eals, M. (1992). Sex differences in spatial abilities: Evolutionary theory and data. In J. H. Barkow, L. Cosmides, & J. Tooby (Eds.), *The adapted mind.* Oxford University Press.

Silverman, J. G., Raj, A., Mucci, L. A., & Hathaway, J. E. (2001). Dating violence against adolescent girls and associated substance use, unhealthy weight control, sexual risk behavior, pregnancy, and suicidality. *JAMA, 286,* 572–579.

Silverstein, C., & Picano, F. (1992). *The new joy of gay sex.* HarperCollins.

Silverstein, J. L. (1989). Origins of psychogenic vaginismus. *Psychotherapy and Psychosomatics, 52,* 197–204.

Simon, S. (2002). AIDS scare at tiny college shakes town. *Los Angeles Times,* April 30.

Simon, W., & Gagnon, J. H. (1986). Sexual scripts: Permanence and change. *Archives of Sexual Behavior, 15,* 97–120.

Simon, W., & Gagnon, J. H. (1987). A sexual scripts approach. In J. H. Geer & W. T. O'Donohue (Eds.), *Theories of human sexuality.* Plenum Press.

Simons, G. L. (1984). *The illustrated book of sexual records.* Bell.

Simons, J. S., & Carey, M. P. (2001). Prevalence of sexual dysfunctions: Results from a decade of research. *Archives of Sexual Behavior, 30,* 177–219.

Simpson, J. A. (1986). The association between romantic love and marriage. *Personality and Social Psychology Bulletin, 12,* 363–372.

Sinclair, A. H., Berta, P., Palmer, M. S., Hawkins, J. R., Griffiths, B. L., Smith, M. J., Foster, J. W., Frischauf, A. M., Lovell-Badge, R., & Goodfellow, P. N. (1990). A gene from the human sex-determining region encodes a protein with homology to a conserved DNA-binding motif. *Nature, 346,* 240–244.

Singer, J., & Singer, I. (1972). Types of female orgasm. *Journal of Sex Research, 8,* 255–267.

Singh, D. (1994a). Ideal female body shape: Role of body weight and waist-to-hip ratio. *International Journal of Eating Disorders, 16,* 283–288.

Singh, D. (1994b). Waist-to-hip ratio and judgment of attractiveness and healthiness of female figures by male and female physicians. *International Journal of Obesity and Related Metabolic Disorders, 18,* 731–737.

Singh, D. (1995). Female judgment of male attractiveness and desirability for relationships: Role of waist-to-hip ratio and financial status. *Journal of Personality and Social Psychology, 69,* 1089–1101.

Sipski, M. L., & Alexander, C. J. (Eds.). (1997). *Sexual function in people with disability and chronic illness: A health professional's guide.* Aspen Publications.

Sipski, M. L., Alexander, C. J., & Rosen, R. (2001). Sexual arousal and orgasm in women: Effects of spinal cord injury. *Annals of Neurology, 49,* 35–44.

Skjaerven, R., Wilcox, A. J., & Lie, R. T. (1999). A population-based study of survival and childbearing among female subjects with birth defects and the risk of recurrence in their children. *New England Journal of Medicine, 340,* 1057–1062.

Sloan, P. (1996). Underwear ads caught in bind over sex appeal. *Advertising Age,* July 8.

Small, M. F. (1988). Female primate sexual behavior and conception: Are there really sperm to spare? *Current Anthropology, 29,* 81–100.

Smith, A. D. (2001). Where men love big women. *Marie Claire,* September.

Smith, E. A., Borgerhoff Mulder, M., & Hill, K. (2001). Controversies in the evolutionary social sciences: A guide for the perplexed. *Trends in Ecology and Evolution, 16,* 128–135.

Smith, M. W., Dean, M., Carrington, M., Winkler, C., Huttley, G. A., Lomb, D. A., Goedert, J. J., O'Brien, T. R., Jacobson, L. P., Kaslow, R., Buchbinder, S., Vittinghoff, E., Vlahov, D., Hoots, K., Hilgartner, M. W., & O'Brien, S. J. (1997). Contrasting genetic influence of CCR2 and CCR5 variants on HIV-1 infection and disease progression. Hemophilia Growth and Development Study (HGDS), Multicenter AIDS Cohort Study (MACS), Multicenter Hemophilia Cohort Study (MHCS), San Francisco City Cohort (SFCC), ALIVE Study. *Science, 277,* 959–965.

Smith, S. M. (1988). Extra-pair copulation in black-capped chickadees: The role of the female. *Behaviour, 107,* 15–23.

Smith, T. D., & Bhatnagar, K. P. (2000). The human vomeronasal organ: Part II. Prenatal development. *Journal of Anatomy, 197* (Pt. 3), 421–436.

Smithsonian Institution. (2002). *Our primate origins: An introduction.* Located at http://www.mnh.si.edu/anthro/humanorigins/ha/primate.html.

Smock, P. J. (1993). The economic costs of marital disruption for young women over the past two decades. *Demography, 30,* 353–371.

Socarides, C. W. (1995). *Homosexuality: A freedom too far.* Adam Margrave Books.

Sommer, F., Konig, D., Graft, C., Schwarzer, U., Bertram, C., Klotz, T., & Engelmann, U. (2001). Impotence and genital numbness in cyclists. *International Journal of Sports Medicine, 22,* 410–413.

Sonfield, A., & Gold, R. B. (2001). States' implementation of the Section 510 abstinence education program, FY 1999. *Family Planning Perspectives, 33,* 166–171.

Spalding, L. R., & Peplau, L. A. (1997). The unfaithful lover: Heterosexuals' stereotypes of bisexuals and their relationships. *Psychology of Women Quarterly, 21,* 611–625.

Spector, I. P., & Fremeth, S. M. (1996). Sexual behaviors and attitudes of geriatric residents in long-term care facilities. *Journal of Sex and Marital Therapy, 22,* 235–246.

Spence, J. T., & Helmreich, R. L. (1978). *Masculinity and femininity: Their psychological dimensions, correlates, and antecedents.* University of Texas Press.

Spohn, C., & Horney, J. (1992). *Rape law reform: A grassroots movement and its impact.* Plenum.

St. Lawrence, J. S., Brasfield, T. L., Jefferson, K. W., Alleyne, E., O'Bannon, R. E., III, & Shirley, A. (1995). Cognitive-behavioral intervention to reduce African American adolescents' risk for HIV infection. *Journal of Consulting and Clinical Psychology, 63,* 221–237.

St. Paul Police. (2002). *This week's prostitution arrest photographs.* Located at http://www.stpaul.gov/depts/police/prostitution_photos_current.html.

Stacey, J., & Biblarz, T. J. (2001). (How) does the sexual orientation of parents matter? *American Sociological Review,* April. Retrieved from http://www.asanet.org/pubs/stacey.pdf.

Stack, S., & Gundlach, J. H. (1992). Divorce and sex. *Archives of Sexual Behavior, 21,* 359–367.

Stammer, L. B., & Lobdell, W. (2002). Mahony ousts priests in sex abuse cases. *Los Angeles Times,* March 4.

Stavis, P. F. (1991). *Sexual activity and the law of consent.* Located at http://www.cqc.state.ny.us/cc50.htm.

Stavnezer, A. J., McDowell, C. S., Hyde, L. A., Bimonte, H. A., Balogh, S. A., Hoplight, B. J., & Denenberg, V. H. (2000). Spatial ability of XY sex-reversed female mice. *Behavioural Brain Research, 112,* 135–143.

Steadman, M. (1969). How sexy illustrations affect brand name recall. *Journal of Advertising, 9,* 15–19.

Stein, M. D., Freedberg, K. A., Sullivan, L. M., Savetsky, J., Levenson, S. M., Hingson, R., & Samet, J. H. (1998). Sexual ethics: Disclosure of HIV-positive status to partners. *Archives of Internal Medicine, 158,* 253–257.

Stein, N. (1999). *Incidence and implications of sexual harassment in K-12 schools.* Located at http://www.hamfish.org/pub/nan.pdf.

Steinberg, L. (2002). *Adolescence* (6th ed.). McGraw-Hill.

Stengers, J., & Van Neck, A. (2001). *Masturbation: The history of a great terror* (K. A. Hoffmann, Trans.). Palgrave.

Stepp, L. S. (1999). Parents are alarmed by an unsettling new fad in middle schools: Oral sex. *Washington Post,* July 8.

Stern, K., & McClintock, M. K. (1998). Regulation of ovulation by human pheromones. *Nature, 392,* 177–179.

Sternberg, R. J. (1986). A triangular theory of love. *Psychological Review, 93,* 119–135.

Sternberg, R. J., & Barnes, M. (1985). Real and ideal others in romantic relationships: Is four a crowd? *Journal of Personality and Social Psychology, 47,* 1586–1608.

Stimpson, D., Jensen, L. C., & Neff, W. (1991). Cross-cultural gender differences in preference for a caring morality. *Journal of Social Psychology, 132,* 317–322.

Stokes, D., Damon, W., & McKirnan, D. J. (1997). Predictors of movement toward homosexuality: A longitudinal study of bisexual men. *Journal of Sex Research, 34,* 304–312.

Stoleru, S., Gregoire, M. C., Gerard, D., Decety, J., Lafarge, E., Cinotti, L., Lavenne, F., Le Bars, D., Vernet-Maury, E., Rada, H., Collet, C., Mazoyer, B., Forest, M. G., Magnin, F., Spira, A., & Comar, D. (1999). Neuroanatomical correlates of visually evoked sexual arousal in human males. *Archives of Sexual Behavior, 28,* 1–21.

Stoller, R. J. (1975). *Perversion: The erotic form of hatred,* Pantheon.

Stoller, R. J. (1977). Sexual deviations. In F. A. Beach (Ed.), *Human sexuality in four perspectives.* Johns Hopkins University Press.

Stolley, K. S. (1993). *Statistics on adoption in the United States.* Located at http://www.futureofchildren.org/adp/ADP_03.PDF.

Stone, L. (1988). Passionate attachments in the West in historical perspective. In W. Gaylin & E. Person (Eds.), *Passionate attachments: Thinking about love.* Free Press.

Stone, T. H., Winslade, W. J., & Klugman, C. M. (2000). Sex offenders, sentencing laws and pharmaceutical treatment: A prescription for failure. *Behavioral Sciences and the Law, 18,* 83–110.

Stowers, L., Holy, T. E., Meister, M., Dulac, C., & Koentges, G. (2002). Loss of sex discrimination and male-male aggression in mice deficient for TRP2. *Science, 295,* 1493–1500.

Strassberg, D. S., & Lockerd, L. K. (1998). Force in women's sexual fantasies. *Archives of Sexual Behavior, 27,* 403–414.

Strassmann, B. I. (1992). The function of menstrual taboos among the Dogon: Defense against cuckoldry? *Human Nature, 3,* 89–131.

Strassmann, B. I. (1996). Menstrual hut visits by Dogon women: A hormonal test distinguishes deceit from honest signaling. *Behavioral Ecology, 7,* 304–315.

Strassmann, B. I. (1997). The biology of menstruation in *Homo sapiens*: Total lifetime menses, fecundity, and nonsynchrony in a natural fertility population. *Current Anthropology, 38,* 123–129.

Strassmann, B. I. (1999). Menstrual synchrony pheromones: Cause for doubt. *Human Reproduction, 14,* 579–580.

Strassmann, B. I., & Warner, J. H. (1998). Predictors of fecundability and conception waits among the Dogon of Mali. *American Journal of Physical Anthropology, 105,* 167–184.

Straus, M. (1992). Children as witnesses to marital violence: A risk factor for lifelong problems among a nationally representative sample of American men and women. In D. F. Schwartz (Ed.), *Children and violence.* Ross Laboratories.

Straus, M. A., Gelles, R. J., & Steinmetz, S. K. (1980). *Behind closed doors: Violence in the American family.* Anchor/Doubleday.

Streib, V. L. (2001). *Death penalty for female offenders.* Located at http://www.law.onu.edu/faculty/streib/femdeath.htm.

Streissguth, A. P., Barr, H. M., & Sampson, P. D. (1990). Moderate prenatal alcohol exposure: Effects on child IQ and learning problems at age 7 1/2 years. *Alcoholism, Clinical and Experimental Research, 14,* 662–669.

Strossen, N. (1995). *Defending pornography: Free speech, sex, and the fight for women's rights.* Scribner.

Strube, M. J., & Barbour, L. S. (1983). The decision to leave an abusive relationship: Economic dependence and psychological commitment. *Journal of Marriage and the Family, 45,* 785–793.

Stumpf, H., & Jackson, D. N. (1994). Gender-related differences in cognitive abilities: Evidence from a medical school admissions program. *Personality and Individual Differences, 17,* 335–344.

Suggs, D. N., & Miracle, A. W. (Eds.) (1999). *Culture, biology, and sexuality.* University of Georgia Press.

Sullivan, A. (1995). *Virtually normal: An argument about homosexuality.* Knopf.

Supreme Court of Arkansas. (2002). *Jegley v. Picado.* Located at http://courts.state.ar.us/opinions/2002a/20020705/01-815.html.

Survive-UK. (2001). *It happened to me.* Located at http://survive.org.uk/stories.html.

Swain, A., & Lovell-Badge, R. (1999). Mammalian sex determination: A molecular drama. *Genes and Development, 13,* 755–767.

Swan, S. H., Elkin, E. P., & Fenster, L. (2000). The question of declining sperm density revisited: An analysis of 101 studies published 1934–1996. *Environmental Health Perspectives, 108,* 961–966.

Syed, R. (1999). Knowledge of the "Grafenberg zone" and female ejaculation in ancient Indian sexual science: A medical history contribution. *Sudhoffs Archiv; Zeitschrift fur Wissenschaftsgeschichte, 83,* 171–190.

Szasz, T. S. (1970). *The manufacture of madness: A comparative study of the Inquisition and the mental health movement.* Harper and Row.

Szasz, T. S. (2000). Remembering Krafft-Ebing. *Ideas on Liberty, 50,* 31–32 (January).

Talimini, J. T. (1982). *Boys will be girls: The hidden world of the heterosexual male transvestite.* University Press of America.

Tanfer, K., & Aral, S. O. (1996). Sexual intercourse during menstruation and self-reported sexually transmitted disease history among women. *Sexually Transmitted Diseases, 23,* 395–401.

Tanfer, K., Wierzbicki, S., & Payn, B. (2000). Why are US women not using long-acting contraceptives? *Family Planning Perspectives, 32,* 176–183, 191.

Tay, J. I., Moore, J., & Walker, J. J. (2000). Ectopic pregnancy. *BMJ, 320,* 916–919.

Taylor, H. (1993). Number of gay men more than 4 times higher than the 1 percent reported in a recent survey. *The Harris Poll, 20,* 1–4.

Tempest, R. (1995). Sex-orientation references cut in deference to Vatican, Muslims. *Los Angeles Times,* September 15.

Templeman, T. L., & Stinnett, R. D. (1991). Patterns of sexual arousal and history in a "normal" sample of young men. *Archives of Sexual Behavior, 20,* 137–150.

Tenn, W. (1968). *The seven sexes.* Ballantine Books.

Tennov, D. (1979). *Love and limerence.* Stein & Day.

Terrorism Research Center. (1998). *Trafficking in women and children.* Located at http://www.terrorism.com/documents/pub45270/pub45270chap2.html#5.

Terry, D. (2000). A.C.L.U. will defend group that advocates legalizing sex between men and boys. *New York Times,* September 1.

Testa, R. J., Kinder, B. N., & Ironson, G. (1987). Heterosexual bias in the perception of loving relationships of gay males and lesbians. *Journal of Sex Research, 16,* 245–257.

Thackray, H., & Tifft, C. (2001). Fetal alcohol syndrome. *Pediatrics in Review, 22,* 47–55.

Thienhaus, O. J. (1988). Practical overview of sexual function and advancing age. *Geriatrics, 43,* 63–67.

Thomas, S. L., & Ellertson, C. (2000). Nuisance or natural and healthy: Should monthly menstruation be optional for women? *Lancet, 355,* 922–924.

Thompson, J. K., & Tantleff, S. (1992). Female and male ratings of upper torso: Actual, ideal, and stereotypical conceptions. *Journal of Social Behavior and Personality, 7,* 345–354.

Thompson, M. (Ed.) (1991). *Leatherfolk: Radical sex, people, politics, and practice.* Alyson.

Thompson, M. (1995). *Gay soul: Finding the heart of gay spirit and nature.* Harper San Francisco.

Thomson, J. A., Itskovitz-Eldor, J., Shapiro, S. S., Waknitz, M. A., Swiergiel, J. J., Marshall, V. S., & Jones, J. M. (1998). Embryonic stem cell lines derived from human blastocysts. *Science, 282,* 1145–1147.

Thorne-Finch, R. (1991). *Ending the silence: The origins and treatment of male violence against women.* University of Toronto Press.

Thorneycroft, I. H., & Cariati, S. L. (2001). Ultra-low-dose oral contraceptives: Are they right for your patient? Located at http://www.medscape.com/Medscape/WomensHealth/journal/2001/v06.n04/wh0703.thor/wh0703.thor-01.html.

Thornhill, R. (1980). Rape in *Panorpa* scorpionflies and a general rape hypothesis. *Animal Behavior, 28,* 52–59.

Thornhill, R., & Gangestad, S. W. (1999). Facial attractiveness. *Trends in Cognitive Science, 3*, 452–460.

Thornhill, R., Gangestad, S. W., & Comer, R. (1995). Human female orgasm and mate fluctuating asymmetry. *Animal Behaviour, 50*, 1601–1615.

Thornhill, R., & Palmer, C. T. (2000). *A natural history of rape: Biological bases of sexual coercion.* MIT Press.

Tiihonen, J., Kuikka, J., Kupila, J., Partanen, K., Vainio, P., Airaksinen, J., Eronen, M., Hallikainen, T., Paanila, J., Kinnunen, I. (1994). Increase in cerebral blood flow of right prefrontal cortex in man during orgasm. *Neuroscience Letters, 170*, 241–243.

Tilghman, S. M. (1999). The sins of the fathers and mothers: Genomic imprinting in mammalian development. *Cell, 96*, 185–193.

Tjaden, P., & Thoennes, N. (1998). *Stalking in America: Findings from the National Violence against Women survey.* Located at http://www.ncjrs.org/pdffiles/169592.pdf.

Tomlinson, P. S. (1987). Spousal differences in marital satisfaction during transition to parenthood. *Nursing Research, 36*, 239–243.

Toppari, J., & Kaleva, M. (1999). Maldescendus testis. *Hormone Research, 51*, 261–269.

Torfs, C. P., & Christianson, R. E. (2000). Effect of maternal smoking and coffee consumption on the risk of having a recognized Down syndrome pregnancy. *American Journal of Epidemiology, 152*, 1185–1191.

Townsend, L. (1997). *The leatherman's handbook* (Silver jubilee ed.). Masquerade Books.

Tran, M. (2001). 60 years in prison for boys' molester. *Los Angeles Times*, July 28.

Travin, S. (1995). Compulsive sexual behaviors. *Psychiatric Clinics of North America, 18*, 155–169.

Trevathan, W. R., Burleson, M. H., & Gregory, W. L. (1993). No evidence for menstrual synchrony in lesbian couples. *Psychoneuroendocrinology, 18*, 425–435.

Trivers, R. L. (1974). Parent-offspring conflict. *American Zoologist, 14*, 249–264.

Trivers, R. L., & Hare, H. (1976). Haplodiploidy and the evolution of the social insects. *Science, 191*, 249–263.

Troiden, R. R. (1989). The formation of homosexual identities. *Journal of Homosexuality, 17*, 43–73.

Trotier, D., Eloit, C., Wassef, M., Talmain, G., Bensimon, J. L., Doving, K. B., & Ferrand, J. (2000). The vomeronasal cavity in adult humans. *Chemical Senses, 25*, 369–380.

Trudel, G., & Saint-Laurent, S. (1983). A comparison between the effects of Kegel's exercises and a combination of sexual awareness relaxation and breathing on situational orgasmic dysfunction in women. *Journal of Sex and Marital Therapy, 9*, 204–209.

True, L. D., Berger, R. E., Rothman, I., Ross, S. O., & Krieger, J. N. (1999). Prostate histopathology and the chronic prostatitis/chronic pelvic pain syndrome: A prospective biopsy study. *Journal of Urology, 162*, 2014–2018.

Tucker, M. B., & Mitchell-Kernan, C. (Eds.) (1995). *The decline in marriage among African Americans.* Russell Sage.

Tugwell, P., Wells, G., Peterson, J., Welch, V., Page, J., Davison, C., McGowan, J., Ramroth, D., & Shea, B. (2001). Do silicone breast implants cause rheumatologic disorders? A systematic review for a court-appointed national science panel. *Arthritis and Rheumatism, 44*, 2477–2484.

Turner, T., & Loder, K. (1993). *I, Tina: My life story.* Avon.

Twenge, J. M. (1999). Mapping gender: The multifactorial approach and the organization of gender-related attributes. *Psychology of Women Quarterly, 23*, 485–502.

Tyring, S. K., Douglas, J. M., Jr., Corey, L., Spruance, S. L., & Esmann, J. (1998). A randomized, placebo-controlled comparison of oral valacyclovir and acyclovir in immunocompetent patients with recurrent genital herpes infections. The Valaciclovir International Study Group. *Archives of Dermatology, 134*, 185–191.

Udry, J. R., Billy, J. O., Morris, N. M., Groff, T. R., & Raj, M. H. (1985). Serum androgenic hormones motivate sexual behavior in adolescent boys. *Fertility and Sterility, 43*, 90–94.

Udry, J. R., & Talbert, L. M. (1988). Sex hormone effects on personality at puberty. *Journal of Personality and Social Psychology, 54*, 291–295.

Uitti, R. J., Tanner, C. M., Rajput, A. H., Goetz, C. G., Klawans, H. L., & Thiessen, B. (1989). Hypersexuality with antiparkinsonian therapy. *Clinical Neuropharmacology, 12*, 375–383.

Ullian, D. Z. (1981). Why boys will be boys: A structural perspective. *American Journal of Orthopsychiatry, 51*, 493–501.

UNAIDS. (2001). 20 years of HIV/AIDS. Located at http://www.unaids.org/publications/graphics/20years/Eng/HIV.time.chart.e.jpg.

United Methodist Church. (2000). *The book of discipline of the United Methodist Church.* United Methodist Publishing House.

U.S. Census Bureau. (2001). *America's families and living arrangements—2000.* Located at http://www.census.gov/prod/2001pubs/p20–537.pdf.

U.S. Department of Defense. (1995). *1995 sexual harassment study.* Located at http://www.defenselink.mil/news/fact_sheets/sxhas95.html.

U.S. Department of Health and Human Services. (2001). *Guidelines for the use of antiretroviral agents in HIV-infected adults and adolescents.* Located at http://www.hivatis.org/trtgdlns.html#Adult.

U.S. Department of Justice. (1998). *Prevalence, incidence, and consequences of violence against women: Findings from the National Violence against Women Survey.* Located at http://ncjrs.org/pdffiles/172837.pdf.

U.S. Department of Justice. (1999a). *1999 report on cyberstalking: A new challenge for law enforcement and industry.* Located at http://www.usdoj.gov/criminal/cybercrime/cyberstalking.htm.

U.S. Department of Justice. (1999b). *Marital rape.* Located at http://www.vaw.umn.edu/Vawnet/mrape.htm.

U.S. Department of Justice. (2000a). *Full report of the prevalence, incidence, and consequences of violence against women.* Located at http://www.ncjrs.org/pdffiles1/nij/183781.pdf.

U.S. Department of Justice. (2000b). *National crime victimization survey.* Located at http://www.ojp.usdoj.gov/bjs/pub/pdf/cv99.pdf.

U.S. Equal Employment Opportunity Commission. (2001). *Sexual harassment charges.* Located at http://www.eeoc.gov/stats/harass.html.

U.S. Food and Drug Administration. (1999). *Toxic shock syndrome: Reducing the risk.* Located at http://www.fda.gov/bbs/topics/consumer/con00116.html.

U.S. Public Health Service. (2001). *Guidelines for the prevention of opportunistic infections in persons infected with human immunodeficiency virus.* Located at http://www.hivatis.org/guidelines/OIGuidelinesJuly2001.pdf.

Vagell, M. E., & McGinnis, M. Y. (1997). The role of aromatization in the restoration of male rat reproductive behavior. *Journal of Neuroendocrinology, 9*, 415–421.

Valenti, W. M. (1998). Managing managed care: Strategies to manage costs. *The AIDS Reader, 8*, 157–159.

Valentine, G. H. (1986). *The chromosomes and their disorders: An introduction for clinicians* (4th Ed.). W. Heineman Medical Books.

Vance, E. B., & Wagner, N. N. (1976). Written descriptions of orgasms: A study of sex differences. *Archives of Sexual Behavior, 5,* 87–98.

Van Goozen, S. H., Wiegant, V. M., Endert, E., Helmond, F. A., & Van de Poll, N. E. (1997). Psychoendocrinological assessment of the menstrual cycle: The relationship between hormones, sexuality, and mood. *Archives of Sexual Behavior, 26,* 359–382.

van Kesteren, P. J., Gooren, L. J., & Megens, J. A. (1996). An epidemiological and demographic study of transsexuals in The Netherlands. *Archives of Sexual Behavior, 25,* 589–600.

VanOss Marin, B., Coyle, K. K., Gómez, C. A., Carvajal, S. C., & Kirby, D. B. (2000). Older boyfriends and girlfriends increase risk of sexual initiation in young adolescents. *Journal of Adolescent Health, 27,* 409–418.

Varney, H. (1997). *Varney's midwifery* (3rd ed.). Jones and Bartlett.

Varsano, I. B., Jaber, L., Garty, B. Z., Mukamel, M. M., & Grunebaum, M. (1984). Urinary tract abnormalities in children with supernumerary nipples. *Pediatrics, 73,* 103–105.

Vatsyayana. (1991). *The Kama Sutra of Vatsyayana* (R. F. Burton, Trans.). Arkana.

Verkauf, B. S., Von Thron, J., & O'Brien, W. F. (1992). Clitoral size in normal women. *Obstetrics and Gynecology, 80,* 41–44.

Vincent, A., & Fitzpatrick, L. A. (2000). Soy isoflavones: Are they useful in menopause? *Mayo Clinic Proceedings, 75,* 1174–1184.

Virginia Commonwealth University. (2001). *Sexual assault survivor's handbook.* Located at http://www.students.vcu.edu/health/sasa/SHB4.html.

Voyer, D., Voyer, S., & Bryden, M. P. (1995). Magnitude of sex differences in spatial abilities: A meta-analysis and consideration of critical variables. *Psychological Bulletin, 117,* 250–270.

Vrana, P. B., Guan, X. J., Ingram, R. S., & Tilghman, S. M. (1998). Genomic imprinting is disrupted in interspecific *Peromyscus* hybrids. *Nature Genetics, 20,* 362–365.

Waage, J., & Gowaty, P. A. (1997). Myths of genetic determinism. In P. A. Gowaty (Ed.), *Feminism and evolutionary biology.* Chapman Hall.

Waite, L. J., & Joyner, K. (2001). Emotional and physical satisfaction with sex in married, cohabiting, and dating sexual unions: Do men and women differ? In E. O. Laumann & R. T. Michael (Eds.), *Sex, love, and health in America: Private choices and public policies.* University of Chicago Press.

Wald, A., Zeh, J., Selke, S., Warren, T., Ryncarz, A. J., Ashley, R., Krieger, J. N., & Corey, L. (2000). Reactivation of genital herpes simplex virus type 2 infection in asymptomatic seropositive persons. *New England Journal of Medicine, 342,* 844–850.

Waldinger, M. D., Zwinderman, A. H., & Olivier, B. (2001). Antidepressants and ejaculation: A double-blind, randomized, placebo-controlled, fixed-dose study with paroxetine, sertraline, and nefazodone. *Journal of Clinical Psychopharmacology, 21,* 293–297.

Walen, S. R., & Roth, D. (1987). A cognitive approach. In J. H. Geer & W. T. O'Donohue (Eds.), *Theories of human sexuality.* Plenum Press.

Walker, B. G. (1983). *Woman's encyclopedia of myths and secrets.* Harper San Francisco.

Walker, L. E. (1979). *The battered woman.* Harper and Row.

Walker, L. E. A. (2000). *The battered woman syndrome* (2nd ed.). Springer.

Walker, L. J. (1989). A longitudinal study of moral reasoning. *Child Development, 60,* 157–166.

Wallen, K. (1996). Nature needs nurture: The interaction of hormonal and social influences on the development of behavioral sex differences in rhesus monkeys. *Hormones and Behavior, 30,* 364–378.

Wallen, K. (2000). The development of hypothalamic control of sexual behavior. In J.-P. Bourguignon & T. M. Plant (Eds.), *The onset of puberty in perspective.* Elsevier.

Wallen, K., & Lovejoy, J. (1993). Sexual behavior: Endocrine function and therapy. In J. Schulkin (Ed.), *Hormonally induced changes in mind and brain.* Academic Press.

Wallerstein, J. S., & Blakeslee, S. (1998). *The good marriage: How and why love lasts.* Houghton Mifflin.

Walsh, A. (1991). *The science of love: Understanding love and its effects on mind and body.* Prometheus.

Walsh, R. N., Budtz-Olsen, I., Leader, C., & Cummins, R. A. (1981). The menstrual cycle, personality, and academic performance. *Archives of General Psychiatry, 38,* 219–221.

Walster, E., Walster, G. W., & Berscheid, E. (1978). *Equity: Theory and research.* Allyn and Bacon.

Wang, C., Swedloff, R. S., Iranmanesh, A., Dobs, A., Snyder, P. J., Cunningham, G., Matsumoto, A. M., Weber, T., & Berman, N. (2000). Transdermal testosterone gel improves sexual function, mood, muscle strength, and body composition parameters in hypogonadal men. Testosterone Gel Study Group. *Journal of Clinical Endocrinology and Metabolism, 85,* 2839–2853.

Ward, I. L., Ward, O. B., Winn, R. J., & Bielawski, D. (1994). Male and female sexual behavior potential of male rats prenatally exposed to the influence of alcohol, stress, or both factors. *Behavioral Neuroscience, 108,* 1188–1195.

Ward, I. L., & Weisz, J. (1984). Differential effects of maternal stress on circulating levels of corticosterone, progesterone, and testosterone in male and female rat fetuses and their mothers. *Endocrinology, 114,* 1635–1644.

Ward, S. L., Newcombe, N., & Overton, W. F. (1986). Turn left at the church, or three miles north: A study of direction giving and sex differences. *Environment and Behavior, 18,* 192–213.

Ward, T., & Siegert, R. (2002). Rape and evolutionary psychology. *Aggression and Violent Behavior, 2,* 145–168.

Warner, M. (2000). *The trouble with normal: Sex, politics, and the ethics of gay life.* Harvard University Press.

Warshaw, R. (1994). *I never called it rape: The Ms. report on recognizing, fighting, and surviving date and acquaintance rape.* Harperperennial.

Wasserman, S., & Watson, A. (2000). *HIV/AIDS partner notification programs.* Located at http://www.stateserv.hpts.org/HPTS2001/issueb2001.nsf/970e745f9e50ddca852564f0007b3abd/eea526bbe0ff0cee852568ab00693be4?OpenDocument.

Watkins, D., Dong, Q., & Xia, Y. (1997). Age and gender differences in the self-esteem of Chinese children. *Journal of Social Psychology, 137,* 374–379.

Watson, N. V., & Kimura, D. (1991). Nontrivial sex differences in throwing and intercepting: Relation to psychometrically-defined spatial functions. *Personality and Individual Differences, 12,* 375–385.

Waynforth, D., & Dunbar, R. I. M. (1995). Conditional mate choice strategies in humans: Evidence from lonely hearts advertisements. *Behaviour, 132,* 755–779.

Webby, S. (2001). Molester's castration could set precedent. *San Jose Mercury News,* August 23.

Wedekind, C., Chapuisat, M., Macas, E., & Rulicke, T. (1996). Non-random fertilization in mice correlates with the MHC and something else. *Heredity, 77,* 400–409.

Weeks, G. R., & Gambescia, N. (2002). *Hypoactive sexual desire: Integrating sex and couple therapy.* W.W. Norton.

Wegesin, D. J. (1998). A neuropsychologic profile of homosexual and heterosexual men and women. *Archives of Sexual Behavior, 27*, 91–108.

Weinberg, M. S., Shaver, F. M., & Williams, C. J. (1999). Gendered sex work in the San Francisco Tenderloin. *Archives of Sexual Behavior, 28*, 503–521.

Weinberg, M. S., Williams, C. J., & Calhan, C. (1994). Homosexual foot fetishism. *Archives of Sexual Behavior, 23*, 611–626.

Weinberg, M. S., Williams, C. J., & Pryor, D. W. (1995). *Dual attraction: Understanding bisexuality.* Oxford University Press.

Weinberg, T. S. (Ed.). (1995). *S and M: Studies in dominance and submission.* Prometheus Books.

Weinrich, J. D. (1987). A new sociobiological theory of homosexuality applicable to societies with universal marriage. *Behavioral Ecology and Sociobiology, 8*, 37–47.

Weise, E. R. (1991). Bisexuality, *The Rocky Horror Picture Show*, and me. In L. Hutchins & L. Kaahumanu (Eds.), *Bi any other name: Bisexual people speak out.* Alyson.

Weise, E. R. (1992). *Closer to home: Bisexuality and feminism.* Seal Press.

Weiss, K. R. (2001). Eggs buy a college education. *Los Angeles Times*, May 27, 2001.

Weissman, M. M., & Olfson, M. (1995). Depression in women: Implications for health care research. *Science, 269*, 799–801.

Weller, A., & Weller, L. (1997). Menstrual synchrony under optimal conditions: Bedouin families. *Journal of Comparative Psychology, 111*, 143–151.

Weller, A., & Weller, L. (1998). Prolonged and very intensive contact may not be conducive to menstrual synchrony. *Psychoneuroendocrinology, 23*, 19–32.

Weller, L., Weller, A., & Avinir, O. (1995). Menstrual synchrony: Only in roommates who are close friends? *Physiology and Behavior, 58*, 883–889.

Wellings, K., Field, J., Johnson, A. M., & Wadsworth, J. (1994). *Sexual behavior in Britain: The National Survey of Sexual Attitudes and Lifestyles.* Penguin Books.

Wells, B. (1986). Predictors of female nocturnal orgasm. *Journal of Sex Research, 23*, 421–427.

Wessells, H., Lue, T. F., & McAninch, J. W. (1996a). Complications of penile lengthening and augmentation seen at 1 referral center. *Journal of Urology, 155*, 1617–1620.

Wessells, H., Lue, T. F., & McAninch, J. W. (1996b). Penile length in the flaccid and erect states: Guidelines for penile augmentation. *Journal of Urology, 156*, 995–997.

Westneat, D. F. (1994). To guard or go forage: Conflicting demands affect the paternity of red-winged blackbirds. *American Naturalist, 144*, 343–354.

Whipple, B., Ogden, G., & Komisaruk, B. R. (1992). Physiological correlates of imagery-induced orgasm in women. *Archives of Sexual Behavior, 21*, 121–133.

Whisman, V. (1996). *Queer by choice: Lesbians, gay men, and the politics of identity.* Routledge.

Whitam, F. L. (1980). The prehomosexual male child in three societies: The United States, Guatemala, Brazil. *Archives of Sexual Behavior, 9*, 87–99.

Whitam, F. L. (1983). Culturally invariant properties of male homosexuality: Tentative conclusions from cross-cultural research. *Archives of Sexual Behavior, 12*, 207–226.

Whitam, F. L., & Dizon, M. J. (1979). Occupational choice and sexual orientation in cross-cultural perspective. *International Review of Modern Sociology, 9*, 137–149.

Whitam, F. L., & Mathy, R. M. (1991). Childhood cross-gender behavior of homosexual females in Brazil, Peru, Philippines, and the United States. *Archives of Sexual Behavior, 20*, 151–170.

White, G. L., Fishbein, S., & Rutstein, J. (1981). Passionate love and the misattribution of arousal. *Journal of Personality and Social Psychology, 41*, 56–62.

White, L. K. (1991). Determinants of divorce: A review of research in the eighties. In A. Booth (Ed.), *Contemporary families: Looking forward, looking back.* National Council on Family Relations.

Wilcox, A. J., Weinberg, C. R., & Baird, D. D. (1995). Timing of sexual intercourse in relation to ovulation: Effects on the probability of conception, survival of the pregnancy, and sex of the baby. *New England Journal of Medicine, 333*, 1517–1521.

Wiley, D., & Bortz, W. M., II. (1996). Sexuality and aging—usual and successful. *Journals of Gerontology. Series A, Biological Sciences and Medical Sciences, 51*, M142–146.

Wilgoren, J. (2002). Scholar's pedophilia essay stirs outrage and revenge. *New York Times*, April 30.

Williams, T. J., Pepitone, M. E., Christensen, S. E., Cooke, B. M., Huberman, A. D., Breedlove, N. J., Breedlove, T. J., Jordan, C. L., & Breedlove, S. M. (2000). Finger-length ratios and sexual orientation. *Nature, 404*, 455–456.

Williams, W. L. (1986). *The spirit and the flesh: Sexual diversity in American Indian culture.* Beacon Press.

Wilson, M., & Daly, M. (1992). The man who mistook his wife for a chattel. In J. H. Barkow, L. Cosmides, & J. Tooby (Eds.), *The adapted mind: Evolutionary psychology and the evolution of culture.* Oxford University Press.

Wilson, M., & Daly, M. (1997). Relationship-specific social psychological adaptations. *Ciba Foundation Symposium, 208*, 253–263.

Winters, S. J., Brufsky, A., Weissfeld, J., Trump, D. L., Dyky, M. A., & Hadeed, V. (2001). Testosterone, sex hormone-binding globulin, and body composition in young adult African American and Caucasian men. *Metabolism: Clinical and Experimental, 50*, 1242–1247.

Wisborg, K., Kesmodel, U., Henriksen, T. B., Olsen, S. F., & Secher, N. J. (2000). A prospective study of smoking during pregnancy and SIDS. *Archives of Disease in Childhood, 83*, 203–206.

Wise, T. N., & Kalyanam, R. C. (2000). Amputee fetishism and genital mutilation: Case report and literature review. *Journal of Sex and Marital Therapy, 26*, 339–344.

Wiswell, T. E., Enzenauer, R. W., Holton, M. E., Cornish, J. D., & Hankins, C. T. (1987). Declining frequency of circumcision: Implications for changes in the absolute incidence and male to female sex ratio of urinary tract infections in early infancy. *Pediatrics, 79*, 338–342.

Wolff, C. (1986). *Magnus Hirschfeld: A portrait of a pioneer in sexology.* Quartet Books.

Wolinsky, H. (1997). Steps still being taken to undo damage of "America's Nuremberg." *Annals of Internal Medicine, 127*, I43–44.

Women's Health Initiative. (2002). Risks and benefits of estrogen plus progestin in healthy postmenopausal women: Principal results from the Women's Health Initiative randomized controlled trial. *JAMA, 288*, 321–333.

Won, J., Mair, E. A., Bolger, W. E., & Conran, R. M. (2000). The vomeronasal organ: An objective anatomic analysis of its prevalence. *Ear, Nose, and Throat Journal, 79*, 600–605.

Woods, N. F. (1987). Premenstrual symptoms: Another look. *Public Health Reports* (Suppl.) 106–112.

World Health Organization. (1993). *The ICD-10 classification of mental and behavioural disorders* (4th ed.). World Health Organization.

World Health Organization. (1998). *Female genital mutilation: An overview.* Located at http://www.who.int/dsa/cat98/fgmbook.htm.

World Health Organization. (2001a). *Estimated prevalence rates for FGM, updated May 2001.* Located at http://www.who.int/frh-whd/FGM/FGM%20prev%20update.html.

World Health Organization. (2001b). Medical abortion at 57 to 63 days' gestation with a lower dose of mifepristone and gemeprost: A randomized controlled trial. *Acta Obstetricia et Gynecologica Scandinavica, 80*, 447–451.

Wright, K. (2000). Totally unacceptable to cultural norms: Gays in Zimbabwe fight institutionalized homophobia. *Washington Blade*, April 28. Retrieved from http://ww2.aegis.com/news/wb/2000/WB000402.html.

Wright, L. (Ed.) (1997). *The bear book: Readings in the history and evolution of a gay male subculture*. Haworth Press.

Wu, F. C., Balasubramanian, R., Mulders, T. M., & Coelingh-Bennink, H. J. (1999). Oral progestogen combined with testosterone as a potential male contraceptive: Additive effects between desogestrel and testosterone enanthate in suppression of spermatogenesis, pituitary-testicular axis, and lipid metabolism. *Journal of Clinical Endocrinology and Metabolism, 84*, 112–122.

Wyatt, R. C. (2001). *An interview with John Gottman, Ph.D.* Located at http://www.psychotherapistresources.com/bios/totmframe.html.

Yankelovich Partners. (1994). *A Yankelovich MONITOR perspective on gays/lesbians*. Yankelovich Partners.

Yarab, P. E., Sensibaugh, C. C., & Allgeier, E. R. (1998). More than just sex: Gender differences in the incidence of self-defined unfaithful behavior in heterosexual dating relationships. *Journal of Psychology and Human Sexuality, 10*, 45–57.

Yllö, K., & Bograd, M. (Eds.) (1988). *Feminist perspectives on wife abuse*. Sage.

Yoshizaki, A. (1991). I am who I am: A married bisexual teacher. In L. Hutchins & L. Kaahumanu (Eds.), *Bi any other name: Bisexual people speak out*. Alyson.

Young, C. (1998). Don't shield juries from the truth in sex cases. *Wall Street Journal*, April 20.

Young, L. J., Nilsen, R., Waymire, K. G., MacGregor, G. R., & Insel, T. R. (1999). Increased affiliative response to vasopressin in mice expressing the V1a receptor from a monogamous vole. *Nature, 400*, 766–768.

Young-Bruehl, E. (1996). *The anatomy of prejudices*. Harvard University Press.

Zahavi, A., & Zahavi, A. (1997). *The handicap principle: A missing piece of Darwin's puzzle*. Oxford University Press.

Zaviacic, M., & Whipple, B. (1993). Update on the female prostate and the phenomenon of female ejaculation. *Journal of Sex Research, 30*, 148–151.

Zbar, R. I., Zbar, L. I., Dudley, C., Trott, S. A., Rohrich, R. J., & Moss, R. L. (2000). A classification schema for the vomeronasal organ in humans. *Plastic and Reconstructive Surgery, 105*, 1284–1288.

Zilbergeld, B. (1999). *The new male sexuality* (Rev. ed.). Bantam.

Zourlas, P. A. & Jones, H. W. (1965). Clinical, histologic, and cytogenetic findings in male hermaphroditism. *Obstetrics and Gynecology, 25*, 768–778.

Zucker, K. J., & Blanchard, R. (1997). Transvestic fetishism: Psychopathology and theory. In R. Laws and W. O'Donohue (Eds.), *Sexual deviance: Theory, assessment, and treatment*. Guilford Press.

Zucker, K. J., Bradley, S. J., Oliver, G., Blake, J., Fleming, S., & Hood, J. (1996). Psychosexual development of women with congenital adrenal hyperplasia. *Hormones and Behavior, 30*, 300–318.

Zumpe, D., Bonsall, R. W., & Michael, R. P. (1993). Effects of the nonsteroidal aromatase inhibitor, fadrozole, on the sexual behavior of male cynomolgus monkeys (*Macaca fascicularis*). *Hormones and Behavior, 27*, 200–215.

Zverina, J., Hampl, R., Sulocava, J., & Starka, L. (1990). Hormonal status and sexual behaviour of 16 men after surgical castration. *Archivio Italiano di Urologia, Nefrologia, Andrologia, 62*, 55–58.

Author Index

Subject Index

Italic page numbers refer to illustrations.